Canadian Bibliography of International Law

Christian L. Wiktor

UNIVERSITY OF TORONTO PRESS
Toronto Buffalo London

© University of Toronto Press 1984
Toronto Buffalo London
Printed in Canada

ISBN 0-8020-5615-6

Canadian Cataloguing in Publication Data
Wiktor, Christian L.
Canadian bibliography of international law

Includes indexes.
ISBN 0-8020-5615-6

1. International law – Canada – Bibliography.   I. Title.

Z6465.C2W54 1984   016.341'0971   C84-098261-5

Published with the assistance of the Canadian Council on International Law
and the Canadian Law Information Council and with the help of a grant to
University of Toronto Press from the Andrew W. Mellon Foundation.

To Bodil

CONTENTS

FOREWORD BY PROFESSOR R. ST. J. MACDONALD xvii

INTRODUCTION xix

PART ONE:

PUBLIC INTERNATIONAL LAW: DOCTRINE AND INSTITUTIONS

I. REFERENCE WORKS

    A. Bibliographies and Indexes 3
    B. Periodicals and Continuations 7
    C. Biographies (Selected) 12
    D. Directories 15
    E. Associations and Societies 16
    F. Primary Sources
        1. General 18
        2. Collections of Documents 18
        3. Treaties and Agreements 20
        4. Annual Surveys 21
        5. State Practice 22
        6. Judicial Decisions 25
        7. International Organizations 26
        8. International Conferences 27
        9. Others 27

II. GENERAL WORKS 29

III. INTERNATIONAL LAW IN GENERAL

    A. General Nature 33
    B. History of International Law 41
    C. Relation to Municipal Law 42
    D. Codification of International Law 43
    E. Study and Teaching 43

IV. SOURCES OF INTERNATIONAL LAW 46

V. SUBJECTS OF INTERNATIONAL LAW

A. States
  1. General Nature of the State 47
  2. Sovereignty in General....................................... 47
  3. International Status
     (a) British Dominions 48
     (b) Canada 51
     (c) Others 55
  4. Self-Determination.. 56
  5. Recognition of States and Governments 57
  6. State Succession and Continuity 58
  7. Types of States
     (a) Federal States and Federalism 58
     (b) Canadian Federalism
         (i) General 60
         (ii) Admission into Confederation (Newfoundland) 65
         (iii) Quebec Separatism 66
         (iv) International Relations of Provinces 73
     (c) Associations of States
         (i) Commonwealth of Nations........................... 77
         (ii) Union Française and Francophonie 86
     (d) Permanently Neutral States 87
     (e) Divided States (Germany)................................ 87
     (f) Special Entities (Berlin, Cyprus, Etc.) 88
B. Other Subjects of International Law
  1. National Liberation Movements 89
  2. Holy See 89
  3. Mandated and Trust Territories 90
  4. Colonies.. 92
  5. Miscellaneous (Indian Tribes, Etc.) 93

VI. INDIVIDUALS

A. General 94
B. Nationality and Citizenship...................................... 94
C. Aliens and Non-Nationals....................................... 97
D. Diplomatic Protection.. 100
E. Passports and Visas 100
F. Minorities 101
G. Statelessness, Refugees 104
H. Slavery.. 106
I. Immigration and Emigration 107
J. Extradition, Expulsion and Asylum 115
K. Human Rights and Fundamental Freedoms 118

VII. ORGANS OF THE STATE

   A. Administration of External Affairs 133
   B. Diplomatic Service 140
   C. Consular Service 144
   D. Privileges and Immunities 145
   E. Trade and Special Missions, Etc. 146

VIII. LAW OF TREATIES

   A. General 147
   B. Treaty-Making Power 150
   C. Conclusion and Entry into Force of Treaties 154
   D. Interpretation of Treaties 155
   E. Termination of Treaties 156
   F. Succession to Treaties 156
   G. Treaties and National Law 157
   H. Indian Treaties 158
   I. Specific Treaties (by Subject)
      1. Labour 159
      2. Trade 161

IX. JURISDICTION OF THE STATE

   A. Personal Jurisdiction (Military) 163
   B. Territorial Jurisdiction
      1. Territorial Sovereignty 163
      2. Limitations (Servitudes, Leases, Etc.) 164
      3. Immunity of Foreign States 164

X. STATE TERRITORY

   A. Boundaries of Canada
      1. General 166
      2. Early History 168
      3. Eastern Boundary 170
      4. Inland Water Boundary 172
      5. Western Boundary
         (a) General (49th Parallel, Oregon Territory, Etc.) 172
         (b) San Juan Dispute 174
      6. Alaska Boundary 175
      7. Labrador Boundary 178
   B. Boundary Delimitation and Demarcation 180
   C. Transboundary Relations
      1. General 183
      2. International Joint Commission 184
   D. Acquisition and Loss of Territory
      1. General (Purchase of Alaska, Etc.) 191

2. Oregon Question... 192
3. Annexation (Proposals)...................................... 194

XI. POLAR REGIONS

A. General 196
B. Arctic
   1. General... 197
   2. Legal Régime 200
   3. Other Legal Aspects 205

XII. INLAND WATERWAYS

A. General 208
B. Great Lakes 209
C. Rivers, River Basins and Canals
   1. General... 211
   2. St. Lawrence River and Seaway 215
   3. Columbia River 224
D. Inland Seas (Hudson Bay) 228
E. Interoceanic Canals 229

XIII. LAW OF THE SEA

A. General 230
B. Territorial Sea 238
C. Functional Zones (Extended Jurisdiction)
   1. General... 239
   2. Exclusive Economic Zones 241
   3. Fishing Zones 242
D. Submerged Areas
   1. Seabed in General....................................... 243
   2. Continental Shelf 245
E. High Seas
   1. Freedom of the Sea 248
   2. Nationality of Vessels.................................. 249
   3. Hot Pursuit 249
F. Bays, Gulfs, Straits and Archipelagos 250
G. Marine Resources
   1. General... 251
   2. Living Resources
     (a) General 251
     (b) Fisheries
        (i) General 252
        (ii) History 258
     (c) Marine Mammals...................................... 262
   3. Non-Living Resources
     (a) Oil and Gas Exploitation 263

(b) Deep Sea Mining	264
H. Marine Pollution	264

XIV. MARITIME NAVIGATION AND TRANSPORTATION

A. General	270
B. Admiralty Courts and Procedure	274
C. Collision (Safety at Sea, Etc.)	276
D. Carriage of Goods	276
E. Marine Insurance	278

XV. AIRSPACE AND OUTER SPACE

A. General	280
B. Sovereignty over Airspace	281
C. International Air Transportation	
1. General	284
2. Air Carrier's Liability (Warsaw Convention, Etc.)	297
3. Navigation and Air Traffic Control	305
4. Legal Status of Aircraft	
(a) Civilian Aircraft	307
(b) Military Aircraft	310
5. Airports	310
D. National Air Law	
1. Canada	311
2. Other Countries	314
E. Outer Space	315

XVI. INTERNATIONAL ORGANIZATIONS

A. General	332
B. Universal Intergovernmental Organizations	
1. General	334
2. League of Nations	337
3. United Nations	
(a) General	340
(b) Legal Aspects	345
(c) Organs	346
(d) Membership and Representation	347
(e) Participation of Members	348
4. Specialized Agencies	
(a) General (Incl. Individual Agencies)	353
(b) International Civil Aviation Organization	357
(c) International Labour Organization	359
(d) United Nations Educational, Scientific and Cultural Organization	361
C. Regional Intergovernmental Organizations	
1. General	362

2. Western Europe and North Atlantic
     (a) General 363
     (b) European Economic Community 367
  3. Eastern Europe 379
  4. Western Hemisphere
     (a) General 379
     (b) Inter-American Organizations 380
     (c) Central American and Caribbean Organizations 383
  5. Africa 384
  6. Other Regions 385
 D. International Administration
  1. General... 386
  2. Officials and Employees 386
  3. Headquarters.. 388
 E. Nongovernmental Organizations 388

XVII. INTERNATIONAL CONFERENCES........................... 389

XVIII. STATE RESPONSIBILITY 391

XIX. PACIFIC SETTLEMENT OF DISPUTES

 A. General 392
 B. Arbitration
  1. General... 394
  2. Specific Cases
     (a) 'I'm Alone'... 396
     (b) Gut Dam 397
     (c) Trail Smelter 397
     (d) Fisheries 398
 C. Judicial Settlement
  1. International Courts and Tribunals 402
  2. Specific Cases 405
 D. Settlement within International Organizations 407

XX. COERCION AND USE OF FORCE

 A. Unilateral Acts (Intervention, Etc.) 408
 B. Collective Measures
  1. Sanctions in General 409
  2. United Nations Action in Korea (1950-53) 410
  3. Peace-Keeping Operations
     (a) General 411
     (b) Canadian Contribution 415

XXI. CONTROL AND PREVENTION OF CONFLICT

 A. General 419

B. Peace Movements 421
C. Arms Control and Disarmament
   1. General 422
   2. Nuclear Testing and Control 430
D. Collective Security
   1. General 434
   2. North American Defence 436
   3. North Atlantic Treaty Organization 441

XXII. CONDUCT OF ARMED CONFLICT (LAW OF WAR)

A. Resort to War in General (Ius ad Bellum) 447
B. Definition of War, Aggression, Etc. 448
C. Conduct of War in General (Ius in Bello) 448
D. Use of Weapons of Mass Extermination 449
E. Sea Warfare 450
F. Air and Space Warfare 451
G. Humanitarian Law (Prisoners of War, Etc.) 451
H. Effects of War
   1. General 453
   2. Enemy Aliens 453
I. Military Occupation 454
J. Termination of War, Peace Treaties, Armistices 454
K. Reparations and War Claims 455
L. Civil War and Guerrilla Warfare 456

XXIII. NEUTRALITY 458

XXIV. INTERNATIONAL CRIMINAL LAW

A. General 459
B. War Crimes
   1. General 461
   2. International Military Tribunals 462
   3. Superior Orders 462
C. Terrorism 463
D. Hijacking 466

PART TWO:

INTERNATIONAL RELATIONS: LEGAL IMPLICATIONS

I. INTERNATIONAL RELATIONS

A. Diplomatic History in General 475

B. Canadian Diplomatic History
  1. General.. 481
  2. Colonial Period (Before 1867) 496
  3. Relations with the British Empire and the Commonwealth 501
  4. Relations with the United States
     (a) General 510
     (b) Historical
         (i) American Revolution and the Treaty of Peace of 1783 ... 522
         (ii) Jay Treaty of November 19, 1794 523
         (iii) War of 1812 and the Treaty of Ghent of 1814 524
         (iv) Naval Forces on the Great Lakes (Rush-Bagot
              Agreement of 1817) 524
         (v) Webster-Ashburton Treaty of August 9, 1842 525
         (vi) Reciprocity Treaty of June 5, 1854 526
         (vii) American Civil War (1861-65) 528
         (viii) Treaty of Washington of May 8, 1871 529
         (ix) Reciprocity Agreement of January 21, 1911 530
  5. Relations with Other Countries (Selected) 534

II. INTERNATIONAL ECONOMIC RELATIONS

A. General (Incl. New International Economic Order) 539
B. International Trade
  1. General.. 545
  2. Multilateral Trade (GATT, Etc.) 550
  3. Foreign Trade of Canada
     (a) General 553
     (b) Tariffs and Customs 563
     (c) Trade with the United States
         (i) General 567
         (ii) Historical 572
         (iii) Specific Issue: Automotive Agreement 573
     (d) Multilateral Trade 576
C. Commodities
  1. General.. 580
  2. Specific Products
     (a) Wheat 581
     (b) Coffee, Tea, Sugar 582
     (c) Oil and Gas 583
     (d) Other Minerals 585
D. Foreign Investment
  1. General 586
  2. Foreign Investment in Canada 589
E. Multinational and Foreign Corporations
  1. General 599
  2. Foreign Corporations in Canada 604

F. Nationalization and Expropriation 610
G. International Finance (Foreign Exchange, Etc.) 611
H. International Taxation (Incl. Double Taxation) 617
I. Economic and Technical Assistance 627
J. Industrial and Intellectual Property 636

III. INTERNATIONAL TRANSPORTATION AND COMMUNICATION

A. Transportation in General 641
B. Telecommunications 643
C. Postal Service 649

IV. INTERNATIONAL SCIENTIFIC AND TECHNOLOGICAL AFFAIRS

A. General 650
B. Natural Resources 652
C. Energy Issues
   1. General.. 653
   2. Nuclear Energy 656
   3. Other Sources of Energy 659
D. Weather Information (Meteorology)............................. 659
E. Weights and Measures 660

V. INTERNATIONAL ENVIRONMENTAL COOPERATION

A. General 661
B. Pollution
   1. General.. 664
   2. Water Pollution (Non-Marine)................................. 666
   3. Air Pollution (Transboundary)................................. 667
   4. Other Forms of Pollution (Noise) 669
C. International Parks 670
D. Wildlife Protection (Migratory Birds, Etc.) 670

VI. INTERNATIONAL SOCIAL AFFAIRS

A. General 672
B. Population.. 672
C. Health 673
D. Labour and Trade Unions 673
E. Food and Nutrition 676
F. Narcotic Drugs 677
G. Alcoholic Beverages.. 678

VII. INTERNATIONAL CULTURAL RELATIONS

A. General 679
B. Protection of Cultural Property 681

VIII. INTERNATIONAL LEGAL COOPERATION

A. General 682
B. Execution of Penal Sentences Agreements 684
C. Commercial Arbitration 685

INDEX OF AUTHORS 689

INDEX OF CORPORATE NAMES, CONFERENCES
AND SERIES 749

FOREWORD

Whether they serve as government officials, scholars, researchers or practitioners, modern international lawyers are extraordinarily information-dependent: they need knowledge and information about international law in order to synthesize new data with known information, to anticipate problems, formulate policies, draft recommendations, refine decision-making, and, generally, develop an enlightened position within their professional groupings. They need information for their continuing education, for increasing their productivity, for the better performance of their institutional duties, and as part of the on-going creative process. They usually need it quickly.

From the standpoint of the well-being and development of the state itself, specialized information is a national resource of great importance. The state's capacity to adapt to changing international conditions and to find solutions to major problems is enhanced by the availability of sophisticated information: the right information, provided by competent experts at the right time and place, improves the likelihood that informed decisions will be made and particular goals achieved. It is no exaggeration to say that the availability of information about public international law promotes a wider understanding of the particular interpretations of the subject preferred by the state in question: it also encourages the idea of a law-oriented international society.

In the context of these few preliminary observations, it is now a pleasure to introduce Professor Christian L. Wiktor's *Canadian Bibliography of International Law* to lawyers, scholars, students and practitioners in Canada and abroad. Professor Wiktor's splendid book organizes a vast amount of specialized information and knowledge for use. It will induce Canadians to build on the past, to make use of a rich storehouse of material that was in danger of being lost or remaining forever untapped, and it will inevitably stimulate the production of new knowledge and more effective programmes of information transfer particularly but certainly not exclusively in the domain of public international law.

Officials, judges, scholars, students and practitioners outside as well as inside Canada will find that this major reference work is an essential tool for any serious consideration of the application of international law in relation to Canada, its policies, problems and prospects. Abroad, as at home, there will be delight and astonishment at the sheer quantity and variety of writing on international law that was produced in Canada in the past. Who would have suspected that the pioneer scholars had written so much in, and about, Canada? More, much more, useful work has been done than we once thought, and Professor Wiktor's dedicated efforts have made possible its wider utilization.

All international lawyers, particularly those in Canada, who want to get at the interior of the Canadian past, without which the country cannot have a future at all, will need to have this foundation volume at hand. Hopefully the new technologies will enable the editor to update this essential book, in various form of print and other media, at regular intervals. Hopefully too scholars in countries which have not already done so will be heartened to produce similar volumes of their own national literature as a further step towards the realization of more complete and comprehensive world-wide bibliographic services needed to sustain the expanding responsibilities of international lawyers.

R. St. J. Macdonald
Professor of International Law
Dalhousie University, Halifax
Judge at the European Court
of Human Rights, Strasbourg

INTRODUCTION

Since its creation as a federal state in 1867, Canada has gradually increased its role in the international community. Emerging from the rivalries of French and British colonial powers on the North American continent beginning in the late sixteenth century, it did not attain fully independent international status until the mid 1920s. The traditional ties between Canada and the United Kingdom, the Commonwealth and the United States slowly extended to other regions beyond Canada's natural border on the Atlantic and Pacific oceans. The nation's contributions to the Second World War led to an active involvement in the building of the post-war international organizations, to acceptance of the role of host to ICAO in Montreal, and to the adoption of a special peacekeeping role for the United Nations. In other contexts Canada began to make important - sometimes pioneering - contributions, particularly in "frontier" areas such as the Arctic, the oceans, and airspace and outer space. All this and more is reflected in the proliferation of Canadian writings on international law and relations, especially during the last twenty years.

BIBLIOGRAPHICAL CONTROL OF INTERNATIONAL LAW PUBLICATIONS

The amount of international law materials published in various forms (textbooks, monographs, articles, parts of books, dissertations, and official documents) now average about 400 titles a year. Much of this literature has become difficult to find and is in danger of being lost. Because international law deals with a wide range of topics published in many languages, international law material is not easy to locate, and world wide bibliographies on the subject are indeed rare. Among existing ones are those by Karl Strupp (1938), Robinson (1967), Gould and Barkun (1972), Delupis (1975), and Merrills (1978). For current material, the Max Planck Institute in Heidelberg has published the *Public International Law* bibliography quarterly since 1975. In addition, printed catalogues of international law collections, such as the Peace Palace at The Hague, Harvard, Cambridge, the Foreign Office in London or the United Nations at Geneva (in progress) are very helpful research tools. Publications of international organizations are more complex and are listed in specialized indexes.

On a national level, some countries have quite recently initiated the compilations of their own bibliographies of writings on international law. Examples of these are: Durdenevski of the Soviet Union in 1957 (covering 1917-1957), Feldman also of the Soviet Union in 1976 (for 1917-1972), and Rausching of Germany in 1966 (covering

1945-1964). Rausching's work was continued by Gascard in 1972 (for 1965-1971). Other nations have resorted to providing current listings of their writings in their journals or yearbooks of international law. Examples of these countries are: France, Germany, the Netherlands, Poland, Switzerland, and the Soviet Union.

In Canada, there is no current or retrospective bibliography on international law. However, some publications can be found listed in bibliographies on foreign relations, such as Thibaut published in 1972, covering the years 1600-1969 (No. 47), Motiuk and Grant covering the period 1945-1971 (No. 37), and Page for the years 1945-1975 (Nos. 39 and 40), continued by Barrett and Beaumont until 1980 (No. 1). In 1978, the Canadian Council on International Law issued in its *Bulletin* a short bibliography on international law, mainly containing writings of its members covering ten years (1967-1977) (No. 27). At that time, Professor Ronald St.John Macdonald, founding President of the Council and former Dean of the University of Toronto and Dalhousie Law Schools, expressed his concern with the inadequate bibliographical control of international law publications in Canada, and suggested the preparation of a full-scale bibliography on the subject. Further support for this bibliography has been in the form of grants from the Canadian Council on International Law, and the Canadian Law Information Council.

The *Canadian Bibliography of International Law* is the first comprehensive and retrospective Canadian bibliography on the subject. It is hoped that it will facilitate further research in international law, a subject of growing multinational interest, and that it will be an important working tool making a storehouse of information available to scholars, practitioners, officials, students of international law and relations, and everyone interested in world affairs affecting Canada. At the same time, it serves to reveal the scope of Canada's contribution to international law and to suggest the degree of its significance in the international community.

SCOPE

The *Canadian Bibliography of International Law* contains 9040 entries, of which 332 are duplicated under more than one heading. This represents 8708 individual publications, of which 2612 are monographs, 5627 are articles, and 469 are parts of books. Chronologically, the first listed publication was printed in 1755 in London and deals with the boundaries of British and French possessions in America (No. 2183). The next publication appeared in 1828, and during the colonial period until 1867, only a total of 22 titles dealing with Canada are included in this bibliography. For the period from Confederation in 1867 to the end of the nineteenth century 111 titles are listed, representing an annual average of 3.3 titles. During the first twenty years of the twentieth century (1900-1919) marked by the end of World War I, the annual average reached 16.3 titles, with a total of 326 items. From 1920 on, the number of publications in each decade illustrates steady growth. In 1920-29 there were 296 titles; in 1930-39 - 470 titles; in 1940-49 - 586 titles; in 1950-59 - 883 titles; in 1960-69 - 1671 titles; in 1970-79 - 3401 titles, and in 1980-81 (2 years) - 731 titles. While the bibliography has been checked up to March 1, 1983, the figure for 1982 is not complete. As the figures show, since 1950 the number of publications has doubled during each of the decades, with the busiest years being 1978 (435 titles), and 1979 (432 titles). It will be interesting to follow the trend in the future.

This bibliography has been compiled through a wide range of sources: collected files of Canadiana, legal and general bibliographies, catalogues and indexes, library catalogues both printed and on cards, lists of theses, catalogues of official documents, and others. Articles were selected primarily from original periodicals. They include scholarly, legal, and law related journals, with only a very few articles from more popular magazines, usually on less represented subjects. All entries have been verified with the original publication or reliable sources, such as *Canadiana*, the *National Union Catalog*, or the issuing agency. This was done for dissertations and over 50 libraries in Canada and elsewhere were contacted and replies were received from all of them. As to form, the type of material selected, both in English and French, includes treatises and monographs, parts of books, pamphlets, official documents, proceedings of conferences, publications of associations, theses and periodical articles.

The first part of the bibliography includes publications on international law in a wide sense, encompassing some subjects on the borderline with other legal disciplines, such as constitutional law (federalism, human rights and fundamental freedoms, treaties), administrative law, or criminal law. With some exceptions it does not include conflict of laws (private international law). The second part, comprising publications on international relations, is more selective, and more interdisciplinary in character, especially in such topics as foreign trade and investment, foreign corporations, communication and transport, scientific or technological affairs, and social and cultural relations.

The continuing subdivision of publications illustrates the widening interest of Canada in more and more detailed aspects of international law. The 134 publications printed before 1900 primarily deal with topics concerned with relations with the United States in such matters as boundaries (39 entries), fishery rights and arbitration (29 entries), and bilateral relations between the two countries (13 entries). Today publications fall into all 269 subdivisions of the 32 main subjects listed in the table of contents. In descending order, the subject profile looks as follows: *Part 1* - international organizations (832 entries), airspace and outer space (706), subjects of international law (688), individuals (576), law of the sea (532), control and prevention of conflict (416), state territory (375), inland waterways (294), reference works (233), organs of the state (219), law of treaties (204), pacific settlement of disputes (193), international law in general (175), polar regions (175), international criminal law (163), coercion and use of force (154), conduct of armed conflict (law of war) (145), maritime navigation and transportation (134), jurisdiction of the state (27), general works (22), international conferences (16), neutrality (12), sources of international law (7), and state responsibility (6); *Part 2* - international economic relations (1408 entries), international relations (794), international aspects of scientific and technological affairs (141), environmental cooperation (123), communication and transport (107), social affairs (86), legal cooperation (41), and cultural relations (36).

The bibliography includes Canadian writings defined in a broad sense. It lists publications published in Canada, irrespective of the status of the writer, and published abroad by Canadian nationals and permanent residents, including publications of those who published before their coming to Canada. Publications of temporary residents are included for the period while they resided in Canada, but those of former Canadians are included for the longer period during which they maintained a close association with Canada. Single works by several authors, one of whom at least is Canadian, are also included. It should be mentioned that because of the mobility of an educated population, the Canadian status of an author is sometimes a difficult one to determine. Inacurracies and omissions are probably impossible to avoid entirely.

Finally, the bibliography includes a small number of non-Canadian publications dealing specifically with subjects of special interest to Canada. The last category includes publications which fall mainly into two groups: (a) those dealing with *Commonwealth matters*, such as the international status of British Dominions (23 entries), the Commonwealth of Nations (44 entries), Canadian relations with the British Empire and the Commonwealth (16 entries), and a handful of common topics concerning citizenship, extradiction, treaties and trade; and (b) those dealing with *Canadian-American relations*, such as boundaries (58 entries), boundary waters, including the Great Lakes, and the St. Lawrence and Columbia rivers (62 entries), the Arctic (14 entries), fisheries (23 entries), pacific settlements of disputes (26 entries), relations with the United States in general (47 entries), and a few specific topics of mutual interest such as trade, foreign investment and corporations or environmental cooperation.

METHODOLOGY AND ORGANIZATION

The bibliography is arranged by subject, and is divided into two parts: 1) public international law: doctrine and institutions; and 2) international relations: legal implications. The two parts are subdivided into 32 main topics, and further into 269 sections. The classification scheme used in the first part follows, with some modifications, the Model Plan for Classification of Documents Concerning State Practice in the Field of Public International Law, adopted by the Council of Europe in June 1968. This scheme is increasingly being accepted as a standard classification on the subject, especially in Europe. The second part follows a logical arrangement from the more general writings on international relations to the more specific topics dealing with economic relations, transportation and communication, science and technology, the environment, social, cultural and legal cooperation. This part interprets international relations more broadly, listing many entries which may be viewed as policy oriented, but nevertheless may have legal implications. This is done mainly to assist the user with what is available. Some subject headings contain cross references to other related topics. When a subject has been more selective, such as "Biographies" or "Relations with other Countries," it is indicated in the heading.

Each entry has a full bibliographical description, including the main entry under author(s), corporate name or conference, followed by title and imprint, although author entries were preferred. Inconsistencies in the spelling of authors names were eliminated when possible, generally by adopting the latest form used by the writer. In some cases, however, it was not possible to solve the conflict and names were left as they appear on publications. Titles in English are capitalized, while those in French are not. Each entry has a consecutive number in bold type face for ease of identification in the indexes. When necessary, useful annotations were added, referrring to previous editions, title in the other language, historical background, as well as contents notes and book reviews. The entries are arranged alphabetically by author and title, usually under one subject, the more specific one. Only a small number of entries (332), namely those dealing with more than one subject, are listed under more than one heading.

The bibliography contains an index of authors, with numerical references to writings and reviews, and a combined index of corporate names, conferences and series. It has been produced by computer, which made many publishing improvements possible, including the cut-off date as recently as March 1, 1983.

ACKNOWLEDGEMENTS

In the preparation of this bibliography I would like to convey my gratitude to a number of persons. In addition to Professor Ronald St. John Macdonald, I am indebted to other colleagues for their unfailing encouragement and interest, especially Professors Douglas M. Johnston, and Edgar Gold, as well as Mr. Rik Davidson of the University of Toronto Press. I am also particularly grateful to Leslie A. Foster for invaluable assistance with computer programming, to Mary Boite, Debbie Kilpatrick, Sarah Martin, Marie Wiktor, and Jane Lombard for technical contribution and research support. Last but not least, I wish to express my sincere appreciation to the many custodians of human knowledge, the librarians, who all responded to my many queries, some of them with valuable additional information.

Dalhousie University
Halifax, Nova Scotia
October 2, 1983

Christian L. Wiktor
Professor of Law
and Law Librarian

PART ONE

PUBLIC INTERNATIONAL LAW: DOCTRINE AND INSTITUTIONS

I. REFERENCE WORKS

A. Bibliographies and Indexes

Barrett, Jane R., and Beaumont, Jane. *A Bibliography of Works on Canadian Foreign Relations, 1976-1980.* Toronto: Canadian Institute of International Affairs; Ottawa: Norman Paterson School of International Affairs, Carleton University, 1981. xii, 306 p. **1**
Continues Page, Donald M., *A Bibliography of Works on Canadian Foreign Relations, 1971-1975* (Toronto, 1977. ix, 300 p.).
Review: Hélène Galarneau in (1982), 13 *Études Internationales* 407.

Barrett, Jane R., and McTavish, Mary. *Reference Aids in International Relations.* Toronto: University of Toronto Library, 1981. iv, 155 p. (University of Toronto. Library. Reference Series, No. 25) **2**

Brassard, Hélène. *Bibliographie sélective sur les politiques d'immigration dans la Communauté économique européenne.* Étude effectuée pour la Direction de la recherche du Ministère de l'immigration du Québec. Montréal: Direction de la recherche, 1978. 57 p. (Études et documents, no 7) **3**

Canada. Dept. of External Affairs. *Arctic Sovereignty: A Bibliography.* Ottawa, 1974. 6 leaves. **4**

Canada. Human Rights Commission. *Bibliography on Human Rights / Bibliographie sur les droits de la personne.* Ottawa: Canadian Human Rights Commission, 1979. iv, 262 p. (loose-leaf) **5**

"Canada and Foreign Affairs." 1st-17th, 1935-51. Toronto. **6**
This is a series of review articles of publications on Canada and foreign affairs, including a short bibliography, published annually in the *Canadian Historical Review* during 1935-1951.

Carleton University. Norman Paterson School of International Affairs. *Bibliography Series.* 1—, 1975—. Ottawa: Norman Paterson School of International Affairs, Carleton University. **7**
Individual bibliographies are listed separately.

Centre québécois de relations internationales. *Relations extérieures du Canada et du Québec: bibliographie.* 1978—. Québec: 1979—. Annual. **8**

Chew, Anne Rose (Cushman), and Churchill, Arthur Chester. *References on the Great Lakes-Saint Lawrence Waterway Project.* Prepared under the direction of Everett E. Edwards. Washington: Dept. of Agriculture, 1940. v, 189 p. (U.S. Dept. of Agriculture. Library. Bibliographical Contributions, No. 30, Ed. 2) **9**

Clark, Margaret, and Carroll, Francis M. *A Guide to Documents on International Relations in the University of Manitoba, Provincial and University of Winnipeg Libraries.* Winnipeg: University of Manitoba Libraries, 1972. iv, 129 p. (University of Manitoba. Libraries. Reference Series, No. 8) **10**

Cohen, Maxwell. "Some Bibliographical Problems of Public International Law." (1959-60), 6 *McGill Law Journal* 277-291. **11**

Deener, David R. "Canada-United States Treaties and Agreements: Including Those between the United States and the United Kingdom Affecting Canada (Bilateral - Excluding Postal Arrangements) 1782-1960." *In* Deener, David R., ed., *Canada-United States Treaty Relations* (Durham, N.C., 1963), pp. 196-231. **12**
This is a list of treaties.

Demers, Henri. *Les investissements étrangers au Canada et au Québec: essai de bibliographie.* Québec: Ministère de l'industrie et du commerce, Direction générale de l'administration, Centre de documentation, 1977. 83 p. **13**

Donneur, André P. *Politique étrangère canadienne: bibliographie 1972-1975.* Montréal: Université du Québec à Montréal, Département de science politique, 1976. iii, 50 leaves. (Université du Québec à Montréal. Département de science politique. Notes de recherche, no 1) **14**

Donneur, André P. *Politique étrangère du Canada: bibliographie 1976-1977.* Montréal: Université du Québec à Montréal, Département de science politique, 1978. vi, 26 leaves. (Université du Québec à Montréal. Département de science politique. Notes de recherche, no 14) **15**

Edwards, Everett Eugene, and Lowe, Edith (Johnston). *References on the Great Lakes-Saint Lawrence Waterway Project.* Washington: Dept. of Agriculture, 1936. v, 185 p. (U.S. Dept. of Agriculture. Library. Bibliographical Contributions, No. 30) **16**

Ervin, Linda. *The Council for Mutual Economic Assistance: A Selective Bibliography.* Ottawa: Norman Paterson School of International Affairs, Carleton University, 1975. ii, 97 p. (Carleton University. Norman Paterson School of International Affairs. Bibliography Series, 2) **17**

Flenley, Ralph. *Post-War Problems, a Reading List; a Select Bibliography on Post-War Settlement and Reconstruction.* Toronto: Canadian Institute of International Affairs, 1943. 62 p. **18**

Glazebrook, G.P. de T. "Canada and Foreign Affairs." (1935), 16 *Canadian Historical Review* 179-190. **19**
Contents: Survey of Materials on Canada and Foreign Affairs: Sources.- Later Works (General Books.- The Peace Settlement and the League.- Relations with the United States.- Relations with Europe.- Relations with the Far East.- Economic Relations.- Contemporary Problems.- Bibliography).

Granatstein, J.L. "Foreign and Defence Policy." *In* Granatstein, J.L., and Stevens, Paul, eds., *Canada since 1867: A Bibliographical Guide* (2d ed., Toronto, 1977), pp. 37-63. **20**

Green, Leslie C. "Selected Bibliography on International Law as Applied by International Courts and Tribunals." *In* Schwarzenberger, Georg, *International Law* (2d ed., London, 1949), vol.1, pp. 631-667. **21**

Green, Leslie C. "Selected Bibliography on Some Aspects of the Principle of Self-Defence." (1958), 48 *International Law Association, Report of Conference* 622-628. **22**

Hajnal, Peter I. *Guide to United Nations Organization, Documentation & Publishing for Students, Researchers, Librarians.* Dobbs Ferry, N.Y.: Oceana Publications, 1978. xxviii, 450 p. **23**
Review: Patricia J. Appavoo in (1979), 34 *International Journal* 736-738.

Hajnal, Peter I. *The United Nations and Its Publications: A Bibliographical Guide.* Toronto: Reference Dept., University of Toronto Library, 1976. vi, 37 p. (University of Toronto. Library. Reference Series, No. 20) **24**

Hymer, Stephen. "La firme plurinationale; une bibliographie sélective." (1971), 2 *Études Internationales* 115-129. **25**

Kohler, Gernot. *Arms Control and Disarmament: A Bibliography of Canadian Research, 1965-1980.* Ottawa: Dept. of National Defence, Operational Research and Analysis Establishment, 1981. v, xiii, 168 p. (ORAE Extra-Mural Paper, No. 15) **26**

Langlois, Micheline. *Canadian Bibliography on International Law / Bibliographie canadienne en droit international (1967-1977).* Ottawa: Canadian Council on International Law, 1978. iv, 53 p. **27**
Published as a special issue of the *Canadian Council on International Law Bulletin*, Vol. 5, No. 2 (1978).

Le Garignon, John P. *Relations internationales: bibliographie-guide.* Cap-Rouge, Québec: Séminaire St-Augustin, Bibliothèque, 1975? v, 98 p. (Séminaire St-Augustin. Bibliothèque. Document, 221) **28**

Legault, Albert. *Peace-Keeping Operations: Bibliography.* Paris: International Information Center on Peace-Keeping Operations, 1967. 203 p. **29**

Li, Kuo Lee. "Air and Space Law Research and Materials: A Bibliographical Essay." (1980), 5 *Annals of Air and Space Law* 720-743. **30**

Li, Kuo Lee. *World Wide Space Law Bibliography.* Preface by Nicolas Mateesco Matte. Montreal: McGill, Institute and Center of Air and Space Law; Toronto: distributed by Carswell, 1978. lviii, 700 p. **31**
At head of title: McGill, Institute and Center of Air and Space Law.
Reviews: Eilene Galloway in (1980), 74 *American Journal of International Law* 253-254; Ludwig Weber in (1980), 40 *Zeitschrift für Ausländisches Öffentliches Recht und Völkerrecht* 652-653; unsigned in (1979), 7 *Journal of Space Law* 81.

Lodrup, P. "Air Law: Bibliography 1966-67." (1967), *Yearbook of Air and Space Law* 265-277. **32**

McDorman, Ted L. "Researching Law of the Sea." (1982), 10 *International Journal of Legal Information* 147-157. **33**

McDorman, Ted L.; Beauchamp, Kenneth P.; and Johnston, Douglas M. *Maritime Boundary Delimitation: An Annotated Bibliography.* Lexington, Mass.: Lexington Books, c1983. xiii, 207 p. **34**

McGill University. Institute of Air and Space Law. *Catalogue of Air and Space Law Materials, July 1, 1965.* Montreal: McGill University, 1965. 103 leaves. **35**

A revision and up-dating of the first *Catalogue of Air and Space Law Materials*, prepared by Professor Peter Sand and issued in July 1963. Prepared by the staff of the McGill Law Library.

McGill University. Library. Reference Dept. *International Relations: A Student's Guide to Reference Resources.* Montreal: McGill University, McLennan Library, Reference Dept., 1973. 15 p. **36**

Motiuk, Laurence, and Grant, Madeline. *A Reading Guide to Canada in World Affairs, 1945-1971.* Toronto: Canadian Institute of International Affairs, c1972. x, 313 p. **37**

"Orientation bibliographique." *In* Painchaud, Paul, ed., *Le Canada et le Québec sur la scène internationale* (Québec, 1977), pp. 575-602. **38**

Page, Donald M. *A Bibliography of Works on Canadian Foreign Relations, 1945-1970.* Toronto: Canadian Institute of International Affairs, 1974 (c1973). x, 442 p. **39**

Review: G.P. de T. Glazebrook in (1975), 56 *Canadian Historical Review* 80-81.

Page, Donald M. *A Bibliography of Works on Canadian Foreign Relations, 1971-1975.* Toronto: Canadian Institute of International Affairs, 1977. ix, 300 p. **40**

Continues the author's *A Bibliography of Works on Canadian Foreign Relations, 1945-1970.* Continued by Barrett, Jane R., and Beaumont, Jane, *A Bibliography of Works on Canadian Foreign Relations, 1976-1980* (Toronto, 1981. xii, 306 p.).

Pépin, Eugène. *Bibliographie du droit aérien et questions connexes/ Bibliography of Air Law and Related Problems.* Montreal: The Author, 1959. ix, 69 leaves. **41**

Roberts, Debra. *Selected Bibliography on East-West Commercial Relations.* Ottawa: East-West Project, Carleton University, 1980. 134 p. **42**

Roseman, Daniel. "European Community/Canada Relations: A Selected Bibliography, 1976-1981." (1980-81), 4 *Revue d'Intégration Européenne* 327-334. **43**

"Selected Bibliography of Literature on Canadian-American Relations." (1974), 28 *International Organization* 1015-1023. **44**

Reprinted in Fox, Annette Baker, and others, *Canada and the United States* (New York, 1976), pp. 421-429.

Smith, Gaddis G. "Selected Readings on Canadian External Policy." *In* Keenleyside, Hugh L., and others, *The Growth of Canadian Policies in External Affairs* (Durham, N.C., 1960), pp. 164-168. **45**

Smith, Gordon S. *A Selected Bibliography on International Peace-Keeping.* Ottawa, 1964. 24 p. (SAG Memorandum, 64/M.2) **46**

At head of title: Defence Research Board, Department of National Defence, Systems Analysis Group.

Thibault, Claude J. *Canada's External Relations / Les relations extérieures du Canada, 1600-1969: A Bibliography/ Une bibliographie.* Rochester, N.Y., 1972. 2 vols. (xlii, 969 leaves) **47**

Thesis (Ph.D.), University of Rochester, 1973. Abstracted in (1973), 34 *Dissertation Abstracts International* 2538-A. (University Microfilms, Ann Arbor, No. 73-25859). See also the author's *Bibliographia Canadiana* (Don Mills, Ont., Longman Canada, c1973. lxiv, 795 p.).

Thomson, Jennifer. *The Law of the Sea: With Special Reference to Canada: A Select Bibliography.* Ottawa: Norman Paterson School of International Affairs, Carleton University, 1976. ii, 74 p. (Carleton University. Norman Paterson School of International Affairs. Bibliography Series, 4) **48**

Vogel, Robert. *A Breviate of British Diplomatic Blue Books, 1919-1939.* Montreal: McGill University Press, 1963. xxxv, 474 p. **49**
Continues the task undertaken by Temperley and Penson in their *A Century of Diplomatic Blue Books, 1814-1914.*
Reviews: Michael G. Fry in (1963), 44 *Canadian Historical Review* 359-360; Lionel Groulx in (1962-63), 16 *Revue d'Histoire de l'Amérique Française* 598-599.

Wiktor, Christian L. *Canadian Bibliography of International Law.* Issued for the Canadian Council on International Law. Halifax: Dalhousie Law School, 1981. xxvi, 861 p. (computer print-out) **50**
Review: Leslie C. Green in (1980), 28 *Chitty's Law Journal* 154.

Wiktor, Christian L., and Foster, Leslie A. *Marine Affairs Bibliography: A Comprehensive Index to Marine Law and Policy Literature.* v.1—, 1980—. Halifax: Dalhousie Law School, c1980—. Quarterly, with annual cumulation. **51**
Prepared under the auspices of Dalhousie Ocean Studies Programme.
Reviews: Donald M. McRae in (1981), 19 *Canadian Yearbook of International Law* 448-449; Pauline N. Richards in (1981), 8 *Maritime Policy and Management* 65-66; Adolf Sprudzs in (1981), 9 *International Journal of Law Libraries* 40.

B. Periodicals and Continuations

Annals of Air and Space Law / Annales de droit aérien et spatial. v.1—, 1976—. Montreal: Institute and Centre of Air and Space Law; Toronto: Carswell; Paris: A. Pedone. Annual. **52**
Editor: 1976—, Nicolas Mateesco Matte.
Reviews:
Volume 1: Leslie C. Green in (1978), 16 *Canadian Yearbook of International Law* 447-449; Kay Hailbronner in (1977), 37 *Zeitschrift für Ausländisches Öffentliches Recht und Völkerrecht* 805-806; Oliver J. Lissitzyn in (1977), 71 *American Journal of International Law* 833-834; Chin-Shih Tang in (1978), 10 *Ottawa Law Review* 467-471; Aart van Wijk in (1977), 2 *Air Law* 58-60.
Volume 2: Isabella H.Ph. Diederiks-Verschoor in (1978), 25 *Netherlands International Law Review* 297-298; Isabella H.Ph. Diederiks-Verschoor in (1978), 3 *Air Law* 136; Maurice Tancelin in (1979), 20 *Cahiers de Droit* 656-657.
Volume 3: Aart van Wijk in (1979), 4 *Air Law* 125-126.
Volume 4: Harry H. Almond, Jr., in (1982), 76 *American Journal of International Law* 707; Isabella H.Ph. Diederiks-Verschoor in (1981), 28 *Netherlands International Law Review* 101; Olivier Nicoloff in (1980), 11 *Études Internationales* 578-579; Aart van Wijk in (1980), 5 *Air Law* 125-126.
Volume 5: Aart van Wijk in (1981), 6 *Air Law* 123-124.
Volume 6: Aart van Wijk in (1982), 7 *Air Law* 135-136.

Behind the Headlines. v.1—, 1940—. Toronto: Canadian Institute of International Affairs. Six issues a year. **53**
A series of pamphlets on current problems, most of them of international interest.

Canada in World Affairs. v.1—. Toronto: Published under the auspices of the Canadian Institute of International Affairs by Oxford University Press, 1941—. Each volume covers about two years. **54**
Contents: v. 1. The Pre-War Years, by Frederic H. Soward, J.F. Parkinson, Norman A.M. MacKenzie, and T.W.L. MacDermot (1941. 343 p.).- v. 2. Two Years of War, 1939-1941, by Robert MacGregor Dawson (1943. 432 p.).- v. 3. September 1941 to May 1944, by Charles Cecil Lingard, and Reginald George Trotter (1950. 240 p.).- v. 4. From Normandy to Paris, 1944-1946, by Frederic Hubert Soward (1950. 359 p.).- v. 5. From UN to NATO, 1946-1949, by Robert A. Spencer (1959. 447 p.).- v. 6. 1949 to 1950, by W.E.C. Harrison (1957. 374 p.).- v. 7. September 1951 to October 1953, by B.S. Keirstead (1956. 268 p.).- v. 8. 1953 to 1955, by Donald C. Masters (1959. 223 p.).- v. 9. October 1955 to June 1957, by James George Eayrs (1959. 291 p.).- v. 10. 1957 to 1959, by Trevor Lloyd (1968. 253 p.).- v. 11. 1959-1961, by Richard A. Preston (1965. 300 p.).- v. 12. 1961-1963, by Peyton V. Lyon (1968. 555 p.).- v. 13. 1963-1965, by Charlotte Girard (1980. 372 p.).
Reviews:
Volume 1: Thomas-A. Birch in (1941-42), 17/2 *Actualité Économique* 489; Robert A. MacKay in (1942-43), 22 *Dalhousie Review* 128-129; Francis R. Scott in (1940-41), 10 *University of Toronto Quarterly* 120-122; unsigned in (1941-42), 4 *University of Toronto Law Journal* 440.
Volume 2: Thomas-A. Birch in (1945-46), 21/1 *Actualité Économique* 492-493; Samuel Mack Eastman in (1944), 38 *American Journal of International Law* 316-317; W.B. MacKinnon in (1944), 10 *Canadian Journal of Economics and Political Science* 114-115; William L. Morton in (1943), 24 *Canadian Historical Review* 308-311.
Volume 3: H.F. Angus in (1951), 17 *Canadian Journal of Economics and Political Science* 262-263; Thomas-A. Birch in (1951-52), 27 *Actualité Économique* 181-183; John Bartlet Brebner in (1950-51), 6 *International Journal* 152-155; F.P. Chambers in (1951), 27 *International Affairs* 373-374; Edgar McInnis in (1951), 32 *Canadian Historical Review* 66-67.
Volume 4: Thomas-A. Birch in (1951-52), 27 *Actualité Économique* 182-183; John Bartlet Brebner in (1950-51), 6 *International Journal* 152-155; H.S. Ferns in (1951), 27 *International Affairs* 497; Frank MacKinnon in (1951), 17 *Canadian Journal of Economics and Political Science* 263-265; Edgar McInnis in (1951), 32 *Canadian Historical Review* 66-67.
Volume 5: H.S. Ferns in (1960), 36 *International Affairs* 147-148; Nicholas Mansergh in (1960), 41 *Canadian Historical Review* 73-74; William L. Morton in (1958-59), 14 *International Journal* 307-308.
Volume 6: George W. Brown in (1958-59), 14 *International Journal* 218-219; Gerald S. Graham in (1957), 33 *International Affairs* 488; Nicholas Mansergh in (1958), 39 *Canadian Historical Review* 76-78.
Volume 7: J.H. Aitchison in (1957-58), 37 *Dalhousie Review* 296-302; John Bartlet Brebner in (1955-56), 11 *International Journal* 225-226; Charles E. Carrington in (1957), 33 *International Affairs* 104; Kenneth McNaught in (1956), 37 *Canadian Historical Review* 276-278; John Meisel in (1958), 24 *Canadian Journal of Economics and Political Science* 283-284.
Volume 8: Douglas G. Anglin in (1958-59), 14 *International Journal* 308-310; H.S. Ferns in (1960), 36 *International Affairs* 414-415; G.S. French in (1960), 41 *Canadian Historical Review* 79-80; Mason Wade in (1960), 26 *Canadian Journal of Economics and Political Science* 164-165.
Volume 9: John C. Campbell in (1959-60), 15 *International Journal* 155-157; H.S. Ferns in (1960), 36 *International Affairs* 553-554; Nicholas Mansergh in (1960), 26 *Canadian Journal of Economics and Political Science* 643.
Volume 10: R.B. Byers in (1970), 51 *Canadian Historical Review* 91-94; H.S. Ferns in

(1970), 46 *International Affairs* 622-623; Jon B. McLin in (1968-69), 24 *International Journal* 378-382.
Volume 11: Lloyd Axworthy in (1965-66), 21 *International Journal* 133-134; David Cox in (1966), 47 *Canadian Historical Review* 293-294; H.S. Ferns in (1967), 43 *International Affairs* 414-415.
Volume 12: R.B. Byers in (1970), 51 *Canadian Historical Review* 92-94; H.S. Ferns in (1970), 46 *International Affairs* 622-623; Ronald Harvey Wagenberg in (1969), 2 *Canadian Journal of Political Science* 133.
Volume 13: H.S. Ferns in (1980-81), 57 *International Affairs* 528-529; Tobias Fisher under title: "Gerard's Canada in World Affairs," in (1981), *International Perspectives* 31-32 (July/Aug.); George Ignatieff in (1981), 62 *Canadian Historical Review* 220-222; Paul Pilisi in (1981), 12 *Études Internationales* 823-824; Donald C. Story in (1982), 15 *Canadian Journal of Political Science* 162-163.

Canadian Annual Review of Politics and Public Affairs. 1971— . Toronto: University of Toronto Press. **55**
Continues *Canadian Annual Review of Public Affairs,* 1901-1938, and *Canadian Annual Review,* 1960-70. Contains a regular section on "External Affairs and Defence," and other topics of international interest.

Canadian Yearbook of International Law / Annuaire Canadien de Droit International. v.1— , 1963— . Vancouver, B.C.: University of British Columbia Press. Annual. **56**
Published under the auspices of the Canadian Branch, International Law Association. Editor: 1963— , Charles B. Bourne. Contains: articles; notes and comments, including an annual section on Canadian practice in international law as reflected by the Dept. of External Affairs and in the House of Commons, and digest of important Canadian cases in public international law and conflict of laws; book reviews; index.
Reviews:
Volume 1: L. Erades in (1965), 12 *Netherlands International Law Review* 167-168; Pierre Fayon in (1965), 92 *Journal du Droit International* 818; Wolfgang G. Friedmann under title: "Canadian Approaches in International Law," in (1963-64), 19 *International Journal* 77-83; Leslie C. Green in (1964), 42 *Canadian Bar Review* 520-522; Charles Rousseau in (1964), 68 *Revue Générale de Droit International Public* 261; G.P.R. Tallin in (1962-65), 1 *Manitoba Law School Journal* 216-221; Robert R. Wilson in (1964), 58 *American Journal of International Law* 1044-1046.
Volume 2: L. Erades in (1965), 12 *Netherlands International Law Review* 315; Pierre Fayon in (1965), 92 *Journal du Droit International* 818; Leslie C. Green in (1965), 43 *Canadian Bar Review* 685-688; Robert R. Wilson in (1966), 60 *American Journal of International Law* 421-423.
Volume 3: Jacob Austin in (1964-66), 2 *University of British Columbia Law Review* 601-604; L. Erades in (19), 15 *Netherlands International Law Review* 68; Pierre Fayon in (1967), 94 *Journal du Droit International* 211; Leslie C. Green in (1966), 44 *Canadian Bar Review* 707-709; Robert R. Wilson in (1967), 61 *American Journal of International Law* 233-235.
Volume 4: Pierre Fayon in (1968), 95 *Journal du Droit International* 496-497; Leslie C. Green in (1967), 45 *Canadian Bar Review* 210-212; Harry R. Johnson in (1966-67), 5 *Alberta Law Review* 372-374; Robert R. Wilson in (1968), 62 *American Journal of International Law* 219-221; unsigned in (1970), 18 *American Journal of Comparative Law* 214.
Volume 5: Pierre Fayon in (1969), 96 *Journal du Droit International* 549-550; Robert R. Wilson in (1969), 63 *American Journal of International Law* 174-177; unsigned in (1970), 18 *American Journal of Comparative Law* 214.
Volume 6: Leslie C. Green in (1970), 48 *Canadian Bar Review* 199-202; Robert R. Wilson

in (1970), 64 *American Journal of International Law* 210-212 unsigned in (1970), 18 *American Journal of Comparative Law* 214.
Volume 7: Mahomed Ali Adam in (1971), 9 *Alberta Law Review* 157-163; Leslie C. Green in (1970), 48 *Canadian Bar Review* 824-826; Robert R. Wilson in (1971), 65 *American Journal of International Law* 229-232.
Volume 8: Mahomed Ali Adam in (1972), 10 *Alberta Law Review* 380-383; Robert R. Wilson in (1972), 66 *American Journal of International Law* 444-445.
Volume 9: Leslie C. Green in (1973), 51 *Canadian Bar Review* 725-727; K.R. Simmonds in (1973), 22 *International and Comparative Law Quarterly* 585-586; Robert R. Wilson in (1973), 67 *American Journal of International Law* 183-184.
Volume 10: Leslie C. Green in (1973), 51 *Canadian Bar Review* 725-727; D.V. Kerig in (1974), 12 *Alberta Law Review* 296-297; Edward G. Lee in (1974), 9 *University of British Columbia Law Review* 207-212; Robert R. Wilson in (1974), 68 *American Journal of International Law* 175-176.
Volume 11: Leslie C. Green in (1975), 53 *Canadian Bar Review* 446-448; Robert R. Wilson in (1975), 69 *American Journal of International Law* 228-229.
Volume 12: Forest L. Grieves in (1976), 70 *American Journal of International Law* 887-888; Michael F. Rutter in (1976), 14 *Alberta Law Review* 376-377.
Volume 13: Forest L. Grieves in (1977), 71 *American Journal of International Law* 388-389.
Volumes 13-14: Mohammad Ghouse in (1979), 19 *Indian Journal of International Law* 464-466.
Volume 14: Michael Bothe in (1979), 39 *Zeitschrift für Ausländisches Öffentliches Recht und Völkerrecht* 138-139; Marc Hilary Gold in (1978), 12 *University of British Columbia Law Review* 365-373.
Volume 15: Michael Bothe in (1979), 39 *Zeitschrift für Ausländisches Öffentliches Recht und Völkerrecht* 815-81.
Volume 16: Forest L. Grieves in (1980), 74 *American Journal of International Law* 985-986; D.H.N. Johnson in (1980), 14 *University of British Columbia Law Review* 381-383.
Volume 17: Forest L. Grieves in (1982), 76 *American Journal of International Law* 700-701; Rosalyn Higgins in (1981), 15 *University of British Columbia Law Review* 504-508; Edward G. Hudon in (1981), 11 *American Review of Canadian Studies* 121-123 (No. 1); Errol P. Mendes in (1981), 19 *Alberta Law Review* 330-331.
Volume 18: Forest L. Grieves in (1982), 76 *American Journal of International Law* 700-701.

Carleton University. Norman Paterson School of International Affairs. *Occasional Papers.* Ottawa: Norman Paterson School of International Affairs, 1974— . **57**
Began publication in 1974. Continues: Carleton University. School of International Affairs. Occasional Papers. Individual papers are listed separately.

Conference on Canadian-American Affairs. *Proceedings. 1st-4th, 1935-1941.* Boston, etc.: Published for the Carnegie Endowment for International Peace by Ginn, 1936-1941. **58**
Contains proceedings of the first conference held at St. Lawrence University, Canton, N.Y., June 17-22, 1935 (301 p.).- 2d held at Queen's University, Kingston, Ont., June 14-18, 1937 (274 p.).- 3d held at St. Lawrence University, Canton, N.Y., June 19-22, 1939 (250 p.).- 4th held at Queen's University, Kingston, Ont., June 23-26, 1941 (287 p.). In 1972, the St. Lawrence University at Canton, N.Y., inaugurated the 'Canada Week Programs,' with papers presented annually on various aspects of Canadian-American relations, a selection of which is listed separately.

Conflict Quarterly. Journal of the Centre for Conflict Studies, University of New Brunswick. v.1—, Summer 1980—. Fredericton, N.B. Quarterly. **59**

Études Internationales. v.1—, 1970—. Québec: Centre québécois de relations internationales, affilié à l'Institut canadien des affaires internationales. Quarterly.
60

External Affairs. v.1-23, 1949-1971. Ottawa: Dept. of External Affairs. Monthly.
61
Also published in French under title: *Affaires extérieures.* Superseded by *International Perspectives.*

International Journal. v.1—, 1946—. Toronto: Canadian Institute of International Affairs. Quarterly. **62**
See also J.L. Granatstein's "Looking Backwards: The *Journal's* First Year," in (1977-78), 33 *International Journal* 115-127.

International Perspectives. Jan./Feb. 1972—. Ottawa: Dept. of External Affairs. Bi-monthly. **63**
Contains a very useful Reference Section, which includes 'Treaty Information.' Also published in French under title: *Perspectives internationales.* Supersedes *External Affairs.*

New Directions in Ocean Law, Policy and Management. v.1—, 1980—. Halifax: Dalhousie Ocean Studies Programme. Quarterly. **64**

Ocean Yearbook. 1—, 1978—. Chicago: University of Chicago Press. Annual. **65**
Sponsored by the International Ocean Institute. Editors: Elisabeth Mann Borgese (Dalhousie University), and Norton Ginsburg (University of Chicago).

Revue d'Intégration Européenne / Journal of European Integration. v.1—, Sept. 1977—. Montréal: Centre d'études et de documentation européennes de l'Université de Montréal. Three times a year. **66**

University of Windsor Seminar on Canadian-American Relations. *Proceedings.* 1st—, 1959—. Windsor: University of Windsor Press. **67**
The seminars are held annually, usually at the University of Windsor. The 7th in 1965 was called *Conference.* The proceedings of the first seminar were not published; some were called *Papers*; later volumes have a distinctive title; editors vary.

Yearbook of Air and Space Law / Annuaire de Droit Aérien et Spatial. 1965-67. Montreal: McGill-Queen's University Press. 1967-70. Annual. **68**
Issued by the Institute of Air and Space Law, McGill University. Editor: 1965-67, René H. Mankiewicz.
Reviews:
Volume 1965: J.E.S. Fawcett in (1968), 44 *International Affairs* 90-91; C. Granger in (1968), 46 *Canadian Bar Review* 332-336; Paul de La Pradelle in (1967), 30 *Revue Générale de l'Air et de l'Espace* 441-442; Eugène Pépin in (1968), 95 *Journal du Droit International* 217; A. Beatty Rosevear in (1969), 19 *University of Toronto Law Journal* 102-104; Howard J. Taubenfeld in (1967-68), 66 *Michigan Law Review* 1321-1325; Robert K. Woetzel in (1968), 62 *American Journal of International Law* 804-805.
Volume 1966: Bozidar Bakotić in (1971), 18 *Jugoslovenska Revija za Medunarodno Pravo* 143; S. Bhatt in (1969), 9 *Indian Journal of International Law* 281-283.
Volume 1967: S. Houston Lay in (1972), 66 *American Journal of International Law* 695; K. Venkata Raman in (1972), 12 *Indian Journal of International Law* 510-511.

C. Biographies (Selected)

Aulis, Hartley L. *Loring Christie: Canada's Unknown Influential Diplomat.* Lennoxville, Que., 1972. 145 leaves. **69**
    Thesis (M.A.), Bishop's University, 1973.

Ayre, William Burton. *Mr. Pearson and Canada's Revolution by Diplomacy.* Montreal, c1966. x, 285 p. **70**

Bruchési, Jean. *Souvenirs d'ambassade: mémoires 1959-1972.* Montréal: Fides, 1976. 183 p., 12 leaves of plates, maps. **71**
    Canadian diplomat. Ambassador to Spain, 1959-64, and to Morocco 1962-69. Continues: *Souvenirs à vaincre (1901-1959),* published in 1974.

Cadieux, Marcel. *Premières armes.* Montréal: Le Cercle du Livre de France, 1951. 206 p. **72**
    Reminiscences of a member of the Canadian diplomatic corps at London and Brussels, 1944-46.

Chevrier, Lionel. "The Practical Diplomacy of Lester Pearson." (1973-74), 29 *International Journal* 122-135. **73**

Claxton, Brooke. "Vincent Massey: High Commissioner for Canada." (1936), 139 *Fortnightly* 295-301. **74**

Côté, Yvon. "Alejandro Alvarez et son droit de la vie." (1952-53), 3 *Thémis* 156-170. **75**

Dobell, Peter C., and Willmot, Robert. "John Holmes." (1977-78), 33 *International Journal* 104-114. **76**

Dupuy, Pierre. "Mission à Vichy: Novembre 1940." (1966-67), 22 *International Journal* 395-401. **77**

Garner, Joseph John Saville. "Canadian Diplomacy; the Memoirs of Two Public Servants." (1974), 64 *Round Table* 85-94. **78**
    This is a review article of Lester B. Pearson, *Mike* (Toronto, 1972, vol. 1); and Arnold Heeney, *The Things That Are Caesar's* (Toronto, 1972).

Granatstein, J.L. *A Man of Influence: Norman A. Robertson and Canadian Statecraft 1929-68.* Ottawa: Deneau Publishers, c1981. xv, 488 p., 16 p. of plates. **79**
    Reviews: Arthur J. Andrew in (1981), 61 *Dalhousie Review* 366-368; James George Eayrs in (1981), 62 *Canadian Historical Review* 525-528; John Starnes under title: "Granatstein's Norman Robertson" in (1981), *International Perspectives* 28-29 (July/Aug.); Burke Trend in (1981-82), 37 *International Journal* 480-483.

Heeney, Arnold D.P. *The Things That Are Caesar's ; Memoirs of a Canadian Public Servant.* Edited by Brian D. Heeney. Foreword by John W. Holmes. Toronto: University of Toronto Press, 1972. xiv, 218 p. **80**
    Arnold Danford Patrick Heeney (1902-1970), a Canadian diplomat, was Under Secretary of State for External Affairs from 1949 to 1952, Canada's representative to the North Atlantic Council and the O.E.E.C. from 1952 to 1953, and Canada's Ambassador to the United States during 1953-57, and 1959-62. At the time of his death in 1970, he was Chairman of the Canadian sections of the International Joint Commission and the Canada-United States Permanent Joint Board on Defence (See *Macmillan Dictionary of Canadian Biography,* Toronto, 1978, pp. 348-349).

Ignatieff, George. "General A.G.L. McNaughton: A Soldier in Diplomacy." (1966-67), 22 *International Journal* 402-414. **81**

Keenleyside, Hugh L. *Memoirs of Hugh L. Keenleyside.* Toronto: McClelland and Stewart, 1981-82. 2 vols. **82**
Contents: v.1. Hammer the Golden Day (526 p.).- v.2. On the Bridge of Time (647 p.).
Review: Donald C. Story in (1981-82), 37 *International Journal* 483-485 (of vol. 1).

LePan, Douglas. *Bright Glass of Memory: A Set of Four Memoirs.* Toronto: McGraw-Hill Ryerson, c1979. 245 p. **83**

Manion, James Patrick. *A Canadian Errant; Twenty-Five Years in the Canadian Foreign Service.* Edited by Guy Sylvestre. Toronto: Ryerson Press, 1960. 196 p. **84**
Reviews: Gaddis G. Smith in (1960-61), 16 *International Journal* 184-185; Melville H. Watkins in (1962), 43 *Canadian Historical Review* 352.

Massey, Vincent. *What's Past Is Prologue; the Memoirs of the Right Honourable Vincent Massey.* Toronto: Macmillan, 1963. 540 p. **85**
Charles Vincent Massey (1887-1967), was appointed first Canadian Minister to the United States (1926-30), Canadian High Commissioner in London (1935-1946), and later Governor General of Canada (1952-1959).

McGillicuddy, Owen E. "Canada's First Envoy." (1928), *North American Review* 257-264. **86**
A sketch of the life of Vincent Massey, Canada's first Minister to the United States.

McNally, George Frederick. *Odlum: Canada's First Ambassador to China.* Edmonton, 1977. vi, 185 leaves. **87**
Thesis (M.A.), University of Alberta, 1977.

McWhinney, Edward. "Wolfgang Friedmann and Eclectic Legal Philosophy." (1972-73), 6 *Indiana Law Review* 169-171. **88**

Munro, John A., and Inglis, Alex I. "The Atomic Conference 1945 and the Pearson Memoirs." (1973-74), 29 *International Journal* 90-109. **89**

Pearson, Lester B. *Mike; the Memoirs of the Right Honourable Lester B. Pearson.* Toronto: University of Toronto Press, c1972-75. 3 vols. **90**
Memoirs of Lester Bowles Pearson (1897-1972), Canadian diplomat, and Prime Minister of Canada (1963-68). He joined the Department of External Affairs in 1928, and after serving in various positions became the Secretary of State for External Affairs from 1948 to 1957. Mr. Pearson was very active in international organizations and conferences and became Chairman of the Commission on International Development for the World Bank in August 1968. Also published New York, Quadrangle Books, 1972-75. Volumes 2 and 3 edited by John Munro and Alex I. Inglis.
Contents: v. 1. 1897-1948.- v. 2. 1948-1957.- v. 3. 1957-1968.
Reviews: Peter C. Dobell under title: "A Matter of Balance," in (1972-73), 28 *International Journal* 315-324 (of vol. 1); Denis Stairs in a review article under title: "Present in Moderation: Lester Pearson and the Craft of Diplomacy," in (1973-74), 29 *International Journal* 143-153 (of vol. 2); Bruce Thordarson in a review article under title: "Posture and Policy: Leadership in Canada's External Affairs," in (1975-76), 31 *International Journal* 666-691 (of vol. 3).

Pickersgill, J.W. *My Years with Louis St. Laurent: A Political Memoir.* Toronto: University of Toronto Press, c1975. viii, 334 p. **91**
Reviews: Bruce Thordarson in a review article under title: "Posture and Policy: Leadership in Canada's External Affairs," in (1975-76), 31 *International Journal* 666-691.

Pope, Maurice Arthur. *Soldiers and Politicians; Memoirs.* Toronto: University of Toronto Press, 1962. viii, 462 p. **92**
Memoirs of Lieut.-Gen. Maurice Arthur Pope (born in 1889), diplomat and army officer, Chairman of the Canadian Joint Staff Mission in Washington (1942-44), Chief of the Canadian Military Mission to Berlin (1945-50), and Ambassador to Belgium (1950-53), and Spain (1953-56).

Rankin, Bruce. "Personal Reflections on the Life of a Canadian Diplomat." *In* Splete, Allen P., ed., *Canadian-American Relations: Continuing a Needed Dialogue* (Canton, N.Y., 1975), pp. 76-90. **93**
Bruce Rankin was Consul General of Canada in New York.

Reid, Escott. *Envoy to Nehru.* Delhi: Oxford University Press, 1981. x, 301 p., 5 p. of plates. **94**
Reviews: Milton Israel in (1981-82), 37 *International Journal* 485-487; Jean Roch Perron in (1982), 13 *Études Internationales* 594-596; Arthur G. Rubinoff in (1982), 15 *Canadian Journal of Political Science* 606-608.

Reid, Escott. "Memories of Louis St. Laurent, 1946-9." *In* Penlington, Norman, ed., *On Canada: Essays in Honour of Frank H. Underhill* (Toronto, 1971), pp. 71-82. **95**

Ritchie, Charles. *Diplomatic Passport: More Undiplomatic Diaries, 1946-1962.* Toronto: Macmillan of Canada, 1981. 200 p. **96**
Also published in First Laurentian Library edition, 1982 (Laurentian Library, 70).
Reviews: Robert Bothwell in (1981), 62 *Canadian Historical Review* 523-525; Terence A. Keenleyside in (1982), 15 *Canadian Journal of Political Science* 608-610.

Ritchie, Charles. *The Siren Years: A Canadian Diplomat Abroad, 1937-1945.* Toronto: Macmillan of Canada, 1974. 216 p. **97**
See also the author's *An Appetite for Life: The Education of a Young Diarist, 1924-1927* (Toronto, MacMillan, 1981. x, 173 p.; Laurentian Library, 68).
Reviews: Claude Bissell in (1974-75), 30 *International Journal* 162-163; Lovat Dickson in (1975), 56 *Canadian Historical Review* 215-217.

Roberts, James Alan. *The Canadian Summer: The Memoirs of James Alan Roberts.* Toronto: University of Toronto Press, 1981. viii, 253 p. **98**
Review: Robert Spencer in (1981-82), 37 *International Journal* 487-488.

Sherfield, Roger Mellor Makins. "On the Diplomatic Trail with LBP: Some Episodes 1930-1972." (1973-74), 29 *International Journal* 71-89. **99**

Smith, Arnold. *Stitches in Time: The Commonwealth in World Politics.* With Clyde Sanger. Don Mills, Ont.: General Pub., 1981. xix, 322 p., map. **100**
Reviews: Margaret P. Doxey in (1981-82), 37 *International Journal* 489-491; John English in (1982), 63 *Canadian Historical Review* 61-62; Philip Stuchen in (1982), 89 *Queen's Quarterly* 648-651.

Soward, Frederic H. "Inside a Canadian Triangle: The University, the CIIA, and the Department of External Affairs - A Personal Record." (1977-78), 33 *International Journal* 66-87. **101**

Speaight, Robert. *Vanier: Soldier, Diplomat and Governor General: A Biography.* London: Collins, 1970. 488 p., 15 plates, map. **102**
Biography of George Philias Vanier (1888-1967).
Review: James R. Mallory in (1971-72), 27 *International Journal* 325-328.

Stairs, Denis. "Present in Moderation: Lester Pearson and the Craft of Diplomacy." (1973-74), 29 *International Journal* 143-153. **103**

Thomson, Dale C. *Louis St. Laurent, Canadian.* Toronto: Macmillan of Canada, 1967. x, 564 p. **104**

Louis Stephen St. Laurent (1882-1973), was Prime Minister of Canada from 1948 to 1957. He was appointed Secretary of State for External Affairs in 1946, and participated in the U.N. Conference at San Francisco in 1945, and in U.N. General Assembly sessions in 1946 (London), and 1947 (New York). Also published in French, Montréal, Cercle du Livre de France, 1968.

Thordarson, Bruce. *Lester Pearson: Diplomat and Politician.* Toronto: Oxford University Press, 1974. ix, 245 p. (Canadian Lives) **105**

Thornton, A.P. "A Reserved Occupation." (1974-75), 30 *International Journal* 1-14. **106**

Willms, Abraham Martin. *Sir Robert Borden at the Paris Peace Conference.* Toronto, 1950. 198 leaves. **107**

Thesis (M.A.), University of Toronto, 1950.

D. Directories

Canadian Representatives Abroad. Dec. 1968—. Ottawa: Dept. of External Affairs. **108**

Irregular. Text in English and French; French text on inverted pages under title: *Représentants du Canada à l'étranger.* Continues in part: *Canadian Representatives Abroad and Representatives of Other Countries in Canada.*

Diplomatic Corps and Consular and Other Representatives in Canada. June 1969—. Ottawa: Dept. of External Affairs. **109**

Frequency varies. Text in English and French on inverted pages, each with separate paging. The French text has title: *Corps diplomatique et représentants consulaires et autres au Canada* (juin 1971—). Formerly *British and Foreign Government Representatives in Canada.- Canadian Representatives Abroad and Representatives in Canada of the British Commonwealth and Foreign Governments* (until March 1949).- *Diplomatic and Consular Representatives in Ottawa* (1949-1954).- *Diplomatic Corps* (1955-1969).

Ryback, P. *Canada: Non-Governmental Agencies in International Aid and Development, 1966/67.* Ottawa: External Aid Office, 1967. xiii, 113 leaves. **110**

University of British Columbia. Institute of International Relations. *Canadian Professors Concerned with International Problems: A Survey / Professeurs canadiens intéressés par des problèmes internationaux: résultats d'un sondage.* Vancouver, 1973. 286 p. **111**

Introduction signed by Mark W. Zacher.

University of British Columbia. Institute of International Relations. *Federal Government Departments and Agencies Concerned with International Problems: A Survey / Services gouvernementaux intéressés par des problèmes internationaux: résultats d'un sondage.* Vancouver, 1973. 75 p. **112**

E. Associations and Societies

Bowlby, Kathleen E. "The United Nations Association in Canada." (1952), 4 *External Affairs* 144-146. **113**

Canadian Bar Association. Committee on International Law. *Reports, 1922-36.* Ottawa, etc. **114**
   The reports of the Committee on International Law were printed in the *Proceedings of the Canadian Bar Association* for the following years: 1922 (vol. 7, pp. 271-276); 1925 (vol. 10, pp. 217-222); 1926 (vol. 11, pp. 354-357); 1927 (vol. 12, pp. 339-341); 1928 (vol. 13, pp. 223-237); 1929 (vol. 14, pp. 229-235); 1930 (vol. 15, pp. 209-223); 1931 (vol. 16, pp. 196-201); 1932 (vol. 17, pp. 129-133); 1933 (vol. 18, pp. 207-216); 1934 (vol. 19, pp. 204-207); 1935 (vol. 20, pp. 197-204); and 1936 (vol. 21, pp. 191-199).

Canadian Council on International Law. *Bulletin.* v.1—, 1974—. Ottawa. Quarterly. **115**

Canadian Council on International Law. *Proceedings of the Annual Conference / Conseil canadien de droit international. Travaux du congrès annuel.* 1st—, 1972—. Ottawa: Université d'Ottawa, Faculté de droit. **116**
   Each annual conference is devoted to a specific topic. Individual papers are listed separately.
   Contents: 1st (October 13-14, 1972): New Approaches to International Law.- 2d (October 12-13, 1973): The Next 25 Years in the International Law of Human Rights.- 3d (October 18-19, 1974): International Terrorism / Le terrorisme international.- 4th (October 24-25, 1975): The International Law of Development / Le droit international du développement.- 5th (October 22-23, 1976): Avoiding International Conflicts: 1) Law of the Sea Issues; 2) Non-Proliferation / Évitons les différends internationaux: 1) Le droit de la mer; 2) La non-prolifération nucléaire.- 6th (October 20-22, 1977): Canada-U.S. Relations - Cooperation and Dispute Settlement in the North American Context / Relations canado-américaines - coopération et règlement de différends dans le contexte nord-américain (joint proceedings with the Canada-United States Institute, published in (1978), 1 *Canada-United States Journal,* pp. 1-169).- 7th (October 22-28, 1978): International Human Rights / Les droits de la personne au plan international.- 8th (October 25-27, 1979): International Economic Law - Canadian Perspectives / Le droit économique international - perspectives canadiennes.- 9th (October 23-25, 1980): International Law and Canadian Foreign Policy in the 1980s / Le droit international et la politique étrangère du Canada au cours des années 80 (jointly sponsored with the United Nations Association in Canada).- 10th (October 29-31, 1981): International Law and the Practice of Law in Canada / Le droit international et la pratique du droit au Canada.- 11th (October 21-23, 1982): Communications and Information - International Legal Aspects.

Canadian Institute of International Affairs. *Annual Report / Rapport annuel.* 1933—. Toronto. **117**
   Now published in English and French. Report year ends June 30. Title varies: *Report on the Work; Annual Report.* The Institute was established in 1928, with Sir Robert Borden as its first elected president.

"The Canadian Institute of International Affairs." (1950), 2 *External Affairs* 55-57. **118**

Centre québécois de relations internationales. *Rapport d'activités.* Québec, 1974—. Annual. **119**
   Cover title: *Rapport annuel.*

"Conference of the International Law Association." (1964), 16 *External Affairs* 493-496. **120**

Green, Leslie C. "The International Law Association Conference at Copenhagen, 1950 (44th)." (1951), 4 *International Law Quarterly* 115-119. **121**

Green, Leslie C. "The International Legal Conference - New Delhi (December 28, 1953-January 2, 1954)." (1954), 3 *International and Comparative Law Quarterly* 484-489. **122**

Herperger, Donald John. *The League of Nations Society in Canada During the 1930's*. Regina, 1978. iii, 191 leaves. **123**
Thesis (M.A.), University of Regina, 1978. (National Library of Canada. Canadian Theses on Microfiche, No. 36950).

Inglis, Alex I. "The Institute and the Department." (1977-78), 33 *International Journal* 88-103. **124**
Refers to the Canadian Institute of International Affairs and the Dept. of External Affairs.

"International Law Association." (1910), 30 *Canadian Law Times* 628-630. **125**

Loranger, Louis J. "The International Congress of Law." (1907), 6 *Canadian Law Review* 386-397. **126**
The Congress was held at Portland, Maine, in 1907.

MacKenzie, Norman A.M. "The International Law Association: 34th Congress, 1926." (1927), 5 *Canadian Bar Review* 106-111. **127**

Manny, Carter. *The Canadian Institute of International Affairs, 1928 to 1939; an Attempt to Enlighten Canada's Foreign Policy*. Cambridge, Mass., 1971. 107 leaves. **128**
Thesis (B.A.), Harvard College, 1971.

McRae, Donald M. "Annual Conference of the Canadian Council on International Law." (1972), 10 *Canadian Yearbook of International Law* 278-282. **129**
Review of the first annual conference held in Ottawa on October 13 and 14, 1972.

McRae, Donald M. "Annual Conference of the Canadian Council on International Law." (1973), 11 *Canadian Yearbook of International Law* 280-284. **130**
Review of the second annual conference held in Ottawa on October 12 and 13, 1973.

McRae, Donald M. "Annual Conference of the Canadian Council on International Law." (1974), 12 *Canadian Yearbook of International Law* 267-271. **131**
Review of the third annual conference held in Ottawa on October 18 and 19, 1974.

McRae, Donald M. "Annual Conference of the Canadian Council on International Law." (1975), 13 *Canadian Yearbook of International Law* 323-328. **132**
Review of the fourth annual conference held in Ottawa on October 24 and 25, 1975.

McRae, Donald M. "Annual Conference of the Canadian Council on International Law." (1976), 14 *Canadian Yearbook of International Law* 317-322. **133**
Review of the fifth annual conference held in Ottawa on October 22 and 23, 1976.

McWhinney, Edward. "Coexistence, National and International: The First Annual Scientific Meeting of the International Law Association (Canadian Branch)." (1966), 4 *Canadian Yearbook of International Law* 216-219. **134**

Millar, Thomas B. "Commonwealth Institutes of International Affairs." (1977-78), 33 *International Journal* 5-27. **135**

Normand, Wilfrid Guild. "International Law Association Edinburgh Conference 1954: Address by the President." (1955), 5 *Chitty's Law Journal* 40-42, 50. **136**

Page, Donald M. "The Institute's 'Popular Arm': The League of Nations Society in Canada." (1977-78), 33 *International Journal* 28-65. **137**

Raffo, Peter. "The Founding of the League of Nations Union." (1977-78), 12 *Canadian Journal of History* 193-206. **138**

Samuels, Joseph W. "The Manila Conference on the Law of the World: Some Personal Reflections." (1978), 10 *Case Western Reserve Journal of International Law* 503-509. **139**

Weis, Paul. "The Development of International Law: Conference in Britain." (1946-47), 16 *Fortnightly Law Journal* 121-122. **140**

F. Primary Sources

For arbitration awards, see "Arbitration: Specific Cases" (p. 396); for publications of international organizations and conferences, see also "International Organizations" (p. 332), and "International Conferences" (p. 389).

1. GENERAL

"Canada's Treaty Records." (1958), 10 *External Affairs* 162-165. **141**

"Canadian Archives Service." (1952), 4 *External Affairs* 335-338. **142**

"Department of External Affairs Records." (1960), 12 *External Affairs* 791-797. **143**

Green, Leslie C. "The Raw Materials of International Law." (1980), 29 *International and Comparative Law Quarterly* 187-205. **144**

Nicholas, H.G. "Public Records: The Historian, the National Interest and Public Policy." (1964-65), 20 *International Journal* 33-44. **145**

Page, Donald M. "Unlocking Canada's Diplomatic Record." (1978-79), 34 *International Journal* 251-280. **146**

"The Problem of Records in External Affairs." (1952), 4 *External Affairs* 178-182. **147**

Stacey, Charles P. "Some Pros and Cons of the Access Problem." (1964-65), 20 *International Journal* 45-53. **148**

2. COLLECTIONS OF DOCUMENTS

Blanchette, Arthur E., ed. *Canadian Foreign Policy 1955-1965: Selected Speeches and Documents*. Toronto: McClelland and Stewart; Ottawa: Institute of Canadian Studies, Carleton University, c1977. xxv, 424 p. (Carleton Library, No. 103) **148a**

Continuation of R.A. MacKay's *Canadian Foreign Policy 1945-1954* (Toronto, c1970). Continued by the author's *Canadian Foreign Policy 1966-1976* (Toronto, c1980).
Review: Kim Richard Nossal in (1977-78), 33 *International Journal* 457-458.

Blanchette, Arthur E., ed. *Canadian Foreign Policy 1966-1976: Selected Speeches and Documents*. Toronto: Gage in association with the Institute of Canadian Studies, Carleton University, c1980. xvii, 366 p. (Carleton Library, No. 118) **149**
Continuation of the author's *Canadian Foreign Policy 1955-1965* (Toronto, c1977).

Canada. Dept. of External Affairs. *Documents on Canadian External Relations / Documents relatifs aux relations extérieures du Canada*. v.1—, 1909—. Ottawa: Dept. of External Affairs, 1967—. **150**
Volumes 1 and 2 were published separately in English and French; beginning with volume 3, the French and English editions are published in combined volumes.
Contents: v. 1. 1909-1918 (1967. ix, 906 p.).- v. 2. Conference of 1919, by Robert A. MacKay (1969. xxx, 237 p.).- v. 3. 1919-1925, by Lovell C. Clark (1970. cxviii, 1007 p.).-v. 4. 1926-1930, edited by Alex I. Inglis (1971. cxix, 1038 p.).- v. 5. 1931-1935, by Alex I. Inglis (1973. cxv, 818 p.).- v. 6. 1936-1939, by John A. Munro (1972. cxlv, 1334 p.).- v. 7. 1939-1941, pt. 1, by David R. Murray (1974. cxcix, 1167 p.).- v. 8. 1939-1941, pt. 2, by David R. Murray (1976. ccxlii, 1604 p.).- v. 9. 1942-1943, by John F. Hilliker (1980. xxxix, 1891 p.).- v. 12. 1946, edited by Donald M. Page (1977. xliv, 2120 p.).
Reviews: Ramsay Cook under title: "From Lord Grey to Lloyd George," in *International Journal* 186-193 (of vols. 1 and 2); J.L. Granatstein in (1975), 56 *Canadian Historical Review* 212-215 (of vol. 5); J.L. Granatstein in (1975), 56 *Canadian Historical Review* 212-215 (of vol. 6); J.L. Granatstein in (1977), 58 *Canadian Historical Review* 520-521 (of vols. 7 and 8); J.L. Granatstein in (1979), 60 *Canadian Historical Review* 109-110 (of vol. 12); Allison Taylor Hardy in (1978), *International Perspectives* 32-34 (Sept./Oct.) (of vol. 12); Norman Hillmer in (1973), 54 *Canadian Historical Review* 308-309 (of vol. 4); Frederic H. Soward in (1970), 51 *Canadian Historical Review* 324-325 (of vol. 2); Frederic H. Soward in (1972), 53 *Canadian Historical Review* 329-331 (of vol. 3); Charles P. Stacey in (1968), 49 *Canadian Historical Review* 423-424 (of vol. 1); unsigned under title: "After Versailles," in (1970), 22 *External Affairs* 449-451 (of vol. 3).

Canada. Dept. of External Affairs. *Documents relatifs aux relations entre le Canada et Terre-Neuve / Documents on Relations between Canada and Newfoundland*. Ottawa: Dept. of External Affairs, 1974—. **151**
Issued to mark the 25th anniversary of the confederation of Newfoundland with Canada.
Contents: v. 1. 1935-1949, edited by Paul Bridle (1974. lxxiv, 1446 p., maps).
Review: G.E. Panting in (1976), 57 *Canadian Historical Review* 217-218 (of vol. 1).

Canada. Dept. of External Affairs. *Reference Papers*. Ottawa: Information Services Division, Dept. of External Affairs, 1946?—. **152**
Irregular. A continuously numbered series of papers on various topics of public interest, including international affairs (e.g. No. 69. *The Department of External Affairs* (1953); No. 85. *Canada and the International Labour Organization* (1956); No. 87. *Canada and the World Meteorological Organization* (1956); No. 88. *Canada and I.C.A.O.* (1956); etc.). Some papers are reissued in revised editions. Also issued in French under title: *Pages documentaires*.

Canada. Dept. of External Affairs. *Statements and Speeches*. Ottawa: Information Services Division, Dept. of External Affairs, 1946—. **153**
A collection of statements and speeches by Canadian government officials on various topics relating to foreign relations of Canada. Includes indexes. For a chronological list,

see *A Bibliography of Works on Canadian Foreign Relations*, by Donald M. Page for 1945-1970 (Toronto, 1973), pp. 319-350, and for 1971-1975 (Ottawa, 1977), pp. 155-161, and by Jane R. Barrett, and Jane Beaumont for 1976-1980 (Toronto, 1982), pp. 231-273. Also issued in French under title: *Déclarations et discours*.

Canada. Parliament. *Papers Relating to the Conference Held at Washington in February, 1892, between Canadian Delegates and the U.S. Secretary of State upon the Several Subjects Mentioned*. Ottawa, 1893. 8 p. (Canada. Parliament, 1893. Sessional Papers, No. 52) **154**

Documents juridiques internationaux. v. 1—, sept. 1982—. Montréal: Société québécoise de droit international; Québec: Éditions Yvon Blais. Three times a year. Editors: Francis Rigaldies, Daniel Turp, and Carole Belleau. **155**
Contents: Actes des organisations et conférences internationales.- Accords internationaux.- Actes juridictionnels internationaux.- Actes unilatéraux étatiques.

MacKay, Robert A., ed. *Canadian Foreign Policy, 1945-1954; Selected Speeches and Documents*. Toronto: McClelland and Stewart, c1970. xxix, 407 p. **155a**
Continued by A.E. Blanchette's *Canadian Foreign Policy, 1955-1965* (Toronto, c1977).
Review: Clarence G. Redekop in (1972-73), 28 *International Journal* 375-380.

Manning, William Ray. *Diplomatic Correspondence of the United States: Canadian Relations, 1784-1860*. Washington: Carnegie Endowment for International Peace, 1940-1945. 4 vols., maps. (Carnegie Endowment for International Peace. Division of International Law. Publications) **156**
Reprinted Millwood, N.Y., Kraus Reprint, 1975.
Contents: I. 1784-1820. Documents 1-661.- II. 1821-1835. Documents 662-1192.- III. 1836-1848. Documents 1193-1853.- IV. 1849-1860. Documents 1854-2460.
Reviews: C. John Colombos in (1948), 2 *International Law Quarterly* 102-104 (of vols. 1-4); Albert B. Corey in (1941), 22 *Canadian Historical Review* 323-326 (of vol. 1); Albert B. Corey in (1942), 23 *Canadian Historical Review* 422-423 (of vol. 2); H. Lauterpacht in (1944), 21 *British Year Book of International Law* 245-246 (of vols. 1-3); Norman A.M. MacKenzie in (1941), 35 *American Journal of International Law* 421 (of vol. 1); Norman A.M. MacKenzie in (1942), 36 *American Journal of International Law* 748-749 (of vol. 2); unsigned in (1941), 19 *Canadian Bar Review* 699-700 (of vol. 1); and (1942), 20 *Canadian Bar Review* 888-889 (of vol. 2).

Riddell, Walter Alexander, ed. *Documents on Canadian Foreign Policy, 1917-1939*. Toronto: Oxford University Press, 1962. liii, 806 p. **157**
Reviews: Ramsay Cook in (1961-62), 17 *International Journal* 311-312; P.G. Cornell in (1963), 44 *Canadian Historical Review* 51-52; Rachel F. Wall in (1963), 39 *International Affairs* 150.

Swanson, Roger Frank, ed. *Canadian-American Summit Diplomacy, 1923-1973: Selected Speeches and Documents*. Toronto: McClelland and Stewart, c1975. xxii, 314 p. (Carleton Library, No. 81) **158**
Review: Donald J. Munton in (1976), 9 *Canadian Journal of Political Science* 331-332.

3. TREATIES AND AGREEMENTS

Canada. Dept. of External Affairs. *Treaties and Agreements Affecting Canada in Force between His Majesty and the United States of America, with Subsidiary Documents 1814-1913*. Compiled under the direction of Sir Robert Borden,

Secretary of State for External Affairs. Ottawa: Printed by J. de L. Taché, 1915. 301 p. **159**

Canada. Dept. of External Affairs. *Treaties and Agreements Affecting Canada in Force between His Majesty and the United States of America with Subsidiary Documents 1814-1925.* Compiled in the Department of External Affairs. Ottawa: Printed by F.A. Acland, 1927. viii, 578 p. **160**

Canada. Dept. of Trade and Commerce. *Papers Relating to Commercial Arrangements between Canada and Foreign Countries* (Collected to July 1, 1910). Ottawa, 1910. 84 p. **161**

Canada Treaty Series / Recueil des traités du Canada. 1928—. Ottawa: Queen's Printer, 1929—. **162**

Published in slip form, in a series numbered annually. Text in English and French on opposite pages. A French version was published separately until 1947/48. Indexes are issued annually, usually bearing the first number for the year (e.g. CTS 1975/1); some indexes are cumulated, and the years 1928-1964 are covered by a cumulated index published separately in 1967 (Ottawa: Queen's Printer, 1967. 388 p., bilingual, prepared by Marie-Louise Myrand). The years 1965-1974 are covered by a cumulated index published as CTS 1974/1. However, not all treaties concluded by Canada are published. A list of treaties concluded by Canada during a year can be found in the *Annual Review* of the Dept. of External Affairs. The texts of treaties negotiated before 1928 are to be found mainly in British sources. For more information, see Christian L. Wiktor, *Canadian Treaty Calendar / Répertoire des traités du Canada, 1928-1978* (London, etc., Oceana, 1982), vol. 1, pp. xvii, and subs.

Wiktor, Christian L. *Canadian Treaty Calendar / Répertoire des traités du Canada: 1928-1978.* London, Rome, New York: Oceana Publications, 1982 (c1983). 2 vols. **163**

Contents: v.1. Chronological Index; Numerical List.- v.2. Bilateral Treaty Index; Multilateral Treaty Index; Subject Index.

4. ANNUAL SURVEYS

Chen, Tung-Pi. "Annual Survey of Canadian Law: International Law." (1968-69), 3 *Ottawa Law Review* 573-590. **164**

Chen, Tung-Pi. "Annual Survey of Canadian Law: International Law." (1970-71), 4 *Ottawa Law Review* 525-539. **165**

Chen, Tung-Pi. "Annual Survey of Canadian Law: International Law." (1971-72), 5 *Ottawa Law Review* 499-510. **166**

Pharand, Donat. "Annual Survey of Canadian Law: International Law." (1977), 9 *Ottawa Law Review* 505-567. **167**

Covers a period of nearly five years, from 1972 to mid-1977.
Contents: I. Introduction.- II. Law of the Sea (pp. 507-526).- III. Sovereign, Diplomatic and Consular Immunities (pp. 526 536).- IV. Human Rights (pp. 536-552).- V. Treaty Ratification and Entry Into Force (pp. 552-567).

5. STATE PRACTICE

Beesley, J. Alan, ed. "Canadian Practice in International Law During 1969 as Reflected Mainly in Public Correspondence and Statements of the Department of External Affairs." (1970), 8 *Canadian Yearbook of International Law* 337-384. **168**

Beesley, J. Alan, ed. "Canadian Practice in International Law During 1972 as Reflected Mainly in Public Correspondence and Statements of the Department of External Affairs." (1973), 11 *Canadian Yearbook of International Law* 285-313. **169**

Beesley, J. Alan, and Bourne, Charles B., eds. "Canadian Practice in International Law During 1970 as Reflected Mainly in Public Correspondence and Statements of the Department of External Affairs." (1971), 9 *Canadian Yearbook of International Law* 276-311. **170**

Beesley, J. Alan, and Bourne, Charles B., eds. "Canadian Practice in International Law During 1971 as Reflected Mainly in Public Correspondence and Statements of the Department of External Affairs." (1972), 10 *Canadian Yearbook of International Law* 287-316. **171**

Carsen, Gary L., and Tanner, Susan. "Human Rights." In *Canadian Encyclopedic Digest (Ontario)*, 3d ed., 1979, title 74, vol. 14, 112 p. **172**

Copithorne, M.D., ed. "Canadian Practice in International Law During 1975 as Reflected Mainly in Public Correspondence and Statements of the Department of External Affairs." (1976), 14 *Canadian Yearbook of International Law* 323-343. **173**

Copithorne, M.D., ed. "Canadian Practice in International Law During 1976 as Reflected Mainly in Public Correspondence and Statements of the Department of External Affairs." (1977), 15 *Canadian Yearbook of International Law* 315-336. **174**

Copithorne, M.D., ed. "Canadian Practice in International Law During 1977 as Reflected Mainly in Public Correspondence and Statements of the Department of External Affairs." (1978), 16 *Canadian Yearbook of International Law* 359-377. **175**

Copithorne, M.D., ed. "Canadian Practice in International Law During 1978 as Reflected Mainly in Public Correspondence and Statements of the Department of External Affairs." (1979), 17 *Canadian Yearbook of International Law* 334-356. **176**

"Copyright." In *Canadian Encyclopedic Digest (Ontario)*, 3d ed., 1974, title 34, vol. 5, 82 p. **177**

De Mestral, Armand L.C., ed. "Canadian Practice in International Law During 1972 as Reflected in Resolutions of the House of Commons and in Government Statements in the House of Commons." (1973), 11 *Canadian Yearbook of International Law* 314-346. **178**

De Mestral, Armand L.C., ed. "Canadian Practice in International Law During 1973 as Reflected in Resolutions of the House of Commons and in Government

Statements in the House of Commons." (1974), 12 *Canadian Yearbook of International Law* 304-332. **179**

De Mestral, Armand L.C., ed. "Canadian Practice in International Law During 1974 as Reflected in Resolutions of the House of Commons and in Government Statements in the House of Commons." (1975), 13 *Canadian Yearbook of International Law* 374-395. **180**

De Mestral, Armand L.C., ed. "Canadian Practice in International Law During 1975 as Reflected in Resolutions of the House of Commons and in Government Statements in the House of Commons." (1976), 14 *Canadian Yearbook of International Law* 344-370. **181**

De Mestral, Armand L.C., ed. "Canadian Practice in International Law During 1976 as Reflected in Resolutions of the House of Commons and in Government Statements in the House of Commons." (1977), 15 *Canadian Yearbook of International Law* 337-372. **182**

De Mestral, Armand L.C., ed. "Canadian Practice in International Law During 1977 as Reflected in Resolutions of the House of Commons and in Government Statements in the House of Commons." (1978), 16 *Canadian Yearbook of International Law* 378-405. **183**

De Mestral, Armand L.C., ed. "Canadian Practice in International Law During 1978 as Reflected in Resolutions of the House of Commons and in Government Statements in the House of Commons." (1979), 17 *Canadian Yearbook of International Law* 357-395. **184**

De Mestral, Armand L.C., ed. "Canadian Practice in International Law During 1979 as Reflected in Resolutions of the House of Commons and in Government Statements in the House of Commons." (1980), 18 *Canadian Yearbook of International Law* 337-358. **185**

De Mestral, Armand L.C., ed. "Canadian Practice in International Law During 1980 as Reflected in Resolutions of the House of Commons and in Government Statements in the House of Commons." (1981), 19 *Canadian Yearbook of International Law* 347-375. **186**

Ettinger, Michael L. "Shipping." In *Canadian Encyclopedic Digest (Ontario)*, 3d ed., 1981, title 134, vol. 30, 281 p. **187**

Goldsmith, Immanuel. "Patents of Invention." In *Canadian Encyclopedic Digest (Ontario)*, 3d ed., 1981, title 107, vol. 24, 288 p. **188**

Gotlieb, Allan E., ed. "Canadian Practice in International Law During 1964 as Reflected in Correspondence and Statements of the Department of External Affairs." (1965), 3 *Canadian Yearbook of International Law* 315-348. **189**

Gotlieb, Allan E., ed. "Canadian Practice in International Law During 1965 as Reflected Mainly in Public Correspondence and Statements of the Department of External Affairs." (1966), 4 *Canadian Yearbook of International Law* 260-306. **190**

Gotlieb, Allan E., ed. "Canadian Practice in International Law During 1966 as Reflected Mainly in Public Correspondence and Statements of the Department of External Affairs." (1967), 5 *Canadian Yearbook of International Law* 253-293. **191**

Gotlieb, Allan E., ed. "Canadian Practice in International Law During 1967 as Reflected Mainly in Public Correspondence and Statements of the Department of External Affairs." (1968), 6 *Canadian Yearbook of International Law* 252-278. **192**

Gotlieb, Allan E., and Beesley, J. Alan, eds. "Canadian Practice in International Law During 1968 as Reflected Mainly in Public Correspondence and Statements of the Department of External Affairs." (1969), 7 *Canadian Yearbook of International Law* 298-339. **193**

Lawford, Hugh J., ed. "Canadian Practice in International Law During 1963." (1964), 2 *Canadian Yearbook of International Law* 271-315. **194**

Lawford, Hugh J., ed. "Canadian Practice in International Law During 1964 as Reflected in Public Statements." (1966), 4 *Canadian Yearbook of International Law* 220-259. **195**

Lawford, Hugh J., ed. "Canadian Practice in International Law During 1965 and 1966 as Reflected in Public Statements." (1967), 5 *Canadian Yearbook of International Law* 294-352. **196**

Lawford, Hugh J., ed. "Canadian Practice in International Law During 1965 and 1966 as Reflected in Public Statements." (1968), 6 *Canadian Yearbook of International Law* 279-329. **197**

Lee, Edward G., ed. "Canadian Practice in International Law During 1973 as Reflected Mainly in Public Correspondence and Statements of the Department of External Affairs." (1974), 12 *Canadian Yearbook of International Law* 272-303. **198**

Lee, Edward G., ed. "Canadian Practice in International Law During 1974 as Reflected Mainly in Public Correspondence and Statements of the Department of External Affairs." (1975), 13 *Canadian Yearbook of International Law* 329-373. **199**

Legault, L.H., ed. "Canadian Practice in International Law During 1979 as Reflected Mainly in Public Correspondence and Statements of the Department of External Affairs." (1980), 18 *Canadian Yearbook of International Law* 301-336. **200**

Legault, L.H., ed. "Canadian Practice in International Law During 1980 as Reflected Mainly in Public Correspondence and Statements of the Department of External Affairs." (1981), 19 *Canadian Yearbook of International Law* 320-347. **201**

Mintah, Gloria. "International Law." In *Canadian Encyclopedic Digest (Ontario)*, 3d ed., 1977, title 81, vol. 17, 123 p. **202**

Scott, Janet V., and Stonehouse, Robert C. "Citizens, Aliens and Immigration." In *Canadian Encyclopedic Digest (Ontario)*, 3d ed., 1980, title 27, vol. 4, 154 p.
Review: Laurence Kearley in (1981), 59 *Canadian Bar Review* 595-598. **203**

Stonehouse, Robert C. "Extradition." In *Canadian Encyclopedic Digest (Ontario)*, 3d ed., 1976, title 61, vol. 12, 51 p. **204**

6. JUDICIAL DECISIONS

Blom, Joost, ed. "Digest of Important Canadian Cases Reported in 1979 in the Fields of Public International Law and Conflict of Laws." (1980), 18 *Canadian Yearbook of International Law* 359-383. **205**

Blom, Joost, ed. "Digest of Important Canadian Cases Reported in 1980 in the Fields of Public International Law and Conflict of Laws." (1981), 19 *Canadian Yearbook of International Law* 376-400. **206**

Castel, Jean-Gabriel, ed. "Digest of Important Canadian Cases Decided in 1968 in the Fields of Public International Law and Conflict of Laws." (1969), 7 *Canadian Yearbook of International Law* 340-351. **207**

Castel, Jean-Gabriel, ed. "Digest of Important Canadian Cases Decided in 1969 in the Fields of Public International Law and Conflict of Laws." (1970), 8 *Canadian Yearbook of International Law* 385-399. **208**

Castel, Jean-Gabriel, ed. "Digest of Important Canadian Cases Decided in 1970 in the Fields of Public International Law and Conflict of Laws." (1971), 9 *Canadian Yearbook of International Law* 312-325. **209**

Castel, Jean-Gabriel, ed. "Digest of Important Canadian Cases Decided in 1971 in the Fields of Public International Law and Conflict of Laws." (1972), 10 *Canadian Yearbook of International Law* 317-346. **210**

Castel, Jean-Gabriel, ed. "Digest of Important Canadian Cases Reported in 1972 in the Fields of Public International Law and Conflict of Laws." (1973), 11 *Canadian Yearbook of International Law* 347-381. **211**

Castel, Jean-Gabriel, ed. "Digest of Important Canadian Cases Reported in 1973 in the Fields of Public International Law and Conflict of Laws." (1974), 12 *Canadian Yearbook of International Law* 333-365. **212**

Williams, Sharon A., ed. "Digest of Important Canadian Cases Reported in 1974 in the Fields of Public International Law and Conflict of Laws." (1975), 13 *Canadian Yearbook of International Law* 396-434. **213**

Williams, Sharon A., ed. "Digest of Important Canadian Cases Reported in 1975 in the Fields of Public International Law and Conflict of Laws." (1976), 14 *Canadian Yearbook of International Law* 371-395. **214**

Williams, Sharon A., ed. "Digest of Important Canadian Cases Reported in 1976 in the Fields of Public International Law and Conflict of Laws." (1977), 15 *Canadian Yearbook of International Law* 373-394. **215**

Williams, Sharon A., ed. "Digest of Important Canadian Cases Reported in 1977 in the Fields of Public International Law and Conflict of Laws." (1978), 16 *Canadian Yearbook of International Law* 406-428. **216**

Williams, Sharon A., ed. "Digest of Important Canadian Cases Reported in 1978 in the Fields of Public International Law and Conflict of Laws." (1979), 17 *Canadian Yearbook of International Law* 396-416. **217**

7. INTERNATIONAL ORGANIZATIONS

Great Lakes Fishery Commission. *Report.* 1956—. Ann Arbor, Mich. Annual.
218

The commission was established under the convention on Great Lakes fisheries between Canada and the United States of September 10, 1954 (CTS 1955/19), implemented by the *Great Lakes Fisheries Convention Act* (R.S.C. 1970, c. F-15). The commission was organized in April 1956, and began its activities on July 1, 1956. French name: *Commission des pêcheries des Grands Lacs*; headquarters at Ann Arbor, Michigan; membership limited to Canada and the United States. Canada actively participates in a number of international fisheries commissions, *bilateral:* 1) International Pacific Salmon Fisheries Commission; 2) International Pacific Halibut Commission (formerly International Fisheries Commission); 3) Great Lakes Fishery Commission (all three with the U.S.); 4) Canada/Norway Sealing Commission; *trilateral:* 5) International North Pacific Fisheries Commission; *multilateral:* 6) International Whaling Commission; 7) Inter-American Tropical Tuna Commission; 8) International Commission for the Conservation of Atlantic Tuna; 9) North Pacific Fur Seal Commission; 10) Northwest Atlantic Fisheries Organization (formerly ICNAF); 11) International Council for the Exploration of the Seas. Canada's activities in these commissions are coordinated by the International Directorate of Fisheries and Oceans of the Dept. of Fisheries and Oceans. Selected publications of some of the commissions of special interest to Canada are listed below.

International Commission for the Northwest Atlantic Fisheries. *Annual Report.* v.1-29, 1950/51-1979. Dartmouth, N.S. **219**

Title varies: *Annual Proceedings*, v.3-22, 1952/53-1971/72; *Annual Report*, v.23-29, 1972/73-1979. This commission (ICNAF), was established in 1950 by the convention of February 8, 1949 (CTS 1950/10), implemented by the *Northwest Atlantic Fisheries Convention Act* (R.S.C. 1970, c. F-18). French name: *Commission internationale pour les pêcheries de l'Atlantique Nord-Ouest*; headquarters at Dartmouth, N.S.; members were governments of 17 countries. The commission was replaced in 1979 by the Northwest Atlantic Fisheries Organization (NAFO).

International Commission for the Northwest Atlantic Fisheries. *Proceedings of the Annual Meeting.* 1st-29th, 1951-1979. Dartmouth, N.S. **220**

This commission (ICNAF) was replaced in 1979 by the Northwest Atlantic Fisheries Organization (NAFO).

International North Pacific Fisheries Commission. *Annual Report.* 1st—, 1954—. Vancouver, B.C. **221**

The commission was established by the convention of May 9, 1952, signed by Canada, Japan and the United States (CTS 1953/3), implemented by the *North Pacific Fisheries Convention Act* (R.S.C. 1970 c. F-16). French name: *Commission internationale concernant les pêcheries hauturières de l'océan Pacifique Nord*; headquarters at Vancouver, B.C.; membership limited to Canada, Japan and the United States.

International Pacific Halibut Commission. *Annual Report.* 1969—. Seattle. **222**

Supersedes *Report of the International Fisheries Commission*, Nos. 1-20, 1928-1953; and *Report of the International Pacific Halibut Commission*, Nos. 21-52, 1954-1969. The commission was established in 1923 under the halibut fishery convention between Canada and the United States, signed at Washington on March 2, 1923 (BTS 18(1925); 117 BFSP 382; 43 Stat. 1841; TS 701; 12 Bevans 394; 32 LNTS 94), implemented by the *Northern Pacific Halibut Fishery Convention Act* (R.S.C. 1970, c. F-17). It was known until 1953 as the International Fisheries Commission (see Article 3 of the convention). French name: *Commission internationale du flétan du Pacifique*; headquarters at Seattle; membership limited to Canada and the United States.

International Pacific Salmon Fisheries Commission. *Annual Report.* 1937/38—.
New Westminster, B.C. **223**

The commission was established in 1937 under the sockeye salmon fisheries convention between Canada and the United States of May 26, 1930 (CTS 1937/10), implemented by an act of Parliament (S.C. 1930, c. 10). French name: *Commission internationale de la pêche du saumon dans le Pacifique*; headquarters at New Westminster, B.C.; membership limited to Canada and the United States.

North Pacific Fur Seal Commission. *Proceedings of the Annual Meeting.* 1st—, 1958—. Washington, D.C. **224**

The commission was established in January 1958, pursuant to the convention of February 9, 1957 (CTS 1957/26), implemented by the *Pacific Fur Seals Convention Act* (R.S.C. 1970, c. F-33). French name: *Commission du phoque à fourrure du Pacifique Nord*; headquarters at Washington, D.C.; members: Canada, Japan, U.S.A., and U.S.S.R.

Northwest Atlantic Fisheries Organization. *Annual Report.* v.1—, 1979—. Dartmouth, N.S. **225**

Continues: International Commission for the Northwest Atlantic Fisheries. *Annual Report*, 1st-29th, 1951-1979.

Northwest Atlantic Fisheries Organization. *Proceedings of the Annual Meeting.* 1st—, 1979—. Dartmouth, N.S. **226**

This organization, replacing the International Commission for the Northwest Atlantic Fisheries (ICNAF), was created by the NAFO convention of October 24, 1978 (CTS 1979/11). It held its first inaugural meeting in Montreal on March 8 and 9, 1979. French name: *Organisation des pêches de l'Atlantique Nord-Ouest*.

8. INTERNATIONAL CONFERENCES

Canada. Parliament. *Conference on the Limitation of Armament, Held at Washington, November 12, 1921, to February 6, 1922; Report of the Canadian Delegate Including Treaties and Resolutions.* Ottawa, 1922. 222 p. (Canada. Parliament, 1922. Sessional Papers, No. 47) **227**
Sir Robert Borden, Delegate.

Canada. Parliament. *The Genoa Conference for the Economic and Financial Reconstruction of Europe, April 10 to May 19, 1922. Joint Report of the Canadian Delegates.* Ottawa, 1922. 101 p. (Canada. Parliament, 1923. Sessional Papers, No. 35) **228**

Canada. Parliament. *Imperial Economic Conference, Held in October and November, 1923. Record of Proceedings and Documents. Summary of Conclusions. Appendices to the Summary of Proceedings.* Ottawa, 1924. 491, 20, 127 p. (Canada. Parliament, 1924. Sessional Papers, Nos. 35, 37, and 37a) **229**

9. OTHERS

Johnston, Douglas M., and Chiu, Hungdah. *Agreements of the People's Republic of China, 1949-1967: A Calendar.* Cambridge: Harvard University Press, 1968. xvii, 286 p. (Harvard Studies in East Asian Law, 3) **230**

Reviews: William E. Butler in (1969), 10 *Harvard International Law Journal* 395-397; George Ginsburgs in (1970), 18 *American Journal of Comparative Law* 653; Luke T. Lee in (1970), 64 *American Journal of International Law* 199-201.

Wiktor, Christian L. *Unperfected Treaties of the United States of America, 1776-1976.* Dobbs Ferry, N.Y.: Oceana Publications, 1976—.   **231**
Contents: v.1. 1776-1855.- v.2. 1856-1882.- v.3. 1883-1904.- v.4. 1905-1918.- v.5. 1919.
Reviews: Charles I. Bevans in (1977), 71 *American Journal of International Law* 812-813; Leslie C. Green in (1976), 14 *Canadian Yearbook of International Law* 416-418; Igor I. Kavass in (1977), 70 *Law Library Journal* 114-116; Lin Murphy in (1977), 5 *International Journal of Law Libraries* 135-136.

II. GENERAL WORKS

Bernard, Mathieu A. *Manuel de droit international, public et privé. Ouvrage basé sur le droit international de Charles Calvo et contenant les dispositions du Code civil de la province de Québec et des statuts impériaux et fédéraux applicables à la matière.* Montréal: C. Théoret, 1901. xxix, 256 p. **232**

Bourne, Charles B., and Jahnke, L. Gordon. *Cases and Materials on Public International Law.* Vancouver: University of British Columbia, 1969. 1 vol. (various pagings) **233**
Also published in 1972.

Castel, Jean-Gabriel. *International Law, Chiefly as Interpreted and Applied in Canada.* Toronto: University of Toronto Press, c1965. xxii, 1402 p., maps. **234**
Reviews: Pedro Pablo Camargo in (1967), 20 *Boletin del Instituto de Derecho Comparado de Mexico* 269-270; René-Jean Dupuy in (1968), 95 *Journal du Droit International* 495-496; L. Erades in (1968), 15 *Netherlands International Law Review* 69; Gerald F. FitzGerald in (1966), *Australian Year Book of International Law* 171-174; H. Patrick Glenn in (1967), 8 *Harvard International Law Journal* 211-212; Leslie C. Green in (1966), 4 *Canadian Yearbook of International Law* 310-314; William Andrew MacKay in (1967), 45 *Canadian Bar Review* 379-383; Charles Rousseau in (1966), 70 *Revue Générale de Droit International Public* 215-216; K.R. Simmonds in (1967), 16 *International and Comparative Law Quarterly* 559; Helmut Strebel in (1966), 26 *Zeitschrift für Ausländisches Recht und Völkerrecht* 174-175; Robert R. Wilson in (1966), 60 *American Journal of International Law* 874-875.

Castel, Jean-Gabriel. *International Law, Chiefly as Interpreted and Applied in Canada.* 2d rev. ed. Downsview, Ont.: York University, Osgoode Hall Law School, 1973. 3 vols. (xii, 1175 p.), maps. **235**

Castel, Jean-Gabriel. *International Law, Chiefly as Interpreted and Applied in Canada.* 3d ed. Toronto: Butterworths, 1976. xxxi, 1268 p. (Canadian Legal Casebook Series) **236**
Reviews: Claude C. Emanuelli in (1977-78), 25 *University of New Brunswick Law Journal* 64-68; Claude C. Emanuelli in (1977-78), 4 *Dalhousie Law Journal* 236-240; Gerald F. FitzGerald in (1976), 54 *Canadian Bar Review* 476-486; Wesley L. Gould in (1977), 71 *American Journal of International Law* 175-176; Leslie C. Green in (1976), 14 *Canadian Yearbook of International Law* 396-399; Annemarie Jacomy-Millette in (1976), 7 *Études Internationales* 463-464; Hugh M. Kindred in (1977-78), 4 *Dalhousie Law Journal* 233-236; Charles Rousseau in (1976), 80 *Revue Générale de Droit International Public* 661-662; Joseph W. Samuels in (1976), 15 *University of Western Ontario Law Review* 265-267; Daniel C. Turack in (1977-78), 13 *Texas International Law Journal* 160-162.

De Mestral, Armand L.C., and Williams, Sharon A. *Introduction au droit international public.* Toronto: Butterworths, 1981. 340 p. **237**
Originally published in English under title: *An Introduction to International Law.* Translated by Ethel Groffier-Atala.

Dufour, André, and Langlumé, Patrice Michel. *Cours de droit international public; recueil de textes et d'arrêts.* Québec: Presses de l'Université Laval, 1971. 4 vols. (2239, 359 p.) **238**
Contents: t.1-2, titre 1: La notion de droit international public.- t.3, titre 2: Les traités, titre 3: Les états, titre 4: Les juridictions internationales.- t.4, titre 5: Le domaine public international.

Emanuelli, Claude C. *Droit international public.* Sherbrooke: Université de Sherbrooke, Faculté de droit, 1979. 2 vols. **239**

Green, Leslie C. *International Law through the Cases.* London: Stevens; New York: Praeger, 1951. xxviii, 913 p. (Library of World Affairs, No. 17) **240**
First edition. Published under the auspices of the London Institute of World Affairs.
Reviews: Herbert W. Briggs in (1952), 46 *American Journal of International Law* 372; F. Honig in (1951), 27 *International Affairs* 484-485; A.B. Lyons in (1951), 28 *British Year Book of International Law* 425-426; F.A. Mann in (1951), 14 *Modern Law Review* 523-524; Barry Nicholas in (1951), 33 *Journal of Comparative Legislation and International Law* 105-106 (3d Ser.); Hans-Jürgen Schlochauer in (1951-52), 3 *Archiv des Völkerrechts* 499-500; unsigned in (1951), 4 *International Law Quarterly* 437-438; (1952), 79 *Journal du Droit International* 726; (1951), 21 *Nordisk Tidsskrift for International Ret og Jus Gentium* 77; and (1952), 56 *Revue Générale de Droit International Public* 107.

Green, Leslie C. *International Law through the Cases.* 2d ed. London: Stevens; New York: Praeger, 1959. 885 p. (Library of World Affairs, No. 17) **241**
Reviews: R.K. Dixit in (1960-61), 1 *Indian Journal of International Law* 338-339; L. Erades in (1960), 7 *Netherlands International Law Review* 397; Leo Gross in (1961), 55 *American Journal of International Law* 205; F. Honig in (1960), 36 *International Affairs* 360; Roger Pinto in (1960), 87 *Journal du Droit International* 902; K. Narayana Rao in (1962), 4 *Journal of the Indian Law Institute* 467-470; Charles Rousseau in (1960), 64 *Revue Générale de Droit International Public* 416-417; Hans-Jürgen Schlochauer in (1961-62), 9 *Archiv des Völkerrechts* 367; Helmut Strebel in (1961), 21 *Zeitschrift für Ausländisches Öffentliches Recht und Völkerrecht* 123-125; D.G. Valentine in (1960), 23 *Modern Law Review* 349; signed S. M. in (1960-61), 9-10 *Indian Year Book of International Affairs* 307-308.

Green, Leslie C. *International Law through the Cases.* 3d ed. London: Stevens; Dobbs Ferry, N.Y.: Oceana Publications, 1970. xxiii, 855 p. (Library of World Affairs, No. 17) **242**
Published under the auspices of the London Institute of World Affairs.
Reviews: Yehuda Z. Blum in (1971), 19 *American Journal of Comparative Law* 798-799; D.J. Harris in (1971), 20 *International and Comparative Law Quarterly* 380; John Hopkins in (1971), 29 *Cambridge Law Journal* 327-329; D.H.N. Johnson in (1971), 25 *Year Book of World Affairs* 244; Andreas F. Lowenfeld in (1971), 65 *American Journal of International Law* 837-839; Hans-Jürgen Schlochauer in (1974-75), 16 *Archiv des Völkerrechts* 481; D. Colwyn Williams in (1970), 35 *Saskatchewan Law Review* 223-224

Green, Leslie C. *International Law through the Cases.* 4th ed. Toronto: Carswell Dobbs Ferry, N.Y.: Oceana, 1978. xxix, 836 p. **243**

Reviews: M.J. Peterson in (1980), 74 *American Journal of International Law* 244-245; Hans-Jürgen Schlochauer in (1980), 19 *Archiv des Völkerrechts* 117; K.R. Simmonds in (1979), 28 *International and Comparative Law Quarterly* 154; Derrick Wyatt in (1980), 96 *Law Quarterly Review* 315-316.

Kindred, Hugh M. *International Law: A Canadian Coursebook*. Halifax: Dalhousie University, Faculty of Law, 1981. 371 p. (various pagings) **244**

Kindred, Hugh M. *International Law: A Canadian Coursebook*. 1982 ed. Halifax: Dalhousie University, Faculty of Law, 1982. 1 vol. (various pagings) **245**

Lebel, Michel; Rigaldies, Francis; and Woehrling, José. *Droit international public: sources et sujets*. Montréal: Éditions Thémis, 1977. xxxv, 708 p., maps. (Éditions Thémis. Notes et documents) **246**
This is a collection of materials for students.
Reviews: Armand L.C. de Mestral in (1977), 55 *Canadian Bar Review* 782-783; Annemarie Jacomy-Millette in (1978), 9 *Études Internationales* 565-566.

Lebel, Michel; Rigaldies, Francis; and Woehrling, José. *Droit international public: sources et sujet*. 2. éd. Montréal: Éditions Thémis, 1978. 2 vols. (xxix, 930 p.) (Éditions Thémis. Notes et documents) **247**

Macdonald, Ronald St. John; Morris, Gerald L.; and Johnston, Douglas M., eds. *Canadian Perspectives on International Law and Organization*. Toronto: University of Toronto Press, 1974. xx, 972 p. **248**
Contains thirty-eight papers in English and French by different authors, listed individually in this bibliography.
Reviews: Richard R. Baxter in (1974), 12 *Canadian Yearbook of International Law* 366-369; Craig Brown in (1976), 8 *Victoria University of Wellington Law Review* 230-233; Ian Brownlie in (1977), 23 *McGill Law Journal* 152; Ronald C.K. Cheng in (1975), 33 *University of Toronto Faculty of Law Review* 113-115; John Claydon under title: "Canadian Perspectives on International Law and Organization: Toward an Expanding Role in World Order," in (1975-76), 2 *Dalhousie Law Journal* 533-552; J. Duthiel de la Rochère in (1976), 28 *Revue Internationale de Droit Comparé* 404-406; Thomas M. Franck under title: "International Law in Canadian Practice: The State of the Art and the Art of the State," in (1975-76), 31 *International Journal* 180-214; Leslie C. Green under title: "Focus on International Law," in (1974), *International Perspectives* 52-55 (Sept./Oct.); Leslie C. Green under title: "Is There a Canadian International Law?," in (1974), 22 *Chitty's Law Journal* 289-291; C.A. Hopkins in (1976-77), 48 *British Year Book of International Law* 425-428; Gerard V. La Forest in (1975), 53 *Canadian Bar Review* 442-445; Donald M. McRae in (1974), 24 *University of Toronto Law Journal* 457-463; Edward McWhinney in (1975), 8 *Canadian Journal of Political Science* 335-337; A. Clayton Rice under title: "Canadian Perspectives on International Law and Organization: Systems-Building and the Role of Law," in (1976), 14 *Alberta Law Review* 344-361; Charles Rousseau in (1974), 78 *Revue Générale de Droit International Public* 1215-1216; Ko Swan Sik in (1976), 23 *Netherlands International Law Review* 107-109; Stanislas Slosar in (1975-76), 6 *Revue de Droit, Université de Sherbrooke* 223-231; Daniel C. Turack in (1975), 4 *Capital University Law Review* 363-370; unsigned in (1975), 6 *Études Internationales* 293 (brief notice).

MacKenzie, Norman A.M., and Laing, Lionel H., eds. *Canada and the Law of Nations; a Selection of Cases in International Law, Affecting Canada or Canadians, Decided by Canadian Courts, by Certain of the Higher Courts in the United States and Great Britain and by International Tribunals*. Foreword by Sir Robert Borden. Introduction by James Brown Scott. Toronto: Ryerson

Press; New Haven: Yale University Press; etc., 1938. xxvii, 567 p. (Relations of Canada and the United States) **249**
Published for the Carnegie Endowment for International Peace, Division of Economics and History. Reprinted New York, Kraus Reprint, 1972.
Reviews: Elbridge Colby in (1940), 9 *Fordham Law Review* 443-444; G.S. Cowan in (1938-39), 18 *Dalhousie Review* 274-275; Wilhelm Friede in (1939-40), 9 *Zeitschrift für Ausländisches Öffentliches Recht und Völkerrecht* 190-191; Manley O. Hudson under title: "Twelve Casebooks on International Law," in (1938), 32 *American Journal of International Law* 447-456; A. Berriedale Keith in (1939), 18 *International Affairs* 690-691; John Willis in (1939-40), 3 *University of Toronto Law Journal* 461-463; Lester H. Woolsey in (1938), 32 *American Journal of International Law* 624-625; signed J.A.C. in (1939-40), 46 *Queen's Quarterly* 104-105; unsigned in (1938), 19 *Canadian Historical Review* 326-329; and under title: "Canada and the World," in (1938), 185 *Law Times* 371-373.

Morin, Jacques-Yvan. *Cours de droit international public.* Montréal: Librairie de l'Université de Montréal, 1972. 3 vols., maps. **250**

Slosar, Stanislas. *Droit international public: recueil de textes.* Montréal: Librairie de l'Université de Montréal, 1980. 260 p. **251**
Notes de cours.

Vincke, Christian. *Cours de droit international public: jurisprudence, textes, notes et documents.* Montréal: Librairie de l'Université de Montréal, 1974. 2 vols. (viii, 530 p.), maps. **252**
At head of title: Université de Montréal. Faculté de droit.
Contents: t.1. 1973.- t.2. 1974.

Williams, Sharon A., and De Mestral, Armand L.C. *An Introduction to International Law: Chiefly as Interpreted and Applied in Canada.* Toronto: Butterworths, 1979. xix, 338 p. (Butterworth Basic Text Series) **253**
Also published in French under title: *Introduction au droit international public.*
Reviews: Maxwell Cohen in (1980), 25 *McGill Law Journal* 632-635; James Ellis in (1981), 19 *Canadian Yearbook of International Law* 431-433; Donald J. Fleming in (1981), 30 *University of New Brunswick Law Journal* 299-301; Wesley L. Gould in (1981), 75 *American Journal of International Law* 399-402; L.H. Legault, and François Mathys in (1980), 58 *Canadian Bar Review* 706-708; K. Venkata Raman in (1979), 5 *Queen's Law Journal* 183-185; Joseph W. Samuels in (1980), 18 *University of Western Ontario Law Review* 553; Stanislas Slosar in (1979), 10 *Revue de Droit, Université de Sherbrooke* 289-291; Friedl Weiss in (1980), 43 *Modern Law Review* 605-606.

III. INTERNATIONAL LAW IN GENERAL

A. General Nature

Bai, Kui-mei. *Contemporary Theoretical Approaches to International Law.* Halifax, 1982. vi, 203 leaves. **254**
Thesis (LL.M.), Dalhousie University, 1982.

Beaudoin, Rosario. *Le droit international.* Ottawa, 1936. 131 leaves. **255**
Thesis (M.A.), Université d'Ottawa, 1936.

Boisvert, René. "Droit international en progression." (1951), 11 *Revue du Barreau* 40-46. **256**

Cadieux, Marcel. "La coexistence pacifique et le droit international." (1963), 23 *Revue du Barreau* 501-520. **257**

Canada. Dept. of External Affairs. *Some Examples of Current Issues of International Law of Particular Importance to Canada / Quelques exemples de questions courantes de droit international d'une importance particulière pour le Canada.* Ottawa: Dept. of External Affairs, 1977. 45 p. In English and French. **258**

Carignan, Pierre. "Le droit de se faire justice dans l'ordre politique national et international." (1952-53), 3 *Thémis* 137-155. **259**

Cohen, Maxwell. "Basic Principles of International Law." (1963), *World Peace Through Law* 759-771. **260**

Cohen, Maxwell. "'Basic Principles' of International Law - A Revaluation." (1964), 42 *Canadian Bar Review* 449-462. **261**

Cohen, Maxwell. "Canada and the International Legal Order: An Inside Perspective." *In* Macdonald, Ronald St. John, and others, *Canadian Perspectives on International Law and Organization* (Toronto, 1974), pp. 3-32. **262**

Cohen, Maxwell. "Expanding Structure of International Law: Peacekeeping, General Principles and International Organizations. (Report of Rapporteur)." (1965), *World Peace Through Law* 565-569. **263**

Cohen, Maxwell. "From Diversity to Unity: International Law in a Bipolar World." (1959), 53 *American Society of International Law, Proceedings* 98-107. **264**

Cohen, Maxwell. "Reflections on the Comparative Law Element of Public International Law." *In* Popovici, Adrian, ed., *Problèmes de droit contemporain: mélanges Louis Baudouin* (Montréal, 1974), pp. 485-488. **265**

Cohen, Maxwell. "Some International Law Problems of Interest to Canada and to Canadian Lawyers." (1955), 33 *Canadian Bar Review* 389-423. **266**
Also published in (1954), *Canadian Bar Association, Papers,* 24 p.

Cohen, Maxwell. "Some Main Directions of International Law: A Canadian Perspective." (1963), 1 *Canadian Yearbook of International Law* 15-39. **267**

Corbett, Percy E. *From International to World Law.* Bethlehem, Pa.: Dept. of International Relations, Lehigh University, 1969. 40 p. (Lehigh University, Bethlehem, Pa. Dept. of International Relations. Research Monograph, No. 1) **268**
Review: Charles G. Fenwick in (1970), 64 *American Journal of International Law* 724-725.

Corbett, Percy E. "Fundamentals of a New Law of Nations." (1935-36), 1 *University of Toronto Law Journal* 3-16. **269**

Corbett, Percy E. *The Growth of World Law.* Princeton, N.J.: Princeton University Press, 1971. xii, 216 p. **270**
Review: Leslie C. Green in (1972), 35 *Modern Law Review* 219-222.

Corbett, Percy E. *Law and Society in the Relations of States.* New York: Harcourt, Brace, 1951. x, 337 p. **271**
At head of half-title: Institute of International Studies, Yale University.
Reviews: Leslie C. Green in (1953), 16 *Modern Law Review* 262-263; H. Lauterpacht in (1951), 28 *British Year Book of International Law* 424-425; Julius Stone under title: "International Law and International Society," in (1952), 30 *Canadian Bar Review* 164-174; Edgar Turlington in (1951), 45 *American Journal of International Law* 803-805.

Corbett, Percy E. *Law in Diplomacy.* Princeton, N.J.: Princeton University Press, 1959. xii, 290 p. **272**
Published for the Center of International Studies, Princeton University.
Reviews: P. Barandon in (1959-60), 8 *Archiv des Völkerrechts* 308-313; Jasper Yeates Brinton in (1960), 16 *Revue Egyptienne de Droit International* 149-152; John M. Flackett in (1962), 40 *Canadian Bar Review* 520-522; John Foster in (1960), 36 *International Affairs* 226-227; Wesley L. Gould in (1959), 53 *American Journal of International Law* 996-997.

Corbett, Percy E. "Social Basis of a Law of Nations." (1954), 85 *Académie de Droit International, Recueil des Cours* 471-544. **273**

Corbett, Percy E. "Some Thoughts on the Contemporary International Lawlessness and What Lawyers Are or Might Be Doing about It." (1972), 1 *Canadian Council on International Law, Proceedings* 259-262. **274**

"Current Notes on International Laws." (1913), 33 *Canadian Law Times* 907-911. **275**

D'Amato, Anthony A. "On Consensus." (1970), 8 *Canadian Yearbook of International Law* 104-122. **276**

Dubé, Georges. "Le rapport entre la politique et le droit dans l'ordre international." (1962-63), 5 *Cahiers de Droit* 47-56 (no 2) **277**

Falk, Richard A. "The Domains of Law and Justice." (1975-76), 31 *International Journal* 1-13. **278**

Falk, Richard A. "The International Order and the Prospects for Humanity in the 1980's." (1980), 9 *Canadian Council on International Law, Proceedings* 75-83.
279

Focsaneanu, Lazar. "Esquisse d'un droit international sans obligation, ni sanction: un essai de droit des gens phénoménologique." (1977), 8 *Études Internationales* 447-477.
280

Fowler, R.M. "A Wider Range of Law." (1946), 1 *International Journal* 285-287.
281

Friedmann, Wolfgang G. "Canada and the International Legal Order: An Outside Perspective." *In* Macdonald, Ronald St. John, and others, *Canadian Perspectives on International Law and Organization* (Toronto, 1974), pp. 33-54. **282**

Friedmann, Wolfgang G. "The Role of International Law in the Conduct of International Affairs." (1964-65), 20 *International Journal* 158-172. **283**

"Friendly Relations: A Study of Principles of International Law." (1964), 16 *External Affairs* 610-612.
284

Green, Leslie C. "De l'influence des nouveaux états sur le droit international." (1970), 74 *Revue Générale de Droit International Public* 78-106. **285**

Green, Leslie C. "The Impact of the New States on International Law." (1969), 4 *Israel Law Review* 27-60.
286
See also the author's *Law and Society* (Leyden, 1975), pp. 183-240.

Green, Leslie C. "International Law and the Control of Barbarism." *In* Macdonald, Ronald St. John, and others, *The International Law and Policy of Human Welfare* (Alphen aan den Rijn, 1978), pp. 239-271. **287**

Green, Leslie C. "Is International Law Law?" (1966), 1 *International Journal of Legal Research* 23-50.
288
See also the author's *Law and Society* (Leyden, 1975), pp. 133-182.

Green, Leslie C. "Law and Morality in a Changing Society." (1970), 20 *University of Toronto Law Journal* 422-447.
289

Green, Leslie C. *Law and Society.* Leyden: A.W. Sijthoff; Dobbs Ferry, N.Y.: Oceana, c1975. xviii, 502 p.
290
Partial contents of essays originally issued separately: "Is International Law Law?" (pp. 133-182).- "The Impact of the New States on International Law" (pp. 183-240).- "The Individual in International Law" (pp. 241-282).- "Human Rights and the General Principles of Law" (pp. 283-320).- "The Right of Asylum in International Law" (pp. 321-362) - "Hijacking, Extradition and Asylum" (pp. 363-395).- "Aftermath of Vietnam: War and the Soldier" (pp. 397-432).
Reviews: C.M. Chinkin in (1977), 40 *Modern Law Review* 117; Percy E. Corbett in (1976), 70 *American Journal of International Law* 893; G.I.A.D. Draper in (1977-78), 33 *International Journal* 640-642; A.B. Edwards in (1977), 10 *Comparative and International Law Journal of Southern Africa* 371-373; René H. Mankiewicz in (1976), 7 *Études Internationales* 634-636; Robert Martin in (1976), 15 *University of Western Ontario Law Review* 245-251; Edward McWhinney in (1977), 15 *Canadian Yearbook of International Law* 395-396; Francis J. Nicholson in (1979), 2 *Boston College International and Comparative Law Review* 534-540; Hans-Jürgen Schlochauer in (1976-78), 17 *Archiv des Völkerrechts* 455-456; Norman J. Singer in (1976), 69 *Law Library Journal* 112-113; Egbert W. Vierdag in (1977), 63 *Archiv für Rechts- und Sozialphilosophie* 441-443; unsigned in (1976), 80 *Revue Générale de Droit International Public* 352-353.

Green, Leslie C. "The Nature of International Law." (1961-62), 14 *University of Toronto Law Journal* 176-193. **291**

Head, Ivan L., ed. *'This Fire-Proof House'; Canadians Speak Out about Law and Order in the International Community.* Edited by Ivan L. Head for the World Law Foundation. Dobbs Ferry, N.Y.: Oceana Publications; Toronto: Canadian Institute of International Affairs, 1967. xi, 176 p. **292**

Papers presented at the Banff Conference on Law and Order in the International Community held June 7-8, 1965, and three papers from other conferences. Individual papers are listed separately.
Review: John P.S. McLaren in (1967), 32 *Saskatchewan Law Review* 154-158.

Hendry, James M. "Canada and Modern International Law." (1961), 39 *Canadian Bar Review* 59-77. **293**

Hendry, James M. "Ethics, Values and the Common Good as Guidelines for a World Community." (1975), 7 *Ottawa Law Review* 330-383. **294**

Hudson, Manley O. "The Post-War Development of International Law and Some Contributions by the United States of America." (1934), 12 *Canadian Bar Review* 191-208. **295**

Humphrey, John P. "On the Foundations of International Law." (1945), 39 *American Journal of International Law* 231-243. **296**

"International Law." (1916), 52 *Canada Law Journal* 329-331. **297**

"International Law and the Practice of Law in Canada / Le droit international et la pratique du droit au Canada." (1981), 10 *Canadian Council on International Law, Proceedings*, 219 p. **298**

This is the general theme of the tenth annual conference held at Ottawa, October 29-31, 1981. Individual papers are listed separately.

Jacomy-Millette, Annemarie. "Quelques jalons de l'apport canadien au droit international: en guise de présentation." (1980), 11 *Études Internationales* 371-374. **299**

Johnston, Douglas M. "The Foundations of Justice in International Law." In Macdonald, Ronald St. John, and others, *The International Law and Policy of Human Welfare* (Alphen aan den Rijn, 1978), pp. 111-146. **300**

Johnston, Douglas M. "The Scottish Tradition in International Law." (1978), 16 *Canadian Yearbook of International Law* 3-45. **301**

Kleffens, Eelco N. van. "The Place of Law in International Relations." (1955), 5 *Chitty's Law Journal* 15-17. **302**

Macdonald, Ronald St. John; Johnston, Douglas M.; and Morris, Gerald L., eds. *The International Law and Policy of Human Welfare.* Alphen aan den Rijn: Sijthoff & Noordhoff, 1978. xviii, 690 p. **303**

Contains 25 essays, some of which are listed separately.
Reviews: Hedley Bull in (1980-81), 57 *International Affairs* 140; Maxwell Cohen in (1981), 59 *Canadian Bar Review* 613-619; Michel Distel in (1980), 32 *Revue Internationale de Droit Comparé* 247; H. Scott Fairley in (1981), 19 *University of Western Ontario Law Review* 371-380; Jens Foerkel in (1981), 50 *Nordisk Tidsskrift for International Ret* 96-97; Julian R. Friedman in (1979-80), 7 *Syracuse Journal of International Law and Commerce* 299-302; Ved P. Nanda in (1980-81), 10 *Denver Journal of International Law and Policy* 185-192; Haji N.A. Noor Muhammad in (1981), 21 *Indian Journal of*

International Law 331-332; Clark C. Siewert in (1981), 14 *Vanderbilt Journal of Transnational Law* 457-460; K.R. Simmonds in (1980), 29 *International and Comparative Law Quarterly* 539-540; Detlev Vagts in (1981), 75 *American Journal of International Law* 680-681; P.J.I.M. de Waart in (1980), 27 *Netherlands International Law Review* 258-261; Friedl Weiss in (1980), 51 *British Year Book of International Law* 288-290; Anne M. Williams in (1980), 15 *Texas International Law Journal* 611-623; José Woehrling in (1980), 11 *Études Internationales* 349-350; unsigned in (1979), 25 *Annuaire Français de Droit International* 1083.

Macdonald, Ronald St. John; Johnston, Douglas M.; and Morris, Gerald L. "The International Law of Human Welfare: Concept, Experience, and Priorities." *In* Macdonald, Ronald St. John, and others, *The International Law and Policy of Human Welfare* (Alphen aan den Rijn, 1978), pp. 3-79. **304**

Macdonald, Ronald St. John; Morris, Gerald L.; and Johnston, Douglas M. "Canadian Approaches to International Law." *In* Macdonald, Ronald St. John, and others, *Canadian Perspectives on International Law and Organization* (Toronto, 1974), pp. 940-954. **305**

Macdonald, Ronald St. John; Morris, Gerald L.; and Johnston, Douglas M. "International Law and Society in the Year 2000." (1973), 51 *Canadian Bar Review* 316-332. **306**

MacKenzie, Norman A.M. "American Contributions to International Law." (1939), 33 *American Society of International Law, Proceedings* 104-117. **307**

MacKenzie, Norman A.M. "Canada and the Law of Nations." (1938), 19 *British Year Book of International Law* 225-226. **308**

MacKenzie, Norman A.M. "International Law and the Contemporary World Situation." (1959-63), 1 *University of British Columbia Law Review* 679-687. **309**

MacKenzie, Norman A.M. "The Nature, Place and Function of International Law." (1939-40), 3 *University of Toronto Law Journal* 114-131. **310**

Martin, Paul. "International Law in a Changing World: Value of the Old and the New." (1964), 16 *External Affairs* 586-596. **311**
Text of a speech by the Secretary of State for External Affairs to the Toronto Branch of the International Law Association, October 14, 1964. Also issued in the French edition under title: "Le droit international dans un monde en évolution."

Martin, Paul. "Philosophy of Internationalism." (1934), 12 *Canadian Bar Review* 227-241. **312**

Martin, Paul. "Recent Developments in International Law." (1954), 32 *Canadian Bar Review* 304-323. **313**

Matte, Nicolas Mateesco. *Le droit international nouveau*. Préface d'Alejandro Alvarez. Paris: A. Pedone, 1948. 174 p. **314**
Review: R.R. Oglesby in (1949), 43 *American Journal of International Law* 211-212.

Mayrand, Léon. "Introduction à l'étude du droit international." (1937), 7 *Revue de l'Université d'Ottawa* 307-319. **315**

McWhinney, Edward. "Changing International Law Method and Objectives in the Era of the Soviet-Western *Détente*." (1965), 59 *American Journal of International Law* 1-15. **316**

McWhinney, Edward. "Changing Science and Technology and International Law." (1972-73), 6 *Indiana Law Review* 172-181. **317**

McWhinney, Edward. " 'Coexistence,' the Cuba Crisis, and Cold War International Law." (1962-63), 18 *International Journal* 67-74. **318**

McWhinney, Edward. "Le concept soviétique de 'coexistence pacifique' et les rapports juridiques entre l'U.R.S.S. et les états occidentaux." (1963), 67 *Revue Générale de Droit International Public* 545-562. **319**

McWhinney, Edward. *Conflict and Compromise: International Law and World Order in a Revolutionary Age.* Toronto: CBC Merchandising, 1981. 160 p. **320**

Texts of seven half-hour talks first broadcast during December, 1966, and January, 1967, on the radio series *Ideas*; revised edition of: *International Law and World Revolution, 1967.*
Reviews: Roger Fisher in (1982), 76 *American Journal of International Law* 658-660; Leslie C. Green in (1982), 20 *Alberta Law Review* 369-371; Leslie C. Green in (1982), 15 *Canadian Journal of Political Science* 198-200.

McWhinney, Edward. *Conflit idéologique et ordre public mondial.* Paris: A. Pedone, 1970. 159 p. **321**

This is a series of lectures delivered in April 1968, at Institut des hautes études internationales, Université de Paris.
Reviews: André Dufour in (1970), 1 *Études Internationales* 123-124 (no 4); Kazimierz Grzybowski in (1971), 65 *American Journal of International Law* 237-238; Alberto José Lleonart y Amselem in (1970), 23 *Revista Española de Derecho Internacional* 147-148; Alain Pellet in (1967), 13 *Annuaire Français de Droit International* 1007-1008; Charles Rousseau in (1970), 74 *Revue Générale de Droit International Public* 538.

McWhinney, Edward. "Federalism and International Law Making in a World Community in Revolution." (1965), 11 *Lucknow Law Journal* 60-69. **322**

McWhinney, Edward. "Friendly Relations and Cooperation among States (Coexistence), and the Principle of Non-Intervention." *In The Legal Principles Governing Friendly Relations and Cooperation Among States* (Leyden, 1966), pp. 69-88. **323**

McWhinney, Edward. "From Bipolarity to Polypolarity: The International Law of the Post-Détente Era." *In* Tittel, Josef, ed., *Multitudo Legum Ius Unum: Mélanges en l'honneur de Wilhelm Wengler* (Berlin, 1973), vol. 1, pp. 289-304. **324**

McWhinney, Edward. "Ideological Conflict and the Special Soviet Approach to International Law." (1971), 3 *University of Toledo Law Review* 215-232. **325**

McWhinney, Edward. *International Law and World Revolution.* Toronto: Canadian Broadcasting Corporation, c1967. 101 p. **326**

Contains the texts of seven half-hour talks first broadcast during December, 1966, and January, 1967, in the radio series *Ideas*. Also published Leiden, A.W. Sijthoff, 1967. 116 p. Revised edition published in 1981 under title: *Conflict and Compromise.*
Reviews: George Ginsburgs in (1970), 18 *American Journal of Comparative Law* 644-650; Manuel Pérez Gonzalez in (1970), 23 *Revista Española de Derecho Internacional* 145-147; John N. Hazard in (1969), 63 *American Journal of International Law* 370-371; Jean Klein in (1970), 97 *Journal du Droit International* 510-512; Jean Touscoz in (1968), 95 *Journal du Droit International* 495; unsigned in (1968), 72 *Revue Générale de Droit*

International Public 272 (brief notice); and (1968), 21 *Revue Hellénique de Droit International* 346.

McWhinney, Edward. "International Law in the Nuclear Age: Soviet-Western, Inter-Bloc, International Law." (1963), 57 *American Society of International Law, Proceedings* 68-72. **327**

McWhinney, Edward. "The Moscow Summit Meeting and the Post-Détente International Law." (1972-73), 6 *Indiana Law Review* 202-219. **328**

McWhinney, Edward. "Le 'nouveau' droit international et la 'nouvelle' communauté mondiale." (1968), 72 *Revue Générale de Droit International Public* 323-345. **329**

McWhinney, Edward. "Objectives and Method in International Law and the East-West *Détente.*" In McWhinney, Edward, ed., *Law, Foreign Policy, and the East-West Détente* (Toronto, 1964), pp. 33-45. **330**

McWhinney, Edward. "Operational Methodology and Philosophy for Accommodation of the Contending Systems of International Law." (1964), 50 *Virginia Law Review* 36-57. **331**

McWhinney, Edward. " 'Pax Metternichea?' International Law and Power in the Era of Detente." In *Festskrift til Professor Alf Ross* (København, 1969), pp. 335-350. **332**

McWhinney, Edward. " 'Peaceful Co-Existence' and Soviet-Western International Law." (1962), 56 *American Journal of International Law* 951-970. **333**

McWhinney, Edward. *'Peaceful Coexistence' and Soviet-Western International Law.* Leyden: A.W. Sythoff, 1964. 135 p. **334**
Reviews: S.K. Agrawala in (1965), 7 *Journal of the Indian Law Institute* 164-167; John N. Hazard in (1965), 3 *Canadian Yearbook of International Law* 352-354; Ivo Lapenna in (1965), 14 *International and Comparative Law Quarterly* 1045-1047; Oliver J. Lissitzyn in (1965), 59 *American Journal of International Law* 956-959; F. Münch in (1965), 25 *Zeitschrift für Ausländisches Öffentliches Recht und Völkerrecht* 142-143; A.N. Papacostas in (1965), 18 *Revue Hellénique de Droit International* 498; T.S. Rama Rao in (1964), 13 *Indian Year Book of International Affairs* 488-489; Charles Rousseau in (1965), 69 *Revue Générale de Droit International Public* 267-268; Surya P. Sharma in (1965), 5 *Indian Journal of International Law* 52-55; A.M. Stuyt in (1965), 12 *Netherlands International Law Review* 313; signed B.D.S. in (1965), 1 *Revue Belge de Droit International* 545-546.

McWhinney, Edward. "Soviet Bloc Publicists and the East-West Legal Debate." (1964), 2 *Canadian Yearbook of International Law* 172-183. **335**

McWhinney, Edward. "Soviet and Western International Law and the Cold War in the Era of Bipolarity." In Falk, Richard A., and Mendlovitz, Saul H., eds., *The Strategy of World Order* (New York, 1966), vol. 2, pp. 189-231. **336**

McWhinney, Edward. "Soviet and Western International Law and the Cold War in the Era of Bipolarity: Inter-Block Law in a Nuclear Age." (1963), 1 *Canadian Yearbook of International Law* 40-81. **337**

Morse, Charles. "Some Notes on International Law." (1912), 32 *Canadian Law Times* 964-971. **338**

"New Approaches to International Law." (1972), 1 *Canadian Council on International Law, Proceedings*, 262 p. **339**

This is the general theme of the first annual conference held at Ottawa, October 13-14, 1972. Individual papers are listed separately.

Padjen, Ivan. *Marxism and Positivism in Soviet Theories on the Foundations of International Law*. Halifax, 1975. 220 leaves. **340**
Thesis (LL.M.), Dalhousie University, 1975.

Patry, André. "La conception soviétique du droit international." (1971), 9 *Canadian Yearbook of International Law* 102-113. **341**

Pearson, Lester B. "International Law and International Politics." (1966), 18 *External Affairs* 387-393. **342**
Excerpts from an address by the Prime Minister to the American Bar Association convention in Montreal, August 9, 1966.

Pearson, Lester B. "Toward Effective International Law." (1966), 52 *A.B.A. Journal* 1017-1020. **343**

Perrault, Antonio. "Si Vis Pacem, Para ... Pacem." (1944), 4 *Revue du Barreau* 188-198, 322-327 (Letter of Antonio Langlais). **344**

"Principles of International Law concerning Friendly Relations." (1971), 23 *External Affairs* 39-40. **345**

Read, John E. "Place for International Law and Justice in the Years to Come." (1958), 48 *International Law Association, Report of Conference* 660-667. **346**

Read, John E. "Problems of International Law and Justice." (1956), 6 *Chitty's Law Journal* 43-48. **347**

Sarbadhikari, Pradip. "Non-Alignment, International System and International Law." (1971), 43 *Canadian Political Science Association, Papers*, 24 p. **348**

Sharp, Mitchell. "Canadian Foreign Policy and International Law." (1971), 23 *External Affairs* 175-181. **349**
Speech by the Secretary of State for External Affairs to the International Law Association and the Canadian Institute of International Affairs in Montreal, on March 29, 1971.

Sharp, Mitchell. "The Rule of Law in International Affairs." (1969), 21 *External Affairs* 183-188. **350**
Speech by the Secretary of State for External Affairs to Osgoode Hall Law students, Toronto, March 4, 1969.

St. Laurent, Renault. "The Rule of Law Applied between Nations." (1961), 4 *Canadian Bar Journal* 216-222. **351**

Strong, Maurice F. "Le droit international et la morale internationale." (1976), 10 *Law Society of Upper Canada Gazette* 90-98. **352**

Strong, Maurice F. "International Law and International Morality." (1976), 10 *Law Society of Upper Canada Gazette* 83-89. **353**

Suy, Erik, "Innovations in International Law-Making Processes." *In* Macdonald, Ronald St. John, and others, *The International Law and Policy of Human Welfare* (Alphen aan den Rijn, 1978), pp. 187-200. **354**

Tammelo, Ilmar. "World Order and the 'Enclaves of Justice.'" (1966), 1 *Ottawa Law Review* 1-35. **355**

B. History of International Law

Birkenhead, Frederick Edwin Smith. "International Law as the Great War Has Left It." (1923), 1 *Canadian Bar Review* 763-773. **356**
Also printed in (1923), 8 *Canadian Bar Association, Proceedings* 239-249.

Cave, George. "Growth of International Law Unretarded by the War." (1921), 41 *Canadian Law Times* 107-114. **357**

Clément, Laurent. "Le 'Jus Gentium.'" (1940), 10 *Revue de l'Université d'Ottawa* 100-124, 177-195 (section spéciale) **358**

Connelly, Alpha M. *International Law Across the Ages: A Comparison of the Legal Relations of the Greek City-States and of Modern Nation-States.* Montreal, 1975 (c1976). xii, 710 leaves. **359**
Thesis (LL.M.), McGill University, 1975. (National Library of Canada. Canadian Theses on Microfiche, No. 27108).

Costigan, Richard F. "A Rationalist Critique of Grotius." (1963), 33 *Revue de l'Université d'Ottawa* 289-307. **360**

Deutsch, Karl W. "Medieval Unity and the Economic Conditions for an International Civilization." (1944), 10 *Canadian Journal of Economics and Political Science* 18-35. **361**

Duthoit, Eugène. "Le droit international: leçons du passé - perspective d'avenir." (1917-18), 3 *Revue Trimestrielle Canadienne* 341-372. **362**
Two lectures given at Université Laval, January 8 and 18, 1918.

Finlay, Robert Bannatyne. "Two Addresses to the Canadian Bar Association, Chiefly concerning Certain Phases of International Law." (1919), 39 *Canadian Law Times* 557-593. **363**

"The Grotius Legend." (1919), 39 *Canadian Law Times* 277-281. **364**

Jacobs, Gunther. *Christian Contributions Towards the Abolition of War and the Problem of Property, with Special Emphasis on St. Thomas, Martin Luther and John Calvin.* Edmonton, 1951. vi, 140 leaves. **365**
Thesis (M.A.), University of Alberta, 1951.

Langlais, Antonio. "Un précurseur du droit international: Francisco de Vitoria." (1946), 6 *Revue du Barreau* 257-279. **366**

MacDougall, A.R. "Hugo de Grotte (Grotius)." (1946), 4 *Advocate* 194-200. **367**

Matte, Nicolas Mateesco. *La coutume dans les cycles juridiques internationaux.* Préface de Marcel Sibert. Paris: A. Pedone, 1947. 302 p. **368**
Review: Alejandro Herrero y Rubio in (1949), 2 *Revista Española de Derecho Internacional* 615-655.

Morin, Jacques-Yvan. "Hugo Grotius fut-il un traître." (1958-59), 9 *Thémis* 68-80. **369**

C. Relation to Municipal Law

Claydon, John. "The Application of International Human Rights Law by Canadian Courts." (1981), 30 *Buffalo Law Review* 727-752.   **370**

Gotlieb, Allan E., and Dalfen, Charles M. "National Jurisdiction and International Responsibility: New Canadian Approaches to International Law." (1972), 1 *Canadian Council on International Law, Proceedings* 18-91.   **371**
The address is followed by a discussion (pp. 92-193).

Gotlieb, Allan E., and Dalfen, Charles M. "National Jurisdiction and International Responsibility: New Canadian Approaches to International Law." (1973), 67 *American Journal of International Law* 229-258.   **372**

Howell, John M. "The Commonwealth and the Concept of Domestic Jurisdiction." (1967), 5 *Canadian Yearbook of International Law* 14-44.   **373**

"Integrating International Law into Canadian Domestic Law: Sovereign Immunities / L'incorporation du droit international au droit canadien: le cas des immunités des états." (1981), 10 *Canadian Council on International Law, Proceedings,* 201-212.   **374**
This is a panel. Chairman: Stanislas Slosar.
Contents: "Integrating International Law into Canadian Domestic Law: Sovereign Immunities," by M.L. Jewett (pp. 201-206).- "Sovereign Immunity Law," by Leonard B. Boudin (pp. 207-209).- Discussion (pp. 210-212).

Kindred, Hugh M. "Acts of State and the Application of International Law in Canadian Courts." (1979-80), 10 *Revue de Droit, Université de Sherbrooke* 271-288.   **375**

Kindred, Hugh M. "Acts of State and the Application of International Law in English Courts." (1981), 19 *Canadian Yearbook of International Law* 271-286.   **376**

Lawton, William N. "The Desirability of Giving International Law Primacy over State Law." (1958), 23 *Saskatchewan Bar Review* 46-49.   **377**

Lederman, William R. "The Private International Law System: Some Thoughts on Objectives, Methods, and Relations to Public International Law." *In* Macdonald, Ronald St. John, and others, *Canadian Perspectives on International Law and Organization* (Toronto, 1974), pp. 137-150.   **378**

Macdonald, Ronald St. John. "International Law and the Domestic Law of Canada." *In* Wilner, Gabriel M., ed., *Jus et Societas; Essays in Tribute to Wolfgang Friedmann* (The Hague, 1979), pp. 220-240.   **379**

Macdonald, Ronald St. John. "Public International Law Problems Arising in Canadian Courts." (1955-56), 11 *University of Toronto Law Journal* 224-247.   **380**

Macdonald, Ronald St. John. "The Relationship between International Law and Domestic Law in Canada." *In* Macdonald, Ronald St. John, and others, *Canadian Perspectives on International Law and Organization* (Toronto, 1974), pp. 88-136.   **381**

Morris, Gerald L. "Foreign Relations and the Constitution." (1968), *Canadian Bar Association, Papers,* 10 p. **382**

Rigaldies, Francis, and Woehrling, José. "Le juge interne canadien et le droit international." (1980), 21 *Cahiers de Droit* 293-329. **383**

Vanek, D.C. "Is International Law Part of the Law of Canada?" (1949-50), 8 *University of Toronto Law Journal* 251-297. **384**

Wingler, Wilhelm. "Réflexions sur l'application du droit international public par les tribunaux nationaux." (1967-68), 2 *Ottawa Law Review* 265-319. **385**

D. Codification of International Law

Baxter, Richard R. "The Quest for Certainty and Simplicity in International Law." (1959-63), 1 *University of British Columbia Law Review* 321-332. **386**

"International Law: Canadian and American Associations Cooperate for Its Development." (1946), 32 *A.B.A. Journal* 853-855. **387**

"International Law Commission." (1949), 1 *External Affairs* 21-23 (Sept.) **388**

"International Law Commission." (1962), 14 *External Affairs* 10-12. **389**

Langlais, Antonio. "Les Nations-Unies et la codification du droit international." (1947), 7 *Revue du Barreau* 458-462. **390**

MacKenzie, Norman A.M. "The Progressive Codification of International Law." (1926), 4 *Canadian Bar Review* 302-306. **391**

Wang, Erik B., and Stanford, Joseph S. "Making Progress in Codifying Body of International Law." (1977), *International Perspectives* 10-13 (May/June) **392**

Wickersham, George W. "The Codification of International Law." (1925), 10 *Canadian Bar Association, Proceedings* 94-101. **393**

E. Study and Teaching

Abonyi, Arpad; Sylvain, Ivan J.; and Tomlin, Brian W. "L'état des études internationales au Canada: un survol de la recherche scientifique." (1978), 9 *Études Internationales* 337-359. **394**

Beres, Louis René. "Ends, Means and Methods: The Vital Triad in International Legal Studies." (1979), 27 *Chitty's Law Journal* 145-155. **395**

Brown, Craig. "The Jessup Mooting Competition as a Vehicle for Teaching Public International Law." (1978), 16 *Canadian Yearbook of International Law* 332-341. **396**

Castel, Jean-Gabriel. "Public International Law and Comparative Law." (1961-62), 14 *University of Toronto Law Journal* 108-114. **397**

Corbett, Percy E. *The Study of International Law*. Garden City, N.Y.: Doubleday, 1955. vi, 55 p. (Short Studies in Political Science, 22) **398**

Fleming, Donald J. "The Canadian Round of the Philip C. Jessup International Law Moot Court Competition: Team Preparation, the National Value of the Event, and Its Place in the Curricula of Law Schools in Canada." (1981), 30 *University of New Brunswick Law Journal* 187-197. **399**

Green, Leslie C. "McGill's Institute of Air and Space Law at Twenty-Five." (1977), 25 *Chitty's Law Journal* 244-245. **400**

Hadjidimoulas, Constantine C. "The McGill Institute of Air and Space Law." (1958), 11 *Revue Hellénique de Droit International* 409-410. **401**

Harrison, W.E.C. "The University Teaching of International Affairs." (1936), 2 *Canadian Journal of Economics and Political Science* 431-436. **402**
Discussion follows (pp. 436-439).

Kilgour, Arthur R. *Resources for the Study of International Relations in Canadian Universities: From a Survey Made for the Department of External Affairs and the Canadian Institute of International Affairs- 1968-1969*. Ottawa: Dept. of External Affairs, Information Division, Academic Relations Section, 1969. xi, 350 p. **403**

Macdonald, Ronald St. John. "An Historical Introduction to the Teaching of International Law in Canada." (1974), 12 *Canadian Yearbook of International Law* 67-110. **404**

Macdonald, Ronald St. John. "An Historical Introduction to the Teaching of International Law in Canada: Part II." (1975), 13 *Canadian Yearbook of International Law* 255-280. **405**

Macdonald, Ronald St. John. "An Historical Introduction to the Teaching of International Law in Canada: Part III." (1976), 14 *Canadian Yearbook of International Law* 224-256. **406**

Macdonald, Ronald St. John. "International Organization Courses in Law Schools - A Canadian Comment." (1965), 59 *American Society of International Law, Proceedings* 84-87. **407**

Macdonald, Ronald St. John; Morris, Gerald L.; and Johnston, Douglas M. "The New Lawyer in a Transnational World." (1975), 25 *University of Toronto Law Journal* 343-357. **408**

MacKenzie, Norman A.M. "The Teaching of International Law and International Relations in Canadian Universities, 1931." (1932), 10 *Canadian Bar Review* 519-523. **409**

McGill University. Institute of Air and Space Law. *A Brief History and Bibliography, 1951-70*. Montreal: McGill University, 1970. 32 p. **410**
Review: Unsigned in (1970), 11 *Cahiers de Droit* 863 (brief notice).

McGill University. Institute of Air and Space Law. *The Institute of Air and Space Law, 1951-1976: Historical Background and General Information, Conferences, and Symposium, Books and Other Publications, Students by Classes and Dissertations*. Montreal: McGill University, 1976. 32 p. **411**

McWhinney, Edward. "The Teaching of International Law." (1972), 2 *Georgia Journal of International and Comparative Law* 103-110. **412**

McWhinney, Edward. "The Teaching of Public Law and Public International Law in an Era of Revolutionary Change." *In* Agrawala, S.K., ed., *Legal Education in India: Problems and Perspectives* (Bombay, 1973), pp. 290-296. **413**

Painchaud, Paul. "L'étude de la politique étrangère canadienne et des relations internationales du Québec." *In* Painchaud, Paul, ed., *Le Canada et le Québec sur la scène internationale* (Québec, 1977), pp. 3-27. **414**

Parry, D. Hughes. "The Place of Constitutional Law and International Law in Legal Education." (1950), 28 *Canadian Bar Review* 189-196. **415**

Pépin, Eugène. "L'enseignement du droit aérien dans le monde." (1957-58), 4 *McGill Law Journal* 111-143. **416**

Pépin, Eugène. "L'enseignement du droit aérien dans le monde (addendum)." (1958-59), 5 *McGill Law Journal* 79-83. **417**

"Phase canadienne du procès simulé en droit international - 1979: The 1979 Philip C. Jessup International Law Moot Court Competition." (1979-80), 10 *Revue de Droit, Université de Sherbrooke* 293-368. **418**

"The Philip C. Jessup International Law Moot Court Competition." (1981), 13 *Ottawa Law Review* 822-881. **419**

Pratt, Geoffrey N. "The Institute of Air and Space Law." (1963), 1 *Canadian Yearbook of International Law* 298-300. **420**

Pratt, Geoffrey N. "The Institute of Air and Space Law, McGill University." (1964-68), 1 *Canadian Legal Studies* 22-24. **421**

Rosevear, A. Beatty. "John Cobb Cooper and McGill's Institute of Air and Space Law." (1961-62), 28 *Journal of Air Law and Commerce* 346-350. **422**

Rosevear, A. Beatty. "McGill's Institute of Air and Space Law." (1961-62), 14 *University of Toronto Law Journal* 257-260. **423**

Slosar, Stanislas. "Procès simulé en droit international: leçons d'une courte expérience." (1979-80), 10 *Revue de Droit, Université de Sherbrooke* 369-379. **424**

United Nations Association in Canada. *Teaching about the United Nations.* Vancouver: University of British Columbia, 1963. 43 p. **425**
A report on four workshops for teachers on teaching about the United Nations, conducted under the sponsorship of the United Nations Association in Canada, the British Columbia Teachers' Federation, the Extension Department, University of British Columbia, during October and November 1962, in Castlegar, Kelowna, Vancouver, and Nanaimo, British Columbia.

Vanek, D.C. "Report on the Institute in the Teaching of International and Comparative Law." (1949-50), 8 *University of Toronto Law Journal* 97-102. **426**
Conducted under the auspices of the Association of American Law Schools, New York City, August 23-September 4, 1948.

Warnock, John W. "International Relations as a Canadian Academic Discipline." (1973), 8 *Journal of Canadian Studies* 46-57 (No. 1) **427**

Wiseman, Henry. *Introductory Courses in International Relations in Canadian Universities.* Guelph, Ont., 1970. 170 leaves. **428**
Collection of twenty-nine syllabi prepared at the Dept. of Political Studies, University of Guelph, for the Canadian Political Science Association.

IV. SOURCES OF INTERNATIONAL LAW

Corbett, Percy E. "The Consent of States and the Sources of the Law of Nations." (1925), 6 *British Year Book of International Law* 20-30. **429**

Green, Leslie C. "Comparative Law as a 'Source' of International Law." (1967-68), 42 *Tulane Law Review* 52-66. **430**
    Also printed in Butler, William E., ed., *International Law in Comparative Perspective* (Alphen aan den Rijn, 1980), pp. 139-151.

Green, Leslie C. "An International Lawyer Looks at Comparative Law." (1966), 1 *Israel Law Review* 580-592. **431**
    Annual breakfast address to the joint session of the International and Comparative Law Sections of the American Bar Association, Montreal, August, 1966.

McWhinney, Edward. "Equity in International Law." *In* Newman, Ralph A., ed., *Equity in the World's Legal Systems* (Brussels, 1973), pp. 581-588. **432**

"Principles of International Law: Special United Nations Study." (1966), 18 *External Affairs* 234-237. **433**

Rigaldies, Francis. "Contribution à l'étude de l'acte juridique unilatéral en droit international public." (1980-81), 15 *Revue Juridique Thémis* 417-451. **434**

Sinha, S. Prakash. "Identifying a Principle of International Law Today." (1973), 11 *Canadian Yearbook of International Law* 106-122. **435**

V. SUBJECTS OF INTERNATIONAL LAW

A. States

1. GENERAL NATURE OF THE STATE

Cameron, David M., ed. *Regionalism and Supranationalism: Challenges and Alternatives to the Nation-State in Canada and Europe.* Montreal: Institute for Research on Public Policy, and Policy Studies Institute, c1981. xxv, 138 p. **436**

Revised papers from a seminar held at the Policy Studies Institute, London, March 1980.

Fox, Annette Baker. "The Small States in the International System, 1919-1969." (1968-69), 24 *International Journal* 751-764. **437**

Gilbert, Sidney Norman. *The Status of Nations and Conformity to International Norms.* Ottawa, 1970. 1 vol. (various pagings) **438**

Thesis (M.A.), Carleton University, 1970.

Janssen, Friedrich-Wilhelm. "L'importance de la forme d'état." (1951-52), 2 *Thémis* 210-215. **439**

McWhinney, Edward. "The Effects of Regional Cooperation on the Traditional Conception of the State." *In* Popovici, Adrian, ed., *Problèmes de droit contemporain: mélanges Louis Baudouin* (Montréal, 1974), pp. 401-409. **440**

2. SOVEREIGNTY IN GENERAL

Brosseau, Richard. *Société des états et souveraineté.* Montréal, 1959. 76 leaves. **441**

Thesis, Université de Montréal, Faculté de Théologie. Extract from *Studia Montis Regii,* vol. 1, 1958, pp. 185-212, and vol. 2, 1959, pp. 77-104.

Chipman, Warwick. "Sovereignty." (1925), 3 *Canadian Bar Review* 530-536, 607-613. **442**

Corbett, Percy E. "Sovereignty the Wrecker." (1934), 41 *Queen's Quarterly* 466-474. **443**

Klein, Robert A. *Sovereign Equality among States: The History of an Idea.* Toronto: University of Toronto Press, c1974. xix, 198 p. **444**

Reviews: Leslie C. Green in (1975), 53 *Canadian Bar Review* 448-450; Carston Holbraad in (1977-78), 33 *International Journal* 644-645; Daniel Klang in (1976), 57 *Canadian Historical Review* 311-313; Carol A.L. Prager in (1976), 9 *Canadian Journal of Political Science* 179; Howard Weinroth in (1975), 10 *Canadian Journal of History* 261-262.

Lee, R.W. "On Sovereignty." (1915), 35 *Canadian Law Times* 677-680.   **445**

MacIntyre, Malcolm M. "The Rationale of Separate National Sovereignty." (1942-44), 5 *Alberta Law Quarterly* 155-168.   **446**

McRae, Donald M. "Sovereignty and the International Legal Order." (1971), 10 *Western Ontario Law Review* 56-86.   **447**

Ross, Charles R. "National Sovereignty in International Environmental Decisions." (1972), 12 *Natural Resources Journal* 242-254.   **448**

Wood, John R. "Secession: A Comparative Analytical Framework." (1981), 14 *Canadian Journal of Political Science* 107-134.   **449**

3. INTERNATIONAL STATUS

(a) BRITISH DOMINIONS

See also *"Commonwealth of Nations" (p. 77), and "Relations with the British Empire and the Commonwealth" (p. 501).*

Allin, C.D. "The International Status of the British Dominions with Respect to the League of Nations." (1919-20), 4 *Minnesota Law Review* 190-218.   **450**

Allin, C.D. "Recent Developments in the Constitutional and International Status of the British Dominions." (1925-26), 10 *Minnesota Law Review* 100-122. **451**

Anderson, J.C. "Dominion Status." (1930), 8 *Canadian Bar Review* 32-48, 112-125, 196-212.   **452**

Baker, Philip John Noel. *The Present Juridical Status of the British Dominions in International Law*. London: Longmans, Green, 1929. xii, 421 p.   **453**
Half-title: *Contributions to International Law and Diplomacy*. English version of: *Le statut juridique actuel des Dominions britanniques dans le domaine du droit international*, published in (1927), 19 *Académie de Droit International, Recueil des Cours* 247-391.
Reviews: Norman A.M. MacKenzie in (1930), 24 *American Journal of International Law* 414-415; Norman A.M. MacKenzie in (1929), 10 *Canadian Historical Review* 356-358.

Buchet, Edmond Édouard. *Le 'status' des Dominions britanniques en droit constitutionnel et en droit international*. Paris: Recueil Sirey, 1928. 137 p.   **454**
Reviews: Edwin M. Borchard in (1929), 23 *American Journal of International Law* 706-707; A. Berriedale Keith in a review article under title: "The British Empire," in (1929), 11 *Journal of Comparative Legislation and International Law* 142-145 (3d Ser.); M. MacWhite in (1928), 5 *Revue de Droit International, de Sciences Diplomatiques et Politiques* 375-377; Charles Rousseau in (1929), 36 *Revue Générale de Droit International Public* 369-371.

Chevallier, Jean-Jacques. "L'évolution du statut de dominion." (1932), 39 *Revue Générale de Droit International Public* 458-497.   **455**

Chevallier, Jean-Jacques. "Les origines et le sens du Statut de Westminster." (1936), 17 *Revue de Droit International* 413-441. **456**

Crabitès, Pierre. "The Balfour Declaration." (1930), 8 *Canadian Bar Review* 479-482. **457**

Cross, Hartley William. *Dominion Status*. Worcester, Mass., 1924. 176 leaves.
Thesis (M.A.), Clark University, 1924. **458**

Cross, Hartley William. *The Status of the British Dominions*. Worcester, Mass., 1929. 282, (7), 4 leaves. **459**
Thesis (Ph.D.), Clark University, 1929.

Dawson, Robert MacGregor, ed. *The Development of Dominion Status, 1900-1936*. London: Oxford University Press, 1937. xiv, 466 p. **460**
Reviews: Charles J. Burchell in (1938), 16 *Canadian Bar Review* 71-72; Percy E. Corbett in (1938), 4 *Canadian Journal of Economics and Political Science* 113-114; A. Berriedale Keith in (1938), 17 *International Affairs* 420-421; W.P.M. Kennedy in (1938), 19 *Canadian Historical Review* 65; Escott Reid in (1938-39), 18 *Dalhousie Review* 408-409.

Dumon, Laurence. *La situation juridique des Dominions britanniques depuis 1926*. Bordeaux: J. Bière, 1935. 120 p. **461**
Thesis, Université de Bordeaux.
Review: Charles Rousseau in (1936), 43 *Revue Générale de Droit International Public* 226-227.

Dunn, Frederick Sherwood. "The New International Status of the Dominions." (1926-27), 13 *Virginia Law Review* 354-379. **462**

Ewart, John S. "Dominion Autonomy at the Imperial Conference 1926." (1926-27), 34 *Queen's Quarterly* 285-297. **463**

Fitzhardinge, L.F. "Hughes, Borden, and Dominion Representation at the Paris Peace Conference." (1968), 49 *Canadian Historical Review* 160-169. **464**

Francis, R. "The End of Dominion Status." (1945), 23 *Canadian Bar Review* 725-744. **465**

Hall, Hessel Duncan. "The Genesis of the Balfour Declaration of 1926." (1961-63), 1 *Journal of Commonwealth Political Studies* 169-193. **466**

Hall, Hessel Duncan. "The Imperial Crown and the Foreign Relations of the Dominions." (1921), 41 *Canadian Law Times* 33-44. **467**
Reprinted from (1920), 2 *Journal of Comparative Legislation and International Law* 196-205 (3d Ser.).

Hudson, Manley O. "Notes on the Statute of Westminster, 1931." (1932-33), 46 *Harvard Law Review* 261-289. **468**

Johnston, V. Kenneth. "Dominion Status in International Law." (1927), 21 *American Journal of International Law* 481-489. **469**

Johnston, V. Kenneth. *The International Status of the British Dominions*. Chicago, 1926. 298 leaves. **470**
Thesis (Ph.D.), University of Chicago, 1926.

Keith, A. Berriedale. *Dominion Autonomy in Practice*. London: Oxford University Press; H. Milford, 1929. vi, 92 p. **471**
Review: John S. Ewart in (1930), 8 *Canadian Bar Review* 394-396.

Keith, A. Berriedale. *The Dominions as Sovereign States; Their Constitutions and Governments.* London: Macmillan, 1938. xiv, 769 p. **472**
Reviews: Percy E. Corbett in (1939), 33 *American Journal of International Law* 407-408; Kenneth Clinton Wheare in (1938), 17 *International Affairs* 842-844; unsigned in (1939-40), 3 *University of Toronto Law Journal* 209-210.

Keith, A. Berriedale. "The International Status of the Dominions." (1923), 5 *Journal of Comparative Legislation and International Law* 161-168 (3d Ser.) **473**

Keith, A. Berriedale. *The Sovereignty of the British Dominions.* London: Macmillan, 1929. xxvi, 524 p. **474**
Review: Norman A.M. MacKenzie in (1930), 24 *American Journal of International Law* 835-836.

Keith, A. Berriedale, ed. *Speeches and Documents on the British Dominions, 1918-1931; from Self-Government to National Sovereignty.* London: Oxford University Press; H. Milford, 1932. xlvii, 501 p. (World's Classics) **475**

Kennedy, W.P.M. "The Imperial Conferences, 1926-1930: The Statute of Westminster." (1932), 48 *Law Quarterly Review* 191-216. **476**
Review: Norman McL. Rogers in (1932), 13 *Canadian Historical Review* 199-200.

Kennedy, W.P.M. "Status of South Africa." (1935-36), 1 *University of Toronto Law Journal* 147-158. **477**

Kidwai, M.H.M. "External Affairs Power and the Constitutions of the British Dominions." (1975-76), 9 *University of Queensland Law Journal* 167-187. **478**
Refers to Canada, Australia and New Zealand.

Kidwai, M.H.M. "International Personality and the British Dominions: Evolution and Accomplishment." (1975-76), 9 *University of Queensland Law Journal* 76-117. **479**

Laing, Lionel H. "The Struggle for the Recognition of Dominion Authority." (1939), 33 *American Journal of International Law* 747-753. **480**

Lewis, Malcolm M. "The International Status of the British Self-Governing Dominions." (1922-23), 3 *British Year Book of International Law* 21-41. **481**

Madden, A.F. "How Colonies Grow into Dominions." (1950), 41 *United Empire* 159-164. **482**

Mallory, James R. "Seals and Symbols: From Substance to Form in Commonwealth Equality." (1956), 22 *Canadian Journal of Economics and Political Science* 281-291. **483**

Marriott, J.A.R. "Dominion Status." (1930), 107 *Nineteenth Century* 56-69. **484**

McWhinney, Edward. " 'Sovereignty' in the United Kingdom and the Commonwealth Countries at the Present Day." (1953), 68 *Political Science Quarterly* 511-525. **485**

Morgan, J.H. "Dominion Status." (1929-30), 9 *Dalhousie Review* 131-156. **486**

Morse, Charles. "Dominions Old and New." (1922-23), 2 *Dalhousie Review* 53-58. **487**

Nathan, Manfred. "Dominion Status." (1922), 8 *Grotius Society, Transactions* 117-132. **488**

Nelson, Herbert Ira. *The British Dominions at the Paris Peace Conference, 1919: An Essay on Their Role in the Colonial and in the Racial Equality Negotiations.* Ithaca, N.Y., 1949. 11, 127 leaves. **489**
Thesis (A.M.), Cornell University, 1949.

Porritt, Edward. *The Fiscal and Diplomatic Freedom of the British Overseas Dominions.* Oxford: Clarendon Press; London, New York, etc.: H. Milford, 1922. xvi, 492 p. (Carnegie Endowment for International Peace. Division of Economics and History. Publications) **490**
Reviews: John S. Ewart in (1922), 16 *American Journal of International Law* 735-741; W.P.M. Kennedy in (1922), 3 *Canadian Historical Review* 367-371.

Scott, Francis R. "The End of Dominion Status." (1944), 38 *American Journal of International Law* 34-49. **491**

Smith, Herbert A. "The British Dominions and Foreign Relations." (1926-27), 12 *Cornell Law Quarterly* 1-12. **492**

Sweeney, Joseph. "The Status of the Irish Free State in the British Commonwealth of Nations." (1944), 22 *Canadian Bar Review* 183-195. **493**

Tariff Commission, London. *The Status of the Dominions and Their Relations with Foreign Countries.* London: Published for the Tariff Commission by P.S. King, 1920. 21 p. **494**
Review: Unsigned in (1920), 1 *Canadian Historical Review* 331-332.

Wheare, Kenneth Clinton. *The Statute of Westminster and Dominion Status.* 5th ed. London: Oxford University Press, 1953. xvi, 347 p. **495**
Reviews: Robert MacGregor Dawson in (1939), 5 *Canadian Journal of Economics and Political Science* 267-268 (of 1938 ed.); W.P.M. Kennedy in (1938), 20 *Journal of Comparative Legislation and International Law* 287-288 (3d Ser.) (of 1938 ed.); unsigned in (1939-40), 46 *Queen's Quarterly* 105-107 (of 1938 ed.).

(b) CANADA

Anderson, Edward. "Canada's National Status." (1921), 41 *Canadian Law Times* 248-254. **496**
Address delivered to the Manitoba Bar Association.

Bertrand, Charles-Auguste. "Le Canada est-il une nation?" (1946), 6 *Revue du Barreau* 401-409. **497**

Bonenfant, Jean-Charles. "Le développement du statut international du Canada." In Painchaud, Paul, ed., *Le Canada et le Québec sur la scène internationale* (Québec, 1977), pp. 31-49. **498**

Brière, Marc. "Souveraineté au Canada." (1952-53), 3 *Thémis* 125-136. **499**

Burchell, Charles J. *The Statute of Westminster and Its Effect on Canada.* Foreword by Sir Edward Harding. Johannesburg: South African Institute of International Affairs, 1945. 16 p. **500**
Review: E.C.S. Wade in (1946), 28 *Journal of Comparative Legislation and International Law* 150 (3d Ser.).

Buron, Edmond. "Où va le Canada?" (1932), 2 *Revue de l'Université d'Ottawa* 298-315, 434-452. **501**

Castro-Rial, Juan M. "L'exercice de la souveraineté externe du Canada." (1950), 3 *Revue Hellénique de Droit International* 199-204. **502**

Castro-Rial, Juan M. *La personnalité internationale du Canada.* Montréal, 1950. 132 leaves. **503**
Thesis (Ph.D.), Université de Montréal, 1950.
Review: André Patry in (1950), 56/2 *Revue Dominicaine* 139-144.

Christie, Loring C. "Canada's International Status: Developments at the Paris Peace Conference, 1919." (1964), 16 *External Affairs* 163-172. **504**

Clokie, H. McD. "Canada's National Status in Recent Years." (1947), 253 *Annals of the American Academy of Political and Social Science* 22-31. **505**

Crofton, F. Blake. "Our Unworthy Status." (1908-09), 16 *Journal of the Canadian Bankers' Association* 29-37. **506**

Cronin, Maureen P. *Canada and the Conference on the Limitation of Armament, 1921-2.* Stanford, Calif., 1954. ii, 156 leaves. **507**
Thesis (M.A.), Stanford University, 1954.

Dawson, Robert MacGregor, ed. *The Development of Dominion Status, 1900-1936.* London: Oxford University Press, 1937. xiv, 466 p. **508**
Reviews: Charles J. Burchell in (1938), 16 *Canadian Bar Review* 71-72; Percy E. Corbett in (1938), 4 *Canadian Journal of Economics and Political Science* 113-114; A. Berriedale Keith in (1938), 17 *International Affairs* 420-421; W.P.M. Kennedy in (1938), 19 *Canadian Historical Review* 65; Escott Reid in (1938-39), 18 *Dalhousie Review* 408-409.

"Dominion Status: The French Canadian View (From a French Canadian Pen)." (1928-29), 19 *Round Table.* 620-625. **509**

Dumouchel, Jean. "Le Canada au Cabinet impérial de guerre." (1941-42), 17/1 *Actualité Économique* 456-466. **510**

Dumouchel, Jean. "Le Canada en marche vers son status international; de 1914 au Cabinet de guerre (1917)." (1941-42), 17/1 *Actualité Économique* 220-240. **511**

Dumouchel, Jean. *Première étape du Canada vers son status international 1914-1919.* Ottawa, 1940. 115 leaves. **512**
Thesis (M.A.), University of Ottawa, 1940.

Ewart, John S. "Canada: Colony to Kingdom." (1913), 7 *American Journal of International Law* 268-284. **513**
Includes a section on treaties (pp. 275-278).

Ewart, John S. "Canada and War." (1932), 10 *Canadian Bar Review* 495-506. **514**

Ewart, John S. "Canada Breaks Her Shell." (1923-24), 3 *Dalhousie Review* 304-316. **515**

Ewart, John S. "Canada's Political Status." (1928), 9 *Canadian Historical Review* 194-205. **516**
Comments on an article by A. Berriedale Keith entitled: "Recent Changes in Canada's Constitutional Status," published in (1928), 9 *Canadian Historical Review* 102-116.

FitzGerald, Gerald F. "Canada, a Self-Governing Nation." (1945), 15 *Revue de l'Université d'Ottawa* 317-333. **517**

Frith, Elizabeth Aldon (Stewart). *The Growth of Canadian Control over External Affairs, 1867-1939.* Vancouver, 1955. 258 leaves. **518**
Thesis (M.A.), University of British Columbia, 1955.

Gagnon, Onésime. "The Evolution of Canadian Autonomy." (1933), 18 *Canadian Bar Association, Proceedings* 163-187. **519**
Also published in French under title: "L'évolution de l'autonomie canadienne," in (1934-35), 10 *Actualité Économique* 94-109.

Gibson, James A. "Mr. Mackenzie King and Canadian Autonomy, 1921-46." (1951), *Canadian Historical Association, Historical Papers* 12-21. **520**

Herman, Lawrence L. "International Law Aspects of Patriation." (1982), 31 *University of New Brunswick Law Journal* 69-86. **521**

Hougham, George Millard. *The Development of Dominion Status Canada, 1931-1945.* Toronto, 1946 (c1976). 219 leaves. **522**
Thesis (M.A.), University of Toronto, 1948. (National Library of Canada. Canadian Theses on Microfiche, No. 24583).

Keith, A. Berriedale. "The Canadian Constitution and External Relations." (1919), 1 *Journal of Comparative Legislation and International Law* 7-16 (3d Ser.)
Review: W.P.M. Kennedy in (1920), 1 *Canadian Historical Review* 107-109. **523**

Keith, A. Berriedale. "Growth of Canadian Independence." (1919), 39 *Canadian Law Times* 372-373. **524**

Keith, A. Berriedale. "Recent Changes in Canada's Constitutional Status." (1928), 9 *Canadian Historical Review* 102-116. **525**
See comments by John S. Ewart under title: "Canada's Political Status," in (1928), 9 *Canadian Historical Review* 194-205.

Kennedy, W.P.M. " 'The Kingdom of Canada.' " (1939), 17 *Canadian Bar Review* 1-6. **526**
See also reply by T.S. Ewart in (1939), 17 *Canadian Bar Review* 178-180.

Lapointe, Ernest. "La situation internationale du Canada." (1927-28), 6 *Revue du Droit* 193-216. **527**
Conférence donnée à un déjeuner-causerie du Jeune Barreau de Québec, le 19 novembre 1927.

Lapointe, Ernest. "Le Statut de Westminster et l'évolution nationale du Canada." (1932), 18 *Revue Trimestrielle Canadienne* 1-18. **528**
Lecture given at the 'Cercle Universitaire' of Montreal, January 16, 1932.

Lapointe, L.-A. "Le statut international du Canada." (1927), 13 *Revue Trimestrielle Canadienne* 349-366. **529**
Lecture given at the 'Cercle Universitaire' of Montreal, October 29, 1927.

Lavoie, Paul. "L'autonomie du Canada et sa nouvelle situation internationale." (1927), 34 *Revue Générale de Droit International Public* 171-209. **530**
Reviewed by "Un professeur" in (1927-28), 6 *Revue du Droit* 65-68.

Lemieux, Rodolphe. "L'évolution du Canada." (1931), 1 *Revue de l'Université d'Ottawa* 32-42. **531**

Levadie, Meyer. *John W. Dafoe and the Evolution of Canadian Autonomy, 1918-1926.* Winnipeg, 1952. vi, 173 leaves. **532**
Thesis (M.A.), University of Manitoba, 1952.

Martin, Chester B. "The United States and Canadian Nationality." (1937), 18 *Canadian Historical Review* 1-11. **533**

Mazer, Brian M. "Sovereignty and Canada: An Examination of Canadian Sovereignty from a Legal Perspective." (1977-78), 42 *Saskatchewan Law Review* 1-15. **534**

Mignault, P.B. "Quelques aperçus sur le développement du principe de l'autonomie au Canada avant et depuis le 'Statute of Westminster' de 1931." (1932), 26 *Royal Society of Canada, Transactions* 45-64 (3d Ser., Sec. 1) **535**

Morse, Charles. "Status of Canada." (1906), 5 *Canadian Law Review* 379-382. **536**

Mowat, H.M. "Greater Canadian Independence." (1903-04), 11 *Queen's Quarterly* 34-45. **537**

Ollivier, Maurice. *Le Canada, pays souverain? Le statut de Westminster.* Montréal: Éditions Albert Lévesque, 1935. 229 p. (Documents politiques) **538**

Ollivier, Maurice. *Problems of Canadian Sovereignty from the British North America Act, 1867, to the Statute of Westminster, 1931.* Toronto: Canada Law Book, 1945. xi, 491 p. **539**
Discusses both constitutional and international aspects of sovereignty.
Reviews: Henry F. Angus in (1947), 28 *Canadian Historical Review* 72-75; Bora Laskin in (1946), 24 *Canadian Bar Review* 249-251.

Ollivier, Maurice. "Le Statut de Westminster: étude de l'évolution politique au Canada." (1933), 19 *Revue Trimestrielle Canadienne* 12-44. **540**
A résumé of a doctoral thesis presented before the Faculty of Law of the University of Montreal in 1933; includes international aspects of Canadian sovereignty.

Ollivier, Maurice. "Structure juridique de l'État canadien." (1948), 18 *Revue de l'Université d'Ottawa* 280-293. **541**

Pange, Jean de. "Roi du Canada." (1948), 62 *Revue d'Histoire Diplomatique* 1-7. **542**

Pelland, Léo. "Notre 'status' international." (1926-27), 5 *Revue du Droit* 5-13, 65-74, 129-141, 193-208. **543**

Pierce, Clifford James. *Sovereignty as an Issue in Canadian Defence Policy: 1940 to 1968.* Fredericton, 1976 (c1977). xi, 234 leaves. **544**
Thesis (M.A.), University of New Brunswick, 1976. (National Library of Canada. Canadian Theses on Microfiche, No. 30448).

Riddell, William Renwick. "The Status of Canada." (1921), 7 *A.B.A. Journal* 293-296. **545**

Riddell, William Renwick. "What Is Canada, Anyway?" (1921), 1 *Boston University Law Review* 13-20. **546**

Rowell, Newton W. "Recent Constitutional Developments in Canada: Three Great Steps in Canada's Progress from Dependent Colonies of Great Britain to the Full Equality of Status in the Britannic Commonwealth Which It Now Enjoys." (1924), 10 *A.B.A. Journal* 427-433. **547**

Russell, Benjamin. "Canada's International Status." (1928), 22 *American Society of International Law, Proceedings* 19-26. **548**

Sandwell, B.K. "Sovereignty in Canada." (1932), 39 *Queen's Quarterly* 193-209.
   549

Shields, Robert A. "Imperial Policy and the Ripon Circular of 1895." (1966), 47 *Canadian Historical Review* 119-135.
   550

Siegfried, André. "Le statut international du Canada." (1937), 1 *Revue d'Histoire Politique et Constitutionnelle* 39-54.
   551

"Situation internationale du Canada." (1927-28), 6 *Revue du Droit* 304-309. **552**
Contains mainly the speech of Raoul Dandurand given at the 'Cercle Universitaire' of Montreal on January 21, 1928.

Smith, Herbert A. "Diplomacy and International Status." (1924), 2 *Canadian Bar Review* 231-242.
   553

"Statut international du Canada." (1927-28), 6 *Revue du Droit* 442-448. **554**
Extracts from debates in the House of Commons.

"Le statut international du Canada." (1928-29), 7 *Revue du Droit* 65-75. **555**
This is a review of an article by André Siegfried in (1928), 46 *Revue des Deux-Mondes* 187-202.

Stevenson, John A. "Canada and Downing Street." (1924-25), 3 *Foreign Affairs* 135-146.
   556

Thompson, Bram. "Canada's National Status." (1928), 6 *Canadian Bar Review* 759-772.
   557

Thompson, Bram. "Canada's Status." (1922), 42 *Canadian Law Times* 513-519.
   558

Tupper, Charles Hibbert. "Canada's International Status." (1898), 11 *Canadian Magazine* 409-412.
   559

(c) OTHERS

Castro-Rial, Juan M. "La situation internationale de l'Espagne." (1949), 19 *Revue de l'Université d'Ottawa* 319-334.
   560

Crean, Frank Leo van de. *The Legal Status of Israel Revisited: A Study in International Law of the Legality of Its Genesis and of the Reality of Its Statehood.* Montreal, 1978. xviii, 224 leaves. **561**
Thesis (LL.M.), McGill University, 1978.

Doxcy, Margaret P. "The Making of Zimbabwe: From Illegal to Legal Independence." (1982), 36 *Year Book of World Affairs* 151-165.
   562

Green, Leslie C. "Rhodesian Independence - Legal or Illegal?" (1967-68), 6 *Alberta Law Review* 37-66.
   563

Green, Leslie C. "Southern Rhodesian Independence." (1969-70), 14 *Archiv des Völkerrechts* 155-191.
   564

Matthews, Robert O. "Talking Without Negotiating: The Case of Rhodesia." (1979-80), 35 *International Journal* 91-117.
   565

4. SELF-DETERMINATION

Claydon, John. "Reflections on Self-Determination, Minorities, and Northern Ireland." (1973), 2 *Canadian Council on International Law, Proceedings* 41-59.
566

Cooper, John A. "Self-Government and Imperialism." (1903-04), 11 *Queen's Quarterly* 243-246.
567

Franck, Thomas M., and Hoffman, Paul. "The Right of Self-Determination in Very Small Places." (1975-76), 8 *New York University Journal of International Law and Politics* 331-386.
568

Friedlander, Robert A. "Proposed Criteria for Testing the Validity of Self-Determination as It Applies to Disaffected Minorities." (1977), 25 *Chitty's Law Journal* 335-338.
569

Green, Leslie C. "Self-Determination and Settlement of the Arab-Israeli Conflict." (1971), 65 *American Society of International Law, Proceedings* 40-48.
570

Hanham, H.J. "The Scottish Nation Faces the Post-Imperial World." (1967-68), 23 *International Journal* 570-584.
571

"The International Law of Human Rights: Future of Self-Determination / Les droits de la personne en droit international: l'avenir de l'auto-détermination." (1978), 7 *Canadian Council on International Law, Proceedings* 83-95.
572
   This is a panel. Chairman: Brian Crane.- Speakers: Gerald L. Morris (pp. 83-86), and Ivan Bernier (pp. 86-88).- Discussion (pp. 89-95).

Kaida, Lawrence. *Self-Determination and the United Nations*. Edmonton, 1980. viii, 131 leaves.
573
   Thesis (M.A.), University of Alberta, 1980. (National Library of Canada. Canadian Theses on Microfiche, No. 48989).

Kusi, Jonathan Atta. *The Right of Self-Determination in International Law*. Montreal, 1970. 120, vii leaves.
574
   Thesis (LL.M.), McGill University, 1970. (National Library of Canada. Canadian Theses on Microfilm, No. 6414).

McWhinney, Edward. "Non-Intervention and Self-Determination." (1974), 56 *International Law Association, Report of Conference* 295-301.
575

Meissner, Boris. "The Soviet Concept of Nation and the Right of National Self-Determination." (1976-77), 32 *International Journal* 56-81.
576

Pomerance, Michla. "Methods of Self-Determination and the Argument of 'Primitiveness.' " (1974), 12 *Canadian Yearbook of International Law* 38-66.
577

Sinha, S. Prakash. "Is Self-Determination Passé?" (1973), 12 *Columbia Journal of Transnational Law* 260-273.
578

Williams, Colin H. *National Separatism*. Vancouver: University of British Columbia Press, 1982. ix, 317 p., maps.
579

5. RECOGNITION OF STATES AND GOVERNMENTS

Bilsland, A.W. "International Law - Doctrine of Immunity, Impleading Foreign Sovereign Government by Special Order - Doctrine of Retroactive Recognition, Effect of De Jure Recognition on Title to Property Acquired by Foreign Government in Breach of Municipal Law of Recognizing Power." (1953-58), 2 *U.B.C. Legal Notes* 131-136. **580**

Binavince, Emilio S. "The Canadian Practice in Matters of Recognition." *In* Macdonald, Ronald St. John, and others, *Canadian Perspectives on International Law and Organization* (Toronto, 1974), pp. 153-183. **581**

Brookfield, F.M. "The Courts, Kelsen, and the Rhodesian Revolution." (1969), 19 *University of Toronto Law Journal* 326-352. **582**

"Canadian Recognition of the Czechoslovak Government-in-Exile, 1939-1940." (1971), 23 *External Affairs* 496-502. **583**

"Canadian Recognition of the People's Republic of China; the Course of Negotiations." (1970), 22 *External Affairs* 414-417. **584**

Cohen, Maxwell. "Communist China - To Recognize or not to Recognize." (1952-53), 8 *International Journal* 266-273. **585**

Dai, Poeliu. "Recognition of States and Governments under International Law with Special Reference to Canadian Postwar Practice and the Legal Status of Taiwan (Formosa)." (1965), 3 *Canadian Yearbook of International Law* 290-305. **586**

Frenette, Claude. "De la reconnaissance d'état en droit international." (1956-57), 7 *Thémis* 240-254. **587**

Gill, W.B. "International Law - The Doctrine of Retroactive Recognition, Its Effects in Municipal Law - Offer of Former Government Binding on New Government - Limitations on Doctrine of Retroactive Recognition." (1949-52), 1 *U.B.C. Legal Notes* 182-190. **588**

Green, Leslie C. "New States, Regionalism and International Law." (1967), 5 *Canadian Yearbook of International Law* 118-141. **589**

Green, Leslie C. "The Recognition of Communist China. (*Civil Air Transport Inc. v. Chennault and Others*)." (1950), 3 *International Law Quarterly* 418-422. **590**

Hankin, Janet G. *Silence and Perception: A Case Study of Swedish Recognition of the Democratic Republic of Vietnam.* Montreal, 1972. 184 leaves. **591**
Thesis (M.A.), McGill University, 1972.

Harbron, John D. "Canada Recognizes China: The Trudeau Round 1968-1973." (1974-75), 33 *Behind the Headlines* No. 5 (29 p.) **592**

Jolicoeur, André. "De la reconnaissance en droit international." (1964-65), 6 *Cahiers de Droit* 85-92 (no 2) **593**

Lyon, Peyton V. "A Case for the Recognition of East Germany." (1959-60), 15 *International Journal* 337-346. **594**

Macpherson, Marion A. "Looking at the 20-Year Debate over China's Voice at the UN." (1972), *International Perspectives* 3-6 (Jan./Feb.) **595**

Merrills, J.G. "Law, Politics and the Legislation of the Unrecognized Government." (1968-69), 3 *Ottawa Law Review* 1-24. **596**

Nisot, Joseph. "Is the Recognition of a Government Retroactive." (1943), 21 *Canadian Bar Review* 617-643. **597**

Theuman, Richard. *An Analysis of Tanzania's Recognition of Biafra.* Montreal, 1970 (c1971). xii, 124 leaves. **598**
 Thesis (M.A.), McGill University, 1971. (National Library of Canada. Canadian Theses on Microfilm, No. 9501).

Wagenberg, Ronald Harvey. *Canada and Red China: Problems of Recognition.* Windsor, 1962. 69 leaves. **599**
 Thesis (M.A.), Assumption University of Windsor, 1962.

Woolsey, Theodore S. "The Recognition of Panama and Its Results." (1904), 3 *Canadian Law Review* 91-101. **600**

Yee, Herbert Sun-Jun. *Decisions to Establish Diplomatic Relations with China: Environmental Variables in Foreign Policy Decision-Making.* Honolulu, 1976. xiv, 248 leaves. **601**
 Thesis (Ph.D.), University of Hawaii, 1976. Abstracted in (1977), 38 *Dissertation Abstracts International* 467-A. (University Microfilms, Ann Arbor, No. 77-14606).

Yee, Herbert Sun-Jun. *The Making of Canadian and Japanese Policies in Establishing Diplomatic Relations with China.* Windsor, 1973. v, 341 leaves. **602**
 Thesis (M.A.), University of Windsor, 1973. (National Library of Canada. Canadian Theses on Microfiche, No. 19990).

6. STATE SUCCESSION AND CONTINUITY

Arbour, Jean-Maurice. "Secession and International Law: Some Economic Problems in Relation to State Succession." (1978), 19 *Cahiers de Droit* 285-338. **603**

Green, Leslie C. "Malaya/Singapore/Malaysia: Comments on State Competence, Succession and Continuity." (1966), 4 *Canadian Yearbook of International Law* 3-42. **604**

La Forest, Gerard V. "Towards a Reformulation of the Law of State Succession." (1966), 60 *American Society of International Law, Proceedings* 103-111. **605**

Misra, K.P. "Succession of States: Pakistan's Membership in the United Nations." (1965), 3 *Canadian Yearbook of International Law* 281-289. **606**

7. TYPES OF STATES

(a) FEDERAL STATES AND FEDERALISM

Azab, Nagulb. *Theoretical Problems of Integration, a Case Study: The Egyptian-Syrian Union.* Edmonton, 1970. v, 161 leaves. **607**
 Thesis (M.A.), University of Alberta, 1970.

Bernier, Ivan. *International Legal Aspects of Federalism.* London: Longman, 1973. xi, 308 p. **608**
A revision of the author's thesis, University of London, 1969.
Reviews: Jean-Maurice Arbour in (1973), 14 *Cahiers de Droit* 704-707; C. Lloyd Brown-John in (1974), 7 *Canadian Journal of Political Science* 386-387; Leslie C. Green in (1974), 68 *American Journal of International Law* 772-773; Peter W. Hogg in (1974), 52 *Canadian Bar Review* 618-619; Annemarie Jacomy-Millette in (1974), 5 *Études Internationales* 573-575; Thomas Allen Levy in (1973-74), 1 *Dalhousie Law Journal* 634-638.

"The Constitution of Switzerland." (1950), 2 *External Affairs* 212-217. **609**

Fédéralisme et nations. Montréal: Presses de l'Université du Québec, 1971. 290 p., maps. (Cahiers de l'Université du Québec, C-27) **610**
Edited by Roman Serbyn.
Review: Jean-Charles Bonenfant in (1971), 2 *Études Internationales* 493-494.

Ibrahim, Muhammad Khalil. *The Application of International Law in Disputes between Member-States of Federal Unions, with Special Reference to the United States, Australia and Canada.* Leiden: Prytaneum, 1952. xi, 160 p.**611**
Review: Charles Fairman in (1953), 47 *American Journal of International Law* 515.

Leisner, Walter. "The Foreign Relations of the Member States of the Federal Republic of Germany." (1965-66), 16 *University of Toronto Law Journal* 346-360. **612**

McWhinney, Edward. *Comparative Federalism; States' Rights and National Power.* Toronto: University of Toronto Press, c1962. ix, 103 p. **613**
Reviews: J.A. Corry in (1964), 42 *Canadian Bar Review* 649-651; Zelman Cowen in (1962-63), 23 *Louisiana Law Review* 819-820; Peter H. Russell in (1964), 30 *Canadian Journal of Economics and Political Science* 278-279; S.A. de Smith in (1964), 27 *Modern Law Review* 754-756; Joseph Szabó in (1964), 13 *American Journal of Comparative Law* 98-100; Dennis Thompson in (1964), 13 *International and Comparative Law Quarterly* 360-361; Herman Walker in (1964), 58 *American Journal of International Law* 223-224.

McWhinney, Edward. *Comparative Federalism; States' Rights and National Power.* 2d ed. Toronto: University of Toronto Press, 1965. xii, 114 p. **614**

McWhinney, Edward. *Federal Constitution-Making for a Multi-National World.* Leyden: A.W. Sijthoff, 1966. xii, 150 p. **615**
Reviews: J.E.S. Fawcett in (1967), 43 *International Affairs* 735-736; Thomas M. Franck in (1968), 62 *American Journal of International Law* 214-216.

McWhinney, Edward. "The Relevance of 'Classical' Federalism to Contemporary Constitution-Making in the 'New Countries.'" (1963), 57 *American Society of International Law, Proceedings* 249-250. **616**

McWhinney, Edward, and Pescatore, Pierre, eds. *Federalism and Supreme Courts and the Integration of Legal Systems / Fédéralisme et cours suprêmes et l'intégration des systèmes juridiques.* With the assistance of Raymond Baeyens. Heule: UGA, 1973. xi, 266 p. **617**
Contains papers presented at a special international seminar held in Luxembourg in July and August of 1972, under the auspices of Centre international d'études et de recherches européennes, and Faculté internationale de droit comparé, in Luxembourg.
Reviews: R. Taylor Cole in (1976), 9 *Canadian Journal of Political Science* 153-154; Leslie C. Green in (1975), 69 *American Journal of International Law* 720-721.

Morin, Jacques-Yvan. *L'état fédéral en droit international.* Paris: Association des études internationales, 1962? 77, iii p. **618**
At head of title: Université de Paris. Institut des hautes études internationales, 1961-1962.

Trudeau, André. "La capacité internationale de l'état fédéré et sa participation au sein des organisations et conférences internationales." (1968), 3 *Revue Juridique Thémis* 223-276. **619**

Wildhaber, Luzius. "External Relations of the Swiss Cantons." (1974), 12 *Canadian Yearbook of International Law* 211-221. **620**

(b) CANADIAN FEDERALISM

(i) GENERAL

Beaudoin, Gérald. "Nationalismes et fédéralisme renouvelé." (1978), 16 *Royal Society of Canada, Transactions* 293-300 (4th Ser.) **621**

Bergeron, Gérard. "Projet d'un nouveau Commonwealth canadien." (1977), 8 *Études Internationales* 240-253. **622**
Also published in (1977), 12 *Journal of Canadian Studies* 8-17 (No. 3).

Bergeron, Gérard. "Une solution 'super-fédéraliste' à la crise canadienne: un Canadian Commonwealth Canadien." (1979), 57 *Canadian Bar Review* 609-625. **623**

Bernier, Ivan. "Législation et pratiques relatives à la libre circulation des marchandises, personnes, services et capitaux au Canada." (1979-80), 3 *Revue d'Intégration Européenne* 267-282. **624**

Black, Edwin R. *Canadian Concepts of Federalism.* Durham, N.C., 1962. xi, 305 leaves. **625**
Thesis (Ph.D.), Duke University, 1962. Abstracted in (1963), 24 *Dissertation Abstracts* 365-366. (University Microfilms, Ann Arbor, No. 63-4369).

Brossard, Jacques. "Fédéralisme et statut particulier." *In* Popovici, Adrian, ed., *Problèmes de droit contemporain: mélanges Louis Baudouin* (Montréal, 1974), pp. 425-444. **626**

Brossard, Jacques. "La révolution fédéraliste." (1972), 7 *Revue Juridique Thémis* 1-12. **627**

Brown, Douglas McK. "Constitutional and International Law Consequences of the 'New' Canadian Federalism." (1965), *Canadian Bar Association, Papers* 81-86. **628**

Cameron, David R. "The Political Impact of the Free Movement of Goods, Persons, Services and Capital on the General Process of Integration: A Comment on the Canadian Case." (1979-80), 3 *Revue d'Intégration Européenne* 357-361. **629**

Canada. Dept. of External Affairs. *Federalism and International Conferences on Education: A Supplement to Federalism and International Relations / Fédéralisme et conférences internationales sur l'éducation: supplément à Fédéralisme et relations internationales.* Ottawa: Queen's Printer, 1968. 73 p. **630**
English and French text on opposite pages.

Cohen, Maxwell. "The Search for a Viable Federalism." (1968-69), 3 *Manitoba Law Journal* 1-18. **631**

Crépeau, Paul André, and Macpherson, Crawford Brough, eds. *The Future of Canadian Federalism / L'avenir du fédéralisme canadien.* Toronto: University of Toronto Press, 1965. x, 188 p. **632**

Contains the papers and some of the commentaries presented at the annual meeting of the Association of Canadian Law Teachers and the Canadian Political Science Association held at Charlottetown in June 1964.
Reviews: Michel Brunet in (1966), 47 *Canadian Historical Review* 165-166; R. Taylor Cole in (1966-67), 22 *International Journal* 532-533; Roland J. Lamontagne in (1966-67), 20 *Revue d'Histoire de l'Amérique Française* 117-125; Bora Laskin in (1965-66), 16 *University of Toronto Law Journal* 470-472; Elizabeth Nish in (1966-67), 42 *Actualité Économique* 691-694.

Dacks, Gurston. *Integration, Federalism and Authority: The Canadian Case.* Princeton, N.J., 1975. x, 308 leaves. **633**

Thesis (Ph.D.), Princeton University, 1975. Abstracted in (1976), 36 *Dissertation Abstracts International* 4727-A. (University Microfilms, Ann Arbor, No. 76-244).

Dufour, André. "Fédéralisme canadien et droit international." *In* Macdonald, Ronald St. John, and others, *Canadian Perspectives on International Law and Organization* (Toronto, 1974), pp. 72-87. **634**

Fairley, H. Scott. "Canadian Federalism, Fisheries and the Constitution: External Constraints on Internal Ordering." (1980), 12 *Ottawa Law Review* 257-318.
635

Fairweather, Gordon. "Canada: A Faltering Exemplar of Federalism." (1977), 12 *Journal of Canadian Studies* 126-127 (No. 3) **636**

Forsey, Eugene. "Canada: Two Nations or One?" (1962), 28 *Canadian Journal of Economics and Political Science* 485-501. **637**

"French and English in Canada; a Crisis of Confederation?" (1963-64), 54 *Round Table* 155-162. **638**

Head, Ivan L. "The 'New Federalism' in Canada: Some Thoughts on the International Legal Consequences." (1965-66), 4 *Alberta Law Review* 389-394. **639**
Also published in (1965), *Canadian Bar Association, Papers* 87-93.

Hertz, Allen Zangwil. *The Constitutional Basis of Canadian Foreign Relations.* Toronto, c1981. 171 leaves. **640**
Thesis (LL.M.), University of Toronto, 1981.

Hogg, Peter W. "Freedom of Movement of Goods, Persons, Services and Capital: Canadian Case-Law." (1979-80), 3 *Revue d'Intégration Européenne* 301-311.
641

Holmes, John W. "Canadian Unity: The International Dimension." (1979), 17 *Royal Society of Canada, Transactions* 99-109 (4th Ser.) **642**

Jacomy-Millette, Annemarie. "L'état fédéré dans les relations internationales contemporaines: le cas du Canada." (1976), 14 *Canadian Yearbook of International Law* 3-56. **643**

Kear, Allan R. "The Canadian Confederation as a Quasi-International System of Constitutional Government: Pre-1867 Phase." (1970), 42 *Canadian Political Science Association, Papers,* 33, 9 p. **644**

Kennedy, W.P.M. "The Nature of Canadian Federalism." (1921), 2 *Canadian Historical Review* 106-125. **645**

Knopff, Rainer. "Nationalism, Liberalism, and Federalism: Elements of Canada's Constitutional Crisis." (1979-80), 59 *Dalhousie Review* 651-658. **646**

Lalande, Gilles. *In Defence of Federalism: A View from Quebec.* Toronto: McClelland and Stewart, c1978. 128 p. **647**
Translation by Jo LaPierre of *Pourquoi le fédéralisme.*
Review: André Bernard in (1979), 5 *Canadian Public Policy* 144-145.

Lamontagne, Maurice A. *Le fédéralisme canadien: évolution et problèmes.* Québec: Presses universitaires Laval, 1954. x, 298 p. **648**
Review: Wilfrid Eggleston in (1955), 36 *Canadian Historical Review* 162-163.

Lamontagne, Maurice A. "Fédéralisme ou association d'états indépendants." (1977), 8 *Études Internationales* 208-230. **649**

Laski, H.J. "Sovereignty and Federalism." (1915), 35 *Canadian Law Times* 891-896. **650**

Laskin, Bora. "Some International Legal Aspects of Federalism: The Experience of Canada." *In* Currie, David P., ed., *Federalism and the New Nations of Africa* (Chicago, 1964), pp. 390-414. **651**

Leeson, Howard A., and Vanderelst, Wilfrid. *External Affairs and Canadian Federalism: The History of a Dilemma.* Toronto: Holt, Rinehart and Winston of Canada, 1973. v, 138 p. **652**
Reviews: J. Murray Beck in (1974), 7 *Canadian Journal of Political Science* 177; Thomas Allen Levy in (1974), 17 *Canadian Public Administration* 338-339.

Lower, Arthur R.M., and others. *Evolving Canadian Federalism.* Durham, N.C.: Duke University Press, 1958. xvi, 187 p. (Duke University. Commonwealth-Studies Center. Publication, No. 9) **653**
Contents: 1. "Theories of Canadian Federalism - Yesterday and Today," by Arthur R.M. Lower (pp. 3-53).- 2. "French-Canada and Canadian Federalism," by Francis R. Scott (pp. 54-91).- 3. "Constitutional Trends and Federalism," by J.A. Corry (pp. 92-125).- 4. "External Affairs and Canadian Federalism," by Frederic H. Soward (pp. 126-160).- 5. "Federations: The Canadian and British West Indies," by Alexander Brady (pp. 161-180).
Reviews: Eugene Forsey in (1959), 40 *Canadian Historical Review* 162-163; Edward McWhinney in (1959), 37 *Canadian Bar Review* 523-524.

Lysyk, Kenneth M. "Reshaping Canadian Federalism." (1979), 13 *University of British Columbia Law Review* 1-37. **654**

Macfarlane, R.O. "Provinces versus Dominion." (1935-36), 42 *Queen's Quarterly* 203-214. **655**

MacGuigan, Mark. "Le fédéralisme et les relations internationales du Canada." (1981), 12 *Politique Internationale* 189-200. **656**

Martin, Paul. *Federalism and International Relations,* by Paul Martin, Secretary of State for External Affairs. Ottawa: Queen's Printer, 1968. 56 p. **657**
Also issued in French under title: *Fédéralisme et relations internationales.*

Mathie, William. "Political Community and the Canadian Experience: Reflections on Nationalism, Federalism and Unity." (1979), 12 *Canadian Journal of Political Science* 3-20. **658**

McWhinney, Edward. "Canadian Federalism, and the Foreign Affairs and Treaty Power: The Impact of Quebec's 'Quiet Revolution.' " (1969), 7 *Canadian Yearbook of International Law* 3-32. **659**

McWhinney, Edward. "Federalism, Biculturalism, and International Law." (1965), 3 *Canadian Yearbook of International Law* 100-126. **660**

McWhinney, Edward. "The New, Pluralistic Federalism in Canada." (1967), 2 *Revue Juridique Thémis* 139-149. **661**

McWhinney, Edward. "Pluralistic Federalism in Canada." *In Le fédéralisme et le développement des ordres juridiques* (Bruxelles, 1971), pp. 23-57. **662**

Morris, Gerald L. "Canadian Federalism and International Law." *In* Macdonald, Ronald St. John, and others, *Canadian Perspectives on International Law and Organization* (Toronto, 1974), pp. 55-71. **663**

Painchaud, Paul. "Fédéralisme et théories de politique étrangère." (1974), 5 *Études Internationales* 25-44. **664**

Piotrowski, G. "La structure fédérative de l'état dans la jurisprudence canadienne en matière de droit international public / The Federative Structure of the State in Canadian Court Decisions as Regards Public International Law." (1956), 83 *Journal du Droit International* 824-885. **665**
In French and English on opposite sides.

Proulx, Pierre-Paul. "Les effets socio-économiques de la libre circulation des marchandises, personnes, services et capitaux sur les unités membres et la structure intégrative du Canada." (1979-80), 3 *Revue d'Intégration Européenne* 325-347. **666**

Rémillard, Gil. "Souveraineté et fédéralisme." (1979), 20 *Cahiers de Droit* 237-246. **667**

Roy, Richard. "De la structure fédérative et des entités spacio-politiques et sectorio-professionnelles." (1972), 7 *Revue Juridique Thémis* 25-60. **668**

Saba, John. *The Canadian Federal System in the Continental Parameter: Disintegration or Adaptation.* Montreal, 1975 (c1976). v, 202 leaves. **669**
Thesis (M.A.), McGill University, 1975. (National Library of Canada. Canadian Theses on Microfiche, No. 27246).

Sabourin, Louis. *Canadian Federalism and International Organizations: A Focus on Quebec.* New York, 1971 (c1974). 502 leaves. **670**
Thesis (Ph.D.), Columbia University, 1971. Abstracted in (1974), 34 *Dissertation Abstracts International* 7861-A. (University Microfilms, Ann Arbor, No. 74-12760).

Sandwell, B.K. "The Future of Unity in Canada: Two Views. Part 2: As Seen by an English-Speaking Canadian." (1944-45), 14 *University of Toronto Quarterly* 125-132. **671**

Schlegel, John P. "Federalism and Canadian Foreign Policy." (1981), 71 *Round Table* 179-192. **672**

Simoneau, Pierre. "Les principes du fédéralisme." (1972), 7 *Revue Juridique Thémis* 13-23. **673**

Smiley, Donald V. *Canada in Question: Federalism in the Seventies.* 2d ed.

Toronto, New York: McGraw-Hill Ryerson, c1976. xiv, 248 p. (McGraw-Hill Ryerson Series in Canadian Politics) **674**
First edition published in 1972.
Reviews: Clare F. Beckton in (1976-77), 3 *Dalhousie Law Journal* 861-865; Ronald I. Cheffins in (1973-74), 1 *Dalhousie Law Journal* 386-391 (of 1st ed.); Richard H. Leach in (1973), 16 *Canadian Public Administration* 315-317 (of 1st ed.); James R. Mallory in (1973), 6 *Canadian Journal of Political Science* 315-316 (of 1st ed.); Denis Smith in (1978), 59 *Canadian Historical Review* 110-111; Garth Stevenson in (1977), 10 *Canadian Journal of Political Science* 411-412.

Stevenson, Garth. *Unfulfilled Union: Canadian Federalism and National Unity.* Toronto: Macmillan of Canada, 1979. x, 257 p. (Canadian Controversies Series) **675**
See also revised edition published Toronto, Gage, 1982.
Review: Denis Smith in (1980), 13 *Canadian Journal of Political Science* 166-168.

Stursberg, Peter. *Lester Pearson and the Dream of Unity.* Toronto: Doubleday Canada; Garden City, N.Y.: Doubleday, 1978. xv, 456 p., 8 leaves of plates.
676

Taylor, Martin R. "Some Quebec Views on the Nature of Canadian Federalism: A Summary of the Tremblay Report." (1959-63), 1 *University of British Columbia Law Review* 646-654. **677**

Thatcher, Max B. *The Political Island of Quebec: A Study in Federalism.* Chicago, 1953. vi, 644 leaves. **678**
Thesis (Ph.D.), Northwestern University, 1953. Abstracted in (1953), 13 *Dissertation Abstracts* 1241. (University Microfilms, Ann Arbor, No. 6250).

Tremblay, Arthur. "Les nationalismes et les états." (1978), 16 *Royal Society of Canada, Transactions* 141-149 (4th Ser.) **679**

Trotter, Reginald G. "Why Confederation Came." (1938-39), 45 *Queen's Quarterly* 22-29. **680**

Trudeau, Pierre Elliott. *Federalism and the French Canadians.* With an Introduction by John T. Saywell. Toronto: Macmillan of Canada, 1968. xxvi, 212 p.
Translation of: *Le fédéralisme et la société canadienne-française.* **681**
Review: Norman Ward in (1968-69), 48 *Dalhousie Review* 127-129.

Trudeau, Pierre Elliott. *Le fédéralisme et la société canadienne-française.* Montréal: Éditions HMH, 1967. xiii, 227 p. (Collection Constantes, vol. 10) **682**
Also published in English under title: *Federalism and the French Canadians.*
Reviews: James Ross Hurley in (1968), 1 *Canadian Journal of Political Science* 361-362; Leslie Katz in (1968-69), 3 *Manitoba Law Journal* 89-92 (No. 2); Donald V. Smiley in (1968), 49 *Canadian Historical Review* 413-415; Michael Stein in (1968-69), 24 *International Journal* 610-612.

Turcotte, Edmond. "The Future of Unity in Canada: Two Views. Part 1: As Seen by a French-Speaking Canadian." (1944-45), 14 *University of Toronto Quarterly* 117-124. **683**

Van der Esch, Bastiaan. *Canadian Federalism and the Common Market Formula.* Ottawa: School of International Affairs, Carleton University, 1971. 46 p. (Carleton University. Norman Paterson School of International Affairs. Occasional Papers, 15) **684**

(ii) ADMISSION INTO CONFEDERATION (NEWFOUNDLAND)

Canada. Dept. of External Affairs. *Report and Documents Relating to the Negotiations for the Union of Newfoundland with Canada.* Ottawa: King's Printer, 1949. 91 p. (Canada. Dept. of External Affairs. Conference Series, 1948, No. 2) **685**

Canada. Parliament. *Minutes of the Proceedings of a Conference between the Representatives of Canada and Newfoundland to Achieve the Union of Newfoundland with the Dominion, with Copies of Correspondence, etc.* Ottawa, 1895. 30 p. (Canada. Parliament, 1895. Sessional Papers, No. 48) **686**

Chadwick, Gerald William St. John. *Newfoundland; Island into Province.* Cambridge: University Press, 1967. xiv, 268 p., maps. **687**
Review: J. Murray Beck in (1967-68), 47 *Dalhousie Review* 591-595.

Chatwood, Andrew. "The Death of a Dominion, and the Prenatal Years and Birth of a Canadian Province." (1974-75), 71 *Newfoundland Quarterly* 8-9 (No. 1) **688**

Eggleston, Wilfrid. *Newfoundland: The Road to Confederation.* Ottawa: Dept. of External Affairs, 1974. x, 117 p., maps. **689**
Also issued in French under title: *Terre-Neuve en route vers la confédération.*

Fraser, A.M. "The Nineteenth-Century Negotiations for Confederation of Newfoundland with Canada." (1949), *Canadian Historical Association, Historical Papers* 14-21. **690**

Lacey, A. "Canada's Tenth Province." (1942-43), 12 *University of Toronto Quarterly* 435-445. **691**

Langlois, P. *Le rattachement de Terre-Neuve au Canada.* Paris, 1972. 293 leaves. Thesis, Université de Paris II, 1972. **692**

Mayo, H.B. "Newfoundland's Entry into the Dominion." (1949), 15 *Canadian Journal of Economics and Political Science* 505-522. **693**

McGrath, Sir Patrick T. "Will Newfoundland Join Canada?" (1929), 36 *Queen's Quarterly* 253-266. **694**

Mitchell, Harvey. "Canada's Negotiations with Newfoundland, 1887-1895." (1959), 40 *Canadian Historical Review* 277-293. **695**

Newell, I. "Newfoundland, Canada." (1949-50), 56 *Queen's Quarterly* 268-276. **696**

"Newfoundland and Canada: Terms of Union Signed." (1949), 1 *External Affairs* 3-8 (Jan.) **697**

"Newfoundland Looks at Her Future: The Question of Federal Union with Canada." (1947-48), 38 *Round Table* 551-558. **698**

Turewich, Larry Andrew. *Economic Factors Behind the Newfoundland-Canada Confederation Movement, 1864-1895.* Montreal, c1978. ix, 297 leaves. **699**
Half-title: *Newfoundland-and-Canada Confederation Movement, 1864-1895.* Thesis (M.A.), McGill University, 1977. (National Library of Canada. Canadian Theses on Microfiche, No. 35812).

"Union of Newfoundland with Canada." (1949), 1 *External Affairs* 25-31 (Apr.) **700**

(iii) QUEBEC SEPARATISM

Appavoo, Patricia J., ed. "Alternatives Canada: A Conference Report." (1977-78), 36 *Behind the Headlines* No. 3 (28 p.)   **701**

Beaudoin, Gérald. "Les aspects constitutionnels du référendum." (1977), 8 *Études Internationales* 197-207.   **702**

Bergeron, Gérard. "Le Canada français: du provincialisme à l'internationalisme." In Keenleyside, Hugh L., and others, *The Growth of Canadian Policies in External Affairs* (Durham, N.C., 1960), pp. 99-130.   **703**

Bergeron, Gérard. *L'indépendance, oui, mais...* Montréal: Éditions Quinze, 1977. 198 p.   **704**
Review: Maurice Poncelet in (1978), 11 *Canadian Journal of Political Science* 185-186.

Bernard, André. *What Does Quebec Want?* Toronto: J. Lorimer, 1978. 160 p., map.   **705**

Brachet, Bernard. "Canada: la crise du fédéralisme canadien et le problème québécois." (1972), 88 *Revue du Droit Public et de la Science Politique en France et à l'Étranger* 303-324.   **706**

Brady, Alexander. "Quebec and Canadian Federalism." (1959), 25 *Canadian Journal of Economics and Political Science* 259-270.   **707**

Breton, Albert. "French Separatism and the Canadian Federation." (1964), 6 *University of Windsor Seminar on Canadian-American Relations, Proceedings* 207-213.   **708**

Brossard, Jacques. *L'accession à la souveraineté et le cas du Québec: conditions et modalités politico-juridiques.* Montréal: Presses de l'Université de Montréal, 1976. 800 p.   **709**
Reviews: Michael Bothe in (1979), 39 *Zeitschrift für Ausländisches Öffentliches Recht und Völkerrecht* 812-814; William H. Bryant in (1979), 9 *American Review of Canadian Studies* 88-89 (No. 1); Eric David in (1976), 12 *Revue Belge de Droit International* 719-720; Michel Distel in (1977), 29 *Revue Internationale de Droit Comparé* 431-432; Claude C. Emanuelli, and Stanislas Slosar in (1978), 56 *Canadian Bar Review* 365-374; V. Di Gregorio in (1976), 31 *Comunità Internazionale* 642-643; Annemarie Jacomy-Millette in (1977), 8 *Études Internationales* 404-405; Jean-Paul Lacasse in (1977), 37 *Revue du Barreau* 384-389; Maurice Poncelet in (1977), 10 *Canadian Journal of Political Science* 408-411; Charles Rousseau in (1976), 80 *Revue Générale de Droit International Public* 1288-1289; unsigned in (1979), 33 *Revue Juridique et Politique, Indépendance et Coopération* 230-231.

Brossard, Jacques. "Le droit du peuple québécois à l'autodétermination et à l'indépendance." (1977), 8 *Études Internationales* 151-171.   **710**

Brossard, Jacques. "Le droit du peuple québécois de disposer de lui-même au regard du droit international." (1977), 15 *Canadian Yearbook of International Law* 84-145.   **711**

Brunet, Michel. "Continentalism and Quebec Nationalism: A Double Challenge to Canada." (1969), 76 *Queen's Quarterly* 511-527.   **712**

Burns, Ronald M., ed. *One Country or Two?* Introduction by John J. Deutsch. Montreal: McGill-Queen's University Press, 1971. vii, 287 p.   **713**
Collection of essays.

Reviews: Alexander Brady, André Dufour, and P.B. Waite (separately) in (1973-74), 1 *Dalhousie Law Journal* 370-386.

Byers, R.B., and Leyton-Brown, David. "The Strategic and Economic Implications for the United States of a Sovereign Quebec." (1980), 6 *Canadian Public Policy* 325-341. **714**

Cameron, David R. *Nationalism, Self-Determination and the Quebec Question.* Toronto: Macmillan of Canada, 1974. xiii, 177 p. (Canadian Controversies Series) **715**
Review: Donald V. Smiley in (1976), 9 *Canadian Journal of Political Science* 138-139.

Carey, Thomas C. "Self-Determination in the Post-Colonial Era: The Case of Quebec." (1977), 1 *A.S.I.L.S. International Law Journal* 47-71. **716**

Chaput, Roger. "Du rapport Durham au 'rapport' Brossard: le droit des Québécois à disposer d'eux-mêmes." (1979), 20 *Cahiers de Droit* 289-313. **717**

Clift, Dominique. *Quebec Nationalism in Crisis.* Kingston, McGill-Queen's University Press, 1982. viii, 155 p. **718**
Translation of: *Le déclin du nationalisme au Québec.*
Review: Sylvie Arend in (1982), 15 *Canadian Journal of Political Science* 812-814.

Cohen, Maxwell. "Canada and Quebec in North America: A Pattern for Fulfillment." (1968), 75 *Queen's Quarterly* 389-400. **719**

Cook, Ramsay. *Canada and the French-Canadian Question.* Toronto: Macmillan of Canada, 1966. 219 p. **720**
Contains nine essays, most of which were previously published in various periodicals.
Reviews: Claude Julien in (1966-67), 22 *International Journal* 113-115; Gordon Winter in (1967), 43 *International Affairs* 413-414.

Cook, Ramsay. "Quebec and Confederation: Past and Present." (1964), 71 *Queen's Quarterly* 468-484. **721**

Corbett, Edward M. *Québec Confronts Canada.* Baltimore: Johns Hopkins Press, 1967. xi, 336 p., maps. **722**
Review: Michael Stein in (1968-69), 24 *International Journal* 610-612.

Corry, J.A. "Notes to English Canadians." (1977), 12 *Journal of Canadian Studies* 33-38 (No. 3) **723**

Crenna, Dave. "A Separate Quebec - What Would it Mean to Canada and to the United States?" (1963), 5 *University of Windsor Seminar on Canadian-American Relations, Proceedings* 277-280. **724**

Croisat, Maurice. *Le fédéralisme canadien et l'autonomie de la province de Québec.* Grenoble, 1964. 487 leaves. **725**
Thesis (Doctorat), Université de Grenoble, 1964.

Croisat, Maurice. *Le fédéralisme canadien et la question du Québec.* Paris: Éditions Anthropos, 1979. 397 p. **726**

DeBane, Pierre, and Asselin, Martial. "Quebec's Right to Secede." *In* Meekison, J. Peter, ed., *Canadian Federalism: Myth or Reality* (3d ed., Toronto, 1977), pp. 497-507. **727**

Dion, Léon. *Le Québec et le Canada: les voies de l'avenir.* Montréal: Éditions Québécor, 1980. 236 p. (Collection Politique) **728**

Dumont, Georges. "American-Canadian Views on Present Separatist Movements in Quebec." (1963), 5 *University of Windsor Seminar on Canadian-American Relations, Proceedings* 37-42. **729**

Dunton, Davidson. "Recognized, Equitable Duality." (1977), 12 *Journal of Canadian Studies* 106-108 (No. 3) **730**

Forsey, Eugene. "Special Status for Quebec: The Separatists Define Their Aims." (1967), 57 *Round Table* 198-203. **731**

Fortin, Pierre; Paquet, Gilles; and Rabeau, Yves. "Quebec in the Canadian Federation: A Provisional Evaluative Framework." (1978), 21 *Canadian Public Administration* 558-578. **732**
This article is followed by a commentary by Gérard Bélanger (pp. 579-583).

Fox, Paul. "French Separatism and the Canadian Federation." (1964), 6 *University of Windsor Seminar on Canadian-American Relations, Proceedings* 187-194. **733**

Fraser, Blair. "De Gaulle Acclaims Free Quebec; English Anger and French Pride." (1967), 57 *Round Table* 423-425. **734**

Fullerton, Douglas H. *The Dangerous Delusion: Quebec's Independence Obsession: As Seen by Former Adviser to René Lévesque and Jean Lesage.* Toronto: McClelland and Stewart, c1978. 240 p. **735**
Review: Gregory Mahler in (1980), 10 *American Review of Canadian Studies* 134-136 (No. 1).

Gauthier, François. "The English Response to the Prospect of the Separation of Quebec: A Comment." (1978), 4 *Canadian Public Policy* 385-387. **736**

Greenwood, F. Murray. "The Legal Secession of Québec - A Review Note." (1978), 12 *University of British Columbia Law Review* 71-84. **737**

Griffin, Elizabeth Anne. *Six Functions of Separatism in Quebec.* New York, 1975 (viii), 258 leaves. **738**
Thesis (Ph.D.), New York University, 1975. Abstracted in (1975), 36 *Dissertation Abstracts International* 3981-A. (University Microfilms, Ann Arbor, No. 75-28536).

Hagy, James William. *The Quebec Separatists: An American Viewpoint.* Athens Ga., 1969. 163 leaves. **739**
Thesis (Ph.D.), University of Georgia, 1969. Abstracted in (1970), 30 *Dissertation Abstracts International* 3885-A. (University Microfilms, Ann Arbor, No. 70-1158).

Hagy, James William. "Quebec Separatists: The First Twelve Years." (1969), 76 *Queen's Quarterly* 229-238. **740**

Harbron, John D. *Canada Without Québec.* Don Mills, Ont.: Musson Book, 1977 164 p., maps. **741**
Also published in French under title: *Le Québec sans le Canada* (Montréal, Quinze 1979).
Reviews: R.K. Carty in (1978), 4 *Canadian Public Policy* 581-582; Kenneth McRobert in (1979), 86 *Queen's Quarterly* 143-147.

Heintzman, Ralph. "A Future as Well as a Past." (1977), 12 *Journal of Canadian Studies* 1-2, 128-135 (No. 3) **742**

Hodgins, Bruce W., and Smith, Denis. "Canada and Québec: Facing the Reality." (1977), 12 *Journal of Canadian Studies* 124-126 (No. 3) **743**

Jacobs, Jane. *The Question of Separatism: Quebec and the Struggle over Sovereignty.* New York: Random House, c1980. 134 p., map. **744**

Kwavnick, David. "Quebec and the Two Nations Theory: A Re-Examination." (1974), 81 *Queen's Quarterly* 357-376. **745**

Kwavnick, David. "Québécois Nationalism and Canada's National Interest." (1977), 12 *Journal of Canadian Studies* 53-68 (No. 3) **746**

Lallier, Adalbert. *La souveraineté-association: réalisme économique ou utopie.* Montréal: Cercle du livre de France, c1980. 47 p. **747**

Latouche, Daniel. "It Takes Two to...Divorce and Remarry." (1977), 12 *Journal of Canadian Studies* 24-32 (No. 3) **748**

Latouche, Daniel. "Quebec and the North American Subsystem: One Possible Scenario." (1974), 28 *International Organization* 931-960. **749**
Reprinted in Fox, Annette Baker, and others, *Canada and the United States* (New York, 1976), pp. 337-366.

Lemay, Valère. *Notre choix: souveraineté ou fédéralisme.* Montréal: Éditions Charmay, c1977. xviii, 158 p., 12 leaves of plates. **750**

Lentner, Howard H. "Canadian Separatism and Its Implications for the United States." (1978), 22 *Orbis* 375-393. **751**

Lévesque, René. "For an Independent Québec." (1975-76), 54 *Foreign Affairs* 734-744. **752**

Lévesque, René. *An Option for Quebec.* Toronto, Montreal: McClelland and Stewart, c1968. 128 p. **753**
Translation of *Option Québec.*
Review: Michael Stein in (1986-69), 24 *International Journal* 610-612.

Lithwick, N.H., and Winer, Stanley L. "Faltering Federalism and French Canadians." (1977), 12 *Journal of Canadian Studies* 44-52 (No. 3) **754**

Lower, Arthur R.M. "The Problem of Québec." (1977), 12 *Journal of Canadian Studies* 93-97 (No. 3) **755**

Mallen, Pierre-Louis. *Vivre le Québec libre.* Préface de René Lévesque. Montréal: Presses de la Cité; Paris: Plon, c1978. 378 p. **756**

Mallory, James R. "Confederation: The Ambiguous Bargain." (1977), 12 *Journal of Canadian Studies* 18-23 (No. 3) **757**

Matas, David. "Can Quebec Separate?" (1975), 21 *McGill Law Journal* 387 403. **758**

Mayer, R.A. "Legal Aspects of Secession." (1968-69), 3 *Manitoba Law Journal* 61-74 (No. 1) **759**

McKinsey, Lauren S. "Dimensions of National Political Integration and Disintegration: The Case of Quebec Separation, 1960-1975." *In* Meekison, J. Peter, ed., *Canadian Federalism: Myth or Reality* (3d ed., Toronto, 1977), pp. 460-483. **760**

McRoberts, Kenneth. "English Canada and the Québec Referendum; the Stakes and the Dangers." (1977), 12 *Journal of Canadian Studies* 108-113 (No. 3)**761**

McWhinney, Edward. "The 'French Fact' in Quebec and the Future of Canadian

Federalism." *In* Blumenwitz, Dieter, and Randelzhofer, Albrecht, eds., *Festschrift für Friedrich Berber* (München, 1973), pp. 339-349. **762**

McWhinney, Edward. "French-Canadian Nationalism and Separatism and Contemporary Canadian Federalism." (1972), 21 *Jahrbuch des Öffentlichen Rechts der Gegenwart* 571-590. **763**

McWhinney, Edward. "Nationalism and Self-Determination and Contemporary Canadian Federalism." *In Miscellanea W.J. Ganshof van der Meersch* (Bruxelles, 1972), vol. 3, pp. 219-240. **764**

McWhinney, Edward. *Quebec and the Constitution, 1960-1978*. Toronto: University of Toronto Press, 1979. xvi, 170 p. **765**

Reviews: Alexander Brady under title: "Quebec, Canada and the Constitution," in (1980), 87 *Canadian Banker and ICB Review* 25-27, 58-59 (No. 2); Kenneth Bryden in (1980), 35 *International Journal* 618-620; Eugene Forsey in (1979), 60 *Canadian Historical Review* 523-524; William H. McConnell in (1981), 29 *American Journal of Comparative Law* 723-727; John D. Whyte in (1980), 87 *Queen's Quarterly* 126-128.

Mitchell, John Stirling. *Views on International Affairs of 14 Quebec Separatist Groups, an Exploratory Analysis*. Ottawa, 1973. 204 leaves. **766**
Research essay (M.A.), Carleton University, 1973.

Monnet, François Marie. *Le défi québécois*. Montréal: Quinze; Saint-Léonard: distributeur Nouvelles messageries internationales du livre, 1977. xx, 258 p. **767**

Reviews: André Bernard in (1979), 5 *Canadian Public Policy* 299; Gérard Loriot in (1978), 11 *Canadian Journal of Political Science* 671-672.

Moore, A. Milton. "Fact and Fantasy in the Unity Debate." (1979), 5 *Canadian Public Policy* 206-222. **768**

Morin, Wilfrid. *L'avenir du Canada; nos droits à l'indépendance politique*. Préface de Yves de La Brière. Paris: F. Sorlot, 1938. 253 p. **769**

Later edition published under title: *L'indépendance du Québec; le Québec aux Québécois* (Montréal, 1960).
Review: Unsigned in (1939-40), 15/2 *Actualité Économique* 378.

Morin, Wilfrid. *L'indépendance du Québec; le Québec aux Québécois!* 2. éd. Montréal: Alliance Laurentienne, 1960, c1938. 253 p. **770**

First published under title: *L'avenir du Canada; nos droits à l'indépendance politique* (Paris, F. Sorlot, 1938). This edition was also published Paris, Nouvelles éditions latines.

Morris, Gerald L. "Quebec and Sovereignty: The Interface between Constitutional and International Law." (1978) *Law Society of Upper Canada, Special Lectures* 47-64. **771**

Le nationalisme québécois à la croisée des chemins. Québec: Centre québécois de relations internationales; Toronto: Institut canadien des affaires internationales; Québec: Université Laval, 1975. 375 p. (Collection Choix, 7) **772**

Review: Brian Young in (1976), 6 *American Review of Canadian Studies* 151-152 (No. 1).

O'Grady, William. *The Quebec Problem: An Inquiry into the Ethics of Sovereignty and Secession*. Ottawa: Borealis Press, 1980. 53 p., maps. **773**

Orban, Edmond. "Canada-Québec: pour un processus accéléré de créativité." (1977), 12 *Journal of Canadian Studies* 39-43 (No. 3) **774**

Ouellet, Fernand. "Les fondements historiques de l'option séparatiste dans le Québec." (1962), 43 *Canadian Historical Review* 185-203. **775**

Paddock, Harold. "Canadian Unity: The Dream Redreamt." (1978-79), 74 *Newfoundland Quarterly* 9-11 (No. 1) **776**

Pagé, Carole. *Décolonisation et question nationale québécoise.* Montréal, 1978. 170 frames. **777**
   Thesis (M.A.), Université du Québec à Montréal, 1978. (National Library of Canada. Canadian Theses on Microfiche, No. 46533).

Parizeau, Jacques. "Separatism and Confederation." (1964), 6 *University of Windsor Seminar on Canadian-American Relations, Proceedings* 195-206. **778**

Patry, Richard. *Le séparatisme québécois, 1960-1970: l'idée et le mouvement.* Québec, 1976 (c1978). x, 149 leaves. **779**
   Thesis (M.A.), Université Laval, 1976. (National Library of Canada. Canadian Theses on Microfiche, No. 35476).

Québec (Province). Conseil exécutif. *La nouvelle entente Québec-Canada: proposition du gouvernement du Québec pour une entente d'égal à égal: la souveraineté-association.* Québec: Éditeur officiel, 1979. viii, 118 p. **780**
   Also published in English under title: *Québec-Canada: A New Deal.*
   Review: Stephen Kenny under title: "Sovereignty Association: A Critical Commentary," in (1980), 10 *American Review of Canadian Studies* 142-144 (No. 1).

Quenneville, Jean-Guy R. *The Emergence of French Canada in Domestic and External Politics.* Notre Dame, Ind., 1974. x, 318 leaves, maps. **781**
   Thesis (Ph.D.), University of Notre Dame, 1974. Abstracted in (1974), 35 *Dissertation Abstracts International* 2368-A. (University Microfilms, Ann Arbor, No. 74-20593).

Rioux, Marcel. *Quebec in Question.* Toronto: J. Lorimer, 1978. 209 p. **782**
   Translation by James Boake of *La question du Québec.*

Robert, Jean-Claude. *Du Canada français au Québec libre: histoire d'un mouvement indépendantiste.* Paris: Flammarion, 1975. 323 p., maps. (Histoire vivante) (Autonomismes-nationalités) **783**
   Review: René Durocher in (1975-76), 29 *Revue d'Histoire de l'Amérique Française* 437-439.

Rowat, Donald C., ed. *The Referendum and Separation Elsewhere: Implications for Quebec.* Ottawa: Dept. of Political Science, Carleton University, 1978. xiv, 197 p. **784**
   Review: Arthur Siegel in (1979), 12 *Canadian Journal of Political Science* 388-390.

Roy, Jean-Louis. *Le choix d'un pays: le débat constitutionnel Québec-Canada, 1960-1976.* Montréal: Leméac, 1978. 366 p. **785**
   Review: Dorval Brunelle in (1979-80), 33 *Revue d'Histoire de l'Amérique Française* 478-480.

Sabourin, Louis. "La recherche d'un statut endogène québécois: trois stades de connaissance mutuelle." (1977), 8 *Études Internationales* 231-239. **786**

Sabourin, Louis. " 'Vive le Québec libre,' deux ans après." (1970), 7 *Québec* 69-79 (mars) **787**

Shaw, William F., and Albert, Lionel. *Partition: The Price of Quebec's Independence: A Realistic Look at the Possibility of Quebec Separating from Canada* and *Becoming An Independent State.* Foreword by Eugene Forsey. Montreal: Thornhill Pub., 1980. 205 p., maps. **788**

Simeon, Richard, ed. *Must Canada Fail?* Montreal: McGill-Queen's University Press, 1977. x, 307 p. **789**
Reviews: J.R. Happy in (1978), 4 *Canadian Public Policy* 582-584; Kenneth McRoberts in (1979), 86 *Queen's Quarterly* 143-147.

Simeon, Richard. "Scenarios for Separation." *In* Meekison, J. Peter, ed., *Canadian Federalism: Myth or Reality* (3d ed., Toronto, 1977), pp. 442-459. **790**

Singer, Howard Lewis. *Institutionalization of Protest: The Quebec Separatist Movement.* New York, 1977. v, 300 leaves. **791**
Thesis (Ph.D.), New York University, 1976. Abstracted in (1977), 38 *Dissertation Abstracts International* 1002-A. (University Microfilms, Ann Arbor, No. 77-16525).

Smiley, Donald V. "As the Options Narrow: Notes on Post-November 15 Canada." (1977), 12 *Journal of Canadian Studies* 3-7 (No. 3) **792**

Soldatos, Panayotis. *Souveraineté-association: l'urgence de réfléchir.* Montréal: Éditions France-Amérique, 1979. 207 p. **793**
Reviews: Guy Héraud in (1980), 3 *Revue d'Intégration Européenne* 253; Charles Pentland in (1981), 14 *Canadian Journal of Political Science* 836-837; Jacques Zylberberg in (1980), 11 *Études Internationales* 542-543.

Thibodeau, Marc Arthur. "The Legality of an Independent Quebec: Canadian Constitutional Law and Self-Determination in International Law." (1979), 3 *Boston College International and Comparative Law Review* 99-142. **794**

Treddenick, John M. "Quebec and Canada: Some Economic Aspects of Independence." (1973), 8 *Journal of Canadian Studies* 16-31 (No. 4) **795**

Tremblay, André. "Some Elements of a Third Constitutional Option for Canada." (1979), 13 *University of British Columbia Law Review* 38-51. **796**

Tremblay, Marc-Adélard. "Le 15 novembre et ses lendemains: les défis de la souveraineté politique." (1977), 12 *Journal of Canadian Studies* 100-105 (No. 3) **797**

Tremblay, Rodrigue. *Indépendance et marché commun Québec-E.-U.; manifeste économique.* Montréal: Éditions du Jour, 1970. 127 p., map. (Collection Les idées du jour, D-56) **798**
Review: Michel Boucher in (1971-72), 47 *Actualité Économique* 192-194.

Usher, D. "The English Response to the Prospect of the Separation of Quebec." (1978), 4 *Canadian Public Policy* 57-70. **799**
This article is followed by comments by David L. Emerson (pp. 71-76).

Valaskakis, Kimon. *'L'option Europe': analyse de la plausibilité d'une association Québec/Canada/Europe.* Québec: Ministère des affaires intergouvernementales, 1978. xxi, 176 p. **800**
Review: Panayotis Soldatos in (1980), 6 *Canadian Public Policy* 421-422.

Valaskakis, Kimon. *Le Québec et son destin international: les enjeux géopolitiques.* Montréal: Quinze, c1980. 149 p. **801**

Wade, Mason. "An American View of Quebec Separatism." (1963), 5 *University of Windsor Seminar on Canadian-American Relations, Proceedings* 68-73. **802**

Watts, Ronald L. "The High Price of Separation." (1977), 12 *Journal of Canadian Studies* 97-100 (No. 3). **803**

Whalen, Hugh. "Québec and Post-Canada: The Imagery of Separation." (1978-79), 74 *Newfoundland Quarterly* 6-7 (No. 1) **804**

Wilson, F.J. "Canada's Ireland." (1936-37), 43 *Queen's Quarterly* 201-203. **805**

Wilson, Frank L. "French-Canadian Separatism." (1967), 20 *Western Political Quarterly* 116-131. **806**

Young, Robert Andrew. "National Identification in English Canada: Implications for Québec Independence." (1977), 12 *Journal of Canadian Studies* 69-84 (No. 3) **807**

Young, Robert Andrew. *Prospects for Quebec Independence: A Study of National Identification in English Canada.* Montreal, 1974 (c1975). viii, 208 leaves. **808**
Half-title: *A Study of National Identification in English Canada.* Thesis (M.A.), McGill University, 1974. (National Library of Canada. Canadian Theses on Microfiche, No. 23239).

Zebroff, George. "A Separate Quebec - What Would It Mean to Canada and to the United States?" (1963), 5 *University of Windsor Seminar on Canadian-American Relations, Proceedings* 281-289. **809**

(iv) INTERNATIONAL RELATIONS OF PROVINCES

Atkey, Ronald G. "Provincial Transnational Activity: An Approach to a Current Issue in Canadian Federalism." *In* Ontario, Advisory Committee on Confederation, *Background Papers and Reports* (Toronto, 1970), vol. 2, pp. 153-188.
810

Atkey, Ronald G. "The Role of the Provinces in International Affairs." (1970-71), 26 *International Journal* 249-273. **811**

Beaudoin, Louise. "Origines et développement du rôle international du gouvernement du Québec." *In* Painchaud, Paul, ed., *Le Canada et le Québec sur la scène internationale* (Québec, 1977), pp. 441-470. **812**

Beaudoin, Louise. *Les relations France-Québec: deux époques, 1855-1910, 1960-1972.* Québec, 1974. viii, 196 leaves. **813**
Thesis (M.A.), Université Laval, 1974. (National Library of Canada. Canadian Theses on Microfiche, No. 35331).

Bergeron, Gérard. *Incertitudes d'un certain pays: le Québec et le Canada dans le monde, 1958-1978.* Québec: Presses de l'Université Laval, 1979. 270 p. **814**

Bissonnette, Lise. "Orthodoxie fédéraliste et relations régionales transfrontières - une menace illusoire." (1981), 12 *Études Internationales* 635-655. **815**

Bissonnette, Lise. "Québec-Ottawa-Washington, the Pre-Referendum Triangle." (1972), 79 *Canadian Banker* 64-76 (No. 1) **816**

Brossard, Jacques; Patry, André; and Weiser, Elisabeth. *Les pouvoirs extérieurs du Québec.* Montréal: Presses de l'Université de Montréal, 1967. 463 p. **817**
Études rédigées pour le compte du Comité parlementaire de la Constitution formé en juin 1963 par l'Assemblée législative du Québec.

Reviews: A.F. Bisson in (1968), 28 *Revue du Barreau* 612-615; Pierre Blache in (1968), 1 *Canadian Journal of Political Science* 365-367; Thierry Godechot in (1969), 83 *Revue d'Histoire Diplomatique* 94-95.

Caron, Maximilien. "La province de Québec est-elle un état?" (1938-39), 14/1 *Actualité Économique* 121-132. **818**

Chapdelaine, Jean. "Esquisse d'une politique extérieure d'un Québec souverain - genèse et prospective." (1977), 8 *Études Internationales* 342-355. **819**

Gariépy, Henri. *Sondage d'opinion publique dans la région de Québec sur les relations du gouvernement du Québec avec l'extérieur.* Québec, 1974. x, 120 leaves. **820**
Thesis (M.Soc.Sc.), Université Laval, 1975.

Ghent, Jocelyn Maynard. "The Participation of Provincial Governments in International Science and Technology." (1980), 10 *American Review of Canadian Studies* 48-62 (No. 1) **821**

Giroux, Lorne. "La capacité internationale des provinces en droit constitutionnel canadien." (1967-68), 9 *Cahiers de Droit* 241-271. **822**

Goyer, Jean-Pierre. "Foreign Policy and the Provinces." (1969), 21 *External Affairs* 387-394. **823**
Statement made to the House of Commons on October 30, 1969.

Jacomy-Millette, Annemarie. "Aspects juridiques des activités internationales du Québec." *In* Painchaud, Paul, ed., *Le Canada et le Québec sur la scène internationale* (Québec, 1977), pp. 515-544. **824**

Jacomy-Millette, Annemarie. "International 'Diplomatic' Activity of Canadian Provinces, with Emphasis on Quebec Behaviour." (1976), 7 *Revue Générale de Droit* 7-23. **825**

Jacomy-Millette, Annemarie. "Le rôle des provinces dans les relations internationales." (1979), 10 *Études Internationales* 285-320. **826**

Johannson, Peter Roff. *British Columbia's Inter-Governmental Relations with the United States.* Baltimore, Md., 1975. viii, 425 leaves. **827**
Thesis (Ph.D.), Johns Hopkins University, 1975. Abstracted in (1978/79), 39 *Dissertation Abstracts International* 3123-A. (University Microfilms, Ann Arbor).

Johannson, Peter Roff. "British Columbia's Relations with the United States." (1978), 21 *Canadian Public Administration* 212-233. **828**

Johannson, Peter Roff. "Provincial International Activities." (1977-78), 33 *International Journal* 357-378. **829**

Johannson, Peter Roff. "A Study in Regional Strategy: The Alaska-British Columbia-Yukon Conferences." (1975-76), 28 *B.C. Studies* 29-52. **830**

Kachanov, V.A. "Participation of Canadian Provinces in International Agreements and Organizations." (In Russian). (1969), *Soviet Year Book of International Law* 315-320. **831**

Kelly, Mark Stewart. *The International Relations of Quebec.* Windsor, 1971. vii, 113 leaves. **832**
Thesis (M.A.), University of Windsor, 1971.

Kettner, Bonni Raines. *Canadian Federalism and the International Activities of*

Three Provinces: Alberta, Ontario and Quebec. Burnaby, B.C., 1980. 207 leaves. **833**
Thesis (M.A.), Simon Fraser University, 1980. (National Library of Canada. Canadian Theses on Microfiche, No. 44917).

Keyserlingk, Robert H. "France and Quebec: The Psychological Basis for Their Co-operation." (1968), 75 *Queen's Quarterly* 21-32. **834**

La Forest, Gerard V. "May the Provinces Legislate in Violation of International Law." (1961), 39 *Canadian Bar Review* 78-91. **835**

Lande, Ellen Beth. "Quebec's International Personality." (1979), 3 *Fletcher Forum* 22-45 (No. 2) **836**

Landey, Deborah. *Quebec as a Non-State Nation Actor in International Relations.* Ottawa, 1978. vii, 273 leaves. **837**
Thesis (M.A.), Carleton University, 1978. (National Library of Canada. Canadian Theses on Microfiche, No. 39041). Abstracted in (1979), 17 *Masters Abstracts* 222.

Leach, Richard H., and Walker, Donald E. "Province-State Relations Across the International Boundary: A Preliminary Assessment." (1972), 44 *Canadian Political Science Association, Papers,* 20 p. **838**

Leach, Richard H.; Walker, Donald E.; and Levy, Thomas Allen. "Province-State Trans-Border Relations: A Preliminary Assessment." (1973), 16 *Canadian Public Administration* 468-482. **839**

Leeson, Howard A. "Foreign Relations and Quebec." *In* Meekison, J. Peter, ed., *Canadian Federalism: Myth or Reality* (3d ed., Toronto, 1977), pp. 510-525. **840**

Lemieux, Vincent. "Quel État du Québec?" (1977), 8 *Études Internationales* 254-265. **841**

Levy, Thomas Allen. *The International Status of Provinces.* Montreal, 1970 (c1971). iv, 131 leaves. **842**
Thesis (M.A.), McGill University, 1970. (National Library of Canada. Canadian Theses on Microfilm, No. 7086).

Levy, Thomas Allen. "Provincial International Status Revisited." (1976-77), 3 *Dalhousie Law Journal* 70-103. **843**

Levy, Thomas Allen. "Le rôle des provinces." *In* Painchaud, Paul, ed., *Le Canada et le Québec sur la scène internationale* (Québec, 1977), pp. 109-145. **844**

Levy, Thomas Allen. "The Role of the Canadian Provinces in External Affairs: A Study in Canadian Federalism." (1972), 44 *Canadian Political Science Association, Papers,* 32, 7 p. **845**
Tentative draft of a paper presented at the 1972 annual meeting.

Levy, Thomas Allen. *Some Aspects of the Role of the Canadian Provinces in External Affairs: A Study in Canadian Federalism.* Durham, N.C., 1974. xiv, 504 leaves. **846**
Thesis (Ph.D.), Duke University, 1974. Abstracted in (1975), 35 *Dissertation Abstracts International* 6222-A. (University Microfilms, Ann Arbor, No. 75-6780).

Levy, Thomas Allen, and Munton, Donald J. "Canada and the United-States: Federal-Provincial Dimensions of State-Provincial Relations." (1976), *International Perspectives* 23-27 (Mar./Apr.) **847**

Levy, Thomas Allen, and Munton, Donald J. "Federal-Provincial Aspects of Canadian-American Relations: Some Possible Futures." (1975), 47 *Canadian Political Science Association, Papers*, 38 p. **848**

Malone, Christopher Paul. *La politique québécoise en matière de relations internationales: changement et continuité, 1960-1972.* Ottawa, 1974. xvii, 337 leaves. Thesis (M.A.), Université d'Ottawa, 1974. **849**

Masse, Marcel. "La vocation internationale du Québec." (1967), 2 *Journal of Canadian Studies* 40-45 (No. 3) **850**

McLaren, Robert I. "Management of Foreign Affairs Reflects Provincial Priorities: The Case of Saskatchewan." (1978), *International Perspectives* 28-30 (Sept./Oct.) **851**

Meekison, J. Peter. "Provincial Activity Adds New Dimension to Federalism." (1977), *International Perspectives* 8-11 (Mar./Apr.) **852**

Morin, Claude. "La politique extérieure du Québec." (1978), 9 *Études Internationales* 281-289. **853**

Morin, Claude. "Quebec's Foreign Policy: An Interview with Claude Morin, Minister for Intergovernmental Affairs, Province of Québec." (1980), 4 *Fletcher Forum* 127-134 (No. 1) **854**
Questions prepared by Stephen Davis, a doctoral candidate at the Fletcher School of Law and Diplomacy.

Painchaud, Paul. "Le rôle international du Québec: possibilités et contraintes." (1977), 8 *Études Internationales* 374-392. **855**

Patry, André. *Le Québec dans le monde.* Montréal: Leméac, 1980. 167 p. (Ouvrages historiques) **856**
Reviews: John English in (1982), 63 *Canadian Historical Review* 264-265; Monique Lachance in (1981), 12 *Études Internationales* 227-228.

Québec (Province). Ministère des affaires intergouvernementales. Direction générale de la coopération internationale. *La coopération franco-québécoise.* Québec: Direction générale de la coopération internationale, 1976. 108 p. **857**

Rand, Michael C. "International Agreements between Canadian Provinces and Foreign States." (1967), 25 *University of Toronto Faculty of Law Review* 75-86. **858**

Riley, Richard B., and Leach, Richard H. "Province-State Transborder Relations from the American Perspective: A Preliminary Assessment." (1974), 46 *Canadian Political Science Association, Papers*, 33 p. **859**

Roy, Jean-Louis. "Les relations du Québec et des États-Unis (1945-1970)." In Painchaud, Paul, ed., *Le Canada et le Québec sur la scène internationale* (Québec, 1977), pp. 497-514. **860**

Rutan, Gerard F. "Legislative Interaction of a Canadian Province and an American State: Thoughts upon Sub-National Cross-Border Relations." (1981), 11 *Canadian Banker* 67-79 (No. 2) **861**

Rutan, Gerard F. "Provincial Participation in Canadian Foreign Relations." (1971), 13 *Journal of Inter-American Studies and World Affairs* 230-245. **862**

Sabourin, Louis. "La participation des provinces canadiennes aux organisations internationales." (1965), 3 *Canadian Yearbook of International Law* 73-99. **863**

Sabourin, Louis. "Politique étrangère et 'État du Québec.' " (1964-65), 20 *International Journal* 350-361. **864**

Sabourin, Louis. "Quebec's International Activity Rests on Idea of Competence." (1977), *International Perspectives* 3-7 (Mar./Apr.) **865**

St.-Aubin, Michel. "La province de Québec est-elle un état?" (1963), 13 *Thémis* 51-59. **866**

Starnes, John. "Foreign Policy in the 'New' Quebec." (1980), *International Perspectives* 3-5 (Mar./Apr.) **867**

Swanson, Roger Frank. "Canada and the United States: The Range of Direct Relations between States and Provinces." (1976), *International Perspectives* 18-23 (Mar./Apr.) **868**

Swanson, Roger Frank. *State/Provincial Interaction: A Study of Relations between U.S. States and Canadian Provinces.* Washington: Canus Research Institute, 1974. 509 p., maps. **869**
Prepared for the U.S. Department of State.

Tellier, Luc-Normand. *Étude des possibilités de rapprochement économique entre le Québec, le Canada et les pays scandinaves.* Préparé pour le compte du Ministère des affaires intergouvernementales du Québec. Québec: Éditeur officiel du Québec, 1979. 139 p. **870**

Torrelli, Maurice. "Les relations extérieures du Québec." (1970), 16 *Annuaire Français de Droit International* 275-303. **871**

Vaugeois, Denis. "La coopération du Québec avec l'extérieur." (1974), 5 *Études Internationales* 376-387. **872**

Walsh, David Francis. *The External Relations of Quebec, 1960-1970: An Aspect of the Jurisdictional Crisis within the Canadian Federal System.* Storrs, Conn., 1975. iii, 482 leaves. **873**
Thesis (Ph.D.), University of Connecticut, 1975. Abstracted in (1975-76), 36 *Dissertation Abstracts International* 4747-A. (University Microfilms, Ann Arbor, No. 76-1721).

(c) ASSOCIATIONS OF STATES

(i) COMMONWEALTH OF NATIONS

See also *"International Status: British Dominions" (p. 48), and "Relations with the British Empire and the Commonwealth" (p. 501).*

Ball, M. Margaret. *The 'Open' Commonwealth.* Durham, N.C.: Duke University Press, 1971. xiv, 286 p. (Duke University. Commonwealth-Studies Center. Publication, No. 39) **874**
Reviews: John Flint in (1973), 54 *Canadian Historical Review* 323; Leslie C. Green in (1973), 67 *American Journal of International Law* 188-189; David Smith in (1972), 15

Canadian Public Administration 658-659; Elisabeth Wallace in (1972), 5 Canadian Journal of Political Science 469-470.

Baxter, Neil Himrod. *The Influence of Sir Wilfrid Laurier on the Formation of the British Commonwealth of Nations.* Iowa City, 1937. 2 vols. **875**
Thesis (Ph.D.), University of Iowa, 1937.

Beauchesne, Arthur. "La Grande-Bretagne et ses Dominions." (1931), 25 *Royal Society of Canada, Transactions* 101-113 (3d Ser., Sec. 1) **876**

Beloff, Max. "Commonwealth Without Common Power." (1970-71), 26 *International Journal* 291-302. **877**

Boehm, Peter Michael. *Canada and the Commonwealth: Aspects of a Notable Role.* Ottawa, 1978. 133 leaves. **878**
Research essay (M.A.), Carleton University, 1978.

Borden, *Sir* Robert L. "A Study of the Commonwealth." (1929), 7 *Canadian Bar Review* 629-634. **879**

Brady, Alexander. "Canada and the Commonwealth." (1949), 4 *International Journal* 189-211. **880**

Brady, Alexander. "The Commonwealth." (1945-46), 15 *University of Toronto Quarterly* 148-169. **881**

Brady, Alexander. "The Modern Commonwealth." (1960), 26 *Canadian Journal of Economics and Political Science* 62-73. **882**

Brock, William Ranulf. *Britain and the Dominions.* Cambridge, Eng.: University Press, 1951. xxi, 521 p., 47 plates, maps. (British Commonwealth Series, Book 1) **883**

Burchell, Charles J. "The British Commonwealth of Nations." (1930), 8 *Canadian Bar Review* 492-497. **884**

Carter, Gwendolen M. *The British Commonwealth and International Security; the Role of the Dominions, 1919-1939.* Toronto: Ryerson Press, 1947. xx, 326 p. **885**
Issued under the auspices of the Canadian Institute of International Affairs. Reprinted Westport, Conn., Greenwood Press, 1971.
Reviews: J.L. Morison in (1947), 23 *International Affairs* 579-580; William L. Morton in (1946-47), 2 *International Journal* 262-263; Ulrich Scheuner in (1950-51), 13 *Zeitschrift für Ausländisches Öffentliches Recht und Völkerrecht* 861-863; H. Gordon Skilling in (1948), 14 *Canadian Journal of Economics and Political Science* 129-132.

Carter, Gwendolen M. "The Evolving Commonwealth." (1949), 4 *International Journal* 261-270. **886**

Carter, Gwendolen M. "The Expanding Commonwealth." (1956-57), 35 *Foreign Affairs* 131-143. **887**

Cheng, Seymour Ching-Yuan. *Schemes for the Federation of the British Empire.* New York: Columbia University Press; London: P.S. King, 1931. 313 p. (Studies in History, Economics and Public Law, No. 335) **888**
Also published as a thesis (Ph.D.), Columbia University.
Review: Robert A. MacKay in (1932), 13 *Canadian Historical Review* 201.

Chevallier, Jean-Jacques. "L'Empire britannique à la croisée des chemins (1919-1921)." (1930), 6 *Revue de Droit International* 462-505. **889**
Extract from the author's *L'évolution de l'Empire britannique* (Paris, 1930. 2 vols.).

Chevallier, Jean-Jacques. *L'évolution de l'Empire britannique.* Paris: Éditions internationales, 1930. 2 vols. (1068 p.) **890**
Review: G. Revel in (1932), 39 *Revue Générale de Droit International Public* 219-220.

Chevallier, Jean-Jacques. "Le mécanisme de coopération et de consultation dans l'Empire britannique." (1935), 15 *Revue de Droit International* 347-387. **891**

Chevallier, Jean-Jacques. "La Société des Nations britanniques." (1938), 64 *Académie de Droit International, Recueil des Cours* 237-345. **892**

Chipman, Warwick. "The Empire at the Cross-Roads." (1923-24), 3 *Dalhousie Review* 317-329. **893**

Claxton, Brooke. "The Commonwealth and South Africa." (1935-36), 42 *Queen's Quarterly* 110-120. **894**

"The Commonwealth: A Canadian View; A Member of Two Continents." (1959-60), 50 *Round Table* 341-348. **895**

Conway, John S. "The Changing Concept of the Commonwealth." (1956-57), 12 *International Journal* 34-41. **896**

Conway, John S. "The Dynamic Commonwealth. (Review Article)." (1960), 41 *Canadian Historical Review* 224-231. **897**

Conway, John S. " 'In Her Other Realms and Territories.' " (1958-59), 14 *International Journal* 175-181. **898**

Copland, Douglas. "Australia's Attitude to British Commonwealth Relations." (1948), 3 *International Journal* 39-48. **899**

Corbett, Percy E. "British Colonials and the Commonwealth." (1930-31), 20 *Yale Review* 727-736 (N.S.) **900**

Corbett, Percy E. "The Status of the British Commonwealth in International Law." (1939-40), 3 *University of Toronto Law Journal* 348-359. **901**

Cross, J.A. "The Colonial Office and the Dominions Before 1914." (1966), 4 *Journal of Commonwealth Political Studies* 138-148. **902**

Currey, Charles Herbert. *The British Commonwealth since 1815.* Sydney: Angus and Robertson, 1950-51. 2 vols., maps. **903**

Dale, William. "Is the Commonwealth an International Organisation?" (1982), 31 *International and Comparative Law Quarterly* 451-473. **904**

De Smith, Stanley A. *The New Commonwealth and Its Constitutions.* London: Stevens, 1964. xvi, 312 p. **905**
Review: J.H. Aitchison in (1965), 31 *Canadian Journal of Economics and Political Science* 297-299.

Dewey, Alexander Gordon. "Canada's Part in the Britannic Question." (1927), 8 *Canadian Historical Review* 284-301. **906**

Dohle, Gordon Carl. *Commonwealth Secretariat, 1965-1973: a Descriptive Analysis.* Ottawa, 1973 (i.e. 1974). v, 202 leaves. **907**
Thesis (M.A.), Carleton University, 1974.

Dorland, Arthur G. "The Republican Tradition in the British Empire and the Commonwealth." (1950), 44 *Royal Society of Canada, Transactions* 1-18 (3d Ser., Sec. 2) **908**

Doxey, Margaret P. "Canada and the Evolution of the Modern Commonwealth." (1982), 40 *Behind the Headlines* No. 2 (20 p.) **909**

Doxey, Margaret P. "The Commonwealth in the 1970s." (1973), 27 *Year Book of World Affairs* 90-109. **910**

Doxey, Margaret P. "The Commonwealth Secretariat." (1976), 30 *Year Book of World Affairs* 69-96. **911**

Dumouchel, Jean. "La décentralisation de l'Empire; les accords de Locarno de 1924 et la conférence impériale de 1926." (1946-47), 22 *Actualité Économique* 688-707. **912**

Dumouchel, Jean. "Le retour à la décentralisation de l'Empire; de l'incident de Tchanak aux accords de Locarno." (1946-47), 22 *Actualité Économique* 315-337. **913**

Dumouchel, Jean. "Les tentatives de centralisation de l'Empire de 1920 à 1922." (1946-47), 22 *Actualité Économique* 102-127. **914**

Dupras, Maurice. "Réflexions sur la fonction politique du Commonwealth et de la francophonie." *In* Jacomy-Millette, Annemarie, ed., *Francophonie et Commonwealth: mythe ou réalité?* (Québec, 1978), pp. 250-254. **915**

Elliott, W.Y. "The Riddle of the British Commonwealth." (1929-30), 8 *Foreign Affairs* 442-464. **916**

Fawcett, J.E.S. *The British Commonwealth in International Law*. London: Stevens, 1963. xvii, 243, viii p. (Library of World Affairs, No. 61) **917**
Published under the auspices of the London Institute of World Affairs.
Reviews: Louis Blom-Cooper in (1964), 40 *International Affairs* 503-504; C.A. Colliard in (1964), 91 *Journal du Droit International* 469; Charles G. Fenwick in (1965), 59 *American Journal of International Law* 678-679; Brian Flemming in (1965), 3 *Canadian Yearbook of International Law* 364-366; Charles Rousseau in (1964), 68 *Revue Générale de Droit International Public* 580-581; Robert R. Wilson in (1963-64), 19 *International Journal* 393-394.

Forsey, Eugene. "'The Expanding Commonwealth': A Personal Impression." (1958-59), 14 *International Journal* 213-217. **918**

Franck, Thomas M. "The Crown as Head of the Commonwealth - From Unity to Unity." (1953-58), 2 *U.B.C. Legal Notes* 167-176. **919**

Friedmann, Wolfgang G. "The Changing Commonwealth." (1951-52), 58 *Queen's Quarterly* 465-476. **920**

Gottlieb, Paul Herbert. *The Commonwealth of Nations at the United Nations*. Boston, 1962. 307 leaves, maps. **921**
Thesis (Ph.D.), Boston University, 1962. (University Microfilms, Ann Arbor, No. 62-3790).

Green, Leslie C. "De l'évolution historique du Commonwealth." *In* Jacomy-Millette, Annemarie, ed., *Francophonie et Commonwealth: mythe ou réalité?* (Québec, 1978), pp. 101-116. **922**
Comment by Donat Pharand (pp. 117-119).

Green, Leslie C. "From Empire through Commonwealth to ...?" (1978), 16 *Alberta Law Review* 52-69. **923**

Grimal, Henri. *De l'Empire britannique au Commonwealth.* Paris: A. Colin, 1971. 416 p. (Collection U2, 142) (Série Études anglo-américaines) **924**
Reviews: Charles Rousseau in (1971), 75 *Revue Générale de Droit International Public* 1211-1212.

Hall, Hessel Duncan. *The British Commonwealth of Nations; a Study of Its Past and Future Development.* London: Methuen, 1920. xviii, 393 p. **925**
Review: J.L. Morison in (1921), 2 *Canadian Historical Review* 192-194.

Hall, Hessel Duncan. *Commonwealth: A History of the British Commonwealth of Nations.* Introduction by Sir Robert Menzies. London, New York: Van Nostrand Reinhold, 1971. xxxvi, 1015 p., 33 plates, maps. **926**

Hall, Walter Phelps. *Empire to Commonwealth, Thirty Years of British Imperial History.* New York: H. Holt, c1928. x, 526 p., maps. **927**
Review: W.T. Waugh in (1928), 9 *Canadian Historical Review* 162-163.

Hamilton, William Baskerville, and others. *A Decade of the Commonwealth, 1955-1964.* Durham, N.C.: Published for the Duke University Commonwealth-Studies Center by Duke University Press, 1966. xx, 567 p. (Duke University. Commonwealth-Studies Center. Publication, No. 25) **928**
Review: Elisabeth Wallace in (1966), 32 *Canadian Journal of Economics and Political Science* 542-543.

Harvey, Heather Joan. *The British Commonwealth; a Pattern of Cooperation.* New York: Carnegie Endowment for International Peace, 1953. 48 p. (International Conciliation, No. 487) **929**

Heasman, Donald J. "British Politics and Commonwealth Principles: The Case of Central Africa." (1960-61), 67 *Queen's Quarterly* 175-187. **930**

Hennigar, W.J. "The British Commonwealth in the Post-War World." (1947-48), 27 *Dalhousie Review* 281-293. **931**

Hodson, Henry V. "United Kingdom Opinion on a Multi-Racial Commonwealth." (1949-50), 5 *International Journal* 14-21. **932**

Holland, Sir Robert E. "The Commonwealth Today." (1951-52), 31 *Dalhousie Review* 11-18. **933**

Holmes, John W. "A Commonwealth Secretariat - New Style." (1965), 72 *Canadian Banker* 63-68 (No. 1) **934**

Holmes, John W. "Le Commonwealth dans l'histoire." *In* Jacomy-Millette, Annemarie, ed., *Francophonie et Commonwealth: mythe ou réalité?* (Québec, 1978), pp. 67-74. **935**

Holmes, John W. "The Commonwealth and the United Nations." *In* Hamilton, William Baskerville, and others, *A Decade of the Commonwealth, 1955-1964* (Durham, N.C., 1966), pp. 349-365. **936**

Holmes, John W. "The Impact on the Commonwealth of the Emergence of Africa." (1962), 16 *International Organization* 291-302. **937**

Holmested, George S. "What Is an Empire?" (1928), 6 *Canadian Bar Review* 115-116. **938**

Hore, Satchidananda. "The Commonwealth as an International Organisation." (1974), 17 *Indian Year Book of International Affairs* 343-372. **939**

Hudson, G.F. "How Unified Is the Commonwealth?" (1954-55), 33 *Foreign Affairs* 679-688. **940**

Hudson, Manley O. "The Style and Titles of His Britannic Majesty." (1928), 22 *American Journal of International Law* 146-150. **941**

Hurst, *Sir* Cecil. *Great Britain and the Dominions.* Chicago: University of Chicago Press, 1928. x, 510 p. (Harris Foundation Lectures, 1927) **942**
Reviews: A. Berriedale Keith in (1928), 10 *Journal of Comparative Legislation and International Law* 326-329 (3d Ser.); W.P.M. Kennedy in (1928), 9 *Canadian Historical Review* 163-165; Robert A. MacKay in (1928-29), 8 *Dalhousie Review* 430-431.

Ingram, Derek. "Le Commonwealth." *In* Jacomy-Millette, Annemarie, ed., *Francophonie et Commonwealth: mythe ou réalité?* (Québec, 1978), pp. 229-237. **943**

Iwi, Edward F. "The Evolution of the Commonwealth since the Statute of Westminster." (1951), 37 *Grotius Society, Transactions* 83-97. **944**

Jennings, R.Y. "The Commonwealth and International Law." (1953), 30 *British Year Book of International Law* 320-351. **945**

Jennings, *Sir* William Ivor. *The British Commonwealth of Nations.* London, New York: Hutchinson's University Library, 1948. 176 p. (Hutchinson's Library; Politics, No. 4) **946**
Review: Nicholas Mansergh in (1949), 25 *International Affairs* 216.

Jennings, *Sir* William Ivor. *Problems of the New Commonwealth.* Durham, N.C.: Published for the Duke University Commonwealth-Studies Center, Duke University Press, 1958. 114 p. (Duke University. Commonwealth-Studies Center. Publication, No. 7) **947**
Reviews: Edward McWhinney in (1958), 36 *Canadian Bar Review* 278-280.

Kavic, Lorne. "Canada and the Commonwealth; Sentiment, Symbolism and Self-Interest." (1975), 65 *Round Table* 37-49. **948**

Keith, A. Berriedale. "The Imperial War Cabinet and the Dominions." (1918), 38 *Canadian Law Times* 695-705. **949**

Kennedy, W.P.M. "British Possessions." (1937-38), 2 *University of Toronto Law Journal* 114-116. **950**

Keppel-Jones, Arthur. "South Africa and the Commonwealth." (1954-55), 61 *Queen's Quarterly* 2-12. **951**

Kerr, Philip Henry, and Kerr, A.C. *The Growth of the British Commonwealth.* London, New York, etc.: Longmans, Green, 1937. viii, 214 p., plates, maps. **952**

Leach, Richard A. "The Secretariat." (1970-71), 26 *International Journal* 374-400. **953**
Refers to the Commonwealth Secretariat.

Leacock, Stephen Butler. *The British Empire; Its Structure, Its Unity, Its Strength.* New York: Dodd, Mead, 1940. vi, 263 p., maps. **954**

Lowell, Abbott Lawrence, and Hall, Hessel Duncan. *The British Commonwealth of Nations.* Boston, 1927. pp. 573-693. (World Peace Foundation. Pamphlets Series, Vol. 10, No. 6) **955**
Review: W.P.M. Kennedy in (1928), 9 *Canadian Historical Review* 52-57.

MacKay, Robert A. "Changes in the Legal Structure of the British Commonwealth of Nations." (1931), 272 *International Conciliation* 507-587. **956**

MacKay, Robert A. "The Problem of a Commonwealth Tribunal." (1932), 10 *Canadian Bar Review* 338-348. **957**
Also published in (1932), 4 *Canadian Political Science Association, Proceedings* 68-81.

MacKenzie, Norman A.M. "Commonwealth or Empire." (1934), 28 *American Journal of International Law* 559-562. **958**

MacKenzie, Norman A.M. "Constitutional Developments in the Commonwealth of Nations." (1930), 8 *Canadian Bar Review* 213-217. **959**

MacKirdy, Kenneth A. "The Commonwealth Idea." (1965-66), 25 *Behind the Headlines* No. 2 (21 p.) **960**

Manigat, Leslie F. "Réflexions sur la fonction politique du Commonwealth et de la francophonie." *In* Jacomy-Millette, Annemarie, ed., *Francophonie et Commonwealth: mythe ou réalité?* (Québec, 1978), pp. 241-250. **961**

Mansergh, Nicholas. *The Commonwealth Experience.* New York: Praeger, 1969. xix, 471 p., maps. (Praeger History of Civilization) **962**

Mansergh, Nicholas. "The Commonwealth in Asia." (1953), 13 *Behind the Headlines* No. 2 (17 p.) **963**

Mansergh, Nicholas, and others. *Commonwealth Perspectives.* Durham, N.C.: Published for the Duke University Commonwealth-Studies Center by Duke University Press, 1958. vii, 214 p. (Duke University. Commonwealth-Studies Center. Publication, No. 8) **964**
These essays represent revised versions of faculty contributions to a joint seminar conducted at Duke University in the spring of 1957.
Reviews: Alexander Brady in (1960), 41 *Canadian Historical Review* 358-360; A.F. Madden in (1959), 35 *International Affairs* 372; Frank H. Underhill in (1960), 26 *Canadian Journal of Economics and Political Science* 165-167.

Martin, Chester B. "The British Commonwealth." (1944), 25 *Canadian Historical Review* 131-150. **965**

Miller, John Donald Bruce. *The Commonwealth in the World.* 3d ed. Cambridge: Harvard University Press, 1965. 304 p. **966**

Miller, John Donald Bruce. "The Decline of *Inter Se.*" (1968-69), 24 *International Journal* 765-775. **967**

Moore, Rodney Ernest. *The Commonwealth Secretariats of 1965 and 1907; an Analysis of the Secretariat Established in 1965 and an Account of the Failure to Establish a Similar Body at the Colonial Conference of 1907.* Ottawa, 1967. 149, vi leaves. **968**
Thesis (M.A.), Carleton University, 1968.

Murray, Howard. "Reflections on Canada in the Empire." (1939-40), 19 *Dalhousie Review* 323-333. **969**

O'Connell, Daniel Patrick. "The Crown in the British Commonwealth." (1957), 6 *International and Comparative Law Quarterly* 103-125. **970**

Painchaud, Paul. "Commonwealth et francophonie: alliances culturelles?" *In* Jacomy-Millette, Annemarie, ed., *Francophonie et Commonwealth: mythe ou réalité?* (Québec, 1978), pp. 263-268. **971**

Patry, André. "Le Commonwealth et la Couronne." (1949), 55/1 *Revue Dominicaine* 15-22. **972**

Perrault, Antonio. "Le Canada et le Commonwealth: aspect juridique." (1939), 13 *Action Nationale* 225-252. **973**

Potter, Pitman B. "Dominions, Commonwealth, and the Society of Nations." (1931), 25 *American Journal of International Law* 316-318. **974**

Reese, Trevor R. "The Conference System." (1970-71), 26 *International Journal* 361-373. **975**

Reid, Patrick. "The Contemporary Commonwealth." (1954), 9 *International Journal* 208-215. **976**

Richardson, B.T. "The Evolving Commonwealth." (1958-59), 14 *International Journal* 131-138. **977**

Richer, Léopold. "La liberté et l'unité dans le Commonwealth." (1940), 46/1 *Revue Dominicaine* 121-133. **978**

Ross, David J. "Official Canadian Attitudes Toward the Commonwealth." (1980), 26 *Australian Journal of Politics and History* 183-192. **979**

Rowell, Newton W. "Canada's Position in the British Commonwealth of Nations." (1930), 8 *Canadian Bar Review* 570-586. **980**

Scott, Francis R. "Canada's Future in the British Commonwealth." (1936-37), 15 *Foreign Affairs* 429-442. **981**

Scott, Francis R. "The Redistribution of Imperial Sovereignty." (1950), 44 *Royal Society of Canada, Transactions* 27-34 (3d Ser., Sec. 2) **982**

Scott, James Brown. "The British Commonwealth of Nations." (1927), 21 *American Journal of International Law* 95-101. **983**

Shatzky, Boris. "L'Angleterre et les Dominions." (1933), 11 *Revue de Droit International, de Sciences Diplomatiques et Politiques* 1-21. **984**

Shearman, Hugh. "The British Commonwealth and Its Members." (1950), 4 *Year Book of World Affairs* 105-129. **985**

Shiels, Sir Drummond, ed. *The British Commonwealth; a Family of Peoples.* London: Odhams Press, 1952. 384 p. (New Educational Library) **986**

Shinn, Ridgway Foulks. *The Right of Secession in the Development of the British Commonwealth of Nations.* New York, 1958. (9), 278 leaves. **987**
Thesis (Ph.D.), Columbia University, 1958. Abstracted in (1958), 19 *Dissertation Abstracts* 127-128. (University Microfilms, Ann Arbor, No. 58-2477).

Smith, Arnold. "Le Commonwealth, instrument de consultation et de collaboration." *In* Jacomy-Millette, Annemarie, ed., *Francophonie et Commonwealth, mythe ou réalité?* (Québec, 1978), pp. 45-54. **988**

Smith, Arnold. "Commonwealth of Nations after 25 Years of Change." (1975) *International Perspectives* 43-50 (Nov./Dec.) **989**

Smith, S.A. de. "Fundamental Rules - Forty Years On." (1970-71), 26 *International Journal* 347-360. **990**

Soward, Frederic H. "The Changing Commonwealth." (1950), 44 *Royal Society of Canada, Transactions* 19-26 (3d Ser., Sec. 2) **991**

Stanton, Stephen B. "Is the British Empire Constitutionally a Nation?" (1904), 3 *Canadian Law Review* 149-166. **992**

Thorson, Joseph T. "The British Commonwealth of Nations." (1929), 7 *Canadian Bar Review* 96-110. **993**

Trotter, Reginald G. "Bigwig and the Changing Commonwealth." (1949-50), 5 *International Journal* 22-30. **994**

Trotter, Reginald G. *The British Empire-Commonwealth; a Study in Political Evolution.* New York: H. Holt, c1932. viii, 131 p. (Berkshire Studies in European History) **995**

Trotter, Reginald G. "National Interests within the British Commonwealth." (1944), 51 *Queen's Quarterly* 439-452. **996**

Underhill, Frank H. *The British Commonwealth; an Experiment in Co-operation among Nations.* Durham, N.C.: Duke University Press, 1956. xxiii, 127 p. (Duke University. Commonwealth-Studies Center. Publications) **997**
Published for the Duke University Commonwealth-Studies Center. Lectures delivered by the author at Duke University in 1955, under the sponsorship of the Duke University Commonwealth-Studies Center.
Reviews: Alfred LeRoy Burt in (1956), 37 *Canadian Historical Review* 370-371; Donald J. Heasman in (1957-58), 37 *Dalhousie Review* 98-100; Nicholas Mansergh in (1957), 33 *International Affairs* 224-225; R.C. Pratt in (1957), 23 *Canadian Journal of Economics and Political Science* 431-432.

Watts, Ronald L. *New Federations: Experiments in the Commonwealth.* Oxford: Clarendon Press, 1966. xii, 419 p., 7 plates (maps). **998**
Reviews: F.M. Fraser in (1966-67), 47 *Dalhousie Review* 103-105; Kenneth A. MacKirdy in (1966-67), 22 *International Journal* 694-695.

Wheare, Kenneth Clinton. *The Constitutional Structure of the Commonwealth.* Oxford: Clarendon Press, 1960. xiv, 201 p. **999**

Wilson, Robert R. *International Law and Contemporary Commonwealth Issues.* Durham, N.C.: Duke University Press, 1971. ix, 245 p. (Duke University. Commonwealth-Studies Center. Publication, No. 38) **1000**
Reviews: Thomas M. Franck in (1972), 66 *American Journal of International Law* 672-674; Elisabeth Wallace in (1972), 5 *Canadian Journal of Political Science* 469-470.

Wilson, Robert R. "International Law and the Commonwealth, 1907-1967." (1966), 60 *American Journal of International Law* 770-781. **1001**
Reprinted Duke University. Commonwealth-Studies Center. Reprint Series, No. 19.

Wilson, Robert R., and others. *International and Comparative Law of the Commonwealth.* Durham, N.C.: Published for the Duke University Commonwealth-Studies Center by Duke University Press, 1968. vii, 247 p. (Duke University. Commonwealth-Studies Center. Publication, No. 33) **1002**
Reviews: Gerald F. FitzGerald in (1970), 64 *American Journal of International Law* 990-991; Brian Flemming in (1967-68), 47 *Dalhousie Review* 102-103; F. Honig in (1970), 46 *International Affairs* 795-796; S.A. de Smith in (1969-70), 25 *International Journal* 645-646.

Wilson, Robert R., and others. *The International Law Standard and Commonwealth Developments.* Durham, N.C.: Published for the Duke University Commonwealth-Studies Center by Duke University Press, 1966. ix, 306 p.

(Duke University. Commonwealth-Studies Center. Publication, No. 27) **1003**
Reviews: Louis M. Bloomfield in (1968), 62 *American Journal of International Law* 541-542; Leslie C. Green in (1968), 6 *Canadian Yearbook of International Law* 339-342; Otto C. Kitsinger in (1967), 3 *Texas International Law Journal* 412-415; Gerald L. Morris in (1966-67), 22 *International Journal* 674-675.

(ii) UNION FRANÇAISE AND FRANCOPHONIE

Brossard, Jacques. "Le Québec et la francophonie." *In* Popovici, Adrian, ed., *Problèmes de droit contemporain: mélanges Louis Baudouin* (Montréal, 1974), pp. 445-462. **1004**

Cousin, Marie-Elisabeth. "Quelques aspects formels des conventions de coopération entre pays francophones." (1974), 5 *Études Internationales* 326-341. **1005**

Dan Dicko, Dankoulodo. "L'Agence de coopération culturelle et technique, clef de voûte de la francophonie." *In* Jacomy-Millette, Annemarie, ed., *Francophonie et Commonwealth: mythe ou réalité?* (Québec, 1978), pp. 11-18. **1006**

Dupras, Maurice. "Réflexions sur la fonction politique du Commonwealth et de la francophonie." *In* Jacomy-Millette, Annemarie, ed., *Francophonie et Commonwealth: mythe ou réalité?* (Québec, 1978), pp. 250-254. **1007**

Flory, Maurice. "Aspects culturels de la coopération francophone." (1974), 5 *Études Internationales* 244-251. **1008**

Hugon, Philippe. "Vers une théorie économique de la coopération entre les pays francophones." (1974), 5 *Études Internationales* 252-268. **1009**

Jacomy-Millette, Annemarie, ed. *Francophonie et Commonwealth: mythe ou réalité?* Québec: Centre québécois de relations internationales, Université Laval; Toronto: Institut canadien des affaires internationales, 1978. 288 p. (Collection Choix, 9) **1010**
Proceedings of a conference organized by the Centre québécois de relations internationales held March 31-April 2, 1977, at Université Laval, Québec; some papers are listed separately.

Léger, Jean-Marc. "La francophonie, une grande aventure spirituelle." *In* Jacomy-Millette, Annemarie, ed., *Francophonie et Commonwealth: mythe ou réalité?* (Québec, 1978), pp. 19-31. **1011**

Manigat, Leslie F. "Réflexions sur la fonction politique du Commonwealth et de la francophonie." *In* Jacomy-Millette, Annemarie, ed., *Francophonie et Commonwealth: mythe ou réalité?* (Québec, 1978), pp. 241-250. **1012**

Morrison, Jean. "Canada's Role in a French Commonwealth." (1967-68), 27 *Behind the Headlines* No. 1 (37 p.) **1013**
Review: H.S. Ferns in (1968), 44 *International Affairs* 833-834.

Painchaud, Paul. "Commonwealth et francophonie: alliances culturelles?" *In* Jacomy-Millette, Annemarie, ed., *Francophonie et Commonwealth: mythe ou réalité?* (Québec, 1978), pp. 263-268. **1014**

Sabourin, Louis. "La coopération entre pays francophones dans une perspective globale." (1974), 5 *Études Internationales* 195-207. **1015**

Sabourin, Louis. "Dimensions politiques de la francophonie: de la problématique culturelle à la dynamique internationale." *In* Jacomy-Millette, Annemarie, ed.,

Francophonie et Commonwealth: mythe ou réalité? (Québec, 1978), pp. 221-226. **1016**

Savard, Pierre. "Les Canadiens français et la France: de la 'cession' à la 'révolution tranquille.' " *In* Painchaud, Paul, ed., *Le Canada et le Québec sur la scène internationale* (Québec, 1977), pp. 471-495. **1017**

Savary, Alan. "The French Union: Centralism or Federalism?" (1951-52), 7 *International Journal* 258-264. **1018**

Touscoz, Jean. "La 'normalisation' de la coopération bilatérale de la France avec les pays africains 'francophones' (aspects juridiques)." (1974), 5 *Études Internationales* 208-225. **1019**

(d) PERMANENTLY NEUTRAL STATES

See also *"Neutrality" (p. 458).*

Aksim, Rudi Ervin. *Switzerland and the Second World War; a Study of Neutrality.* Ottawa, 1970. xi, 215 leaves. **1020**
Research essay (B.A.), Carleton University, 1970.

Baumgartner, F.W. "The Neutralization of States." (1917-18), 25 *Queen's Quarterly* 54-89, 172-203. **1021**

(e) DIVIDED STATES (GERMANY)

Dorscht, Axel. *The Origin of the Division and the Subsequent Development of Post-World War II Germany: A Study in Linkage Politics.* Burnaby, B.C., 1977. ix, 167 leaves. **1022**
Thesis (M.A.), Simon Fraser University, 1977. (National Library of Canada. Canadian Theses on Microfiche, No. 35904).

Knudson, Charles A. "One or More Germanies: The Economics of Partition." (1948), 3 *International Journal* 56-66. **1023**

Pelletier, Luc. *La réunification de l'Allemagne dans la politique extérieure de la R.F.A.* Montréal, 1975 (c1977). xiii, 152 leaves. **1024**
Thesis (M.A.), Université du Québec à Montréal, 1976. (National Library of Canada. Canadian Theses on Microfiche, No. 32364).

Smith, Jean Edward. "The German Democratic Republic and the West." (1966-67), 22 *International Journal* 231-252. **1025**

Smith, Jean Edward. "The United States, German Unity, and the Deutsche Demokratische Republik." (1967), 74 *Queen's Quarterly* 21-35. **1026**

Spencer, Robert A. "Divided Germany and the Thaw." (1958-59), 14 *International Journal* 250-258. **1027**

Warburg, J.P. "Deadlock over Germany." (1948), 8 *Behind the Headlines* No. 2 (27 p.) **1028**

(f) SPECIAL ENTITIES (BERLIN, CYPRUS, ETC.)

"Agreement on the Saar." (1956), 8 *External Affairs* 290-295. **1029**

Boreham, Gordon F. "Two Chinas, One World." (1982), *International Perspectives* 21-26 (July/Aug.) **1030**

Corrigan, Beatrice. "Trieste and the Empires." (1946-47), 53 *Queen's Quarterly* 137-146. **1031**

"The Cyprus Agreements." (1959), 11 *External Affairs* 70-75. **1032**

Dai, Poeliu. "Recognition of States and Governments under International Law with Special Reference to Canadian Postwar Practice and the Legal Status of Taiwan (Formosa)." (1965), 3 *Canadian Yearbook of International Law* 290-305. **1033**

Deutsch, Harold C. "New Crisis on Berlin." (1959), 19 *Behind the Headlines* No. 2 (17 p.) **1034**

Dobell, William M. "Division over Cyprus." (1966-67), 22 *International Journal* 278-292. **1035**

Dobell, William M. "Policy or Law for Cyprus? (Review Article)." (1975-76), 31 *International Journal* 146-158. **1036**

Dobell, William M. "A Respite for Cyprus." (1964-65), 24 *Behind the Headlines* No. 4 (20 p.) **1037**

"East-West Relations in Berlin." (1949), 1 *External Affairs* 3-9 (June) **1038**

Evans, J.A.S. "Cyprus in Hazard - Large Stakes in a Small Island." (1956-57), 63 *Queen's Quarterly* 366-374. **1039**

"Formosa." (1953), 5 *External Affairs* 114-123. **1040**

George, James. "Jerusalem: The Holy City - A Religious Solution for a Political Problem." (1978), *International Perspectives* 18-24 (Mar./Apr.) **1041**

Green, Leslie C. "Berlin and the United Nations." (1949), 3 *World Affairs* 23-42 (N.S.) **1042**

Green, Leslie C. "The Legal Status of Berlin." (1963), 10 *Netherlands International Law Review* 113-138. **1043**

Heasman, Donald J. "The Gibraltar Affair." (1966-67), 22 *International Journal* 265-277. **1044**

Hsiao, Frank S.T., and Sullivan, Lawrence R. "The Chinese Communist Party and the Status of Taiwan, 1928-1943." (1979), 52 *Pacific Affairs* 446-467. **1045**

"Jerusalem and the Holy Places." (1950), 2 *External Affairs* 7-11. **1046**

Kalogeropoulos, George A. *The Cyprus Question: A Problem of External Interests.* Halifax, 1974 (c1975). iii, 257 leaves. **1047**
  Thesis (M.A.), Dalhousie University, 1974. (National Library of Canada. Canadian Theses on Microfiche, No. 22839).

Kirkham, D. Barry. "The International Legal Status of Formosa." (1968), 6 *Canadian Yearbook of International Law* 144-163. **1048**

Lucy, R.V. "Jerusalem: The Holy City - Problem Can Only Be Resolved as Part of

General Settlement: Canadian Position." (1978), *International Perspectives* 24-28 (Mar./Apr.) **1049**

Macdonald, Ronald St. John. "International Law and the Conflict in Cyprus." (1981), 19 *Canadian Yearbook of International Law* 3-49. **1050**

Preston, Richard A. "The Gibraltar Question." (1954-55), 61 *Queen's Quarterly* 179-188. **1051**

Rosenbaum, Naomi. "Cyprus and the United Nations: An Appreciation of Parliamentary Diplomacy." (1967), 33 *Canadian Journal of Economics and Political Science* 218-231. **1052**
   Contains a résumé in French under title: "Chypre et les Nations Unies: une appréciation de la diplomatie parlementaire."

Taylor, A.J.P. "France, Germany, and the Saar." (1952-53), 8 *International Journal* 27-31. **1053**

"Trieste." (1954), 6 *External Affairs* 294-298. **1054**

"The Trusteeship Council's Statute for Jerusalem." (1950), 2 *External Affairs* 171-174. **1055**

B. Other Subjects of International Law

For international organizations, see "International Organizations" (p. 332).

1. NATIONAL LIBERATION MOVEMENTS

See also *"Civil War and Guerilla Warfare" (p. 456).*

Green, Leslie C. "The Status of Rebel Armies." (1961), 3 *University of Malaya Law Review* 25-45. **1056**

Green, Leslie C. "Le statut des forces rebelles en droit international." (1962), 66 *Revue Générale de Droit International Public* 5-33. **1057**

Krauss, Michel. "Les conflits internes et les états-tiers: à la recherche de l'état du droit." (1979-80), 10 *Revue de Droit, Université de Sherbrooke* 1-65. **1058**

2. HOLY SEE

Bergeron, Désiré. "La personnalité internationale du Saint-Siège." (1942), 12 *Revue de l'Université d'Ottawa* 185-207 (section spéciale) **1059**

Cardinale, Igino. *The Holy See and the International Order*, by Hyginus Eugene Cardinale. Toronto: Macmillan of Canada, Niagara Falls, N.Y.: Maclean-Hunter Press, 1976. xx, 557 p., 2 leaves of plates. **1060**
   Reviews: John S. Conway in (1977-78), 12 *Canadian Journal of History* 411-412; John Jay Hughes in (1979), 34 *International Journal* 503-504.

Caron, Arthur. "Le rôle de l'Église dans l'ordre international." (1945), 15 *Revue de l'Université d'Ottawa* 5-15. **1061**

Conway, John S. "Vatican Diplomacy Today: The Legacy of Paul VI." (1978-79), 34 *International Journal* 457-474. **1062**

Greenwood, Thomas. "La souveraineté pontificale." (1953), 59/1 *Revue Dominicaine* 78-89. **1063**

Patry, André. "Le Saint-Siège." (1964-65), 6 *Cahiers de Droit* 21-28 (no 2) **1064**

Phelan, G.B. "The Lateran Treaty." (1929-30), 9 *Dalhousie Review* 427-438. **1065**

Robbins, John E. "The Vatican's Political Role in the International Sphere." (1974), *International Perspectives* 44-46 (Jan./Feb.) **1066**

Valiquette, André. "La condition juridique internationale du Saint-Siège." (1953-54), 4 *Thémis* 202-220. **1067**

3. MANDATED AND TRUST TERRITORIES

Armstrong, Elizabeth. "The United States and Non-Self-Governing Territories." (1948), 3 *International Journal* 327-333. **1068**

Castañeda, Jorge. "La question du Sud-Ouest africain." (1962-63), 5 *Cahiers de Droit* 7-18 (no 1) **1069**

Doxey, G.V., and Doxey, Margaret P. "Whither Southern Africa?" (1966-67), 22 *International Journal* 25-38. **1070**

Faris, Nabil Ahmed. *The Palestine Question Before the United Nations, 1946-1949.* Calgary, 1975. viii, 202 leaves, maps. **1071**
   Thesis (M.A.), University of Calgary, 1975. (National Library of Canada. Canadian Theses on Microfiche, No. 23733).

Fletcher-Cooke, *Sir* John. "The United Nations and the Birth of Israel 1948." (1972-73), 28 *International Journal* 612-629. **1072**

Gelber, Marvin. "The Palestine Mandate: Story of a Fumble." (1946), 1 *International Journal* 302-316. **1073**

Gordon, Daniel. *Juridical Problems of the Mandate System.* Toronto, 1934. 195 leaves. **1074**
   Thesis (M.A.), University of Toronto, 1934.

Grant, Christina Phelps. "Must Palestine Be Partitioned." (1937-38), 44 *Queen's Quarterly* 455-462. **1075**

Green, Leslie C. "South West Africa and the World Court." (1966-67), 22 *International Journal* 39-67. **1076**

Green, Leslie C. "The United Nations, South-West Africa and the World Court." (1967), 7 *Indian Journal of International Law* 491-525. **1077**

Gryger, Elizabeth M. *South West Africa in the United Nations.* Ottawa, 1969. v, 263 leaves, maps. **1078**
   Thesis (M.A.), Carleton University, 1969.

Herman, Lawrence L. "The Legal Status of Namibia and of the United Nations

Council for Namibia." (1975), 13 *Canadian Yearbook of International Law* 306-322. **1079**

Holland, *Sir* Robert E. "Peril in Palestine." (1948-49), 28 *Dalhousie Review* 38-52. **1080**

Los, Laurence John. *The Mandate for South West Africa, 1920-1939.* Toronto, 1969. 153 leaves. **1081**
Thesis (M.Phil.), University of Toronto, 1969.

McCullough, W.S. "Palestine: The Arabs, the Jews, and the Peel Report." (1937-38), 7 *University of Toronto Quarterly* 468-487. **1082**

Meret, Livia. "Canada and Namibia." (1979), 17 *Canadian Yearbook of International Law* 314-323. **1083**

Prince, A.E. "Britain and Palestine." (1930), 37 *Queen's Quarterly* 679-697. **1084**

Prince, A.E. "Canada and the Problem of Palestine." (1946-47), 53 *Queen's Quarterly* 64-68. **1085**

Redekop, Clarence G. "The Limits of Diplomacy: The Case of Namibia." (1979-80), 35 *International Journal* 70-90. **1086**

Rousseau, A. "Colonies et mandats." (1937), 23 *Revue Trimestrielle Canadienne* 188-202. **1087**

Silcox, Claris Edwin. "Impasse in the Holy Land." (1946-47), 16 *University of Toronto Quarterly* 123-132. **1088**

Slonim, S. "The Origins of the South West Africa Dispute: The Versailles Peace Conference and the Creation of the Mandates System." (1968), 6 *Canadian Yearbook of International Law* 115-143. **1089**

Smith, David E. "The International Community and the South West Africa Dispute." (1967), 74 *Queen's Quarterly* 593-609. **1090**

Stuchen, Philip. "The Problem of Palestine." (1947-48), 54 *Queen's Quarterly* 413-420. **1091**

Tschirgi, Robert Daniel. *The Politics of Indecision: American Involvement with the Palestine Problem, 1939-1948.* Toronto, c1975. xlix, 784 leaves. **1092**
Thesis (Ph.D.), University of Toronto, 1976. (National Library of Canada. Canadian Theses on Microfiche, No. 35152).

"United Nations Trusteeship Council." (1959), 11 *External Affairs* 180-184. **1093**

Variawa, Mohamed. *The Namibia Question: A Study of American and British Behaviour in the United Nations.* London, Ont., 1976, c1977. viii, 245 leaves. **1094**
Thesis (M.A.), University of Western Ontario, 1977. (National Library of Canada. Canadian Theses on Microfiche, No. 31660).

Zuijdwijk, Anthony J.M. "The International Court and South West Africa: Latest Phase." (1973), 3 *Georgia Journal of International and Comparative Law* 323-343. **1095**

4. COLONIES

Andrew, C.M., and Kanya-Forstner, A.S. "France and the Repartition of Africa, 1914-1922." (1977-78), 57 *Dalhousie Review* 475-493.   **1096**

Baldwin, John R. "Germany's Bluff and the Colonies Problem." (1939-40), 19 *Dalhousie Review* 318-322.   **1097**

Baty, Thomas. "Sovereign Colonies." (1921), 41 *Canadian Law Times* 677-704.
Also published in (1920-21), 34 *Harvard Law Review* 837-861.   **1098**

"The British Caribbean Colonies." (1951), 3 *External Affairs* 11-17.   **1099**

Higiro, Jean-Marie Vianney. *La décolonisation du Rwanda et le rôle de l'ONU, 1946-1962.* Montréal, 1975. x, 300 leaves.   **1100**
Thesis (M.A.), Université de Montréal, 1975.

Isnard, H. "Problèmes de décolonisation dans le monde arabe." (1973), 43 *Revue de l'Université d'Ottawa* 614-622.   **1101**

Knorr, Klaus E. *British Colonial Theories, 1570-1850.* With a Foreword by H.A. Innis. Toronto: University of Toronto Press, 1963. xix, 429 p.   **1102**
First published in 1944.
Reviews: Thomas-A. Birch in (1944-45), 20/2 *Actualité Économique* 485-486; C.R. Fay in (1945), 11 *Canadian Journal of Economics and Political Science* 628, 630-631.

Kushnin, Slava M. "Mauriac et la politique coloniale de la France." (1966), 36 *Revue de l'Université d'Ottawa* 703-723.   **1103**

Leener, Georges de. "Le problème du statut international des colonies." (1937-38), 13/1 *Actualité Économique* 401-424.   **1104**

MacKay, Robert A. "Foreign Governments and Politics: Newfoundland Reverts to the Status of a Colony." (1934), 28 *American Political Science Review* 895-900.   **1105**

Manheim, Frank J. "The British Colonial System." (1936), 6 *Revue de l'Université d'Ottawa* 204-226.   **1106**

Marmier, Xavier. "La France dans ses colonies." (1873), 10 *Revue Canadienne* 367-384.   **1107**

Mazzeo, Domenico. "Les Nations Unies et la diplomatie de la décolonisation." (1972), 3 *Études Internationales* 330-355.   **1108**

Mazzeo, Domenico. *The United Nations and the Problem of Decolonization: The Special Committee of Twenty-Four.* Ottawa, 1969. 192 leaves.   **1109**
Thesis (M.A.), University of Ottawa, 1970.

Mousaw, Ralph Edgar. *The United Nations and Decolonization: The Declaration on the Granting of Independence to Colonial Countries and Its Special Committee.* Kingston, 1972. v, 146 leaves.   **1110**
Thesis (M.A.), Queen's University, 1972. (National Library of Canada. Canadian Theses on Microfilm, No. 11712).

Namaliu, Rabi Langanai. *Australia and the United Nations Special Committee on Decolonisation.* Victoria, B.C., c1973. ix, 198 leaves.   **1111**
Thesis (M.A.), University of Victoria, 1973.

Patterson, Bruce. "Britain's Caribbean Colonies: Tragic, Doomed Lands?" (1954), 9 *International Journal* 34-40. **1112**

Pell, Claiborne. "Rivalry of Colonial Policies." (1945), 25 *Dalhousie Review* 311-321. **1113**

Robinson, Kenneth Ernest. *The Dilemmas of Trusteeship; Aspects of British Colonial Policy between the Wars.* Preface by Watson Kirkconnell. London, Toronto, etc.: Oxford University Press, 1965. viii, 95 p. (Reid Lectures of Acadia University, 4th Ser., 1963) **1114**
  Lectures delivered at Acadia University, Wolfville, N.S., February, 1963.
  Review: Kenneth A. MacKirdy in (1965-66), 21 *International Journal* 121-122.

Rousseau, A. "Colonies et mandats." (1937), 23 *Revue Trimestrielle Canadienne* 188-202. **1115**

Soward, Frederic H. "Canada and 'Colonialism' in the United Nations." *In* Clark, Robert M., ed., *Canadian Issues: Essays in Honour of Henry F. Angus* (Toronto, 1961), pp. 81-94. **1116**

Thornton, A.P. "Colonialism." (1961-62), 17 *International Journal* 335-357. **1117**

Thornton, A.P. "Decolonisation." (1963-64), 19 *International Journal* 7-29. **1118**

Tupper, Charles Hibbert. "Colonies and Constitutional Law." (1922-23), 2 *Dalhousie Review* 438-443. **1119**

5. MISCELLANEOUS (INDIAN TRIBES, ETC.)

See also *"Minorities" (p. 101), and "Indian Treaties" (p. 158).*

Gough, Barry M. "The Hudson's Bay Company and the Imperialism of Monopoly: A Review Article." (1973), 18 *B.C. Studies* 70-78. **1120**

Green, Leslie C. "North America's Indians and the Trusteeship Concept." (1975), 4 *Anglo-American Law Review* 137-162. **1121**

Sampat-Mehta, Ramdeo. *The Jay Treaty as It Affects North American Indians: The International Boundary between the U.S.A. and Canada.* Ottawa?: Canada Research Bureau?, c1972. 20 p. **1122**

Scott, Duncan C. "Traditional History of the Confederacy of the Six Nations." Prepared by a Committee of the Chiefs. (1911), 5 *Royal Society of Canada, Transactions* 195-246 (3d Ser., Sec. 2) **1123**

VI. INDIVIDUALS

A. General

Cohen, Maxwell. "The Individual in International Law." *In* Gotlieb, Allan E., ed., *Human Rights, Federalism and Minorities* (Toronto, 1970), pp. 111-120. **1124**

Green, Leslie C. "The Individual and His Status in International Law." (1960-61), 1 *Indian Journal of International Law* 415-428. **1125**

MacKenzie, Norman A.M. "Problems of Population and Persons." (1936), 30 *American Society of International Law, Proceedings* 87-96. **1126**

Mathur, Athakattu Mathew. *International Law and the Individual.* Toronto, 1967. 219 leaves. **1127**
Thesis (LL.M.), University of Toronto, 1967.

Poulantzas, Nicholas M. "The Individual Before International Jurisdictions (Recent Practice)." (1962), 15 *Revue Hellénique de Droit International* 375-390. **1128**

Tardu, Maxime. "L'individu et l'état en Afrique tropicale." (1967), 13 *McGill Law Journal* 277-302. **1129**

Tripet, André. *L'individu: sujet de droits et d'obligations dans le droit international moderne et de l'avenir.* Ottawa, 1955. 308 leaves. **1130**
Thesis (M.A.), University of Ottawa, 1956.

B. Nationality and Citizenship

Andrew, G.C. "Citizenship." (1947), 34 *Canadian Geographical Journal* 53. **1131**

Baty, Thomas. "The History of Canadian Nationality." (1936), 18 *Journal of Comparative Legislation and International Law* 195-203 (3d Ser.) **1132**

Beaudoin, Gérald. "La perte de la nationalité canadienne." (1971), 25 *Revue Juridique et Politique, Indépendance et Coopération* 627-632. **1133**

Campbell, Betty. *Becoming a Canadian: A Guide through Citizenship Court.* Vancouver: Self-Counsel Press, 1978. xvii, 123 p. (Self-Counsel Series) **1134**

Canada. Dept. of the Secretary of State. *Annual Report.* 1st—, 1868—. Ottawa.
1135

Established in 1867 (R.S.C. 1970, c. S-15), initially as an official channel of communication with the imperial government. It has been responsible for state protocol and ceremonial, naturalization and citizenship (except in the years 1950-1966, during the existence of the Dept. of Citizenship and Immigration), and cultural affairs. It administers the *Citizenship Act* (S.C. 1974-75-76, c. 108, as amended), including citizenship courts. Its Bureau of Translations assists in the implementation of the official languages policy.

Canada. Dept. of the Secretary of State. *Citizenship as Legal Access: An Annotated Index to Statutes in Force in Canada That Convey Privileges on the Basis of Citizenship / La citoyenneté et la loi: index annoté des lois en vigueur au Canada qui confèrent des privilèges fondés sur la citoyenneté.* Ottawa: Secretary of State, 1979. 22, 22 p., 133 leaves (various pagings) **1136**

Canada. Parliament. *Copy of a Despatch from the Secretary of State for the Colonies on the Subject of Naturalization Treaties.* Ottawa, 1874. 4 p. (Canada. Parliament, 1874. Sessional Papers, No. 54) **1137**

"The Canadian Citizenship Act." (1947), 25 *Canadian Bar Review* 364-372. **1138**
Prepared by the Canadian Citizenship Branch of the Department of the Secretary of State. Refers to the act, effective January 1, 1947 (S.C. 1946, c. 15; R.S.C. 1970, c. C-19).

Clarke, A.H. "Citizenship and Naturalization." (1915), 35 *Canadian Law Times* 317-323. **1139**

Copithorne, M.D. "International Claims and the Rule of Nationality." (1969), 63 *American Society of International Law, Proceedings* 30-35. **1140**

Dyer, Louis. "Anglo-Saxon Citizenship: A Proposition by Prof. Dicey Looking to This End - How Englishmen and Americans Would Be Affected by It." (1897), 3 *Barrister* 107-111. **1141**

Edwards, F.B. "Naturalisation. (1) Natural-Born British Subjects at Common Law." (1914), 14 *Journal of Comparative Legislation* 314-326 (N.S.) **1142**

Ewart, John S. "Naturalization." (1911), 31 *Canadian Law Times* 837-850. **1143**

Fawcett, J.E.S. "British Nationality and the Commonwealth: An Historical Survey." (1973), 63 *Round Table* 259-269. **1144**

Flournoy, Richard W., Jr. "The New British Imperial Law of Nationality." (1915), 9 *American Journal of International Law* 870-882. **1145**

Fraser, Charles Frederick. "Transfer of Sovereignty and Non-Recognition as Affecting Nationality." (1940-42), 4 *Alberta Law Quarterly* 138-155. **1146**

Gey van Pittius, Ernst F.W. " 'Dominion' Nationality." (1931), 13 *Journal of Comparative Legislation and International Law* 199-202 (3rd Ser.) **1147**

Gey van Pittius, Ernst F.W. *Nationality within the British Commonwealth of Nations.* London: P.S. King, 1930. xvi, 238 p. **1148**
Originally presented as a thesis (Ph.D.), University of London.
Reviews: Manley O. Hudson in (1931), 25 *American Journal of International Law* 187-188; W.P.M. Kennedy in (1930), 8 *Canadian Bar Review* 764-765.

Ginsburgs, George. "Soviet Law and the Acquisition of Citizenship at Birth." (1970), 20 *University of Toronto Law Journal* 71-80. **1149**

Howell, Alfred. *Naturalization and Nationality in Canada; Expatriation and Repatriation of British Subjects: Aliens, Their Disabilities and Their Privileges in Canada, etc.* Toronto, Edinburgh: Carswell, 1884. vi, 132 p. **1150**

Hoyles, N.W. "Naturalization of Aliens." (1905), 25 *Canadian Law Times* 181-199. **1151**

"International Law - Citizenship - Expatriation of Child upon Father's Naturalization in Canada - Constitutionality of Treaty. *(United States* v. *Reid)."* (1936-37), 14 *New York University Law Quarterly Review* 404-406. **1152**

Kennedy, W.P.M. "Nationality." (1935-36), 1 *University of Toronto Law Journal* 139-146. **1153**

Kiefe, Robert. *La nationalité des personnes dans l'Empire britannique.* Paris: Rousseau, 1926. viii, 190 p. (Collection d'études théoriques et pratiques de droit étranger, de droit comparé et de droit international, no 4) **1154**
Reviews: Henry B. Hazard in (1927), 21 *American Journal of International Law* 830-831; W.P.M. Kennedy in (1927), 8 *Canadian Historical Review* 322-323.

Lamarche, Thomas. "'Je suis citoyen canadien.'" (1947), 53/1 *Revue Dominicaine* 15-18. **1155**

Lenoir, Robert L. "Citizenship as a Requirement for the Practice of Law in Ontario." (1981), 13 *Ottawa Law Review* 527-548. **1156**

MacKenzie, Norman A.M. "Citizenship in Canada." (1934), 15 *British Year Book of International Law* 159-161. **1157**

Millstone, Maurice Shelly. *How to Become a Canadian Citizen; the Law Relating to Naturalization in Canada.* Toronto: Francis White Publishers, 1939. 30 p. **1158**

Millstone, Maurice Shelly. *The Law of Naturalization in Canada.* Toronto: Blackstone Publishing, 1942. 45 p. **1159**

Morel, André. "Nationalité et immigration au Canada." (1971), 25 *Revue Juridique et Politique, Indépendance et Coopération* 615-626. **1160**

Parry, Clive. *Nationality and Citizenship Laws of the Commonwealth and of the Republic of Ireland.* London: Stevens, 1957-60. 2 vols. (liv, 1285 p.) **1161**
Reviews: H. Ridder in (1953-54), 4 *Archiv des Völkerrechts* 119; unsigned in (1963), 90 *Journal du Droit International* 296-299.

Piscopo, Franco A. *Canadian Citizenship.* Montreal, 1954. iii, 105 leaves. **1162**
Thesis (M.A.), McGill University, 1954.

Riddell, William Renwick. "The First Naturalized Canadian." (1931), 9 *Canadian Bar Review* 119-121. **1163**

Sargant, E.B. "Naturalisation. (2) Naturalisation in the British Dominions, with Special Reference to the British Nationality and Status of Aliens Bill, 1914." (1914), 14 *Journal of Comparative Legislation* 327-336 (N.S.) **1164**

Schwartz, Mildred A. "Citizenship in Canada and the United States." (1976), 14 *Royal Society of Canada, Transactions* 83-96 (4th Ser.) **1165**

Scott, Janet V., and Stonehouse, Robert C. "Citizens, Aliens and Immigration." In *Canadian Encyclopedic Digest (Ontario),* 3d ed., 1980, title 27, vol. 4, 154 p. **1166**
Review: Laurence Kearley in (1981), 59 *Canadian Bar Review* 595-598.

Slosar, Stanislas. "La citoyenneté canadienne et ses effets juridiques." (1979), 10 *Revue de Droit, Université de Sherbrooke* 157-196. **1167**

Tamaki, George T. "The Canadian Citizenship Act, 1946." (1947-48), 7 *University of Toronto Law Journal* 68-97. **1168**

Tamaki, George T. "The Canadian Citizenship Bill." (1946), 4 *School of Law Review* 3, 6 (No. 1) **1169**

Tamaki, George T. *The Law Relating to Nationality in Canada.* Toronto, 1944. 175 leaves. **1170**
Thesis, (LL.M.), University of Toronto, 1944.

Tamaki, George T. "Legal Consequences of British Nationality in Canada." (1945), 3 *School of Law Review* 2 (No. 2) **1171**

Toxey, Walter W. "Restrictive Citizenship Policies within the Commonwealth." (1967), 13 *McGill Law Journal* 494-502. **1172**

Vallat, Frank A. "The Nationality of Married Women." (1934), 12 *Canadian Bar Review* 283-292. **1173**

Walton, F.P. "Nationality and Citizenship." (1912), 11 *University Magazine* 12-26. **1174**

Wilkinson, W.E. "Marriage and Nationality." (1915), 35 *Canadian Law Times* 906-916. **1175**

Wilson, Robert R., and Clute, Robert E. "Commonwealth Citizenship and Common Status." (1963), 57 *American Journal of International Law* 566-587.
1176

C. Aliens and Non-Nationals

See also *"Enemy Aliens" (p. 453).*

Avery, Donald H. *Canadian Immigration Policy and the Alien Question, 1896-1919: The Anglo-Canadian Perspective.* London, Ont., 1973. vi, 653 leaves.
1177
Thesis (Ph.D.), University of Western Ontario, 1973. (National Library of Canada. Canadian Theses on Microfiche, No. 20475).

Boudreau, Joseph A. *The Enemy Alien Problem in Canada, 1914-1921.* Los Angeles, 1965. v, 213 leaves. **1178**
Thesis (Ph.D.), University of California, Los Angeles, 1965. (University Microfilms, Ann Arbor, No. 65-7320).

Carruthers, James R. "The Great War and Canada's Enemy Alien Policy." (1978), 4 *Queen's Law Journal* 43-110. **1179**

Clark, Dorothy M. *Restrictions on Aliens in the United Kingdom, 1914-1919: A Study of the Origins and Political Background of the Aliens Restriction Acts of 1914 and 1919.* Kingston, c1979. v, 84 leaves. **1180**
Thesis (M.A.), Queen's University, 1979. (National Library of Canada. Canadian Theses on Microfiche, No. 42418).

Davis, Morris, and Krauter, Joseph F. "U.S. Citizens as Canadian Aliens." (1980-81), 60 *Dalhousie Review* 251-263. **1181**

Dawson, Frank Griffith, and Head, Ivan L. *International Law, National Tribu-*

nals, and the Rights of Aliens. With the collaboration of Peter E. Herzog. Syracuse, N.Y.: Syracuse University Press, 1971. xvi, 334 p. (Procedural Aspects of International Law Series, Vol. 10) **1182**
Reviews: Peter Z.R. Finkle in (1975), 8 *Canadian Journal of Political Science* 159-160; Leslie C. Green in (1971-72), 27 *International Journal* 632-633; James N. Hyde in (1972), 66 *American Journal of International Law* 663-664; Donald M. McRae in (1972), 10 *Canadian Yearbook of International Law* 349-355; David Suratgar in (1971-72), 3 *Journal of Maritime Law and Commerce* 835-837.

Desjardins, Alice. "La condition des étrangers au regard de l'immigration, de la citoyenneté et de quelques autres lois fédérales au Canada." (1980), 34 *Revue Juridique et Politique, Indépendance et Coopération* 269-282. **1183**

Fraser, Charles Frederick. "Administrative Control over Aliens in Canada." (1938-39), 7 *George Washington Law Review* 433-474. **1184**

Fraser, Charles Frederick. *Control of Aliens in the British Commonwealth of Nations.* London: Hogarth Press, 1940. 304 p. **1185**
Reviews: E. Russell Hopkins in (1941-42), 4 *University of Toronto Law Journal* 437-439; Bora Laskin in (1941), 19 *Canadian Bar Review* 153-154; Norman A.M. MacKenzie in (1941), 35 *American Journal of International Law* 407-408; signed A.E.P. in (1941-42), 48 *Queen's Quarterly* 302; and M.M.M. in (1940-42), 4 *Alberta Law Quarterly* 27-28.

Grey, Julius H. "The Status of Foreign Students under the *Immigration Act, 1976.*" (1982), 27 *McGill Law Journal* 556-562. **1186**

Head, Ivan L. "The Alien's Access to Local Remedies: The African Commonwealth Countries' Experience." (1967-68), 21 *Vanderbilt Law Review* 701-711. **1187**

Head, Ivan L. "A Fresh Look at the Local Remedies Rule." (1967), 5 *Canadian Yearbook of International Law* 142-158. **1188**

Head, Ivan L. "International Standards of Civil Procedure: The Alien in the Courts of Ghana." (1967-68), 12 *Saint Louis University Law Journal* 392-417. **1189**

Head, Ivan L. "The Stranger in Our Midst: A Sketch of the Legal Status of the Alien in Canada." (1964), 2 *Canadian Yearbook of International Law* 107-140. **1190**

Hodgins, Thomas. "The Prerogative Right of Revoking Treaty Privileges to Alien-Subjects." (1909), 29 *Canadian Law Times* 105-129. **1191**
Reprinted from *The Nineteenth Century and After*. Also published separately, 2d ed., Toronto, Carswell, 1909. 27 p., map. Reviewed by Amos S. Hershey in (1910), 4 *American Journal of International Law* 770.

Hodgins, Thomas. "The Revocation of Treaty Privileges to Alien-Subjects." (1908), 44 *Canada Law Journal* 633-651. **1192**

International Institute for the Unification of Private Law. *Compilation of Laws on the Legal Status of Aliens: Canada.* Rome, 1953. 3, 97 p. **1193**
At head of title: Unidroit. Contains legislation in effect in 1952.

International Institute for the Unification of Private Law. *Legal Status of Aliens; Systematic Compilation of International Instruments: Canada.* Rome, 1954. ii, 134 p. **1194**
At head of title: Unidroit. Cover title: *Systematic Compilation of International Instruments Relating to the Legal Status of Aliens. Canada.*

Janach, Monica Ann. *Foreign Ownership of Land in Canada: The Ontario Case.* Ottawa, 1977. 202 leaves. **1195**
   Research essay (M.A.), Carleton University, 1977.

Jones, Douglas W. "Status of American Draft Evaders and Deserters in Canada and Sweden." (1972), 13 *Harvard International Law Journal* 90-107. **1196**

Kelly, Ian F. "Immigration Parole and the Alien Offender." (1977), 3 *Queen's Law Journal* 450-495. **1197**

Leermakers, Dirk J. *Compensation for the Expropriation of Alien Property in International Law.* Montreal, 1979. 268 frames. **1198**
   Thesis (LL.M.), McGill University, 1979. (National Library of Canada. Canadian Theses on Microfiche, No. 50485).

MacKenzie, Norman A.M., ed. *The Legal Status of Aliens in Pacific Countries; an International Survey of Law and Practice concerning Immigration, Naturalization and Deportation of Aliens and Their Legal Rights and Disabilities.* London, New York, etc.: Oxford University Press, 1937. xii, 374 p. **1199**
   A report in the International Research Series of the Institute of Pacific Relations; issued under the auspices of the Secretariat.
   Contents: Introduction, by Norman A.M. MacKenzie.- Australia.- Canada.- China.- Indo-China.- Pacific Dependencies of Great Britain.- Japan.- Netherlands.- India.- New Zealand.- Philippine Islands.- Russia.- United States of America.
   Reviews: F.C. Cronkite in (1938), 4 *Canadian Journal of Economics and Political Science* 573-576; Clyde Eagleton in (1938), 32 *American Journal of International Law* 651-652; G.W. Paton in (1939-40), 3 *University of Toronto Law Journal* 188-189; Cheng Tien-Hsi in (1939), 20 *British Year Book of International Law* 181-182; unsigned in (1938), 19 *Canadian Historical Review* 326-329.

MacKenzie, Norman A.M., and Finkleman, J. "The Status of Aliens in Canada." (1934), 6 *Canadian Political Science Association, Proceedings* 60-93. **1200**

McFadyen, Stuart. "The Control of Foreign Ownership of Canadian Real Estate." (1976), 2 *Canadian Public Policy* 65-77. **1201**

Meunier, M., and Pérusse, S. "Les résidents permanents du Canada." (1981), 41 *Revue du Barreau* 469-482. **1202**

Morse, Charles. "Deportation of Aliens." (1906), 5 *Canadian Law Review* 383. **1203**

Morton, Desmond. "Sir William Otter and Internment Operations in Canada During the First World War." (1974), 55 *Canadian Historical Review* 32-58. **1204**

Pellonpää, Matti Päävo. *International Law and Expulsion of Aliens.* Toronto, c1979. iv, 257 leaves. **1205**
   Thesis (LL.M.), University of Toronto, 1979.

Spencer, John. "The Alien Landowner in Canada." (1973), 51 *Canadian Bar Review* 389-418. **1206**

Wydrzynski, Christopher J. *Civil Liberties of Aliens in the Canadian Immigration Process.* Downsview, Ont., 1976. vii, 231 leaves. **1207**
   Thesis (LL.M.), York University, 1976. (National Library of Canada. Canadian Theses on Microfiche, No. 30964).

Yachetti, Roger D. "Natural Justice and the Alien." (1965), 4 *Western Law Review* 68-89. **1208**

D. Diplomatic Protection

See also *"Consular Service" (p. 144)*.

Emanuelli, Claude C. "La protection internationale du voyageur non-privilégié." *In* Macdonald, Ronald St. John, and others, *The International Law and Policy of Human Welfare* (Alphen aan den Rijn, 1978), pp. 373-396. **1209**

Maybee, J.R. "The Problems in Providing Aid to Canadians in Trouble Abroad." (1974), *International Perspectives* 39-44 (May/June) **1210**

E. Passports and Visas

Batshaw, Harry. "The Right to Leave and Re-Enter Canada." (1973), 21 *Chitty's Law Journal* 164-166. **1211**

"Canada's Passport Office." (1960), 12 *External Affairs* 527-532. **1212**

"Canadian Passports." (1953), 5 *External Affairs* 75-78. **1213**

Turack, Daniel C. "A Brief Review of the Provisions in Recent Agreements concerning Freedom of Movement Issues in the Modern World." (1979), 11 *Case Western Reserve Journal of International Law* 95-115. **1214**

Turack, Daniel C. "Freedom of Movement: The Right of a United Kingdom Citizen to Leave His Country." (1970), 31 *Ohio State Law Journal* 247-303. **1215**

Turack, Daniel C. "Freedom of Movement and Aircraft Personnel." (1968), 34 *Journal of Air Law and Commerce* 223-232. **1216**

Turack, Daniel C. "Freedom of Movement and the International Regime of Passports." (1968), 6 *Osgoode Hall Law Journal* 230-251. **1217**

Turack, Daniel C. "Freedom of Movement and the Seaman." (1966-68), 1 *Philippine Yearbook of International Law* 233-250. **1218**

Turack, Daniel C. "Freedom of Movement and the Seaman." (1970), 3 *Revue des Droits de l'Homme* 465-486. **1219**

Turack, Daniel C. "Freedom of Movement and the Travel Document." (1973-74), 4 *California Western International Law Journal* 8-42. **1220**

Turack, Daniel C. "Freedom of Movement and the Travel Document in Benelux." (1968), 17 *International and Comparative Law Quarterly* 191-206. **1221**

Turack, Daniel C. "Freedom of Movement and Travel Documents in Community Law." (1967-68), 17 *Buffalo Law Review* 435-453. **1222**

Turack, Daniel C. "Freedom of Movement in Latin America." (1968-69), 7 *Duquesne University Law Review* 80-106. **1223**

Turack, Daniel C. "Freedom of Movement in the Caribbean Community." (1981), 11 *Denver Journal of International Law and Policy* 37-49. **1224**

Turack, Daniel C. "Freedom of Movement within the British Commonwealth." (1968), 1 *Comparative and International Law Journal of Southern Africa* 476-484. **1225**

Turack, Daniel C. "International Judges and Travel Documents." (1968-69), 6 *Houston Law Review* 454-470. **1226**

Turack, Daniel C. "Officials of International Organizations in the United Nations System and Their Travel Documents." (1968-69), 5 *California Western Law Review* 167-200. **1227**

Turack, Daniel C. *The Passport in International Law.* Lexington, Mass.: Lexington Books, 1972. xviii, 360 p. **1228**

Turack, Daniel C. "Passports Issued by Some Non-State Entities." (1968-69), 43 *British Year Book of International Law* 209-216. **1229**

Turack, Daniel C. "Regional Developments Towards Freedom of Movement: The O.E.C.D." (1969), 5 *Revue Belge de Droit International* 516-534. **1230**

Turack, Daniel C. "The Right to Travel as a Human Right." (1968), 8 *Indian Journal of International Law* 348-366. **1231**

Turack, Daniel C. "The Scandinavian Passport Union." (1968), 38 *Nordisk Tidsskrift for International Ret og Jus Gentium* 171-181. **1232**

Turack, Daniel C. "Selected Aspects of International and Municipal Law concerning Passports." (1970-71), 12 *William and Mary Law Review* 805-837. **1233**

F. Minorities

See also *"Human Rights and Fundamental Freedoms" (p. 118).*

Adachi, Ken. *The Enemy That Never Was: A History of the Japanese-Canadians.* Toronto: McLelland and Stewart, c1976. vi, 456 p. **1234**
Commissioned by the National Japanese Canadian Citizens Association.
Reviews: Ellen Baar in (1977), 10 *Canadian Journal of Political Science* 425-426; Patricia E. Roy in (1978), 59 *Canadian Historical Review* 255-257.

Angus, Henry F. "The Effect of the War on Oriental Minorities in Canada." (1941), 7 *Canadian Journal of Economics and Political Science* 506-516. **1235**

Angus, Henry F. "The Legal Status in British Columbia of Residents of Oriental Race and Their Descendants." (1931), 9 *Canadian Bar Review* 1-12. **1236**

Angus, Henry F. "Underprivileged Canadians." (1931), 38 *Queen's Quarterly* 445-460. **1237**

Barsh, Russell Lawrence, and Henderson, James Youngblood. "Aboriginal Rights, Treaty Rights, and Human Rights: Indian Tribes and 'Constitutional Renewal.'" (1982), 17 *Journal of Canadian Studies* 55-81 (No. 2) **1238**

Broadfoot, Barry. *Years of Sorrow, Years of Shame: The Story of the Japanese Canadians in World War II.* Toronto: Doubleday Canada; Garden City, N.Y.: Doubleday, 1977. viii, 370 p., 12 leaves of plates. **1239**

Claydon, John. "Internationally Uprooted People and the Transnational Protection of Minority Culture." (1978), 24 *New York Law School Law Review* 125-151. **1240**

Claydon, John. "The Transnational Protection of Ethnic Minorities: A Tentative Framework for Inquiry." (1975), 13 *Canadian Yearbook of International Law* 25-60. **1241**

Cumming, Peter A., and Mickenberg, Neil H., eds. *Native Rights in Canada.* 2d ed. Toronto: Indian-Eskimo Association of Canada, Legal Committee, 1972. xxiv, 352 p., maps. **1242**
Includes the law of Indian treaties.
Review: Leslie C. Green in (1972), 7 *University of British Columbia Law Review* 327-330.

De Montigny, Yves. "L'O.N.U. et la protection internationale des minorités depuis 1945." (1978), 13 *Revue Juridique Thémis* 389-447. **1243**

Green, Leslie C. "Aboriginal Rights or Vested Rights?" (1974), 22 *Chitty's Law Journal* 219-224. **1244**

Green, Leslie C. "Canada's Indians: Federal Policy, International and Constitutional Law." (1970-71), 4 *Ottawa Law Review* 101-131. **1245**

Green, Leslie C. "The Canadian Bill of Rights, Indian Rights, and the United Nations." (1974), 22 *Chitty's Law Journal* 22-28. **1246**

Green, Leslie C. "Human Rights and Canada's Indians." (1971), 1 *Israel Yearbook on Human Rights* 156-190. **1247**

Green, Leslie C. "Protection of Minorities in the League of Nations and the United Nations." *In* Gotlieb, Allan E., ed., *Human Rights, Federalism and Minorities* (Toronto, 1970), pp. 180-210. **1248**

Green, Leslie C. "Tribal Rights and Equal Rights." (1974), 22 *Chitty's Law Journal* 97-101. **1249**

Green, Leslie C. "Trusteeship and Canada's Indians." (1976-77), 3 *Dalhousie Law Journal* 104-135. **1250**

Hayakawa, S. Ichiye. "The Japanese Canadian: An Experiment in Citizenship." (1936-37), 16 *Dalhousie Review* 16-22. **1251**

Hudon, Edward G. "The Status of Persons of Japanese Ancestry in the United States and Canada During World War II: A Tragedy in Three Parts." (1977), 18 *Cahiers de Droit* 61-90. **1252**

Humphrey, John P. "The United Nations Sub-Commission on the Prevention of Discrimination and the Protection of Minorities." (1968), 62 *American Journal of International Law* 869-888. **1253**

Isajiw, W.W. "Civil Rights and Ethnic Pluralism." (1967-68), 3 *University of Windsor Review* 20-26 (No. 1) **1254**

Jennes, Desmond. "Canada's Eskimo Problem." (1924-25), 32 *Queen's Quarterly* 317-329. **1255**

Jennes, Desmond. "The Eskimos: Their Past and Future." (1944), 51 *Queen's Quarterly* 132-148. **1256**

Kallen, Evelyn. *Ethnicity and Human Rights in Canada.* Introduction by David R. Hughes. Toronto: Gage, 1982. xiv, 268 p. **1257**

Koch, Eric. *Deemed Suspect: A Wartime Blunder.* Toronto: Methuen, 1980. xv, 272 p., 16 p. of plates. **1258**

Krauter, Joseph F. *Civil Liberties and the Canadian Minorities.* Urbana, Ill., 1968. 227 leaves. **1259**
   Thesis, University of Illinois, 1968. Abstracted in (1969), 30 *Dissertation Abstracts International* 370-A. (University Microfilms, Ann Arbor, No. 69-10753).

La Violette, Forrest E. "The American-Born Japanese and the World Crisis." (1941), 7 *Canadian Journal of Economics and Political Science* 517-527. **1260**

La Violette, Forrest E. *The Canadian Japanese and World War II, a Sociological and Psychological Account.* Issued under the auspices of the Canadian Institute of International Affairs and the Institute of Pacific Relations. Toronto: University of Toronto Press, 1948. x, 332 p., map. **1261**
   Reviews: G. Gordon Brown in (1949), 4 *International Journal* 72-74; H.B. Hawthorn in (1949), 15 *Canadian Journal of Economics and Political Science* 99-101; John A. Irving in (1949), 30 *Canadian Historical Review* 160-162; F.C. Jones in (1949), 25 *International Affairs* 89-90; A.H. MacLean in (1948-49), 28 *Dalhousie Review* 424-425.

La Violette, Forrest E. "The Japanese Canadians." (1946), 6 *Behind the Headlines* No. 2 (20 p.) **1262**

La Violette, Forrest E. "War and the Japanese in Canada." (1944-45), 8 *Public Affairs* 243-247. **1263**

Lee, Carol F. "The Road to Enfranchisement: Chinese and Japanese in British Columbia." (1976), 30 *B.C. Studies* 44-76. **1264**

Lysyk, Kenneth M. "Human Rights and the Native Peoples of Canada. (Comment)." (1968), 46 *Canadian Bar Review* 695-705. **1265**

McRae, K.D. "The Constitutional Protection of Linguistic Rights in Bilingual and Multilingual States." *In* Gotlieb, Allan E., ed., *Human Rights, Federalism and Minorities* (Toronto, 1970), pp. 211-227. **1266**

Montigny, Yves de. "L'O.N.U. et la protection internationale des minorités depuis 1945." (1978), 13 *Revue Juridique Thémis* 389-447. **1267**

Monture, G.C. "The Indians of the North." (1959-60), 66 *Queen's Quarterly* 556-563. **1268**

Morin, Wilfrid. *Nos droits minoritaires; les minorités françaises au Canada.* Montréal: Éditions Fides, 1943. 431 p. (Philosophie et problèmes contemporains, 2) **1269**
   Reviews: H. McD. Clokie in (1944), 25 *Canadian Historical Review* 428-432; Roger Duhamel in (1945-46), 21/2 *Actualité Économique* 393-394.

Niedermeier, Lynn. "Aboriginal Rights: Definition or Denial?" (1981), 6 *Queen's Law Journal* 568-586. **1270**

Phillips, R.A.J. "The Arctic: Its Human Resources." (1959-60), 66 *Queen's Quarterly* 564-574. **1271**

"The Rights of Indigenous Peoples: A Comparative Analysis." (1974), 68 *American Society of International Law, Proceedings* 265-301. **1272**
   This is a panel. Louis B. Sohn, Chairman. Includes remarks by Peter A. Cumming on Canada's Native Peoples and Treaty Rights (pp. 265-276).

Roy, Patricia E. "Educating the 'East': British Columbia and the Oriental Question in the Interwar Years." (1973), 18 *B.C. Studies* 50-69. **1273**

Roy, Patricia E. "The Soldiers Canada Didn't Want: Her Chinese and Japanese Citizens." (1978), 59 *Canadian Historical Review* 341-358. **1274**

Sampat-Mehta, Ramdeo. *Minority Rights and Obligations.* Ottawa: Canada Research Bureau, 1973. xiv, 233 p. **1275**
Reviews: Leslie C. Green in (1973-74), 29 *International Journal* 663-665.

Sissons, C.B. "The Rights of Minorities in a Democracy." (1954), 48 *Royal Society of Canada, Transactions* 99-102 (3d Ser., Sec. 2) **1276**

Sunahara, Ann Gomer. *Federal Policy and the Japanese Canadians: 1942-1950.* Calgary, 1977. 190 frames. **1277**
Thesis (M.A.), University of Calgary, 1977. (National Library of Canada. Canadian Theses on Microfiche, No. 44643).

Sunahara, Ann Gomer. *The Politics of Racism: The Uprooting of Japanese Canadians During the Second World War.* Toronto: Lorimer, 1981. xii, 222 p., 18 p. of plates. **1278**
Review: J.L. Granatstein in (1982), 53 *BC Studies* 66-68.

Touret, Bernard. *L'aménagement constitutionnel des états de peuplement composite.* Québec: Presses de l'Université Laval, 1973, c1972. xx, 259 p. (Centre international de recherches sur le bilinguisme. Travaux, 6) **1279**
Published for the Centre international de recherches sur le bilinguisme. Based on a dissertation (doctorat), presented at Faculté de droit et des sciences politiques de Strasbourg in 1968.

Upton, L.F.S. "The Origins of Canadian Indian Policy." (1973), 8 *Journal of Canadian Studies* 51-61 (No. 4) **1280**

Ward, William Peter. "British Columbia and the Japanese Evacuation." (1976), 57 *Canadian Historical Review* 289-308. **1281**

Ward, William Peter. *White Canada Forever: British Columbia's Response to Orientals, 1858-1914.* Kingston, 1972. vii, 292 leaves. **1282**
Thesis (Ph.D.), Queen's University, 1973. (National Library of Canada. Canadian Theses on Microfiche, No. 21172).

Ward, William Peter. *White Canada Forever: Popular Attitudes and Public Policy Toward Orientals in British Columbia.* Montreal: McGill-Queen's University Press, c1978. xi, 205 p. **1283**
Reviews: Roger Daniels in (1980), 61 *Canadian Historical Review* 104-106; Jean A. Laponce in (1980), 13 *Canadian Journal of Political Science* 177-178.

G. Statelessness, Refugees

Abella, Irving, and Troper, Harold M. " 'The Line Must Be Drawn Somewhere': Canada and Jewish Refugees, 1933-9." (1979), 60 *Canadian Historical Review* 178-209. **1284**

Brazeau, J.A.R. "The Great Immigration Debate: Special Problem of Refugees Receives Special Attention." (1975), *International Perspectives* 13-17 (Sept./Oct.) **1285**

Canada. Task Force on Immigration Practices and Procedures. *The Refugee Status Determination Process: A Report.* Ottawa: Supply and Services Canada, 1981. xxiii, 132 p. **1286**
   Chairman: W.G. Robinson. Also issued in French under title: *Reconnaissance du statut de réfugié.*

Coldwell, M.J. "Refugees and the United Nations." (1946-47), 2 *International Journal* 102-105. **1287**

Dirks, Gerald E. "Canada's Refugee Admissions Policy: Three Differing Responses." (1974), 46 *Canadian Political Science Association, Papers,* 17, 3 p. **1288**

Dirks, Gerald E. *Canada's Refugee Policy: Indifference or Opportunism?* Montreal: McGill-Queen's University Press, 1977. xii, 316 p. **1289**
   Reviews: Freda E. Hawkins in (1979), 22 *Canadian Public Administration* 317-320; Peyton V. Lyon in (1978), 11 *Canadian Journal of Political Science* 911-912; Howard Palmer in (1979), 60 *Canadian Historical Review* 239-242; David Staines in (1980), 87 *Queen's Quarterly* 317-318.

Dirks, Gerald E. *Canadian Policies and Programmes Toward Political Refugees.* Toronto, c1972. iii, 432 leaves. **1290**
   Thesis (Ph.D.), University of Toronto, 1972. (National Library of Canada. Canadian Theses on Microfiche, No. 35198).

Dirks, Gerald E. "The Green Paper and Canadian Refugee Policy." (1975), 7 *Canadian Ethnic Studies* 61-64 (No. 1; Special Issue) **1291**

Dirks, Gerald E. "The Plight of the Homeless: The Refugee Phenomenon." (1980-81), 38 *Behind the Headlines* No. 3 (26 p.) **1292**

Domanski, Robert P. *While Millions Cried: Canada and the Refugee Question, 1938-1941.* Ottawa, 1975. 88 leaves. **1293**
   Thesis (M.A.), Carleton University, 1975.

Gotlieb, Allan E. "Canada and the Refugee Question in International Law." (1975), 13 *Canadian Yearbook of International Law* 3-24. **1294**

Hanff, George. "Decision-Making under Pressure: A Study of the Admittance of Chilean Refugees by Canada." (1979), 4 *North/South Canadian Journal of Latin American Studies* 116-135. **1295**

Holborn, Louise W. "The Palestine Arab Refugee Problem." (1967-68), 23 *International Journal* 82-96. **1296**

Howard, Rhoda. "Contemporary Canadian Refugee Policy: A Critical Assessment." (1980), 6 *Canadian Public Policy* 361-373. **1297**

"Immigration and Refugees / L'immigration et les réfugiés." (1981), 10 *Canadian Council on International Law, Proceedings,* 117-156. **1298**
   This is a panel. Chairman: John Hucker.
   Contents: "The Refugee Process in Canada," by James R. Aldridge (pp. 117-135).- "Certain Aspects of Determining Refugee Status in Present Canadian Immigration Appeal Board Practice," by G.W. Alexandrowicz (pp. 136-156).

MacDonald, John A.G. "The Refugee Problem." (1946), 4 *School of Law Review* 2 (No. 2) **1299**

Matthews, Robert O. "Refugees and Stability in Africa." (1972), 26 *International Organization* 62-83. **1300**

Mayrand, Léon. "Personnes déplacées." (1948), 18 *Revue de l'Université d'Ottawa* 226-233. **1301**

Passaris, Constantine. "Canada's Record in Assisting Refugee Movements." (1981), *International Perspectives* 6-9 (Sept./Oct.) **1302**

Ristelhueber, René. "L'aide aux réfugiés depuis la disparition de l'Organisation internationale pour les réfugiés." (1955-56), 10 *Revue de l'Université Laval* 610-618. **1303**
In operation from July 1, 1947 to March 1, 1952.

"Statelessness." (1959), 11 *External Affairs* 176-179. **1304**

Stuchen, Philip. "Canada's Newcomers: The Displaced Persons." (1948-49), 55 *Queen's Quarterly* 197-205. **1305**

Stuchen, Philip. "Mass-Employment for Displaced Persons." (1947-48), 54 *Queen's Quarterly* 360-365. **1306**

"UN Relief for Palestine Refugees." (1961), 13 *External Affairs* 303-305. **1307**

"United Nations High Commissioner for Refugees." (1958), 10 *External Affairs* 56-58. **1308**

"United Nations High Commissioner for Refugees (UNHCR)." (1961), 13 *External Affairs* 279-283. **1309**

"United Nations Relief and Works Agency for Palestine Refugees." (1959), 11 *External Affairs* 230-235. **1310**

Walmsley, Norma Eleanor. *Canada's Response to the International Problem of Displaced Persons, 1947-51*. Montreal, 1954. vii, 230 leaves. **1311**
Thesis (M.A.), McGill University, 1954.

"World Refugee Year." (1959), 11 *External Affairs* 344-349. **1312**
June 28, 1959-June 30, 1960.

"World Refugee Year." (1960), 12 *External Affairs* 688-696. **1313**

Wydrzynski, Christopher J. "Refugees and the Immigration Act." (1979), 25 *McGill Law Journal* 154-192. **1314**

H. Slavery

Brode, Patrick. "In the Matter of John Anderson: Canadian Courts and the Fugitive Slave." (1980), 14 *Law Society of Upper Canada Gazette* 92-97. **1315**

Landon, Fred. "The Canadian Anti-Slavery Group." (1918), 17 *University Magazine* 540-547. **1316**

McDermott, Gordon Bryan. *Britain and the Struggle for the Universal Abolition of the Slave Trade, 1814-1821*. Fredericton, 1975. vi, 105 leaves. **1317**
Thesis (M.A.), University of New Brunswick, 1975. (National Library of Canada. Canadian Theses on Microfiche, No. 27410).

Murray, Alexander L. *Canada and the Anglo-American Anti-Slavery Movement: A Study in International Philanthropy*. Philadelphia, 1960. xxvi, 576 leaves.
Thesis (Ph.D.), University of Pennsylvania, 1960. **1318**

Paquet, L.A. "L'esclavage au Canada." (1913), 7 *Royal Society of Canada, Transactions* 139-149 (3d Ser., Sec. 1) **1319**

Pemberton, Ian Cleghorn Blanshard. *The Anti-Slavery Society of Canada.* Toronto, 1967 (c1973). 148 leaves. **1320**
Thesis (M.A.), University of Toronto, 1967. (National Library of Canada. Canadian Theses on Microfilm, No. 16122).

Riddell, William Renwick. "Le Code Noir." (1925), 19 *Royal Society of Canada, Transactions* 33-38 (3d Ser., Sec. 2) **1321**
Refers to the 'Black Code' concerning the slave trade, published in Paris in 1770.

Ryan, H.R.S. "Ex Parte John Anderson." (1981), 6 *Queen's Law Journal* 382-388. **1322**

Trudel, Marcel. "L'esclavage au Canada français." (1959-60), 14 *Revue de l'Université Laval* 99-115. **1323**

Withrow, W.H. "The Underground Railway." (1902), 8 *Royal Society of Canada, Transactions* 49-77 (2d Ser., Sec. 2) **1324**

Zorn, Roman J. "Criminal Extradition Menaces the Canadian Haven for Fugitive Slaves, 1841-1861." (1957), 38 *Canadian Historical Review* 284-294. **1325**

I. Immigration and Emigration

Angus, Henry F. "Canadian Immigration: The Law and Its Administration." (1934), 28 *American Journal of International Law* 74-89. **1326**

Angus, Henry F. "A Contribution to International Ill-Will: The Immigration Act and the Chinese Immigration Act and Certain Orders-in-Council." (1933-34), 13 *Dalhousie Review* 23-33. **1327**

Angus, Henry F. "The Future of Immigration into Canada." (1946), 12 *Canadian Journal of Economics and Political Science* 379-386. **1328**

Angus, Henry F. "Immigration." (1946), 1 *International Journal* 65-67. **1329**

Angus, Henry F. "Need for an Immigration Policy." (1947), 253 *Annals of the American Academy of Political and Social Science* 16-21. **1330**

Avery, Donald H. *Canadian Immigration Policy and the Alien Question, 1896-1919: The Anglo-Canadian Perspective.* London, Ont., 1973. vi, 653 leaves. **1331**
Thesis (Ph.D.), University of Western Ontario, 1973. (National Library of Canada. Canadian Theses on Microfiche, No. 20475).

Avery, Donald H. "Canadian Immigration Policy and the 'Foreign' Navy, 1896-1914." (1972), *Canadian Historical Association, Historical Papers* 135-156. **1332**

Avery, Donald H., and Neary, Peter F. "Laurier, Borden and a White British Columbia." (1977), 12 *Journal of Canadian Studies* 24-34 (No. 4) **1333**

Barkway, Michael. "Turning Point for Immigration?" (1957), 17 *Behind the Headlines* No. 4 (16 p.) **1334**

Barnett, John. "Post-War Immigration to Canada." (1945), 25 *Dalhousie Review* 22-30. **1335**

Berrocal Martin, Luciano. "Intégration européenne et libre circulation des travailleurs: quelques éléments d'analyse pour le cas espagnol." (1980-81), 4 *Revue d'Intégration Européenne* 335-362. **1336**

Best, J. Calbert. "Canadian Immigration Patterns and Policies." (1950), 50 *Labour Gazette* 1512-1522. **1337**

Bicha, Karel Denis. *Canadian Immigration Policy and the American Farmer, 1896-1914.* Minneapolis, 1963. 201 leaves. **1338**
Thesis (Ph.D.), University of Minnesota, 1963. (University Microfilms, Ann Arbor, No. 64-07288).

Black, Warren. "Novel Features of the Immigration Act, 1976." (1978), 56 *Canadian Bar Review* 561-578. **1339**

Bonavia, George. *Focus on Canadian Immigration.* Ottawa: Dept. of Manpower and Immigration, 1977. iii, 170 p. **1340**
Originally published in *Ethnic Kaleidoscope Canada.* Also issued in French under title: *Coup d'oeil sur l'immigration canadienne.*

Bonin, Bernard. "L'immigration étrangère au Québec." (1975), 1 *Canadian Public Policy* 296-301. **1341**

Bonin, Bernard, ed. *Immigration: Policy-Making Process and Results / Immigration: processus d'élaboration de la politique et résultats.* Toronto: Institute of Public Administration of Canada, 1976. 103 p. **1342**

Brossard, Jacques. *L'immigration; les droits et pouvoirs du Canada et du Québec.* Montréal: Presses de l'Université de Montréal, 1967. 208 p. **1343**
Étude commanditée par le Comité parlementaire de la Constitution de l'Assemblée législative du Québec.
Reviews: A.F. Bisson in (1967), 27 *Revue du Barreau* 490-492; Jules Brière in (1968), 1 *Canadian Journal of Political Science* 369-370; Thierry Godechot in (1969), 83 *Revue d'Histoire Diplomatique* 96.

Cameron, John Duncan. *The Development of Legislation Relating to Emigration to Canada.* Toronto, 1943. 2 vols. in 4. **1344**
Thesis (Ph.D.), University of Toronto, 1945. Titles of volumes vary slightly.

Canada. Dept. of Manpower and Immigration. *Annual Report / Rapport annuel.* 1968/69—. Ottawa. Bilingual. **1345**
This department was created in 1966, replacing the Dept. of Citizenship and Immigration, in existence during 1950-1966. It was reconstituted in 1977 into the Dept. of Employment and Immigration, and the Employment and Immigration Commission (S.C. 1976-77, c. 54). The commission has an Immigration and Demographic Policy Group which is responsible for the administration of the *Immigration Act* (S.C. 1976-77, c. 52), immigration regulations, and the implementation of the federal immigration policy. The Immigration Appeal Board reports to Parliament through the Minister of Employment and Immigration. The annual report contains a section on immigration.

Canada. Dept. of Manpower and Immigration. *Highlights from the Green Paper on Immigration and Population / Points saillants du Livre vert sur l'immigration et les objectifs démographiques.* Ottawa: Manpower and Immigration, 1975. 53, 53 p. (Canadian Immigration and Population Study) **1346**
Text in English and French on inverted pages, each with a separate title page and paging.

Canada. Dept. of Manpower and Immigration. *The Immigration Bill: Explanatory Notes of an Office Consolidation of the Immigration Bill / Le projet de Loi concernant l'immigration: notes explicatives sur une consolidation administrative du projet de Loi concernant l'immigration.* Ottawa: Manpower and Immigration, 1976. 75, 75 p. **1347**
Text in English and French on inverted pages, each with a separate title page and paging.

Canada. Dept. of Manpower and Immigration. *A Report of the Canadian Immigration and Population Study.* Ottawa: Manpower and Immigration, 1974—. v.1—. **1348**
Also issued in French under title: *Études sur l'immigration et les objectifs démographiques du Canada.*
Contents (Partial): 1. Imigration Policy Perspectives (xi, 77 p.).- 2. The Immigration Program (233 p.).- 3. Immigration and Population Statistics (111 p.).- Effect of Immigration on Population, by Warren E. Kalbach (93 p.).- The Economic Impact of Immigration, by Louis Parai (118 p.).- Canadian Views on Immigration and Population: An Analysis of Post-War Gallup Polls, by N. Tienhaara (102 p.).

Canada. Dept. of Manpower and Immigration. *White Paper on Immigration.* Ottawa: Queen's Printer, 1966. 42, 45 p. **1349**
Cover title: *Canadian Immigration Policy.* Added title page in French: *Livre blanc sur l'immigration.* Text bilingual, in English and French.

Canada. Parliament. Special Joint Committee on Immigration Policy. *Minutes of Proceedings and Evidence of the Special Joint Committee of the Senate and of the House of Commons on Immigration Policy / Procès-verbaux et témoignages du Comité mixte spécial du Sénat et de la Chambre des communes sur la politique de l'immigration.* Ottawa: Queen's Printer, 1975?—. v.1—. In English and French. **1350**

Canada. Parliament. Special Joint Committee on Immigration Policy. *Report to Parliament, Special Joint Committee of the Senate and of the House of Commons on Immigration Policy.* Ottawa, 1975. vi, 111 p. **1351**
Also issued in French under title: *Rapport au Parlement, Comité spécial mixte du Sénat et de la Chambre des communes sur la politique de l'immigration* (vi, 124 p.).

"Canadian Immigration Policy and Its Administration." (1949), 1 *External Affairs* 3-11 (May) **1352**

Carlsen, Sigurd Camillo. *Immigration and the Rule of Law.* Ottawa, 1961. 228, (10) leaves. **1353**
Thesis (M.A.), Carleton University, 1961.

Carrothers, W.A. "The Immigration Problem in Canada." (1929), 36 *Queen's Quarterly* 517-531. **1354**

Chaput, Donald. "Some 'Repatriement' Dilemmas." (1968), 49 *Canadian Historical Review* 400-412. **1355**

Chicanot, E.L. "The Future of Immigration." (1936-37), 16 *Dalhousie Review* 28-35. **1356**

Chicanot, E.L. "The New Immigration." (1926-27), 6 *Dalhousie Review* 312-326. **1357**

Claydon, John. "International Protection of the Welfare of Migrant Workers." In Macdonald, Ronald St. John, and others, *The International Law and Policy of Human Welfare* (Alphen aan den Rijn, 1978), pp. 347-371. **1358**

Cohen, Maxwell. "The Immigration Act and Limitations upon Judicial Power: Bail." (1936), 14 *Canadian Bar Review* 405-411. **1359**

Conn, J.R. "Immigration." (1900-01), 8 *Queen's Quarterly* 117-131. **1360**

Corbett, David C. *Canada's Immigration Policy; a Critique*. Toronto: University of Toronto Press, 1957. 215 p. **1361**
Published under the auspices of the Canadian Institute of International Affairs.
Reviews: Antoine-Elie Immarigeon in (1958-59), 34 *Actualité Économique* 328-330; Frank H. Underhill in (1958), 39 *Canadian Historical Review* 79-80; Dennis H. Wrong in (1957), 12 *International Journal* 138-140.

Corbett, David C. "Canada's Immigration Policy, 1957-1962." (1962-63), 18 *International Journal* 166-180. **1362**

Corbett, David C. "Immigration and Canadian Politics." (1950-51), 6 *International Journal* 207-216. **1363**

Corbett, David C. "Immigration and Foreign Policy in Australia and Canada." (1957-58), 13 *International Journal* 110-123. **1364**

Cousineau, René. "Pour une politique canadienne d'immigration." (1947-48), 23 *Actualité Économique* 542-558. **1365**

Cowan, Helen. "Early Canadian Emigration to the United States." (1928-29), 8 *Dalhousie Review* 73-81. **1366**

"The Determinants of Canadian Immigration Policy." (1946-47), 37 *Round Table* 51-57. **1367**

Dobell, Peter C., and D'Aquino, Susan. "The Special Joint Committee on Immigration Policy 1975: An Exercise in Participatory Democracy." (1975-76), 34 *Behind the Headlines* No. 6 (24 p.) **1368**

Drummond, Andrew T. "State Directed Emigration to the Overseas Dominions -A Policy for the Imperial Government after the War." (1916-17), 24 *Queen's Quarterly* 297-301. **1369**

Friedmann, Wolfgang G. "Migration and World Politics." (1951-52), 7 *International Journal* 197-203. **1370**

Green, Alan G. *Immigration and the Postwar Canadian Economy*. Toronto: Macmillan of Canada, c1976. xvi, 312 p. **1371**
Reviews: Isabel B. Anderson in (1977), 10 *Canadian Journal of Economics* 522-524; Spencer Star in (1978), 4 *Canadian Public Policy* 135-136; F. Richard Swann in (1977), 7 *American Review of Canadian Studies* 67-68 (No. 2).

Greening, W. "Is the French-Canadian Attitude Toward Immigration Changing?" (1951-52), 31 *Dalhousie Review* 43-47. **1372**

Grey, Julius H. "The New Immigration Law: A Technical Analysis." (1978), 10 *Ottawa Law Review* 103-113. **1373**

Gunther, Peter. "Canada's Immigration Policy: Some Comments." (1975), 1 *Canadian Public Policy* 580-583. **1374**

Hallett, Mary E. "A Governor-General's Views on Oriental Immigration to British Columbia, 1904-1911." (1972), 14 *B.C. Studies* 51-72. **1375**

Hawkins, Freda E. *Canada and Immigration; Public Policy and Public Concern* Montreal: McGill-Queen's University Press, 1972. xvi, 444 p. (Canadian Public Administration Series) **1376**

Reviews: Clive Lloyd Brown-John in (1975), 8 *Canadian Journal of Political Science* 328-330; David C. Corbett in (1972-73), 28 *International Journal* 382-384; Gerald E. Dirks in (1974), 17 *Canadian Public Administration* 155-158; W.W. Isajiw in (1974), 8 *International Migration Review* 437; unsigned in (1973), 4 *Études Internationales* 585-586 (notice).

Hawkins, Freda E. *Canadian Immigration: A Study in Public Policy, 1946-1968.* Toronto, 1969. 2 vols. (iv, 518 leaves) **1377**
Thesis (Ph.D.), University of Toronto, 1969. (National Library of Canada. Canadian Theses on Microfilm, No. 15397).

Hawkins, Freda E. "Canadian Immigration; Present Policies, Future Options." (1977), 67 *Round Table* 50-63. **1378**

Hawkins, Freda E. "Destination Unknown: Difficult Decisions in Immigration Policy." (1975), 82 *Queen's Quarterly* 589-599. **1379**

Hawkins, Freda E. "The Great Immigration Debate: Demographic Studies Needed to Supplement Green Paper." (1975), *International Perspectives* 3-9 (Sept./Oct.) **1380**

Hawkins, Freda E. "Immigration and Population: The Canadian Approach." (1975), 1 *Canadian Public Policy* 285-295. **1381**

Holborn, Louise W. "Canada and the ICEM." (1962-63), 18 *International Journal* 211-214. **1382**
ICEM refers to the Intergovernmental Committee for European Migration.

Holborn, Louise W. "International Organizations for Migration of European Nationals and Refugees." (1964-65), 20 *International Journal* 331-349. **1383**

Hucker, John. "Immigration, Natural Justice and the Bill of Rights." (1975), 13 *Osgoode Hall Law Journal* 649-692. **1384**

Hucker, John. "Migration and Resettlement under International Law." *In* Macdonald, Ronald St. John, and others, *The International Law and Policy of Human Welfare* (Alphen aan den Rijn, 1978), pp. 327-345. **1385**

Hucker, John. "A Synopsis of Canadian Immigration Law." (1975), 3 *Syracuse Journal of International Law and Commerce* 47-76. **1386**

Hunter, Ian A., and Kelly, Ian F. *The Immigration Appeal Board: A Study.* Prepared for the Law Reform Commission of Canada. Ottawa: Law Reform Commission of Canada, 1976. ix, 88 p. (Administrative Law Series) **1387**
Also issued in French under title: *La Commission d'appel de l'immigration.*

Hurd, W. Burton. "The Case for a Quota." (1929), 36 *Queen's Quarterly* 145-159. **1388**

Hurtubise, René. "L'immigration des travailleurs au Canada, et plus spécialement au Québec." (1980), 34 *Revue Juridique et Politique, Indépendance et Coopération* 291-311. **1389**

Imai, Shin. "Deportation in the Depression." (1981), 7 *Queen's Law Journal* 66-94. **1390**

"Immigration for the Sixties." (1966), 18 *External Affairs* 131-132. **1391**

Janzen, William, and Hunter, Ian A. "The Interpretation of Section 15 of the Immigration Appeal Board Act." (1973), 11 *Alberta Law Review* 260-278. **1392**

Jarry, G. Michel. *L'enquêteur spécial et l'enquête en matière d'immigration.* Montréal, 1976. vii, 299 leaves. **1393**
Thesis (LL.M.), Université de Montréal, 1976.

Johnson, Caswell Lewington. *The Structure of Immigration and the Labour Force: An Enquiry into the Economic Characteristics of Canada's Postwar Immigration, 1946-1962.* New York, 1967 (c1971). v, 707 leaves. **1394**
Thesis (Ph.D.), Columbia University, 1967. Abstracted in (1971), 31 *Dissertation Abstracts International* 6231-A. (University Microfilms, Ann Arbor, 1976).

Kalbach, Warren E. "Demographic Concerns and the Control of Immigration." (1975), 1 *Canadian Public Policy* 302-310. **1395**

Kalbach, Warren E. "The National Conference on Canadian Immigration and the Green Paper in Retrospect." (1975), 7 *Canadian Ethnic Studies* 71-79 (No. 1; Special Issue) **1396**

Keenleyside, Hugh L. "Canadian Immigration Policy." (1948), 3 *International Journal* 222-238. **1397**

Kokas, Louis. "Quelques aspects économiques de l'immigration au Canada." (1957-58), 33 *Actualité Économique* 271-283. **1398**

Kronby, Malcolm. "The Administration of the Immigration Act." (1958-59), 1 *Osgoode Hall Law Journal* 1-9 (No. 2) **1399**

Kung, S.W. "Chinese Immigration into North America: With Special Reference to the Problem of Illegal Entry." (1961), 68 *Queen's Quarterly* 610-620. **1400**

Levine, Martin. *Compassion When Convenient: Canadian Attitudes Toward Immigration in 1946 and 1947.* Ottawa, 1975. 134 leaves. **1401**
Thesis (M.A.), Carleton University, 1975.

Ligue des droits de l'homme, Montréal. *Immigration et droits de l'homme: rapport sur la politique de l'immigration.* Montréal: Ligue des droits de l'homme, 1976. 113, 15 p. **1402**

Linden, Allen M. "Race and Nationality Restrictions in the Immigration Act: Is a Revision Overdue?" (1960-63), 2 *Osgoode Hall Law Journal* 243-254. **1403**

Lower, Arthur R.M. "The Case Against Immigration." (1930), 37 *Queen's Quarterly* 557-574. **1404**

Marchand, Jean. "White Paper on Immigration." (1967), 19 *External Affairs* 97-100. **1405**

Marcus, Stephen. "Note on the New Immigration Act, 1977." (1977), 3 *Queen's Law Journal* 496-507. **1406**

Marr, William L. "Canadian Immigration Policies since 1962." (1975), 1 *Canadian Public Policy* 196-203. **1407**

Marr, William L. "Employment Visas and the Canadian Labour Force." (1977), 3 *Canadian Public Policy* 518-524. **1408**

Marr, William L. *Labour Market and Other Implications of Immigration Policy for Ontario.* Toronto: Ontario Economic Council, 1976. iv, 241 p. (Ontario Economic Council. Working Paper Series, No. 1/76) **1409**

McDougall, Duncan M. "Immigration into Canada, 1851-1920." (1961), 27 *Canadian Journal of Economics and Political Science* 162-175. **1410**

McGinnis, David. "At the Banquet of Life, or Neo-Malthusians on Immigration Policy." (1975), 7 *Canadian Ethnic Studies* 55-60 (No. 1; Special Issue) **1411**

McMillan, Anthony J. "Canadian Immigration." (1928-29), 8 *Dalhousie Review* 179-187. **1412**

Mercier, Jean. "Immigration and Provincial Rights." (1944), 22 *Canadian Bar Review* 856-869. **1413**
Originally published in French in (1944), 4 *Revue du Barreau* 149-163.

Mercier, Jean. "Immigration et droits des provinces." (1944), 4 *Revue du Barreau* 149-163. **1414**

Morgan, Lucy Ingram. "Immigration, Emigration, and External Trade." (1949), 56 *Canadian Banker* 110-118 (No. 3) **1415**

Morin, Rosaire. *L'immigration au Canada*. Montréal: Éditions de l'Action nationale, 1966. xi, 172 p. **1416**
Review: Denis Bertrand in (1969-70), 23 *Revue d'Histoire de l'Amérique Française* 630-632.

Munro, John A. "British Columbia and the 'Chinese Evil': Canada's First Anti-Asiatic Immigration Law." (1971), 6 *Journal of Canadian Studies* 42-51 (No. 4) **1417**

National Conference on Immigration Policy, Victoria College, University of Toronto, 1975. *Immigration, 1975-2001: Report of the National Conference on Immigration Policy, May 22-24, 1975 / Immigration, 1975-2001: rapport du Colloque national sur la politique d'immigration, 22-24 mai, 1975*. Toronto: Canadian Association for Adult Education, c1975. 41, 44 p. **1418**
Sponsored by the Canadian Association for Adult Education and the Toronto Committee on Immigration and Migration. Text in English and French.

Nord, Douglas C. *Immigration as an International Problem: Canada, the United States and East Asia*. Durham, N.C., 1979. 293 frames. **1419**
Thesis (Ph.D.), Duke University, 1979. (University Microfilms, Ann Arbor, No. 80-3634).

Nord, Douglas C. "The 'Problem' of Immigration: The Continuing Presence of the Stranger within Our Gates." (1978), 8 *American Review of Canadian Studies* 116-133 (No. 2) **1420**

Parai, Louis. "Canada's Immigration Policy, 1962-74." (1975), 9 *International Migration Review* 449-477. **1421**

Parai, Louis. *Canadian International Immigration, 1953-1965; an Empirical Study*. New Haven, Conn., 1969 (c1970). vi, 276 leaves. **1422**
Thesis, Yale University, 1969. Abstracted in (1970), 30 *Dissertation Abstracts International* 3157-A. (University Microfilms, Ann Arbor, No. 70-2785).

Passaris, Constantine. "The Immigration Debate: The Cost-Benefit Impact of Immigrants on Economy." (1975), *International Perspectives* 9-13 (Sept./Oct.) **1423**

Passaris, Constantine. " 'Input' of Foreign Policy to Immigration Equation." (1976), *International Perspectives* 23-28 (Nov./Dec.) **1424**

Paul, Gurbachan Singh. "The Green Paper and Third World Immigrants: A Subjective Analysis." (1975), 7 *Canadian Ethnic Studies* 40-49 (No. 1; Special Issue) **1425**

Pelletier, Georges. "Le partage de l'immigration canadienne depuis 1900." (1918), 12 *Royal Society of Canada, Transactions* 33-39 (3d Ser., Sec. 1)   **1426**

Phelan, Vincent C. "Organisation of Migration into Canada." (1952), 65 *International Labour Review* 321-347.   **1427**

Piggott, Eleanora. *Dominion Government Policy on Immigration and Colonization.* Vancouver, 1950. 185 leaves.   **1428**
Thesis (M.A.), University of British Columbia, 1950.

Rawlyk, George A. "Canada's Immigration Policy, 1945-1962." (1962-63), 42 *Dalhousie Review* 287-300.   **1429**

Richmond, Anthony H. "The Green Paper: Reflections on the Canadian Immigration and Population Study." (1975), 7 *Canadian Ethnic Studies* 5-21 (No. 1; Special Issue)   **1430**

Roddick, Paul M. "Canadian Immigration Policy: The Hard Facts." (1955-56), 11 *International Journal* 122-128.   **1431**

Roddick, Paul M. "Canadian Immigration: Policy and Practice." (1955), 62 *Queen's Quarterly* 529-538.   **1432**

"Round Table on the Green Paper on Immigration." (1975), 7 *Canadian Ethnic Studies* 1-79 (No. 1; Special Issue)   **1433**
Some individual articles are listed separately.

Sampat-Mehta, Ramdeo. *International Barriers.* Ottawa: Canada Research Bureau, 1973. xxxiii, 338 p.   **1434**
Cover title: *International Barriers; Aliens, Immigration and Citizenship in Canada.* Also published by Harpell's Press.

Sandwell, B.K. "Our Immigration Problem: Some Facts and Fallacies." (1946-47), 53 *Queen's Quarterly* 502-510.   **1435**

Sandwell, B.K. "Population: A Canadian Problem." (1947-48), 54 *Queen's Quarterly* 312-322.   **1436**

Scott, Janet V., and Stonehouse, Robert C. "Citizens, Aliens and Immigration." In *Canadian Encyclopedic Digest (Ontario),* 3d ed., 1980, title 27, vol. 4, 154 p.
Review: Laurence Kearley in (1981), 59 *Canadian Bar Review* 595-598.   **1437**

"Should People Stay Home? Regulation of Free Movement and Right of Establishment between the U.S., Canada, and Mexico." (1974), 68 *American Society of International Law, Proceedings* 38-58.   **1438**
This is a panel. E. (Kika) De La Garza, Chairman.

Smith, William George. *A Study in Canadian Immigration.* Toronto: Ryerson Press, 1920. 406 p., map.   **1439**
Review: H. Michell in (1920), 1 *Canadian Historical Review* 415-416.

Spowart, Ann. *The Immigration Laws of the United Kingdom and of Canada.* Halifax, 1976. 223 leaves.   **1440**
Thesis (LL.M.), Dalhousie University, 1976.

Star, Spencer. "In Search of a Rational Immigration Policy." (1975), 1 *Canadian Public Policy* 328-342.   **1441**

Sugimoto, Howard Hiroshi. *Japanese Immigration, the Vancouver Riots, and*

Canadian Diplomacy. New York: Arno Press, 1978. 263 p. (Asian Experience in North America: Chinese and Japanese) **1442**
Originally presented as the author's thesis (M.A.), University of Washington, 1966.

Timlin, Mabel F. "Canada's Immigration Policy, 1896-1910." (1960), 26 *Canadian Journal of Economics and Political Science* 517-532. **1443**

Timlin, Mabel F. *Does Canada Need More People?* Toronto: Oxford University Press, 1951. xii, 143 p. **1444**
Issued under the auspices of the Canadian Institute of International Affairs.
Reviews: Allan G. Bogue in (1951), 32 *Canadian Historical Review* 281-282; Brinley Thomas in (1952), 28 *International Affairs* 222.

Timlin, Mabel F. "Recent Changes in Government Attitudes Towards Immigration." (1955), 49 *Royal Society of Canada, Transactions* 95-105 (3d Ser., Sec. 2) **1445**

Toxey, Walter W. *Immigration and Citizenship in the Commonwealth of Nations.* Austin, Tex., 1964 (c1967). 204 leaves. **1446**
Thesis (Ph.D.), University of Texas, 1964. (University Microfilms, Ann Arbor, No. 64-11849).

Troper, Harold M. *Official Canadian Government Encouragement of American Immigration 1896-1911.* Toronto, c1971. 311 leaves. **1447**
Thesis (Ph.D.), University of Toronto, 1971. (National Library of Canada. Canadian Theses on Microfiche, No. 31354).

Whiteley, A.S. "What Need of Immigrants?" (1929-30), 9 *Dalhousie Review* 225-231. **1448**

Whitton, Charlotte. "The Immigration Problem for Canada." (1923-24), 31 *Queen's Quarterly* 388-420. **1449**

Wood, John R. "East Indians and Canada's New Immigration Policy." (1978), 4 *Canadian Public Policy* 547-567. **1450**

Wydrzynski, Christopher J. "Immigration Law: Ten Years of Increasing Pessimism." *In* Menezes, Julio, ed., *Decade of Adjustment* (Toronto, 1980), pp. 123-145. **1451**

Ziskind, David, and Horney, Esther. "Laws Affecting Migratory Labor: United States, Mexico, and Canada." (1981), 4 *Comparative Labor Law* 1-25. **1452**

J. Extradition, Expulsion and Asylum

April, Serge. "Examining the Right of Asylum: The Choices and the Limitations." (1974), *International Perspectives* 44-47 (May/June) **1453**

Armour, Eric. "Extradition and Fugitive Offenders." (1925), 2 *Dominion Law Reports* 169-199. **1454**

Baldwin, William H. "The Canadian Extradition Treaty and Family Deserters." (1921-22), 12 *Journal of Criminal Law, Criminology and Police Science* 199-212. **1455**

Bedi, Satya Deva. "Law and Practice of Extradition within the Commonwealth Countries." (1977), 19 *Journal of the Indian Law Institute* 419-437. **1456**

Brown-John, Clive Lloyd. "Commonwealth 'Extradition': The Case of Duncan Crux." (1970), 8 *Canadian Yearbook of International Law* 324-331. **1457**

Canada. Dept. of the Secretary of State. *Documents Relating to Extradition Procedure*. Ottawa: King's Printer, 1923. 52 p. **1458**
Extradition under the *Extradition Act* (R.S.C. 1970, c. E-21), falls within the jurisdiction of the Dept. of Justice.

Castel, Jean-Gabriel, and Edwardh, Marlys. "Political Offences: Extradition and Deportation - Recent Canadian Developments." (1975), 13 *Osgoode Hall Law Journal* 89-148. **1459**

"The Cohen Extradition Proceedings." (1902-03), 2 *Canadian Law Review* 74-76. **1460**

Cole, Charles V. "Extradition Treaties Abound but Unlawful Seizures Continue." (1975), *International Perspectives* 40-44 (Mar./Apr.) **1461**
Also published in (1975), 9 *Law Society of Upper Canada Gazette* 177-184.

"A Complexity in International Law." (1906), 42 *Canada Law Journal* 174-176. **1462**

Delisle, R.J. "Sufficiency of Evidence: The Implications of *Sheppard*." (1978), 4 *Queen's Law Journal* 111-123. **1463**

"Extradition." (1960), 12 *External Affairs* 784-788. **1464**

"The Extradition of Lamirande." (1866-67), 2 *Lower Canada Law Journal* 73-76, 97-98. **1465**

Fera, Norma M. "A Critical Examination of the LRC's Proposals for Reform of Extradition Review." (1977), 20 *Criminal Law Quarterly* 103-120. **1466**

"The Gaynor and Greene Extradition Proceedings." (1901-02), 1 *Canadian Law Review* 537-547; (1902-03), 2 *Canadian Law Review* 9-15, 594-604. **1467**

Green, Leslie C. "Extradition v. Asylum for Aerial Hijackers." (1975), 10 *Israel Law Review* 207-224. **1468**

Green, Leslie C. "Hijacking, Extradition and Asylum." (1974), 22 *Chitty's Law Journal* 135-143. **1469**
See also the author's *Law and Society* (Leyden, 1975), pp. 321-362.

Green, Leslie C. "Immigration, Extradition, and Asylum in Canadian Law and Practice." *In* Macdonald, Ronald St. John, and others, *Canadian Perspectives on International Law and Organization* (Toronto, 1974), pp. 244-303. **1470**

Green, Leslie C. "International Court of Justice." (1951), 4 *International Law Quarterly* 229-239. **1471**
Refers to the *Right of Asylum Case (Colombia* v. *Peru),* (1950) *I.C.J. Reports* 266.

Green, Leslie C. "The Legal Aspects of the Problem of Asylum." (1966), 52 *International Law Association, Report of Conference* 730-743. **1472**
Progress report by Leslie C. Green, Rapporteur.

Green, Leslie C. "The Nature of Political Offences." (1964), 3 *Solicitor Quarterly* 213-238. **1473**
Also printed in (1965), 7 *Journal of the Indian Law Institute* 1-26.

Green, Leslie C. "Recent Practice in the Law of Extradition." (1953), 6 *Current Legal Problems* 274-296. **1474**

Green, Leslie C. "The Right of Asylum in International Law." (1961), 3 *University of Malaya Law Review* 223-242. **1475**

Keith, B.C. "Asylum or Accessory: The Non-Surrender of Political Offenders by Canada." (1973), 31 *University of Toronto Faculty of Law Review* 93-102. **1476**

Koenigsberg, M. "A Unique Defense: 'Politics Made Me Do It.' " (1973), 12 *Western Ontario Law Review* 223-227. **1477**

La Forest, Gerard V. *Extradition to and from Canada.* New Orleans: Hauser Press, 1961. vii, 200 p. (Galleon Book) **1478**
Appendices (p. 129-182): 1. Legislation.- 2. Treaties.- 3. Extradition Crimes.
Review: Charles B. Bourne in (1963), 41 *Canadian Bar Review* 473-474.

La Forest, Gerard V. *Extradition to and from Canada.* With the Assistance of Sharon A. Williams. 2d ed. Toronto: Canada Law Book, 1977. xxv, 289 p.
Appendices (pp. 197-272): 1. Legislation.- 2. Treaties.- 3. Extradition Crimes. **1479**
Reviews: Robert A. Friedlander in (1979), 27 *Chitty's Law Journal* 20-22; Leslie C. Green in (1978), 56 *Canadian Bar Review* 359-361; Donald J. Rosenbloom in (1979), 17 *Canadian Yearbook of International Law* 441-443; I.A. Shearer in (1979), 73 *American Journal of International Law* 547-548.

Lee, Edward G. "Criminal Law - Extradition of Fugitives - Canadian Procedure. (Comment)." (1959), 37 *Canadian Bar Review* 377-381. **1480**

MacGregor, James Patrick. "Extradition from Canada." (1934), 39 *Commercial Law Journal* 371-374. **1481**

Magone, C.R. "Extradition." (1925), 3 *Canadian Bar Review* 179-186. **1482**

Morrison, Stephen R. "Extradition from Canada: Rights of the Fugitive Following Committal for Surrender." (1977), 19 *Criminal Law Quarterly* 366-404. **1483**

Morse, Charles. "Political Offenses and the Right of Asylum." (1910), 30 *Canadian Law Times* 786-787. **1484**

Murray, Alexander L. "The Extradition of Fugitive Slaves from Canada: A Re-Evaluation." (1962), 43 *Canadian Historical Review* 298-314. **1485**

Noto, Mario T. "Comparative Analysis of the Deportation Process in the United States and Canada." (1961), *American Bar Association, Section of International and Comparative Law, Proceedings* 49-55. **1486**

O'Hearn, W.J. "Extradition." (1930), 8 *Canadian Bar Review* 175-183. **1487**

O'Higgins, Paul. "Extradition within the Commonwealth." (1960), 9 *International and Comparative Law Quarterly* 486-494. **1488**

Pomerant, Joseph Baer. "The Extradition Act: A 'Renewal of Phraseology' Reconsidered." (1960), 3 *Criminal Law Quarterly* 215-226. **1489**

Popple, A.E. "Extradition." (1922), 42 *Canadian Law Times* 122-123. **1490**

"The Right of Asylum." (1911), 47 *Canada Law Journal* 408-414. **1491**

Sinha, S. Prakash. "An Anthropocentric View of Asylum in International Law." (1971), 10 *Columbia Journal of Transnational Law* 78-110. **1492**

Sinha, S. Prakash. *Asylum and International Law*. The Hague: Nijhoff, 1971. xii, 366 p. **1493**

Stonehouse, Robert C. "Extradition." In *Canadian Encyclopedic Digest (Ontario)*, 3d ed., 1976, title 61, vol. 12, 51 p. **1494**

Timbers, William H., and Pollack, Irving M. "Extradition from Canada to the United States for Securities Fraud: Frustration of the National Policies of Both Countries." (1956), 16 *Federal Bar Journal* 31-61; (1955-56), 24 *Fordham Law Review* 301-325. **1495**

U.S. Congress. Senate. Committee on Foreign Relations. *Supplementary Extradition Convention with Canada. Report on Ex. G, 82-2, Accompanied by Appendix with Hearings*. Washington: Govt. Print. Off., 1952. ii, 18 p. (U.S. 82d Cong., 2d sess. Senate. Ex. Rept. 5) **1496**
Refers to the convention of October 26, 1951 (CTS 1952/12).

Weis, Paul. "The United Nations Declaration on Territorial Asylum." (1969), 7 *Canadian Yearbook of International Law* 92-149. **1497**

Winston, Milton W. *The Role of Extradition in International Civil Aviation*. Montreal, 1973. (6), 242 leaves. **1498**
Thesis (LL.M.), McGill University, 1973. (National Library of Canada. Canadian Theses on Microfilm, No. 16045).

Zorn, Roman J. "Criminal Extradition Menaces the Canadian Haven for Fugitive Slaves, 1841-1861." (1957), 38 *Canadian Historical Review* 284-294. **1499**

K. Human Rights and Fundamental Freedoms

See also *"Minorities" (p. 101)*.

Addy, Andrews. *Socio-Economic Rights and Measures of Implementation under the International Covenant on Economic, Social and Cultural Rights*. Montreal, 1981. 168 frames. **1500**
Thesis (LL.M.), McGill University, 1981. (National Library of Canada. Canadian Theses on Microfiche, No. 51837). Refers to the covenant of October 5, 1977.

Anglin, Douglas G. "Canada and Apartheid." (1959-60), 15 *International Journal* 122-137. **1501**

Angus, Henry F. "The Dangers of Declaring Human Rights." (1951), 17 *Canadian Journal of Economics and Political Science* 218-221. **1502**

Armour, Leslie. "Human Rights: A Canadian View." In Rosenbaum, Alan S., ed. *The Philosophy of Human Rights: International Perspectives* (Westport, Conn., 1980), pp. 195-205. **1503**

Arthurs, H.W. "Hate Propaganda: An Argument Against Attempts to Stop It by Legislation." (1970), 18 *Chitty's Law Journal* 1-5. **1504**

Barsh, Russell Lawrence, and Henderson, James Youngblood. "Aboriginal Rights, Treaty Rights, and Human Rights: Indian Tribes and 'Constitutional Renewal.'" (1982), 17 *Journal of Canadian Studies* 55-81 (No. 2) **1505**

Batshaw, Harry. "The Individual - His Rights and Responsibilities. (Report of Rapporteur)." (1971), 5 *World Law Review* 334-335. **1506**

Batshaw, Harry. "Infringement of Human Rights by Individuals or State Organs: A Report on the Canadian Scene." *In René Cassin Amicorum Discipulorumque Liber* (Paris, 1969-1971), vol. 1, pp. 3-15. **1507**

Batshaw, Harry. "A Landmark Decision Against Discrimination in Canada." (1971), 4 *Revue des Droits de l'Homme* 207-211. **1508**

Bayefsky, Anne F. "The Impact of the European Convention on Human Rights in the United Kingdom: Implications for Canada." (1981), 13 *Ottawa Law Review* 507-526. **1509**

Beaudoin, Gérald. "De la protection législative et constitutionnelle des droits de la personne au Canada en général et au Québec." (1981), 12 *Revue Générale de Droit* 299-309. **1510**

Beres, Louis René. "Nation Without a Soul, Policy Without a Purpose." (1981), 29 *Chitty's Law Journal* 1-12. **1511**

Beres, Louis René. "An Open Letter to the Secretary of State." (1981), 29 *Chitty's Law Journal* 13-17. **1512**

Berger, Thomas R. *Fragile Freedoms: Human Rights and Dissent in Canada.* Toronto: Clarke, Irwin, 1982. xviii, 298 p. **1513**

Binavince, Emilio S. "The Impact of the Mobility Rights: The Canadian Economic Union - A Boom or a Bust?" (1982), 14 *Ottawa Law Review* 340-365. **1514**

Blache, Pierre. "Les tribunaux et la protection des droits de la personne au Canada." (1981), 12 *Revue Générale de Droit* 311-322. **1515**

Bolté, Paul-Émile. *Les droits de l'homme et la papauté contemporaine: synthèse et textes.* Montréal: Fides, 1975. 428 p. (Pensée chrétienne, 1) **1516**

Bonenfant, Jean-Charles. "Les influences étatsuniennes sur la conception canadienne des droits de l'homme." (1973), 11 *Royal Society of Canada, Transactions* 85-96 (4th Ser.) **1517**

Bromke, Adam. "The Impact of Human Rights on the Process of Détente." (1978), *International Perspectives* 12-15 (July/Aug.) **1518**

Cadieux, Marcel. "Les droits de l'homme au regard du droit international." (1962), 22 *Revue du Barreau* 18-39. **1519**

Cadieux, Marcel. "Human Rights and International Law: Some Problems." (1962), 69 *Queen's Quarterly* 276-293. **1520**

Cadieux, Rita. "La Loi canadienne sur les droits de la personne et sa mise en application par la Commission." (1981), 12 *Revue Générale de Droit* 323-333. **1521**

Canada. Dept. of External Affairs. *International Year for Action to Combat Racism and Racial Discrimination / Année internationale de la lutte contre le racisme et la discrimination raciale.* Ottawa: Dept. of External Affairs, 1971. 23, 23 p. **1522**

Canada. Dept. of the Secretary of State. *International Convention on the Elimination of All Forms of Racial Discrimination: Report of Canada.* 1st—, 1971—. Ottawa. **1523**

Canada. Dept. of the Secretary of State. *International Covenant on Civil and Political Rights: Report of Canada on Implementation of the Provisions of the Covenant*. Ottawa: Supply and Services Canada, 1979. 479 p. **1524**
Also issued in French under title: *Pacte international relatif aux droits civils et politiques: rapport du Canada sur l'application des dispositions du pacte* (577 p.).

Canada. Dept. of the Secretary of State. *Notes for a Conference on Human Rights, Tehran, Iran, 1968*. Ottawa: Queen's Printer, 1970. 97 p. **1525**
Prepared by the Citizenship Branch for the use of the Canadian Delegation to the Conference. Also published in French under title: *Dossier relatif à la Conférence sur les droits de l'homme, Téhéran, Iran, 1968*.

Canada. Human Rights Commission. *Annual Report / Rapport annuel*. 1st—, 1977/78—. Ottawa. Bilingual. **1526**
The Canadian Human Rights Commission was created in 1977 under the *Canadian Human Rights Act* (S.C. 1977, c. 33). It is responsible for the enforcement of the prohibition of all forms of discrimination. The commission has wide powers, including the establishment of human rights tribunals. It reports to Parliament through the Minister of Justice.

Canada. Human Rights Commission. *Final Report on the National Conference 'Human Rights in Canada ... the Years Ahead.'* Ottawa: Canadian Human Rights Commission, 1979. 55, 55 p. **1527**
The conference was held in Ottawa, December 8-10, 1978, sponsored by the Canadian Human Rights Commission in collaboration with the Dept. of External Affairs, on the occasion of the 30th Anniversary of the Universal Declaration of Human Rights. French title: *Rapport final de la Conférence 'Les droits de la personne au Canada...L'avenir.'* Text in English and French on inverted pages, each with a separate title page and paging.

Canada. Special Committee on Hate Propaganda in Canada. *Report to the Minister of Justice*. Ottawa: Queen's Printer, 1966. xi, 327 p. **1528**
Maxwell Cohen, Chairman. Also issued in French under title: *Rapport soumis au ministre de la justice, par le Comité spécial de la propagande haineuse au Canada*. Reviews: Andrew Brewin in (1967), 17 *University of Toronto Law Journal* 235-238; W. Gunther Plaut in (1967), 5 *Osgoode Hall Law Journal* 313-317.

Caron, Madeleine. "La Commission des droits de la personne du Québec: cinq années de lutte pour le droit à l'égalité." (1981), 12 *Revue Générale de Droit* 335-357. **1529**

Carsen, Gary L., and Tanner, Susan. "Human Rights." In *Canadian Encyclopedic Digest (Ontario)*, 3d ed., 1979, title 74, vol. 14, 112 p. **1530**

Castel, Jean-Gabriel. "International Year for Human Rights - 1968 - Année internationale des droits de l'homme." (1968), 46 *Canadian Bar Review* 543-553.
1531

Chambers, L.P. "The Armenian Deportations." (1917-18), 25 *Queen's Quarterly* 1-9. **1532**

Clark, Roger S. "Enforcement of International Human Rights: The Role of Lawyers." (1980), 28 *Chitty's Law Journal* 4-12. **1533**

Claydon, John. "The Application of International Human Rights Law by Canadian Courts." (1981), 30 *Buffalo Law Review* 727-752. **1534**

Claydon, John. "The Treaty Protection of Religious Rights: U.N. Draft Conven tion on the Elimination of All Forms of Intolerance and of Discrimination Based on Religion or Belief." (1971-72), 12 *Santa Clara Lawyer* 403-423. **1535**

Cohen, Maxwell. "Bill C-60 and International Law - The United Nations Charter - Declaration of Human Rights." (1959), 37 *Canadian Bar Review* 228-233.
1536

Cohen, Maxwell. "The Hate Propaganda Amendments: Reflections on a Controversy." (1972), 4 *Canadian Communications Law Review* 243-259. **1537**

Cohen, Maxwell. "Human Rights: Programme or Catchall? A Canadian Rationale." (1968), 46 *Canadian Bar Review* 554-564. **1538**

Cohen, Maxwell. "Human Rights; the Individual and International Law." *In René Cassin Amicorum Discipulorumque Liber* (Paris, 1969-1971), vol. 3, pp. 69-77.
1539

Cohen, Maxwell. "Human Rights and Hate Propaganda: A Controversial Canadian Experiment." *In* Shoham, Shlomo, ed., *Of Law and Man: Essays in Honour of Haim H. Cohn* (New York, 1971), pp. 59-78. **1540**

Colard, Daniel. "Détente, dissidence et droits de l'homme." (1977), 8 *Études Internationales* 549-599. **1541**

Colas, Émile. "Les droits de l'homme et la constitution canadienne." (1958), 18 *Revue du Barreau* 317-335. **1542**

"La Conférence européenne sur l'individu et l'état." (1969), 4 *Revue Juridique Thémis* 133-142. **1543**

Conklin, William E. *In Defence of Fundamental Rights*. Alphen aan den Rijn: Sijthoff & Noordhoff, 1979. xix, 307 p. **1544**
Review: John P. Humphrey in (1981), 7 *Canadian Public Policy* 135-136.

"Convention on the Elimination of Racial Discrimination, Ratification by Canada." (1970), 22 *External Affairs* 453-460. **1545**
Contains substantial parts of the convention.

Copithorne, M.D. "Note sur l'élaboration des pactes de 1966 sur les droits de l'homme." (1978), 9 *Études Internationales* 531-537. **1546**

Copithorne, M.D. "The Structural Law of the International Human Welfare System." *In* Macdonald, Ronald St. John, and others, *The International Law and Policy of Human Welfare* (Alphen aan den Rijn, 1978), pp. 147-185.**1547**

Copithorne, M.D. "What Are Human Rights?" (1978), *International Perspectives* 30-33 (Nov./Dec.) **1548**

Cotler, Irwin. "Intrusion on Individual Liberties in the Eighties." (1980), 62 *Canadian Bar Association, Proceedings* 150-158. **1549**
Discusses international human rights in the eighties.

Das, Kamleshwar, and Bilder, Richard. "The Options Ahead (In the International Law of Human Rights)." (1973), 2 *Canadian Council on International Law, Proceedings* 146-195. **1550**
The panel includes Maxwell Cohen, Chairman; the presentations were made by the two panelists, followed by a general discussion (pp. 171-195).

Day, Brigham. *Le Canada et les droits de l'homme. Le concept des droits de*

l'homme dans la politique étrangère et la Constitution du Canada. Préface de J.-J. Chevallier. Paris: Recueil Sirey, 1953. 154 p. **1551**
Also issued as thesis, Faculté de droit, Paris, under title: *Les droits de l'homme au Canada.*
Reviews: J.M. Bowie in (1954), 30 *International Affairs* 368; Guy Frégault in (1954), 35 *Canadian Historical Review* 253-254.

Desjardins, Alice. "Des normes régionales et universelles pour les droits de la personne." (1978), 16 *Canadian Yearbook of International Law* 46-91. **1552**

Desjardins, Alice. "La mise en oeuvre au Canada des traités relatifs aux droits de la personne." (1981), 12 *Revue Générale de Droit* 359-374. **1553**

Dinstein, Yoram. "Science, Technology and Human Rights." (1979), 5 *Dalhousie Law Journal* 155-168. **1554**

Doxey, Margaret P. "Human Rights and Canadian Foreign Policy." (1978-79), 37 *Behind the Headlines* No. 4 (20 p.) **1555**

Drieger, Elmer A. "The Canadian Charter of Rights and Freedoms." (1982), 14 *Ottawa Law Review* 366-378 **1556**

"Editorial on the Universal Declaration of Human Rights." (1956), 28 *Manitoba Bar News* 65-71. **1557**

Edmondson, Locksley G.E. *Race, Politics and the International System: Aspects of Research and Behaviour.* Kingston, 1973. xiv, 720 leaves, maps. **1558**
Half-title: *Aspects of Research and Behaviour.* Thesis (Ph.D.), Queen's University, 1973. (National Library of Canada. Canadian Theses on Microfiche, No. 17913).

Fischer, Hugo. "The Human Rights Covenants and Canadian Law." (1977), 15 *Canadian Yearbook of International Law* 42-83. **1559**

Forest, Réal. "Quelques aspects de la mise en oeuvre au Canada des pactes de l'O.N.U. relatifs aux droits de l'homme." (1981), 12 *Revue Générale de Droit* 375-395. **1560**

Gall, Gerald L., ed. *Civil Liberties in Canada: Entering the 1980s.* Toronto: Butterworths, c1982. xv, 259 p. **1561**
Contains nine essays.

Gibson, Dale. "Charter or Chimera: A Comment on the Proposed Canadian Charter of Rights and Freedoms." (1978-79), 9 *Manitoba Law Journal* 363-391.
1562

Glenn, Jane *Le pacte international relatif aux droits civils et politiques et la convention européenne des droits de l'homme: étude comparative.* Montréal: Presses de l'Université de Montréal, 1975. xi, 625 p. **1563**

Golsong, Heribert. "Regional Approaches to Human Rights: The European Experiment." (1973), 2 *Canadian Council on International Law, Proceedings* 81-86. **1564**

Gormley, W. Paul. "The Development of International Law through Cases from the European Court of Human Rights: Linguistic and Detention Disputes." (1967-68), 2 *Ottawa Law Review* 382-442. **1565**

Gotlieb, Allan E. "The Changing Canadian Attitude to the United Nations Role in

Protecting and Developing Human Rights." *In* Gotlieb, Allan E., ed., *Human Rights, Federalism and Minorities* (Toronto, 1970), pp. 16-53. **1566**

Gotlieb, Allan E., ed. *Human Rights, Federalism and Minorities / Les droits de l'homme, le fédéralisme et les minorités.* Toronto: Canadian Institute of International Affairs, 1970. x, 268 p. (Contemporary Affairs, No. 43) **1567**
A collection of ten essays listed separately.
Reviews: Peter Z.R. Finkle in (1971), 65 *American Journal of International Law* 869-870; Joseph W. Samuels in (1971), 49 *Canadian Bar Review* 494-496; Douglas A. Schmeiser in (1971), 21 *University of Toronto Law Journal* 579-580.

Green, Leslie C. "Derogation of Human Rights in Emergency Situations." (1978), 16 *Canadian Yearbook of International Law* 92-115. **1568**

Green, Leslie C. "The European Convention of Human Rights." (1951), 5 *World Affairs* 432-444 (N.S.) **1569**

Green, Leslie C. "General Principles of Law and Human Rights." (1955), 8 *Current Legal Problems* 162-184. **1570**

Green, Leslie C. "Human Rights and Colour Discrimination. (*Sei Fujii* v. *The State of California*)." (1950), 3 *International Law Quarterly* 422-426. **1571**

Green, Leslie C. "Human Rights and State Survival." (1979), 27 *Chitty's Law Journal* 121-127. **1572**

Green, Leslie C. "Human Rights and the Colour Problem." (1950), 3 *Current Legal Problems* 236-262. **1573**

Green, Leslie C. "Human Rights and the United Nations." (1968), 2 *Patterns of Prejudice (London)* 6-10. **1574**

Green, Leslie C. "Human Rights in Public International Law." *In* Singhvi, Laxmi Mall, ed., *Horizons of Freedom* (Delhi, 1969), pp. 59-105. **1575**

Grenier, Bernard. *La déclaration canadienne des droits, une loi bien ordinaire?* Québec: Presses de l'Université Laval, 1979. xxviii, 172 p. (Bibliothèque juridique, D-2.) **1576**

Grenon, Jean-Yves. "De la mise en oeuvre du futur pacte international des droits de l'homme dans l'état fédératif canadien: clause fédérale." (1951-52), 2 *Thémis* 195-209. **1577**

Head, Ivan L. "Regional Developments Respecting Human Rights: The Implications for Canada." *In* Gotlieb, Allan E., ed., *Human Rights, Federalism and Minorities* (Toronto, 1970), pp. 228-243. **1578**

Hérisson, Charles-D. "L'économie et les problèmes raciaux des Rhodésies." (1946-47), 22 *Actualité Économique* 515-531. **1579**

Hiscocks, C. Richard. "The United Nations and Anti-Semitism." (1959-60), 15 *International Journal* 143-146. **1580**

Hommel, Maurice W. *Capricorn Blues: The Struggle for Human Rights in South Africa.* Introduction by Paul Roubaix. Toronto: Culturama, c1981. 251 p. **1581**

Howard, Rhoda. "The Dilemma of Human Rights in Sub-Saharan Africa." (1979-80), 35 *International Journal* 724-747. **1582**

Hucker, John, and McDonald, Bruce C. "Securing Human Rights in Canada." (1969), 15 *McGill Law Journal* 220-243. **1583**

"Human Rights and Foreign Policy: (i) The Traditional Policy of Minding Your Own Business; (ii) Factors of Change / Les droits de la personne et la politique extérieure: (i) L'approche traditionnelle: se mêler de ses affaires; (ii) Facteurs de changements." (1978), 7 *Canadian Council on International Law, Proceedings* 48-61. **1584**

This is a panel. Speakers: Charles B. Bourne (pp. 48-53), and Michel Lebel (pp. 54-56).-Discussion (pp. 56-61).

"Human Rights and Foreign Policy: Canada - in Search of an International Human Rights Policy / Les droits de la personne et la politique extérieure: Le Canada - à la recherche d'une politique internationale des droits de la personne." (1978), 7 *Canadian Council on International Law, Proceedings* 62-82. **1585**

This is a panel. Speakers: Allan E. Gotlieb (pp. 62-67), and David MacDonald (pp. 68-71).- Discussion (pp. 72-82).

"Human Rights and Foreign Policy: Nations Are Their Brothers' Keepers - Carter's Human Rights Policy / Les droits de la personne et la politique extérieure: la politique du Président Carter en matière des droits de la personne." (1978), 7 *Canadian Council on International Law, Proceedings* 13-40. **1586**

This is a panel. Speakers: William J. Butler (pp. 13-20), and Louis Balthazar (pp. 21-24).-Discussion (pp. 25-40).

Humphrey, John P. "Human Rights: New Directions in the U.N. Program." (1958), 4 *New York Law Forum* 391-397. **1587**

Humphrey, John P. "Human Rights, the United Nations and 1968." (1968), 9 *Journal of the International Commission of Jurists* 1-13. **1588**

Humphrey, John P. "Human Rights and Authority." (1970), 20 *University of Toronto Law Journal* 412-421. **1589**

Humphrey, John P. "Human Rights Committee - Interim Report." (1966), 52 *International Law Association, Report of Conference* 758-764. **1590**

Humphrey, John P. "The International Bill of Rights: Scope and Implementation." (1975-76), 17 *William and Mary Law Review* 527-541. **1591**

Humphrey, John P. "International Committee on Human Rights. Report." (1968), 53 *International Law Association, Report of Conference* 437-458. **1592**

Humphrey, John P. "International Committee on Human Rights. Report." (1972), 55 *International Law Association, Report of Conference* 571-583. **1593**

Humphrey, John P. "International Committee on Human Rights. Report." (1974), 56 *International Law Association, Report of Conference* 205-216. **1594**

Humphrey, John P. "International Committee on Human Rights. Report." (1976), 57 *International Law Association, Report of Conference* 507-518. **1595**

Humphrey, John P. "International Law of Human Rights: Present Realities and Future Prospects. (La protection internationale des droits de l'homme, réalité présente et perspective de l'avenir)." (1973), 2 *Canadian Council on International Law, Proceedings* 7-30. **1596**

Humphrey, John P. "The International Law of Human Rights in the Middle Twentieth Century." *In* Bos, Maarten, ed., *The Present State of International Law and Other Essays* (Deventer, 1973), pp. 75-105. **1597**
This address is followed by papers of panelists (listed separately), and a general discussion (pp. 60-80).

Humphrey, John P. "La nature juridique de la Déclaration universelle des droits de l'homme." (1981), 12 *Revue Générale de Droit* 397-400. **1598**

Humphrey, John P. "The Revolution in the International Law of Human Rights." (1974-75), 4 *Human Rights* 205-216. **1600**

Humphrey, John P. "The Right of Petition in the United Nations." (1971), 4 *Revue des Droits de l'Homme* 463-475. **1601**

Humphrey, John P. "The Role of Canada in the United Nations Program for the Promotion of Human Rights." *In* Macdonald, Ronald St. John, and others, *Canadian Perspectives on International Law and Organization* (Toronto, 1974), pp. 612-619. **1602**

Humphrey, John P. "The U.N. Charter and the Universal Declaration of Human Rights." *In* Luard, Evan, ed., *The International Protection of Human Rights* (London, 1967), pp. 39-58. **1603**

Humphrey, John P. "The United Nations and Human Rights." (1963-64), 23 *Behind the Headlines* No. 1 (26 p.) **1604**

Humphrey, John P. "The United Nations and Human Rights." (1965), 11 *Howard Law Journal* 373-378. **1605**

Humphrey, John P. "The United Nations Commission on Human Rights and Its Parent Body." *In René Cassin Amicorum Discipulorumque Liber* (Paris, 1969-1971), vol. 1, pp. 108-113. **1606**

Humphrey, John P. "A United Nations High Commissioner for Human Rights: The Birth of an Initiative." (1973), 11 *Canadian Yearbook of International Law* 220-225. **1607**

Humphrey, John P. "The Universal Declaration of Human Rights." (1949), 27 *Canadian Bar Review* 203-210. **1608**

Humphrey, John P. "The Universal Declaration of Human Rights." (1949), 4 *International Journal* 351-361. **1609**

Humphrey, John P. "The Universal Declaration of Human Rights. Its History, Impact and Juridical Character." *In* Ramcharan, B.G., ed., *Human Rights: Thirty Years after the Universal Declaration* (The Hague, 1979), pp. 21-37. **1610**

Humphrey, John P. "The World Revolution and Human Rights." *In* Gotlieb, Allan E., ed., *Human Rights, Federalism and Minorities* (Toronto, 1970), pp. 147-179. **1611**

Hunter, Ian A. "Anti-Discrimination Legislation in Great Britain and Ontario." (1981), 59 *Canadian Bar Review* 427-446. **1612**

Hunter, Ian A. "Human Rights Legislation in Canada: Its Origin, Development and Interpretation." (1976), 15 *University of Western Ontario Law Review* 21-58. **1613**

"Integrating International Law into Canadian Domestic Law: Human Rights as a Case Study / L'incorporation du droit international au droit interne canadien: le cas des droits de l'homme." (1981), 10 *Canadian Council on International Law, Proceedings,* 1-52. **1614**
  This is a panel. Chairman: John P. Humphrey.
  Contents: "The International Law of Human Rights and Canadian Courts," by John Claydon (pp. 1-21).- "Le pacte international relatif aux droits civils et politiques et sa mise en oeuvre au Canada," by Michel Lebel (pp. 22-31).- "Integrating International Human Rights Law into Domestic Law - U.S. Experience," by Richard B. Bilder (pp. 32-42).- Discussion (pp. 43-52).

"International Human Rights / Les droits de la personne au plan international." (1978), 7 *Canadian Council on International Law, Proceedings,* 188 p. **1615**
  This is the general theme of the seventh annual conference held jointly with the Canadian Human Rights Foundation (Fondation canadienne des droits de l'homme); and the International Commission of Jurists, Canadian Section (Commission internationale de juristes, section canadienne), at Ottawa, October 25-28, 1978. Individual papers are listed separately. The panels were grouped into two sections: "Human Rights and Foreign Policy / Les droits de la personne et la politique extérieure," with John P. Humphrey as General Chairman (pp. 13-82); and "The International Law of Human Rights / Les droits de la personne en droit international," with Ronald St. John Macdonald as General Chairman (pp. 83-182).

"The International Law of Human Rights: Derogation of Human Rights in Emergency Situations / Les droits de la personne en droit international: les dérogations aux droits de la personne en situations d'urgence." (1978), 7 *Canadian Council on International Law, Proceedings* 96-123. **1616**
  This is a panel. Chairman: J. W. Samuels.- Speakers: Leslie C. Green (pp. 96-106), Pierre Chénier (pp. 107-110), and K. Venkata Raman (pp. 111-118).- Discussion (pp. 119-123).

"The International Law of Human Rights: Future of Self-Determination / Les droits de la personne en droit international: l'avenir de l'auto-détermination." (1978), 7 *Canadian Council on International Law, Proceedings* 83-95. **1617**
  This is a panel. Chairman: Brian Crane.- Speakers: Gerald L. Morris (pp. 83-86), and Ivan Bernier (pp. 86-88).- Discussion (pp. 89-95).

"The International Law of Human Rights: Helsinki Accords - Disputed Rights / Les droits de la personne en droit international: les accords d'Helsinki - droits contestés." (1978), 7 *Canadian Council on International Law, Proceedings* 124-141. **1618**
  This is a panel. Chairman: Gordon Blair.- Speakers: Gabriel I. Warren (pp. 124-128), Bozidar Bakotić (pp. 129-134), and Irwin Cotler (pp. 135-141).

"The International Law of Human Rights: Human Rights Standards - Regional and Universal / Les droits de la personne en droit international: des normes régionales et universelles pour les droits de la personne." (1978), 7 *Canadian Council on International Law, Proceedings* 142-182. **1619**
  This is a panel. Chairman: Mark MacGuigan.- Speakers: Alice Desjardins (pp. 142-153), Robert Martin (pp. 154-164), and Michel de Salvia (pp. 165-173).- Discussion (pp. 173-177).- Paper submitted by Heribert Golsong (pp. 179-182).

Jacomy-Millette, Annemarie. "La Femme Nouvelle dans la vie sociale internationale des années 1970." *In* Macdonald, Ronald St. John, and others, *The*

International Law and Policy of Human Welfare (Alphen aan den Rijn, 1978), pp. 291-325. **1620**

Jamieson, Don. "Human Rights and Foreign Policy / Les droits de la personne et la politique extérieure. (Luncheon Address)." (1978), 7 *Canadian Council on International Law, Proceedings* 41-47. **1621**

Kiwanuka, Richard Ntege. *The Law of Nations and Human Rights in Uganda.* Toronto, c1979. x, 194 leaves. **1622**
Thesis (LL.M.), University of Toronto, 1976.

Kly, Yussuf Naim. *The U.S. Human Rights Foreign Policy, the Black Minority in the U.S., and International Law.* Quebec, 1979. 420 frames, map. **1623**
Thesis (Ph.D.), Université Laval, 1979. (National Library of Canada. Canadian Theses on Microfiche, No. 48006).

Lachance, Louis. *Le droit et les droits de l'homme.* Paris: Presses Universitaires de France, 1959. 238 p. (Bibliothèque de philosophie contemporaine) **1624**
Review: Paul Lacoste in (1961), 21 *Revue du Barreau* 300-303.

Lachs, Manfred. "The Gathering Concern for Human Rights." (1973), 2 *Canadian Council on International Law, Proceedings* 139-145. **1625**

Langlais, Antonio. "La Commission internationale de juristes et le Congrès d'Athènes." (1957), 17 *Revue du Barreau* 275-281. **1626**

Lebel, Michel. "Le choix de la langue d'enseignement et le droit international." (1974), 9 *Revue Juridique Thémis* 221-248. **1627**

Lebel, Michel. "Les tribunaux canadiens et la protection des droits de la personne." (1981), 12 *Revue Générale de Droit* 401-412. **1628**

Lemieux, Denis; Lachapelle, Andrée; and Lévesque, Suzanne. "La 'Loi canadienne sur les droits de la personne': une Charte méconnue." (1982), 23 *Cahiers de Droit* 277-324. **1629**

Leville, G. "Pius XII and Religious Freedom." (1967), 37 *Revue de l'Université d'Ottawa* 11-25, 269-286. **1630**

Lillich, Richard B. "Intervention to Protect Human Rights." (1969), 15 *McGill Law Journal* 205-219. **1631**

MacDermot, Niall. "The Credibility Gap in Human Rights." (1976-77), 3 *Dalhousie Law Journal* 262-274. **1632**

Macdonald, Ronald St. John. "Petitioning an International Authority." *In* Gotlieb, Allan E., ed., *Human Rights, Federalism and Minorities* (Toronto, 1970), pp. 121-144. **1633**

Macdonald, Ronald St. John. "The United Nations and the Promotion of Human Rights." *In* Macdonald, Ronald St. John, and others, *The International Law and Policy of Human Welfare* (Alphen aan den Rijn, 1978), pp. 203-237.**1634**

Macdonald, Ronald St. John. "The United Nations High Commissioner for Human Rights." (1967), 5 *Canadian Yearbook of International Law* 84-117. **1635**

Macdonald, Ronald St. John. "A United Nations High Commissioner for Human Rights: The Decline and Fall of an Initiative." (1972), 10 *Canadian Yearbook of International Law* 40-64. **1636**

Macdonald, Ronald St. John, and Humphrey, John P., eds. *The Practice of Freedom: Canadian Essays on Human Rights and Fundamental Freedoms.* Toronto: Butterworths, 1979. xx, 460 p. **1637**
Contains 24 essays by various authors.
Reviews: William E. Conklin in (1980), 6 *Canadian Public Policy* 690-692; Rainer Knopff in (1980), 13 *Canadian Journal of Political Science* 624-625; Noel Lyon in (1980), 6 *Queen's Law Journal* 318-322; David A. Townsend in (1981), 30 *University of New Brunswick Law Journal* 257-258.

Malik, Charles. "The Challenge of Human Rights." (1949), 9 *Behind the Headlines* No. 6 (17 p.) **1638**

Malik, Charles. "Human Rights in the United Nations." (1950-51), 6 *International Journal* 274-280. **1639**

McArthur, Ernest. *The International Right of Petition and the Optional Protocol to the International Covenant on Civil and Political Rights.* Montreal, 1977. viii, 199 leaves. **1640**
Thesis (LL.M.), McGill University, 1977.

McCracken, George W. "World Security and Freedom of Information." (1945), 52 *Queen's Quarterly* 91-99. **1641**

McDonald, David C. *Legal Rights in the Canadian Charter of Rights and Freedoms: A Manual of Issues and Sources.* Toronto: Carswell, 1982. xxv, 275 p. **1642**

McInnis, Edgar. "Apartheid in Action." (1955-56), 11 *International Journal* 235-242. **1643**

McRae, Donald M. "Non-Western Approaches to Human Rights." (1973), 2 *Canadian Council on International Law, Proceedings* 89-97. **1644**
See also general discussion (pp. 103-108).

McRae, K.D. "The Constitutional Protection of Linguistic Rights in Bilingual and Multilingual States." *In* Gotlieb, Allan E., ed., *Human Rights, Federalism and Minorities* (Toronto, 1970), pp. 211-227. **1645**

Mendes, Errol P. "Interpreting the Canadian Charter of Rights and Freedoms: Applying International and European Jurisprudence on the Law and Practice of Fundamental Rights." (1982), 20 *Alberta Law Review* 383-433. **1646**

Morin, Jacques-Yvan. "Une charte des droits de l'homme pour le Québec." (1963), 9 *McGill Law Journal* 273-316. **1647**

Myhal, Patricia J. "Canada's Unjustified Ratification of the Race Convention." (1972), 30 *University of Toronto Faculty of Law Review* 31-46. **1648**

New Brunswick. Human Rights Commission. *United Nations' Basic Human Rights Documents.* Fredericton: New Brunswick Human Rights Commission, 1981. 85, 90 p. **1649**
Text in English and French on inverted pages. Title in French: *Principaux documents des Nations-Unies sur les droits de l'homme.*

"The Next 25 Years in the International Law of Human Rights." (1973), 2 *Canadian Council on International Law, Proceedings,* 195 p. **1650**
This is the general theme of the second annual conference held at Ottawa, October 12-13, 1973. Individual papers are listed separately.

Nossal, Kim Richard. "Les droits de la personne et la politique étrangère canadienne: le cas de l'Indonésie." (1980), 11 *Études Internationales* 223-238. **1651**

Pearson, Geoffrey. "Emergence of Human Rights in International Relations." (1978), *International Perspectives* 9-12 (July/Aug.) **1652**

Perez-Jimenez, Fabian. *Les droits de l'homme.* Fredericton: Commission des droits de l'homme du Nouveau-Brunswick, 1971. 4 vols. in 1. **1653**

Petrenko, Alex. "The Human Rights Provisions of the United Nations Charter." (1978-79), 9 *Manitoba Law Journal* 53-92. **1654**

Pilling, A.M. "The European Convention on Human Rights: A Study in Regionalism." (1963), 21 *University of Toronto Faculty of Law Review* 93-116. **1655**

Poulantzas, Nicholas M. "International Protection of Human Rights: Implementation Procedures within the Framework of the International Labour Organization." (1972), 25 *Revue Hellénique de Droit International* 110-141. **1656**

Power, W. Kent. "Rights of Individuals in Peace and War." (1917), 37 *Canadian Law Times* 33-48. **1657**

Proulx, Daniel. "Égalité et discrimination dans la Charte des droits et libertés de la personne: étude comparative." (1979-80), 10 *Revue de Droit, Université de Sherbrooke* 381-568. **1658**
First presented as the author's thesis (LL.M.), Université de Montréal.

Proulx, Daniel. "La suprématie des droits et libertés de la personne et la question constitutionnelle au Canada." (1981), 12 *Revue Générale de Droit* 413-429. **1659**

Ramcharan, B.G. "The Emerging Jurisprudence of the Human Rights Committee." (1980-81), 6 *Dalhousie Law Journal* 7-40. **1660**

Ramcharan, B.G. "Equity in the International Law of Human Rights." (1979), 5 *Dalhousie Law Journal* 45-72. **1661**

Ryan, H.R.S. "Seeking Relief under the United Nations International Covenant on Civil and Political Rights." (1981), 6 *Queen's Law Journal* 389-407. **1662**

Sabourin, Louis. "Le fédéralisme et les conventions internationales des droits de l'homme." *In* Gotlieb, Allan E., ed., *Human Rights, Federalism and Minorities* (Toronto, 1970), pp. 67-107. **1663**

Samek, Robert A. "Untrenching Fundamental Rights." (1982), 27 *McGill Law Journal* 755-787. **1664**

Samuels, Joseph W. "A Paradox of Time: Human Rights - Late Twentieth Century." (1973), 2 *Canadian Council on International Law, Proceedings* 37-40. **1665**

Sandwell, B.K. "The State and Human Rights." (1947), 7 *Behind the Headlines* No. 2 (16 p.) **1666**

Sanon, Pierre J. "Les Nations Unies et les droits de l'homme (exposé) / The United Nations and Human Rights. (Address)." (1978), 7 *Canadian Council on International Law, Proceedings* 183-188. **1667**

Scarman, Leslie George. "Human Rights in a Plural Society: the Constitutional Problem." (1979), 13 *Law Society of Upper Canada Gazette* 281-296. **1668**

Short, David E. "Restrictions on Access to English Language Schools in Quebec: An International Human Rights Analysis." (1981), 4 *Canada-United States Law Journal* 1-38. **1669**

Sinha, S. Prakash. "The Anthropocentric Theory of International Law as a Basis for Human Rights." (1978), 10 *Case Western Reserve Journal of International Law* 469-502. **1670**

Skilling, H. Gordon. "CSCE Review Conference: Belgrade and Human Rights - Success or Failure?" (1978), *International Perspectives* 19-22 (July/Aug.) **1671**

Skilling, H. Gordon. "Organizing Hatred." (1943-44), 23 *Dalhousie Review* 11-22. **1672**

Smiley, Donald V. *The Canadian Charter of Rights and Freedoms, 1981*. Toronto: Ontario Economic Council, c1981. 71 p. (Ontario Economic Council. Discussion Paper Series) **1673**

Stripinis, Daniel, and others. "Human Rights in the Modern World." (1980), 2 *Canadian Criminology Forum* 73-80 (Spring) **1674**

Szawlowski, Richard. "The International Protection of Human Rights - A Soviet and a Polish View." (1979), 28 *International and Comparative Law Quarterly* 775-781. **1675**

Tardu, Maxime. "La conception occidentale des droits de l'homme." (1973), 2 *Canadian Council on International Law, Proceedings* 98-102. **1676**
See also general discussion (pp. 103-108).

Tarnopolsky, Walter S. "A Bill of Rights and Future Constitutional Change." (1979), 57 *Canadian Bar Review* 626-639. **1677**

Tarnopolsky, Walter S. *The Canadian Bill of Rights*. 2d rev. ed. Toronto: McClelland and Stewart, 1975. xii, 436 p. (Carleton Library, No. 83) **1678**
First edition published by Carswell in 1966.
Reviews: Gerald L. Gall in (1976), 14 *Alberta Law Review* 192-197; Herbert Marx in (1975), 53 *Canadian Bar Review* 832-837; W.A. McKean in (1976), 92 *Law Quarterly Review* 127-130; John D. Whyte in (1977), 23 *McGill Law Journal* 144-149; John D. Whyte under title: "Civil Liberties and the Courts," in (1976), 83 *Queen's Quarterly* 655-663.

Tarnopolsky, Walter S. *Discrimination and the Law in Canada*. Toronto: Richard De Boo, 1982. vii, 595 p. **1679**

Tarnopolsky, Walter S. "Freedom of Expression v. Right to Equal Treatment: The Problem of Hate Propaganda and Racial Discrimination." (1967), *University of British Columbia Law Review / Cahiers de Droit* 43-68 (Centennial ed.) **1680**

Tarnopolsky, Walter S. "The Historical and Constitutional Context of the Proposed Canadian Charter of Rights and Freedoms." (1981), 44 *Law and Contemporary Problems* 169-193. **1681**

Tarnopolsky, Walter S. "The Impact of United Nations Achievements on Canadian Laws and Practices." *In* Gotlieb, Allan E., ed., *Human Rights, Federalism and Minorities* (Toronto, 1970), pp. 54-66. **1682**

Tarnopolsky, Walter S. "The Iron Hand in the Velvet Glove: Administration and Enforcement of Human Rights Legislation in Canada." (1968), 46 *Canadian Bar Review* 565-590. **1683**

Tarnopolsky, Walter S., and Beaudoin, Gérald, eds. *The Canadian Charter of Rights and Freedoms: Commentary.* Toronto: Carswell, 1982. liii, 590 p. **1684**
Contains sixteen studies by various authors. Also issued in French.

Torrelli, Maurice, and Baudouin, Renée. *Les droits de l'homme et les libertés publiques par les textes.* Montréal: Presses de l'Université du Québec, 1972. xxv, 387 p. **1685**
Reviews: Jean-Charles Bonenfant in (1972), 13 *Cahiers de Droit* 469-470; Leslie C. Green in (1973-74), 1 *Dalhousie Law Journal* 628-632; Panayotis Soldatos in (1973), 6 *Canadian Journal of Political Science* 547-548.

Tremblay, Guy. "Les situations d'urgence qui permettent en droit international de suspendre les droits de l'homme." (1977), 18 *Cahiers de Droit* 3-60. **1686**

Tremblay, Paul. "Convention internationale sur l'élimination de toutes les formes de discrimination raciale." (1966), 26 *Revue du Barreau* 360-367. **1687**

Trudeau, Pierre Elliott. "Les droits de l'homme et la suprématie parlementaire." *In* Gotlieb, Allan E., ed., *Human Rights, Federalism and Minorities* (Toronto, 1970), pp. 3-15. **1688**

United Nations Association in Canada. *Summary of United Nations Conventions and Covenants on Human Rights / Résumé des conventions et pactes des Nations Unies sur les droits de l'homme.* Ottawa: United Nations Association in Canada, 1968? 39 p. (United Nations Association in Canada. Reference Paper, No. 1) **1689**
Contains full text of the Universal Declaration of Human Rights as well as summaries of the UN conventions based on this declaration. Text in English and French in parallel columns.

"United Nations Commission on the Status of Women." (1959), 11 *External Affairs* 140-144. **1690**

Valero, Juan J. *Implementation of Human Rights under the Covenant and Protocol on Civil and Political Rights.* Montreal, 1969. 131 leaves. **1691**
Short title: *Human Rights Implementation, Covenant and Protocol.* Thesis (LL.M.), McGill University, 1969. (National Library of Canada. Canadian Theses on Microfilm, No. 4165). Refers to the covenant and protocol adopted by the U.N. General Assembly in December 1966.

Valero, Juan J. *International Human Rights Conventions and the Canadian Context / Conventions internationales de droits de l'homme et le contexte canadien.* Ottawa: United Nations Association in Canada, 1974. 13, 13 p.
Cover title: *Ratification: Why? Why Not?* Text in English and French. **1692**

Vincke, Christian. "La mise en oeuvre des droits de l'homme dans le cadre des Nations Unies." (1973), 2 *Canadian Council on International Law, Proceedings* 31-36. **1693**

Weber, Ludwig. "Grundrechtsschutz in Kanada: Ungeschriebene Grundrechte und die kanadische Bill of Rights." (1980), 40 *Zeitschrift für Ausländisches Öffentliches Recht und Völkerrecht* 727-758. **1694**

Weiler, Paul C. "Of judges and Rights, or Should Canada Have a Constitutional Bill of Rights?" (1980-81), 60 *Dalhousie Review* 205-237. **1695**

Wilberforce, Richard Orme. "Human Rights." (1979), 13 *Law Society of Upper Canada Gazette* 124-140. **1696**

Zuijdwijk, Anthony J.M. *Petitioning in the United Nations: A Study in Human Rights.* New York: St. Martins' Press, 1982. xv, 397 p. **1697**
Originally presented as the author's thesis (D.Jur.), University of Toronto, 1979.

Zuijdwijk, Anthony J.M. *Petitions to the United Nations about Violations of Human Rights.* Toronto, 1979. vii, 635 leaves. **1698**
Thesis (D.Jur.), University of Toronto, 1979.

Zuijdwijk, Anthony J.M. "The Right to Petition the United Nations Because of Alleged Violations of Human Rights." (1981), 59 *Canadian Bar Review* 103-123. **1699**

VII. ORGANS OF THE STATE

A. Administration of External Affairs

"The Administrative Services Division." (1961), 13 *External Affairs* 257-260.
1700
Also issued in the French edition under title: *La Division des services administratifs* (pp. 261-264).

Beesley, J. Alan. "The Sixties to the Seventies: The Perspective of the Legal Adviser." *In* Macdonald, Ronald St. John, and others, *Canadian Perspectives on International Law and Organization* (Toronto, 1974), pp. 918-939. **1701**

Boyce, Peter J. "Foreign Offices and New States." (1974-75), 30 *International Journal* 141-161. **1702**

Breen, Urban. *The Canadian Parliamentary Question Period with Particular Reference to External Affairs.* Halifax, 1977 (c1978). iii, 105 leaves. **1703**
Thesis (M.A.), Dalhousie University, 1977. (National Library of Canada. Canadian Theses on Microfiche, No. 36045).

Cadieux, Marcel. "Les avocats et le ministère des Affaires extérieures." (1961), 21 *Revue du Barreau* 244-246. **1704**

Cadieux, Marcel. *Le ministère des Affaires extérieures; conseils aux étudiants qui se destinent à la carrière.* Montréal: Éditions Variétés, 1950 (c1949). 111 p.
1705

Cadieux, Marcel. "La tâche du sous-secrétaire d'État aux Affaires extérieures." (1966-67), 22 *International Journal* 512-529. **1706**

Canada. Dept. of External Affairs. *Annual Review.* 1909/10—. Ottawa. Annual.
1707
Title varies: *Report* or *Annual Report*, 1909/10-1971. *Annual Review*, 1972—. The annual reports were also issued for some time in the Sessional Papers series of Parliament. Also published in French under title: *Revue annuelle*. The annual review for 1972 also has a distinctive title: *Canadian Foreign Relations* ('Relations étrangères du Canada,' in the French edition). The English and French versions of the annual review for 1978 are bound together. Contains a very useful list of international agreements concluded by Canada during the year. The Department of External Affairs was established in 1909 (S.C. 1909, c. 13; R.S.C. 1970, c. E-20). This department is responsible for the conduct of foreign relations of Canada. It also administers the following statutes: *High Commissioners in the United Kingdom Act* (R.S.C. 1970, c. H-5); *United Nations Act* (R.S.C. 1970, c. U-3); *Territorial Sea and Fishing Zones Act* (R.S.C. 1970, c. T-7);

International Boundary Waters Treaty Act (R.S.C. 1970, c. 1-20), establishing the International Joint Commission; acts dealing with diplomatic privileges and immunities (R.S.C. 1970, cc. D-4, P-22, P-23), and others. The following autonomous agencies report to Parliament through the Secretary of State for External Affairs: Foreign Claims Commission (founded in 1970), International Boundary Commission, International Joint Commission, Canadian International Development Agency, and others.

Canada. Dept. of External Affairs. *The Department of External Affairs.* Ottawa: Supply and Services Canada, 1980. 40 p. (Canada. Dept. of External Affairs. Reference Series, No. 17) **1708**

Canada. Parliament. House of Commons. Standing Committee on External Affairs and National Defence. *Minutes of Proceedings and Evidence.* Ottawa: Queen's Printer, 1968/69—. **1709**
Formerly Standing Committee on External Affairs (1945-1968/69). Also issued in French under title: *Procès-verbaux et témoignages, Comité permanent des affaires extérieures et de la défense nationale.*

Canada. Parliament. Senate. Standing Committee on Foreign Affairs. *Proceedings of the Standing Senate Committee on Foreign Affairs / Délibérations du Comité sénatorial permanent des affaires étrangères.* Ottawa: Queen's Printer, 1968/69—. **1710**
In English and French; also issued separately.

"Canada's Passport Office." (1960), 12 *External Affairs* 527-532. **1711**

"Canada's Treaty Records." (1958), 10 *External Affairs* 162-165. **1712**

"The Canadian Foreign Service." (1953), 5 *External Affairs* 243-249. **1713**

"The Canadian Immigration Service Abroad." (1962), 14 *External Affairs* 269-271.
1714

Coghlan, F.A. "James Bryce and the Establishment of the Department of External Affairs." (1968), *Canadian Historical Association, Historical Papers* 84-93.
1715

Cohen, Maxwell. "Secrecy in Law and Policy: The Canadian Experience and International Relations." *In* Franck, Thomas M., and Weisband, Edward, eds., *Secrecy and Foreign Policy* (New York, 1974), pp. 355-376. **1716**

"Co-ordination of Canadian Policy at the United Nations." (1953), 5 *External Affairs* 12-16. **1717**

Corbett, Percy E. "Public Opinion and Canada's External Affairs." (1931), 38 *Queen's Quarterly* 1-12. **1718**

Cousineau, Rosario. "Organisation administrative publique au Canada: le ministère des Affaires extérieures." (1945), 15 *Revue de l'Université d'Ottawa* 144-156. **1719**

Dahamni, Ahmed. "Quelques aspects du management du ministère des Affaires extérieures du Canada." (1975), 18 *Canadian Public Administration* 171-188.
1720

De Pauw, Richard James. *The Changing Role of the Bureaucratic Elite in the Canadian Foreign Policy Formulation Process from 1909 to 1970; an Analysis* Ottawa, 1970. 169 leaves. **1721**
Research essay (M.A.), Carleton University, 1970.

"The Department of External Affairs." (1963), 15 *External Affairs* 178-189. **1722**

"Department of External Affairs Records." (1960), 12 *External Affairs* 791-797.
1723

Dewey, Alexander Gordon. "Parliamentary Control of External Relations in the British Dominions." (1931), 25 *American Political Science Review* 285-310.
1724

Dobell, Peter C. "The Management of a Foreign Policy for Canadians." (1970-71), 26 *International Journal* 202-220.
1725

Dobell, William M. "Interdepartmental Management in External Affairs." (1978), 21 *Canadian Public Administration* 83-102.
1726

Dobell, William M. "Is External Affairs a Central Agency? - A Question of Leadership Controls." (1979), *International Perspectives* 8-12 (May/June)
1727

Duhamel, Roger. "Le ministère canadien des Affaires extérieures." (1943), 22 *Action Nationale* 204-211.
1728

Eayrs, James George. *The Art of the Possible; Government and Foreign Policy in Canada*. Toronto: University of Toronto Press, 1966. viii, 232 p. (Canadian University Paperbooks, 49)
1729

First published in 1961. Also reprinted in 1971.
Reviews: Max Beloff in (1961-62), 17 *International Journal* 60-61; Frederic H. Soward in (1962), 43 *Canadian Historical Review* 69-70.

Eayrs, James George. "Canada: The Department of External Affairs." *In* Steiner, Zara, ed., *The Times Survey of Foreign Ministries of the World* (London, 1982), pp. 95-117.
1730

Eayrs, James George. "The Origins of Canada's Department of External Affairs." (1959), 25 *Canadian Journal of Economics and Political Science* 109-128.
1731

A revised version of this article is published in Keenleyside, Hugh L., and others, *The Growth of Canadian Policies in External Affairs* (Durham, N.C., 1960), pp. 14-32.

Eayrs, James George. "The Origins of Canada's Department of External Affairs." *In* Keenleyside, Hugh L., and others, *The Growth of Canadian Policies in External Affairs* (Durham, N.C., 1960), pp. 14-32.
1732

This paper is a revised version of the author's article published in (1959), 25 *Canadian Journal of Economics and Political Science* 109-128.

"Estimates and Their Preparation." (1951), 3 *External Affairs* 374-376. **1733**

"External Affairs Finances." (1961), 13 *External Affairs* 100-104. **1734**

"External Affairs Finances." (1963), 15 *External Affairs* 327-331. **1735**

"External Affairs Headquarters." (1970), 22 *External Affairs* 243-245. **1736**

"External Affairs Inspection Service." (1960), 12 *External Affairs* 824-826. **1737**

"External Affairs Inspection Service." (1963), 15 *External Affairs* 305-307. **1738**

"External Affairs Protocol Division." (1961), 13 *External Affairs* 69-71. **1739**

Also issued in the French edition under title: "La Division du protocole aux Affaires extérieures."

Fairweather, R. Gordon L. "The Role of Parliament in the Review and Planning of Canadian National Defence and External Affairs." *In* Franck, Thomas M., and

Weisband, Edward, eds., *Secrecy and Foreign Policy* (New York, 1974), pp. 144-162. **1740**

Farrell, Robert Barry. *Planning and Control of Canadian Foreign Policy.* Cambridge, Mass., 1953. 251 p. **1741**
Thesis (Ph.D.), Harvard University, 1953.

"The Foreign Service Officer Competition." (1953), 5 *External Affairs* 218-222. **1742**

Franck, Thomas M., and Weisband, Edward, eds. *Secrecy and Foreign Policy.* New York: Oxford University Press, 1974. xvii, 453 p. (Studies in Peaceful Change) **1743**
Includes Canada. Some individual papers are listed separately.

Fraser, Charles Frederick. "Canada's Foreign Relations." (1942-43), 22 *Dalhousie Review* 48-54. **1744**

Freifeld, Sidney A. "The Press Officer and External Affairs." (1975-76), 31 *International Journal* 255-269. **1745**

Freymond, Bernard. "Au service du Département fédéral suisse des Affaires étrangères." (1981-82), 37 *International Journal* 413-440. **1746**

Gordon, Sheldon E. *Ottawa's International Affairs Establishment: A Study of Opinion-Makers and the Mass Media.* Ottawa, 1972 (i.e. 1973). 107 leaves.
Research essay (M.A.), Carleton University, 1973. **1747**

Gotlieb, Allan E. "Legal Advisers and Foreign Affairs: A Comment." (1965-66), 16 *University of Toronto Law Journal* 158-165. **1748**

Henderson, Michael D. "La gestion des politiques internationales du gouvernement fédéral." *In* Painchaud, Paul, ed., *Le Canada et le Québec sur la scène internationale* (Québec, 1977), pp. 81-107. **1749**

Henderson, Michael D. "Planning in Canadian External Affairs." (1974), 46 *Canadian Political Science Association, Papers,* 50 p. **1750**

Hillmer, Norman. "A British High Commissioner for Canada, 1927-28." (1972-73), 1 *Journal of Imperial and Commonwealth History* 339-356. **1751**

Ignatieff, George. "Secrecy and Democratic Participation in the Formulation and Conduct of Canadian Foreign Policy." *In* Franck, Thomas M., and Weisband, Edward, eds., *Secrecy and Foreign Policy* (New York, 1974), pp. 53-68. **1752**

"Integration of the Government's External Operations." (1970), 22 *External Affairs* 354-356. **1753**

"The International Service of the Canadian Broadcasting Corporation." (1961), 13 *External Affairs* 328-333. **1754**

Keenleyside, Hugh L. "Canada's Department of External Affairs." (1946), 1 *International Journal* 189-214. **1755**

Keenleyside, Hugh L. "The Department of External Affairs." (1937-38), 44 *Queen's Quarterly* 483-495. **1756**

Keenleyside, Terence A. "The Generalist versus the Specialist: The Department of External Affairs." (1979), 22 *Canadian Public Administration* 51-71. **1757**

Keenleyside, Terence A. "Lament for a Foreign Service: The Decline of Canadian Idealism." (1980-81), 15 *Journal of Canadian Studies* 75-84 (No. 4) **1758**

Kirton, John J. *The Conduct and Coordination of Canadian Government Decision-Making Towards the United States.* Baltimore, Md., 1977. 364 leaves. **1759**
Thesis (Ph.D.), Johns Hopkins University, 1977. Abstracted in (1977/78), 38 *Dissertation Abstracts International* 463-A. (University Microfilms, Ann Arbor, No. 77-15079).

Kirton, John J. "Foreign Policy Decision-Making in the Trudeau Government: Promise and Performance." (1977-78), 33 *International Journal* 287-311. **1760**

Kohler, Larry Robert. *Parliamentary Questions, External Affairs, and the Canadian House of Commons.* Ottawa, 1970. vi, 65 leaves. **1761**
Research essay (M.A.), Carleton University, 1970.

Lalande, Gilles. *The Department of External Affairs and Biculturalism: Diplomatic Personnel (1945-1965) and Language Use (1964-1965).* Ottawa: Queen's Printer, 1969. xv, 210 p. (Canada. Royal Commission on Bilingualism and Biculturalism. Studies, 3) **1762**
Issued by the Royal Commission on Bilingualism and Biculturalism. Also published in French under title: *Le ministère des Affaires extérieures et la dualité culturelle: personnel diplomatique, 1945-1965, emploi du français, 1964-1965.*

"The Law and Diplomacy." (1944-45), 14 *Fortnightly Law Journal* 186-188. **1763**

Long, Morden H. "Sir John Rose and the Informal Beginnings of the Canadian High Commissionership." (1931), 12 *Canadian Historical Review* 23-43. **1764**

Macdonald, Flora. "Ministers, Civil Servants, and Parliamentary Democracy." (1980-81), 60 *Dalhousie Review* 238-250. **1765**

Macdonald, Ronald St. John. "The Role of the Legal Adviser of Ministries of Foreign Affairs." (1977), 156 *Académie de Droit International, Recueil des Cours* 377-482. **1766**

Mace, Gordon. *Les activités transnationales du ministère de l'Industrie et Commerce, 1960-1970.* Québec, 1974, c1978. xi, 291 leaves. **1767**
Thesis (M.Sc.Soc.), Université Laval, 1974. (National Library of Canada. Canadian Theses on Microfiche, No. 35453).

Madar, Daniel R. *Foreign Policy Planning: Its Practice and Problems in the U.S. Department of State.* Toronto, 1974. 270 leaves. **1768**
Thesis (Ph.D.), University of Toronto, 1974. (National Library of Canada. Canadian Theses on Microfiche, No. 31273).

Madar, Daniel R. "Planners, Influence, and Burcaucracy." (1974-75), 30 *International Journal* 57-79. **1769**

Madar, Daniel R., and Stairs, Denis. "Alone on Killers' Row: The Policy Analysis Group and the Department of External Affairs." (1976-77), 32 *International Journal* 727-755. **1770**

March, Roman Robert. *The Canadian Department of External Affairs; Growth and Organization, 1944-1958.* Ottawa, 1958. 152 leaves. **1771**
Thesis (M.A.), Carleton University, 1958.

Martin, Paul. "Bilingualism in the Department of External Affairs." (1967), 19 *External Affairs* 320-323. **1772**

McNaught, Kenneth. "Parliamentary Control of Foreign Policy." (1955-56), 11 *International Journal* 251-260. **1773**

McNaught, Kenneth. "Who Controls Foreign Policy? American and Canadian Contrasts." (1954), 14 *Behind the Headlines* No. 3 (17 p.) **1774**

Merillat, Herbert Christian Laing, ed. *Legal Advisers and Foreign Affairs.* Dobbs Ferry, N.Y.: Oceana Publications, 1964. x, 162 p. **1775**
Summary report and background papers of a conference on legal advisers and foreign affairs, sponsored by the American Society of International Law, held at Princeton, N.J., September 1963. Published for the American Society of International Law.

Merillat, Herbert Christian Laing, ed. *Legal Advisers and International Organizations.* Dobbs Ferry, N. Y.: Published for the American Society of International Law by Oceana Publications, 1966. xviii, 124 p. **1776**
Summary report and background papers of a conference held in Bellagio, Italy, August 1965, sponsored by the American Society of International Law.
Review: Leslie C. Green in (1966-67), 5 *Alberta Law Review* 369-370.

Millar, Thomas B. "Managing the Australian Foreign Affairs Department." (1981-82), 37 *International Journal* 441-452. **1777**

Morton, Desmond. *A Peculiar Kind of Politics: Canada's Overseas Ministry in the First World War.* Toronto: University of Toronto Press, c1982. xii, 267 p., 8 p. of plates. **1778**

Nossal, Kim Richard. "Allison through the (Ottawa) Looking Glass: Bureaucratic Politics and Foreign Policy in a Parliamentary System." (1979), 22 *Canadian Public Administration* 610-626. **1779**

"The Operations Centre of the Department of External Affairs." (1971), 23 *External Affairs* 3-5. **1780**

Osbaldeston, Gordon. "Reorganizing Canada's Department of External Affairs." (1981-82), 37 *International Journal* 453-466. **1781**

Piper, Donald C. "The Role of Intergovernmental Machinery in Canadian-American Relations." (1963), 62 *South Atlantic Quarterly* 551-574. **1782**

Plumptre, Timothy. "Diplomacy: Obsolete or Essential?" (1973), 80 *Queen's Quarterly* 503-520. **1783**

"Preparations for a Session of the General Assembly." (1959), 11 *External Affairs* 331-333. **1784**

Price, Trevor. *The Role of the House of Commons in External Affairs; a Study of Democratic Influences in Canada's Foreign Policy.* Windsor, 1968. 229 leaves. Thesis (M.A.), University of Windsor, 1968. **1785**

"The Problem of Records in External Affairs." (1952), 4 *External Affairs* 178-182. **1786**

"Protocol: Its Nature and Function." (1949), 1 *External Affairs* 8-11 (Sept.) **1787**

Read, John E. " 'The Practising Lawyer and External Affairs.' " (1939), 24 *Canadian Bar Association, Proceedings* 100-111. **1788**
The "Analysis of Civil Procedure Conventions" is annexed to this article (pp. 111-122).

Read, John E. "Problems of an External Affairs Legal Adviser, 1928-1946." (1966-67), 22 *International Journal* 376-394. **1789**

Rendel, A.M. "Policy-Makers and Opinion." (1974-75), 30 *International Journal* 80-91. **1790**

Richards, Peter Godfrey. *Parliament and Foreign Affairs.* Toronto: University of Toronto Press, 1967. 191 p. **1791**
Reviews: Marvin Gelber in (1967-68), 23 *International Journal* 298-299.

Ritchie, A.E. "Department of External Affairs Headquarters Organization." (1971), 23 *External Affairs* 194-197. **1792**

Rizos, E.J. "The Technical Assistance Project Officer: Qualities and Quandaries." (1966), 9 *Canadian Public Administration* 475-483. **1793**

Sharp, Mitchell. "How the Department of External Affairs Serves the Nation." (1970), 22 *External Affairs* 94-100. **1794**

Smith, Arnold. "The New Department of External Affairs." (1982), *International Perspectives* 13-14 (May/June) **1795**

Soward, Frederic H. *The Department of External Affairs and Canadian Autonomy, 1899-1939.* Ottawa: Canadian Historical Association, 1972. 24 p. (Canadian Historical Association. Booklets, No. 7) **1796**
Reviews: John S. Conway in (1958), 39 *Canadian Historical Review* 73-74.

Spicer, Keith. "Quelques problèmes des experts techniques canadiens à l'étranger." (1962), 5 *Canadian Public Administration* 209-218. **1797**

Steiner, Zara. "Foreign Ministries Old and New." (1981-82), 37 *International Journal* 349-377. **1798**

Stevenson, Garth. "L'élaboration de la politique étrangère canadienne." *In* Painchaud, Paul, ed., *Le Canada et le Québec sur la scène internationale* (Québec, 1977), pp. 51-79. **1799**

"The Supplies and Properties Division." (1961), 13 *External Affairs* 131-141.
This is one of five administrative divisions in the Dept. of External Affairs. **1800**

"The Supplies and Properties Division." (1963), 15 *External Affairs* 368-378. **1801**

"The Supplies and Properties Division." (1967), 19 *External Affairs* 272-278. **1802**

"Training in the Department of External Affairs." (1971), 23 *External Affairs* 316-318. **1803**

Turner, Wesley Barry. *Colonial Self-Government and the Colonial Agency; Changing Concepts of Permanent Canadian Representation in London, 1848 to 1880.* Durham, N.C., 1970 (c1971). x, 325 leaves. **1804**
Thesis (Ph.D.), Duke University, 1971. Abstracted in (1971), 32 *Dissertation Abstracts International* 1459-A. (University Microfilms, Ann Arbor, No. 71-24209).

Willoughby, William R. "Joint Canadian-American Agencies Concerned with Natural Resources and Trade." *In* Splete, Allen P., ed., *Toward a Better Understanding of Canadian-American Relations* (Canton, N.Y., 1973), pp. 84-88. **1805**
Discusses five of the sixteen joint organizations in existence: 1) the International Pacific Halibut Commission, 2) the International Pacific Salmon Fisheries Commission, 3) the Great Lakes Fishery Commission, 4) the Canada-United States Joint Committee on Trade and Economic Affairs (created in 1953), and 5) the Joint Senior Policy Committee on Production-Development Sharing (created in 1959).

Willoughby, William R. *The Joint Organizations of Canada and the United States.* Foreword by John W. Holmes. Toronto: University of Toronto Press, 1979. xi, 289 p. **1806**
Reviews: Alfred O. Hero in (1980), 11 *Études Internationales* 568-569; Peter Roff Johannson in (1980-81), 36 *International Journal* 245-247; John J. Kirton in (1981), 62 *Canadian Historical Review* 102-104; Robert I. McLaren in (1980), 23 *Canadian Public Administration* 662-663; John P. Schlegel in (1980), 10 *American Review of Canadian Studies* 98-99 (No. 2).

Winham, Gilbert R. "Negotiation as Art and Science." (1980), *International Perspectives* 24-27 (Mar./Apr.) **1807**

Wiper, James. *Le Comité permanent des Affaires extérieures: une analyse prospective (1945-1964).* Montréal, 1966. vii, 158 leaves. **1808**
Thesis (M.A.), Université de Montréal, 1966.

"Work of a Canadian Immigration Office Abroad." (1952), 4 *External Affairs* 285-287. **1809**

B. Diplomatic Service

"An Ambassador's Day." (1950), 2 *External Affairs* 206-211. **1810**

Andrew, Arthur J. "The Diplomat and the Manager." (1974-75), 30 *International Journal* 45-56. **1811**

Andrew, Arthur J. "His Ex or Telex?" (1969-70), 25 *International Journal* 676-684. **1812**

Andrew, Arthur J. "Probing the Raison d'Être of a Canadian Diplomat Abroad." (1974), *International Perspectives* 54-57 (Mar./Apr.) **1813**

Bergeron, Désiré. "La représentation diplomatique et le Canada." (1945), 15 *Revue de l'Université d'Ottawa* 77-87. **1814**

Bonardelli, Peter M. "Canada's Foreign Service: Some Notes on Its Origins to Modern Times." (1956), 17 *Culture* 31-38. **1815**

Bothwell, Robert. "Canadian Representation at Washington: A Study in Colonial Responsibility." (1972), 53 *Canadian Historical Review* 125-148. **1816**

Cadieux, Marcel. *The Canadian Diplomat; an Essay in Definition.* Toronto: University of Toronto Press, c1963. x, 113 p. **1817**
Translation of: *Le diplomate canadien; éléments d'une définition* (Montréal, Fides, c1962. 125 p.; Bibliothèque économique et sociale). Translated by Archibald Day. Published under the auspices of the Canadian Institute of International Affairs.
Reviews: Sir William Hayter in (1963-64), 19 *International Journal* 389-399; Frederic H. Soward in (1964), 45 *Canadian Historical Review* 324.

Cadieux, Marcel. "La formation juridique et la carrière diplomatique." (1955-56), 6 *Thémis* 240-244. **1818**

Canada. Royal Commission on Conditions of Foreign Service. *Report.* Ottawa: Supply and Services Canada, 1981. xi, 443 p. **1819**

Pamela A. McDougal, Commissioner. Also issued in French under title: *Commission royale d'enquête sur la situation dans le service extérieur.*
Contents: Part I. Report of the Royal Commission on Conditions of Foreign Service.- Part II. Staff Reports.- Part III. Background Papers.- Appendices.

"Canadian Ambassador at Washington." (1921-22), 12 *Round Table* 170-173. **1820**

"The Canadian Diplomatic Service." (1928-29), 19 *Round Table* 837-845. **1821**

Chevallier, Jean-Jacques. "Le droit de représentation diplomatique distincte des Dominions britanniques et de l'État libre d'Irlande." (1932), 13 *Revue de Droit International et de Législation Comparée* 277-301 (3. sér.) **1822**

Cohen, Martin Bernard. *The First Legation: Canadian Diplomacy and the Opening of Relations with the United States.* Washington, D.C., 1975. iv, 292 leaves, maps. **1823**
 Thesis (Ph.D.), George Washington University, 1975. Abstracted in (1976), 37 *Dissertation Abstracts International* 513-A. (University Microfilms, Ann Arbor, No. 76-10606).

"Diplomatic Dress." (1967), 19 *External Affairs* 439-442. **1824**

Donneur, André P. "Advocating Scientific Approach for Diplomats and Academics." (1974), *International Perspectives* 47-49 (Jan./Feb.) **1825**

Eayrs, James George. *Diplomacy and Its Discontents.* Toronto: University of Toronto Press, c1971. xi, 198 p. **1826**
 Review: Andrew Brewin in (1972), 79 *Queen's Quarterly* 551-552.

Eayrs, James George. "The Diplomatic Eye." (1976-77), 56 *Dalhousie Review* 205-220. **1827**

Eltscher, Louis Robert, III. *A Study of Various Problems Encountered in Establishing a Canadian Legation in Washington, D.C.* Washington, D.C., 1959. 1 vol. **1828**
 Thesis (M.A.), American University, 1959. Abstracted in (1962/63), 1 *Masters Abstracts* 41 (No. 1). (University Microfilms, Ann Arbor, No. M-127).

Fleury, Serge. "Diplomatie courtoise et foraine." (1948-49), 3 *Revue de l'Université Laval* 707-710. **1829**

Fleury, Serge. "La diplomatie courtoise et la diplomatie foraine." (1948-49), 3 *Revue de l'Université Laval* 499-503. **1830**

Fleury, Serge. "La diplomatie de plein vent." (1948-49), 3 *Revue de l'Université Laval* 609-616. **1831**

"The Foreign Service Officer Competition." (1958), 10 *External Affairs* 225-229. **1832**

Fraser, Blair. "Our Diplomats at Work." (1945), 5 *Behind the Headlines* No. 3 (31 p.) **1833**

Galbraith, John S. *The Establishment of Canadian Diplomatic Status at Washington.* Berkeley: University of California Press, 1951. 119 p. (University of California. Publications in History, Vol. 41) **1834**
 Review: H. Gordon Skilling in (1952), 33 *Canadian Historical Review* 292-293.

Greenwood, J.W. "Scientists as Diplomats." (1971), 23 *External Affairs* 125-140. **1835**

"Growth of the Canadian Foreign Service." (1966), 18 *External Affairs* 240-242. **1836**

Hardy, Allison Taylor. "Women: Always Diplomatic and More Recently Diplomats." (1976), *International Perspectives* 26-32 (July/Aug.) **1837**

Jackson, *Sir* Geoffrey, and others. "Canada's Royal Commission on Conditions of Foreign Service." (1981-82), 37 *International Journal* 378-412. **1838**
Contributions by Lord Garner, Rufus Z. Smith, Martin F. Herz, and J.L. Granatstein.

Kasurak, Peter C. *The United States Legation at Ottawa, 1927-1941: An Institutional Study.* Durham, N.C., 1976. vi, 249 leaves, maps. **1839**
Thesis (Ph.D.), Duke University, 1976. Abstracted in (1977), 37 *Dissertation Abstracts International* 4562-A. (University Microfilms, Ann Arbor, No. 77-1074).

Keenleyside, Terence A. "Career Attitudes of Canadian Foreign Service Officers." (1976), 19 *Canadian Public Administration* 208-226. **1840**

Kyer, Clifford Ian. *The Papal Legate and the 'Solemn' Papal Nuncio 1243-1378: The Changing Pattern of Papal Representation.* Toronto, c1979. vi, 248 leaves. **1841**
Thesis (Ph.D.), University of Toronto, 1979. (National Library of Canada. Canadian Theses on Microfiche, No. 42247).

Lavenir, Hervé. "Le français, langue diplomatique." (1951), 21 *Revue de l'Université d'Ottawa* 484-493. **1842**

Leclerc, Marc. "Notre représentation commerciale à l'étranger." (1940-41), 16/1 *Actualité Économique* 239-254. **1843**

MacDermot, T.W.L. "Training for the Foreign Service." (1949), 4 *International Journal* 24-32. **1844**

Malabard, Jean. "Langues internationales: langue française." (1947-48), 2 *Revue de l'Université Laval* 41-50. **1845**

Maybee, Jack. "Foreign Service Consolidation." (1980), *International Perspectives* 17-20 (July/Aug.) **1846**

Mayrand, Léon. "La carrière diplomatique." (1949), 19 *Revue de l'Université d'Ottawa* 174-186. **1847**

Mayrand, Léon. "Notre droit de légation." (1935-36), 11/2 *Actualité Économique* 247-261. **1848**

Murray, David R. "Canada's First Diplomatic Missions in Latin America." (1974), 16 *Journal of Inter-American Studies and World Affairs* 153-172. **1849**

"Notre représentation aux États-Unis." (1926-27), 5 *Revue du Droit* 621. **1850**

Parent, Georges-Henri. "La représentation commerciale du Canada à l'étranger." (1953-54), 29 *Actualité Économique* 105-137. **1851**

Patry, André. "Le Canada dans les capitales du Commonwealth." (1948), 54/1 *Revue Dominicaine* 40-47. **1852**

Patry, André. *Étude sur l'origine et l'évolution du service diplomatique et consulaire canadien.* Québec, 1947. 65 leaves. **1853**
Thesis (M.Sc.Soc.), Université Laval, 1947.

Pelletier, Jean, and Adams, Claude. *The Canadian Caper.* Toronto: Macmillan of Canada, 1981. 239 p., 16 p. of plates. **1854**

Also published in French under title: *Evadés d'Iran* (Montréal: Éditions La Presse, 1981).
Review: John Starnes under title: "Pelletier's Canadian Caper," in (1980-81), *International Perspectives* 29-30 (May/June).

Penisson, Bernard. "Le Commissariat canadien à Paris (1882-1928)." (1980), 34 *Revue d'Histoire de l'Amérique Française* 357-376. **1855**

Pilon, Raphaël. *La représentation canadienne à l'étranger.* Ottawa, 1946. x, 120 leaves. **1856**
Thesis (M.A.), University of Ottawa, 1946.

"The Recruiting of Foreign Service Officers." (1960), 12 *External Affairs* 778-783. **1857**

"Recruitment of University Graduates." (1966), 18 *External Affairs* 344-349. **1858**

Reid, Escott. "The Conscience of the Diplomat: A Personal Testament." (1967), 74 *Queen's Quarterly* 574-592. **1859**

Ritchie, Charles. "What Are Diplomats Made Of?" (1974-75), 30 *International Journal* 15-23. **1860**

Savard, Pierre. "L'ambassade de Francisque Gay au Canada en 1948-49." (1974), 44 *Revue de l'Université d'Ottawa* 5-31. **1861**

Sharp, Mitchell. "The Languages of Canadian Diplomacy." (1968), 20 *External Affairs* 410-414. **1862**
An address to officers of the Department of External Affairs.

Skilling, H. Gordon. "Canada's Foreign Trade Service." (1946-47), 2 *International Journal* 325-337. **1863**

Skilling, H. Gordon. "The Canadian Diplomatic Service." (1945-46), 9 *Public Affairs* 23-27. **1864**

Skilling, H. Gordon. *Canadian Representation Abroad, from Agency to Embassy.* Toronto: Ryerson Press, 1945. 359 p. (Studies in International Affairs, No. 1) Published under the auspices of the Canadian Institute of International Affairs. **1865**
Reviews: Henry F. Angus in (1946), 1 *International Journal* 370-371; G.P. de T. Glazebrook in (1947), 13 *Canadian Journal of Economics and Political Science* 126-127; D.C. Harvey in (1946-47), 26 *Dalhousie Review* 390-391; Heather Joan Harvey in (1947), 23 *International Affairs* 101; Francis R. Scott in (1946), 24 *Canadian Bar Review* 639-640; Frederic H. Soward in (1946), 27 *Canadian Historical Review* 437-438; unsigned in (1947-48), 7 *University of Toronto Law Journal* 287-288.

Skilling, H. Gordon. "The Development of Canada's Permanent External Representation." (1943), *Canadian Historical Association, Historical Papers* 82-93. **1866**

Skilling, H. Gordon. "The Rise of a Canadian Diplomatic Service." (1947), 9 *Journal of Politics* 211-225. **1867**

"Some Aspects of Foreign Service Administration." (1952), 4 *External Affairs* 62-66. **1868**

Stambrook, F. " 'Resourceful in Expedients' - Some Examples of Ambassadorial Policy-Making in the Inter-War Period." (1973), *Canadian Historical Association, Historical Papers* 301-320. **1869**

Stigger, Philip. "A Study in Confusion: Canadian Diplomatic Staffing Practices in

Africa and the Middle East." (1971), 5 *Canadian Journal of African Studies* 241-262. **1870**

Swanson, Roger Frank. "Canadian Diplomatic Representation in the United States." (1975), 18 *Canadian Public Administration* 366-398. **1871**

Sylvestre, Guy. "Canada's First Legation." (1952-53), 59 *Queen's Quarterly* 53-62. **1872**
On February 18, 1927, Vincent Massey became the first chief of a Canadian diplomatic mission formally accredited to a foreign Chief of State (U.S. President Coolidge), and the Canadian Legation in Washington became the first permanent diplomatic mission established abroad by Canada.

C. Consular Service

Audet, Francis-J. "Les représentants de la France au Canada au XIXe siècle." (1939), 4 *Cahiers des Dix* 197-222. **1873**

Buick, Glen. "Consuls Lend a Helping Hand to Innocents Abroad - and Others." (1977), *International Perspectives* 23-27 (July/Aug.) **1874**

"The Canadian Consular Service." (1949), 1 *External Affairs* 25-27 (June) **1875**

"Canadian Consular Work Abroad." (1959), 11 *External Affairs* 334-338. **1876**

"Canadian Consular Work Abroad." (1963), 15 *External Affairs* 205-210. **1877**

Cederbalk, S. "Consular Formalities." (1957), 64 *Canadian Banker* 140-143 (No. 2) **1878**

Chappell, Joseph J. "A United States Consulate in Canada." (1962), 5 *Canadian Public Administration* 200-208. **1879**

"Consular Status, Immunities and Privileges, Vienna Conference, 1963." (1963), 15 *External Affairs* 244-248. **1880**

"Neutral Consuls in War-Time." (1913), 33 *Canadian Law Times* 300-302. **1881**

Patry, André. "Le service consulaire du Canada." (1947), 53/2 *Revue Dominicaine* 230-236. **1882**

Portes, Jacques. "L'établissement du réseau d'agences consulaires françaises au Canada (1850-1970)." (1977), 3 *Études Canadiennes (France)* 59-71. **1883**

Renton, A. Wood. "The Development of the Commercial Consulate." (1931), 9 *Canadian Bar Review* 718-723. **1884**

Savard, Pierre. *Le consulat général de France à Québec et à Montréal de 1859 à 1914.* Québec: Presses de l'Université Laval, 1970. 132 p. (Cahiers de l'Institut d'histoire, 15) **1885**
Reviews: Robert Bothwell in (1972), 53 *Canadian Historical Review* 325-326; G. Dethan in (1970), 84 *Revue d'Histoire Diplomatique* 375.

Shields, Robert A. "Imperial Policy and the Role of Foreign Consuls in Canada 1870-1911." (1979-80), 59 *Dalhousie Review* 717-747. **1886**

Swanson, Roger Frank. "Canadian Consular Representation in the United States." (1977), 20 *Canadian Public Administration* 342-369. **1887**

D. Privileges and Immunities

See also *"Immunity of Foreign States" (p. 164).*

Arbour, Jean-Maurice. "Aspects juridiques de la crise américano-iranienne." (1980), 21 *Cahiers de Droit* 367-397. **1888**

Baillie, C.P.F. "Beyond Cannon Shot: Taxation of Foreign Governments." (1966), 14 *Canadian Tax Journal* 182-185. **1889**

"The Canadian Spy Case: Admissibility in Evidence of Stolen Embassy Documents *(Rose* v. *The King,* (1947) 3 D.L.R. 618)." (1947-48), 15 *University of Chicago Law Review* 404-409. **1890**

"Diplomatic Immunities and Privileges: Vienna Conference, 1961." (1961), 13 *External Affairs* 226-229. **1891**

"Diplomatic Immunity." (1949), 1 *External Affairs* 23-24 (July) **1892**

"Diplomatic Privileges and Immunities." (1959), 11 *External Affairs* 374-378. **1893**

Dufour, André. "La protection des immunités diplomatiques et consulaires au Canada." (1973), 11 *Canadian Yearbook of International Law* 123-165. **1894**

Dufour, André. "La protection des immunités diplomatiques et consulaires au Canada: II - Les problèmes que soulève la mise en oeuvre des conventions de Vienne." (1974), 12 *Canadian Yearbook of International Law* 3-37. **1895**

Freifeld, Sidney A. "Diplomatic Hostage-Taking: A Retrospective Look at Bogota." (1980), *International Perspectives* 13-18 (Sept./Oct.) **1896**

Green, Leslie C. "Niceties and Necessities - the Case for Diplomatic Immunity." (1980), *International Perspectives* 19-23 (Mar./Apr.) **1897**

Green, Leslie C. "The Tehran Embassy Incident - Legal Aspects." (1980-81), 19 *Archiv des Völkerrechts* 1-22. **1898**

Green, Leslie C. "The Tehran Embassy Incident and International Law." (1980-81), 38 *Behind the Headlines* No. 1 (22 p.) **1899**

Green, Leslie C. "Trends in the Law concerning Diplomats." (1981), 19 *Canadian Yearbook of International Law* 132-157. **1900**

"Hostage Taking and Diplomatic Immunity / Les prises d'otage et l'immunité diplomatique." (1980), 62 *Canadian Bar Association, Proceedings* 227-261. **1901**

This is a Panel. Addresses by David Matas (pp. 227-231), Kenneth Taylor (pp. 231-238), L.H. Legault (pp. 238-247), John Jones, Jr. (pp. 248-255), and Robert H. Simmonds (pp. 256-261).

Laskin, Bora. "International Law - Liability of Foreign Legations and High Commissioners' Residences to Local Taxation. *(Reference re Powers of Municipalities to Levy Rates on Foreign Legations and High Commissioners' Residences,* (1943) 2 D.L.R. 481; (1943) S.C.R. 208). (Case Note)." (1943), 21 *Canadian Bar Review* 506-509. **1902**

Lee, Edward G., and April, Serge. "Behind-the-Scenes Negotiation of Treaty to Protect Diplomats." (1975), *International Perspectives* 3-7 (May/June) **1903**

Lee, Edward G., and Vechsler, Michael J. "Sovereign, Diplomatic, and Consular Immunities." *In* Macdonald, Ronald St. John, and others, *Canadian Perspectives on International Law and Organization* (Toronto, 1974), pp. 184-206.
1904

Legault, L.H. "Hostage Taking and Diplomatic Immunity." (1980-81), 11 *Manitoba Law Journal* 359-365. **1905**

Poulantzas, Nicholas M. "Some Problems of International Law Connected with Urban Guerrilla Warfare: The Kidnapping of Members of Diplomatic Missions, Consular Offices and Other Foreign Personnel." (1972), 3 *Annales d'Études Internationales* 137-167. **1906**

Przetacznik, Franciszek. "Les pouvoirs découlant pour l'état accréditaire de l'inviolabilité personelle de l'agent diplomatique." (1971), 17 *McGill Law Journal* 360-404. **1907**

Read, Horace E. "International Law - Diplomatic Privilege - Waiver - Legal Liability. Dickinson v. Del Solar, (1930) 1 K.B. 376. (Case Note)." (1931), 9 *Canadian Bar Review* 444-447. **1908**

Smith, Ernest H. "Tax Immunities. Part I - Tax Immunities of Diplomats under Canadian Federal Law." (1960), 8 *Canadian Tax Journal* 318-324. **1909**

Taylor, Kenneth. "Kenneth Taylor's Press Conference after Escape of 'the Six' from Iran." (1980), *International Perspectives* 5-13 (Jan./Feb.) **1910**

Vaillancourt, Benoit. "De la possibilité de contraindre consuls et diplomates à comparaître en cour comme témoins ou accusés ou de les incarcérer." (1961), 21 *Revue du Barreau* 421-430. **1911**

E. Trade and Special Missions, Etc.

Boyer, J. MacLeod. "Some Experiences of a Canadian Trade Commissioner." (1952), 59 *Canadian Banker* 117-125 (No. 3) **1912**

Douglas, Dudley G.W. "Canadian Trade Missions and Canadian Participation in Trade Fairs Abroad." (1962), 69 *Canadian Banker* 96-101 (No. 4) **1913**

Duncan, James S. "The Canadian Trade Mission to the United Kingdom." (1958), 56 *Canadian Geographical Journal* 202-209. **1914**

"Representation of Canada at Washington." (1920-21), 11 *Round Table* 153-160.
1915

Ryan, Michael H. "The Status of Agents on Special Mission in Customary International Law." (1978), 16 *Canadian Yearbook of International Law* 157-196.
1916

Smith, David E. "Provincial Representation Abroad: The Office of Agent General in London." (1975-76), 55 *Dalhousie Review* 315-327. **1917**

Turner, John H.F. "The Canadian Trade Mission to the United Kingdom." (1958), 65 *Canadian Banker* 23-32 (No. 1) **1918**

VIII. LAW OF TREATIES

A. General

Baldwin, John R. *Canada and the International Political Agreements of the Post-War Period, 1918-1932.* Toronto, 1934. 220 leaves. **1919**
Thesis (M.A.), University of Toronto, 1934.

Borchard, Edwin M. *Opinion on the Question Whether the St. Lawrence Waterway and Power Project Can Be Concluded by Executive Agreement with Canada or Requires a Treaty.* Washington: B.S. Adams, 1944. 63 p. **1920**

Burchill, R.W. "Commentary on Some Treaties Signed by Canada in 1979." (1980), 18 *Canadian Yearbook of International Law* 384-392. **1921**

Choquette, Guy. "Commentary on Some Treaties Signed by Canada in 1980." (1981), 19 *Canadian Yearbook of International Law* 401-425. **1922**

Coffin, William F. "How Treaty-Making Unmade Canada." (1876), 9 *Canadian Monthly and National Review* 349-359. **1923**

Cohen, Maxwell. "Canada-United States Treaty Relations: Trends and Future Problems." *In* Deener, David R., ed., *Canada-United States Treaty Relations* (Durham, N.C., 1963), pp. 185-195. **1924**

Constas, Dimitrios C. "Legal and Political Aspects of Intra-Community Conventions." (1981-82), 5 *Revue d'Intégration Européenne* 201-220. **1925**

De Blois, Denis Grégoire. "Commentary on Some Treaties Signed by Canada in 1977." (1978), 16 *Canadian Yearbook of International Law* 429-444. **1926**

Deener, David R., ed. *Canada-United States Treaty Relations.* Durham, N.C.: Published for the Duke University Commonwealth-Studies Center, by Duke University Press; London: Cambridge University Press, 1963. xiv, 250 p. (Duke University. Commonwealth-Studies Center. Publication, No. 19) **1927**
Several of the contributors are Canadians. Contains ten papers by individual authors, and a list of Canada-United States treaties and agreements (1782-1960), a bibliographical note, and an index. Individual papers are listed separately
Reviews: Peter W. Brown in (1964), 40 *British Year Book of International Law* 396-398; L. Erades in (1965), 12 *Netherlands International Law Review* 166-167; J.E.S. Fawcett in (1964), 13 *International and Comparative Law Quarterly* 1503; H.S. Ferns in (1964), 40 *International Affairs* 569; Wolfgang G. Friedmann under title: "Canadian Approaches in International Law," in (1963-64), 19 *International Journal* 77-83; J. Frowein in (1964), 24 *Zeitschrift für Ausländisches Öffentliches Recht und Völkerrecht* 318; Charles Rousseau in (1964), 68 *Revue Générale de Droit International Public* 260-261; Albert E. Utton in (1965), 59 *American Journal of International Law* 675-677.

"Entente on Cultural Co-operation between France and Quebec." (1965), 17 *External Affairs* 520-523. **1928**
Includes the text of the entente of November 24, 1965, assented to by the Canadian Government the same day.

Fawcett, J.E.S. "Treaty Relations of British Overseas Territories." (1949), 26 *British Year Book of International Law* 86-107. **1929**

Gotlieb, Allan E. "Canadian Treaty-Making: Informal Agreements and Interdepartmental Arrangements." *In* Macdonald, Ronald St. John, and others, *Canadian Perspectives on International Law and Organization* (Toronto, 1974), pp. 229-243. **1930**

Graham, A.M. "The Effects of Domestic Hostilities on Public and Private International Agreements: A Tentative Approach." (1964), 3 *Western Law Review* 128-149. **1931**

Hackworth, Green Haywood. "General Aspects of Canadian-United States Treaty Relations: Their Import for the Conduct of Relations between Nations on the Basis of Respect for Law and Mutual Interests." *In* Deener, David R., ed., *Canada-United States Treaty Relations* (Durham, N.C., 1963), pp. 123-134. **1932**

Humphrey, John P. "La nature juridique de la Déclaration universelle des droits de l'homme." (1981), 12 *Revue Générale de Droit* 397-400. **1933**

Jacomy-Millette, Annemarie. "Les accords bilatéraux du Canada en matière d'assistance au développement international avant l'élaboration de la nouvelle stratégie: fluidité et pragmatisme des concepts juridiques." (1975), 6 *Revue Générale de Droit* 165-184. **1934**

Jacomy-Millette, Annemarie. *L'introduction et l'application des traités internationaux au Canada.* Paris, 1966. 290 leaves. **1935**
Thesis (Doctorat), Université de Paris, 1966.

Jacomy-Millette, Annemarie. *L'introduction et l'application des traités internationaux au Canada.* Préface de Charles Rousseau. Paris: Librairie générale de droit et de jurisprudence, 1971. viii, 357 p. (Bibliothèque de droit international, t. 61) **1936**
Translated into English under title: *Treaty Law in Canada* (Ottawa, 1975).
Reviews: C. Lloyd Brown-John in (1974), 5 *Études Internationales* 730-731; André Dufour in (1972), 10 *Canadian Yearbook of International Law* 347-349; Kenneth James Keith in (1972), 66 *American Journal of International Law* 881-882; J.G. Merrills in (1971), 45 *British Year Book of International Law* 464-465; Francis Rigaldies in (1972), 7 *Revue Juridique Thémis* 413-418; Charles Rousseau in (1971), 75 *Revue Générale de Droit International Public* 889-890; signed D. S. in (1973), 9 *Revue Belge de Droit International* 385-386.

Jacomy-Millette, Annemarie. *Treaty Law in Canada.* Ottawa: University of Ottawa Press, 1975. xviii, 431 p. (Université d'Ottawa. Faculté de droit. Collection des travaux. Monographies juridiques, no 8) **1937**
Translation by Thomas V. Helwig of: *L'introduction et l'application des traités internationaux au Canada.*
Reviews: Jean-Charles Bonenfant in (1976), 17 *Cahiers de Droit* 554-556; Michel Distel in (1976), 28 *Revue Internationale de Droit Comparé* 422; Leslie C. Green in (1976), 8 *Ottawa Law Review* 678-682; Gerald V. La Forest in (1976), 14 *Canadian Yearbook of*

International Law 399-401; René H. Mankiewicz in (1977), 8 *Études Internationales* 119-121; Christopher J. Wydrzynski in (1977), 23 *McGill Law Journal* 562-564; unsigned in (1976), 80 *Revue Générale de Droit International Public* 662-663 (brief notice).

Jennings, *Sir* William Ivor. "Dominion Legislation and Treaties." (1937), 15 *Canadian Bar Review* 455-463. **1938**

Johnston, Douglas M. "Chinese Treaty Behaviour: Experiments in Analysis." *In* Dial, Roger L, ed., *Advancing and Contending Approaches to the Study of Chinese Foreign Policy* (Halifax, 1974), pp. 385-396. **1939**

Johnston, Douglas M. "Treaty Analysis and Communist China: Preliminary Observations." (1967), 61 *American Society of International Law, Proceedings* 126-134. **1940**

Knox, *Sir* Geoffrey. "Treaty Revision and Revisionism." (1945-46), 15 *University of Toronto Quarterly* 27-36. **1941**

Lawford, Hugh J. "Commonwealth Treaty Research Programme." (1970), 64 *American Journal of International Law* 925-927. **1942**

MacKenzie, Norman A.M. "Two Recent Canadian Treaties." (1925), 6 *British Year Book of International Law* 191-192. **1943**
Refers to the halibut fisheries treaty with the United States of March 2, 1923 (BTS 18(1925); 117 BFSP 382; 43 Stat. 1841; TS 701; 12 Bevans 394; 32 LNTS 93), and the commercial convention with Belgium of July 3, 1924 (BTS 7(1925); 32 LNTS 36), both concluded by Canada on its own behalf.

McRae, Donald M. "Co-operation Agreements and the Law Relating to Agreements Concluded by International Organizations." *In* Zemanek, K., ed., *Agreements of International Organizations and the Vienna Convention on the Law of Treaties* (New York, 1971), pp. 1-55. **1944**

Parry, Jack O. "Commentary on Some Treaties Signed by Canada in 1978." (1979), 17 *Canadian Yearbook of International Law* 417-430. **1945**

Read, John E. "International Agreements." (1948), 26 *Canadian Bar Review* 520-532. **1946**

Rohn, Peter H. "Canada in the United Nations Treaty Series: A Global Perspective." (1966), 4 *Canadian Yearbook of International Law* 102-130. **1947**

Shields, Robert A. "The Canadian Treaty Negotiations with France: A Study in Imperial Relations, 1878-83." (1967), 40 *Bulletin of the Institute of Historical Research* 186-202. **1948**

"Some Aspects of Canadian Treaty Law and Practice." (1967), 19 *External Affairs* 369-376. **1949**
This article is based on lectures given by a former head of the Treaty Section to university students in the Ottawa area.

Stanford, Joseph S. "United Nations Law of Treaties Conference: First Session." (1969), 19 *University of Toronto Law Journal* 59-68. **1950**

Stanford, Joseph S. "The Vienna Convention on the Law of Treaties." (1970), 20 *University of Toronto Law Journal* 18-47. **1951**

Stewart, Robert B. *Treaty Relations of the British Commonwealth of Nations.* Foreword by W.Y. Elliott. Published for the Bureau of International Research, Harvard University and Radcliffe College. New York: Macmillan, 1939. xxi, 503 p., map. **1952**

Includes Canada. Originally presented as a dissertation (Ph.D.), Harvard University, 1938.
Reviews: Percy E. Corbett in (1939), 33 *American Journal of International Law* 806-807; Norman A.M. MacKenzie in (1941), 7 *Canadian Journal of Economics and Political Science* 127-129; unsigned in (1939-40), 3 *University of Toronto Law Journal* 506-507.

Wilson, Robert R. "Canada-United States Treaty Relations and International Law." *In* Deener, David R., ed., *Canada-United States Treaty Relations* (Durham, N.C., 1963), pp. 3-27. **1953**

B. Treaty-Making Power

Allin, C.D. "Canada's Treaty Making Power." (1925-26), 24 *Michigan Law Review* 249-276. **1954**

Cameron, J.D. "International Treaties in Relation to Legislative Power." (1922), 42 *Canadian Law Times* 10-17. **1955**

Canada. Parliament. "Treaties." Ottawa, 1911. (Canada. Parliament, 1911. Sessional Papers, No. 208, pp. 344-350) **1956**
Discussion at the Imperial Conference, June 16, 1911.

"Le Canada et les traités." (1926-27), 5 *Revue du Droit* 235-240. **1957**

Chevallier, Jean-Jacques. "Les Dominions britanniques et le droit de traiter." (1929), 4 *Revue de Droit International* 67-134. **1958**

Das, S.K. "Canadian Experience and the Treaty-Making Power in the Government of India Act, 1935." (1938), 20 *Journal of Comparative Legislation and International Law* 204-209 (3d Ser.) **1959**

Deener, David R. "The Treaty Power in Canada." *In* Keenleyside, Hugh L., and others, *The Growth of Canadian Policies in External Affairs* (Durham, N.C., 1960), pp. 81-98. **1960**

Deener, David R. "Treaty Powers in a Federal-Parliamentary System: Case of Canada." (1959), 53 *American Society of International Law, Proceedings* 288-293. **1961**
See also comments by Gertrude C.K. Leighton at pp. 311-314.

Delisle, R.J. "Treaty-Making Power in Canada." *In* Ontario Advisory Committee on Confederation, *Background Papers and Reports* (Toronto, 1967), pp. 115-147. **1962**

Di Marzo, Luigi. *Component Units of Federal States and International Agreements.* Alphen aan den Rijn: Sijthoff & Noordhoff, 1980. xxvi, 244 p. **1963**
Revised and up-dated thesis (Ph.D.), submitted at the Graduate Institute of International Studies at Geneva in December 1977.

Di Marzo, Luigi. "The Legal Status of Agreements Concluded by Component Units of Federal States with Foreign Entities." (1978), 16 *Canadian Yearbook of International Law* 197-229. **1964**

Dumouchel, Jean. "La conquête de notre droit de traiter avant la Grande-Guerre." (1940-41), 16/2 *Actualité Économique* 1-24. **1965**

Dumouchel, Jean. "Le status international du Canada et les traités d'après-guerre (1918-1930)." (1941-42), 17/2 *Actualité Économique* 248-264. **1966**

Edmonds, William L. "Canada and the Treaty-Making Power." (1920-21), 13 *Current History* 467-469. **1967**

Elkin, Alexander B. "De la compétence du Canada pour conclure les traités internationaux; étude sur le statut juridique des Dominions britanniques." (1938), 45 *Revue Générale de Droit International Public* 658-693. **1968**

FitzGerald, Gerald F. "Educational and Cultural Agreements and Ententes: France, Canada, and Quebec - Birth of a New Treaty-Making Technique for Federal States?" (1966), 60 *American Journal of International Law* 529-537.
1969

Gotlieb, Allan E. *Canadian Treaty-Making.* Toronto: Butterworths, 1968. xi, 107 p.
1970

Reviews: Ian Brownlie in (1969), 18 *International and Comparative Law Quarterly* 1029-1030; David R. Deener in (1969-70), 25 *International Journal* 223-224; L. Erades in (1971), 18 *Netherlands International Law Review* 248 (in Dutch); L. Gordon Jahnke in (1969), 7 *Canadian Yearbook of International Law* 361-362; D.P. O'Connell in (1969), 15 *McGill Law Journal* 357-358; Joseph W. Samuels in (1967-68), 7 *Alberta Law Review* 171-172; Robert R. Wilson in (1970), 64 *American Journal of International Law* 465.

Gotlieb, Allan E. "The Method of Canadian Treaty-Making." (1964-68), 1 *Canadian Legal Studies* 181-215. **1971**

Hartmann, Gunther. "The Capacity of International Organizations to Conclude Treaties." *In* Zemanek, K., ed., *Agreements of International Organizations and the Vienna Convention on the Law of Treaties* (New York, 1971), pp. 127-163.
1972

Hendry, James M. "Constitutionalism and the Treaty." (1953-54), 10 *University of Toronto Law Journal* 176-189. **1973**

Hendry, James M. *Treaties and Federal Constitutions.* Foreword by William W. Bishop, Jr. Washington: Public Affairs Press, 1955. v, 186 p. **1974**
A study of the constitutional limits of Canada, Australia, the United States, and Switzerland with regard to treaty-making.
Reviews: Robert B. Looper in (1956), 50 *American Journal of International Law* 704-707; Ronald St. John Macdonald in (1956), 34 *Canadian Bar Review* 489-490; Ronald St. John Macdonald in (1957), 23 *Canadian Journal of Economics and Political Science* 590-591.

Hill, Edward Albert. *The Extension of the Canadian Treaty-Making Power.* Toronto, 1924 (c1977). 277 leaves. **1975**
Thesis (M.A.), University of Toronto, 1924. (National Library of Canada. Canadian Theses on Microfiche, No. 31236).

Hodgins, Thomas. "Canada and the Treaty-Making Power." (1903-04), 22 *Canadian Magazine* 479-482. **1976**

Ianni, Ronald W. *Le 'treaty-making power' de la province de Québec.* Paris, 1968. 129 leaves. **1977**
Thesis, Institut des hautes études internationales, 1968.

Jacomy-Millette, Annemarie. *Les traités internationaux et le pouvoir législatif dans l'état fédéral.* Ottawa: Université d'Ottawa, 1973. 379 leaves (various pagings) **1978**

Notes de cours et documents de travail; Université d'Ottawa, Section de droit civil, Maîtrise en droit public, mai-juillet 1973.

Jacomy-Millette, Annemarie. "Treaty-Making Power and the Provinces: From the 'Quiet Revolution' to Economic Claims." (1973), 4 *Revue Générale de Droit* 131-153. **1979**

Jenks, C. Wilfred. "The Constitutional Capacity of Canada to Give Effect to International Labour Conventions." (1934), 16 *Journal of Comparative Legislation and International Law* 201-215 (3rd Ser.) **1980**
Continued in (1935), 17 *Journal of Comparative Legislation and International Law* 12-30 (3rd Ser.).

Keith, A. Berriedale. "The Dominions and the Treaty Power." (1924), 6 *Journal of Comparative Legislation and International Law* 193-194, 197, 201-202 (3d Ser.) **1981**

LaPierre, Laurier L. "Quebec and Treaty-Making." (1964-65), 20 *International Journal* 362-366. **1982**

Laskin, Bora. "The Provinces and International Agreements." *In* Ontario Advisory Committee on Confederation, *Background Papers and Reports* (Toronto, 1967), pp. 101-113. **1983**

League of Nations Society in Canada. *The Treaty Making Power in Canada; a Brief Presented to the Royal Commission on Dominion-Provincial Relations.* Ottawa, 1938. 49, 5, 38 leaves. **1984**

Lewis, Malcolm M. "The Treaty-Making Power of the Dominions." (1925), 6 *British Year Book of International Law* 31-43. **1985**

Lowell, Abbott Lawrence. "The Treaty-Making Power of Canada." (1923-24), 2 *Foreign Affairs* 12-22. **1986**

MacDonald, Vincent C. "Canada's Power to Perform Treaty Obligations." (1933), 11 *Canadian Bar Review* 581-599, 664-680. **1987**

MacKenzie, Norman A.M. "Canada: The Treaty-Making Power." (1937), 18 *British Year Book of International Law* 172-175. **1988**

MacKenzie, Norman A.M. "Canada and the Treaty-Making Power." (1937), 15 *Canadian Bar Review* 436-454. **1989**

MacKenzie, Norman A.M. "The Treaty-Making Power in Canada." (1925), 19 *American Journal of International Law* 489-504. **1990**

Martin, Paul. "The Provinces and Treaty-Making Powers." (1965), 17 *External Affairs* 306-307. **1991**

Matas, R.J. "Treaty Making in Canada." (1947), 25 *Canadian Bar Review* 458-477. **1992**

McDonald, Susan A. "The Problem of Treaty-Making and Treaty Implementation in Canada." (1981), 19 *Alberta Law Review* 293-302. **1993**

McWhinney, Edward. "Canadian Federalism: Foreign Affairs and Treaty Power: The Impact of Quebec's 'Quiet Revolution.'" *In* Ontario Advisory Committee on Confederation, *Background Papers and Reports* (Toronto, 1970), vol. 2, pp. 115-152. **1994**

McWhinney, Edward. "Canadian Federalism, and the Foreign Affairs and Treaty

Power: The Impact of Quebec's 'Quiet Revolution.' " (1969), 7 *Canadian Yearbook of International Law* 3-32. **1995**

McWhinney, Edward. "The Constitutional Competence within Federal Systems as to International Agreements." (1964-68), 1 *Canadian Legal Studies* 145-151.
1996
Reprinted in Ontario Advisory Committee on Confederation, *Background Papers and Reports* (Toronto, 1967), pp. 149-157.

McWhinney, Edward. "Federal Constitutional Law and the Treaty-Making Power: Conflict between Legislation Passed by Member-State of Federation and Treaty Obligations of Federal Government - German-Vatican Concordat of 1933 - Decision of West German Federal Constitutional Court. (Case Note)." (1957), 35 *Canadian Bar Review* 842-848. **1997**

Milani, Michael. "The Canadian Treaty Power: Decidedly Anachronistic; Potentially Antagonistic." (1980-81), 44 *Saskatchewan Law Review* 195-217. **1998**

Moore, *Sir* William Harrison. "The Dominions and Treaties." (1926), 8 *Journal of Comparative Legislation and International Law* 21-37 (3d Ser.) **1999**

Morin, Jacques-Yvan. "La conclusion d'accords internationaux par les provinces canadiennes à la lumière du droit comparé." (1965), 3 *Canadian Yearbook of International Law* 127-186. **2000**

Morin, Jacques-Yvan. "International Law - Treaty-Making Power - Constitutional Law - Position of the Government of Quebec. (Comment)." (1967), 45 *Canadian Bar Review* 160-173. **2001**

Morin, Jacques-Yvan. "Le Québec et le pouvoir de conclure des accords internationaux." (1964-68), 1 *Canadian Legal Studies* 136-144. **2002**

Morris, Gerald L. "The Treaty-Making Power: A Canadian Dilemma." (1967), 45 *Canadian Bar Review* 478-512. **2003**

Northey, John F. "Constitutional Limitations as Affecting the Validity of Treaties." (1955-56), 11 *University of Toronto Law Journal* 175-201. **2004**

Ollivier, Maurice. "Treaties." *In* Ollivier, Maurice, *Problems of Canadian Sovereignty* (Toronto, 1945), pp. 82-98. **2005**

Rand, Michael C. "International Agreements between Canadian Provinces and Foreign States." (1967), 25 *University of Toronto Faculty of Law Review* 75-86.
2006

Read, Horace E. "Canada as a Treaty Maker." (1927), 5 *Canadian Bar Review* 229-238, 301-310. **2007**

Rice, William Gorham, Jr. "Can Canada Ratify International Labor Conventions? - A Problem of the Division of Power between Central-State and Member-States in a Federal Union." (1936-37), 12 *Wisconsin Law Review* 185-197.
2008

Rodgers, Raymond S. "Conclusion of Quebec-Louisiana Agreement on Cultural Co-operation." (1970), 64 *American Journal of International Law* 380. **2009**
Refers to the agreement contained in the joint communiqué of September 1969.

Rogers, Norman McL. "Notes on the Treaty-Making Power." (1926), 7 *Canadian Historical Review* 27-33. **2010**

Sandwell, B.K. "The Provinces and the Supremacy of the Treaty Power." (1930), 37 *Queen's Quarterly* 543-556. **2011**

Senécal, Nicole. "Les accords conclus par les organisations internationales." (1971), 2 *Revue de Droit, Université de Sherbrooke* 207-257. **2012**

Shortt, Adam. "The Treaty-Making Power." (1903-04), 11 *Queen's Quarterly* 326-328. **2013**

Smith, Goldwin. "Can Canada Make Her Own Treaties?" (1903-04), 22 *Canadian Magazine* 331-335. **2014**

Smith, Herbert A. "Diplomacy and International Status." (1924), 2 *Canadian Bar Review* 231-242. **2015**

Stewart, Robert B. "Canada and International Labor Conventions." (1938), 32 *American Journal of International Law* 36-62. **2016**

Stewart, Robert B. "The Great Seal and Treaty-Making in the British Commonwealth."(1937), 15 *Canadian Bar Review* 745-759. **2017**

Stewart, Robert B. "Treaty-Making Procedure in the British Dominions." (1938), 32 *American Journal of International Law* 467-487. **2018**

Sumichrast, Frederick Caesar de. "Independence and the Treaty-Making Power." (1904), 23 *Canadian Magazine* 26-31. **2019**

Szablowski, G.J. "Creation and Implementation of Treaties in Canada." (1956), 34 *Canadian Bar Review* 28-59. **2020**

"The Treaty-Making Power." (1909), 10 *Journal of Comparative Legislation* 186-192 (N.S.) **2021**

Tupper, Charles Hibbert. "Treaty-Making Powers of the Dominions." (1917), 17 *Journal of Comparative Legislation* 5-18 (N.S.) **2022**

Willison, *Sir* John S. "A Treaty and a Signature." (1923), 4 *Canadian Historical Review* 145-149. **2023**

C. Conclusion and Entry into Force of Treaties

Brandon, Michael. "International Law - Legal Nature of a Reservation to a Multilateral Convention - Genocide Convention - Reference to the International Court of Justice. (Comment)." (1951), 29 *Canadian Bar Review* 428-434. **2024**

Camara, José Sette. *The Ratification of International Treaties.* Foreword by Hans Kelsen. Toronto: Ontario Pub., 1949. xii, 173 p. **2025**
Thesis (M.C.L.), McGill University. The author was vice consul of Brazil at Toronto. Reviews: E. Russell Hopkins in (1950), 28 *Canadian Bar Review* 827-828; Josef L. Kunz in (1951), 45 *American Journal of International Law* 215-216.

Cheffins, Ronald I. "The Negotiation, Ratification, and Implementation of Treaties in Canada and Australia." (1955-61), 1 *Alberta Law Review* 312-324, 410-430. **2026**

FitzGerald, Gerald F. "The Development of the Authentic Trilingual Text of the Convention on International Civil Aviation." (1970), 64 *American Journal of International Law* 364-371. **2027**

Grenon, Jean-Yves. "De la conclusion des traités et de leur mise en oeuvre au Canada." (1962), 40 *Canadian Bar Review* 151-164. **2028**

Jenks, C. Wilfred. "Can the Obligation to Ratify International Labour Conventions Be Time-Barred?" (1937), 15 *Canadian Bar Review* 86-92. **2029**

Jenks, C. Wilfred. "The Present Status of the Bennett Ratifications of International Labour Conventions." (1937), 15 *Canadian Bar Review* 464-477. **2030**

McDorman, Ted L. "Reservations and the Law of the Sea Treaty." (1982), 13 *Journal of Maritime Law and Commerce* 481-519. **2031**

"Negotiation and Conclusion of Treaties Affecting Any Part of the British Empire." (1924), 5 *British Year Book of International Law* 193-195. **2032**

"The Negotiation and Signature of International Agreements." (1949), 1 *External Affairs* 23-25 (Aug.) **2033**

"Reservations to Multilateral Conventions." (1952), 4 *External Affairs* 111-112. **2034**

"Reservations to Multilateral Conventions." (1960), 12 *External Affairs* 510-513. **2035**

"The Signing of the Treaty." (1905), 4 *Canadian Law Review* 465-466. **2036**

Woehrling, José. "La conclusion et la mise en oeuvre des traités dans le fédéralisme allemand (première partie)." (1979-80), 14 *Revue Juridique Thémis* 73-108. **2037**

D. Interpretation of Treaties

Emanuelli, Claude C., and Slosar, Stanislas. "L'application et l'interprétation des traités internationaux par le juge canadien." (1978), 13 *Revue Juridique Thémis* 69-83. **2038**

Also published in (1978), 29 *Assosiation Henri Capitant des Amis de la Culture Juridique Française, Travaux* 328-343.

Lenoir, James J. "Treaty Interpretation - A Comparative Study of Views Expressed by the United States and Canadian Courts on the Webster-Ashburton Treaty (1842)." (1934-35), 7 *Mississippi Law Journal* 197-202. **2039**

McRae, Donald M. "The Legal Effect of Interpretative Declarations." (1978), 49 *British Year Book of International Law* 155-173. **2040**

E. Termination of Treaties

Hodgins, Thomas. "The Prerogative Right of Revoking Treaty Privileges to Alien-Subjects." (1909), 29 *Canadian Law Times* 105-129. **2041**
  Reprinted from *The Nineteenth Century and After*. Also published separately, 2d ed., Toronto, Carswell, 1909. 27 p., map. Reviewed by Amos S. Hershey in (1910), 4 *American Journal of International Law* 770.

Hodgins, Thomas. "The Revocation of Treaty Privileges to Alien-Subjects." (1908), 44 *Canada Law Journal* 633-651. **2042**

Macdonald, Ronald St. John. "International Law - Jay Treaty of 1794 - Abrogation of Treaties by Outbreak of War - Review of Canadian and Foreign Decisions. Francis v. The Queen, (1954) Ex. C.R. 590; (1955) 4 D.L.R. 760). (Case Note)." (1956), 34 *Canadian Bar Review* 602-612, 760-762 (Letter) **2043**

Marsh, A.H. "Has the 29th Article of the Treaty of Washington Been Terminated?" (1888), 8 *Canadian Law Times* 229-241. **2044**
  Article 29 concerns the conveyance of merchandise through the United States.

Sastry, K.R.R. "*Clausula Rebus Sic Stantibus* in International Law." (1935), 13 *Canadian Bar Review* 227-229. **2045**

F. Succession to Treaties

Lawford, Hugh J. "The Practice concerning Treaty Succession in the Commonwealth." (1967), 5 *Canadian Yearbook of International Law* 3-13. **2046**

Lester, A.P. "State Succession to Treaties in the Commonwealth." (1963), 12 *International and Comparative Law Quarterly* 475-507. **2047**

Udokang, Okon. *Succession of New States to International Treaties.* Edmonton, 1970. iv, 525 leaves. **2048**
  Thesis (Ph.D.), University of Alberta, 1970. (National Library of Canada. Canadian Theses on Microfilm, No. 6244).

Udokang, Okon. *Succession of New States to International Treaties.* Dobbs Ferry, N.Y.: Oceana Publications, 1972. 525 p. **2049**
  First issued as a thesis (Ph.D.), University of Alberta, 1970.
  Reviews: Leslie C. Green in (1974), 37 *Modern Law Review* 236-237; Leslie C. Green in (1975), 8 *Canadian Journal of Political Science* 178; Joseph W. Samuels in (1973), 11 *Canadian Yearbook of International Law* 402-403.

Udokang, Okon. "The Succession of New States to Multilateral Treaties." (1971), 9 *Alberta Law Review* 118-140. **2050**

Udokang, Okon. "Succession to Treaties in New States." (1970), 8 *Canadian Yearbook of International Law* 123-157. **2051**

G. Treaties and National Law

Bonenfant, Jean-Charles. "L'étanchéité de l'A.A.N.B. est-elle menacée?" (1977), 18 *Cahiers de Droit* 383-396. **2052**

Bourne, Charles B. "International Law - Unimplemented Treaties - Their Effect on Municipal Law - Public Policy. (Comment)." (1951), 29 *Canadian Bar Review* 969-974. **2053**

Daggett, Athern P. "Treaty Legislation in Canada." (1938), 16 *Canadian Bar Review* 159-184. **2054**

Desjardins, Alice. "La mise en oeuvre au Canada des traités relatifs aux droits de la personne." (1981), 12 *Revue Générale de Droit* 359-374. **2055**

Dufour, J.A. *Les conflits de compétences et leurs conséquences dans la mise en oeuvre des traités au Canada.* Paris, 1973. 634 leaves. **2056**
Thesis, Université de Paris II, 1973.

Forest, Réal. "Quelques aspects de la mise en oeuvre au Canada des pactes de l'O.N.U. relatifs aux droits de l'homme." (1981), 12 *Revue Générale de Droit* 375-395. **2057**

Gagnon, Guy. *L'introduction des conventions multilatérales maritimes dans l'ordre interne canadien.* Ottawa, 1975. 110, (42) leaves. **2058**
Thesis (M.A.), Université d'Ottawa, 1975.

Holmes, J.D. "A Note on the Implementing of Treaties in Australia and Canada." (1936-37), 10 *Australian Law Journal* 482-483. **2059**

Kos-Rabcewicz-Zubkowski, Ludwik. "Clause fédérale dans les conventions internationales." (1980), 11 *Revue de Droit, Université de Sherbrooke* 253-266. **2060**

Lederman, William R. "Legislative Power to Implement Treaty Obligations in Canada." *In* Aitchison, J.H., ed., *The Political Process in Canada* (Toronto, 1963), pp. 171-181. **2061**

Macdonald, Ronald St. John. "International Treaty Law and the Domestic Law of Canada." (1975-76), 2 *Dalhousie Law Journal* 307-329. **2062**

Mankiewicz, René H. "Solutions jurisprudentielles des divergences entre le texte authentique d'une convention d'unification de droit privé et la loi nationale de sa mise en oeuvre, ou une loi postérieure." (1974), 5 *Revue de Droit, Université de Sherbrooke* 275-311. **2063**

Martinez Ruiz, L.F. "De la force obligatoire des traités dans l'ordre juridique interne; des conflits entre dispositions conventionnelles et dispositions législatives internes." (1972), 3 *Revue Générale de Droit* 100-124. **2064**

McDonald, Susan A. "The Problem of Treaty-Making and Treaty Implementation in Canada." (1981), 19 *Alberta Law Review* 293-302. **2065**

Nettl, J.P. "The Treaty Enforcement Power in Federal Constitutions." (1950), 28 *Canadian Bar Review* 1051-1070. **2066**

Rogers, A.W. "Some Aspect of Treaty Legislation." (1926), 4 *Canadian Bar Review* 40-45. **2067**

"Treaties in Municipal Law - Canadian Authorities." (1932), 13 *British Year Book of International Law* 122-125. **2068**

Vallat, Frank A. "Treaties: When Do British (Including Canadian) Treaties Need Legislation?" (1933), 11 *Canadian Bar Review* 385-391. **2069**

H. Indian Treaties

Barsh, Russell Lawrence, and Henderson, James Youngblood. "Aboriginal Rights, Treaty Rights, and Human Rights: Indian Tribes and 'Constitutional Renewal.'" (1982), 17 *Journal of Canadian Studies* 55-81 (No. 2) **2070**

Burrell, Gordon; Young, Robert; and Price, Richard, eds. *Indian Treaties and the Law: An Interpretation for Laymen*. Edmonton: Indian Association of Alberta, c1975. iii, 58, (10) p. **2071**

Chalmers, John W. "Treaty No. Six." (1977), 25 *Alberta History* 22-27 (No. 2) **2072**

Dempsey, Hugh A. "The Centennial of Treaty Seven, and Why Indians Think Whites Are Knaves." (1977-78), 95 *Canadian Geographical Journal* 10-19 (Oct./Nov.) **2073**

Duff, Wilson. "The Fort Victoria Treaties." (1969), 3 *B.C. Studies* 3-57. **2074**
Comments on eleven treaties concluded at Fort Victoria in 1850 and 1852.

Fumoleau, René. *As Long as This Land Shall Last: A History of Treaty 8 and Treaty 11, 1870-1939*. Toronto: McClelland and Stewart, 1975. 415 p., 8 leaves of plates. **2075**

Green, Leslie C. "Legal Significance of Treaties Affecting Canada's Indians." (1972), 1 *Anglo-American Law Review* 119-135. **2076**

Indian Treaties and Surrenders, from 1680 to 1890 (i.e. 1902). Toronto: Coles, 1971. 3 vols., maps. (Coles Canadiana Collection) **2077**
Facsimile reprint of 1891 and 1912 edition (Ottawa, Queen's Printer).
Contents: v.1. Treaty numbers 1-138.- v.2. Treaty numbers 140-280.- v.3. Treaty numbers 281-483.

Kennedy, J. de N. "Reparation for Breach of Indian Treaties." (1966), 14 *Chitty's Law Journal* 119-120. **2078**

Kerr, John Andrew. "The Indian Treaties of 1876." (1937-38), 17 *Dalhousie Review* 187-195. **2079**

Long, John S. *Treaty No. 9: The Indian Petitions, 1889-1927*. Cobalt, Ont.: Highway Book Shop, c1978. 35 p., maps. **2080**

Lysyk, Kenneth M. "Indian Hunting Rights: Constitutional Considerations and the Role of Indian Treaties in British Columbia." (1964-66), 2 *University of British Columbia Law Review* 401-421. **2081**

McInnes, R.W. "Indian Treaties and Related Disputes." (1969), 27 *University of Toronto Faculty of Law Review* 52-71. **2082**

McKay, Raoul J. *A History of Indian Treaty Number Four and Government Policies in Its Implementation.* Winnipeg, 1973. vii, 147 leaves. **2083**
Thesis (M.A.), University of Manitoba, 1973. (National Library of Canada. Canadian Theses on Microfiche, No. 13751).

Morin, Victor. "Les traités du Gouvernement canadien avec les Indiens du Nord-Ouest." (1932), 26 *Royal Society of Canada, Transactions* 181-190 (3d Ser., Sec. 2) **2084**

Morris, Alexander. *The Treaties of Canada with the Indians of Manitoba and the North-West Territories, Including the Negotiations on Which They Were Based, and Other Information Relating Thereto.* Toronto: Belfords, Clarke, 1880. Reprinted Toronto: Coles, c1971. 375 p. (Coles Canadiana Collection) **2085**

Price, Richard, ed. *The Spirit of the Alberta Indian Treaties.* Montreal: Institute for Research on Public Policy; distributed by Butterworth, 1979. xxvii, 202 p. **2086**
Review: Gurston Dacks in (1980), 13 *Canadian Journal of Political Science* 621-622.

Raby, S. "Indian Treaty No. 5 and the Pas Agency, Saskatchewan, N.W.T." (1972), 25 *Saskatchewan History* 92-114. **2087**

Torrelli, Maurice. "Les Indiens du Canada et le droit des traités dans la jurisprudence canadienne." (1974), 20 *Annuaire Français de Droit International* 227-249. **2088**

"Treaty No. Seven in Pictures." (1977), 25 *Alberta History* 15-22 (No. 3) **2089**

Whitehead, G.R.B. "Indian Treaties and the Indian Act - The Sacredness of Treaties?" (1966), 14 *Chitty's Law Journal* 121-125. **2090**

I. Specific Treaties (by Subject)

See also *"Boundaries of Canada" (p. 166), "Law of the Sea: Fisheries" (p. 252), and "Arbitration: Specific Cases: Fisheries" (p. 398).*

1. LABOUR

Assaly, Louis C. *Canada and the International Labour Conventions.* Cambridge, Mass., 1949. iii, 130 leaves. **2091**
Paper submitted at Harvard Law School for a course in international organization, May 25, 1949.

Bonenfant, Jean-Charles. "L'étanchéité de l'A.A.N.B. est-elle menacée?" (1977), 18 *Cahiers de Droit* 383-396. **2092**

Gagnon, Jean Dunis. "L'influence des conventions internationales du travail sur les législations canadienne et québécoise." (1970), 30 *Revue du Barreau* 329-346. **2093**

Hyde, Charles Cheney. "Canada's 'Water-Tight Compartments.' " (1937), 31 *American Journal of International Law* 466-468. **2094**

Jenks, C. Wilfred. "Are International Labour Conventions Agreements between Governments? (Case Note)." (1937), 15 *Canadian Bar Review* 574-578. **2095**

Jenks, C. Wilfred. "Can the Obligation to Ratify International Labour Conventions Be Time-Barred?" (1937), 15 *Canadian Bar Review* 86-92. **2096**

Jenks, C. Wilfred. "The Constitutional Capacity of Canada to Give Effect to International Labour Conventions." (1934), 16 *Journal of Comparative Legislation and International Law* 201-215 (3rd Ser.) **2097**
Continued in (1935), 17 *Journal of Comparative Legislation and International Law* 12-30 (3rd Ser.).

Jenks, C. Wilfred. "The Present Status of the Bennett Ŕ(1935), 13 *Canadian Bar Review* 448-462. **2099**

La Forest, Gerard V. "The *Labour Conventions* Case Revisited." (1974), 12 *Canadian Yearbook of International Law* 137-152. **2100**

Mainwaring, John. *A Review of International Labour Conventions.* Ottawa: International Labour Affairs Branch, Canada Department of Labour, 1974. ii, 45 p. **2101**
Also published in French under title: *Étude des conventions internationales du travail.*

Pelland, Léo. "Problèmes de droit constitutionnel. IV. Traités et accords internationaux." (1936-37), 15 *Revue du Droit* 194-214. **2102**
Refers to I.L.O. conventions and the decision of the Supreme Court regarding the validity of three statutes of 1935.

Rice, William Gorham, Jr. "Can Canada Ratify International Labor Conventions? - A Problem of the Division of Power between Central-State and Member-States in a Federal Union." (1936-37), 12 *Wisconsin Law Review* 185-197. **2103**

Scott, Francis R., and MacKinnon, B.J. "Labour Conventions Case: Lord Wright's Undisclosed Dissent? (Correspondence)." (1956), 34 *Canadian Bar Review* 114-117. **2104**

Stewart, Bryce Morrison. *Canadian Labor Laws and the Treaty.* New York: Columbia University Press, 1926. 501 p. (Studies in History, Economics and Public Law, No. 278) **2105**
Also published as thesis (Ph.D.), Columbia University, 1926. Reprinted New York, AMS Press, 1968.
Review: Norman A.M. MacKenzie in (1927), 8 *Canadian Historical Review* 164-165.

Stewart, Robert B. "Canada and International Labor Conventions." (1938), 32 *American Journal of International Law* 36-62. **2106**

Stewart, Robert B. "International Labor Conventions in India." (1938), 16 *Canadian Bar Review* 792-802. **2107**

Stewart, Robert B. "International Labour Conventions in Australia." (1938), 4 *Canadian Journal of Economics and Political Science* 34-46. **2108**

Wanczycki, Jan K. "Les aspects constitutionnels de la ratification des conventions de l'O.I.T." (1969), 24 *Relations Industrielles* 727-735. **2109**
Also contains an English version under title: "Constitutional Aspects of Ratification of I.L.O. Conventions" (pp. 735-744).

Weinfeld, Abraham Chaim. "Canadian Constitutional Problems in Connection with Conventions of the International Labor Organization - Comparison with Problems in the United States." (1935-36), 4 *George Washington Law Review* 326-335. **2110**

2. TRADE

See also *"Reciprocity Treaty of June 5, 1854" (p. 526), "Reciprocity Agreement of January 21, 1911" (p. 530), and "Foreign Trade of Canada" (p. 553), including "Trade with the United States: Specific Issue: Automotive Agreement" (p. 573).*

Canada. Parliament. *Agreement between Canada and France in Respect of Customs Tariffs, with Related Correspondence.* Ottawa, 1893. 55 p. (Canada. Parliament, 1893. Sessional Papers, Nos. 51 to 51c) **2111**
The agreement was signed at Paris, February 6, 1893 (BTS 15(1895); 85 BFSP 28; 20 Hertslet 281; 178 Parry 193). See also related correspondence printed in 1895, as Sessional Papers, No. 89 (11 p.).

Canada. Parliament. *Convention Respecting the Commercial Relations between Canada and France / Convention de commerce entre le Canada et la France.* Ottawa, 1907. 47 p. (Canada. Parliament, 1907-1908. Sessional Papers, No. 10a) **2112**
This is one of the first important commercial conventions signed by Canada with a foreign country. The convention was signed at Paris on September 19, 1907, for Canada by Sir Francis Bertie, British Ambassador to France, William S. Fielding, Canadian Minister of Finance, and Louis-Philippe Brodeur, Canadian Minister of Marine and Fisheries. See text in BTS 4(1910); 102 BFSP 77; 25 Hertslet 800; 1 LNTS 96; 205 Parry 22.

Canada. Parliament. *Correspondence and Memoranda in Connection with the Convention of 1907, Respecting the Commercial Relations between Canada and France.* Ottawa, 1908. 29 p. (Canada. Parliament, 1907-1908. Sessional Papers, No. 10b) **2113**

Canada. Parliament. *Correspondence with Reference to the Abrogation of Certain Articles in the Treaties of Commerce, etc.* Ottawa, 1892. 7, 2 p. (Canada. Parliament, 1892. Sessional Papers, Nos. 24, and 24a) **2114**

Canada. Parliament. *List of Treaties of Commerce and Navigation between Great Britain and Foreign Powers, Containing Most-Favoured Nation Clauses; Stating the Period When Terminable; and Showing Whether They Apply to the British Colonies.* Ottawa, 1880. 85 p. (Canada. Parliament, 1880. Sessional Papers, No. 26) **2115**

Canada. Parliament. *Supplementary Convention Respecting Commercial Relations between France and Canada / Convention complémentaire de commerce*

entre le Canada et la France; with Related Correspondence. Ottawa, 1909. 8, 27 p. (Canada. Parliament, 1909. Sessional Papers, Nos. 101, and 102) **2116**
The convention was signed at Paris on January 23, 1909 (BTS 4(1910); 102 BFSP 81; 25 Hertslet 821: 1 LNTS 128; 208 Parry 248).

Goldenberg, H. Carl. "The Canada-United States Trade Agreement, 1935." (1936), 2 *Canadian Journal of Economics and Political Science* 209-212. **2117**
Refers to the trade agreement of November 15, 1935 (CTS 1936/9).

Grenon, Jean-Yves. "Les traités de commerce, cadre de la libéralisation des échanges." (1972), 10 *Canadian Yearbook of International Law* 65-101. **2118**

Hardy, J.E.G. *Le rôle des traités dans la politique commerciale du Canada, 1923-1939.* Ottawa, 1949. 105 leaves. **2119**
Thesis (M.A.), University of Ottawa, 1949.

Shields, Robert A. "The Canadian Tariff and the Franco-Canadian Treaty Negotiations 1907-1909: A Study in Imperial Relations." (1977-78), 57 *Dalhousie Review* 300-321. **2120**

Shields, Robert A. "Sir Charles Tupper and the Franco-Canadian Treaty of 1895: A Study of Imperial Relations." (1968), 49 *Canadian Historical Review* 1-23.
2121

Skelton, O.D. "Canada and the Most Favored Nation Treaties." (1911-12), 19 *Queen's Quarterly* 231-252. **2122**

IX. JURISDICTION OF THE STATE

A. Personal Jurisdiction (Military)

See also *"North American Defence" (p. 436)*, and *"North Atlantic Treaty Organization" (p. 441)*.

Ginsburgs, George. "Soviet Status-of-Forces Agreements: Pre-War and Wartime Experience." (1965-66), 16 *University of Toronto Law Journal* 368-395. **2123**

Meron, Theodor. "Civil Jurisdiction of Canadian Courts over United States Military Personnel in Canada." (1957-58), 12 *University of Toronto Law Journal* 67-78. **2124**

"NATO Forces in Germany." (1959), 11 *External Affairs* 274-275. **2125**

Vince, Donald M.A.R. "Development in the Legal Status of the Canadian Military Forces, 1914-19, as Related to Dominion Status." (1954), 20 *Canadian Journal of Economics and Political Science* 357-370. **2126**

Wilson, H.J. "International Law - Jurisdiction over Foreign Armed Forces Which Enter Canada with the Consent of the Government of Canada. (Case Note)." (1943), 21 *Canadian Bar Review* 593-597, 665. **2127**

B. Territorial Jurisdiction

See also *"State Territory" (p. 166)*, *"Polar Regions" (p. 196)*, *"Law of the Sea (p. 230)*, and *"Airspace and Outer Space" (p. 280)*.

1. TERRITORIAL SOVEREIGNTY

"Admiralty Jurisdiction over Maritime Treaty Rights." (1907), 43 *Canada Law Journal* 345-349. **2128**

Johnson, Walter S. "Extra-Territorial Criminal Legislation." (1935), 13 *Canadian Bar Review* 127-142. **2129**

MacKenzie, Norman A.M. "International and Constitutional Law Legislative Jurisdiction within Territorial Waters - The Three Mile Limit - *The King* v.

Boutilier, (1929) 2 D.L.R. 849. (Case Note)." (1929), 7 *Canadian Bar Review* 736-738. **2130**

Morse, Charles. "International Law - Criminal Jurisdiction of National Courts over Foreigners. *The Franconia Case (Reg.* v. *Keyn,* (1876) 2 Ex. D. 63). (Case Note)." (1927), 5 *Canadian Bar Review* 622-623. **2131**

Smith, Herbert A. "Extra-Territorial Legislation." (1923), 1 *Canadian Bar Review* 338-350. **2132**

2. LIMITATIONS (SERVITUDES, LEASES, ETC.)

Langer, S. Joshua. "International Leases, Licenses, and Servitudes." *In* Macdonald, Ronald St. John, and others, *Canadian Perspectives on International Law and Organization* (Toronto, 1974), pp. 544-552. **2133**

Melvin, A. Gordon. "Why China's 'Unequal Treaties' Must Go." (1927-28), 7 *Dalhousie Review* 211-218. **2134**

O'Connell, Daniel Patrick. "A Re-Consideration of the Doctrine of International Servitude." (1952), 30 *Canadian Bar Review* 807-818. **2135**

Straus, Richard. *The Diplomatic Negotiations Leading to the Establishment of American Bases in Newfoundland, June 1940-April 1941.* St. John's, 1972. iii, 164 leaves. **2136**
Thesis (M.A.), Memorial University of Newfoundland, 1972. (National Library of Canada. Canadian Theses on Microfilm, No. 11898).

3. IMMUNITY OF FOREIGN STATES

See also *"Privileges and Immunities" (p. 145).*

Castel, Jean-Gabriel. "Exemption from the Jurisdiction of Canadian Courts." (1971), 9 *Canadian Yearbook of International Law* 159-188. **2137**

Hendry, James M. "Sovereign Immunities from the Jurisdiction of the Courts." (1958), 36 *Canadian Bar Review* 145-174. **2138**

"Integrating International Law into Canadian Domestic Law: Sovereign Immunities / L'incorporation du droit international au droit canadien: le cas des immunités des états." (1981), 10 *Canadian Council on International Law, Proceedings,* 201-212. **2139**
This is a panel. Chairman: Stanislas Slosar.
Contents: "Integrating International Law into Canadian Domestic Law: Sovereign Immunities," by M.L. Jewett (pp. 201-206).- "Sovereign Immunity Law," by Leonard B. Boudin (pp. 207-209).- Discussion (pp. 210-212).

Kelsey, Brian A. "Recent Trends in Sovereign Immunity from Taxation." (1959), 17 *University of Toronto Faculty of Law Review* 81-95. **2140**

Kindred, Hugh M. "Foreign Governments Before the Courts." (1980), 58 *Canadian Bar Review* 602-629. **2141**

Kos-Rabcewicz-Zubkowski, Ludwik. "Immunité de juridiction. État ou gouvernement étranger. Exposition universelle de 1967." (1968), 6 *Canadian Yearbook of International Law* 242-251. **2142**

Kos-Rabcewicz-Zubkowski, Ludwik. "Immunité de juridiction de l'état ou du gouvernement étranger." (1974), 34 *Revue du Barreau* 53-60. **2143**

Macdonald, Ronald St. John. "International Law - Impleading Foreign Sovereign State - Immunity from Suit - New Method to Test Sovereign Immunity Doctrine. (*Rahimtoda* v. *Nizam of Hyderabad*, (1957) 3 All E.R. 441). (Case Note)." (1958), 36 *Canadian Bar Review* 549-558. **2144**

Marasinghe, M.L. "A Reassessment of Sovereign Immunity." (1977), 9 *Ottawa Law Review* 474-504. **2145**

McRae, Donald M. *"Le Gouvernement de la République Démocratique du Congo* v. *Venne* - Sovereign Immunity - The Role of the Courts. (1971) S.C.R. 997; 22 D.L.R. (3d) 669. (Case Comment)." (1973), 11 *Osgoode Hall Law Journal* 326-334. **2146**

Molot, Henry L. "Suability, Taxability and Sovereign Immunity in Canada: A Brief Glance." (1974), 22 *Chitty's Law Journal* 314-318. **2147**

Simmonds, K.R. "Limits of Sovereign Jurisdictional Immunity: The *Petrol Shipping Corporation* and *Victory Transport* Cases." (1965), 11 *McGill Law Journal* 291-309. **2148**

Vincke, Christian. "Certain aspects de l'évolution récente du problème de l'immunité de juridiction des états." (1969), 7 *Canadian Yearbook of International Law* 224-254. **2149**

X. STATE TERRITORY

A. Boundaries of Canada

1. GENERAL

For Arctic boundaries, see *"Arctic: Legal Régime" (p. 200); for maritime boundaries,* see *"Law of the Sea" (p. 230); for airspace limits,* see *"Airspace and Outer Space" (p. 280).*

Brossard, Jacques, and others. *Le territoire québécois.* Montréal: Presses de l'Université de Montréal, 1970. xiii, 412 p. **2150**
On cover: Faculté de droit. Institut de recherche en droit public.
Review: Jacques Benjamin in (1971), 4 *Canadian Journal of Political Science* 574.

Brun, Henri. *Le territoire du Québec: six études juridiques.* Québec: Presses de l'Université Laval, 1974. 288 p. (Droit et science politique, 6) **2151**
Includes international aspects.
Reviews: James Iain Gow in (1975), 8 *Canadian Journal of Political Science* 566-568; Jean-Paul Lacasse in (1974), 5 *Revue Générale de Droit* 415-416.

Canada. Parliament. *Report on Treaty Relating to Boundary Waters and Questions Arising along the Boundary between Canada and the United States.* Ottawa, 1910. 86 p. (Canada. Parliament, 1910. Sessional Papers, No. 19e)
2152

Classen, H. George. *Thrust and Counterthrust: The Genesis of the Canada-United States Boundary.* Toronto: Longmans Canada, c1965. 386 p., maps. **2153**
Reprinted Chicago, Rand McNally, 1967.
Review: Norman Penlington in (1967), 48 *Canadian Historical Review* 67-68.

Correspondence and Other Papers Relating to the Boundary between the British Possessions in North America and the United States of America, with Appendices, 1857-94. Shannon, Ire.: Irish University Press, c1971. 324 p., maps. (Irish University Press Series of British Parliamentary Papers. Colonies. Canadian Boundary, 3) **2154**
Also in IUP Library of Fundamental Source Books Series.

Emanuelli, Claude C. "Boundary and Resource Issues: Modes de règlement des différends entre le Canada et les États-Unis en matière de frontières et de ressources maritimes." (1978), 1 *Canada-United States Law Journal* 36-66.
2155

Hackworth, Green Haywood. "Boundaries: United States-Canada." *In* Hackworth, Green Haywood, *Digest of International Law* (Washington, 1940), vol. 1, pp. 755-771. **2156**

International Boundary Commission. *Joint Report upon the Maintenance of the Boundary between the United States and Canada under the Provisions of Article 4 of the Treaty Signed at Washington, February 24, 1925. Revised Data from the Mouth of Niagara River to the Head of St. Clair River, and Maintenance on This Section from 1925 to 1956.* Ottawa, 1957. v, 269 p. (International Boundary Commission. Special Report, No. 2) **2157**

"The International Boundary Commission." (1950), 2 *External Affairs* 447-450. **2158**

Lacasse, Jean-Paul. "L'état des frontières du Québec." (1977), 8 *Revue Générale de Droit* 119-127. **2159**

Mayrand, Léon. "Nos frontières." (1936), 6 *Revue de l'Université d'Ottawa* 162-176. **2160**

Minghi, Julian Vincent. *Some Aspects of the Impact of an International Boundary on Spatial Patterns; an Analysis of the Pacific Coast Lowland Region of the Canada-United States Boundary.* Seattle, 1962. 209 leaves. **2161**
Thesis, University of Washington, 1962. Abstracted in (1963), 23 *Dissertation Abstracts* 4307. (University Microfilms, Ann Arbor, No. 63-3130).

Moore, John Bassett. "Boundaries of the United States: With the British Possessions." *In* Moore, John Bassett, *Digest of International Law* (Washington, 1906), vol. 1, pp. 749-753. **2162**

Nicholson, Norman L. *The Boundaries of Canada, Its Provinces and Territories.* Ottawa: Queen's Printer, 1964. 142 p. (Canada. Dept. of Mines and Technical Surveys. Geographical Branch. Memoir, 2) **2163**
This is a reissue of the same book first published in 1954.

Nicholson, Norman L. *Boundaries of the Canadian Confederation.* Toronto: Macmillan of Canada, 1979. x, 252 p. (Carleton Library, No. 115) **2164**
Revision and enlargement of the author's *The Boundaries of Canada, Its Provinces and Territories,* published by the Government of Canada in 1954.
Review: J. William Brennan in (1980), 61 *Canadian Historical Review* 88-89.

Nicholson, Norman L. *A Dissertation on Canadian Boundaries: Their Evolution, Establishment and Significance.* Ottawa, 1951. xxiii, 252 leaves, maps. **2165**
Thesis (Ph.D.), University of Ottawa, 1951.

"Our Northern Boundary." (1908), 2 *American Journal of International Law* 634-637. **2166**

Poole, A.F.N. "The Boundaries of Canada." (1964), 42 *Canadian Bar Review* 100-139. **2167**

Ramsay, Robert A. *Treaties Affecting the Boundaries and the Fisheries of Canada; a Lecture.* Montreal, 1885. 15 p. **2168**
Reprinted from (1885), 8 *Legal News* 84, 91.

Richards, J. Howard. "Changing Canadian Frontiers." (1961), 5 *Canadian Geographer* 23-29. **2169**
Includes some international aspects.

Stacey, Charles P. *The Undefended Border; The Myth and the Reality.* Ottawa: Canadian Historical Association, 1967. 18 p. (Canadian Historical Association. Booklets, No. 1) **2170**
Review: Peter Waite in (1954-55), 34 *Dalhousie Review* 215-216.

Trotter, Reginald G. "The Canadian Back Fence in Anglo-American Relations." (1933), 40 *Queen's Quarterly* 383-397. **2171**

Whiteman, Marjorie M. "United States Boundary Relations: United States-Canadian Boundary." *In* Whiteman, Marjorie M., *Digest of International Law* (Washington, 1964), vol. 3, pp. 722-871. **2172**
Includes summaries of cases of the International Joint Commission (Docket Nos. 1-80).

Wiktor, Christian L., and Tanguay, Guy. "Boundaries." *In* Wiktor, Christian L., and Tanguay, Guy, eds., *Constitutions of Canada: Federal and Provincial* (Dobbs Ferry, N.Y., 1978), vol. 1, pp. C1-C282. **2173**

2. EARLY HISTORY

See also *"Relations with the United States: Historical" (p. 522).*

Bemis, Samuel Flagg. "Jay's Treaty and the Northwest Boundary Gap." (1921-22), 27 *American Historical Review* 465-484. **2174**

Blue, George Verne. "Anglo-French Diplomacy During the Critical Period of the Nootka Controversy, 1790." (1938), 39 *Oregon Historical Quarterly* 162-179. **2175**

Boissonnault, Charles-Marie. "Mirabeau donne la Colombie 'espagnole' à l'Angleterre." (1972), 10 *Royal Society of Canada, Transactions* 103-113 (4th Ser.) **2176**

"British Diplomacy and Canada: I. The Ashburton Treaty: A Diplomatic Victory.-II. The Alaska Boundary Award." (1907), 6 *University Magazine* 291-298, 412-426. **2177**
Part II is signed by D.A. MacArthur.

Brown, George W. "The St. Lawrence in the Boundary Settlement of 1783." (1928), 9 *Canadian Historical Review* 223-238. **2178**

Burpee, Lawrence J. "John Cabot, Who Sought Cipangu and Found Canada." (1938), 16 *Canadian Geographical Journal* 258-267. **2179**

Cazes, P. de. "La frontière nord de la province de Québec." (1885), 3 *Royal Society of Canada, Transactions* 89-99 (Sec. 1) **2180**

Davis, John W. "The Unguarded Boundary." (1922), 12 *Geographical Review* 585-601. **2181**

Delafield, Joseph. *The Unfortified Boundary; a Diary of the First Survey of the Canadian Boundary Line from St. Regis to the Lake of the Woods.* Edited by Robert McElroy, and Thomas Riggs. New York: Privately printed, 1943. 490 p., maps. **2182**
Review: Ralph H. Brown in (1945), 35 *Geographical Review* 162-163.

Gt. Brit. Commissioners for Adjusting the Boundaries for the British and French Possessions in America. *The Memorials of the English and French Commissaries concerning the Limits of Nova Scotia or Acadia.* London: Printed in the year 1755. 2 vols., map. **2183**
Volume 2 has title: *The Memorials of the English and French Commissaries concerning St. Lucia.* Also published in French under title: *Mémoires des commissaires de Sa Majesté très-chrétienne et de ceux de Sa Majesté britannique, sur les possessions & les droits respectifs des deux couronnes en Amérique* (Amsterdam, J. Schreuder & P. Mortier, 1755).

Hanson, Stan D. "Policing the International Boundary Area in Saskatchewan, 1890-1910." (1966), 19 *Saskatchewan History* 61-73 (No. 2) **2184**

Jost, Isabelle. "Territorial Evolution of Canada." (1967), 75 *Canadian Geographical Journal* 134-141. **2185**

Klitscher, K.R. "How to Settle a Boundary Line Without a War." (1980), 100 *Canadian Geographic* 66-72 (No. 2) **2186**

Laplante, Corinne. "Le traité d'Utrecht et la question des limites territoriales de l'Acadie." (1975), 6 *Société Historique Acadienne, Cahiers* 5-24. **2187**

Maclaren, J.J. "Our International Boundary: An Object Lesson." (1909-10), 17 *Queen's Quarterly* 23-27. **2188**

Macphail, Andrew. "British Diplomacy and Canada: V. Concluded." (1909), 8 *University Magazine* 188-214. **2189**

Martin, Lawrence, and Bemis, Samuel Flagg. "Franklin's Red-Line Map Was a Mitchell." (1937), 10 *New England Quarterly* 105-111. **2190**

Mulligan, Wm. Orr. "Sir Charles Bagot and Canadian Boundary Questions." (1936), *Canadian Historical Association, Historical Papers* 40-52. **2191**

Osborn, Chase Salmon, and Osborn, Stella Brunt. *The Conquest of a Continent.* Lancaster, Pa.: Science Press, 1939. 190 p. **2192**

Paradis, Roger. "John Baker and the Republic of Madawaska: An Episode in the Northeast Boundary Controversy." (1972-73), 52 *Dalhousie Review* 78-95. **2193**

Pease, Theodore Calvin, ed. *Anglo-French Boundary Disputes in the West, 1749-1763.* Springfield, Ill.: Trustees of the Illinois State Historical Library, c1936. clxxi, 607 p., maps. (Illinois State Historical Library. Collections, Vol. 27; French Series, Vol. 2) **2194**
Review: Max Savelle in (1937), 18 *Canadian Historical Review* 436-437.

Prud'Homme, L.A. "La baie d'Hudson." (1909), 3 *Royal Society of Canada, Transactions* 3-36 (3d Ser., Sec. 1) **2195**

Prud'Homme, L.A. "La baie d'Hudson." (1910), 4 *Royal Society of Canada, Transactions* 17-40 (3d Ser., Sec. 1) **2196**

Prud'Homme, L.A. "La baie d'Hudson - Notes préliminaires." (1911), 5 *Royal Society of Canada, Transactions* 119-165 (3d Ser., Sec. 1) **2197**

Savelle, Max. *The Diplomatic History of the Canadian Boundary, 1749-1763.* New York: Russell & Russell, 1968. xiv, 172 p., maps. **2198**

First published New Haven: Yale University Press; Toronto: Ryerson, 1940. xiv, 172 p., maps (Relations of Canada and the United States).
Reviews: Albert B. Corey in (1941), 22 *Canadian Historical Review* 323-326; D.C. Harvey in (1940-41), 20 *Dalhousie Review* 513-514.

Slattery, Brian. "French Claims in North America, 1500-59." (1978), 59 *Canadian Historical Review* 139-169. **2199**
Reprinted Saskatoon, Sask., University of Saskatchewan, Native Law Centre, 1980. 31 p. (Studies in Aboriginal Rights, No. 1)

Verreau, Hospice. "Jacques Cartier: Questions de droit public, de législation et d'usages maritimes." (1891), 9 *Royal Society of Canada, Transactions* 77-83 (Sec. 1) **2200**

Verreau, Hospice. "Jacques Cartier - Questions de lois et coutumes maritimes." (1897), 3 *Royal Society of Canada, Transactions* 119-133 (2d Ser., Sec. 1) **2201**

White, James. "Boundary Disputes and Treaties." *In* Shortt, Adam, and Doughty, Arthur G., eds., *Canada and Its Provinces* (Toronto, 1914-1916), vol. 8, pp. 751-958. **2202**
Contents: I. From Fundy to Juan de Fuca.- II. Ontario-Manitoba Boundary.- III. Labrador-Canada Boundary.- IV. Alaska Boundary.

3. EASTERN BOUNDARY

Baldwin, John R. "The Ashburton-Webster Boundary Settlement." (1938), *Canadian Historical Association, Historical Papers* 121-133. **2203**

"British Diplomacy and Canada: IV. The Ashburton Treaty: An Afterword." (1908), 7 *University Magazine* 560-563, map. **2204**

Burrage, Henry Sweetser. "The Attitude of Maine in the Northeastern Boundary Controversy." (1904), 1 *Maine Historical Society, Collections* 353-368 (3d Ser.) **2205**

Burrage, Henry Sweetser. *Maine in the Northeastern Boundary Controversy.* Portland, Me.: Printed for the State, 1919. xiv, 398 p., maps. **2206**

Burrage, Henry Sweetser. "The St. Croix Commission, 1796-1798." (1895), 6 *Maine Historical Society, Collections* 225-251 (2d Ser.) **2207**
Concerning the commission, see Article 5 of the Jay Treaty of November 19, 1794 (1 BFSP 784; 8 Stat. 116; TS 105; 12 Bevans 13; 52 Parry 243).

Chipman, Ward. *Remarks upon the Disputed Points of Boundary under the Fifth Article of the Treaty of Ghent, Principally Compiled from the Statements Laid by the Government of Great Britain Before the King of the Netherlands, as Arbiter.* Saint John, N.B.: Printed by D.A. Cameron, at the Observer Office, 1838. 81, xxiv p., map. **2208**
Published anonymously.

Gallatin, Albert. *A Memoir on the North-Eastern Boundary, in Connexion with Mr. Jay's Map, together with a Speech on the Same Subject, by Daniel Webster.* New York: Printed for the New York Historical Society, 1843. iii, 74 p., map. (New York Historical Society. Proceedings for the Year 1843. Appendix) **2209**

Gallatin, Albert. *The Right of the United States of America to the Northeastern Boundary Claimed by Them.* New York: S. Adams, 1840. x, 179 p., 8 maps. **2210**

Ganong, William F. "A Monograph of the Evolution of the Boundaries of the Province of New Brunswick." (1901), 7 *Royal Society of Canada, Transactions* 139-449 (2d Ser., Sec. 2). (Contributions to the History of New Brunswick, No. 5) **2211**

See also "Additions and Corrections," in (1906), 12 *Royal Society of Canada, Transactions* 151-152 (2d Ser., Sec. 2).

Gluek, Alvin Charles. "The Passamaquoddy Bay Treaty, 1910: A Diplomatic Side-Show in Canadian-American Relations." (1966), 47 *Canadian Historical Review* 1-21. **2212**

Hasse, A.R. "The Northeastern Boundary." (1900), 4 *New York Public Library Bulletin* 391-411. **2213**

Irish, Maria M. "The Northeastern Boundary of Maine." (1922), 16 *Journal of American History* 311-322. **2214**

Jones, Wilbur Devereux. "Lord Ashburton and the Maine Boundary Negotiations." (1953-54), 40 *Mississippi Valley Historical Review* 477-490. **2215**

Lawrence, William Beach. *The History of the Negotiations in Reference to the Eastern and Northeastern Boundaries of the United States.* New York: R. Craighead, 1841. 68 p., map. **2216**

Published anonymously. A Review of Albert Gallatin's *Right of the United States of America to the Northeastern Boundary Claimed by Them* (New York, 1840).

Le Duc, Thomas H. "The Maine Frontier and the Northeastern Boundary Controversy." (1947-48), 53 *American Historical Review* 30-41. **2217**

Lenentine, Charlotte. *Madawaska: A Chapter in Maine-New Brunswick Relations.* Madawaska, Me.: Madawaska Historical Society, 1975. vii, 86, xxvi p., maps. **2218**

Lucey, William L. "Some Correspondence of the Maine Commissioners Regarding the Webster-Ashburton Treaty." (1942), 15 *New England Quarterly* 331-348. **2219**

Maine. Legislature. Committee on Northeastern Boundary. *Report of the Committee on the North-Eastern Boundary.* Augusta: Severance & Dorr, 1841. 88 p., maps. **2220**

At head of title: Twenty-First Legislature. No. 19. Senate. Signed: Charles S. Daveis.

Mayo, Lawrence Shaw. "The Forty-Fifth Parallel: A Detail of the Unguarded Boundary." (1923), 13 *Geographical Review* 255-265. **2221**

Reid, R.L. "The Indian Stream Territory: An Episode of the North-East Boundary Dispute." (1940), 34 *Royal Society of Canada, Transactions* 143-171 (3d Ser., Sec. 2) **2222**

Ross, Eleanor. *The Diplomatic Controversy with Great Britain Regarding the Northeast Boundary of the United States.* Berkeley, Calif., 1932. 140 leaves. Thesis (M.A.), University of California, 1932. **2223**

Washburn, Israel. *The North-Eastern Boundary.* Portland, 1881. 106 p. (Maine Historical Society. Collections, Vol. 8, pp. 1-106) **2224**

Weatherbe, R.L. "The Acadian Boundary Disputes and the Ashburton Treaty." (1887-88), 6 *Nova Scotia Historical Society, Collections* 2-51. **2225**

Winsor, Justin. *The Cartographical History of the North-Eastern Boundary between the United States and Great Britain.* Cambridge, Mass.: J. Wilson, 1887. 24 p. **2226**
Reprinted from the proceedings of the Massachusetts Historical Society, October 1887.

Winter, Carl George. "A Note on the Passamaquoddy Boundary Affair." (1953), 34 *Canadian Historical Review* 46-53. **2227**

4. INLAND WATER BOUNDARY

"Boundary Waters between the United States and Canada." (1910), 4 *American Journal of International Law* 668-673. **2228**
Refers to the boundary waters treaty of January 11, 1909 (BTS 23(1910); 102 BFSP 137; 36 Stat. 2448; TS 548; 12 Bevans 319; 208 Parry 213).

Dreisziger, Nandor A.F. "Wrangling over the St. Mary and Milk." (1980), 28 *Alberta History* 6-15 (No. 2) **2229**
Refers to the boundary waters treaty of January 11, 1909.

Gibbons, Alan O. "Sir George Gibbons and the Boundary Waters Treaty of 1909." (1953), 34 *Canadian Historical Review* 124-138. **2230**

Gibbons, George. "Boundary Waters Treaty of 1909." (1916), 2 *Canadian Bar Association, Proceedings* 167-184. **2231**

Griffin, William L. "A History of the Canadian-United States Boundary Waters Treaty of 1909." (1959-60), 37 *University of Detroit Law Journal* 76-95. **2232**
Refers to the boundary waters treaty of January 11, 1909.

La Forest, Gerard V. "Boundary Waters Problems in the East." *In* Deener, David R., ed., *Canada-United States Treaty Relations* (Durham, N.C., 1963), pp. 28-50. **2233**

Scott, Robert Day. "The Canadian-American Boundary Waters Treaty: Why Article II?" (1958), 36 *Canadian Bar Review* 511-547. **2234**

Whitney, Harriet Eleanor. "Sir George C. Gibbons, Canadian Diplomat; and Canadian-American Boundary Water Resources 1905-1910." (1973), 3 *American Review of Canadian Studies* 65-75 (No. 1) **2235**

5. WESTERN BOUNDARY

(a) GENERAL (49TH PARALLEL, OREGON TERRITORY, ETC.)

Anderson, Samuel. "The North-American Boundary from the Lake of the Woods to the Rocky Mountains." (1876), 46 *Royal Geographical Society, Journal* 228-262. **2236**

Bashford, James Whitford. *The Oregon Missions; the Story of How the Line Was Run between Canada and the United States.* New York, Cincinnati: Abingdon Press, c1918. 311 p., map. **2237**

STATE TERRITORY

Culkin, W.E. "Northern Minnesota Boundary Surveys in 1822 to 1826, under the Treaty of Ghent." (1915), 15 *Minnesota Historical Society, Collections* 379-392. **2238**
See especially Article 7 of the Treaty of Ghent of December 24, 1814 (2 BFSP 357; 8 Stat. 218; TS 109; 12 Bevans 41; 63 Parry 421).

Deutsch, Herman J. "The Evolution of Territorial and State Boundaries in the Inland Empire of the Pacific Northwest." (1960), 51 *Pacific Northwest Quarterly* 115-131. **2239**

Deutsch, Herman J. "The Evolution of the International Boundary in the Inland Empire of the Pacific Northwest." (1960), 51 *Pacific Northwest Quarterly* 63-79. **2240**

Elliott, T.C. "The Northern Boundary of Oregon." (1919), 20 *Oregon Historical Quarterly* 25-34. **2241**

Hill, A.J. "How the Mississippi River and the Lake of the Woods Became Instrumental in the Establishment of the North-Western Boundary of the United States." (1893), 7 *Minnesota Historical Society, Collections* 305-317. **2242**
See also Article 2 of the Peace Treaty of September 3, 1783 (1 BFSP 779; 8 Stat. 80; TS 104; 12 Bevans 8; 48 Parry 437), and Article 4 of the Jay Treaty of November 19, 1794 (1 BFSP 784; 8 Stat. 116; TS 105; 12 Bevans 13; 52 Parry 243).

Ireland, Willard E. "The Evolution of the Boundaries of British Columbia." (1939), 3 *B.C. Historical Quarterly* 263-282. **2243**

Klotz, Otto. "The Forty-Ninth Parallel." (1908), 2 *Royal Astronomical Society of Canada, Journal* 282-292. **2244**

Klotz, Otto. "The Forty-Ninth Parallel." (1917), 16 *University Magazine* 422-430. **2245**

Lass, William E. "How the Forty-Ninth Parallel Became the International Boundary." (1974-75), 44 *Minnesota History* 209-219. **2246**

Martig, Ralph Richard. *The Hudson's Bay Company Claims, 1846-1869*. Urbana, Ill., 1934. 245, xiv leaves. **2247**
Thesis (Ph.D.), University of Illinois, 1934. Refers to the claims of the Hudson's Bay Company, from the signing of the Oregon Treaty on June 15, 1846 (34 BFSP 14; 9 Stat. 869; TS 120; 12 Bevans 95; 5 Miller 3; 100 Parry 39; Article 3), to the date of the final settlement of claims on September 10, 1869 (See 12 Bevans 154, Note 1).

McCabe, James O. *Great Britain and the Evolution of the Western Part of the International Boundary of Canada*. Glasgow, 1941. 2 vols. (175, 114 p., maps) Thesis (Ph.D.), University of Glasgow, 1941. **2248**

Merk, Frederick. "The Ghost River Caledonia in the Oregon Negotiation of 1818." (1949-50), 55 *American Historical Review* 530-551. **2249**

Merk, Frederick. "The Oregon Pioneers and the Boundary." (1923-24), 29 *American Historical Review* 681-699. **2250**

Miller, David Hunter, ed. *Northwest Water Boundary; Report of the Experts Summoned by the German Emperor as Arbitrator under Articles 34-42 of the Treaty of Washington of May 8, 1871, Preliminary to His Award Dated October 21, 1872*. Seattle: University of Washington, 1942. vii, 75 p. (University of Washington. Publications in the Social Sciences, Vol. 13, No. 1) **2251**
Review: Willard E. Ireland in (1942), 23 *Canadian Historical Review* 330-332.

Morris, Grace Parker. *The Relationship of the Hudson's Bay Company to the Settlement of the Oregon Boundary Dispute in 1846.* Eugene, 1941. 153 leaves. Thesis (M.A.), University of Oregon, 1941. **2252**

Nicholson, Norman L. "The U.S. Northwest Angle: East of Manitoba." (1978), 96 *Canadian Geographical Journal* 54-59 (Feb./Mar.) **2253**

Paullin, Charles O. "The Early Choice of the Forty-Ninth Parallel as a Boundary Line." (1923), 4 *Canadian Historical Review* 127-131. **2254**

Savelle, Max. "The Forty-Ninth Degree of North Latitude as an International Boundary, 1719: The Origin of an Idea." (1957), 38 *Canadian Historical Review* 183-201. **2255**

U.S. Dept. of State. *The Northwest Boundary: Discussion of the Water Boundary Question; Geographical Memoir of the Islands in Dispute; and History of the Military Occupation of San Juan Island; Accompanied by Map and Cross-Sections of Channels.* Washington: Govt. Print. Off., 1868. x, 270 p., maps. **2256**

Also issued as Senate Ex. Doc. No. 29, 40th Cong., 2d sess. (Serial No. 1316). Archibald Campbell, Commissioner on the part of the United States; James C. Prevost, Commissioner on the part of Great Britain. The Northwestern Boundary Commission, 1857-1869, was appointed under the act of August 11, 1856 (11 Stat. 42; ch. 87), in order to establish the boundary line west of the Rocky Mountains, in accordance with Article I of the Oregon Treaty of June 15, 1846. The commissioners were not successful and the Treaty of Washington of May 8, 1871, referred the matter to the Emperor of Germany for arbitration, who rendered the award at Berlin, October 21, 1872 (See *Checklist of United States Public Documents, 1789-1909,* 3d ed., 1911, pp. 912, 916).

White, James. "British Diplomacy and Canada: III. Oregon and San Juan Boundaries." (1908), 7 *University Magazine* 398-414. **2257**

White, James. "The Oregon and San Juan Boundaries." (1908), 7 *University Magazine* 398-414. **2258**

Winchell, Alexander N. "Minnesota Northern Boundary." (1898), 8 *Minnesota Historical Society, Collections* 185-212. **2259**

(b) SAN JUAN DISPUTE

"The Beginning of the San Juan Dispute." (1907), 2 *Washington Historical Quarterly* 352-356. **2260**

Dallas, Alexander Grant. *San Juan, Alaska, and the North-West Boundary.* London: H.S. King, 1873. 11 p. **2261**

Dawson, Will. *The War That Was Never Fought.* Princeton, N.J.: Auerbach Publishers, c1971. ix, 118 p., map. (Great Events in World History) **2262**

Fish, Andrew. "The Last Phase of the Oregon Boundary Question; the Struggle for San Juan Island." (1921), 22 *Oregon Historical Quarterly* 161-224. **2263**
Review: F.W. Howay in (1922), 3 *Canadian Historical Review* 286-288.

Gough, Barry M. "British Policy in the San Juan Boundary Dispute, 1854-72." (1971), 62 *Pacific Northwest Quarterly* 59-68. **2264**

Jordon, Mabel E. "The British on San Juan Island." (1959), 59 *Canadian Geographical Journal* 14-19. **2265**

Long, John W. "The Origin and Development of the San Juan Island Water Boundary Controversy." (1952), 43 *Pacific Northwest Quarterly* 187-213.
2266

Long, John W. *The San Juan Island Boundary Controversy: A Phase of Nineteenth Century Anglo-American Relations.* Durham, N.C., 1949. 595 p. **2267**
Thesis (Ph.D.), Duke University, 1949.

McCabe, James O. *The San Juan Water Boundary Question.* Toronto: University of Toronto Press, 1965 (c1964). 163 p., map. (Canadian Studies in History and Government, No. 5) **2268**
Reviews: Charles B. Bourne in (1964-65), 20 *International Journal* 539; Alvin Charles Gluek, Jr. in (1966), 47 *Canadian Historical Review* 163-164.

Miller, David Hunter. *San Juan Archipelago; Study of the Joint Occupation of San Juan Island.* Bellows Falls, Vt.: Windham Press, 1943. 203 p., map. **2269**
Reviews: James Morton Callahan in (1943), 37 *American Journal of International Law* 553; F.W. Howay in (1943), 24 *Canadian Historical Review* 316-317.

Milton, William Fitzwilliam. *A History of the San Juan Water Boundary Question, as Affecting the Division of Territory between Great Britain and the United States.* London and New York: Cassell, Petter, and Galpin, 1869. 442 p., 2 maps. **2270**

Richardson, David Blair. *Pig War Islands.* Eastsound, Wash.: Orcas Pub., 1971. 362 p., maps. **2271**
Story of the 1859 clash between British and U.S. forces over the ownership of San Juan Islands, on the Canadian-U.S. boundary.

Smith, Goldwin A. "Notes on the Problem of San Juan." (1940), 31 *Pacific Northwest Quarterly* 181-186. **2272**

Tunem, Alfred. "The Dispute over the San Juan Island Water Boundary." (1932), 23 *Washington Historical Quarterly* 38-46, 133-137, 196-204, 286-300. **2273**

6. ALASKA BOUNDARY

Alaskan Boundary Tribunal. *Proceedings of the Alaskan Boundary Tribunal, Concluded at Washington, January 24, 1903.* Washington: Govt. Print. Off., 1904. 7 vols., plates, and atlas (3 vols.) (U.S. 58th Cong., 2d sess. Senate. Doc. 162) **2274**
The tribunal was convened in London under provisions of the treaty of January 24, 1903 (BTS 4(1903); 96 BFSP 84; 32 Stat. 1961; TS 419; 12 Bevans 263; 192 Parry 336). Individual documents, such as cases, counter cases, arguments, were also published separately.

Alaskan-Canadian Boundary Commission. *Joint Report of the United States and British Commissioners on the Alaskan-Canadian Boundary. December 31, 1895.* Washington: Govt. Print. Off., 1898. 15 p., 16 maps. **2275**

Alway, Richard Martin Holden. *Anatomy of a Dispute; the Alaska Boundary Controversy as a Chapter in Canadian-American Relations.* Toronto, 1967. 90 leaves. **2276**
Thesis (Phil.M.), University of Toronto, 1967.

Bailey, Thomas Andrew. "Theodore Roosevelt and the Alaska Boundary Settlement." (1937), 18 *Canadian Historical Review* 123-130. **2277**

Baker, Marcus. *The Alaskan Boundary.* New York, 1896. 16 p., maps. **2278**
Reprinted from the *Bulletin of the American Geographical Society* (1896), vol. 28, pp. 130-145.

Balch, Thomas Willing. *The Alaska Frontier.* Philadelphia: Allen, Lane and Scott, 1903. xv, 198 p., maps. **2279**

Balch, Thomas Willing. *The Alasko-Canadian Frontier.* Philadelphia: Press of Allen, Lane and Scott, 1902. 45 p., maps. **2280**
Read at the annual meeting of the Franklin Institute, January 15, 1902, and reprinted from the *Journal of the Franklin Institute* for March, 1902.

Ball, Georgiana. "The Peter Martin Case and the Provisional Settlement of the Stikine Boundary." (1971), 10 *B.C. Studies* 35-55. **2281**

Bourne, Charles B., and McRae, Donald M. "Maritime Jurisdiction in the Dixon Entrance: The Alaska Boundary Re-Examined." (1976), 14 *Canadian Yearbook of International Law* 175-223. **2282**

Callahan, James Morton. *The Alaska Purchase and Americo-Canadian Relations.* Morgantown, W. Va.: Department of History and Political Science, West Virginia University, 1908. 44 p. (West Virginia University. Studies in American History. Series 1, Diplomatic History, Nos. 2 and 3) **2283**

Canada. Parliament. *Boundary between Alaska and Canada. Protocol No. LXIII of the Joint High Commission, Washington, Respecting the Boundary between Alaska and Canada, Dated February 18, 1899.* Ottawa, 1899. 6 p. (Canada. Parliament, 1899. Sessional Papers, No. 99) **2284**

Canada. Parliament. *Convention Regarding the Alaskan Boundary Line, Signed at Washington, April 21, 1906, with Related Documents.* Ottawa, 1907. 5 p. (Canada. Parliament, 1907-1908. Sessional Papers, No. 54) **2285**

Canada. Parliament. *Correspondence and Papers in Relation to the Alaska Boundary Question.* Ottawa, 1903. 11 p. (Canada. Parliament, 1903. Sessional Papers, No. 149) **2286**
Includes the text of the convention of January 24, 1903.

Canada. Parliament. *Correspondence Regarding the Settlement of the Boundary Line between Alaska and British Columbia.* Ottawa, 1876. 5 p. (Canada. Parliament, 1876. Sessional Papers, No. 110) **2287**

Canada. Parliament. *Report of Major General Cameron on the Proposed Convention in Reference to a Portion of the Alaskan Boundary, with a Memorandum.* Ottawa, 1897. 9 p. (Canada. Parliament, 1897. Sessional Papers, No. 77) **2288**

Canada. Parliament. *Report of the Engineer Employed on the Boundary Line between British Columbia and Alaska, with Accompanying Documents.* Ottawa, 1878. 171 p., map. (Canada. Parliament, 1878. Sessional Papers, No. 125) **2289**

Canada's Alaskan Dismemberment: An Analytical Examination of the Fallacies Underlying the Tribunal Award. Niagara-on-the-Lake, Ont.: Printed by C. Thonger, 1904. 76 p. **2290**

Cole, Douglas. "Allen Aylesworth on the Alaska Boundary Award." (1971), 52 *Canadian Historical Review* 472-477. **2291**

Davidson, Donald C. *The Alaska Boundary*. Berkeley, Calif., 1938. **2292**
Thesis (Ph.D.), University of California at Berkeley, 1916. Listed in (1937-38), 5 *Doctoral Dissertations Accepted by American Universities* 76.

Davidson, George. *The Alaska Boundary*. San Francisco: Alaska Packers Association, 1903. 235 p., 2 maps. **2293**

Ewart, John S. "The Alaska Boundary." *In* Ewart, John S., *The Kingdom of Canada* (Toronto, 1908), pp. 299-347. **2294**

Foster, John W. *The Alaskan Boundary*. Washington: National Geographic Society, 1899. **2295**
Excerpt from (1899), 10 *National Geographic Magazine* 425-456.

Foster, John W. *The Alaskan Boundary Tribunal*. Washington, D.C.: Judd & Detweiler, 1903. 14 p., map. **2296**
A lecture delivered at Washington, D.C., December 8, 1903.

Garraty, John A., ed. "Henry Cabot Lodge and the Alaskan Boundary Tribunal." (1951), 24 *New England Quarterly* 469-494. **2297**

Gibson, F.W. "The Alaskan Boundary Dispute." (1945), *Canadian Historical Association, Historical Papers* 25-41. **2298**
Includes a discussion (pp. 40-41).

Glass, David. "The Alaskan Boundary Line." (1899), 2 *Anglo-American Magazine* 315-325, 464-472, 548-573. **2299**

Gosnell, R.E. "The Alaska Boundary Question." (1895-96), 6 *Canadian Magazine* 248-258. **2300**

Hodgins, Thomas. "The Alaska Boundary Commission." (1903), 23 *Canadian Law Times* 150-153. **2301**

Hodgins, Thomas. "The Alaska-Canada Boundary Dispute." (1902), 38 *Canada Law Journal* 571-588. **2302**

Hodgins, Thomas. "The Alaska-Canada Boundary Dispute." (1901-02), 1 *Canadian Law Review* 525-537. **2303**

Hodgins, Thomas. *The Alaska-Canada Boundary Dispute, under the Anglo-Russian Treaty of 1825; the Russian-American Alaska Treaty of 1867; and the Anglo-American Conventions of 1892, 1894 and 1897. An Historical and Legal Review*. Toronto: R.G. McLean, 1902. 24 p., map. **2304**

Hodgins, Thomas. *The Alaska-Canada Boundary Dispute, under the Anglo-Russian Treaty of 1825; the Russian-American Alaska Treaty of 1867; and the Anglo-American Conventions of 1892, 1894 and 1897. An Historical and Legal Review*. 2d ed. Toronto: W. Tyrrell, 1903. 26 p., map. **2305**

Hodgins, Thomas. "The Alaska Tribunal and International Law." (1903), 23 *Canadian Law Times* 435-454. **2306**

Holmested, George S. "The Alaskan Boundary." (1904), 3 *Canadian Law Review* 59-69. **2307**

Huculak, Michael. *When Russia Was in America; the Alaska Boundary Treaty*

Negotiations, 1824-25, and the Role of Pierre de Poletica. Vancouver: Mitchell Press, c1971. xv, 149 p., map. **2308**

Hyde, Charles Cheney. "Concerning the Alaskan Boundary." (1902-03), 16 *Harvard Law Review* 418-435. **2309**

Jebb, Richard. "The Alaska Boundary." (1903), 5 *Empire Review* 185-193. **2310**

Lowry, Bullitt. "The Canadian 'Dalmatia' at the Paris Peace Conference, 1919." (1972), 14 *B.C. Studies* 47-50. **2311**

MacArthur, D.A. "British Diplomacy and Canada: II. The Alaska Boundary Award." (1907), 6 *University Magazine* 412-426, maps. **2312**

Miller, David Hunter. *The Alaska Treaty*. Kingston, Ont.: Limestone Press, 1981. vi, 221 p., 4 p. of plates. (Alaska History, No. 18) **2313**

Moore, John Bassett. "The Alaskan Boundary." (1899), 169 *North American Review* 501-515. **2314**

Munro, John A., ed. *The Alaska Boundary Dispute*. Toronto: Copp Clark, c1970. 169 p., maps. (Issues in Canadian History) **2315**

Munro, John A. "English-Canadianism and the Demand for Canadian Autonomy: Ontario's Response to the Alaska Boundary Decision, 1903." (1965), 57 *Ontario History* 189-203. **2316**

Penlington, Norman. *The Alaska Boundary Dispute: A Critical Reappraisal*. Toronto: McGraw-Hill Ryerson, 1972. ix, 141 p., maps. (Frontenac Library, No. 5) **2317**
Review: Charles S. Campbell in (1975), 56 *Canadian Historical Review* 73-74.

Smith, Gaddis G. "The Alaska Panhandle at the Paris Peace Conference, 1919." (1961-62), 17 *International Journal* 25-29. **2318**

Tompkins, Stuart R. "Drawing the Alaskan Boundary." (1945), 26 *Canadian Historical Review* 1-24. **2319**

Vexler, Robert Irwin. *The Alaskan Boundary Dispute*. Rochester, N.Y., 1960. 179 leaves. **2320**
Thesis (M.A.), University of Rochester, 1961.

Wade, F.C. "Some Comments on the Alaskan Award." (1903-04), 22 *Canadian Magazine* 336-342. **2321**

White, James. "Henry Cabot Lodge and the Alaska Boundary Award." (1925), 6 *Canadian Historical Review* 332-347. **2322**

White, James. "Treaty of 1825 - Correspondence Respecting the Boundary between Russian America (Alaska) and British North America." (1915), 9 *Royal Society of Canada, Transactions* 65-78 (3d Ser., Sec. 2) **2323**

7. LABRADOR BOUNDARY

Bédard, Roger Jean. *L'affaire du Labrador, anatomie d'une fraude. Synthèse et conclusion d'une étude sur l'arrière-plan économique et politique de l'affaire du Labrador*. Montréal: Éditions du Jour, 1968. 124 p. (Collection Les idées du jour, D-39) **2324**

Dorion, Henri. "L'affaire du Labrador entre le droit constitutionnel et le droit international." (1967), 2 *Revue Juridique Thémis* 93-97. **2325**

Dorion, Henri. *La frontière Québec-Terreneuve; contribution à l'étude systématique des frontières.* Québec: Presses de l'Université Laval, 1963. 316 p., maps. (Université Laval. Institut de géographie. Publications, 2) (Université Laval. Centre d'études nordiques. Travaux et documents, 1) **2326**
  Review: Fernand Grenier in (1963-64), 17 *Revue d'Histoire de l'Amérique Française* 601-603.

Gardner, Gérard. "La frontière Canada-Labrador." (1938), 24 *Revue Trimestrielle Canadienne* 272-289. **2327**

Gt. Brit. Privy Council. Judicial Committee. *In the Matter of the Boundary between the Dominion of Canada and the Colony of Newfoundland in the Labrador Peninsula, between the Dominion of Canada of the One Part and the Colony of Newfoundland of the Other Part.* London, Printed by W. Clowes, 1927. 12 vols., maps. **2328**

Howley, M.F. "The Labrador Boundary Question." (1907), 1 *Royal Society of Canada, Transactions* 291-305 (3d Ser., Sec. 2) **2329**

McGrath, *Sir* Patrick T. "The Labrador Boundary Decision." (1927), 17 *Geographical Review* 643-660. **2330**
  Refers to the decision of March 1, 1927, rendered by the Judicial Committee of the imperial Privy Council in London.

Patenaude, Luce. *Le Labrador à l'heure de la contestation.* Montréal: Presses de l'Université de Montréal, 1972. xvii, 434 p., maps. (Collection Centre de recherche en droit public) **2331**
  Thesis (LL.D.), University of Ottawa.
  Reviews: Jean-Maurice Arbour in (1972), 13 *Cahiers de Droit* 459-462; Giovanni Scarangella Arpino in (1972-75), 9 *Jus Gentium (Rome)* 220-221; Clive Lloyd Brown-John in (1975), 69 *American Journal of International Law* 933; Henri Brun in (1973), 6 *Canadian Journal of Political Science* 518-520; James M. Mabbutt in (1972), 7 *University of British Columbia Law Review* 331-333; Jean Provencher in (1973-74), 27 *Revue d'Histoire de l'Amérique Française* 292-293; Jean-K. Samson in (1972), 7 *Revue Juridique Thémis* 255-256; Joe Verhoeven in (1974), 10 *Revue Belge de Droit International* 390-391.

Rothney, Gordon O. "L'annexion de la côte du Labrador à Terre-Neuve en 1763." (1963-64), 17 *Revue d'Histoire de l'Amérique Française* 213-243. **2332**

Smith, William. "The Labrador Boundary Case." (1929), 36 *Queen's Quarterly* 267-281. **2333**

White, James. "The Labrador Boundary." (1909), 8 *University Magazine* 215-224, map. **2334**

B. Boundary Delimitation and Demarcation

Anderson, Chandler P. *Northern Boundary of the United States; the Demarcation of the Boundary between the United States and Canada, from the Atlantic to the Pacific, with Particular Reference to the Portions Thereof Which Require More Complete Definition and Marking.* Report Prepared for the Dept. of State. Washington: Govt. Print. Off., 1906. iv, 85 p. **2335**

Boggs, S. Whittemore. "Problems of Water-Boundary Definition: Median Lines and International Boundaries through Territorial Waters." (1937), 27 *Geographical Review* 445-456. **2336**

Canada. Parliament. *Joint Report on the Survey and Remonumenting of the Quebec-New York International Boundary.* Ottawa, 1903. 31 p. (Canada. Parliament, 1903. Sessional Papers, No. 65) **2337**

Canada. Parliament. *Treaty Providing for the Demarcation of the International Boundary between Canada and the States, Signed at Washington, April 11, 1908, with Related Correspondence.* Ottawa, 1908. 10, 25 p. (Canada. Parliament, 1907-1908. Sessional Papers, Nos. 54a, and 54b) **2338**

Classen, H. George. "Keepers of the Boundary." (1962), 65 *Canadian Geographical Journal* 122-129. **2339**

Cuyvers, Luc. "Maritime Boundaries: Canada vs. United States." (1979-80), 2 *Marine Policy Reports* No. 1 (5 p.) **2340**

Deutsch, Herman J. "A Contemporary Report on the 49^0 Boundary Survey." (1962), 53 *Pacific Northwest Quarterly* 17-33. **2341**

Eggleston, Ellen K. "The Gulf of Maine Maritime Boundary Dispute." (1982), 12 *Denver Journal of International Law and Policy* 120-127. **2342**

Frédérick, Michel. "La délimitation du plateau continental entre le Canada et les États-Unis dans la mer de Beaufort." (1979), 17 *Canadian Yearbook of International Law* 30-98. **2343**

Frédérick, Michel. *La délimitation du plateau continental entre le Canada et les États-Unis dans la mer de Beaufort.* Ottawa, 1980. 138 frames. **2344**
Thesis (LL.M.), Université d'Ottawa, 1980. (National Library of Canada. Canadian Theses on Microfiche, No. 48528).

Green, Lewis. *The Boundary Hunters: Surveying the 141st Meridian and the Alaska Panhandle.* Vancouver: University of British Columbia Press, 1982. xii, 214 p., 24 p. of plates, maps. **2345**

"The International Boundary Commission." (1962), 14 *External Affairs* 126-130. **2346**

International Boundary Commission. *Annual Joint Report.* 1st–, 1905?–. Ottawa; Washington. **2347**
The commission operates under the Alaska boundary convention of April 21, 1906 (BTS 5(1906); 99 BFSP 177; 34 Stat. 2948; TS 452; 12 Bevans 279; 201 Parry 104), the boundary convention of April 11, 1908 (BTS 18(1908); 101 BFSP 210; 35 Stat. 2003; TS 497; 12 Bevans 297; 206 Parry 377), implemented by the *International Boundary Commission Act* (R.S.C. 1970, c. I-19), and the boundary convention (Lake Superior-Lake of

the Woods) of February 24, 1925 (BTS 37(1927); 121 BFSP 933; 44 Stat. 2102; TS 720; 6 Bevans 7; 43 LNTS 239). The International Boundary Commission has had commissioners appointed since 1904, and a full time commission was appointed in 1925. Its purpose is to define, mark, and maintain the demarcation of the international boundary line between Canada and the United States. The 53d annual report covers the year 1978 (28 p.).

International Boundary Commission. *Joint Report upon the Survey and Demarcation of the Boundary between Canada and the United States from Tongass Passage to Mount St. Elias.* Ottawa, 1952. xiv, 365 p., maps. **2348**
Accompanied by *Joint Maps of the International Boundary between United States and Canada from Cape Muzon to Mount St. Elias*, Ottawa?, 1952. 13 maps. This is one of a series of seven final reports on the survey and demarcation of the several sections of the international boundary line between Canada and the United States.

International Boundary Commission. *Joint Report upon the Survey and Demarcation of the Boundary between the United States and Canada from the Gulf of Georgia to the Northwesternmost Point of Lake of the Woods, etc.* Washington: Govt. Print. Off., 1937. xv, 477 p., map, and atlas (61 maps) **2349**
The atlas has title: *Joint Maps of the International Boundary between United States and Canada from the Gulf of Georgia to the Northwesternmost Point of the Lake of the Woods* (59 sheets).

International Boundary Commission. *Joint Report upon the Survey and Demarcation of the Boundary between the United States and Canada from the Northwesternmost Point of Lake of the Woods to Lake Superior, etc.* Washington: Govt. Print. Off., 1931. xiv, 621 p., maps, and atlas (37 maps) **2350**
Accompanied by *Triangulation and Traverse Sketches*, Washington, Govt. Print. Off., 1931. 41 maps.

International Boundary Commission. *Joint Report upon the Survey and Demarcation of the Boundary between the United States and Canada from the Source of the St. Croix River to the Atlantic Ocean, etc.* Washington: Govt. Print. Off., 1934. xiv, 318 p., maps, and atlas (19 maps) **2351**
The atlas has title: *Joint Maps of the International Boundary between United States and Canada from the Source of the St. Croix River to the Atlantic Ocean.*

International Boundary Commission. *Joint Report upon the Survey and Demarcation of the Boundary between the United States and Canada from the Source of the St. Croix River to the St. Lawrence River, etc.* Washington: Govt. Print. Off., 1925. xv, 512 p., maps, and atlas (62 maps) **2352**
The atlas has title: *Joint Maps of the International Boundary between United States and Canada from the St. Lawrence River to the Source of the St. Croix River* (61 sheets). Accompanied by *Triangulation and Precise Traverse Sketches*, Washington, Govt. Print. Off., 1924. 15 maps.

International Boundary Commission. *Joint Report upon the Survey and Demarcation of the Boundary between the United States and Canada from the Western Terminus of the Land Boundary along the Forty-Ninth Parallel, on the West Side of Point Roberts, through Georgia, Haro, and Juan de Fuca Straits, to the Pacific Ocean.* Washington: Govt. Print. Off., 1921. 104 p., map. **2353**
Review: F.W. Howay in (1921), 2 *Canadian Historical Review* 382-383.

International Boundary Commission. *Joint Report upon the Survey and Demarcation of the International Boundary between the United States and Canada along the 141st Meridian from the Arctic Ocean to Mount St. Elias.* Washington: Govt. Print. Off., 1918. 305 p., maps, and atlas (41 maps) **2354**

International Boundary Commission. *Maintenance of the Boundary between Canada and the United States under the Provisions of Article 4 of the Treaty of 1925. Revised Data from the Source of St. Croix River to the Mouth of St. Francis River: Together with an Account of Maintenance Operations on This Section from 1927 to 1952, Inclusive.* Ottawa; Washington, 1955. 182 p. (International Boundary Commission. Special Report, No. 1) **2355**

See also *Revised Data from the Source of St. Croix River to the Atlantic Ocean and Maintenance on This Section from 1925 to 1961*, published in 1962 (*Its* Special Report No. 3).

Klotz, Otto. "The History of the Forty-Ninth Parallel Survey West of the Rocky Mountains." (1917), 3 *Geographical Review* 382-387. **2356**

La Forest, Gerard V. "The Delimitation of National Territory: *Re Dominion Coal Company and County of Cape Breton.*" (1964), 2 *Canadian Yearbook of International Law* 233-244. **2357**

Lawson, Karin L. "Delimiting Continental Shelf Boundaries in the Arctic: The United States-Canada Beaufort Sea Boundary." (1981), 22 *Virginia Journal of International Law* 222-246. **2358**

McDorman, Ted L.; Beauchamp, Kenneth P.; and Johnston, Douglas M. *Maritime Boundary Delimitation: An Annotated Bibliography.* Lexington, Mass.: Lexington Books, c1983. xiii, 207 p. **2359**

McRae, Donald M. "Proportionality and the Gulf of Maine Maritime Boundary Dispute." (1981), 19 *Canadian Yearbook of International Law* 287-302. **2360**

Nesham, E.W. "The Alaska Boundary Demarcation." (1927), 69 *Geographical Journal* 49-61. **2361**

Nied, G. David. "International Adjudication: Settlement of the United States-Canada Maritime Boundary Dispute - *Delimitation of the Maritime Boundary in the Gulf of Maine Area (U.S. v. Can.),* (1982) *I.C.J. Reports* 3." (1982), 23 *Harvard International Law Journal* 138-143. **2362**

North American Boundary Commission, 1872-1876. *Reports upon the Survey of the Boundary between the Territory of the United States and the Possessions of Great Britain from the Lake of the Woods to the Summit of the Rocky Mountains.* Washington: Govt. Print. Off., 1878. 624 p., maps. (U.S. 44th Cong., 2d sess. Senate. Ex. Doc. 41) **2363**

At head of title: Dept. of State.

Parsons, John E. *West on the 49th Parallel; Red River to the Rockies, 1872-1876.* New York: W. Morrow, 1963. xiv, 208 p., maps. **2364**

Account of the surveying of the boundary between the United States and Canada.

Rigaldies, Francis. "La délimitation du plateau continental entre états voisins." (1976), 14 *Canadian Yearbook of International Law* 116-174. **2365**

Riggs, Thomas. "Surveying the 141st Meridian." (1912), 23 *National Geographic Magazine* 685-713. **2366**

Swan, George S. "That Gulf of Maine Dispute: Canada and the United States Delimit the Atlantic Continental Shelf." (1977-78), 10 *Natural Resources Lawyer* 405-456. **2367**

STATE TERRITORY   183

Tait, W.McD. "Fixing the Border Line." (1915), 45 *Canadian Magazine* 209-216.
2368

Turner, Allan R. "Surveying the International Boundary: The Journal of George M. Dawson, 1873." (1968), 21 *Saskatchewan History* 1-23. **2369**

U.S. Congress. House. Committee on Merchant Marine and Fisheries. *Oversight Report on the U.S.-Canada East Coast Fishery Agreement and Boundary Treaty.* Submitted by John B. Breaux, Chairman, Subcommittee on Fisheries and Wildlife Conservation and the Environment. Washington: Govt. Print. Off., 1980. ii, 23 p. (Serial No. 96-C) **2370**

U.S. Congress. Senate. Committee on Foreign Relations. *Maritime Boundary Settlement Treaty and East Coast Fishery Resources Agreement: Hearings, 96th Cong., 2d sess., on Ex. U, 96-1, and Ex. V, 96-1, April 15 and 17, 1980.* Washington: Govt. Print. Off., 1980. iv, 223 p., maps. **2371**
Refers to the maritime boundary treaty (S.Ex. U. 96-1), and the fishery agreement (S.Ex. V. 96-1), both signed at Washington on March 29, 1979.

U.S. Congress. Senate. Committee on Foreign Relations. *The Maritime Boundary Treaty with Canada: Hearing, 97th Cong., 1st sess., on Ex. U, 96-1, March 18, 1981.* Washington: Govt. Print. Off., 1981. iii, 46 p. **2372**

Weeks, Kathleen. "Monuments Mark This Boundary." (1945), 31 *Canadian Geographical Journal* 120-133. **2373**

Wilson, *Sir* Charles William. *Mapping the Frontier; Charles Wilson's Diary of the Survey of the 49th Parallel, 1858-1862, While Secretary of the British Boundary Commission.* Edited with an introduction by George F.G. Stanley. Toronto: Macmillan of Canada, 1970. 182 p., maps. **2374**
Review: Ian McClymont in (1972-73), 52 *Dalhousie Review* 149-150.

C. Transboundary Relations

See also *"Air Pollution (Transboundary)" (p. 667).*

1. GENERAL

"Entente Cordiale? Bilateral Commissions and International Legal Methods of Adjustment." (1974), 68 *American Society of International Law, Proceedings* 226-250. **2375**
This is a panel; Richard B. Lillich, Chairman.
Contents: "The International Joint Commission: United States-Canada," by Charles R. Ross (pp. 229-236).- "The International Joint Commission: United States-Canada," by Maxwell Cohen (pp. 236-239).- "The Case for Cross Border Litigation: The Continent that Sues Together Hews Together," by Charles N. Brower (pp. 239-243).

McDougall, Ian A. "The Development of International Law with Respect to Trans-Boundary Water Resources: Co-operation for Mutual Advantage or Continentalism's Thin Edge of the Wedge?" (1971), 9 *Osgoode Hall Law Journal* 261-311. **2376**

Munro, Gordon R. "The Optimal Management of Transboundary Renewable Resources." (1979), 12 *Canadian Journal of Economics* 355-376. **2377**

Scott, Anthony D. "Fisheries, Pollution and Canadian-American Transnational Relations." (1974), 28 *International Organization* 827-848. **2378**
Reprinted in Fox, Annette Baker, and others, *Canada and the United States* (New York, 1976), pp. 234-255.

Stein, Murray. "Aspects of United States and Canadian Water Law." (1970), 20 *University of Toronto Law Journal* 69-71. **2379**

2. INTERNATIONAL JOINT COMMISSION

Beaupré, Bernard. "Le rôle de la Commission mixte internationale dans la gestion du bassin des Grands Lacs et du fleuve Saint-Laurent." (1977), 3 *Études Canadiennes (France)* 19-32. **2380**

Bloomfield, Louis M., and FitzGerald, Gerald F. *Boundary Waters Problems of Canada and the United States. (The International Joint Commission 1912-1958).* Toronto: Carswell, 1958. x, 264 p., map. **2381**
Reviews: Juraj Andrassy in (1959-60), 20 *Zeitschrift für Ausländisches Öffentliches Recht und Völkerrecht* 699-700; Charles B. Bourne in (1958-59), 14 *International Journal* 145-146; William L. Griffin in (1959), 53 *American Journal of International Law* 728-729; Roger Pinto in (1960), 87 *Journal du Droit International* 313 (brief notice); Charles Rousseau in (1959), 63 *Revue Générale de Droit International Public* 376-377 (brief notice).

Burpee, Lawrence J. "From Sea to Sea." (1938), 16 *Canadian Geographical Journal* 3-32. **2382**

Burpee, Lawrence J. "An International Experiment." (1923-24), 3 *Dalhousie Review* 163-179. **2383**

Burpee, Lawrence J. "The International Joint Commission." (1915), 14 *University Magazine* 362-374. **2384**

Burpee, Lawrence J. "The International Joint Commission." (1916), 16 *Journal of Comparative Legislation* 5-12 (N.S.) **2385**

Canada. Parliament. *Documents concerning the Appointment of Commissioners under the Treaty with the United States Relating to Boundary Waters of January 11, 1909, with Related Papers.* Ottawa, 1912. 23 p. (Canada. Parliament, 1912. Sessional Papers, No. 119) **2386**

Canada. Water Resources Branch. *The Activities of the International Joint Commission, 1909-1956.* Ottawa, 1956. 1 vol. (various pagings), maps. **2387**

Carter, Arthur T. "The Boundary Waters Treaty of 1909: Does It Provide an Environmental Cause of Action?" (1975), 20 *South Dakota Law Review* 147-180. **2388**

Chacko, Chirakaikaran Joseph. *The International Joint Commission between the United States of America and the Dominion of Canada.* New York: Columbia University Press; London: P.S. King, 1932. 431 p., map. (Studies in History Economics and Public Law, No. 358) **2389**
Series statement also appears as: Columbia University Studies in the Social Sciences

358. Originally presented as the author's thesis (Ph.D.), Columbia University, 1932. Reprinted New York, AMS Press, 1968.
Reviews: Robert A. MacKay in (1933), 11 *Canadian Bar Review* 66-68; Norman A.M. MacKenzie in (1932), 13 *Canadian Historical Review* 437-439; J.S. Reeves in (1933), 27 *American Journal of International Law* 187-188.

Chacko, Chirakaikaran Joseph. *International Waterways, with Special Reference to the International Joint Commission between the United States and Canada.* New York, 1927. 55 leaves. **2390**
Thesis (M.A.), Columbia University, 1927.

Cohen, Maxwell. "Canada and the United States: Dispute Settlement and the International Joint Commission - Can This Experience Be Applied to Law of the Sea Issues?" (1976), 8 *Case Western Reserve Journal of International Law* 69-83. **2391**

Cohen, Maxwell. "The International Joint Commission: United States-Canada." (1974), 68 *American Society of International Law, Proceedings* 236-239. **2392**

Cohen, Maxwell. "The Régime of Boundary Waters: The Canadian-United States Experience." (1975), 146 *Académie de Droit International, Recueil des Cours* 219-339. **2393**

Cohen, Maxwell. "Le traité canado-américain des eaux limitrophes et la Commission mixte internationale." (1980), 11 *Études Internationales* 375-392. **2394**

"Control of Pollution in Canada-United States Boundary Waters." (1951), 3 *External Affairs* 425. **2395**

Dreisziger, Nandor A.F. *The International Joint Commission of the United States and Canada, 1895-1920: A Study in Canadian-American Relations.* Toronto, 1974. vi, 420 leaves. **2396**
Thesis (Ph.D.), University of Toronto, 1974. (National Library of Canada. Canadian Theses on Microfiche, No. 27831).

Dunlop, Charles Clifford. *The Origin and Development of the International Joint Commission as a Judicial Tribunal.* Kingston, 1960. 221 leaves, maps. **2397**
Thesis (M.A.), Queen's University, 1960.

Dwivedi, O.P. "The International Joint Commission: Its Role in the United States-Canada Boundary Pollution Control." (1974), 40 *International Review of Administrative Sciences* 369-376. **2398**
Includes a résumé in French under title: "Le rôle de la Commission mixte Canada-États-Unis en matière de lutte contre la pollution" (pp. vii-viii).

Heeney, Arnold D.P. "Along the Common Frontier: The International Joint Commission." (1966-67), 26 *Behind the Headlines* No. 5 (18 p.) **2399**

Heeney, Arnold D.P. "External Affairs in Parliament: International Joint Commission." (1966), 18 *External Affairs* 350-358. **2400**

Heeney, Arnold D.P. "The International Joint Commission." (1963), 15 *External Affairs* 141-145. **2401**

International Joint Commission. *Annual Report.* 1st—, 1974—. Washington; Ottawa. **2402**
The International Joint Commission between the United States and Canada was set up in 1911, pursuant to the boundary waters treaty of January 11, 1909 (BTS 23(1910); 102

BFSP 137; 36 Stat. 2448; TS 548; 12 Bevans 319; 208 Parry 213), implemented by the *International Boundary Waters Treaty Act* (S.C. 1911, c. 28; R.S.C. 1970, c. I-20), and held its first meeting in January 1912. It precedes the short lived International Waterways Commission founded in 1905. It is an autonomous agency, whose Canadian Co-Chairman reports to Parliament through the Secretary of State for External Affairs. The International Joint Commission deals with matters relating to boundary waters and rivers crossing the boundary line, and carries out work through international boards and working committees. The projects received by the I.J.C., either by *application* for approval, or by *reference* for investigation, are listed in its annual report, starting with Docket No. 1 in 1912 (the last project in 1977 is Docket No. 107). Summaries of cases can be found in a number of publications: e.g. Dockets 1-72 are outlined in Bloomfield, L.M., and FitzGerald, Gerald F., *Boundary Waters Problems of Canada and the United States* (Toronto, 1958), pp. 65-205. Only a selection of the most important I.J.C. publications will be listed in this bibliography. These, in almost all cases, fall in the category of references, i.e. investigations and studies of specific problems of differences referred to it by the United States or the Canadian government, or both. Some of these references resulted in the conclusion of additional agreements, such as the convention regulating the level of Lake of the Woods of February 24, 1925 (See Docket No. 3), the unperfected treaty regarding the St. Lawrence project of July 18, 1932 (See Docket No. 17), the Columbia River treaty of January 17, 1961 (See Docket No. 51), and the Great Lakes water quality agreement of April 15, 1972 (See Docket No. 83).

International Joint Commission. *Annual Report on Great Lakes Water Quality.* 1st—, 1973—. Windsor, Ont.: International Joint Commission. **2403**

International Joint Commission. *Champlain Waterway: Interim Report of the International Joint Commission on the Champlain Waterway.* Washington; Ottawa. 1937. Ottawa: King's Printer, 1938. 187 p., maps. **2404**

Reference for investigation of deep waterway from St. Lawrence to Hudson River, filed in 1936 (Docket No. 37); project completed; it recommended a new study after the St. Lawrence Seaway was built. See also Docket No. 77 (1962).

International Joint Commission. *Columbia River: Water Resources of the Columbia River Basin; Report to the Joint Commission from the International Columbia River Engineering Board.* n.p., 1959. 110 p., map. **2405**

Reference filed in 1944 (Docket No. 51); completed; it resulted in the conclusion of the Columbia River treaty signed January 17, 1961 (CTS 1964/2).

International Joint Commission. *Functions, Powers and Duties of the International Joint Commission and of the International Boards Operating under Its Jurisdiction.* Ottawa: King's Printer, 1935. 11 p. **2406**

International Joint Commission. *Garrison Diversion Unit: Transboundary Implications of the Garrison Diversion Unit.* Ottawa; Washington: International Joint Commission, 1977. v, 153 p. **2407**

Reference filed in 1975 (Docket No. 101); completed. This report was presented to the governments of Canada and the United States.

International Joint Commission. *Great Lakes Levels: Regulation of Great Lakes Water Levels, Report by the International Great Lakes Levels Board.* n.p., 1973. 294 p. **2408**

Reference filed in 1964 (Docket No. 82); completed. See also its *Interim Report* (1968. 20 p.), and *Further Regulation* (1976. ix, 96 p., maps).

International Joint Commission. *Great Lakes Pollution: New and Revised Great Lakes Water Quality Objectives.* Windsor, Ont.: International Joint Commission, 1977—. **2409**

International Joint Commission. *The International Joint Commission: Organization, Jurisdiction and Operation under the Treaty of January 11, 1909, between the United States and Great Britain.* Washington: Govt. Print. Off., 1924. v, 55 p.
2410

International Joint Commission. *Lake of the Woods: Final Report of the International Joint Commission on the Lake of the Woods Reference.* Washington-Ottawa. Washington: Govt. Print. Off., 1917. ii, 261 p., 54 plates. **2411**
Reference for investigation filed in 1912 (Docket No. 3); project completed; it resulted in the conclusion of the convention to regulate the level of Lake of the Woods, signed February 24, 1925 (BTS 38(1925); 121 BFSP 939; 44 Stat. 2108; TS 721; 6 Bevans 41; 43 LNTS 251).

International Joint Commission. *Lake of the Woods: Report to International Joint Commission Relating to Official Reference re Lake of the Woods Levels,* by Adolph F. Meyer, and Arthur V. White, Consulting Engineers. Washington-Ottawa, 1916. Washington: Govt. Print. Off., 1916-17. 3 vols., plates, maps.
Contents: v.1. Text.- v.2. Plates.- v.3. Tables. **2412**

International Joint Commission. *Papers Relating to the Work of the International Joint Commission.* Ottawa, 1929. 171 p., map. **2413**
Contents: "International Relations," by George Gibbons (pp. 7-17).- "The International Joint Commission of the United States and Canada," by Wesley L. Jones (pp. 18-26).-"A Successful Experiment in International Relations," by Lawrence J. Burpee (pp. 27-42).- "The International Joint Commission," by Charles S. MacInnes (pp. 43-47).-"An International Experiment," by Lawrence J. Burpee (pp. 48-62).- "Insurance for Peace," by Lawrence J. Burpee (pp. 63-70).- "The International Joint Commission between the United States and Canada," by Robert A. MacKay (pp. 71-100).- "International Joint Commission," by William H. Smith (pp. 101-147); includes a summary of cases (Docket Nos. 1-25).- List of Documents of the International Joint Commission.

International Joint Commission. *Passamaquoddy Tidal Power: Report of the International Joint Commission, United States and Canada, on the Investigation of the International Passamaquoddy Tidal Power Project.* Washington, 1961. 35 p. **2414**
References for investigation filed in 1948 (Docket No. 60), and 1956 (Docket No. 72); completed. See also hearings held in U.S. Congress, House, Committee on Foreign Affairs, July 14 and 22, 1953 (Washington, Govt. Print. Off., 1953. iv, 93 p., maps).

International Joint Commission. *Pollution of Boundary Waters: Final Report of the International Joint Commission on the Pollution of Boundary Waters Reference.* Washington-Ottawa. Washington: Govt. Print. Off., 1918. 56 p.
2415
Reference for investigation filed in 1912 (See Docket No. 4); project completed; recommendations not implemented.

International Joint Commission. *Pollution of Boundary Waters: Progress Report of the International Joint Commission on the Reference re the Pollution of Boundary Waters.* Washington, 1914. iv, (4), 388 p., plates, maps. **2416**

International Joint Commission. *Pollution of Boundary Waters: Report of the Consulting Sanitary Engineer, upon Remedial Measures. March 8, 1916.* Washington: Govt. Print. Off., 1916. 159 p., maps. **2417**

International Joint Commission. *Pollution of Boundary Waters: Report of the*

International Joint Commission on the Pollution of Boundary Waters.
Washington, 1951. 312 p., maps. **2418**
See also *Report,* 1950. 10 p.

International Joint Commission. *Pollution of Lower Great Lakes: Pollution of Lake Erie, Lake Ontario and the International Section of the St. Lawrence River.* Ottawa: Information Canada, 1970 (i.e. 1971). 105 p., maps. **2419**
Also issued in French under title: *La pollution dans le lac Erié, le lac Ontario, et le secteur international du fleuve Saint-Laurent* (1971. 116 p., maps). Also published Washington: Govt. Print. Off., 1970 (i.e. 1971). iv, 174 p., maps.

International Joint Commission. *Pollution of Lower Great Lakes: Report to the International Joint Commission on the Pollution of Lake Erie, Lake Ontario and the International Section of the St. Lawrence River.* n.p., 1969. 3 vols., maps. **2420**
Reference for investigation filed in 1964 (Docket No. 83); completed; it led to the conclusion of the Great Lakes water quality agreement of April 15, 1972 (CTS 1971/12). See also *Interim Report* (1965. 18 p., map), the *Second Interim Report* (1968. 5, 16 p., maps), and the *Third Interim Report on Potential Oil Pollution* (1970. 36 p., map).

International Joint Commission. *Rainy Lake: Final Report of the International Joint Commission on the Rainy Lake Reference.* Washington-Ottawa, 1934. Ottawa: King's Printer, 1934. 82 p., map. **2421**
Reference for investigation filed in 1925 (Docket No. 20); project completed; it resulted in the conclusion of the convention of September 15, 1938 (CTS 1940/9).

International Joint Commission. *Rainy Lake: Hearings of the International Joint Commission on the Reference re Levels of Rainy Lake and Other Upper Waters of the Lake of the Woods Watershed and Their Future Regulation and Control, Being Public Hearings at International Falls, Minn., September 28, 29, 30, 1925.* Washington: Govt. Print. Off., 1926. ii, 407 p. **2422**

International Joint Commission. *Rainy Lake: Preliminary Report to International Joint Commission Relating to Official Reference re Levels of Rainy Lake and Other Upper Waters.* Ottawa: King's Printer, 1929-30. 3 vols., 41 plates. **2423**
Running title: *Report of Engineers, Rainy Lake Investigation.*

International Joint Commission. *Rainy River and Lake of the Woods Pollution: Report on the Pollution of Rainy River and Lake of the Woods.* Washington-Ottawa, February 1965. Ottawa: Queen's Printer, 1965. 68, 19 p., maps. **2424**
Reference for investigation filed in 1959 (Docket No. 73); completed.

International Joint Commission. *Rules of Procedure and Text of Treaty.* Ottawa-Washington, 1971. 22 p. **2425**
Revised from time to time since 1912. Refers to the treaty of January 11, 1909.

International Joint Commission. *St. Croix River: Reports on Development of the Water Resources of the St. Croix River Basin.* Ottawa, 1959. 22 leaves. **2426**
Reference filed in 1955 (Docket No. 71); completed.

International Joint Commission. *St. Lawrence Waterway: Message from the President of the United States to the Senate, Transmitting the Report of the International Joint Commission concerning the Improvement of the St. Lawrence River between Montreal and Lake Ontario for Navigation and Power.* Washington: Govt. Print. Off., 1922. 184 p., 8 charts. (U.S. 67th Cong., 2d sess. Senate. Doc. 114) **2427**

Reference for investigation filed in 1920 (Docket No. 17); completed; it resulted in the conclusion of a treaty signed July 18, 1932 (unperfected); revived in 1952 (Docket No. 68). The Great Lakes-St. Lawrence Waterway operates under a number of agreements concluded between Canada and the United States. The St. Lawrence Seaway Authority established in 1954 (R.S.C. 1970, c. S-1), cooperates with its American counterpart, the Saint Lawrence Seaway Development Corporation, established by an act of Congress of May 13, 1954 (68 Stat. 92).

International Joint Commission. *St. Lawrence Waterway: Report of the United States and Canadian Government Engineers on the Improvement of the St. Lawrence River from Montreal to Lake Ontario Made to the International Joint Commission.* Washington: Govt. Print. Off., 1922. ii, 104 p. (U.S. 67th Cong., 2d sess. Senate. Doc. 179) **2428**
Supplementary to S. Doc. 114, 67th Cong., 2d sess.

International Joint Commission. *Trail Smelter Reference. In the Matter of the Investigation of Alleged Damage in the State of Washington Caused by Fumes from the Smelter of the Consolidated Mining & Smelting Company of British Columbia. Hearings.* n.p., 1928-29. 223, 69 leaves. **2429**
Reference filed in 1928 (Docket No. 25); report completed February 28, 1931, but not accepted by the United States. Claims settled by an international tribunal established under the convention of April 15, 1935 (CTS 1935/20). See also published statements and briefs of both governments under "Arbitration: Trail Smelter" (p. 397).

International Joint Commission. *Water Quality of the Upper Great Lakes.* Windsor, Ont.: Great Lakes Regional Office, International Joint Commission, 1979. 91 p. **2430**
Cover title: *An I.J.C. Report to the Governments of Canada and the United States.*

"The International Joint Commission." (1914-15), 5 *Round Table* 851-856; (1924-30), 20 *Round Table* 381-393. **2431**

"The International Joint Commission." (1951), 3 *External Affairs* 90-95. **2432**

"The International Joint Commission: The IJC: A Canadian View, by Bernard Beaupré; The IJC: A U.S. View, by Charles R. Ross." *In* Splete, Allen P., ed., *Toward a Better Understanding of Canadian-American Relations* (Canton, N.Y., 1973), pp. 66-76. **2433**

"The International Joint Commission between the United States and Canada." (1912), 6 *American Journal of International Law* 191-197. **2434**

"The International Joint Commission in Action: Measures to Control Pollution of Niagara River." (1968), 20 *External Affairs* 383-388. **2435**

Jordan, Frederick J.E. "The International Joint Commission and Canada-United States Boundary Relations." *In* Macdonald, Ronald St. John, and others, *Canadian Perspectives on International Law and Organization* (Toronto, 1974), pp. 522-543. **2436**

Kasta, Donald. "Successful Canadian-American Relations." (1964), 6 *University of Windsor Seminar on Canadian-American Relations, Proceedings* 374-381.
2437

Kyte, George William. *Organization and Work of the International Joint Commission.* Ottawa: King's Printer, 1937. 14 p. **2438**
Delivered as an address, over the coast-to-coast network of the Canadian Broadcasting Corporation, from Sydney, N.S., on January 5, 1937.

MacCallum, J.L. "The International Joint Commission." (1966), 72 *Canadian Geographical Journal* 76-87. **2439**

MacKay, Robert A. "The International Joint Commission between the United States and Canada." (1928), 22 *American Journal of International Law* 292-318. **2440**

Mignault, P.B. "Un essai d'arbitrage international." (1916), 10 *Royal Society of Canada, Transactions* 49-63 (3d Ser., Sec. 1) **2441**

Moore, Dorothy Louise. *The Role of the International Joint Commission in Columbia River Basin Development.* Berkeley, Calif., 1962. iii, 172 leaves. Thesis (M.A.), University of California, 1962. **2442**

Nossal, Kim Richard. "International Joint Commission and the Garrison Diversion." (1978), *International Perspectives* 22-25 (Nov./Dec.) **2443**

Pantaleo, Peter. "A Primer on the Boundary Waters Treaty and the International Joint Commission." (1974-75), 51 *North Dakota Law Review* 493-508. **2444**

Perrault, Joseph-Édouard. "Commission conjointe internationale." (1944), 4 *Revue du Barreau* 1-9. **2445**

Piper, Donald C. "Two International Waterways Commissions: A Comparative Study." (1965), 6 *Virginia Journal of International Law* 98-112. **2446**
Refers to the International Joint Commission between the United States and Canada, and the International Boundary and Water Commission between the United States and Mexico.

Ross, Charles R. "The International Joint Commission: United States-Canada." (1974), 68 *American Society of International Law, Proceedings* 229-235. **2447**

Smedresman, Peter S. "The International Joint Commission (United States-Canada) and the International Boundary and Water Commission (United States-Mexico): Potential for Environmental Control along the Boundaries." (1973), 6 *New York University Journal of International Law and Politics* 499-531. **2448**

Spencer, Robert; Kirton, John J.; and Nossal, Kim Richard. *The International Joint Commission Seventy Years on.* Toronto: Centre for International Studies, University of Toronto, c1981. xiv, 158 p. **2449**

Stephens, D.M. "The IJC as an Analogy." (1966), 8 *University of Windsor Seminar on Canadian-American Relations, Proceedings* 100-109. **2450**

Sugarman, Robert J. "The International Joint Commission and Principles of International Law." In *Common Boundary/Common Problems: The Environmental Consequences of Energy Production* (Washington, D.C., c1982), pp. 48-55. **2451**

U.S. Congress. Senate. Committee on Foreign Relations. *Treaty between the United States and Canada concerning Boundary Waters Ratified 1910. Hearings and Proceedings January-February 1909.* Washington, 1909, pp. 269-298. **2452**
Refers to the boundary waters treaty of January 11, 1909 (BTS 23(1910); 102 BFSP 137; 36 Stat. 2448; TS 548; 12 Bevans 319; 208 Parry 213).

Waite, G. Graham. "The International Joint Commission - Its Practice and Its Impact on Land Use." (1963-64), 13 *Buffalo Law Review* 93-118.   **2453**

Wex, Samuel. "The Legal Status of the International Joint Commission under International and Municipal Law." (1978), 16 *Canadian Yearbook of International Law* 276-303.   **2454**

Whitney, Harriet Eleanor. *Sir George C. Gibbons and the Boundary Waters Treaty of 1909*. East Lansing, Mich., 1968. iv, 150 leaves.   **2455**
  Thesis (Ph.D.), Michigan State University, 1968. Refers to the treaty of January 11, 1909.

Willoughby, William R. "The Appointment and Removal of Members of the International Joint Commission." (1969), 12 *Canadian Public Administration* 411-428.   **2456**

Winter, Carl George. "The Boundary Waters Treaty." (1954), 17 *Historian* 76-96. Refers to the treaty of January 11, 1909.   **2457**

"The Work of the International Joint Commission." (1971), 23 *External Affairs* 208-214.   **2458**

D. Acquisition and Loss of Territory

1. GENERAL (PURCHASE OF ALASKA, ETC.)

Adamkiewicz, George. "If Alaska Were Still Russian." (1947-48), 27 *Dalhousie Review* 468-476.   **2459**

Caron, Arthur. "Les droits de la civilisation et l'occupation des terres non-civilisées." (1938), 8 *Revue de l'Université d'Ottawa* 165-182 (section spéciale)   **2460**

McMenemy, Frank S. *The Attitude of the Canadian Government to the Acquisition of the North West, 1856-1859*. Calgary, 1972. vi, 106 leaves.   **2461**
  Thesis (M.A.), University of Calgary, 1972. (National Library of Canada. Canadian Theses on Microfilm, No. 13907).

Mitchell, David Joseph. *The American Purchase of Alaska and Canadian Expansion to the Pacific*. Burnaby, B.C., 1976. viii, 114 leaves.   **2462**
  Thesis (M.A.), Simon Fraser University, 1976. (National Library of Canada. Canadian Theses on Microfiche, No. 30295).

Tarnovecky, Joseph. *The Purchase of Alaska; Backgrounds and Reactions*. Montreal, 1968. xi, 225 leaves, map.   **2463**
  Thesis (Ph.D.), McGill University, 1968. (National Library of Canada. Canadian Theses on Microfilm, No. 3230).

2. OREGON QUESTION

Barrows, William. *Oregon: The Struggle for Possession*. Boston: Houghton, Mifflin, 1884. viii, 363 p., map. (American Commonwealth, Vol. 2) **2464**

Benson, Kenneth Merrill. *The Influence of Exploration, Trade and Settlement on the Final Determination of the Oregon Boundary*. Saskatoon, 1940. 215 leaves. Thesis (M.A.), University of Saskatchewan, 1940. **2465**

Blue, George Verne. "France and the Oregon Question." (1933), 34 *Oregon Historical Quarterly* 39-54, 144-163. **2466**

Cail, Robert E. "The Oregon Treaty: Finis to Joint Occupation." (1946), 10 *B.C. Historical Quarterly* 217-234. **2467**

Carey, Charles H. "British Side of the Oregon Question, 1846." (1935), 36 *Oregon Historical Quarterly* 263-294. **2468**

Commager, Henry. "England and the Oregon Treaty of 1846." (1927), 28 *Oregon Historical Quarterly* 18-38. **2469**

Doherty, Edward J. *The Oregon Boundary Settlement: 1840-1846*. Chicago, 1956. 539 leaves, maps. **2470**
Thesis (Ph.D.), Loyola University, 1956.

Falconer, Thomas. *The Oregon Question; or, a Statement of the British Claims to the Oregon Territory, in Opposition to the Pretensions of the Government of the United States of America*. London: Samuel Clarke, 1845. iv, (5)-46 p. **2471**

Galbraith, John S. "France as a Factor in the Oregon Negotiations." (1953), 44 *Pacific Northwest Quarterly* 69-73. **2472**

Gallatin, Albert. *Letters of Albert Gallatin, upon the Oregon Question*. Washington: Office of the National Intelligencer, 1846. 40 p. **2473**
Originally published in the *National Intelligencer*, January, 1846.

Gallatin, Albert. *The Oregon Question*. New York: Bartlett & Welford, 1846. 75 p. **2474**
Also published in Washington, 1846, under title: *Letters of Albert Gallatin, upon the Oregon Question*.

Gluek, Alvin Charles. *The Struggle for the British Northwest: A Study in Canadian-American Relations*. Minneapolis, 1953. vi, 498 leaves. **2475**
Thesis (Ph.D.), University of Minnesota, 1953. Abstracted in (1953), 13 *Dissertation Abstracts* 776-777. (University Microfilms, Ann Arbor, No. 5532).

Gough, Barry M. "The Royal Navy and the Oregon Crisis, 1844-1846." (1971), 9 *B.C. Studies* 15-37. **2476**

Graebner, Norman A. "Maritime Factors in the Oregon Compromise." (1951), 20 *Pacific Historical Review* 331-345. **2477**

Graebner, Norman A. "Politics and the Oregon Compromise." (1961), 52 *Pacific Northwest Quarterly* 7-14. **2478**

Gt. Brit. Foreign Office. *Correspondence Relative to the Negotiation of the Question of Disputed Right to the Oregon Territory, on the North-West Coast of*

America; Subsequent to the Treaty of Washington of August 9, 1842. London: Printed by T.R. Harrison, 1846. iv, 71 p. **2479**

Kingston, C.S. "The Oregon Convention of 1843." (1931), 22 *Washington Historical Quarterly* 163-171. **2480**
Refers to the Oregon Convention held at Cincinnati in July 1843, calling for the occupation of the Oregon Territory.

Levirs, Franklin P. *The British Attitude to the Oregon Question.* Vancouver, 1931. vii, 195 leaves. **2481**
Thesis (M.A.), University of British Columbia, 1931.

Marshall, William Isaac. *Acquisition of Oregon and the Long Suppressed Evidence about Marcus Whitman.* Seattle: Lowman & Hanford, 1911. 2 vols. **2482**

McCabe, James O. "Arbitration and the Oregon Question." (1960), 41 *Canadian Historical Review* 308-327. **2483**

McLeod, Malcolm. *Oregon Indemnity: Claim of Chief Factors and Chief Traders of the Hudson's Bay Company, Thereto, as Partners, under Treaty of 1846.* Ottawa, 1892. 57 p. **2484**

Merk, Frederick. *Albert Gallatin and the Oregon Problem; a Study in Anglo-American Diplomacy.* Cambridge: Harvard University Press, 1950. xi, 97 p. (Harvard Historical Monographs, 23) **2485**
Review: Walter N. Sage in (1951), 32 *Canadian Historical Review* 84-85.

Merk, Frederick. "The British Corn Crisis of 1845-46 and the Oregon Treaty." (1934), 8 *Agricultural History* 95-123. **2486**

Merk, Frederick. "British Government Propaganda and the Oregon Treaty." (1934-35), 40 *American Historical Review* 38-62. **2487**

Merk, Frederick. "British Party Politics and the Oregon Treaty." (1931-32), 37 *American Historical Review* 653-677. **2488**

Merk, Frederick. "The Genesis of the Oregon Question." (1949-50), 36 *Mississippi Valley Historical Review* 583-612. **2489**

Merk, Frederick. *The Oregon Question; Essays in Anglo-American Diplomacy and Politics.* Cambridge: Belknap Press of Harvard University Press, 1967. xiv, 427 p., map. **2490**

Merk, Frederick. "The Oregon Question in the Webster-Ashburton Negotiations." (1956-57), 43 *Mississippi Valley Historical Review* 379-404. **2491**

Pratt, Julius W. "James K. Polk and John Bull." (1943), 24 *Canadian Historical Review* 341-349. **2492**

Sage, Walter N. "The Oregon Treaty of 1846." (1946), 27 *Canadian Historical Review* 349-367. **2493**

Schafer, Joseph. "The British Attitude Toward the Oregon Question, 1815-1846." (1910-11), 16 *American Historical Review* 273-299. **2494**

Shippee, Lester Burrell. "Oregon and the Diplomacy of 1821-1827." (1918), 19 *Oregon Historical Quarterly* 189-214. **2495**

Soward, Frederic H. "President Polk and the Canadian Frontier." (1930), *Canadian Historical Association, Historical Papers* 71-80. **2496**

Stacey, Charles P. "The Hudson's Bay Company and Anglo-American Military Rivalries During the Oregon Dispute." (1937), 18 *Canadian Historical Review* 281-300. **2497**

Thom, Adam. *The Claims to the Oregon Territory Considered.* By Adam Thom, Recorder of Rupert's Land. London: Smith, Elder, 1844. iv, 44 p. **2498**

Twiss, Sir Travers. *The Oregon Question Examined, in Respect to Facts and the Law of Nations.* London: Longman, Brown, Green, and Longmans, 1846. ix, 391 p., map. **2499**

Wallace, Edward J. *The Oregon Question Determined by the Rules of International Law.* London: A. Maxwell, 1846. 39 p. (Political Pamphlets, Vol. 83, No. 4) **2500**

3. ANNEXATION (PROPOSALS)

Aitken, William B. *The Dominion of Canada: A Study of Annexation.* New York, 1890. 106 leaves. **2501**
Thesis (Ph.D.), Columbia University, 1890.

Allin, C.D., and Jones, George Mallory. *Annexation, Preferential Trade and Reciprocity; an Outline of the Canadian Annexation Movement of 1849-50, with Special Reference to the Questions of Preferential Trade and Reciprocity.* Toronto: Musson, 1912. xii, 398 p. **2502**

Blegen, Theodore C. "A Plan for the Union of British North America and the United States, 1866." (1917-18), 4 *Mississippi Valley Historical Review* 471-483. **2503**

Cross, Michael Sean. *Free Trade, Annexation and Reciprocity, 1846-54.* Toronto: Holt, Rinehart and Winston of Canada, c1971. viii, 88 p. (Canadian History Through the Press Series) **2504**

De Ricci, James Herman. *The Fisheries Dispute, and Annexation of Canada.* London: S. Low, Marston, Searle & Rivington, 1888. viii, 310 p., map. **2505**

Desjardins, Louis Georges. *Considérations sur l'annexion.* Québec: s.l., 1891. 58 p. **2506**

Dessaulles, Louis Antoine. *Six lectures sur l'annexion du Canada aux États-Unis.* New York: Johnson Reprint; The Hague: Mouton, 1968 (1969). xi, 204 p. (Canadiana avant 1867) **2507**
Reprint of the 1851 edition published in Montreal by P. Gendron.

Dubé, Paul-André. *La crise annexionniste à Québec, 1848-1850.* Québec, 1974 (c1978). xxvi, 291 leaves. **2508**
Thesis (M.A.), Université Laval, 1975. (National Library of Canada. Canadian Theses on Microfiche, No. 35380).

Fittro, Mary E. *Proposals for the Annexation of Canada to the United States.* Baltimore, 1926. 96, xi leaves. **2509**
Thesis (M.A.), Johns Hopkins University, 1926.

Gluek, Alvin Charles. "The Riel Rebellion and Canadian-American Relations." (1955), 36 *Canadian Historical Review* 199-221. **2510**

Griffin, Watson. *The Provinces and the States. Why Canada Does not Want Annexation.* Toronto: J. Moore, 1884. 85 p. **2511**

Lawson, Murray G. "Canada and the Articles of Confederation." (1952-53), 58 *American Historical Review* 39-54. **2512**
Refers to Article 11 of the first version of the *Articles of Confederation* of the United States, approved November 15, 1777.

MacRae, A.O. "When Annexation Was in Flower." (1929-30), 9 *Dalhousie Review* 282-286. **2513**

Mills, George Hampden Stanley. *The Annexation Movement of 1849-50 as Seen through Lower Canadian Press.* Rochester, N.Y.: University of Rochester Press, c1956. 208, 8 leaves. (University of Rochester. Canadian Studies Series, No. 18) **2514**
Thesis (M.A.), McGill University, 1947.

Monet, Jacques. "French Canada and the Annexation Crisis, 1848-1850." (1966), 47 *Canadian Historical Review* 249-264. **2515**

Penny, Arthur G. "The Annexation Movement, 1849-50." (1924), 5 *Canadian Historical Review* 236-261. **2516**

Sage, Walter N. "The Annexationist Movement in British Columbia." (1927), 21 *Royal Society of Canada, Transactions* 97-110 (3d Ser., Sec. 2) **2517**

Smith, Goldwin A. "The Gospel of Annexation on the Eve of the Treaty of Washington." (1937), 31 *Royal Society of Canada, Transactions* 79-86 (3d Ser., Sec. 2) **2518**

Smith, Joe Patterson. "American Republican Leadership and the Movement for the Annexation of Canada in the Eighteen-Sixties." (1935), *Canadian Historical Association, Historical Papers* 67-75. **2519**

Tallman, Ronald D. "Annexation in the Maritimes? The Butler Mission to Charlottetown." (1973-74), 53 *Dalhousie Review* 97-112. **2520**

Wager-Smith, Elizabeth. "Historic Attempt to Annex Canada to the United States." (1911), 5 *Journal of American History* 215-230. **2521**

Warner, Donald F. "Drang Nach Norden: The United States and the Riel Rebellion." (1952-53), 39 *Mississippi Valley Historical Review* 693-712. **2522**

Warner, Donald F. *The Idea of Continental Union; Agitation for the Annexation of Canada to the United States, 1849-1893.* Lexington: Published for the Mississippi Valley Historical Association by the University of Kentucky Press, 1960. xi, 276 p., map. **2523**
Reviews: J.M.S. Careless in (1962), 43 *Canadian Historical Review* 153-154; Patrick C.T. White in (1961), 27 *Canadian Journal of Economics and Political Science* 301-302.

Warner, Donald F. *The Movement for the Annexation of Canada to the United States, 1849-1893.* New Haven, Conn., 1940. 114 leaves. **2524**
Thesis (Ph.D.), Yale University, 1940.

XI. POLAR REGIONS

A. General

"Antarctica." (1962), 14 *External Affairs* 167-173.   **2525**
Also issued in the French edition under title: "L'Antarctique" (pp. 171-177).

Balch, Thomas Willing. "The Arctic and Antarctic Regions and the Law of Nations." (1910), 4 *American Journal of International Law* 265-275.   **2526**

Bankes, Nigel D. "Environmental Protection in Antarctica: A Comment on the Convention on the Conservation of Antarctic Marine Living Resources." (1981), 19 *Canadian Yearbook of International Law* 303-319.   **2527**

Dollot, René. "Le droit international des espaces polaires." (1949), 75 *Académie de Droit International, Recueil des Cours* 121-200.   **2528**

Hyde, Charles Cheney. "Acquisition of Sovereignty over Polar Areas." (1933-34), 19 *Iowa Law Review* 286-294.   **2529**

Lillie, Harry R. "The Antarctic in World Affairs." (1948), 36 *Canadian Geographical Journal* 282-295.   **2530**

Lonergan, Stephen J. *The Legal Status of the Antarctic Airspace.* Montreal, 1972. 115 leaves.   **2531**
Thesis (LL.M.), McGill University, 1972. (National Library of Canada. Canadian Theses on Microfilm, No. 12747).

McKitterick, T.E.M. "The Validity of Territorial and Other Claims in Polar Regions." (1939), 21 *Journal of Comparative Legislation and International Law* 89-97 (3d Ser.)   **2532**

Moore, Joan E. "The Polar Regions and the Law of the Sea." (1976), 8 *Case Western Reserve Journal of International Law* 204-219.   **2533**

Pallone, Frank. "Resource Exploitation: The Threat to the Legal Regime of Antarctica." (1977-78), 8 *Manitoba Law Journal* 597-610.   **2534**

Pharand, Donat. "L'Arctique et l'Antarctique: patrimoine commun de l'humanité?" (1982), 7 *Annals of Air and Space Law* 415-430.   **2535**

"A Treaty for Antarctica." (1960), 12 *External Affairs* 514-515.   **2536**

B. Arctic

1. GENERAL

Baird, P.D., and Robinson, J. Lewis. "A Brief History of Exploration and Research in the Canadian Eastern Arctic." (1945), 30 *Canadian Geographical Journal* 136-157. **2537**

Bloomfield, Lincoln P. "The Arctic: Last Unmanaged Frontier." (1981-82), 60 *Foreign Affairs* 87-105. **2538**
Initiated at a workshop on Arctic questions held on MacKinac Island, Michigan, June 10-12, 1981, co-sponsored by the Dalhousie Ocean Studies Programme and the Law of the Sea Institute.

Britton, M.E. "Special Problems of the Arctic Environment." *In* Alexander, Lewis M., and Hawkins, Gordon R.S., eds., *Canadian-U.S. Maritime Problems* (Kingston, R.I., 1972), pp. 9-28. **2539**

Bryce, James Scott. *Security Considerations in the Canadian Arctic.* Kingston, 1975. 97 leaves. **2540**
Thesis (M.A.), Queen's University, 1975. (National Library of Canada. Canadian Theses on Microfiche, No. 26231).

Canada. Dept. of Energy, Mines and Resources. *Islands in the Midnight Sun: The Story of the Polar Continental Shelf Project.* Ottawa: Energy, Mines and Resources Canada, c1974. 20 p. **2541**
Prepared for the Polar Continental Shelf Project by the Public Relations and Information Services Branch.

Canadian Arctic Resources Committee. *The Arctic Pilot Project: A Submission to the Environmental Assessment and Review Process.* Ottawa: The Committee, 1980. 71 p. **2542**

Cohen, Maxwell. "The Arctic and the National Interest." (1970-71), 26 *International Journal* 52-81. **2543**

Collin, A.E. "Oceanography in the Canadian Arctic." (1962), 6 *Canadian Geographer* 120-128. **2544**

Critchley, W. Harriet. "Canadian Security Policy in the Arctic: The Context for the Future." *In Marine Transportation and High Arctic Development* (Ottawa, 1979), pp. 181-209. **2545**

Dosman, Edgar J., and Abele, Frances. "Offshore Diplomacy in the Canadian Arctic: The Beaufort Sea and Lancaster Sound." (1981), 16 *Journal of Canadian Studies* 3-15 (No. 2) **2546**

Dunbar, M.J. "Common Cause in the North." (1946), 1 *International Journal* 353-364. **2547**

Fingland, F.B. "Administrative and Constitutional Changes in Arctic Territories: Canada." *In* Macdonald, Ronald St. John, ed., *The Arctic Frontier* (Toronto, 1966), pp. 130-159. **2548**

Gardner, Gérard. "La valeur stratégique du Grand-Nord." (1953-54), 29 *Actualité Économique* 525-547. **2549**

Griffiths, Franklyn. *A Northern Foreign Policy.* Toronto: Canadian Institute of International Affairs, 1979. 90 p. (Wellesley Papers, 7) **2550**
Reviews: C.E.S. Franks in (1981), 14 *Canadian Journal of Political Science* 195-196; Roger Suffling in (1980), 6 *Canadian Public Policy* 416-417.

Holt, Wayne G. "Problems Relating to Arctic Farmout and Joint Operating Agreements." (1972), 10 *Alberta Law Review* 450-476. **2551**

Keating, Bern. "North for Oil: 'Manhattan' Makes the Historic Northwest Passage." (1970), 137 *National Geographic Magazine* 374-391. **2552**

Keenleyside, Hugh L. "Recent Developments in the Canadian North." (1949), 39 *Canadian Geographical Journal* 156-176. **2553**

Lindsey, George R. "Strategic Aspects of the Polar Regions." (1976-77), 35 *Behind the Headlines* No. 6 (24 p.) **2554**

Lloyd, Trevor. "Canada's Arctic in the Age of Ecology." (1969-70), 48 *Foreign Affairs* 726-740. **2555**

Lloyd, Trevor. "Canada's Northland." (1959-60), 66 *Queen's Quarterly* 529-537. **2556**

Lloyd, Trevor. "Canada's Strategic North." (1946-47), 2 *International Journal* 144-149. **2557**

Lloyd, Trevor. "Frontier of Destiny - The Canadian Arctic." (1946), 6 *Behind the Headlines* No. 7 (16 p.) **2558**

Macdonald, Ronald St. John, ed. *The Arctic Frontier.* Published in association with the Canadian Institute of International Affairs and the Arctic Institute of North America. Toronto: University of Toronto Press, 1966. 311 p., maps.
Some essays are listed separately. **2559**
Reviews: Kenneth Rea in (1966), 32 *Canadian Journal of Economics and Political Science* 531-532; I. Norman Smith in (1965-66), 21 *International Journal* 385-386; Gordon Winter in (1967), 43 *International Affairs* 806-807.

Marine Transportation and High Arctic Development: Policy Framework and Priorities; Symposium Proceedings. Ottawa: Canadian Arctic Resources Committee, 1979. viii, 271 p. **2560**
Symposium held at Montebello, Quebec, March 21-23, 1979. M.J. Dunbar, Chairman.

Minotto, Claude. *La frontière arctique du Canada: les expéditions de Joseph-Elzéar Bernier, 1895-1925.* Montréal, 1975 (c1976). xxi, 311 (i.e. 341) leaves, map. **2561**
Thesis (M.A.), McGill University, 1975. (National Library of Canada. Canadian Theses on Microfiche, No. 27213).

Nelson, James Gordon, and Jessen, Sabine. *The Scottish and Alaskan Offshore Oil and Gas Experience and the Canadian Beaufort Sea.* Ottawa: Canadian Arctic Resources Committee, c1981. xix, 155 p., maps. **2562**
Published jointly with the University of Waterloo, Faculty of Environmental Studies.

Nergaard, Paul. "Ecological Problems of the Canadian Arctic." (1972-73), 1 *Syracuse Journal of International Law and Commerce* 223-225. **2563**

"North of Seventy-Four." (1952), 4 *External Affairs* 280-284, 309-315. **2564**

Ørvik, Nils, and Patterson, Kirk R., eds. *The North in Transition.* Kingston, Ont. Centre for International Relations, Queen's University, 1976. 168 p. **2565**

See especially Chapter 6: "The Theory and Practice of Home Rule in the International North," by Kirk R. Patterson (pp. 113-159).

Ough, John P. "The Polar Continental Shelf Project." (1962), 65 *Canadian Geographical Journal* 3-13. **2566**

Patriarche, V.H. "The Strategy of the Arctic." (1949), 25 *International Affairs* 466-474. **2567**

Pearson, Lester B. "Canada Looks 'Down North.' " (1945-46), 24 *Foreign Affairs* 638-647. **2568**

Pharand, Donat. "Soviet Union Warns United States Against Use of Northeast Passage." (1968), 62 *American Journal of International Law* 927-935. **2569**

Phillips, R.A.J. "Canada and Russia in the Arctic." (1956), 16 *Behind the Headlines* No. 4 (12 p.) **2570**

Phillips, R.A.J. *Canada's North*. Toronto: Macmillan of Canada, 1967. xiv, 306 p., maps. **2571**
Contains a chapter on sovereignty.
Review: Richard J. Diubaldo in (1968), 49 *Canadian Historical Review* 64-65.

Pullen, T.C. "Canada and Future Shipping Operations in the Arctic." (1973-74), 3 *Canadian Defence Quarterly* 8-13 (No. 2) **2572**

Richards, J. Howard. "Northland or Promised Land?" (1959-60), 66 *Queen's Quarterly* 538-547. **2573**

Roberts, Brian Birley. *The Arctic Ocean: Report of a Conference at Ditchley Park, 14-17 May 1971*. Ditchley Park, Eng.: Ditchley Foundation, 1971. 49 p. (Ditchley Paper, No. 37) **2574**

Robinson, J. Lewis. "Canada's Western Arctic." (1948), 37 *Canadian Geographical Journal* 242-260. **2575**
Subject of some international law interest.

Rohmer, Richard Heath. *The Arctic Imperative: An Overview of the Energy Crisis*. Toronto: McClelland and Stewart, c1973. 224 p., maps. **2576**
Review: T.L. Burton, and L.M. Burton in (1973), 16 *Canadian Public Administration* 700-701.

Rowley, G.W. "International Scientific Relations in the Arctic." *In* Macdonald, Ronald St. John, ed., *The Arctic Frontier* (Toronto, 1966), pp. 279-292. **2577**

Sater, John E., ed. *The Arctic Basin*. Rev. ed. Washington: Arctic Institute of North America, 1969. viii, 337 p., maps. **2578**

Sater, John E.; Ronhovde, Andreas G.; and Van Allen, L.C. *Arctic Environment and Resources*. Washington: Arctic Institute of North America, 1971. viii, 309 p. **2579**

Smith, Brian D. *United States Arctic Policy*. Charlottesville: Published for the Center for Oceans Law and Policy, University of Virginia, by Mitchie, 1978. 40 p. (Oceans Policy Study, 1:1) **2580**

Solem, Erik. "Energy and Changing Strategic Aspects of Canada's Arctic Regions." (1981-82), 11 *Canadian Defence Quarterly* 18-25 (No. 3) **2581**

Stead, Gordon W. "Arctic Probes by the Canadian Coast Guard." (1963), 66 *Canadian Geographical Journal* 176-188. **2582**

Storrs, A.H.G., and Pullen, T.C. " 'S.S. Manhattan' in Arctic Waters." (1970), 80 *Canadian Geographical Journal* 166-181. **2583**

Taylor, Andrew. "Our Polar Islands - The Queen Elizabeths." (1956), 52 *Canadian Geographical Journal* 233-251. **2584**

Tynan, Thomas M. *The Role of the Arctic in Canadian-American Relations.* Washington, D.C., 1976. 512 leaves. **2585**
Thesis (Ph.D.), Catholic University of America, 1976. Abstracted in (1976/77), 37 *Dissertation Abstracts International* 1784-A. (University Microfilms, Ann Arbor, No. 76-21497).

Zaslow, Morris, ed. *A Century of Canada's Arctic Islands / Un siècle des îles arctiques du Canada, 1880-1980.* Ottawa: Royal Society of Canada, c1981. xix, 358 p. **2586**
Proceedings of the 23rd symposium organized by the Royal Society of Canada.

2. LÉGAL RÉGIME

Auburn, F.M. "International Law - Sea-Ice - Jurisdiction. (Comment)." (1970), 48 *Canadian Bar Review* 776-782. **2587**

Auburn, F.M. "International Law and the Sea-Ice Jurisdiction in the Arctic Ocean (Based on *U.S. v. Escamilla).*" (1973), 22 *International and Comparative Law Quarterly* 552-557. **2588**

Baird, P.D. "Planting the Flag North." (1971), 83 *Canadian Geographical Journal* 74-83. **2589**

Baird, W.J. *Sovereignty in the Arctic Territorial Waters Law of the Sea; File Guide to the Indian Affairs and Northern Development and Its Predecessors.* Ottawa: Dept. of Indian Affairs and Northern Development, 1971. 56 leaves. **2590**

Beesley, J. Alan. "Rights and Responsibilities of Arctic Coastal States: The Canadian View." (1971-72), 3 *Journal of Maritime Law and Commerce* 1-12. **2591**

Bériault, Yvon. *Les problèmes politiques du Nord canadien. Le Canada et le Groenland. À qui appartient l'archipel arctique?* Préface de Maurice Ollivier. Montréal: B. Valiquette; Ottawa: Université d'Ottawa, 1942. 291 p., map. (University of Ottawa. Publications, 15) **2592**
Thesis (Doctorat), University of Ottawa, 1942.
Reviews: Percy E. Corbett in (1942), 36 *American Journal of International Law* 530; Roger Duhamel in (1943-44), 19/1 *Actualité Économique* 413; G.S. Graham in (1948), 24 *International Affairs* 272-273; Harold A. Innis in (1942), 8 *Canadian Journal of Economics and Political Science* 639.

Breitfuss, Leonid. "Territorial Division of the Arctic." (1928-29), 8 *Dalhousie Review* 456-470. **2593**
Translated from the original German text.

Browne, Evan. "Sovereignty Questions Remain after Century in the Arctic." (1980), *International Perspectives* 7-11 (July/Aug.) **2594**

Byrne, John. "Canada and the Legal Status of Ocean Space in the Canadian Arctic Archipelago." (1970), 28 *University of Toronto Faculty of Law Review* 1-16. **2595**

Canada. Dept. of the Interior. *Report upon the Title of Canada to the Islands North of the Mainland of Canada,* by W.F. King, Chief Astronomer. Ottawa: Government Printing Bureau, 1905. 77 p. **2596**

Chen, Tung-Pi. "International Law - Arctic Sovereignty - Northwest Territories Act, R.S.C., 1906, c. 62 - Regina v. *Tootalik*, (1970) 71 W.W.R. 435. (Case Note)." (1970), 8 *Alberta Law Review* 456-459. **2597**

Clute, A.R. "The Ownership of the North Pole." (1927), 5 *Canadian Bar Review* 19-26. **2598**

Cruickshank, David A. "Arctic Ice and International Law: The Escamilla Case." (1971), 10 *Western Ontario Law Review* 178-194. **2599**

Dehner, Joseph W. "Creeping Jurisdiction in the Arctic: Has the Soviet Union Joined Canada?" (1972), 13 *Harvard International Law Journal* 271-288.
2600

Dellapenna, Joseph W. "Canadian Claims in Arctic Waters." (1972), 7 *Land and Water Law Review* 383-420. **2601**

Dinwoodie, D.H. "Arctic Controversy: The 1925 Byrd-MacMillan Expedition Example." (1972), 53 *Canadian Historical Review* 51-65. **2602**

Diubaldo, Richard J. "Wrangling over Wrangel Island." (1967), 48 *Canadian Historical Review* 201-226. **2603**

Dorion-Robitaille, Yolande. *Captain J.E. Bernier's Contribution to Canadian Sovereignty in the Arctic.* Ottawa: Dept. of Indian and Northern Affairs, 1978. 110 p. **2604**

Dosman, Edgar J., ed. *The Arctic in Question.* Contributors, P. A. Brennan, and others. Toronto: Oxford University Press, 1976. 206 p. **2605**
Reviews: Rita R. Capon in (1977), 8 *Journal of Maritime Law and Commerce* 531-532; Valentin R. Livada in (1977), 71 *American Journal of International Law* 186; Nils Ørvik in (1977), 10 *Canadian Journal of Political Science* 637-638; Erik B. Wang under title: "Canadian Sovereignty in the Arctic: A Comment on *The Arctic in Question,"* in (1976), 14 *Canadian Yearbook of International Law* 307-316.

Eggleston, Wilfrid. "Canada's Northernmost Island." (1935), 10 *Canadian Geographical Journal* 289-297. **2606**
Refers to the Ellesmere Island. Subject of some international law interest.

Eyre, Kenneth C. "Canadian Sovereignty 1922 Style." (1976), 23 *North/Nord* 2-5 (No. 3) **2607**

Feder, Barnaby J. "A Legal Regime for the Arctic." (1977-78), 6 *Ecology Law Quarterly* 785-829. **2608**

Forget, Claude E. "Pollution and Territorial Sovereignty in the Arctic." (1970), 77 *Canadian Banker* 15-17 (No. 5) **2609**

Francis, Daniel. "Staking Canada's Claim to the Arctic Islands." (1977-78), 95 *Canadian Geographical Journal* 60-69 (No. 1) **2610**

Gagné, Maud. "The Legal Status of the Waters Met by the Manhattan During Her Voyage through the Arctic." (1970), 11 *Cahiers de Droit* 66-73. **2611**

Galway, Michael A. "Arctic Sovereignty." (1969-70), 49 *Canadian Forum* 179-181.
2612

Green, Leslie C. "Canada and Arctic Sovereignty. (Comments)." (1970), 48 *Canadian Bar Review* 740-775.　　　　　　　　　　　　　　　　　　　　　**2613**

Green, Leslie C. "Canada's Jurisdiction over the Arctic and the Littoral Sea." In Yates, George T., and Young, John Hardin, eds., *Limits to National Jurisdiction over the Sea* (Charlottesville, 1974), pp. 207-229.　　　　　　　　　**2614**

Head, Ivan L. *Canadian Claims to Territorial Sovereignty in the Arctic Regions.* Cambridge, Mass., 1960. 153 leaves.　　　　　　　　　　　　　　　　　　**2615**
Thesis (LL.M.), Harvard University, 1960.

Head, Ivan L. "Canadian Claims to Territorial Sovereignty in the Arctic Regions." (1963), 9 *McGill Law Journal* 200-226.　　　　　　　　　　　　　　　　　**2616**

Inch, Donald R. "An Examination of Canada's Claim to Sovereignty in the Arctic." (1962-65), 1 *Manitoba Law School Journal* 31-35.　　　　　　　　**2617**
Based on a thesis (LL.M.), Manitoba Law School.

Johnston, V. Kenneth. "Canada's Title to the Arctic Islands." (1933), 14 *Canadian Historical Review* 24-41.　　　　　　　　　　　　　　　　　　　　　　　**2618**

Jones, Kenneth. "How Canada Almost Claimed Wrangel Island." (1982), 102 *Canadian Geographic* 56-63 (No. 4)　　　　　　　　　　　　　　　　　　**2619**

Konan, Raymond H. "The *Manhattan's* Arctic Conquest and Canada's Response in Legal Diplomacy." (1970), 3 *Cornell International Law Journal* 189-204.
　　　　　　　　　　　　　　　　　　　　　　　　　　　　　　　　　　　　　2620

Lakhtine, W. "Rights over the Arctic." (1930), 24 *American Journal of International Law* 703-717.　　　　　　　　　　　　　　　　　　　　　　　　　　**2621**

Larmour, W.T. " 'Symbol of Sovereignty.' " (1954), 49 *Canadian Geographical Journal* 82-89.　　　　　　　　　　　　　　　　　　　　　　　　　　　　**2622**

Lawson, Karin L. "Delimiting Continental Shelf Boundaries in the Arctic: The United States-Canada Beaufort Sea Boundary." (1981), 22 *Virginia Journal of International Law* 222-246.　　　　　　　　　　　　　　　　　　　　　　　**2623**

Legault, Albert. *Problèmes de souveraineté et de défense.* Québec: Centre québécois de relations internationales; Institut canadien des affaires internationales, 1971-72. 2 vols., maps. (Centre québécois de relations internationales. Notes de recherche, nos 1, 3)　　　　　　　　　　　　　　　　　　　　　　　　　　**2624**
Based on reports by Yves Brissy, and Elisabeth Langlois.

Lloyd, Trevor. "Some International Aspects of Arctic Canada." (1969-70), 25 *International Journal* 717-725.　　　　　　　　　　　　　　　　　　　　　**2625**

Lucas, Alastair R. "Regulation of Marine Operations in the Far North." (1980), 3 *Canadian Issues* 175-186.　　　　　　　　　　　　　　　　　　　　　　　**2626**

Maxim, James M. *Canada's Sovereignty Claim: The Arctic.* Calgary, 1976. vi, 126 leaves, maps.　　　　　　　　　　　　　　　　　　　　　　　　　　　　**2627**
Thesis (M.A.), University of Calgary, 1976. (National Library of Canada. Canadian Theses on Microfiche, No. 28545).

McConnell, William H. *Canadian Sovereignty over the Arctic Archipelago.* Saskatoon, 1970. ii, 147 leaves, map.　　　　　　　　　　　　　　　　　　　　**2628**
Thesis (LL.M.), University of Saskatchewan, 1970.

McConnell, William H. "The Dispute on Arctic Sovereignty: A Canadian Appraisal." (1972-73), 25 *University of Florida Law Review* 465-493.　　　　**2629**

Meredith, Brian. "A Plan for the Arctic: Mr. Trudeau's International Regime." (1970), 60 *Round Table* 177-182. **2630**

Meyers, John E. "Political Rights in the Canadian Arctic." (1969-70), 4 *International Lawyer* 666-672. **2631**

Miller, David Hunter. "Political Rights in the Arctic." (1925-26), 4 *Foreign Affairs* 47-60. **2632**

Milsten, Donald E. "Arctic Passage - Legal Heavy Weather." (1972), 15 *Orbis* 1173-1193. **2633**

Morris, Margaret W. "Boundary Problems Relating to the Sovereignty of the Arctic." (1969), 6 *Musk-Ox* 32-58. **2634**

O'Brien, William V., and Chapelli, Armando C. "The Law of the Sea in the 'Canadian' Arctic: The Pattern of Controversy. (Part I and II)." (1973), 19 *McGill Law Journal* 322-366, 477-542. **2635**

Pharand, Donat. "The Arctic Regions in International Law." *In* Girardot, Rafael Gutiérrez, and others, *New Directions in International Law: Essays in Honour of Wolfgang Abendroth* (Frankfurt/Main, 1982), pp. 257-277. **2636**

Pharand, Donat. "The Arctic Waters in Relation to Canada." *In* Macdonald, Ronald St. John, and others, *Canadian Perspectives on International Law and Organization* (Toronto, 1974), pp. 434-448. **2637**

Pharand, Donat. "Aspects of International Law Concerning Two Questions of Jurisdiction Relating to Natural Resource Conservation and Development in Canada." *In* Crabbé, Philippe, and Spry, Irene M., eds., *Natural Resource Development in Canada: Multi-Disciplinary Seminar* (Ottawa, 1973), pp. 231-242. **2638**
Includes a discussion (pp. 235-242).

Pharand, Donat. "Canada's Jurisdiction in the Arctic." *In* Zaslow, Morris, ed., *A Century of Canada's Arctic Islands / Un siècle des îles arctiques du Canada, 1880-1980* (Ottawa, c1981), pp. 111-130. **2639**

Pharand, Donat. "The Continental Shelf Redefinition, with Special Reference to the Arctic." (1972), 18 *McGill Law Journal* 536-559. **2640**

Pharand, Donat. "Freedom of the Seas in the Arctic Ocean." (1969), 19 *University of Toronto Law Journal* 210-233. **2641**

Pharand, Donat. "Historic Waters in International Law with Special Reference to the Arctic." (1971), 21 *University of Toronto Law Journal* 1-14. **2642**

Pharand, Donat. "The Implications of Canadian Marine and Arctic Legislation for the Development of International Law." *In* Alexander, Lewis M., and Hawkins, Gordon R.S., eds., *Canadian-U.S. Maritime Problems* (Kingston, R.I., 1972), pp. 75-81. **2643**

Pharand, Donat. "The Implications of Changes in the 'North American' Arctic Ocean." *In* Gamble, John King, ed., *Law of the Sea: Neglected Issues* (Honolulu, 1979), pp. 183-192. **2644**

Pharand, Donat. "Innocent Passage in the Arctic." (1968), 6 *Canadian Yearbook of International Law* 3-60. **2645**

Pharand, Donat. *The Law of the Sea of the Arctic, with Special Reference to Canada.* Ottawa: University of Ottawa Press, 1973. xxii, 367 p., maps. (Univer-

sité d'Ottawa. Faculté de droit. Collection des travaux. Monographies juridiques, no 7) **2646**
Expanded version of the author's dissertation (S.J.D.), University of Michigan, 1972.
Reviews: Jean-Maurice Arbour in (1974), 15 *Cahiers de Droit* 209-211; Brian Flemming in (1974), 12 *Canadian Yearbook of International Law* 369-371; J. Michel Marcoux in (1974), 68 *American Journal of International Law* 755-756; Francis Rigaldies in (1975), 6 *Études Internationales* 409-411; René Rodière in (1975), 27 *Revue Internationale de Droit Comparé* 290-291; Charles Rousseau in (1974), 78 *Revue Générale de Droit International Public* 538; Michael F. Rutter in (1975), 13 *Alberta Law Review* 371-372; Kim Traavik in (1974-75), 30 *International Journal* 796-798.

Pharand, Donat. "The Legal Status of Ice Shelves and Ice Islands in the Arctic." (1969-70), 10 *Cahiers de Droit* 461-475. **2647**

Pharand, Donat. "The Legal Status of the Arctic Regions." (1979), 163 *Académie de Droit International, Recueil des Cours* 49-115. **2648**

Pharand, Donat. "Le passage du Nord-Ouest, un souci des Canadiens." (1974), 5 *Revue Générale de Droit* 185-189. **2649**

Pharand, Donat. "Quel sera l'avenir du passage du Nord-Ouest?" (1980), 27 *North/-Nord* 2-9 (No. 2), 2-7 (No. 3) **2650**

Pharand, Donat. "State Jurisdiction over Ice Island T-3: The Escamilla Case." (1971), 24 *Arctic* 83-89. **2651**

Pharand, Donat. "Studying the Law of the Sea of the Arctic." (1978), 3 *Hearsay* 10-12 (No. 2) **2652**

Pharand, Donat. *La théorie des secteurs dans l'Arctique à l'égard du droit international.* Paris, 1955. 166 leaves. **2653**
Thesis (Doctorat), Université de Paris, 1955.

Pharand, Donat. "The Waters of the Canadian Arctic Islands." (1968-69), 3 *Ottawa Law Review* 414-432. **2654**

Plischke, Elmer. *Jurisdiction in the Polar Regions: A Study of the Juridical Principles Governing the Original Acquisition of Polar Territory in the Arctic, with Special Reference to the Sector Principle.* Worcester, Mass., 1943. 627 leaves. **2655**
Thesis (Ph.D.), Clark University, 1943.

Reid, Robert S. "The Canadian Claim to Sovereignty over the Waters of the Arctic." (1974), 12 *Canadian Yearbook of International Law* 111-136. **2656**

Ronhovde, Andreas G. *Jurisdiction over Ice Islands: The Escamilla Case in Retrospect.* Ottawa: Arctic Institute of North America, 1972. 18 p. (Arctic Development and the Environment Program) **2657**

Rousseau, Charles. *Le régime juridique des espaces polaires.* Paris: Institut des hautes études internationales, 1957. 1 vol. in 2. (Association des études internationales. Cours, 1956/57, no 3) **2658**

Scott, James Brown. "Arctic Exploration and International Law." (1909), 3 *American Journal of International Law* 928-941. **2659**

Smith, Brian D. "Canadian and Soviet Arctic Policy: An Icy Reception for the Law of the Sea?" (1975-76), 16 *Virginia Journal of International Law* 609-634. **2660**

Smith, Gordon W. *Canada's Arctic Archipelago: 100 Years of Canadian Jurisdiction.* Ottawa: Indian and Northern Affairs Canada, c1980. 19, 19 p. **2661**
Text in English and French on inverted pages. Title in French: *L'archipel arctique: territoire canadien depuis un siècle.*

Smith, Gordon W. "Canada's Arctic Archipelago: 100 Years of Canadian Jurisdiction." (1980), 27 *North/Nord* 10-15 (No. 1), 10-17 (No. 2) **2662**

Smith, Gordon W. *The Historical and Legal Background of Canada's Arctic Claims.* New York, 1952. vi, 496 leaves, map. **2663**
Thesis (Ph.D.), Columbia University, 1952. Abstracted in (1953), 13 *Dissertation Abstracts* 85-86. (University Microfilms, Ann Arbor, No. 4597).

Smith, Gordon W. "Sovereignty in the North: The Canadian Aspect of an International Problem." *In* Macdonald, Ronald St. John, ed., *The Arctic Frontier* (Toronto, 1966), pp. 194-255. **2664**

St. Pierre, Paul. "The Arctic: Problems of Sovereignty and Development." (1970), 43 *Canadian Business* 50-51, 53 (No. 1) **2665**

Svarlien, Oscar. "The Legal Status of the Arctic." (1958), 52 *American Society of International Law, Proceedings* 136-143. **2666**

Trudeau-Bérard, Nicole. "Souveraineté et passage du Nord-Ouest." (1970), 5 *Revue Juridique Thémis* 47-63. **2667**

Tynan, Thomas M. "Canadian-American Relations in the Arctic: The Effect of Environmental Influence upon Territorial Claims." (1979), 41 *Review of Politics* 402-427. **2668**

Utton, Albert E. "The Arctic Waters Pollution Prevention Act, and the Right of Self-Protection." *In* Teclaff, Ludwik A., and Utton, Albert E., eds., *International Environmental Law* (New York, 1974), pp. 140-153. **2669**

Waultrin, René. "Le problème de la souveraineté des pôles." (1909), 16 *Revue Générale de Droit International Public* 649-660. **2670**

Yogis, John A. "Canada: Sovereignty in the Arctic." (1970), 2 *Ansul* 8-10 (No. 3) **2671**

3. OTHER LEGAL ASPECTS

Almond, Harry H., Jr. "Canada's Legislative and Regulatory Scheme to Control Pollution in Arctic Waters." (1972-73), 1 *Syracuse Journal of International Law and Commerce* 236-249. **2672**

Beesley, J. Alan. "The Arctic Pollution Prevention Act: Canada's Perspective." (1972-73), 1 *Syracuse Journal of International Law and Commerce* 226-235. **2673**

Bilder, Richard B. "The Canadian Arctic Waters Pollution Prevention Act." *In* Alexander, Lewis M., ed., *The Law of the Sea: The United Nations and Ocean Management* (Kingston, R.I., 1971), pp. 204-223. **2674**

Bilder, Richard B. "The Canadian Arctic Waters Pollution Prevention Act: New Stresses on the Law of the Sea." (1970-71), 69 *Michigan Law Review* 1-54. **2675**

"Canadian Legislation on Arctic Pollution and Territorial Sea and Fishing Zones."
(1970), 9 *International Legal Materials* 543-554. **2676**
Reproduces the text of bills C-202 and C-203, which have been passed (See R.S.C. 1970, c. 2 (1st Supp.); and R.S.C. 1970, c. T-7).

Carnahan, Burt K. "The Canadian Arctic Waters Pollution Prevention Act: An Analysis." (1970-71), 31 *Louisiana Law Review* 632-649. **2677**

Flemming, Brian. "Canadian Pollution Control over Arctic and Coastal Waters." (1970), *Canadian Bar Association, Papers*, 17 p. **2678**

Graham, Gerald Francis. *The Canadian Arctic Waters Pollution Prevention Act of 1970 and the Concept of Self-Protection.* Ottawa, 1974. vi, 220 leaves. **2679**
Thesis (M.A.), Carleton University, 1974. (National Library of Canada. Canadian Theses on Microfiche, No. 19481). Abstracted in (1975), 13 *Masters Abstracts* 34. (University Microfilms, Ann Arbor, No. M-6481).

Henkin, Louis. "Arctic Anti-Pollution: Does Canada Make - or Break - International Law?" (1971), 65 *American Journal of International Law* 131-136. **2680**

Johnston, Douglas M. "The Arctic Marine Environment: A Managerial Perspective." *In* Alexander, Lewis M., ed., *The Law of the Sea: The United Nations and Ocean Management* (Kingston, R.I., 1971), pp. 312-318. **2681**

Johnston, Douglas M., ed. *Arctic Ocean Issues in the 1980's.* Honolulu: Law of the Sea Institute, University of Hawaii, c1982. iii, 60 p. **2682**
Proceedings, Law of the Sea Institute, University of Hawaii, and Dalhousie Ocean Studies Programme, Dalhousie University, Halifax, Nova Scotia: Workshop June 10-12, 1981, Mackinac Island, Michigan.

Johnston, Douglas M. "Canada's Arctic Marine Environment: Problems of Legal Protection." (1970), 29 *Behind the Headlines* Nos. 5-6, pp. 1-7. **2683**

Legault, L.H. "Canadian Arctic Waters Pollution Prevention Legislation." *In* Alexander, Lewis M., ed., *The Law of the Sea: The United Nations and Ocean Management* (Kingston, R.I., 1971), pp. 294-300. **2684**
Commentary by John E. McCracken (pp. 301-306), and Leigh Ratiner (pp. 307-311).

Lewis, D.E. "Legal Liability in the Canadian Arctic Relating to Oil Spills and Blowouts." (1972), 10 *Alberta Law Review* 440-449. **2685**

M'Gonigle, R. Michael. "Unilateralism and International Law: The Arctic Waters Pollution Prevention Act." (1976), 34 *University of Toronto Faculty of Law Review* 180-198. **2686**

McRae, Donald M., and Goundrey, D.J. "Environmental Jurisdiction in Arctic Waters: The Extent of Article 234." (1982), 16 *University of British Columbia Law Review* 197-228. **2687**

Morin, Jacques-Yvan. "Le progrès technique, la pollution et l'évolution récente du droit de la mer au Canada, particulièrement à l'égard de l'Arctique." (1970), 8 *Canadian Yearbook of International Law* 158-248. **2688**

Newbury, Philip. "The International Environmental Law of the Sea: The Canadian Arctic Waters Pollution Prevention Act and Its Effects, 1970-1980." (1979-80), 4 *Suffolk Transnational Law Journal* 139-161. **2689**

Pharand, Donat. "La contribution du Canada au développement du droit international pour la protection du milieu marin: le cas spécial de l'Arctique." (1980), 11 *Études Internationales* 441-466. **2690**

Pharand, Donat. "International Regulation and Control of Oil Pollution of the High Seas, with Special Reference to the Arctic." (1971), 5 *World Law Review* 93-110. **2691**

Pharand, Donat. "Oil Pollution Control in the Canadian Arctic." (1971-72), 7 *Texas International Law Journal* 45-72. **2692**

Rogers, George W. "The International Implications of Arctic Exploitation." *In* Macdonald, Ronald St. John, ed., *The Arctic Frontier* (Toronto, 1966), pp. 293-311. **2693**

Ronhovde, Andreas G. *Legal and Regulatory Framework for Arctic Marine Commerce: With Special Reference to the United States.* Ottawa: Arctic Institute of North America, 1974. 36 p. (Arctic Institute of North America. Technical Papers, No. 27) **2694**

Sherrin, Jeffrey J. "International Law and Canadian Arctic Pollution Control." (1973-74), 38 *Albany Law Review* 921-942. **2695**

Sutton, Gary. "Pollution Prevention in the Arctic: National and Multinational Approaches Compared." (1971-72), 5 *Ottawa Law Review* 32-64. **2696**

Thompson, Andrew R. "The Arctic Environment and Legislation." (1972), 10 *Alberta Law Review* 431-439. **2697**

Utton, Albert E. "The Arctic Waters Pollution Prevention Act and the Right of Self-Protection." (1972), 7 *University of British Columbia Law Review* 221-234. **2698**

Wilkes, Daniel. "International Administrative Due Process and Control of Pollution - The Canadian Arctic Waters Example." (1970-71), 2 *Journal of Maritime Law and Commerce* 499-539. **2699**

XII. INLAND WATERWAYS

A. General

See also *"Water Pollution (Non-Marine)" (p. 666).*

Glazebrook, G.P. de T. "Nationalism and Internationalism on Canadian Waterways." *In* Innis, Harold A., *Essays in Transportation* (Toronto, 1941), pp. 1-16. **2700**

Graham, Gerald. "International Rivers and Lakes: The Canadian-American Regime." *In* Zacklin, Ralph, and others, *The Legal Regime of International Rivers and Lakes / Le régime juridique des fleuves et des lacs internationaux* (The Hague, 1981), pp. 3-21. **2701**

International Waterways Commission. *Compiled Reports of the International Waterways Commission, 1905-1913.* Ottawa, 1913. 1224 p., maps. (Canada. Parliament, 1913. Sessional Papers, No. 19a) **2702**

    The stenographic notes of several public hearings of the commission on important questions are included in this compilation. The International Waterways Commission between the United States and Canada, created in 1905, was the predecessor to the International Joint Commission. Its purpose was to regulate the navigation and use of all the waters of the lakes and rivers whose natural outlet is the St. Lawrence River. It held its first meeting May 25, 1905 (See *Checklist of United States Public Documents, 1789-1909,* 3d ed., 1911, p. 1449).

International Waterways Commission. *Reports of the International Waterways Commission, 1905-1906.* Ottawa, 1906. 104, 6, 293 p. (Canada. Parliament, 1906. Sessional Papers, Nos. 19b, and 19d) **2703**
See also Canada. Parliament, 1906-1907. Sessional Papers, No. 19.

International Waterways Commission. *Supplement to Report of 1907; and Supplementary Report 1908.* Ottawa, 1908. 36, 5 p. (Canada. Parliament, 1907-1908. Sessional Papers, Nos. 19b, and 19c) **2704**

International Waterways Commission. *Supplementary Report of the International Waterways Commission 1909 / Rapport supplémentaire de la Commission des voies navigables internationales.* Ottawa, 1910. 12 p. (Canada. Parliament, 1910. Sessional Papers, No. 19c) **2705**

B. Great Lakes

Beaupré, Bernard. "The International Joint Commission (Canada - United States) and the Great Lakes." *In Environmental Protection in Frontier Regions* (Paris, OECD, 1979), pp. 431-438. **2706**

Bédard, Charles. "Les Grands Lacs de l'Amérique du Nord et le fleuve Saint-Laurent: frontière, voie de navigation commerciale, nature juridique." (1976), 3 *Annuaire de Droit Maritime et Aérien* 139-150. **2707**

Bédard, Charles. "Le régime juridique des Grands Lacs." *In* Macdonald, Ronald St. John, and others, *Canadian Perspectives on International Law and Organization* (Toronto, 1974), pp. 500-521. **2708**

Bédard, Charles. *Le régime juridique des Grands Lacs de l'Amérique du Nord et du Saint-Laurent.* Québec: Presses de l'Université Laval, 1966. 178 p., map. **2709**
Reviews: Charles Rousseau in (1966), 70 *Revue Générale de Droit International Public* 1071-1072; Jean-K. Samson in (1966-67), 8 *Cahiers de Droit* 109-110; Peter Wright in (1966-67), 22 *International Journal* 675-677.

Bédard, Charles. "Les relations canado-américaines et le régime juridique des Grands Lacs." (1953), 14 *Culture* 111-142. **2710**

Bilder, Richard B. "Controlling Great Lakes Pollution: A Study in United States-Canadian Environmental Cooperation." (1971-72), 70 *Michigan Law Review* 469-556. **2711**

Burns, Douglas. "U.S. Position on Negotiations concerning the Great Lakes." (1972-73), 1 *Syracuse Journal of International Law and Commerce* 199-204. **2712**

Burpee, Lawrence J. "The Great Lakes: An International Heritage." (1939), 19 *Canadian Geographical Journal* 156-183. **2713**

Canada-United States University Seminar, 1971-1972. *A Proposal for Improving the Management of the Great Lakes of the United States and Canada: A Report.* Waterloo, Ont.: Dept. of Man-Environment Studies, University of Waterloo, 1973. vii, 76 p. **2714**

Donnelly, Murray S. "Progress and Problems in Environmental Controls with Special Reference to the Great Lakes." (1979), 17 *Royal Society of Canada, Transactions* 187-200 (4th Ser.) **2715**

Dworsky, Leonard B.; Francis, George R.; and Swezey, Charles F. "Management of the International Great Lakes." (1974), 14 *Natural Resources Journal* 103-138. **2716**

Easterhay, Carl A. "Restoring the Water Quality of the Great Lakes: The Joint Commitment of Canada and the United States." (1981), 4 *Canada-United States Law Journal* 208-231. **2717**

Hunt, Harry E. "How the Great Lakes Became 'High Seas,' and Their Status Viewed from the Standpoint of International Law." (1910), 4 *American Journal of International Law* 285-313. **2718**

Jordan, Frederick J.E. "Great Lakes Pollution: A Framework for Action." (1971-72), 5 *Ottawa Law Review* 65-83. **2719**

Kiss, Alexandre Charles, and Lambrechts, Claude. "L'accord entre le Canada et les États-Unis relatif à la qualité des eaux dans les Grands Lacs." (1974), 20 *Annuaire Français de Droit International* 797-807. **2720**

Laidlaw, John B. "Control the Lakes." (1953), 60 *Canadian Banker* 93-98 (No. 1) **2721**

Landis, Henry. "Legal Control of Pollution in the Great Lakes Basin." (1970), 48 *Canadian Bar Review* 66-157. **2722**

Lee, T.R. "Water Use in the Great Lakes Basin." (1971), 82 *Canadian Geographical Journal* 200-205. **2723**

Moore, John Bassett. "The Great Lakes." *In* Moore, John Bassett, *Digest of International Law* (Washington, 1906), vol. 1, pp. 670-698. **2724**

Moseley, Frederick E. *The United States-Canadian Great Lakes Pollution Agreement: A Study in International Water Pollution Control.* Kent, Ohio, 1978. v, 266 leaves, map. **2725**
Thesis (Ph.D.), Kent State University, 1978. Abstracted in (1978/79), 39 *Dissertation Abstracts International* 3124-A. (University Microfilms, Ann Arbor, No. 78-21087).

Piper, Donald C. *The International Law of the Great Lakes.* Durham, N.C., 1961. 295 leaves. **2726**
Thesis (Ph.D.), Duke University, 1961. Abstracted in (1962), 22 *Dissertation Abstracts* 3730. (University Microfilms, Ann Arbor, No. 62-2004).

Piper, Donald C. *The International Law of the Great Lakes; a Study of Canadian-United States Co-operation.* Durham, N.C.: Duke University Press, 1967. xiv, 165 p. (Duke University. Commonwealth-Studies Center. Publication, No. 30) **2727**
Originally issued as the author's thesis (Ph.D.), Duke University, 1961. Published for the Duke University Commonwealth-Studies Center.
Reviews: Gordon B. Baldwin in (1968), 62 *American Journal of International Law* 804; Yehuda Z. Blum in (1969), 17 *American Journal of Comparative Law* 489-490; Charles B. Bourne in (1967), 5 *Canadian Yearbook of International Law* 380-381; Brian Flemming in (1967-68), 47 *Dalhousie Review* 253-254; Donald S. Macdonald in (1967), 33 *Canadian Journal of Economics and Political Science* 612-613; Peter Wright in (1966-67), 22 *International Journal* 675-677.

"Pollution of the Great Lakes." (1966), 18 *External Affairs* 552-554. **2728**

Pondaven, Philippe. *Les lacs-frontière.* Préface de Charles Rousseau. Paris: A. Pedone, 1972. x, 451 p. (Revue générale de droit international public; Publications, Nouv. sér., no 16) **2729**
Includes the Great Lakes.

Pratt, Gibson E. "Pollution of the Great Lakes: A Joint Approach by Canada and the United States." (1971), 2 *California Western International Law Journal* 109-127. **2730**

Rasmussen, Eric K. "The 1978 Great Lakes Water Quality Agreement and Prospects for U.S.-Canada Pollution Control." (1979), 2 *Boston College International and Comparative Law Review* 499-520. **2731**
Refers to the agreement of November 22, 1978.

Smith, R.H. "Great Lakes Water Levels: A Look at the Problem of Control." (1966), 72 *Canadian Geographical Journal* 113-123. **2732**

U.S. Congress. House. Committee on Foreign Affairs. Subcommittee on Inter-American Affairs. *The Great Lakes: Hearings, 93d Cong., 1st sess., March 23, 26, and May 1, 1973*. Washington: Govt. Print. Off., 1973–, pt. 1–. **2733**
Contents: Pt. 1. The 1973 Floods, and Activities of the International Joint Commission, United States and Canada.

U.S. Congress. Senate. Committee on Foreign Relations. *The Great Lakes Basin: Hearings Before a Subcommittee of the Committee on Foreign Relations, 84th Cong., 2d sess.* Washington: Govt. Print. Off., 1956. iv, 172 p., maps. **2734**
Hubert H. Humphrey, Chairman of Subcommittee. Hearing held August 27-30, 1956.

U.S. Congress. Senate. Committee on Foreign Relations. *Great Lakes Fisheries Convention: Hearing Before a Subcommittee, 84th Cong., 1st sess., on Great Lakes Fisheries Convention, April 27, 1955.* Washignton: Govt. Print. Off., 1955. iii, 76 p. **2735**
Hubert H. Humphrey, Chairman of Subcommittee. See also its report (S.Ex.Rept. 7, 84th Cong., 1st sess., 6 p., to accompany Ex.B, 84-1).

U.S. General Accounting Office. *A More Comprehensive Approach is Needed to Clean Up the Great Lakes: Report to the Congress by the Comptroller General of the United States.* Washington: General Accounting Office, 1982. v, 137 p., maps. **2736**

U.S. Great Lakes Basin Commission. *Great Lakes Basin Framework Study.* Ann Arbor, Mich.: Great Lakes Basin Commission, 1974-1976. 27 vols., maps.
Extensive study; includes some international aspects. **2737**

Wardroper, Kenneth. "Canada's Interests as Regards Protection and Regulation in the Great Lakes." (1972-73), 1 *Syracuse Journal of International Law and Commerce* 205-222. **2738**

Welch, Ronald M. *An Empirical Study of Great Lakes Water Quality Management; the Experience in the St. Clair River, Lake St. Clair, and the Detroit River.* London, Ont., 1970 (c1971). ix, 181 leaves, maps. **2739**
Thesis (M.A.), University of Western Ontario, 1970. (National Library of Canada. Canadian Theses on Microfilm, No. 7245).

C. Rivers, River Basins and Canals

1. GENERAL

Austin, Jacob. "Canadian-United States Practice and Theory Respecting the International Law of International Rivers: A Study of the History and Influence of the Harmon Doctrine." (1959), 37 *Canadian Bar Review* 393-443.
2740

Bloomfield, Louis M. "The Jordan-Negev Project of Israel." (1964), 2 *Canadian Yearbook of International Law* 184-190. **2741**

Bourne, Charles B. "Canada and the Law of International Drainage Basins." *In* Macdonald, Ronald St. John, and others, *Canadian Perspectives on International Law and Organization* (Toronto, 1974), pp. 486-499. **2742**

Bourne, Charles B. "The Development of International Water Resources: The 'Drainage Basin Approach.'" (1969), 47 *Canadian Bar Review* 62-87. **2743**

Bourne, Charles B. "Procedure in the Development of International Drainage Basins." (1972), 22 *University of Toronto Law Journal* 172-206. **2744**

Bourne, Charles B. "Procedure in the Development of International Drainage Basins: The Duty to Consult and to Negotiate." (1972), 10 *Canadian Yearbook of International Law* 212-234. **2745**

Bourne, Charles B. "The Right to Utilize the Waters of International Rivers." (1965), 3 *Canadian Yearbook of International Law* 187-264. **2746**

Bourne, Charles B. *Some Aspects of the International Law on International Drainage Basins.* Cambridge, Mass., 1969. 1 vol. (various pagings) **2747**
Thesis (S.J.D.), Harvard University, 1970.

Bourne, Charles B. "The Suspension of Disputed Works or Utilizations of the Waters of International Drainage Basins." *In* Blumenwitz, Dieter, and Randelzhofer, Albrecht, eds., *Festschrift für Friedrich Berber* (München, 1973), pp. 109-125. **2748**

Bruncken, Ernest. "The Chicago Water Diversion." (1928-29), 13 *Marquette Law Review* 191-200. **2749**

Canada. Dept. of External Affairs. *Correspondence and Documents Relating to St. Lawrence Deep Waterway Treaty 1932, Niagara Convention 1929, Ogoki River and Kenogami River (Long Lake) Projects, and Export of Electrical Power.* Ottawa: King's Printer, 1938. 144 p. **2750**
Refers to the unperfected treaty of July 18, 1932 (UTS J-12), and convention of January 2, 1929 (UTS H-12). Includes Supplement (16 p.).

Canada. Dept. of External Affairs. *Correspondence and Documents Relating to the Great Lakes-St. Lawrence Basin Development, 1938-1941.* Ottawa: King's Printer, 1941. vi, 73 p., map. **2751**
Supplementary to *Correspondence and Documents Relating to St. Lawrence Deep Waterway Treaty, 1932* (Ottawa, 1938. 144 p.).

Canada. Parliament. *Correspondence Relating to Diversion of the Waters of the Great Lakes by the Sanitary District of Chicago; from March 27, 1912, to October 17, 1927.* Ottawa: King's Printer, 1928. 70 p. (Canada. Parliament, 1928. Sessional Papers, No. 227) **2752**

Carroll, John E., and Logan, Roderick M. *The Garrison Diversion Unit: A Case Study in Canadian-U.S. Environmental Relations.* Montreal: C.D. Howe Research Institute; Washington: National Planning Association, 1980. 56 p., map. (Canada-U.S. Prospects) **2753**
Review: Bruce Mitchell in (1981), 7 *Canadian Public Policy* 479-480.

Chapman, John Doneric, ed. *The International River Basin; Proceedings of a Seminar on the Development and Administration of the International River Basin Held under the Auspices of the Regional Training Centre for United*

Nations Fellows, University of British Columbia. Vancouver: Publications Centre, University of British Columbia, 1963. xvi, 53 p. **2754**
Review: Larratt T. Higgins in (1963-64), 19 *International Journal* 133.

Cohen, Maxwell. "Reflections on International Rivers." *In* Nawaz, M.K., ed., *Essays on International Law in Honour of Krishna Rao* (Leyden, 1976), pp. 141-144. **2755**

Dealey, J.Q., Jr. "The Chicago Drainage Canal and St. Lawrence Development." (1929), 23 *American Journal of International Law* 307-328. **2756**

Dreisziger, Nandor A.F. "The Canadian-American Irrigation Frontier Revisited: The International Origins of Irrigation in Southern Alberta." (1975), *Canadian Historical Association, Historical Papers* 211-229. **2757**

Eagleton, Clyde. "Le canal de drainage de Chicago et autres détournements de cours d'eau aux États-Unis." (1932), 13 *Revue de Droit International et de Législation Comparée* 398-409 (3. sér.) **2758**

Eagleton, Clyde. "The Use of the Waters of International Rivers." (1955), 33 *Canadian Bar Review* 1018-1034. **2759**

FitzGerald, Gerald F. "Legal Aspects of the Power Development of the Saint John River Basin." (1959), 12 *University of New Brunswick Law Journal* 7-38.
2760

Goldberg, Charlotte K. "The Garrison Diversion Project: New Solutions for Transboundary Pollution Disputes." (1981), 4 *Canada-United States Law Journal* 177-189. **2761**

Goldie, D.M.M. "Effect of Existing Uses on the Equitable Apportionment of International Rivers. II: A Canadian View." (1959-63), 1 *University of British Columbia Law Review* 399-408. **2762**

Goldie, D.M.M. "International Law and the Development of International River Basins." (1959-63), 1 *University of British Columbia Law Review* 763-776.
2763

Griffin, William L. "Problems Respecting the Availability of Remedies in Cases Relating to the Uses of International Rivers." (1957), 51 *American Society of International Law, Proceedings* 36-42. **2764**

Harrington, Lyn, and Harrington, Richard. "The Welland Canal." (1947), 34 *Canadian Geographical Journal* 203-215. **2765**

Hyde, Charles Cheney. "Notes on Rivers and Navigation in International Law." (1910), 4 *American Journal of International Law* 145-155. **2766**
Includes rivers in North America.

"International Highways." (1882), 2 *Canadian Law Times* 173-174. **2767**

International Law: Rivers and Marginal Seas, Foreword by N.A.M. MacKenzie. Vancouver: University of British Columbia, 1956. ii, 45 p. (University of British Columbia. Publications; Lecture Series, No. 27) **2768**
Contains four papers presented at the Pacific Northwest Regional Meeting of the American Society of International Law, held at Seattle, April 18-19, 1956. Individual papers are listed separately.

Johnson, Ralph W. "Effect of Existing Uses on the Equitable Apportionment of

International Rivers. I: An American View." (1959-63), 1 *University of British Columbia Law Review* 389-398. **2769**

Kenworthy, William E. "Joint Development of International Waters." (1960), 54 *American Journal of International Law* 592-602. **2770**

La Forest, Gerard V. "International Rivers." *In* La Forest, Gerard V., and others, *Water Law in Canada: The Atlantic Provinces* (Ottawa, 1973), pp. 342-370. **2771**

La Forest, Gerard V. "Interprovincial Rivers." (1972), 50 *Canadian Bar Review* 39-49. **2772**
Subject of some international law interest.

Lawrence, Henry. "Waterways Problems on the Canadian Boundary." (1925-26), 4 *Foreign Affairs* 556-573. **2773**

LeMarquand, David G. *International Rivers: The Politics of Cooperation.* Vancouver: Westwater Research Centre, University of British Columbia, 1977. 143 p., maps. **2774**
Review: John G. Laylin in (1978), 72 *American Journal of International Law* 686-687.

Mackenzie, Kenneth C. "Interprovincial Rivers in Canada: A Constitutional Challenge." (1959-63), 1 *University of British Columbia Law Review* 499-512.
Subject of some international law interest. **2775**

Morse, Anita. "Model Water Resources Program for International Boundaries of the United States and Canada." (1972), 12 *Natural Resources Journal* 388-412. **2776**

Nossal, Kim Richard. "The Unmaking of Garrison: United States Politics and the Management of Canadian-American Boundary Waters." (1978-79), 37 *Behind the Headlines* No. 1 (30 p.) **2777**

Oetting, R.B. "How the Garrison Dam Project Affects Canada." (1977-78), 95 *Canadian Geographical Journal* 38-45 (No. 2) **2778**

Patry, André. *Le régime des cours d'eau internationaux.* Québec: Presses Universitaires Laval, 1960. 72 p. **2779**

Patry, André. "Le régime des cours d'eau internationaux." (1963), 1 *Canadian Yearbook of International Law* 172-212. **2780**

Ryan, William F. "Saint John River Power Development: Some International Law Problems." (1958), 11 *University of New Brunswick Law Journal* 20-25. **2781**

Simsarian, James. "Diversion of Waters - United States and Canada." (1938), 32 *American Journal of International Law* 488-518. **2782**

Smith, Herbert A. "The Chicago Diversion." (1930), 8 *Canadian Bar Review* 330-343. **2783**
Reprinted from (1929), 10 *British Year Book of International Law* 144-157. Refers to the diversion of the waters of Lake Michigan at Chicago.

Smith, Herbert A. "Diversion of International Waters." (1930), 11 *British Year Book of International Law* 195-196. **2784**

Williams, Gardner S. "The Sanitary District of Chicago in the Supreme Court of the United States." (1929-30), 28 *Michigan Law Review* 1-25. **2785**
Refers to the boundary waters treaty of January 11, 1909.

Willmann, Hildegard. "The Chicago Diversion from Lake Michigan." (1932), 10 *Canadian Bar Review* 575-583. **2786**

Wolfe, Larry Dennis Sturm. *The High Ross Dam/Skagit River Controversy: The Use of Public Hearings in the Management of an International River.* Vancouver, 1974 (c1975). xvii, 232 leaves, maps. **2787**
Thesis (M.Sc.), University of British Columbia, 1974. (National Library of Canada. Canadian Theses on Microfiche, No. 22266).

Yates, George W. "The Welland Canal." (1931), 2 *Canadian Geographical Journal* 23-38. **2788**

2. ST. LAWRENCE RIVER AND SEAWAY

Aikin, J. Alexander. "The St. Lawrence Waterway Project." (1922-23), 30 *Queen's Quarterly* 53-65. **2789**

Aikin, J. Alexander. "The St. Lawrence Waterway Project." (1932), 39 *Queen's Quarterly* 111-129. **2790**

Anderson, Chandler P. "The St. Lawrence Waterway Project." (1932), 26 *American Journal of International Law* 110-113. **2791**

Angel, Arthur D. "The Great Lakes-St. Lawrence Project." (1950), 26 *Land Economics* 222-231. **2792**

Aziz, Muhammed Abdul. *The St. Lawrence Seaway: Its History, Administration and Economics.* Kingston, 1961. 163 leaves. **2793**
Thesis (M.A.), Queen's University, 1961.

Baxter, Richard R., ed. *Documents on the St. Lawrence Seaway; a Selection.* New York: Praeger, 1961. vi, 85 p. (Books That Matter) **2794**
Published under the auspices of the British Institute of International and Comparative Law. First published London, Stevens; New York, Praeger, 1960.

Beck, Mary Celeste. *An Historical Evaluation of the St. Lawrence Seaway Controversy 1950-1953.* Brooklyn, N.Y., 1954. 141 leaves. **2795**
Thesis (Ph.D.), St. John's University, 1954.

Bédard, Charles. "Canalisation du Saint-Laurent." (1953), 14 *Culture* 3-14. **2796**

Bédard, Charles. "En marge du nouveau projet canadien de canalisation et d'aménagement hydro-électrique du réseau Grands Lacs-Saint-Laurent." (1953-54), 29 *Actualité Économique* 229-270. **2797**

Borchard, Edwin M. "The St. Lawrence Waterway and the Power Project." (1949), 43 *American Journal of International Law* 411-434. **2798**

Boyd, Hugh. "Seaway of Destiny." (1951), 11 *Behind the Headlines* No. 7 (16 p.) **2799**

Brown, Andrew H. "New St. Lawrence Seaway Opens the Great Lakes to the World." (1959), 115 *National Geographic Magazine* 299-339. **2800**

Brown, George W. "Some Aspects of the St. Lawrence Deepening Project." (1928-29), 36 *Journal of the Canadian Bankers' Association* 177-185. **2801**

Brown, George W. *The St. Lawrence Waterway as a Factor in International Trade and Politics, 1783-1854.* Chicago, 1924. 1923 leaves. **2802**
Thesis (Ph.D.), University of Chicago, 1924.

Brown, Mannie. *An Introduction to the Legal Aspects of the St. Lawrence Waterway Project.* Toronto, 1935. 166 leaves. **2803**
Thesis (M.A.), University of Toronto, 1935.

Cahan, C.H. "The St. Lawrence Waterways." (1928-29), 8 *Dalhousie Review* 490-499. **2804**

Calvin, D.D. "Navigation and the 'Seaway.' " (1937-38), 44 *Queen's Quarterly* 66-70. **2805**

Canada. Dept. of External Affairs. *St. Lawrence Waterway Project: 1. Correspondence between the Governments of Canada and the United States, 1927-28. 2. Report of the Canadian National Advisory Committee, January, 1928, and Observations Thereupon by Certain of Its Members. 3. Orders in Council Referring to the Supreme Court of Canada. Certain Questions as to Water Power Rights of the Dominion and the Provinces.* Ottawa: King's Printer, 1928. 32 p. **2806**

Canada. Parliament. *Correspondence between the United States Government and the Canadian Government concerning the St. Lawrence River Improvement Scheme.* Ottawa, 1922. 6 p. (Canada. Parliament, 1922. Sessional Papers, No. 89a) **2807**

Canada. Parliament. *Deeper Waterways from the Great Lakes to the Atlantic. Reports of the Canadian Members of the International Commission.* Ottawa, 1897. 62 p., map. (Canada. Parliament, 1898. Sessional Papers, No. 16a) **2808**

Canada. Parliament. *Papers Relating to the St. Lawrence Waterway Project and the Chicago Drainage Canal.* Ottawa, 1924. 149 p. (Canada. Parliament, 1924. Sessional Papers, Nos. 101c, 101d, 101e, 101f, 101g, 157 and 180) **2809**

Chevrier, Lionel. "The Seaway in the Canadian Economy." (1956-57), 36 *Dalhousie Review* 207-211. **2810**

Chevrier, Lionel. *The St. Lawrence Seaway.* Toronto: Macmillan of Canada, 1959. x, 174 p., maps. **2811**

Chevrier, Lionel. "The St. Lawrence Seaway." (1952), 4 *External Affairs* 20-32. **2812**

Cohen, Maxwell, and Nadeau, Gilbert. "The Legal Framework of the St. Lawrence Seaway." (1959), *University of Illinois Law Forum* 29-50. **2813**

Comstock, Rudolph Swayne. *The St. Lawrence Seaway and Power Project: A Case Study in Presidential Leadership.* Columbus, Ohio, 1956. 2 vols. (536 leaves) **2814**
Thesis (Ph.D.), Ohio State University, 1956. (University Microfilms, Ann Arbor, No. 21427).

Craig, Sydney G., and others. "The St. Lawrence Seaway and the Law." (1957), 38 *Chicago Bar Record* 351-373, 409-437. **2815**

Cumming, R. Stanley. "The St. Lawrence Seaway and Nova Scotia's Economy: A Preliminary Study." (1956-57), 36 *Dalhousie Review* 212-229. **2816**

Currie, A.W. "The St. Lawrence Waterway." (1951-52), 58 *Queen's Quarterly* 558-572. **2817**

Duncan, James S. "Highway to the Inland Seas." (1959), 58 *Canadian Geographical Journal* 152-160. **2818**

Francis, Thomas L. "Highway to the Sea." (1949), 56 *Canadian Banker* 91-98 (No. 3) **2819**

Freeman, R.E. "The St. Lawrence-Great Lakes Deep Waterway." (1925), 97 *Nineteenth Century* 815-822. **2820**

"From Lakes to Ocean: The St. Lawrence Seaway." (1958-59), 49 *Round Table* 233-239. **2821**

Gerity, F.O. "Treaties and Rights of Transit on the St. Lawrence. (Letter to the Editor)." (1962), 40 *Canadian Bar Review* 146-148. **2822**

Goforth, William Wallace. "The Economic Consequences of the St. Lawrence Project: A Canadian View." (1927-28), 35 *Queen's Quarterly* 148-155. **2823**

"Great Lakes-St. Lawrence Waterway and Power Project." (1948-49), 1 *External Affairs* 3-9 (No. 2) **2824**

Gregg, Eugene Stuart, and Cricher, Aaron Lane. *Great Lakes-to-Ocean Waterways: Some Economic Aspects of the Great Lakes-St. Lawrence, Lakes-to-Hudson, and All-American Waterway Projects.* Reviewed and Revised by Norman F. Titus, and Reuben B. Sleight. Washington: Govt. Print. Off., 1927. vi, 134 p., map. (U.S. Dept. of Commerce. Bureau of Foreign and Domestic Commerce. Domestic Commerce Series, No. 4) **2825**

Hamel, Philippe. "La canalisation du Saint-Laurent." (1941), 17 *Action Nationale* 546-579. **2826**

Henderson, J.M. "Accounting for the St. Lawrence Seaway: The First Phase." (1964), 7 *Canadian Public Administration* 182-188. **2827**

Henry, Philip W. "The Great Lakes-St. Lawrence Waterway." (1927), 17 *Geographical Review* 258-277. **2828**

Hills, Theodore Lewis. *The St. Lawrence Seaway.* London: Methuen, 1959. 157 p., maps. **2829**
Concise history of the Seaway and Power projects.

Hoan, Daniel W. "The St. Lawrence Seaway - Navigation Aspects." (1948), 36 *Canadian Geographical Journal* 53-69. **2830**

Holgate, Henry. "The Upper St. Lawrence River: Its International History, Development of Navigation, and Future Possibilities." (1910-11), 18 *Journal of the Canadian Bankers' Association* 184-197. **2831**

Howard, William Ralph. *The Problem of the St. Lawrence Waterway.* Toronto, 1934. 188 leaves. **2832**
Thesis (M.A.), University of Toronto, 1934.

Hurry, Margaret Isabel. *The St. Lawrence Waterway Project.* Berkeley, Calif., 1929. 90 leaves. **2833**
Thesis (M.A.), University of California, 1930.

Ireland, Tom. *The Great Lakes-St. Lawrence Deep Waterway to the Sea.* New York, London: G.P. Putnam, c1934. xiv, 19-223 p., maps. **2834**

Jackman, W.T. "The St. Lawrence Waterway Project." (1932), 4 *Canadian Political Science Association, Proceedings* 213-244. **2835**

Jessup, Philip C. "The Great Lakes-St. Lawrence Deep Waterway Treaty." (1932), 26 *American Journal of International Law* 814-819. **2836**

Kerr, Donald A. "The St. Lawrence Seaway and Trade on the Great Lakes, 1958-63." (1964), 8 *Canadian Geographer* 188-196. **2837**

King, Francis. "The Problem of the Upper St. Lawrence." (1929), 36 *Queen's Quarterly* 2-19. **2838**

Knox, Frank A. "The Seaway and Trade: Getting on the World's Front Street." (1954-55), 61 *Queen's Quarterly* 160-166. **2839**

Kottman, Richard N. "Herbert Hoover and the St. Lawrence Seaway Treaty of 1932." (1975), 56 *New York History* 314-346. **2840**
Refers to the treaty of July 18, 1932 (unperfected).

Kunen, James L. "International Negotiations concerning the St. Lawrence Project." (1955-56), 33 *University of Detroit Law Journal* 14-36. **2841**

Lasserre, Jean-Claude. "Le rôle d'un fleuve-frontière: le cas des deux rives du Saint-Laurent Supérieur." (1972), 16 *Canadian Geographer* 199-210. **2842**
Includes international aspects.

Lawford, Hugh J. "Treaties and Rights of Transit on the St. Lawrence." (1961), 39 *Canadian Bar Review* 577-602. **2843**

Lawford, Hugh J. "Treaties and Rights of Transit on the St. Lawrence. (Letter to the Editor)." (1962), 40 *Canadian Bar Review* 148-150. **2844**

Lefebvre, Olivier. "La canalisation du St-Laurent." (1928), 14 *Revue Trimestrielle Canadienne* 229-247. **2845**

Lefebvre, Olivier. "Le Saint-Laurent et son aménagement." (1941), 27 *Revue Trimestrielle Canadienne* 117-146. **2846**

Legget, Robert Ferguson. *The Seaway: In Commemoration of the 20th Anniversary of the Seaway and the 150th Anniversary of the First Welland Canal, 1829, 1959, 1979.* Foreword by Lionel Chevrier. Toronto: Clarke, Irwin; St. Lawrence Seaway Authority, 1979. 92 p. **2847**
Also issued in French under title: *La voie maritime.*

Loriot, François. *Le régime juridique de la région du golfe St-Laurent et la théorie des eaux historiques.* Paris, 1971. 249 leaves. **2848**
Thesis, Université de Paris II, 1971.

MacGibbon, D.A. "Economic Aspects of the Proposed St. Lawrence Shipway." (1929), 36 *Queen's Quarterly* 449-467. **2849**

Mahood, Harry Richard. *The St. Lawrence Seaway Bill of 1954; a Case Study of Decision-Making in American Foreign Policy.* Urbana-Champaign, Ill., 1960. iv, 176 leaves. **2850**
Thesis (Ph.D.), University of Illinois, 1960. Abstracted in (1961), 21 *Dissertation Abstracts* 3152. (University Microfilms, Ann Arbor, No. 61-164).

Maxwell, Norman James. *The Development of the St. Lawrence Waterway: A Factor in Canadian-American Relations.* Hamilton, Ont., 1960. vii, 204 leaves. Thesis (M.A.), McMaster University, 1960. **2851**

McKee, Samuel, Jr. "Canada's Bid for the Traffic of the Middle West: A Quarter-Century of the History of the St. Lawrence Waterway, 1849-1874." (1940), *Canadian Historical Association, Historical Papers* 26-35. **2852**

Menefee, Ferdinand Northrup. *The St. Lawrence Seaway.* Ann Arbor, Mich.: Edwards, 1940. xiv, 325 p., maps. **2853**
Review: Earle H. Ketcham in (1941), 35 *American Journal of International Law* 177-178.

Moulton, Harold Glenn; Morgan, Charles Stillman; and Lee, Adah L. *The St. Lawrence Navigation and Power Project.* Washington: Brookings Institution, 1929. xvi, 675 p., maps. (Brookings Institution. Institute of Economics. Publication, No. 33) **2854**
Review: George W. Brown in (1930), 11 *Canadian Historical Review* 76-77.

Nadeau, Jean-Marie. "La canalisation du Saint-Laurent." (1942-43), 18/1 *Actualité Économique* 31-56. **2855**

Ontario. Provincial Great Lakes/Seaway Task Force. *The Great Lakes/Seaway: Setting a Course for the '80s - A Report.* Toronto: The Task Force, 1981. 88 p. R. S. Misener, Chairman. **2856**

Paint, Henry M. "The St. Lawrence Seaway: Part One - The Fulfillment of a Dream." (1957), 64 *Canadian Banker* 34-49 (No. 1) **2857**

Paint, Henry M. "The St. Lawrence Seaway: Part Two - Tolls and Traffic Patterns." (1957), 64 *Canadian Banker* 23-28 (No. 2) **2858**

Paint, Henry M. "The St. Lawrence Seaway: Part Three - The Port of Montreal." (1957), 64 *Canadian Banker* 21-37 (No. 3) **2859**

Peel, David. *Le régime international du Saint-Laurent.* Paris, 1959. 315 leaves. Thesis (Doctorat), Université de Paris, 1959. **2860**

Rainbow, Edwin D. *The St. Lawrence Seaway: Shipping and Marine Insurance Aspects.* London: Witherby, 1957. 50 p., maps. (Valiant Series) **2861**
Includes Appendices A-E in a pocket.

Rainville, J.-H. "La canalisation du Saint-Laurent." (1932-33), 8 *Actualité Économique* 7-16. **2862**

Sandwell, B.K. "American Rights and the Proposed St. Lawrence Canal." (1928), 103 *Nineteenth Century* 468-474. **2863**

Sandwell, B.K. "Can We Make a St. Lawrence Treaty?" (1929-30), 9 *Dalhousie Review* 12-17. **2864**

Sandwell, B.K. "The St. Lawrence Waterway." (1930), 1 *Canadian Geographical Journal* 619-634. **2865**

The Seaway-Great Lakes Transportation System: Shoals Ahead. Toronto: Financial Post Conference, 1979. 108 p. **2866**
Contains the texts of thirteen speeches delivered at the Seaway-Great Lakes Conference held in Toronto, October 17, 1979.

Sinclair, Clayton. "A Realist Looks at the Seaway." (1958), 65 *Canadian Banker* 70-75 (No. 2) **2867**

Smith, Herbert A. "The St. Lawrence Waterway Treaty." (1934), 15 *British Year Book of International Law* 150-151. **2868**
Refers to the treaty of July 18, 1932, rejected by the U.S. Senate on March 14, 1934.

"The St. Lawrence Deep Waterway." (1923-24), 14 *Round Table* 578-584. **2869**

"The St. Lawrence Deep Waterway." (1927-28), 18 *Round Table* 623-630. **2870**

"The St. Lawrence Seaway." (1959), 11 *External Affairs* 147-151. **2871**

"St. Lawrence Seaway: Historical Document." (1952), 4 *External Affairs* 241-248, 390-391. **2872**

"The St. Lawrence Seaway and Power Project." (1954), 6 *External Affairs* 332-343. **2873**

St. Lawrence Seaway Authority. *Annual Report.* 1st—, 1954—. Ottawa. **2874**
Also published in French under title: Administration de la voie maritime du Saint-Laurent. *Rapport annuel*. Established in 1954 by the *St. Lawrence Seaway Authority Act* (R.S.C. 1970, c. S-1). It reports to Parliament through the Minister of Transport. It cooperates with its American counterpart, the Saint Lawrence Seaway Development Corporation, in controling the operation of the Seaway.

"The St. Lawrence Waterway." (1933-34), 24 *Round Table* 548-562. **2875**
Discusses the treaty of July 18, 1932, rejected by the U.S. Senate on March 14, 1934 (See text in 76 *Cong. Record* 2096-2098). It was replaced by a similar agreement of March 19, 1941, also unperfected (See text in (1941), 4 *U.S. Dept. of State Bulletin* 307-313).

"The St. Lawrence Waterway Agreement." (1940-41), 31 *Round Table* 567-571. **2876**
Briefly describes the agreement of March 19, 1941 (See text in (1941), 4 *U.S. Dept. of State Bulletin* 307-313). It replaces a similar treaty of July 18, 1932, rejected by the U.S. Senate.

Stead, Robert J.C. "Taming the St. Lawrence." (1955), 51 *Canadian Geographical Journal* 176-189. **2877**

Stephens, George Washington. *The St. Lawrence Waterway Project; the Story of the St. Lawrence River as an International Highway for Water-Borne Commerce.* Montreal: L. Carrier, 1930. 460 p., maps. **2878**
Reviews: George W. Brown in (1930), 11 *Canadian Historical Review* 359-361; Norman A.M. MacKenzie in (1931), 10 *International Affairs* 265-266.

Sussman, Gennifer. *Quebec and the St. Lawrence Seaway*. Montreal: C.D. Howe Research Institute, 1979. iii, 46 p. (Accent Québec, AQ11) **2879**
Also published in French under title: *Le Québec et la voie maritime du Saint-Laurent*.

Tallamy, Bertram Dailey, and Sedweek, T.M. *The St. Lawrence Seaway Project.* Buffalo: Niagara Frontier Planning Board, 1940. 129 p., maps. **2880**
This report has been prepared by the executive staff of the Niagara Frontier Planning Board.

Tanghe, Raymond. "La canalisation du St-Laurent." (1928), 14 *Revue Trimestrielle Canadienne* 82-94. **2881**

Tearney, Thomas W. "Common Admiralty Problems Arising from the Opening of the Saint Lawrence Seaway." (1960), *Canadian Bar Association, Papers* 275-297. **2882**

Thompson, Dwayne Thomas. *The St. Lawrence Project: A Case Study in American Politics.* Nashville, Tenn., 1957. iv, 263 leaves, maps. **2883**
Thesis (Ph.D.), George Peabody College for Teachers, 1957. Abstracted in (1958), 18 *Dissertation Abstracts* 1402-1403. (University Microfilms, Ann Arbor, No. 24491).

Thompson, Ralph. "The St. Lawrence Waterway Treaty." (1932), 36 *Current History* 693-696. **2884**
Refers to the treaty of July 18, 1932, rejected by the U.S. Senate on March 14, 1934.

Thomson, Lesslie R. "The St. Lawrence Navigation and Power Project." (1930), 38 *Journal of Political Economy* 86-107. **2885**

Thomson, Lesslie R. "The St. Lawrence Navigation and Power Project: A Rejoinder." (1930), 38 *Journal of Political Economy* 479-482. **2886**

Thomson, Lesslie R. "The St. Lawrence Waterway and the Canadian Railways." (1929), 36 *Queen's Quarterly* 729-738. **2887**

Tucker, Albert Victor. *The Sectional Controversy in Congress over the St. Lawrence Seaway 1895 to 1932*. Toronto, 1952. 212 leaves. **2888**
Thesis (M.A.), University of Toronto, 1952.

U.S. Congress. House. Committee on Interstate and Foreign Commerce. *St. Lawrence River: Hearing, 93d Cong., 1st sess., on H.J. Res. 157, Joint Resolution Providing for the Use of the Water of the St. Lawrence River for the Generation of Power by the State of New York under and in Accordance with the Provisions of the Great Lakes-St. Lawrence Deep Waterway Treaty between the United States and Canada. April 20, 1933.* Washington: Govt. Print. Off., 1933. iii, 44 p. **2889**

U.S. Congress. House. Committee on Public Works. *Great Lakes-St. Lawrence Basin: Hearings, 81st Cong., 2d sess., on H.J. Res. 271, Approving the Agreement between the United States and Canada Relating to the Great Lakes-St. Lawrence Basin with Exception of Certain Provisions, etc.* Washington: Govt. Print. Off., 1950. ix, 567 p., maps. **2890**
Hearings held April 24-May 10, 1950.

U.S. Congress. House. Committee on Public Works. *St. Lawrence Seaway: Hearings, 82d Cong., 1st sess., on H.J. Res. 2, and Others.* Washington: Govt. Print. Off., 1951. 3 pts. (vi, 1691 p.), maps. **2891**
Hearings held February 20-October 10, 1951.

U.S. Congress. House. Committee on Public Works. *St. Lawrence Seaway: Hearings, 83d Cong., 1st sess., on H.J. Res. 104, Providing for Creation of the St. Lawrence Seaway Development Corporation to Construct Part of the St. Lawrence Seaway in United States Territory in the Interest of National Security; Authorizing the Corporation to Consummate Certain Arrangements with the St. Lawrence Seaway Authority of Canada Relative to Construction and Operation of the Seaway; etc.* Washington: Govt. Print. Off., 1953. vi, 539 p., map. **2892**

U.S. Congress. House. Committee on Public Works. *The St. Lawrence Seaway; Report on S. 2150, a Bill Providing for Creation of the St. Lawrence Seaway Development Corporation to Construct Part of the St. Lawrence Seaway in United States Territory and for Other Purposes.* Washington: Govt. Print. Off., 1954. iii, 121 p., maps. (U.S. 83d Cong., 2d sess. House. Rept. 1215) **2893**

U.S. Congress. House. Committee on Rivers and Harbors. *Great Lakes-St. Lawrence Basin: Hearings, 77th Cong., 1st sess., on the Improvement of the Great*

Lakes-St. Lawrence Seaway and Power Project. Washington: Govt. Print. Off., 1941. 18 pts., map. **2894**
Joseph J. Mansfield, Chairman. Hearings held June 17-August 6, 1941. Also published in a revised edition, 1942. 2 vols. (1104, 1179 p.).

U.S. Congress. Senate. Committee on Commerce. *Great Lakes-St. Lawrence Basin: Hearings Before a Subcommittee of the Committee on Commerce, 78th Cong., 2d sess., on S. 1385, a Bill to Provide for the Improvement of the Great Lakes-St. Lawrence Basin in the Interest of National Defense, and for Other Purposes.* Washington: Govt. Print. Off., 1945. iii, 308 p. **2895**
Hearings held November 21-30, 1944.

U.S. Congress. Senate. Committee on Commerce. *Great Lakes-St. Lawrence Seaway Transportation Study: Hearings Before a Special Subcommittee of the Committee on Commerce, 88th Cong., 1st sess., in Connection with a Study of Transportation on the Great Lakes-St. Lawrence Seaway.* Washington: Govt. Print. Off., 1964. 3 pts., maps. **2896**
F.J. Lausche, Chairman, Special Subcommittee on the Study of Transportation on the Great Lakes-St. Lawrence Seaway. Hearings held December 10, 1963-July 15, 1964.

U.S. Congress. Senate. Committee on Foreign Relations. *Great Lakes-St. Lawrence Basin: Hearings Before a Subcommittee of the Committee on Foreign Relations, 79th Cong., 2d sess., on S.J. Res. 104, a Joint Resolution Approving the Agreement between the United States and Canada Relating to the Great Lakes-St. Lawrence Basin with the Exception of Certain Provisions, etc.* Washington: Govt. Print. Off., 1946. v, 1404 p., maps. **2897**
Hearings held February 18-March 9, 1946. Carl A. Hatch, Chairman of Subcommittee.

U.S. Congress. Senate. Committee on Foreign Relations. *Great Lakes-St. Lawrence Basin. Report to Accompany S.J. Res. 104, with Minority Views.* Washington: Govt. Print. Off., 1946. 97 p. (U.S. 79th Cong., 2d sess. Senate. Rept. 1499) **2898**

U.S. Congress. Senate. Committee on Foreign Relations. *The St. Lawrence Seaway. Report on S. 2150, a Bill Providing for Creation of the St. Lawrence Seaway Development Corporation to Construct Part of the St. Lawrence Seaway in United States Territory, etc.* Washington: Govt. Print. Off., 1953. iii 63 p., maps. (U.S. 83d Cong., 1st sess. Senate. Rept. 441) **2899**

U.S. Congress. Senate. Committee on Foreign Relations. *St. Lawrence Seaway Hearings Before a Subcommittee, 83d Cong., 1st sess., on S. 589, S. 1065, and S.J. Res. 45, Bills and Joint Resolution Relating to the St. Lawrence Seaway and Power Project.* Washington: Govt. Print. Off., 1953. viii, 565 p., maps. **2900**

U.S. Congress. Senate. Committee on Foreign Relations. *St. Lawrence Seaway and Power Project: Hearings, 82d Cong., 2d sess., on S.J. Res. 27, and S.J. Res 111.* Washington: Govt. Print. Off., 1952. vii, 872 p., maps. **2901**
Hearings held February 25-29, 1952. Tom Connally, Chairman.

U.S. Congress. Senate. Committee on Foreign Relations. *St. Lawrence Seaway Project: Hearings Before a Subcommittee of the Committee on Foreign Relations, 80th Cong., 1st sess., on S.J. Res. 111, a Joint Resolution Approving the Agreement between the United States and Canada Relating to the Great*

Lakes-St. Lawrence Basin, with the Exception of Certain Provisions, etc. Washington: Govt. Print. Off., 1947. iv, 603 p., maps. **2902**
Hearings held May 28-June 20, 1947. Alexander Wiley, Chairman of Subcommittee. See also Digest of Hearings (ii, 92 p.), Report of the Subcommittee (21 p.), and Report of the Committee, with Minority Views (S.Rept. No. 810, 80th Cong., 2d sess., 2 pts.).
Hearings held April 14-May 21, 1963. Alexander Wiley, Chairman of Subcommittee.

U.S. Congress. Senate. Committee on Foreign Relations. *St. Lawrence Waterway: Hearings Before a Subcommittee of the Committee on Foreign Relations, 72d Cong., 2d sess., on S. Res. 278, a Resolution Authorizing the Committee on Foreign Relations to Make an Investigation and to Hold Hearings Respecting Matters Touching the St. Lawrence Waterways Treaty.* Washington: Govt. Print. Off., 1932-33. 2 vols. (iv, 1074 p.), map. **2903**
Contents: Pt. 1. Hearings, November 14 to December 8, 1932.- Pt. 2. Hearings, December 13, 14, and 20, 1932, and February 10, 1933.

U.S. Dept. of Commerce. *The St. Lawrence Survey.* N.R. Danielian, Director, St. Lawrence Survey. Washington: Govt. Print. Off., 1941. 7 vols., maps. **2904**
See also *Supplement, Official Statements on the St. Lawrence Project* (1942. xiv, 43 p.). Contents: I. History of the St. Lawrence Project.- II. Shipping Services on the St. Lawrence River.- III. Potential Traffic on the St. Lawrence Seaway.- IV. The Effect of the St. Lawrence Seaway upon Existing Harbors.- V. The St. Lawrence Seaway and Future Transportation Requirements.- VI. The Economic Effects of the St. Lawrence Power Project.- VII. Summary Report of the St. Lawrence Survey, Including the National Defense Aspects of the St. Lawrence Project.

U.S. Dept. of State. *Great Lakes-St. Lawrence Deep Waterway Treaty. Text of the Treaty between the United States and Canada, Signed at Washington July 18, 1932; Statements of the President and the Department of State; and Report of the Joint Board of Engineers of April 9, 1932.* Washington: Govt. Print. Off., 1932. iii, 25 p. (U.S. Dept. of State. Publication, No. 347) **2905**

U.S. Dept. of State. *Navigation of the St. Lawrence: Message from the President, Transmitting a Report from the Secretary of State, and the Correspondence with the Government of Great Britain, Relative to the Free Navigation of the River St. Lawrence, January 7, 1828.* Washington: Gales & Seaton, 1828. 54 p. (U.S. 20th Cong., 1st sess. House. Ex. Doc. 43) **2906**

U.S. Library of Congress. Legislative Reference Service. *St. Lawrence Seaway Manual; a Compilation of Documents on the Great Lakes Seaway Project and Correlated Power Development.* By C. Frank Keyser. Washington. Govt. Print. Off., 1955. v, 254 p., maps. (U.S. 83d Cong., 2d sess. Senate. Doc. 165) **2907**

U.S. President. *St. Lawrence Waterway: Message from the President of the United States Requesting the Consideration of Ratification by the Senate of the So-Called 'St. Lawrence Treaty with Canada,' and Transmitting a Summary of Data Prepared by the Interdepartmental Board on the Great Lakes-St. Lawrence Project.* Washington: Govt. Print. Off., 1954. v, 21 p., maps. (U.S. 73d Cong., 2d sess. Senate. Doc. 110) **2908**

U.S. President. *Survey of the Great Lakes-St. Lawrence Seaway and Power Project: Message from the President of the United States Transmitting Reports on the Proposed Great Lakes-St. Lawrence Project.* Washington: Govt. Print.

Off., 1934. 2 vols. (706 p.), maps. (U.S. 73d Cong., 2d sess. Senate. Doc. 116) **2909**

Pages 3-27, with addition of two maps, are printed separately as S.Doc. 110, 73d Cong., 2d sess. (21 p.).

Van Allen, W.H. "Opening of Navigation in the St. Lawrence." (1962), 64 *Canadian Geographical Journal* 150-160. **2910**

Vignes, Daniel. "Les travaux du Saint-Laurent." (1957), 3 *Annuaire Français de Droit International* 119-133. **2911**

Warner, Fayette S. "The St. Lawrence Waterway Project." (1928), 135 *Annals of the American Academy of Political and Social Science* 60-67. **2912**

Willis, R.B. "St. Lawrence Seaway." (1941), 8 *Quarterly Review of Commerce* 249-303. **2913**

Willoughby, William R. "Power along the St. Lawrence." (1958), 34 *Current History* 283-290. **2914**

Willoughby, William R. "The St. Lawrence Seaway - A Study in Pressure Politics." (1960-61), 67 *Queen's Quarterly* 1-10. **2915**

Willoughby, William R. *The St. Lawrence Waterway; a Study in Politics and Diplomacy.* Madison: University of Wisconsin Press, 1961. xiv, 381 p., plates, map. **2916**

Reviews: Hugh Boyd in (1961-62), 17 *International Journal* 174-176; H.S. Ferns in (1962), 38 *International Affairs* 291-292; Theodore Lewis Hills in (1962), 5 *Canadian Public Administration* 237-239; Donald Q. Innis in (1962), 43 *Canadian Historical Review* 77-78; Don C. Piper in (1962), 56 *American Journal of International Law* 869-870.

Willoughby, William R. "The St. Lawrence Waterway Understandings." (1954-55), 10 *International Journal* 242-252. **2917**

Wright, Conrad Payling. *The St. Lawrence Deep Waterway; a Canadian Appraisal.* Toronto: Macmillan of Canada, 1935. xx, 450 p., maps. **2918**

Reviews: Mannie Brown in (1936), 14 *Canadian Bar Review* 559-561; A.K. Griffin in (1937-38), 17 *Dalhousie Review* 381-382; W.C. Keirstead in (1936), 17 *Canadian Historical Review* 198-199; Earle H. Ketcham in (1936), 30 *American Journal of International Law* 751-752; D.A. MacGibbon in (1936), 2 *Canadian Journal of Economics and Political Science* 226-231; signed N. McK. in (1937), 16 *International Affairs* 146-147.

3. COLUMBIA RIVER

Adelman, Maurice. "The Columbia River Problem." (1960), 2 *University of Windsor Seminar on Canadian-American Relations, Proceedings* 74-87. **2919**

Armstrong, T.E.; Langford, J.A.; and Pennington, A.C. "Columbia River Dispute." (1958-59), 1 *Osgoode Hall Law Journal* 1-36 (No. 1) **2920**

Bourne, Charles B. "The Columbia River Controversy." (1959), 37 *Canadian Bar Review* 444-472. **2921**

Bourne, Charles B. "Columbia River Diversion: The Law Determining Rights of Injured Parties." (1953-58), 2 *U.B.C. Legal Notes* 610-622. **2922**

Bourne, Charles B. "The Columbia River Treaty: Another View." (1961-62), 17 *International Journal* 137-140. **2923**

Bourne, Charles B. "Development of the Columbia River: Its International Legal Aspects." (1957), *Canadian Bar Association, Papers* 90-98. **2924**

Bourne, Charles B. "International Law and the Diversion of the Columbia River in Canada." *In International Law: Rivers and Marginal Seas* (Vancouver, 1956), pp. 17-25. **2925**

Canada. Dept. of External Affairs. *The Columbia River Treaty; Protocol and Related Documents.* Ottawa: Queen's Printer, 1964. 180 p., maps. **2926**
Issued by the Dept. of External Affairs and the Dept. of Northern Affairs and National Resources. The Columbia Treaty was signed at Washington on January 17, 1961 (CTS 1964/2).

Canada. Dept. of External Affairs. *The Columbia River Treaty and Protocol; a Presentation.* Ottawa: Queen's Printer, 1964. 172 p., maps. **2927**
Issued by the Dept. of External Affairs and the Dept. of Northern Affairs and National Resources. Prepared in consultation with Maxwell Cohen, the staff of the Montreal Engineering Company Ltd., and officials of the Government of British Columbia and the British Columbia Hydro and Power Authority.

Canada. Parliament. House of Commons. Standing Committee on External Affairs. *Minutes of Proceedings and Evidence: Columbia River Treaty and Protocol.* Ottawa: Queen's Printer, 1964. 1506 p. **2928**
Also issued in French under title: Comité permanent des Affaires extérieures. *Délibérations: Traité du fleuve Columbia et le protocole* (1964. 1553 p.).

Canadian-American Committee. *Cooperative Development of the Columbia River Basin: a Statement.* Montreal, 1960. 12 p. **2929**

Cohen, Maxwell. "The Columbia River Problem: Canadian Aims." (1960), 2 *University of Windsor Seminar on Canadian-American Relations, Proceedings* 88-97. **2930**

Cohen, Maxwell. "The Columbia River Treaty - A Comment." (1961-62), 8 *McGill Law Journal* 212-215. **2931**
Attached is *A précis* on the Columbia River Treaty by Philippe R. de Massy (pp. 216-218).

Cohen, Maxwell. "International Legal Problems of the Columbia River." (1957), *Canadian Bar Association, Papers* 99-119. **2932**

Cohen, Maxwell. "Some Legal and Policy Aspects of the Columbia River Dispute." (1958), 36 *Canadian Bar Review* 25-41. **2933**

"The Columbia River Treaty and Protocol." (1964), 16 *External Affairs* 98-110. **2934**

"Columbia River Treaty Ratified." (1964), 16 *External Affairs* 546-547. **2935**

Diefenbaker, John G. "The Columbia River Treaty." (1961), 13 *External Affairs* 34-49. **2936**
Statement by the Prime Minister after the signature of the treaty in Washington on January 17, 1961.

Eagleton, Clyde. "Panel Discussion on the Columbia River." (1957), *Canadian Bar Association, Papers* 120-134. **2937**

Epstein, Martin. "The Columbia River Treaty: A Chronological Study." (1966), 5 *Columbia Journal of Transnational Law* 167-172. **2938**

Higgins, Larratt T. "The Columbia River Treaty: A Critical View." (1960-61), 16 *International Journal* 399-404. **2939**

Higgins, Larratt T. "The Columbia River Treaty: A Reply to Professor Bourne." (1961-62), 17 *International Journal* 141-144. **2940**

Inglis, Peter. "Columbia River Crisis." *In International Law: Rivers and Marginal Seas* (Vancouver, 1956), pp. 26-34. **2941**

"International Agreement of Columbia River." (1960), 12 *External Affairs* 870-877. **2942**

International Columbia River Engineering Board. *Annual Report to the Governments of the United States and Canada.* Washington; Ottawa, 1965?—. **2943**

Johnson, Ralph W. "The Canada-United States Controversy over the Columbia River." (1966), 41 *Washington Law Review* 676-763. **2944**

Johnson, Ralph W. "The Columbia River System." (1960), 54 *American Society of International Law, Proceedings* 120-133. **2945**

Keenleyside, Hugh L. "Columbia River Power Development." (1965), 71 *Canadian Geographical Journal* 148-161. **2946**

Krutilla, John V. *The Columbia River Treaty: An International Evaluation.* Washington: Resources for the Future, 1963. 22 p., maps. (Resources for the Future. Reprint, No. 42) **2947**
A lecture given on July 9 and 10, 1963, at a programme jointly sponsored by the University of British Columbia, and the University of Washington.

Krutilla, John V. *The Columbia River Treaty; the Economics of an International River Basin Development.* Baltimore: Published for Resources for the Future by Johns Hopkins Press, 1967. xv, 211 p., maps. **2948**
Reviews: Anthony D. Scott in (1969), 2 *Canadian Journal of Economics* 619-627; Albert E. Utton in (1968), 62 *American Journal of International Law* 792-793.

Ladner, Leon J. "Diversion of Columbia River Waters." *In International Law: Rivers and Marginal Seas* (Vancouver, 1956), pp. 1-16. **2949**

Ladner, Leon J. "International Legal Implications of the Columbia River Development." (1957), *Canadian Bar Association, Papers* 135-158. **2950**

Marr, Norman. "The Columbia River Basin." (1952), 45 *Canadian Geographical Journal* 68-83. **2951**

Martin, Charles E. "The Diversion of Columbia River Waters." (1957), 51 *American Society of International Law, Proceedings* 2-10. **2952**

Martin, Charles E. "International Waters Problems in the West: The Columbia Basin Treaty between Canada and the United States." *In* Deener, David R., ed., *Canada-United States Treaty Relations* (Durham, N.C., 1963), pp. 51-71.
2953

McDougall, Ian A. "Report on the Proposed Fraser-Columbia Water Transfer: Some Economic and Legal Implications for the Upstream Riparians." (1970), 8 *Osgoode Hall Law Journal* 301-327. **2954**

McMenemy, John Murray. *The Columbia River Treaty, 1961-1964: A Study of Opposition and Representation in the Canadian Political System.* Toronto, c1969. 2 vols. (xiv, 586 leaves, maps) **2955**
Thesis (Ph.D.), University of Toronto, 1969. (National Library of Canada. Canadian Theses on Microfiche, No. 19722).

McNaughton, A.G.L. "The Proposed Columbia River Treaty." (1962-63), 18 *International Journal* 148-165. **2956**

Murphy, Wallace S. "The Function of International Law in the International Community: The Columbia River Dispute." (1961), *Military Law Review* 181-196 (July) **2957**

Plain, Richard Hayward McVicar. *An Economic Critique of the Columbia River Treaty and Protocol.* Edmonton, 1968. vii, 87 leaves. **2958**
Thesis (M.A.), University of Alberta, 1968.

Sewell, W.R. Derrick. "The Columbia River Treaty: Some Lessons and Implications." (1966), 10 *Canadian Geographer* 145-156. **2959**

Swainson, Neil A. *Conflict over the Columbia: The Canadian Background to an Historic Treaty.* Toronto: Institute of Public Administration of Canada; Montreal: McGill-Queen's University Press, c1979. xxiv, 476 p. (Canadian Public Administration Series) **2960**
Based on the author's thesis (Ph.D.), Stanford University, 1973.
Reviews: Peter Roff Johannson in (1980), 13 *Canadian Journal of Political Science* 173-174; John J. Kirton in (1979-80), 35 *International Journal* 188-189; H.V. Nelles in (1980), 47 *BC Studies* 79-84.

Swainson, Neil A. *The Evolution of the Canadian Position on the International Development of the Columbia River: A Study in Political and Administrative Behaviour.* Stanford, Calif., 1973. xvi, 635 leaves, maps. **2961**
Thesis (Ph.D.), Stanford University, 1974. Abstracted in (1974), 34 *Dissertation Abstracts International* 7850-A. (University Microfilms, Ann Arbor, No. 74-13694).

U.S. Congress. Senate. Committee on Foreign Relations. *Columbia River Treaty: Hearing, 87th Cong., 1st sess., on Ex. C, 87-1, March 8, 1961.* Washington: Govt. Print. Off., 1961. iv, 80 p., map. **2962**

U.S. Congress. Senate. Committee on Foreign Relations. *Columbia River Treaty; Report to Accompany Ex. C, 87-1.* Washington: Govt. Print. Off., 1961. iv, 14 p., map. (U.S. 87th Cong., 1st sess. Senate. Ex. Rept. 2) **2963**
Report on the Columbia River Basin Treaty signed at Washington on January 17, 1961 (CTS 1964/2).

U.S. Dept. of State. *Legal Aspects of the Use of Systems of International Waters, with Reference to Columbia-Kootenay River System under Customary International Law and the Treaty of 1909.* Memorandum Prepared by William Griffin, of the State Dept. Washington: Govt. Print. Off., 1958. v, 92 p. (U.S. 85th Cong., 2d sess. Senate. Doc. 118) **2964**

Utton, Albert E. "The Columbia River Treaty and Protocol." (1966), 1 *Land and Water Law Review* 181-199. **2965**

"Water Resources of the Columbia River Basin." (1955), 7 *External Affairs* 218-223. **2966**

Waterfiled, Donald Cresswell. *Continental Waterboy; the Columbia River Controversy.* Toronto: Clarke, Irwin, 1970. 250 p., maps. **2967**
Diagrams by R. Deane.
Reviews: H.V. Nelles in (1970-71), 26 *International Journal* 284-286; Everett B. Peterson in (1971), 6 *University of British Columbia Law Review* 298-301.

Watkins, Ernest. "The Columbia River: A Gordian Knot." (1956-57), 12 *International Journal* 250-261. **2968**

D. Inland Seas (Hudson Bay)

See also *"Bays, Gulfs, Straits, and Archipelagos" (p. 250).*

Balch, Thomas Willing. "The Hudsonian Sea Is a Great Open Sea." (1913), 7 *American Journal of International Law* 546-565. **2969**
This is largely an English version of a paper: "La baie d'Hudson est une grande mer ouverte," published in (1913), 15 *Revue de Droit International et de Législation Comparée* 153-172 (2. sér.).

Balch, Thomas Willing. "Is Hudson Bay a Closed or an Open Sea?" (1912), 32 *Canadian Law Times* 469-484, 560-578, 632-648. **2970**
Also published in (1912), 6 *American Journal of International Law* 409-459. This is the English version, with variations, of an article in French: "La baie d'Hudson, est-elle une mer libre ou une mer fermée?," published in (1911), 13 *Revue de Droit International et de Législation Comparée* 539-586 (2. sér.).

Birt, Charles. "Who Owns the Mineral Rights in Hudson Bay?" (1968-69), 3 *Manitoba Law Journal* 41-52 (No. 2) **2971**

Johnston, V. Kenneth. "Canada's Title to Hudson Bay and Hudson Strait." (1934), 15 *British Year Book of International Law* 1-20. **2972**

Kester, William Cameron. *Territorial Waters at International Law, with Special Reference to Hudson Bay.* Toronto, 1915. 76 leaves. **2973**
Thesis (M.A.), University of Toronto, 1915.

McGrath, *Sir* Patrick T. "A New Anglo-American Dispute: Is Hudson Bay a Closed Sea?" (1903), 177 *North American Review* 883-896. **2974**

Prud'Homme, L.A. "La baie d'Hudson." (1909), 3 *Royal Society of Canada, Transactions* 3-36 (3d Ser., Sec. 1) **2975**

Prud'Homme, L.A. "La baie d'Hudson." (1910), 4 *Royal Society of Canada, Transactions* 17-40 (3d Ser., Sec. 1) **2976**

Prud'Homme, L.A. "La baie d'Hudson - Notes préliminaires." (1911), 5 *Royal Society of Canada, Transactions* 119-165 (3d Ser., Sec. 1) **2977**

Wright, Barbara. *The Hudson Bay in French Colonial Policy, 1670-1715.* Lennoxville, Que., 1973. 129, x leaves. **2978**
Thesis (M.A.), Bishop's University, 1974.

E. Interoceanic Canals

Briggs, E. Donald. "Crisis and World Opinion: Suez in Retrospect." (1967), 74 *Queen's Quarterly* 610-626. **2979**

Evans, W. Sanford. "Canadian Traffic through the Panama." (1929), 36 *Queen's Quarterly* 326-337. **2980**

Kaliski, Stephan F. "The Demand for Passages through the Kiel Canal: A Comment." (1959), 25 *Canadian Journal of Economics and Political Science* 507-508. **2982**

Lenschow, Gerhard. "The Demand for Passages through the Kiel Canal: Some Results of an Involuntary Economic Experiment." (1959), 25 *Canadian Journal of Economics and Political Science* 65-70. **2983**

Maduro, Morris F. *The Law of International Straits and Inter-Oceanic Canals.* Edmonton, 1978. xi, 262 leaves. **2984**
    Thesis (Ph.D.), University of Alberta, 1978. (National Library of Canada. Canadian Theses on Microfiche, No. 40237).

Maduro, Morris F. *The Panama Question in the Light of International Law.* Edmonton, 1969. vi, 139 leaves. **2985**
    Thesis (M.A.), University of Alberta, 1969.

Munro, Henry F. "The Panama Canal." (1913), 12 *University Magazine* 598-608. **2986**

"The Panama Canal Act, American Reply to the British Protest." (1913), 33 *Canadian Law Times* 81-83. **2987**

"Panama Canal Act, Protest by the British Government." (1913), 33 *Canadian Law Times* 77-81. **2988**

"The Panama Canal Bill." (1912), 32 *Canadian Law Times* 800-803. **2989**

"Panama Canal Tolls." (1913), 33 *Canadian Law Times* 212-237. **2990**

"Should the Panama Canal Tolls Controversy Be Arbitrated." (1913), 33 *Canadian Law Times* 70-76. **2991**

Stewart, Herbert L. "The Suez Canal in World Politics." (1942-43), 22 *Dalhousie Review* 37-47. **2992**

"The Suez Canal Question." (1957), 9 *External Affairs* 195-202. **2993**

XIII. LAW OF THE SEA

See also *"Arbitration: Specific Cases" (p. 396), and "Sea Warfare" (p. 450).*

A. General

Alexander, Lewis M. "The Nature of Offshore Boundaries." *In* Alexander, Lewis M., and Hawkins, Gordon R.S., eds.; *Canadian-U.S. Maritime Problems* (Kingston, R.I., 1972), pp. 56-62. **2994**

Alexander, Lewis M., and Hawkins, Gordon R.S., eds. *Canadian-U.S. Maritime Problems.* Kingston, R.I.: University of Rhode Island, Law of the Sea Institute, 1972. 88 p., maps. **2995**

First of a series of international regional workshops held by the Law of the Sea Institute. The workshop was held June 15-17, 1971, in Toronto, with the cooperation of the Canadian Institute of International Affairs and the University of Toronto Faculty of Law. Individual papers are listed separately.

Review: Richard Young in (1972-73), 4 *Journal of Maritime Law and Commerce* 645-646.

Auburn, F.M. "The 1973 Conference on the Law of the Sea in the Light of Current Trends in State Seabed Practice." (1972), 50 *Canadian Bar Review* 87-109. **2996**

Auger, Robert. "Law of the Sea: Prelude to a Finale Provided by Single Negotiating Text?" (1975), *International Perspectives* 34-40 (July/Aug.) **2997**

"Avoiding International Conflicts: 1) Law of the Sea Issues; 2) Nuclear Non-Proliferation / Évitons les différends internationaux: 1) Le droit de la mer; 2) La non-prolifération nucléaire." (1976), 5 *Canadian Council on International Law, Proceedings,* 182 p. **2998**

This is the general theme of the fifth annual conference held at Ottawa, October 22-23, 1976. Individual papers are listed separately.

Beesley, J. Alan. "Conflicting Approaches to the Control and Exploitation of the Ocean." (1971), 65 *American Society of International Law, Proceedings* 117-121. **2999**

Comments on an address by John R. Stevenson.

Beesley, J. Alan. "The Law of the Sea Conference: Factors Behind Canada's Stance." (1972), *International Perspectives* 28-35 (July/Aug.) **3000**

Beesley, J. Alan. "Some Unresolved Issues on the Law of the Sea." (1971), 4 *Natural Resources Lawyer* 629-638. **3001**

Boardman, Robert. "Ocean Politics in Western Europe." *In* Johnston, Douglas M., ed., *Marine Policy and the Coastal Community* (New York, 1976), pp. 183-214. **3002**

Borgese, Elisabeth Mann. "The Draft Convention." (1982), 3 *Ocean Yearbook* 1-12 **3003**

Borgese, Elisabeth Mann. "Introduction to the IOI." *In* Pacem in Maribus X, *Proceedings* (Vienna, 1980), pp. 10-13. **3004**
Refers to the International Ocean Institute at Msida, Malta.

Borgese, Elisabeth Mann. "Man and the Oceans." (1978), 1 *Ocean Yearbook* 1-8. **3005**

Broeren, Wilma M.J. *Canada's Role in the Law of the Sea: 1927-1975.* Halifax, 1977, c1978. iii, 327, 20 leaves, maps. **3006**
Thesis (M.A.), Dalhousie University, 1977. (National Library of Canada. Canadian Theses on Microfiche, No. 36047).

Buzan, Barry G. "Canada and the Law of the Sea." (1982), 11 *Ocean Development and International Law* 149-180. **3007**

Buzan, Barry G. "Caracas 1974: Time-Lag Could Jeopardize Progress Toward Law of the Sea." (1974), *International Perspectives* 25-29 (Nov./Dec.) **3008**

Buzan, Barry G. "Law of the Sea: Necessities of Compromise Forced Idealism's Retreat; Assessment of the Geneva Session." (1975), *International Perspectives* 41-44 (July/Aug.) **3009**

Buzan, Barry G. *A Sea of Troubles? Sources of Dispute in the New Ocean Regime.* London: International Institute for Strategic Studies, 1978. 50 p., maps. (Adelphi Papers, No. 143) **3010**

Buzan, Barry G., and Johnson, Barbara. *Canada at the Third Law of the Sea Conference: Policy, Role, and Prospects.* Kingston, R.I.: Law of the Sea Institute, University of Rhode Island, 1975. iii, 25 p., map. (Law of the Sea Institute. Occasional Paper, No. 29) **3011**

Buzan, Barry G., and Johnson, Barbara. "Canada at the Third Law of the Sea Conference: Strategy, Tactics, and Policy." *In* Johnson, Barbara, and Zacher, Mark W., eds., *Canadian Foreign Policy and the Law of the Sea* (Vancouver, 1977), pp. 255-310. **3012**

Canada. Dept. of External Affairs. *Canada and the Law of the Sea; Resource Information.* Ottawa: Dept. of External Affairs, c1978. 158 p. **3013**
Also published in French under title: *Canada, le droit de la mer.*

Canada. Dept. of External Affairs. *The Future of the Oceans.* Prepared in collaboration with the Canadian Hydrographic Service. Ottawa, 1974. 29 p., maps. **3014**

"Canadian Legislation on Arctic Pollution and Territorial Sea and Fishing Zones." (1970), 9 *International Legal Materials* 543-554. **3015**
Reproduces the text of bills C-202 and C-203, which have been passed (See R.S.C. 1970, c. 2 (1st Supp.); and R.S.C. 1970, c. T-7).

Clouden, Anselm Bertram. *Grenada and the Law of the Sea.* Halifax, 1980. vii, 238 leaves. **3016**

Thesis (LL.M.), Dalhousie University, 1980. (National Library of Canada. Canadian Theses on Microfiche, No. 48170).

Cole, M. Sanford D. "Maritime Dominion." (1913), 33 *Canadian Law Times* 333-340. **3017**

Critchley, W. Harriet. "Canada's Maritime Forces and the Law of the Sea." (1978), *International Perspectives* 3-8 (Mar./Apr.) **3018**

De Mestral, Armand L.C., and Legault, L.H. "Multilateral Negotiation - Canada and the Law of the Sea Conference." (1979-80), 35 *International Journal* 47-69. **3019**

Dupuy, René-Jean. "The Law of the Sea Conference: A Bid to Resolve Contradictions." (1974), *International Perspectives* 63-72 (Mar./Apr.) **3020**

Emanuelli, Claude C. "Canadian Approach to the Third Law of the Sea Conference." (1975), 24 *University of New Brunswick Law Journal* 3-28. **3021**

Fenrick, W.J. "Legal Limits on the Use of Force by Canadian Warships Engaged in Law Enforcement." (1980), 18 *Canadian Yearbook of International Law* 113-145. **3022**

Flemming, Brian. "Customary International Law and the Law of the Sea: A New Dynamic." *In* Clingan, Thomas A., Jr., ed., *Law of the Sea: State Practice in Zones of Special Jurisdiction* (Honolulu, 1982), pp. 489-505. **3023**

Flemming, Brian. "The Legal Future of the Oceans." (1972), *Canadian Bar Association, Papers*, 14 p. **3024**
Also published in (1973), 4 *Canadian Bar Association Journal* 4-8 (Apr.).

Gold, Edgar. "Conference Report: The Third United Nations Conference on the Law of the Sea." (1975-76), 3 *Maritime Studies and Management* 117-122.
3025

Gold, Edgar. "Law of the Sea: Conference Outcomes and Problems of Implementation (Report of the 10th Annual Conference of the Law of the Sea Institute, Kingston, R.I., 21-25 June 1976)." (1976-77), 4 *Maritime Policy and Management* 167-169. **3026**

Gold, Edgar. "Law of the Sea and Ocean Resources: A Short Summary of the International Legal Problems Relating to the Uses of the Seas." *In* King, Cuchlaine A.M., *Introduction to Physical and Biological Oceanography* (London, 1975), pp. 323-344. **3027**

Gold, Edgar, ed. *New Directions in Maritime Law, 1976*. Halifax: Public Services Committee, Faculty of Law, Dalhousie University, 1976. vii, 193 p. (Dalhousie Continuing Legal Education Series, No. 12) **3028**
Proceedings of a conference sponsored by the Nova Scotia Subsection of the Maritime Law Section of the Canadian Bar Association, in co-operation with the Public Services Committee of the Faculty of Law, Dalhousie University, held at the Faculty of Law, January 23-24, 1976.
Review: W.E. Scobie in (1977), 8 *Journal of Maritime Law and Commerce* 413-415.

Gold, Edgar, ed. *New Directions in Maritime Law 1978: Proceedings of an International Conference*. Halifax: Public Services Committee, Faculty of Law, Dalhousie University, 1978. ii, 286 p. (Dalhousie Continuing Legal Education Series, No. 18) **3029**

Review: W.E. Scobie in (1978-79), 10 *Journal of Maritime Law and Commerce* 463-464.

Gold, Edgar. "The Rise of the Coastal State in the Law of the Sea." *In* Johnston, Douglas M., ed., *Marine Policy and the Coastal Community* (New York, 1976), pp. 13-33. **3030**

Gold, Edgar. "The Third United Nations Conference on the Law of the Sea: The Caracas Session, 1974." (1974-75), 2 *Maritime Studies and Management* 102-109. **3031**

Gold, Edgar. "The Third United Nations Conference on the Law of the Sea: The Geneva Session, 1975. (Conference Report)." (1975-76), 3 *Maritime Studies and Management* 117-122. **3032**

Gold, Edgar. "The Third United Nations Conference on the Law of the Sea: The 4th and 5th Sessions, New York, 1976." (1976-77), 4 *Maritime Policy and Management* 171-182. **3033**

Gold, Edgar. "The Third United Nations Conference on the Law of the Sea: The Sixth Session, New York, 1977." (1978), 5 *Maritime Policy and Management* 63-71. **3034**

Gold, Edgar, and Letalik, Norman G., eds. *New Directions in Maritime Law 1980: Proceedings of an International Conference.* Halifax: Faculty of Law, Dalhousie University, 1980. ii, 324 p. (Dalhousie Continuing Legal Education Series, No. 20) **3035**
Proceedings of an international conference held at the Dalhousie Law School, May 30-31, 1980.
Reviews: W.E. Scobie in (1982), 13 *Journal of Maritime Law and Commerce* 403-405; W.E. Scobie in (1982), 9 *Maritime Policy and Management* 236.

Gotlieb, Allan E. "Canadian Diplomatic Initiatives: The Law of the Sea." *In* Fry, Michael G., ed., *'Freedom and Change': Essays in Honour of Lester B. Pearson* (Toronto, 1975), pp. 136-151. **3036**

Green, Leslie C. "The *Santa Maria*: Rebels or Pirates?" (1961), 37 *British Year Book of International Law* 496-505. **3037**
Refers to the seizure on the high seas in 1961 of the Portuguese liner *Santa Maria.*

Green, Leslie C. "Sovereignty, Resources and the Law of the Sea." *In* Hillmer, Norman, and Stevenson, Garth, eds., *A Foremost Nation: Canadian Foreign Policy and a Changing World* (Toronto, 1977), pp. 126-149. **3038**

Hamilton, Alvin. "Report on Law of Sea Conference." (1958), 10 *External Affairs* 195-202. **3039**

Harrison, Peter. "Managing Our Vast New 3-Ocean Domain." (1979-80), 99 *Canadian Geographic* 10-17 (No. 3) **3040**

Hawkins, Gordon R.S. "Science and Political Will at Sea." (1969-70), 25 *International Journal* 704-716. **3040a**

Hayden, Gene. "Reopening the Negotiations on the Law of the Sea Treaty." (1981), *International Perspectives* 8-12 (July/Aug.) **3041**

Hodgins, Thomas. "Ancient Law of Nations Respecting the Sea and Sea-Shore." (1893), 13 *Canadian Law Times* 14-21. **3042**

Hollick, Ann L. "Canadian-American Relations: Law of the Sea." (1974), 28 *International Organization* 755-780. **3043**

Reprinted in Fox, Annette Baker, and others, *Canada and the United States* (New York, 1976), pp. 162-187.

Hollick, Ann L. "United States and Canadian Policy Processes in the Law of the Sea." (1974-75), 12 *San Diego Law Review* 518-552. **3044**

"The International Conference on the Law of the Sea." (1958), 10 *External Affairs* 21-25, 86-89, 111, 195-202. **3045**
   Also issued in the French edition under title: "Conférence internationale sur le droit de la mer."

Johnson, Barbara. "Regionalism and the Law of the Sea: New Aspects of Dominance and Dependency." *In* Johnston, Douglas M., ed., *Regionalization of the Law of the Sea* (Cambridge, Mass., 1978), pp. 103-127. **3046**

Johnson, Barbara, and Langdon, Frank. "The Impact of the Law of the Sea Conference upon the Pacific Region." (1978), 51 *Pacific Affairs* 5-23, 216-229. **3047**

Johnson, Barbara, and Zacher, Mark W., eds. *Canadian Foreign Policy and the Law of the Sea.* Vancouver: University of British Columbia Press, c1977. xx, 387 p. **3048**
   This is a collection of eight essays listed separately.
   Reviews: Edward D. Brown in (1978), 49 *British Year Book of International Law* 239; Edward Collins, Jr., in (1980), 10 *American Review of Canadian Studies* 117-118 (No. 1); H. Scott Fairley in (1978), 12 *University of British Columbia Law Review* 355-361; Gerhard Hafner in (1978), 38 *Zeitschrift für Ausländisches Öffentliches Recht und Völkerrecht* 983-985; Mark W. Janis in (1978), 19 *Harvard International Law Journal* 413-418; Douglas M. Johnston in (1978), 4 *Canadian Public Policy* 414-415; Valentin R. Livada in (1979), 73 *American Journal of International Law* 315-316; J.G. Merrills in (1979), 29 *University of Toronto Law Journal* 192-194; Daniel G. Partan in (1978), 2 *Boston College International and Comparative Law Journal* 190-196.

Johnson, Barbara, and Zacher, Mark W. "An Overview of Canadian Ocean Policy." *In* Johnson, Barbara, and Zacher, Mark W., eds., *Canadian Foreign Policy and the Law of the Sea* (Vancouver, 1977), pp. 356-379. **3049**

Johnston, Douglas M. "The Conduct of Oceanographic Research in the '80s." *In* Pacem in Maribus X, *Proceedings* (Vienna, 1980), pp. 37-44. **3050**

Johnston, Douglas M. "Environment at the Seventh Session." (1978), 4 *Environmental Policy and Law* 78-79. **3051**

Johnston, Douglas M. "Equity and Efficiency in Marine Law and Policy." *In* Johnston, Douglas M., ed., *Marine Policy and the Coastal Community* (New York, 1976), pp. 297-327. **3052**

Johnston, Douglas M. "Impact of the New Law of the Sea on Japanese-Canadian Relations." *In* Hay, Keith A.J., ed., *Canadian Perspectives on Economic Relations with Japan* (Montreal, 1980), pp. 95-127. **3053**
   See also "Comment" by B. Applebaum (pp. 128-132).

Johnston, Douglas M. "Law, Technology and the Sea." (1967), 55 *California Law Review* 449-472. **3054**

Johnston, Douglas M. "The Law of the Sea: Recent Trends in the Literature." (1977), 71 *American Journal of International Law* 539-555. **3055**
   This is a review article of nine books on law of the sea.

Johnston, Douglas M. "The New Equity in the Law of the Sea." (1975-76), 31 *International Journal* 79-99. **3056**

Johnston, Douglas M. "The Options for LOS III: Appraisal and Proposal." *In* Christy, Francis T., and others, *Law of the Sea: Caracas and Beyond* (Cambridge, Mass., 1975), pp. 357-372. **3057**

Johnston, Douglas M. "Recent Canadian Marine Legislation: An Historical Perspective." *In* Alexander, Lewis M., and Hawkins, Gordon R.S., eds., *Canadian U.S. Maritime Problems* (Kingston, R.I., 1972), pp. 63-67. **3058**

Johnston, Douglas M., ed. *Regionalization of the Law of the Sea.* Cambridge, Mass.: Ballinger, 1978. ix, 346 p. **3059**
Proceedings, Law of the Sea Institute, Eleventh Annual Conference, November 14-17, 1977, University of Hawaii, Honolulu.
Review: W.R. Edeson in (1981), 12 *Journal of Maritime Law and Commerce* 284-287.

Johnston, Douglas M., and Gold, Edgar. "Extended Jurisdiction: The Impact of UNCLOS III on Coastal State Practice." *In* Clingan, Thomas A., Jr., ed., *Law of the Sea: State Practice in Zones of Special Jurisdiction* (Honolulu, 1982), pp. 4-56. **3060**

Kingham, J.D., and McRae, Donald M. "Competent International Organizations and the Law of the Sea." (1979), 3 *Marine Policy* 106-132. **3061**

Krieger, David. *The Oceans: A Common Heritage.* Oakville, Ont.: Canadian Peace Research Institute, 1974. 63 p. (Peace Research Reviews, Vol. 5, No. 6) **3062**

Krueger, Robert B. "An Evaluation of United States Oceans Policy." (1971), 17 *McGill Law Journal* 603-698. **3063**

"LOS III: Canadian Interests and Common Concerns / Les intérêts canadiens dans la 3e Conférence du droit de la mer." (1976), 5 *Canadian Council on International Law, Proceedings* 13-52. **3064**
This is a panel. Opening remarks: Ronald St. John Macdonald (pp. 13-15).- Chairman: Max Wershof (p. 16).- Speaker: J. Alan Beesley (pp. 17-23).- Commentators: Douglas M. Johnston (pp. 23-26), and Donat Pharand (pp. 26-28).- General discussion (pp. 32-52).

Lapointe, Paul A. "Caracas 1974 - Law of the Sea Advanced but Much Remains to Be Done: New Conference Rules Emerge." (1974), *International Perspectives* 19-24 (Nov./Dec.). **3065**

Lapointe, Paul A. "Law of the Sea Conference: Report on New York Session." (1976), *International Perspectives* 22-25 (July/Aug.) **3066**

Lapointe, Paul A. "Report on the Course of Negotiations at Caracas: Commentary." *In* Christy, Francis T., and others, *Law of the Sea: Caracas and Beyond* (Cambridge, Mass., 1975), pp. 26-29. **3067**

"Law of the Sea." (1970), 22 *External Affairs* 250-257. **3068**

"The Law of the Sea: A Canadian Proposal." (1960), 12 *External Affairs* 435-446. **3069**

"The Law of the Sea: Second United Nations Conference." (1960), 12 *External Affairs* 656-659. **3070**

Legault, L.H. "Maritime Claims." *In* Macdonald, Ronald St. John, and others,

Canadian Perspectives on International Law and Organization (Toronto, 1974), pp. 377-397. **3071**

Lehoux, Grégoire. "La Troisième Conférence sur le droit de la mer et le règlement obligatoire des différends." (1980), 18 *Canadian Yearbook of International Law* 31-90. **3072**

Logan, Roderick M. *Canada, the United States, and the Third Law of the Sea Conference.* Montreal, Washington, D.C.: Canadian-American Committee, 1974. viii, 122 p. (CAC, 37) **3073**
   Study commissioned by the Canadian-American Committee. Sponsored by the C.D. Howe Research Institute (Canada), and the National Planning Association (U.S.A.). Reviews: Brian Flemming in (1976), 70 *American Journal of International Law* 181-182; Edward Miles in (1975), 5 *American Review of Canadian Studies* 185-186 (No. 2).

MacGuigan, Mark R. "Beyond the Law of the Sea Conference." (1980), 9 *Canadian Council on International Law, Proceedings* 85-88. **3074**

Matte, Nicolas Mateesco. "The Law of the Sea and Outer Space: A Comparative Survey of Specific Issues." (1982), 3 *Ocean Yearbook* 13-37. **3075**

Matte, Nicolas Mateesco. *Vers un nouveau droit international de la mer.* Préface de J.G. Guerrero. Paris: A. Pedone, 1950. viii, 162 p. **3076**
   Reviews: C. John Colombos in (1951), 27 *International Affairs* 221; Léon Lalande in (1951-52), 7 *International Journal* 167.

Mawhinney, Barry. "Law of the Sea: Nine Years of Negotiation May Be Reaching Conclusion." (1978), *International Perspectives* 33-39 (Jan./Feb.) **3077**

McDorman, Ted L. "Researching Law of the Sea." (1982), 10 *International Journal of Legal Information* 147-157. **3078**

McDorman, Ted L. "Reservations and the Law of the Sea Treaty." (1982), 13 *Journal of Maritime Law and Commerce* 481-519. **3079**

McDorman, Ted L.; Beauchamp, Kenneth P.; and Johnston, Douglas M. *Maritime Boundary Delimitation: An Annotated Bibliography.* Lexington, Mass.: Lexington Books, c1983. xiii, 207 p. **3080**

McDorman, Ted L., and others. *The Marine Environment and the Caracas Convention on the Law of the Sea: A Study of the Third United Nations Conference on the Law of the Sea and Other Related Marine Environmental Activities.* Halifax: Dalhousie University, Dalhousie Ocean Studies Programme, 1981. ix, 127 p. **3081**
   Prepared by Ted L. McDorman, Norman G. Letalik, Hal Mills, Douglas M. Johnston, and Edgar Gold.

McRae, Donald M. "Canada and the Law of the Sea: Some Multilateral and Bilateral Issues." (1980), 3 *Canadian Issues* 161-173. **3082**

McRae, Donald M. "The Law of the Sea Draft Convention and International Organizations." (1980), 3 *Marine Policy Reports* No. 2 (5 p.) **3083**

McWhinney, Edward. "The Codifying Conference and International Law-Making: From the 'Old' Law of the Sea to the 'New.'" *In* Dorsey, Gray, ed., *Equality & Freedom: International and Comparative Jurisprudence* (Dobbs Ferry, N.Y., 1977), vol. 2, pp. 453-474. **3084**

McWhinney, Edward. "The Codifying Conference as an Instrument of International Law-Making: From the 'Old' Law of the Sea to the 'New.' " (1975), 3 *Syracuse Journal of International Law and Commerce* 301-318. **3085**

Middlemiss, Danford W. "Canadian Maritime Enforcement Policies." *In* Johnson, Barbara, and Zacher, Mark W., eds., *Canadian Foreign Policy and the Law of the Sea* (Vancouver, 1977), pp. 311-355. **3086**

Miles, Edward. "The Dynamics of Global Ocean Politics." *In* Johnston, Douglas M., ed., *Marine Policy and the Coastal Community* (New York, 1976), pp. 147-181. **3087**

Milsten, Donald E. "The Law of the Sea: Implications for North American Neighbors." (1973), 3 *American Review of Canadian Studies* 2-13 (No. 2) **3088**

Morin, Jacques-Yvan. "Les nouvelles utilisations du milieu marin et l'avenir du droit de la mer." (1973), 51 *Canadian Bar Review* 333-388. **3089**

Muli'aumaseali'i, Saverivi. *New Trends in the Law of the Sea: Implications for the Regime of the Airspace.* Montreal, c1977. xi, 154 leaves. **3090**
Thesis (LL.M.), McGill University, 1976. (National Library of Canada. Canadian Theses on Microfiche, No. 31846).

Munro, Donald W. "Law of the Sea: A Canadian Dilemma." (1982) *International Perspectives* 14-17 (Sept./Oct.) **3091**

Murray, Ronald Charles. *Towards a New Model of International Maritime Relations: The Contribution of Existential Phenomenology and General Systems Theory.* Kingston, 1975. xxiii, 520 (i.e. 528) leaves, maps. **3092**
Half-title: *International Maritime Relations.* Thesis (Ph.D.), Queen's University, 1975. (National Library of Canada. Canadian Theses on Microfiche, No. 24872).

North-South Institute. *Canada, the Third World and the Law of the Sea.* Ottawa: North-South Institute, 1981. 5 p. (North-South Institute. Briefing, 2) **3093**

Ochan, Ralph W. *Marine Policy and Developing Landlocked States: The Search for a New Equity in the Law of the Sea.* Halifax, 1977. xvi, 372 leaves. **3094**
Thesis (LL.M.), Dalhousie University, 1977. (National Library of Canada. Canadian Theses on Microfiche, No. 36151).

Pardo, Arvid, and Borgese, Elisabeth Mann. *The New International Economic Order and the Law of the Sea: A Projection.* Msida: Malta University Press, 1975? 223 p. (International Ocean Institute. Occasional Papers, No. 4) **3095**
Prepared in cooperation with RIO Reviewing the International Order and the Center for the Study of Democratic Institutions.

Pharand, Donat. "Le droit de la mer: où en sommes-nous?" (1980), 5 *Annuaire de Droit Maritime et Aérien* 132a-1321 **3096**

Pharand, Donat. "The Northwest Passage in International Law." (1979), 17 *Canadian Yearbook of International Law* 99-133. **3097**

Pharand, Donat. "Vers un nouveau droit de la mer." (1976), 7 *Revue Générale de Droit* 279-286. **3098**

Rigaldies, Francis. "Les deux premières sessions de la Troisième Conférence sur le droit de la mer." (1975), 10 *Revue Juridique Thémis* 179-204. **3099**

Rigaldies, Francis. "La préparation de la Troisième Conférence sur le droit de la mer." (1974), 9 *Revue Juridique Thémis* 435-507. **3100**

Rigaldies, Francis. "La quatrième session de la Troisième Conférence sur le droit de la mer." (1979-80), 14 *Revue Juridique Thémis* 41-71. **3101**

Rigaldies, Francis. "La troisième session de la Troisième Conférence sur le droit de la mer." (1977), 12 *Revue Juridique Thémis* 285-340. **3102**

Rolston, Susan J. *The Scandinavian Nations' Foreign Policies and the Law of the Sea.* Halifax, 1982. iv, 129 leaves. **3103**
Thesis (M.A.), Dalhousie University, 1982.

Slimman, Donald J. "The Parting of the Waves: Canada-United States Differences on the Law of the Sea." (1974-75), 33 *Behind the Headlines* No. 6 (21 p.)**3104**

Thomson, Jennifer. *Role of International Organizations in Light of a New Law of the Sea Convention.* Ottawa, 1977. 1 vol. (various pagings) **3105**
Research essay (M.A.), Carleton University, 1977.

Trilateral Commission. *A New Regime for the Oceans: A Report of the Trilateral Task Force on the Oceans to the Committee of the Trilateral Commission.* Rapporteurs: Michael Hardy, Douglas M. Johnston, and others. New York, 1975. viii, 54 p. (Trilateral Commission. Triangle Papers, 9) **3106**

B. Territorial Sea

Austin, Jacob, and MacKenzie, Norman A.M. "A Canadian View of Territorial Seas and Fisheries." *In International Law: Rivers and Marginal Seas* (Vancouver, 1956), pp. 35-45. **3107**

Baird, W.J. *Sovereignty in the Arctic Territorial Waters Law of the Sea; File Guide to the Indian Affairs and Northern Development and Its Predecessors.* Ottawa, Dept. of Indian Affairs and Northern Development, 1971. 56 leaves. **310**

"Coastal State Jurisdiction / La juridiction des états côtiers." (1976), 5 *Canadian Council on International Law, Proceedings* 124-141. **310**
This is a workshop. Animateur: Paul Lapointe. The transcript is incomplete.

Conboy, Martin. "The Territorial Sea." (1924), 2 *Canadian Bar Review* 8-23.
Also published in (1923), 8 *Canadian Bar Association, Proceedings* 276-292. **311**

Green, Leslie C. "The Territorial Sea and the Anglo-Icelandic Dispute." (1960), *Journal of Public Law* 53-72. **311**

Gushue, Raymond. "The Territorial Waters of Newfoundland." (1949), 15 *Canadian Journal of Economics and Political Science* 344-352. **311**

Herman, Lawrence L. "Proof of Offshore Territorial Claims in Canada." (1982), *Dalhousie Law Journal* 3-38. **311**

La Forest, Gerard V. "Coastal Waters at Common Law." *In* La Forest, Gerard V. and others, *Water Law in Canada: The Atlantic Provinces* (Ottawa, 1973), pp. 462-468. **311**

La Forest, Gerard V. "Offshore Submarine Resources." *In* La Forest, Gerard V.

Natural Resources and Public Property under the Canadian Constitution (Toronto, 1969), pp. 85-107. **3115**

MacKenzie, Norman A.M. "International and Constitutional Law - Legislative Jursidiction within Territorial Waters - The Three Mile Limit - *The King* v. *Boutilier*, (1929) 2 D.L.R. 849. (Case Note)." (1929), 7 *Canadian Bar Review* 736-738. **3116**

Martial, Jean A. "State Control of the Air Space over the Territorial Sea and the Contiguous Zone." (1952), 30 *Canadian Bar Review* 245-263. **3117**

Martin, Paul. "Canada Regulates Its Coastal Waters." (1964), 16 *External Affairs* 282-288. **3118**

Matte, Nicolas Mateesco. *Deux frontières invisibles: de la mer territoriale à l'air 'territorial.'* Paris: A. Pedone, 1965. 295 p. **3119**

Reviews: Charles Chaumont in (1967), 3 *Revue Belge de Droit International* 337-338; C. John Colombos in (1966), 42 *International Affairs* 475-476; Karl Doehring in (1966), 26 *Zeitschrift für Ausländisches Öffentliches Recht und Völkerrecht* 423-424; Gerald F. FitzGerald in (1966-67), 12 *McGill Law Journal* 334-336; Euthymène Georgiades in (1966), 20 *Revue Française de Droit Aérien* 112-113; Juan José López Gutiérrez in (1966), 19 *Revista Española de Derecho Internacional* 148-149; F. Münch in (1969-70), 14 *Archiv des Völkerrechts* 122-123; Nicholas M. Poulantzas in (1966), 19 *Revue Hellénique de Droit International* 467-469; Charles Rousseau in (1966), 70 *Revue Générale de Droit International Public* 225-226; Jean Touscoz in (1966), 93 *Journal du Droit International* 518.

Morin, Jacques-Yvan. "Les eaux territoriales du Canada au regard du droit international." (1963), 1 *Canadian Yearbook of International Law* 82-148. **3120**

Roberts, E.M. *"Re Dominion Coal Co. Ltd.:* Constitutional Law - Property Rights in *Solum* of Canada's Territorial Sea." (1964), 22 *University of Toronto Faculty of Law Review* 203-210. **3121**

"Statutes Respecting Coastal Waters." *In* La Forest, Gerard V., and others, *Water Law in Canada: The Atlantic Provinces* (Ottawa, 1973), pp. 469-480. **3122**

Thompson, Bram. "The Territorial Water Belt." (1920), 40 *Canadian Law Times* 470-490. **3123**

C. Functional Zones (Extended Jurisdiction)

See also *"Marine Pollution (p. 264), and "Arctic: Other Legal Aspects" (p. 205).*

1. GENERAL

Albert, Joan E. McCabe; Harrison, Albert; and Harrison, Peter. *Jurisdictional Problems of New Brunswick Coastal Zones.* Ottawa: University of Ottawa, Faculty of Arts, Geography and Regional Planning, 1974. 32 p. (University of Ottawa. Research Notes, Geography and Regional Planning, No. 4) **3124**

Alexander, Lewis M., and Norton, Virgil. "Maritime Problems between the U.S. and Canada." (1977), 20 *Oceanus* 24-34 (No. 3) **3125**

Beauchamp, Kenneth P. *The Management Function of Ocean Boundaries: Prospects for Co-operative Ocean Management between Canada and the United States.* Halifax, 1981. vii, 328 leaves. **3126**
Thesis (LL.M.), Dalhousie University, 1981.

Clingan, Thomas A., Jr. "Third-Party Imitations of Canadian Legislation and the Implications for International Law Development." *In* Alexander, Lewis M., and Hawkins, Gordon R.S., eds., *Canadian-U.S. Maritime Problems* (Kingston, R.I., 1972), pp. 68-74. **3127**

Dorcey, Anthony H.J. "Coastal Zone Management in Western Canada." (1980), 3 *Canadian Issues* 37-42. **3128**

Feldman, Mark B., and Colson, David. "The Maritime Boundaries of the United States: III. The Gulf of Maine Area." (1981), 75 *American Journal of International Law* 754-763. **3129**

Ferguson, Alan John. *Institutional Aspects of the Coastal Zone: The Case of Estuarine Management on Vancouver Island.* Victoria, B.C., 1977. ix, 120 leaves. **3130**
Thesis (M.A.), University of Victoria, 1977. (National Library of Canada. Canadian Theses on Microfiche, No. 37200).

Johnston, Douglas M. "Coastal Zone Management: National and International Aspects." *In* Miles, Edward, and Gamble, John King, eds., *Law of the Sea: Conference Outcomes and Problems of Implementation* (Cambridge, Mass., 1977), pp. 61-62. **3131**

Johnston, Douglas M. "Coastal Zone Management in Canada: Purposes and Prospects." (1977), 20 *Canadian Public Administration* 140-151. **3132**

Johnston, Douglas M., ed. *Marine Policy and the Coastal Community: The Impact of the Law of the Sea.* New York: St. Martin's Press; London: Croom Helm, 1976. 338 p. **3133**
Contains thirteen essays on the marine economy, ocean politics and the coastal community. Some individual essays are listed separately.
Reviews: Lewis M. Alexander in (1977), 8 *Journal of Maritime Law and Commerce* 521-522; Edward D. Brown in (1976-77), 4 *Maritime Policy and Management* 183-184; Elizabeth Young in (1977), 1 *Marine Policy* 82-83.

Johnston, Douglas M.; Pross, A. Paul; and McDougall, Ian A. *Coastal Zone: Framework for Management in Atlantic Canada.* With special assistance by Norman G. Dale. Halifax: Institute of Public Affairs, Dalhousie University, 1975. xiii, 201, 48 p., maps. **3134**
Commissioned by Inland Waters Directorate, Environmental Management Service, Department of Environment, Ottawa, Canada.
Reviews: Mary L. Barker in (1976), 20 *Canadian Geographer* 345-346; Donald M. McRae in (1976), 2 *Canadian Public Policy* 651-653.

Macdonald, Ronald St. John; Morris, Gerald L.; and Johnston, Douglas M. "The Canadian Initiative to Establish a Maritime Zone for Environmental Protection: Its Significance for Multilateral Development of International Law." (1971), 21 *University of Toronto Law Journal* 247-251. **3135**

A statement circulated and discussed at the annual conference of the American Society of International Law, meeting in New York on April 24, 1970. Annexed to a symposium on the International Legal Aspects of Pollution, held in Vancouver, September 1970.

Maritimes' Coastal Zone Seminar, Mount Allison University, 1973. *Proceedings.* Sackville, N.B.: Mt. Allison University, 1973. 24 p. **3136**

Pharand, Donat. "Contiguous Zones of Pollution Prevention." (1972-73), 1 *Syracuse Journal of International Law and Commerce* 257-263. **3137**

Pharand, Donat. "The Implications of Canadian Marine and Arctic Legislation for the Development of International Law." *In* Alexander, Lewis M., and Hawkins, Gordon R.S., eds., *Canadian-U.S. Maritime Problems* (Kingston, R.I., 1972), pp. 75-81. **3138**

Rhee, Sang-Myon. "Equitable Solutions to the Maritime Boundary Dispute between the United States and Canada in the Gulf of Maine." (1981), 75 *American Journal of International Law* 590-628. **3139**

2. EXCLUSIVE ECONOMIC ZONES

Cooper, John. "Boundaries of the Economic Zone: Commentary." *In* Miles, Edward, and Gamble, John King, eds., *Law of the Sea: Conference Outcomes and Problems of Implementation* (Cambridge, Mass., 1977), pp. 210-211.
3140

Edwards, G.L. "The 200-mile Economic Zone: New Territory, New Commitments, New Worries." (1976-77), 6 *Canadian Defence Quarterly* 32-36 (No. 3) **3141**

Johnson, Barbara. "Governing Canada's Economic Zone." (1977), 20 *Canadian Public Administration* 152-173. **3142**

Johnston, Douglas M. "The Economic Zone in North America: Scenarios and Options." (1975-76), 3 *Ocean Development and International Law Journal* 53-68. **3143**

Johnston, Douglas M., and Gold, Edgar. *The Economic Zone in the Law of the Sea: Survey, Analysis, and Appraisal of Current Trends.* Kingston, R. I.: Law of the Sea Institute, 1973. iii, 53 leaves. (Law of the Sea Institute. Occasional Paper, No. 17) **3144**

Leger, Georges Antoine. "Droit de la mer: la contribution du Canada au nouveau concept de la zone économique." (1980), 11 *Études Internationales* 421-440.
3145

Munro, Gordon R. "North America, Extended Jurisdiction and the Northwest Atlantic: A Canadian Perspective." *In* Miles, Edward, and Gamble, John King, eds., *Law of the Sea: Conference Outcomes and Problems of Implementation* (Cambridge, Mass., 1977), pp. 29-45. **3146**
Commentary by Douglas M. Johnston (pp. 51-54).

Okidi, C. Odidi. "The Role of the OAU Member States in the Evolution of the Concept of the Exclusive Economic Zone in the Law of the Sea: The First Phase." (1982), 7 *Dalhousie Law Journal* 39-71. **3147**

Sanguin, André-Louis. "La zone canadienne des 200 milles dans l'Atlantique: un exemple de la nouvelle géographie des océans." (1980), 11 *Études Internationales* 239-251. **3148**

Stanford, Gerald B. "Canadian Perspectives on the Future Enforcement of the Exclusive Economic Zone: A Paper in Diplomacy and the Law of the Sea." (1979), 5 *Dalhousie Law Journal* 73-120. **3149**

Zama, Charles Cho. *The Exclusive Economic Zone and the Developing Countries.* Kingston, 1981. 424 frames. **3150**
Thesis (LL.M.), Queen's University, 1981. (National Library of Canada. Canadian Theses on Microfiche, No. 50219).

3. FISHING ZONES

Copes, Parzival. "British Columbia Fisheries and the 200-mile Limit: Perverse Effects for the Coastal State." (1980), 4 *Marine Policy* 205-214. **3151**

Copes, Parzival. "Fisheries on Canada's Pacific East Coast: The Impact of Extended Jurisdiction on Exploitation Patterns." (1981), 6 *Ocean Management* 279-297. **3152**

Gotlieb, Allan E. "The Canadian Contribution to the Concept of a Fishing Zone in International Law." (1964), 2 *Canadian Yearbook of International Law* 55-76. **3153**

Gudmundsson, Thordur Ingvi. *The Canadian 200-mile Fishery Limit: A Study of Fisheries Regulations in the 1960's and 1970's.* Kingston, 1980. 235 leaves. **3154**
Thesis (M.A.), Queen's University, 1980. (National Library of Canada. Canadian Theses on Microfiche, No. 46420).

Johnson, Barbara, and Langdon, Frank. "Two Hundred Mile Zones: The Politics of North Pacific Fisheries." (1976-77), 49 *Pacific Affairs* 5-27. **3155**

Johnson, Barbara, and Middlemiss, Danford W. "Canada's 200-Mile Fishing Zone: The Problem of Compliance." (1977), 4 *Ocean Development and International Law Journal* 67-110. **3156**

LeBlanc, Romeo. "Beyond the 200-Mile Limit." *In* Patton, Donald J., and others, *The Future of the Offshore* (Halifax, 1978), pp. 91-99. **3157**

Lucas, Kenneth C., and Loftas, Tony. "FAO's EEZ Program: Helping to Build the Fisheries of the Future." (1982), 3 *Ocean Yearbook* 38-76. **3158**

McRae, Donald M. "Adjudication of the Maritime Boundary in the Gulf of Maine." (1979), 17 *Canadian Yearbook of International Law* 292-303. **3159**

Morin, Jacques-Yvan. "La zone de pêche exclusive du Canada." (1964), 2 *Canadian Yearbook of International Law* 77-106 **3160**

Morin, Jacques-Yvan. "Les zones de pêche de Terre-Neuve et du Labrador à la lumière de l'évolution du droit international." (1968), 6 *Canadian Yearbook of International Law* 91-114. **3161**

Munro, Gordon R. "Canada and Fisheries Management with Extended Jurisdiction: A Preliminary View." *In* Anderson, Lee G., ed., *Economic Impacts of Extended Fisheries Jurisdiction* (Ann Arbor, Mich., 1977), pp. 29-50. **3162**

Munro, Gordon R. "Extended Fisheries Jurisdiction and International Co-operation." (1978), *International Perspectives* 12-18 (Mar./Apr.) **3163**

Munro, Gordon R. "Extended Fisheries Jurisdiction in a Regional Setting: Problems of Conflicting Goals and Interests." *In* Johnston, Douglas M., ed., *Regionalization of the Law of the Sea* (Cambridge, Mass., 1978), pp. 233-253. **3164**

Munro, Gordon R. "Fisheries, Extended Jurisdiction and the Economics of Common Property Resources." (1982), 15 *Canadian Journal of Economics* 405-425. **3165**

Poulantzas, Nicholas M. "Recent Developments in Canada Relating to Enforcement Measures in an Expanded Fisheries Zone." (1977), 30 *Revue Hellénique de Droit International* 109-119. **3166**

Snow, Rodney A. "Extended Fishery Jurisdiction in Canada and the United States." (1978), 5 *Ocean Development and International Law Journal* 291-344. **3167**

Symmons, C.R. "The Canadian 200-Mile Fishery Limit and the Delimitation of Maritime Zones Around St. Pierre and Miquelon." (1980), 12 *Ottawa Law Review* 145-165. **3168**

Travis, Ralph. "Policing Our Enlarged Coastal Fishing Zones." (1978), 97 *Canadian Geographic* 46-51 (No. 2) **3169**

Wang, Erik B. "Canada-United States Fisheries and Maritime Boundary Negotiations: Diplomacy in Deep Water." (1981), 38(6)/39(1) *Behind the Headlines* (47 p.) **3170**

D. Submerged Areas

1. SEABED IN GENERAL

Alexandrowicz, G.W. "Canadian Approaches to the Seabed Regime." *In* Macdonald, Ronald St. John, and others, *Canadian Perspectives on International Law and Organization* (Toronto, 1974), pp. 410-433. **3171**

Angrand, Jean. "Essai d'analyse de quelques problèmes soulevés par l'exploitation des ressources minérales du fond des mers." (1976), 54 *Revue de Droit International, de Sciences Diplomatiques et Politiques* 81-95. **3172**

Angrand, Jean. "Law of the Sea: Adapting International Law to Handle Seabed Resources." (1975), *International Perspectives* 45-48 (July/Aug.) **3173**

Bagambiire, Davies Birenzo Namiti. *The New Law of the Sea: The Non-National Sea-Bed Area and the International Sea-Bed Authority: With a Critique on the Approach of the African and Latin American States.* Halifax, 1977. xi, 231 leaves. **3174**
Thesis (LL.M.), Dalhousie University, 1977.

Borgese, Elisabeth Mann. *The Enterprises: A Proposal to Reconceptualize the*

Operational Arm of the International Seabed Authority to Manage the Common Heritage of Mankind. Malta: International Ocean Institute, 1978. x, 23 p. (International Ocean Institute. Occasional Papers, No. 6) **3175**
Review: Roderick C. Ogley in (1979), 3 *Marine Policy* 247-248.

Borgese, Elisabeth Mann. "The Role of the International Seabed Authority in the 1980's." (1981) 18 *San Diego Law Review* 395-407. **3176**

Buzan, Barry G. "Seabed Issues at the Law of the Sea Conference: The Caracas Session." (1974), 12 *Canadian Yearbook of International Law* 222-238. **3177**

Buzan, Barry G. *Seabed Politics.* New York: Praeger, 1976. xviii, 311 p. (Praeger Special Studies in International Politics and Government) **3178**
Review: V.S. Mani in (1978), 18 *Indian Journal of International Law* 258-259.

Buzan, Barry G., and Middlemiss, Danford W. "Canadian Foreign Policy and the Exploitation of the Seabed." *In* Johnson, Barbara, and Zacher, Mark W., eds., *Canadian Foreign Policy and the Law of the Sea* (Vancouver, 1977), pp. 1-51. **3179**

Crommelin, Michael. "An Evaluation of Proposals for a Regime for the Deep Sea-Bed in the Light of National Experience." (1975), 13 *Canadian Yearbook of International Law* 281-294. **3180**

De Mestral, Armand L.C. "Le régime juridique du fond des mers: inventaire et solutions possibles." (1970), 74 *Revue Générale de Droit International Public* 640-667. **3181**

Dupuy, René-Jean. "Le régime des fonds marins internationaux: la communauté inaccessible." (1982), 7 *Annals of Air and Space Law* 283-293. **3182**

Franck, Thomas M., and Chesler, Evan R. "International Regime for the Sea-Bed Beyond National Jurisdiction." (1975), 13 *Osgoode Hall Law Journal* 579-601. **3183**
Also printed in (1976), 6 *Georgia Journal of International and Comparative Law* 151-179.

Franck, Thomas M.; Kennedy, Thomas M.; and Trinko, Curtis V. "An Equitable Regime for Seabed and Ocean Subsoil Resources." (1974), 4 *Denver Journal of International Law and Policy* 161-186. **3184**

Gotlieb, Allan E. "Recent Developments concerning the Exploration and Exploitation of the Ocean Floor." (1969), 15 *McGill Law Journal* 260-278. **3185**

Hawkins, Gordon R.S. "The Pressing Implications of Canada as a Seabed Power." (1972), *International Perspectives* 35-39 (July/Aug.) **3186**

Head, Ivan L. "Whose Is the Bed of the Sea? (A Panel. Remarks)." (1968), 62 *American Society of International Law, Proceedings* 241-243. **3187**

Keller, Joseph. *The Law of the Seabed Beyond the Limits of National Jurisdiction: A Study of an International Regime and an International Authority.* Halifax, 1976 (c1977). xiv, 237 leaves. **3188**
Thesis (LL.M.), Dalhousie University, 1976. (National Library of Canada. Canadian Theses on Microfiche, No. 31512).

Kirsch, Philippe. *Le régime juridique applicable à l'exploitation des ressources minérales des grands fonds marins.* Montréal, 1972. 190 leaves. **3189**
Thesis (LL.M.), Université de Montréal, 1972.

Legault, L.H. "Peace and Security on the Ocean Floor." (1970), 22 *External Affairs* 161-166. **3190**

Nesgos, Peter D. "The Proposed International Sea-Bed Authority as a Model for the Future Outer Space International Régime." (1980), 5 *Annals of Air and Space Law* 549-573. **3191**

Paget, D. "Towards a Regime for the Sea-Bed: An Examination of Official Proposals." (1971-72), 1 *Queen's Law Journal* 484-512. **3192**

Purver, Ronald G. "Canada and the Control of Arms on the Seabed." (1975), 13 *Canadian Yearbook of International Law* 195-230. **3193**

Ruddick, Valley. "Can the UN Agree upon Undersea Rights?" (1975), 90 *Canadian Geographical Journal* 12-21 (No. 3) **3194**

2. CONTINENTAL SHELF

Anderson, Catherine. "Off-Shore Rights Deal Faces Legal Hurdles." (1979), 6 *Canadian Business Review* 23-26 (No. 3) **3195**

Arvay, Joseph. "Newfoundland's Claim to Offshore Mineral Resources: An Overview of the Legal Issues." (1979), 5 *Canadian Public Policy* 32-44. **3196**

Beauchamp, K.; Crommelin, Michael; and Thompson, Andrew R. "Jurisdictional Problems in Canada's Offshore." (1973), 11 *Alberta Law Review* 431-469.
3197

Beesley, J. Alan. "Offshore Mineral Rights Considered from an International and Constitutional Point of Law." (1972), *Canadian Bar Association, Papers*, 37 p.
3198

Brière, Jules. "La Cour suprême du Canada et les droits sous-marins." (1967-68), 9 *Cahiers de Droit* 735-776. **3199**

Caplan, Neil. "Legal Issues of the Offshore Mineral Rights Dispute in Canada." (1968), 14 *McGill Law Journal* 475-493. **3200**

Caplan, Neil. "Offshore Mineral Rights: Anatomy of a Federal-Provincial Conflict." (1970), 5 *Journal of Canadian Studies* 50-61 (No. 1) **3201**

Caplan, Neil. *The Offshore Mineral Rights Dispute in Canada.* Ottawa, 1968. ii, 129 leaves. **3202**
Thesis (M.A.), Carleton University, 1968.

Cole, Charles V. "The Continental Shelf." (1955), 20 *Saskatchewan Bar Review* 22-23. **3203**

"Continental Shelf and International Sea-Bed / Le plateau continental et la zone internationale des grands fonds marins." (1976), 5 *Canadian Council on International Law, Proceedings* 142-151. **3204**
This is a workshop. Animateur: D.G. Crosby. The transcript is incomplete.

Cosford, Edwin G. "The Continental Shelf and the Abu Dhabi Award." (1952-55), 1 *McGill Law Journal* 109-127. **3205**

Cosford, Edwin G. "The Continental Shelf 1910-1945." (1957-58), 4 *McGill Law Journal* 245-266. **3206**

Crommelin, Michael. *Allocation of Rights over Offshore Oil and Gas Resources: A Study of the Legal Systems in Force in the United States, the United Kingdom, Canada and Australia.* Vancouver, 1972. 256 leaves. **3207**
Thesis (LL.M.), University of British Columbia, 1972.

Crommelin, Michael. "Jurisdiction over Offshore Oil and Gas in Canada." (1975), 10 *University of British Columbia Law Review* 86-144. **3208**

Cumyn, A. Peter. "Can Canada Levy Tax on the Continental Shelf?" (1981), 4 *Canada-United States Law Journal* 165-170. **3209**

Cuyvers, Luc. "Maritime Boundaries: Canada vs. United States." (1979-80), 2 *Marine Policy Reports* No. 1 (5 p.) **3210**

De Mestral, Armand L.C. "The Law Applicable to the Canadian East-Coast Offshore." (1983), 21 *Alberta Law Review* 63-81. **3211**

Douglas, Colin. "Conflicting Claims to Oil and Natural Gas Resources Off the Eastern Coast of Canada." (1980), 18 *Alberta Law Review* 54-69. **3212**

Foley, Edward C. "Nova Scotia's Case for Coastal and Offshore Resources." (1981), 13 *Ottawa Law Review* 281-308. **3213**

Frédérick, Michel. "La délimitation du plateau continental entre le Canada et les États-Unis dans la mer de Beaufort." (1979), 17 *Canadian Yearbook of International Law* 30-98. **3214**

Frédérick, Michel. *La délimitation du plateau continental entre le Canada et les États-Unis dans la mer de Beaufort.* Ottawa, 1980. 138 frames. **3215**
Thesis (LL.M.), Université d'Ottawa, 1980. (National Library of Canada. Canadian Theses on Microfiche, No. 48528).

Gault, Ian Townsend. "Recent Developments in the Federal-Provincial Dispute Concerning Jurisdiction Over Offshore Petroleum Resources." (1983), 21 *Alberta Law Review* 97-113. **3216**

Green, Leslie C. "The Continental Shelf." (1951), 4 *Current Legal Problems* 54-80. **3217**

Harrison, Rowland J. "Jurisdiction over the Canadian Offshore: A Sea of Confusion." (1979), 17 *Osgoode Hall Law Journal* 469-505. **3218**

Harrison, Rowland J. "The Offshore Mineral Resources Agreement in the Maritime Provinces." (1977-78), 4 *Dalhousie Law Journal* 245-276. **3219**

Head, Ivan L. "The Canadian Offshore Minerals Reference: The Application of International Law to a Federal Constitution." (1968), 18 *University of Toronto Law Journal* 131-157. **3220**

Head, Ivan L. "The Legal Clamour over Canadian Off-Shore Minerals." (1966-67), 5 *Alberta Law Review* 312-327. **3221**

Herman, Lawrence L. "The Need for a Canadian Submerged Lands Act: Some Further Thoughts on Canada's Offshore Mineral Rights Problems." (1980), 58 *Canadian Bar Review* 518-544. **3222**

Inions, Noela J. "Newfoundland Offshore Claims." (1981), 19 *Alberta Law Review* 461-482. **3223**

Ippolito, Joseph T. "Newfoundland and the Continental Shelf: From Cod to Oil and Gas." (1976), 15 *Columbia Journal of Transnational Law* 138-162. **3224**

Kovach, A.J. "An Assessment of the Merits of Newfoundland's Claim to Offshore Mineral Resources." (1975), 23 *Chitty's Law Journal* 18-23. **3225**

Lacasse, Jean-Paul. "The Development of Canada's Offshore Mineral Resources and Its Legal Environment." (1969), *Canadian Bar Association, Papers,* 13 p. **3226**

Lacasse, Jean-Paul. "Fédéralisme et ressources sous-marines." (1975), 6 *Revue Générale de Droit* 475-477. **3227**

Lacasse, Jean-Paul. "La territorialisation de la notion de plateau continental." (1976), 7 *Revue Générale de Droit* 91-93. **3228**

Lawson, Karin L. "Delimiting Continental Shelf Boundaries in the Arctic: The United States-Canada Beaufort Sea Boundary." (1981), 22 *Virginia Journal of International Law* 222-246. **3229**

MacLauchlan, H. Wade. "Newfoundland's Continental Shelf: The Jurisdictional Issue." (1981), 30 *University of New Brunswick Law Journal* 91-120. **3230**

Martin, Cabot. "Newfoundland's Case on Offshore Minerals: A Brief Outline." (1975), 7 *Ottawa Law Review* 34-61. **3231**

McKenna, Frank J. "New Brunswick and Offshore Mineral Rights." (1973), 22 *University of New Brunswick Law Journal* 69-88. **3232**

McRae, Donald M. "Delimitation of the Continental Shelf between the United Kingdom and France: The Channel Arbitration." (1977), 15 *Canadian Yearbook of International Law* 173-197. **3233**

Mesaritis, Panayiotis. *An Historical Examination of the Development of Legal Claims to the Continental Shelf.* Edmonton, 1979. xii, 233 leaves. **3234**
Thesis (LL.M.), University of Alberta, 1979. (National Library of Canada. Canadian Theses on Microfiche, No. 40458).

Mestier du Bourg, Hubert de. *Droit pétrolier et plateau continental.* Montréal, 1970 (c1971). v, 97 leaves, map. **3235**
Thesis (LL.M.), McGill University, 1970. (National Library of Canada. Canadian Theses on Microfilm, No. 7296).

Mestier du Bourg, Hubert de. "Droit pétrolier et plateau continental." (1970), 1 *Revue de Droit, Université de Sherbrooke* 1-53. **3236**

Mills, Hal. "Eastern Canada's Offshore Resources and Boundaries: A Study in Political Geography." (1971), 6 *Journal of Canadian Studies* 36-50 (No. 3) **3237**

Morris, Hugh G. "Continental Shelf - An International Dilemma." (1958-59), 1 *Osgoode Hall Law Journal* 37-46 (No. 1) **3238**

Pearcy, G. Etzel. "The Continental Shelf: Physical vs. Legal Definition." (1961), 5 *Canadian Geographer* 26-29. **3239**

Pharand, Donat. "Aspects of International Law Concerning Two Questions of Jurisdiction Relating to Natural Resource Conservation and Development in Canada." *In* Crabbé, Philippe, and Spry, Irene M., eds., *Natural Resource Development in Canada: Multi-Disciplinary Seminar* (Ottawa, 1973), pp. 231-242. **3240**
Includes a discussion (pp. 235-242).

Pharand, Donat. "The Continental Shelf Redefinition, with Special Reference to the Arctic." (1972), 18 *McGill Law Journal* 536-559. **3241**

Rigaldies, Francis. "La délimitation du plateau continental entre états voisins." (1976), 14 *Canadian Yearbook of International Law* 116-174. **3242**

Swan, George S. "The Newfoundland Offshore Claims: Interface of Constitutional Federalism and International Law." (1976), 22 *McGill Law Journal* 541-573.
3243

Swan, George S. *Northwest Atlantic Offshore Claims: International and Interfederal Challenges Confronting Canada and the U.S.A.* Toronto, 1976. iii, 188 leaves. **3244**
Thesis (LL.M.), University of Toronto, 1976.

Swan, George S. "Remembering *Maine:* Offshore Federalism in the United States and Canada." (1976), 6 *California Western International Law Journal* 296-322.
3245

Swan, George S. "That Gulf of Maine Dispute: Canada and the United States Delimit the Atlantic Continental Shelf." (1977-78), 10 *Natural Resources Lawyer* 405-456. **3246**

E. High Seas

1. FREEDOM OF THE SEA

"The Freedom of the Seas." (1919), 55 *Canada Law Journal* 77-79. **3247**

Gold, Edgar. "Navigation: The 'Not-So-Sacred' Freedom of the Sea. (Commentary)." *In* Miles, Edward, and Gamble, John King, eds., *Law of the Sea: Conference Outcomes and Problems of Implementation* (Cambridge, Mass., 1977), pp. 120-123. **3248**

Green, Leslie C. "The Geneva Conventions and the Freedom of the Seas." (1959), 12 *Current Legal Problems* 224-246. **3249**

Keith, A. Berriedale. "The Freedom of the Sea." (1918), 38 *Canadian Law Times* 230-241. **3250**

Law, Carl Edgar. "Freedom of Innocent Passage versus Territorial Expansion." (1980), *International Perspectives* 13-16 (July/Aug.) **3251**

MacKenzie, Norman A.M. "The Freedom of the Seas." (1929), 36 *Queen's Quarterly* 420-436. **3252**

Mackneson, Stephen Wayne. *Freedom of Flight over the High Seas.* Montreal 1959. 114 leaves. **3253**
Thesis (LL.M.), McGill University, 1959.

Ogunbanwo, Ogunsola Olaniyi. *The Exercise of State Authority in the Air-Space over the High Seas.* Montreal, 1966. 149 leaves, maps. **3255**
Thesis (LL.M.), McGill University, 1966. (National Library of Canada. Canadian Theses on Microfilm, No. 275).

2. NATIONALITY OF VESSELS

Herman, Lawrence L. "Flags of Convenience: New Dimensions to an Old Problem." (1978), 24 *McGill Law Journal* 1-28. **3255**

McDougal, Myres S.; Burke, William T.; and Vlasic, Ivan A. "The Maintenance of Public Order at Sea and the Nationality of Ships." (1960), 54 *American Journal of International Law* 25-116. **3256**
Review: Unsigned in (1960), 16 *Revue Égyptienne de Droit International* 135-141.

3. HOT PURSUIT

Beck, J. Stafford H. "The Doctrine of Hot Pursuit." (1931), 9 *Canadian Bar Review* 85-114, 176-202, 249-270, 341-365. **3257**
Based on a thesis (S.J.D.), University of Michigan.

Poulantzas, Nicholas M. "The Right of Hot Pursuit Especially under the Geneva Convention on the High Seas." (1961), 14 *Revue Hellénique de Droit International* 196-224. **3258**

Poulantzas, Nicholas M. *The Right of Hot Pursuit in International Law.* Leyden: A.W. Sijthoff, 1969. xv, 451 p. (Nova et Vetera Iuris Gentium. Series A: Modern International Law, No. 5) **3259**
Reviews: Alfred Connor Bowman in (1973), 59 *A.B.A. Journal* 237-238; Martí Bravo Navarro in (1969), 22 *Revista Española de Derecho Internacional* 645-646; Burdick H. Brittin in (1972), 66 *American Journal of International Law* 426-427; Eric David in (1971), 7 *Revue Belge de Droit International* 378-379; Jochen Erler in (1970), 8 *Canadian Yearbook of International Law* 414-415; W. Paul Gormley in (1969-70), 1 *Journal of Maritime Law and Commerce* 505-508; W. Paul Gormley in (1970), 23 *Revue Hellénique de Droit International* 463-468; W. Paul Gormley in (1969-70), 14 *St. Louis University Law Journal* 355-364; Leslie C. Green in (1970), 48 *Canadian Bar Review* 828-831; Frits Kalshoven in (1971). 18 *Netherlands International Law Review* 247 (in Dutch); James J. Knicely in (1969), 10 *Harvard International Law Journal* 583-589; Howard S. Levie in (1970), 9 *Columbia Journal of Transnational Law* 453-457; F.A. Mann in (1970), 46 *International Affairs* 799-800; F. Münch in (1971), 31 *Zeitschrift für Ausländisches Öffentliches Recht und Völkerrecht* 394-395; K. Venkata Raman in (1970), 10 *Indian Journal of International Law* 388-391; Charles Rousseau in (1970), 74 *Revue Générale de Droit International Public* 208; Ignaz Seidl-Hohenveldern in (1976), 27 *Österreichische Zeitschrift für Öffentliches Recht* 380-381; Michel Smirnoff in (1970), 24 *Revue Française de Droit Aérien* 370-372; signed D.R. in (1970), 97 *Journal du Droit International* 514.

F. Bays, Gulfs, Straits and Archipelagos

See also *"Inland Seas (Hudson Bay)" (p. 228).*

Barros, James. *The Aland Islands Question: Its Settlement by the League of Nations.* New Haven: Yale University Press, 1968. xiii, 362 p. **3260**
Review: Frederic H. Soward in (1969-70), 25 *International Journal* 209.

Bloomfield, Louis M. *Egypt, Israel, and the Gulf of Aqaba in International Law.* Toronto: Carswell, 1957. 240 p., maps. **3261**
Reviews: Richard R. Baxter in (1957), 51 *American Journal of International Law* 843-845; Jasper Yeates Brinton in (1957), 13 *Revue Égyptienne de Droit International* 153-154; Reinhardt Freudenberg in (1957-58), 18 *Zeitschrift für Ausländisches Öffentliches Recht und Völkerrecht* 771-772; Ronald St. John Macdonald in (1958), 36 *Canadian Bar Review* 127-129.

La Forest, Gerard V. "Canadian Inland Waters of the Atlantic Provinces and the Bay of Fundy Incident." (1963), 1 *Canadian Yearbook of International Law* 149-171. **3262**

Lamontagne, Roland. *La baie James dans l'histoire du Canada.* Montréal: Librairie Beauchemin, 1974. 115 p., map. **3263**
Review: Louis-Edmond Hamelin in (1974-75), *Revue d'Histoire de l'Amérique Française* 434-436.

Loriot, François. *La théorie des eaux historiques et le régime juridique du golfe Saint-Laurent en droit interne et international.* Québec: s.n., 1972 (i.e. 1973). 705 p. **3264**

Maduro, Morris F. *The Law of International Straits and Inter-Oceanic Canals.* Edmonton, 1978. xi, 262 leaves. **3265**
Thesis (Ph.D.), University of Alberta, 1978. (National Library of Canada. Canadian Theses on Microfiche, No. 40237).

McConchie, Roger D., and Reid, Robert S. "Canadian Foreign Policy and International Straits." *In* Johnson, Barbara, and Zacher, Mark W., eds., *Canadian Foreign Policy and the Law of the Sea* (Vancouver, 1977), pp. 158-201. **3266**

McConnell, William H. "The Legal Regime of Archipelagoes." (1970), 35 *Saskatchewan Law Review* 121-145. **3267**

McKelvey, E. Neil. "Some Domestic Law Aspects of the Obstruction to Navigation Involved in the Proposed International Passamaquoddy Tidal Power Project.' (1960), *Canadian Bar Association, Papers* 257-274. **3268**

Pharand, Donat. "International Straits." (1977), 7 *Thesaurus Acroasium* (Thessaloniki) 64-100 **3269**

Turnquest, Harcourt Lowell. *Possible Archipelagic Claims for the Bahamas: An Appraisal.* Ottawa, 1976. 218 leaves, maps. **3270**
Research essay (M.A.), Carleton University, 1976.

"United States Rights in British Bays." (1911), 31 *Canadian Law Times* 289-298.
3271

G. Marine Resources

1. GENERAL

Anderson, Lee G. "The Economics of Marine Resource Management." *In* Johnston, Douglas M., ed., *Marine Policy and the Coastal Community* (New York, 1976), pp. 65-84. **3272**

Couper, Alistair D. "The Economic Geography of the Sea." *In* Johnston, Douglas M., ed., *Marine Policy and the Coastal Community* (New York, 1976), pp. 37-63. **3273**

Devine, D.J. "The Protection of Maritime Environment by the Courts of Third States: Some Difficulties." (1973), 19 *McGill Law Journal* 279-283. **3274**

Park, Choon-ho. "Marine Resource Conflicts in the North Pacific." *In* Johnston, Douglas M., ed., *Marine Policy and the Coastal Community* (New York, 1976), pp. 215-232. **3275**

Patton, Donald J.; Beckton, Clare F.; and Johnston, Douglas M., eds. *The Future of the Offshore: Legal Developments and Canadian Business.* Halifax: Centre for International Business Studies, Dalhousie University, 1978. viii, 243 p., maps. **3276**
Proceedings of a conference sponsored by the Centre for International Business Studies, School of Business Administration, and the Public Services Committee of the Faculty of Law, Dalhousie University, Halifax, Nova Scotia.
Review: G.W. Haight in (1979), 5 *Ocean Management* 346-347.

Pontecorvo, Giulio, and Mesznik, Roger. "Economic Organization and the Exploitation of Marine Resources." *In* Johnston, Douglas M., ed., *Marine Policy and the Coastal Community* (New York, 1976), pp. 85-102. **3277**

Stewart, Robert William, and Dickie, Lloyd Merlin. *Ad Mare: Canada Looks to the Sea; a Study on Marine Science and Technology.* Ottawa: Information Canada, 1971. 175 p. (Background Study for the Science Council of Canada. Special Study, No. 16) **3278**

University of Rhode Island. Center for Ocean Management Studies. *Comparative Marine Policy: Perspectives from Europe, Scandinavia, Canada, and the United States.* New York: Praeger, 1981. xi, 260 p., maps. (Praeger Special Studies) (Praeger Scientific) **3279**
Proceedings of a conference sponsored by the Center for Ocean Management Studies at the University of Rhode Island.

2. LIVING RESOURCES

(a) GENERAL

Canada. Fisheries and Marine Service. *The Marine Environment and Renewable Resources.* Ottawa: Fisheries and Marine Service, Dept. of the Environment, 1973. 10 leaves. **3280**

At head of title: *Law of the Sea Discussion Paper.* Also issued in French under title: *L'environnement marin et les ressources renouvelables.*

"Living Resources of the Sea: Protective Legislation Announced by Canada." (1970), 22 *External Affairs* 130-160. **3281**

(b) FISHERIES

(i) GENERAL

Alhéritière, Dominique. "La compétence fédérale sur les pêcheries et la lutte contre la pollution des eaux: réflexions sur le nouveau règlement de la loi sur les pêcheries." (1972), 13 *Cahiers de Droit* 53-78. **3282**

Allen, Edward W. "The North Pacific Fisheries." (1937), 10 *Pacific Affairs* 136-151. **3283**

Ball, James T. "Fisheries: Canada-United States Reciprocal Fisheries Relations under the Interim Fisheries Agreement of 1978." (1979), 11 *Case Western Reserve Journal of International Law* 201-210. **3284**

Canada. Dept. of Fisheries and Oceans. *Policy for Canada's Atlantic Fisheries in the 1980's: A Discussion Paper.* Ottawa: Dept. of Fisheries and Oceans, Communications Branch, 1981. 60 p. **3285**

Canada. Dept. of Fisheries and the Environment. *Annual Report / Rapport annuel.* 1976/77—. Ottawa. Bilingual. **3286**

This department, reorganized in 1976, is responsible for fisheries, renewable resources, water, meteorology, environment protection, and others, as well as the enforcement of rules or regulations made by the International Joint Commission. It administers a number of fisheries statutes, including those implementing international conventions, as well as the *Territorial Sea and Fishing Zones Act* (R.S.C. 1970, c. T-7). The annual report briefly describes some activities of international interest. The federal government has jurisdiction over all fisheries (marine and freshwater) in Nova Scotia, New Brunswick, Newfoundland, P.E.I., and the Northwest and Yukon Territories; it has jurisdiction over marine fisheries in British Columbia, while Quebec manages both marine and fresh fisheries with some exceptions; in the four inland provinces of Ontario, Manitoba, Saskatchewan, and Alberta, all fisheries are a provincial responsibility.

Canada. Fisheries and Marine Service. *Policy for Canada's Commercial Fisheries.* Ottawa: Fisheries and Marine Service, Dept. of the Environment, 1976. 1 vol. (various pagings) **3287**

Also issued in French under title: *Politique canadienne pour la pêche commerciale.*

Carroz, J.E. "La Commission internationale des pêches pour l'Atlantique Sud-Est." (1971), 9 *Canadian Yearbook of International Law* 3-29. **3288**

Carroz, J.E., and Roche, A.G. "The International Policing of High Sea Fisheries." (1968), 6 *Canadian Yearbook of International Law* 61-90. **3289**

Chaussade, Jean. "Quelques considérations sur l'expansion des pêches mondiales." (1973), 6 *Revue de l'Université de Moncton* 235-246 (no 2) **3290**

Commission on Pacific Fisheries Policy. *Conflict and Opportunity: Toward a New Policy for Canada's Pacific Fisheries: A Preliminary Report.* Vancouver: Commission on Pacific Fisheries Policy, 1981. 148 p. **3291**
Peter H. Pearse, Commissioner.

Copes, Parzival. "Canada's Atlantic Coast Fisheries: Policy Development and the Impact of Extended Jurisdiction." (1978), 4 *Canadian Public Policy* 155-171.
3292

Copes, Parzival. "The Economics of Marine Fisheries Management in the Era of Extended Jurisdiction: The Canadian Perspectives." (1979), 69 *American Economic Review* 256-260. **3293**

Copes, Parzival. *The Evolution of Marine Fisheries Policy in Canada.* Burnaby, B.C.: Dept. of Economics and Commerce, Simon Fraser University, 1979. 45 p. (Simon Fraser University. Dept. of Economics and Commerce. Discussion Paper, 79-3-1) **3294**

Copes, Parzival. "Fisheries on Canada's Pacific East Coast: The Impact of Extended Jurisdiction on Exploitation Patterns." (1981), 6 *Ocean Management* 279-297. **3295**

Copes, Parzival. *The Impact of UNCLOS III on Management of the World's Fisheries.* Burnaby, B.C.: School of Business Administration and Economics, Simon Fraser University, 1981. 39 p. (Simon Fraser University. School of Business Administration and Economics. Discussion Paper, 81-08-01) **3296**

Copes, Parzival. "Implementing Canada's Marine Fisheries Policy: Objectives, Hazards and Constraints." (1982), 6 *Marine Policy* 219-235. **3297**

Copes, Parzival. *Marine Fisheries Management in Canada: Policy Objectives and Institutional Constraints.* Burnaby, B.C.: Dept. of Economics and Commerce, Simon Fraser University, 1979. 21 p. (Simon Fraser University. Dept. of Economics and Commerce. Discussion Paper, 79-7-2) **3298**

De Mestral, Armand L.C. "Accord entre le Canada et la Norvège sur leurs relations en matière de pêche." (1976), 14 *Canadian Yearbook of International Law* 270-282. **3299**

De Mestral, Armand L.C. "Deux récents accords bilatéraux en matière de pêche en 1977." (1977), 15 *Canadian Yearbook of International Law* 287-300. **3300**

Dickie, Lloyd Merlin. "The Gulf of St. Lawrence: Requirements for Fishery Management." (1980), 3 *Canadian Issues* 15-24. **3301**

Donaldson, John, and Pontecorvo, Giulio. "Economic Rationalization of Fisheries: The Problem of Conflicting National Interests on Georges Bank." (1980), 8 *Ocean Development and International Law Journal* 149-169. **3302**
Paper presented at Powell River Symposium, Powell River, B.C., August 1978.

Fairley, H. Scott. "Canadian Federalism, Fisheries and the Constitution: External Constraints on Internal Ordering." (1980), 12 *Ottawa Law Review* 257-318.
3303

Fairley, H. Scott. "Fisheries Jurisdiction and the Atlantic Salmon: Fact and Law from a Canadian Point of View." (1977-78), 4 *Dalhousie Law Journal* 609-646.
3304

Finkle, Peter Z.R. "Canadian Foreign Policy for Marine Fisheries: An Alternate Perspective." (1975), 10 *Journal of Canadian Studies* 10-24 (No. 1) **3305**

Finkle, Peter Z.R. *Fisheries Management in the Northwest Atlantic: Canadian Perspectives.* Toronto, 1975. xv, 307 leaves. **3306**

Thesis (Ph.D.), University of Toronto, 1975. Abstracted in (1977/78), 38 *Dissertation Abstracts International* 3713-A.

Finkle, Peter Z.R. "The International Commission for the Northwest Atlantic Fisheries: An Experiment in Conservation." (1973-74), 1 *Dalhousie Law Journal* 526-550. **3307**

Finkle, Peter Z.R. "Realities of Environmental Management: The Case of Marine Fisheries." (1974), 81 *Queen's Quarterly* 240-246. **3308**

Gillespie, G.J. "Canada's Commercial Fisheries." (1970), 81 *Canadian Geographical Journal* 110-123. **3309**

Green, Leslie C. "The Anglo-Norwegian Fisheries Case, (1951) *I.C.J. Reports* 116." (1952), 15 *Modern Law Review* 373-377. **3310**

Greene, Stephen, and Keating, Thomas. "Domestic Factors and Canada-United States Fisheries Relations." (1980), 13 *Canadian Journal of Political Science* 731-750. **3311**

Hackworth, Green Haywood. "Fisheries: Miscellaneous Fisheries." *In* Hackworth, Green Haywood, *Digest of International Law* (Washington, 1940), vol. 1, pp. 798-803. **3312**

Herrington, William C. "Canadian-U.S. Fishery Problems." *In* Alexander, Lewis M., and Hawkins, Gordon R.S., eds., *Canadian-U.S. Maritime Problems* (Kingston, R.I., 1972), pp. 47-49. **3313**

Hewison, George. "A National Fishery Policy for Canada: Dream or Debacle." (1980), 3 *Canadian Issues* 87-93. **3314**

"The International Commission for the Northwest Atlantic Fisheries." (1955), 7 *External Affairs* 198-200. **3315**

Also issued in the French edition under title: "La Commission internationale des pêches du Nord-Ouest de l'Atlantique."

Ireland, Gordon. "The North Pacific Fisheries." (1942), 36 *American Journal of International Law* 400-424. **3316**

Johnson, Barbara. "Canadian Foreign Policy and Fisheries." *In* Johnson, Barbara, and Zacher, Mark W., eds., *Canadian Foreign Policy and the Law of the Sea* (Vancouver, 1977), pp. 52-99. **3317**

Johnson, Barbara. "Technocrats and the Management of International Fisheries." (1975), 29 *International Organization* 745-770. **3318**

Johnston, Douglas M. *The International Law of Fisheries: A Framework for Policy-Oriented Inquiries.* New Haven: Yale University Press, 1965. xxiv, 554 p. **3319**

Based on the author's thesis (J.S.D.), Yale University, 1962.
Reviews: Edward W. Allen in (1966), 4 *Canadian Yearbook of International Law* 316-318; J.A. Andrews in (1966), 42 *International Affairs* 474-475; Yehuda Z. Blum in (1969), 17 *American Journal of Comparative Law* 489-490; E.D. Brown in (1967), 83 *Law Quarterly Review* 150-153; Thomas Ehrlich in (1966-67), 19 *Stanford Law Review* 1394-1399; L.F.E. Goldie in (1968), 7 *Western Ontario Law Review* 213-219; Leslie C. Green in (1966), 44 *Canadian Bar Review* 716-718; F.G. Jacobs in (1967), 30 *Modern Law Review* 470-471; D.H.N. Johnson in (1966), 15 *International and Comparative Law Quarterly* 912-913; James A.R. Nafziger in (1965-66), 7 *Harvard International Law Journal* 396-398; D.P. O'Connell in (1968-71), 6 *Sydney Law Review* 139-140; Stefan A.

Riesenfeld in (1969), 63 *American Journal of International Law* 648-652; Albert E. Utton in (1967), 7 *Natural Resources Journal* 463-465; Peter Wright in (1966-67), 22 *International Journal* 101-102; John A. Yogis in (1966-67), 46 *Dalhousie Review* 397-399.

Johnston, Douglas M. "The International Law of Fisheries: A Policy-Oriented Inquiry in Outline." (1960), 1 *Current Law and Social Problems* 19-67; (1963), 3 *Current Law and Social Problems* 146-237.   **3320**
The two articles form a summary version of a doctoral dissertation submitted at Yale Law School.

Johnston, Douglas M. *A Juridical Approach to the Problems of the World Fisheries.* Montreal, 1958. 312 leaves.   **3321**
Thesis (M.C.L.), McGill University, 1958.

Johnston, Douglas M. "Legal and Diplomatic Developments in the Northwest Atlantic Fisheries." (1977-78), 4 *Dalhousie Law Journal* 37-61.   **3322**

Johnston, Douglas M. "The Legal Theory of Fishery Organization." *In* Alexander, Lewis M., ed., *The Law of the Sea: International Rules and Organization of the Sea* (Kingston, R.I., 1969), pp. 431-435.   **3323**

Johnston, Douglas M. "New Uses of International Law in the North Pacific." (1967-68), 43 *Washington Law Review* 77-114.   **3324**

Johnston, Douglas M. "The Regional Consequences of a Global Fisheries Convention." *In* Pontecorvo, Giulio, ed., *Fisheries Conflicts in the North Atlantic: Problems of Management and Jurisdiction* (Cambridge, Mass., 1974), pp. 35-51.   **3325**

Johnston, Douglas M. "Some Treaty Law Aspects of a Future International Fishing Convention." *In* Knight, H. Gary, ed., *The Future of International Fisheries Management* (St. Paul, Minn., 1975), pp. 103-157.   **3326**

Labrie, Arthur. "Notre territoire de pêche maritime." (1943-44), 19/2 *Actualité Économique* 105-158.   **3327**
Includes international aspects.

Leger, Georges Antoine. "Les accords bilatéraux régissant la pêche étrangère dans les eaux canadiennes." (1978), 16 *Canadian Yearbook of International Law* 116-156.   **3328**

Leger, Georges Antoine. "La guerre du thon n'aura pas lieu." (1981), 19 *Canadian Yearbook of International Law* 257-270.   **3329**

Lotz, Jim. "200-Mile Limit Revives Atlantic Fisheries." (1978), 97 *Canadian Geographic* 40-45 (No. 2)   **3330**

Lucas, Kenneth C., and Loftas, Tony. "FAO's EEZ Program: Helping to Build the Fisheries of the Future." (1982), 3 *Ocean Yearbook* 38-76.   **3331**

Macdonald, R.D.S. "Inshore Fishing Interests on the Atlantic Coast: Their Response to Extended Jurisdiction by Canada." (1979), 3 *Marine Policy* 171-189.   **3332**

Macdonald, Ronald St. John. "Some Aspects of International Fisheries Control in United States-Canadian Relations." (1954), 7 *Revue Hellénique de Droit International* 194-213.   **3333**

MacKay, Robert A. "International Conservation of Fisheries in the North Pacific." *In* Holland, William Lancelot, ed., *Commodity Control in the Pacific Area* (London, 1935), pp. 426-448. 3334

MacKenzie, W.C. "Problems of the Fisheries in the Atlantic Provinces." *In* Alexander, Lewis M., and Hawkins, Gordon R.S., eds., *Canadian-U.S. Maritime Problems* (Kingston, R.I., 1972), pp. 50-55. 3335

Manchester, Lorne. "Harvest of the Waters." (1949), 39 *Canadian Geographical Journal* 2-17. 3336

Mitchell, C.L. "The 200-Mile Limit: New Issues, Old Problems for Canada's East Coast Fisheries." (1978), 4 *Canadian Public Policy* 172-183. 3337

Munro, Gordon R. "Fisheries, Extended Jurisdiction and the Economics of Common Property Resources." (1982), 15 *Canadian Journal of Economics* 405-425. 3338

Munro, Gordon R. *A Promise of Abundance: Extended Fisheries Jurisdiction and the Newfoundland Economy.* Ottawa: Supply and Services Canada, 1980. vi, 111 p. 3339
A study prepared for the Economic Council of Canada.

"The North Pacific Fisheries: Regulation by International Agreement." (1963), 15 *External Affairs* 297-301. 3340

"North Pacific Fisheries Convention." (1952), 4 *External Affairs* 67-71. 3341

"North Pacific Fisheries Convention: Third Meeting of Parties, 1964." (1964), 16 *External Affairs* 550-552. 3342

Ottenheimer, Gerald R. "Patterns of Development in International Fishery Law." (1973), 11 *Canadian Yearbook of International Law* 37-47. 3343

Ozere, S.V. "Needed: Sea Law to Protect Sea Resources." (1973), 87 *Canadian Geographical Journal* 4-10 (No. 3) 3344

Parsons, R.A. "The Menace of Foreign Ships to Newfoundland's Sealing and Fishing Industry." (1966), 14 *Chitty's Law Journal* 42-47. 3345

Pearse, Peter H. "Fishing Rights, Regulations and Revenues." (1981), 5 *Marine Policy* 135-146. 3346

Pepper, Donald A. "The Future of the World's Fisheries." *In* Johnston, Douglas M., ed., *Marine Policy and the Coastal Community* (New York, 1976), pp. 119-143. 3347

Pontecorvo, Giulio; Johnston, Douglas M.; and Wilkinson, Maurice. "Conditions for Effective Fisheries Management in the Northwest Atlantic." *In* Anderson, Lee G., ed., *Economic Impacts of Extended Fisheries Jurisdiction* (Ann Arbor, Mich., 1977), pp. 51-103. 3348

Redding, Forest William, Jr. *Sharing the Living Resources of the Sea: An Analysis of Contemporary American-Canadian Fisheries Relations.* Norman, Okla., 1979. 429 leaves. 3349
Thesis (Ph.D.), University of Oklahoma, 1979. Abstracted in (1980), 40 *Dissertation Abstracts International* 5582-A. (University Microfilms, Ann Arbor, No. 80-8660).

Resources of the Sea Conference, Fish and Oil, St. John's, Nfld., 1973. *Resources of the Sea Conference, Fish and Oil.* Sponsored by the Extension Service,

Memorial University of Newfoundland in Co-operation with the Canadian International Development Agency. St. John's: Memorial University, 1973. 2 vols. **3350**

Rhee, Sang-Myon. "The Application of Equitable Principles to Resolve the United States-Canada Dispute over East Coast Fishery Resources." (1980), 21 *Harvard International Law Journal* 667-683. **3351**

Rosenow, Beverly J. "North Pacific Fisheries Treaties and International Law of the Seas." (1963), 38 *Washington Law Review* 223-248. **3352**

Scott, Anthony D. "Fisheries, Pollution and Canadian-American Transnational Relations." (1974), 28 *International Organization* 827-848. **3353**
Reprinted in Fox, Annette Baker, and others, *Canada and the United States* (New York, 1976), pp. 234-255.

Selak, Charles B. "The United States-Canadian Great Lakes Fisheries Convention." (1956), 50 *American Journal of International Law* 122-129. **3354**

Surette, Ralph. "200-Mile Limit Brings More Offshore Problems." (1981), 101 *Canadian Geographic* 44-51 (No. 5) **3355**

Tomlinson, J.W.C., and Brown, P.S. "Joint Ventures with Foreigners as a Method of Exploiting Canadian Fishery Resources under Extended Fisheries Jurisdiction." (1979), 5 *Ocean Management* 251-261. **3356**

Tomlinson, J.W.C., and Vertinsky, I. "International Joint Ventures in Fishing and 200-Mile Economic Zones." (1975), 32 *Journal of the Fisheries Research Board of Canada* 2569-2579. **3357**

U.S. Congress. House. Committee on Merchant Marine and Fisheries. *Oversight Report on the U.S.-Canada East Coast Fishery Agreement and Boundary Treaty.* Submitted by John B. Breaux, Chairman, Subcommittee on Fisheries and Wildlife Conservation and the Environment. Washington: Govt. Print. Off., 1980. ii, 23 p. (Serial No. 96-C) **3358**

U.S. Congress. House. Committee on Merchant Marine and Fisheries. *United States-Canadian Reciprocal Fisheries Agreement: Report, together with Dissenting Views (To Accompany H.R. 5638).* Washington: Govt. Print. Off., 1977. 26 p. (U.S. 95th Cong., 1st sess. House. Rept. 95-193) **3359**

U.S. Congress. Senate. Committee on Commerce, Science, and Transportation. *Reciprocal Fisheries Agreement for 1978 between the United States and Canada: Hearings, 95th Cong., 1st sess., May 10, 1978.* Washington: Govt. Print. Off., 1978. iii, 28 p. (Serial No. 95-79) **3360**

U.S. Congress. Senate. Committee on Foreign Relations. *Maritime Boundary Settlement Treaty and East Coast Fishery Resources Agreement: Hearings, 96th Cong., 2d sess., on Ex. U, 96-1, and Ex. V, 96-1, April 15 and 17, 1980.* Washington: Govt. Print. Off., 1980. iv, 223 p., maps. **3361**
Refers to the maritime boundary treaty (S.Ex. U. 96-1), and the fishery agreement (S.Ex. V. 96-1), both signed at Washington on March 29, 1979.

Vander Zwaag, David L. *American and Canadian Fisheries Management in the Georges Bank/Gulf of Maine Region: Options for Bridging Troubled Waters.* Halifax, 1982. vi, 283 leaves. **3362**
Thesis (LL.M.), Dalhousie University, 1982.

Yogis, John A. "Canadian Fisheries and International Law." *In* Macdonald, Ronald St. John, and others, *Canadian Perspectives on International Law and Organization* (Toronto, 1974), pp. 398-409. **3363**

(ii) HISTORY

Adler, H.H. "The French Fishery Rights in Newfoundland." (1901-02), 1 *Canadian Law Review* 33-37. **3364**

Anglo-American Association. *Report on the Questions between Great Britain and the United States with Respect to the North American Fisheries.* London, Cambridge: Macmillan, 1871. 35, 6 p., map. **3365**

Armerding, H.T. *The Halibut Treaty of 1923 between Canada and the United States.* Worcester, Mass., 1942. 118 leaves. **3366**
> Thesis (M.A.), Clark University, 1942. Refers to the halibut fishery convention signed at Washington on March 2, 1923 (BTS 18(1925); 117 BFSP 382; 43 Stat. 1841; TS 701; 12 Bevans 394; 32 LNTS 94).

Balch, Thomas Willing. "The American-British Atlantic Fisheries Question." (1909), 48 *American Philosophical Society, Proceedings* 319-353. **3367**

"The Boundary-Fisheries Treaty." (1908), 2 *American Journal of International Law* 637-640. **3368**
> Refers to the treaty of April 11, 1908 (BTS 17(1908); 101 BFSP 224; 35 Stat. 2000; TS 498; 12 Bevans 311; 206 Parry 392).

Brown, Vera Lee. "Spanish Claims to a Share in the Newfoundland Fisheries." (1925), *Canadian Historical Association, Annual Report* 64-82. **3369**

Caix, Robert de. *Terre-Neuve, Saint-Pierre et le French-Shore. La question des pêcheries et le traité du 8 avril 1904; enquête.* Paris: Société française d'imprimerie et de librairie, 1904. 100 p. **3370**

Campbell, Charles S. "American Tariff Interests and the Northeastern Fisheries, 1882-1888." (1964), 45 *Canadian Historical Review* 212-228. **3371**

Canada. Parliament. *Correspondence: Halibut Fisheries Treaty.* Ottawa, 1923. 16 p. (Canada. Parliament, 1923. Sessional Papers, No. 111a) **3372**

Canada. Parliament. *Correspondence on the Subject of the Fisheries.* Ottawa, 1871. 67, 5 p. (Canada. Parliament, 1871. Sessional Papers, No. 12) **3373**

Canada. Parliament. *Correspondence Relative to the Admission or Exclusion of American Fishing Vessels from the Waters of the Dominion.* Ottawa, 1870. 19 p. (Canada. Parliament, 1870. Sessional Papers, No. 81) **3374**

Canada. Parliament. *Treaty concerning Fisheries in Waters Contiguous to Canada and the United States, Signed at Washington, April 11, 1908, with Related Correspondence.* Ottawa, 1908. 2, 11 p. (Canada. Parliament, 1907-1908. Sessional Papers, Nos. 215, and 215a) **3375**

Cayley, Charles Everett. *The North Atlantic Fisheries in United States-Canadian Relations.* Chicago, 1931. 437 leaves. **3376**
> Thesis (Ph.D.), University of Chicago, 1931.

Comeau, Roger. *Pêche et traite en Acadie jusqu'en 1713.* Ottawa, 1949. iv, 265 leaves. **3377**
> Thesis (Ph.D.), University of Ottawa, 1949.

Daggett, Athern P. "The Regulation of Maritime Fisheries by Treaty." (1934), 28 *American Journal of International Law* 693-717. **3378**

Davis, David John. *The Bond-Blaine Negotiations, 1890-1891.* St. John's, 1970. 190 leaves, maps. **3379**
Thesis (M.A.), Memorial University of Newfoundland, 1970. (National Library of Canada. Canadian Theses on Microfilm, No. 14291).

De Ricci, James Herman. *The Fisheries Dispute, and Annexation of Canada.* London: S. Low, Marston, Searle & Rivington, 1888. viii, 310 p., map. **3380**

Doran, Joseph Ingersoll. *Our Fishery Rights in the North Atlantic.* Philadelphia: Allen, Lane & Scott, 1888. 67 p. **3381**

Geffcken, H. "Question des pêcheries de Terre-Neuve et sur les côtes des États-Unis d'Amérique et du Canada." (1890), 22 *Revue de Droit International et de Législation Comparée* 217-233. **3382**

Graham, Gerald S. "Fisheries and Sea-Power." (1941), *Canadian Historical Association, Historical Papers* 24-31. **3383**

Graham, Wallace. "The Fisheries of British North America and the American Fishermen." (1910), 14 *Nova Scotia Historical Society, Collections* 1-39. **3384**

Guichard, Léon. *La question de Terre-Neuve.* Paris: Éditions Liber, 1902. 112 p. Thesis, Université de Paris. **3385**

"The Halibut Treaty and the Commonwealth." (1922-23), 13 *Round Table* 628-633. **3386**
Refers to the treaty between Canada and the United States of March 2, 1923 (BTS 18(1925); 117 BFSP 382; 43 Stat. 1841; TS 701; 12 Bevans 394; 32 LNTS 93).

Harvey, D.C. "Nova Scotia and the Convention of 1818." (1933), 27 *Royal Society of Canada, Transactions* 57-73 (3d Ser., Sec. 2) **3387**
Refers to the convention between Great Britain and the United States of October 20, 1818 (6 BFSP 3; 2 Hertslet 392; 8 Stat. 248; TS 112; 12 Bevans 57; 2 Miller 658; 69 Parry 293).

Hignette, Marcel. *La question de Terre-Neuve avant et après la convention du 8 avril 1904 entre la France et l'Angleterre.* Paris: F. Pichon et Durand-Auzias, 1905. 215 p. **3388**
Thesis, Université de Paris. See the text of the convention in BTS 5(1905); 97 BFSP 31; 24 Hertslet 392; and 195 Parry 205. It did not apply to Canada.

Hodghead, Helen Mari. *The Northeastern Fishery Negotiations, 1783-1855.* Berkeley, Calif., 1929. v, 203 leaves. **3389**
Thesis (M.A.), University of California, 1929.

Hodgins, Thomas. "The Coercion of Newfoundland: Agreement between Great Britain and the United States concerning Fishing on the Newfoundland Coast." (1908), 28 *Canadian Law Times* 867-873. **3390**

Hodgins, Thomas. *Fishery Concessions to the United States in Canada and Newfoundland.* 2d ed. Toronto: W. Briggs, 1907. 34 p., map. **3391**
Reprinted from the *Contemporary Review.*

Innis, Harold A. *The Cod Fisheries: The History of an International Economy.* Rev. ed. Toronto: University of Toronto Press, 1978. xviii, 522 p., maps. (Canadian University Paperbooks, 212) **3392**
First edition published in 1940, New Haven, Yale University Press; Toronto, Ryerson, in

the series: Relations of Canada and the United States. Reprint of the revised edition published in 1954.

Reviews: Herbert Heaton in (1941), 22 *Canadian Historical Review* 60-63; Abbott Payson Usher under title: "The Influence of the Cod Fishery upon the History of the North American Seaboard," in (1940), 6 *Canadian Journal of Economics and Political Science* 591-599; signed P.R. in (1940-41), 16/1 *Actualité Économique* 489.

Innis, Harold A. "The Rise and Fall of the Spanish Fishery in Newfoundland." (1931), 25 *Royal Society of Canada, Transactions* 51-70 (3d Ser., Sec. 2) **3393**

Irvine, Dallas D. "The Newfoundland Fishery: A French Objective in the War of American Independence." (1932), 13 *Canadian Historical Review* 268-284.
3394

Isham, Charles. *The Fishery Question: Its Origin, History and Present Situation, with a Map of the Anglo-American Fishing Grounds and a Short Bibliography.* New York, London: G.P. Putnam, 1887. 89 p., map. (Questions of the Day, No. 41) **3395**

Judah, Charles Barnet. *The North American Fisheries and British Policy to 1713.* Urbana: University of Illinois, 1933. 183 p. (University of Illinois. Illinois Studies in the Social Sciences, Vol. 18, Nos. 3-4) **3396**
Reviews: Harold A. Innis in (1935), 16 *Canadian Historical Review* 326-327.

Kerr, William Hastings. *The Fishery Question; or, American Rights in Canadian Waters, etc.* Montreal: Mitchell & Wilson, 1871. 31 p. **3397**
Reprinted from (1871), 1 *Revue Critique de Législation et de Jurisprudence du Canada* 38-67.

Laing, Lionel H. "American Fishing Vessels in Canadian Waters of the Pacific." (1932), 26 *American Journal of International Law* 374-379. **3398**

La Morandière, Charles de. *Histoire de la pêche française de la morue dans l'Amérique septentrionale, des origines à 1789.* Paris: G.-P. Maisonneuve et Larose, 1962. 2 vols. (xviii, 1023 p.), maps. **3399**

Lewis, John. "The Fisheries Question." *In* Shortt, Adam, and Doughty, Arthur G., eds., *Canada and Its Provinces* (Toronto, 1914-1916), vol. 6, pp. 172-175.
3400

Lewis, Malcolm M. "The Canadian-American Halibut Fisheries Treaty." (1923-24), 4 *British Year Book of International Law* 168-169. **3401**

Longley, Ronald S. "Peter Mitchell, Guardian of the North Atlantic Fisheries 1867-1871." (1941), 22 *Canadian Historical Review* 389-402. **3402**

Lounsbury, Ralph Greenlee. *The British Fishery at Newfoundland, 1634-1763.* New Haven: Yale University Press; London: H. Milford, Oxford University Press, 1934. viii, 398 p., maps. (Yale Historical Publications; Miscellany, 27)
3403
Originally prepared as a doctoral dissertation, submitted at Yale University in 1928, revised, and completely rewritten. Reprinted Hamden, Conn., Archon Books, 1969.
Reviews: Harold A. Innis in (1935), 16 *Canadian Historical Review* 326-327; S.A Saunders in (1935), 1 *Canadian Journal of Economics and Political Science* 127.

Mérignhac, A. "Les pêcheries de Terre-Neuve et la jurisprudence du Conseil d'État français au sujet des actes de gouvernement." (1894), 1 *Revue Générale de Droit International Public* 305-323. **3404**

Moncharville, M. "La question de Terre-Neuve (avec une carte)." (1899), 6 *Revue Générale de Droit International Public* 141-168. **3405**

Morine, Alfred B. "Newfoundland and Her Fishing Rights." (1906), 42 *Canada Law Journal* 737-741. **3406**

Morine, Alfred B. "The Newfoundland Fisheries' Dispute." (1906), 5 *Canadian Law Review* 414-417. **3407**

Morse, Charles. "Newfoundland's Grievance." (1907), 6 *Canadian Law Review* 257-258, 339-340. **3408**

Murphy, Orville T. "The Comte de Vergennes, the Newfoundland Fisheries, and the Peace Negotiation of 1783: A Reconsideration." (1965), 46 *Canadian Historical Review* 32-46. **3409**

Neary, Peter F. "The French and American Shore Questions as Factors in Newfoundland History." *In* Miller, James, and Neary, Peter F., eds., *Newfoundland in the Nineteenth and Twentieth Centuries: Essays in Interpretation* (Toronto, 1980), pp. 95-122. **3410**

Neary, Peter F. *The French Shore Question, 1865-1878.* St. John's, 1961. 263 leaves. **3411**
Thesis (M.A.), Memorial University of Newfoundland, 1961.

"The Newfoundland Fisheries." (1907), 1 *American Journal of International Law* 144-148. **3412**

"The Newfoundland Fisheries Question." (1909), 3 *American Journal of International Law* 461-464. **3413**

"The North Atlantic Coast Fisheries." (1910), 4 *American Journal of International Law* 903-908. **3414**

Prowse, D.W. "The Settlement of the French Shore Question and Union between Canada and Newfoundland." (1904), 3 *Canadian Law Review* 343-349. **3415**

Prowse, D.W. "The Treaty Shore Question in Newfoundland." (1901-02), 1 *Canadian Law Review* 329-335. **3416**

Reeves, William George. *The Fortune Bay Dispute: Newfoundland's Place in Imperial Treaty Relations under the Washington Treaty, 1871-1885.* St. John's, 1971. vi, 159 leaves. **3417**
Thesis (M.A.), Memorial University of Newfoundland, 1971. (National Library of Canada. Canadian Theses on Microfilm, No. 15667).

"Renewal of 'Modus Vivendi' concerning Newfoundland Fisheries." (1909), 3 *American Journal of International Law* 953-954. **3418**

Tallman, Ronald D. *Warships and Mackerel: The North Atlantic Fisheries in Canadian-American Relations, 1867-1877.* Orono, Maine, 1971 (c1973). 593 leaves. **3419**
Thesis (Ph.D.), University of Maine, 1971. Abstracted in (1973), 34 *Dissertation Abstracts International* 714-A. (University Microfilms, Ann Arbor, No. 73-13082).

Thompson, Frederic Fraser. *The Background to the Newfoundland Clauses of the Anglo-French Agreement of 1904.* Oxford, 1954. xviii, 535 leaves. **3420**
Thesis (Ph.D.), Oxford University, 1954. Refers to the convention between Great Britain and France respecting Newfoundland and West and Central Africa signed April 8, 1904 (BTS 5(1905); 97 BFSP 31; 24 Hertslet 392; 195 Parry 205). Concerns mainly fisheries.

Thompson, Frederic Fraser. *The French Shore Problem in Newfoundland; an Imperial Study.* Toronto: University of Toronto Press, 1961. 222 p., maps. (Canadian Studies in History and Government, No. 2) **3421**
Originally prepared as a doctoral thesis at the University of Oxford.
Reviews: Robert Craig Brown in (1962), 43 *Canadian Historical Review* 73-74; Jean Comtois in (1962-63), 38 *Actualité Économique* 471-472; W.S. McNutt in (1962-63), 42 *Dalhousie Review* 532-535.

U.S. Congress. House. Committee on Foreign Affairs. *United States-Canada Fisheries: Hearings, 63d Cong., 2d sess., on H.R. 13005. February 20, 1914.* Statement of Miller Freeman, of Seattle. Washington: Govt. Print. Off., 1914. 39 p. **3422**

Whiteley, William H. "Governor Hugh Palliser and the Newfoundland and Labrador Fishery, 1764-1768." (1969), 50 *Canadian Historical Review* 141-163.
3423

Whiteley, William H. "James Cook and British Policy in the Newfoundland Fisheries, 1763-7." (1973), 54 *Canadian Historical Review* 246-272. **3424**

Yogis, John A. *Canadian Fishery Treaties and International Law.* Halifax, 1966. 235 leaves. **3425**
Thesis (LL.M.), Dalhousie University, 1966.

Young, George Renny. *The British North American Colonies. Letters upon the Existing Treaties with France and America, as Regards Their 'Rights of Fishery' upon the Coasts of Nova Scotia, Labrador and Newfoundland, with a General View of the Colonial Policy.* London: J. Ridgway, 1834. iii, 193 p., map. **3426**

(c) MARINE MAMMALS

Canada. Parliament. *Convention for the Preservation and Protection of the Fur Seal, of July 7, 1911, with Related Correspondence.* Ottawa, 1912. 37 p. (Canada. Parliament, 1912. Sessional Papers, No. 84) **3427**

Clark, C.W., and Lamberson, R. "An Economic History and Analysis of Pelagic Whaling." (1982), 6 *Marine Policy* 103-120. **3428**

Duncan, Bingham. "A Letter on the Fur Seal in Canadian-American Diplomacy." (1962), 43 *Canadian Historical Review* 42-47. **3429**

Gluek, Alvin Charles. "Canada's Splendid Bargain: the North Pacific Fur Seal Convention of 1911." (1982), 63 *Canadian Historical Review* 179-201. **3430**

Lavigne, D.M. "The Harp Seal Controversy Reconsidered." (1978-79), 85 *Queen's Quarterly* 377-388. **3431**

Lillie, Harry R. "Whaling and Its Antarctic Problems Today." (1949), 38 *Canadian Geographical Journal* 105-113. **3432**

"North Pacific Fur Seals Convention." (1957), 9 *External Affairs* 176-178. **3433**

Pike, Gordon C. "Whaling in the North Pacific - the End of an Era." (1968), 76 *Canadian Geographical Journal* 128-137. **3434**
Subject of some international law interest.

"Protecting the North Pacific Fur Seal: An International Conservation Effort." (1962), 14 *External Affairs* 90-92. **3435**

Robichaud, Hédard J. "The Control of Sealing in the Gulf of St. Lawrence." (1967), 19 *External Affairs* 66-69. **3436**

Tansill, Charles Callan. "The Fur-Seal Fisheries and the Doctrine of the Freedom of the Seas." (1942), *Canadian Historical Association, Historical Papers* 71-81.
3437

3. NON-LIVING RESOURCES

(a) OIL AND GAS EXPLOITATION

See also *"Continental Shelf" (p. 245),* and *"Commodities: Oil and Gas" (p. 583).* For pipelines, see *"Transportation in General" (p. 641).*

Black, Edwin R. "Oil Offshore Troubles the Waters." (1965-66), 72 *Queen's Quarterly* 589-603. **3438**

De Mestral, Armand L.C. "The Law Applicable to the Canadian East-Coast Offshore." (1983), 21 *Alberta Law Review* 63-81. **3439**

Finnie, Robert S. "North American Arctic Petroleum Development." (1971), 83 *Canadian Geographical Journal* 146-161. **3440**

Gault, Ian Townsend. "Recent Developments in the Federal-Provincial Dispute Concerning Jurisdiction Over Offshore Petroleum Resources." (1983), 21 *Alberta Law Review* 97-113. **3441**

Killey, J.M. "Drilling and Service Contracts in Offshore Oil and Gas Operations." (1973), 11 *Alberta Law Review* 480-502. **3442**

Little, C.H. "Off-Shore Exploration for Gas and Oil." (1968), 77 *Canadian Geographical Journal* 108-115. **3443**

Loutfi, M.A. *Canadian Maritime Oil Exploration, Exploitation and Transport: A Multidisciplinary Study.* Montreal: Office of Industrial Research, McGill University, 1973. xiii, 364 p., maps. **3444**
Prepared for Environment Canada through the Office of Industrial Research, McGill University, Montreal, by a multidisciplinary team of McGill faculty members.

MacWilliam, D.A., and Muir, R.C. "Offshore Operating Agreements." (1973), 11 *Alberta Law Review* 503-516. **3445**

Mestier du Bourg, Hubert de. *Droit pétrolier et plateau continental.* Montréal, 1970 (c1971). v, 97 leaves, map. **3446**
Thesis (LL.M.), McGill University, 1970. (National Library of Canada. Canadian Theses on Microfilm, No. 7296).

Mestier du Bourg, Hubert de. "Droit pétrolier et plateau continental." (1970), 1 *Revue de Droit, Université de Sherbrooke* 1-53. **3447**

Pimlott, Douglas H.; Brown, Dougald; and Sam, Kenneth P. *Oil under the Ice.* Ottawa: Canadian Arctic Resources Committee, 1976. xix, 178 p. **3448**

Spicer, W. Wylie. "Some Admiralty Law Issues in Offshore Oil and Gas Development." (1982), 20 *Alberta Law Review* 153-178. **3449**

Warbrick, Colin. "Off-Shore Petroleum Exploitation in Federal Systems: Canadian and Australian Action." (1968), 17 *International and Comparative Law Quarterly* 501-513. **3450**

Wonder, Edward F. "Energy Bargaining in North America: Oil and Gas in Canadian-American Relations." *In International Energy Policy* (Lexington, Mass., 1980), pp. 81-109. **3451**

(b) DEEP SEA MINING

Chopra, Sudhir K. *Deep Ocean Mining: Prospects for a New International Regime.* Halifax, 1979. xv, 504 leaves. **3452**
Thesis (LL.M.), Dalhousie University, 1979. (National Library of Canada. Canadian Theses on Microfiche, No. 44206).

Herman, Lawrence L. "The Niceties of Nickel - Canada and the Production Ceiling Issue at the Law of the Sea Conference." (1978-79), 6 *Syracuse Journal of International Law and Commerce* 265-294. **3453**

Johnston, Douglas M. "Deep Ocean Mining: Interim Arrangements and Alternative Outcomes." *In* Allen, Scott, and Craven, John P., eds., *Alternatives in Deepsea Mining* (Honolulu, c1979), pp. 57-74. **3454**

Ontario. Mineral Resources Branch. *The Future of Nickel and the Law of the Sea.* Toronto: Ministry of Natural Resources, 1980. iv, 28 p. (Ontario. Ministry of Natural Resources. Mineral Policy Background Paper, No. 10) **3455**

H. Marine Pollution

See also *"Arctic: Other Legal Aspects" (p. 205).*

Almond, Harry H., Jr. "Canada's Legislative and Regulatory Scheme to Control Pollution in Arctic Waters." (1972-73), 1 *Syracuse Journal of International Law and Commerce* 236-249. **3456**

Beesley, J. Alan. "The Arctic Pollution Prevention Act: Canada's Perspective." (1972-73), 1 *Syracuse Journal of International Law and Commerce* 226-235.
3457

Bilder, Richard B. "The Canadian Arctic Waters Pollution Prevention Act: New Stresses on the Law of the Sea." (1970-71), 69 *Michigan Law Review* 1-54.
3458

Carnahan, Burt K. "The Canadian Arctic Waters Pollution Prevention Act: An Analysis." (1970-71), 31 *Louisiana Law Review* 632-649. **3459**

Davies, Gareth John. *Civil Liability for Oil Pollution from Ships.* Downsview, Ont., 1974. xii, 175 leaves. **3460**

Thesis (LL.M.), York University, 1974. (National Library of Canada. Canadian Theses on Microfiche, No. 21534).

De Mestral, Armand L.C. "La convention internationale de 1973 sur la prévention de la pollution par les navires." (1974), 12 *Canadian Yearbook of International Law* 239-254. **3461**

De Mestral, Armand L.C. "La convention sur la prévention de la pollution résultant de l'immersion de déchets." (1973), 11 *Canadian Yearbook of International Law* 226-243. **3462**

De Mestral, Armand L.C. "The Prevention of Pollution of the Marine Environment Arising from Offshore Mining and Drilling." (1979), 20 *Harvard International Law Journal* 469-518. **3463**

Donnelly, Brian Eugene. *International Law: Canada's Effort to Protect Itself from Marine Pollution*. Athens, Ga., 1977. vii, 265 leaves. **3464**
Thesis (Ph.D.), University of Georgia, 1977. Abstracted in (1978/79), 39 *Dissertation Abstracts International* 1820-A. (University Microfilms, Ann Arbor, No. 78-14938).

Dunn, James David, and Hargrave, John A. "Oil Pollution Problems on the Pacific Coast." (1971), 6 *University of British Columbia Law Review* 137-165. **3465**

Emanuelli, Claude C. "Le droit international et la responsabilité civile pour les dommages dus à la pollution des mers par les hydrocarbures: la convention de Bruxelles de 1969 et ses développements ultérieurs." (1973), 4 *Revue de Droit, Université de Sherbrooke* 25-54. **3466**

Emanuelli, Claude C. *L'élaboration du droit international et la protection des intérêts côtiers contre les risques de pollution résultant de la navigation maritime*. Toronto, 1975. x, 470 leaves. **3467**
Thesis (D.Jur.), University of Toronto, 1975.

Emanuelli, Claude C. "La pollution maritime et la notion de passage inoffensif." (1973), 11 *Canadian Yearbook of International Law* 13-36. **3468**

Emanuelli, Claude C. "Les principes généraux de droit et la protection des états côtiers contre les risques de pollution des eaux navigables." (1975), 13 *Canadian Yearbook of International Law* 231-254. **3469**

Emanuelli, Claude C. "The Right of Intervention of Coastal States on the High Seas in Cases of Pollution Casualties." (1976), 25 *University of New Brunswick Law Journal* 79-96. **3470**

Flemming, Brian. "Canadian Pollution Control over Arctic and Coastal Waters." (1970), *Canadian Bar Association, Papers,* 17 p. **3471**

Gold, Edgar. "Compensation for Ship-Source Marine Pollution: A Hypothetical Case Study." *In Shipping, Energy, and Environment: Southeast Asian Perspectives for the Eighties* (Halifax, 1982), pp. 261-283. **3472**

Gold, Edgar. "IMCO International Marine Pollution Conference, London, 1973. (Report)." (1973-74), 1 *Maritime Studies and Management* 161-177. **3473**

Gold, Edgar. *Oil Pollution; a Survey of Worldwide Legislation*. Arendal, Norway: Assuranceforeningen GARD(gjensidig), 1971. 1 vol. (loose-leaf) **3474**
New edition published in 1978 under title.

Gold, Edgar. "Pollution of the Sea and International Law: A Canadian Perspective." (1971-72), 3 *Journal of Maritime Law and Commerce* 13-44. **3475**

Gold, Edgar, and Johnston, Douglas M. "Ship-Generated Pollution: The Creator of Regulated Navigation." *In* Clingan, Thomas A., Jr., ed., *Law of the Sea: State Practice in Zones of Special Jurisdiction* (Honolulu, 1982), pp. 156-197. **3476**

Graham, Gerald Francis. *The Canadian Arctic Waters Pollution Prevention Act of 1970 and the Concept of Self-Protection.* Ottawa, 1974. vi, 220 leaves. **3477**
Thesis (M.A.), Carleton University, 1974. (National Library of Canada. Canadian Theses on Microfiche, No. 19481). Abstracted in (1975), 13 *Masters Abstracts* 34. (University Microfilms, Ann Arbor, No. M-6481).

Green, Leslie C. "Canada, Pollution Control and the Law." *In* Dwivedi, O.P., ed., *Protecting the Environment* (Toronto, 1974), pp. 139-158, 311-313. **3478**

Green, Leslie C. "International Law and Canada's Anti-Pollution Legislation." (1970-71), 50 *Oregon Law Review* 462-490. **3479**

Harrison, W. "The Fate of Crude Oil Spills and the Siting of Four Super-Tanker Ports." (1974), 18 *Canadian Geographer* 211-231. **3480**

Henkin, Louis. "Arctic Anti-Pollution: Does Canada Make - or Break - International Law?" (1971), 65 *American Journal of International Law* 131-136. **3481**

Hoult, David P. "Marine Pollution, Concentrating on the Effects of Hydrocarbons in Seawater." *In* Alexander, Lewis M., and Hawkins, Gordon R.S., eds., *Canadian-U.S. Maritime Problems* (Kingston, R.I., 1972), pp. 29-31. **3482**

Johnston, Douglas M. "Canada's Arctic Marine Environment: Problems of Legal Protection." (1970), 29 *Behind the Headlines* Nos. 5-6, pp. 1-7. **3483**

Johnston, Douglas M. "Environment at the Seventh Session." (1978), 4 *Environmental Policy and Law* 78-79. **3484**

Johnston, Douglas M., ed. *The Environmental Law of the Sea.* Gland, Switzerland: International Union for Conservation of Nature and Natural Resources, 1981. 419 p. (IUCN Environmental Policy and Law Paper, No. 18) **3485**
Individual contributions are listed separately.
Reviews: A.V. Lowe in (1982), 6 *Marine Policy* 337-338; Charles Rousseau in (1982), 86 *Revue Générale de Droit International Public* 631.

Johnston, Douglas M. "The Environmental Law of the Sea: Historical Development." *In* Johnston, Douglas M., ed., *The Environmental Law of the Sea* (Gland, Switzerland, 1981), pp. 17-70. **3486**

Johnston, Douglas M. *Environmental Management in the South China Sea: Legal and Institutional Developments.* Honolulu, Hawaii: East-West Center. 1982. vii, 114 p. (East-West Environment and Policy Institute. Research Report, No. 10) **3487**

Johnston, Douglas M. "Facts and Value in the Prevention and Control of Marine Pollution." *In* Reisman, William Michael, and Weston, Burns H., eds., *Towards World Order and Human Dignity: Essays in Honor of Myres S. McDougal* (New York, 1976), pp. 534-561. **3488**

Johnston, Douglas M. "Marine Pollution Control: Law, Science, and Politics." (1972-73), 28 *International Journal* 69-102. **3489**

Johnston, Douglas M. "UNCLOS III: Environmental Issues in Southeast Asia." *In Shipping, Energy, and Environment: Southeast Asian Perspectives for the Eighties* (Halifax, 1982), pp. 209-214. **3490**

Johnston, Douglas M., and Enomoto, Lawrence M.G. "Regional Approaches to the Protection and Conservation of the Marine Environment." *In* Johnston, Douglas M., ed., *The Environmental Law of the Sea* (Gland, Switzerland, 1981), pp. 285-385. **3491**

Johnston, Douglas M., and Klemm, Cyrille de. "The Environmental Law of the Sea: Conclusions and Recommendations." *In* Johnston, Douglas M., ed., *The Environmental Law of the Sea* (Gland, Switzerland, 1981), pp. 387-419. **3492**

Klotz, John C. "Are Ocean Polluters Subject to Universal Jurisdiction - Canada Breaks the Ice." (1972), 6 *International Lawyer* 706-717. **3493**

Legault, L.H. "The Freedom of the Seas: A Licence to Pollute?" (1971), 21 *University of Toronto Law Journal* 211-221. **3494**
Paper prepared for a symposium on the international legal aspects of pollution held at Vancouver in September 1970.

Letalik, Norman G. "Prevention and Control of Marine Pollution: Pollution from Dumping." *In* Johnston, Douglas M., ed., *The Environmental Law of the Sea* (Gland, Switzerland, 1981), pp. 217-230. **3495**

Lewis, D.E. "Legal Liability in the Canadian Arctic Relating to Oil Spills and Blowouts." (1972), 10 *Alberta Law Review* 440-449. **3496**

Lowry, P. Donovan. "Maritime Pollution: The Canada Shipping Act Amended. (Comment)." (1973), 8 *University of British Columbia Law Review* 197-204.
3497

Lowry, P. Donovan. "The Shipowner and Oil Pollution Liability." (1972), 18 *McGill Law Journal* 577-591. **3498**
Also published in (1972), *Canadian Bar Association, Papers*, 24, 4 p.

Macdonald, Ronald St. John; Morris, Gerald L.; and Johnston, Douglas M. "The Canadian Initiative to Establish a Maritime Zone for Environmental Protection: Its Significance for Multilateral Development of International Law." (1971), 21 *University of Toronto Law Journal* 247-251. **3499**
A statement circulated and discussed at the annual conference of the American Society of International Law, meeting in New York on April 24, 1970. Annexed to a symposium on the International Legal Aspects of Pollution, held in Vancouver, September 1970.

McDorman, Ted L., and others. *The Marine Environment and the Caracas Convention on the Law of the Sea: A Study of the Third United Nations Conference on the Law of the Sea and Other Related Marine Environmental Activities.* Halifax: Dalhousie University, Dalhousie Ocean Studies Programme, 1981. ix, 127 p. **3500**
Prepared by Ted L. McDorman, Norman G. Letalik, Hal Mills, Douglas M. Johnston, and Edgar Gold.

McLaren, Robert I. "Pollution Probe in the Global Village." (1974-75), 30 *International Journal* 127-140. **3501**

McRae, Donald M., and Goundrey, D.J. "Environmental Jurisdiction in Arctic Waters: The Extent of Article 234." (1982), 16 *University of British Columbia Law Review* 197-228. **3502**

M'Gonigle, R. Michael. "Unilateralism and International Law: The Arctic Waters Pollution Prevention Act." (1976), 34 *University of Toronto Faculty of Law Review* 180-198. **3503**

M'Gonigle, R. Michael, and Zacher, Mark W. "Canadian Foreign Policy and the Control of Marine Pollution." *In* Johnson, Barbara, and Zacher, Mark W., eds., *Canadian Foreign Policy and the Law of the Sea* (Vancouver, 1977), pp. 100-157. **3504**

M'Gonigle, R. Michael, and Zacher, Mark W. "International Problem of Marine Pollution." (1978), *International Perspectives* 8-12 (Mar./Apr.) **3505**

M'Gonigle, R. Michael, and Zacher, Mark W. *Pollution, Politics, and International Law: Tankers at Sea.* Berkeley: University of California Press, 1979. xviii, 394 p. **3506**
Reviews: Günther Handl in (1980), 15 *Texas International Law Journal* 409-412; Paul C. Szasz in (1981), 75 *American Journal of International Law* 387-388; Ludwik A. Teclaff in (1980), 20 *Natural Resources Journal* 952-954; Patricia Louise Vassil in (1981), 59 *Canadian Bar Review* 237-240; Donald C. Watt in (1981), 5 *Marine Policy* 162.

Morin, Jacques-Yvan. "La pollution des mers au regard du droit international." (1973), *Académie de Droit International, Colloque* 239-352. **3507**

Morin, Jacques-Yvan. "Le progrès technique, la pollution et l'évolution récente du droit de la mer au Canada, particulièrement à l'égard de l'Arctique." (1970), 8 *Canadian Yearbook of International Law* 158-248. **3508**

Newbury, Philip. "The International Environmental Law of the Sea: The Canadian Arctic Waters Pollution Prevention Act and Its Effects, 1970-1980." (1979-80), 4 *Suffolk Transnational Law Journal* 139-161. **3509**

Onorato, William T. "A Regional Remedial Approach to Offshore-Sourced Oil Pollution Damage: The North Sea Voluntary Compensation Scheme (OPOL)." *In Shipping, Energy, and Environment: Southeast Asian Perspectives for the Eighties* (Halifax, 1982), pp. 284-315. **3510**

Pharand, Donat. "Contiguous Zones of Pollution Prevention." (1972-73), 1 *Syracuse Journal of International Law and Commerce* 257-263. **3511**

Pharand, Donat. "La contribution du Canada au développement du droit international pour la protection du milieu marin: le cas spécial de l'Arctique." (1980), 11 *Études Internationales* 441-466. **3512**

Pharand, Donat. "International Regulation and Control of Oil Pollution of the High Seas, with Special Reference to the Arctic." (1971), 5 *World Law Review* 93-110. **3513**

Qing-nan, Meng. *The International Law on Vessel-Source Pollution and the Caracas Convention.* Halifax, 1982. xv, 303 leaves. **3514**
Thesis (LL.M.), Dalhousie University, 1982.

Reycraft, L.S. "The 'Torrey Canyon.'" (1967), *Canadian Bar Association, Papers* 85-89. **3515**
The "Torrey Canyon" was a large tanker (118,000 ton) which went aground on Seven Stones Reef, eight miles from the Scilly Isles off the Coast of England, releasing into the Atlantic Ocean a great part of her cargo of crude oil, which spread along the coast of Cornwall and crossed to Normandy and Brittany.

Rigaldies, Francis. "Le Canada et la pollution de la mer par les navires." (1977), 23 *McGill Law Journal* 334-370. **3516**

Ross, William Michael. *Oil Pollution as a Developing International Problem: A Study of the Puget Sound and Strait of Georgia Regions of Washington and British Columbia.* Seattle, 1972. xiii, 273 leaves, maps. **3517**
Thesis (Ph.D.), University of Washington, 1972. Abstracted in (1972), 33 *Dissertation Abstracts International* 2146-B. (University Microfilms, Ann Arbor, No. 72-28658).

Ross, William Michael. *Oil Pollution as an International Problem: A Study of Puget Sound and the Strait of Georgia.* Seattle: University of Washington Press, 1973. xiii, 279 p. **3518**
First issued as a dissertation (Ph.D.), University of Washington, 1972. Also published Victoria, B.C., University of Victoria, 1973 (Western Geographical Series, Vol. 6).
Review: Bentley LeBaron in (1974), 17 *Canadian Public Administration* 352-354.

Sautier, Jérôme. *L'Organisation inter-gouvernementale consultative de la navigation maritime et la pollution des mers par les hydro-carbures.* Montréal, 1972. 147 leaves. **3519**
Thesis (LL.M.), Université de Montréal, 1972.

Sherrin, Jeffrey J. "International Law and Canadian Arctic Pollution Control." (1973-74), 38 *Albany Law Review* 921-942. **3520**

Stone, A.J. "Legal Aspects of Maritime Pollution." (1968), *Canadian Bar Association, Papers,* 14 p. **3521**

Stone, A.J. "Pollution des mers, liberté de navigation et le droit canadien." (1972), *Canadian Bar Association, Papers,* 9 p. **3522**

Sutton, Gary. "Pollution Prevention in the Arctic: National and Multinational Approaches Compared." (1971-72), 5 *Ottawa Law Review* 32-64. **3523**

Utton, Albert E. "The Arctic Waters Pollution Prevention Act and the Right of Self-Protection." (1972), 7 *University of British Columbia Law Review* 221-234. **3524**

Young, Charles A. *Liability for Marine Pollution by Ships.* Vancouver, 1976. iv, 174 leaves. **3525**
Thesis (LL.M.), University of British Columbia, 1977. (National Library of Canada. Canadian Theses on Microfiche, No. 34984).

XIV. MARITIME NAVIGATION AND TRANSPORTATION

See also *"High Seas" (p. 248).*

A. General

Abrahamsson, Bernhard J. *International Ocean Shipping: Current Concepts and Principles.* Boulder, Colo.: Westview Press, 1980. xv, 232 p. **3526**
Published in cooperation with the Canadian Marine Transportation Centre, Dalhousie University, Halifax, Nova Scotia.
Reviews: L. Juda in (1982), 8 *Ocean Management* 90; Chia Lin Sien in (1981-82), 13 *Journal of Maritime Law and Commerce* 119-120; unsigned in (1980-81), 10 *Denver Journal of International Law and Policy* 397.

Benton, Mark A. *Routes: Vessel Traffic Regulation and Maritime Law.* Halifax, 1979. viii, 220 leaves. **3527**
Thesis (LL.M.), Dalhousie University, 1979. (National Library of Canada. Canadian Theses on Microfiche, No. 44192).

Bowman, Donald Fox. *The Influence and Implications of Containerization upon the Use of the Great Lakes-St. Lawrence Seaway in International Trade.* Ann Arbor, 1972. xvi, 511 leaves. **3528**
Thesis (Ph.D.), University of Michigan, 1972. Abstracted in (1972), 33 *Dissertation Abstracts International* 1895-A.

Bryan, Ingrid A. *Canadian Deep Sea Shipping Policy and the Merchant Marine Issue.* Toronto: Joint Program in Transportation, 1977. 24, 9 leaves. (University of Toronto/York University Joint Program in Transportation. Transportation Paper, No. 3) **3529**

Bryan, Ingrid A., and Kotowitz, Yehuda. *Shipping Conferences in Canada.* Ottawa: Consumer and Corporate Affairs Canada, 1978. 106 p. (Canada. Bureau of Competition Policy. Research Branch. Research Monograph, No. 2)
Also issued in French under title: *Les conférences maritimes au Canada.* **3530**
Review: J.J. Evans in (1979), 6 *Maritime Policy and Management* 233-234.

Burley, Kevin H. "Canada and the Imperial Shipping Committee." (1974-75), 3 *Journal of Imperial and Commonwealth History* 349-368. **3531**

Bush, Edward F. "The Canadian Fast Line on the North Atlantic, 1851-1915." (1973-74), 53 *Dalhousie Review* 479-500. **3532**

Cameron, E.R. "The Canada Shipping Act." (1929), 7 *Canadian Bar Review* 111-116. **3533**

Canada. Dept. of Marine. *International Rules of the Road in Force in All Navigable Waters within Canada or within the Jurisdiction of the Parliament Thereof, etc.* Ottawa: King's Printer, 1936. 24 p.   **3534**

Canada. Marine Transportation Administration. *A Shipping Policy for Canada / Une politique canadienne de transport maritime.* Ottawa: Transport Canada, Marine, 1979. 51, 56 p. (TP-1676)   **3535**
> Text in English and French on inverted pages, each with a separate title page and paging.

"Canadian Deep Seas Fleet." (1978), 61 *Canadian Bar Association, Proceedings* 108-142.   **3536**
> This is a panel. Address by J. Graham Day, Chairman (pp. 108-111), Louis R. Desmarais (pp. 111-115), Joseph Nuss (pp. 116-122), and Robert Timbrell (pp. 123-127). Question-Answer Period (pp. 127-142).

Cheng, Wei-Lien. *The American Ocean Shipping Policy.* Ottawa, 1952. 145 leaves. Thesis (M.A.), University of Ottawa, 1952.   **3537**

Clerget, Pierre. "L'état actuel et la crise des transports maritimes." (1934-35), 10 *Actualité Économique* 623-626.   **3538**

Conley, Marshall W. "Canadian Shipping Policies and the United Nations Conference on Trade and Development: An Analysis of UNCTAD V." (1982), 9 *Maritime Policy and Management* 35-43.   **3539**

Cushman, Dawn. "*Canadian Transport Company* v. *United States:* An Avenue Toward a Remedy for a Treaty Violation." (1979), 9 *California Western International Law Journal* 377-404.   **3540**

Darling, H.J. *The Elements of an International Shipping Policy for Canada.* Ottawa: Information Canada, 1974. ix, 62 p.   **3541**
> Also published in French under title: *Les éléments d'une politique internationale canadienne en matière de navigation.*

Day, J. Graham. "UNCTAD: Southeast Asia and the Future of Shipping Policy." *In Shipping, Energy, and Environment: Southeast Asian Perspectives for the Eighties* (Halifax, 1982), pp. 217-225.   **3542**

Djalal, Hasjim. "UNCLOS III: Navigational Issues in Southeast Asia." *In Shipping, Energy, and Environment: Southeast Asian Perspectives for the Eighties* (Halifax, 1982), pp. 201-208.   **3543**

Erler, Jochen. "The New Conventions on Facilitation of International Maritime Traffic." (1967), 13 *McGill Law Journal* 323-328.   **3544**

Ettinger, Michael L. "Shipping." In *Canadian Encyclopedic Digest (Ontario),* 3d ed., 1981, title 134, vol. 30, 281 p.   **3545**

Ewart, John S. "Merchant Shipping." (1912), 32 *Canadian Law Times* 337-378.   **3546**

Gold, Edgar. "The 'Freedom' of Ocean Shipping and Commercial Viability: Myths and Realities in the Aftermath of UNCLOS III." *In* Gamble, John King, ed., *Law of the Sea: Neglected Issues* (Honolulu, 1979), pp. 248-258.   **3547**

Gold, Edgar. *The International Law and Policy of Ocean Transportation: A Historical Examination of Marine Policy and Shipping Law with Particular Reference to the Third World.* Cardiff, 1979. xxiv, 768 leaves.   **3548**
> Thesis (Ph.D.), University of Wales, 1980.

Gold, Edgar. "Marine Salvage Law, Supertankers and Oil Pollution: New Pressures on Ancient Law." (1980), 11 *Revue de Droit, Université de Sherbrooke* 127-153. **3549**

Gold, Edgar. *Maritime Transport: The Evolution of International Marine Policy and Shipping Law.* Lexington, Mass.: Lexington Books, 1981. xxi, 425 p.
Based on the author's thesis (Ph.D.), University of Wales, 1980. **3550**
Reviews: Andrew Ashley in (1982), 6 *Marine Policy* 251-252; Boleslaw A. Boczek in (1982), 76 *American Journal of International Law* 906-908; Gary Edwards in (1981), 13 *Law and Policy in International Business* 879-885; Trevor D. Heaver in (1982), 16 *University of British Columbia Law Review* 188-191; S. Mankabady in (1982), 9 *Maritime Policy and Management* 235; Elliott B. Nixon in (1982), 13 *Journal of Maritime Law and Commerce* 391-393.

Gold, Edgar. "Monitoring and Surveillance with Respect to Navigation." *In* Pacem in Maribus X, *Proceedings* (Vienna, 1980), pp. 94-98. **3551**

Gold, Edgar. "The Surveillance and Control of Navigation in the New Law of the Sea: A Comment." (1982), 3 *Ocean Yearbook* 126-134. **3552**
Based on a commentary presented to the Pacem in Maribus X Conference, Vienna, October 1980.

Gold, Edgar, and Letalik, Norman G. *Canadian Admiralty Law: Introductory Materials.* 3d ed. Halifax: Dalhousie University, Faculty of Law, 1979. xxiv, 706 p. (various pagings) **3553**

Herman, Lawrence L. "The Code of Conduct for Liner Conferences: Frustrations on the Road to Utopia." (1976), 14 *Canadian Yearbook of International Law* 257-269. **3554**

Hohmann, W.; Higgs, G.R.L.; and Gillanders, D.E. "Are Offshore Drilling Rigs 'Ships' under Canadian Maritime Law?" (1967), *Canadian Bar Association, Papers* 115-121. **3555**

Hope, Ronald. "The Political Economy of Marine Transportation." *In* Johnston, Douglas M., ed., *Marine Policy and the Coastal Community* (New York, 1976), pp. 103-117. **3556**

Howell, Alfred. "Seamen's Wages - Maritime Law." (1884), 4 *Canadian Law Times* 153-164, 213-223. **3557**

Johnston, Douglas M., and Letalik, Norman G. "Emerging Legislative Trends in Southeast Asia." *In Shipping, Energy, and Environment: Southeast Asian Perspectives for the Eighties* (Halifax, 1982), pp. 231-250. **3558**

Koller, Philip Alexander. "Canada's Maritime Prospects under ERP." (1948), 3 *International Journal* 146-155. **3559**
ERP - refers to "European Recovery Programme" - or Marshall Plan.

Lawes, A.L. "Ocean Shipping and Canada." (1947), 54 *Canadian Banker* 58-70 (No. 3) **3560**

Lewis, Edward Norman. *Lewis' Law of Shipping, Being a Treatise on the Law Respecting the Inland and Sea-Coast Shipping of Canada and the United States.* Toronto: Carswell, 1885. 512 p. **3561**

Lucas, F.G.T. "Empire Shipping and the Imperial Conference." (1928), 6 *Canadian Bar Review* 525-529. **3562**

MacKenzie, Charles H.C., and Power, Michael E. *Liner Shipping Conferences: An Annotated Bibliography of Selected Economic, Commercial and Government Materials.* Halifax: Dalhousie University, Canadian Marine Transportation Centre, 1982. 180 p. (Dalhousie University. Canadian Marine Transportation Centre. Research Report, No. 6)   **3563**

Mapp, Wayne Daniel. *The Legal and Documentary Problems of International Containerized and Intermodal Transport.* Toronto, 1977. xi, 226, (102) leaves. Thesis (LL.M.), University of Toronto, 1977.   **3564**

McDorman, Ted L. *The Development of Shipping Law and Policy in Canada: An Historical Examination of the British Influence.* Halifax, 1982. v, 218 leaves. Thesis (LL.M.), Dalhousie University, 1982.   **3565**

Morin, William. "Le transport maritime à travers les âges de l'humanité." (1945), 5 *Revue du Barreau* 11-22.   **3566**
Continued by: "Des ventes maritimes."

Morin, William. "Des ventes maritimes." (1945), 5 *Revue du Barreau* 53-68, 168-184.   **3567**
Continues: "Le transport maritime à travers les âges de l'humanité."

Pineau, Jean. "La législation maritime canadienne et le Code civil québécois." (1968), 14 *McGill Law Journal* 26-58.   **3568**

Pineau, Jean. "Quelques réflexions sur la formule Lloyd du contrat d'assistance maritime." (1964), 24 *Revue du Barreau* 528-542.   **3569**

Popp, Alfred H.E. "Maritime Law - Brussels Convention - International Conference - Recent Developments." (1978), 56 *Canadian Bar Review* 150-162. **3570**

Popp, Alfred H.E. "Recent Developments in Tanker Control in International Law." (1980), 18 *Canadian Yearbook of International Law* 3-30.   **3571**

Pourcelet, Michel. *Transport maritime: recueil d'arrêts.* Montréal: Librairie de l'Université de Montréal, 1974. viii, 360 leaves. (various pagings)   **3572**
Lecture-notes for 1974-1975, Université de Montréal, Faculté de droit. Text in French and English.

Prabhu, M.A. "International Freight Rate Regulation." (1972), 18 *McGill Law Journal* 60-104.   **3573**

Prussing, Eugene E. "Law and Custom Binds Sailors to Die at Sea to Save Others." (1914), 34 *Canadian Law Times* 618-619.   **3574**

"Salvage at Sea." (1931-32), 1 *Fortnightly Law Journal* 83-84.   **3575**

Shipping, Energy, and Environment: Southeast Asian Perspectives for the Eighties. Edited by Mark J. Valencia, Edgar Gold, Lin Sien Chia, and Norman G. Letalik. Halifax: Dalhousie Ocean Studies Programme, 1982. xi, 333 p. **3576**
Proceedings of a Workshop held in Honolulu, Hawaii, December 10-12, 1980.

Silverstein, Harvey B. "International Cooperation in Surveillance and Enforcement." *In* Pacem in Maribus X, *Proceedings* (Vienna, 1980), pp. 125-135.
   3577

Silverstein, Harvey B. *Superships and Nation-States: The Transnational Politics of the Intergovernmental Maritime Consultative Organization.* Boulder, Colo.: Westview Press, 1978. xiii, 251 p. (Westview Replica Edition)   **3578**

Sletmo, Gunnar K. *Liner Conferences: International Aspects.* Ottawa: Transport Canada, 1982. 141 p. (Canada. Transport Canada. Marine, TP 3891E) **3579**

Smith, Sidney A. "Rules of the Road at Sea." (1932), 10 *Canadian Bar Review* 630-644. **3580**

Spicer, W. Wylie. "Some Admiralty Law Issues in Offshore Oil and Gas Development." (1982), 20 *Alberta Law Review* 153-178. **3581**

Stone, A.J. "International Maritime Law." *In* Macdonald, Ronald St. John, and others, *Canadian Perspectives on International Law and Organization* (Toronto, 1974), pp. 449-467. **3582**

Tetley, William. *Liner Conferences in Canada under Canadian Law and the U.N. Code of Conduct for Liner Conferences.* With the assistance of David J. Peippo. Ottawa: Transport Canada, 1982. 148 p. (Canada. Transport Canada. Marine, TP 3892E) **3583**

Tetley, William. "Navigation and Management of the Vessel." (1964), 7 *Canadian Bar Journal* 244-249. **3584**

Tetley, William. "Peril of the Sea." (1963), 6 *Canadian Bar Journal* 148-153, 172, 174. **3585**

B. Admiralty Courts and Procedure

Aylesworth, Allen B., and others. "Admiralty Jurisdiction." (1908), 28 *Canadian Law Times* 404-414, 472-483, 553-561, 627-634. **3586**

Bradley, Martin A. "The Ranking of Privileged Claims in Admiralty." (1972), *Canadian Bar Association, Papers,* 34 p. **3587**

Braen, André. "Cour fédérale - Compétence en amirauté - Problème de l'existence d'une législation fédérale applicable - Droit maritime canadien." (1981), 59 *Canadian Bar Review* 579-588. **3588**

Braen, André. "La juridiction en amirauté de la Cour fédérale du Canada." (1981), 41 *Revue du Barreau* 367-414. **3589**

Burchell, Charles J. *Admiralty Law in Canada.* Montreal: McGill University, 1935. 47 p. **3590**

A series of lectures delivered at McGill University, Montreal.
Reviews: F.H. Barlow in (1935-36), 1 *University of Toronto Law Journal* 441; W.C. MacDonald in (1935-36), 15 *Dalhousie Review* 392.

Burchell, Charles J. "Canadian Admiralty Jurisdiction and Shipping Laws." (1929), 45 *Law Quarterly Review* 370-377. **3591**

Burchell, Charles J. "Uniformity of Merchant Shipping Legislation and Admiralty Jurisdiction Throughout the British Empire." (1932), 10 *Canadian Bar Review* 179-181. **3592**

Cantin, Serge A. *Juridiction d'amirauté canadienne et compétence de la Cour fédérale en matière maritime.* Ottawa, 1980. 718 frames. **3593**

Thesis (LL.D.), Université d'Ottawa, 1979. (National Library of Canada. Canadian Theses on Microfiche, No. 43983).

Cox, R. Gregory. "The Maritime Court of Ontario." (1888), 8 *Canadian Law Times* 1-13. **3594**

Cox, R. Gregory. "Maritime Law: Necessaries and Repairs." (1885), 5 *Canadian Law Times* 529-538. **3595**

Cox, R. Gregory. "Vice-Admiralty Jurisdiction - Damage." (1886), 6 *Canadian Law Times* 457-469, 505-512. **3596**

Howell, Alfred. *Admiralty Law, Canada; the Rules, 1893, Annotated with Forms, Tables of Fees, and Statutes, and a Treatise on the Matters Subject to the Jurisdiction of Admiralty Courts in Canada.* Toronto: Carswell, 1893. xxvi, 11, 356 p. **3597**

Kerr, Robert W. "Constitutional Limitations on the Admiralty Jurisdiction of the Federal Court." (1979), 5 *Dalhousie Law Journal* 568-583. **3598**

Laing, Lionel H. "Nova Scotia's Admiralty Court as a Problem of Colonial Administration." (1935), 16 *Canadian Historical Review* 151-161. **3599**

Lash, Z.A., and Cox, R. Gregory. "Vice-Admiralty Jurisdiction: Possession - Restraint - Co-Ownership." (1887), 7 *Canadian Law Times* 21-34. **3600**

Letalik, Norman G. *Canadian Maritime Liens.* Halifax, 1980. vii, 221 leaves.
3601
Thesis (LL.M.), Dalhousie University, 1980. (National Library of Canada. Canadian Theses on Microfiche, No. 48218).

Marston, Geoffrey. "Historical Aspects of Colonial Criminal Legislation Applying to the Sea." (1980), 14 *University of British Columbia Law Review* 299-328.
3602

Mayers, Edward Courtenay. *Admiralty Law and Practice in Canada; etc.* Toronto: Carswell, 1916. xxx, 574 p. **3603**

Meagher, Arthur J. "Memorandum of the Proposed Revision of the Admiralty Act, Chapter 1, of the Revised Statutes of Canada, 1952." (1968), *Canadian Bar Association, Papers,* 6 p. **3604**

Meagher, Arthur J. "The Revision of the Admiralty Act." (1955), *Canadian Bar Association, Papers,* 22 p. **3605**

Merriman, *Sir* Boyd. " 'The Admiralty Court ' " (1935), 20 *Canadian Bar Association, Proceedings* 74-89. **3606**

Morin, William. "Juridiction maritime de nos tribunaux." (1943), 3 *Revue du Barreau* 3-13, 53-60, 103-117, 178-187. **3607**

Ryan, Edward F. "Admiralty Jurisdiction and the Maritime Lien: An Historical Perspective." (1968), 7 *Western Ontario Law Review* 173-200. **3608**

Tetley, William. "Against Whom Should Cargo Claimant Take Suit." (1962), *Canadian Bar Association, Papers* 217-232. **3609**

Tetley, William. "Maritime Law Judgments in Canada - 1979." (1980-81), 6 *Dalhousie Law Journal* 676-689. **3610**

Tetley, William. "The *Pennsylvania* Rule - An Anachronism? The *Pennsylvania*

Judgment - An Error?" (1981-82), 13 *Journal of Maritime Law and Commerce* 127-146. **3611**

Tetley, William. "Repairmen's Liens." (1981-82), 13 *Journal of Maritime Law and Commerce* 177-221. **3612**

Thanos, Panagiotis G. *Canadian Maritime Liens*. Toronto, 1975. 123 leaves. Thesis (LL.M.), University of Toronto, 1975. **3613**

C. Collision (Safety at Sea, Etc.)

Bernard, Marc. "De la responsabilité en matière d'abordage." (1967), 2 *Revue Juridique Thémis* 345-390. **3614**

Gerity, F.O. "Radar Information Applied to Rules for Avoiding Collisions." (1962), 5 *Canadian Bar Journal* 290-303. **3615**

Gold, Edgar, and Letalik, Norman G. *Admiralty II: Marine Collisions and Salvage: Cases and Materials*. 3d ed. Halifax: Dalhousie University, Faculty of Law, Marine and Environmental Law Programme, 1982. v, 319 p. **3616**

Healy, Nicholas J. "Radar and the New Collisions Regulations." (1962), *Canadian Bar Association, Papers* 189-216. **3617**

Hyndman, Patricia. "Adequacy of Canadian Concentrates Code in Light of the Experience of M.V. Erwin Shroder." (1967), *Canadian Bar Association, Papers* 91-107. **3618**

D. Carriage of Goods

Angus, W. David. "Legal Implications of 'the Container Revolution' in International Carriage of Goods." (1968), 14 *McGill Law Journal* 395-429. **3619**

Côté, Pierre G. "A Personal View of the Legal Status of the Himalaya Clause in the Light of Recent Jurisprudence." (1972), *Canadian Bar Association, Papers*, 27 p. **3620**

Delpuer, Jean. "Le marché du fret maritime et l'évolution récente des taux." (1957-58), 33 *Actualité Économique* 514-523. **3621**

Kindred, Hugh M., and others. *The Future of Canadian Carriage of Goods by Water Law*. (A Study of the Hague Rules, the Hague/Visby Rules, and the Hamburg Rules on the Carriage of Goods by Sea). Halifax: Dalhousie Ocean Studies Programme, 1982. xiv, 387 p. **3622**

Lauzon, Yves. "Les connaissements émis sous l'empire des chartes-parties." (1973), 8 *Revue Juridique Thémis* 65-96. **3623**

McInnes, Hector. "Bills of Lading and the Hague Convention of 1922." (1922-23), 30 *Journal of the Canadian Bankers' Association* 324-328. **3624**

Mukherjee, P.K. "The Charting and Safekeeping of Oceans and Waterways." (1980-81), 6 *Dalhousie Law Journal* 578-630. **3625**

Pinsonnault, Marcel, Jr. "Affrètement, arrimage et fret." (1940-41), 16/1 *Actualité Économique* 134-149. **3626**

Pourcelet, Michel. "Clauses attributives de compétence et clauses d'arbitrage dans le transport maritime sous connaissement." *In* Popovici, Adrian, ed., *Problèmes de droit contemporain: mélanges Louis Baudouin* (Montréal, 1974), pp. 349-365. **3627**

Pourcelet, Michel. *Le transport maritime sous connaissement: droit canadien, américain et anglais.* Montréal: Presses de l'Université de Montréal, 1972. xvii, 280 p. **3628**
Review: Unsigned in (1973), 36 *Revue Générale de l'Air et de l'Espace 140*.

Reycraft, L.S. "'A Careless and Slovenly Document' - A Discussion of the Effect of the Incorporation of the Clause Paramount (Canadian, United States or Hague Rules) in a Charter Party." (1966), *Canadian Bar Association, Papers* 189-195. **3629**

Reycraft, L.S. "Comments on '*Muncaster Castle'* and '*Mauriene'* Decisions: Hague Rules, Should They Be Amended?" (1963), *Canadian Bar Association, Papers* 348-361. **3630**

Reycraft, L.S. "*Muncaster Castle* Dilemma." (1967), *Canadian Bar Association, Papers* 81-83. **3631**

Tetley, William. "The Application of the Hague Rules and the *Vita Food* Case." (1960), *Canadian Bar Association, Papers* 244-256. **3632**

Tetley, William. "Canadian Comments on the Proposed Uncitral Rules: An Analysis of the Proposed UNCITRAL Text." (1977-78), 9 *Journal of Maritime Law and Commerce* 251-268. **3633**

Tetley, William. "The Himalaya Clause - Heresy or Genius?" (1977-78), 9 *Journal of Maritime Law and Commerce* 111-130. **3634**

Tetley, William. "The Himalaya Clause, 'Stipulation pour Autrui,' Non-Responsibility Clauses and Gross Negligence under the Civil Code." (1979), 20 *Cahiers de Droit* 449-483. **3635**

Tetley, William. *Marine Cargo Claims.* Toronto: Carswell; London: Stevens, 1965. xxxix, 404 p. **3636**
More than twenty of the chapters in this book have been published previously in legal journals in Canada, Great Britain, France, and Italy.
Review: Léon Lalande in (1967), 27 *Revue du Barreau* 207-209.

Tetley, William. *Marine Cargo Claims.* With Assistance from Marc Nadon. 2d ed. Toronto: Butterworths, c1978. xlii, 664 p. (Canadian Legal Manual Series) **3637**
Reviews: J.R. Cunningham in (1979), 13 *University of British Columbia Law Review* 165-167; Hugh M. Kindred in (1980), 6 *Dalhousie Law Journal* 191-193; Alex L. Parks in (1978-79), 10 *Journal of Maritime Law and Commerce* 465-467; Jean Pineau in (1978),

13 *Revue Juridique Thémis* 219-220; René Rodière in (1979), 31 *Revue Internationale de Droit Comparé* 255; Maurice Tancelin in (1979), 20 *Cahiers de Droit* 651-652.

Tetley, William. "The Muncaster Castle Amendment." (1964), *Canadian Bar Association, Papers* 148-150. **3638**

Tetley, William. "Per Package Limitation and Containers under the Hague Rules, Visby and Uncitral." (1977-78), 4 *Dalhousie Law Journal* 685-707. **3639**

Tetley, William. "Selected Problems of Maritime Law under the Hague Rules." (1963), 9 *McGill Law Journal* 53-65. **3640**

Tetley, William. "Selected Problems under the Hague Rules." (1965), 11 *McGill Law Journal* 19-34. **3641**

Tetley, William. "Who May Claim under the Hague Rules." (1964), *Canadian Bar Association, Papers* 142-147. **3642**

Ward, Les. "The SDR in Transport Liability Conventions: Some Clarification." (1981-82), 13 *Journal of Maritime Law and Commerce* 1-20. **3643**

E. Marine Insurance

Canada. Transport Commission. Directorate of Transport Industries Analysis. Research Branch. *The Marine Insurance Industry in Canada.* Ottawa: Canadian Transport Commission, 1978. xvii, 226 p. **3644**
Project members: Les Ward, B.F. Kelso, and H. Kurasawa. Also published in French under title: *L'industrie de l'assurance maritime au Canada.*

Famula, Paul F. "Shipowner's Limitation of Liability in Canada and the United States: Problematic Aspects under Private International Law." (1982), 27 *McGill Law Journal* 372-380. **3645**

Forbes, Wm.O.M. "Report on the 'Convention on the Liability of Operators of Nuclear Ships.' " (1963), *Canadian Bar Association, Papers* 298-341. **3646**
Includes the text of the convention adopted at Brussels, May 25, 1962 (pp. 320-341).

Hadjis, Dimitris. *Liability Limitations in the Carriage of Passengers and Goods by Air and Sea.* Montreal, 1958. 167 leaves. **3647**
Thesis (LL.M.), McGill University, 1958.

Kerr, Donald A. "Proposed Revision of Canada Shipping Act - Limitation of Ship Owners' Liability." (1959), *Canadian Bar Association, Papers* 219-256. **3648**

Macaulay, Wallace D. "The Liability of a Carrier by Sea." (1952), 5 *University of New Brunswick Law Journal* 26-35 (No. 2) **3649**

Meagher, Arthur J. "Limitations of Shipowner's Liability in Collision Cases." (1954), *Canadian Bar Association, Papers,* 17 p. **3650**

Morin, William. "Assurance maritime et transport par mer." (1935-36), 14 *Revue du Droit* 259-270, 321-336, 389-400. **3651**
Parts 2 (pp. 321-336), and 3 (pp. 389-400) have title: "Du transport par mer."

Morin, William. "Clause 'Inchmaree' dans l'assurance maritime." (1944), 4 *Revue du Barreau* 124-128. **3652**

Morin, William. "Les périls de la mer." (1935-36), 14 *Revue du Droit* 454-471. **3653**

Pourcelet, Michel. "La limitation légale de responsabilité dans le transport de marchandises sous connaissement." (1967), 2 *Revue Juridique Thémis* 569-585. **3654**

Powell, R. "The Gold Clause Agreement." (1954), *Canadian Bar Association, Papers*, 8 p. **3655**

Québec (Province). Civil Code Revision Office. *Report on Marine Insurance / Rapport sur l'assurance maritime.* Montréal, 1976. v, 113 p. (Québec (Province). Civil Code Revision Office. Report, Vol. 47) **3656**

Tetley, William. "Loss and Damage under Marine Claims." (1964), 10 *McGill Law Journal* 105-125. **3657**

Tetley, William. "Responsibility for Sweat Damage to Cargo." (1959), *Canadian Bar Association, Papers* 257-265. **3658**

Tremeear, W.J. "The 'Amen' in Marine Insurance Policies." (1926), 4 *Canadian Bar Review* 386. **3659**

XV. AIRSPACE AND OUTER SPACE

For air pollution, see "Air Pollution (Transboundary)" (p. 667); for telecommunications, see "Telecommunications" (p. 643); for weather information, see "Weather Information (Meteorology)" (p. 659). See also "Air and Space Warfare" (p. 451), "Hijacking" (p. 466), and "International Civil Aviation Organization" (p. 357).

A. General

Cooper, John Cobb. "Backgrounds of International Public Air Law." (1965), *Yearbook of Air and Space Law* **3660**

FitzGerald, Gerald F. "Air Law 1972-2022." (1973), 51 *Canadian Bar Review* 264-279. **3661**
Also published in (1972), *Canadian Bar Association, Papers*, 23 p.

FitzGerald, Gerald F. "International Law Association - Fifty-Third Conference -Buenos Aires." (1969), 35 *Journal of Air Law and Commerce* 245-248. **3662**

Guldimann, Werner. "Air Law - An Autonomous System?" (1980), 5 *Annals of Air and Space Law* 119-132. **3663**

Mankiewicz, René H. "L'unification du droit aérien; organes et techniques de l'unification du droit aérien (public et privé)." (1970), 16 *McGill Law Journal* 419-459. **3664**

Martin, Paul. "New Frontiers in the Law of the Air." (1967), 19 *External Affairs* 521-526. **3665**
Speech to the second International Conference on Air and Space Law, McGill University, November 3, 1967.

Martin, Paul. "New Frontiers in the Law of the Air." *In* McWhinney, Edward, and Bradley, Martin A., eds., *The Freedom of the Air* (Leyden, 1968), pp. 238-245. **3666**

Matte, Nicolas Mateesco. *Traité de droit aérien-aéronautique*. 3. éd. Montréal: ICDAS, McGill University; Paris: A. Pedone, 1980. 844 p. **3667**
At head of title: Institut et centre de droit aérien et spatial.
Reviews: George A. Codding, Jr., in (1982), 76 *American Journal of International Law* 214-215; Isabella H.Ph. Diederiks-Verschoor in (1981), 28 *Netherlands International Law Review* 100; Gerald F. FitzGerald in (1980), 58 *Canadian Bar Review* 805-809; Euthymène Georgiades in (1980), 34 *Revue Française de Droit Aérien* 353-354; Aart van Wijk in (1980), 5 *Air Law* 190-192.

Matte, Nicolas Mateesco. *Treatise on Air-Aeronautical Law*. Montreal: ICASL,

McGill University; Toronto: distributed by Carswell, 1981. 832 p. **3668**
English edition of the author's *Traité de droit aérien-aéronautique*.
Reviews: W. Paul Gormley in (1981), 6 *Annals of Air and Space Law* 642-647; Aart van Wijk in (1981), 6 *Air Law* 123.

McWhinney, Edward, and Bradley, Martin A., eds. *The Freedom of the Air.* Leyden: A.W. Sijthoff; Dobbs Ferry, N.Y.: Oceana Publications, 1968 (1969). 260 p. **3669**
Contains 17 papers presented at a closed conference held in November 1967 in the Institute of Air and Space Law at McGill University, Montreal. Individual papers are listed separately.
Reviews: Isabella H.Ph. Diederiks-Verschoor in (1970), 17 *Netherlands International Law Review* 81-82 (in Dutch); Euthymène Georgiades in (1969), 23 *Revue Française de Droit Aérien* 103-104; Werner Guldimann in (1969), 17 *American Journal of Comparative Law* 648-649; Kay Hailbronner in (1971), 31 *Zeitschrift für Ausländisches Öffentliches Recht und Völkerrecht* 599-600; Andreas F. Lowenfeld in (1969), 15 *McGill Law Journal* 510-515; E. Roucounas in (1969), 22 *Revue Hellénique de Droit International* 204; Joseph W. Samuels in (1969), 7 *Canadian Yearbook of International Law* 362-363; unsigned in (1968), 14 *Annuaire Français de Droit International* 996 (brief notice).

Milde, C. Michael. "Conflicts of Laws in the Law of the Air: Some Remarks on the Resolution of the 51st Session of the Institut de Droit International of September 11, 1963." (1965), 11 *McGill Law Journal* 220-262. **3670**

Milde, C. Michael. "International Organizations: United Nations." (1982), 7 *Annals of Air and Space Law* 528-531. **3671**

Mishra, Shantnu, and Pavlasek, Tomas J.F. "On the Lack of Physical Bases for Defining a Boundary between Air Space and Outer Space." (1982), 7 *Annals of Air and Space Law* 399-414. **3672**

Muli'aumaseali'i, Saverivi. *New Trends in the Law of the Sea: Implications for the Regime of the Airspace.* Montreal, (c1977). xi, 154 leaves. **3673**
Thesis (LL.M.), McGill University, 1976. (National Library of Canada. Canadian Theses on Microfiche, No. 31846).

Sand, Peter H.; Lyon, James T.; and Pratt, Geoffrey N. "An Historical Survey of International Air Law since 1944." (1960-61), 7 *McGill Law Journal* 125-160. **3674**

Sand, Peter H.; Sousa Freitas, Jorge de; and Pratt, Geoffrey N. "An Historical Survey of International Air Law Before the Second World War." (1960-61), 7 *McGill Law Journal* 24-42. **3675**

Wassenbergh, H.A. "Reality and Value in Air and Space Law." (1978), 3 *Annals of Air and Space Law* 323-354. **3676**

B. Sovereignty over Airspace

Abramovitch, Yehuda. "The Maxim *'Cujus Est Solum Ejus Usque ad Coelum'* as Applied in Aviation." (1961-62), 8 *McGill Law Journal* 247-269. **3677**

Abramovitch, Yehuda. *Property Rights in Airspace, (Landowners and the Right of Flight).* Montreal, 1962. iv, 164 leaves. **3678**
Thesis (LL.M.), McGill University, 1962.

Ahmed, Saiyed Ehtasham. *The Airspace in International Air Law.* Montreal, 1957. 135 leaves. **3679**
Thesis (LL.M.), McGill University, 1957.

Arnold, Stanley Richard. *Sovereign Rights in Space.* Montreal, 1957. vi, 129 leaves. **3680**
Thesis (LL.M.), McGill University, 1957.

Cheng, Bin. "The Legal Regime of Airspace and Outer Space: The Boundary Problem. Functionalism versus Spatialism: The Major Premises." (1980), 5 *Annals of Air and Space Law* 323-361. **3681**

Cooper, John Cobb. *Roman Law and the Maxim 'Cujus Est Solum' in International Air Law.* Montreal: Institute of International Air Law, McGill University. 1952. 43 p. (McGill University. Institute of Air and Space Law. Publication, No. 1) **3682**
Also published in (1952-55), 1 *McGill Law Journal* 23-65; (1952), 6 *Revue Française de Droit Aérien* 339-389 (in French), and in the author's *Explorations in Aerospace Law* (Montreal, 1968), pp. 54-102.

Diop, Charles M. *Les implications juridico-politiques de la présence irrégulière d'un aéronef étranger dans l'espace aérien d'un état.* Montréal, 1978. vi, 297 leaves. **3683**
Thesis (LL.M.), McGill University 1978.

Dohan, David J. "Airspace and Article 414 C.C." (1955-56), 2 *McGill Law Journal* 114-127. **3684**

Eubank, John A. "What about the Airspace?" (1930), 8 *Canadian Bar Review* 126-143. **3685**

Fedele, Frank. *Peacetime Reconnaissance from Air Space and Outer Space; a Study of Defensive Rights in Contemporary International Law.* Montreal, 1965. ix, 251 leaves. **3686**
Thesis (LL.M.), McGill University, 1965.

Flynn, Frank Joseph. *The Legal Status of the Airspace of Trusteeship Territory.* Montreal, 1956. vii, 230 leaves. **3687**
Thesis (LL.M.), McGill University, 1956.

Gunatilaka, Visty Charles. *Problems of Air Space Sovereignty in the Seventies.* Montreal, 1972 (c1973). ii, 148 leaves. **3688**
Thesis (LL.M.), McGill University, 1972. (National Library of Canada. Canadian Theses on Microfilm, No. 14459).

Hailbronner, Kay. *Protection of Aerial Frontiers.* Montreal, 1969. ii, 112 leaves. **3689**
Thesis (LL.M.), McGill University, 1969. (National Library of Canada. Canadian Theses on Microfilm, No. 4826).

Head, Ivan L. "ADIZ, International Law, and Contiguous Airspace." (1960), 2 *Harvard International Law Journal* 28-51. **3690**

Also published in (1962-64), 2-3 *Alberta Law Review* 182-196. ADIZ refers to Air Defence Identification Zone (U.S.), and CADIZ (Canadian).

Li, Kuo Lee. *For a More Rational Legal Regime of Aerospace Continuum: A Proposal.* Montreal, 1968. ix, 192 leaves. **3691**
Thesis (LL.M.), McGill University, 1968. (National Library of Canada. Canadian Theses on Microfilm, No. 2839).

Lonergan, Stephen J. *The Legal Status of the Antarctic Airspace.* Montreal, 1972. 115 leaves. **3692**
Thesis (LL.M.), McGill University, 1972. (National Library of Canada. Canadian Theses on Microfilm, No. 12747).

Loriot, François, and Parizeau, Micheline. "L'influence de l'aéronautique sur l'évolution de la notion de souveraineté nationale." (1964), 14 *Thémis* 7-36. **3693**

MacBrayne, Sheila F. "The Right of Innocent Passage." (1952-55), 1 *McGill Law Journal* 270-276. **3694**

MacBrayne, Sheila F. *Right of Innocent Passage.* Montreal, 1956. iv, 267 leaves. Thesis (LL.M.), McGill University, 1956. **3695**

Mackneson, Stephen Wayne. *Freedom of Flight over the High Seas.* Montreal, 1959. 114 leaves. **3696**
Thesis (LL.M.), McGill University, 1959.

Martial, Jean A. "State Control of the Air Space over the Territorial Sea and the Contiguous Zone." (1952), 30 *Canadian Bar Review* 245-263. **3697**

Matte, Nicolas Mateesco. "À qui appartient le milieu aérien?" (1980), 5 *Annals of Air and Space Law* 223-247. **3698**

Matte, Nicolas Mateesco. "À qui appartient le milieu aérien?" (1952), 12 *Revue du Barreau* 227-242. **3699**
Reviewed by José Luis de Azcárraga in (1952), 5 *Revista Española de Derecho Internacional* 308-309.

McWhinney, Edward. "International Law and the Freedom of the Air - The Chicago Convention and the Future." (1969), 1 *Rutgers Camden Law Journal* 229-242. **3700**

Murchison, John Taylor. *The Contiguous Air Space Zone in International Law.* Ottawa: Queen's Printer, 1957. 113 p., map. **3701**
First issued as the author's thesis (LL.M.), McGill University, 1955. Published by the Dept. of National Defence, Ottawa.
Review: Ivan A. Vlasic in (1958), 36 *Canadian Bar Review* 129-134, and 443-444 (Letter by J.T. Murchison).

Ogunbanwo, Ogunsola Olaniyi. *The Exercise of State Authority in the Air-Space over the High Seas.* Montreal, 1966. 149 leaves, maps. **3702**
Thesis (LL.M.), McGill University, 1966. (National Library of Canada. Canadian Theses on Microfilm, No. 275).

"Passing of Air Ship over Property as Trespass." (1913), 33 *Canadian Law Times* 749-751. **3703**

Peng, Ming-Min. "Le vol à haute altitude et l'article 1 de la convention de Chicago, 1944." (1952), 12 *Revue du Barreau* 277-292. **3704**

Pépin, Eugène. "The Legal Status of the Airspace in the Light of Progress in Aviation and Astronautics." (1956-57), 3 *McGill Law Journal* 70-77.   3705

Richardson, Jack E. "Private Property Rights in the Air Space at Common Law." (1953), 31 *Canadian Bar Review* 117-149.   3706

Richardson, Jack E. *State Sovereignty over the Airspace with Particular Reference to the Status of Airspace above Australia and Australian Territories.* Montreal, 1971 (c1973). 90 leaves.   3707
  Half-title: *Australian Territories Status of Airspace.* Thesis (LL.M.), McGill University, 1972. (National Library of Canada. Canadian Theses on Microfilm, No. 13376).

Ritchie, Jean Harris. *Prohibited Areas in International Air Law.* Montreal, 1969. ii, 106 leaves, maps.   3708
  Thesis (LL.M.), McGill University, 1969. (National Library of Canada. Canadian Theses on Microfilm, No. 4855).

Tamm, John R. *The Status of States' Rights in the Airspace of the United States: The Sovereign Powers of and the Powers Exercised by the Several States at Airports and in the Airspace Superjacent to Their Territory.* Montreal, 1978. xi, 388 leaves.   3709
  Thesis (D.C.L.), McGill University, 1978.

"Trespass by Aeroplane." (1910), 46 *Canada Law Journal* 728-733.   3710

Zhukov, Gennady P. "Space Flights and the Problem of Altitude Frontier of Sovereignty." (1966), *Yearbook of Air and Space Law* 485-491.   3711

C. International Air Transportation

1. GENERAL

Abdeh, Ibrahim Ahmad. *Bilateral Air Transport Agreements of Jordan.* Montreal, 1977 (c1978). xiv, 190 leaves.   3712
  Thesis (LL.M.), McGill University, 1977. (National Library of Canada. Canadian Theses on Microfiche, No. 35999).

Abraham, Claude. "Politiques aériennes internationales vues par la France." *In* Matte, Nicolas Mateesco, ed., *International Air Transport: Law, Organization and Policies for the Future* (Toronto, 1976), pp. 3-11.   3713

Adelfio, Antonio. *Particular Aspects of the Rome Convention of 1952 on Damages at the Surface.* Montreal, 1955. ii, 139 leaves.   3714
  Thesis (LL.M.), McGill University, 1955.

Alam, Mahmud. *Pakistan-Iran-Turkey (RCD) Collaboration in Air Transport: Formation of a Joint International Airline and Its Legal Aspects.* Montreal, 1970. xii, 752 leaves.   3715
  Half-title: *RCD Collaboration in Air Transport.* Thesis (LL.M.), McGill University, 1971. (National Library of Canada. Canadian Theses on Microfilm, No. 12745).

Archer, Ian Dev. *Multinational Co-operation in Air Transport in the Commonwealth Caribbean.* Montreal, 1968. iii, 107 leaves.   3716

Thesis (LL.M.), McGill University, 1968. (National Library of Canada. Canadian Theses on Microfilm, No. 2600).

Aryal, Puskar Raj. *Bilateral Air Transport Agreements of Nepal.* Montreal, 1978. viii, 281 leaves. **3717**
Thesis (LL.M.), McGill University, 1978.

Assum, Baudouin M.A.J.B. van den. *International Air Charter Transportation: Its Legal Regulations and Implications.* Montreal, 1975 (c1976). 226 leaves. **3718**
Thesis (LL.M.), McGill University, 1975. (National Library of Canada. Canadian Theses on Microfiche, No. 27083).

Azzie, Ralph. "Second Special Air Transport Conference and Bilateral Air Transport Agreements." (1980), 5 *Annals of Air and Space Law* 3-15. **3719**

Azzie, Ralph. "Specific Problems Solved by the Negotiation of Bilateral Air Agreements." (1967), 13 *McGill Law Journal* 303-308. **3720**

Berle, A.A. "The Air Transportation Crisis and the Future." *In* McWhinney, Edward, and Bradley, Martin A., eds., *The Freedom of the Air* (Leyden, 1968), pp. 13-16. **3721**

Biggar, O.M. "The Law Relating to the Air." (1921), 6 *Canadian Bar Association, Proceedings* 196-205. **3722**

Biggar, O.M. "The Law Relating to the Air." (1921), 41 *Canadian Law Times* 667-676. **3723**

Biggar, O.M. "The Law Relating to the Air." (1922), 58 *Canada Law Journal* 57-69. **3724**

Biggar, O.M. "Legislative Jurisdiction over Flying." (1930), 8 *Canadian Bar Review* 587-592. **3725**

Böckstiegel, Karl-Heinz. "Coordinating Aviation Liability." (1977), 2 *Annals of Air and Space Law* 15-29. **3726**

Bogolasky, José. "International Organizations: LACAC - Latin American Civil Aviation Commission: A Report on the Third LACAC Assembly and 1979 Developments." (1979), 4 *Annals of Air and Space Law* 677-685. **3727**

Bogolasky, José. "International Organizations: LACAC - A Report on the Activities of the Latin American Civil Aviation Commission During 1980." (1980), 5 *Annals of Air and Space Law* 655-657. **3728**

Bogolasky, José. "International Organizations: Latin American Civil Aviation Commission." (1978), 3 *Annals of Air and Space Law* 597-600. **3729**

Bogolasky, José. "International Organizations: The Latin American Civil Aviation Commission." (1977), 2 *Annals of Air and Space Law* 464-468. **3730**

Bogolasky, José. "International Organizations: Latin American Civil Aviation Commission (LACAC)." (1981), 6 *Annals of Air and Space Law* 576-585. **3731**

Bradley, Martin A. "International Air Cargo Services: The Italy-U.S.A. Air Transport Agreement Arbitration." (1966-67), 12 *McGill Law Journal* 312-326. **3732**

Browne, Secor D. "Internal Problems of U.S. International Aviation Policy." *In* Matte, Nicolas Mateesco, ed., *International Air Transport: Law, Organization and Policies for the Future* (Toronto, 1976), pp. 19-21. **3733**

Canada. Wartime Information Board. *Canada and International Civil Aviation.* Ottawa, 1945. 29 p., map. **3734**

Caplan, Kenneth Gary. *The Tort Liability of the United States Government for Its Aviation and Space Activities.* Montreal, 1970. 120 leaves. **3735**
Thesis (LL.M.), McGill University, 1970. (National Library of Canada. Canadian Theses on Microfilm, No. 7257).

Carpenter, *Lord* Boyd. "International Air Transport Policies as Viewed by the United Kingdom." *In* Matte, Nicolas Mateesco, ed., *International Air Transport: Law, Organization and Policies for the Future* (Toronto, 1976), pp. 13-18. **3736**

Catibog, José Rosa. *Some Legal Problems in International Law on Aerial Collisions.* Montreal, 1964. iii, 147 leaves. **3737**
Thesis (LL.M.), McGill University, 1964.

Cavdar, Arif. *Regionalization in International Civil Aviation.* Montreal, 1969. 171, 7 leaves. **3738**
Thesis (LL.M.), McGill University, 1969. (National Library of Canada. Canadian Theses on Microfilm, No. 4812).

Chauveau, Paul. "La faute inexcusable." (1979), 4 *Annals of Air and Space Law* 3-9. **3739**

Chauveau, Paul. "Interprétation judiciaire des conventions portant loi uniforme." (1977), 2 *Annals of Air and Space Law* 47-54. **3740**

Cheng, Bin. "Beyond Bermuda." *In* Matte, Nicolas Mateesco, ed., *International Air Transport: Law, Organization and Policies for the Future* (Toronto, 1976), pp. 81-99. **3741**

Coulibaly, Seydou. *Les accords des Bermudes et les accords bilatéraux des états membres du traité de Yaoundé.* Montréal, 1978. vi, 296 leaves. **3742**
Thesis (LL.M.), McGill University, 1978.

Culver, Howard L. *Route Schedules in Canadian-American Civil Air Relations: The 1966 Air Transport Services Agreement.* Montreal, 1968 (c1972). iii, 97 leaves. **3743**
Half-title: *Route Schedules in the 1966 Canadian-U.S. Air Transport Agreement.* Thesis (LL.M.), McGill University, 1968. (National Library of Canada. Canadian Theses on Microfilm, No. 11788). Refers to the agreement signed at Ottawa, January 17, 1966 (CTS 1966/2).

Deák, Francis. "The Balance-Sheet of Bilateralism." *In* McWhinney, Edward, and Bradley, Martin A., eds., *The Freedom of the Air* (Leyden, 1968), pp. 159-173. **3744**

DeDongo, Paul J. *Progress Toward the Multilateral Exchange of Commercial Air Transport Rights.* Montreal, 1954. iv, 316 leaves. **3745**
Thesis (LL.M.), McGill University, 1954.

Diersch, Wolfdieter. *International Non-Scheduled Air Transportation: A Study of International Agreements and Government Regulation in the United States of America, Canada, the United Kingdom of Great Britain and the Federal Republic of Germany.* Montreal, 1976 (c1977). 588 leaves. **3746**
Thesis (LL.M.), McGill University, 1976. (National Library of Canada. Canadian Theses on Microfiche, No. 31751).

DuCrest, Maxime M. *L'état et les compagnies de navigation aérienne: les interventions économiques gouvernementales pour l'organisation de la profession de transporteur aérien.* Montréal, 1959. 171 leaves. **3747**
Thesis (LL.M.), McGill University, 1959.

Ewart, John S. "The Aeronautics Case." (1931), 9 *Canadian Bar Review* 724-728. **3748**

FitzGerald, Gerald F. "Aviation - Liability Rules Governing Damages Caused by Foreign Aircraft to Third Parties on the Surface - Rome Convention of 1952. (Comment)." (1953), 31 *Canadian Bar Review* 90-98. **3749**

FitzGerald, Gerald F. "Concerted Action Against States Found in Default of Their International Obligations in Respect of Unlawful Interference with International Civil Aviation." (1972), 10 *Canadian Yearbook of International Law* 261-277. **3750**

FitzGerald, Gerald F. "Convention on International Civil Aviation: Lease, Charter and Interchange of Aircraft in International Operations." (1975-76), 1 *Air Law* 20-24. **3751**

FitzGerald, Gerald F. "The Development of International Liability Rules concerning Aerial Collisions." (1954), 21 *Journal of Air Law and Commerce* 203-210. **3752**

FitzGerald, Gerald F. "The Development of International Liability Rules Governing Aerial Collisions." (1961), 2 *Current Law and Social Problems* 154-176. **3753**

FitzGerald, Gerald F. "The Implications of the United Nations Convention on International Multimodal Transport of Goods (Geneva, 1980) for International Civil Aviation." (1982), 7 *Annals of Air and Space Law* 41-80. **3754**

FitzGerald, Gerald F. "International Air Law in the 1970s." *In* Macdonald, Ronald St. John, and others, *Canadian Perspectives on International Law and Organization* (Toronto, 1974), pp. 307-336. **3755**

FitzGerald, Gerald F. "The Lease, Charter and Interchange of Aircraft in International Operations: Amendments to the Chicago and Rome Conventions." (1977), 2 *Annals of Air and Space Law* 103-137. **3756**

FitzGerald, Gerald F. "Proposed Convention on the International Combined Transport of Goods: Implications for International Civil Aviation." (1973), 11 *Canadian Yearbook of International Law* 166-192. **3757**

FitzGerald, Gerald F. "The Protocol to Amend the Convention on Damage Caused by Foreign Aircraft to Third Parties on the Surface (Rome, 1952) Signed at Montreal, September 23, 1978." (1979), 4 *Annals of Air and Space Law* 29-73. **3758**

Fraino, Carlos. *Venezuela's Bilateral Air Transport Agreements on Threshold of the Supersonic Era.* Montreal, 1977 (c1978). vii, 249 leaves. **3759**
Thesis (LL.M.), McGill University, 1977. (National Library of Canada. Canadian Theses on Microfiche, No. 35713).

Frank, Pierre. "Le droit aérien." (1929), 7 *Canadian Bar Review* 491-499. **3760**

"The Future of Air Transport." (1944), 4 *Behind the Headlines* No. 1 (36 p.) **3761**

Revision of "Canada - Crossroads of the Airways," published in (1942), 3 *Behind the Headlines* No. 3.

Gamacchio, Giampiero. *Les premiers résultats de la coopération aéronautique européenne.* Montréal, 1957. 49 leaves. **3762**
Thesis (LL.M.), McGill University, 1957.

Gautier, Pierre, and Bédard, Charles. "L'aube du transport supersonique." (1979), 4 *Annals of Air and Space Law* 75-92. **3763**

Gertler, Z. Joseph. "Order in the Air and the Problem of Real and False Options." (1979), 4 *Annals of Air and Space Law* 93-125. **3764**

Gillilland, Whitney. "Bilateral Agreements." *In* McWhinney, Edward, and Bradley, Martin A., eds., *The Freedom of the Air* (Leyden, 1968), pp. 140-158. **3765**

Gonzales-Rodas, Aster. *The Reciprocity Clause in Latin America Bilateral Air Transport Agreements.* Montreal, 1963. ii, 113 leaves. **3766**
Thesis (LL.M.), McGill University, 1963.

Guillaume, Gilbert. "La responsabilité des constructeurs de matériel aéronautique en droit européen." (1979), 4 *Annals of Air and Space Law* 127-134. **3767**

Guldimann, Werner. "Bilateral Agreements as Regulatory Instruments in International Commercial Aviation." *In* Matte, Nicolas Mateesco, ed., *International Air Transport: Law, Organization and Policies for the Future* (Toronto, 1976), pp. 113-126. **3768**

Guldimann, Werner. "The Distinction between Scheduled and Non-Scheduled Air Services: Another Exercise in International Frustration." (1979), 4 *Annals of Air and Space Law* 135-149. **3769**

Haanappel, Peter P.C. "Background of the Dutch-American Aviation Conflict." (1976), 1 *Annals of Air and Space Law* 63-81. **3770**

Haanappel, Peter P.C. "Bermuda II: A First Impression." (1977), 2 *Annals of Air and Space Law* 139-149. **3771**

Haanappel, Peter P.C. "Bilateral Air Transport Agreements - 1913-1980." (1979-80), 5 *International Trade Law Journal* 241-267. **3772**

Haanappel, Peter P.C. "Bilateral Air Transport Agreements between Canada and the U.S.A." (1980), 5 *Annals of Air and Space Law* 133-154. **3773**

Haanappel, Peter P.C. "International Air Transport Association: Quo Vadis?" *In* Matte, Nicolas Mateesco, ed., *International Air Transport: Law, Organization and Policies for the Future* (Toronto, 1976), pp. 67-78. **3774**

Haanappel, Peter P.C. "The International Air Transport Association (IATA) and the International Charter Airlines." (1978), 3 *Annals of Air and Space Law* 143-153. **3775**

Haanappel, Peter P.C. *Ratemaking in International Air Transport: A Legal Analysis of International Air Fares and Rates.* Montreal, 1976. xi, 340 leaves. **3776**

Thesis (D.C.L.), McGill University, 1976. (National Library of Canada. Canadian Theses on Microfiche, No. 32951).

Haanappel, Peter P.C. *Ratemaking in International Air Transport: A Legal Analysis of International Air Fares and Rates.* Deventer: Kluwer, 1978. xii, 172 p. Based on the author's thesis (D.C.L.), McGill University, 1976. **3777**
Reviews: Gerald F. FitzGerald in (1978), 24 *McGill Law Journal* 509-512; Wybo P. Heere in (1978), 3 *Air Law* 136; Jean-Louis Magdelénat in (1978), 3 *Annals of Air and Space Law* 645-646; H.A. Wassenbergh in (1978), 25 *Netherlands International Law Review* 270-276.

Haanappel, Peter P.C. *The Scheduled International Airlines and the Aviation Consumer.* Montreal, 1974. vii, 204 leaves. **3778**
Thesis (LL.M.), McGill University, 1974. (National Library of Canada. Canadian Theses on Microfiche, No. 20722).

Hackford, R.R. "The *Colonial Airlines* Challenge to U.S.-Canadian Transport Agreement." (1952), 19 *Journal of Air Law and Commerce* 1-10. **3779**

Hammarskjöld, Knut. "The Rôle of IATA." *In* McWhinney, Edward, and Bradley, Martin A., eds., *The Freedom of the Air* (Leyden, 1968), pp. 30-36. **3780**

Heller, Paul Peter. *The Grant and Exercise of Transit Rights in Respect of Scheduled International Air Services.* Montreal, 1954. 214 leaves. **3781**
Thesis (LL.M.), McGill University, 1954.

Hesse, Nicky E. "Some Questions on Aviation Cabotage." (1952-55), 1 *McGill Law Journal* 129-140. **3782**

Illich, Michael John. *Development of International Measures for the Control of Civil Aviation.* Fredericton, 1954. (iii), 156, (15) leaves. **3783**
Thesis (M.A.), University of New Brunswick, 1954.

Imam, Abbas Imam Ibràhim. *Transnational Cooperation in Air Transport: Towards the Establishment of International Airlines.* Montreal, 1966. 187 leaves. **3784**
Thesis (LL.M.), McGill University, 1966.

Jakhu, Ram S. *The Legal Effects of Airline Tariffs.* Montreal, 1978. viii, 252 leaves. Thesis (LL.M.), McGill University, 1978. **3785**

Jiménez de Aréchaga, Eduardo. "South American Attitudes Towards the Regulation of International Air Transportation." *In* McWhinney, Edward, and Bradley, Martin A., eds., *The Freedom of the Air* (Leyden, 1968), pp. 70-86. **3786**

Kakkar, Gul Mohammed. *The Settlement of Disputes in International Civil Aviation.* Montreal, 1968. iv, 206 leaves. **3787**
Thesis (LL.M.), McGill University, 1968. (National Library of Canada. Canadian Theses on Microfilm, No. 2819).

Kanaan, Issam Y. *Air Transport Bilateralism in the Arab Middle East (Iraq, Jordan, Kuwait, Lebanon, Syria).* Montreal, 1970. vi, 317 leaves. **3788**
Thesis (LL.M.), McGill University, 1970. (National Library of Canada. Canadian Theses on Microfilm, No. 6408).

Keenan, John T. *The Aircraft Manufacturer's Liability for Damage to Third Parties.* Montreal, 1969. vii, 224 leaves. **3789**
Thesis (LL.M.), McGill University, 1969. (National Library of Canada. Canadian Theses on Microfilm, No. 4833).

Koffi, Aoussou. "Contribution africaine au développement du transport aérien international." *In* Matte, Nicolas Mateesco, ed., *International Air Transport: Law, Organization and Policies for the Future* (Toronto, 1976), pp. 23-32.
3790

Kotaite, Assad. "Le processus d'élaboration des conventions internationales de droit aérien privé adoptées sous les auspices de l'Organisation de l'aviation civile internationale (OACI)." (1979), 4 *Annals of Air and Space Law* 157-169.
3791

Kotaite, Assad. "Security of International Civil Aviation - Role of ICAO." (1982), 7 *Annals of Air and Space Law* 95-101.
3792

Koval, Josef. *Liability to Third Parties on the Surface in Air Law.* Montreal, 1954. xi, 253 leaves.
3793
Thesis (LL.M.), McGill University, 1954.

Lafleur, Gérard. *The Law of Aviation Insurance: Fundamentals.* Montreal, 1971 (c1972). 110, (46) leaves.
3794
Thesis (LL.M.), McGill University, 1971. (National Library of Canada. Canadian Theses on Microfilm, No. 11876).

Larose-Aubry, Huguette. "International Organizations: IATA." (1980), 5 *Annals of Air and Space Law* 643-645.
3795

Larose-Aubry, Huguette. "International Organizations: IATA." (1981), 6 *Annals of Air and Space Law* 538-541.
3796

Larose-Aubry, Huguette. "International Organizations: IATA." (1982), 7 *Annals of Air and Space Law* 500-503.
3797

Larose-Aubry, Huguette. "International Organizations: IATA - Proposed UNCTAD Convention on International Multimodal Transport." (1979), 4 *Annals of Air and Space Law* 674-677.
3798

Larose-Aubry, Huguette. "International Organisations: IATA and the Changing Industry Environment." (1976), 1 *Annals of Air and Space Law* 263-268.
3799

Larose-Aubry, Huguette. "International Organizations: IATA Legal Activities." (1977), 2 *Annals of Air and Space Law* 445-452.
3800

Larose-Aubry, Huguette. "International Organizations: Reorganisation and Restructuring of IATA." (1978), 3 *Annals of Air and Space Law* 582-583.
3801

Latchford, Stephen. "Aviation Relations between the United States and Canada Prior to Negotiation of the Air Navigation Arrangement of 1929." (1931), 2 *Journal of Air Law and Commerce* 335-341.
3802

Lee, Roy S.K. *Liability for Nuclear Damage Caused by Flight Instrumentalities.* Montreal, 1964. x, 227 leaves.
3803
Thesis (LL.M.), McGill University, 1964.

Leshem, Moshe. *The International Air Transport Policy of Israel.* Montreal, 1978. xii, 260 leaves.
3804
Thesis (LL.M.), McGill University, 1978. (National Library of Canada. Canadian Theses on Microfiche, No. 38287).

Liang, Irene Ai-Yum. *International Non-Scheduled Air Transport.* Montreal, 1978. iii, 148 leaves.
3805
Thesis (LL.M.), McGill University, 1978.

Lissitzyn, Oliver J. "Freedom of the Air: Scheduled and Non-Scheduled Air Services." *In* McWhinney, Edward, and Bradley, Martin A., eds., *The Freedom of the Air* (Leyden, 1968), pp. 89-105. **3806**

Lowenfeld, Andreas F. "Beyond the Bermuda Agreement." *In* Matte, Nicolas Mateesco, ed., *International Air Transport: Law, Organization and Policies for the Future* (Toronto, 1976), pp. 101-112. **3807**

Loy, Frank E. "Bilateral Air Transport Agreements: Some Problems of Finding a Fair Route Exchange." *In* McWhinney, Edward, and Bradley, Martin A., eds., *The Freedom of the Air* (Leyden, 1968), pp. 174-189. **3808**

Lyon, James T. "Principles, Policies and Practices in International Air Transport: A Canadian View." *In* Matte, Nicolas Mateesco, ed., *International Air Transport: Law, Organization and Policies for the Future* (Toronto, 1976), pp. 33-44. **3809**

MacKenzie, Norman A.M. "Congress on Laws of Aviation." (1926), 4 *Canadian Bar Review* 29-34. **3810**

Magdelénat, Jean-Louis. "Ballons et dirigeables: technologie renaissante et réglementation réadaptée." (1979), 4 *Annals of Air and Space Law* 171-186. **3811**

Magdelénat, Jean-Louis. "Le fret aérien." (1976), 1 *Annals of Air and Space Law* 97-108. **3812**

Magdelénat, Jean-Louis. *Le fret aérien: contribution du droit aérien au développement du transport aérien de marchandises.* Montréal, 1974 (c1975). vi, 188 leaves. **3813**
Thesis (M.A.), McGill University, 1974. (National Library of Canada. Canadian Theses on Microfiche, No. 23139).

Magdelénat, Jean-Louis. *Le fret aérien: réglementation, responsabilités.* Toronto: Carswell; Paris: A. Pedone, 1979. xi, 214 p. **3814**
At head of title: Institute and Centre of Air and Space Law.
Reviews: Isabella H.Ph. Diederiks-Verschoor in (1979), 4 *Air Law* 245; Peter P.C. Haanappel in (1979), 4 *Annals of Air and Space Law* 703; Nicolas Mateesco Matte in (1979), 17 *Canadian Yearbook of International Law* 436-439; Jean Pineau in (1979-80), 14 *Revue Juridique Thémis* 141-142; Emmanuel du Pontavice in (1977), 31 *Revue Française de Droit Aérien* 218.

Magdelénat, Jean-Louis. "Le transport aérien en 1977: espoirs d'éclaircies dans un ciel nuageux." (1977), 2 *Annals of Air and Space Law* 151-162. **3815**

Magdelénat, Jean-Louis. "Le transport par air des matières dangereuses et la nouvelle annexe 18 de la convention de Chicago." (1981), 6 *Annals of Air and Space Law* 75-88. **3816**

Malabard, Jean. "L'essor mondial des transports aériens." (1952-53), 28 *Actualité Économique* 243-262. **3817**

Mankiewicz, René H. "À propos d'une convention unique sur la responsabilité en droit aérien." (1976), 57 *International Law Association, Report of Conference* 115-118. **3818**

Mankiewicz, René H. "Air Law Conventions and the New States." (1963), 29 *Journal of Air Law and Commerce* 52-64. **3819**

Mankiewicz, René H. "La convention de Tokyo et l'escale en territoire étranger." (1965), 28 *Revue Générale de l'Air et de l'Espace* 247-252. **3820**

Mankiewicz, René H. "Interprétation et application de l'article 77 de la convention de Chicago; travaux du Comité juridique et décision du Conseil." (1969), 23 *Revue Française de Droit Aérien* 355-368. **3821**

Mankiewicz, René H. "Notes sur l'utilité d'un recueil international des décisions judiciaires intéressant l'aviation civile internationale." (1949), 9 *Revue du Barreau* 226-240. **3822**

Mankiewicz, René H. "Les nouveaux états et les conventions de droit aérien." (1961), 7 *Annuaire Français de Droit International* 752-760. **3823**

Mankiewicz, René H. "Le projet de convention relative à l'abordage aérien élaboré par le Comité juridique de l'O.A.C.I. en 1964." (1965), 19 *Revue Française de Droit Aérien* 34-105. **3824**

Mapelli, Enrique. "Point de vue sur la pratique de l'overbooking." (1979), 4 *Annals of Air and Space Law* 213-232. **3825**

Mapelli, Enrique. "Le transport aérien des handicapés." (1980), 5 *Annals of Air and Space Law* 171-188. **3826**

Martinelli, Jean-Claude. *Les troubles de voisinage en matière aéronautique.* Montréal, 1970. iii, 24, 6 leaves. **3827**
Thesis (LL.M.), McGill University, 1970. (National Library of Canada. Canadian Theses on Microfilm, No. 7294).

Masse, Barthélémy. "L'aviation commerciale." (1939-40), 15/2 *Actualité Économique* 318-330. **3828**

Matte, Nicolas Mateesco. "La convention de Rome vingt-cinq ans après." (1976), 3 *Annuaire de Droit Maritime et Aérien* 335-364. **3829**

Matte, Nicolas Mateesco. *Droit aérien-aéronautique (évolution - nouvelle orientation).* Paris: A. Pedone, 1954. 312 p. **3830**
Second edition published in 1964 under title: *Traité de droit aérien-aéronautique (évolution - problèmes spatiaux).*
Reviews: André-J. Clermont in (1954-55), 5 *Thémis* 61-62; Edward Mroz in (1955), 59 *Revue Générale de Droit International Public* 289-290.

Matte, Nicolas Mateesco, ed. *International Air Transport: Law, Organization and Policies for the Future / Le transport aérien international: droit, organisation et principes directeurs pour l'avenir.* Montreal: Institute of Air and Space Law, McGill University, 1977. xi, 172 p. **3831**
Proceedings of the Institute of Air and Space Law 25th Anniversary Conference, held November 17-19, 1976, in the Moot Court Room, Faculty of Law, McGill University, Montreal. Distributed Toronto: Carswell; Paris: A. Pedone. Contains sixteen papers listed separately.
Reviews: Edward McWhinney in (1978), 72 *American Journal of Law* 443-444; Aleksander Tobolewski in (1977), 2 *Annals of Air and Space Law* 480-481.

Matte, Nicolas Mateesco. "Les services aériens réguliers et non réguliers dans le système de Chicago." (1980), 5 *Annuaire de Droit Maritime et Aérien* 355-383.
3832

Matte, Nicolas Mateesco. *Traité de droit aérien-aéronautique (évolution - problèmes spatiaux).* 2. éd. Paris: A. Pedone, 1964. 1021 p. **3833**
First edition published in 1954 under title: *Droit aérien-aéronautique (évolution - nouvelle orientation).*

Reviews: DeForest Billyou in (1964), 30 *Journal of Air Law and Commerce* 221-222; C. John Colombos in (1965), 41 *International Affairs* 515-516; Isabella H.Ph. Diederiks-Verschoor in (1965), 12 *Netherlands International Law Review* 78; J. Frowein in (1965), 25 *Zeitschrift für Ausländisches Öffentliches Recht und Völkerrecht* 383; Euthymène Georgiades in (1964), 18 *Revue Française de Droit Aérien* 252-254; Arnold W.G. Kean in (1965-66), 41 *British Year Book of International Law* 477; Paul de La Pradelle in (1964), 27 *Revue Générale de l'Air et de l'Espace* 211; Eugène Pépin in (1968), 95 *Journal du Droit International* 217; Michel Pourcelet in (1964), 24 *Revue du Barreau* 416-418; A. Beatty Rosevear in (1964), 2 *Canadian Yearbook of International Law* 325-328; Charles Rousseau in (1964), 68 *Revue Générale de Droit International Public* 578-579; Miguel Sáenz Sagaseta de Ilùrdoz in (1965), *Revista Española de Derecho Internacional* 273-274; Ivan A. Vlasic in (1965), 59 *American Journal of International Law* 680-682.

McKim, Anson C. "World Order in Air Transport." (1946-47), 2 *International Journal* 226-236. **3834**

McMaster, Glen F. "The Draft Convention on Aerial Collisions." (1965), *Canadian Bar Association, Papers* 25-29. **3835**

McNairn, Colin H. "Aeronautics and the Constitution." (1971), 49 *Canadian Bar Review* 411-445. **3836**

McPherson, Ian E. *The Participation of Canada in International Aviation Agreements.* Montreal, 1955. 165 leaves. **3837**
Thesis (LL.M.), McGill University, 1955.

McPherson, Ian E. "The Rome Convention 1952." (1955), *Canadian Bar Association, Papers,* 13 p. **3838**

Miller, Anthony John. *International Carriage of Cargo by Air.* Montreal, 1972. viii, 223 leaves. **3839**
Thesis (LL.M.), McGill University, 1972. (National Library of Canada. Canadian Theses on Microfilm, No. 11941).

Monlaü, Michel B. "Le transport aérien en Afrique noire francophone et les accords bilatéraux franco-africains." (1976), 1 *Annals of Air and Space Law* 133-149. **3840**

Moursi, Fouad Kamel. *Conflict in the Competence and Jurisdiction of Courts of Different States to Deal with Acts and Occurrences on Board Aircraft.* Montreal, 1955. v, 395 leaves. **3841**
Thesis (LL.M.), McGill University, 1955.

Nesgos, Peter D. "International Organizations: ILA." (1982), 7 *Annals of Air and Space Law* 516-527. **3842**

Nicholson, T.A.C. "Report on Draft Convention on Aerial Collisions." (1961), *Canadian Bar Association, Papers* 81-106. **3843**
Includes the text of the draft convention as Appendix A (pp. 97-106).

Noel, Roderick Aldwin David. *A Survey of Accident Investigation in International Air Law.* Montreal, 1967. 256 leaves. **3844**
Thesis (LL.M.), McGill University, 1967. (National Library of Canada. Canadian Theses on Microfilm, No. 1386).

Odubayo, Wilberforce O. *Legal Regulation of Civil Aviation in Commonwealth Africa: A Comparative Study.* Montreal, 1973. xviii, 357 leaves, map. **3845**
Thesis (D.C.L.), McGill University, 1973. (National Library of Canada. Canadian Theses on Microfilm, No. 15951).

Paterson, Alastair R. "Carriage by Air." (1964-65), 13 *Chitty's Law Journal* 10-12, 46-50, 82-86, 111-114.   **3846**

Paterson, Alastair R. "An Outline of the Law on Carriage by Air." (1954), 32 *Canadian Bar Review* 982-993.   **3847**

Pépin, Eugène. "La Conférence de Paris de 1910 ou le premier essai de réglementer l'aviation internationale." (1978), 3 *Annals of Air and Space Law* 185-206.   **3848**

Pépin, Eugène. "Development of the National Legislation on Aviation since the Chicago Convention." (1957), 24 *Journal of Air Law and Commerce* 1-23.   **3849**

Pineau, Jean. "Transport aérien international. De l'art d'éviter l'application d'une législation internationale qui déplait." (1977), 37 *Revue du Barreau* 665-669.   **3850**

Popescu, Dumitra. *Bilateral Air Agreements of Socialist Countries and International Law; a Comparative Study.* Montreal, 1970 (c1971). iv, 189 leaves.   **3851**

Thesis (LL.M.), McGill University, 1970. (National Library of Canada. Canadian Theses on Microfilm, No. 7309).

Pourcelet, Michel. "La responsabilité pour les dommages résultant des vols supersoniques." (1970), 5 *Revue Juridique Thémis* 413-439.   **3852**

Ranadive, Ramesh V. *Inclusive Tours in International Air Transport.* Montreal, 1968 (c1969). ii, 54, xv, iv leaves.   **3853**

Half-title: *Inclusive Tours by Air.* Thesis (LL.M.), McGill University, 1968. (National Library of Canada. Canadian Theses on Microfilm, No. 3203).

Richardson, B.V. "Aeroplane Accident Cases in Canada." (1959), 26 *Insurance Counsel Journal* 544-547.   **3854**

Robert-Andino, Luis Fernando. *The Scheduled and Non-Scheduled International Air Transport Service: A Need for a Definition.* Montreal, 1972 (c1973). (7), 113, (48) leaves.   **3855**

Short title: *The Scheduled and Non-Scheduled Air Transport Services.* Thesis (LL.M.), McGill University, 1973. (National Library of Canada. Canadian Theses on Microfilm, No. 15981).

Romanelli, Gustavo, and Miszerak, Martin A. "Charter Flights and the Role of the Tour Operator." (1978), 3 *Annals of Air and Space Law* 207-217.   **3856**

Rosevear, A. Beatty. "Scheduled International Air Transport: A Canadian Analysis." *In* McWhinney, Edward, and Bradley, Martin A., eds., *The Freedom of the Air* (Leyden, 1968), pp. 123-139.   **3857**

Saba, John E. "Aircraft Crashworthiness and the Manufacturer's Tort Liability in the United States." (1982), 7 *Annals of Air and Space Law* 171-211.   **3858**

Saleh, Samir. *Collision entre aéronefs.* Montréal, 1955. 156 leaves.   **3859**

Thesis (LL.M.), McGill University, 1955.

Saljooqi, Hamid S. *Air Transport Regulation; an Analytical Approach with Reference to Selected Countries Including Afghanistan.* Montreal, 1967. x, 298 leaves.   **3860**

Thesis (LL.M.), McGill University, 1967. (National Library of Canada. Canadian Theses on Microfilm, No. 1410).

Sampaio de Lacerda, J.C. "The Intermodal Transport Contract." (1977), 2 *Annals of Air and Space Law* 163-180. **3861**

Sand, Peter H. *Choice of Law in Contracts of International Carriage by Air.* Montreal, 1962. 173 leaves. **3862**
Thesis (LL.M.), McGill University, 1962.

Sand, Peter H. "Legislation Relating to Air Accident Investigation: International and Comparative Legal Problems." (1964), *Canadian Bar Association, Papers* 27-34. **3863**

Sand, Peter H.; Pratt, Geoffrey N.; and Lyon, James T. *An Historical Survey of the Law of Flight.* Montreal: Institute of Air and Space Law, McGill University, 1961. 74 p. (McGill University. Institute of Air and Space Law. Publication, No. 7) **3864**

Seldon, Zena Aronoff. *The Economic Implication of Alternative Air Transport Regulatory Practices: A Canada-United States Comparison.* Winnipeg, 1978. xiv, 571 leaves. **3865**
Thesis (Ph.D.), University of Manitoba, 1979. (National Library of Canada. Canadian Theses on Microfiche, No. 40047).

Sprokkreeff, Hans Pieter. *The Regulation of Capacity in International Air Transport.* Montreal, 1976 (c1977). viii, 188 leaves. **3866**
Thesis (LL.M.), McGill University, 1976. (National Library of Canada. Canadian Theses on Microfiche, No. 31892).

Sundberg, Jacob. "Air Chartering: The Scandinavian Contribution." (1979), 4 *Annals of Air and Space Law* 323-347. **3867**

Swan, John Harold. *Liability for the Acts of Agents and Servants in International Air Law.* Montreal, 1954. vii, 330 leaves. **3868**
Thesis (LL.M.), McGill University, 1954.

Taylor, Claude. "Towards New Policies for the Airline Industry." (1981), 6 *Annals of Air and Space Law* 219-222. **3869**

Thomka-Gazdik, Julian G. *Analysis of Certain Aspects of the Law of Contracts Relating to International Carriage of Goods by Air.* Montreal, 1949. 267 leaves. Thesis (M.C.L.), McGill University, 1949. **3870**

Thomka-Gazdik, Julian G. "Are Inclusive Tour Charters Scheduled or Non-Scheduled Services?" *In* McWhinney, Edward, and Bradley, Martin A., eds., *The Freedom of the Air* (Leyden, 1968), pp. 106-122. **3871**

Thomka-Gazdik, Julian G. "Multilaterism in Civil Aviation." (1979), 4 *Air Law* 130-136. **3872**

Thomka-Gazdik, Julian G. "Questions Relating to Hire, Charter and Interchange of Aircraft in Connection with the Chicago and Warsaw Conventions." (1957), *Canadian Bar Association, Papers* 251-265. **3873**

Tobolewski, Aleksander. "The Berlin Agreement." (1977), 2 *Annals of Air and Space Law* 211-216. **3874**

Toepper, Anton. *The Single Forum Method and the Unification of International Private Air Law: Article 20 of the Rome Convention, 1952.* Montreal, 1955. 233 leaves. **3875**
Thesis (LL.M.), McGill University, 1955.

Troncoso, Francisco M. "The Concorde Litigation: Catch 22 Breaks the Sound Barrier." (1977), 2 *Annals of Air and Space Law* 217-231. **3876**

Tsai, Shaopan. *The Legal Status of Passenger Ticket for International Carriage by Air.* Montreal, 1968 (c1969). iii, 92 leaves. **3877**
Thesis (LL.M.), McGill University, 1968. (National Library of Canada. Canadian Theses on Microfilm, No. 2938).

Vellas, Pierre. "Le développement des transports aériens en Afrique." (1981), 6 *Annals of Air and Space Law* 223-233. **3878**

Verploeg, Elias Alexander G. *The Road Towards a European Common Air Market.* Montreal, 1963. 323, 17 leaves. **3879**
Thesis (LL.M.), McGill University, 1963.

Videla Escalada, Federico. "Réflexions sur la condition juridique du constructeur d'aéronefs et ses responsabilités." (1978), 3 *Annals of Air and Space Law* 287-322. **3880**

Vlasic, Ivan A. *The Grant of Passage and Exercise of Commercial Rights in International Air Transport.* Montreal, 1955. 280 leaves. **3881**
Thesis (LL.M.), McGill University, 1955.

Vlasic, Ivan A., and Bradley, Martin A. *The Public International Law of Air Transport: Materials and Documents.* Montreal: McGill University, 1974. 2 vols. (xii, 994 p.) **3882**
Prepared for the use of students attending the Institute of Air and Space Law.

Wassenbergh, H.A. "Aspect of the Exchange of International Air Transportation Rights." (1981), 6 *Annals of Air and Space Law* 235-255. **3883**

Wassenbergh, H.A. "Bilateralism Ad Absurdum in International Air Transportation?" *In* Matte, Nicolas Mateesco, ed., *International Air Transport: Law, Organization and Policies for the Future* (Toronto, 1976), pp. 127-132. **3884**

Wassenbergh, H.A. "Liberal Bilateral Air Agreements between the U.S. and Europe and Their Impact on Latin America." (1979), 4 *Annals of Air and Space Law* 367-383. **3885**

Weber, Ludwig. "Air Transport in the Common Market and the Public Air Transport Enterprises." (1980), 5 *Annals of Air and Space Law* 283-305. **3886**

Weber, Ludwig. "The Application of European Community Law to Air Transport." (1977), 2 *Annals of Air and Space Law* 233-252. **3887**

Weber, Ludwig. "Les éléments de la coopération dans le cadre de la Commission européenne de l'aviation civile." (1977), 31 *Revue Française de Droit Aérien* 388-412. **3888**

Weber, Ludwig. *European Integration and Air Transport.* Montreal, 1976 (c1977). xiii, 228 leaves. **3889**
Thesis (LL.M.), McGill University, 1976. (National Library of Canada. Canadian Theses on Microfiche, No. 31917).

Weber, Ludwig. "International Organizations: CEAC/ECAC." (1981), 6 *Annals of Air and Space Law* 542-555. **3890**

Weber, Ludwig. "International Organizations: The European Civil Aviation Conference - Activities and Orientation 1976/77." (1977), 2 *Annals of Air and Space Law* 461-464. **3891**

Weber, Ludwig. "International Organizations: The European Civil Aviation Conference (ECAC)." (1978), 3 *Annals of Air and Space Law* 593-597. **3892**

Weber, Ludwig. "International Organizations: The European Civil Aviation Conference (ECAC); Its Work During 1978-1980." (1980), 5 *Annals of Air and Space Law* 649-654. **3893**

Weber, Ludwig. "International Organizations: The European Communities." (1980), 5 *Annals of Air and Space Law* 646-648. **3894**

Weber, Ludwig. "International Organizations: The European Communities." (1981), 6 *Annals of Air and Space Law* 556-574. **3895**

Weber, Ludwig. "Laker Airways v. the Ten Governments of the EEC: Comments on a Pending Case." (1981), 6 *Annals of Air and Space Law* 257-276. **3896**

Wijesinha, Samson Sena. *Legal Status of the Annexes to the Chicago Convention.* Montreal, 1960. viii, 273 leaves. **3897**
Thesis (LL.M.), McGill University, 1960.

Wijk, Aart van. "International Organizations: IFALPA - 32nd Annual Conference, Brighton, England, 17th to 22nd March, 1977." (1977), 2 *Annals of Air and Space Law* 452-461. **3898**

Wijk, Aart van. "International Organizations: IFALPA - 33rd Annual Conference." (1978), 3 *Annals of Air and Space Law* 584-593. **3899**

Wijk, Aart van. "International Organizations: IFALPA - 34th Annual Conference." (1979), 4 *Annals of Air and Space Law* 661-674. **3900**

Wijk, Aart van. "International Organizations: IFALPA - 35th Annual Conference." (1980), 5 *Annals of Air and Space Law* 633-642. **3901**

Wijk, Aart van. "International Organizations: IFALPA - 36th Annual Conference." (1981), 6 *Annals of Air and Space Law* 516-537. **3902**

Wijk, Aart van. "International Organizations: IFALPA - 37th Annual Conference." (1982), 7 *Annals of Air and Space Law* 476-499 **3903**

Wijk, Aart van. "International Organizations: The Legal Study Group of IFALPA, 1969-1976." (1976), 1 *Annals of Air and Space Law* 269-271. **3904**

Winnipeg Air Law Committee. "Current Air Law Problems." (1956), *Canadian Bar Association, Papers* 222-243. **3905**

2. AIR CARRIER'S LIABILITY (WARSAW CONVENTION, ETC.)

Aberkane, Abès. *La mise en cause de la responsabilité illimitée du transporteur aérien.* Montréal, 1970. 140 leaves. **3906**
Thesis (LL.M.), McGill University, 1971. (National Library of Canada. Canadian Theses on Microfilm, No. 9664).

Bailey, Edwin O. *Air Carrier Liability for Nuclear Damage Occuring During the Carriage of the Source of Nuclear Energy: A Comparison of the O.E.C.D., I.A.E.A., and the I.A.N.E.C. Draft Conventions.* Montreal, 1968. ii, 57 leaves. **3907**
Thesis (LL.M.), McGill University, 1968. (National Library of Canada. Canadian Theses on Microfilm, No. 2962).

Bailey, Edwin O. "Air Carrier Liability for Nuclear Risks, under Paris and Vienna Conventions." (1967), *Canadian Bar Association, Papers* 1-7. **3908**

Balachandran, Ponniah. *Vicarious Liability in Air Law*. Montreal, 1955. 261 leaves. **3909**
Thesis (LL.M.), McGill University, 1955.

Bédard, Charles. "Le système de Varsovie: complexités, flexibilité." (1977), 2 *Annals of Air and Space Law* 3-14. **3910**

Bloomfield, Louis M. "La convention de Varsovie dans une optique canadienne." (1961), 11 *Thémis* 7-25. **3911**

Bloomfield, Louis M. "La convention de Varsovie dans une optique canadienne." (1974), 9 *Revue Juridique Thémis* 91-106. **3912**

Blumenthal, Mitchell. *The Cause of Action Provisions of Article 17 of the Warsaw Convention and the Attendant Problems of Conflict of Laws and Federal Jurisdiction in the United States*. Montreal, 1979. v, 231 leaves. **3913**
Thesis (LL.M.), McGill University, 1979. (National Library of Canada. Canadian Theses on Microfiche, No. 47307).

Böckstiegel, Karl-Heinz. "Some Recent Efforts for a Fundamental Reconsideration of the International Aviation Liability System." (1980), 5 *Annals of Air and Space Law* 17-36. **3914**

Chauveau, Paul. "Responsabilité du transporteur aérien et compétence juridictionnelle." (1978), 3 *Annals of Air and Space Law* 19-23. **3915**

Cheng, Bin. "La convention de Varsovie fête son cinquantième anniversaire: comment s'annonce l'avenir?" (1979), 4 *Annals of Air and Space Law* 11-27. **3916**

Cheng, Bin. "A Reply to Charges of Having Inter Alia Misused the Term Absolute Liability in Relation to the 1966 Montreal Inter-Carrier Agreement in my Plea for an Integrated System of Aviation Liability." (1981), 6 *Annals of Air and Space Law* 3-13. **3917**
See also a reply by Mircea Mateesco-Matte published in (1982), 7 *Annals of Air and Space Law* 103-126.

Cheng, Bin. "Wilful Misconduct: From Warsaw to The Hague and from Brussels to Paris." (1977), 2 *Annals of Air and Space Law* 55-102. **3918**

Chevrette, François. "La responsabilité du transporteur aérien et la Constitution." (1981), 26 *McGill Law Journal* 607-613. **3919**

Colas, Émile. "La responsabilité du transporteur aérien pour retard dans la livraison d'un colis." (1981), 6 *Annals of Air and Space Law* 15-30. **3920**

Cooper, John Cobb. "Canada and the Warsaw Convention." (1953), 13 *Revue du Barreau* 68-76. **3921**

Corrigan, John M. "The Right of the Air Carrier to Refuse Carriage." (1978), 3 *Annals of Air and Space Law* 25-40. **3922**

Diederiks-Verschoor, Isabella H.Ph. "Observations on the Registration of Deaths and Missing Persons Resulting from Aircraft Accidents." (1978), 3 *Annals of Air and Space Law* 41-49. **3923**

Diederiks-Verschoor, Isabella H.Ph. "Observations sur la déclaration de valeur." (1980), 5 *Annals of Air and Space Law* 37-49. **3924**

Drion, Huibert. *Limitation of Liabilities in International Air Law.* Montreal, 1954. xxiii, 389 leaves. **3925**
Thesis (LL.M.), McGill University, 1954. Also published, The Hague, Nijhoff.

Elashiv, Arlazar. *Article 28(1) of the Warsaw Convention.* Montreal, 1972. iv, 94 leaves. **3926**
Thesis (LL.M.), McGill University, 1972. (National Library of Canada. Canadian Theses on Microfilm, No. 11805).

FitzGerald, Gerald F. "Aviation - Liabilities Rules in the International Carriage of Passengers, Luggage or Goods by Aircraft - Warsaw Convention - The Carriage by Air Act, 1939. (Comment)." (1948), 26 *Canadian Bar Review* 861-867. **3927**

FitzGerald, Gerald F. "Current Developments in the Revision of Rules Governing the Liability of the Aircraft in the Respect of the International Carriage of Passengers by Air." (1968), 6 *Canadian Yearbook of International Law* 188-211. **3928**

FitzGerald, Gerald F. "The Development of New Liability Rules Governing International Carriage by Air." (1952), 5 *University of New Brunswick Law Journal* 13-20 (No. 2) **3929**

FitzGerald, Gerald F. "The Four Montreal Protocols to Amend the Warsaw Convention Regime Governing International Carriage by Air." (1976), 42 *Journal of Air Law and Commerce* 273-350. **3930**
The International Conference on Air Law under the auspices of I.C.A.O., met at Montreal September 3-25, 1975. The conference adopted 4 protocols (Nos. 1-4), pertaining to the Warsaw Convention of October 12, 1929 (CTS 1947/15).

FitzGerald, Gerald F. "The Guatemala City Protocol to Amend the Warsaw Convention." (1971), 9 *Canadian Yearbook of International Law* 217-251. **3931**

FitzGerald, Gerald F. "Liability Rules in the International Carriage of Passengers by Air and the Notice of Denunciation of the Warsaw Convention by the United States of America." (1966), 4 *Canadian Yearbook of International Law* 194-215. **3932**

FitzGerald, Gerald F. "The Revision of the Warsaw Convention." (1970), 8 *Canadian Yearbook of International Law* 284-306. **3933**

FitzGerald, Gerald F. "The Warsaw Convention as Amended by the Montreal Convention on International Air Law (1975)." (1976), 1 *Annals of Air and Space Law* 49-62. **3934**

Gruszczynski, Alfred J. *Warsaw System of Limited Liability in the Seventies (Passenger Provisions).* Montreal, 1978. viii, 185 leaves. **3935**
Thesis (LL.M.), McGill University, 1978. (National Library of Canada. Canadian Theses on Microfiche, No. 39681).

Guerreri, Giuseppe. *American Jurisprudence on the Warsaw Convention.* Montreal: Institute of Air and Space Law, McGill University, 1960. 72 p. (McGill University. Institute of Air and Space Law. Publication, No. 6) **3936**
Thesis, McGill University. Also published in part under title: "Wilful Misconduct in the Warsaw Convention; a Stumbling Block?," in (1960), 6 *McGill Law Journal* 267-276. Review: Oliver J. Lissitzyn in (1961), 54 *American Journal of International Law* 922.

Guerreri, Giuseppe. "Wilful Misconduct in the Warsaw Convention: A Stumbling Block?" (1959-60), 6 *McGill Law Journal* 267-276. **3937**

Haanappel, Peter P.C. "L'affaire *Marier* v. *Air Canada* à la lumière de l'article 24, alinéa 2, de la convention de Varsovie." (1981), 26 *McGill Law Journal* 590-606. **3938**

Haanappel, Peter P.C. "The Right to Sue in Death Cases under the Warsaw Convention." (1981), 6 *Air Law* 66-78. **3939**

Hadjis, Dimitris. *Liability Limitations in the Carriage of Passengers and Goods by Air and Sea.* Montreal, 1958. 167 leaves. **3940**
Thesis (LL.M.), McGill University, 1958.

Hesse, Nicky E. *The Aircraft Operator's Liability in International Conventions.* Montreal, 1953. 408 leaves. **3941**
Thesis (LL.M.), McGill University, 1953.

Hjalsted, Finn. *The Air Carrier's Liability in Cases of Unknown Cause of Damage in International Air Law.* Montreal, 1960. xii, 154 leaves. **3942**
Thesis (LL.M.), McGill University, 1959. Reprinted in (1960), 27 *Journal of Air Law and Commerce* 1-28, 119-149.

Irwin, Clare J. "Passenger Liability Limits in International and Domestic Air Carriage." (1962), *Canadian Bar Association, Papers* 16-41. **3943**

Kose, Yasuyuki. *Liability for Death or Personal Injury under the Guatemala City Protocol.* Montreal, 1973. (10), 195 leaves. **3944**
Short title: *Liability under the Guatemala City Protocol.* Thesis (LL.M.), McGill University, 1973. (National Library of Canada. Canadian Theses on Microfiche, No. 18274).

Lafleur, Gérard. *The Law of Aviation Insurance: Fundamentals.* Montreal, 1971 (c1972). 110, (46) leaves. **3945**
Thesis (LL.M.), McGill University, 1971. (National Library of Canada. Canadian Theses on Microfilm, No. 11876).

Lureau, Daniel. *Exonération et limitation de responsabilité du transporteur aérien en droit international et en droit comparé.* Montréal, 1959. xi, 414 leaves.
Thesis (LL.M.), McGill University, 1959. **3946**

MacBrayne, Sheila F. "Draft Protocol to Amend the Warsaw Convention (1929) - International Carriage by Air." (1955-56), 2 *McGill Law Journal* 67-68. **3947**

MacDonald, Elliott B. "New Liability Basis for International Air Carriage." (1966), *Canadian Bar Association, Papers* 53-58. **3948**

Mankiewicz, René H. "Air Transport Liability: Present and Future Trends." (1969), 3 *Journal of World Trade Law* 32-48. **3949**

Mankiewicz, René H. "De l'application au Québec, de la convention de Varsovie et du protocole de La Haye." (1974), 28 *Revue Française de Droit Aérien* 61-78. Commentaires sur des décisions de jurisprudence canadienne. **3950**

Mankiewicz, René H. "L'application de la convention de Varsovie dans certains pays de l'Europe et de l'Amérique du Nord." (1975), 10 *European Transport Law* 276-324. **3951**

Mankiewicz, René H. "The Application of Article 17 of the Warsaw Convention to

Mental Suffering not Related to Physical Injury." (1979), 4 *Annals of Air and Space Law* 187-211. **3952**

Mankiewicz, René H. "Les applications nationales de la convention de Varsovie." *In* International Congress of Comparative Law, 9th, Tehran, 1974, *Rapports généraux* (Bruxelles, 1977), pp. 521-569. **3953**

Mankiewicz, René H. "Charter and Interchange of Aircraft and the Warsaw Convention: A Study of the Problems Arising from the National Application of Conventions for the Unification of Private Law." (1961), 10 *International and Comparative Law Quarterly* 707-725. **3954**

Mankiewicz, René H. "Conflits entre la convention de Varsovie et le protocole de La Haye." (1956), *Revue Générale de l'Air* 239-246. **3955**

Mankiewicz, René H. "La convention de Varsovie devant la Constitution des États-Unis d'Amérique." (1969), 23 *Revue Française de Droit Aérien* 256-260. **3956**

Sub-title: "Jugement de la Cour de Circuit de Cook County, Illinois du 7 novembre 1968 dans l'affaire *Burdell* contre *Canadian Pacific Airlines*."

Mankiewicz, René H. "La convention de Varsovie et le droit comparé." (1969), 23 *Revue Française de Droit Aérien* 136-150. **3957**

Sub-title: "Interprétation de l'article 8(i) de l'annexe au *Carriage by Air Act, 1932*, correspondant à l'article 8(i) de la convention de Varsovie.- Recours au texte authentique français de la convention et aux lois étrangères.- La convention de Varsovie primant 'la loi du contrat.' "

Mankiewicz, René H. "Difficulties with the Montreal Agreement and the Future of the Air Carrier's Liability." (1968), 7 *Diritto Aereo* 353-374. **3958**

Mankiewicz, René H. "A Galaxy of Unified Laws Will Replace the Uniform Regime Created in 1929 in Warsaw or The Death-Blow to the Uniform Regime of Liability in International Carriage by Air." (1975-76), 1 *Air Law* 157-160. **3959**

Mankiewicz, René H. "L'irrégularité des titres de transport et la responsabilité du transporteur aérien international." (1972), 3 *Revue de Droit, Université de Sherbrooke* 171-181. **3960**

Mankiewicz, René H. "The Judicial Diversification of Uniform Private Law Conventions: The Warsaw Convention's Days in Court." (1972), 21 *International and Comparative Law Quarterly* 718-757. **3961**

Mankiewicz, René H. *The Liability Regime of the International Air Carrier: A Commentary on the Present Warsaw System*. Deventer: Kluwer, 1981. xxvii, 259 p. **3962**

Reviews: Arnold W.G. Kean in (1982), 31 *International and Comparative Law Quarterly* 591-592; Jean-Louis Magdelénat in (1982), 7 *Annals of Air and Space Law* 618-619; H.A. Wassenbergh in (1982), 29 *Netherlands International Law Review* 136-138; Aart van Wijk in (1981), 6 *Air Law* 265-266.

Mankiewicz, René H. "Modification de la 'clause-or' de la convention de Varsovie de 1929 et des protocoles d'amendement." (1975), 21 *Annuaire Français de Droit International* 784-791. **3963**

Mankiewicz, René H. "The 1971 Protocol of Guatemala City to Further Amend

the 1929 Warsaw Convention." (1972), 38 *Journal of Air Law and Commerce* 519-545. **3964**
The protocol of Guatemala City, signed on March 8, 1971, further amends the Warsaw Convention for the Unification of Certain Rules Relating to International Carriage by Air of October 12, 1929 (CTS 1947/15).

Mankiewicz, René H. "Post-scriptum dans l'affaire *Burdell* contre *Canadian Pacific Airlines."* (1971), 25 *Revue Française de Droit Aérien* 198. **3965**

Mankiewicz, René H. "Pourquoi les États-Unis d'Amérique n'ont pas ratifié le protocole de La Haye." (1967), 30 *Revue Générale de l'Air et de l'Espace* 349-359. **3966**

Mankiewicz, René H. "Le protocole de Guatemala du 8 mars 1971 portant modifications de la convention de Varsovie." (1972), 26 *Revue Française de Droit Aérien* 15-27. **3967**

Mankiewicz, René H. "Protocole de La Haye de 1955 amendant la convention de Varsovie de 1929." (1956), 16 *Revue du Barreau* 253-264. **3968**

Mankiewicz, René H. "Le sort de la convention de Varsovie en droit écrit et en common law." In *Mélanges en l'honneur de Paul Roubier* (Paris, 1961), tome 2, pp. 105-148. **3969**

Mankiewicz, René H. "Le statut de l'arrangement de Montréal (mai 1966) et la décision du Civil Aeronautics Board du 13 mai 1966 concernant la responsabilité de certains transporteurs aériens à l'égard de leurs passagers." (1967), 21 *Revue Française de Droit Aérien* 384-413. **3970**

Mankiewicz, René H. "Vers la refonte de la convention de Varsovie et la révision de la convention de Rome?" (1976), 11 *European Transport Law* 854-861. **3971**

Mankiewicz, René H. "The Warsaw Convention." (1971), 2 *Revue de Droit, Université de Sherbrooke* 163-206. **3972**

Mankiewicz, René H. "Warsaw Convention: The 1971 Protocol of Guatemala City." (1972), 20 *American Journal of Comparative Law* 335-342. **3973**

Mapelli, Enrique. "Air Carriers' Liability in Cases of Delay." (1976), 1 *Annals of Air and Space Law* 109-131. **3974**

Margalioth, Eliahu. *A New Liability System for the International Air Carrier.* Montreal, 1968 (c1969). 149 leaves. **3975**
Thesis (LL.M.), McGill University, 1968. (National Library of Canada. Canadian Theses on Microfilm, No. 2857).

Martin, Peter. "Fifty Years of the Warsaw Convention: A Practical Man's Guide." (1979), 4 *Annals of Air and Space Law* 233-252. **3976**

Martin, Peter. "Recent Trends in International Aviation Accident Litigation - A Practical View." (1980), 5 *Annals of Air and Space Law* 189-199. **3977**

Mateesco-Matte, Mircea. "À propos du système varsovien: un mauvais procès pour de faux problèmes." (1982), 7 *Annals of Air and Space Law* 103-126. **3978**
This is a reply to a reply by Bin Cheng published in (1981), 6 *Annals of Air and Space Law* 3-13.

Mateesco-Matte, Mircea. "Should the Warsaw System Be Denounced or 'Integrated?' " (1980), 5 *Annals of Air and Space Law* 201-221. **3979**

Matte, Nicolas Mateesco. "De Varsovie à Montréal, avec escale à La Haye." (1966), 29 *Revue Générale de l'Air et de l'Espace* 348-373. **3980**

Matte, Nicolas Mateesco. "De Varsovie à Montréal, avec escale à La Haye (problèmes posés par l'augmentation de la responsabilité du transporteur aérien international)." (1966), 1 *Revue Juridique Thémis* 165-186. **3981**

Matte, Nicolas Mateesco. "La dernière révision de la convention de Varsovie: les protocoles de Montréal de 1975." (1975), 2 *Annuaire de Droit Maritime et Aérien* 327-342. **3982**

Matte, Nicolas Mateesco. "The Most Recent Revision of the Warsaw Convention: The Montreal Protocols of 1975." (1976), 11 *European Transport Law* 822-841. **3983**

Milde, C. Michael. "International Organisations: Consolidation of the 'Warsaw System.'" (1976), 1 *Annals of Air and Space Law* 257-261. **3984**

Nishigori, Hou. *Passengers' Accident Compensation Schemes under the Warsaw Convention.* Montreal, 1966. 147 leaves. **3985**
Thesis (LL.M.), McGill University, 1966. (National Library of Canada. Canadian Theses on Microfilm, No. 932).

O'Brien, John David. *Passenger Liability of International Air Carriers.* Vancouver, 1974 (c1975). vii, 129 leaves. **3986**
Thesis (M.B.A.), University of British Columbia, 1974. (National Library of Canada. Canadian Theses on Microfiche, No. 22190).

"On the Application of National Law under and in Margin of the Warsaw Convention." (1981), 6 *Air Law* 79-82. **3987**

Ostlund, Raymond E. "Limitation of Liability of a Canadian Carrier by Air." (1952), 2 *Chitty's Law Journal* 10-16. **3988**

Patterson, Walter T., and MacDonald, Elliott B. "Air Carriers Liability." (1960), 3 *Canadian Bar Journal* 297-314. **3989**

Patterson, Walter T., and MacDonald, Elliott B. "Current Air Law Problems - Air Carriers' Liability." (1959), *Canadian Bar Association, Papers* 31-58. **3990**

Pontavice, Emmanuel du. "L'interprétation des conventions internationales portant loi uniforme dans les rapports internationaux. (À propos de la convention relative au transport aérien international signée à Varsovie en 1929)." (1982), 7 *Annals of Air and Space Law* 3-39. **3991**

Popp, Alfred H.E. "Air Law - Warsaw Convention - International Conference - Recent Developments. (Comment)." (1976), 54 *Canadian Bar Review* 438-449. **3992**

Pourcelet, Michel. "L'accord du 4 mai 1966 sur les limites de responsabilité dans le transport aérien international de passagers." (1966), 29 *Revue Générale de l'Air et de l'Espace* 247-260. **3993**

Pourcelet, Michel. "Les applications nationales de la convention de Varsovie." (1973), 8 *Revue Juridique Thémis* 253-273. **3994**

Pourcelet, Michel. *La responsabilité du transporteur aérien international: de Varsovie (1929) à Guadalajara (1961). Étude critique doctrinale et jurisprudentielle.* Montréal, 1963. 272 leaves. **3995**
Thesis (LL.M.), McGill University, 1963.

Pourcelet, Michel. "La responsabilité illimitée du transporteur aérien dans la convention de Varsovie de 1929 et le protocole de La Haye de 1955." (1963), 23 *Revue du Barreau* 148-165. **3996**

Pourcelet, Michel. *Transport aérien international et responsabilité.* Montréal: Presses de l'Université de Montréal, 1964. xii, 269 p. **3997**
Review: Jean Pineau in (1964), 24 *Revue du Barreau* 414-416.

Pourcelet, Michel. "Transporteur contractuel et transporteur de fait dans la convention de Guadalajara (18 septembre 1961)." (1963), 9 *McGill Law Journal* 317-336. **3998**

Pourcelet, Michel. "Vers une nouvelle limite de responsabilité dans le transport aérien international." (1964), 2 *Canadian Yearbook of International Law* 3-20. **3999**

Rajkhan, Siraj Mohammad. *The General Principles Governing the Liability of International Air Carriers for Damages to Persons and Property.* Montreal, 1972 (c1973). iv, 201 leaves. **4000**
Half-title: *Principles of Air Carrier's Liability Towards Person and Property.* Thesis (LL.M.), McGill University, 1972. (National Library of Canada. Canadian Theses on Microfilm, No. 14537).

Redgwell, J.F. "Why Limit Carrier Liability?" (1965), *Canadian Bar Association, Papers* 39-42. **4001**

Robbins, Charles E. "Jurisdiction under Article 28 of the Warsaw Convention." (1963), 9 *McGill Law Journal* 352-356. **4002**

Rosevear, A. Beatty. "The Future of the Warsaw Convention." (1968), 14 *McGill Law Journal* 161-173. **4003**

Senkiko-Kasara, Pauline. *The Trend from Fault Liability to Strict Liability in Private International Law and Its Relationship to Developments in the Law of Torts.* Montreal, 1978. 224 leaves. **4004**
Thesis (LL.M.), McGill University, 1978.

Sözer, Bülent. "Consolidation of the Warsaw/Hague System." (1979), 25 *McGill Law Journal* 217-235. **4005**

Sukonthapan, Pisawat. *The Liability of the Carrier for Passengers and Baggage in the Warsaw Convention with Particular Stress on Articles 17 and 18.* Montreal, 1977 (c1978). ix, 230 leaves. **4006**
Half-title: *Article 17 of the Warsaw Convention.* Thesis (LL.M.), McGill University, 1977. (National Library of Canada. Canadian Theses on Microfiche, No. 36021).

Thomka-Gazdik, Julian G. "Comments on the Tokyo Draft Convention Dealing with Certain Aspects of Carriers' Liability in International Carriage." (1958), *Canadian Bar Association, Papers* 1-18. **4007**

Thomka-Gazdik, Julian G. "Observations on the Draft Protocol to Amend the Warsaw Convention for the Unification of Certain Rules Relating to International Carriage by Air, (1929)." (1955), *Canadian Bar Association, Papers,* 48, 10 p. **4008**

Tobolewski, Aleksander. "Against Limitation of Liability: A Radical Proposal." (1978), 3 *Annals of Air and Space Law* 261-267. **4009**

Tobolewski, Aleksander. *The Evolution of the Provisions of the Warsaw Convention Relating to the Carriage of Cargo.* Montreal, 1976 (c1977). vi, 153 leaves. **4010**
Short title: *The Warsaw Convention: Evolution of the Cargo Provisions.* Thesis (LL.M.), McGill University, 1976. (National Library of Canada. Canadian Theses on Microfiche, No. 31899).

Tobolewski, Aleksander. "Limits of Liability in the Present Economic Situation." (1980), *Lloyd's Maritime and Commercial Law Quarterly* 47-54. **4011**

Travis, Samuel L. *Uniformity Has Its Limits: Article 3 of the Warsaw Convention as an Exercise in Comparative United States and Canadian Law.* Montreal, 1971 (c1972). ix, 289 leaves. **4012**
Half-title: *Warsaw's Article 3 in Comparative U.S. and Canadian Law.* Thesis (LL.M.), McGill University, 1972. (National Library of Canada. Canadian Theses on Microfilm, No. 12063).

Tsai, Shaopan. *The Legal Status of Passenger Ticket for International Carriage by Air.* Montreal, 1968 (c1969). iii, 92 leaves. **4013**
Thesis (LL.M.), McGill University, 1968. (National Library of Canada. Canadian Theses on Microfilm, No. 2938).

Villeneuve, Jacques G. de. "Compétence juridictionnelle et *lex fori* dans la convention de Varsovie." (1961-62), 8 *McGill Law Journal* 284-299. **4014**

Wojcik, Tadeusz L. *La période de transport dans ses relations avec la responsabilité du transporteur de personnes.* Montréal, 1957. 116 leaves. **4015**
Thesis (LL.M.), McGill University, 1957.

3. NAVIGATION AND AIR TRAFFIC CONTROL

"Air Navigation in Canadian-American Diplomacy." (1937-38), 28 *Round Table* 595-603. **4016**

Bogolasky, José. *Government Regulation of Aircraft and Air Navigation Facilities in Latin America.* Montreal, 1976 (c1977). xi, 344 leaves. **4017**
Half-title: *Aircraft and Air Navigation Facilities in Latin America.* Thesis (LL.M.), McGill University, 1976. (National Library of Canada. Canadian Theses on Microfiche, No. 31876).

Guillaume, Gilbert. "La responsabilité des services de la circulation aérienne en droit français." (1978), 3 *Annals of Air and Space Law* 133-141. **4018**

Huner, Jan. *The Responsibility of States for the Provision of Air Traffic Control Service: the Eurocontrol Experiment.* Montreal, 1978. vii, 122 leaves. **4019**
Thesis (LL.M.), McGill University, 1978.

Jaworski, Adam. "International Route Air Navigation Facilities and Services - Its Financial Aspects from a Canadian Point of View." (1959), 26 *Journal of Air Law and Commerce* 137-157. **4020**

Karpishka, Roman B. "Recording Procedures in Aircraft Security Registration System." (1967), *Canadian Bar Association, Papers* 9-29. **4021**

Kos-Rabcewicz-Zubkowski, Ludwik. "Le règlement des différends internationaux relatifs à la navigation aérienne." (1948), 2 *Revue Française de Droit Aérien* 340-396. **4022**

See also thesis, Université de Paris, 1948. 70 p.

Kreindler, Lee S. "Safety of Flight in the Subsonic and Supersonic Air Transport Systems: Passengers' Expectations." *In* Matte, Nicolas Mateesco, ed., *International Air Transport: Law, Organization and Policies for the Future* (Toronto, 1976), pp. 135-139. **4023**

Larsen, Paul B. *The Regulation of Air Traffic Control Liability by International Convention.* Montreal, 1965. 252 leaves. **4024**

Thesis (LL.M.), McGill University, 1965.

Mankiewicz, René H. "Le rôle de l'O.A.C.I. comme administrateur des services de la navigation aérienne." (1954), 8 *Revue Française de Droit Aérien* 223-236. **4025**

McPherson, Ian E. "Attitude of the Airlines: The Regime of Law." *In* Matte, Nicolas Mateesco, ed., *International Air Transport: Law, Organization and Policies for the Future* (Toronto, 1976), pp. 149-157. **4026**

Pandya, Rajnikant. *Joint Support Arrangements for Air Navigation Facilities in International Civil Aviation.* Montreal, 1961. 186 leaves. **4027**

Thesis (LL.M.), McGill University, 1961.

Richard, Ghislaine. "The DC-10 Chicago Crash and the Legality of SFAR 40." (1981), 6 *Annals of Air and Space Law* 195-218. **4028**

Roper, Albert. "L'unification des réglementations relatives à la navigation aérienne." (1951-52), 2 *Thémis* 189-194. **4029**

Rowell, F.N.A. "Obstructions to Navigable Air Space." (1957), *Canadian Bar Association, Papers* 286-306. **4030**

Turcat, André. "Sécurité du vol dans le système de transport supersonique: le point de vue d'un pilote d'essais." *In* Matte, Nicolas Mateesco, ed., *International Air Transport: Law, Organization and Policies for the Future* (Toronto, 1976), pp. 145-147. **4031**

Vallejo Sàenz, Arturo. *The Central American Air Navigation Services Corporation (COCESNA).* Montreal, 1978. xii, 154 leaves. **4032**

Thesis (LL.M.), McGill University, 1978. (National Library of Canada. Canadian Theses on Microfiche, No. 39822).

Weber, Ludwig. "The Eurocontrol Route Charges Litigation Before the Court of Justice of the European Communities." (1978), 3 *Annals of Air and Space Law* 355-369. **4033**

Wijk, Aart van. "Thirteen Aviation Safety Theses." *In* Matte, Nicolas Mateesco, ed., *International Air Transport: Law, Organization and Policies for the Future* (Toronto, 1976), pp. 141-144. **4034**

4. LEGAL STATUS OF AIRCRAFT

(a) CIVILIAN AIRCRAFT

Bahary, Alfred. *Le droit de suite sur les aéronefs en droit québécois.* Montréal, 1969. 112 leaves. **4035**
Thesis (LL.M.), McGill University, 1969. (National Library of Canada. Canadian Theses on Microfilm, No. 4799).

Cheng, Bin. "Nationality of Aircraft Operated by Joint or International Agencies." (1966), *Yearbook of Air and Space Law* 5-31. **4036**

Damiano, Piercarlo. *An Outline of Responsibilities of the Aircraft Commander in Italian and International Law.* Montreal, 1974 (c1975). iv, 195 leaves. **4037**
Half-title: *Responsibilities of the Aircraft Commander.* Thesis (LL.M.), McGill University, 1974. (National Library of Canada. Canadian Theses on Microfiche, No. 23053).

De Boer, Gerrit B. *Nationality and Interchange of Aircraft.* Montreal, 1969 (c1970). ii, 118 leaves. **4038**
Thesis (LL.M.), McGill University, 1970. (National Library of Canada. Canadian Theses on Microfilm, No. 6380).

Fenston, John, and DeSaussure, Hamilton. "Conflict in the Competence and Jurisdiction of Courts of Different States to Deal with Crimes Committed on Board Aircraft and the Persons Involved Therein." (1952-55), 1 *McGill Law Journal* 66-89. **4039**

FitzGerald, Gerald F. "Convention on International Civil Aviation: Lease, Charter and Interchange of Aircraft in International Operations." (1975-76), 1 *Air Law* 20-24. **4040**

FitzGerald, Gerald F. "The Development of International Rules concerning Offences and Certain Other Acts Committed on Board Aircraft." (1963), 1 *Canadian Yearbook of International Law* 230-251. **4041**

FitzGerald, Gerald F. "The Lease, Charter and Interchange of Aircraft in International Operations: Amendments to the Chicago and Rome Conventions." (1977), 2 *Annals of Air and Space Law* 103-137. **4042**

FitzGerald, Gerald F. "The Lease, Charter and Interchange of Aircraft in International Operations - Article 84 bis of the Chicago Convention on International Civil Aviation." (1981), 6 *Annals of Air and Space Law* 49-65. **4043**

FitzGerald, Gerald F. "Nationality and Registration of Aircraft Operated by International Operating Agencies and Article 77 of the Convention on International Civil Aviation, 1944." (1967), 5 *Canadian Yearbook of International Law* 193-216. **4044**

FitzGerald, Gerald F. "Offences and Certain Other Acts Committed on Board Aircraft: The Tokyo Convention of 1963." (1964), 2 *Canadian Yearbook of International Law* 191-204. **4045**
Refers to the convention signed at Tokyo, September 14, 1963 (CTS 1970/5).

Fortier, Jean-Marc. *Real Rights in Aircraft: An International Comparative Study.* Montreal, 1980. 390 frames. **4046**

Thesis (LL.M.), McGill University, 1980. (National Library of Canada. Canadian Theses on Microfiche, No. 50441).

Freitas, Jorge Alberto de Sousa. *Jurisdiction over Events Aboard an Aircraft.* Montreal, 1962. 162 leaves. **4047**
Thesis (LL.M.), McGill University, 1962.

Gardner, Daniel L. *Supersonic Aircraft in International and National Legal Order.* Montreal, c1978. vii, 154 leaves. **4048**
Thesis (LL.M.), McGill University, 1977. (National Library of Canada. Canadian Theses on Microfiche, No. 35716).

Goreish, Ishaq R. *The Problem of Registration and Nationality of Aircraft of International Operating Agencies and the I.C.A.O. Council's Resolution on the Problem.* Montreal, 1970. xii, 205 leaves. **4049**
Thesis (LL.M.), McGill University, 1970. (National Library of Canada. Canadian Theses on Microfilm, No. 6392).

Guerreri, Giuseppe. *The Status of the Aircraft Commander in Italian and International Law.* Montreal, 1961. 158 leaves. **4050**
Thesis (LL.M.), McGill University, 1961.

Hermoso, Justino. *Jurisdiction over Acts and Occurrences on Board an Aircraft.* Montreal, 1955. 184 leaves. **4051**
Thesis (LL.M.), McGill University, 1955.

Kean, Arnold W.G. "Nationality and Interchange of Aircraft." *In* McWhinney, Edward, and Bradley, Martin A., eds., *The Freedom of the Air* (Leyden, 1968), pp. 190-207. **4052**

Keenan, John T. *The Legal Status of the Canadian Aircraft Commander: The Maintenance of Law and Order on Board Aircraft.* Montreal: Canadian Air Line Pilots Association, 1973. 24 p. **4053**

Magdelénat, Jean-Louis. "Negotiating an Aircraft Purchase Contract." (1980), 5 *Annals of Air and Space Law* 155-170. **4054**

Magdelénat, Jean-Louis. "Négociation d'un contrat d'achat d'aéronef." (1980), 5 *Annuaire de Droit Maritime et Aérien* 413-423. **4055**

Mankiewicz, René H. "Aéronefs internationaux." (1962), 8 *Annuaire Français de Droit International* 685-717. **4056**

Mankiewicz, René H. "Aircraft Operated by International Operating Agencies." (1965), 31 *Journal of Air Law and Commerce* 304-310. **4057**

Mankiewicz, René H. "International Civil Aviation Organization: Interpretation and Implementation of Article 77 of the Chicago Convention: Nationality and Registration of Aircraft Operated by International Agencies." (1968), 34 *Journal of Air Law and Commerce* 83-91. **4058**

Mankiewicz, René H. "Some Aspects of Civil Law Regarding Nuisance and Damage Caused by Aircraft." (1958), 25 *Journal of Air Law and Commerce* 44-54. **4059**

Matte, Nicolas Mateesco. "La convention de Genève relative à la reconnaissance internationale des droits sur l'aéronef, trente ans après." (1979), 4 *Annuaire de Droit Maritime et Aérien* 349-384. **4060**

Matte, Nicolas Mateesco. *The International Legal Status of the Aircraft Commander / Le statut juridique international du commandant d'aéronef.* Distributed Toronto: Carswell, and Paris: A. Pedone, 1975. 119 p. **4061**
Parallel texts in English and French. Includes draft convention on the legal status of the aircraft commander.
Reviews: Isabella H.Ph. Diederiks-Verschoor in (1976), 23 *Netherlands International Law Review* 221-222; Alona E. Evans in (1976), 42 *Journal of Air Law and Commerce* 497-499; Euthymène Georgiades in (1976), 30 *Revue Française de Droit Aérien* 155; Kay Hailbronner in (1977), 37 *Zeitschrift für Ausländisches Öffentliches Recht und Völkerrecht* 337-338; Wybo P. Heere in (1975-76), 1 *Air Law* 144; Jean-Louis Magdelénat in (1976), 1 *Annals of Air and Space Law* 281-282; Jean-Louis Magdelénat in (1976), 14 *Canadian Yearbook of International Law* 412-413; William E. O'Connor in (1977), 71 *American Journal of International Law* 576.

Matte, Nicolas Mateesco. "Le statut juridique international du commandant d'aéronef." (1974), 1 *Annuaire de Droit Maritime et Aérien* 207-245. **4062**

Nemeth, John. *The Nationality of Aircraft.* Montreal, 1953. ii, 111 leaves. **4063**
Thesis (LL.M.), McGill University, 1953.

Nowak, Tadeusz Cieplak. *Real Rights in Aircraft and Vessels.* Montreal, 1955. 181 leaves. **4064**
Thesis (LL.M.), McGill University, 1955.

Razanamparany, Voahangy Vaonindrina. *Les droits réels affectant l'aéronef en droit civil.* Montréal, 1979. x, 186 leaves. **4065**
Thesis (LL.M.), McGill University, 1979. (National Library of Canada. Canadian Theses on Microfiche, No. 47425).

Richardson, Jack E. "Nationality and Registration of Aircraft Operated by International Agencies." *In* McWhinney, Edward, and Bradley, Martin A., eds., *The Freedom of the Air* (Leyden, 1968), pp. 208-225. **4066**

Ritchie, Marguerite E. *Crimes Aboard Aircraft.* Montreal, 1958. 277 leaves. **4067**
Thesis (LL.M.), McGill University, 1958.

Rosevear, A. Beatty. "Crimes Committed on Board an Aircraft in Flight Outside Canada." (1956), *Canadian Bar Association, Papers* 214-221. **4068**

Saba, John E. "Aircraft Crashworthiness and the Manufacturer's Tort Liability in the United States." (1982), 7 *Annals of Air and Space Law* 171-211. **4069**

Sirag-Eldin, Yahya. *Aircraft: Nationality and Cooperative Arrangements.* Montreal, 1977. xiv, 223 leaves. **4070**
Thesis (LL.M.), McGill University, 1977.

Thorne, E.S. "Anticipated Problems in Interpretation and Application of 'Foreign Aircraft Third Party Damage Act.'" (1960), *Canadian Bar Association, Papers* 111-121. **4071**

Troncoso, Francisco M., and Feldman, Arlene Butler. "Wake Turbulence and the Jumbo Jets: Whose Responsibility, Pilot or Controller?" (1978), 3 *Annals of Air and Space Law* 269-285. **4072**

(b) MILITARY AIRCRAFT

See also *"Air and Space Warfare" (p. 451).*

Peng, Ming-Min. *Le statut juridique de l'aéronef militaire.* The Hague: M. Nijhoff, 1957. 129 p. **4073**
First issued as a thesis (LL.M.), McGill University, 1953.

Rippon, Clive L. *The Legal Status of Military Air Transport.* Montreal, 1957. xvi, 224 leaves. **4074**
Thesis (LL.M.), McGill University, 1957.

Thaher, Abu Kasim. *International Law and the Legal Status of Military Aircraft in Peacetime.* Montreal, 1969. 173 leaves. **4075**
Thesis (LL.M.), McGill University, 1969. (National Library of Canada. Canadian Theses on Microfilm, No. 4162).

Ward, Donald William S. *The Law of Military Aircraft in War and Peace.* Montreal, 1970 (c1971). iii, 99 leaves. **4076**
Thesis (LL.M.), McGill University, 1970. (National Library of Canada. Canadian Theses on Microfilm, No. 7326).

5. AIRPORTS

Baccelli, Guido Rinaldi. *La collaboration internationale en matière aéroportuaire.* Préface de Giuseppe Fassina. Montréal: McGill University, Institute and Centre of Air and Space Law, 1979. xxiii, 150 p. **4077**
Published version of the author's thesis (LL.M.), McGill University, 1976.
Review: Wybo P. Heere in (1980), 5 *Air Law* 63-64.

Baccelli, Guido Rinaldi. *La collaboration internationale en matière d'aéroports.* Montréal, 1976 (c1977). 186 leaves. **4078**
Thesis (LL.M.), McGill University, 1976. (National Library of Canada. Canadian Theses on Microfiche, No. 31703). Also published by McGill University, Institute and Centre of Air and Space Law, 1979.

Baccelli, Guido Rinaldi. "L'entreprise aéroportuaire: son rôle dans l'aviation civile, ses perspectives dans la collaboration internationale." (1978), 3 *Annals of Air and Space Law* 3-18. **4079**

Corrigan, John M. *Legal Aspects of Airport Operations in Canada.* Montreal, 1978. xi, 189 leaves. **4080**
Thesis (LL.M.), McGill University, 1978. (National Library of Canada. Canadian Theses on Microfiche, No. 39643).

Dupuis, Lionel-Alain. "Mirabel: vers le parachèvement du scénario." (1981), 6 *Annals of Air and Space Law* 31-47. **4081**

Fujita, Katsutoshi. "Tokyo's New Narita Airport: An Illusion." (1978), 3 *Annals of Air and Space Law* 121-132. **4082**

Paquette, Richard. "Étude sur les compétences constitutionnelles en matière d'aéronautique et d'aménagement aéro-portuaire au Canada." (1979), 57 *Canadian Bar Review* 281-300. **4083**

Pontavice, Emmanuel du. "Le bruit aux abords des aérodromes dans la jurisprudence et la législation françaises récentes." (1981), 6 *Annals of Air and Space Law* 115-146. **4084**

Roy, Jean-Denis. *Les conséquences juridiques de l'implantation et de la gestion par l'état de l'aéroport international de Mirabel.* Montréal, 1979. 139 frames. **4085**
Thesis (L.L.M.), McGill University, 1979. (National Library of Canada. Canadian Theses on Microfiche, No. 50552).

Schwenk, Walter. "Problems of Airports in the Vicinity of Foreign States." (1978), 3 *Annals of Air and Space Law* 225-235. **4086**

Smith, James J. "Considerations in Local Administration of Airports in Canada." (1978), 3 *Annals of Air and Space Law* 237-260. **4087**

Smith, James J. "Considerations in Setting Airport User Charges in Canada." (1976), 1 *Annals of Air and Space Law* 151-179. **4088**

Varty, David L. "The Re-Organization of Airport Administration in Canada." (1979), 4 *Annals of Air and Space Law* 359-365. **4089**

D. National Air Law

1. CANADA

Canada. Civil Aeronautics Directorate. *Air Regulations and Aeronautics Act.* 7th ed. Ottawa: Supply and Services Canada, 1980. 89 p. **4090**
Kept up to date with amendments. Issued by Transport Canada, Civil Aeronautics Directorate.

Canada. Transport Commission. *Handbook of Air Transport Legislation / Manuel de législation sur le transport aérien.* Ottawa: Canadian Transport Commission, 1979. 1 vol. (loose-leaf) **4091**
Kept up to date by loose-leaf amendments.

Chevrette, François. "La responsabilité du transporteur aérien et la Constitution." (1981), 26 *McGill Law Journal* 607-613. **4092**

FitzGerald, Gerald F. "Notes on the Development of Canadian Air Law." (1947), 1 *University of New Brunswick Law Journal* 12-15 (No. 1) **4093**
Includes "Annex - Canadian Cases on Air Law" (p. 15).

Haanappel, Peter P.C. "Concentration de transporteurs aériens régionaux au Canada." (1979), 4 *Annals of Air and Space Law* 151-156. **4094**

Hubscher, Frank Frederick. *Aviation Law in Canada.* Montreal, 1953. 118 leaves. Thesis (LL.M.), McGill University, 1953. **4095**

Juvet, David C. *The Economic Regulation of Civil Aviation in Canada.* Montreal, 1973 (c1974). 169 leaves. **4096**
Thesis (LL.M.), McGill University, 1973. (National Library of Canada. Canadian Theses on Microfiche, No. 18261).

Laforet, Joseph. *An Analysis of the Effect of the Canadian Federal Structure on Domestic Unit-Toll Air Transportation Policy.* Kingston, 1978. v, 134 leaves. **4097**

Thesis (M.A.), Queen's University, 1979. (National Library of Canada. Canadian Theses on Microfiche, No. 39514).

Lane, Eric M., and Garrow, D. Bruce. "Canadian Procedural Law in Aviation Litigation." (1981), 46 *Journal of Air Law and Commerce* 295-328. **4098**

Legal, Economic and Socio-Political Implications of Canadian Air Transport. Montreal: Centre for Research of Air and Space Law, 1980. ix, 692 p. **4099**

MacKenzie, Norman A.M. "Legislative Control over Aviation in Canada." (1932), 3 *Air Law Review* 407-416. **4100**

Martial, Jean A. *Government Control of Aviation in Canada.* Montreal, 1953. 128 leaves. **4101**

Thesis (LL.M.), McGill University, 1953.

Matte, Nicolas Mateesco. "Les notions de volonté et de liberté dans le droit aérien-aéronautique canadien." (1967), 21 *Revue Française de Droit Aérien* 15-28. **4102**

See also *Livre du centenaire du Code civil* (Montréal, 1970), vol. 2, pp. 253-269.

Matte, Nicolas Mateesco. "Rôle de la volonté et de la liberté comme éléments créateurs d'obligations juridiques dans le droit aérien-aéronautique canadien." (1967), 27 *Revue du Barreau* 520-535. **4103**

Nadeau, G.W. "Comments on the Aeronautics Act." (1956), *Canadian Bar Association, Papers* 206-213. **4104**

Nerbas, Grant H. "National Transportation Act, 1967 and Air Law Problems." (1967), *Canadian Bar Association, Papers* 31-42. **4105**

Nesgos, Peter D. "Aeronautics Law and the Canadian Constitution." (1981), 6 *Annals of Air and Space Law* 89-113. **4106**

Nesgos, Peter D. "A Call for Labour Protective Provisions in Canadian Aviation." (1982), 7 *Annals of Air and Space Law* 127-159. **4107**

Paquette, Richard. "Étude sur les compétences constitutionnelles en matière d'aéronautique et d'aménagement aéro-portuaire au Canada." (1979), 57 *Canadian Bar Review* 281-300. **4108**

Paquette, Richard. *La responsabilité en droit aérien canadien.* Montréal, c1978. 409 leaves. **4109**

Thesis (LL.M.), McGill University, 1977. (National Library of Canada. Canadian Theses on Microfiche, No. 33352).

Paquette, Richard. *La responsabilité en droit aérien canadien.* Montréal: Wilson & Lafleur, c1979. xiv, 246 p. **4110**

Review: Wybo P. Heere in (1981), 6 *Air Law* 121.

Pourcelet, Michel. "Le droit aérien canadien." (1965), 28 *Revue Générale de l'Air et de l'Espace* 253-279. **4111**

Rajotte, Jacques. "Vers une clarification de la juridiction de la Cour fédérale canadienne en matière de responsabilité civile aérienne." (1979), 4 *Annals of Air and Space Law* 275-293. **4112**

Reschenthaler, G.B., and Roberts, Bruce, eds. *Perspectives on Canadian Airline Regulations.* Toronto: Butterworths for the Institute for Research on Public Policy, 1979. xiv, 266 p. **4113**
Includes a summary in French.

Reukema, Barbara. "The *Air Canada Act* - The Reasons for Change." (1981), 6 *Annals of Air and Space Law* 147-194. **4114**

Richard, Ghislaine. "Les critères de commodité et/ou nécessité publiques dans la délivrance d'un permis de service aérien au Canada." (1982), 7 *Annals of Air and Space Law* 161-169. **4115**

Richardson, B.V. "The Canadian Law of Civil Aviation." (1938), 9 *Journal of Air Law and Commerce* 201-219. **4116**

Richardson, B.V. "The Canadian Law of Civil Aviation." (1940), 18 *Canadian Bar Review* 292-302. **4117**

Richardson, B.V. "The Canadian Law of Civil Aviation." (1941), 19 *Canadian Bar Review* 576-585. **4118**

Richardson, B.V. "Canadian Law of Civil Aviation." (1945), 27 *Journal of Comparative Legislation and International Law* 31-45 (3d Ser.) **4119**

Richardson, B.V. "Canadian Law of Civil Aviation 1937-1942." (1942), 13 *Journal of Air Law and Commerce* 195-211. **4120**

Richardson, B.V. "Liability of Aircraft Passenger under Canadian Law." (1939), 10 *Air Law Review* 292-297. **4121**

Rosevear, A. Beatty. "Should Canada Have an Air Code?" (1960), *Canadian Bar Association, Papers* 45-68. **4122**

Roy, Jean-Denis. "La protection de l'aviation civile: l'exemple canadien." (1979), 4 *Annals of Air and Space Law* 295-306. **4123**

Sandell, Harold. *Government Regulation of Air Carriers in Canada.* Montreal, 1976 (c1977). x, 290 leaves. **4124**
Thesis (LL.M.), McGill University, 1976. (National Library of Canada. Canadian Theses on Microfiche, No. 31878).

Varty, David L. *The Law and Practice of Domestic Air Charter Operations in Canada.* Montreal, 1978. vi, 173 leaves. **4125**
Thesis (LL.M.), McGill University, 1978.

Vary, Michel Jacques. *Sources and Problems of Air Law in Canada.* Montreal, 1961. xvii, 327 leaves. **4126**
Thesis (LL.M.), McGill University, 1961.

Williams, Ray, and Wright, Scott. "Some Aspects of the 1959 Amendments to the Canadian Criminal Code Pertaining to Crimes Committed on Aircraft." (1960), *Canadian Bar Association, Papers* 90-110. **4127**

2. OTHER COUNTRIES

Bradley, Martin A. "Licensing of International Air Services in Britain." (1977), 2 *Annals of Air and Space Law* 31-45. **4128**

Dahl, Christen Sverdrup. *Air Traffic Control Liability in Norway and from a Viewpoint of International Unification.* Montreal, c1974. x, 126 leaves. **4129**
Thesis (LL.M.), McGill University, 1973. (National Library of Canada. Canadian Theses on Microfiche, No. 18187).

Gagné, Roland-Yves. "Les agences de voyages et la déréglementation américaine." (1982), 7 *Annals of Air and Space Law* 81-93. **4130**

Gillilland, Whitney. "The Significance of 'Competition' as One of the Regulatory Criteria Applied by the U.S. Civil Aeronautics Board." (1967), *Yearbook of Air and Space Law* 15-34. **4131**

Intravia, L.R. *American Aviation Policy: Capacity, Competition and Regulation.* Montreal, 1977. v, 257 leaves. **4132**
Thesis (LL.M.), McGill University, 1977. (National Library of Canada. Canadian Theses on Microfiche, No. 38257).

Kean, Arnold W.G. "Confidentiality of Civil Aviation Information in the United Kingdom." (1976), 1 *Annals of Air and Space Law* 83-96. **4133**

Langlois, Juan Pablo, and Bogolasky, José. "The Aviation Policy of Chile Air Transport Liberalization." (1981), 6 *Annals of Air and Space Law* 67-73. **4134**

Magdelénat, Jean-Louis. "L'affaire du 'Show Cause Order' du C.A.B. américain." (1980), 34 *Revue Française de Droit Aérien* 250-274. **4135**

Magdelénat, Jean-Louis. "The Story of the Life and Death of the CAB Show Cause Order." (1980), 5 *Air Law* 83-98. **4136**

Margo, Roderick David. *Aviation Insurance in the United Kingdom: Law and Practice.* Montreal, 1979. xv, 480 leaves. **4137**
Thesis (D.C.L.), McGill University, 1979.

Menon, P.K. "Government Control of the Air Transport System in India." (1978), 3 *Annals of Air and Space Law* 163-183. **4138**

Menon, P.K. "Some Aspects of the Civil Aviation Law in the Commonwealth Caribbean-Jamaica." (1979), 4 *Annals of Air and Space Law* 253-273. **4139**

Popescu, Dumitra. "Development of Air Law and Aviation Organization in the Socialist Republic of Roumania." (1980), 5 *Annals of Air and Space Law* 249-281. **4140**

Schwenk, Walter. "Air Law and Aviation Administration in the Federal Republic of Germany." (1977), 2 *Annals of Air and Space Law* 181-197. **4141**

Tolle, Paulo Ernesto. *Air Law in Latin America.* Montreal, 1960. 2 vols. (xviii, 309 v, 201 leaves) **4142**
Thesis (LL.M.), McGill University, 1960.

E. Outer Space

Arnopoulos, Paris J. "The International Politics of the Orbit-Spectrum Issue." (1982), 7 *Annals of Air and Space Law* 215-240. **4143**

Bhatt, S. "Contribution of Aerospace Law to the Evolution of Man and Global Society." (1980), 5 *Annals of Air and Space Law* 309-321. **4144**

Bhatt, S. "An Ecological Approach to Aerospace Law." (1979), 4 *Annals of Air and Space Law* 385-396. **4145**

Binet, Henri T.P. "Canada and Space Law." (1959), 19 *Revue du Barreau* 194-198. **4146**

Binet, Henri T.P. "Sovereignty in Outer Space." (1960), 3 *Canadian Bar Journal* 144-151. **4147**

Bissonnette, Pierre André. "International Co-operation in Outer Space." (1970), 22 *External Affairs* 364-367. **4148**
Intervention delivered by the Canadian delegate to the U.N. Outer Space Committee on September 3, 1970.

Böckstiegel, Karl-Heinz. "Present and Future Regulation of Space Activities by Private Industry." *In Space Activities and Implications: Where from and Where to at the Threshold of the 80's* (Montreal, 1981), pp. 133-149. **4149**

Bourély, Michel. "Les activités de l'Agence spatiale européenne depuis sa création." (1978), 3 *Annals of Air and Space Law* 373-382. **4150**

Bourély, Michel. "Le Canada et l'Agence spatiale européenne." (1979), 4 *Annals of Air and Space Law* 397-411. **4151**

Bourély, Michel. *Contribution des organisations internationales à la formation et au développement du droit de l'espace: rapport soumis au Centre de recherches en droit aérien et spatial.* Montréal: McGill University, Centre for Research of Air and Space Law, 1980. 40, (9) leaves. **4152**

Bourély, Michel. "Le droit de l'espace et les organisations internationales." (1982), 7 *Annals of Air and Space Law* 241-259. **4153**

Bourély, Michel. "Europe and Remote Sensing." *In* Matte, Nicolas Mateesco, and DeSaussure, Hamilton, eds., *Legal Implications of Remote Sensing from Outer Space* (Leiden, 1976), pp. 43-61. **4154**

Bourély, Michel. "L'Europe et l'espace." *In Space Activities and Implications: Where from and Where to at the Threshold of the 80's* (Montreal, 1981), pp. 223-259. **4155**

Bourély, Michel. "La participation du Canada aux programmes de l'Agence spatiale européenne." (1980), 5 *Annals of Air and Space Law* 363-373. **4156**

Caen, Jacques P., and Drouet, Ludovic O. "Les vaisseaux dans l'espace." (1981), 6 *Annals of Air and Space Law* 315-331. **4157**

"Canada's First Space Satellite." (1963), 15 *External Affairs* 12-15. **4158**

Christol, Carl Q. "The Case for a Possible Integrated North-American Landsat

Program." *In* Matte, Nicolas Mateesco, and DeSaussure, Hamilton, eds., *Legal Implications of Remote Sensing from Outer Space* (Leiden, 1976), pp. 131-140.
4159

Christol, Carl Q. "Inventory of Space Activities: Legal Aspects." *In Space Activities and Implications: Where from and Where to at the Threshold of the 80's* (Montreal, 1981), pp. 69-95. **4160**

Christol, Carl Q. "Protection of Space from Environmental Harms." (1979), 4 *Annals of Air and Space Law* 433-458. **4161**

Cocca, Aldo Armando. "Fundamental Principles of Space Law: A Latin-American Viewpoint." *In* McWhinney, Edward, and Bradley, Martin A., eds., *New Frontiers in Space Law* (Leyden, 1969), pp. 61-72. **4162**

Cocca, Aldo Armando. "Remote Sensing of Natural Resources by Means of Space Technology: A Latin American Point of View." *In* Matte, Nicolas Mateesco, and DeSaussure, Hamilton, eds., *Legal Implications of Remote Sensing from Outer Space* (Leiden, 1976), pp. 63-68. **4163**

Cohen, Maxwell, ed. *Law and Politics in Space; Specific and Urgent Problems in the Law of Outer Space.* Montreal: McGill University Press, 1964. 221 p.
4164
Proceedings of the first McGill Conference on the Law of Outer Space, held at the Faculty of Law of McGill University April 12-13, 1963. Sponsored by the Institute of Air and Space Law. Individual papers are listed separately.
Reviews: J.A. Andrews in (1965), 28 *Modern Law Review* 613-614; Giovanni Scarangella Arpino in (1962-66), 7 *Jus Gentium (Rome)* 214-215; David R. Deener in (1965), 59 *American Journal of International Law* 977; Euthymène Georgiades in (1964), 18 *Revue Française de Droit Aérien* 254; Leslie C. Green in (1964), 42 *Canadian Bar Review* 657-661; D.H.N. Johnson in (1964), 13 *International and Comparative Law Quarterly* 1119-1121; Oliver J. Lissitzyn in (1965-66), 16 *University of Toronto Law Journal* 214-216; Brunson MacChesnay in (1964), 10 *McGill Law Journal* 269-270; Eugène Pépin in (1968), 95 *Journal du Droit International* 217; Charles Rousseau in (1964), 68 *Revue Générale de Droit International Public* 580; J.G. Sauveplanne in (1965), 12 *Netherlands International Law Review* 175-176; Juliaan G. Verplaetse in (1964), 24 *Zeitschrift für Ausländisches Öffentliches Recht und Völkerrecht* 762-764; D. Colwyn Williams in (1963-64), 19 *International Journal* 562-563.

Cohen, Maxwell. "Towards a Legal Regime in Space." (1962-65), 1 *Manitoba Law School Journal* 147-154. **4165**

Cooper, John Cobb. *Explorations in Aerospace Law; Selected Essays by John Cobb Cooper, 1946-1966.* Edited by Ivan A. Vlasic. Montreal: McGill University Press, 1968. xx, 480 p. **4166**
Includes a bibliography of aerospace law writings of John Cobb Cooper, 1931-1967 (pp. 459-465).
Reviews: Gerald F. FitzGerald in (1969), 7 *Canadian Yearbook of International Law* 364-366; Ethymène Georgiades in (1968), 22 *Revue Française de Droit Aérien* 479-480; C. Granger in (1969), 47 *Canadian Bar Review* 147-149; Jack E. Richardson in (1967), *Australian Year Book of International Law* 272-285; Joseph W. Samuels in (1968-69), 7 *Alberta Law Review* 165-166; Robert K. Woetzel in (1969), 63 *American Journal of International Law* 371.

Cooper, John Cobb. "Legal Problems of Upper Space." (1956), 23 *Journal of Air Law and Commerce* 308-316. **4167**
Reprinted from (1956), 50 *American Society of International Law, Proceedings* 85-93.

Dalfen, Charles M. "Towards an International Convention on the Registration of Space Objects: The Gestation Process." (1971), 9 *Canadian Yearbook of International Law* 252-268. **4168**

Danielsson, Sune. "An Interdisciplinary Approach in the Regulation by the United Nations of Activities in Outer Space: Some Technical Considerations." *In Space Activities and Implications: Where from and Where to at the Threshold of the 80's* (Montreal, 1981), pp. 99-118. **4169**

Dembling, Paul G. "Commercial Utilization of Space and the Law." (1967), *Yearbook of Air and Space Law* 283-295. **4170**

Dembling, Paul G. "A Liability Convention: Next Step in the Legal Regime for Outer Space Activities." *In* McWhinney, Edward, and Bradley, Martin A., eds., *New Frontiers in Space Law* (Leyden, 1969), pp. 89-102. **4171**

DeSaussure, Hamilton. "An International Right to Reorbit Earth Threatening Satellites." (1978), 3 *Annals of Air and Space Law* 383-394. **4172**

DeSaussure, Hamilton, and Haanappel, Peter P.C. "A Unified Multinational Approach to the Application of Tort and Contract Principles to Outer Space." (1978), 21 *Colloquium on the Law of Outer Space, Proceedings* 138-147.**4173** Also printed in (1978), 6 *Syracuse Journal of International Law and Commerce* 1-15.

Deschênes, Pierre-A. "Le Québec et les satellites de communication au seuil des années '80." *In Space Activities and Implications: Where from and Where to at the Threshold of the 80's* (Montreal, 1981), pp. 179-202. **4174**

Diederiks-Verschoor, Isabella H.Ph. "Global Use and Regulations of Space Activities." *In Space Activities and Implications: Where from and Where to at the Threshold of the 80's* (Montreal, 1981), pp. 151-162. **4175**

Diederiks-Verschoor, Isabella H.Ph. "The Legal Aspects of the Space Shuttle." (1976), 1 *Annals of Air and Space Law* 197-204. **4176**

Diederiks-Verschoor, Isabella H.Ph. "Observations on Remote Sensing Satellites." *In* Matte, Nicolas Mateesco, and DeSaussure, Hamilton, eds., *Legal Implications of Remote Sensing from Outer Space* (Leiden, 1976), pp. 69-74. **4177**

Diederiks-Verschoor, Isabella H.Ph. "Registration of Spacecraft." *In* McWhinney, Edward, and Bradley, Martin A., eds., *New Frontiers in Space Law* (Leyden, 1969), pp. 124-132. **4178**

Doyle, Stephen E. "Remote Sensing by Satellite: Technical and Operational Implications for International Cooperation." *In* Matte, Nicolas Mateesco, and DeSaussure, Hamilton, eds., *Legal Implications of Remote Sensing from Outer Space* (Leiden, 1976), pp. 3-11. **4179**

DuCharme, Edward D.; Bowen, Robert R.; and Irwin, Matthew J.R. "The Genesis of the 1985/87 ITU World Administrative Radio Conference on the Use of the Geostationary-Satellite Orbit and the Planning of Space Services Utilizing It." (1982), 7 *Annals of Air and Space Law* 261-282. **4180**

Dupuy, René-Jean. "Les structures et le rôle d'une agence internationale de satellites de contrôle: aspects juridiques." (1981), 6 *Annals of Air and Space Law* 333-343. **4181**

Farand, André. "L'apport du Canada en matière de responsabilité internationale pour les dommages d'origine spatiale: l' 'Affaire du satellite Cosmos 954.' " (1980), 11 *Études Internationales* 467-487. **4182**

Farmer, Margaret E. "International Regime in Outer Space." (1966), 31 *Saskatchewan Bar Review* 32-40. **4183**

Fauteux, Paul. "Radiodiffusion directe par satellites: adieu au consensus?" (1981), 6 *Annals of Air and Space Law* 345-380. **4184**

Fauteux, Paul. "Souveraineté fonctionnelle et consentement préalable: déblocage possible en droit spatial." (1980), 18 *Canadian Yearbook of International Law* 248-266. **4185**

Fenema, Peter van. *The 1972 Convention on International Liability for Damage Caused by Space Objects.* Montreal, 1973 (c1974). (8), 271 leaves. **4186**
Short title: *The 1972 Outer Space Liability Convention.* Thesis (LL.M.), McGill University, 1973. (National Library of Canada. Canadian Theses on Microfiche, No. 18209).

FitzGerald, Gerald F. "The Participation of International Organizations in the Proposed International Agreement on Liability for Damage Caused by Objects Launched into Outer Space." (1965), 3 *Canadian Yearbook of International Law* 265-280. **4187**

Foster, William Fraser. "The Convention on International Liability for Damage Caused by Space Objects." (1972), 10 *Canadian Yearbook of International Law* 137-185. **4188**

Fox, Francis. "Space Policies for the 80's: Keeping Pace with the Technology / La politique spatiale des années 80: au diapason de la technologie. (Closing Address)." In *Space Activities and Implications: Where from and Where to at the Threshold of the 80's* (Montreal, 1981), pp. 353-367. **4189**

Gaggero, Eduardo D., and Ripoll, Roberto Puceiro. "Accord régissant les activités des états sur la lune et les autres corps célestes." (1980), 5 *Annals of Air and Space Law* 449-480. **4190**

Galicki, Zdzislaw Waclaw. *Nationality of Spacecraft and Liability for Space Activities.* Montreal, 1969. 109 leaves. **4191**
Thesis (LL.M.), McGill University, 1969. (National Library of Canada. Canadian Theses on Microfilm, No. 4823).

Galloway, Eilene. "Agreement Governing the Activities of States on the Moon and Other Celestial Bodies." (1980), 5 *Annals of Air and Space Law* 481-508. **4192**

Galloway, Eilene. "Applicability of Space Treaties to Uses of Outer Space." (1976), 1 *Annals of Air and Space Law* 205-212. **4193**

Galloway, Eilene. "The History and Development of Space Law: International Law and United States Law." (1982), 7 *Annals of Air and Space Law* 295-318. **4194**

Galloway, Eilene. "Nuclear Powered Satellites: The U.S.S.R. Cosmos 954 and the Canadian Claim." (1979), 12 *Akron Law Review* 401-415. **4195**

Galloway, Eilene. "Recent Developments in United States Space Policy." (1979), 4 *Annals of Air and Space Law* 483-504. **4196**

Galloway, Eilene. "Remote Sensing from Outer Space: Legal Implications of

Worldwide Utilisation and Dissemination of Data." *In* Matte, Nicolas Mateesco, and DeSaussure, Hamilton, eds., *Legal Implications of Remote Sensing from Outer Space* (Leiden, 1976), pp. 91-104. **4197**

Galloway, Eilene. "The United States Congress and Space Law." (1978), 3 *Annals of Air and Space Law* 395-407. **4198**

Gibson, Roy. "Future Space Activities and Implications: Political Aspects." *In Space Activities and Implications: Where from and Where to at the Threshold of the 80's* (Montreal, 1981), pp. 309-314. **4199**

Goedhuis, Daniel. "The International Law Association and the Development of a Legal Regime of Outer Space." *In* McWhinney, Edward, and Bradley, Martin A., eds., *New Frontiers in Space Law* (Leyden, 1969), pp. 31-45. **4200**

Goedhuis, Daniel. "Some Observations on the Problem of the Definition and/or the Delimitation of Outer Space." (1977), 2 *Annals of Air and Space Law* 287-309. **4201**

Golden, David A. "The Launching Powers and Space Utilization for the Benefit of Mankind - A Canadian Commercial Perspective." *In Space Activities and Implications: Where from and Where to at the Threshold of the 80's* (Montreal, 1981), pp. 165-177. **4202**

Gorove, Stephen. "Implications of International Space Law for Private Enterprise." (1982), 7 *Annals of Air and Space Law* 319-331. **4203**

Gorove, Stephen. "Legal and Economic Implications of Remote Sensing from Outer Space - Focus on Latin America." *In* Matte, Nicolas Mateesco, and DeSaussure, Hamilton; eds., *Legal Implications of Remote Sensing from Outer Space* (Leiden, 1976), pp. 75-84. **4204**

Gorove, Stephen. "Legal Aspects of International Space Flight." (1978), 3 *Annals of Air and Space Law* 409-419. **4205**

Gorove, Stephen. "Solar Power Satellites and the ITU: Some U.S. Policy Options." (1979), 4 *Annals of Air and Space Law* 505-517. **4206**

Gorove, Stephen. "Sovereignty and the Law of Outer Space Re-Examined." (1977), 2 *Annals of Air and Space Law* 311-321. **4207**

Gorove, Stephen. "The Space Shuttle: Some of Its Features and Legal Implications." (1981), 6 *Annals of Air and Space Law* 381-398. **4208**

Gotlieb, Allan E., and Dalfen, Charles M. "International Relations and Outer Space: The Politics of Cooperation." (1969-70), 25 *International Journal* 685-703. **4209**

Granier, Elisabeth Mireille. *L'Agence spatiale européenne: une analyse de l'intégration régionale dans le domaine spatial.* Montréal, 1975. 202 leaves. **4210**
Thesis (LL.M.), McGill University, 1975. (National Library of Canada. Canadian Theses on Microfiche, No. 24330).

Haanappel, Peter P.C. "Airspace, Outer Space and Mesospace." (1976), 19 *Colloquium on the Law of Outer Space, Proceedings* 160-163. **4211**

Haanappel, Peter P.C. "Article II of the Outer Space Treaty and the Status of the Geostationary Orbit." (1978), 21 *Colloquium on the Law of Outer Space, Proceedings* 28-30. **4212**

Haanappel, Peter P.C. "Article XI of the Moon Treaty." (1980), 23 *Colloquium on the Law of Outer Space, Proceedings* 29-33. **4213**

Haanappel, Peter P.C. "Definition of Outer Space and Outer Space Activities." (1977), 20 *Colloquium on the Law of Outer Space, Proceedings* 53-55. **4214**

Haanappel, Peter P.C. "Product Liability in Space Law." (1979), 2 *Houston Journal of International Law* 55-64. **4215**

Haanappel, Peter P.C. "Some Observations on the Crash of Cosmos 954." (1978), 6 *Journal of Space Law* 147-149. **4216**

Haanappel, Peter P.C. "Space Law Colloquium IV: Comments." (1979), 22 *Colloquium on the Law of Outer Space, Proceedings* 305-306. **4217**

Haanappel, Peter P.C. "The Stagnating Development of International Space Law and Its Causes." (1979), 22 *Colloquium on the Law of Outer Space, Proceedings* 149-152. **4218**

Haley, Andrew G. "Space Law - Some Current Problems and Solutions." (1958), *Canadian Bar Association, Papers* 19-37. **4219**

Henein, Jean-Claude. "Notes on the 'Real World' Framework for Space Law as Applied to Remote Sensing." *In* Matte, Nicolas Mateesco, and DeSaussure, Hamilton, eds., *Legal Implications of Remote Sensing from Outer Space* (Leiden, 1976), pp. 141-145. **4220**

Hitt, William R. *A Treaty on Remote Sensing Activities.* Montreal, 1975 (c1976). viii, 177 leaves. **4221**
Thesis (LL.M.), McGill University, 1975. (National Library of Canada. Canadian Theses on Microfiche, No. 27165).

Hosenball, S. Neil. "Free Acquisition and Dissemination of Data through Remote Sensing." *In* Matte, Nicolas Mateesco, and DeSaussure, Hamilton, eds., *Legal Implications of Remote Sensing from Outer Space* (Leiden, 1976), pp. 105-111. **4222**

Hosenball, S. Neil. "United States Space Activities - The Practical Returns from Space for the Benefit of All Mankind." *In Space Activities and Implications: Where from and Where to at the Threshold of the 80's* (Montreal, 1981), pp. 203-208. **4223**

Jacquemin, Georges. "Droit orbital terrestre ou droit spatial cosmique?" (1978), 3 *Annals of Air and Space Law* 421-443. **4224**

Jakhu, Ram S. "The Legal Status of the Geostationary Orbit." (1982), 7 *Annals of Air and Space Law* 333-352. **4225**

Jakhu, Ram S., and Singal, Ramesh. "Satellite Technology and Education." (1981), 6 *Annals of Air and Space Law* 399-404. **4226**

Jankowitsch, Peter. "The U.N.: Framework for a Consensus on Remote Sensing." *In* Matte, Nicolas Mateesco, and DeSaussure, Hamilton, eds., *Legal Implications of Remote Sensing from Outer Space* (Leiden, 1976), pp. 159-166. **4227**

Jasentuliyana, Nandasiri. "International Organizations: UNISPACE '82." (1982), 7 *Annals of Air and Space Law* 510-515. **4228**

Jasentuliyana, Nandasiri. "A Perspective of the Use of Nuclear Power Sources in Outer Space." (1979), 4 *Annals of Air and Space Law* 519-552. **4229**

Jasentuliyana, Nandasiri. "Third-World Perspectives of Space Technology." *In Space Activities and Implications: Where from and Where to at the Threshold of the 80's* (Montreal, 1981), pp. 261-277. **4230**

Johnson, John A. "Pollution and Contamination in Space." *In* Cohen, Maxwell, ed., *Law and Politics in Space* (Montreal, 1964), pp. 37-50. **4231**

Kaplan, Irving E., and Jakhu, Ram S. "Global Climate Space Reflector Systems: Some Legal Issues." (1982), 7 *Annals of Air and Space Law* 353-361. **4232**

Kingstone, H. Courtney. "The Future of the Law of Outer Space." (1960), 38 *Canadian Bar Review* 226-237. **4233**

Kopal, Vladimir. "The Agreement on Rescue of Astronauts and Return of Space Objects." *In* McWhinney, Edward, and Bradley, Martin A., eds., *New Frontiers in Space Law* (Leyden, 1969), pp. 103-123. **4234**

Kopal, Vladimir. "Treaty on Principles Governing the Activities of States in the Exploration and Use of Outer Space, Including the Moon and Other Celestial Bodies." (1966), *Yearbook of Air and Space Law* 463-484. **4235**

Kos-Rabcewicz-Zubkowski, Ludwik. "Los puntos de vista soviéticos sobre el derecho internacional del espacio." (1963), 16 *Boletin del Instituto de Derecho Comparado de Mexico* 597-610 (no. 48) **4236**

Kos-Rabcewicz-Zubkowski, Ludwik. "La notion soviétique du droit international spatial." (1965), 19 *Revue Française de Droit Aérien* 190-200. **4237**

Lachs, Manfred. "The Freedom of the Air. The Relevance of the Developing Law of Outer Space." *In* McWhinney, Edward, and Bradley, Martin A., eds., *The Freedom of the Air* (Leyden, 1968), pp. 246-254. **4238**

Lachs, Manfred. "The Law-Making Process for Outer Space." *In* McWhinney, Edward, and Bradley, Martin A., eds., *New Frontiers in Space Law* (Leyden, 1969), pp. 13-30. **4239**

Lazarev, Marklen I. "Future Space Cities (International Legal Aspects)." (1980), 5 *Annals of Air and Space Law* 529-536. **4240**

Leigh, Monroe. "United States Policy of Collecting and Disseminating Remote Sensing Data." *In* Matte, Nicolas Mateesco, and DeSaussure, Hamilton, eds., *Legal Implications of Remote Sensing from Outer Space* (Leiden, 1976), pp. 147-150. **4241**

Leister, Valnora. *Transfer of Space Application Technology: Legal Implications*. Montreal, c1978. ix, 186 leaves. **4242**
  Thesis (LL.M.), McGill University, 1977. (National Library of Canada. Canadian Theses on Microfiche, No. 35748).

Léger, Brigitte. "La lune: patrimoine commun de l'humanité." (1979), 17 *Canadian Yearbook of International Law* 280-291. **4243**

Logsdon, John M. "The Evolution of the U.S. Space Program: An Inventory of Policy Issues." *In Space Activities and Implications: Where from and Where to at the Threshold of the 80's* (Montreal, 1981), pp. 53-67. **4244**

Logsdon, John M. "International Dimensions of Solar Power Satellites: Collaboration or Competition?" (1980), 5 *Annals of Air and Space Law* 537-547. **4245**

Loriot, François. "Propriété intellectuelle et droit spatial." (1978), 3 *Annals of Air and Space Law* 445-466. **4246**

Loriot, François. "Propriété intellectuelle et droit spatial: la convention 'satellites' de Bruxelles." (1979), 4 *Annals of Air and Space Law* 553-566. **4247**

Lustgarten, Lionel S. *Legal and Organizational Aspects of Remote Sensing of Earth Resources from Outer Space.* Montreal, 1972 (c1973). vii, 198 leaves. **4248**
  Short title: *Law & Organizations for Remote Sensing from Space.* Thesis (LL.M.), McGill University, 1972. (National Library of Canada. Canadian Theses on Microfilm, No. 14500).

Lyon, James T. "Space Vehicles, Satellites, and the Law." (1960-61), 7 *McGill Law Journal* 271-286. **4249**

MacDonald, David. "Space, Communications and the New Information Order." (1980), 9 *Canadian Council on International Law, Proceedings* 57-61. **4250**

Magdelénat, Jean-Louis. "Energie solaire via satellites et la coopération internationale." (1978), 3 *Annals of Air and Space Law* 467-482. **4251**

Magdelénat, Jean-Louis. "Perspectives du droit spatial." (1980), 9 *Canadian Council on International Law, Proceedings* 63-72. **4252**

Magdelénat, Jean-Louis. "Spacecraft Insurance." (1982), 7 *Annals of Air and Space Law* 363-377. **4253**

Malik, Sushma. *Space Law as Inter-Systems Consensus; Contributions of the Third World to Soviet Bloc and Western Approaches to the Emerging Principles of Space Law.* Montreal, 1967 (c1968). 85 leaves. **4254**
  Thesis (LL.M.), McGill University, 1967. (National Library of Canada. Canadian Theses on Microfilm, No. 2197).

Mankiewicz, René H. "De l'ordre juridique dans l'espace extra-aéronautique." (1959), 5 *Annuaire Français de Droit International* 103-160. **4255**

Mankiewicz, René H. "Des problèmes que soulève l'utilisation pacifique de l'espace extra-aéronautique: essai d'une mise au point." (1959), 19 *Revue du Barreau* 384-389. **4256**

Mankiewicz, René H. "L'état des doctrines sur le droit de l'espace extra-aéronautique après le quatrième Colloque sur le droit de l'espace." (1962), 16 *Revue Française de Droit Aérien* 19-42. **4257**
Colloquium held in Washington, October 3 and 4, 1961.

Mankiewicz, René H. "Interpretation of the Treaty on Outer Space." (1968), 11 *Colloquium on the Law of Outer Space, Proceedings* 82-84. **4258**

Mankiewicz, René H. "Interventions with Respect to Permanent Stations on the Moon." (1968), 11 *Colloquium on the Law of Outer Space, Proceedings* 163-165. **4259**

Mankiewicz, René H. "The Legal Status of Space Vehicles." (1968), 53 *International Law Association, Report of Conference* 170-185. **4260**

Mankiewicz, René H. "Notes concernant le régime international de responsabilité pour les dommages causés par des engins spatiaux." (1963), 17 *Revue Française de Droit Aérien* 34-44. **4261**

Mankiewicz, René H. "Questionnaire on the Legal Status of Spacecraft." (1966), 52 *International Law Association, Report of Conference* 215-223. **4262**

Mankiewicz, René H. "The Regulation of Activities in Extra-Aeronautical Space, and Some Related Problems." (1961-62), 8 *McGill Law Journal* 193-211.
4263

Mankiewicz, René H. "Satellites, agents de paix." (1960), 30 *Revue de l'Université d'Ottawa* 95-100. **4264**

Mankiewicz, René H. "Some Thoughts on Law and Public Order in Space." (1964), 2 *Canadian Yearbook of International Law* 258-269. **4265**

Mateesco-Matte, Mircea. "Cosmos 954: pour une 'zone orbitale de sécurité.' " (1978), 3 *Annals of Air and Space Law* 483-509. **4266**

Mateesco-Matte, Mircea. "Des agents très spatiaux: quel régime juridique?: au vingtième anniversaire de l'ère spatiale." (1977), 2 *Annals of Air and Space Law* 351-374. **4267**

Mateesco-Matte, Mircea. "Le droit extra-atmosphérique: *de lege ferenda.*" In *Space Activities and Implications: Where from and Where to at the Threshold of the 80's* (Montreal, 1981), pp. 315-351. **4268**

Mateesco-Matte, Mircea. "Droit spatial ou droit aéro-orbital? Quelques réflexions en marge de l'opération 'Viking.' " (1976), 1 *Annals of Air and Space Law* 213-229. **4269**

Mateesco-Matte, Mircea. "Un *jus communicationis* et un *jus navigationis.*" (1981), 6 *Annals of Air and Space Law* 405-438. **4270**

Matte, Nicolas Mateesco. *Aerospace Law.* London: Sweet & Maxwell; Toronto: Carswell, 1969. 501 p. **4271**

Also published in French under title: *Droit aérospatial* (Paris, A. Pedone, 1969).
Reviews: R.P. Anand in (1970), 12 *Journal of the Indian Law Institute* 712-715; Bozidar Bakotič in (1970), 17 *Jugoslovenska Revija za Medunarodno Pravo* 158-159; Bin Cheng in (1970), 24 *Year Book of World Affairs* 280-281; Carl Q. Christol in (1970), 43 *Southern California Law Review* 383-387; Isabella H.Ph. Diederiks-Verschoor in (1970), 17 *Netherlands International Law Review* 84-85 (in Dutch); L.F.E. Goldie in (1971), 10 *Columbia Journal of Transnational Law* 172-175; C. Granger in (1970), 48 *Canadian Bar Review* 358-361; Robert Reed Gray in (1970), 36 *Journal of Air Law and Commerce* 175-177; D.H.N. Johnson in (1970), 19 *International and Comparative Law Quarterly* 178; Edward G. Lee in (1970), 8 *Canadian Yearbook of International Law* 411-413; C. Michael Milde in (1970), 16 *McGill Law Journal* 183-185; Ivan A. Vlasic in (1971), 65 *American Journal of International Law* 843-844.

Matte, Nicolas Mateesco. *Aerospace Law: From Scientific Exploration to Commercial Utilization.* Distributed Toronto: Carswell, and Paris: A. Pedone, 1977. 354 p. **4272**

Continues: *Aerospace Law* (London, Sweet & Maxwell, 1969). Also published in French under title: *Droit aérospatial: de l'exploration scientifique à l'utilisation commerciale* (Paris, A. Pedone, 1976).
Reviews: Carl Q. Christol in (1978), 24 *McGill Law Journal* 158-160; Stephen Gorove in (1979), 7 *Journal of Space Law* 189-190; Jerzy Rajski in (1977), 2 *Annals of Air and Space Law* 475; Chin-Shih Tang in (1978), 10 *Ottawa Law Review* 224-227.

Matte, Nicolas Mateesco. *Aerospace Law: Telecommunication Satellites.* Toronto:

Butterworths in cooperation with the Institute of Air and Space Law, McGill University, c1982. xxi, 354 p. **4273**
Also published in French under title: *Droit aérospatial: les télécommunications par satellites.*
Review: Ludwik Kos-Rabcewicz-Zubkowski in (1982), 7 *Annals of Air and Space Law* 622.

Matte, Nicolas Mateesco. "The Convention on Registration of Objects Launched into Outer Space." (1976), 1 *Annals of Air and Space Law* 231-241. **4274**

Matte, Nicolas Mateesco. "The Draft Treaty on the Moon, Eight Years Later." (1978), 3 *Annals of Air and Space Law* 511-544. **4275**

Matte, Nicolas Mateesco. *Droit aérospatial.* Paris: A. Pedone, 1969. 607 p. **4276**
Also published in English under title: *Aerospace Law* (London, Sweet & Maxwell, 1969).
Reviews: Euthymène Georgiades in (1970), 24 *Revue Française de Droit Aérien* 120-121; Paul de La Pradelle in (1970), 33 *Revue Générale de l'Air et de l'Espace* 229-231; Hans von Mangoldt in (1970), 30 *Zeitschrift für Ausländisches Öffentliches Recht und Völkerrecht* 561-564; Eugène Pépin in (1972), 99 *Journal du Droit International* 172-173; Alain Pellet in (1969), 15 *Annuaire Français de Droit International* 994-995; Jean Pineau in (1970), 1 *Études Internationales* 86, 84 (no 1); Paul Robitaille in (1970), 30 *Revue du Barreau* 243; Edgar Tomson in (1969), *Internationales Recht und Diplomatie* 283-286.

Matte, Nicolas Mateesco. *Droit aérospatial: de l'exploration scientifique à l'utilisation commerciale.* Paris: A. Pedone, 1976. 436 p. **4277**
Continues: *Droit aérospatial* (Paris, A. Pedone, 1969). Also published in English under title: *Aerospace Law: From Scientific Exploration to Commercial Utilization* (Toronto, Carswell, 1977).
Reviews: Hélène Brassard in (1977-78), 1 *Revue d'Intégration Européenne* 408-409; Isabella H.Ph. Diederiks-Verschoor in (1977), 24 *Netherlands International Law Review* 597; Kay Hailbronner in (1979), 39 *Zeitschrift für Ausländisches Öffentliches Recht und Völkerrecht* 152-153; Marco Marcoff in (1978), 34 *Schweizerisches Jahrbuch für Internationales Recht* 243-246; Charles Rousseau in (1976), 80 *Revue Générale de Droit International Public* 1288; Maurice Tancelin in (1978), 19 *Cahiers de Droit* 279-280; G. Thompson in (1977), 104 *Journal du Droit International* 542-543.

Matte, Nicolas Mateesco. *Droit aérospatial: les télécommunications par satellites.* Paris: A. Pedone, 1982. 472 p. **4278**
Also published in English under title: *Aerospace Law: Telecommunication Satellites.*
Review: Michel Bourély in (1982), 7 *Annals of Air and Space Law* 620-622.

Matte, Nicolas Mateesco. "Institutional Arrangements for Space Activities: An Appraisal." (1981), 6 *Annals of Air and Space Law* 439-459. **4279**

Matte, Nicolas Mateesco. "Institutional Arrangements for Space Activities: An Appraisal." (1981), 24 *Colloquium on the Law of Outer Space, Proceedings* 211-218. **4280**

Matte, Nicolas Mateesco. "Introductory Comments on the Aerospace Medium." (1977), 20 *Colloquium on the Law of Outer Space, Proceedings* 47-52. **4281**

Matte, Nicolas Mateesco. "The Law of the Sea and Outer Space: A Comparative Survey of Specific Issues." (1982), 3 *Ocean Yearbook* 13-37. **4282**

Matte, Nicolas Mateesco. "Limited Aerospace Natural Resources and Their Regulation." (1982), 7 *Annals of Air and Space Law* 379-398. **4283**

Matte, Nicolas Mateesco. "Product Liability of the Manufacturer of Space Objects." (1977), 2 *Annals of Air and Space Law* 375-421. **4284**

Matte, Nicolas Mateesco. "Remote Sensing by Satellites and Aerospace Law." (1976), 19 *Colloquium on the Law of Outer Space, Proceedings* 325-340. **4285**

Matte, Nicolas Mateesco. "Space Policy: Today and Tomorrow: The Vanishing Duopole." (1979), 4 *Annals of Air and Space Law* 567-616. **4286**

Matte, Nicolas Mateesco. *Space Policy and Programmes Today and Tomorrow: The Vanishing Duopole.* Montreal: ICASL, McGill University; Toronto: distributed by Carswell, 1980. xiii, 183 p. **4287**
At head of title: Institute and Centre of Air and Space Law.
Reviews: Hamilton DeSaussure in (1982), 76 *American Journal of International Law* 471; Panos C. Spiliakos in (1980), 1 *Hellenic Review of International Relations* 579-580; Chin-Shih Tang in (1981), 59 *Canadian Bar Review* 619-622.

Matte, Nicolas Mateesco, and DeSaussure, Hamilton, eds. *Legal Implications of Remote Sensing from Outer Space.* Leiden: Sijthoff, 1976. xiv, 197 p. **4288**
Contains twenty-one papers presented at a symposium organized in October 1975 by the Institute of Air and Space Law, McGill University. The papers are listed separately.
Reviews: W. Paul Gormley in (1977-78), 1 *Hastings International and Comparative Law Review* 225-234; V. di Gregorio in (1976), 31 *Comunità Internazionale* 642; Michel Guinchard in (1976), 30 *Revue Française de Droit Aérien* 552; Peter P.C. Haanappel in (1976), 1 *Annals of Air and Space Law* 280-281; Kay Hailbronner in (1977), 37 *Zeitschrift für Ausländisches Öffentliches Recht und Völkerrecht* 338-339; Velon H. Minshew in (1976), 4 *Journal of Space Law* 183-185; Chin-Shih Tang in (1979), 25 *McGill Law Journal* 129-134; Georges Thomson in (1976), 103 *Journal du Droit International* 1015.

Matte, Nicolas Mateesco, and Mateesco-Matte, Mircea, eds. *Telesat, symphonie et la coopération spatiale régionale.* Montréal: Institute of Air and Space Law; Paris: A. Pedone, 1978. viii, 133 p. **4289**
Jointly published with Centre de droit maritime et aérien de l'Université de Nantes.
Reviews: Peter P.C. Haanappel in (1978), 3 *Annals of Air and Space Law* 646-647; Louise Louthood in (1979), 10 *Études Internationales* 867-868; Ludwig Weber in (1980), 40 *Zeitschrift für Ausländisches Öffentliches Recht und Völkerrecht* 666-667.

McDougal, Myres S. "The Prospects for a Regime in Outer Space." *In* Cohen, Maxwell, ed., *Law and Politics in Space* (Montreal, 1964), pp. 105-123. **4290**

McDougal, Myres S., Lasswell, Harold D.; and Vlasic, Ivan A. *Law and Public Order in Space.* New Haven: Yale University Press, 1963. xxvi, 1147 p. **4291**
Reviews: J.A. Andrews in (1965), 28 *Modern Law Review* 613-614; James Milton Brown in (1964-65), 36 *Mississippi Law Journal* 116-120; Charles M. Chaumont in (1964-65), 3 *Columbia Journal of Transnational Law* 271-274; Bin Cheng in (1965-66), 16 *University of Toronto Law Journal* 210-213; Stephen E. Doyle in (1964), 10 *McGill Law Journal* 197-202; J.E.S. Fawcett in (1963), 39 *British Year Book of International Law* 531-532; J.E.S. Fawcett in (1965), 41 *International Affairs* 107-108; D.H.N. Johnson in (1964), 13 *International and Comparative Law Quarterly* 1121-1122; G. Vernon Leopold in (1964-65), 42 *University of Detroit Law Journal* 238-240; J. Noel Lyon in (1964), 42 *Canadian Bar Review* 653-657; Manuel Medina Ortega in (1964), 17 *Revista Española de Derecho Internacional* 289-290; Kenneth L. Penegar in (1964-65), 43 *North Carolina Law Review* 1032-1036; Courtland H. Peterson in (1965-66), 18 *Journal of Legal Education* 115-118; Richard Posner in (1963-64), 77 *Harvard Law Review* 1370-1374; Charles Rousseau in (1964), 68 *Revue Générale de Droit International Public* 761-762; Allison L. Scafuri in (1965), 18 *Vanderbilt Law Review* 863-866; Hans-Jürgen Schlo-

chauer in (1964-65), 12 *Archiv des Völkerrechts* 465-469; Cameron K. Wehringer in (1964-65), 31 *Brooklyn Law Review* 197-200; Robert K. Woetzel in (1967), 61 *American Journal of International Law* 626-629.

McDougal, Myres S.; Lasswell, Harold D.; and Vlasic, Ivan A. "Potential Interactions with Advanced Forms of Non-Earth Life." (1962), 18 *Revue Égyptienne de Droit International* 33-101. **4292**

McWhinney, Edward, and Bradley, Martin A., eds. *New Frontiers in Space Law.* Leyden: A.W. Sijthoff; Dobbs Ferry, N.Y.: Oceana Publications, 1969. 134 p. **4293**

Contains ten working papers, most of them originally presented in a closed gathering of specialists in the emerging Law of Outer Space, held at the Institute of Air and Space Law in Montreal on October 21-22, 1968. Individual essays are listed separately.
Reviews: William E. Butler in (1971), 65 *American Journal of International Law* 234; Alexandre Charles Kiss in (1970), 97 *Journal du Droit International* 1034-1035; Vladimir Kopal in (1970), 14 *Casopis pro Mezinarodni Pravo* 373; Carl E.B. McKenry in (1970), 36 *Journal of Air Law and Commerce* 375-376; unsigned in (1970), 6 *Annuaire Français de Droit International* 1065.

Meeker, Leonard C. "Observation in Space." *In* Cohen, Maxwell, ed., *Law and Politics in Space* (Montreal, 1964), pp. 75-84. **4294**

Menter, Martin. "The United Nations Contribution Towards an International Agreement on Remote Sensing." *In* Matte, Nicolas Mateesco, and DeSaussure, Hamilton, eds., *Legal Implications of Remote Sensing from Outer Space* (Leiden, 1976), pp. 173-185. **4295**

Morley, Lawrence W. "International Organization for Remote Sensing - A Gordian Knot." (1977), 2 *Annals of Air and Space Law* 423-428. **4296**

Morley, Lawrence W. "Remote Sensing Satellites - What Do They Actually Measure and How Sensitive Is the Information." *In* Matte, Nicolas Mateesco, and DeSaussure, Hamilton, eds., *Legal Implications of Remote Sensing from Outer Space* (Leiden, 1976), pp. 13-18. **4297**

Nesgos, Peter D. "The Proposed International Sea-Bed Authority as a Model for the Future Outer Space International Régime." (1980), 5 *Annals of Air and Space Law* 549-573. **4298**

Niciu, Martian. "Le droit cosmique: un droit de la paix et de la coopération internationale (la doctrine roumaine de droit cosmique)." (1980), 5 *Annals of Air and Space Law* 575-587. **4299**

"Peaceful Uses of Outer Space." (1959), 11 *External Affairs* 220-225. **4300**

"The Peaceful Uses of Outer Space: UN Committee Meeting, March 1962." (1962), 14 *External Affairs* 192-195. **4301**

Pépin, Eugène. "French Proposals with Respect to Remote Sensing of Earth Resources by Satellite." *In* Matte, Nicolas Mateesco, and DeSaussure, Hamilton, eds., *Legal Implications of Remote Sensing from Outer Space* (Leiden, 1976), pp. 85-87. **4302**

Pépin, Eugène. "A Legal Order for Outer Space: The Next Steps." *In* McWhinney, Edward, and Bradley, Martin A., eds., *New Frontiers in Space Law* (Leyden, 1969), pp. 1-7. **4303**

Pépin, Eugène. "Legal Problems Created by the Sputnik." (1957-58), 4 *McGill Law Journal* 66-71. **4304**

Pépin, Eugène. "Les problèmes juridiques de l'espace." (1959-60), 6 *McGill Law Journal* 30-43. **4305**
Also published in (1959), 13 *Revue Française de Droit Aérien* 307-325. Reprinted, Paris, Sirey, 1959. 46 p.

Pépin, Eugène. "Space Penetration." (1958), 52 *American Society of International Law, Proceedings* 229-235. **4306**

Poulantzas, Nicholas M. "Development or Retrogression of International Law in View of Outer Space Activities?" (1965), 8 *Colloquium on the Law of Outer Space, Proceedings* 272-278. **4307**

Poulantzas, Nicholas M. "Development or Retrogression of International Law in View of Outer Space Activities?" (1965), 4 *Diritto Aereo* 151-175. **4308**

Poulantzas, Nicholas M. "Imperium or Dominium (within the Framework of Space Law)." (1962), 15 *Revue Hellénique de Droit International* 95-97. **4309**

Poulantzas, Nicholas M. "International Law in View of Outer Space Activities." (1965), 35 *Annuaire de l'A.A.A.* 171-176. **4310**

Poulantzas, Nicholas M. "Legal Problems Arising Out of Environmental Protection of the Earth." (1971), 14 *Colloquium on the Law of Outer Space, Proceedings* 75-78. **4311**

Poulantzas, Nicholas M. "The Outer Space Treaty of January 27, 1967, a Decisive Step Towards Arms Control, Demilitarization of Outer Space and International Supervision." (1967), 10 *Colloquium on the Law of Outer Space, Proceedings* 209-221. **4312**
Also printed in (1967), 20 *Revue Hellénique de Droit International* 66-83.

Poulantzas, Nicholas M. "The Outer Space Treaty of January 27, 1967 ; and Its Aftermath." (1968), 11 *Colloquium on the Law of Outer Space, Proceedings* 50-56. **4313**

Poulantzas, Nicholas M. "The Problem of 'Peaceful Purposes' Revisited." (1969), 12 *Colloquium on the Law of Outer Space, Proceedings* 270-274. **4314**
Also printed in (1969), 22 *Revue Hellénique de Droit International* 140-144.

Poulantzas, Nicholas M. "Synopsis of Recent Developments in Extra Atmospheric Law and Some Relevant Theoretical Problems." (1964), 7 *Colloquium on the Law of Outer Space, Proceedings* 24-28. **4315**
Also printed in (1964), 17 *Revue Hellénique de Droit International* 97-101.

Poulantzas, Nicholas M. "World Law and Space Law." (1961), 14 *Revue Hellénique de Droit International* 229-231. **4316**

Poulantzas, Nicholas M. "World Peace through the Law of Outer Space." (1963), *World Peace Through Law* 548-549. **4317**
Also printed in (1963), 16 *Revue Hellénique de Droit International* 307-309.

Pourcelet, Michel. "La création de bases spatiales dans l'espace extra-atmosphérique." (1962), 12 *Thémis* 33-45. **4318**

Probst, Samuel E. "Future Space Activities and Implications: The Technical Viewpoint." In *Space Activities and Implications: Where from and Where to at the Threshold of the 80's* (Montreal, 1981), pp. 289-292. **4319**

Reed, Walter Dudley. *The Legal Status of Spacecraft with Reference to Nationality and Regions of Operation.* Montreal, 1964. 112 leaves. **4320**
   Thesis (LL.M.), McGill University, 1964.

Reijnen, G.C.M. "Remote Sensing by Satellites and Legality." *In* Matte, Nicolas Mateesco, and DeSaussure, Hamilton, eds., *Legal Implications of Remote Sensing from Outer Space* (Leiden, 1976), pp. 19-32. **4321**

Reiskind, Jason. "Towards a Responsible Use of Nuclear Power in Outer Space -The Canadian Initiative in the United Nations. (With Preceding Note and Commentary by Maxwell Cohen)." (1981), 6 *Annals of Air and Space Law* 461-474. **4322**

Robinson, George S. *Contamination of Earth's Ecosystem by Extra-Terrestrial Matter; United States Authority to Promulgate and Enforce Quarantine Regulations.* Montreal, 1970 (c1971). vii, 265 leaves. **4323**
   Short title: *Earth Exposure to Alien Matter; Quarantine Law.* Thesis (D.C.L.), McGill University, 1970. (National Library of Canada. Canadian Theses on Microfilm, No. 7313).

Robinson, George S. "For a Worldwide Utilisation and Dissemination of Data Acquired through Remote Sensing." *In* Matte, Nicolas Mateesco, and DeSaussure, Hamilton, eds., *Legal Implications of Remote Sensing from Outer Space* (Leiden, 1976), pp. 113-124. **4324**

Robinson, George S. "Frontier Law at L-5." (1979), 4 *Annals of Air and Space Law* 617-638. **4325**

Robinson, George S. *Jurisprudence for Man and His Alien Sentient Counterpart in Space.* Montreal, 1967 (c1968). iii, 109 leaves. **4326**
   Thesis (LL.M.), McGill University, 1967. (National Library of Canada. Canadian Theses on Microfilm, No. 2232).

Robinson, Marvin. "The United Nations as an International Forum for Developing Consensus." *In* Matte, Nicolas Mateesco, and DeSaussure, Hamilton, eds., *Legal Implications of Remote Sensing from Outer Space* (Leiden, 1976), pp. 187-193. **4327**

Rosevear, A. Beatty. "The Search for Agreement on the Rule of Law in Outer Space." (1961-62), 8 *McGill Law Journal* 29-37. **4328**

Saint-Lager, Olivier de. "L'organisation des activités spatiales françaises: une combinaison dynamique du secteur public et du secteur privé." (1981), 6 *Annals of Air and Space Law* 475-487. **4329**

Saleh, Saleh Tewfik. *The Liability for Damage Caused by Space Activities.* Montreal, 1967 (c1968). vii, 206 leaves. **4330**
   Thesis (LL.M.), McGill University, 1967. (National Library of Canada. Canadian Theses on Microfilm, No. 2241).

Samuelli, Antoine Louis. *La nationalité comme base de juridiction sur les engins spatiaux.* Montréal, 1967 (c1969). i, 104 leaves. **4331**
   Thesis (LL.M.), McGill University, 1967. (National Library of Canada. Canadian Theses on Microfilm, No. 2912).

Schachter, Oscar. "The Prospects for a Regime in Outer Space and International Organization." *In* Cohen, Maxwell, ed., *Law and Politics in Space* (Montreal, 1964), pp. 95-102. **4332**

Schnee, Jerome E. "Inventory of Space Activities (Economic)." *In Space Activities and Implications: Where from and Where to at the Threshold of the 80's* (Montreal, 1981), pp. 35-51. **4333**

Schwartz, Bryan, and Berlin, Mark L. "After the Fall: An Analysis of Canadian Legal Claims for Damage Caused by Cosmos 954." (1982), 27 *McGill Law Journal* 676-720. **4334**

Simon, H. Paul. "Man in Space: Beyond the Reach of the Law?" (1969), 76 *Queen's Quarterly* 252-268, 401-411. **4335**

Sloup, George Paul. "Liability and Insurance Aspects of the Space Transportation System under the New Section 308 of the National Aeronautics and Space Act." (1979), 4 *Annals of Air and Space Law* 639-651. **4336**

Soraghan, Joseph R. "Reconnaissance Satellites: Legal Characterization and Possible Utilization for Peacekeeping." (1967), 13 *McGill Law Journal* 458-493. **4337**

Space Activities and Implications: Where from and Where to at the Threshold of the 80's: Proceedings of the Symposium Held on October 16-17, 1980 / Les activités spatiales et leurs implications: d'où vient-on et où va-t-on à l'aube des années 80: rapports du symposium tenu les 16 et 17 octobre 1980. Montreal: Centre for Research of Air & Space Law, McGill University; Toronto: Carswell; Paris: A. Pedone, 1981. xvi, 367 p. **4338**
Most papers are listed separately.
Review: Martin A. Bradley in (1981), 6 *Annals of Air and Space Law* 655-656.

Stoebner, André W. "Remote Sensing of Earth Resources: Technique and Law." *In* Matte, Nicolas Mateesco, and DeSaussure, Hamilton, eds., *Legal Implications of Remote Sensing from Outer Space* (Leiden, 1976), pp. 33-40. **4339**

Strome, W. Murray. "Remote Sensing from Space in the 1980's." *In Space Activities and Implications: Where from and Where to at the Threshold of the 80's* (Montreal, 1981), pp. 281-287. **4340**

Tamm, John R. *An Analysis and Concept for the Law of Space.* Montreal, 1960. v, 98 leaves. **4341**
Thesis (LL.M.), McGill University, 1960.

Tang, Chin-Shih. "The Boundary Question in Space Law: A Balance Sheet." (1973-74), 6 *Ottawa Law Review* 266-276. **4342**

Tang, Chin-Shih. *The Influence of Publicists on the Development of Space Law.* Montreal, 1967. 163 leaves. **4343**
Thesis (LL.M.), McGill University, 1967. (National Library of Canada. Canadian Theses on Microfilm, No. 1431).

Thomson, Georges. *Régime juridique des activités humaines au regard des corps célestes.* Montréal, 1972 (c1973). xiii, 246 leaves. **4344**
Thesis (LL.M.), McGill University, 1972. (National Library of Canada. Canadian Theses on Microfilm, No. 14582).

"United Nations Committee on the Peaceful Uses of Outer Space." (1971), 23 *External Affairs* 123-124. **4345**

Vencatassin, J.L. "Le champ d'application du droit de l'espace." *In* McWhinney, Edward, and Bradley, Martin A., eds., *New Frontiers in Space Law* (Leyden, 1969), pp. 9-12. **4346**

Vereshchetin, V.S. "Intercosmos: Present and Future." (1976), 1 *Annals of Air and Space Law* 243-254. **4347**

Vereshchetin, V.S. "Legal Status of International Space Crews." (1978), 3 *Annals of Air and Space Law* 545-560. **4348**

Vereshchetin, V.S. "On the Principle of State Sovereignty in International Space Law." (1977), 2 *Annals of Air and Space Law* 429-436. **4349**

Vereshchetin, V.S. "The Principle of Cooperation in International Space Law and Its Implementation in the Soviet Union." *In Space Activities and Implications: Where from and Where to at the Threshold of the 80's* (Montreal, 1981), pp. 209-222. **4350**

Vicas, Alexander G. "Efficiency, Equity and the Optimum Utilization of Outer Space as a Common Resource." (1980), 5 *Annals of Air and Space Law* 589-609. **4351**

Vicas, Alexander G. "The New International Economic Order and the Emerging Space Regime." *In Space Activities and Implications: Where from and Where to at the Threshold of the 80's* (Montreal, 1981), pp. 293-307. **4352**

Vlasic, Ivan A. "The Developing Law of Outer Space." (1966), 14 *Chitty's Law Journal* 241-249. **4353**

Vlasic, Ivan A. "Disarmament Decade, Outer Space and International Law." (1981), 26 *McGill Law Journal* 135-206. **4354**

Vlasic, Ivan A. "The Evolution of the International Code of Conduct to Govern Remote Sensing by Satellite: Progress Report." (1978), 3 *Annals of Air and Space Law* 561-574. **4355**

Vlasic, Ivan A. "The Growth of Space Law 1957-65: Achievements and Issues." (1965), *Yearbook of Air and Space Law* 365-405. **4356**

Vlasic, Ivan A. "Law and Public Order in Space: A Balance Sheet." (1965), *World Peace Through Law* 164-181. **4357**

Vlasic, Ivan A. "The Space Treaty: A Preliminary Evaluation." (1967), 55 *California Law Review* 507-519. **4358**

Vlasic, Ivan A. *Studies in the Law of Outer Space.* New Haven, Conn., 1961. **4359**

Thesis (Ph.D.), Yale University, 1961. Listed in (1960-61), *Index to American Doctoral Dissertations* 103.

Walsh, Kevin B. "Controversial Issues under Article XI of the Moon Treaty." (1981), 6 *Annals of Air and Space Law* 489-498. **4360**

Wang, Erik B. "Canada and the International Principles Governing Remote Sensing." *In* Matte, Nicolas Mateesco, and DeSaussure, Hamilton, eds., *Legal Implications of Remote Sensing from Outer Space* (Leiden, 1976), pp. 151-155. **4361**

Wassenbergh, H.A. "Speculation on the Law Governing Space Resources." (1980), 5 *Annals of Air and Space Law* 611-626. **4362**

Wijkman, Per Magnus, and Wihlborg, Clas G. "Global Use and Regulation of Space Activities under the Common Heritage Principle." *In Space Activities* and Implications: Where from and Where to at the Threshold of the 80's (Montreal, 1981). pp. 119-131. **4363**

Zhukov, Gennady P. "Problems of Legal Regulation of Using Information concerning Remote Sensing of the Earth from Space." *In* Matte, Nicolas Mateesco, and DeSaussure, Hamilton, eds., *Legal Implications of Remote Sensing from Outer Space* (Leiden, 1976), pp. 125-128. **4364**

Zhukov, Gennady P. "Tendencies and Prospects of the Development of Space Law: The Soviet Viewpoint." *In* McWhinney, Edward, and Bradley, Martin A., eds., *New Frontiers in Space Law* (Leyden, 1969), pp. 73-88. **4365**

XVI. INTERNATIONAL ORGANIZATIONS

A. General

Arès, Richard. *L'Église catholique et l'organisation de la société internationale contemporaine, 1939-1949; les faits, les principes, le programme.* Montréal: Facultés de philosophie et de théologie de la Compagnie de Jésus, 1949? 269 p. (Studia Collegii Maximi Immaculatae Conceptionis) **4366**
Reviews: François-Albert Angers in (1949-50), 25 *Actualité Économique* 363-364; Samuel Mack Eastman in (1949-50), 5 *International Journal* 372-373.

Bailey, Lance. "Le Concert européen et l'époque actuelle." (1963), 33 *Revue de l'Université d'Ottawa* 417-439. **4367**

Bedwell, C.E.A. "Everyman's Part in International Unity." (1949), 4 *International Journal* 147-155. **4368**

Bidmead, Harold S. "World Federalists' Congress, Stockholm, 1949." (1949-50), 29 *Dalhousie Review* 411-418. **4369**

Boisvert, Michael A. *Les implications économiques de la souveraineté-association: le Canada face à l'expérience des pays nordiques.* Montréal: Presses de l'Université de Montréal, 1980. 211 p. **4370**
Reviews: Charles Pentland in (1981), 12 *Études Internationales* 420-422; Luc-Normand Tellier in (1980), 56 *Actualité Économique* 341-343.

Bourély, Michel. "Le droit de l'espace et les organisations internationales." (1982), 7 *Annals of Air and Space Law* 241-259. **4371**

Claude, Innis L., Jr. "The Collectivist Theme in International Relations." (1968-69), 24 *International Journal* 639-656. **4372**

Clavet, Adrien. *Essai d'analyse de l'intégration des organisations internationales intergouvernementales.* Québec, 1973 (c1978). viii, 139 leaves. **4373**
Thesis (M.A.), Université Laval, 1976. (National Library of Canada. Canadian Theses on Microfiche, No. 35360).

Claxton, Brooke. "The Place of Canada in Post-War Organization." (1944), 10 *Canadian Journal of Economics and Political Science* 409-421. **4374**

Clayton, Graham. *Economic Integration among Less-Developed Countries.* Windsor, 1974. ix, 308 leaves. **4375**
Thesis (M.A.), University of Windsor, 1974. (National Library of Canada. Canadian Theses on Microfiche, No. 19875).

Corbett, Percy E. *Post-War Worlds.* New York: Farrar and Rinehart, 1942. ix, 233 p. (I.P.R. Inquiry Series) **4376**
Also published in French under title: *L'après-guerre* (Montréal, B. Valiquette, 1944).
Review: Roger Duhamel in (1945-46), 21/1 *Actualité Économique* 490-491.

Cox, Robert W. "The Crisis of World Order and the Problem of International Organization in the 1980's." (1979-80), 35 *International Journal* 370-395. **4377**

Dauphin, Roma. "Les unions douanières." (1971), 2 *Études Internationales* 147-164. **4378**

Doxey, Margaret P. "International Organisation in Foreign Policy Perspective." (1975), 29 *Year Book of World Affairs* 173-195. **4379**

Duncan, Lewis. "Blueprint of World Order." (1944), 22 *Canadian Bar Review* 405-411. **4380**

Erler, Jochen. "International Legislation." (1964), 2 *Canadian Yearbook of International Law* 153-163. **4381**

Ferguson, George V. "The Challenging World Crisis." (1946-47), 2 *International Journal* 281-286. **4382**

Gordenker, Leon. "International Organization and the Cold War." (1967-68), 23 *International Journal* 357-368. **4383**

Holmes, John W. "Les institutions internationales et la politique extérieure." (1970), 1 *Études Internationales* 20-40 (no 2) **4384**

Lawler, James, and Laulicht, Jerome. *International Integration in Developing Regions.* Oakville, Ont.: Canadian Peace Research Institute, c1970. 95 p. (Peace Research Reviews, Vol. 3, No. 4) **4385**

MacKenzie, Norman A.M. "International Notes." (1926), 4 *Canadian Bar Review* 241-246. **4386**

Mahant, E.E. "An Application of Structural-Functional Theory to the Study of International Organizations." (1976), 48 *Canadian Political Science Association, Papers,* 29 p. **4387**

McLin, Jon. "Are There Alternatives to Public International Agencies?" (1979-80), 35 *International Journal* 357-369. **4388**

McLin, Jon. "Surrogate International Organization and the Case of World Food Security, 1949-1969." (1979), 33 *International Organization* 35-55. **4389**

Miller, Anthony John. "Doomsday Politics: Prospects for International Cooperation." (1972-73), 28 *International Journal* 121-133. **4390**

Pentland, Charles. "Neofunctionalism." (1973), 27 *Year Book of World Affairs* 345-371. **4391**

Pollock, Sidney. "The International Allocation of Resources: New Concepts and Problems of Administration." (1956), 22 *Canadian Journal of Economics and Political Science* 461-466. **4392**

Prat, Henri. "L'avenir de l'organisation de l'union franco-britannique." (1940), 26 *Revue Trimestrielle Canadienne* 385-403. **4393**

Rosenau, James N. "Le touriste et le terroriste ou les deux extrêmes du continuum transnational." (1979), 10 *Études Internationales* 219-252. **4394**

Sabourin, Louis. "Pour un nouveau droit international opérationel." (1969), 4 *Revue Juridique Thémis* 11-16 (no 3) **4395**

Siddiqui, Norma. *A Survey of Customs Union Theory.* Montreal, 1970 (c1971). iv, 93 leaves. **4396**
Thesis (M.A.), McGill University, 1970. (National Library of Canada. Canadian Theses on Microfilm, No. 7757).

Wallace, Michael D., and Singer, J. David. "The Use and Abuse of Imagination; a Reply to Samuel A. Bleicher." (1971), 25 *International Organization* 953-957. **4397**

B. Universal Intergovernmental Organizations

1. GENERAL

Akindele, Rafiu Ayo. *The Organization and Promotion of World Peace: A Study of Universal-Regional Relationships.* Toronto: University of Toronto Press, 1976. xiii, 209 p. **4398**
This is a revision of the author's thesis (Ph.D.), University of Alberta, 1970, presented under title: *Regional Organizations and World Order.*
Reviews: Robert W. Cox in (1978), 11 *Canadian Journal of Political Science* 238-239; George Ignatieff in (1977), 84 *Queen's Quarterly* 503-504; Annemarie Jacomy-Millette in (1978), 9 *Études Internationales* 290-293.

Akindele, Rafiu Ayo. *Regional Organizations and World Order: A Study of the Problems of Universal-Regional Relationship in the Organization of International Peace and Security.* Edmonton, 1970. xi, 531 leaves. **4399**
Thesis (Ph.D.), University of Alberta, 1970. (National Library of Canada. Canadian Theses on Microfilm, No. 6459).

Barrett, Carol, and Newcombe, Hanna. *Weighted Voting in International Organizations.* Oakville, Ont.: Canadian Peace Research Institute, 1968. 110 p. (Peace Research Reviews, Vol. 2, No. 2) **4400**

Bergeron, Gérard. *La Société des Nations et les Nations Unies (étude comparative de deux essais d'organisation internationale).* Québec, 1947. 2 vols. **4401**
Thesis (M.Sc.Soc.), Université Laval, 1947.

Bernier, Robert. *L'autorité politique internationale et la souveraineté des états; fondements philosophiques de l'ordre politique.* Montréal: Institut social populaire, 1951. 201 p. **4402**
First issued as a dissertation (Ph.D.), Université de Montréal, 1949.

Borgese, Elisabeth Mann. "The Role of the International Seabed Authority in the 1980's." (1981) 18 *San Diego Law Review* 395-407. **4403**

Corbett, Percy E. "World Government - in Whose Time?" (1949), 25 *International Affairs* 426-433. **4404**

Cox, Robert W., ed. *International Organisation: World Politics - Studies in*

Economic and Social Agencies. Papers Prepared under the Auspices of the International Political Science Association. London: Macmillan, 1969. 319 p.
Review: Mark W. Zacher in (1969-70), 25 *International Journal* 791-793. **4405**

Cox, Robert W., and Jacobson, Harold K. *The Anatomy of Influence; Decision Making in International Organization.* New Haven: Yale University Press, 1973. xiii, 497 p. **4406**
Review: Mark W. Zacher in (1973-74), 29 *International Journal* 665-667.

Da Costa, Richard Cochrane. *International Integration: Delineation of an Analytical Framework and an Application in the Context of the International Financial Community.* Ottawa, 1978. v, 83 leaves. **4407**
Research essay (M.A.), Carleton University, 1978.

Doxey, Margaret P. "Strategies in Multilateral Diplomacy: The Commonwealth, Southern Africa, and the NIEO." (1979-80), 35 *International Journal* 329-356. **4408**

Foster, *Sir* George. "The New Internationalism." (1929), 36 *Queen's Quarterly* 369-379. **4409**

Gordenker, Leon. "The Superpowers and International Organization." (1979-80), 35 *International Journal* 448-477. **4410**

Gregor, Richard. *Domestic Jurisdiction and International Organization; a Study of Article 15, Paragraph 8, of the League of Nations Covenant, and Article 2, Paragraph 7, of the United Nations Charter.* Toronto, 1956. 156 leaves. **4411**
Thesis (M.A.), University of Toronto, 1956.

Hackett, W.T.G. *Bretton Woods.* Toronto: Canadian Institute of International Affairs, 1945. 56 p. **4412**

Harrison, Eric. "Riders to the Covenant." (1934), 41 *Queen's Quarterly* 341-355. **4413**

Heaton, H. "From Versailles to Locarno." (1925-26), 33 *Queen's Quarterly* 234-260. **4414**

Hendry, James M. *Canada in International Organization.* Cambridge, Mass., 1948. 35, 12 leaves. **4415**
Thesis (LL.M.), Harvard University, 1948.

Holmes, John W. "Canada's Role in International Organizations." (1967), 74 *Canadian Banker* 115-130 (No. 1) **4416**

Humphrey, John P. "Les fonctions gouvernementales dans la société internationale." (1946), 16 *Revue de l'Université d'Ottawa* 172-186. **4417**

Kingham, J.D., and McRae, Donald M. "Competent International Organizations and the Law of the Sea." (1979), 3 *Marine Policy* 106-132. **4418**

Lindgren, William. *Canada: The League of Nations and the United Nations.* Vancouver, 1946. ii, 11, 169 leaves. **4419**
Thesis (M.A.), University of British Columbia, 1946.

Macdonald, Ronald St. John. "Relaciones crecientes entre las Naciones Unidas y la Organización de los Estados Americanos." (1969), 2 *Boletin Mexicano de Derecho Comparado* 293-325. **4420**
Translated by Héctor Cuadra.

MacLean, Donald A. "The World Commonwealth: Its Christian Basis." (1944), 38 *Royal Society of Canada, Transactions* 103-116 (3d Ser., 2d Sec.) **4421**

Martin, Paul. "L'ordre international nouveau." (1948), 18 *Revue de l'Université d'Ottawa* 405-412. **4422**

Matte, Nicolas Mateesco. "Les précurseurs de l'O.N.U." (1953), 13 *Revue du Barreau* 262-274. **4423**

McRae, Donald M. "Legal Obligations and International Organizations." (1973), 11 *Canadian Yearbook of International Law* 87-105. **4424**

Meyer, Cord, Jr., and Brinton, Crane. "World Government - Necessity or Utopia?" (1949), 9 *Behind the Headlines* No. 5 (17 p.) **4425**

Newcombe, Hanna. *National Patterns in International Organizations.* Oakville, Ont.: Canadian Peace Research Institute, 1975. 3 vols. (367 p.) (Peace Research Reviews, Vol. 6, Nos. 4-6) **4426**

Nogaro, Bertrand. "La Banque des règlements internationaux." (1929-30), 5 *Actualité Économique* 361-365. **4427**

Pearson, Lester B. "National Sovereignty and International Organization." (1952), 4 *External Affairs* 166-175. **4428**

"Permanent Foundations of World Peace." (1920), 56 *Canada Law Journal* 170-171. **4429**

Piplani, S.S. "International Co-operation." (1965-66), 45 *Dalhousie Review* 127-136. **4430**

Pugsley, William Howard. *The Bank for International Settlements.* Montreal, 1950. 1 vol. (various pagings) **4431**
Thesis (Ph.D.), McGill University, 1950.

Ralph, Michael. *The Diplomacy of Developing States in International Organizations: A Comparison of the Strategies Used by the LDCs in UNCTAD and in UNCLOS III.* Vancouver, 1979. 73 frames. **4432**
Thesis (M.A.), University of British Columbia, 1979. (National Library of Canada. Canadian Theses on Microfiche, No. 46239).

Renouf, Alan. "The Abortive Charter for an International Trade Organization." (1951), 29 *Canadian Bar Review* 53-69. **4433**

Sewell, James P. "Canada and the Functional Agencies: the NIEO's Challenge, Trudeau's Response." (1977-78), 33 *International Journal* 339-356. **4434**
Refers to the New International Economic Order (NIEO).

Simoni, Arnold. *Beyond Repair; the Urgent Need for a New World Body.* Don Mills, Ont.: Collier-Macmillan Canada, c1972. xxii, 210 p. **4435**
Review: Marvin Gelber in (1974-75), 30 *International Journal* 181-182.

Singer, J. David, and Wallace, Michael D. "Intergovernmental Organization and the Preservation of Peace, 1816-1964: Some Bivariate Relationships." (1970), 24 *International Organization* 520-547. **4436**

Soldatos, Panayotis. "La sociologie de l'intégration internationale: essai de bilan critique." (1974), 5 *Études Internationales* 519-541. **4437**

Taylor, Alastair M. "Canada and the Principle of Universality." (1966-67), 22 *International Journal* 17-24. **4438**

Tritt, Robert Walter. *International Telecommunications Satellite Organization (INTELSAT): A Case Study in the Evolution of an International Operating Agency.* Ottawa, 1971. 117 leaves. **4439**
Research essay (M.A.), Carleton University, 1971.

Trotter, Reginald G. "Canada and World Organization." (1945), 26 *Canadian Historical Review* 128-147. **4440**

Viner, Jacob. *The Customs Union Issue.* New York: Carnegie Endowment for International Peace, 1950. viii, 221 p. (Carnegie Endowment for International Peace. Studies in the Administration of International Law and Organization, No. 10) **4441**
Review: J. R. Petrie in (1950), 28 *Canadian Bar Review* 1160-1163.

Wallace, Michael D., and Singer, J. David. "Intergovernmental Organization in the Global System, 1815-1964: A Quantitative Description." (1970), 24 *International Organization* 239-287. **4442**

"The World Is Our Oyster." (1944), 4 *Behind the Headlines* No. 7 (28 p.) **4443**

2. LEAGUE OF NATIONS

Argue, Dorothy F. *The Political Activities of the League of Nations, 1920-1932.* Edmonton, 1935. ii, 59 leaves. **4444**
Thesis (M.A.), University of Alberta, 1935.

Armstrong, William E. *Canada and the League of Nations: The Problem of Peace.* Genève: Imprimerie Jent, 1930. 222 p. **4445**
Thesis (Doctorat), Université de Genève.
Review: Samuel Mack Eastman in (1931), 12 *Canadian Historical Review* 321-323.

Barros, James. *Betrayal from Within: Joseph Avenol, Secretary-General of the League of Nations, 1933-1940.* New Haven: Yale University Press, 1969. xii, 289 p. **4446**
Review: Henri Reymond in (1969-70), 25 *International Journal* 641-642.

Barros, James. *The Corfu Incident of 1923; Mussolini and the League of Nations.* Princeton, N.J.: Princeton University Press, 1965. xxi, 339 p., maps. **4447**

Barros, James. *The League of Nations and the Great Powers: The Greek-Bulgarian Incident, 1925.* Oxford: Clarendon Press, 1970. xiv, 143 p. **4448**
Reviews: Ulrich Trumpener in (1972), 53 *Canadian Historical Review* 103-104; Richard Veatch in (1971-72), 27 *International Journal* 611-612.

Bell, G.F. "Force Behind the League." (1935-36), 42 *Queen's Quarterly* 22-30.
4449

Briquet, Pierre E. "Sanctions, the League and British Prestige." (1935-36), 43 *Journal of the Canadian Bankers' Association* 279-283. **4450**

Burtt, Judith. *The Reaction of the Quebec Press to the American Debate on the League of Nations.* Quebec, 1972. vii, 115 leaves. **4451**
Thesis (M.A.), Université Laval, 1972. (National Library of Canada. Canadian Theses on Microfiche, No. 18927).

Canada. Dept. of External Affairs. *Report of the Canadian Delegates to the*

Assembly of the League of Nations. 1st-21st, 1920-1946. Ottawa: King's Printer, 1920-1946. **4452**

Canada. Parliament. *League of Nations: The Covenant of the League of Nations and the Protocol for the Pacific Settlement of International Disputes.* Ottawa, 1925. 53 p. (Canada. Parliament, 1925. Sessional Papers, No. 116) **4453**

Carter, Gwendolen M. "Consider the Record: Canada and the League of Nations." (1941-42), 2 *Behind the Headlines* No. 6 (25 p.) **4454**

Dafoe, John W. "Canada, the Empire and the League." (1935-36), 14 *Foreign Affairs* 297-308. **4455**

Dafoe, John W. "Canada's Interest in the World Crisis." (1935-36), 15 *Dalhousie Review* 477-484. **4456**

Darling, H. Maurice. "Who Kept the United States Out of the League of Nations." (1929), 10 *Canadian Historical Review* 196-211. **4457**

Désy, Jean. "La Société des Nations et l'opposition américaine." (1920), 6 *Revue Trimestrielle Canadienne* 357-368. **4458**

Eastman, Samuel Mack. *Canada at Geneva; an Historical Survey and Its Lessons.* Published under the auspices of the Canadian Institute of International Affairs. Toronto: Ryerson Press, 1946. x, 117 p. (Contemporary Affairs, No. 20) **4459**
Reviews: William E. Armstrong in (1947), 41 *American Journal of International Law* 712-713; Eric W. More in (1946-47), 2 *International Journal* 263-264.

Egerton, George W. *The British Government and the Evolution of the League of Nations: A Study in Official Attitudes and Policies with Regard to the Creation of an International Organization for Peace, Co-operation and Security, 1914-1919.* Toronto, 1970. 475 leaves. **4460**
Thesis (Ph.D.), University of Toronto, 1970. (National Library of Canada. Canadian Theses on Microfiche, No. 27835).

Egerton, George W. *Great Britain and the Creation of the League of Nations: Strategy, Politics, and International Organization, 1914-1919.* Chapel Hill: University of North Carolina Press, c1978. xiii, 273 p. (Papers of Woodrow Wilson; Supplementary Volumes) **4461**
Review: P.F. Clarke in (1980), 15 *Canadian Journal of History* 318-319.

Forbes, Frederic J. *Canada in the League of Nations.* Montreal, 1927. 291 leaves. Thesis (M.A.), McGill University, 1927. **4462**

Germain, Victorin. *La Société des Nations: étude doctrinale.* Québec: Action sociale, 1923. 214 p. **4463**
Thesis (Doctorat), Rome, Collège Angélique.
Review: Unsigned in (1923-24), 2 *Revue du Droit* 30-32.

Gilmore, William C. "Newfoundland and the League of Nations." (1980), 18 *Canadian Yearbook of International Law* 201-217. **4464**

Glazebrook, G.P. de T. "International Anarchy?" (1934-35), 14 *Dalhousie Review* 148-154. **4465**

Gordon, Shirley Saul. *Canadian Public Opinion and the League of Nations, 1914-1920.* Toronto, 1936. 403 leaves. **4466**
Thesis (M.A.), University of Toronto, 1936.

Hamelin, Marcel. *L'honorable Raoul Dandurand et la participation du Canada à*

la Société des Nations dans les années 1920. Québec, 1964, xviii, 172 leaves.
Thesis (D.E.S.), Université Laval, 1965.   **4467**

Harrison, W.E.C. "Rebuilding Geneva." (1936-37), 43 *Queen's Quarterly* 309-316.   **4468**

Holcombe, Arthur N. "Americanizing the League of Nations." (1921-22), 1 *Dalhousie Review* 281-292.   **4469**

Kierstead, Stella. "The League and Abyssinia." (1936-37), 16 *Dalhousie Review* 324-336.   **4470**

Lapointe, Ernest. "The League of Nations." (1928), 6 *Canadian Bar Review* 278-282.   **4471**

Manning, Charles Anthony Woodward. *The Policies of the British Dominions in the League of Nations.* London: Oxford University Press, 1932. 159 p. (Graduate Institute of International Studies, Geneva. Publications, No. 3)   **4472**
Review: Norman A.M. MacKenzie in (1933), 14 *Canadian Historical Review* 336-337.

McInnis, Edgar. "The Stimson Policy and the League." (1932-33), 12 *Dalhousie Review* 369-377.   **4473**

McInnis, Edgar. "What Is Left of the League?" (1936-37), 16 *Dalhousie Review* 337-343.   **4474**

McKercher, Brian. *The Golden Gleam, 1916-1920: Britain and the Origins of the League of Nations.* Edmonton, 1975. ix, 185 leaves.   **4475**
Thesis (M.A.), University of Alberta, 1975. (National Library of Canada. Canadian Theses on Microfiche, No. 24090).

Moore, *Sir* William Harrison. "The Dominions of the British Commonwealth in the League of Nations." (1931), 10 *International Affairs* 372-391.   **4476**
The author represented Australia in the League of Nations.

Nkiwane, Solomon Moyo. *The Role of the Rapporteur in the League of Nations.* Montreal, 1975 (c1976). viii, 278 leaves.   **4477**
Thesis (Ph.D.), McGill University, 1975. (National Library of Canada. Canadian Theses on Microfiche, No. 24392).

Page, Donald M. *Canadians and the League of Nations Before the Manchurian Crisis.* Toronto, c1972. 568 leaves.   **4478**
Thesis (Ph.D.), University of Toronto, 1972. (National Library of Canada. Canadian Theses on Microfiche, No. 31301).

Pijoan, J. "The Second Assembly of the League of Nations." (1921-22), 29 *Queen's Quarterly* 219-242.   **4479**

Pillai, Nilakandan Perumal. *Unit Voting of the British Empire in the League of Nations (Assembly).* New York, 1928. 66 leaves.   **4480**
Thesis (A.M.), Columbia University, 1928.

Shumate, Roger Vernon. *The British Dominions and the League of Nations.* Berkeley, Calif., 1929. vii, 11, 136 leaves.   **4481**
Thesis (M.A.), University of California, 1930.

Soward, Frederic H. "Canada and the League of Nations." (1932), 283 *International Conciliation* 353-395.   **4482**
First published Ottawa, League of Nations Society in Canada, 1931.
Review: Samuel Mack Eastman in (1931), 12 *Canadian Historical Review* 321-323.

Soward, Frederic H. "The Election of Canada to the League of Nations Council in 1927." (1929), *Canadian Historical Association, Historical Papers* 31-40. **4483**
Also published in (1929), 23 *American Journal of International Law* 753-765.

Soward, Frederic H. "Ten Years of the League of Nations." (1930), 37 *Queen's Quarterly* 350-369. **4484**

Story, Donald C. "Canada, the League of Nations and the Far East, 1931-33: The Cahan Incident." (1981), 3 *International History Review* 236-255. **4485**

Story, Donald C. *Canada's Covenant: The Bennett Government, the League of Nations and Collective Security, 1930-1935.* Toronto, 1977. vi, 387 leaves.
4486
Thesis (Ph.D.), University of Toronto, 1977. (National Library of Canada. Canadian Theses on Microfiche, No. 40965).

Taft, William H. "The League of Nations." (1920), 40 *Canadian Law Times* 1025-1040. **4487**
Address by W.H. Taft, ex-President of the United States, delivered at the annual meeting of the Canadian Bar Association at Ottawa, September 1, 1920.

Veatch, Richard. *Canada and the League of Nations.* Toronto: University of Toronto Press, c1975. xi, 224 p. **4488**
Originally presented as the author's thesis, Université de Genève, 1973, under title: *Canadian Foreign Policy and the League of Nations 1919-1939.*
Reviews: John English under title: "Aura of Predestination Pervades Discussion of League's Future," in (1976), *International Perspectives* 49-51 (Mar./Apr.); Thierry Godechot in (1979), *Revue d'Histoire Diplomatique* 361-362; John C. Kendall in (1976), 6 *American Review of Canadian Studies* 122-124 (No. 2); Robert A. MacKay in (1977), 10 *Canadian Journal of Political Science* 641-642; Denis Stairs in (1977), 58 *Canadian Historical Review* 517-518; Donald C. Story in (1975-76), 31 *International Journal* 550-552.

Walmsley, Percival B. "Enforced Peace." (1917), 37 *Canadian Law Times* 629-631.
4489

3. UNITED NATIONS

(a) GENERAL

Anderson, Peter Robert P. *The United Nations as a Mechanism for Preserving the Peace: The Soviet View.* Ottawa, 1967. x, 149 leaves. **4490**
Added title: *The Soviet View of the UN as a Mechanism for Preserving Peace.* Thesis (M.A.), Carleton University, 1967. (National Library of Canada. Canadian Theses on Microfilm, No. 1545).

Angus, Henry F. "The United Nations." (1948), 14 *Canadian Journal of Economics and Political Science* 312-320. **4491**
Paper presented at the annual meeting of the Canadian Political Science Association in Vancouver, June 15, 1948.

Antoine, Aristide. "Les Nations Unies et la technique." (1948-49), 34 *Revue Trimestrielle Canadienne* 454-458. **4492**

Barros, James, ed. *The United Nations: Past, Present, and Future.* London: Collier-Macmillan; New York: Free Press, 1972. 279 p. **4493**
Reviews: George Ignatieff in (1972-73), 28 *International Journal* 555-556; Mark W. Zacher in (1975), 8 *Canadian Journal of Political Science* 588-589.

Barton, William H. "The Best United Nations We Have." (1982), *International Perspectives* 3-5 (July/Aug.) **4494**

Bernardin-Haldemann, Verena. "L'idéologie de la Cépal." (1974), 5 *Études Internationales* 123-142. **4495**
Cépal refers to the U.N. Economic Commission for Latin America (in French: Commission économique pour l'Amérique latine), created in 1948.

Boyd, Andrew. "The Role of the Great Powers in the United Nations System." (1969-70), 25 *International Journal* 356-369. **4496**

Boyd, Andrew. "The Unknown United Nations." (1963-64), 19 *International Journal* 202-212. **4497**

Burn, Henry Pelham. "United Nations Development and the Future." (1971), 78 *Canadian Banker* 21-25 (No. 2) **4498**

"The Commonwealth; We Need the United Nations." (1944), 4 *Behind the Headlines* No. 5 (40 p.) **4499**

Comtois, Robert. "La signification de l'ONU." (1954), 60/2 *Revue Dominicaine* 225-234. **4500**

Côté, Ernest-A. "Le travail des Nations-Unies." (1947-48), 2 *Revue de l'Université Laval* 122-135. **4501**

Davy, Grant R. "The United Nations and the Problem of Change." (1955-56), 11 *International Journal* 292-296. **4502**

Eayrs, James George. "Canadian Federalism and the United Nations." (1950), 16 *Canadian Journal of Economics and Political Science* 172-183. **4503**

"The Establishment of a General International Organization: Canadian Views on the Dumbarton Oaks Proposals, 1945." (1965), 17 *External Affairs* 58-61. **4504**

Friedmann, Wolfgang G. "The United Nations and National Loyalties." (1952-53), 8 *International Journal* 17-26. **4505**

Friedmann, Wolfgang G. "The United Nations and the Development of International Law." (1969-70), 25 *International Journal* 272-286. **4506**

Frowein, Jochen A. "The United Nations and the Non-Member States." (1969-70), 25 *International Journal* 333-344. **4507**

Glazebrook, G.P. de T. "The Middle Powers in the United Nations System." (1947), 1 *International Organization* 307-315. **4508**

Goldberg, Arthur. "The Rule of Law in an Unruly World." (1970-71), 4 *Manitoba Law Journal* 1-7. **4509**

Goldie, D.M.M. "Korea and the United Nations." (1949-52), 1 *U.B.C. Legal Notes* 125-134. **4510**

Goodrich, Leland M. "San Francisco in Retrospect." (1969-70), 25 *International Journal* 239-260. **4511**

Green, Leslie C. "The Double Standard of the United Nations." (1957), 11 *Year Book of World Affairs* 104-137. **4512**

Green, Leslie C. "The 'Little Assembly.' " (1949), 3 *Year Book of World Affairs* 169-187. **4513**

Green, Leslie C. "Recent Issues at Lake Success." (1947), 1 *World Affairs* 340-356 (N.S.) **4514**

Green, Leslie C. "The United Nations at 25: Prospects for the Future." (1972), 3 *Lawasia* 471-482. **4515**

Greenwood, Thomas. "La Conférence de San Francisco." (1945), 31 *Revue Trimestrielle Canadienne* 224-234. **4516**

Greenwood, Thomas. "L'héritage de la guerre et les étapes de la paix." (1945), 31 *Revue Trimestrielle Canadienne* 113-122. **4517**

Hadwen, John G., and Kaufmann, Johan. *How United Nations Decisions Are Made.* Foreword by Paul G. Hoffman. Leyden: A.W. Sythoff, 1960. 144 p. **4518**

Reviews: Morris Davis in (1961-62), 41 *Dalhousie Review* 96-97; Frederic H. Soward in (1960-61), 16 *International Journal* 79-80.

Hadwen, John G., and Kaufmann, Johan. *How United Nations Decisions Are Made.* Foreword by Paul G. Hoffman. 2d rev. ed. Leyden: A.W. Sythoff; New York: Oceana Publications, 1962. 179 p., map. **4519**

Review: Peter V. Bishop in (1961-62), 17 *International Journal* 329.

Heathcote, Nina. "United Nations and Nation-Building." (1964-65), 20 *International Journal* 20-32. **4520**

Hodgetts, John E. "The San Francisco Conference: Old Worlds for New?" (1944-45), 14 *University of Toronto Quarterly* 431-440. **4521**

Holly, Daniel A. "L'ONU et le système international dans la littérature spécialisée: pertinence ou non-pertinence d'une relation." (1974), 5 *Études Internationales* 502-518. **4522**

Holmes, John W. "Sadder but Wiser: The UN at Thirty." (1975), *International Perspectives* 19-23 (Nov./Dec.) **4523**

Holmes, John W. "The Way of the World." (1979-80), 35 *International Journal* 211-225. **4524**

Humphrey, John P. "The Main Functions of the United Nations in the Year 2,000 A.D." (1971), 17 *McGill Law Journal* 219-231. **4525**

Humphrey, John P. "The Parent of Anarchy." (1946), 1 *International Journal* 11-21. **4526**

James, Robert Rhodes. "International Crises, the Great Powers, and the United Nations." (1969-70), 25 *International Journal* 345-355. **4527**

Kent, William. *Diplomacy at the United Nations.* Hamilton, Ont., 1966. v, 195 leaves. **4528**

Thesis (M.A.), McMaster University, 1966.

Langlais, Antonio. "À propos des Nations Unies." (1947-48), 2 *Revue de l'Université Laval* 446-453, 536-543. **4529**

Langlais, Antonio. "Babel n'est pas un mythe." (1946), 1 *International Journal* 134-143. **4530**
Also published in (1946), 6 *Revue du Barreau* 183-192.

Langlais, Antonio. "Les Nations Unies." (1947-48), 2 *Revue de l'Université Laval* 224-236, 321-332. **4531**

Langlais, Antonio. "Les Nations Unies." (1948), 8 *Revue du Barreau* 165-173. **4532**

Macdonald, Ronald St. John. "The Developing Relationship between Superior and Subordinate Political Bodies at the International Level: A Note on the Experience of the United Nations and the Organization of American States." (1964), 2 *Canadian Yearbook of International Law* 21-54. **4533**

Macdonald, Ronald St. John. "Hungary, Egypt and the United Nations." (1957), 35 *Canadian Bar Review* 38-71, 603-604 (Letter from Edward G. Lee). **4534**

Mackintosh, W.A. "The Problem of the United Nations." (1947-48), 54 *Queen's Quarterly* 90-99. **4535**

MacKirdy, Kenneth A. "United Nations: Some Thoughts on Changing Perspectives." (1960-61), 67 *Queen's Quarterly* 557-567. **4536**

Maes, Albert. "The European Community and the United Nations General Assembly." (1979-80), 3 *Revue d'Intégration Européenne* 73-83. **4537**

McLaren, Robert I. "The UN System and Its Quixotic Quest for Coordination." (1980), 34 *International Organization* 139-148. **4538**
This is a review article of three books.

McNaught, Kenneth. "Ottawa and Washington Look at the U.N." (1954-55), 33 *Foreign Affairs* 663-678. **4539**

McWhinney, Edward. "Friendly Relations and Co-operation among States: Debate at the Twentieth General Assembly, United Nations." (1966), 60 *American Journal of International Law* 356-361. **4540**

McWhinney, Edward. "The 'New' Countries and the 'New' International Law: The United Nations' Special Conference on Friendly Relations and Co-operation among States." (1966), 60 *American Journal of International Law* 1-33. **4541**

Metz, Homer. "The United Nations." (1947), 7 *Behind the Headlines* No. 4 (36 p.) **4542**

Mohammed, Franklyn. *The Role of the United Nations in the Establishment of Israel.* London, Ont., 1973. vii, 162 leaves. **4543**
Thesis (M.A.), University of Western Ontario, 1973. (National Library of Canada. Canadian Theses on Microfiche, No. 17093).

Monk, Richard C. "United Nations Library." (1960), 12 *External Affairs* 626-628. **4544**

Morillo-Ferrer, Consuelo. *Le développement communautaire et les Nations Unies; étude conceptuelle à partir de l'analyse de quatre documents des Nations Unies sur le développement communautaire.* Montréal, 1970. vi, 256 leaves. **4545**
Thesis (M.A.), Université de Montréal, 1970.

Morton, William L. "Behind Dumbarton Oaks." (1945), 5 *Behind the Headlines* No. 2 (28 p.) **4546**

Naidu, Mumulla Venkat Rao. *Collective Security and the United Nations: A Definition of the UN Security System.* Delhi: Macmillan of India, 1974. xv, 164 p. **4547**

Naidu, Mumulla Venkat Rao. "Collective Security and the United Nations: A Politico-Legal Analysis." (1971), 43 *Canadian Political Science Association, Papers,* 32, 12 p. **4548**

Nicholas, H.G. "The United Nations as a Political Institution: A Personal Retrospect." (1969-70), 25 *International Journal* 261-271. **4549**

O'Hearn, Walter. "U.N. Struggle for Peace." (1950), 10 *Behind the Headlines* No. 2 (20 p.) **4550**

Pearson, Lester B.; Gross, Ernest A.; and Dean, Patrick. *A Critical Evaluation of the United Nations.* Vancouver: University of British Columbia, 1961. 55 p. (University Lecture Series) **4551**
Contains three lectures.

Robinson, Marvin. "The United Nations as an International Forum for Developing Consensus." *In* Matte, Nicolas Mateesco, and DeSaussure, Hamilton, eds., *Legal Implications of Remote Sensing from Outer Space* (Leiden, 1976), pp. 187-193. **4552**

Rosenbaum, Naomi. "Cyprus and the United Nations: An Appreciation of Parliamentary Diplomacy." (1967), 33 *Canadian Journal of Economics and Political Science* 218-231. **4553**
Contains a résumé in French under title: "Chypre et les Nations Unies: une appréciation de la diplomatie parlementaire."

Rosenthal, Abraham Michael. *The United Nations, Its Record and Prospects.* New York: Manhattan Pub., 1953. 64 p. **4554**
Prepared for the Carnegie Endowment for International Peace.

Russell, Ruth B. "'Power Politics' and the United Nations." (1969-70), 25 *International Journal* 321-332. **4555**

Russell, Ruth B. "The United Nations at Thirty-Five." (1979-80), 35 *International Journal* 226-239. **4556**

"The San Francisco Meeting." (1955), 7 *External Affairs* 235-238. **4557**
Summary of speeches made at the tenth anniversary meeting.

Scott, Francis R. "Roads to Peace and Security." (1946), 1 *International Journal* 349-357. **4558**

Smith, I. Norman. "San Francisco - First Step to Peace." (1945), 5 *Behind the Headlines* No. 6 (32 p.) **4559**

Smouts, Marie-Claire. "L'ONU et ses membres: recherches d'un cadre d'analyse comparative." (1974), 5 *Études Internationales* 673-692. **4560**

Spitzer, Tadeusz B. "Dumbarton Oaks Project of World Democracy." (1945), 25 *Dalhousie Review* 1-13. **4561**

Stairs, Denis. "The United Nations and the Politics of the Korean War." (1969-70), 25 *International Journal* 302-320. **4562**

Tabor, Hans. "Stepping Beyond Idealism to See the United Nations." (1978), *International Perspectives* 15-19 (Sept./Oct.) **4563**

Woodside, Willson. "UN Progress?" (1946-47), 2 *International Journal* 118-123.
4564

Zacher, Mark W. *Dag Hammarskjold's Conception of the Political Role of the United Nations.* New York, 1966. iii, 357 leaves. **4565**
Thesis, Columbia University, 1966.

Zacher, Mark W. *Dag Hammarskjold's United Nations.* New York: Columbia University Press, 1970. 295 p. (Columbia University. Studies in International Organization, No. 7) **4566**
Review: James Barros in (1970-71), 26 *International Journal* 439-440.

(b) LEGAL ASPECTS

Amerasinghe, Chittharanjan Felix. "The Charter *Travaux Préparatoires* and United Nations Powers to Use Armed Force." (1966), 4 *Canadian Yearbook of International Law* 81-101. **4567**

Anglin, Douglas G. "Revision of the United Nations Charter." (1954-55), 24 *University of Toronto Quarterly* 162-174. **4568**

Angus, Henry F. "The Canadian Constitution and the United Nations Charter." (1946), 12 *Canadian Journal of Economics and Political Science* 127-135.
4569

Bell, Joel I. "A Legal Analysis of Article 19 of the United Nations Charter." (1965), 11 *McGill Law Journal* 148-162. **4570**

Cadieux, Marcel. "L'affaire des obligations financières des membres des Nations Unies." (1963), 23 *Revue du Barreau* 114-137. **4571**
Sub-title: "Demande d'avis consultatif à la Cour internationale de justice."

Cohen, Maxwell. "Bill C-60 and International Law - The United Nations Charter - Declaration of Human Rights." (1959), 37 *Canadian Bar Review* 228-233.
4572

Cohen, Maxwell. "Reflections on Law and the United Nations System." (1960), 54 *American Society of International Law, Proceedings* 243-253. **4573**

Day, Brigham. "Should the U.N. Charter Be Changed?" (1954), 14 *Behind the Headlines* No. 5 (17 p.) **4574**

Dubé, Georges. "Les sanctions du droit international public dans la Charte des Nations Unies." (1962-63), 5 *Cahiers de Droit* 98-103 (no 1) **4575**

Gibson, J. Douglas. "The Financial Problem of the United Nations." (1966-67), 22 *International Journal* 182-194. **4576**

Holland, *Sir* Robert E. "Amendment of the United Nations Charter." (1948-49), 28 *Dalhousie Review* 233-245. **4577**

Langlais, Antonio. "La Charte des Nations Unies." (1945-46), 33 *Canada Français* 190-194. **4578**

Langlais, Antonio. "La Charte des Nations Unies et le Canada." (1945-46), 33 *Canada Français* 129-134. **4579**

McWhinney, Edward. "The Changing United Nations Constitutionalism: New

Arenas and New Techniques for International Law-Making." (1967), 5 *Canadian Yearbook of International Law* 68-83. **4580**

Ogden, Suzanne. "China's Position on U.N. Charter Review." (1979), 52 *Pacific Affairs* 210-240. **4581**

Pharand, Donat. "Analysis of the Opinion of the International Court of Justice on Certain Expenses of the United Nations." (1963), 1 *Canadian Yearbook of International Law* 272-297. **4582**

Rendall, James A. "The *Special Assessments Case* - International Law - United Nations Charter - Article 17. (Case Comment)." (1960-63), 2 *Osgoode Hall Law Journal* 539-560. **4583**

"Report of the Committee on Legal Problems of International Organization for the Maintenance of Peace." (1945), 27 *Canadian Bar Association, Proceedings* 110-128. **4584**

Sayre, Paul. "United Nations Law." (1947), 25 *Canadian Bar Review* 809-822. **4585**

St. Laurent, Louis S. "The Charter of the United Nations." (1948), 26 *Canadian Bar Review* 363-372. **4586**

Verma, Dhirendra P. *The United Nations Charter: Review and Revision.* Halifax, 1977. xi, 466 leaves. **4587**
   Thesis (LL.M.), Dalhousie University, 1977. (National Library of Canada. Canadian Theses on Microfiche, No. 36190).

(c) ORGANS

Barton, William H. "Ambassador Barton Recalls Term on Security Council: A Personal Reminiscence." (1979), *International Perspectives* 12-17 (May/June) **4588**

Doe, John. "International Law - Korea - United Nations - Validity of Resolutions of the Security Council - Two Views. (Comment)." (1950), 28 *Canadian Bar Review* 902-908. **4589**

Edmondson, Locksley G.E. *The Trusteeship Council of the United Nations: Purposes, Evolution and Future.* Kingston, 1965. 371 leaves. **4590**
   Thesis (M.A.), Queen's University, 1965.

Freedman, Max. "The General Assembly." (1946-47), 2 *International Journal* 106-117. **4591**

Gotlieb, Allan E. "The International Law Commission." (1966), 4 *Canadian Yearbook of International Law* 64-80. **4592**

Green, Leslie C. "Gentlemen's Agreements and the Security Council." (1960), 13 *Current Legal Problems* 255-275. **4593**

Green, Leslie C. "Representation in the Security Council: A Survey." (1962), 11 *Indian Year Book of International Affairs* 48-75. **4594**

Green, Leslie C. "The Security Council in Action." (1948), 2 *Year Book of World Affairs* 125-161. **4595**

Green, Leslie C. "The Security Council in Retreat." (1954), 8 *Year Book of World Affairs* 95-117. **4596**

Ignatieff, George. "Canada at the United Nations: Sitting on the Hot Seat of the UN Security Council." (1976), *International Perspectives* 7-11 (Sept./Oct.) **4597**

"Legal Work of the UN General Assembly." (1968), 20 *External Affairs* 109-113. **4598**

Mizouni, Mohamed Hédi. *The Work of the United Nations General Assembly's Committee on Information and Special Committee on the Granting of Independence in 1962 and 1963.* London, Ont., 1966. vi, 116 leaves. **4599**
Thesis (M.A.), University of Western Ontario, 1966.

Newcombe, Hanna. *Reform of the U.N. Security Council.* Dundas, Ont.: Peace Research Institute, 1979. 104 p. (Peace Research Reviews, Vol. 8, No. 3) **4600**

Richardson, B.T. "The First Assembly of the United Nations." (1946), 32 *Canadian Geographical Journal* 226-233. **4601**

Smith, I. Norman. "Security Council Membership - A Challenge to Canada." (1948), 3 *International Journal* 111-119. **4602**

"United Nations General Assembly." (1960), 12 *External Affairs* 762-766. **4603**

(d) MEMBERSHIP AND REPRESENTATION

Advani, Gotam Motiram. *The Problem of Membership in the United Nations.* Toronto, 1961. 139, (31) leaves. **4604**
Thesis (LL.M.), University of Toronto, 1961.

Choi, Chung Su. *Chinese Representation: A Study of U.S. Policy in the United Nations, 1949-1971.* Halifax, 1972 (c1973). 123 leaves. **4605**
Thesis (M.A.), Dalhousie University, 1972. (National Library of Canada. Canadian Theses on Microfilm, No. 13117).

Cole, Charles V. "Expulsion of Russia from the United Nations." (1951), 16 *Saskatchewan Bar Review* 58-60. **4606**

Dai, Poeliu. "Canada and the Two-China Formula at the United Nations." (1967), 5 *Canadian Yearbook of International Law* 217-228. **4607**

Green, Leslie C. "Admission of a State to the United Nations (Charter, Article 4), Advisory Opinion, (1948) *I.C.J. Reports* 57." (1949), 12 *Modern Law Review* 485-487. **4608**

Green, Leslie C. "China and the United Nations." (1971), 40 *Malayan Law Journal* 22-29. **4609**

Green, Leslie C. "The Dissolution of States and Membership of the United Nations." (1967), 32 *Saskatchewan Law Review* 93-112. **4610**
Also published in *Law, Justice and Equity; Essays in Tribute to G. W. Keeton* (London, 1967), pp. 152-167.

Green, Leslie C. "Indonesia, the United Nations and Malaysia." (1965), 6 *Journal of South-East Asian History* 71-86 (No. 2) **4611**

Green, Leslie C. "Membership in the United Nations." (1949), 2 *Current Legal Problems* 258-282. **4612**

Green, Leslie C. "Membership in the United Nations: China, Taiwan and Bangladesh." (1972), 22 *Annales de la Faculté de Droit d'Istanbul* 415-461. **4613**

Green, Leslie C. "Representation versus Membership: The Chinese Precedent in the United Nations." (1972), 10 *Canadian Yearbook of International Law* 102-136. **4614**

McWhinney, Edward. "Credentials of State Delegations to the U.N. General Assembly: A New Approach to Effectuation of Self-Determination for Southern Africa." (1975-76), 3 *Hastings Constitutional Law Quarterly* 19-35. **4615**

Simpson, Robert Vernon. *The History of the Membership Controversy in the United Nations.* Vancouver, 1951. 173 leaves. **4616**
Thesis (M.A.), University of British Columbia, 1951.

Tadros, Michel-Charles. *Canada and the Membership Question of the United Nations, 1946-1970.* Halifax, 1971. v, 123 leaves. **4617**
Thesis (M.A.), Dalhousie University, 1971.

(e) PARTICIPATION OF MEMBERS

Beesley, J. Alan. "Canadian Initiatives in East-West Legal Relations in the United Nations." *In* McWhinney, Edward, ed., *Law, Foreign Policy, and the East-West Détente* (Toronto, 1964), pp. 69-82. **4618**

Button, Roger William. *The Afro-Asian Commonwealth and the United Nations.* Ottawa, 1969. 104 leaves. **4619**
Research essay (B.A.), Carleton University, 1969.

"Canada and the United Nations." (1953), 5 *External Affairs* 124-130. **4620**

"Canada and the United Nations - the Record after Fourteen Years." (1959), 11 *External Affairs* 253-260. **4621**

"Canada and the United Nations - the Record after Ten Years." (1955), 7 *External Affairs* 150-158. **4622**

"Canada's Contribution to the United Nations." (1962), 14 *External Affairs* 361-374. **4623**

"Canada's Contributions to United Nations." (1957), 9 *External Affairs* 31-34.
4624

Canada. Dept. of External Affairs. *Canada and the United Nations, 1945-1965.* Ottawa: Queen's Printer, 1966. 108 p. **4625**
At head of title: *We the peoples.* Also issued in French under title: *Le Canada et les Nations Unies, 1945-1965.*

Canada. Dept. of External Affairs. *Canada and the United Nations, 1946-66.* Ottawa: Queen's Printer, 1946-68. 21 vols. **4626**
Published annually in its *Conference Series.* Reviews the work of the United Nations and specialized agencies. Title varies slightly. Also published in French under title: *Le Canada et les Nations Unies.*
Contents: 1946, Pt. 1 (96 p.).- 1946, Pt. 2 (290 p.).- 1947 (276 p.).- 1948 (279 p.).- 1949 (319 p.).- 1950 (ix, 190 p.).- 1951-52 (xv, 165 p.).- 1952-53 (xi, 114 p.).- 1953-54 (x, 116 p.).-

1954-55 (118 p.).- 1956-57 (xii, 132 p.).- 1957 (ix, 105 p.).- 1958 (ix, 116 p.).- 1959 (ix, 93 p.).- 1960 (ix, 117 p.).- 1961 (xi, 133 p.).- 1962 (x, 93 p.).- 1963 (xi, 97 p.).- 1964 (ix, 95 p.).-1965 (x, 123 p.).- 1966 (x, 140 p.).
Reviews: Thomas-A. Birch in (1951-52), 27 *Actualité Économique* 178-179 (of 1949; French ed.); James George Eayrs in (1953), 8 *International Journal* 200-201 (of 1951-52); G.P. de T. Glazebrook in (1948), 14 *Canadian Journal of Economics and Political Science* 150 (of 1946, Pt. 2); G.P. de T. Glazebrook in (1948), 3 *International Journal* 362-365 (of 1947); C. Richard Hiscocks in (1954), 35 *Canadian Historical Review* 156 (of 1952-53); A.H. MacLean in (1948-49), 28 *Dalhousie Review* 424 (of 1947); Camille Martin in (1955-56), 31 *Actualité Économique* 172 (of 1953-54; French ed.); Walter Alexander Riddell in (1946-47), 2 *International Journal* 360-361 (of 1946, Pt. 2); Walter Alexander Riddell in (1946-47), 16 *University of Toronto Quarterly* 436-442 (of 1946, Pt. 2); Albert A. Shea in (1949), 15 *Canadian Journal of Economics and Political Science* 439-440 (of 1948).

Canada. Dept. of External Affairs. *Canada and the United Nations, 1945-1975.* Ottawa: Supply and Services Canada, 1977. xv, 202 p. **4627**
Also issued in French under title: *Le Canada et les Nations Unies, 1945-1975* (c1976. xv, 207 p.).

Canada. Dept. of External Affairs. *Canada at the 31st Regular Session of the United Nations General Assembly.* Ottawa, 1977. 96 p. **4628**

Canada. Dept. of External Affairs. *Canada at the 32nd Regular Session of the United Nations General Assembly / Le Canada à la XXXIIe session de l'Assemblée générale des Nations Unies.* Ottawa: External Affairs Canada, 1980. (7), 120, 127 (7) p. **4629**
The 32nd session was held in 1977. Text in English and French on inverted pages.

Canada. Dept. of External Affairs. *Canada at the 33rd Regular Session of the United Nations General Assembly.* Prepared by the United Nations Political and Institutional Division. Ottawa: External Affairs Canada, 1979. iii, 82, 92, iii p. **4630**
Also contains the French version on inverted pages, under title: *Le Canada à la XXXIIIe session de l'Assemblée générale des Nations Unies.*

Canada. Dept. of External Affairs. *Canada's Financial Contribution to the United Nations.* Ottawa: Supply and Services Canada, 1979. 23 p. (Canada. Dept. of External Affairs. Reference Series, No. 21) **4631**
Also issued in French under title: *Apport financier du Canada aux Nations Unies.*

Canada. Dept. of External Affairs. *Report on the United Nations Conference on International Organization Held at San Francisco, 25th April-26th June, 1945.* Ottawa: King's Printer, 1945. 138 p. (Canada. Dept. of External Affairs. Conference Series, 1945, No. 2) **4632**
Also published in French.

Carter, Gwendolen M. "The Commonwealth in the United Nations." (1950), 4 *International Organization* 247-260. **4633**

Conner, Barbara Ann. *Canada at the United Nations Conference on International Organization, San Francisco, 1945.* Stanford, Calif., 1948. 131 leaves. **4634**
Thesis (A.M.), Stanford University, 1948.

"A Day with the Canadian Delegation at the United Nations." (1949), 1 *External Affairs* 22-24 (Dec.) **4635**

Eagleton, Clyde. "The Share of Canada in the Making of the United Nations." (1947-48), 7 *University of Toronto Law Journal* 329-356. **4636**

Fotheringham, Peter. *Voting Patterns in the General Assembly of the United Nations.* Winnipeg, 1963. 302 leaves. **4637**
Thesis (M.A.), University of Manitoba, 1963.

Gelber, Lionel. "The Commonwealth and the United Nations." (1953), 13 *Behind the Headlines* No. 5 (17 p.) **4638**

Gordon, J. King. "Canada at the United Nations: Specific Policies Must Reflect a Return of Global Perspective." (1976), *International Perspectives* 3-6 (Sept./ Oct.) **4639**

Gupta, Aditya N. *The Egyptian Crisis and the United Nations General Assembly: With Special Emphasis on the Role of Canada, Colombia, India and Norway.* Washington, D.C., 1967. 165 leaves. **4640**
Thesis (M.A.), American University, 1967. Abstracted in (1967), 5 *Masters Abstracts* 21 (No. 3). (University Microfilms, Ann Arbor, No. M-1154).

Holmes, John W. "Canada's Role in the United Nations." (1966-67), 18 *Air University Review* 18-27 (May/June) **4641**

Jacomy-Millette, Annemarie. "Canada at the United Nations: Canada's Voting Pattern at 30th General Assembly." (1976), *International Perspectives* 21-26 (Sept./Oct.) **4642**

Keating, Thomas F., and Keenleyside, Terence A. "United Nations: Voting Patterns as a Measure of Foreign Policy Independence." (1980), *International Perspectives* 21-26 (May/June) **4643**

King, William Lyon Mackenzie, and others. *Canada and the United Nations.* Toronto: Canadian Institute of International Affairs, 1947. 31 p. (Canadian Institute of International Affairs. Special Series) **4644**

Kinsman, Jeremy. "United Nations: Recap of 34th General Assembly." (1980), *International Perspectives* 15-20 (May/June) **4645**

MacKay, Robert A. "Canada and the United Nations." (1956-57), 36 *Dalhousie Review* 120-128. **4646**

Macquarrie, Heath. "The Thirteenth General Assembly." (1958-59), 14 *International Journal* 122-130. **4647**

Martin, Paul. "Canada and the United Nations." (1953-54), 33 *Dalhousie Review* 211-226. **4648**

McInnis, Edgar. "Canada at the United Nations." (1953), 13 *Behind the Headlines* No. 1 (17 p.) **4649**

Merrick, John Robert. *Canada and the Origins of the United Nations, 1941-1945.* Kingston, 1974. ix, 251 leaves. **4650**
Half-title: *Origins of the United Nations.* Thesis (M.A.), Queen's University, 1974. (National Library of Canada. Canadian Theses on Microfiche, No. 20266).

Millar, Thomas B. "The Commonwealth and the United Nations." (1962), 16 *International Organization* 736-757. **4651**

Miller, Anthony John. *Functionalism and Foreign Policy; an Analysis of Cana-*

dian Voting Behaviour in the General Assembly of the United Nations, 1946-1966. Montreal, 1970 (c1971). vi, 447 leaves. **4652**
Thesis (Ph.D.), McGill University, 1971. (National Library of Canada. Canadian Theses on Microfilm, No. 9428).

Newcombe, Hanna. "Inter-Bloc Shifts in U.N. Voting in Relation to International Events Outside the U.N., 1946-71." (1976), 48 *Canadian Political Science Association, Papers,* 28 p. **4653**

Newcombe, Hanna, and Allett, John. *Nations in Groups: Typical Analyses of Roll-Call Votes in the U.N. General Assembly (1946-1973).* Dundas, Ont.: Peace Research Institute, c1981. 155 p. **4654**
Also supplement (1974-1977). 29 p.

Newcombe, Hanna, and Mahoney, Terry. *The Affinities of Nations: Tables of Pearson Correlation Coefficients of U.N. General Assembly Roll-Call Votes, (1974-1977). Supplement.* Dundas, Ont.: Peace Research Institute-Dundas, 1981. 161 p. **4655**
Supplement to: Newcombe, Hanna, *The Affinities of Nations: Tables of Pearson Correlation Coefficients of U.N. General Assembly Roll-Call Votes, (1946-1973).*

Newcombe, Hanna; Ross, Michael; and Newcombe, Alan G. "United Nations Voting Patterns." (1970), 24 *International Organization* 100-121. **4656**

Newcombe, Hanna; Young, Christopher; and Suaiko, Elia. "Alternative Pasts: A Study of Weighted Voting at the United Nations." (1975), 47 *Canadian Political Science Association, Papers,* 34 p. **4657**

Pearson, Lester B. "Canada, the United Nations and a Two-Power World." (1951), 3 *External Affairs* 154-160. **4658**

Petrusa, Seraph M. *Canadian Participation in the United Nations.* New York, 1959. 146 leaves. **4659**
Thesis (M.A.), Columbia University, 1959.

Reford, Robert W. "Le Canada et les Nations Unies." *In* Painchaud, Paul, ed., *Le Canada et le Québec sur la scène internationale* (Québec, 1977), pp. 421-438. **4660**

Richard, John. *Le Canada et certains problèmes de sécurité aux Nations Unies de 1946 à 1956.* Louvain, 1960. 189 leaves. **4661**
Thesis, École des sciences politiques, 1960.

Schopen, Lynn, and others. *Nations on Record: United Nations General Assembly Roll-Call Votes (1946-1973).* Oakville, Ont.: Canadian Peace Research Institute, c1975. x, 515, 19 p. **4662**

Simon, Pierre A. *Rapports de dépendance en politique étrangère: le comportement de vote des états latino-américains à l'Assemblée générale des Nations Unies.* Montréal, 1974. 184 leaves. **4663**
Thesis (M.A.), Université de Montréal, 1974.

Soward, Frederic H. "Canada, the Eleventh General Assembly and Trusteeship." (1956-57), 12 *International Journal* 167-181. **4664**

Soward, Frederic H., and McInnis, Edgar. *Canada and the United Nations.* With

the assistance of Walter O'Hearn. New York: Manhattan Pub., 1956 (i.e. 1957). 285 p. (National Studies on International Organization) **4665**
Prepared for the Canadian Institute of International Affairs and the Carnegie Endowment for International Peace. This is one of a series of studies dealing with the respective national experiences in the United States.
Reviews: Wolfgang G. Friedman in (1957), 12 *International Journal* 309-311; Lionel H. Laing in (1958), 52 *American Journal of International Law* 561-562; Arthur R.M. Lower in (1958), 39 *Canadian Historical Review* 157-158; Robert Rie in (1958-59), 7 *Archiv des Völkerrechts* 358-359; Ignaz Seidl-Hohenveldern in (1958), 7 *American Journal of Comparative Law* 109-111; Gordon Winter in (1957), 33 *International Affairs* 343-344.

Stevenson, Garth. "Canada in the United Nations." *In* Hillmer, Norman, and Stevenson, Garth, eds., *A Foremost Nation: Canadian Foreign Policy and a Changing World* (Toronto, 1977), pp. 150-177. **4666**

Tanguay, J.F. "Controversial Resolutions Marked 35th UN Assembly." (1981), *International Perspectives* 15-20 (May/June) **4667**

Tanguay, J.F. "Recap of Canada's Activities at Thirty-Third General Assembly." (1979), *International Perspectives* 17-21 (May/June) **4668**

Taylor, Alastair M. "Canada and Competitive Coexistence: Our Rôle in the U.N." (1956-57), 63 *Queen's Quarterly* 1-18. **4669**

Tomalin, Beth. "Canada at the Opening Sessions of UNO." (1946), 1 *International Journal* 243-265. **4670**

Tomlin, Brian W. *United Nations Supranationalism: An Analysis of Roll-Call Voting in the General Assembly.* Downsview, Ont., 1972. xi, 273 leaves. **4671**
Thesis (Ph.D.), York University, 1972. (National Library of Canada. Canadian Theses on Microfilm, No. 12610).

Turi, Giuseppe. *Le Canada et le droit de veto aux Nations-Unies.* Montréal, 1968. v, 253 leaves. **4672**
Thesis (M.A.), Université de Montréal, 1968.

United Nations Association in Canada. *Canada and the United Nations in a Changing World: The Report of a Conference Held in Winnipeg, Manitoba May 12-14, 1977.* Ottawa: United Nations Association in Canada, c1977. 146 p. J. King Gordon, Chairman. **4673**

Van Praagh, David. "United States Holds the Key to Central Issues at U.N." (1981), *International Perspectives* 6-7 (July/Aug.) **4674**

Vincent, Jack E. *Empirical Studies of Behavioral Patterns at the United Nations.* Oakville, Ont.: Canadian Peace Research Institute, 1978. 120 p. (Peace Research Reviews, Vol. 7, No. 4) **4675**

Waters, Maurice. "Canada's Role in the United Nations and Its Effects on Interdependence." (1964), 6 *University of Windsor Seminar on Canadian-American Relations, Proceedings* 221-229. **4676**

Western, Maurice. "Canada's Rôle in the Second Assembly." (1948), 3 *International Journal* 120-131. **4677**

4. SPECIALIZED AGENCIES

(a) GENERAL (INCL. INDIVIDUAL AGENCIES)

Acheson, A.L. Keith; Chant, John F.; and Prachowny, Martin F.J., eds. *Bretton Woods Revisited: Evaluations of the International Monetary Fund and the International Bank for Reconstruction and Development.* Toronto: University of Toronto Press, 1972. xxiv, 138 p. **4678**
Papers delivered at a conference held at Queen's University, Kingston, Ont., June 2-3, 1969. Also published in London, Macmillan, 1972.
Reviews: H.H.F. Binhammer in (1973), 6 *Canadian Journal of Economics* 459-460; John Helliwell in (1974), 55 *Canadian Historical Review* 204-205; H.R.C. Wright in (1976), 7 *Études Internationales* 617-618.

"An Achievement in International Co-operation: The World Health Organization." (1968), 20 *External Affairs* 335-340. **4679**
Contains a brief history of W.H.O.

Baum, Warren C. "World Bank Offers a Rich Potential." (1974), 81 *Canadian Banker and ICB Review* 42-47 (No. 1) **4680**

Beattie, Laura. "Gateway to a New World." (1945), 31 *Canadian Geographical Journal* 304-308. **4681**

Belfie, Michael Arthur. *The World Bank; an Overview.* Burnaby, B.C., 1970. vi, 42, v, 30 leaves. **4682**
Thesis (M.A.), Simon Fraser University, 1970. Contains two extended essays, each with a title page. (National Library of Canada. Canadian Theses on Microfilm, No. 6643).

Broadley, James Ashley. *The Reform of the I.M.F.: The Exchange Stability Problem: The Pareto Optimum.* Burnaby, 1968. xiii, 16, 17, 17 leaves. **4683**
Thesis (M.A.), Simon Fraser University, 1968. (National Library of Canada. Canadian Theses on Microfilm, No. 1777).

Cameron, Duncan Charles. "Le Fonds monétaire international, la réforme monétaire et le tiers-monde." (1979), 55 *Actualité Économique* 28-45. **4684**

Camps, Miriam. "The New Bretton Woods." (1979-80), 35 *International Journal* 240-262. **4685**

Canada. Dept. of External Affairs. *Canada and the Intergovernmental Maritime Consultative Organization.* Ottawa: Supply and Services Canada, 1979. 5 p. (Canada. Dept. of External Affairs. Reference Series, No. 15) **4686**
Also issued in French under title: *Le Canada et l'Organisation intergouvernementale consultative de la navigation maritime.*

Canada. Dept. of External Affairs. *Canada and the International Atomic Energy Organization.* Ottawa: Supply and Services Canada, 1979. 6 p. (Canada. Dept. of External Affairs. Reference Series, No. 14) **4687**
Also issued in French under title: *Le Canada et l'Agence internationale de l'énergie atomique.*

Canada. Dept. of External Affairs. *Canada and the World Intellectual Property Organization.* Ottawa: Supply and Services Canada, 1979. 4 p. (Canada. Dept. of External Affairs. Reference Series, No. 12) **4688**

Also issued in French under title: *Le Canada et l'Organisation mondiale de la propriété intellectuelle.*

Canada. Dept. of External Affairs. *Canada and the World Meteorological Organization.* Ottawa: Supply and Services Canada, 1979. 6 p. (Canada. Dept. of External Affairs. Reference Series, No. 16) **4689**
Also issued in French under title: *Le Canada et l'Organisation météorologique mondiale.*

Canada. Dept. of Finance. *Report on Operations under the Bretton Woods Agreements Act and International Development Association Act / Rapport sur les opérations effectuées en vertu de la Loi sur les accords de Bretton Woods et de la Loi sur l'Association internationale de développement.* Ottawa, 1954/55–. Annual. **4690**
Reviews the operations of the International Monetary Fund, the World Bank, the International Development Association, and the International Finance Corporation. Text in French and English.

Canada. Parliament. House of Commons. Standing Committee on Banking and Commerce. *Bill No. 238, an Act for Carrying into Effect the Agreements for an International Monetary Fund and an International Bank for Reconstruction and Development. Minutes of Proceedings and Evidence and Report to the House.* Ottawa: King's Printer, 1945. xii, 152 p. **4691**
Minutes taken December 11-13, 1945. Hughes Cleaver, Chairman.

"Canada and the Specialized Agencies." (1955), 7 *External Affairs* 116-121. **4692**

"Canada and the World Health Organization." (1968), 20 *External Affairs* 389-392. **4693**

"Canada and the World Meteorological Organization." (1956), 8 *External Affairs* 205-208. **4694**

"The Food and Agriculture Organization." (1954), 6 *External Affairs* 230-234. **4695**

"Food and Agriculture Organization of the United Nations." (1952), 4 *External Affairs* 56-61. **4696**

Girard, Roger. "Réalisations et perspectives du Fonds monétaire international." (1955-56), 31 *Actualité Économique* 388-407. **4697**

Granatstein, J.L. "The Road to Bretton Woods: International Monetary Policy and the Public Servant." (1981-82), 16 *Journal of Canadian Studies* 174-185. **4698**

Halim, Md. Abdul. *Lending Policy of the World Bank with Special Reference to Its Contribution to the Economic Development of Bangladesh from 1972 to 1978.* Ottawa, 1980. 243 leaves. **4699**
Thesis (M.A.), Carleton University, 1980. (National Library of Canada. Canadian Theses on Microfiche, No. 44404).

Healey, Derek. "The World Bank in the Sixties." (1964), 71 *Canadian Banker* 51-70 (No. 3) **4700**

Herchak, Gayle. "World Bank Energy Affiliate - An Idea Whose Time May Come." (1981), *International Perspectives* 13-15 (July/Aug.) **4701**

"The International Atomic Energy Agency." (1956), 8 *External Affairs* 192-196.
4702

"International Atomic Energy Agency: First General Conference." (1957), 9 *External Affairs* 385-390. **4703**

"International Atomic Energy Agency Statute." (1956), 8 *External Affairs* 346-351.
4704

"The International Bank for Reconstruction and Development." (1949), 1 *External Affairs* 3-10 (Mar.) **4705**

Jacobson, Harold K. "International Institutions for Telecommunications. The ITU's Rôle." *In* McWhinney, Edward, ed., *The International Law of Communications* (Leyden, 1971), pp. 51-68. **4706**

Khalid, El Rashid Osman. *An Evaluation of the Development Programmes of the International Bank for Reconstruction and Development, with Special Reference to the Iraqi and Syrian Programmes.* Saskatoon, 1959. (5), 134 leaves.
Thesis (M.A.), University of Saskatchewan, 1959. **4707**

Kitazawa, Kimiko. *McNamara's World Bank and Prebisch's UNCTAD: A Comparison.* Kingston, 1981. 243 leaves. **4708**
Thesis (M.A.), Queen's University, 1980. (National Library of Canada. Canadian Theses on Microfiche, No. 46365).

MacGibbon, D.A. "International Monetary Control." (1945), 11 *Canadian Journal of Economics and Political Science* 1-13. **4709**

McNaughton, A.G.L. "The International Control of Atomic Energy." (1949), 38 *Canadian Geographical Journal* 238-241. **4710**

Miller, Anthony John. *The Food and Agriculture Organisation of the United Nations; a Systems Analysis.* Hamilton, Ont., 1966. iv, 85 leaves. **4711**
Thesis (M.A.), McMaster University, 1966.

Pineo, C.C. "The International Bank for Reconstruction and Development." (1947), 54 *Canadian Banker* 26-32 (No. 3) **4712**

Plosz, D.J. "The International Telecommunications Union." (1966), 31 *Saskatchewan Bar Review* 41-53. **4713**

Plumptre, A.F.W. "International Monetary Reform." (1966), 73 *Canadian Banker* 37-44 (No. 4) **4714**

"The Present and Future Role of the ITU in the Management of International Telecommunications." (1973), 5 *Canadian Communications Law Review* 175-205. **4715**
Panel discussion: Harold K. Jacobson, Chairman; David M. Leive, Samuel D. Estep, David M. Miller, and J.R. Marchand, participants.

Pritchard, David A. *International Telecommunication Union: Adapting to Technological and Geopolitical Change.* Ottawa, 1975. vii, 152 leaves. **4716**
Thesis (M.A.), Carleton University, 1975.

Reid, Escott. *Strengthening the World Bank.* Chicago: Adlai Stevenson Institute of International Affairs, 1973. xviii, 289 p. **4717**
Reviews: Theodore H. Cohn in (1973-74), 29 *International Journal* 646-649; Margaret P.

Doxey in (1976), 2 *Canadian Public Policy* 125-126; Colin Leys in (1976), 83 *Queen's Quarterly* 131-132; Douglas J. McCready in (1976), 9 *Canadian Journal of Political Science* 525-526; James Pickett in (1976), 9 *Canadian Journal of Economics* 736-738.

Sautier, Jérôme. *L'Organisation inter-gouvernementale consultative de la navigation maritime et la pollution des mers par les hydro-carbures.* Montréal, 1972. 147 leaves. **4718**
Thesis (LL.M.), Université de Montréal, 1972.

Scammell, W.M. "Have We Reformed the International Monetary System?" (1976), 83 *Canadian Banker and ICB Review* 24-28 (No. 4) **4719**

Shefrin, Frank. "The Agricultural Agencies: Objectives and Performance." (1979-80), 35 *International Journal* 263-291. **4720**

Silverstein, Harvey B. *Superships and Nation-States: The Transnational Politics of the Intergovernmental Maritime Consultative Organization.* Boulder, Colo.: Westview Press, 1978. xiii, 251 p. (Westview Replica Edition) **4721**

Sinclair, Adelaide. "Progress and Achievements of UNICEF." (1954), 6 *External Affairs* 46-50. **4722**

Szawlowski, Richard. *Les finances et le droit financier d'une organisation internationale intergouvernementale: examen sur la base de l'Organisation mondiale de la santé et certaines autres organisations.* Préface de Georges Langrod. Paris: Éditions Cujas, 1970. 223 p. **4723**
Reviews: Herbert R. Balls in (1972), 15 *Canadian Public Administration* 510-511; Ludwik Kos-Rabcewicz-Zubkowski in (1971), 9 *Canadian Yearbook of International Law* 334-336.

Thompson, Dale Edward. *Selected Issues in the Canadian Participation with the United Nations Relief and Rehabilitation Administration (UNRRA), 1942-47.* Ottawa, 1978. 159 leaves. **4724**
Thesis (M.A.), Carleton University, 1978.

Tomkinson, Grace. "Our Share in 'UNRRA.' " (1945), 25 *Dalhousie Review* 183-189. **4725**

"The United Nations International Children's Emergency Fund." (1951), 3 *External Affairs* 249-251. **4726**

"The Universal Postal Union." (1952), 4 *External Affairs* 134-138. **4727**

"The Universal Postal Union." (1957), 9 *External Affairs* 256-259. **4728**

Verdon, Christiane. "L'UIT et quelques problèmes existant au sein de cette organisation." (1970), 20 *University of Toronto Law Journal* 386-388. **4729**

Williams, John S. *Extraterritorial Enforcement of Exchange Control Regulations under the International Monetary Fund Agreement.* Montreal, 1973 (c1974). 198, xxxv leaves. **4730**
Thesis (LL.M.), McGill University, 1973. (National Library of Canada. Canadian Theses on Microfiche, No. 18415).

Wilson, Kenneth R. "Geneva and the I.T.O." (1946-47), 2 *International Journal* 242-249. **4731**
Refers to the proposed International Trade Organization.

"World Health Organization." (1950), 2 *External Affairs* 135-138. **4732**

"The World Meteorological Organization." (1953), 5 *External Affairs* 68-74.**4733**

"The World Meteorological Organization." (1961), 13 *External Affairs* 306-311.
4734

(b) INTERNATIONAL CIVIL AVIATION ORGANIZATION

See also *"Airspace and Outer Space" (p. 280).*

Binaghi, Walter. "The International Civil Aviation Organization (ICAO) after Twenty Years: Its Activities in the Technical, Economic, and Legal Fields." (1967), *Yearbook of Air and Space Law* 5-14. **4735**

Binaghi, Walter. "The Rôle of ICAO." *In* McWhinney, Edward, and Bradley, Martin A., eds., *The Freedom of the Air* (Leyden, 1968), pp. 17-29. **4736**

Bogolasky, José. "International Organizations: ICAO Panel of Experts on Regulation of Air Transport Services." (1978), 3 *Annals of Air and Space Law* 600-605.
4737

Bogolasky, José. "International Organizations: ICAO Second Meeting of the Panel on Regulation of Air Transport Services." (1979), 4 *Annals of Air and Space Law* 655-661. **4738**

Canada. Dept. of External Affairs. *Canada and the International Civil Aviation Organization.* Ottawa: Supply and Services Canada, 1979. 5 p. (Canada. Dept. of External Affairs. Reference Series, No. 13) **4739**
    Also issued in French under title: *Le Canada et l'Organisation de l'aviation civile internationale.*

"Canada and ICAO." (1956), 8 *External Affairs* 413-416. **4740**

Doehring, Karl. "ICAO and the European Economic Community." *In* McWhinney, Edward, and Bradley, Martin A., eds., *The Freedom of the Air* (Leyden, 1968), pp. 54-69. **4741**

Edge, Frederick. "PICAO into ICAO - International Civil Aviation Organization." (1947), 34 *Canadian Geographical Journal* 286-293. **4742**

Erler, Jochen. *The Regulatory Functions of ICAN and ICAO: A Comparative Study.* Montreal, 1964. ix, 178 leaves. **4743**
    Thesis (LL.M.), McGill University, 1964.

Erler, Jochen. "Regulatory Procedures of ICAO as a Model for IMCO." (1964), 10 *McGill Law Journal* 262-268. **4744**

FitzGerald, Gerald F. "I.C.A.O. Now and in the Coming Decades." *In* Matte, Nicolas Mateesco, ed., *International Air Transport: Law, Organization and Policies for the Future* (Toronto, 1976), pp. 47-58. **4745**

FitzGerald, Gerald F. "The International Civil Aviation Organization: A Case Study in the Implementation of Decisions of a Functional International Organization." *In* Schwebel, Stephen M., ed., *The Effectiveness of International Decisions* (Leyden, 1971), pp. 156-205. **4746**

FitzGerald, Gerald F. "The International Civil Aviation Organization - a Case

Study in Functional International Organization." (1966), *Canadian Bar Association, Papers* 31-51. **4747**

FitzGerald, Gerald F. "The International Civil Aviation Organization and the Development of Conventions on International Air Law (1947-1978)." (1978), 3 *Annals of Air and Space Law* 51-120. **4748**

Hildred, *Sir* William. "The Interdependence of ICAO and IATA." *In* McWhinney, Edward, and Bradley, Martin A., eds., *The Freedom of the Air* (Leyden, 1968), pp. 40-51. **4749**

"ICAO: A Review of Five Years' Activity." (1950), 2 *External Affairs* 12-15. **4750**

Jasentuliyana, Nandasiri. *Role of International Organizations in the Development of a Legal Order in Space.* Montreal, 1965. 233 leaves. **4751**
Thesis (LL.M.), McGill University, 1965.

Kotaite, Assad. "ICAO's Concern and Recent Work in the Legal Field to Meet the Present Requirements of International Air Transport." (1978), 3 *Annals of Air and Space Law* 155-162. **4752**

Kotaite, Assad. "Security of International Civil Aviation - Role of ICAO." (1982), 7 *Annals of Air and Space Law* 95-101. **4753**

Mankiewicz, René H. "Augmentation du nombre des membres du Conseil de l'O.A.C.I." (1961), 7 *Annuaire Français de Droit International* 445-450. **4754**

Mankiewicz, René H. "Comparative Law and the International Civil Aviation Organization." *In* Butler, William E., ed., *International Law in Comparative Perspective* (Alphen aan den Rijn, 1980), pp. 269-276. **4755**

Mankiewicz, René H. "International Civil Aviation Organization: The Legal Committee - Its Organization and Working Methods." (1966), 32 *Journal of Air Law and Commerce* 94-98. **4756**

Mankiewicz, René H. "L'Organisation de l'aviation civile internationale. (Chroniques)." (1956), 2 *Annuaire Français de Droit International* 643-666. **4757**
Continued in vol. 3, pp. 383-417 (1957); vol. 13, pp. 482-531 (1967); vol. 14, pp. 483-529 (1968); vol. 15, pp. 462-489 (1969); vol. 18, pp. 804-835 (1972); vol. 20, pp. 637-658 (1974); and vol. 23, pp. 625-647 (1977).

Mankiewicz, René H. "L'Organisation de l'aviation civile internationale: mode d'élection et composition du Conseil; interprétation de l'article 50 de la convention de Chicago." (1959), 5 *Annuaire Français de Droit International* 549-568.
4758

Mankiewicz, René H. "Organisation de l'aviation civile internationale (O.A.C.I): I. Résolution de la 21e session de l'Assemblée de l'O.A.C.I. (Montréal, 22 septembre-16 octobre 1974).- II. Résumé des travaux du Comité juridique de l'O.A.C.I. (21e session, Montréal, 3 au 22 octobre 1974)." (1975), 29 *Revue Française de Droit Aérien* 88-104. **4759**

Milde, C. Michael. "International Organizations: ICAO - Legal Work in 1980." (1980), 5 *Annals of Air and Space Law* 629-632. **4760**

Milde, C. Michael. "International Organizations: ICAO - Legal Work of ICAO in 1978." (1978), 3 *Annals of Air and Space Law* 577-581. **4761**

Milde, C. Michael. "International Organizations: OACI/ICAO." (1981), 6 *Annals of Air and Space Law* 500-515. **4762**

Milde, C. Michael. "International Organizations: OACI/ICAO." (1982), 7 *Annals of Air and Space Law* 470-475. **4763**

Milde, C. Michael. "International Organizations: UN and ICAO." (1977), 2 *Annals of Air and Space Law* 439-445. **4764**

Rajski, Jerzy. "I.C.A.O. and the Development of Air Law." *In* Matte, Nicolas Mateesco, ed., *International Air Transport: Law, Organization and Policies for the Future* (Toronto, 1976), pp. 59-66. **4765**

Sampaio de Lacerda, J.C. "A Study about the Decisions of the ICAO Council, the Admissible Appeals and Their Effects." (1978), 3 *Annals of Air and Space Law* 219-223. **4766**

Sheffy, Menachem. *The Air Navigation Commission of the International Civil Aviation Organization.* Montreal, 1957. v, 122 leaves. **4767**
Thesis (LL.M.), McGill University, 1957. Also published in (1958), 25 *Journal of Air Law and Commerce* 281-328, 428-443.

Tobolewski, Aleksander. "ICAO's Legal Syndrome or; International Air Law in the Making." (1979), 4 *Annals of Air and Space Law* 349-357. **4768**

(c) INTERNATIONAL LABOUR ORGANIZATION

See also *"Labour and Trade Unions" (p. 673), "Law of Treaties: Specific Treaties: Labour" (p. 159), and "Treaties and National Law" (p. 157).*

Beigbeder, Yves. "The United States' Withdrawal from the International Labour Organization." (1979), 34 *Relations Industrielles* 223-239. **4769**
Summary in French under title: "Le retrait des États-Unis de l'Organisation internationale du travail" (p. 240).

Binet, Henri. "International Labour Legislation." (1946), 24 *Canadian Bar Review* 847-860. **4770**

Binet, Henri. "L'Organisation internationale du travail." (1931), 17 *Revue Trimestrielle Canadienne* 177-185. **4771**

Burke, Frank E., and Munro, John A. *Canada and the Founding of the International Labour Organization.* Ottawa: Dept. of External Affairs, 1969. 22, 24 p. **4772**
Published in English and French; at head of title: *Fiftieth Anniversary of the I.L.O.*

Canada. International Labour Affairs Branch. *The ILO Today: Some Observations on Its Present Role and Problems.* Ottawa: Dept. of Labour, 1968. 35 p. **4773**

"Canada and the International Labour Organization." (1956), 8 *External Affairs* 119-122. **4774**

Carter, Thomas Le Mesurier. *Canada in the International Labour Organization (1919-1938).* London, Eng., 1940. 246 leaves. **4775**
Thesis (M.Sc.), University of London, 1940.

Conroy, Pat. "Canada and the I.L.O." (1944-45), 8 *Public Affairs* 146-150. **4776**

Després, Jean-Pierre. *Le Canada et l'Organisation internationale du travail.* Québec, 1946. 372 leaves. **4777**
> Thesis (Ph.D.), Université Laval, 1946. Listed in (1945/46), 13 *Doctoral Dissertations Accepted by American Universities* 53.

Després, Jean-Pierre. *Le Canada et l'Organisation internationale du travail.* Preface by Georges-Henri Lévesque. Published under the auspices of the Canadian Institute of International Affairs. Montréal: South Bend, Fides, 1947. 273 p. **4778**
> Originally presented for the Doctorat de sciences sociales, Université Laval, 1946.
> Reviews: Samuel Mack Eastman in (1948), 3 *International Journal* 277; Eugene Forsey in (1949), 15 *Canadian Journal of Economics and Political Science* 272; Camille Martin in (1949-50), 25 *Actualité Économique* 371-372.

Després, Jean-Pierre. "Les Commissions d'industrie du Bureau international du travail." (1946), 52/2 *Revue Dominicaine* 73-82. **4779**

George, Pierre. "L'Organisation internationale du travail et les relations industrielles." (1948), 54/2 *Revue Dominicaine* 109-115. **4780**

Goodrich, Carter. "The I.L.O. at Montreal." (1941), 7 *Canadian Journal of Economics and Political Science* 267-269. **4781**

Green, Leslie C. "The International Labour Organisation under Pressure." (1957), 10 *Current Legal Problems* 57-84. **4782**

Hardy, Edith H. *Canada and the International Labour Organization.* Ottawa: Dept. of Labour, 1951. 55 p. **4783**

Haythorne, George V. "The International Labour Organization: A Canadian Appraisal after Fifty Years." (1971), 14 *Canadian Public Administration* 173-192. **4784**

"The International Labor Organization." (1970), 22 *External Affairs* 29-31, 63-65. **4785**
> Contents: Development of Technical Assistance Programs.- Protection for Women and Young Workers.

"International Labour Organization." (1960), 12 *External Affairs* 730-733. **4786**

"The International Labour Organization." (1969), 21 *External Affairs* 259-263, 266-268, 315-317, 351-353, 377-379, 422-424, 457-459. **4787**
> Contents: History and Development.- Structure and Function.- History of Canadian Participation.- International Standards for Social Justice.- Human Resources Development.- World Employment Program.- International Labor Standards.

Langlais, Antonio. "Le gouvernement Kadar, l'O.I.T. et la C.I.J." (1957-58), 12 *Revue de l'Université Laval* 359-364. **4788**
> Refers to "Organisation internationale du travail," and "Commission internationale de juristes."

Macdonnell, H.W. "The International Labour Organization." (1964-65), 13 *Chitty's Law Journal* 258-260. **4789**

Mainwaring, John. "Canada and the ILO: The Past Quarter Century." (1975), 75 *Labour Gazette* 618-623. **4790**

Mainwaring, John. "Canada and the World Movement Towards Social Justice." (1950), 50 *Labour Gazette* 1460-1487. **4791**

Mainwaring, John. "Le Canada en tant que membre de l'O.I.T.: réalisations et possibilités." (1969), 24 *Relations Industrielles* 680-704. **4792**

Maurette, Fernand. "L'Organisation internationale du travail." (1930-31), 6 *Actualité Économique* 209-216. **4793**

National Tripartite Conference, Ottawa, 1969. *National Tripartite Conference in Honour of the 50th Anniversary of the International Labour Organization, October 26-29, 1969, Ottawa: A Summary of Highlights.* Ottawa, 1970. 350 p. Also issued in French. **4794**

Phelan, Vincent C. "Human Welfare and the ILO." (1954), 9 *International Journal* 24-33. **4795**

Sturmthal, Adolf. "Labour and World Affairs." (1951), 11 *Behind the Headlines* No. 6 (18 p.) **4796**

(d) UNITED NATIONS EDUCATIONAL, SCIENTIFIC AND CULTURAL ORGANIZATION

Campbell, Duncan Darroch. *UNESCO: An Examination of the Development of Its Philosophy, Purposes, Programming, and Policies, 1945-1952.* Edmonton, 1960. 189 leaves. **4797**
Thesis (M.A.), University of Alberta, 1960.

Canada. National Commission for UNESCO. *Dialogue 1961; New Dimensions in International Relations.* Report of the Second National Conference Held at the Royal York Hotel, Toronto, on 22 to 24 February 1961. Ottawa, 1961. 55 p. **4798**

Canadian Commission for UNESCO. *Unesco Programme: Objectives, Alternatives and Priorities: A Canadian Commentary / Le programme de l'Unesco: objectifs, alternatives et priorités: un commentaire canadien.* Ottawa: Canadian Commission for Unesco, 1973. vi, 30, 32, vi p. Irregular. **4799**
Text in English and French on inverted pages, each with a separate title page and paging.

Conway, Myrtle R. "Impressions of a UNESCO Conference." (1953), 5 *External Affairs* 7-11. **4800**

Dirks, Gerald E. *The Canadian National Commission for UNESCO; an Analysis and Evaluation.* Kingston, 1965. 114 leaves. **4801**
Thesis (M.A.), Queen's University, 1965.

Douglas, A. Vibert. "Report on UNESCO: What Will Canada Do?" (1955), 62 *Queen's Quarterly* 89-99. **4802**

Dussault, Paul N. *Le rôle de l'UNESCO dans le développement des systèmes d'information pour les pays en voie de développement.* Ottawa, 1967. iv, 112 leaves. **4803**
Thesis (M.A.), University of Ottawa, 1967.

Fowlie, E.L. "Canadian National Commission for UNESCO." (1958), 10 *External Affairs* 78-79, 84. **4804**

Fraser, Charles Frederick. "The Functional Approach to UNESCO." (1947-48), 27 *Dalhousie Review* 143-157. **4805**

Holly, Daniel A. *L'Unesco, le tiers-monde et l'économie mondiale.* Montréal: Presses de l'Université de Montréal, 1981. 176 p. **4806**
Reviews: Paris J. Arnopoulos in (1982), 15 *Canadian Journal of Political Science* 852-853; Guy Gosselin in (1982), 13 *Études Internationales* 384-386.

Kidd, J.R. "Canada's Stake in UNESCO - A National Commission Now?" (1956-57), 63 *Queen's Quarterly* 248-264. **4807**

LeBlanc, Napoleon. "Measuring UNESCO's Progress in Wake of Nairobi Meeting." (1977), *International Perspectives* 13-19 (May/June) **4808**

Leddy, John Francis. *Canada and UNESCO.* Ottawa: Canadian National Commission for UNESCO, 1961. 10, 10 p. **4809**
Presidential address by J.F. Leddy delivered at the third annual meeting of the National Commission, Toronto, February 21, 1961. In English and French.

Page, Garnet T. "Canadian Council for Reconstruction through UNESCO." (1953), 5 *External Affairs* 154-160. **4810**

Sewell, James P. *UNESCO and World Politics: Engaging in International Relations.* Princeton, N. J.: Princeton University Press, 1975. 384 p. **4811**
Reviews: Robert Boardman in (1976-77), 56 *Dalhousie Review* 769-771; Guy Gosselin in (1976), 7 *Études Internationales* 137-140; Brian W. Tomlin in (1977-78), 33 *International Journal* 656-659; Mark W. Zacher in (1977), 10 *Canadian Journal of Political Science* 188-189.

Turcotte, Edmond. "The World of UNESCO." (1946), 1 *International Journal* 365-369. **4812**

Voaden, Herman. "The Arts and UNESCO." (1947-48), 17 *University of Toronto Quarterly* 161-167. **4813**

Wallace, R.C. "UNESCO." (1945), 52 *Queen's Quarterly* 385-389. **4814**

C. Regional Intergovernmental Organizations

1. GENERAL

Gosztonyi, Paul Marie Joseph. *Some Constitutional Problems of the Regional Organizations.* Montreal, 1953. vii, 213 leaves. **4815**
Thesis (M.C.L.), McGill University, 1953.

Killam, Ronald W.B. *Regional Integration and Less Developed Countries; a General Survey.* Fredericton, 1969 (c1971). iii, 65 leaves. **4816**
Thesis (M.A.), University of New Brunswick, 1970. (National Library of Canada. Canadian Theses on Microfilm, No. 8201).

McRae, Donald M. "Regional Organisation Involving South East Asia and the Western Pacific: ECAFE, the Colombo Plan and the Asian Development Bank." (1969-72), 2 *Otago Law Review* 393-407. **4817**

Pentland, Charles. "The Regionalization of World Politics: Concepts and Evidence." (1974-75), 30 *International Journal* 599-630. **4818**

"Regional Organization Without Big-Power Participation: A Suggestion for a Total World Development System." (1974-75), 30 *International Journal* 768-784. **4819**

"UN Regional Economic Commissions." (1962), 14 *External Affairs* 205-207. **4820**

2. WESTERN EUROPE AND NORTH ATLANTIC

See also *"North Atlantic Treaty Organization" (p. 441).*

(a) GENERAL

Bareau, Paul. "Britain and the European Free Trade." (1956-57), 12 *International Journal* 128-137. **4821**

Birrenbach, Kurt. "Europe, the European Economic Community, and the Outer Seven." (1959-60), 15 *International Journal* 59-65. **4822**

Bourély, Michel. "L'Agence spatiale européenne." (1976), 1 *Annals of Air and Space Law* 183-196. **4823**

Bourély, Michel. "La coordination des organisations européennes de coopération spatiale." *In* McWhinney, Edward, and Bradley, Martin A., eds., *New Frontiers in Space Law* (Leyden, 1969), pp. 47-60. **4824**

Brebner, John Bartlet. *North Atlantic Triangle: The Interplay of Canada, the United States and Great Britain.* New York: Russell & Russell, 1970 (c1945). xxii, 344, (43) p., maps. (Relations of Canada and the United States) **4825**
First published New Haven, Yale University Press; Toronto, Ryerson Press, 1945. Edited under the auspices of the Carnegie Endowment for International Peace. Also reprinted New York, Columbia University Press, 1958, and Toronto, McClelland and Stewart, 1966 (Carleton Library, No. 30), with an introduction by Donald G. Creighton. Reviews: Henry F. Angus in (1946), 12 *Canadian Journal of Economics and Political Science* 219-220; S. Whittemore Boggs in (1947), 41 *American Journal of International Law* 348-349; Alexander Brady in (1946), 1 *International Journal* 173-174; Harold Butler in (1947), 23 *International Affairs* 405; D.C. Harvey in (1945), 25 *Dalhousie Review* 514-515; Frederic H. Soward in (1946), 27 *Canadian Historical Review* 58-60.

"Brussels Treaty Organization." (1949), 1 *External Affairs* 21-24 (May) **4826**

Caves, Richard E. "Europe's Unification and Canada's Trade." (1959), 25 *Canadian Journal of Economics and Political Science* 249-258. **4827**

Chevallard, Francine Charbonneau. *Quelques expériences étrangères d'intégration économique.* Québec: Ministère des affaires intergouvernementales, 1979, c1978. 1 vol. (625 leaves) **4828**

Constas, Dimitrios C. *Exercise of Political Pressure by International Organizations: Greece and the Council of Europe.* Ottawa, 1975. vii, 327 leaves. **4829**
Thesis (M.A.), Carleton University, 1975.

Corriveau, Patrice. "L'unité européenne et le christianisme." (1951), 21 *Revue de l'Université d'Ottawa* 259-286. **4830**

"The Council of Europe and European Unity." (1951), 3 *External Affairs* 309-312. **4831**

"The Council of Europe." (1950), 2 *External Affairs* 167-170. **4832**

De Planelles, Margarita. "Does U.S.A. Want a 'U.S. of Europe?' " (1945), 25 *Dalhousie Review* 465-468. **4833**

Dimitriu, Paul. "De la mise en veilleuse de l'intégration à l'épanouissement de la coopération en Europe." (1974), 5 *Études Internationales* 623-636. **4834**

Donneur, André P. "Le système paneuropéen: un modèle d'analyse." (1973), 4 *Études Internationales* 6-30. **4835**

Duroselle, Jean Baptiste. "The Future of the Atlantic Community." (1965-66), 21 *International Journal* 421-446. **4836**

Eayrs, James George. "Canada and the Enlarged Community: 'Tradition, Trust and Trade.' " (1971), 61 *Round Table* 543-546. **4837**

Eayrs, James George. "North America and the Atlantic Community." (1967), 9 *University of Windsor Seminar on Canadian-American Relations, Proceedings* 27-33. **4838**

"The European Free Trade Association." (1959), 11 *External Affairs* 270-273. **4839**

Franck, Christian. "Évolution des relations inter-Atlantiques: Europe-États-Unis." (1976), 7 *Études Internationales* 572-598. **4840**

Friedmann, Wolfgang G. "The European Coal and Steel Community." (1954-55), 10 *International Journal* 12-25. **4841**

Galbraith, J. William. "Les relations entre le Canada et l'Euratom." (1981-82), 5 *Revue d'Intégration Européenne* 53-78. **4842**

Gelber, Lionel. "The Schuman Plan and German Revival." (1950-51), 6 *International Journal* 180-188. **4843**

Goffart, Lionel J. "Some Legal Aspects of the Schuman Plan." (1952), 10 *School of Law Review* 46-51. **4844**

Gow, James Iain. *The European Coal and Steel Community*. Kingston, 1958. 193 leaves. **4845**
Thesis (M.A.), Queen's University, 1959.

Green, Leslie C. "Legal Aspects of the Schuman Plan." (1952), 5 *Current Legal Problems* 274-294. **4846**

Greenwald, Joseph. "Canada and the United States in a Changing Atlantic Community." (1963), 5 *University of Windsor Seminar on Canadian-American Relations, Proceedings* 215-220. **4847**

Grenon, Jean-Yves. "Canada's Developing Relations with the Europe of 'Eighteen.' " (1976), *International Perspectives* 37-42 (Mar./Apr.) **4848**

Harrison, Eric. "Atlantic Partnership." (1949), 9 *Behind the Headlines* No. 3 (17 p.) **4849**

Healey, Denis. "Western Europe - the Challenge of Unity." (1949), 9 *Behind the Headlines* No. 7 (23 p.) **4850**

Heckscher, Kay. "Une communauté économique des pays du Nord." (1955-56), 31 *Actualité Économique* 70-90. **4851**

Henderson, Michael D. "Current Economic Stresses Strain the Fabric of OECD." (1978), *International Perspectives* 3-6 (Sept./Oct.) **4852**

Henderson, Michael D. "The OECD as an Instrument of National Policy." (1980-81), 36 *International Journal* 793-814. **4853**

Humphreys, David. "Canada's Link with Europe Still not Widely Understood." (1976), *International Perspectives* 32-36 (Mar./Apr.) **4854**

"Inter-Scandinavian Co-operation." (1955), 7 *External Affairs* 246-252. **4855**

"Intergovernmental Committee for European Migration." (1957), 9 *External Affairs* 391-393. **4856**

Kogan, Norman. "Italy, the European Community, and the Alliances." (1976-77), 32 *International Journal* 272-287. **4857**

Krosby, Hans Peter. "Denmark, EFTA and EEC." (1965-66), 21 *International Journal* 508-520. **4858**

Kruijtbosch, E.D.J. "L'expérience acquise par plus de trente ans d'intégration économique dans le cadre du Benelux." (1980-81), 4 *Revue d'Intégration Européenne* 43-58. **4859**

Laing, Lionel H. "Canada and the United States in a Changing Atlantic Community." (1963), 5 *University of Windsor Seminar on Canadian-American Relations, Proceedings* 221-229. **4860**

Latey, Maurice. "What the Council of Europe Has Achieved in Five Years." (1954-55), 34 *Dalhousie Review* 235-237. **4861**

Marshall, Richard Eugene. *Canada in the Role of a Middle Power; a Study of Canadian Non-Military Collaboration Vis-à-Vis the Organization for Economic Cooperation and Development and the North Atlantic Treaty Organization, 1960-1967.* Philadelphia, 1971. xxxvi, 315 leaves. **4862**

Thesis (Ph.D.), University of Pennsylvania, 1971. Abstracted in (1972), 32 *Dissertation Abstracts International* 4694-A. (University Microfilms, Ann Arbor, No. 72-6202).

Mhun, Henry. "Les difficultés du Plan Schuman: la Communauté européenne du charbon et de l'acier après l'ouverture du marché commun." (1953-54), 29 *Actualité Économique* 727-738. **4863**

Miljan, Toivo. "Problems of Nordic Integration." (1974-75), 30 *International Journal* 707-731. **4864**

Molot, Maureen Appel, and Haskel, Barbara G. *Problems of Inter-State Economic Integration in North America and Northern Europe.* Ottawa: School of International Affairs, Carleton University, 1972. 59 p. (Carleton University. Norman Paterson School of International Affairs. Occasional Papers, 24) **4865**

Contents: The Role of Institutions in Canada-United States Relations, by M.A. Molot.- Disparities, Strategies, and Opportunity Costs: The Example of Scandinavian Economic Market Negotiations in the 1950s and 1960s, by B.G. Haskel.

Nanes, Allan. "The Evolution of EURATOM." (1957-58), 13 *International Journal* 12-20. **4866**

Nicol, Eric Patrick. *L'idée de l'Europe.* Vancouver, 1948. 113 leaves. **4867**
Thesis (M.A.), University of British Columbia, 1948.

"Nordic Co-operation in the Cultural and Social Fields." (1952), 4 *External Affairs* 212-215. **4868**

Orban, Edmond. *Un modèle de souveraineté-association?: le Conseil nordique.* Montréal: Hurtubise HMH, c1978. 152 p., maps. (Cahiers du Québec, 38) (Collection Science politique) **4869**
Reviews: Miren A. Letemendia in (1979), 2 *Revue d'Intégration Européenne* 344-346; Panayotis Soldatos in (1979-80), 33 *Revue d'Histoire de l'Amérique Française* 270-272.

"Organization for Economic Co-operation and Development." (1961), 13 *External Affairs* 64-68. **4870**

"The Organization for European Economic Co-operation." (1951), 3 *External Affairs* 63-66. **4871**

Pearson, Lester B. "Western European Union: Implications for Canada and NATO." (1954-55), 10 *International Journal* 1-11. **4872**

Picard, Roger. "L'Union douanière européenne." (1930-31), 6 *Actualité Économique* 81-84. **4873**

Reboud, Louis. "Où en est la construction européenne?" (1966), 1 *Revue Juridique Thémis* 55-75. **4874**

Sandwell, B.K. "North Atlantic - Community or Treaty?" (1951-52), 7 *International Journal* 169-172. **4875**

"The Schuman Plan." (1951), 3 *External Affairs* 279-285. **4876**

Shenstone, Michael. "The Schuman Plan - 'A Leap into the Unknown.'" (1951-52), 7 *International Journal* 116-126. **4877**

Smithers, *Sir* Peter. "Some Thoughts of a Secretary-General." (1974-75), 30 *International Journal* 758-767. **4878**
Refers to the Secretary General of the Council of Europe.

Soloveytchik, George. "BENELUX." (1956), 16 *Behind the Headlines* No. 6 (22 p.) **4879**

Sussman, Edmond. *Some Implications of a Customs Union: The Benelux Case.* Montreal, 1954. 140 leaves. **4880**
Thesis (M.Com.), McGill University, 1954.

"Tenth Anniversary of OEEC." (1958), 10 *External Affairs* 101-109. **4881**

Touscoz, Jean. "Les diverses formes de la coopération Est-Ouest en Europe." (1973), 4 *Études Internationales* 235-252. **4882**

Velay, Clément C. *An Economic Study of the Schuman Plan.* Montreal, 1955. viii, 128 leaves. **4883**
Thesis (M.A.), McGill University, 1955.

Warren, Jake. "Canada and the United States in a Changing Atlantic Community." (1963), 5 *University of Windsor Seminar on Canadian-American Relations, Proceedings* 230-237. **4884**

Wilgress, Dana. "Canada and the United States in a Changing Atlantic Community." (1963), 5 *University of Windsor Seminar on Canadian-American Relations, Proceedings* 238-246. **4885**

(b) EUROPEAN ECONOMIC COMMUNITY

Abraham, J.P., and Lemineur-Toumson, C. "Les choix monétaires européens 1950-1980." (1981), 12 *Études Internationales* 499-512. **4886**

Adler, Gerald M. "The E.E.C. Court of Justice." (1964), 7 *Canadian Bar Journal* 102-127. **4887**

Arias, Francisco. *Le processus d'intégration de l'Espagne dans les Communautés européennes à la lumière de la politique économique extérieure: 1959-1977.* Montréal: Université de Montréal, Centre d'études et de documentation européennes, 1978. iii, 88 p. (CEDE, Note de recherches, no 1) **4888**

Bahcheli, Tozun S. "Turkey and the EC: the Strains of Association." (1979-80), 3 *Revue d'Intégration Européenne* 221-237. **4889**

Bélanger, France. *De la pratique à la légitimation: la théorie des trois mondes dans les rapports entre la R.P.C. et les pays de la C.E.E.* Québec, 1980. 141 frames. **4890**

Thesis (M.A.), Université Laval, 1980. (National Library of Canada. Canadian Theses on Microfiche, No. 47897).

Bird, Richard M. "Regional Policies in the European Economic Community." (1966-67), 46 *Dalhousie Review* 200-214. **4891**

Black, Naomi. "Feminism and Integration: The European Communities' Surveys 'European Men and Women.' " (1980-81), 4 *Revue d'Intégration Européenne* 83-103. **4892**

Boardman, Robert. "British Public Opinion and the Common Market Issue." (1972-73), 52 *Dalhousie Review* 34-46. **4893**

Boardman, Robert. "Initiatives and Outcomes: The European Community and Canada's 'Third Option.' " (1979-80), 3 *Revue d'Intégration Européenne* 5-28. **4894**

Boegler-Bogdanow, George W. *Monetary Integration in the Common Market. (An Analysis of the Management Rights Controversy).* Burnaby, B.C., 1969. vi, 33, vi, 45 leaves. **4895**

Thesis (M.A.), Simon Fraser University, 1969. Contains two essays, each with a separate title page. (National Library of Canada. Canadian Theses on Microfilm, No. 4193).

Bonvicini, Gianni. "A Mismanaged Community." (1980-81), 36 *International Journal* 815-826. **4896**

Boulanger, Claude. *Communauté économique européene: le traité de Rome: objectifs, pouvoirs, institutions, droit communautaire, financement.* Ottawa: Faculté de droit, Université d'Ottawa, 1975. 266 p. **4897**

Boulanger, Claude. "La Communauté économique européenne à travers le traité de Rome." (1974), 5 *Revue Générale de Droit* 254-297. **4898**

Boulanger, Claude. "La Communauté économique européenne à travers le traité de Rome." (1975), 6 *Revue Générale de Droit* 93-163. **4899**

Bridge, John W. "National and Transnational Regulation of Equal Pay for Equal Work in England and the European Community." (1981-82), 5 *Revue d'Intégration Européenne* 117-144. **4900**

Busch, Peter A. "Germany in the European Community: Theory and Case Study." (1978), 11 *Canadian Journal of Political Science* 545-573. **4901**

Cacopardo, Massimo. *Le Canada et la Communauté économique européenne; étude des effets probables du marché commun européen sur le commerce extérieur du Canada.* Montréal, 1960. ix, 180 leaves. **4902**
Thesis (M.A.), Université de Montreal, 1960.

Canada. Dept. of External Affairs. *Canada and the European Community.* Ottawa: Dept. of External Affairs, 1980. 24 p. **4903**
Jointly published with the Commission of the European Communities.

Canada. Dept. of External Affairs. *Canada and the European Community: Trade Flows, 1962-1977.* Ottawa: Dept. of External Affairs, 1980. 32 p. **4904**

Canada. Parliament. Senate. Standing Committee on Foreign Affairs. *Canadian Relations with the European Community / Les relations du Canada avec la Communauté européenne.* Ottawa: Queen's Printer, 1973. 52, 52 p. In English and French. **4905**

"Canada and the European Community: A Conference Organized by the CIIA in Co-operation with the Department of External Affairs and the Commission of the European Community." (1973-74), 32 *Behind the Headlines* No. 6 (34 p.) **4906**

Caporaso, James A. "The European Community in the World System: Prolegomena to a Political Economy of the European Community." (1978-79), 2 *Revue d'Intégration Européenne* 415-440. **4907**

Carson, George Barr, Jr. "The Spinning Wheel, the Stone Axe, and Sovereignty." (1974), 7 *Canadian Journal of Political Science* 70-85. **4908**
Contains a résumé in French under title: "Le concept de souveraineté à l'ère du marché commun."

Carty, R.K. "Towards a European Politics: The Lessons of the European Parliament Election in Ireland." (1980-81), 4 *Revue d'Intégration Européenne* 211-241. **4909**

Cermakian, Jean. "Les échanges commerciaux entre le Canada et la Communauté économique européenne." (1972), 16 *Canadian Geographer* 119-127. **4910**

Chabot, Marc. "L'harmonisation des législations en matière de faillite et d'insolvabilité au sein du marché commun." (1982), 6 *Revue d'Intégration Européenne* 43-73. **4911**

Christensen, Rolf Buschardt. *Denmark and the European Community: Relations Vis-à-Vis Germany and Britain.* Ottawa, 1979. 171 frames. **4912**
Thesis (M.A.), Carleton University, 1979. (National Library of Canada. Canadian Theses on Microfiche, No. 49482).

Clark, Andrew Charles. *The Non-Contractual Liability of the European Communities.* Montreal, 1972. xii, 140 leaves. **4913**
Thesis (LL.M.), McGill University, 1972. (National Library of Canada. Canadian Theses on Microfilm, No. 15814).

Coffey, Peter. *The External Economic Relations of the EEC.* Toronto: Macmillan of Canada; Maclean-Hunter Press, c1976. xii, 118 p. **4914**
Also published London, Macmillan, 1976.
Reviews: Charles Pentland in (1978-79), 34 *International Journal* 130-134; Cecil Rajana in (1977-78), 1 *Revue d'Intégration Européenne* 257-259.

Colloque sur les relations du Canada et du Québec avec les Communautés européennes, Québec, 1978. *Actes du Colloque sur les relations du Canada et du Québec avec les Communautés européennes.* Québec: Centre québécois de relations internationales; Toronto: Institut canadien des affaires internationales; Québec: Université Laval, 1979. 154 p. (Collection Choix, 10) **4915**
Organized by Centre québécois de relations internationales (Québec), and Institut européen des hautes études internationales (Nice).

Constas, Dimitrios C. "Legal and Political Aspects of Intra-Community Conventions." (1981-82), 5 *Revue d'Intégration Européenne* 201-220. **4916**

Coudevylle, Andrée. "L'efficacité du Comité économique et social des Communautés européennes." (1979-80), 3 *Revue d'Intégration Européenne* 51-71.
4917

Courtis, Kenneth S. "La politique industrielle dans la Communauté économique européenne: crise et changement." (1981), 12 *Études Internationales* 269-320.
4918

Crawford, Malcolm. "When Uniting Europe, Money Helps." (1972), 79 *Canadian Banker* 21-23 (No. 6) **4919**

Dauphin, Roma. "Les effets socio-économiques de la libre circulation des marchandises, personnes, services et capitaux sur les unités membres et la structure intégrative de la CEE: quelques commentaires." (1979-80), 3 *Revue d'Intégration Européenne* 349-355. **4920**

Decaluwé, Bernard. "Le système monétaire européen: où en sommes-nous?" (1981), 12 *Études Internationales* 445-463. **4921**

Dehem, Roger. "Le système monétaire européen à la lumière de l'expérience et de la théorie monétaires." (1981), 12 *Études Internationales* 465-474. **4922**

Denis, Jean-Émile, and Lindekens, Emmanuel. "Perspectives de coopération industrielle dans le contexte de l'accord cadre entre le Canada et les Communautés européennes." (1977-78), 1 *Revue d'Intégration Européenne* 107-124.
4923

Desmarais, Ginette. *Politique agricole de la Communauté économique européenne et estimations empiriques des effets d'une union économique sur les flux d'échanges.* Québec, 1973. 184 leaves. **4924**
Thesis (M.Soc.Sc.), Université Laval, 1973. (National Library of Canada. Canadian Theses on Microfiche, No. 18949).

Dodd, Rosemarie A. *Le Canada et la Communauté européenne.* Montréal, 1974. vii, 277 leaves. **4925**
Thesis (M.A.), Université de Montréal, 1974.

Easson, Alex J. "Approximation and Unification of Laws in the EEC." (1978-79), 2 *Revue d'Intégration Européenne* 375-390. **4926**

Easson, Alex J. "The 'Direct Effect' of EEC Directives." (1979), 28 *International and Comparative Law Quarterly* 319-353. **4927**

Easson, Alex J. "The Free Movement of Goods, Persons, Services, and Capital in Canada and in the European Community. (Introduction)." (1979-80), 3 *Revue d'Intégration Européenne* 263-266. **4928**

"The Economic Integration of Western Europe." (1959), 11 *External Affairs* 7-15. **4929**

"European Integration." (1958), 10 *External Affairs* 10-13. **4930**

Feld, Werner J. "Les effets des tensions économiques sur le mouvement d'intégration européenne." (1978-79), 2 *Revue d'Intégration Européenne* 183-201. **4931**

Feld, Werner J., and Wagner, Helmut. "West Germany and European Unification: Economic and Political Interests and Policy Motivations." (1980-81), 4 *Revue d'Intégration Européenne* 59-81. **4932**

Fischer, Lewis A. "The Common Agricultural Policy of the EC: Its Impact on Canadian Agriculture." (1979-80), 3 *Revue d'Intégration Européenne* 29-50. **4933**

Forest, Pierre-Gerlier. "Les relations transnationales et l'intégration européenne: notes pour un modèle." (1981), 12 *Études Internationales* 343-360. **4934**

Fortin, L. Yves, and Perron, Martin. "Le système monétaire européen: un point de vue Nord américain." (1981), 12 *Études Internationales* 513-532. **4935**

"The Free Movement of Goods, Persons, Services and Capital in Canada and in the European Community: A Comparison between Federalism and Supra-National Integration." (1979-80), 3 *Revue d'Intégration Européenne* 261-392. **4936**
Individual articles are listed separately.

Geise, Conrad David. *A Quantitative Analysis of National Leadership Commitment to Collective Decision-Making within the Framework of the European Communities, 1959-1972*. Ottawa, 1978. ix, 159 leaves. **4937**
Thesis (M.A.), Carleton University, 1978. (National Library of Canada. Canadian Theses on Microfiche, No. 39036).

Gherson, A.R.A. "Notes on Some Implications of the EEC for Canada." (1973-74), 6 *Case Western Reserve Journal of International Law* 116-120. **4938**

Grenon, Jean-Yves. "L'accord-cadre entre le Canada et les Communautés européennes: une première juridique." (1978), 16 *Canadian Yearbook of International Law* 304-314. **4939**

Grenon, Jean-Yves. "Au-delà de la Communauté, vers l'Union européenne: le rapport Tindemans." (1976), 7 *Études Internationales* 252-265. **4940**

Grenon, Jean-Yves. "Le droit des relations extérieures de la CEE et le Canada." (1975), 13 *Canadian Yearbook of International Law* 61-97. **4941**

Grenon, Jean-Yves. "Principales étapes et conséquences juridiques de l'adhésion du Royaume-Uni au traité de Rome." (1972), 7 *Revue Juridique Thémis* 93-100. **4942**

Griffith, N. Patrick. *Economic Integration and Industrial Policy in Canada and the European Community*. Ottawa, 1980. 154 frames. **4943**

Thesis (M.A.), Carleton University, 1980. (National Library of Canada. Canadian Theses on Microfiche, No. 49499).

Grima, J. Peter. *Britain and European Community, 1947-1963: The Political-Economic Imperatives of a Long Recessional.* Halifax, 1972 (1974). iv, 145 leaves. **4944**
Thesis (M.A.), Dalhousie University, 1972. (National Library of Canada. Canadian Theses on Microfiche, No. 18619).

Hartzer, Craig E. "A Study of Integration Behaviour in the Committees of the European Parliament: 1959-1976." (1982), 6 *Revue d'Intégration Européenne* 75-106 **4945**

Héraud, Guy. "La Communauté européenne et la question linguistique." (1981-82), 5 *Revue d'Intégration Européenne* 5-28. **4946**

Heywood, Robert W. "West European Community and the Eurafrica Concept in the 1950's." (1980-81), 4 *Revue d'Intégration Européenne* 199-210. **4947**

Holmes, John W. "Political Implications of the European Economic Community." (1962), 69 *Queen's Quarterly* 1-10. **4948**

Hoy, Gerald E. "Common Market Regional Incentives." (1961), 9 *Canadian Tax Journal* 207-214. **4949**

Hunter, Louis Clare, and Reid, G.L. *European Economic Integration and the Movement of Labour.* Kingston: Industrial Relations Centre, Queen's University, 1970. 38 p. (Queen's University. Industrial Relations Centre. Research Series, No. 9) **4950**

Hurt, Leslie John. *Britain and the Common Market, 1955-1963.* Edmonton, 1975. vi, 154 leaves. **4951**
Thesis (M.A.), University of Alberta, 1975. (National Library of Canada. Canadian Theses on Microfiche, No. 26786).

Inohana, Terue. *The External Relations of the European Community and Its Member States: A Study of Alternative Perspectives.* Kingston, 1978. v, 112 leaves. **4952**
Thesis (M.A.), Queen's University, 1978. (National Library of Canada. Canadian Theses on Microfiche, No. 39498).

Jacquemin, Alex. "Politique de concurrence ou politique industrielle au sein de la Communauté économique européenne." (1971), 2 *Études Internationales* 303-308. **4953**

Jahnke, L. Gordon. "The European Economic Community and the Most-Favoured-Nation Clause." (1963), 1 *Canadian Yearbook of International Law* 252-271. **4954**

Jenson, Jane. "Strategic Divisions within the French Left: The Case of the First Elections to the European Parliament." (1980-81), 4 *Revue d'Intégration Européenne* 5-28. **4955**

Kaliski, Stephan F. "Canada, the United Kingdom and the Common Market." (1961-62), 17 *International Journal* 17-24. **4956**

Knuth, Harald Wolfgang W. *The European Economic Community in the Federalizing Process of Western Europe.* Ottawa, 1972 (c1973). xv, 137 leaves. **4957**

Thesis (M.A.), Carleton University, 1973. (National Library of Canada. Canadian Theses on Microfilm, No. 16536).

Laabi, Abdelhai. *Association CEE-Maghreb.* Montréal, 1973. vi, 163, iv, (263) leaves. **4958**
Thesis (M.A.), Université de Montréal, 1973.

Lane, Robert C. *Nature and Role of Law in the European Community.* Ottawa, 1977 (i.e. 1978). viii, 130 leaves. **4959**
Research essay (M.A.), Carleton University, 1978.

Langley, James. "European Community Continues Its Momentum Towards Union." (1976), *International Perspectives* 28-32 (Mar./Apr.) **4960**

La Serre, Françoise de. "Élargissement des Communautés européennes et intégration régionale." (1973), 4 *Études Internationales* 276-285. **4961**

Lasok, Dominik. "La Cour de justice, instrument de l'intégration communautaire." (1978-79), 2 *Revue d'Intégration Européenne* 391-413. **4962**

Lasok, Dominik. "Involvement with the European Economic Community: Some Canadian Considerations." (1976), 22 *McGill Law Journal* 574-604. **4963**

Lasok, Dominik. "Leading Cases on the Movement of Goods, Persons, Services and Capital in the European Economic Community." (1979-80), 3 *Revue d'Intégration Européenne* 313-325. **4964**

Leavy, James. "Législation et pratiques relatives à la libre circulation des marchandises, personnes, services et capitaux dans la CEE." (1979-80), 3 *Revue d'Intégration Européenne* 283-300. **4965**

Lehart, Michel. "Le système monétaire européen: le point de vue européen." (1981), 12 *Études Internationales* 533-547. **4966**

Letemendia, Miren A. "Les accords de coopération commerciale et économique de la CEE: contenu et base juridique." (1981-82), 5 *Revue d'Intégration Européenne* 145-158. **4967**

Lisein Norman, Margaretha. "La participation des organisations de travailleurs au processus de décision dans la Communauté européenne." (1981-82), 5 *Revue d'Intégration Européenne* 221-258. **4968**

Lodenstein, John Peter. *Some Problems of Political Integration in the European Community.* Waterloo, Ont., 1974. 149 leaves. **4969**
Thesis (M.A.), University of Waterloo, 1974.

Lodge, Juliet. "The European Parliament after Direct Elections: Talking-Shop or Putative Legislature?" (1981-82), 5 *Revue d'Intégration Européenne* 259-284. **4970**

Lodge, Juliet. "Nation-States versus Supranationalism: The Political Future of the European Community." (1978-79), 2 *Revue d'Intégration Européenne* 161-181. **4971**

Lodge, Juliet, and Herman, Valentine. "Institutional Reform in the European Community: The Case for Bicameralism." (1978), 11 *Canadian Journal of Political Science* 575-599. **4972**

Louis, Jean-Victor. "La Cour de justice comme facteur d'intégration dans les relations extérieures des Communautés européennes." (1978), 9 *Études Internationales* 43-56. **4973**

Louis, Jean-Victor. "Quelques réflexions sur la répartition des compétences entre la Communauté européenne et ses états membres." (1978-79), 2 *Revue d'Intégration Européenne* 355-374. **4974**

Lyon, Peyton V. "The Quest for Counterweight: Canada, Britain and the EEC." (1972), *International Perspectives* 26-31 (Mar./Apr.) **4975**

Macdonald, H. Ian. "The European Common Market." (1958), 18 *Behind the Headlines* No. 4 (16 p.) **4976**

Macdonald, H. Ian. "The European Economic Community: Background and Bibliography." (1962-63), 22 *Behind the Headlines* No. 2 (15 p.) **4977**

Maes, Albert. "The European Community and the United Nations General Assembly." (1979-80), 3 *Revue d'Intégration Européenne* 73-83. **4978**

Mahant, E.E. "Canada and the European Community: The First Twenty Years." (1980-81), 4 *Revue d'Intégration Européenne* 263-279. **4979**

Mahant, E.E. "Canada and the European Community: The New Policy." (1976), 52 *International Affairs* 551-564. **4980**

Mahant, E.E. "Canada and the European Economic Community: A Policy-Making Case Study." (1975), 47 *Canadian Political Science Association, Papers*, 79 p. **4981**

Manoogian, Peter R. "Transnational Interaction Levels in the European Communities: A Longitudinal Analysis." (1979-80), 3 *Revue d'Intégration Européenne* 163-180. **4982**

Matas, David. "The EEC as a Model for Canada." (1979-80), 10 *Manitoba Law Journal* 241-257. **4983**

Matthews, Roy A. "Britain and the Common Market: A Contemporary Canadian View." (1967-68), 27 *Behind the Headlines* No. 3 (14 p.) **4984**
Also printed in French on the reverse side under title: *La Grande-Bretagne et le marché commun: opinion canadienne actuelle* (16 p.).

Matthews, Roy A. "Britain's Move into Europe: The Implications for Canada." (1972), 31 *Behind the Headlines* Nos. 5-6 (15 p.) **4985**

Mayhew, Daniel Richard. *Europeanism: A Study of Public Opinion and Attitudinal Integration in the European Community.* Ottawa, 1980. 234 frames. **4986**
Thesis (M.A.), Carleton University, 1980. (National Library of Canada. Canadian Theses on Microfiche, No. 49519).

McAllister, Ian. *Regional Development and the European Community: A Canadian Perspective.* Montreal: Institute for Research on Public Policy, 1982. xvii, 243 p., maps. **4987**
Review: Guy Beaulieu in (1982), 5 *Revue d'Intégration Européenne* 303-305.

McFarlane, William James. *The European Community and Summit Diplomacy: A Case of Federal Resurgence.* London, Ont., c1975. viii, 144 leaves. **4988**
Thesis (M.A.), University of Western Ontario, 1976.

McIvor, R. Craig. "Canadian Foreign Trade and the European Common Market." (1957-58), 13 *International Journal* 1-11. **4989**

McWhinney, Edward. " 'Classical' Federalism and Supra-National Integration or Treaty-Based Association: The European Community Movement as a Case-Study." (1963), 57 *American Society of International Law, Proceedings* 241-249. **4990**

McWhinney, Edward. "Soviet and American Responses to the Emerging European Community in the Post-Détente Era." *In* Alting von Geusau, Frans A.M., ed., *The External Relations of the European Community* (Lexington, Mass., 1974), pp. 117-123. **4991**

Mendez, Joseph-M. "La politique agricole de la Communauté économique européenne. I. La situation de départ." (1965-66), 41 *Actualité Économique* 226-268. **4992**

Mendez, Joseph-M. "La politique agricole de la Communauté économique européenne. II. Traité de Rome." (1966-67), 42 *Actualité Économique* 82-113. **4993**

Mhun, Henry. "L'intégration de l'agriculture européenne." (1951-52), 27 *Actualité Économique* 500-511. **4994**

Michelmann, Hans J. "Credentials, Jurisdiction and Mobility: Physicians in the European Community." (1978-79), 2 *Revue d'Intégration Européenne* 203-229. **4995**

Miljan, Toivo. *The Reluctant Europeans: The Attitudes of the Nordic Countries Towards European Integration.* Montreal: McGill-Queen's University Press, 1977. viii, 325 p. **4996**
Also published London, England, C. Hurst, 1977.
Reviews: Niels J. Haagerup in (1979), 34 *International Journal* 318-320; Charles Pentland in (1979), 12 *Canadian Journal of Political Science* 390-391.

Modak, N.D. "The Growing Power of Europe." (1980), 87 *Canadian Banker and ICB Review* 24-28 (No. 1) **4997**

Mueller, Volkmar. *Coordination and Harmonization of Monetary Policy in the European Economic Community, 1953-1969.* Kingston, 1971 (c1972). iv, 86 (i.e. 96) leaves. **4998**
Half-title: *Monetary Policy.* Thesis (M.A.), Queen's University, 1971. (National Library of Canada. Canadian Theses on Microfilm, No. 11191).

Murray, Ronald Charles. *Canada and Western European Unification; a Case Study of Canadian Political Behaviour Towards the United Kingdom's Application for Membership in the European Economic Community, 1961-1963.* Kingston, 1968. 140 leaves. **4999**
Thesis (M.A.), Queen's University, 1968.

Nadal, François. "La Communauté économique européenne." (1957-58), 33 *Actualité Économique* 472-500. **5000**

Nadal, François. "L'organisation économique de l'Europe et le marché commun." (1957-58), 33 *Actualité Économique* 286-311. **5001**

Ndongko, Wilfred Awung. *The Association of the African and Malagasy States with the European Common Market.* Edmonton, 1967. viii, 142 leaves. **5002**
Thesis (M.A.), University of Alberta, 1967.

Oak, G. Brian. *Canadian Counterweight Foreign Policy: The Example of the*

Framework Agreement with the European Community (1972-76). Ottawa, 1978. v, 251 leaves. **5003**
Thesis (M.A.), Carleton University, 1978. (National Library of Canada. Canadian Theses on Microfiche, No. 37353). Abstracted in (1979), 17 *Masters Abstracts* 222.

Owugah, Lemuel. *Nigeria and the European Economic Community: A Case Study in Decision-Making, 1960-1973.* Toronto, c1980. 532 leaves. **5004**
Thesis (Ph.D.), University of Toronto, 1978. (National Library of Canada. Canadian Theses on Microfiche, No. 43695).

Palk, William L. "European Court and the Common Market." (1967), 10 *Canadian Bar Journal* 290-309. **5005**

Palk, William L. "Harmonization of the Laws of the European Common Market Countries." (1966-67), 2 *Manitoba Law Journal* 173-189. **5006**

Palk, William L. *An Investigation of the Formation and Development of the European Economic Community.* Winnipeg, 1967. iii, 135 leaves. **5007**
Thesis (LL.M.), University of Manitoba, 1967. (National Library of Canada. Canadian Theses on Microfilm, No. 1538).

Patry, André. "L'intégration européenne et le marché commun." (1962-63), 5 *Cahiers de Droit* 19-28. **5008**

Pelkmans, Jacques. "The European Community and the Newly Industrializing Countries." (1980-81), 4 *Revue d'Intégration Européenne* 135-166. **5009**

Pentland, Charles. "L'évolution de la politique étrangère de la Communauté européenne: le contexte transatlantique." (1978), 9 *Études Internationales* 106-125. **5010**

Pentland, Charles. *International Theory and European Integration.* London: Faber, 1973. 283 p. (Studies in International Politics) **5011**
Reviews: George Friesen in (1973-74), 29 *International Journal* 686-687; John H. Sigler in (1976), 9 *Canadian Journal of Political Science* 178-179.

Pentland, Charles. "Linkage Politics: Canada's Contract and the Development of the European Community's External Relations." (1976-77), 32 *International Journal* 207-231. **5012**

Pentland, Charles. "The Political Consequences of Economic Integration: Political Science and the Case of Western Europe." (1979-80), 3 *Revue d'Intégration Européenne* 363-379. **5013**

Pryce, Roy. "Political Aspects of an Enlarged European Community." (1971-72), 27 *International Journal* 98-112. **5014**

Raworth, Philip. "Article 177 of the Treaty of Rome and the Evolution of the Doctrine of the Supremacy of Community Law." (1977), 15 *Canadian Yearbook of International Law* 276-286. **5015**

Les relations extérieures de la Communauté européenne: le cas particulier du Canada: actes des colloques du C.E.D.E. Montréal: Université de Montréal, 1977. 137 p. **5016**
Conference organized by Centre d'études et de documentation européennes, held at Estérel, June 14 and 15, 1975.

Reny, Jean Pierre. *European Economic Integration.* Ottawa, 1961. ix, 164 leaves.
Thesis (M.A.), University of Ottawa, 1961. **5017**

Rieber, Roger A. "The Future of the European Community in International Politics." (1976), 9 *Canadian Journal of Political Science* 206-226. **5018**
Contains a résumé in French under title: "L'avenir de la Communauté européenne en politique internationale."

Roseman, Daniel. "European Community/Canada Relations: A Selected Bibliography, 1976-1981." (1980-81), 4 *Revue d'Intégration Européenne* 327-334.
5019

Rouméliotis, Panayotis. "Les effets de l'adhésion de la Grèce aux Communautés européennes sur le mouvement des capitaux." (1980-81), 4 *Revue d'Intégration Européenne* 187-198. **5020**

Rouquet La Garrigue, Victor. "Les conditions de l'établissement d'un marché commun européen et ses répercussions sur l'économie française." (1957-58), 33 *Actualité Économique* 312-334. **5021**

Rouquet La Garrigue, Victor. "Le marché commun et les problèmes agricoles." (1959-60), 35 *Actualité Économique* 446-462. **5022**

Ryan, Michael H. "The Treaty of Rome and Monetary Policy in the European Community." (1978), 10 *Ottawa Law Review* 535-565. **5023**

Scanteie, Eugene. *Les échanges commerciaux entre l'Afrique noire et la C.E.E. créent-ils des effets de domination?* Montréal, 1974. viii, 183 leaves. **5024**
Thesis (M.Sc.), Université de Montréal, 1974.

Schellenberger, Milton Arthur. *Free Movement of Workers in the European Community: Its Role in the Integration Process.* Ottawa, 1975. ix, 146 leaves.
Thesis (M.A.), Carleton University, 1975. **5025**

Schmitthoff, Clive M. "The Impact of Britain's Accession to the European Communities on the Common Law." (1972-73), 5 *Manitoba Law Journal* 215-228.
5026

Schmitthoff, Clive M. "The Impact of European Community Law on English Law." (1977-78), 8 *Manitoba Law Journal* 461-472. **5027**

Seiler, Daniel Louis. "Les élections européennes de 1979 entre le nationalisme et l'intégration." (1978-79), 2 *Revue d'Intégration Européenne* 441-472. **5028**

Seiler, Daniel Louis. "Ombres et lumières sur les élections européennes des 7 et 10 juin 1979: ébauche d'une première analyse des résultats." (1979), 10 *Études Internationales* 549-589. **5029**

Seymour-Ure, Colin. "Press and Referenda: The Case of the British Referendum of 1975." (1978), 11 *Canadian Journal of Political Science* 601-615. **5030**

Sheridan, Paul Robert. *The Taxation of Cash Dividends within the European Community.* Toronto, c1981. 218 leaves. **5031**
Thesis (LL.M.), University of Toronto, 1981.

Sheridan, Ronald T. "Canada and the Common Market - Black and White." (1962), 69 *Canadian Banker* 111-118 (No. 3) **5032**

Siotis, Jean. "L'Europe communautaire et la Méditerranée: les cheminements tortueux d'un 'grand dessein.' " (1978), 9 *Études Internationales* 57-74. **5033**

Sloane, John H. "Political Integration in the European Community." (1968), 1 *Canadian Journal of Political Science* 442-461. **5034**

Contains a résumé in French under title: "L'intégration politique de la Communauté européenne."

Soldatos, Panayotis. "Réflexions sur l'état de la recherche au Canada dans le domaine de l'intégration européenne." (1979-80), 3 *Revue d'Intégration Européenne* 85-112. **5035**

Soldatos, Panayotis. "La théorie de la politique étrangère et sa pertinence pour l'étude des relations extérieures des Communautés européennes." (1978), 9 *Études Internationales* 7-42. **5036**

Stingelin, Peter, ed. *The European Community and the Outsiders.* Don Mills, Ont.: Longman, 1973. 168 p. **5037**

Contains papers presented at a conference held in 1971 at the Waterloo Lutheran University. Text in English or French.

Stinson, Robert David. *Transnational Business Collaboration within the European Community 1966-1975: An Economic and Geographic Interpretation.* Ottawa, 1978. vii, 305 leaves. **5038**

Thesis (M.A.), Carleton University, 1978. (National Library of Canada. Canadian Theses on Microfiche, No. 39053).

Story, Donald C. "The Framework Agreement for Commercial and Economic Cooperation: A Political Act." (1980-81), 4 *Revue d'Intégration Européenne* 281-297. **5039**

Taylor, Paul. "The European Communities as an Actor in International Society." (1982), 6 *Revue d'Intégration Européenne* 7-41. **5040**

Taylor, Phillip. "Political Cooperation among the EC Member States' Embassies in Washington." (1980-81), 4 *Revue d'Intégration Européenne* 29-41. **5041**

Taylor, Phillip. "Public and Elite Support for European Union: Perceptions and Expectations of General Publics and European Community Administrators." (1978-79), 2 *Revue d'Intégration Européenne* 231-249. **5042**

Tezapsidis, Leonidas. *The Political Economy of Greece's Relations with the European Communities in a Mediterranean Perspective.* Ottawa, 1978. v, 193 leaves. **5043**

Thesis (M.A.), Carleton University, 1979. (National Library of Canada. Canadian Theses on Microfiche, No. 41681).

Tomsa, Branko. "Les relations de la CEE avec les pays de l'Europe de l'Est." (1978), 9 *Études Internationales* 87-105. **5044**

Torrelli, Maurice. "La C.E.E. et l'aide au développement: renouvellement de la convention de Yaoundé." (1969-70), 45 *Actualité Économique* 240-266. **5045**

Torrelli, Maurice. "L'élaboration des relations extérieures de la Communauté économique européenne." (1973), 167 *Revue du Marché Commun* 328-340. **5046**

Torrelli, Maurice. *Great Britain and Europe of the Six: The Failure of Negotiations.* Montréal: Presses de l'École des hautes études commerciales, 1968. 74 p. (Université de Montréal. École des hautes études commerciales. Centre d'études et de documentation européennes. Annals) **5047**

Translated by Cameron Nish.
Review: Jacques Beauroy in (1971), 4 *Canadian Journal of Economics* 420-421.

Torrelli, Maurice. *L'individu et le droit de la Communauté économique européenne* Préface de René-Jean Dupuy. Montréal: Presses de l'Université de Montréal, 1970. xii, 396 p. **5048**
Reviews: Ivan Bernier in (1970), 11 *Cahiers de Droit* 397-398; Ivan Bernier in (1970), 3 *Canadian Journal of Political Science* 491-492; Adrian Popovici in (1971), 14 *Canadian Public Administration* 296-297.

Torrelli, Maurice. "L'influence des accords d'association de la Communauté économique européenne sur les relations internationales des états d'Afrique noire." (1971), 2 *Études Internationales* 182-230. **5049**

Torrelli, Maurice. "Les relations extérieures de la Communauté économique européenne." (1979), 68 *Action Nationale* 378-393. **5050**

Torrelli, Maurice. *Ten Years of European Integration*. Montréal: Presses de l'École des hautes études commerciales, 1968. 116, 121 p. (Université de Montréal. École des hautes études commerciales. Centre d'études et de documentation européennes. Annals, 1) **5051**
Papers presented at the colloquy organized by the C.E.D.E. in Montreal, March 14 and 15, 1968. Papers prepared by Maurice Torrelli; translated by Cameron Nish. Added title page: *Dix ans d'intégration européenne*.
Review: H.G. Hambleton in (1970), 3 *Canadian Journal of Economics* 348-349.

Torrelli, Maurice, and Valaskakis, Kimon. "Le Canada et la Communauté économique européenne." *In* Painchaud, Paul, ed., *Le Canada et le Québec sur la scène internationale* (Québec, 1977), pp. 347-362. **5052**

Triantis, Stephen G. *Common Market and Economic Development; the E. E. C. and Greece*. Athens: Center of Planning and Economic Research, 1965. 232 p. (Center of Planning and Economic Research. Research Monograph Series, 14.) **5053**
Reviews: Tillo E. Kuhn in (1965-66), 21 *International Journal* 234-235; H. Ian Macdonald in (1969), 2 *Canadian Journal of Economics* 152-153.

Université de Montréal. École des hautes études commerciales. Centre d'études et de documentation européennes. *L'élection du Parlement européen au suffrage universel direct: bilan et perspectives intégratives*: colloque organisé le 3 novembre 1979, sous la direction de Panayotis Soldatos et Gilles Rossignol. Montréal, 1980. 112 p. (Université de Montréal. École des hautes études commerciales. Centre d'études et de documentation européennes. Cahiers, 5) **5054**

Valaskakis, Kimon. "La CEE a-t-elle une politique cohérente vis-à-vis du Canada?" (1978), 9 *Études Internationales* 126-136. **5055**

Van Wijk, Alfons Pieter. *Western European Integration*. London, Ont., 1967. vi, 97 leaves. **5056**
Thesis (M.A.), University of Western Ontario, 1967. (National Library of Canada. Canadian Theses on Microfilm, No. 1624).

Wilgress, L.D. *The Impact of European Integration on Canada*. Montreal: Private Planning Association of Canada, 1962. viii, 46 p. **5057**
Sponsored by the Canadian Trade Committee, Private Planning Association of Canada. Review: Bernard Bonin in (1964-65), 40 *Actualité Économique* 195-196.

Windsor, Philip. "European Economic Community Beset by Internal Pressures." (1977), *International Perspectives* 12-16 (Mar./Apr.) **5058**

Yannopoulos, G.N. "The Second Enlargement of the EEC and the Trade Interests of the Developing Countries." (1980-81), 4 *Revue d'Intégration Européenne* 167-186. **5059**

Ziegel, Jacob S. "The Legal Consequences of Britain's Entry into the Common Market." (1964), 29 *Saskatchewan Bar Review* 13-27. **5060**

3. EASTERN EUROPE

Abbondanzio, Francis E. *Middle Level Management Reform and Comecon Integration.* Ottawa, 1974. xiii, 157 leaves. **5061**
Research essay (M.A.), Carleton University, 1974.

Jiranek, Slavomir. "Banque internationale pour la coopération économique à Moscou." (1970-71), 46 *Actualité Économique* 466-471. **5062**

Kovrig, Bennett. "Regionalism and Integration in Eastern Europe." (1974-75), 30 *International Journal* 689-706. **5063**

Pilisi, Paul. "Les pays socialistes de l'Est et l'unité européenne: la tradition dans le socialisme et le socialisme dans la tradition." (1979), 10 *Études Internationales* 351-383, 527-547. **5064**

Séranne, Catherine. "Les situations d'inégalité au sein du Conseil d'assistance économique mutuelle (Comecon)." (1971), 2 *Études Internationales* 250-296.
5065

Szawlowski, Richard. *The System of the International Organizations of the Communist Countries.* Leyden: Sijthoff, 1976. xxix, 322 p. **5066**
Reviews: Leslie C. Green in (1979), 27 *Chitty's Law Journal* 140-144; O. Kimminich in (1979-80), 18 *Archiv des Völkerrechts* 482-485; Ludwik Kos-Rabcewicz-Zubkowski in (1979), 17 *Canadian Yearbook of International Law* 452-454.

Wionczek, Miguel S. "The COMECON Bank: A Step Toward Multilateral Trade and Currency Convertibility within the Soviet Bloc?" (1966), 73 *Canadian Banker* 65-73 (No. 1) **5067**

4. WESTERN HEMISPHERE

(a) GENERAL

Baudin, Louis. "Les projets d'union économique en Amérique du Sud." (1932-33), 8 *Actualité Économique* 1-6. **5068**

Benoit, Marcel Georges Hector. *The Latin American Free Trade Association.* Edmonton, 1970. vii, 149 leaves. **5069**
Thesis (M.A.), University of Alberta, 1970.

Ducatenzeiler, Graciela, and De La Fuente, Manuel. "Acteurs et stratégies dans le processus d'intégration économique en Amérique latine." (1979), 12 *Canadian Journal of Political Science* 775-797. **5070**

"Free Trade in Latin America: The Montevideo Treaty." (1960), 12 *External Affairs* 856-858. **5071**

The treaty, signed on February 18, 1960, instituted the Latin American Free Trade Association (LAFTA).

Gil, Enrique. " 'Significance of Canada's Contribution to Hemispheric Solidarity.' " (1941), 25 *Canadian Bar Association, Proceedings* 85-94. **5072**

Guy, James John. "The Growing Relationship of Canada and the Americas." (1977), *International Perspectives* 3-6 (July/Aug.) **5073**

Lande, Eric P. *The Welfare Theory of Economic Integration with Particular Reference to Developing Countries.* Montreal, 1972 (c1973). 99 leaves. **5074**
Thesis (M.A.), McGill University, 1972. (National Library of Canada. Canadian Theses on Microfilm, No. 14487).

Lower, Arthur R.M. "Canada and the Americas." (1937-38), 17 *Dalhousie Review* 17-21. **5075**

Mace, Gordon. "The Andean Group at the Ten Year Mark." (1979), *International Perspectives* 30-34 (Sept./Dec.) **5076**

Mace, Gordon. *Intégration régionale et pluralisme idéologique au sein du groupe andin.* Québec: Centre québécois de relations internationales, 1981. x, 321 p. **5077**

Tapia Salinas, L. "Tentatives de régionalisation aérienne: la Commission latino-américaine de l'aviation civile." (1977), 2 *Annals of Air and Space Law* 199-210. **5078**

Wionczek, Miguel S. "Integration and Development." (1968-69), 24 *International Journal* 449-462. **5079**

Wionczek, Miguel S. "Towards Latin American Economic Integration." (1963), 70 *Canadian Banker* 83-94 (No. 3) **5080**

Zylberberg, Jacques. "Latin American Economic System: SELA Does Little to Further Latin American Integration." (1976), *International Perspectives* 29-33 (May/June) **5081**
SELA refers to Latin American Economic System.

Zylberberg, Jacques. "Nationalisme-intégration-dépendance: introduction dialectique au cas latino-américain." (1978-79), 2 *Revue d'Intégration Européenne* 251-298. **5082**

(b) INTER-AMERICAN ORGANIZATIONS

Anglin, Douglas G. "United States Opposition to Canadian Membership in the Pan American Union: A Canadian View." (1961), 15 *International Organization* 1-20. **5083**

Banker, Stephen. "The Changing OAS" (1982), *International Perspectives* 23-26 (May/June) **5084**

Beau, Jean Claude. *Organisation des états américains: fondements et expériences (1948-1968).* Montpellier, 1970. 263, 9, 38, xiii leaves. **5085**
Thesis (LL.D.), Université de Montpellier, France, 1970.

Corbett, Percy E. "Address." (1937), 31 *American Society of International Law, Proceedings* 213-216. **5086**
Address on Canada and the Pan American Union.

Crawford, Horace Donald. "Should Canada Join Pan-America?" (1939), 248 *North American Review* 219-233. **5087**

Crean, John G. "Should Canada Join O.A.S." (1961), 3 *University of Windsor Seminar on Canadian-American Relations, Proceedings* 57-64. **5088**

Duplisea, Gerald Hugh. *Canada, Latin America and the Organization of American States.* Fredericton, 1965. xi, 177 leaves. **5089**
Thesis (M.A.), University of New Brunswick, 1965.

Eayrs, James George. "Canadian and American Viewpoints on Closer Canadian Association in Pan Americanism." (1961), 3 *University of Windsor Seminar on Canadian-American Relations, Proceedings* 65-76. **5090**

Eby, John C. "Canada and the Inter-American Development Bank." (1978), 85 *Canadian Banker and ICB Review* 6-14 (No. 2) **5091**

Fenwick, Charles G. "The Question of Canadian Participation in Inter-American Conferences." (1937), 31 *American Journal of International Law* 473-476. **5092**

Harbron, John D. *Canada and the Organization of American States.* Washington: Canadian-American Committee, 1963. vii, 31 p. (Reports on Canada-United States Relations) **5093**
Report prepared for the Canadian-American Committee.
Review: Bernard Bonin in (1964-65), 40 *Actualité Économique* 621-622.

Holmes, John W. "Canada and Pan America." (1968), 10 *Journal of Inter-American Studies and World Affairs* 173-184. **5094**

Hubert, Jean-Paul. "Organisation des états américains, Comité juridique interaméricain: 5ième Séminaire de droit international, Rio de Janeiro, 6 août-1er septembre 1978." (1978), 16 *Canadian Yearbook of International Law* 328-331. **5095**

Humphrey, John P. *The Inter-American System, a Canadian View.* Issued under the auspices of the Canadian Institute of International Affairs. Toronto: Macmillan of Canada, 1942. xi, 329 p. **5096**
Includes a list of special Pan American conferences, and a list of Inter-American organizations (up to September, 1940).
Reviews: Ricardo J. Alfaro in (1942), 36 *American Journal of International Law* 735-736; H. McD. Clokie in (1942), 8 *Canadian Journal of Economics and Political Science* 615-617; Robert A. MacKay in (1943), 24 *Canadian Historical Review* 63-64; Reginald G. Trotter under title: "Canada and Pan-Americanism," in (1942), 49 *Queen's Quarterly* 252-260.

Humphrey, John P. "The Twenty-Second Chair: Is It for Canada?" (1941), 3 *Inter-American Quarterly* 5-13 (No. 4) **5097**

Irwin, W. Arthur. "Should Canada Join the Organization of American States?" (1965-66), 72 *Queen's Quarterly* 289-303. **5098**

Kiervin, Jack Orval. *Canada, Latin America and the Organization of American States.* Windsor, 1969. v, 95 leaves. **5099**
Thesis (M.A.), University of Windsor, 1969.

Klepak, H.P., and Vachon, G.K. "Le Canada et l'Organisation des états américains: les questions militaires." (1975-76), 5 *Canadian Defence Quarterly* 31-34 (No. 3) **5100**

Kos-Rabcewicz-Zubkowski, Ludwik. "Canada and the Organization of American States." (1966-67), 18 *Air University Review* 61-69 (Sept./Oct.) **5101**

Langis, Pierre-Paul. "Une nouvelle institution panaméricaine." (1942), 28 *Revue Trimestrielle Canadienne* 324-337. **5102**

Lawrence, Donald Arthur. *The Organization of American States; Divergent Perspectives in the Western Hemisphere.* Kingston, 1971 (c1972). iv, 121 leaves. **5103**
Half-title: *American States.* Thesis (M.A.), Queen's University, 1971. (National Library of Canada. Canadian Theses on Microfilm, No. 10856).

Macdonald, Ronald St. John. "The Organization of American States in Action." (1963-64), 15 *University of Toronto Law Journal* 358-429. **5104**

Macdonald, Ronald St. John. "Relaciones crecientes entre las Naciones Unidas y la Organización de los Estados Americanos." (1969), 2 *Boletin Mexicano de Derecho Comparado* 293-325. **5105**
Translated by Héctor Cuadra.

Macquarrie, Heath. "Canada and the O.A.S.: The Still Vacant Chair." (1968-69), 48 *Dalhousie Review* 37-45. **5106**

Macquarrie, Heath. *Pan-American Union and Canadian Foreign Policy.* Fredericton, 1949. iii, 164 leaves. **5107**
Thesis (M.A.), University of New Brunswick, 1949.

Massey, Vincent. "Canada and the Inter-American System." (1947-48), 26 *Foreign Affairs* 693-700. **5108**

McShane, King G. *Canadian Legislators and the Inter-American System, 1935-1965.* Ottawa, 1966. iv, 155 leaves. **5109**
Thesis (M.A.), University of Ottawa, 1966.

Miller, Eugene H. "Canada and the Pan American Union." (1948), 3 *International Journal* 24-38. **5110**

Morin, Jacques-Yvan. *Thoughts on Canada and the Inter-American System.* Dallas, Tex.: Law Institute of the Americas, Southern Methodist University School of Law; Southwestern Legal Foundation, 1954. iv, 130 leaves, maps. **5111**

Ogelsby, J.C.M. "Canada and the Pan American Union: Twenty Years On." (1968-69), 24 *International Journal* 571-589. **5112**

"The Organization of American States." (1960), 12 *External Affairs* 878-881. **5113**

Pick, Alfred. "The Americas: Protocol Signed at San José Provides Reform of Rio Treaty." (1975), *International Perspectives* 25-30 (Sept./Oct.) **5114**

Podea, Iris S. "Pan American Sentiment in French Canada." (1948), 3 *International Journal* 334-348. **5115**

Roussin, Marcel. "Au carrefour de l'histoire." (1953-54), 4 *Thémis* 63-75. **5116**

Roussin, Marcel. *Le Canada et le système interaméricain.* Ottawa: Éditions de l'Université d'Ottawa, 1959. ix, 285 p. (Université d'Ottawa. Publications sériées, 59) **5117**
Reviews: Charles G. Fenwick in (1960), 54 *American Journal of International Law*

449-450; John D. Harbron in (1961), 42 *Canadian Historical Review* 153-154; Jean-Marc Léger in (1959-60), 13 *Revue d'Histoire de l'Amérique Française* 445-448.

Roussin, Marcel. "Evolution of the Canadian Attitude Towards the Inter-American System." (1953), 47 *American Journal of International Law* 296-300. **5118**

Santiago, Zeno Marques. *The Organization of American States: A Historical Analysis of Its Development, with Brief Reference to Brazil and Canada in Their Relation to the Organization.* Hamilton, Ont., 1960. 106 leaves. **5119**
Thesis (M.A.), McMaster University, 1960.

Slater, Jerome. "The Decline of the OAS." (1968-69), 24 *International Journal* 497-506. **5120**

Smith, David E. "Should Canada Join the Organization of American States? A Rejoinder to W. Arthur Irwin." (1966), 73 *Queen's Quarterly* 100-114. **5121**

Soward, Frederic H., and Macaulay, A.M. *Canada and the Pan American System.* Toronto: Ryerson Press, 1948. v, 47 p. (Contemporary Affairs, No. 21) **5122**
Published under the auspices of the Canadian Institute of International Affairs.
Reviews: George W. Brown in (1948), 3 *International Journal* 386-387; Clifton J. Child in (1948), 24 *International Affairs* 587; Ronald S. Longley in (1948-49), 28 *Dalhousie Review* 411.

Trembley, William A. "American Viewpoints on Closer Canadian Association in Pan Americanism." (1961), 3 *University of Windsor Seminar on Canadian-American Relations, Proceedings* 77-86. **5123**

Trotman, Gene Thornton Torron. *The Organization of American States; Appraisals, Criticisms and Recommendations.* Toronto, 1963. 177 leaves. **5124**
Thesis (LL.M.), University of Toronto, 1963.

Trotter, Reginald G. "Canada and Pan-Americanism." (1942), 49 *Queen's Quarterly* 252-260. **5125**

Trotter, Reginald G., and MacKay, Robert A. "Pan Americanism Is not Enough - Two Opinions." (1942), 5 *Public Affairs* 118-123. **5126**

(c) CENTRAL AMERICAN AND CARIBBEAN ORGANIZATIONS

Clarke, Hugh W. *The Commonwealth Caribbean: From Federation to Common Market.* Montreal, 1975. i, 128 leaves. **5127**
Thesis (M.A.), McGill University, 1975. (National Library of Canada. Canadian Theses on Microfiche, No. 27104).

Gittens, Thoms Wilton. *Caribbean Community and Common Market: Its Problems and Its Prospects.* Ottawa, 1978. vii, 231 leaves. **5128**
Thesis (M.A.), Carleton University, 1978. (National Library of Canada. Canadian Theses on Microfiche, No. 39037).

Hull, Douglas Gordon. *The Central American Integration Process: Técnicos, Politicos and Interest Groups.* London, Ont., 1973. vii, 148 leaves. **5129**
Thesis (M.A.), University of Western Ontario, 1973. (National Library of Canada. Canadian Theses on Microfilm, No. 16420).

Linton, Neville. "Regional Diplomacy of the Commonwealth Caribbean." (1970-71), 26 *International Journal* 401-417. **5130**

Wallace, Elisabeth. "The West Indies: Improbable Federation." (1961), 27 *Canadian Journal of Economics and Political Science* 444-459. 5131

Wallace, Elisabeth. "The West Indies Federation: Decline and Fall." (1961-62), 17 *International Journal* 269-288. 5132

White, Philip Meltan. *An Integration of the Commonwealth Caribbean with Cuba.* Halifax, 1973. 115 leaves. 5133
Thesis (M.A.), Dalhousie University, 1974. (National Library of Canada. Canadian Theses on Microfiche, No. 18729).

Willmore, Larry N. *Regional Integration and the Process of Industrialization in Central America.* Ottawa, 1970. 100 leaves. 5134
Research essay (M.A.), Carleton University, 1970.

5. AFRICA

"African Groupings and African Unity." (1962), 14 *External Affairs* 210-215. 5135

Akindele, Rafiu Ayo. "The Organization of African Unity and the United Nations: A Study of the Problems of Universal-Regional Relationship in the Organization and Maintenance of International Peace and Security." (1971), 9 *Canadian Yearbook of International Law* 30-58. 5136

Aouedri, Allou Pierre. *Intégration économique et développement agricole en Afrique: le cas de la Communauté économique de l'Afrique de l'Ouest (C.E.A.O.).* Québec, 1978. xvi, 220 leaves, maps. 5137
Thesis (M.Sc.), Université Laval, 1978. (National Library of Canada. Canadian Theses on Microfiche, No. 39089).

Avogan, Mathias Kuami. *Problems of Economic Integration in West Africa.* St. John's, 1971. 246 leaves. 5138
Thesis (M.A.), Memorial University of Newfoundland, 1972.

Ban-Ethat, José Rigobert. *La dépendance des états de l'Union douanière et économique de l'Afrique Centrale (U.D.E.A.C.) à l'égard de la France.* Québec, 1975. xi, 163 leaves. 5139
Thesis (M.Sc.Soc.), Université Laval, 1976.

Embolo, Essama A. *L'intégration monétaire en pays sous-développés: conditions d'intégration: cas de l'U.M.O.A.* Montréal, 1973. xii, 110 leaves. 5140
Thesis (M.A.), Université de Montréal, 1973. Refers to Union monétaire Ouest africaine.

Hérisson, Charles-D. "Le problème agricole en Afrique: la coopération agricole pan-africaine." (1947), 33 *Revue Trimestrielle Canadienne* 319-346. 5141

Kanamby, Paul Mulemeri. *Les dimensions des faiblesses de l'Organisation de l'unité africaine (O.U.A.).* Montréal, 1974. iii, 324 leaves. 5142
Thesis (M.A.), Université de Montréal, 1974.

Noel, Albert John. *Political and Economic Integration in East Africa; from the Attempt at Federation in 1963 to the Treaty for East African Co-operation in 1967.* Ottawa, 1970. 118 leaves, map. 5143
Research essay (M.A.), Carleton University, 1970.

Potholm, Christian P. "The Protectorates, the O.A.U. and South Africa." (1966-67), 22 *International Journal* 68-72. **5144**

"Schemes for Union in Western and Equatorial Africa." (1959), 11 *External Affairs* 236-241. **5145**

Shaw, Timothy M. "Organization of African Unity: Prospects for the Second Decade." (1973), *International Perspectives* 31-34 (Sept./Oct.) **5146**

Shaw, Timothy M. "Regional Co-operation and Conflict in Africa." (1974-75), 30 *International Journal* 671-688. **5147**

Touré, Amadou. "Structures économiques et intégration africaine: les principaux freins et blocages du mécanisme d'intégration de la Communauté économique de l'Afrique de l'Ouest. (Note)." (1982), 13 *Études Internationales* 515-524. **5148**

Tremblay, Rodrigue, ed. *Afrique et intégration monétaire / Africa and Monetary Integration.* Montréal: Éditions HRW, 1972. xvi, 466 p. **5149**
Papers and discussions of an international conference organized by the Research Center in Economic Development of the University of Montreal, held on October 3-4, 1971. Text in French and English.

Yadi, Melchiade. "Promotion du développement industriel équilibré des pays-membres de l'UDEAC et de la CAE." (1975), 6 *Études Internationales* 66-102. **5150**
Refers to Union douanière et économique de l'Afrique centrale (UDEAC), and Communauté de l'Afrique de l'Est (CAE).

6. OTHER REGIONS

Boyce, Raymond. *The Achievements of the Organization of Petroleum Exporting Countries in Relation to the Economic Development of Its Middle Eastern and North African Members.* Montreal, 1974 (c1975). v, 118 leaves. **5151**
Half-title: *The OPEC Agreements and Economic Development.* Thesis (M.A.), McGill University, 1974. (National Library of Canada. Canadian Theses on Microfiche, No. 23032).

Carmichael, Joel. "Projects of Arab Unity." (1945), 25 *Dalhousie Review* 448-457. **5152**

Haifa, Said Jamil. *Arab Economic Integration.* Montreal, 1972. vi, 111 leaves.
Thesis, (M.A.), McGill University, 1972. **5153**

Hervouet, Gérard. "L'ASEAN: une 'communauté' en quête de sécurité et de développement." (1978-79), 2 *Revue d'Intégration Européenne* 299-318. **5154**

"The League of Arab States." (1959), 11 *External Affairs* 363-365. **5155**

Shilling, Nancy Adams. *Ideological Factors in the League of Arab States, 1944-1956.* Montreal, 1965 (c1966). 590 leaves. **5156**
Thesis (Ph.D.), McGill University, 1966. (National Library of Canada. Canadian Theses on Microfilm, No. 388).

D. International Administration

1. GENERAL

Appathurai, E. "Permanent Missions to the United Nations." (1969-70), 25 *International Journal* 287-301. **5157**

Cohen, Maxwell. "The United Nations Secretariat: Some Constitutional and Administrative Developments." (1955), 49 *American Journal of International Law* 295-319. **5158**

Cohen, Maxwell. "The United States and the United Nations Secretariat: A Preliminary Appraisal." (1952-55), 1 *McGill Law Journal* 169-198. **5159**

Keenleyside, Hugh L. "Administrative Problems of the Technical Assistance Administration." (1952), 18 *Canadian Journal of Economics and Political Science* 345-357. **5160**

Renouf, Alan. "The Legal Department of the United Nations: A Survey and a Criticism." (1949), 27 *Canadian Bar Review* 939-946. **5161**

Smith, Ernest H. "Tax Immunities. Part II - International Organizations and Their Staffs." (1960), 8 *Canadian Tax Journal* 404-411. **5162**

Svoboda, Charles Vincent. *Some Administrative Aspects of the United Nations Secretariat*. Ottawa, 1969 (c1970). 123, (14), 11 leaves. **5163**
    Thesis (M.A.), Carleton University, 1970. (National Library of Canada. Canadian Theses on Microfilm, No. 6509).

Turack, Daniel C. "International Regional Organizations and Their Travel Documents." (1968), 6 *Canadian Yearbook of International Law* 164-187 **5164**

2. OFFICIALS AND EMPLOYEES

Anglin, Douglas G. "Lester Pearson and the Office of Secretary-General." (1961-62), 17 *International Journal* 145-150. **5165**

Barros, James. *Betrayal from Within: Joseph Avenol, Secretary-General of the League of Nations, 1933-1940*. New Haven: Yale University Press, 1969. xii, 289 p. **5166**
    Review: Henri Reymond in (1969-70), 25 *International Journal* 641-642.

Barros, James. *Office Without Power: Secretary General Sir Eric Drummond, 1919-1933*. Oxford: Clarendon Press; New York: Oxford University Press, 1979. xii, 423 p. **5167**
    Reviews: Stephen M. Schwebel in (1980), 74 *American Journal of International Law* 695-697; Georgia Tsotsou in (1981), 2 *Hellenic Review of International Relations* 339-340; Richard Veatch in (1980), 35 *International Journal* 400-401.

Barros, James. "Pearson or Lie: The Politics of the Secretary-General's Selection, 1946." (1977), 10 *Canadian Journal of Political Science* 65-92. **5168**

Beigbeder, Yves. "La grève de 1976 à l'Office des Nations Unies à Genève et ses conséquences." (1978), 21 *Canadian Public Administration* 26-50. **5169**

Brumer, Leon. *The Political Development of the Office of the Secretary-General of the United Nations, as Reflected in His Role During the Organization's Peace-Keeping Activities in the Korean, Suez, Congo and Cyprus Crises, 1945-1965.* Kingston, 1967. 139 leaves. **5170**
Thesis (M.A.), Queen's University, 1967.

"Canada and the United Nations: Personnel Policy of the Secretary-General." (1953), 5 *External Affairs* 204-206. **5171**

Gordenker, Leon. "U Thant and the Office of U.N. Secretary-General." (1966-67), 22 *International Journal* 1-16. **5172**

Green, Leslie C. "The International Civil Servant, His Employer, and His State." (1954), 40 *Grotius Society, Transactions* 147-174. **5173**

Green, Leslie C. "Reparation for Injuries Suffered in the Service of the United Nations, Advisory Opinion, (1949) *I.C.J. Reports* 174." (1949), 12 *Modern Law Review* 508-511. **5174**

Green, Leslie C. "The Status of the International Civil Service." (1954), 7 *Current Legal Problems* 192-211. **5175**

Hulmes, Frederick George. *The Changing Political Role of the Secretary-General of the United Nations.* Edmonton, 1959. 174 leaves. **5176**
Thesis (M.A.), University of Alberta, 1959.

McLaren, Robert I. *Civil Servants and Public Policy: A Comparative Study of International Secretariats.* Waterloo, Ont.: Wilfrid Laurier University Press, 1980. xvi, 144 p. **5177**
Reviews: Richard Baker in (1980), 58 *Public Administration* 511-512; Leland M. Goodrich in (1981), 75 *American Journal of International Law* 1038-1039; Lorna Lloyd in (1980-81), 57 *International Affairs* 137; David H. Pollock in (1981), 24 *Canadian Public Administration* 320-321.

Monsma, Edward Bodus. *The Evolution of the Political Role of the Secretary-General in the United Nations.* Edmonton, 1971. (vi), 141 leaves. **5178**
Thesis (M.A.), University of Alberta, 1971.

Sawicki, Manuela Lila. *Some Aspects of the Legal Status of I.C.A.O. Personnel.* Montreal, 1969. 114 leaves. **5179**
Thesis (LL.M.), McGill University, 1969. (National Library of Canada. Canadian Theses on Microfilm, No. 4860).

Scott, Francis R. "The World's Civil Service." (1954), 496 *International Conciliation* 257-320. **5180**

Silver, Jan. *Some Aspects of Personnel Policy and Administration in the United Nations Secretariat.* Windsor, 1970. 127, ix leaves. **5181**
Thesis (M.A.), University of Windsor, 1970.

Walker, Robert Brian James. *The Power and System Paradigms in International Relations; the Case of the Secretary General of the United Nations.* Kingston, 1970 (c1971). ii, 116 leaves. **5182**
Thesis (M.A.), Queen's University, 1971. (National Library of Canada. Canadian Theses on Microfilm, No. 7837).

Zacher, Mark W. "The Secretary-General: Some Comments on Recent Research." (1969), 23 *International Organization* 932-950. **5183**
This is a review article of four books.

Zacher, Mark W. "The Secretary-General and the United Nations' Function of Peaceful Settlement." *In* Wood, Robert S., ed., *The Process of International Organization* (New York, 1971), pp. 255-270. **5184**
Reprinted from (1966), 20 *International Organization* 724-749.

3. HEADQUARTERS

Dai, Poeliu. "The Headquarters Agreement between Canada and the International Civil Aviation Organization." (1964), 2 *Canadian Yearbook of International Law* 205-214. **5185**

"What Goes on in Geneva." (1952), 4 *External Affairs* 339-340. **5186**

E. Nongovernmental Organizations

Borgese, Elisabeth Mann. "Introduction to the IOI." *In* Pacem in Maribus X, *Proceedings* (Vienna, 1980), pp. 10-13. **5187**
Refers to the International Ocean Institute at Msida, Malta.

Laureys, Henry. "La Chambre de commerce internationale." (1935-36), 11/2 *Actualité Économique* 1-33. **5188**

Levy, Gary. "Le Canada, le Québec et l'Association internationale des parlementaires de langue française." (1976), 7 *Études Internationales* 447-456. **5189**

Levy, Gary. "Parliamentary Associations - Useful but Little-Known Forums." (1976), *International Perspectives* 32-35 (July/Aug.) **5190**

Mostafa, Khairy H.Y. *Transnational Commercial Organizations in Public International Air Law*. Montreal, 1969. iv, 243 leaves. **5191**
Thesis (LL.M.), McGill University, 1969. (National Library of Canada. Canadian Theses on Microfilm, No. 4845).

Rahman, A.T.M. Siddiquer. *The Canadian Co-operative Movement and Its Role in International Development*. Ottawa, 1971. ii, 185 leaves. **5192**
Thesis (M.A.), Carleton University, 1971. (National Library of Canada. Canadian Theses on Microfilm, No. 9311).

Raynauld, André. "La doctrine coopérative des échanges internationaux." (1954-55), 30 *Actualité Économique* 614-632. **5193**

Raynauld, André. "Les sociétés coopératives internationales." (1954-55), 30 *Actualité Économique* 223-256. **5194**

Thorson, Joseph T. "The International Commission of Jurists." (1957), 35 *Canadian Bar Review* 898-910. **5195**

Thorson, Joseph T. "The Rule of Law in a Changing World." (1959-63), 1 *University of British Columbia Law Review* 176-184. **5196**

Vasseur, Pierre. "La mission de la Chambre de commerce internationale." (1935-36), 11/2 *Actualité Économique* 401-412. **5197**

XVII. INTERNATIONAL CONFERENCES

For the U. N. Conference on the Law of the Sea, see "Law of the Sea: General" (p. 230).

Bailey, Paul J., and Bailey-Wiebecke, Ilka. "All-European Co-operation: The CSCE's Basket Two and the ECE." (1976-77), 32 *International Journal* 386-407. **5198**

Brown, Wilson. "The Allies at Quebec." (1949-50), 56 *Queen's Quarterly* 465-478. **5199**

Claxton, Brooke. "Canada at the Paris Conference." (1946-47), 2 *International Journal* 124-131. **5200**

Galbraith, John S. "The Imperial Conference of 1921 and the Washington Conference." (1948), 29 *Canadian Historical Review* 143-152. **5201**

Glazebrook, G.P. de T. *Canada at the Paris Peace Conference.* London, Toronto, etc.: Oxford University Press, 1942. vii, 156 p. **5202**
   Issued under the auspices of the Canadian Institute of International Affairs.
   Reviews: H. McD. Clokie in (1944), 10 *Canadian Journal of Economics and Political Science* 104-106; Percy E. Corbett in (1943), 37 *American Journal of International Law* 705; John W. Dafoe under title: "Canada and the Peace Conference of 1919," in (1943), 24 *Canadian Historical Review* 233-248; B.K. Sandwell in (1942-43), 12 *University of Toronto Quarterly* 236-240; signed Sikh in (1940-43), 19 *International Affairs* 575-576.

Holmes, John W. "Geneva: 1954." (1966-67), 22 *International Journal* 457-483. **5203**

Kitsikis, Dimitri. *Le rôle des experts à la Conférence de la paix de 1919; gestation d'une technocratie en politique internationale.* Ottawa: Editions de l'Université d'Ottawa, 1972. x, 227 p. (Cahiers d'histoire de l'Université d'Ottawa, no 4) **5204**
   Reviews: Robert H. Keyserlingk in (1974), 5 *Études Internationales* 177-178; Julien-Maurice Lambert in (1973), 4 *Études Internationales* 572-574; Harold Nelson in (1976), 57 *Canadian Historical Review* 100-102.

Lower, Arthur R.M. "Loring Christie and the Genesis of the Washington Conference of 1921-1922." (1966), 47 *Canadian Historical Review* 38-48. **5205**

Martin, Paul. "The UN Conference on Trade and Development." (1964), 16 *External Affairs* 143-148. **5206**

McGrath, *Sir* Patrick T. "An Inter-Parliamentary Conference." (1926-27), 6 *Dalhousie Review* 177-187. **5207**

Morse, Charles. "The Hague Conference." (1907), 6 *Canadian Law Review* 94-95, 208, 341-342. **5208**

"Moscow Conference." (1942), 3 *Behind the Headlines* No. 10 (28 p.) **5209**

Ouimet, Lise. *La Conférence des Nations Unies sur le commerce et le développement et la théorie fonctionnaliste pour le maintien de la paix.* Ottawa, 1973. xix, 126 leaves. **5210**
Thesis (M.A.), University of Ottawa, 1973.

Picard, Roger. "La Conférence monétaire et bancaire des Nations-Unies." (1944-45), 20/1 *Actualité Économique* 401-431. **5211**

Riddell, Walter Alexander. *World Security by Conference.* Toronto: Ryerson Press, 1947. x, 216 p. **5212**
Reviews: Henry F. Angus in (1948), 14 *Canadian Journal of Economics and Political Science* 395-397; Samuel Mack Eastman in (1948), 3 *International Journal* 165-166; Frederic H. Soward in (1948), 29 *Canadian Historical Review* 84-85; Conrad Payling Wright in (1948-49), 28 *Dalhousie Review* 408-409.

Sandwell, B.K. "The Atlantic Conference." (1941-42), 48 *Queen's Quarterly* 295-299. **5213**

XVIII. STATE RESPONSIBILITY

Adede, A.O. "A Fresh Look at the Meaning of the Doctrine of Denial of Justice under International Law." (1976), 14 *Canadian Yearbook of International Law* 73-95. **5214**

Bissonnette, Pierre André. *La satisfaction comme mode de réparation en droit international.* Geneva: Institut universitaire de hautes études internationales, 1952. vii, 185 p. **5215**
Review: Leslie C. Green in (1953), 31 *Canadian Bar Review* 1179-1180.

Copithorne, M.D. "State Responsibility and International Claims." *In* Macdonald, Ronald St. John, and others, *Canadian Perspectives on International Law and Organization* (Toronto, 1974), pp. 207-228. **5216**

Demain, Bernard. "Compétence territoriale et abus des droits en droit international." (1968-69), 5 *Justinien* 19-85. **5217**

Mayrand, Léon. "La souveraineté et les dettes extérieures." (1934-35), 10 *Actualité Économique* 149-155, 253-259. **5218**

McWhinney, Edward. "Federalism, Pluralism, and State Responsibility - Canadian and American Analogies." (1959), 34 *New York University Law Review* 1079-1095. **5219**

XIX. PACIFIC SETTLEMENT OF DISPUTES

See also *"Commercial Arbitration" (p. 685).*

A. General

Albinski, Henry S. "Australia and the Dutch New Guinea Dispute." (1960-61), 16 *International Journal* 358-382. **5220**

Arnopoulos, Paris J. "Consultation and Conciliation." (1974-75), 30 *International Journal* 102-126. **5221**

Baxter, Richard R. "Settling Our Canadian-United States Differences: An American Perspective." (1978), 1 *Canada-United States Law Journal* 5-11. **5222**

Bourne, Charles B. "Mediation, Conciliation and Adjudication in the Settlement of International Drainage Basin Disputes." (1971), 9 *Canadian Yearbook of International Law* 114-158. **5223**

British and American Joint Commission for the Final Settlement of the Claims of the Hudson's Bay and Puget's Sound Agricultural Companies. *Papers.* Washington: Govt. Print. Off.; Montreal: Printed by J. Lovell, 1865-69. 14 vols. in 13. **5224**

> The commission was appointed under the treaty of July 1, 1863 (53 BFSP 6; 12 Hertslet 932; 13 Stat. 651; TS 128; 12 Bevans 154; 8 Miller 949; 128 Parry 19). The office of the commission was in Washington and meetings were held from January 7, 1865 to September 10, 1869. (See *Checklist of United States Public Documents, 1789-1909,* 3d ed., 1911, p. 911). Caleb Cushing was counsel for the United States, and Charles D. Day was counsel for the Hudson's Bay Company and the Puget Sound Agricultural Company.

"Canada-United States Relations: Cooperation and Dispute Settlement in the North American Context / Relations canado-américaines: coopération et règlement de différends dans le contexte nord-américain." (1977), 6 *Canadian Council on International Law, Proceedings,* 169 p. **5225**

> This is the general theme of the sixth annual conference held jointly with the Canada-United States Institute at Ottawa, October 20-22, 1977, published in (1978), 1 *Canada-United States Law Journal,* pp. 1-169. Individual papers are listed separately.

Cole, Charles V. "A Generation of Canadian Experience with International Claims." (1965-66), 41 *British Year Book of International Law* 368-400. **5226**

Copithorne, M.D. "The Settlement of International Claims between Canada and China: A Status Report." (1975-76), 48 *Pacific Affairs* 230-237. **5227**

Crackanthorpe, Montague. "Notes on a Proposed General Treaty." (1902-03), 2 *Canadian Law Review* 547-551. **5228**

Dalfen, Charles M. "Domestic Models in the International Context. (Review Article)." (1975-76), 31 *International Journal* 44-52. **5229**

Emanuelli, Claude C. "Mode de règlement des différends entre le Canada et les États-Unis en matière de frontières et de ressources maritimes." (1977), 7 *Revue de Droit, Université de Sherbrooke* 319-356. **5230**

Ewart, John S. "The Geneva Protocol." (1924-25), 4 *Dalhousie Review* 456-466.
5231

Gray, Mary A. "Settlement of the Claims in Washington of the Hudson's Bay Company and the Puget's Sound Agricultural Company." (1930), 21 *Washington Historical Quarterly* 95-102. **5232**

Green, Leslie C. "Legal Aspects of the Sino-Indian Border Dispute." (1960), 1 *China Quarterly* 42-58 (No. 3) **5233**

Holmes, John W. "Mediation or Enforcement?" (1969-70), 25 *International Journal* 388-404. **5234**

"International Claims." (1957), 9 *External Affairs* 326-329. **5235**

"International Claims." (1966), 18 *External Affairs* 11-20. **5236**

"An International Court." (1902), 38 *Canada Law Journal* 700-701. **5237**
Refers to 'The Case of the Pious Fund of the Californias,' between the United States and Mexico.

Lehoux, Grégoire. "La Troisième Conférence sur le droit de la mer et le règlement obligatoire des différends." (1980), 18 *Canadian Yearbook of International Law* 31-90. **5238**

Macdonald, Donald S. "Canada's Recent Experience in International Claims." (1965-66), 21 *International Journal* 323-334. **5239**

Macdonald, Ronald St. John. "Settling Our Canadian-United States Differences: A Canadian Perspective." (1978), 1 *Canada-United States Law Journal* 12-18.
5240

McCarney, Rosemary A. "A Proposed Model for Dispute Settlement in North America." (1983), 6 *Canada-United States Law Journal* 89-97. **5241**

Merrills, J.G. "The Justiciability of International Disputes." (1969), 47 *Canadian Bar Review* 241-269. **5242**

Re, Edward D. "International Claims Adjudication: The United States-Canadian Agreement." (1967), 17 *Buffalo Law Review* 125-134. **5243**

Read, John E. "Perspective in the International Plane." *In* Deener, David R., ed., *Canada-United States Treaty Relations* (Durham, N.C., 1963), pp. 72-80.
5244

Riddell, William Renwick. "Settlement of International Disputes by and between the English Speaking Nations." (1912-13), 22 *Yale Law Review* 545-553, 583-589. **5245**

Settlement of International Disputes between Canada and the U.S.A. Chicago:

Published by the Section of International Law of the American Bar Association, 1979. lxii, 113 p. **5246**
At head of title: American Bar Association and Canadian Bar Association. Sub-title: *Resolutions Adopted by the American Bar Association on 15 August 1979, and by the Canadian Bar Association on 30 August 1979, with Accompanying Reports and Recommendations, 20 September 1979.*
Review: Maxwell Cohen in (1982), 60 *Canadian Bar Review* 224-231.

Sichilongo, Mengo D.F. *International Law and the Development of the Ethiopia-Kenya-Somalia Dispute.* Montreal, 1974 (c1978). vii, 241 leaves, maps. **5247**
Half-title: *The Ethiopia-Somalia Dispute.* Thesis (LL.M.), McGill University, 1974. (National Library of Canada. Canadian Theses on Microfiche, No. 35803).

Thomas, Eileen Mitchell. "The Draft Transfrontier Pollution Treaty Adopted by the American and Canadian Bar Associations Relating to Settlement of International Disputes between Canada and the U.S.A." (1981), 9 *International Business Lawyer* 85-87. **5248**

Wang, Erik B. "Nationality of Claims and Diplomatic Intervention - Canadian Practice. (Comment)." (1965), 43 *Canadian Bar Review* 136-150. **5249**

Winham, Gilbert R. "International Negotiation in an Age of Transition." (1979-80), 35 *International Journal* 1-20. **5250**

B. Arbitration

1. GENERAL

Castel, Jean-Gabriel. "Canada and International Arbitration." (1981), 36 *Arbitration Journal* 5-22. **5251**

Corbett, Percy E. *The Settlement of Canadian-American Disputes, a Critical Study of Methods and Results.* New Haven: Yale University Press; Toronto: Ryerson Press, 1937. viii, 134 p., map. (Relations of Canada and the United States) **5252**
Published for the Carnegie Endowment for International Peace, Division of Economics and History. Reprinted New York, Russell & Russell, 1970.
Reviews: Angèle Auburtin in (1938), 8 *Zeitschrift für Ausländisches Öffentliches Recht und Völkerrecht* 206-207; G.F. Curtis in (1937-38), 17 *Dalhousie Review* 395-398; Norman A.M. MacKenzie in (1937), 3 *Canadian Journal of Economics and Political Science* 579-581; W.J.M. Mackenzie in (1938), 17 *International Affairs* 422-423; Harold S. Quigley in (1938), 32 *American Journal of International Law* 643-644; signed 'C.' in (1938), 19 *British Year Book of International Law* 268-269; unsigned in (1937-38), 2 *University of Toronto Law Journal* 457-459.

"International Arbitration Vindicated." (1917), 53 *Canada Law Journal* 321-323. **5253**

Kos-Rabcewicz-Zubkowski, Ludwik. "Central and East European Rules on the Form of International Arbitration Agreements." (1968), 3 *Revue Juridique Thémis* 415-448. **5254**

Lovell, R.I. "The Case for the Alabama." (1935-36), 42 *Queen's Quarterly* 515-522.
5255
Famous Anglo-American case, the subject of the Treaty of Washington of May 8, 1871. The Confederate States ship *Alabama* had destroyed 96 American vessels before she was sunk by the U.S.S. *Kearsage* off Cherbourg, June 19, 1864. For the damage done by her, and others, a tribunal of international arbitration at Geneva in September, 1872, condemned the British government to pay $15,500,000.

McRae, Donald M. "Adjudication of the Maritime Boundary in the Gulf of Maine." (1979), 17 *Canadian Yearbook of International Law* 292-303. **5256**

"Mixed Arbitral Tribunal." (1922), 58 *Canada Law Journal* 69-71. **5257**
Refers to the Anglo-German Mixed Arbitral Tribunal, established under Article 304 of the Treaty of Versailles.

Moore, John Bassett. *History and Digest of the International Arbitrations to Which the United States Has Been a Party, etc.* Washington: Govt. Print. Off., 1898. 6 vols., maps. **5258**
Contents of Volume 1: Ch. 1. The Saint Croix River: Commission under Article 5 of the Jay Treaty (pp. 1-43).- Ch. 2. Islands in the Bay of Fundy: Commission under Article 4 of the Treaty of Ghent (pp. 45-64).- Ch. 3. The Northeastern Boundary: Commission under Article 5 of the Treaty of Ghent (pp. 65-83).- Ch. 4. The Northeastern Boundary: Arbitration under the Convention of September 29, 1827 (pp. 85-161).- Ch. 5. Boundary through the River St. Lawrence and Lakes Ontario, Erie, and Huron: Commission under Article 6 of the Treaty of Ghent (pp. 162-170).- Ch. 6. Boundary from Lake Huron to the Most Northwestern Point of the Lake of the Woods: Commission under Article 7 of the Treaty of Ghent (pp. 171-195).- Ch. 7. The San Juan Water Boundary: Arbitration under Articles 34-42 of the Treaty of May 8, 1871 (pp. 196-236).- Ch. 8. Claims of the Hudson's Bay and Puget's Sound Agricultural Companies: Commission under the Treaty of July 1, 1863 (pp. 237-270).- Ch. 9. Impediments to the Recovery of Debts: Commission under Article 6 of the Jay Treaty (pp. 271-298).- Ch. 10. The Rights and Duties of Neutrals: Commission under Article 7 of the Jay Treaty (pp. 299-349).- Ch. 11. Difference as to the Treaty of Ghent: Award of the Emperor of Russia; Mixed Commissions; Domestic Commissions (pp. 350-390).- Ch. 12. The London Commission of 1853-1855: Convention between the United States and Great Britain of February 8, 1853 (pp. 391-425).- Ch. 13. Reserved Fisheries under the Reciprocity Treaty of 1854 (pp. 426-494).- Ch. 14. The Geneva Arbitration (pp. 495-682).- Ch. 15. Civil War claims: Treaty between the United States and Great Britain, of May 8, 1871 (pp. 683-702).- Ch. 16. The Halifax Commission (pp. 703-753).- Ch. 17. Fur Seal Arbitration (pp. 755-961).- Ch. 18. Question of a Permanent Treaty of Arbitration between the United States and Great Britain (pp. 962-989).

Moore, John Bassett. *International Adjudications, Ancient and Modern: History and Documents, etc.* New York: Oxford University Press, 1929-1931. 6 vols., maps. (Carnegie Endowment for International Peace. Division of International Law. Publications) **5259**
Contents (Partial): v. 1-2. Saint Croix River Arbitration: Mixed Commission under Article 5 of the Treaty between Great Britain and the United States of November 19, 1794 (Jay Treaty).- v. 3. Arbitration of Claims for Compensation for Losses and Damages Resulting from Lawful Impediments to the Recovery of Pre-War Debts: Mixed Commission under Article 6 of the Treaty between Great Britain and the United States of November 19, 1794 (Jay Treaty).- v. 4. Compensation for Losses and Damages Caused by the Violation of Neutral Rights, and by the Failure to Perform Neutral Duties: Mixed Commission under Article 7 of the Treaty between Great Britain and the

United States of November 19, 1794 (Jay Treaty).- v. 6. Arbitration of the Title to Islands in Passamaquoddy Bay and the Bay of Fundy: Mixed Commission under Article 4 of the Treaty between Great Britain and the United States of December 24, 1814 (Treaty of Ghent).
Review: William Renwick Riddell in (1931), 12 *Canadian Historical Review* 446-447 (of vol. 1).

Reid, *Sir* Robert. "International Arbitration." (1902-03), 2 *Canadian Law Review* 277-285. **5260**

Riddell, William Renwick. "When International Arbitration Failed." (1920), 40 *Canadian Law Times* 351-360. **5261**

"Settlement of the Canadian Questions." (1908), 2 *American Journal of International Law* 630-634. **5262**

Taylor, Hannis. "International Arbitration the Product of the Modern International System." (1905), 4 *Canadian Law Review* 210-220. **5263**

Wang, Erik B. "Adjudication of Canada-United States Disputes." (1981), 19 *Canadian Yearbook of International Law* 158-228. **5264**

2. SPECIFIC CASES

See also *"Alaska Boundary" (p. 175)*.

(a) 'I'M ALONE'

Canada. Dept. of External Affairs. *Claim of British Ship 'I'm Alone'; Documents.* Ottawa: King's Printer, 1935. 328 p. (various pagings) **5265**
Each document has a separate title page and pagination.

Canada. Dept. of External Affairs. *The "I'm Alone" Incident: Correspondence between the Governments of Canada and the United States, 1929.* Ottawa: King's Printer, 1929. 23 p. **5266**
Refers to the Canadian schooner *I'm Alone*, registered in Lunenburg, Nova Scotia, sunk by the U.S. Coast Guard on March 22, 1929, in the Gulf of Mexico about 200 miles off the Louisiana coast, while engaged in an attempt to smuggle intoxicating liquors into the United States.

Dennis, William C. "The Sinking of the *'I'm Alone.'*" (1929), 23 *American Journal of International Law* 351-362. **5267**

Fitzmaurice, G.G. "The Case of the *I'm Alone.*" (1936), 17 *British Year Book of International Law* 82-111. **5268**

Frazer, Keener C. "The *'I'm Alone*'s Case and the Doctrine of 'Hot Pursuit.' " (1928-29), 7 *North Carolina Law Review* 413-422. **5269**

Garner, James W. "Hot Pursuit. Illegal Sinking of Vessel on the High Seas. The *I'm Alone* Case." (1935), 16 *British Year Book of International Law* 173-175. **5270**

"The *I'm Alone.*" (1929-30), 7 *New York University Law Quarterly Review* 159-166. **5271**

MacKenzie, Norman A.M. "International Law - Hot Pursuit - The Three Mile Limit. (Comment)." (1929), 7 *Canadian Bar Review* 407-410. **5272**
Refers to the *I'm Alone* case.

U.S. Dept. of State. *'I'm Alone' Case.* Washington: Govt. Print. Off., 1931-35. 7 vols. (U.S. Dept. of State. Publication; Arbitration Series, No. 2) **5273**

(b) GUT DAM

"Arbitration of Lake Ontario (Gut Dam) Claims." (1968), 20 *External Affairs* 507-509. **5274**
Final settlement of the long standing dispute involving some 230 claims by U.S. nationals against the Government of Canada, for damage allegedly caused by the construction of the Gut Dam in the international section of the St. Lawrence River between 1903 and 1907. The *Lake Ontario Claims Tribunal United States and Canada* held meetings from January 11 to September 27, 1968, and awarded the sum of U.S. $350,000 to be paid by Canada.

"Canada-U.S. Agreement on Gut Dam Claims." (1965), 17 *External Affairs* 183-190. **5275**
Includes the text of the Agreement of March 25, 1965 (CTS 1966/22).

"Canada-United States Arbitral Tribunal." (1966), 18 *External Affairs* 73-74.
Claims for damage involving Gut Dam. **5276**

Kerley, Ernest L., and Goodman, Carl F. "The Gut Dam Claims - A Lump Sum Settlement Disposes of an Arbitrated Dispute." (1969-70), 10 *Virginia Journal of International Law* 300-327. **5277**

"Lake Ontario Claims Tribunal." (1967), 19 *External Affairs* 90-94. **5278**
Concerns the Gut Dam claims.

Lillich, Richard B. "The Gut Dam Claims Agreement with Canada." (1965), 59 *American Journal of International Law* 892-898. **5279**

(c) TRAIL SMELTER

See also *"Air Pollution (Transboundary)" (p. 667).*

Dean, Reginald Scott, and Swain, Robert Eckles. *Report Submitted to the Trail Smelter Arbitral Tribunal.* Washington: Govt. Print. Off., 1944. xii, 304 p., maps. (U.S. Bureau of Mines. Bulletin, 453) **5280**
Refers to the arbitration by the *Mixed Arbitration Tribunal* established under the convention of April 15, 1935 (CTS 1935/20), which reported its final decision on March 11, 1941. Published in collaboration with the Meteorological Division of the Air Services Branch, Dept. of Transport, Canada.

Dinwoodie, D.H. "The Politics of International Pollution Control: The Trail Smelter Case." (1971-72), 27 *International Journal* 219-235. **5281**

FitzGerald, Gerald F. "Le Canada et le développement du droit international; la contribution de l'Affaire de la fonderie de Trail à la formation du nouveau droit de la pollution atmosphérique transfrontière." (1980), 11 *Études Internationales* 393-419. **5282**

Kuhn, Arthur K. "The Trail Smelter Arbitration - United States and Canada." (1938), 32 *American Journal of International Law* 785-788. **5283**

Kuhn, Arthur K. "The Trail Smelter Arbitration - United States and Canada." (1941), 35 *American Journal of International Law* 665-666. **5284**

Murray, Keith A. "The Trail Smelter Case: International Air Pollution in the Columbia Valley." (1972), 15 *B.C. Studies* 68-85. **5285**

Read, John E. "The Trail Smelter Dispute." (1963), 1 *Canadian Yearbook of International Law* 213-229. **5286**

"Trail Smelter Arbitral Tribunal. Decision." (1939), 33 *American Journal of International Law* 182-212. **5287**

Trail Smelter Question. Reference of Certain Complaints Arising from the Operation of the Smelter at Trail, B.C., to an International Tribunal for Adjudication. Documents. Ottawa: Printed by J.O. Patenaude, 1936-40. 11 vols. **5288**

(d) FISHERIES

Anderson, Chandler P. "The Final Outcome of the Fisheries Arbitration." (1913), 7 *American Journal of International Law* 1-16. **5289**

"The Atlantic Fisheries Arbitration." (1910), 30 *Canadian Law Times* 670-671. **5290**

Basdevant, Jules. *L'affaire des pêcheries des côtes septentrionales de l'Atlantique entre les États-Unis d'Amérique et la Grande-Bretagne devant la Cour de la Haye.* Paris: A. Pedone, 1912. 170 p., map. **5291**
Reprinted from (1912), 19 *Revue Générale de Droit International Public* 421-582.

Borchard, Edwin M. *North Atlantic Coast Fisheries Arbitration. Coastal Waters; English Translations of Extracts from Works of Publicists, for Use Before the Permanent Court of Arbitration at the Hague, etc.* Washington: Govt. Print. Off., 1910. iv, 362 p. **5292**

Borchard, Edwin M. "The North Atlantic Coast Fisheries Arbitration." (1911), 11 *Columbia Law Review* 1-23. **5293**

Brown, J. Stanley. "Fur Seals and the Bering Sea Arbitration." (1894), 26 *American Geographical Society of New York, Bulletin* 326-372. **5294**

Campbell, Charles S. "The Anglo-American Crisis in the Bering Sea, 1890-1891." (1961-62), 48 *Mississippi Valley Historical Review* 393-414. **5295**

Canada. Parliament. *Correspondence Following the Meeting of the Experts on the Behring Sea Seal Question.* Ottawa, 1898. 5 p. (Canada. Parliament, 1898. Sessional Papers, No. 39) **5296**

Canada. Parliament. *Correspondence Relating to the Seizure of British Vessels in Behring's Sea, with Additional Correspondence.* Ottawa, 1888. (Canada. Parliament, 1888. Sessional Papers, Nos. 65a, 65b, and 65c, pp. 12-114) **5297**

Canada. Parliament. *Correspondence Relative to the Seizure of British American Vessels in Behring's Sea by the United States Authorities in 1886.* Ottawa, 1887. 47 p., map. (Canada. Parliament, 1887. Sessional Papers, No. 48) **5298**

Canada. Parliament. *Papers in Regards to Differences between Canada and the*

United States Referred to the Hague Tribunal, with Amended Fishery Regulations. Ottawa, 1911. 61 p. (Canada. Parliament, 1911. Sessional Papers, Nos. 97a, and 97b) **5299**

Candow, James E. *The North Atlantic Fisheries Dispute of 1886-1888 and Its Perception by the New-York Times and the New-York Tribune.* Halifax, 1977 (c1978). 173 leaves. **5300**
Thesis (M.A.), Dalhousie University, 1977. (National Library of Canada. Canadian Theses on Microfiche, No. 36055).

Cappon, James. "Canada and the Fisheries Dispute." (1906-07), 14 *Queen's Quarterly* 233-235. **5301**

Drago, Luis M. "The North Atlantic Fisheries Arbitration: Questions Submitted to and Answers by the Arbitrators." (1910), 30 *Canadian Law Times* 879-915. **5302**

Elliott, Charles Burke. *The United States and the Northeastern Fisheries: A History of the Fishery Question.* Minneapolis: University of Minnesota, 1887. 151 p., map. **5303**
Also issued as the author's thesis (Ph.D.), University of Minnesota, 1887.

Engelhardt, Ed. "De l'exécution de la sentence arbitrale de 1893 sur les pêcheries de Behring." (1898), 5 *Revue Générale de Droit International Public* 193-207, 347-358. **5304**

"The Final Settlement of the North Atlantic Coast Fisheries Controversy." (1913), 7 *American Journal of International Law* 140-144. **5305**

Foster, John W. "Results of the Bering Sea Arbitration." (1895), 161 *North American Review* 693-702. **5306**

Fur Seal Arbitration. *Proceedings of the Tribunal of Arbitration, Convened at Paris under the Treaty between the United States and Great Britain Concluded at Washington, February 29, 1892, for the Determination of Questions between the Two Governments concerning the Jurisdictional Rights of the United States in the Waters of Bering Sea.* Washington: Govt. Print. Off., 1895. 16 vols., maps. **5307**
This Tribunal, also known as the *Bering* (or Behring) *Sea Tribunal of Arbitration*, held meetings at Paris from February 23 to August 15, 1893. The points of international law involved in the fur seal controversy having been determined by this tribunal, the *Bering Sea Claims Commission* was appointed under the convention of February 8, 1896, for the settlement of damages; sessions of the commission were held at Victoria, B.C., Montreal and Halifax, during 1896-1897. Individual documents, such as cases, counter cases, arguments, were also published separately.

"The Fur Seal Question." (1907), 1 *American Journal of International Law* 742-748. **5308**
Refers to Canadian sealers.

Gluek, Alvin Charles. "Programmed Diplomacy: The Settlement of the North Atlantic Fisheries Question, 1907-12." (1976-77), 6 *Acadiensis* 43-70 (No. 1) **5309**

Goodwin, Frances K. *The Halifax Commission of 1877.* Baltimore, 1959. 184 leaves. **5310**
Thesis (M.A.), Johns Hopkins University, 1959. Refers to the sum of $5,500,000 in gold

awarded to Canada and Newfoundland to be paid by the United States for inshore fishing rights. This award was made at Halifax in June 1877 by a majority vote of two of the three members of the Joint High Commission set up under article 22 of the Treaty of Washington of May 8, 1871 (61 BFSP 40; 13 Hertslet 970; 17 Stat. 863; TS 133; 12 Bevans 170; 143 Parry 145). For documentary sources, see Halifax Commission, 1877, *Record of the Proceedings,* London, 1877, 3 vols., and *Award of the Fishery Commission, Documents and Proceedings,* Washington, Govt. Print. Off., 1878, 3 vols.

Hackworth, Green Haywood. "Fisheries: Northeastern Fisheries." *In* Hackworth, Green Haywood, *Digest of International Law* (Washington, 1940), vol. 1, pp. 783-790. **5311**

Hague. Permanent Court of Arbitration. *North Atlantic Coast Fisheries: Decision in the Permanent Court of Arbitration at the Hague, on the Scope and Meaning of Article 1 of the Convention Signed at London on the 20th of October 1818, etc.* Ottawa: King's Printer, 1924. 50 p. **5312**

Hague. Permanent Court of Arbitration. *North Atlantic Coast Fisheries: Proceedings in the North Atlantic Coast Fisheries Arbitration Before the Permanent Court of Arbitration at the Hague; under the Provisions of the General Treaty of Arbitration of April 4, 1908, and the Special Agreement of January 27, 1909, between the United States of America and Great Britain.* Washington: Govt. Print. Off., 1912-13. 12 vols., maps. (U.S. 61st Cong., 3d sess. Senate. Doc. 870) **5313**

Individual documents, such as cases, counter cases, arguments, various appendices, were also published separately.

Halifax Commission, 1877. *Award of the Fishery Commission. Documents and Proceedings of the Halifax Commission, 1877, under the Treaty of Washington of May 8, 1871.* Washington: Govt. Print. Off., 1878. 3 vols. (U.S. 45th Cong., 2d sess. House. Ex. Doc. 89) **5314**

Also published in London under title: *Record of the Proceedings of the Halifax Fisheries Commission, 1877.* The commission met at Halifax, June 15-November 23, 1877.

Halifax Commission, 1877. *Record of the Proceedings of the Halifax Fisheries Commission, 1877.* Washington, 1877. 440 p., maps. **5315**

Also published in London. Commissioners: Maurice Delfosse, Ensign H. Kellogg, Sir Alexander T. Galt.

Hart, Albert Bushnell, ed. *Extracts from Official Papers Relating to the Bering Sea Controversy. 1790-1892.* New York: A. Lovell, 1892. 26 p. (American History Leaflets, No. 6, November, 1892) **5316**

Hind, Henry Youle. *The Effect of the Fishery Clauses of the Treaty of Washington on the Fisheries and Fishermen of British North America.* Halifax, N.S.: C. Annand, 1877. 2 vols., map. **5317**

At head of title: Confidential. Fishery Commission, Halifax, 1877.

"An Honourable United States Opinion concerning the Behring Sea Dispute." (1897), 3 *Barrister* 6-8. **5318**

Jay, John. *The Fisheries Dispute; a Suggestion for Its Adjustment by Abrogating the Convention of 1818, and Resting on the Rights and Liberties Defined in the Treaty of 1783.* 2d ed. New York: Dodd, Mead, 1887. 52 p. **5319**

The first edition was published the same year (48 p.).

Lammasch, Henri. "Address by President Henri Lammasch on Opening the North Atlantic Fisheries Arbitration at the Hague, June 1, 1910." (1910), 30 *Canadian Law Times* 777-779. **5320**
Also published in (1910), 4 *American Journal of International Law* 567-570.

Lammasch, Henri. "Was the Award in the North Atlantic Fisheries Case a Compromise?" (1912), 6 *American Journal of International Law* 178-180. **5321**

Lansing, Robert. "The North Atlantic Coast Fisheries Arbitration." (1911), 5 *American Journal of International Law* 1-31. **5322**
This article also appeared in (1910-11), 59 *University of Pennsylvania Law Review and American Law Register* 119-150.

Lash, Z.A. "The Behring Sea Question." (1893), 1 *Canadian Magazine* 289-296.
5323

Macmaster, *Sir* Donald. *The Seal Arbitration, 1893.* Montreal: W.F. Brown, 1894. 65 p., map. **5324**

Martens, F. de. "Le Tribunal d'arbitrage de Paris et la mer territoriale." (1894), 1 *Revue Générale de Droit International Public* 32-43. **5325**

McGrath, *Sir* Patrick T. "The Hague Award." (1910), 9 *University Magazine* 542-549. **5326**

Moore, John Bassett. "Northeastern Fisheries." *In* Moore, John Bassett, *Digest of International Law* (Washington, 1906), vol. 1, pp. 767-874. **5327**

Moore, John Bassett. "Seal Fisheries: Bering Sea." *In* Moore, John Bassett, *Digest of International Law* (Washington, 1906), vol. 1, pp. 890-929. **5328**

"The Northeastern Fisheries Question." (1907), 1 *American Journal of International Law* 963-964. **5329**

Paisant, Marcel. "La question de Behring." (1893), 7 *Revue d'Histoire Diplomatique* 375-413, 561-591. **5330**

Renault, L. "Une nouvelle mission donnée aux arbitres dans les litiges internationaux: à propos de l'arbitrage de Behring." (1894), 1 *Revue Générale de Droit International Public* 44-51. **5331**

Root, Elihu. *Argument on Behalf of the United States, Before the North Atlantic Coast Fisheries Arbitration Tribunal at The Hague, 1910.* Edited with introduction and appendix, by James Brown Scott. Boston: World Peace Foundation, 1912. cli, 523 p., map. **5332**

Root, Elihu. *North Atlantic Coast Fisheries Arbitration at the Hague; Argument on Behalf of the United States.* Edited by Robert Bacon and James Brown Scott. Cambridge: Harvard University Press, 1917. cix, 445 p., maps. **5333**
Reprinted Littleton, Colo., Rothman, 1982.

Scott, James Brown, ed. "The North Atlantic Coast Fisheries Case (Great Britain vs. United States)." *In* Scott, James Brown, ed., *The Hague Court Reports, etc.* (New York, 1916), vol. 1, pp. 141-225, maps. **5334**

Shapiro, Samuel. "Problems of International Arbitration: The Halifax Fisheries Commission of 1877." (1959), 95 *Essex Institute Historical Collections* 21-31 (No. 1) **5335**

Stanton, Stephen B. *The Behring Sea Controversy.* New York: A.B. King, 1892. 102 p. **5336**

Stanton, Stephen B. *The Behring Sea Dispute.* New York, 1890. 66 leaves. **5337**
Thesis (Ph.D.), Columbia University, 1890.

Wharton, Francis. "Fisheries: Northeast Atlantic Fisheries." *In* Wharton, Francis, *A Digest of the International Law of the United States* (Washington, 1886), vol. 3, pp. 39-62. **5338**

White, James. *The North Atlantic Fisheries Dispute.* Ottawa: Commission of Conservation, 1911. 62 p., maps. **5339**
Reprinted from the report of the Commission of Conservation entitled: *Lands, Fisheries and Game and Minerals*, 1911.

Williams, William. "Reminiscences of the Bering Sea Arbitration." (1943), 37 *American Journal of International Law* 562-584. **5340**
Refers to the arbitration under the treaty between Great Britain and the United States of February 29, 1892.

Wishart, Andrew. *The Behring Sea Question, the Arbitration Treaty and the Award.* Edinburgh: W. Green, 1893. 54 p., map. **5341**

Wormwith, N.B. "The Fishery Arbitrations." *In* Shortt, Adam, and Doughty, Arthur G., eds., *Canada and Its Provinces* (Toronto, 1914-1916), vol. 8, pp. 681-748. **5342**
Contents: I. The North Atlantic Coast Fishery Disputes. II. The Bering Sea Fur-Seal Disputes.

C. Judicial Settlement

1. INTERNATIONAL COURTS AND TRIBUNALS

Accinelli, R.D. "Peace through Law: The United States and the World Court, 1923-1935." (1972) *Canadian Historical Association, Historical Papers* 247-261. **5343**

Appiah, Ebener Evans. *The Meaning of Domestic Jurisdiction in the Jurisprudence of the International Court of Justice.* Toronto, 1966. 274 leaves. **5344**
Thesis (LL.M.), University of Toronto, 1966.

Arbour, Jean-Maurice. "Quelques réflexions sur les mesures conservatoires indiquées par la Cour internationale de justice." (1975), 16 *Cahiers de Droit* 531-573. **5345**

Aylesworth, Allen B. "The Hague Tribunal." (1911), 31 *Canadian Law Times* 144-172. **5346**

Clermont, Bernard-L. "Le droit international nouveau et la Cour internationale de justice." (1951-52), 2 *Thémis* 179-188. **5347**

Copithorne, M.D. "The Permanent Court of Arbitration and the Election of

Members of the International Court of Justice." (1978), 16 *Canadian Yearbook of International Law* 315-327. **5348**

Crabitès, Pierre. "The World Court not a Judicial Body." (1931), 9 *Canadian Bar Review* 117-118. **5349**

Dalfen, Charles M. "The World Court: Reform or Re-Appraisal." (1968), 6 *Canadian Yearbook of International Law* 212-225. **5350**

Dalfen, Charles M. "The World Court in Idle Splendour: The Basis of States' Attitudes." (1967-68), 23 *International Journal* 124-139. **5351**

Dogra, Hari Krishan. *The Jurisprudence of the International Court of Justice: Customary International Law, State Sovereignty, and the Domestic Jurisdiction.* Vancouver, 1966. 240 leaves. **5352**
Thesis (LL.M.), University of British Columbia, 1966.

"The Enforcement of International Law." (1915), 51 *Canada Law Journal* 472-474. **5353**

Farris, W.B. "A Canadian Tribute to International Justice." (1945), 31 *A.B.A. Journal* 347. **5354**

Farris, W.B. "The World Court." (1945), 3 *Advocate* 80-81. **5355**

Foster, William Fraser. *Fact Finding and the World Court.* Vancouver, 1968. 89 leaves. **5356**
Thesis (LL.M.), University of British Columbia, 1968.

Foster, William Fraser. "Fact Finding and the World Court." (1969), 7 *Canadian Yearbook of International Law* 150-191. **5357**

Fukatsu, Ei'ichi. *The Enforcement of Decisions of International Courts and Tribunals.* Toronto, 1964. 257 leaves. **5358**
Thesis (LL.M.), University of Toronto, 1964. Also issued in Tokyo, 1969 (157, 349 leaves), in English and Japanese.

Grauer, Christopher. "The Role of Equity in the Jurisprudence of the World Court." (1979), 37 *University of Toronto Faculty of Law Review* 101-117. **5359**

Green, Leslie C. "The Jurisdiction of the International Court." (1949), 12 *Modern Law Review* 483-485. **5360**

Head, Ivan L. "The Contribution of the International Court of Justice to the Development of International Organizations." (1965), 59 *American Society of International Law, Proceedings* 177-182. **5361**

Hudson, Manley O. "International Justice According to International Law - the Present Outlook." (1945), 23 *Canadian Bar Review* 527-535. **5362**

Hudson, Manley O. "The New World Court." (1945), 27 *Canadian Bar Association, Proceedings* 79-87. **5363**

"The International Court of the United Nations Organization: A Consensus of American and Canadian Views." (1945), 23 *Canadian Bar Review* 293-308, 317-321. **5364**

"International Justice: Permanent Court of Arbitration and International Court of Justice." (1960), 12 *External Affairs* 774-777. **5365**

Lalonde, Philippe V. "The Death of the Eastern Carelia Doctrine: Has Compulsory Jurisdiction Arrived in the World Court?" (1979), 37 *University of Toronto Faculty of Law Review* 80-100. **5366**

Lombard, Phyllis Ruth. *The Progressives and the World Court Dispute in the Senate, 1920-1936.* Edmonton, 1969. vi, 191 leaves. **5367**
Thesis (M.A.), University of Alberta, 1969.

Macdonald, Ronald St. John. "The New Canadian Declaration of Acceptance of the Compulsory Jurisdiction of the International Court of Justice." (1970), 8 *Canadian Yearbook of International Law* 3-38. **5368**

McWhinney, Edward. "Judicial Opinion-Writing in the World Court and the Western Sahara Advisory Opinion." (1977), 37 *Zeitschrift für Ausländisches Öffentliches Recht und Völkerrecht* 1-42. **5369**

McWhinney, Edward. *The World Court and the Contemporary International Law-Making Process.* Alphen aan den Rijn: Sijthoff and Noordhoff, 1979. vii, 219 p. **5370**
Reviews: E.D. Brown in (1979), 3 *Lloyd's Maritime and Commercial Law Quarterly* 376-377; Michel Distel in (1980), 32 *Revue Internationale de Droit Comparé* 247; Dana D. Fischer in (1980), 74 *American Journal of International Law* 701-702; Leslie C. Green in (1979), 14 *University of British Columbia Law Review* 240-243; Charles Rousseau in (1979), 83 *Revue Générale de Droit International Public* 568.

Morse, Charles. "Canada and the World Court." (1939), 17 *Canadian Bar Review* 196-198. **5371**

Mosler, Hermann. "The International Court of Justice at Its Present Stage of Development." (1979), 5 *Dalhousie Law Journal* 545-567. **5372**

Nordon, Charles L. "The World Court of International Justice - A Draft Protocol." (1944-45), 14 *Fortnightly Law Journal* 263-266. **5373**

"The Permanent Court of International Justice." (1921), 57 *Canada Law Journal* 121-132. **5374**

"The Permanent Court of International Justice." (1922), 58 *Canada Law Journal* 81-82. **5375**

Pharand, Donat. *The International Court of Justice.* Halifax, 1953. 128 leaves.
Thesis (LL.M.), Dalhousie University, 1953. **5376**

Pollak, Walter. "The Eligibility of British Subjects as Judges of the Permanent Court of International Justice." (1926), 20 *American Journal of International Law* 714-725. **5377**

Read, Horace E. "Advisory Opinions in International Justice." (1925), 3 *Canadian Bar Review* 186-195. **5378**

Read, John E. "The International Court of Justice." (1946), 24 *Canadian Bar Review* 561-568. **5379**

Read, John E. "Justice in the New Order." (1948), 6 *Advocate* 168-173. **5380**

Read, John E. "The World Court and the Years to Come." (1964), 2 *Canadian Yearbook of International Law* 164-171. **5381**

Renouf, Alan. "International Court of Justice - Advisory Opinions - Reception by the General Assembly of the United Nations - Opinions Requested by Assembly on Its Own Initiative - Discussion of Legal Merits - Express or Tacit Acceptance. (Comment)." (1950), 28 *Canadian Bar Review* 74-81. **5382**

Rosenne, Shabtai. "Judge John E. Read and the International Court of Justice." (1979), 17 *Canadian Yearbook of International Law* 3-29. **5383**

Rowell, Newton W. "Permanent Court of International Justice." (1921), 6 *Canadian Bar Association, Proceedings* 162-178. **5384**

Rowell, Newton W. "The Permanent Court of International Justice." (1933), 11 *Canadian Bar Review* 435-453. **5385**

"The United Nations' International Court of Justice." (1945-46), 15 *Fortnightly Law Journal* 119-122. **5386**

2. SPECIFIC CASES

Bloomfield, Louis M. *The British Honduras-Guatemala Dispute.* Toronto: Carswell, 1953. 231 p., map. **5387**
Reviews: H.T. Adam in (1955), 55 *Revue Générale de Droit International Public* 292-294; Clyde Eagleton in (1954), 48 *American Journal of International Law* 679-680; W.R. Noble in (1954), 32 *Canadian Bar Review* 350-352.

Feaver, H.F. "The Corfu Channel Case: The Preliminary Objection of Albania." (1948), 26 *Canadian Bar Review* 924-933. **5388**

FitzGerald, Gerald F. "The Judgment of the International Court of Justice in the Appeal Relating to the Jurisdiction of the ICAO Council." (1974), 12 *Canadian Yearbook of International Law* 153-185. **5389**

Flemming, Brian. "Case concerning the *Barcelona Traction, Light and Power Company Limited* (New Application, 1962; *Belgium* v. *Spain).* Preliminary Objections." (1965), 3 *Canadian Yearbook of International Law* 306-314.
5390

Flemming, Brian. "Case concerning the *Northern Cameroons (Cameroon* v. *United Kingdom)."* (1964), 2 *Canadian Yearbook of International Law* 215-232.
5391

Flemming, Brian. "South West Africa Cases. *Ethiopia* v. *South Africa; Liberia* v. *South Africa.* Second Phase." (1967), 5 *Canadian Yearbook of International Law* 241-252. **5392**

Green, Leslie C. "Admission of a State to the United Nations (Charter, Article 4), Advisory Opinion, (1948) *I.C.J. Reports* 57." (1949), 12 *Modern Law Review* 485-487. **5393**

Green, Leslie C. "The Anglo-Norwegian Fisheries Case, (1951) *I.C.J. Reports* 116." (1952), 15 *Modern Law Review* 373 377. **5394**

Green, Leslie C. "The Corfu Channel Case, (1949) *I.C.J. Reports* 4." (1949), 12 *Modern Law Review* 505-508. **5395**

Green, Leslie C. "Reparation for Injuries Suffered in the Service of the United Nations, Advisory Opinion, (1949) *I.C.J. Reports* 174." (1949), 12 *Modern Law Review* 508-511. **5396**

Herman, Lawrence L. "International Law - An Analysis of the World Court Judgment in the Western Sahara Case: *Western Sahara Advisory Opinion.*" (1976-77), 41 *Saskatchewan Law Review* 133-142. **5397**
See also (1975) *I.C.J. Reports* 12.

Herman, Lawrence L. "Nuclear Tests Case: *Australia* v. *France; New Zealand* v. *France.*" (1976-77), 3 *Dalhousie Law Journal* 288-294. **5398**
See also (1974) *I.C.J. Reports* 253.

Macdonald, Ronald St. John. "International Law - Acts Necessary to Prove Sovereignty - Effect of Protests - Admissibility and Evaluation of Evidence. (The Minquiers and Ecrehos Case, (1953) *I.C.J. Reports* 47). (Case Note)." (1952-55), 1 *McGill Law Journal* 277-280. **5399**
Refers to the judgment of the International Court of Justice of November 17, 1953, confirming the sovereignty of the United Kingdom over the islets and rocks of the Ecrehos and Minquiers groups.

Macdonald, Ronald St. John, and Hough, Barbara. "The Nuclear Tests Case Revisited." (1977), 20 *German Yearbook of International Law* 337-357. **5400**

McRae, Donald M. "International Court of Justice - Interim Measures of Protection - Jurisdiction - Nuclear Tests Cases. (Case Note)." (1973), 8 *University of British Columbia Law Review* 375-382. **5401**

McRae, Donald M. "Proportionality and the Gulf of Maine Maritime Boundary Dispute." (1981), 19 *Canadian Yearbook of International Law* 287-302. **5402**

McWhinney, Edward. "International Law-Making and the Judicial Process: The World Court and the French Nuclear Tests Case." (1975), 3 *Syracuse Journal of International Law and Commerce* 9-46. **5403**

Nied, G. David. "International Adjudication: Settlement of the United States-Canada Maritime Boundary Dispute - *Delimitation of the Maritime Boundary in the Gulf of Maine Area (U.S.* v. *Can.),* (1982) *I.C.J. Reports* 3." (1982), 23 *Harvard International Law Journal* 138-143. **5404**

U.S. Congress. Senate. Committee on Foreign Relations. *Maritime Boundary Settlement Treaty and East Coast Fishery Resources Agreement: Hearings, 96th Cong., 2d sess., on Ex. U, 96-1, and Ex. V, 96-1, April 15 and 17, 1980.* Washington: Govt. Print. Off., 1980. iv, 223 p., maps. **5405**
Refers to the maritime boundary treaty (S.Ex. U. 96-1), and the fishery agreement (S.Ex. V. 96-1), both signed at Washington on March 29, 1979.

U.S. Congress. Senate. Committee on Foreign Relations. *The Maritime Boundary Treaty with Canada: Hearing, 97th Cong., 1st sess., on Ex. U, 96-1, March 18, 1981.* Washington: Govt. Print. Off., 1981. iii, 46 p. **5406**

D. Settlement within International Organizations

Archbold, Herbert Seymour Chowne. *United Nations Commissions in the Pacific Settlement of Disputes; the Employment of Military Observers, with Particular Reference to the Canadian Contribution.* Edmonton, 1954. 281 leaves. **5407**
Thesis (M.A.), University of Alberta, 1954.

Dixit, R.K. "Non-Member States and the Settlement of Disputes in the Security Council." (1957-58), 12 *University of Toronto Law Journal* 246-281. **5408**

Kass, Stephen L. "Obligatory Negotiations in International Organizations." (1965), 3 *Canadian Yearbook of International Law* 36-72. **5409**

Noble, Paul C. *Regional Arrangements and the Management of Conflict under the United Nations: The Case of the Arab System.* Montreal, 1972. ix, 702 leaves, map. **5410**
Half-title: *Regionalism and Conflict-Management: The Arab System.* Thesis (Ph.D.), McGill University, 1972. (National Library of Canada. Canadian Theses on Microfilm, No. 11954).

Raman, K. Venkata, ed. *Dispute Settlement through the United Nations.* Dobbs Ferry, N.Y.: Oceana Publications, 1977. xix, 749 p. **5411**
Published under the auspices of the United Nations Institute for Training and Research (UNITAR).
Reviews: Thomas M. Franck in (1978), 72 *American Journal of International Law* 425-426; Leslie C. Green in (1979), 27 *Chitty's Law Journal* 140-144.

Raman, K. Venkata. *The Ways of the Peacemaker: A Study of United Nations Intermediary Assistance in the Peaceful Settlement of Disputes.* New York: United Nations Institute for Training and Research, 1975. viii, 142 p. (UNITAR Peaceful Settlement Study, No. 8) **5412**
Review: Henry Wiseman in (1977-78), 33 *International Journal* 659-660.

XX. COERCION AND USE OF FORCE

A. Unilateral Acts (Intervention, Etc.)

Black, Thomas H. "The Law of Reprisals as Affected by the League Treaty: The Italian Occupation of Corfu." (1923), 1 *Canadian Bar Review* 729-736, 825-834.
5413

Brown, E.A. "The Boycott in International Law." (1933), 11 *Canadian Bar Review* 325-332. **5414**

Claydon, John. "Humanitarian Intervention and International Law." (1968-70), 1 *Queen's Intramural Law Journal* 36-64 (No. 3) **5415**

Coombs, Maurice J. *A Note concerning Some Aspects of Intervention in International Law.* Downsview, 1969 (c1970). iii, 183 leaves. **5416**
Thesis (LL.M.), York University, 1970. (National Library of Canada. Canadian Theses on Microfilm, No. 6870).

Fairley, H. Scott. "State Actors, Humanitarian Intervention and International Law: Reopening Pandora's Box." (1980), 10 *Georgia Journal of International and Comparative Law* 29-63. **5417**

Flinterman, Cees. "Humanitarian Intervention." (1978), 26 *Chitty's Law Journal* 284-288. **5418**

Friedlander, Robert A. "Might Can Also Be Right: The Israeli Nuclear Reactor Bombing and International Law." (1980), 28 *Chitty's Law Journal* 352-358.
5419

Fry, Michael G. "Britain, the Allies, and the Problem of Russia 1918-1919." (1967), 2 *Canadian Journal of History* 62-84 (No. 2) **5420**

Green, Leslie C. "Humanitarian Intervention - 1976 Version." (1976), 24 *Chitty's Law Journal* 217-225. **5421**

Green, Leslie C. "Rescue at Entebbe - Legal Aspects." (1976), 6 *Israel Yearbook on Human Rights* 312-329. **5422**
Based on "Humanitarian Intervention - 1976 Version," published in (1976), 24 *Chitty's Law Journal* 217-225.

Latouche, Daniel Gustave. *The Process and Level of Military Intervention in the States of Tropical Africa, 1960-1971.* Vancouver, 1974. xv, 524 leaves. **5423**
Thesis (Ph.D.), University of British Columbia, 1974. (National Library of Canada. Canadian Theses on Microfiche, No. 19573).

MacLaren, Roy. *Canadians in Russia, 1918-1919.* Toronto: Macmillan of Canada; Lewiston, N.Y.: Maclean-Hunter Press, c1976. viii, 301 p., maps. **5424**
Review: David R. Jones in (1977-78), 57 *Dalhousie Review* 387-388.

Samuels, Joseph W. "Humanitarian Assistance and Intervention: Commentary." In Paxman, John M., and Boggs, George T., eds., *The United Nations: A Reassessment* (Charlottesville, Va., 1973), pp. 135-141. **5425**

Sellen, Robert W. "The British Intervention in Russia, 1917-1920." (1960-61), 40 *Dalhousie Review* 360-371, 520-531. **5426**

Smith, Gaddis G. "Canada and the Siberian Intervention, 1918-1919." (1958-59), 64 *American Historical Review* 866-877. **5427**

Swettenham, John A. *Allied Intervention in Russia, 1918-1919, and the Part Played by Canada.* London: Allen & Unwin, 1967. 315 p., maps. **5428**
Also published Toronto, Ryerson Press, 1967.
Reviews: A.G. Steiger in (1967-68), 47 *Dalhousie Review* 265-267; Richard H. Ullman in (1968-69), 24 *International Journal* 398-399.

Thapa, Dhruba Bar Singh. *Humanitarian Intervention; a Study of the Problems and Practices of Collective Intervention in Contemporary International Law for the Protection of Humanity and Human Rights.* Montreal, 1968 (c1969). 119, xi leaves. **5429**
Thesis (LL.M.),McGill University, 1968. (National Library of Canada. Canadian Theses on Microfilm, No. 3233).

B. Collective Measures

1. SANCTIONS IN GENERAL

Brown-John, Clive Lloyd. *Economic Sanctions: The O.A.S. and the Dominican Republic, 1960-1962.* Toronto, 1971. xv, 481 leaves. **5430**
Thesis (Ph.D.), University of Toronto, 1971. (National Library of Canada. Canadian Theses on Microfilm, No. 11545).

Brown-John, Clive Lloyd. *Multilateral Sanctions in International Law: A Comparative Analysis.* New York: Praeger, 1975. xv, 426 p. (Praeger Special Studies in International Politics and Government) **5431**
Reviews: John Claydon in (1978), 16 *Canadian Yearbook of International Law* 445-447; Paul Gagné in (1976), 7 *Études Internationales* 623-624; Leslie C. Green in (1977), 9 *Ottawa Law Review* 238-242; Gunther Hartmann in (1976), 9 *Canadian Journal of Political Science* 524-525.

Carter, Gwendolen M. "Canada and Sanctions in the Italo-Ethiopian Conflict." (1940), *Canadian Historical Association, Historical Papers* 74-84. **5432**

Corbett, Percy E. "Sanctions - Abyssinia and After." (1935-36), 5 *University of Toronto Quarterly* 482-498. **5433**

Doxey, Margaret P. "Do Sanctions Work?" (1982), *International Perspectives* 13-15 (July/Aug.). **5434**

Doxey, Margaret P. "Economic Sanctions: Past Lessons and the Case of Rhodesia." (1967-68), 27 *Behind the Headlines* No. 2 (24 p.)   **5435**

Doxey, Margaret P. *Economic Sanctions and International Enforcement.* Published for the Royal Institute of International Affairs. London: Oxford University Press, 1971. ix, 162 p. (Oxford Paperbacks, 268)   **5436**
   Reviews: Alan Cassels in (1973-74), 29 *International Journal* 291-292; I.D. Pal in (1972), 5 *Canadian Journal of Economics* 459-461; Charles Pentland in (1972), 5 *Canadian Journal of Political Science* 465-466.

Doxey, Margaret P. "Oil and Food as International Sanctions." (1980-81), 36 *International Journal* 311-334.   **5437**

Doxey, Margaret P. "The Rhodesian Sanctions Experiment." (1971), 25 *Year Book of World Affairs* 142-162.   **5438**

Doxey, Margaret P. "Sanctions Revisited. (Review Article)." (1975-76), 31 *International Journal* 53-78.   **5439**

Fieldhouse, H.N. "The Sanctions Experiment in Retrospect." (1937-38), 17 *Dalhousie Review* 2-15.   **5440**

Goodrich, Leland M. "Peace Enforcement in Perspective." (1968-69), 24 *International Journal* 657-672.   **5441**

Grimes, David A. *United Nations Efforts to Implement Sanctions Against South Africa, Portugal and Rhodesia.* Ottawa, 1967. 183 leaves.   **5442**
   Thesis (M.A.), Carleton University, 1967. (National Library of Canada. Canadian Theses on Microfilm, No. 1546).

Kelsen, Hans. "Sanctions under the Charter of the United Nations." (1946), 12 *Canadian Journal of Economics and Political Science* 429-438.   **5443**

Macdonald, Ronald St. John. "Economic Sanctions in the International System." (1969), 7 *Canadian Yearbook of International Law* 61-91.   **5444**

Macdonald, Ronald St. John. "The Resort to Economic Coercion by International Political Organizations." (1967), 17 *University of Toronto Law Journal* 86-169.   **5445**

Ramcharan, B.G. "Legal Issues Before the United Nations Sanctions Committee." (1976-77), 3 *Dalhousie Law Journal* 540-559.   **5446**

Reid, Escott. "International Sanctions and World Peace. (Review Article)." (1934-35), 4 *University of Toronto Quarterly* 408-417.   **5447**

Saywell, John Tupper. *Canada and League Sanctions, 1919-1936.* Vancouver, 1951. 211, xxxii, xxxvi leaves.   **5448**
   Thesis (M.A.), University of British Columbia, 1951.

2. UNITED NATIONS ACTION IN KOREA (1950-53)

Altstedter, Norman. "Problems of Coalition Diplomacy: The Korean Experience." (1952-53), 8 *International Journal* 256-265.   **5449**

"The Armistice in Korea." (1953), 5 *External Affairs* 262-268.   **5450**

Canada. Dept. of External Affairs. *Canada and the Korean Crisis.* Ottawa: King's Printer, 1950. 36 p. **5451**
Also issued in French under title: *Le Canada et la crise coréenne.*

Canada. Dept. of External Affairs. *Documents on the Korean Crisis.* Ottawa: King's Printer, 1951. vi, 37 p. **5452**

"Canada and the Korean Crisis." (1950), 2 *External Affairs* 288-295. **5453**

Green, Leslie C. "Korea and the United Nations." (1950), 4 *World Affairs* 414-437 (N.S.) **5454**

Green, Leslie C. "The Nature of the 'War' in Korea." (1951), 4 *International Law Quarterly* 462-468. **5455**

"Korea." (1950), 2 *External Affairs* 243-248. **5456**

"The Korean Crisis." (1951), 3 *External Affairs* 410-411. **5457**

Mitchell, C. Clyde. "Political and Economic Significance of the Korean War." (1949-50), 5 *International Journal* 299-303. **5458**

Stairs, Denis. *The Diplomacy of Constraint: Canada, the Korean War, and the United States.* Toronto: University of Toronto Press, 1974. xv, 373 p. **5459**
Reviews: Robert Bothwell in (1976), 57 *Canadian Historical Review* 220-222; Margaret P. Doxey in (1975), 8 *Canadian Journal of Political Science* 152-153; Allen Levy in (1975), 6 *Études Internationales* 289-291; Peyton V. Lyon in (1974), 17 *Canadian Public Administration* 515-516; Robert O'Neill under title: "Constraint with Honour," in (1973-74), 29 *International Journal* 350-355; Richard A. Preston in (1975), 5 *American Review of Canadian Studies* 162-163 (No. 1).

Stairs, Denis. *The Role of Canada in the Korean War.* Toronto, 1969. xii, 561 leaves. **5460**
Thesis (Ph.D.), University of Toronto, 1969. (National Library of Canada. Canadian Theses on Microfilm, No. 4511).

Stairs, Denis. "The United Nations and the Politics of the Korean War." (1969-70), 25 *International Journal* 302-320. **5461**

Stanley, George F.G. "The Korean Dilemma." (1951-52), 7 *International Journal* 278-282. **5462**

3. PEACE-KEEPING OPERATIONS

(a) GENERAL

Barton, William H. "Who Will Pay for Peace? The UN Crisis." (1964-65), 24 *Behind the Headlines* No. 5 (16 p.) **5463**

Beattie, Clayton E. "Preparations for Peacekeeping at the National and International Level." (1978-79), 8 *Canadian Defence Quarterly* 26-29 (No. 2) **5464**

Bishop, Peter V. "Katanga: U.N. Crucible." (1962), 69 *Queen's Quarterly* 113-127. **5465**

Bishop, Peter V. "UNOPAX: A New Name (with a Definition) for U.N. Peace-Keeping Operations." (1962-63), 18 *International Journal* 525-531. **5466**

Brosnan, Vivienne. *The International Control Commission for Vietnam: The Diplomatic and Military Context.* Vancouver, 1975 (c1976). vi, 142 leaves. **5467**
Thesis (M.A.), University of British Columbia, 1975. (National Library of Canada. Canadian Theses on Microfiche, No. 25106).

Buchan, Alastair F. "Concepts of Peacekeeping." *In* Fry, Michael G., ed., *'Freedom and Change': Essays in Honour of Lester B. Pearson* (Toronto, 1975), pp. 16-25. **5468**

Burns, Eedson L.M. "Examining the Possible Tasks for Mideast's Second UNEF." (1974), *International Perspectives* 36-42 (Mar./Apr.) **5469**

Burns, Eedson L.M. "Pearson and the Gaza Strip, 1957." *In* Fry, Michael G., ed., *'Freedom and Change': Essays in Honour of Lester B. Pearson* (Toronto, 1975), pp. 26-42. **5470**

Burns, Eedson L.M. "The Withdrawal of UNEF and the Future of Peacekeeping." (1967-68), 23 *International Journal* 1-17. **5471**

Cohen, Maxwell. "The Demise of UNEF." (1967-68), 23 *International Journal* 18-51. **5472**

Cohen, Maxwell. "The United Nations Emergency Force: A Preliminary View." (1956-57), 12 *International Journal* 109-127. **5473**

"The Cost of Keeping the Peace." (1963), 15 *External Affairs* 125-140. **5474**

Davis, Glen White. *The Peace-Keeping Efforts of the United Nations: A Constitutional Analysis.* London, Ont., 1966. vi, 191 leaves. **5475**
Thesis (M.A.), University of Western Ontario, 1966.

Eastman, Samuel Mack. "A United Nations Guard: Historical Background." (1949), 4 *International Journal* 137-146. **5476**
See also "A United Nations Guard: Postscript" (p. 260).

Edwards, Wayne. *Functional Adaptation of Power and Influence within the International Hierarchy: Analysis of the Special Political Committee on Peacekeeping.* Guelph, Ont., 1979. ii, 152 leaves. **5477**
Thesis (M.A.), University of Guelph, 1979. (National Library of Canada. Canadian Theses on Microfiche, No. 41710).

"Financing UN Peace-Keeping." (1963), 15 *External Affairs* 282-294. **5478**

Gellner, John. "International Peacekeeping: Does It Have Any Future?" (1973), *International Perspectives* 23-26 (Sept./Oct.) **5479**

Gordon, J. King. "Prospects for Peacekeeping." (1969-70), 25 *International Journal* 370-387. **5480**

Gordon, J. King. "The U.N. in Cyprus." (1963-64), 19 *International Journal* 326-347. **5481**

Gordon, J. King. *The United Nations in the Congo; a Quest for Peace.* New York: Carnegie Endowment for International Peace, 1962. 184 p. **5482**
Review: Roland J. Lamontagne in (1962-63), 18 *International Journal* 543.

Goyer, Jean-Pierre. "Peace-Keeping." (1969), 21 *External Affairs* 21-24. **5483**

Granatstein, J.L. "Peacekeeping Is Our Profession? (Review Article)." (1969-70), 25 *International Journal* 414-419. **5484**

Harbottle, Michael. "The Strategy of Third Party Interventions in Conflict Resolution." (1979-80), 35 *International Journal* 118-131.   **5485**

Heine, William. "Of Armies and Politics: Peacekeeping Guidelines the Key to Peacemaking." (1976), *International Perspectives* 34-38 (Jan./Feb.)   **5486**

Holland, Sir Robert E. "Under the United Nations Flag." (1950-51), 6 *International Journal* 136-145.   **5487**

Holmes, John W. "The Political and Philosophical Aspects of U.N. Security Forces." (1963-64), 19 *International Journal* 292-307.   **5488**
Also published in Kay, D.A., ed., *The United Nations Political System* (New York, 1967), pp. 217-229; and Larus, J., *From Collective Security to Preventive Diplomacy* (New York, 1965), pp. 478-489.

Holmes, John W. "Techniques of Peacekeeping in Asia." *In* Buchan, Alastair F., ed., *China and the Peace of Asia* (London, 1965), pp. 231-249.   **5489**

Holmes, John W. "The United Nations in the Congo." (1960-61), 16 *International Journal* 1-16.   **5490**

"In the Cause of Peace." (1962), 14 *External Affairs* 198-204.   **5491**

"Indochina - Membership on International Commissions." (1954), 6 *External Affairs* 257-264.   **5492**

Inglis, Alex I. "Peacekeeping and Peacemaking Should Be Reviewed Together." (1975), *International Perspectives* 31-34 (Jan./Feb.)   **5493**

"International Commission for Supervision and Control in Vietnam: Expulsion of Fixed Teams by North Vietnam." (1965), 17 *External Affairs* 150-157.   **5494**

"International Court of Justice: Opinion on Financing UN Forces." (1962), 14 *External Affairs* 259-262.   **5495**

"The International Supervisory Commission in Vietnam: Fourth Interim Report." (1956), 8 *External Affairs* 55-57.   **5496**

Jonah, James O.C. "Peacekeeping in the Middle East." (1975-76), 31 *International Journal* 100-122.   **5497**

Kenny, L.M. "The United Nations and the Palestine Question: Efforts at Peacemaking." (1972-73), 28 *International Journal* 766-783.   **5498**

Kotani, Hidejiro. "Peace-Keeping: Problems for Smaller Countries." (1963-64), 19 *International Journal* 308-325.   **5499**

Legault, Albert. *Peace-Keeping Operations*. Oakville, Ont.: Canadian Peace Research Institute, 1968. 100 p. (Peace Research Reviews, Vol. 2, No. 4) **5500**
First edition published Paris, International Information Center on Peace-Keeping Operations, 1967, under title: *Research on Peace-Keeping Operations*.

Leslie, E. "Some Thoughts on International Peacekeeping." (1977-78), 7 *Canadian Defence Quarterly* 18-22 (No. 3)   **5501**

Martin, Paul. "International Commission for Supervision and Control in Vietnam." (1965), 17 *External Affairs* 114-118.   **5502**
Comments on the special message of February 13, 1965.

Martin, Paul. "Peace-Keeping and the United Nations: The Broader View." (1964), 40 *International Affairs* 191-204.   **5503**

Martin, Paul. "Peace-Keeping Operations." (1965), 17 *External Affairs* 255-260.
5504

Martin, Paul. "Role of the UN in Maintaining Peace and Security." (1964), 16 *External Affairs* 149-154. **5505**

Martin, Paul. "Some Improvisations in United Nations Peace Keeping." (1964), 16 *External Affairs* 373-377. **5506**

Martin, Paul. "UN Peace-Keeping Operations in Cyprus." (1964), 16 *External Affairs* 130-135. **5507**

Mattar, Gamil A. *The Decision of the U.A.R. Government to Request the Redeployment of UNEF, May 16, 1967; Background to Decision.* Montreal, 1970. 308 leaves. **5508**

Half-title: *U.A.R.'s Request to Redeploy UNEF; Background to Decision.* Thesis (M.A.), McGill University, 1970. (National Library of Canada. Canadian Theses on Microfilm, No. 5954).

Maynard, Bruce H.E. *An Exploratory Application of Factor Analysis to Gain a Conceptual Appreciation of the Countries Which Have Earmarked Forces for United Nations Peacekeeping Purposes.* Ottawa, 1968. viii, 101 leaves. **5509**
Thesis (M.A.), Carleton University, 1968. (National Library of Canada. Canadian Theses on Microfilm, No. 2112). Abstracted in (1970), 8 *Masters Abstracts* 188.

Murray, Geoffrey S. "United Nations Peace-Keeping and Problems of Political Control." (1962-63), 18 *International Journal* 442-457. **5510**

"Peace-Keeping Conference." (1964), 16 *External Affairs* 562-567. **5511**
Meeting convened at Ottawa, November 2-6, 1964.

Pearson, Lester B. "Force for U.N." (1956-57), 35 *Foreign Affairs* 395-404. **5512**
Also published in Kay, David A., ed., *The United Nations Political System* (New York, 1967), pp. 193-200.

Pearson, Lester B. "Keeping the Peace." (1964), 16 *External Affairs* 240-253.
5513
Notes for a lecture by the Prime Minister, in the Dag Hammarskjold Memorial Series, at Carleton College, Ottawa, on May 7, 1964.

Reford, Robert W. "UNIPOM: Success of a Mission." (1971-72), 27 *International Journal* 405-423. **5514**
Concerns the special mission known as the United Nations India Pakistan Observer Mission (UNIPOM), commanded by a Canadian, Major General Bruce F. Macdonald.

Sabia, M.J. "Peace-Keeping Forces and the United Nations Charter." (1965), 23 *University of Toronto Faculty of Law Review* 124-129. **5515**

Tremblay, Paul. "The United Nations Role in Keeping the Peace." (1965), 17 *External Affairs* 399-401. **5516**

"Truce Supervision in Cambodia." (1957), 9 *External Affairs* 310-312. **5517**

United Nations Association in Canada. *The Future of UN Peace-Keeping.* Toronto: United Nations Association in Canada, Policy Committee, c1965. 49 p. (United Nations Association in Canada. Policy Committee. A Policy Paper) **5518**

"United Nations Peace Keeping: Continuing Problems of Financing." (1967), 19 *External Affairs* 119-123. **5519**

"The United Nations Truce Supervision Organization in Palestine." (1959), 11 *External Affairs* 131-135. **5520**

Wiseman, Henry. "Has New Life Been Breathed into U.N. Peace-Keeping?" (1975-76), 5 *Canadian Defence Quarterly* 22-28 (No. 1) **5521**

Wiseman, Henry. "Lebanon: The Latest Example of UN Peacekeeping Action." (1979), *International Perspectives* 3-7 (Jan./Feb.) **5522**

Wiseman, Henry. "Peacekeeping: Début or Dénouement?" (1972), 31 *Behind the Headlines* Nos. 1-2 (15 p.) **5523**

Wiseman, Henry. "UNEF II: New Chance to Set Firm Peace-Keeping Guidelines." (1974), *International Perspectives* 42-48 (Mar./Apr.) **5524**

Wiseman, Henry. "United Nations and UNEF II: A Basis for a New Approach to Future Operations." (1975-76), 31 *International Journal* 123-145. **5525**

Wiseman, Henry. "United Nations and UNEF II: A Basis for a New Approach to Future Operations: Proposal of a Working Model for United Nations Observer Missions and Peace-Keeping Operations." (1974), 46 *Canadian Political Science Association, Papers,* 31 p. **5526**

Wood, Andrew Dartnell B. *United Nations Forces and the Problem of Consent.* Montreal, 1970 (c1971). iii, 136 leaves. **5527**
Thesis (M.A.), McGill University, 1970. (National Library of Canada. Canadian Theses on Microfilm, No. 7164).

"The Work of the International Supervisory Commissions in Indo-China." (1954), 6 *External Affairs* 299-302. **5528**

(b) CANADIAN CONTRIBUTION

Allan, James H. "The Future of Peacekeeping for Canada." (1978-79), 8 *Canadian Defence Quarterly* 30-33, 36 (No. 1) **5529**

Bishop, Peter V. *Canada and the Controversy over the Financing of U.N. Peace-Keeping Operations.* Toronto, 1968. xix, 792 leaves. **5530**
Thesis (Ph.D.), University of Toronto, 1968. (National Library of Canada. Canadian Theses on Microfilm, No. 3891).

Bishop, Peter V. "Canada's Policy on the Financing of U.N. Peace-Keeping Operations." (1964-65), 20 *International Journal* 463-483. **5531**

Bridle, Paul. "Canada and the International Control Commissions in Indochina, 1954-1972." (1973-74), 32 *Behind the Headlines* No. 4 (28 p.) **5532**

Canada. Dept. of External Affairs. *Viet-Nam: Canada's Approach to Participation in the International Commission of Control and Supervision, October 25, 1972-March 27, 1973 / Viet-Nam: participation à la Commission internationale de contrôle et de surveillance telle qu'envisagée par le Canada, du 25 octobre 1972 au 27 mars 1973.* Ottawa: Information Canada, 1973. 51 p. In English and French. **5533**

Canada. Parliament. House of Commons. Standing Committee on External Affairs and National Defence. *Report of the Standing Committee on External Affairs and National Defence Respecting United Nations and Peace-Keeping.* Ottawa: Queen's Printer. **5534**

Eighth report published in 1970. Also issued in French under title: *Rapport du Comité permanent des affaires extérieures et de la défense nationale au sujet des Nations Unies et du maintien de la paix.*

"Canada and the International Commission in Laos." (1958), 10 *External Affairs* 219-221. **5535**

"Canada in Indochina." (1957), 9 *External Affairs* 111-116. **5536**

Dai, Poeliu. "Canada and the Review of United Nations Peacekeeping Operations." (1974), 12 *Canadian Yearbook of International Law* 186-210. **5537**

Dai, Poeliu. "Canada's Reluctant Participation in the International Commission for Control and Supervision in Vietnam in 1973." (1973), 11 *Canadian Yearbook of International Law* 244-257. **5538**

Dai, Poeliu. "Canada's Role in the International Commission for Supervision and Control in Cambodia." (1970), 8 *Canadian Yearbook of International Law* 307-323. **5539**

Dai, Poeliu. "Canada's Role in the International Commission for Supervision and Control in Laos." (1972), 10 *Canadian Yearbook of International Law* 235-260. **5540**

Dai, Poeliu. "Canada's Role in the International Commission for Supervision and Control in Vietnam." (1966), 4 *Canadian Yearbook of International Law* 161-177. **5541**

Dai, Poeliu. "The United Nations Interim Force in Lebanon and Canadian Participation." (1979), 17 *Canadian Yearbook of International Law* 304-313. **5542**

Douglas, W.A.B. "Canada and the Withdrawal of the United Nations Emergency Force." (1972-73), 2 *Canadian Defence Quarterly* 45-52 (No. 3) **5543**

Eyre, Kenneth C. "The Future of U.N. Interpository Peacekeeping under the 1956 Pearson-Hammarskjold Formula." (1982), 12 *Canadian Defence Quarterly* 31-36 (No. 1) **5544**

Gordon, Donald C. "Canada as Peace-Keeper." *In* Gordon, J. King, ed., *Canada's Role as a Middle Power* (Toronto, 1966), pp. 51-65. **5545**

Hill, Roger J. *Command and Control Problems of UN and Similar Peace-Keeping Forces.* Ottawa: Dept. of National Defence, Directorate of Strategic Operational Research, Operational Research Division, 1968. iii, 39, (12) leaves. (ORD Report, No. 68/R5) **5546**

Ichikawa, Akira. "The 'Helpful Fixer': Canada's Persistent International Image." (1978-79), 37 *Behind the Headlines* No. 3 (25 p.) **5547**

Jansen, Gordon W.V. *The Official Rationale for Canadian Participation in International Peacekeeping: Comparison of the Trudeau Administration and the International Era.* Ottawa, 1978. ii, 219 leaves. **5548**
Thesis (M.A.), Carleton University, 1979. (National Library of Canada. Canadian Theses on Microfiche, no. 41668).

Loomis, D.G. "Canada and the United Nations. Relinquishing Sovereignty Is the Key to Peacemaking: The Lesson of Peacekeeping." (1976), *International Perspectives* 15-20 (Sept./Oct.) **5549**

Manor, F.S. "By Abandoning Peace-Keeping NATO Could Be Reinforced." (1977), *International Perspectives* 28-32 (July/Aug.) **5550**

Martin, Paul. "Canada's Role in the United Nations Peace-Keeping Efforts." (1967), 19 *External Affairs* 325-247. **5551**
  First of three Jacob Blaustein Lectures for 1967 delivered to the School of International Affairs, Columbia University, on April 26, 1967.

Milsten, Donald E. *Canadian Peace Keeping Policy; a Meaningful Role for a Middle Power.* Ann Arbor, 1968. ix, 317 leaves. **5552**
  Thesis (Ph.D.), University of Michigan, 1968. Abstracted in (1968), 29 *Dissertation Abstracts* 1268-A. (University Microfilms, Ann Arbor, No. 68-13366).

Murray, John Darrach. *Canada's Military Commitment to International Peacekeeping.* Downsview, Ont., 1975. xi, 261 leaves. **5553**
  Thesis (M.A.), York University, 1975. (National Library of Canada. Canadian Theses on Microfiche, No. 25738).

Patsalides, John George. *The Canadian Response to the Establishment of the United Nations Peace-Keeping Force in Cyprus.* London, Ont., 1974. vi, 110 leaves. **5554**
  Thesis (M.A.), University of Western Ontario, 1975. (National Library of Canada. Canadian Theses on Microfiche, No. 24635).

Ross, Douglas A. *In the Interest of Peace: Perception and Response in the History of Canadian Foreign Policy Decision-Making Concerning the International Commission for Supervision and Control for Vietnam, 1954-65.* Toronto, 1979. 1106 frames, maps. **5555**
  Thesis (Ph.D.), University of Toronto, 1979. (National Library of Canada. Canadian Theses on Microfiche, No. 50339). Abstracted in (1979/80), 40 *Dissertation Abstracts International* 6415-A.

Sheikh, Ahmed. "Canada's Support of the United Nations' Peace-Keeping Operations." (1969), 7 *Journal of Commonwealth Political Studies* 58-65. **5556**

Spry, Graham. "Canada, the United Nations Emergency Force, and the Commonwealth." (1957), 33 *International Affairs* 289-300. **5557**

Tackaberry, R.B. "Keeping the Peace: A Canadian Military Viewpoint on Peace-Keeping Operations." (1966-67), 26 *Behind the Headlines* No. 1 (26 p.) **5558**

Tackaberry, R.B. "Organizing and Training Peace-Keeping Forces: The Canadian View." (1966-67), 22 *International Journal* 195-209. **5559**

Taylor, Alastair M.; Cox, David; and Granatstein, J.L. *Peacekeeping: International Challenge and Canadian Response.* Toronto: Canadian Institute of International Affairs, c1968. 211 p. (Contemporary Affairs, No. 39) **5560**
  Contents: Peacekeeping: The International Content, by A. Taylor.- Peacekeeping: The Canadian Experience.- Issues and Opinions: A Report on the Queen's/CIIA Conference on Peacekeeping, February 24-26, 1967, by D. Cox.- Canada: A Peacekeeper; a Survey of Canada's Participation in Peacekeeping Operations, by J.L. Granatstein.- Bibliography (pp. 205-211).
  Reviews: Willard F. Barber in (1969-70), 49 *Dalhousie Review* 283-287; R.B. Byers in (1970), 51 *Canadian Historical Review* 91-94; C.F. Doxford in (1969-70), 25 *International Journal* 222-223.

Thakur, Ramesh C. *Canada, India and the Vietnam War: Peacekeeping, Foreign Policy and International Politics.* Kingston, 1978. x, 694 leaves, maps. **5561**
  Thesis (Ph.D.), Queen's University, 1978. (National Library of Canada. Canadian Theses on Microfiche, No. 37550). Abstracted in (1978/79), 39 *Dissertation Abstracts International* 5713-A.

Thakur, Ramesh C. "Peacekeeping and Foreign Policy: Canada, India and the International Commission in Vietnam, 1954-1965." (1980), 6 *British Journal of International Studies* 125-153. **5562**

Williams, D. Colwyn. "Canada and International Peace-Keeping Operations." (1964), 29 *Saskatchewan Bar Review* 1-11. **5563**

Williams, D. Colwyn. "International Peacekeeping: Canada's Role." *In* Macdonald, Ronald St. John, and others, *Canadian Perspectives on International Law and Organization* (Toronto, 1974), pp. 645-689. **5564**

Wiseman, Henry. *Theoretical Approaches and Policy Examination of Canada's Role in Peacekeeping.* Kingston, 1970 (c1971). xii, 383 leaves. **5565**
  Half-title: *Peacekeeping.* Thesis (Ph.D.), Queen's University, 1971. (National Library of Canada. Canadian Theses on Microfilm, No. 7839).

Wong, Yau Kwan. *The Genesis of Peacekeeping in Canadian Foreign Policy Postulation and Its Relation to the Principle of Functionalism.* Kingston, 1970 (c1971). ix, 119 leaves. **5566**
  Half-title: *Peacekeeping.* Thesis (M.A.), Queen's University, 1971. (National Library of Canada. Canadian Theses on Microfilm, No. 7586).

XXI. CONTROL AND PREVENTION OF CONFLICT

See also *"Conduct of Armed Conflict (Law of War)" (p. 447)*.

A. General

Alcock, Norman Z. *The War Disease*. Oakville, Ont.: CPRI Press, c1972. 238 p.
5567

Beesley, J. Alan. "Guerre, paix et droit dans un monde divisé." (1974), 5 *Études Internationales* 45-71. **5568**

Bennett, D.C.T. "International Security through the Evolution of Law." (1944-45), 14 *Fortnightly Law Journal* 8-10. **5569**

Bentwich, Norman. "International Security through the Evolution of Law." (1944-45), 14 *Fortnightly Law Journal* 216-217. **5570**

Colard, Daniel. "Problématique internationale de la 'détente.' " (1974), 5 *Études Internationales* 476-501, 599-622. **5571**

Dessauer, F.E. "Peace and Law." (1946-47), 2 *International Journal* 51-58. **5572**

Eckhardt, William, and Lentz, Theodore Ferdinand. *Factors of War/Peace Attitudes*. Clarkson, Ont.: Canadian Peace Research Institute, c1967. 115 p. (Peace Research Reviews, Vol. 1, No. 5) **5573**

Evans, Donald, ed. *Peace, Power and Protest*. Toronto: Ryerson Press, c1967. 314 p. **5574**
Commissioned by the Board of Evangelism and Social Service of the United Church of Canada.
Review: Howard C. Green in (1967-68), 23 *International Journal* 647-648.

Goodhart, A.L. "International Security through the Evolution of Law." (1944-45), 14 *Fortnightly Law Journal* 118-120. **5575**

Gow, James Iain. *The Opinions of French Canadians in Quebec on the Problems of War and Peace, 1945-1960*. Québec, 1969. 3 vols. **5576**
Thesis (Doctorat), Université Laval, 1970.

Granatstein, J.L., and Cuff, Robert D., eds. *War and Society in North America*. Toronto: T. Nelson, c1971. viii, 199 p. **5577**
Papers presented at the Canadian Association for American Studies meeting, Montreal, Fall 1970.

Hughes, Charles E. "The Pathway of Peace." (1923), 1 *Canadian Bar Review* 595-611. **5578**

Also published in (1923), 8 *Canadian Bar Association, Proceedings* 202-218.

Hurst, *Sir* Cecil. "International Security through the Evolution of Law." (1944-45), 14 *Fortnightly Law Journal* 38-40. **5579**

"International Security through the Evolution of Law." (1944-45), 14 *Fortnightly Law Journal* 151-154. **5580**

Keeton, George W. "International Security through the Evolution of Law." (1944-45), 14 *Fortnightly Law Journal* 279-280. **5581**

Kos-Rabcewicz-Zubkowski, Ludwik. "International Justice and Peaceful Coexistence." (1968), 1 *Boletin Mexicano de Derecho Comparado* 197-219. **5582**

L'Heureux, Eugène. "La paix et la guerre: deux fruits de l'éducation." (1955), 49 *Royal Society of Canada, Transactions* 21-29 (3d Ser., Sec. 1) **5583**

MacKay, Robert A. "The Kellogg Peace Pact." (1928-29), 8 *Dalhousie Review* 351-356. **5584**

Maitland, R.L. "Peace - and Afterwards." (1944), 22 *Canadian Bar Review* 561-568. **5585**

Matte, Nicolas Mateesco. "La paix et le droit international." (1967), 2 *Revue Juridique Thémis* 545-556. **5586**

McWhinney, Edward. "The Historical Balance Sheet of 'Peaceful Coexistence' and of the Soviet-Western (Bipolar) Détente." *In* Boasson, Charles, ed., *The Changing International Community: Essays in Honour of Marion Mushkat* (The Hague, 1973), pp. 19-31. **5587**

McWhinney, Edward, ed. *Law, Foreign Policy, and the East-West Détente.* Toronto: University of Toronto Press, 1964. viii, 123 p. **5588**

Contains nine essays based on papers delivered at the Conference on Law and World Affairs held at the University of Toronto, January 17-18, 1964. Relevant essays are listed separately.

Reviews: Rosalyn Higgins in (1966), 42 *International Affairs* 276-279; Ivo Lapenna in (1965), 14 *International and Comparative Law Quarterly* 1423-1426; Oliver J. Lissitzyn in (1965), 59 *American Journal of International Law* 956-959; unsigned in (1965), 69 *Revue Générale de Droit International Public* 556 (brief notice).

McWhinney, Edward. " 'Peaceful Coexistence' and Legal Aspects of the Soviet-Western Détente." (1968), 1 *Boletin Mexicano de Derecho Comparado* 255-268. **5589**

McWhinney, Edward. " 'Peaceful Coexistence' since the Soviet-Western Détente." (1964), 4 *Indian Journal of International Law* 500-521. **5590**

McWhinney, Edward. "The Rule of Law and the Peaceful Settlement of Disputes." *In* Rubinstein, Alvin Z., and Ginsburgs, George, eds., *Soviet and American Policies in the United Nations: A Twenty-Five Year Perspective* (New York, 1971), pp. 165-183. **5591**

McWhinney, Edward. "Statement on 'Codification of the Principles of Peaceful Co-Existence.' " (1962), 50 *International Law Association, Report of Conference* 348-352. **5592**

Melko, Matthew. *52 Peaceful Societies.* Oakville, Ont.: Canadian Peace Research Institute Press, c1973. 223 p., maps. **5593**

Munro, Hector A. "International Security through the Evolution of Law." (1944-45), 14 *Fortnightly Law Journal* 183-186. **5594**

Preston, Richard A. "The Study of War and Its Causes: Part 1: The Long Search for the Right Approach." (1976-77), 6 *Canadian Defence Quarterly* 42-46 (No. 4) **5595**

Read, John E. *The Rule of Law on the International Plane.* With a Foreword by F.C. Cronkite. Toronto: Clarke, Irwin, 1961. 56 p. (W.M. Martin Lectures, 1960) **5596**
Reviews: William H. Charles in (1962-63), 42 *Dalhousie Review* 143-145; Maxwell Cohen in (1961-62), 8 *McGill Law Journal* 317-319.

Rolin, Henri. "International Security through the Evolution of Law." (1944-45), 14 *Fortnightly Law Journal* 314-316. **5597**

Rowan, John Patrick August. *Saint Thomas' Doctrine of Peace.* Toronto, 1947. 307 leaves. **5598**
Thesis (Ph.D.), University of Toronto, 1947.

Spraight, J.M. "International Security through the Evolution of Law." (1945-46), 15 *Fortnightly Law Journal* 25-26. **5599**

Thomson, James S. "War and Human Nature." (1935-36), 15 *Dalhousie Review* 79-84. **5600**

Watt, Lewis. "International Security through the Evolution of Law." (1945-46), 15 *Fortnightly Law Journal* 43-44. **5601**

B. Peace Movements

Babineau, Edmour. "Les religions et la paix du monde." (1970), 3 *Revue de l'Université de Moncton* 54-58. **5602**

Brock, Peter. *Twentieth-Century Pacifism.* New York, Toronto: Van Nostrand Reinhold, c1970. vii, 274 p. (New Perspectives in Political Science, 26) **5603**
Also published Toronto, D. Van Nostrand (Canada), 1970.

Duhamel, Roger. "Les chrétiens devant le problème de la paix." (1949), 4 *International Journal* 11-23. **5604**

Eckhardt, William. "Attitudes of Canadian Peace Groups." (1972), 16 *Journal of Conflict Resolution* 341-352. **5605**

Newberry, Patience Josephine Ruth. *Bertrand Russell and the Pacifists in the First World War.* Hamilton, 1975. xi, 552 leaves. **5606**
Thesis (Ph.D.), McMaster University, 1975. (National Library of Canada. Canadian Theses on Microfiche, No. 29694).

Russell, Bertrand. "Mankind versus the H-Bomb." (1957-58), 13 *International Journal* 175-178. **5607**

Skelton, O.D. "The European War and the Peace Movement." (1914-15), 22 *Queen's Quarterly* 205-214. **5608**

Valpy, Dumaresq Richardson. *The American Peace Movement and the Arbitration Treaties of 1911.* Fredericton, 1980. 153 frames. **5609**
Thesis (M.A.), University of New Brunswick, 1980. (National Library of Canada. Canadian Theses on Microfiche, No. 47816).

Weinroth, Howard. "Peace by Negotiation and the British Anti-War Movement, 1914-1918." (1975), 10 *Canadian Journal of History* 369-392. **5610**

Winterowd, Charles Gregory. *Pacifism and Its Critics; Conceptual Foundations.* Kingston, 1972. v, 173 leaves. **5611**
Thesis (M.A.), Queen's University, 1972. (National Library of Canada. Canadian Theses on Microfilm, No. 11199).

C. Arms Control and Disarmament

1. GENERAL

Ambrose, Paul B. "Canadian Arms Control and Disarmament Policies." (1964), 6 *University of Windsor Seminar on Canadian-American Relations, Proceedings* 305-319. **5612**

Armstrong, Willis C. "Comments on Armament and Disarmament." (1962), 4 *University of Windsor Seminar on Canadian-American Relations, Proceedings* 79-84. **5613**

Brode, Michael J. *Anglo-American Relations and the Geneva Naval Disarmament Conference of 1927.* Edmonton, 1972. vii, 188 leaves. **5614**
Added title: *The 1927 Naval Disarmament Conference and Its Impact on Anglo-American Relations.* Thesis (Ph.D.), University of Alberta, 1972. (National Library of Canada. Canadian Theses on Microfilm, No. 11119).

Burns, Eedson L.M. "Disarmament and Military Policy." (1970-71), 26 *International Journal* 619-634. **5615**

Burns, Eedson L.M. *A Seat at the Table: The Struggle for Disarmament.* Toronto: Clarke, Irwin, 1972. 268 p. **5616**
Reviews: Gerry Dirks in (1973), 6 *Canadian Journal of Political Science* 529-530; John Gellner in (1972-73), 28 *International Journal* 387-388; Colin S. Gray in (1972), 79 *Queen's Quarterly* 550-551; Jonathan Wouk in (1972-73), 52 *Dalhousie Review* 515-519.

Byers, R.B. "The Perils of Superpower Diplomacy: Détente, Defence, and Arms Control." (1979-80), 35 *International Journal* 520-547. **5617**

Byers, R.B. "Seapower and Arms Control: Problems and Prospects." (1980-81), 36 *International Journal* 485-514. **5618**

Byers, R.B. "Understanding SALT - Part 1: The Context of the Debate." (1979-80), 9 *Canadian Defence Quarterly* 11-14 (No. 1) **5619**

Byers, R.B. "Understanding SALT - Part 2: The Issues and the Outcome." (1979-80), 9 *Canadian Defence Quarterly* 7-13 (No. 2) **5620**

Cadieux, Marcel. "Le désarmement." (1957), 17 *Revue du Barreau* 57-72. **5621**

Caldwell, Lawrence T. "The Fate of Strategic Arms Limitation and Soviet-American Relations." (1980-81), 36 *International Journal* 608-634. **5622**

Campsie, John S. *Objection to Murder; the Conscience of a Unilateralist.* Toronto, Montreal: McClelland and Stewart, 1967. 191 p. **5623**

Canada. Dept. of External Affairs. *Conference on Limitation of Naval Armament Held at London, January 21, 1930, to April 22, 1930: Report of the Canadian Delegate, with Annexes.* Ottawa: King's Printer, 1930. 88 p. **5624**

Canada. Dept. of External Affairs. *Report on Disarmament Discussions, 1957.* Ottawa: Queen's Printer, 1958. 40 p. **5625**

Carle, François. "Les pourparlers exploratoires d'Helsinki." (1973), 4 *Études Internationales* 297-361, 502-551. **5626**

Chipman, Warwick. "Canada and the Problem of Naval Disarmament." (1929), 8 *International Affairs* 433-444. **5627**
This is a report made to a Round Table during the winter of 1928-29, at the Canadian Institute of International Affairs, Montreal Branch.

Clemens, Walter C., Jr. "European Arms Control: How, What, and When?" (1971-72), 27 *International Journal* 45-72. **5628**

Conway, John S. "Disarmament Reconsidered." (1957-58), 13 *International Journal* 100-109. **5629**

Corradini, Alessandro. "Organizing for Peace." (1979-80), 35 *International Journal* 292-308. **5630**

Crane, Brian. "Arms Control: A New Approach to Disarmament." (1961-62), 21 *Behind the Headlines* No. 5 (21 p.) **5631**

Davy, Grant R. *Canada's Role in Disarmament Negotiations, 1946-1957.* Medford, Mass., 1962. ix, 476 leaves. **5632**
Thesis (Ph.D.), Fletcher School of Law and Diplomacy, Tufts University, 1962.

DeLisle, Kenneth Edward. *The Eighteen Nation Disarmament Committee and After: The Role and Contributions of the Canadian Delegations.* Winnipeg, 1975. i, 163 leaves. **5633**
Thesis (M.A.), University of Manitoba, 1975.

"Disarmament: Report on the Negotiations in Geneva." (1964), 16 *External Affairs* 202-207, 531-535. **5634**

"Disarmament Negotiations: Geneva, July 27 to September 16, 1965." (1965), 17 *External Affairs* 474-481. **5635**

"Disarmament Negotiations: Geneva, June 14 to August 25, 1966." (1966), 18 *External Affairs* 445-453. **5636**

Dupré, Maurice. "Quelques aspects du problème du désarmement." (1932), 2 *Revue de l'Université d'Ottawa* 399-414. **5637**

Emanuelli, Claude C. "Vers une réglementation du commerce international des armes conventionnelles." (1979-80), 10 *Revue de Droit, Université de Sherbrooke* 89-134. **5638**

Epstein, William. "Canada's Disarmament Initiatives Mark Return to Active Role." (1979), *International Perspectives* 3-8 (Mar./Apr.) **5639**

Epstein, William. *Disarmament: Twenty-Five Years of Effort.* Toronto: Canadian Institute of International Affairs, 1971. 97 p. (Contemporary Affairs, No. 45)
Review: Jean Klein in (1972), 3 *Études Internationales* 283-284. **5640**

Epstein, William. "Failure at UNSSOD II." (1982), *International Perspectives* 26-29 (Nov./Dec.) **5641**
Refers to the United Nations Second Special Session on Disarmament (UNSSOD II).

Epstein, William. "Mounting International Tensions Underline Need for Disarmament." (1980), *International Perspectives* 13-18 (Mar./Apr.) **5642**

Epstein, William, and Toyoda, Toshiyuki, eds. *A New Design for Nuclear Disarmament: Pugwash Symposium, Kyoto, Japan.* Nottingham: Spokesman, 1977. xv, 338 p. **5643**
Proceedings of the 25th Pugwash Symposium.

Finan, J.S. "Arms Control and the Central Strategic Balance: Some Technological Issues." (1980-81), 36 *International Journal* 430-459. **5644**

Finkelstein, Lawrence S. "Defence, Disarmament and World Order." (1962-63), 22 *Behind the Headlines* No. 1 (12 p.) **5645**

Frappier, Monique DesRochers. "Les conséquences économiques du désarmement." (1963-64), 39 *Actualité Économique* 316-322. **5646**

Glasgow, George. "Disarmament and Financial Recovery." (1932), 39 *Queen's Quarterly* 12-28. **5647**

Glasgow, George. "The Naval Conference." (1930), 37 *Queen's Quarterly* 225-245. **5648**

Goetze, Bernd A. *Security through Arms Control.* Kingston, Ont.: Centre for International Relations, Queen's University, 1977. ix, 90, (30) p. (National Security Series, No. 3) **5649**

Goetze, Bernd A. *Security through Arms Control: A Study of SALT as an Instrument of Enhancing International Peace and Security, with Particular Emphasis on the Role of Strategic Weapons Systems Technology.* Kingston, 1977. 124, (26), 7 leaves. **5650**
Thesis (M.A.), Queen's University, 1977. (National Library of Canada, Canadian Theses on Microfiche, No. 32652).

Gotlieb, Allan E. "Appropriate Peacekeeping Machinery Which Would Take Effect During the Process of Disarmament to Protect Disarming States from Attack." (1967), *World Peace Through Law* 126-134. **5651**

Gotlieb, Allan E. *Disarmament and International Law; a Study of the Role of Law in the Disarmament Process.* Toronto: Canadian Institute of International Affairs, c1965. 232 p. (Contemporary Affairs, No. 34) **5652**
Reviews: Richard R. Baxter in (1966), 60 *American Journal of International Law* 621-622; John T. Connor in (1965-66), 7 *Harvard International Law Journal* 389-393; Armand L.C. de Mestral in (1966-67), 12 *McGill Law Journal* 212-213; Arthur H. Dean in (1965-66), 51 *Cornell Law Quarterly* 621-624; C.J.R. Dugard in (1964), 40 *British Year Book of International Law* 402-403; S. Joshua Langer in (1965-66), 21 *International Journal* 238-239; Edward McWhinney in (1965), 3 *Canadian Yearbook of International Law* 360-363; Mariano Aguilar Navarro in (1966), 19 *Revista Española de Derecho Internacional* 484-485; Daniel G. Partan in (1966), 18 *Maine Law Review* 123-126; Jean

Touscoz in (1966), 93 *Journal du Droit International* 238; signed C.M. in (1966), 6 *Indian Journal of International Law* 261-263.

Gotlieb, Allan E. "Remarks on Disarmament." (1965), *World Peace Through Law* 462-465.   **5653**

Gray, Colin S. "Of Bargaining Chips and Building Blocks: Arms Control and Defence Policy." (1972-73), 28 *International Journal* 266-296.   **5654**

Gray, Colin S. "Security through SALT?" (1970-71), 30 *Behind the Headlines* Nos. 3-4 (16 p.)   **5655**

Griffiths, Franklyn. "Inner Tensions in the Soviet Approach to 'Disarmament.'" (1966-67), 22 *International Journal* 593-617.   **5656**

Griffiths, Franklyn. "Limits of the Tabular View of Negotiation." (1979-80), 35 *International Journal* 33-46.   **5657**

Griffiths, Franklyn. "Transnational Politics and Arms Control. (Review Article)." (1970-71), 26 *International Journal* 640-674.   **5658**

Hassner, Pierre. "Faut-il enterrer *l'arms control?"* (1973), 4 *Études Internationales* 411-433.   **5659**

Hewson, John P. *Threat Perception and Negotiating Behavior in Soviet-American Relations in the Eighteen Nation Disarmament Conference: A Quantitative Study.* Ottawa, 1973. v, 101 leaves.   **5660**
Thesis (M.A.), Carleton University, 1973.

Hill, Roger J. "MBFR." (1973-74), 29 *International Journal* 242-255.   **5661**
Refers to Mutual and Balanced Force Reductions (MBFR).

Hirst, Francis W. "Why Civilized Nations Should Disarm: An Economic Preface to the Disarmament Conference." (1921-22), 1 *Dalhousie Review* 243-246.   **5662**

Hunt, Kenneth. "The Problem of Mutual and Balanced Force Reduction." (1971-72), 1 *Canadian Defence Quarterly* 10-16 (No. 3)   **5663**

Ignatieff, George. "Canadian Aims and Perspectives in the Negotiation of International Agreements on Arms Control and Disarmament." *In* Macdonald, Ronald St. John, and others, *Canadian Perspectives on International Law and Organization* (Toronto, 1974), pp. 690-725.   **5664**

Ignatieff, George. "Negotiating Arms Control." (1974-75), 30 *International Journal* 92-101.   **5665**

Ignatieff, George. "The Outlook for Disarmament in the Coming Decade." (1970), 22 *External Affairs* 425-433.   **5666**
Statement of the Canadian representative in the First Committee of the U.N. General Assembly on November 2, 1970.

Jakhu, Ram S., and Trecroce, Riccardo. "International Satellite Monitoring for Disarmament and Development." (1980), 5 *Annals of Air and Space Law* 509-527.   **5667**

Keyston, J.E. "The Nature of the Disarmament Problem." (1961-62), 21 *Behind the Headlines* No. 2 (24 p.)   **5668**

Khan, Mumtaz Ahmed. *Arms Control, Disarmament and Observation in Space, Recent Developments.* Montreal, 1968. ii, 99 leaves.   **5669**

Thesis (LL.M.), McGill University, 1968. (National Library of Canada. Canadian Theses on Microfilm, No. 2824).

Klein, Jean. "Les aspects militaires de la détente en Europe et les perspectives d'une réduction mutuelle des forces dans un cadre régional." (1973), 4 *Études Internationales* 121-158. **5670**

Klein, Jean. "Désarmement ou 'arms control': la position française sous la Ve République." (1972), 3 *Études Internationales* 356-389. **5671**

Kohler, Gernot. *Arms Control and Disarmament: A Bibliography of Canadian Research, 1965-1980*. Ottawa: Dept. of National Defence, Operational Research and Analysis Establishment, 1981. v, xiii, 168 p. (ORAE Extra-Mural Paper, No. 15) **5672**

Kohler, Gernot. "Une théorie structuro-dynamique des armements." (1976), 7 *Études Internationales* 25-50. **5673**

Lachance, Monique, and Legault, Albert. "Les MBFR: l'évolution des négociations et la position des pays participants." (1978), 9 *Études Internationales* 246-280. **5674**
Refers to Mutual Balanced Force Reduction (MBFR).

Lachance, Monique, and Legault, Albert. "Les MBFR: les méthodes de réduction." (1978), 9 *Études Internationales* 405-428. **5675**

Lamb, John, and Mandell, Brian. "How Arms Control Begins at Home: The American and Soviet Cases." (1980-81), 36 *International Journal* 575-607. **5676**

Laulicht, Jerome, and Paul, John. "Issues of Peace and War: Canadian Attitudes on Disarmament and Defense Policy." (1963-64), 11 *Social Problems* 48-62. **5677**

Lawler, William Ralph. *Strategic Arms Limitation Talks: An Evaluation in the Perspective of the Arms Control Experience and Power Politics*. Ottawa, 1973. viii, 155 leaves. **5678**
Thesis (M.A.), Carleton University, 1973.

Legault, Albert. "Les MBFR et l'équilibre des forces en Europe." (1973-74), 3 *Canadian Defence Quarterly* 22-26 (No. 2) **5679**

Legault, Albert. "Les réseaux de la communauté scientifique internationale en matière de désarmement et de contrôle des armements: 1972-1976." (1976), 7 *Études Internationales* 436-446. **5680**

Leitenberg, Milton. *Arms Control and Disarmament: A Short Review of a Thirty Year History and Its Impact on Nuclear Proliferation*. Ottawa: Norman Paterson School of International Affairs, Carleton University, 1978. 53 p. **5681**

Lower, Arthur R.M. "Armament and Disarmament." (1962), 4 *University of Windsor Seminar on Canadian-American Relations, Proceedings* 110-130. **5682**

MacKay, Robert A. "Political Implications of the London Conference." (1930), 37 *Queen's Quarterly* 532-542. **5683**

MacKay, Robert A. "Recent Books on Disarmament." (1932), 39 *Queen's Quarterly* 132-144. **5684**
This is a review article of five books on disarmament.

MacKenzie, Norman A.M. "Disarmament." (1929-30), 7 *Canadian Defence Quarterly* 29-35. **5685**

Martin, Paul. "Disarmament - Canadian Views on the Geneva Discussions." (1964), 16 *External Affairs* 136-142. **5686**

Martin, Paul. "Recent Developments in Disarmament." (1955-56), 11 *International Journal* 79-84. **5687**

Marzari, Frank. "The Derangement of MIRV." (1970-71), 26 *International Journal* 753-770. **5688**
Refers to Multiple Re-entry Vehicles (MIRV).

Marzari, Frank. *The Management of the Strategic Arms Race*. Ottawa: School of International Affairs, Carleton University, 1971. 34 p. (Carleton University. Norman Paterson School of International Affairs. Occasional Papers, 14)
5689
This paper is part of a larger study entitled: *Weapons and Policy; Strategic Options in the 1970s.*

McNaughton, John T. "Space Technology and Arms Control." *In* Cohen, Maxwell, ed., *Law and Politics in Space* (Montreal, 1964), pp. 63-72. **5690**

McWhinney, Edward. *The International Law of Détente: Arms Control, European Security, and East-West Cooperation*. Alphen aan den Rijn: Sijthoff & Noordhoff, 1978. xi, 259 p. **5691**
Reviews: Thomas Bruha in (1981), 41 *Zeitschrift für Ausländisches Öffentliches Recht und Völkerrecht* 901-903; Leslie C. Green in (1979), 57 *Canadian Bar Review* 423-426; Frits Kalshoven in (1982), 29 *Netherlands International Law Review* 135-136; B. Landheer in (1978), 26 *European Yearbook* 654-655; M.J. Peterson in (1979), 73 *American Journal of International Law* 534-535; Charles Rousseau in (1978), 82 *Revue Générale de Droit International Public* 1183; unsigned in (1980-81), 10 *Denver Journal of International Law and Policy* 202-203.

McWhinney, Edward. "International Security and Co-operation. (Comments)." (1968), 53 *International Law Association, Report of Conference* 460-462.
5692

McWhinney, Edward. "International Security and Co-operation. (Comments)." (1970), 54 *International Law Association, Report of Conference* 669-670.
5693

McWhinney, Edward. "Juridical Methods for Ensuring the Control of Disarmament." (1966), 52 *International Law Association, Report of Conference* 645-653. **5694**

Merle, Marcel. "Can the World Bring Itself to Say Farewell to Arms? - A Footnote to the Special Session." (1978), *International Perspectives* 10-14 (Nov./Dec.)
5695

Meyer, Stephen M. "Anti-Satellite Weapons and Arms Control: Incentives and Disincentives from the Soviet and American Perspectives." (1980-81), 36 *International Journal* 460-484. **5696**

Moch, Jules. "Towards a Disarmed Peace." (1955-56), 11 *International Journal* 85-92. **5697**

Munton, Donald J., and Slack, Michael. "Canadian Attitudes on Disarmament." (1982), *International Perspectives* 9-12 (July/Aug.) **5698**

Owen, Walter S. "Legal Problems of Disarmament." (1963), *World Peace Through Law* 427-429. **5699**

Polanyi, John C. "Arms Control." (1961-62), 17 *International Journal* 40-49. **5700**

Potter, G.A. "SALT I: Military Evaluation." (1973-74), 3 *Canadian Defence Quarterly* 29-33 (No. 1) **5701**

Preston, Richard A. "Can We Disarm?" (1957), 17 *Behind the Headlines* No. 6 (16 p.) **5702**

Purver, Ronald G. *The Arms Control Calculus: Factors Affecting the Susceptibility of Military Instruments and Activities to International Regulation.* Vancouver, 1974 (c1975). vi, 117 leaves. **5703**
Thesis (M.A.), University of British Columbia, 1974. (National Library of Canada. Canadian Theses on Microfiche, No. 22202).

Purver, Ronald G. "Canada and the Control of Arms on the Seabed." (1975), 13 *Canadian Yearbook of International Law* 195-230. **5704**

Purver, Ronald G. "Canadian Foreign Policy and the Military Uses of the Seabed." In Johnson, Barbara, and Zacher, Mark W., eds., *Canadian Foreign Policy and the Law of the Sea* (Vancouver, 1977), pp. 202-254. **5705**

Ranger, Robin. "Arms Control in Theory and Practice." (1977), 31 *Year Book of World Affairs* 112-137. **5706**

Ranger, Robin. "Arms Control Negotiations: Progress and Prospects." (1974-75), 4 *Canadian Defence Quarterly* 16-25 (No. 3) **5707**

Ranger, Robin. "Arms Control within a Changing Political Context." (1970-71), 26 *International Journal* 735-752. **5708**

Ranger, Robin. *Arms and Politics, 1958-1978: Arms Control in a Changing Political Context.* Toronto: Macmillan of Canada, 1979. viii, 280 p. **5709**
Reprinted Toronto, Gage, 1981.
Reviews: G.A.H. Pearson under title: "Ranger's Arms and Politics." in (1980), *International Perspectives* 32 (Jan./Feb.); J.L. Richardson in (1980-81), 36 *International Journal* 679-680.

Ranger, Robin. "The Failure of SALT II." (1978-79), 85 *Queen's Quarterly* 626-636. **5710**

Ranger, Robin. "The Politics of Arms Control." (1975), 47 *Canadian Political Science Association, Papers,* 23, 7 p. **5711**

Reford, Robert W. "Merchant of Death?" (1967-68), 27 *Behind the Headlines* No. 4 (28 p.) **5712**

Reford, Robert W. "Our Seat at the Table: A Canadian Menu for Arms Control." (1980-81), 36 *International Journal* 657-677. **5713**

Reford, Robert W. "The UN Disarmament Conference and Canada." (1982), *International Perspectives* 6-8 (July/Aug.) **5714**

Robinson, J.P. Perry. "Chemical Arms Control and the Assimilation of Chemical Weapons." (1980-81), 36 *International Journal* 515-534. **5715**

Rosenbluth, Gideon. *The Canadian Economy and Disarmament.* Toronto: Macmillan of Canada, 1967. x, 189 p. **5716**

Reviews: Bernard Bonin in (1968-69), 44 *Actualité Économique* 338-339; Sam Lanfranco in (1970), 3 *Canadian Journal of Economics* 176-178; John W. Warnock in (1968), 1 *Canadian Journal of Political Science* 225-226.

Sanger, Clyde. *Safe and Sound: Disarmament and Development in the Eighties.* Ottawa: Deneau Publishers, 1982. 122 p. **5717**

This is a "popular version of the study by a United Nations group of governmental experts of the relationship between disarmament and development for the UN General Assembly 1978-81."

Review: Doug Coupar under title: "Disarm Now," in (1982), *International Perspectives* 34 (Sept./Oct.).

Sattler, James F. "The Case for Negotiating with the East on European Security and Mutual Force Reductions." (1972-73), 2 *Canadian Defence Quarterly* 33-36 (No. 3) **5718**

Sherman, Michael E. "Nixon and Arms Control." (1968-69), 24 *International Journal* 327-338. **5719**

Simon, H. Paul. *The German Response to Allied Demands for Disarmament, 1918-1924.* Toronto, c1980. 566 leaves. **5720**

Thesis (Ph.D.), University of Toronto, 1978. (National Library of Canada. Canadian Theses on Microfiche, No. 43726).

Singer, J. David. "From Deterrence to Disarmament." (1960-61), 16 *International Journal* 307-326. **5721**

Skinner, Gerald R. *The Politics of Disarmament: Canada and the Tenth United Nations Special Session on Disarmament.* Ottawa, 1979. 1 vol. **5722**

Thesis (M.A.), Carleton University, 1979. (National Library of Canada. Canadian Theses on Microfiche, No. 49543). Abstracted in (1981), 19 *Masters Abstracts* 265.

Skinner, Gerald R. "Primer on Canada's Approach to UN Disarmament Session." (1978), *International Perspectives* 30-34 (May/June) **5723**

Teilhac, Ernest. "Unité des problèmes de l'or et du désarmement." (1932-33), 8 *Actualité Économique* 122-127. **5724**

"Ten-Nation Disarmament Committee." (1960), 12 *External Affairs* 681-687. **5725**

Tucker, Michael J. "Canada and Arms Control: Perspectives and Trends." (1980-81), 36 *International Journal* 635-656. **5726**

Tucker, Michael J. *Canada's Roles in the Disarmament Negotiations: 1957-1971.* Toronto, c1977. iii, 530 leaves. **5727**

Thesis (Ph.D.), University of Toronto, 1977. (National Library of Canada. Canadian Theses on Microfiche, No. 40970).

Vachon, G.K. "Le contrôle des armements et les armes chimiques." (1982), 13 *Études Internationales* 97-108. **5728**

Vlasic, Ivan A. "Disarmament Decade, Outer Space and International Law." (1981), 26 *McGill Law Journal* 135-206. **5729**

Waddington, George Edwin. *The Search for Security; the Strategic Arms Limitation Talks.* Ottawa, 1970. 106 leaves. **5730**

Research essay (M.A.), Carleton University, 1970.

Watson, Lorna. *History of Disarmament Negotiations.* Clarkson, Ont.: Canadian Peace Research Institute, 1967. 118 p. (Peace Research Reviews, Vol. 1, No. 2) **5731**

Young, Elizabeth. "Hope Springs Eternal..." (1980-81), 36 *International Journal* 413-429. **5732**

2. NUCLEAR TESTING AND CONTROL

See also *"Nuclear Energy" (p. 656).*

"Avoiding International Conflicts: 1) Law of the Sea Issues; 2) Nuclear Non-Proliferation / Évitons les différends internationaux: 1) Le droit de la mer; 2) La non-prolifération nucléaire." (1976), 5 *Canadian Council on International Law, Proceedings,* 182 p. **5733**
This is the general theme of the fifth annual conference held at Ottawa, October 22-23, 1976. Individual papers are listed separately.

Buchan, Alastair F., ed. *A World of Nuclear Powers!* Englewood Cliffs, N.J.: Prentice-Hall, 1966. ix, 176 p. (Spectrum Book, S-AA-19) **5734**
Initially prepared as background reading for the International Assembly on Nuclear Weapons, held at Toronto June 23-26, 1966, sponsored by the Canadian Institute of International Affairs, the Institute for Strategic Studies (London), the Carnegie Endowment for International Peace, and the American Assembly of Columbia University.

Bull, Hedley. "Wider Still and Wider - Nuclear Proliferation 1950-1975." (1975), *International Perspectives* 24-28 (Nov./Dec.) **5735**

Burns, Eedson L.M. "Can the Spread of Nuclear Weapons Be Stopped?" (1965), 19 *International Organization* 851-869. **5736**

Burns, Eedson L.M. *Megamurder.* Toronto: Clarke, Irwin, 1966. xiii, 288 p. **5737**
Also published London, Harrap, 1966.

Burns, Eedson L.M. "The Nonproliferation Treaty: Its Negotiation and Prospects." (1969), 23 *International Organization* 788-807. **5738**

Clayton, Richard H. *On Nuclear Proliferation; the International Political System.* Ottawa, 1970. 165 leaves. **5739**
Thesis (M.A.), Carleton University, 1970.

Dai, Poeliu. "Treaty on the Non-Proliferation of Nuclear Weapons with Special Reference to Canada's Position." (1968), 6 *Canadian Yearbook of International Law* 226-241. **5740**

"Disarmament: Non-Proliferation Treaty." (1968), 20 *External Affairs* 170-180. **5741**

Dunn, Lewis A. "No First Use and Nuclear Proliferation." (1977-78), 33 *International Journal* 573-587. **5742**

Eayrs, James George. "Apocalypse Then: Aspects of Nuclear Weapons-Acquisition Policy Thirty Years Ago." (1979-80), 59 *Dalhousie Review* 635-650. **5743**

This essay was delivered as a public lecture at Dalhousie University, January 31, 1980.

Epstein, William. "Canada and the Problem of Nuclear Proliferation." (1976), 5 *Canadian Council on International Law, Proceedings* 53-83. **5744**
This address was presented during a panel entitled: "Nuclear Non-Proliferation and Safeguards / La non-prolifération nucléaire et les garanties de sécurité" (pp. 53-109).

Epstein, William. "Failure of Review Conference Setback for Non-Proliferation." (1981), *International Perspectives* 21-25 (May/June) **5745**

Epstein, William. *The Last Chance: Nuclear Proliferation and Arms Control* New York: Free Press, c1976. xxiv, 341 p. **5746**
Review: Frank Barnaby in (1976-77), 32 *International Journal* 194-195.

Epstein, William. "Nuclear Proliferation in the Third World." (1975), 29 *Journal of International Affairs* 185-202. **5747**

Epstein, William. "Why States Go - And Don't Go - Nuclear." (1977), 430 *Annals of the American Academy of Political and Social Science* 16-28. **5748**

Fischer, Georges. "Bilan de la non-prolifération." (1977), 8 *Études Internationales* 43-64. **5749**
Refers to the non-proliferation treaty of July 1, 1968 (CTS 1970/7).

Gendron, François. "En marge de Salt II: la logique nucléaire." (1979-80), 9 *Canadian Defence Quarterly* 14-16 (No. 2) **5750**

Ghent, Jocelyn Maynard. *Canadian-American Relations and the Nuclear Weapons Controversy, 1958-1963.* Urbana-Champaign, Ill., 1976. 316 leaves. **5751**
Thesis (Ph.D.), University of Illinois, 1976.

Giner, Marcel M. *Le problème de l'interdiction totale des essais nucléaires souterrains.* Québec, 1974 (c1978). vii, 73 leaves, maps. **5752**
Thesis (M.Sc.Soc.), Université Laval, 1974. (National Library of Canada. Canadian Theses on Microfiche, No. 35407).

Gotlieb, Allan E. "Nuclear Weapons in Outer Space." (1965), 3 *Canadian Yearbook of International Law* 3-35. **5753**

Greenwood, Thomas. "Le berceau de la bombe atomique." (1954), 24 *Revue de l'Université d'Ottawa* 408-420. **5754**

Griffiths, Franklyn. "Preventing the Spread of Nuclear Weapons." (1964-65), 20 *International Journal* 524-529. **5755**

Griffiths, Franklyn, and Polanyi, John C., eds. *The Dangers of Nuclear War: A Pugwash Symposium.* Foreword by Pierre Elliott Trudeau. Toronto: University of Toronto Press, c1979. xii, 197 p. **5756**
Based on papers originally presented at the 30th Pugwash Symposium on the topic: "The Dangers of Nuclear War by the Year 2,000," held in Toronto May 4-7, 1978.
Reviews: Hélène Galarneau in (1980), 11 *Études Internationales* 350-352; Ron Huisken in (1980), 35 *International Journal* 411-413; Robert W. Morrison in (1980), 23 *Canadian Public Administration* 664-666.

Hammond, Thomas. "Canada and the Quest for a Complete Nuclear Test Ban." (1971-72), 1 *Canadian Defence Quarterly* 54-56 (No. 4) **5757**

Ignatieff, George. "Staring Doomsday in the Face. (Review Article)." (1982), 89 *Queen's Quarterly* 352-355. **5758**

"International Assembly on Nuclear Weapons." (1966), 18 *External Affairs* 325-330. **5759**
Report on the Assembly held at Toronto, June 23-26, 1966.

"The International Control of the Military Uses of Atomic Energy." (1955), 7 *External Affairs* 83-94. **5760**

Joynt, Carey B. "Diplomacy and the H-Bomb - Truce Is not Peace." (1956-57), 63 *Queen's Quarterly* 228-235. **5761**

Kapur, Ashok. "Evaluating the Progress of Test Ban Negotiations." (1979), *International Perspectives* 29-33 (Jan./Feb.) **5762**

Kapur, Ashok. *India's Arms Control and Nuclear Policy: A Quest for an Altered World Order.* Ottawa, 1974. vi, v, 485 leaves. **5763**
Thesis (Ph.D.), Carleton University, 1974. (National Library of Canada. Canadian Theses on Microfiche, No. 21227).

Kapur, Ashok. *India's Nuclear Option: Atomic Diplomacy and Decision Making.* New York: Praeger, 1976. xx, 295 p. (Praeger Special Studies in International Politics and Government) **5764**

Kapur, Ashok. *International Nuclear Proliferation: Multilateral Diplomacy and Regional Aspects.* New York: Praeger, c1979. x, 387 p. **5765**

Kapur, Ashok. "Nuclear Proliferation in the 1980s." (1980-81), 36 *International Journal* 535-555. **5766**

Legault, Albert. "Atomic Weapons for Germany?" (1965-66), 21 *International Journal* 445-469. **5767**

Legault, Albert. "Nuclear Policy Should Be More Open and Less Ambiguous." (1976), *International Perspectives* 8-13 (Jan./Feb.) **5768**

Legault, Albert, and Lindsey, George R. *The Dynamics of the Nuclear Balance.* Rev. ed. Ithaca, N.Y.: Cornell University Press, 1976. 283 p. **5769**

Lewis, David Charles. *Nuclear Diplomacy, 1957 to 1962: Eisenhower and Kennedy vs Khruschev from Sputnik to the Cuban Crisis.* London, Ont., 1976. vii, 188 leaves. **5770**
Thesis (M.A.), University of Western Ontario, 1977. (National Library of Canada. Canadian Theses on Microfiche, No. 31614).

Macdonald, Ronald St. John, and Hough, Barbara. "The Nuclear Tests Case Revisited." (1977), 20 *German Yearbook of International Law* 337-357. **5771**

Maltais, Eugene LeRoy. *Rosenau's Pre-Theories: The Diefenbaker Dilemma on Nuclear Warheads.* Edmonton, 1972. 130 leaves. **5772**
Thesis (M.A.), University of Alberta, 1972. (National Library of Canada. Canadian Theses on Microfiche, No. 13476).

Mazer, Brian M. "The Evolution of Canadian Agreements for Co-operation in Nuclear Weapons and Technology." (1980), 18 *Canadian Yearbook of International Law* 267-284. **5773**

Mazer, Brian M. *Manhattan to Missiles: Canada, Nuclear Weapons and International Law (an Interdisciplinary Study).* Edmonton, 1977. xii, 200 leaves. **5774**

Thesis (LL.M.), University of Alberta, 1977. (National Library of Canada. Canadian Theses on Microfiche, No. 32028).

McTaggart, David Fraser. *Outrage! The Ordeal of Greenpeace III*. Vancouver: J.J. Douglas, 1973. xiv, 278 p., maps. **5775**

McWhinney, Edward. "International Law-Making and the Judicial Process: The World Court and the French Nuclear Tests Case." (1975), 3 *Syracuse Journal of International Law and Commerce* 9-46. **5776**

Nellestyn, A. "The Non-Proliferation Treaty and Safeguards Reviewed." (1981-82), 11 *Canadian Defence Quarterly* 27-33 (No. 3) **5777**

"Non-Proliferation Treaty." (1968), 20 *External Affairs* 416-433. **5778**

"Nuclear Non-Proliferation and Safeguards / La non-prolifération nucléaire et les garanties de sécurité." (1976), 5 *Canadian Council on International Law, Proceedings* 53-109. **5779**

> This is a panel. Chairman: M.D. Copithorne (pp. 53-54).- Speaker: William Epstein (Title of address: "Canada and the Problem of Nuclear Proliferation," pp. 55-83).- Commentators: Paul C. Szasz (pp. 84-87), and Michael J. Vechsler (pp. 88-90).- General discussion (pp. 91-109).

"Nuclear Non-Proliferation and Safeguards / La non-prolifération nucléaire et les garanties de sécurité." (1976), 5 *Canadian Council on International Law, Proceedings* 152-182. **5780**

> This is a workshop. Animateurs: Constance D. Hunt, and Stanislas Slosar. The transcript is incomplete.

Ranger, Robin. "NATO's New Great Debate: Theatre Nuclear Force Modernization and Arms Control." (1980-81), 36 *International Journal* 556-574. **5781**

Reford, Robert W. "Problems of Nuclear Proliferation." (1975-76), 34 *Behind the Headlines* No. 1 (22 p.) **5782**

Scheinman, Lawrence. "Pandora's Nuclear Box. (Review Article)." (1969-70), 25 *International Journal* 779-785. **5783**

Sharp, Mitchell. "Non-Proliferation Treaty." (1968), 20 *External Affairs* 263-267. **5784**

Sherman, Michael E. "Guarantees and Nuclear Spread." (1965-66), 21 *International Journal* 484-490. **5785**

Sherman, Michael E. "The Nuclear Club." (1965-66), 25 *Behind the Headlines* No. 5 (18 p.) **5786**

Sherman, Michael E. *Nuclear Proliferation; the Treaty and After*. Toronto: Canadian Institute of International Affairs, c1968. 96 p. (Contemporary Affairs, No. 40) **5787**

Steele, J.A. "The Campaign for Nuclear Disarmament." (1960-61), 67 *Queen's Quarterly* 547-556. **5788**

Wise, S.F. "Balance of Nuclear Terror." (1960-61), 67 *Queen's Quarterly* 337-344. **5789**

D. Collective Security

1. GENERAL

Alcock, Norman Z., and others. "Defence in the 70s: Comments on the White Paper." (1970-71), 30 *Behind the Headlines* Nos. 7-8 (21 p.)   **5790**

Anderson, John Charles. *Mackenzie King and Collective Security: The League of Nations and the United Nations.* Edmonton, 1977. vii, 160 leaves.   **5791**
Thesis (M.A.), University of Alberta, 1977. (National Library of Canada. Canadian Theses on Microfiche, No. 34279).

Andrén, Nils. "The Future of the Scandinavian Security System." (1968-69), 24 *International Journal* 339-348.   **5792**

Beattie, Clayton E. "Defence and Security in the 1980's." (1980), 9 *Canadian Council on International Law, Proceedings* 19-24.   **5793**

Bell, George G. "Canada's Defence Planning and Security Strategies for the 1980's." (1980), 9 *Canadian Council on International Law, Proceedings* 25-35.   **5794**

Bevan, George A. "Canada, a Power Vacuum of World Politics. (A Study in Canadian Defence)." (1947-48), 27 *Dalhousie Review* 196-205.   **5795**

Bishop, Peter V. "ANZUS: Shield or Shroud?" (1960-61), 16 *International Journal* 405-409.   **5796**

Braun, Aurel. "The Evolution of the Warsaw Pact." (1973-74), 3 *Canadian Defence Quarterly* 27-36 (No. 3)   **5797**

Braun, Aurel. *New Dimensions and Directions in the Warsaw Pact.* Kingston, Ont.: Centre for International Relations, Queen's University, 1977. 25 leaves. (National Security Series, No. 1)   **5798**

Burns, Eedson L.M. *Defence in the Nuclear Age: An Introduction for Canadians.* Toronto: Clarke, Irwin, c1976. ix, 133 p., maps.   **5799**
Review: François Gendron in (1979), 10 *Études Internationales* 856-857.

Canada. Dept. of External Affairs. *London and Paris Agreements, September-October 1954.* Ottawa: Queen's Printer, 1955. 40 p. (Canada. Dept. of External Affairs. Conference Series, 1955, No. 1)   **5800**
Also issued in French under title: *Accords de Londres et de Paris, septembre-octobre 1954.*

Carle, François. *Consensus Formation at the Conference on Security and Cooperation in Europe.* Ottawa, 1976. 205 leaves.   **5801**
Thesis (M.A.), Carleton University, 1976.

Carle, François. "La deuxième phase de la Conférence sur la sécurité et la coopération en Europe." (1975), 6 *Études Internationales* 165-187.   **5802**

Crean, G.G. "European Security - the CSCE Final Act: Text and Commentary." (1976-77), 35 *Behind the Headlines* Nos. 2 & 3 (75 p.)   **5803**
Comments on the Conference on Security and Co-operation in Europe (CSCE).

Dabbs, R. Paul. *The European Defence Community.* Ottawa, 1970. 90 (i.e. 102), (14) leaves. **5804**
Research essay (M.A.), Carleton University, 1970. Refers to the proposed European Defence Community Treaty signed at Paris May 27, 1952 (159 BFSP 516).

Eayrs, James George. "Pacific Pact: 'Step in the Right Direction?' " (1951-52), 7 *International Journal* 293-302. **5805**

Gordon, J. King. "Development and Security and the UN Special Session." (1978), *International Perspectives* 14-19 (Nov./Dec.) **5806**

Han, Chin Tack. *Legal Prohibition of War and Its Enforcement through Collective Security Measures by International Organizations as Illustrated by U.N. Intervention in the Korean Conflict.* Ottawa, 1973 (i.e. 1974). iii, v, 191 leaves.
Research essay (M.A.), Carleton University, 1974. **5807**

International Studies Conference, 8th, London, 1935. *Canadian Memorandum No. 1-3.* Toronto, 1935. 3 nos. **5808**
Papers on collective security submitted by members of the Eighth International Studies Conference and the General Study Conference on Collective Security, held in London June 3-8, 1935, under the auspices of the International Institute of Intellectual Cooperation.

Laux, Jeanne Kirk. "Les négociations Est-Ouest: le rôle des états Est-européens à la Conférence sur la sécurité et la coopération en Europe." (1975), 6 *Études Internationales* 478-500. **5809**

Legault, Albert. "La position stratégique du Canada et la décennie 1970." (1970-71), 26 *International Journal* 82-108. **5810**

Legault, Albert, and others. *La sécurité européenne dans les années 1970-1980.* Sillery, Québec: Centre québécois de relations internationales, Institut canadien des affaires internationales, Département de science politique de l'Université Laval, 1973. 167 p. (Collection Choix, 4) **5811**
Rapport d'un colloque organisé conjointement par le Département de science politique de l'Université Laval et le Centre québécois de relations internationales, tenu à Sainte-Foy du 3 au 5 mai 1973.

Lyon, Peter. "Substitutes for SEATO?" (1968-69), 24 *International Journal* 35-46. **5812**

MacKay, Robert A. "Anglo-Russian Alliance." (1942-43), 22 *Dalhousie Review* 337-343. **5813**

Mallory, James R. "What Kind of Post-War Security?" (1944-45), 14 *University of Toronto Quarterly* 90-100. **5814**

Mushkat, Marion. "Le tiers-monde et la sécurité internationale: proposition de recherches." (1978), 9 *Études Internationales* 539-562. **5815**

Ørvik, Nils. "Semi-Neutrality and Canada's Security." (1973-74), 29 *International Journal* 186-215. **5816**

Reford, Robert W. "Making Defence Policy in Canada." (1963-64), 23 *Behind the Headlines* No. 2 (23 p.) **5817**

Ritchie, Ronald S. "Problems of a Defence Policy for Canada." (1958-59), 14 *International Journal* 202-212. **5818**

Ropp, Theodore. "Politics, Strategy, and the Commitments of a Middle Power." *In* Deener, David R., ed., *Canada-United States Treaty Relations* (Durham, N.C., 1963), pp. 81-101. **5819**

Roussin, Marcel. "La sécurité continentale." (1952), 22 *Revue de l'Université d'Ottawa* 37-54. **5820**

Shortt, Adam. "The Significance of Locarno." (1925-26), 5 *Dalhousie Review* 435-443. **5821**

Simon, H. Paul. "The Warsaw Pact and East Germany - Provocation or Response?" (1964), 71 *Queen's Quarterly* 345-364. **5822**

Skilling, H. Gordon. "Who Runs This War?" (1942), 49 *Queen's Quarterly* 220-229. **5823**

Terry, John Charles. *Alliance Cohesion: NATO and the Warsaw Pact.* Vancouver, 1970. 121 leaves. **5824**
Thesis (M.A.), University of British Columbia, 1970.

Zacher, Mark W. *International Conflicts and Collective Security Organization, 1946-77: The United Nations, Organization of American States, Organization of African Unity, and Arab League.* New York: Praeger, 1979. x, 297 p. **5825**

2. NORTH AMERICAN DEFENCE

Arnell, J.C. "The Development of Joint North American Defence." (1970), 77 *Queen's Quarterly* 190-204. **5826**

Axworthy, Thomas Sidney. *Soldiers Without Enemies: A Political Analysis of Canadian Defence Policy, 1945-1975.* Kingston, 1979. viii, 962 leaves. **5827**
Thesis (Ph.D.), Queen's University, 1979. (National Library of Canada. Canadian Theses on Microfiche, No. 42398).

Barry, P.S. "The Prolific Pipeline: Finding Oil for Canol." (1977-78), 57 *Dalhousie Review* 205-223. **5828**

Beatty, David Pierce. *The Canada-United States Permanent Joint Board on Defense.* East Lansing, Mich., 1969. x, 356 leaves. **5829**
Thesis (Ph.D.), Michigan State University, 1969. Abstracted in (1969), 30 *Dissertation Abstracts International,* 2454-A. (University Microfilms, Ann Arbor, No. 69-20821).

"The Canadian-American Defence Agreement and Its Significance." (1940-41), 31 *Round Table* 347-357. **5830**
Refers to the Ogdensburg Declaration of August 18, 1940, concerning the establishment of a permanent Joint Defence Board (CTS 1940/14).

Carr, Wm. K. "Toward a Modernized North American Air Defence System." (1972-73), 2 *Canadian Defence Quarterly* 9-17 (No. 4) **5831**

Chu, Anthony Chun-Chang. *Canadian Attitudes to Continental Defence Co-operation with the United States, 1936-1960, as Expressed in Parliament.* Halifax, 1967. vi, 140 leaves. **5832**
Thesis (M.A.), Dalhousie University, 1967.

Conant, Melvin A. "Canada and Continental Defence: An American View." (1959-60), 15 *International Journal* 219-228. **5833**

Conant, Melvin A. *The Long Polar Watch; Canada and the Defense of North America.* New York: Harper, 1962. 204 p. **5834**
Published for the Council on Foreign Relations.
Reviews: H.S. Ferns in (1963), 39 *International Affairs* 479; R.J. Sutherland in (1961-62), 17 *International Journal* 441-443.

Conant, Melvin A. "A Perspective on Defence: The Canada-United States Compact." (1974-75), 33 *Behind the Headlines* No. 4 (36 p.) **5835**

Conference on 'Canada and the Northern Rim,' Queen's University, 1977. *Report from Conference on 'Canada and the Northern Rim.'* Kingston, Ont.: Centre for International Relations, Queen's University, 1977. vii, 144 leaves, map. (National Security Series, No. 6) **5836**
Conference held at Queen's University, Kingston, Ontario, March 31-April 2, 1977.

Cox, David. "Canadian-American Military Relations: Some Present Trends and Future Possibilities." (1980-81), 36 *International Journal* 91-116. **5837**

Critchley, W. Harriet. "Canadian Security Policy in the Arctic: The Context for the Future." *In Marine Transportation and High Arctic Development* (Ottawa, 1979), pp. 181-209. **5838**

Cuthbertson, Brian. *Canadian Military Independence in the Age of the Superpowers.* Toronto: Fitzhenry & Whiteside, c1977. 282 p. **5839**
Review: H. George Classen in (1979), 86 *Queen's Quarterly* 327-328.

Dickson, J.D. "NORAD: Some Historical Perspectives." (1972-73), 2 *Canadian Defence Quarterly* 18-22 (No. 4) **5840**

Diubaldo, Richard J. "The Canol Project in Canadian-American Relations." (1977), *Canadian Historical Association, Historical Papers* 178-195. **5841**

Dziuban, Stanley W. *Military Relations between the United States and Canada, 1939-1945.* Washington: Office of the Chief of Military History, Dept. of the Army, 1959. xv, 432 p. (United States Army in World War II; Special Studies) **5842**
Reviews: Douglas G. Anglin in (1961), 27 *Canadian Journal of Economics and Political Science* 401-403; Morris Zaslow in (1961), 42 *Canadian Historical Review* 61-63.

Dziuban, Stanley W. *United States Military Collaboration with Canada in World War II.* New York, 1955. 930 leaves. **5843**
Thesis (Ph.D.), Columbia University, 1955.

Gellner, John. "Canada in NATO and NORAD." (1966-67), 18 *Air University Review* 22-37 (Mar./Apr.) **5844**

Goldsman, Alvin. *Canadian-American Relations: Politico-Military Considerations Affecting the Development of a North American Air Defence Policy, 1945-1954.* Ottawa, 1975. 150 leaves. **5845**
Thesis (M.A.), Carleton University, 1975.

Granatstein, J.L. "The Conservative Party and the Ogdensburg Agreement." (1966-67), 22 *International Journal* 73-76. **5846**
Refers to the agreement with the United States establishing a permanent Joint Board on Defence, signed at Ogdensburg, N.Y., August 18, 1940 (CTS 1940/14).

Granatstein, J.L., and Cuff, Robert D. "The Hyde Park Declaration 1941: Origins and Significance." (1974), 55 *Canadian Historical Review* 59-80. **5847**

Refers to the declaration regarding co-operation for war production made on April 20, 1941, at Hyde Park, N.Y. (CTS 1941/14).

Gray, Colin S. "Canada and NORAD: A Study in Strategy." (1972), 31 *Behind the Headlines* Nos. 3-4 (21 p.) **5848**

Gray, Colin S. "Still on the Team: NORAD in 1973." (1973), 80 *Queen's Quarterly* 398-404. **5849**

Green, Colin A. "Some Thoughts on North American Air Defence." (1979-80), 9 *Canadian Defence Quarterly* 16-21 (No. 3) **5850**

Harrison, W.E.C. "Canadian-American Defence." (1949-50), 5 *International Journal* 189-200. **5851**

Hart, John Edward. *Canada and North American Defense, 1940-1965*. Eugene, Oreg., 1967. iv, 85 leaves. **5852**
Thesis (M.A.), University of Oregon, 1967. Abstracted in (1968), 6 *Dissertation Abstracts International* 130. (University Microfilms, Ann Arbor, No. M-1425).

Heeney, Arnold D.P. "Defence and North American Solidarity." (1963), 5 *University of Windsor Seminar on Canadian-American Relations, Proceedings* 107-113. **5853**

Hertzman, Lewis; Warnock, John W.; and Hockin, Thomas A. *Alliances and Illusions; Canada and the NATO-NORAD Question*. With an introduction by Dalton K. Camp. Edmonton: M.G. Hurtig, 1969. xxi, 154 p. **5854**
Reviews: Graham Murray in (1971), 4 *Canadian Journal of Political Science* 575-577; Roger Frank Swanson in (1970-71), 26 *International Journal* 286-288.

Hopkins, Oliver B. "The 'Canol' Project: Canada Provides Oil for the Allies." (1943), 27 *Canadian Geographical Journal* 238-249. **5855**

Jacobson, Harold K. "North American Security in the Nuclear-Missile Era." (1962), 4 *University of Windsor Seminar on Canadian-American Relations, Proceedings* 97-109. **5856**

Jockel, Joseph T. "Un Québec souverain et la défense de l'Amérique du Nord contre une attaque nucléaire." (1980), 11 *Études Internationales* 303-316. **5857**

Jockel, Joseph T. *The United States and Canadian Efforts at Continental Air Defense, 1945-1957*. Baltimore, Md., 1978. ii, 275 leaves. **5858**
Thesis (Ph.D.), Johns Hopkins University, 1978. Abstracted in (1978/79), 39 *Dissertation Abstracts International* 5709-A. (University Microfilms, Ann Arbor, No. 79-6466).

Jones, Dorothy Wendy. *Canada's Search for a Role in Continental Defence since 1945*. Ottawa, 1964. 127, xiii leaves, map. **5859**
Thesis (M.A.), Carleton University, 1964.

Keenleyside, Hugh L. "The Canada-United States Permanent Joint Board on Defence, 1940-1945." (1960-61), 16 *International Journal* 50-77. **5860**

Kirton, John J. *Canadian-American Integration in Defence Production 1941-1971: Causes, Courses, Consequences*. Ottawa, 1973. viii, 188, (8) leaves. **5861**
Research essay (M.A.), Carleton University, 1973.

Kirton, John J. *The Consequences of Integration: The Case of the Defence Production Sharing Agreements*. Ottawa: School of International Affairs, Carleton University, 1972. 30 p. (Carleton University. Norman Paterson School of International Affairs. Occasional Papers, 21) **5862**

La Fay, Howard. "DEW Line: Sentry of the Far North." (1958), 114 *National Geographic Magazine* 128-146. **5863**

Lloyd, Trevor. "Open Skies in the Arctic?" (1958-59), 14 *International Journal* 42-49. **5864**

Magnusson, N.L. "Surveillance and Control of Canadian Air Space." (1973-74), 3 *Canadian Defence Quarterly* 6-13 (No. 1) **5865**

Middlemiss, Danford W. *A Pattern of Co-operation: The Case of the Canadian-American Defence Production and Development Sharing Arrangements, 1958-1963.* Toronto, c1975. iv, 524 leaves. **5866**
Thesis (Ph.D.), University of Toronto, 1976. (National Library of Canada. Canadian Theses on Microfiche, No. 35067). Abstracted in (1978/79), 39 *Dissertation Abstracts International* 1823-A.

Moore, George Bissland. *The Effect on Canada of NORAD, the North American Air Defence Command.* Lawrenceville, N.J., 1967. 260 leaves. **5867**
Thesis (Ph.D.), University of Ottawa, 1967.

Pemberton, J.S.B. "Ogdensburg, Hyde Park - And After: Joint Economic Defence." (1940-41), 1 *Behind the Headlines* No. 7 (23 p.) **5868**

"The Permanent Joint Board on Defence Canada-United States." (1952), 4 *External Affairs* 371-374. **5869**

Pierce, S.D., and Plumptre, A.F.W. "Canada's Relations with War-Time Agencies in Washington." (1945), 11 *Canadian Journal of Economics and Political Science* 402-419. **5870**

Preston, Richard A. "The Nature of Canadian-American Defense Relations." (1964), 6 *University of Windsor Seminar on Canadian-American Relations, Proceedings* 139-148. **5871**

Rosen, S. McKee. *The Combined Boards of the Second World War; an Experiment in International Administration.* New York: Columbia University Press, 1951. 288 p. **5872**

Ross, Douglas A. "American Nuclear Revisionism, Canadian Strategic Interests, and the Renewal of NORAD." (1981-82), 39 *Behind the Headlines* No. 6 (35 p.) **5873**

Rossignol, Michel. *Canada and Continental Defence Co-operation: From Ogdensburg to AWACS.* Ottawa, 1974. 96, (19) leaves, maps. **5874**
Thesis (M.A.), University of Ottawa, 1974.

Schentag, T.R. "An Example of U.S.-Canadian Defence Cooperation: The Strait of Juan de Fuca Defences, 1939-1945." (1976-77), 6 *Canadian Defence Quarterly* 48-53 (No. 3) **5875**

Stacey, Charles P. "The Canadian-American Permanent Joint Board on Defence, 1940-1945." (1954), 9 *International Journal* 107-124. **5876**

Stacey, Charles P. "Twenty-One Years of Canadian-American Military Co-operation." *In* Deener, David R., ed., *Canada-United States Treaty Relations* (Durham, N.C., 1963), pp. 102-122. **5877**

Stewart, Patrick Grattan. *Canada in NORAD: A Small Power's Public Debate over an Alliance with a Great Power.* Fredericton, 1972 (c1973). v, 180 leaves. **5878**

Thesis (M.A.), University of New Brunswick, 1972. (National Library of Canada. Canadian Theses on Microfilm, No. 16288).

Sutherland, R.J. "The Strategic Significance of the Canadian Arctic." *In* Macdonald, Ronald St. John, ed., *The Arctic Frontier* (Toronto, 1966), pp. 256-278. **5879**

Swanson, Roger Frank. "An Analytical Assessment of the United States-Canadian Defense Issue Area." (1974), 28 *International Organization* 781-802. **5880**
Reprinted in Fox, Annette Baker, and others, *Canada and the United States* (New York, 1976), pp. 188-209.

Swanson, Roger Frank. *An Analytical Study of the United States-Canadian Defense Relationship as a Structure, Response and Process: Problems and Potentialities.* Washington, D.C., 1969. vii, 629 leaves. **5881**
Thesis (Ph.D.), American University, 1969.

Swanson, Roger Frank. "NORAD: Choices for Canada." (1972), *International Perspectives* 8-12 (Nov./Dec.) **5882**

Swanson, Roger Frank. "NORAD: Origins and Operations of Canada's Ambivalent Symbol." (1972), *International Perspectives* 3-8 (Nov./Dec.) **5883**

Talmadge, Marian, and Gilmore, Iris. *NORAD: The North American Air Defense Command.* New York: Dodd, Mead, 1967. 79 p., maps. **5884**

Thomas, David Martin. *Canada, NORAD, and Related Problems.* Calgary, 1968. ii, 130 leaves. **5885**
Thesis (M.A.), University of Calgary, 1968.

Wang, Erik B. "Sovereignty and Canada-U.S. Co-operation in North American Defence." *In* Macdonald, Ronald St. John, and others, *Canadian Perspectives on International Law and Organization* (Toronto, 1974), pp. 861-884. **5886**

Warnock, John W. *The Defence Policy of a Middle Power: Canada as a Case Study.* Washington, D.C., 1971. 436 leaves. **5887**
Thesis (Ph.D.), American University, 1971. Abstracted in (1971/72), 32 *Dissertation Abstracts International* 2167-A. (University Microfilms, Ann Arbor, No. 71-24841).

Warnock, John W. *Partner to Behemoth; the Military Policy of a Satellite Canada.* Toronto, Chicago: New Press, 1970. 340 p. **5888**

Willoughby, William R. "Canadian-American Defense Co-operation." (1951), 13 *Journal of Politics* 675-696. **5889**

Willoughby, William R. "The Genesis of Canadian-American Defence Cooperation." (1975-76), 5 *Canadian Defence Quarterly* 42-49 (No. 3) **5890**

3. NORTH ATLANTIC TREATY ORGANIZATION

See also *"Personal Jurisdiction (Military)" (p. 163),* and *"Regional Intergovernmental Organizations: Western Europe and North Atlantic" (p. 363).*

"The Atlantic Congress - The Next Ten Years of NATO." (1959), 11 *External Affairs* 307-315. **5891**

Barkway, Michael. "Canada's Changing Role in NATO Defence." (1958-59), 14 *International Journal* 99-110. **5892**

Bolles, Blair. "NATO - An American View." (1950-51), 6 *International Journal* 281-291. **5893**

Brown, George W. "The 'Atlantic Alliance' in Perspective." (1956-57), 12 *International Journal* 79-82. **5894**

Buchan, Alastair F. "NATO Today." (1959), 19 *Behind the Headlines* No. 1 (14 p.) **5895**

Burrows, Sir Bernard. "The Eurogroup: A Start Toward a Common Western European Defence System?" (1971-72), 1 *Canadian Defence Quarterly* 5-9 (No. 3) **5896**

Buteux, Paul. "Consultation and the Control of Nuclear Weapons in NATO: The Case of the Nuclear Planning Group." (1978), 50 *Canadian Political Science Association, Papers,* 52 p. **5897**

Buteux, Paul. "Theatre Nuclear Weapons and European Security." (1976), 48 *Canadian Political Science Association, Papers,* 43 p. **5898**

Buteux, Paul. "Theatre Nuclear Weapons and European Security." (1977), 10 *Canadian Journal of Political Science* 781-808. **5899**

"Canada and NATO." (1962), 14 *External Affairs* 311-318. **5900**

"Canada and NATO; Technical and Psychological Issues." (1962-63), 53 *Round Table* 154-158. **5901**

Cassie, Lawrence Peter. *NATO Rationale: Challenge of Détente.* London, Ont., 1976. viii, 215 leaves. **5902**
Thesis (M.A.), University of Western Ontario, 1976. (National Library of Canada. Canadian Theses on Microfiche, No. 28181).

Challener, Richard D. "NATO: Contrasts and Similarities in the Canadian and American Viewpoints." (1962), 4 *University of Windsor Seminar on Canadian-American Relations, Proceedings* 85-96. **5903**

Clokie, H. McD., and others. "Canada and the North Atlantic Treaty." (1949), 4 *International Journal* 244-249. **5904**

Conant, Melvin A. "Canada's Role in Western Defense." (1961-62), 40 *Foreign Affairs* 431-442. **5905**

Corry, J.A. "Canada, the North Atlantic Community, and NATO: Domestic Political Implications." (1952), 46 *Royal Society of Canada, Transactions* 27-35 (3d Ser., Sec. 2) **5906**

Cronin, Maureen P. *Canada and NATO.* Stanford, Calif., 1958. iii, 361 leaves. **5907**

Thesis (Ph.D.), Stanford University, 1958. (University Microfilms, Ann Arbor, No. 59-259).

Davis, Jerome D. *To the NATO Review: Constancy and Change in Canadian NATO Policy, 1949-1969*. Baltimore, Md., 1973. 381 leaves. **5908**
Thesis (Ph.D.), Johns Hopkins University, 1973. Abstracted in (1973/74), 34 *Dissertation Abstracts International* 389-A. (University Microfilms, Ann Arbor, No. 73-16639).

Ferguson, George V. "Canada and the 'Atlantic Alliance.'" (1956-57), 12 *International Journal* 83-89. **5909**

Fox, William Thornton Rickert, and Fox, Annette Baker. *NATO and the Range of American Choice*. New York: Columbia University Press, 1967. xii, 352 p. **5910**
Reviews: John W. Holmes in (1967), 33 *Canadian Journal of Economics and Political Science* 616-618; Robert S. Jordan in (1967-68), 23 *International Journal* 297-298.

Freedman, Max. "The Lisbon Conference." (1951-52), 7 *International Journal* 85-93. **5911**

Friedmann, Wolfgang G. "NATO - Shield of Freedom." (1952), 12 *Behind the Headlines* No. 4 (17 p.) **5912**

Friedmann, Wolfgang G. "New Tasks for NATO?" (1955-56), 11 *International Journal* 157-164. **5913**

Garigue, Philippe. "La politique de défense du Canada et ses priorités stratégiques." (1980), 13 *Canadian Journal of Political Science* 537-563. **5914**

Gellner, John. *Canada in NATO*. Toronto: Ryerson Press, 1970. 117 p. (Ryerson Paperbacks, 35) **5915**

Gellner, John. "Canada in NATO and NORAD." (1966-67), 18 *Air University Review* 22-37 (Mar./Apr.) **5916**

Gellner, John. "North America and NATO." (1964-65), 24 *Behind the Headlines* No. 1 (20 p.) **5917**
Also issued in French under title: "L'Amérique du Nord et l'OTAN."

Harrison, Eric. "Canada and the Atlantic Alliance." (1949-50), 56 *Queen's Quarterly* 113-132. **5918**

Hassner, Pierre. "'Plus c'est la même chose, plus ça change: réflexions sur les nouvelles dimensions de la crise Atlantique." (1982), 13 *Études Internationales* 473-496. **5919**

Hastings, Lionel Ismay. "Atlantic Alliance." (1954), 9 *International Journal* 79-86. **5920**

Hertzman, Lewis; Warnock, John W.; and Hockin, Thomas A. *Alliances and Illusions; Canada and the NATO-NORAD Question*. With an introduction by Dalton K. Camp. Edmonton: M.G. Hurtig, 1969. xxi, 154 p. **5921**
Reviews: Graham Murray in (1971), 4 *Canadian Journal of Political Science* 575-577; Roger Frank Swanson in (1970-71), 26 *International Journal* 286-288.

Hill, Roger J. *Political Consultation in NATO*. Toronto: Canadian Institute of International Affairs; Kingston, Ont.: Centre for International Studies, Queen's University, c1978. 143 p. (Wellesley Papers, 6) **5922**
Review: Jean-René Chotard in (1979), 10 *Études Internationales* 627-628.

Hill-Norton, Sir Peter. *No Soft Options: The Politico-Military Realities of NATO.* With a Foreword by J.M.A.H. Luns. Montreal: McGill-Queen's University Press, 1978. 172 p. **5923**
Review: R.B. Byers in (1980), 35 *International Journal* 413-414.

Holmes, John W. "Fearful Symmetry: The Dilemmas of Consultation and Coordination in the North Atlantic Treaty Organization." (1968), 22 *International Organization* 821-840. **5924**

"How NATO Works." (1953), 5 *External Affairs* 224-228. **5925**

"How NATO Works." (1957), 9 *External Affairs* 260-267. **5926**

Ignatieff, George. "NATO, Nuclear Weapons and Canada's Interests." (1978), *International Perspectives* 3-9 (Nov./Dec.) **5927**

Ignatieff, George. "NATO, Nuclear Weapons and Canada's Interests." (1981), *International Perspectives* 14-18 (Nov./Dec.) **5928**

Jordan, Robert S., and Newman, Parley W., Jr. "The Secretary-General of NATO and Multinational Political Leadership." (1974-75), 30 *International Journal* 732-757. **5929**

Klein, Jean. "La France, l'OTAN et la sécurité en Europe." (1977), 8 *Études Internationales* 80-99. **5930**

Knorr, Klaus E. "Canada and Western Defence." (1962-63), 18 *International Journal* 1-16. **5931**

Legault, Albert. *Deterrence and the Atlantic Alliance.* Translated by Archibald Day. Toronto: Canadian Institute of International Affairs, c1966. xv, 103 p. (Contemporary Affairs, No. 37) **5932**
Based on the author's thesis, Institut universitaire de hautes études internationales, Geneva, 1964, entitled: *Le concept de la dissuasion; ses exigences stratégiques et ses incidences sur la politique.*

Lentner, Howard H. "Foreign Policy Decision-Making: The Case of Canada and Nuclear Weapons." (1976-77), 29 *World Politics* 29-66. **5933**

Liesemer, Donald P. *The Nature of Canada's Crusade for NATO.* Lennoxville, Que., 1973. 202 leaves. **5934**
Thesis (M.A.), Bishop's University, 1973.

Ludz, Peter Christian, and others. *Dilemmas of the Atlantic Alliance: Two Germanys, Scandinavia, Canada, NATO and the EEC.* New York: Praeger, 1975. xi, 255 p. (Atlantic Institute Studies, 1) **5935**
Also part of Praeger Special Studies in International Politics and Government Series.

Lyon, Peyton V. "Beyond NATO?" (1973-74), 29 *International Journal* 268-278. **5936**

Lyon, Peyton V. *NATO as a Diplomatic Instrument.* Toronto: Atlantic Council of Canada, c1970. 38 p. **5937**
Slightly revised version of a paper prepared for the annual meeting of the Canadian Political Science Association, held at the University of Manitoba, Winnipeg, June 2, 1970.

Lyon, Peyton V. "NATO as a Diplomatic Instrument." (1970), 42 *Canadian Political Science Association, Papers,* 34 p. **5938**

MacDonald, Hugh. "Canada, NATO and the Neutron Bomb." (1979), *International Perspectives* 9-11 (Mar./Apr.)   **5939**

Marshall, Richard Eugene. *Canada in the Role of a Middle Power; a Study of Canadian Non-Military Collaboration Vis-à-Vis the Organization for Economic Cooperation and Development and the North Atlantic Treaty Organization, 1960-1967.* Philadelphia, 1971. xxxvi, 315 leaves.   **5940**
> Thesis (Ph.D.), University of Pennsylvania, 1971. Abstracted in (1972), 32 *Dissertation Abstracts International* 4694-A. (University Microfilms, Ann Arbor, No. 72-6202).

Martin, Kingsley. "NATO - A British View." (1950-51), 6 *International Journal* 292-299.   **5941**

Martin, L.W. "British Maritime Policy in Transition." (1967-68), 23 *International Journal* 541-550.   **5942**

Martin, Paul. "NATO's Value to Canada." (1967-68), 5 *Atlantic Community Quarterly* 177-185.   **5943**
> A summary of testimony given before the Senate Committee on External Relations, March 15, 1967.

Marwitz, Gustav Peter Axel. *The Effect of Prolonged Non-Crisis upon Alliance Cohesion in International Alliances: A Study of NATO and WTO from 1964 to 1973.* Ottawa, 1978. 1 vol.   **5944**
> Thesis (M.A.), Carleton University, 1978. Abstracted in (1979), 17 *Masters Abstracts* 222.

Marzari, Frank. "Deterrence: NATO's Military Strategy and the European Allies." (1968), 75 *Queen's Quarterly* 410-421.   **5945**

Mayo, H.B. "The Western Alliance - Ideological or Defensive?" (1954), 9 *International Journal* 87-95.   **5946**

Meisel, John. "A Note on NATO." (1952-53), 59 *Queen's Quarterly* 226-234.   **5947**

Moyse, Robert. "No Star for the Wise Men (Some Fiscal Problems of NATO Countries)." (1951-52), 7 *International Journal* 1-11.   **5948**

"NATO Re-Organization." (1951), 3 *External Affairs* 165-167.   **5949**

"NATO's Common Infrastructure Programme." (1953), 5 *External Affairs* 317-320.   **5950**

"North Atlantic Treaty Organization." (1950), 2 *External Affairs* 3-6.   **5951**

"North Atlantic Treaty Re-Organization." (1952), 4 *External Affairs* 130-134.   **5952**

"North Atlantic Treaty Signed at Washington." (1949), 1 *External Affairs* 3-24 (Apr.)   **5953**

Ørvik, Nils. "Canada and North Atlantic Security." *In* Bertram, Christoph, and Holst, Johan J., eds., *New Strategic Factors in the North Atlantic* (Oslo, 1977), pp. 74-85.   **5954**

Ørvik, Nils. "Canada's Security Interests and the European Commitments." (1982), 12 *Canadian Defence Quarterly* 8-17 (No. 2)   **5955**

Ørvik, Nils. "NATO: The Role of the Small Members." (1965-66), 21 *International Journal* 173-185.   **5956**

Pearson, Lester B. "Canada and the North Atlantic Alliance." (1948-49), 27 *Foreign Affairs* 369-378. **5957**

Pearson, Lester B. "NATO: Retrospect and Prospects." (1958-59), 14 *International Journal* 79-84. **5958**

Preston, Richard A. "NATO - A New Departure in International Politics." (1958-59), 65 *Queen's Quarterly* 365-376. **5959**

Ranger, Robin. "NATO's New Great Debate: Theatre Nuclear Force Modernization and Arms Control." (1980-81), 36 *International Journal* 556-574. **5960**

Reid, Escott. "The Birth of the North Atlantic Alliance." (1966-67), 22 *International Journal* 426-440. **5961**

Reid, Escott. "Canada and the Creation of the North Atlantic Alliance, 1948-1949." *In* Fry, Michael G., ed., *'Freedom and Change': Essays in Honour of Lester B. Pearson* (Toronto, 1975), pp. 106-135. **5962**

Reid, Escott. "Canada and the North Atlantic Alliance." (1969), 28 *Behind the Headlines* Nos. 5-6, pp. 13-16. **5963**

Reid, Escott. "Comparing Notes with the British on Negotiating the Atlantic Pact. (Review Article)." (1981), *International Perspectives* 16-19 (Sept./Oct.) **5964**

Reid, Escott. *Time of Fear and Hope: The Making of the North Atlantic Treaty, 1947-1949.* Toronto: McClelland and Stewart, c1977. 315 p. **5965**
Reviews: Robert Bothwell under title: "Canada and the Postwar Quest for Peace," in (1980), 87 *Queen's Quarterly* 709-712; John English in (1979), 60 *Canadian Historical Review* 378-379; Hubert Miles Gladwyn Jebb in (1977-78), 33 *International Journal* 248-261; Richard Jones in (1980), 11 *Études Internationales* 345-346; Richard Veatch in (1978), 11 *Canadian Journal of Political Science* 483-484.

Ritchie, Ronald S. "The Atlantic Condition." (1973-74), 29 *International Journal* 155-165. **5966**

Ritchie, Ronald S. *NATO; the Economics of an Alliance.* Toronto: Ryerson Press, 1956. 147 p. (Contemporary Affairs, No. 25) **5967**
Published under the auspices of the Canadian Institute of International Affairs.
Review: Harry C. Eastman in (1957), 12 *International Journal* 140-141.

Rotvand, Georges. "NATO - A French View." (1951-52), 7 *International Journal* 107-115. **5968**

Smith, Sydney E. "NATO and the Challenge of the Missile Age." (1957-58), 13 *International Journal* 165-174. **5969**

Spaak, Paul-Henri. "NATO and the Communist Challenge." (1957-58), 13 *International Journal* 243-250. **5970**

Spencer, Robert A. "Triangle into Treaty: Canada and the Origins of NATO." (1958-59), 14 *International Journal* 87-98. **5971**

Stewart, Beverley Ann. *Canadian Political Parties and NATO: A Companion of Key Policy Statements of the Liberal, Progressive Conservative and New Democratic Parties.* Kingston, 1979. 125 frames. **5972**
Thesis (M.A.), Queen's University, 1979. (National Library of Canada. Canadian Theses on Microfiche, No. 42527).

Taylor, Kenneth W. "Canada, the North Atlantic Community, and NATO: An

Economic View." (1952), 46 *Royal Society of Canada, Transactions* 19-25 (3d Ser., Sec. 2) **5973**

Thompson, Robert W. "Canada, a United Europe and NATO." (1956-57), 12 *International Journal* 220-226. **5974**

Traquair, Ramsay. "The Atlantic Alliance." (1949-50), 56 *Queen's Quarterly* 313-323. **5975**

Trotman, J.H. "NATO: Uncertainties and Palliatives." (1973-74), 3 *Canadian Defence Quarterly* 15-20 (No. 2) **5976**

Turner, Arthur C. *Bulwark of the West; Implications and Problems of NATO.* Toronto: Ryerson Press, 1953. v, 106 p. (Contemporary Affairs, No. 24) **5977**
Published under the auspices of the Canadian Institute of International Affairs.
Reviews: Marvin Gelber in (1953), 8 *International Journal* 206-208; Eric Harrison in (1953), 34 *Canadian Historical Review* 371-372; Athos G. Tsoutsos in (1953), 6 *Revue Hellénique de Droit International* 282.

Von Riekhoff, Harald. "The Changing Function of NATO." (1965-66), 21 *International Journal* 157-172. **5978**

Von Riekhoff, Harald. *NATO: Issues and Prospects.* Toronto: Canadian Institute of International Affairs, 1967. 170 p. (Contemporary Affairs, No. 38) **5979**
Reviews: Leslie Lipson in (1968-69), 24 *International Journal* 383; J.L. Richardson in (1967), *Australian Year Book of International Law* 286-287; Denis Stairs in (1968-69), 48 *Dalhousie Review* 415-417.

Warren, Reginald A. *Collective Choice and Patterns in NATO Defense Expenditures.* Ottawa, 1978. 165 leaves. **5980**
Research essay (M.A.), Carleton University, 1978.

Willoughby, William R. "Canada and the North Atlantic Pact." (1949), 25 *Virginia Quarterly Review* 429-442. **5981**

Wright, Gerald. "NATO in the New International Order." (1977-78), 36 *Behind the Headlines* No. 4 (27 p.) **5982**

XXII. CONDUCT OF ARMED CONFLICT (LAW OF WAR)

See also *"Control and Prevention of Conflict" (p. 419).*

A. Resort to War in General (Ius ad Bellum)

Alcock, Norman Z. *The War Disease.* Oakville, Ont.: CPRI Press, c1972. 238 p.
5983

Angus, Henry F. "Are We at War?" (1937-38), 17 *Dalhousie Review* 147-154.
5984

Burpee, Lawrence J. "Canada and the War." (1939-40), 46 *Queen's Quarterly* 385-398. **5985**
Canada declared war on Germany on September 10, 1939.

Colton, Timothy. "The 'New Biology' and the Causes of War." (1969), 2 *Canadian Journal of Political Science* 434-447. **5986**
Contains a résumé in French under title: "La 'nouvelle biologie' et les causes de la guerre."

Dean, Edgar Packard. "Canada at War." (1939-40), 18 *Foreign Affairs* 292-304.
5987
The entry of Canada into the Second World War was voted by the Canadian Parliament on September 9, 1939, and proclaimed by King George VI on September 10, 1939.

Gray, Colin S. "New Weapons and the Resort to Force." (1974-75), 30 *International Journal* 238-258. **5988**

Green, Leslie C. "Le rôle du Canada dans le développement du droit en matière de conflit armé." (1980), 11 *Études Internationales* 489-508. **5989**

Klaassen, Walter. "The Just War: A Summary." Oakville, Ont.: Canadian Peace Research Institute, 1978. 70 p. (Peace Research Reviews, Vol. 7, No. 6) **5990**

Lafleur, Eugene. "International Law and the Present War." (1915), 35 *Canadian Law Times* 40-51. **5991**

Morley, Jeremy D. "Approaches to the Law of Armed Conflict." (1971), 9 *Canadian Yearbook of International Law* 269-275. **5992**

Murphy, Ewell E., Jr. "The War Power of the Dominion." (1952), 30 *Canadian Bar Review* 791-806. **5993**

Pelland, Léo. "Saint Thomas d'Aquin et la guerre." (1935-36), 14 *Revue du Droit* 5-35. **5994**
Conférence faite aux Journées Thomistes d'Ottawa, le 6 juin 1935.

Preston, Richard A. "The Study of War and Its Causes: Part 1: The Long Search for the Right Approach." (1976-77), 6 *Canadian Defence Quarterly* 42-46 (No. 4) **5995**

"The Vindication of International Law." (1919), 55 *Canada Law Journal* 41-47. **5996**

Wallace, Michael D. "Alliance Polarization and War in the International System, 1815-1964: A Measurement Procedure and Some Preliminary Findings." (1972), 44 *Canadian Political Science Association, Papers*, 26 p. **5997**

B. Definition of War, Aggression, Etc.

Brown-John, Clive Lloyd. "The 1974 Definition of Aggression: A Query." (1977), 15 *Canadian Yearbook of International Law* 301-305. **5998**

Green, Leslie C. "Armed Conflict, War, and Self-Defence." (1956-57), 6 *Archiv des Völkerrechts* 387-438. **5999**

International Commission of Jurists. "Hungary and the Soviet Definition of Aggression." (1957), 7 *Chitty's Law Journal* 40-41, 52. **6000**

Nyiri, Nicolas A. *The Problem of Aggression in Contemporary Politics.* Kingston, 1966. 2 vols. (323 leaves) **6001**
Thesis (M.A.), Queen's University, 1966.

C. Conduct of War in General (Ius in Bello)

Eayrs, James George. "New Weapons in the Cold War: A Study of Recent Techniques in International Propaganda." (1951-52), 7 *International Journal* 36-47. **6002**

Fenrick, W.J. "The Law of Armed Conflict - The CUSHIE Weapons Treaty." (1981-82), 11 *Canadian Defence Quarterly* 25-30 (No. 1) **6003**

Fenrick, W.J. "New Developments in the Law concerning the Use of Conventional Weapons in Armed Conflict." (1981), 19 *Canadian Yearbook of International Law* 229-256. **6004**

Finlay, Robert Bannatyne. "Address (on Some of the Lessons of the War as to International Law)." (1919), 4 *Canadian Bar Association, Proceedings* 107-118. (See also pp. 89-105). **6005**

Green, Leslie C. "Aftermath of Vietnam: War Law and the Soldier." *In* Falk, Richard A., ed., *The Vietnam War and International Law* (Princeton, 1976), vol. 4, pp. 147-175. **6006**
See also the author's *Law and Society* (Leyden, 1975), pp. 397-432.

Green, Leslie C. "Canada's Role in the Development of the Law of Armed Conflict." (1980), 18 *Canadian Yearbook of International Law* 91-112. **6007**

Green, Leslie C. "The Man in the Field and the Maxim 'Ignorantia Juris Non Excusat.'" (1979-80), 10 *Revue de Droit, Université de Sherbrooke* 135-156. **6008**

Green, Leslie C. "The Man in the Field and the Maxim 'Ignorantia Juris Non Excusat.'" (1980-81), 19 *Archiv des Völkerrechts* 169-187. **6009**

Green, Leslie C. "The New Law of Armed Conflict." (1977), 15 *Canadian Yearbook of International Law* 3-41. **6010**

Green, Leslie C. "The Role of Legal Advisers in the Armed Forces." (1978), 26 *Chitty's Law Journal* 18-24. **6011**
Also printed in (1977), 7 *Israel Yearbook on Human Rights* 154-165.

"International Law - The Spy Mania." (1912), 48 *Canada Law Journal* 378-379. **6012**

"The Laws of War." (1905), 41 *Canada Law Journal* 818-820. **6013**

Read, John E. "Modern Warfare and the Laws of War." (1922-23), 2 *Dalhousie Review* 485-489. **6014**

Shea, Albert A., and Estorick, Eric. "Canada and the Short-Wave War." (1942), 3 *Behind the Headlines* No. 1 (36 p.) **6015**

"Some Points in International Law in War Time." (1914), 50 *Canada Law Journal* 612-614. **6016**

Stacey, Charles P. "Is 'Civilized Warfare' Possible?" (1930), 37 *Queen's Quarterly* 105-121. **6017**

Wolfe, J.P. "War and Military Operations." *In* Macdonald, Ronald St. John, and others, *Canadian Perspectives on International Law and Organization* (Toronto, 1974), pp. 620-645. **6018**

D. Use of Weapons of Mass Extermination

See also *"Arms Control and Disarmament" (p. 422)*.

Basmajian, J.V. "Nuclear Warfare and Morality." (1960-61), 67 *Queen's Quarterly* 329-336. **6019**

"Canadian Scientists Refute Germ Warfare Charges." (1952), 4 *External Affairs* 249-252. **6020**

Conant, Melvin A. "Canada and Nuclear Weapons: An American View." (1962-63), 18 *International Journal* 207-210. **6021**

Gotlieb, Allan E. "Nuclear Weapons in Outer Space." (1965), 3 *Canadian Yearbook of International Law* 3-35. **6022**

Ignatieff, George. "Agents of Chemical and Biological Warfare: Canadian Government Policy." (1970), 22 *External Affairs* 170-174. **6023**

Onwuku, Ralph Iheanyi. *Chemical and Biological Warfare (CBW) and International Law.* Edmonton, 1971. (vii), 137 leaves. **6024**
Thesis (M.A.), University of Alberta, 1971.

Pace, F.C. "Radioactive Fallout from Atomic Weapons." (1956), 16 *Behind the Headlines* No. 5 (11 p.) **6025**

Ranger, Robin. *The Canadian Contribution to the Control of Chemical and Biological Warfare.* Toronto: Canadian Institute of International Affairs, 1976. 66 p. (Wellesley Papers, 5) **6026**

Ross, Patricia Dorothy. *Analysis of the Decision to Use the Atomic Bomb Against Japan.* Vancouver, 1976. xi, 190 leaves. **6027**
Thesis (M.Sc.), University of British Columbia, 1976. (National Library of Canada. Canadian Theses on Microfiche, No. 28793).

Ryan, Stuart. "On Nuclear Warfare." (1962), 69 *Queen's Quarterly* 165-176. **6028**

E. Sea Warfare

"The Declaration of London." (1911), 31 *Canadian Law Times* 441-446. **6029**

Hodgins, Frank E. "Maritime War Rights." (1896), 16 *Canadian Law Times* 77-89. **6030**

"International Law in Relation to Indirect Blockade." (1919), 55 *Canada Law Journal* 323-335. **6031**

Maxey, Edwin. "The Rights of Merchant Vessels." (1916), 36 *Canadian Law Times* 699-707. **6032**

McCurdy, C.A. "The Arming of Merchantmen." (1914), 34 *Canadian Law Times* 1201-1204. **6033**

Morse, Charles. "International Law - Floating Mines." (1906), 5 *Canadian Law Review* 412. **6034**

Power, W. Kent. "Search and Seizure at Sea." (1938-40), 3 *Alberta Law Quarterly* 182-188. **6035**

Stacey, Charles P. "The War: Blockade and Counter-Blockade." (1939-40), 9 *University of Toronto Quarterly* 270-281. **6036**

Wilkinson, W.E. "The Law Administered by Prize Courts." (1916), 36 *Canadian Law Times* 530-543. **6037**

CONDUCT OF ARMED CONFLICT (LAW OF WAR)

F. Air and Space Warfare

See also *"Military Aircraft" (p. 310)*.

DeSaussure, Hamilton. "Belligerent Air Operations and the 1977 Geneva Protocol I." (1979), 4 *Annals of Air and Space Law* 459-482. **6038**

DeSaussure, Hamilton. *International Law and Aerial Warfare.* Montreal, 1953. vii, 188 leaves. **6039**
Thesis (LL.M.), McGill University, 1953.

DeSaussure, Hamilton. "Recent Developments in the Laws of Air Warfare." (1976), 1 *Annals of Air and Space Law* 33-47. **6040**

Gotlieb, Allan E. "Nuclear Weapons in Outer Space." (1965), 3 *Canadian Yearbook of International Law* 3-35. **6041**

Green, Leslie C. "Aerial Considerations in the Law of Armed Conflict." (1980), 5 *Annals of Air and Space Law* 89-117. **6042**

Heinselman, Robert E. "Aerial Warfare." (1913), 33 *Canadian Law Times* 741-748. **6043**

Tager, Thomas Edward. *The Legality of Military Use of Outer Space.* Montreal, 1967 (c1968). 71 leaves. **6044**
Thesis (LL.M.), McGill University, 1967. (National Library of Canada. Canadian Theses on Microfilm, No. 2258).

Ward, Donald William S. *The Law of Military Aircraft in War and Peace.* Montreal, 1970 (c1971). iii, 99 leaves. **6045**
Thesis (LL.M.), McGill University, 1970. (National Library of Canada. Canadian Theses on Microfilm, No. 7326).

Wine, Joseph Raymond. *Aerial Warfare and International Law.* Montreal, 1954. iv, 156 leaves. **6046**
Thesis (LL.M.), McGill University, 1954.

G. Humanitarian Law (Prisoners of War, Etc.)

Bossy, Sanda. "The International Red Cross." (1951-52), 7 *International Journal* 204-212. **6047**

Braithwaite, Max. "Beginning of the Canadian Red Cross." (1952), 44 *Canadian Geographical Journal* 138-139. **6048**

Canada. Dept. of National Defence. *Manual of the Geneva Conventions of August 12, 1949.* Ottawa: Queen's Printer, 1968. 1 vol. (various pagings) (CFP, 122) **6049**

Canada. Royal Commission on Illegal Warfare Claims and for Return of Sequestrated Property in Necessitous Cases. *Reparations, 1930-1931; Report: Maltreatment of Prisoners of War.* Errol M. McDougall, Commissioner. Ottawa: King's Printer, 1932. 332 p. **6050**

Corcelle, Charles. "Les besoins de main-d'oeuvre de l'économie française et les prisonniers de guerre allemands." (1947-48), 23 *Actualité Économique* 486-499.
6051

Green, Leslie C. "The Contemporary Law of Armed Conflict and the Protection of Human Rights." *In* Gall, Gerald L., ed., *Civil Liberties in Canada: Entering the 1980s* (Toronto, c1982), pp. 166-190.
6052

Green, Leslie C. "The Geneva Humanitarian Law Conference 1975." (1975), 13 *Canadian Yearbook of International Law* 295-305.
6053

Green, Leslie C. "Human Rights and the Law of Armed Conflict." (1980), 10 *Israel Yearbook on Human Rights* 9-37.
6054

Green, Leslie C. "Humanitarian Law and the Man in the Field." (1976), 14 *Canadian Yearbook of International Law* 96-115.
6055

Green, Leslie C. "Rewriting the Laws of War: The Geneva Protocols of 1977." (1977), *International Perspectives* 36-43 (Nov./Dec.)
6056

Green, Leslie C. "War Law and the Medical Profession." (1979), 17 *Canadian Yearbook of International Law* 159-205.
6057

Green, Leslie C. "War Law and the Medical Profession." (1979), 3 *Legal Medical Quarterly* 175-196.
6058

"Humanitarian Law of Armed Conflict: Red Cross Conference, Geneva." (1971), 23 *External Affairs* 373-374.
6059

"International Law - Prisoners of War - Criminal Responsibility. Four Cases: *Rex* v. *Krebs*, (1943) 4 D.L.R. 553; *Rex* v. *Shindler*, (1944) 82 Can.C.C. 206; *Rex* v. *Brosig*, (1945) 2 D.L.R. 232; *Rex* v. *Kaehler and Stolski*, (1945) 83 Can.C.C. 353; (1945) 1 W.W.R. 566. (Case Note)." (1945), 23 *Canadian Bar Review* 451-452, 524.
6060

"International Protection for the Victims of War." (1949), 1 *External Affairs* 3-10 (July)
6061

"The International Red Cross Conference in Toronto." (1952), 4 *External Affairs* 298-303.
6062

Kelly, John Joseph. "Intelligence and Counter-Intelligence in German Prisoner of War Camps in Canada During World War II." (1978-79), 58 *Dalhousie Review* 285-294.
6063

Kelly, John Joseph. *The Prisoner of War Camps in Canada, 1939-1947.* Windsor, 1976. xiii, 246 leaves, maps.
6064
Thesis (M.A.), University of Windsor, 1976.

McMurrich, J. Playfair. "The Origins of the Red Cross Movement." (1917), 16 *University Magazine* 204-215.
6065

Miller, D.M. "Next Stage in International Humanitarian Law." (1972), *International Perspectives* 51-57 (Nov./Dec.)
6066

Murphy, Margaret. "The Red Cross International Committee." (1946), 32 *Canadian Geographical Journal* 113-115.
6067

Partsch, Karl Josef. "The Geneva Conventions and Human Rights in Armed Conflicts." (1973), 2 *Canadian Council on International Law, Proceedings* 109-121.
6068
This address is followed by a general discussion (pp. 122-129).

Paslawski, Lou. "The Position of War Prisoners." (1943), 2 *School of Law Review* 3 (No. 1)   **6069**

Silverburg, Sanford R. "Sanctuary and Irregular Warfare: Contortive International Law." (1980), 28 *Chitty's Law Journal* 195-210.   **6070**

Simpson, James M. "Making Humanitarian Law Applicable to Non-International Armed Conflicts." (1971-72), 1 *Canadian Defence Quarterly* 22-28 (No. 2)   **6071**

Wolfe, J.P. "Changes in the Law of Armed Conflict." (1978-79), 8 *Canadian Defence Quarterly* 16-21, 48 (No. 3)   **6072**
Refers to two additional protocols to the Geneva conventions of August 12, 1949, opened for signature at Berne, December 12, 1977.

H. Effects of War

1. GENERAL

Carman, F.A. "Alarming the Foreign Investor." (1927-28), 7 *Dalhousie Review* 23-28.   **6073**

"Contracts and the Outbreak of Peace." (1938-39), 8 *Fortnightly Law Journal* 136-137.   **6074**

"Contracts with the Enemy." (1938-39), 8 *Fortnightly Law Journal* 135-136. **6075**

Corcoran, James I.W. "The Trading with the Enemy Act: The Impact of the Amended Foreign Assets Control Regulations on Canadian Corporations Owned by Americans." (1970), 16 *McGill Law Journal* 460-487.   **6076**

Corcoran, James I.W. "The Trading with the Enemy Act and the Controlled Canadian Corporation." (1968), 14 *McGill Law Journal* 174-208.   **6077**

"The Effect of War on Contracts." (1938-39), 8 *Fortnightly Law Journal* 119-121.   **6078**

2. ENEMY ALIENS

Boudreau, Joseph A. "1914-1919: Interning Canada's 'Enemy Aliens.'" (1974-75), 2 *Canada: An Historical Magazine* 15-27 (No. 1)   **6079**

"Capacity of Enemy Aliens to Sue." (1944-45), 14 *Fortnightly Law Journal* 74-75.   **6080**

Carter, David J. *Behind Canadian Barbed Wire: Alien, Refugee and Prisoner of War Camps in Canada, 1914-1946.* Calgary: Tumbleweed Press, 1980. x, 334 p., map.   **6081**

"Seizure of Property of Enemy Aliens." (1943-44), 13 *Fortnightly Law Journal* 312-314.   **6082**

I. Military Occupation

Gilmore, William C. *Belligerent Occupation, Public Property and War Crimes in Namibia: A New Role for International Law.* Ottawa: Norman Paterson School of International Affairs, Carleton University, 1976. 24 p. (Current Comment, 11) **6083**

Green, Leslie C. "Law and Administration in Present-Day Japan." (1948), 1 *Current Legal Problems* 188-205. **6084**

Green, Leslie C. "The New Regime in Western Germany." (1949), 3 *World Affairs* 368-377 (N.S.) **6085**

Nisan, Mordechai. *Israeli Control of the Administered Territories Acquired in June, 1967.* Montreal, 1975 (c1976). v, 456 leaves. **6086**
   Half-title: *Israeli Control of Territories Acquired in June, 1967.* Thesis (Ph.D.), McGill University, 1975. (National Library of Canada. Canadian Theses on Microfiche, No. 27219).

"The Occupation of Germany (1945-1951)." (1951), 3 *External Affairs* 333-338. **6087**

"Some Aspects of the Occupation of Japan." (1951), 3 *External Affairs* 305-308. **6088**

J. Termination of War, Peace Treaties, Armistices

Canada. Parliament. *Lausanne Conference and Treaty.* Ottawa, 1924. 11 p. (Canada. Parliament, 1924. Sessional Papers, No. 232) **6089**
   Refers to the treaty of peace with Turkey of July 24, 1923 (28 LNTS 12).

"Canadian Accession to the Austrian State Treaty." (1959), 11 *External Affairs* 136-139. **6090**
   Treaty signed at Vienna on May 15, 1955 (CTS 1959/14).

Chettle, H.F. "British Monuments on the Scenes of the Great War." (1934-35), 14 *Dalhousie Review* 444-453. **6091**

Cohen, Bernard Lande. "Is the Versailles Treaty Responsible?" (1935-36), 5 *University of Toronto Quarterly* 334-347. **6092**

Colard, Daniel. "Vers un nouvel ordre politique international: le traité de paix et d'amitié sino-japonais du 12 août 1978." (1980), 11 *Études Internationales* 3-42. **6093**

Ebenstein, William. "Common Sense on the German Problem." (1945), 25 *Dalhousie Review* 284-291. **6094**

Glazebrook, G.P. de T. "The Peace Treaties of 1919-1920." (1929), 36 *Queen's Quarterly* 618-635. **6095**

Glazebrook, G.P. de T. "The Settlement of Germany." (1946-47), 2 *International Journal* 132-143. **6096**
Includes "Canadian submission on the German Peace Settlement."

Green, Leslie C. "Making Peace with Japan." (1952), 6 *Year Book of World Affairs* 1-35. **6097**

Hilliker, John F. "No Bread at the Peace Table: Canada and the European Settlement, 1943-7." (1980), 61 *Canadian Historical Review* 69-86. **6098**

Hiscocks, C. Richard. "Austrian Prospects." (1952-53), 8 *International Journal* 240-248. **6099**

Lee, Chae-Jin. "The Making of the Sino-Japanese Peace and Friendship Treaty." (1979), 52 *Pacific Affairs* 420-445. **6100**

Martin, Charles E. "Prospects for a Japanese Peace Treaty." (1950-51), 6 *International Journal* 13-19. **6101**

McInnis, Edgar. "The German 'Peace Contract': A Brief Analysis." (1951-52), 7 *International Journal* 184-188. **6102**

Oelofsen, Pieter Daniel. *Armistice and the End of War.* Montreal, 1963. v, 165 leaves. **6103**
Thesis (M.C.L.), McGill University, 1963.

Pearson, Lester B. "The Japanese Peace Treaty." (1951), 3 *External Affairs* 330-332. **6104**

Robinson, H. Lukin. "On Terms of Peace with Germany." (1945), 5 *Behind the Headlines* No. 5 (25 p.) **6105**

Samuels, Joseph W. "Middle East Peace: An Examination of Legal Obligation." (1979-80), 10 *Revue de Droit, Université de Sherbrooke* 68-88. **6106**

"Termination of the State of War with Germany." (1951), 3 *External Affairs* 292. **6107**
The state of war between Canada and Germany was terminated by royal proclamation on July 10, 1951.

Williams, R. Hodder. "The Literature of the Peace Conference." (1921), 2 *Canadian Historical Review* 155-171. **6108**

K. Reparations and War Claims

Angus, Henry F. "Beating Swords into Ploughshares: A Suggested Way to Salvage the International War Debts." (1935-36), 15 *Dalhousie Review* 265-274. **6109**

Briquet, Pierre E. "Reparations and Disarmament: The French Point of View." (1931-32), 39 *Journal of the Canadian Bankers' Association* 426-444. **6110**

Canada. Royal Commission on Illegal Warfare Claims and for Return of Sequestrated Property in Necessitous Cases. *Reparations; the Report of the Royal Commissioner, etc.* Ottawa: King's Printer, 1928. 2 vols. **6111**

James Friel, Commissioner. Report dated December 14, 1927. Index of names issued separately (24 p.). See also its *Interim Report* (1931. 172 p.); *Special Report upon Armenian Claims* (1931. 12 p.); *Report on Maltreatment of Prisoners of War* (1932. 332 p.); *Supplementary Report* (1931. 34 p.); *Further Report* (1933. 217 p.), and *Final Report,* March 4, 1933 (211 p.).- See also the index of names and addresses of claimants which appears in volumes I and II of the reparations report, dated December 14, 1927, arranged alphabetically according to provinces, cities and towns (Ottawa, F.A. Acland, 1928).

Canada. War Claims Commission (World War II). *A Consolidation of the Reports of the Commission with Related Documents and Including Cases to Illustrate the Principles and Procedures of Adjudication.* Ottawa: Queen's Printer, 1970. viii, 728 p. **6112**

Also issued in French under title: *Recueil des rapports de la Commission assortis de documents pertinents et de causes mettant en lumière les principes et la procédure d'adjudication.* Commission des réclamations de guerre, Seconde guerre mondiale (1970, c1972. viii, 754 p.).

Goldenberg, H. Carl. "Reparations and the World Crisis." (1931-32), 39 *Journal of the Canadian Bankers' Association* 174-180. **6113**

Gottlieb, Manuel. "The Reparations Problem Again." (1950), 16 *Canadian Journal of Economics and Political Science* 22-41. **6114**

Green, Leslie C. "Civilian War Dead and Reparations Against an Enemy." (1963), 1 *Philippine International Law Journal* 384-405. **6115**

Redler, Richard. "Some Aspects of European Reconstruction." (1943-44), 13 *University of Toronto Quarterly* 367-381. **6116**

L. Civil War and Guerrilla Warfare

See also *"National Liberation Movements, Etc." (p. 89).*

Carpenter, Jacqueline Mary. *Revolutionary Guerrilla Warfare, the Primacy of Politics.* Kingston, 1970. iv, 110 leaves. **6117**
Half-title: *Guerrilla Warfare.* Thesis (M.A.), Queen's University, 1970. (National Library of Canada. Canadian Theses on Microfilm, No. 6324).

Green, Leslie C. "The Indian National Army Trials." (1948), 11 *Modern Law Review* 47-69. **6118**
Also printed in (1947), 1 *Indian Law Review* 290-313.

Green, Leslie C. "The Status of Mercenaries in International Law." (1978-79), 9 *Manitoba Law Journal* 201-246. **6119**
Also printed in (1978), 8 *Israel Yearbook on Human Rights* 9-62.

Hoar, Victor. "Canadians in the Spanish Civil War: The Way Over." (1968-69), 48 *Dalhousie Review* 100-113. **6120**

International Commission of Jurists. "The Hungarian Situation in the Light of the Geneva Conventions." (1957), 7 *Chitty's Law Journal* 64-67. **6121**

Krauss, Michel. "Les conflits internes et les états-tiers: à la recherche de l'état du droit." (1979-80), 10 *Revue de Droit, Université de Sherbrooke* 1-65. **6122**

Lockwood, George H. "Report on the Trial of Mercenaries: Luanda, Angola, June, 1976." (1976-77), 7 *Manitoba Law Journal* 183-202. **6123**

"The Revolution in Portugal and International Law." (1910), 46 *Canada Law Journal* 649-650. **6124**

Ryan, Selwyn D. "Civil Conflict and External Involvement in Eastern Africa." (1972-73), 28 *International Journal* 465-510. **6125**

Saint-Louis, Michel A. "Connaissance du problème indochinois." (1973), 6 *Revue de l'Université de Moncton* 3-8. **6126**

Saint-Louis, Michel A. "Connaissance du problème indochinois: la deuxième guerre du Vietnam." (1974), 7 *Revue de l'Université de Moncton* 117-135 (no 1)
6127

XXIII. NEUTRALITY

See also *"Permanently Neutral States" (p. 87).*

Brecher, Michael. "Neutralism: An Analysis." (1961-62), 17 *International Journal* 224-236. **6128**

Carpenter, Gloria. "The Value of Neutrality." (1944), 2 *School of Law Review* 6 (No. 2) **6129**

Davis, George B. "Neutrality." (1914), 34 *Canadian Law Times* 1191-1200. **6130**

Ionescu, Ghita. "The Austrian State Treaty and Neutrality in Eastern Europe." (1967-68), 23 *International Journal* 408-420. **6131**
The treaty was signed on May 15, 1955 (CTS 1959/14).

Jensen, Kurt F. *Scandinavian Neutrality, 1938-1940.* Edmonton, 1971. v, 177 leaves. **6132**
Thesis (M.A.), University of Alberta, 1971.

MacKay, Robert A. "Revision of Neutrality." (1937-38), 2 *University of Toronto Law Journal* 132-136. **6133**

MacKay, Robert A., and Stanfield, R.L. "A New American Neutrality." (1936-37), 16 *Dalhousie Review* 199-208. **6134**

McConnell, William H. "Neutrality as a 'Balancing' Device: An Unaligned Course for Canada?" (1972-73), 37 *Saskatchewan Law Review* 4-22. **6135**

Reid, Escott. "Can Canada Remain Neutral?" (1935-36), 15 *Dalhousie Review* 135-148. **6136**

Sandwell, B.K. "The Neutrality Act." (1941-42), 48 *Queen's Quarterly* 414-419. **6137**

Trotter, Reginald G. "America's 'New Neutrality.' " (1936-37), 43 *Queen's Quarterly* 68-73. **6138**

Wengler, Wilhelm. "The Meaning of Neutrality in Peacetime." (1964), 10 *McGill Law Journal* 369-379. **6139**

XXIV. INTERNATIONAL CRIMINAL LAW

A. General

Blishchenko, I., and Shdanov, N. "The Problem of International Criminal Jurisdiction." (1976), 14 *Canadian Yearbook of International Law* 283-291. **6140**

Castel, Jean-Gabriel, and Williams, Sharon A. *International Criminal Law; Cases, Notes and Materials.* 1st ed. Toronto: York University, Osgoode Hall Law School, 1974. 756 p. **6141**
On cover: Castel's International Criminal Law 1974-75.

David, Jacques. "La Commission internationale de police criminelle." (1948-49), 3 *Revue de l'Université Laval* 299-308. **6142**

Gingold, Edward Gerald. "An International Penal Code: Why, How, and When." (1976), 24 *Chitty's Law Journal* 350-357. **6143**

Green, Leslie C. "International Crimes and the Legal Process." (1980), 29 *International and Comparative Law Quarterly* 567-584. **6144**

Green, Leslie C. "An International Criminal Code - Now?" (1976-77), 3 *Dalhousie Law Journal* 560-579. **6145**

Green, Leslie C. "Jurisdictional Issues in International Criminal Law." (1979), 27 *Chitty's Law Journal* 356-360. **6146**

Green, Leslie C. "New Trends in International Criminal Law." (1981), 11 *Israel Yearbook on Human Rights* 9-40. **6147**

"International Law and Canadian Criminal Practice / Le droit international et la pratique canadienne du droit criminel." (1981), 10 *Canadian Council on International Law, Proceedings,* 53-84. **6148**
This is a panel. Chairman: S. Williams.
Contents: "Illegal Arrest, Irregular Rendition and Extradition," by Brian H. Greenspan (pp. 53-67).- "International Conventions on Terrorism and Canadian Criminal Law," by Jason Reiskind (pp. 68-78).- Discussion (pp. 79-84).

Kos-Rabcewicz-Zubkowski, Ludwik. "The Creation of an International Criminal Court." *In* Bassiouni, M. Cherif, ed., *International Terrorism and Political Crimes* (Springfield, Ill., 1975), pp. 519-536. **6149**

Kos-Rabcewicz-Zubkowski, Ludwik. "La création d'une cour pénale internationale et l'administration internationale de la justice." (1977), 15 *Canadian Yearbook of International Law* 253-275. **6150**

Kos-Rabcewicz-Zubkowski, Ludwik. "International Criminal Law: Second Interim Report of the Committee." (1978), 58 *International Law Association, Report of Conference* 473-485. **6151**

Kos-Rabcewicz-Zubkowski, Ludwik. "International Criminal Law: Third and Fourth Interim Reports of the Committee, with Appendices." (1980), 59 *International Law Association, Report of Conference* 400-454. **6152**

Kos-Rabcewicz-Zubkowski, Ludwik. "Towards a Feasible International Criminal Court." (1971), 5 *World Law Review* 392-398. **6153**

Low, D. Martin. "The Fifth U.N. Congress on the Prevention of Crime and the Treatment of Offenders." *In* Macdonald, Ronald St. John, and others, *The International Law and Policy of Human Welfare* (Alphen aan den Rijn, 1978), pp. 659-674. **6154**

Marcoux, Laurent, Jr. "Protection from Arbitrary Arrest and Detention under International Law." (1982), 5 *Boston College International and Comparative Law Review* 345-376. **6155**

Radzinowicz, Leon. "International Collaboration in Criminal Science." (1941-42), 4 *University of Toronto Law Journal* 307-337. **6156**

Sinha, S. Prakash. "The Position of the Individual in an International Criminal Law." *In* Bassiouni, M. Cherif, ed., *A Treatise on International Criminal Law* (Springfield, Ill., 1973), vol. 1, pp. 122-143. **6157**

Williams, Sharon A. "Criminal Law - Jurisdiction - Illegal Arrest - Due Process - Violation of International Law. (Comments)." (1975), 53 *Canadian Bar Review* 404-424. **6158**

Williams, Sharon A. *International Criminal Law.* 3d rev. ed. Toronto: York University, Osgoode Hall Law School, 1978. 950 p. **6159**
Review: Leslie C. Green in (1978), 56 *Canadian Bar Review* 749-750.

Williams, Sharon A., and Castel, Jean-Gabriel. *Canadian Criminal Law: International and Transnational Aspects.* Toronto: Butterworths, 1981. xxx, 513 p., maps. **6160**
Review: Gerald F. FitzGerald in (1982), 60 *Canadian Bar Review* 762-767.

Williams, Sharon A., and Castel, Jean-Gabriel. *International Criminal Law; Cases, Notes and Materials.* 2d rev. ed. Toronto: York University, Osgoode Hall Law School, 1975. xiv, 980 p. **6161**
Reviews: Gerald F. FitzGerald in (1976), 54 *Canadian Bar Review* 191-192; Leslie C. Green in (1975), 13 *Canadian Yearbook of International Law* 444-446.

INTERNATIONAL CRIMINAL LAW

B. War Crimes

1. GENERAL

Bellot, Hugh H.L. "War Crimes and War Criminals." (1916), 36 *Canadian Law Times* 754-768. **6162**
Continued in (1917), 37 *Canadian Law Times* 9-22.

Cutler, Phil. "The Eichmann Trial." (1961), 4 *Canadian Bar Journal* 352-371. **6163**

Garstin, L.H. "Recent International Practices." (1946-47), 26 *Dalhousie Review* 319-330. **6164**

Gibbon, W.A. "Some Thoughts on the Eichmann Incident and the International Rule of Law." (1960), 32 *Manitoba Bar News* 79-88. **6165**

Goldenberg, Sydney L. "Crimes Against Humanity: 1945-1970." (1971), 10 *Western Ontario Law Review* 1-55. **6166**

Green, Leslie C. "Aspects juridiques du procès Eichmann." (1963), 9 *Annuaire Français de Droit International* 150-190. **6167**

Green, Leslie C. "Canadian Law and the Punishment of War Crimes." (1980), 28 *Chitty's Law Journal* 249-254. **6168**

Green, Leslie C. "The Eichmann Case." (1960), 23 *Modern Law Review* 507-515. **6169**

Green, Leslie C. "Legal Issues of the Eichmann Trial." (1962-63), 37 *Tulane Law Review* 641-684. **6170**

Green, Leslie C. "The Maxim *Nullum Crimen Sine Lege* and the Eichmann Trial." (1962), 38 *British Year Book of International Law* 457-471. **6171**

Green, Leslie C. "Political Offences, War Crimes and Extradition." (1962), 11 *International and Comparative Law Quarterly* 329-354. **6172**

Green, Leslie C. "The Trials of Some Minor War Criminals." (1950), 4 *Indian Law Review* 249-275. **6173**

Horowitz, Irving Louis. "A Postscript to Genocide." (1980), 28 *Chitty's Law Journal* 90-95. **6174**

Laing, Lionel H. "A Significant Development in International Law." (1945), 23 *Canadian Bar Review* 754-758. **6175**

Maranda, Jean-Gabriel. "Le génocide: du respect de la vie humaine en droit des gens." (1952-53), 3 *Thémis* 5-13. **6176**

McTaggart, Don. "War Crimes and Canada." (1946), 4 *Advocate* 52-53. **6177**

Munro, Hector A. "War Criminals and Neutrals." (1944-45), 14 *Fortnightly Law Journal* 24-27. **6178**

Myerson, Moses Hyman. *Germany's War Crimes and Punishment, the Problem of Individual and Collective Criminality.* Toronto: Macmillan of Canada, 1944. x, 272 p. **6179**
Review: George A. Johnston in (1945), 23 *Canadian Bar Review* 352.

Schick, F.B. "War Criminals and the Law of the United Nations." (1947-48), 7 *University of Toronto Law Journal* 27-67. **6180**

Sokolov, H. "How the Israeli Court Dealt with the Issues of Law and Facts in the Eichmann Case." (1962), 34 *Manitoba Bar News* 1-6. **6181**

"The Trial of Axis War Criminals." (1943-44), 13 *Fortnightly Law Journal* 119-122. **6182**

2. INTERNATIONAL MILITARY TRIBUNALS

Bertrand, Charles-Auguste. "Les procès de Nuremberg." (1948), 8 *Revue du Barreau* 477-488. **6183**

Forbes, Gordon W. "International Trials of the Major German War Criminals." (1946), 11 *Saskatchewan Bar Review* 30-43. **6184**

Forbes, Gordon W. "Some Legal Aspects of the Nuremberg Trial." (1946), 24 *Canadian Bar Review* 584-599. **6185**

Huband, Charles R. "Nuremberg Revisited." (1959), 31 *Manitoba Bar News* 53-58. **6186**

Jackson, Robert H. "Nürnberg in Retrospect." (1949), 27 *Canadian Bar Review* 761-781. **6187**

Lund, T.G. "The Legal Procedure at the Nuremberg Trials." (1946-47), 16 *Fortnightly Law Journal* 41-43. **6188**

"The Nuremberg Trial." (1946-47), 16 *Fortnightly Law Journal* 119-120. **6189**
Article signed P.J.A.C.

"Observations on the Trial of War Criminals in Japan." (1949), 1 *External Affairs* 12-23 (Feb.) **6190**

Seidel, Heinz-Dieter. *The Nuremberg Trials: The Uses and Abuses of Law.* London, Ont., 1975. ix, 211 leaves. **6191**
Thesis (M.A.), University of Western Ontario, 1975. (National Library of Canada. Canadian Theses on Microfiche, No. 24661).

3. SUPERIOR ORDERS

Green, Leslie C. "The Man in the Field and the Maxim 'Ignorantia Juris Non Excusat.'" (1979-80), 10 *Revue de Droit, Université de Sherbrooke* 135-156. **6192**

Green, Leslie C. "The Man in the Field and the Maxim 'Ignorantia Juris Non Excusat.'" (1980-81), 19 *Archiv des Völkerrechts* 169-187. **6193**

Green, Leslie C. "Superior Orders and the Reasonable Man." (1970), 8 *Canadian Yearbook of International Law* 61-103. **6194**

Green, Leslie C. *Superior Orders in National and International Law.* Leyden: A.W. Sijthoff, 1976. xix, 374 p. **6195**
Reviews: Michael Bothe in (1979), 39 *Zeitschrift für Ausländisches Öffentliches Recht*

und Völkerrecht 370; Ian Brownlie in (1978), 49 *British Year Book of International Law* 235-236; James A. Burger in (1977), 78 *Military Law Review* 196-201; Yoram Dinstein in (1977-78), 4 *Dalhousie Law Journal* 221-226; Robert A. Friedlander in (1978), 26 *Chitty's Law Journal* 5-8; Thomas M. Gannon in (1978), 4 *Armed Forces and Society* 353-356; Frits Kalshoven in (1978), 25 *Netherlands International Law Review* 107-109; Ludwik Kos-Rabcewicz-Zubkowski in (1978), 10 *Ottawa Law Review* 237-239; W.A. McKean in (1977), 40 *Modern Law Review* 745-746; Charles Rousseau in (1976), 80 *Revue Générale de Droit International Public* 1291-1292; James M. Simpson under title: "The Defence of Superior Orders in Canada: A Review of *Superior Orders in National and International Law*," in (1977), 15 *Canadian Yearbook of International Law* 306-314; unsigned in (1979), 19 *International Review of the Red Cross* 53-55.

Lawrence, Ivy M. "The Plea of Superior Orders in Defence of the War Criminals." (1945), 3 *School of Law Review* 1, 3, 8 (No. 2) **6196**

C. Terrorism

Adam, Frances Cruchley. "Terrorist Images." (1976), 24 *Chitty's Law Journal* 246-249. **6197**

Alexander, Yonah, and Levine, Herbert M. "Prepare for the Next Entebbe." (1977), 25 *Chitty's Law Journal* 240-242. **6198**

Beres, Louis René. "Terrorism and International Security: The Nuclear Threat." (1978), 26 *Chitty's Law Journal* 73-90. **6199**

Bloomfield, Louis M., and FitzGerald, Gerald F. *Crimes Against Internationally Protected Persons: Prevention and Punishment; an Analysis of the UN Convention.* New York: Praeger, 1975. xviii, 272 p. (Praeger Special Studies in International Politics and Government) **6200**
Reviews: John F. Murphy in (1978), 72 *American Journal of International Law* 183-184; Sharon A. Williams in (1976), 54 *Canadian Bar Review* 197-201.

Carmichael, D.J.C. "Terrorism: Some Ethical Issues." (1976), 24 *Chitty's Law Journal* 233-239. **6201**

Carson, John, ed. *Terrorism in Theory and Practice: Proceedings of a Colloquium.* Toronto: Atlantic Council of Canada, 1978. 56 p. **6202**
Contents: Introductory Note.- Some Thoughts on Contemporary Terrorism: Domestic and International Perspectives, by Jorge Nef.- Sectarian Assassination in Northern Ireland, by Richard Ned Lebov.

Cooper, H.H.A. "Close Encounters of an Unpleasant Kind: Preliminary Thoughts on the Stockholm Syndrome." (1978), 2 *Legal Medical Quarterly* 100-114. **6203**

Cooper, H.H.A. "Hostage Negotiation." (1979), 27 *Chitty's Law Journal* 253-264. **6204**

Cooper, H.H.A. "Hostage Rescue Operations: Denouement at Algeria and Mogadishu Compared." (1978), 26 *Chitty's Law Journal* 91-104. **6205**

Cooper, H.H.A. "Terrorism: The Problem of the Problem of Definition." (1978), 26 *Chitty's Law Journal* 105-108. **6206**

Cooper, H.H.A. "Terrorism and the Intelligence Function." (1976), 24 *Chitty's Law Journal* 73-78. **6207**

Cooper, H.H.A. "Terrorism and the Media." (1976), 24 *Chitty's Law Journal* 226-232. **6208**

Cooper, H.H.A. "Terroristic Fads and Fashions: The Year of the Assassin." (1979), 27 *Chitty's Law Journal* 92-97. **6209**

Cooper, H.H.A. "Whither Now? Terrorism on the Brink." (1977), 25 *Chitty's Law Journal* 181-190. **6210**

Crelinsten, Ronald D., and Laberge-Altmejd, Danielle, eds. *The Impact of Terrorism and Skyjacking on the Operations of the Criminal Justice System: Final Report on Basic Issue Seminar.* Edited under the direction of Denis Szabó. Montréal: Centre international de criminologie comparée, Université de Montréal, 1976. 348 p. **6211**
At head of title: International Centre for Comparative Criminology, Université de Montréal; Institute of Criminal Justice and Criminology, University of Maryland.

Crelinsten, Ronald D.; Laberge-Altmejd, Danielle; and Szabó, Denis. *Terrorism and Criminal Justice: An International Perspective.* Lexington, Mass.: D.C. Heath, 1978. xv, 131 p. **6212**
Derives from a conference entitled: "The impact of terrorism and skyjacking on the operations of the criminal justice system," held in February 1976.

Crelinsten, Ronald D., and Szabó, Denis. *Hostage-Taking.* Lexington, Mass.: Lexington Books, c1979. xii, 160 p. **6213**
Derives from an international multi-disciplinary seminar held in Santa Margherita, Italy, in May 1976.
Review: T.J. Juliani in (1980), 22 *Canadian Journal of Criminology* 487-488.

Derriennic, Jean-Pierre. "The Nature of Terrorism and the Effective Response." (1975), *International Perspectives* 7-10 (May/June) **6214**

Friedlander, Robert A. "Terrorism and Political Violence: Do the Ends Justify the Means?" (1976), 24 *Chitty's Law Journal* 240-245. **6215**

Green, Leslie C. "Double Standards in the United Nations: The Legalization of Terrorism." (1979-80), 18 *Archiv des Völkerrechts* 129-148. **6216**

Green, Leslie C. "International Law and the Suppression of Terrorism." *In* Bartholomew, Geoffrey W., ed., *Malaya Law Review Legal Essays in Memoriam, Bashir Ahmad Mallal* (Singapore, 1975), pp. 129-163. **6217**

Green, Leslie C. "International Terrorism and Its Legal Control." (1973), 21 *Chitty's Law Journal* 289-301. **6218**

Green, Leslie C. "The Legalization of Terrorism." *In* Alexander, Yonah, and others, *Terrorism: Theory and Practice* (Boulder, Colo., 1979), pp. 175-197. **6219**

Green, Leslie C. *The Nature and Control of International Terrorism.* Edmonton: University of Alberta, Dept. of Political Science, 1974. 56 p. (University of Alberta. Dept. of Political Science. Occasional Paper, 1) **6220**
Also printed in (1974), 4 *Israel Yearbook on Human Rights* 134-167.

Green, Leslie C. "The Nature and Control of International Terrorism." (1974), 3 *Canadian Council on International Law, Proceedings* 224-279. **6221**

Green, Leslie C. "Terrorism: The Canadian Perspective." *In* Alexander, Yonah, ed., *International Terrorism: National, Regional, and Global Perspectives* (New York, 1976), pp. 3-29. **6222**

Green, Leslie C. "Terrorism and the Courts." (1980-81), 11 *Manitoba Law Journal* 333-358. **6223**

Groffier-Atala, Ethel. *Terrorisme et guérilla, la révolte armée devant les nations: aspects juridiques.* Montréal: Leméac, 1973. 181 p. (Dossiers Interlex) **6224**
Includes: "Présentation: la violence sans rivages," by Charles Atala (pp. 7-56).

"International Terrorism / Le terrorisme international." (1974), 3 *Canadian Council on International Law, Proceedings*, vii, 282 p. **6225**
This is the general theme of the third annual conference held at Ottawa, October 18-19, 1974. Individual papers are listed separately.
Review: Arnold Beichman in (1976), 9 Canadian Journal of Political Science 521-523.

"International Terrorism and Civil Aviation / Le terrorisme international et l'aviation civile." (1974), 3 *Canadian Council on International Law, Proceedings* 78-150. **6226**
This is a panel. Chairman: Charles B. Bourne.- Speaker: Gerald F. FitzGerald (pp. 79-106).- Commentators: Alona E. Evans (pp. 107-113), Lorne C. Clark (pp. 113-120), and Ivan A. Vlasic (pp. 121-127).- General discussion (pp. 127-150).

Jacomy-Millette, Annemarie. "La violence, le droit et la politique: réflexion sur le problème de la protection internationale des diplomates." (1975), 6 *Études Internationales* 103-109. **6227**

"Kidnapping of Diplomats and Other Forms of International Terrorism / L'enlèvement des diplomates et les autres formes de terrorisme international." (1974), 3 *Canadian Council on International Law, Proceedings* 151-223. **6228**
This is a panel. Chairman: Donat Pharand (p. 151).- Speaker: Edward Lee (pp. 152-166).- Commentators: Annemarie Jacomy-Millette (pp. 167-176), Thomas M. Franck (pp. 177-182), and Irwin Cotler (pp. 183-197).- General discussion (pp. 198-223).

Luk, Kenneth. *A Tripartite Approach to International Terrorism.* London, Ont., 1973. v, 145 leaves. **6229**
Thesis (M.A.), University of Western Ontario, 1974. (National Library of Canada. Canadian Theses on Microfiche, No. 20523).

Miller, Abraham H. "Terrorism and Government Policy." (1979), 27 *Chitty's Law Journal* 44-49. **6230**

Moss, Robert. "International Terrorism and Western Societies." (1972-73), 28 *International Journal* 418-430. **6231**

Norton, Augustus R., and Ben-Gal, Talia. "Terror by Fission: An Analysis and Critique." (1979), 27 *Chitty's Law Journal* 268-278. **6232**

O'Marra, Alfred Joseph Clifford. *Terrorism in Northern Ireland: Origins and Nature.* London, Ont., c1976. vi, 127 leaves, maps. **6233**
Thesis (M.A.), University of Western Ontario, 1976. (National Library of Canada. Canadian Theses on Microfiche, No. 28302).

Poulantzas, Nicholas M. "Some Reflections on International Terrorism." (1980), 58 *Revue de Droit International, de Sciences Diplomatiques et Politiques* 141-147. **6234**

Research Strategies for the Study of International Political Terrorism, Evian, France, 1977. *Final Report on Research Strategies for the Study of International Political Terrorism: Proceedings of the Conference.* Compiled and Edited by Ronald D. Crelinsten. Montréal: Centre international de criminologie comparée, Université de Montréal, 1977. x, 218 p. **6235**
At head of title: International Centre for Comparative Criminology, Université de Montréal; Institute of Criminal Justice and Criminology, University of Maryland. Conference held at the Hotel Lumina, May 30-June 1, 1977. Companion volume to the report on the *Dimensions of Victimization in the Context of Terroristic Acts.*

Smart, I.M.H. "The Power of Terror." (1974-75), 30 *International Journal* 225-237. **6236**

St. John, Peter. "Analysis and Response of a Decade of Terrorism." (1981), *International Perspectives* 2-5 (Sept./Oct.) **6237**

"Le terrorisme international: ses effets sur l'ordre juridique international / International Terrorism: Its Effects on the International Legal Order." (1974), 3 *Canadian Council on International Law, Proceedings* 9-77. **6238**
This is a panel. Chairman: André Dufour.- Speaker: Paul de Visscher (pp. 11-43).- Commentators: Leslie C. Green (pp. 44-52), J. J. Paust (pp. 53-62); and J. M. Simpson (pp. 63-67).- General discussion (pp. 68-77).

Wilder, Shael H. "International Terrorism and Hostage Taking: An Overview." (1980-81), 11 *Manitoba Law Journal* 367-386. **6239**

D. Hijacking

See also *"Airspace and Outer Space" (p. 280).*

Atala, Charles, and Jacquemin, Georges. *Le 'hijacking' aérien; ou, la maîtrise illicite d'aéronef hier, aujourd'hui, demain.* Montréal: Leméac, 1973. 116 p. (Dossiers Interlex) **6240**

Bielinski, Eva Halina. *The Role of Law in the Suppression of Terrorism Against International Civil Aviation.* Montreal, 1978. iii, 226 leaves. **6241**
Thesis (LL.M.), McGill University, 1978. (National Library of Canada. Canadian Theses on Microfiche, No. 39608).

Bissonnette, Pierre André, and Clark, Lorne S. "Securing the Enforcement of International Legal Obligations Relating to Unlawful Interference with International Civil Aviation; Canadian Initiatives." *In* McWhinney, Edward, and others, *Aerial Piracy and International Law* (Leiden, 1971), pp. 72-93. **6242**

Butler, Charles F. "The Path to International Legislation Against Hijacking." *In* McWhinney, Edward, and others, *Aerial Piracy and International Law* (Leiden, 1971), pp. 27-35. **6243**

Clark, Lorne S. "Addendum: Implementation of an International Enforcement System." *In* McWhinney, Edward, and others, *Aerial Piracy and International Law* (Leiden, 1971), pp. 94-96. **6244**

Clark, Lorne S. "Canada's Initiatives to Combat the Latest Scourge of the Skies." (1973), *International Perspectives* 47-51 (Jan./Feb.) **6245**

Cooper, H.H.A. "Aviation: Soft Underbelly of the Corporate World." (1980), 28 *Chitty's Law Journal* 155-161. **6246**

Crelinsten, Ronald D., and Laberge-Altmejd, Danielle, eds. *The Impact of Terrorism and Skyjacking on the Operations of the Criminal Justice System: Final Report on Basic Issue Seminar*. Edited under the direction of Denis Szabó. Montréal: Centre international de criminologie comparée, Université de Montréal, 1976. 348 p. **6247**
At head of title: International Centre for Comparative Criminology, Université de Montréal; Institute of Criminal Justice and Criminology, University of Maryland.

El-Amin, Abdel-Salam. *Concerted Actions Towards Combating Terrorism, with Special Emphasis on Air Transport*. Montreal, 1980. 302 frames. **6248**
Thesis (LL.M.), McGill University, 1980. (National Library of Canada. Canadian Theses on Microfiche, No. 51942).

Emanuelli, Claude C. "Études des moyens de prévention et de sanction en matière d'actes d'interférence illicite dans l'aviation civile internationale." (1973), 77 *Revue Générale de Droit International Public* 577-671, 1081-1134. **6249**

Emanuelli, Claude C. "Legal Aspects of Aerial Terrorism: The Piecemeal vs. the Comprehensive Approach." (1975), 10 *Journal of International Law and Economics* 503-518. **6250**

Emanuelli, Claude C. *Les moyens de prévention et de sanction en cas d'action illicite contre l'aviation civile internationale*. Paris: A. Pedone, 1974. 159 p. **6251**

Eustace, Marilyn D. *Aerial Hijacking: Stimulus to International Collaboration*. Kingston, Ont.: Centre for International Relations, Queen's University, 1976. iii, 77 leaves. (National Security Series, No. 6, 1976) **6252**

FitzGerald, Gerald F. "Development of International Legal Rules for the Repression of the Unlawful Seizure of Aircraft." (1969), 7 *Canadian Yearbook of International Law* 269-297. **6253**

FitzGerald, Gerald F. "The London Draft Convention on Acts of Unlawful Interference Against International Civil Aviation." *In* McWhinney, Edward, and others, *Aerial Piracy and International Law* (Leiden, 1971), pp. 36-54. **6254**

FitzGerald, Gerald F. "Recent Proposals for Concerted Action Against States in Respect of Unlawful Interference with International Civil Aviation." (1974), 40 *Journal of Air Law and Commerce* 161-224. **6255**

FitzGerald, Gerald F. "Toward Legal Suppression of Acts Against Civil Aviation." (1971), 585 *International Conciliation* 42-82. **6256**

Gist, Francis J. *The Aircraft Hijacker and International Law*. Montreal, 1968 (c1969). iii, 157 leaves. **6257**
Thesis (LL.M.), McGill University, 1968. (National Library of Canada. Canadian Theses on Microfilm, No. 3128).

Green, Leslie C. "Extradition v. Asylum for Aerial Hijackers." (1975), 10 *Israel Law Review* 207-224. **6258**

Green, Leslie C. "Hijacking and the Right of Asylum." *In* McWhinney, Edward, and others, *Aerial Piracy and International Law* (Leiden, 1971), pp. 124-145.
 6259

Green, Leslie C. "Hijacking, Extradition and Asylum." (1974), 22 *Chitty's Law Journal* 135-143. 6260
See also the author's *Law and Society* (Leyden, 1975), pp. 321-362.

Green, Leslie C. "Piracy of Aircraft and the Law." (1972), 10 *Alberta Law Review* 72-88. 6261

"The Hague Diplomatic Conference on Unlawful Seizure of Aircraft." (1971), 23 *External Affairs* 74-81. 6262
Includes the text of the convention for the suppression of unlawful seizure of aircraft done at The Hague, December 16, 1970 (CTS 1972/23).

Horvitz, Joanne F. "Arab Terrorism and International Aviation: Deterrence v. the Political Act." (1976), 24 *Chitty's Law Journal* 145-154. 6263

Horvitz, Joanne F. "Update on Hijacking: Ineffectiveness of International Legal Controls." (1977), 25 *Chitty's Law Journal* 88-92. 6264

"International Terrorism and Civil Aviation / Le terrorisme international et l'aviation civile." (1974), 3 *Canadian Council on International Law, Proceedings* 78-150. 6265
This is a panel. Chairman: Charles B. Bourne.- Speaker: Gerald F. FitzGerald (pp. 79-106).- Commentators: Alona E. Evans (pp. 107-113), Lorne C. Clark (pp. 113-120), and Ivan A. Vlasic (pp. 121-127).- General discussion (pp. 127-150).

Kuash, Timothy John. *International Behaviour Relating to Aerial Hijacking in the Context of Theories Dealing with International Integration.* Ottawa, 1975. 93 leaves. 6266
Research essay (B.A.), Carleton University, 1975.

Lissitzyn, Oliver J. "Hijacking, International Law, and Human Rights." *In* McWhinney, Edward, and others, *Aerial Piracy and International Law* (Leiden, 1971), pp. 116-123. 6267

Mankiewicz, René H. "Aspects et problèmes du droit pénal de l'aviation internationale." (1958), 4 *Annuaire Français de Droit International* 112-143. 6268

Mankiewicz, René H. "La convention de Montréal (1971) pour la répression d'actes illicites dirigés contre la sécurité de l'aviation civile." (1971), 17 *Annuaire Français de Droit International* 855-875. 6269

Mankiewicz, René H. "Le détournement d'avions." (1971), 25 *Revue Française de Droit Aérien* 392-413. 6270

Mankiewicz, René H. "Le droit pénal et l'aviation, avec référence au droit canadien." (1957-58), 4 *McGill Law Journal* 13-34. 6271

Mankiewicz, René H. "International Transportation Law (Unlawful Seizure of Aircraft) and International Communications Law. (Report of Rapporteur)." (1971), 5 *World Law Review* 266-267. 6272

Mankiewicz, René H. "Lutte contre les actes d'intervention illicite dans l'aviation civile internationale." (1970), 54 *International Law Association, Report of Conference* 385-404. 6273

Mankiewicz, René H. "The 1970 Hague Convention." (1971), 37 *Journal of Air Law and Commerce* 195-210. **6274**
Refers to the convention for the suppression of unlawful seizure of aircraft done at The Hague, December 16, 1970 (CTS 1972/23).

Mankiewicz, René H. "La problématique de la 'piraterie aérienne.' " (1977), 8 *Études Internationales* 100-112. **6275**

Mankiewicz, René H. "Le projet de convention relative à la capture illicite d'aéronefs élaboré par le Comité juridique de l'O.A.C.I." (1970), 24 *Revue Française de Droit Aérien* 141-158. **6276**

Mankiewicz, René H. "Terrorisme aérien et responsabilité civile du transporteur aérien; note sur la jurisprudence américaine." (1977), 31 *Revue Française de Droit Aérien* 382-387. **6277**

Mankiewicz, René H. "Unlawful Interference with Aircraft." (1970), 54 *International Law Association, Report of Conference* 336-365. **6278**

McWhinney, Edward. "Aerial Piracy and the Problem-Solving Approach to International Law." *In* Nawaz, M.K., ed., *Essays on International Law, in Honour of Krishan Rao* (Leyden, 1976), pp. 145-155. **6279**

McWhinney, Edward. "Le détournement illicite des aéronefs." (1971), 54/2 *Institut de Droit International, Annuaire* 346-403, 455-458, 471-474. **6280**
Includes debates and various documents.

McWhinney, Edward. "Hijacking of Aircraft: (Eighteenth Commission). 1. Provisional Report and Draft Resolution. 2. Final Report." (1971), 54/1 *Institut de Droit International, Annuaire* 520-769. **6281**

McWhinney, Edward. "The Illegal Diversion of Aircraft and International Law." (1973), 138 *Académie de Droit International, Recueil des Cours* 261-372.
6282

McWhinney, Edward. *The Illegal Diversion of Aircraft and International Law.* Leyden: A.W. Sijthoff, 1975. vi, 123 p. **6283**
Reprinted from (1973), 138 *Académie de Droit International, Recueil des Cours* 261-372.
Reviews: Harry H. Almond, Jr., in (1976), 62 *A.B.A. Journal* 294-296; Rodney Brazier in (1975), 38 *Modern Law Review* 604-607; Charles N. Brower in (1976), 42 *Journal of Air Law and Commerce* 269-271; Leslie C. Green in (1976), 9 *Canadian Journal of Political Science* 523-524; Kay Hailbronner in (1977), 37 *Zeitschrift für Ausländisches Öffentliches Recht und Völkerrecht* 153-154; unsigned in (1975), 79 *Revue Générale de Droit International Public* 249 (brief notice); and (1976), 28 *Revue Internationale de Droit Comparé* 191 (brief notice).

McWhinney, Edward. "International Legal Problem-Solving and the Practical Dilemma of Hijacking." *In* McWhinney, Edward, and others, *Aerial Piracy and International Law* (Leiden, 1971), pp. 15-26. **6284**

McWhinney, Edward. "New Developments in the Law of International Aviation: The Control of Aerial Hijacking." (1971), 65 *American Society of International Law, Proceedings* 71-75. **6285**

McWhinney, Edward, and others. *Aerial Piracy and International Law.* Leiden: Sijthoff; Dobbs Ferry, N.Y.: Oceana Publications, 1971. 213 p. **6286**

Contains eight essays presented at the joint meeting of the Institute of the American Society of International Law and the International Law Association (Canadian Branch). Held at the Institute of Air and Space Law at McGill University, Montreal, October 30-31, 1970. Individual essays are listed separately.
Reviews: Kay Hailbronner in (1972), 32 *Zeitschrift für Ausländisches Öffentliches Recht und Völkerrecht* 689-690; Barton T. Jones in (1971-72), 5 *Vanderbilt Journal of Transnational Law* 581-586; Howard J. Taubenfeld in (1972), 66 *American Journal of International Law* 907; Michèle Voisset in (1971), 17 *Annuaire Français de Droit International* 1158-1160.

Miller, Georgette M. *Protection of Victims in the Exercise of Actions Against Air Carriers.* Montreal, 1971 (c1972). vi, 177 leaves. **6287**
Short title: *Protection of Victims Against Air Carriers.* Thesis (LL.M.), McGill University, 1972. (National Library of Canada. Canadian Theses on Microfilm, No. 11942).

Poulantzas, Nicholas M. "The Anti-Hijack Convention of December 6, 1970: An Article-by-Article Appraisal in the Light of Recent Developments." (1973), 2 *Anglo-American Law Review* 4-46. **6288**

Poulantzas, Nicholas M. *Convention for the Suppression of Unlawful Seizure of Aircraft.* Geneva: World Peace Through Law Center, 1971. 59 p. (World Peace Through Law Center. Pamphlets Series, No. 18) **6289**
Includes the text of the convention.

Poulantzas, Nicholas M. "The Hague Convention for the Suppression of Unlawful Seizure of Aircraft (December 16, 1970)." (1971), 18 *Netherlands International Law Review* 25-75. **6290**

Poulantzas, Nicholas M. "Hijacking versus Air Piracy: A Substantial Misunderstanding not a Quarrel over Semantics." (1970), 23 *Revue Hellénique de Droit International* 80-90. **6291**

Pourcelet, Michel. "La capture illicite d'aéronefs (hijacking)." (1969), 32 *Revue Générale de l'Air et de l'Espace* 269-275. **6292**

Pourcelet, Michel. "Comment: Hijacking. The Limitations of the International Treaty Approach." *In* McWhinney, Edward, and others, *Aerial Piracy and International Law* (Leiden, 1971), pp. 55-58. **6293**

Rhinelander, John B. "The International Law of Aerial Piracy: New Proposals for the New Dimension." *In* McWhinney, Edward, and others, *Aerial Piracy and International Law* (Leiden, 1971), pp. 59-71. **6294**

Schwenk, Walter. "The Bonn Declaration on Hijacking." (1979), 4 *Annals of Air and Space Law* 307-322. **6295**

Sharp, John M. "Canada and the Hijacking of Aircraft." (1972-73), 5 *Manitoba Law Journal* 451-464. **6296**

"Unlawful Seizure of Aircraft - Hijacking." (1970), 22 *External Affairs* 21-23.
6297

Valladão, Haroldo. "Piraterie aérienne: nouveau délit international." *In* McWhinney, Edward, and Bradley, Martin A., eds., *The Freedom of the Air* (Leyden, 1968), pp. 226-237. **6298**

Valladão, Haroldo. "Punition internationale de l'actuelle piraterie aérienne." *In*

McWhinney, Edward, and others, *Aerial Piracy and International Law* (Leiden, 1971), pp. 97-115. **6299**

Villamin, Maria Luisa. *Piracy and Air Law.* Montreal, 1962. 157, 24 leaves. **6300**
Thesis (LL.M.), McGill University, 1962.

Warren, Gabriel I. "Assessing Progress in Developing Systems to Curb Aerial Hijackings." (1974), *International Perspectives* 37-39 (Jan./Feb.) **6301**

Zussman, Ephraim Ahron. *International Law Regulating Unlawful Seizure of Aircraft,* by Ephraim A. Zussman (Ben-Yakir). Montreal, 1970 (c1971). iv, 289 leaves. **6302**
Thesis (LL.M.), McGill University, 1971. (National Library of Canada. Canadian Theses on Microfilm, No. 9847).

PART TWO

INTERNATIONAL RELATIONS: LEGAL IMPLICATIONS

I. INTERNATIONAL RELATIONS

A. Diplomatic History in General

Aikins, G.H. " 'The War - And After.' " (1943), 26 *Canadian Bar Association, Proceedings* 78-85. **6303**

Andrew, Arthur J. *Defence by Other Means; Diplomacy for the Underdog.* Toronto: Canadian Institute of International Affairs (1971). xi, 126 p. (Contemporary Affairs, No. 44) **6304**
Review: Annette Baker Fox in (1970-71), 26 *International Journal* 792-794.

Andrew, Arthur J. "A View of the Summit." (1979-80), 35 *International Journal* 21-32. **6305**

Anglin, Douglas G. "Ghana, the West, and the Soviet Union." (1958), 24 *Canadian Journal of Economics and Political Science* 152-165. **6306**

Anglin, Douglas G. *The St. Pierre and Miquelon Affaire of 1941; a Study in Diplomacy in the North Atlantic Quadrangle.* Toronto: University of Toronto Press, 1966. xvi, 219 p., maps. **6307**
Reviews: Charles G. Fenwick in (1967), 61 *American Journal of International Law* 640; Charlotte Girard in (1967), 48 *Canadian Historical Review* 166-168; John W. Holmes in (1967), 33 *Canadian Journal of Economics and Political Science* 476-477; Cameron Nish in (1966-67), 20 *Revue d'Histoire de l'Amérique Française* 311-312; D.C. Watt in (1966-67), 22 *International Journal* 534-535.

Arcand, Arthur. "Nation - nationalité." (1943), 29 *Revue Trimestrielle Canadienne* 347-357. **6308**

Arnopoulos, Paris J. "External Affairs of the Ideal Polis (Foreign Policy According to Plato and Aristotle)." (1976), 48 *Canadian Political Science Association, Papers,* 22 p. **6309**

Azar, Edward E. " 'Les données événementielles': origines et perspectives d'une méthode scientifique en relations internationales." (1974), 5 *Études Internationales* 3-24. **6310**

Barrea, Jean. "Une approche synoptique des théories de la décision, de la puissance et de la négociation." (1981), 12 *Études Internationales* 251-267. **6311**

Bergeron, Gérard. "Internationalisme et régionalisme ou nationalismes et continentalismes." (1946), 52/2 *Revue Dominicaine* 22-44. **6312**

Best, Geoffrey. *Honour Among Men and Nations: Transformation of an Idea.* Toronto: University of Toronto Press, 1982. xiv, 108 p. (Joanne Goodman Lectures, 1981) **6313**

Blaikie, Peter Rutherford. *National Interests and Contractarian Considerations of Justice in International Relations.* Edmonton, 1977. viii, 170 leaves. **6314**

Thesis (Ph.D.), University of Alberta, 1977. (National Library of Canada. Canadian Theses on Microfiche, No. 31940).

Boak, A.E.R. "The American Middle West and the Lease-Lend Bill." (1941-42), 48 *Queen's Quarterly* 106-114. **6315**

Booth, Charles James. *The Dissolution of the Ottoman Empire: The Study of the Political Clauses of the Treaty of Sèvres, August 10, 1920.* Ottawa, 1968. iv, 213 leaves. **6316**

Thesis (M.A.), University of Ottawa, 1968. Refers to the treaty of peace with Turkey signed at Sèvres, August 10, 1920 (BTS 11(1920); 113 BFSP 652; did not come into force).

Brady, Alexander. "Imperialism Old and New." (1947), 41 *Royal Society of Canada, Transactions* 1-21 (3d Ser., 2d Sec.) **6317**

Brons, Janet Wilkinson. *Decision-Makers' Images: Their Use in International Analysis.* Edmonton, 1978. vi, 111 leaves. **6318**

Thesis (M.A.), University of Alberta, 1978. (National Library of Canada. Canadian Theses on Microfiche, No. 40096).

Buchan, Alastair. "The Year That Put an End to the Old Bipolar World." (1981) *International Perspectives* 26-31 (Nov./Dec.) **6319**

Campsie, John S. *Conflict and Co-operation; an Introduction to Some Problems of International Relations in the Twentieth Century.* Toronto: J.M. Dent (Canada), c1967. v, 218 p., maps. (Dent's Canadian Texts) **6320**

Canadian Institute on Public Affairs. *Rights & Liberties in Our Time: Addresses Given at the Canadian Institute on Public Affairs, 1946.* Edited by Martyn Estall. Toronto: Ryerson Press, 1947. viii, 108 p. **6321**

Published under the auspices of the National Council of the Young Men's Christian Associations of Canada.

Contents (Partial): Problems of World Security, by J.K. Gordon.- The United Nations, by E.N. van Kleffens.- International Trusteeship and Accountability: The Problem of Colonies, by R.J. Bunche.- Immigration and Refugees, by R.G. Riddell.- Civil Liberties, by B.K. Sandwell.

Canadian Institute on Public Affairs. *This Is the Peace: Addresses Given at the Canadian Institute on Public Affairs, August 18 to 25, 1945.* Edited by Violet Anderson. Toronto: Ryerson Press, 1945. vi, 118 p. **6322**

Published under the auspices of the National Council of the Young Men's Christian Associations of Canada.

Contents (Partial): Towards a Peaceful World: The San Francisco Charter, by Elizabeth Armstrong.- Human Nature and Enduring Peace, by Goodwin Watson.- Uncertainties in Many Regions: The Reconstruction of Europe, by Frank Munk.- Canadian-American Relations in the Pacific, by Gwendolen M. Carter.- The Constitution and the Problems of Peace, by J.A. Corry.

Caron, Ivanhoë. "La politique coloniale de l'Angleterre aux XVIIe et XVIIIe siècle." (1921), 26 *Revue Canadienne* 241-254 (n.s.) **6323**

Corbett, Percy E. "American Foreign Policy." (1937-38), 7 *University of Toronto Quarterly* 209-227. **6324**

Corbett, Percy E. *Morals, Law & Power in International Relations.* Los Angeles:

John Randolph Haynes and Dora Haynes Foundation, 1956. (5), 51 p. **6325**
Haynes Foundation lectures delivered at the University of California, 1955-56.
Review: John P. Humphrey in (1957), 35 *Canadian Bar Review* 107-109.

Corbett, Percy E. "Power and Law at Suez." (1956-57), 12 *International Journal* 1-12. **6326**

Corriveau, Patrice. "Les origines historiques des attitudes américaines en politique étrangère." (1955), 25 *Revue de l'Université d'Ottawa* 5-33. **6327**

Cowie, Donald. "Pacific Peace Aims." (1944-45), 14 *University of Toronto Quarterly* 256-260. **6328**

Dawson, Samuel Edward. "The Line of Demarcation of Pope Alexander VI in A.D. 1493 and That of the Treaty of Tordesillas in A.D. 1494; with an Inquiry concerning the Metrology of Ancient and Mediaeval Times." (1899), 5 *Royal Society of Canada, Transactions* 467-546 (2d Ser., Sec. 2) **6329**

Dial, Roger L., ed. *Advancing and Contending Approaches to the Study of Chinese Foreign Policy.* Halifax: Centre for Foreign Studies, Dept. of Political Science, Dalhousie University, 1974. viii, 412 p. **6330**

Dial, Roger L. *Chinese Foreign Relations: Toward a Framework for Casual and Comparative Analysis.* Berkeley, Calif., 1973. 1 vol. (various pagings) **6331**
Thesis (Ph.D.), University of California, 1973.

Dickason, Olive Patricia. "Europeans and Amerindians: Some Comparative Aspects of Early Contact." (1979), *Canadian Historical Association, Historical Papers* 182-202. **6332**

Eayrs, James George, ed. *The Commonwealth and Suez; a Documentary Survey.* London, New York: Oxford University Press, 1964. xxi, 483 p. **6333**
Reviews: Peyton V. Lyon in (1964), 30 *Canadian Journal of Economics and Political Science* 474-475; Frederic H. Soward in (1965), 46 *Canadian Historical Review* 54-55.

Fieldhouse, Noel. "The Anglo-German War of 1939-42: Some Movements to End It by a Negotiated Peace." (1971), 9 *Royal Society of Canada, Transactions* 285-312 (4th Ser.) **6334**

Fistié, Pierre. "Le problème territorial des Kouriles du Sud dans les relations nippo-soviétiques." (1982), 13 *Études Internationales* 23-51. **6335**

Fox, Annette Baker. *The Power of Small States: Diplomacy in World War II.* Chicago: University of Chicago Press, 1959. 211 p. **6336**
Review: Douglas G. Anglin in (1959-60), 15 *International Journal* 364-365.

Freymond, Jacques. "The Crisis of the International System." (1968-69), 24 *International Journal* 776-789. **6337**

Fry, Michael G. *Illusions of Security; North Atlantic Diplomacy 1918-22.* Toronto: University of Toronto Press, 1972. xii, 221 p. **6338**
Reviews: Charles Pentland in (1975), 8 *Canadian Journal of Political Science* 585-586; Samuel F. Wells, Jr., in (1974), 55 *Canadian Historical Review* 334-335.

Glubb, John. "The Fate of Empires." (1978), 12 *Law Society of Upper Canada Gazette* 11-41. **6339**

Good, J.W. "The Irish Boundary Question." (1926-27), 6 *Dalhousie Review* 176-187. **6340**

Gotlieb, Allan E., and Kinsman, Jeremy. "North-South or East-West?" (1983), *International Perspectives* 25-28 (Jan./Feb.) **6341**

Green, Leslie C. "European Recovery: Constitutional and Legal Problems." (1947), 2 *World Affairs* 373-386 (N.S.) **6342**

Greenwood, Thomas. "Primauté de l'ordre entre les nations." (1950), 20 *Revue de l'Université d'Ottawa* 220-230. **6343**

Hanna, William. "La prise de Saint-Pierre-et-Miquelon par les forces de la France libre: Noël 1941." (1962), 16 *Revue d'Histoire de l'Amérique Française* 369-387. **6344**

Holland, *Sir* Robert E. "Suez and the U.N.O." (1956-57), 36 *Dalhousie Review* 323-334. **6345**

Holmes, John W. "Everything Has Its Season - And That Adds to Complexity." (1981), *International Perspectives* 10-13 (Nov./Dec.) **6346**

Holsti, Kal J. *Why Nations Realign: Foreign Policy Restructuring in the Postwar World.* London: Allen & Unwin, 1982. xi, 225 p. **6347**
Review: Naomi Black in (1982), 15 *Canadian Journal of Political Science* 864-866.

Ing, Alexius S. *Status Inconsistency and Conflict Behavior in International Relations (A Replication of Wallace's War and Rank among Nations).* Ottawa, 1980. 94 frames. **6348**
Thesis (M.A.), Carleton University, 1980. (National Library of Canada. Canadian Theses on Microfiche, No. 44408).

Jacomy-Millette, Annemarie, and others. *Église et système mondial; la position des églises vis-à-vis des grands problèmes internationaux / The Church and World System: The Position of the Churches in International Affairs.* Québec: Centre québécois de relations internationales, 1980. 244 p. (Collection Choix, 12) **6349**
Proceedings of the 11th Congrès des relations internationales du Québec, held September 27 to 29, 1979; organized by Centre québécois de relations internationales, Institut français des relations internationales, the World Peace Foundation, Institut canadien des affaires internationales, and Université Laval; text in French and English.
Review: Henrique Urbano in (1981), 12 *Études Internationales* 404-405.

Johnston, Douglas M. "Marginal Diplomacy in East Asia." (1971), 26 *International Journal* 469-506. **6350**

Kapp, Richard Ward. *The Failure of the Diplomatic Negotiations between Germany and Austria-Hungary for a Customs Union, 1915-1916.* Toronto, c1977. 380, lvi leaves. **6351**
Thesis (Ph.D.), University of Toronto, 1977. (National Library of Canada. Canadian Theses on Microfiche, No. 36709).

Kim, L. Junchul. *The Manchurian Crisis of 1931 from the Viewpoint of International Law.* Montreal, 1968 (c1969). 75 leaves, map. **6352**
Short title: *The Manchurian Crisis from the Viewpoint of International Law.* Thesis (LL.M.), McGill University, 1969. (National Library of Canada. Canadian Theses on Microfilm, No. 4118).

Kindleberger, Charles P. "The Marshall Plan and the Cold War." (1967-68), 23 *International Journal* 369-382. **6353**

King, Marlene Irma. *The Dominican Crisis (1965) and the Inter-American System*. London, Ont., 1970 (c1971). vii, 145, viii leaves. **6354**
Thesis (M.A.), University of Western Ontario, 1970. (National Library of Canada. Canadian Theses on Microfilm, No. 7214).

Knapton, E.J. "The Holy Alliance: A Retrospect." (1941-42), 48 *Queen's Quarterly* 157-166. **6355**
Refers to the Treaty of the Holy Alliance of September 26, 1815 (3 BFSP 211).

Kohn, Hans. "One World?" (1946-47), 2 *International Journal* 308-315. **6356**

Laabi, Abdelhai. "Les fonctions internes de la détente dans les systèmes politiques du triangle euro-arabo-africain: l'image oubliée de l'interdépendance Nord-Sud." (1980), 11 *Études Internationales* 65-95. **6357**

Legault, Albert, and others. *L'analyse des conflits internationaux: quatre études de cas*. Québec: Centre québécois de relations internationales, Université Laval, c1979. 175 p. **6358**
Review: Jean Barrea in (1980), 11 *Études Internationales* 339-340.

MacKenzie, Norman A.M. "The Crisis in the Far East." (1932-33), 2 *University of Toronto Quarterly* 3-20. **6359**

McInnis, Edgar. *The Atlantic Triangle and the Cold War*. Published under the auspices of the Canadian Institute of International Affairs. Toronto: University of Toronto Press, 1959. 163 p. **6360**

McWhinney, Edward, ed. *Law, Foreign Policy, and the East-West Détente*. Toronto: University of Toronto Press, 1964. viii, 123 p. **6361**
Contains nine essays based on papers delivered at the Conference on Law and World Affairs held at the University of Toronto, January 17-18, 1964. Relevant essays are listed separately.
Reviews: Rosalyn Higgins in (1966), 42 *International Affairs* 276-279; Ivo Lapenna in (1965), 14 *International and Comparative Law Quarterly* 1423-1426; Oliver J. Lissitzyn in (1965), 59 *American Journal of International Law* 956-959; unsigned in (1965), 69 *Revue Générale de Droit International Public* 556 (brief notice).

Munton, Donald J., ed. *Measuring International Behavior: Public Sources, Events and Validity*. Halifax: Centre for Foreign Policy Studies, Dalhousie University, 1978. vi, 348 p. **6362**

Nelson, Harold I. *Land and Power; British and Allied Policy on Germany's Frontiers, 1916-19*. London: Routledge & Paul, 1963. xiv, 402 p. (Studies in Political History) **6363**
Also published Toronto, University of Toronto Press.
Reviews: Ivo J. Lederer in (1965), 46 *Canadian Historical Review* 380-381; Seth P. Tillman in (1963-64), 19 *International Journal* 390-392.

Nomikos, Eugenia V., and North, Robert C. *International Crisis: The Outbreak of World War I*. Montreal: McGill-Queen's University Press, 1976. xv, 339 p.
6364

Pearson, Lester B. *Diplomacy in the Nuclear Age*. Cambridge, Mass.: Harvard University Press; London: Oxford University Press, 1959. vi, 114 p. (William L. Clayton Lectures on International Economic Affairs and Foreign Policy, 1958)
6365
Lecture delivered at Tufts University. Also published Toronto, S.J.R. Saunders, 1959.

Contents: The Clayton Lectures: Diplomacy New and Old.- Coalition Diplomacy.- Negotiation and Diplomacy.- Power and Diplomacy.- Nobel Peace Prize Lecture, 1957: The Four Faces of Peace.
Review: Edgar McInnis in (1958-59), 14 *International Journal* 310-311.

Picard, Roger. "L'affaire de la dette américaine." (1945), 31 *Revue Trimestrielle Canadienne* 1-16. **6366**

Poulantzas, Nicholas M. "Les relations internationales dans un monde en transition." (1979), 57 *Revue de Droit International, de Sciences Diplomatiques et Politiques* 74-80. **6367**

Read, John E. "The Church and the New International Order." (1950-51), 30 *Dalhousie Review* 1-8. **6368**

Ricour, Pierre. "Positions internationalistes au XXe siècle." (1945), 51/1 *Revue Dominicaine* 324-337. **6369**

Rie, Robert. "Austria: The Problem of Complicity and Responsibility." (1947-48), 27 *Dalhousie Review* 167-176. **6370**

Sabourin, Louis. "The Theory of the Four C's: Conflict, Coexistence, Competition, Cooperation - A Conjunctural Approach to International Law and Politics." *In* Boasson, Charles, ed., *The Changing International Community: Essays in Honour of Marion Mushkat* (The Hague, 1973), pp. 33-43. **6371**

Salim, Ziad. *Status Politics in the International System.* Ottawa, 1980. 337 leaves. **6372**
Thesis (Ph.D.), Carleton University, 1980. (National Library of Canada. Canadian Theses on Microfiche, No. 44427).

Samarrai, Alauddin. "Medieval Commerce and Diplomacy: Islam and Europe, A.D. 850-1300." (1980), 15 *Canadian Journal of History* 1-2. **6373**

Soward, Frederic H. *Twenty-Five Troubled Years, 1918-1943.* London, New York, etc.: Oxford University Press, 1943. x, 437 p., maps. **6374**

Toogood, J.D. "Direct Military Implications of the Conference on Security and Co-operation in Europe." (1973-74), 3 *Canadian Defence Quarterly* 40-42 (No. 3) **6375**

Toogood, J.D. "Helsinki 1975: What Was Achieved in the Field of Confidence-Building Measures." (1975-76), 5 *Canadian Defence Quarterly* 28-32 (No. 2) **6376**

Underhill, Frank H. "Trends in American Foreign Policy." (1943-44), 13 *University of Toronto Quarterly* 286-297. **6377**

Warwick, Donald P. "Transnational Participation and International Peace." (1971), 25 *International Organization* 655-674. **6378**

Winham, Gilbert R. "Complexity in International Negotiations." *In* Druckman, Daniel, ed., *Negotiations : Social-Psychological Perspectives* (Beverly Hills, Calif., c1977), pp. 347-366. **6379**

Winham, Gilbert R. "Practitioners' Views of International Negotiation." (1979), 32 *World Politics* 111-135. **6380**

Worswick, Noel Denis. *Roman Relations with Greece and the Hellenistic Empires from c. 475 B.C. to 200 B.C.* Hamilton, 1964. ix, 128 leaves. **6381**
Thesis (M.A.), McMaster University, 1964.

B. Canadian Diplomatic History

1. GENERAL

Adamkiewicz, George. "Canada's International Mission." (1946-47), 26 *Dalhousie Review* 289-303. **6382**

Aitchison, J.H. "Canadian Foreign Policy in the House and on the Hustings." (1956-57), 12 *International Journal* 273-287. **6383**

Alexander, Frederick. *Canadians and Foreign Policy; the Record of an Independent Investigation.* Toronto: University of Toronto Press, 1960. 160 p. **6384**

Anglin, Douglas G.; Shaw, Timothy M.; and Widstrand, Carl., eds. *Canada, Scandinavia, and Southern Africa.* Uppsala: Scandinavian Institute of African Studies, 1978. 190 p. **6385**
Proceedings of a conference sponsored by the Scandinavian Institute of African Studies, the Norman Paterson School of International Affairs of Carleton University, and the Centre for African Studies, Dalhousie University.
Review: Patricia J. Appavoo in (1980), 35 *International Journal* 848-849.

Angus, Henry F. "Canada and a Foreign Policy." (1934-35), 14 *Dalhousie Review* 265-275. **6386**

Barry, Donald J. *Continuity and Change in Canadian Foreign Policy: from the Pre-War to the Post-War Experience, 1935-1957.* Baltimore, Md., 1977. 1 vol. **6387**
Thesis (Ph.D.), Johns Hopkins University, 1977. Abstracted in (1977/78), 38 *Dissertation Abstracts International* 7540-A.

Barry, Donald J. "The United States and the Development of the Canada-European Community Contractual Link Relationship." (1980), 10 *American Review of Canadian Studies* 63-71 (No. 1) **6388**

Beesley, J. Alan. "Law, Diplomacy and Foreign Policy." (1980), 9 *Canadian Council on International Law, Proceedings* 11-17. **6389**

Bertrand, Denis. *La politique extérieure du Canada et la réaction canadienne-française à la veille de la deuxième Grande guerre (1935-1939).* Montréal, 1965. 2 vols. **6390**
Thesis (Ph.D.), Université de Montréal, 1965.

Bothwell, Robert, and Hillmer, Norman, eds. *The In-Between Time: Canadian External Policy in the 1930s.* Vancouver: C. Clark Pub., c1975. 223 p. (Issues in Canadian History) **6392**

Boyd, John. *The Future of Canada: Canadianism or Imperialism.* Montreal: Beauchemin, 1919. 106 p. **6393**
Review: W.P.M. Kennedy in (1920), 1 *Canadian Historical Review* 107, 110-111.

Branscombe, Ralph Eugene. *Canadian External Relations, 1783-1914.* Wolfville, N.S., 1947. 205 leaves. **6394**
Thesis (M.A.), Acadia University, 1947.

Canada. Dept. of External Affairs. *Foreign Policy for Canadians.* Ottawa: Queen's Printer, 1970. 6 parts in a slipcase. **6395**

See also comments in (1969-70), 29 *Behind the Headlines* Nos. 7-8 (23 p.).
Review: Peyton V. Lyon in (1971), 14 *Canadian Public Administration* 161-163.

Canada. Dept. of External Affairs. *Perspectives on World Affairs and Foreign Policy Issues: A Research Report / Perceptions des affaires internationales et des questions de politique étrangère.* Ottawa: External Affairs Canada, 1980. 51, 39 p. **6396**

Canadian Institute on Public Affairs. *Canada: The Empire and the League; Lectures Given at the Canadian Institute on Economics and Politics, July 31st to August 14th, 1936.* Toronto: T. Nelson, c1936. vii, 171 p. **6397**
Published for the National Council of Y.M.C.A.'s of Canada.
Reviews: G.F. Curtis in (1937-38), 17 *Dalhousie Review* 252-254; Lionel Gelber in (1937), 16 *International Affairs* 468; G.P. de T. Glazebrook in (1937), 3 *Canadian Journal of Economics and Political Science* 608-610; Frederic H. Soward in (1937), 18 *Canadian Historical Review* 82-83.

Caron, Jean-Lucien. *Radio-Canada International: reflet de la politique extérieure canadienne, 1945-1975.* Montréal, 1975. 227 leaves. **6398**
Thesis (M.Sc.), Université de Montréal, 1975.

Chapdelaine, Jean. "Le droit international et la politique étrangère du Canada dans les années '80: enjeux politiques et juridiques." (1980), 9 *Canadian Council on International Law, Proceedings* 5-10. **6399**

Chevrier, Bernard. "La politique isolationniste du Canada de 1919 à 1921." (1976), 46 *Revue de l'Université d'Ottawa* 234-241. **6400**

Clarkson, Stephen, ed. *An Independent Foreign Policy for Canada?* Edited for the University League for Social Reform. Toronto: McClelland and Stewart, c1968. xiv, 290 p. (Carleton Contemporary) **6401**
Reviews: H.S. Ferns in (1968), 44 *International Affairs* 833-834; Howard C. Green in (1967-68), 23 *International Journal* 647-648; Frank Marzari in (1968), 49 *Canadian Historical Review* 424-426; David R. Morrison under title: "Independence or Quiet Diplomacy?," in (1968), 3 *Journal of Canadian Studies* 32-39 (No. 4); W.F.W. Neville in (1968), 1 *Canadian Journal of Political Science* 367-368.

Coffin, William F. *Quirks of Diplomacy.* Montreal: J. Lovell, 1874. 31 p. **6402**
Lecture delivered before the Literary and Scientific Society of Ottawa, January 22, 1874.

Congrès des relations internationales du Québec, 12th, 1980. *Le Canada, les États-Unis et l'Europe face à la crise internationale / The International Crisis and the Attitudes of Canada, the United States and Europe.* Québec: Centre québécois de relations internationales, c1981. 141 p. (Collection Choix, 13) **6403**
Proceedings of the 12th Congrès des relations internationales du Québec, held September 25 to 27, 1980; organized by Centre québécois de relations internationales, Institut français des relations internationales, the World Peace Foundation, Institut canadien des affaires internationales, and Université Laval. Text in French and English.

Cook, Ramsay. *The Maple Leaf Forever: Essays on Nationalism and Politics in Canada.* New rev. ed., Toronto: Macmillan of Canada, 1977. xi, 245 p. (Laurentian Library, 54) **6404**
Review: Donald V. Smiley in (1972), 53 *Canadian Historical Review* 75-78.

Corbett, Percy E. "Canada in the Western Hemisphere." (1940-41), 19 *Foreign Affairs* 778-789. **6405**

Corbett, Percy E. "Isolation for Canada?" (1936-37), 6 *University of Toronto Quarterly* 120-131. **6406**

Cruttwell-Vaughn, Adrian. *The Canadian Role in the Suez Crisis of 1958.* Ottawa, 1963. 183 leaves. **6407**
Thesis (M.A.), Carleton University, 1963. Abstracted in (1966), 4 *Masters Abstracts* 19 (No. 2). (University Microfilms, Ann Arbor, No. M-573).

Dafoe, John W. "A Foreign Policy for Canada." (1935-36), 42 *Queen's Quarterly* 161-170. **6408**

D'Auteuil, Maurice. "Pour une politique extérieure canadienne." (1938), 8 *Revue de l'Université d'Ottawa* 314-326. **6409**

Dobell, Peter C. *Canada's Search for New Roles; Foreign Policy in the Trudeau Era.* London, New York: Oxford University Press, 1972. vi, 161 p. (Oxford Paperbacks, 277) **6410**
Published for the Royal Institute of International Affairs.
Reviews: Nicholas D'Ombrain in (1974), 55 *Canadian Historical Review* 454-455; Clarence G. Redekop in (1972-73), 28 *International Journal* 375-380; L.P. Singh in (1973), 4 *Études Internationales* 378-379.

Doxey, Margaret P. "Canada's International Connections." (1978), 32 *Year Book of World Affairs* 43-63. **6411**

Eayrs, James George. "Defining a New Place for Canada in the Hierarchy of World Power." (1981), *International Perspectives* 3-9 (Nov./Dec.) **6412**

Eayrs, James George. *In Defence of Canada.* Toronto: University of Toronto Press, 1964-1980. 4 vols. (Studies in the Structure of Power; Decision Making in Canada, 1, 3, 6, 8) **6413**
Also part of Canadian University Paperbooks Series.
Contents: v. 1. From the Great War to the Great Depression.- v. 2. Appeasement and Rearmament.- v. 3. Peacemaking and Deterrence.- v.4. Growing up Allied.
Reviews:
Volume 1: Gavin Long in (1965), 46 *Canadian Historical Review* 358-360; Theodore Ropp in (1964-65), 20 *International Journal* 402;
Volume 2: H.S. Ferns in (1965), 41 *International Affairs* 768-769; Roger Graham in (1966), 47 *Canadian Historical Review* 369-370; Michael Howard in (1965-66), 21 *International Journal* 386-387; Gordon Winter in (1967), 43 *International Affairs* 199-200;
Volume 3: Alastair F. Buchan in (1972-73), 28 *International Journal* 384-387; J.L. Granatstein in (1974), 55 *Canadian Historical Review* 205-206;
Volume 4: Robert Bothwell under title: "Canada and the Postwar Quest for Peace," in (1980), 87 *Queen's Quarterly* 709-712; Andrew Boyd in (1980-81), 36 *International Journal* 687-689; John English in (1981), 62 *Canadian Historical Review* 105-107; Tobias Fisher under title: "Growing up with Eayrs," in (1980), *International Perspectives* 30-31 (July/Aug.); John Gellner in (1980), 13 *Canadian Journal of Political Science* 834-835; Douglas C. Nord in (1980), 10 *American Review of Canadian Studies* 95-96 (No. 2).

Eayrs, James George. *Northern Approaches; Canada and the Search for Peace.* Toronto: Macmillan, 1961. 195 p. **6414**
Reviews: Alastair F. Buchan in (1961-62), 17 *International Journal* 62-63; H.S. Ferns in (1963), 39 *International Affairs* 150-151.

Edmonds, J. Duncan. "The Implications for Canada of Interdependence." (1964), 6

University of Windsor Seminar on Canadian-American Relations, Proceedings 215-220. **6415**

Ewart, John S. *The Kingdom of Canada, Imperial Federation, the Colonial Conferences, the Alaska Boundary, and Other Essays.* Toronto: Morang, 1908. xv, 370 p., maps. **6416**

Farr, David M.L. "The View of History in the Making of Canada's External Policies." (1978), *Canadian Historical Association, Historical Papers* 1-19. **6417**

Farrell, Robert Barry. *The Making of Canadian Foreign Policy.* Scarborough, Ont.: Prentice-Hall of Canada, 1969. 181 p. **6418**
Reviews: Arthur J. Andrew in (1969-70), 25 *International Journal* 813-814; Zachariah Kay in (1970), 3 *Canadian Journal of Political Science* 333-334; Gilles Lalande in (1970), 1 *Études Internationales* 85-86 (no 1).

Feldman, Elliot J., and Nevitte, Neil, eds. *The Future of North America: Canada, the United States, and Quebec Nationalism.* Cambridge: Center for International Affairs, Harvard University, 1979. 378 p. (Harvard Studies in International Affairs, No. 42) **6419**
Prepared under the auspices of the Center for International Affairs, Harvard University, and the Institute for Research on Public Policy, Montreal.

Filion, Louis Jacques. *De Gaulle: son image du système international et des relations France-Canada-Québec.* Ottawa, 1974. 227 leaves. **6420**
Thesis (M.A.), Université d'Ottawa, 1974.

"A Fireproof House?" (1944), 4 *Behind the Headlines* No. 2 (18 p.) **6421**

Fleming, James MacLean. *Canada and European Security: The C.S.C.E., Helsinki to Belgrade.* Kingston, 1980. 176 frames. **6422**
Thesis (M.A.), Queen's University, 1980. (National Library of Canada. Canadian Theses on Microfiche, No. 50132).

"Foreign Policy for Canadians: Comments on the White Paper." (1969-70), 29 *Behind the Headlines* Nos. 7-8 (23 p.) **6423**
Brief individual contributions by various authors.

Fox, Annette Baker. "The Range of Choice for Middle Powers: Australia and Canada Compared." (1980), 26 *Australian Journal of Politics and History* 193-203. **6424**

Freeman, Linda. "Canada and Africa in the 1970s." (1979-80), 35 *International Journal* 794-820. **6425**

Fry, Michael G., ed. *'Freedom and Change': Essays in Honour of Lester B. Pearson.* Toronto: McClelland and Stewart, 1975. xii, 258 p. **6426**
Collection of fifteen essays.
Contents: Lyon, P.V., and Thordarson, B., "Professor Pearson."- Johnston, G., "Look, a Good Man."- Waldheim, K., "Lester Pearson United Nations."- Buchan, A., "Concepts of Peacekeeping."- Burns, E.L.M., "Pearson and the Gaza Strip, 1957."- Anglin, D.G., "Britain and the Use of Force in Rhodesia."- Smart, I., "The Study of Strategy."- Forcese, D., "Peace Research."- Reid, E., "Canada and the Creation of the North Atlantic Alliance 1948-1949."- Gotlieb, A.E., "Canadian Diplomatic Initiatives."- Plumptre, A.F.W., "The International Development Research Centre and the Role of L.B. Pearson."- Lithwick, N.H., "Selecting an Economic Strategy for Canada."- Curzon, G., "GATT and the Golden Age of Trade Cooperation."- Litvak, I.A., and Maule,

C.J., "Corporate Metamorphosis."- Taylor, D.R.F., "Spatial Organization and Rural Development."- Ward, B., "That Shrewd Yet Visionary Voice."- Lester B. Pearson's Public Address at St. Martin-in-the Fields, London, June 13, 1972, on the Occasion of the Presentation to him of the Victor Gollancz Humanity Award. Some essays are also listed separately.
Reviews: Bruce Thordarson under title: "Posture and Policy: Leadership in Canada's External Affairs," in (1975-76), 31 *International Journal* 666-691; Richard Veatch in (1978), 11 *Canadian Journal of Political Science* 483-484.

Galarneau, Hélène. "Chronique des relations extérieures du Canada et du Québec." (1981), 12 *Études Internationales* 759-790. **6427**
Covers the period from July to September 1981.

Galarneau, Hélène. "Chronique des relations extérieures du Canada et du Québec." (1982), 13 *Études Internationales* 127-171. **6428**
Covers the period from October to December 1981.

Galarneau, Hélène. "Chronique des relations extérieures du Canada et du Québec." (1982), 13 *Études Internationales* 323-364. **6429**
Covers the period from January to March 1982.

Galarneau, Hélène. "Chronique des relations extérieures du Canada et du Québec." (1982), 13 *Études Internationales* 525-557. **6430**
Covers the period from April to June 1982.

Galarneau, Hélène. "Chronique des relations extérieures du Canada et du Québec." (1982), 13 *Études Internationales* 703-731. **6431**
Covers the period from July to September 1982.

Gelber, Lionel. "Canada's New Stature." (1945-46), 24 *Foreign Affairs* 277-289. **6432**

Gelber, Marvin. "Canada's Foreign Policy." (1938-39), 8 *University of Toronto Quarterly* 106-113. **6433**

Gibson, James A. "Canadian Foreign Policy." (1951-52), 58 *Queen's Quarterly* 477-485. **6434**

Glazebrook, G.P. de T. "Canadian External Relations." *In* Martin, Chester B., ed., *Canada in Peace and War* (London, 1941), pp. 150-175. **6435**

Glazebrook, G.P. de T. *Canadian External Relations; an Historical Study to 1914.* London, Toronto, etc.: Oxford University Press, 1942. vii, 312 p. **6436**
Issued under the auspices of the Canadian Institute of International Affairs.
Reviews: H. McD. Clokie in (1944), 10 *Canadian Journal of Economics and Political Science* 104-106; John W. Dafoe in (1943), 24 *Canadian Historical Review* 197; B.K. Sandwell in (1942-43), 12 *University of Toronto Quarterly* 236-240; signed R.N. in (1940-43), 19 *International Affairs* 592.

Glazebrook, G.P. de T. *A History of Canadian External Relations.* Toronto: Oxford University Press, 1950. vii, 449 p. **6437**
Issued under the auspices of the Canadian Institute of International Affairs. Part I is a reprint of the author's *Canadian External Relations; an Historical Study to 1914*, published in 1942.
Reviews: H.F. Angus in (1951), 17 *Canadian Journal of Economics and Political Science* 100-102; Nicholas Mansergh in (1951), 27 *International Affairs* 91-92.

Glazebrook, G.P. de T. *A History of Canadian External Relations.* Rev. ed. Toronto: McClelland and Stewart, c1966. 2 vols. (x, 271; viii, 166 p.) **6438**

Volume 1 was first published Toronto, Oxford University Press, 1942, under title: *Canadian External Relations; an Historical Study to 1914*. The first edition of the whole work was published Toronto, Oxford University Press, 1950.
Contents: v. 1. The Formative Years to 1914.- v. 2. In the Empire and the World 1914-1939.

Gluek, Alvin Charles. "Recent Studies in the History of Canadian External Affairs. (Review Article)." (1979), 8 *Acadiensis* 125-133 (No. 1) **6439**

Gordon, J. King, ed. *Canada's Role as a Middle Power*. Papers given at the Third Annual Banff Conference on World Development, August 1965. Toronto: Canadian Institute of International Affairs, c1966. 212 p. (Contemporary Affairs, No. 35) **6440**
Reviews: H.S. Ferns in (1967), 43 *International Affairs* 414-415; Brian Flemming in (1966-67), 46 *Dalhousie Review* 541-543.

Gotlieb, Allan E. *Canadian Diplomacy in the 1980s: Leadership and Service*. Toronto: Centre for International Studies, University of Toronto, c1979. ii, 22 p. **6441**
A public lecture given in Toronto on February 15, 1979.

Gotlieb, Allan E., and Kinsman, Jeremy. "Reviving the Third Option." (1981), *International Perspectives* 2-5 (Jan./Feb.), 22-25 (Nov./Dec.) **6442**

Gotlieb, Allan E., and Legault, L.H. "Droit et diplomatie: nouvelles frontières du Canada." (1981), 12 *Politique Internationale* 263-285. **6443**

Granatstein, J.L. *Canada's War: The Politics of the Mackenzie King Government, 1939-1945*. Toronto: Oxford University Press, 1975. xi, 436 p. **6444**
Review: John W. Holmes in (1974-75), 30 *International Journal* 802-804.

Granatstein, J.L., ed. *Canadian Foreign Policy since 1945: Middle Power or Satellite?* Rev. ed. Toronto: Copp Clark, 1970, c1969. 221 p. (Issues in Canadian History) **6445**
Review: Zachariah Kay in (1970), 3 *Canadian Journal of Political Science* 333-334.

Granatstein, J.L., ed. *Canadian Foreign Policy since 1945: Middle Power or Satellite?* 2d ed. Toronto: Copp Clark, 1973, c1969. 246 p. (Issues in Canadian History) **6446**

Griffiths, Stuart. "International Shortwave Broadcasting in Canada." (1946), 33 *Canadian Geographical Journal* 219-235. **6447**

Hertz, Allen Zangwil. *The Constitutional Basis of Canadian Foreign Relations*. Toronto, c1981. 171 leaves. **6448**
Thesis (LL.M.), University of Toronto, 1981.

Hettinger, James Frederick. *An Examination of Countervailing Forces in Canadian Foreign Policy*. Kalamazoo, Mich., 1973. 123 leaves. **6449**
Thesis (M.A.), Western Michigan University, 1973. Abstracted in (1973), 11 *Masters Abstracts* 472. (University Microfilms, Ann Arbor, No. M-4935).

Hillmer, Norman, and Stevenson, Garth, eds. *A Foremost Nation: Canadian Foreign Policy and a Changing World*. Toronto: McClelland and Stewart, c1977. 296 p. (Carleton Contemporary) **6450**
Reviews: David Cox in (1978), 4 *Canadian Public Policy* 395; Panayotis Soldatos in (1979), 10 *Études Internationales* 408-409; Donald C. Story in (1977-78), 33 *Interna-*

tional Journal 458-459; J. Richard Wagner in (1977), 7 *American Review of Canadian Studies* 77-79 (No. 2); Gerald Wright in (1978), 11 *Canadian Journal of Political Science* 481-483.

Hockin, Thomas A., and others. *The Canadian Condominium; Domestic Issues and External Policy.* Toronto: McClelland and Stewart, c1972. 176 p. **6451**
Review: Clarence G. Redekop in (1972-73) *International Journal* 375-380.

Holmes, John W. *The Better Part of Valour; Essays on Canadian Diplomacy.* Toronto: McClelland and Stewart, c1970. 239 p. (Carleton Library, No. 49) **6452**
Reviews: André P. Donneur in (1971), 2 *Études Internationales* 143-144; Denis Stairs in (1977), 10 *Canadian Journal of Political Science* 183-184.

Holmes, John W. *Canada, a Middle-Aged Power.* Toronto: McClelland and Stewart, 1976. viii, 293 p. (Carleton Library, No. 98) **6453**
Reviews: Denis Stairs in (1977), 10 *Canadian Journal of Political Science* 183-184; D.H. Stepler in (1976-77), 56 *Dalhousie Review* 791-793.

Holmes, John W. "Canada in Search of Its Role." (1962-63), 41 *Foreign Affairs* 659-672. **6454**

Holmes, John W. "Canadian Foreign Policy and International Law." (1980), 9 *Canadian Council on International Law, Proceedings* 1-3. **6455**

Holmes, John W. *The Shaping of Peace: Canada and the Search for World Order, 1943-1957.* Toronto: University of Toronto Press, 1979-82. 2 vols. **6456**
Reviews:
Volume 1: Robert Bothwell under title: "Canada and the Postwar Quest for Peace," in (1980), 87 *Queen's Quarterly* 709-712; Andrew Boyd in (1980), 35 *International Journal* 396-398; Michael Dunne in (1980-81), 57 *International Affairs* 207-208; Annette Baker Fox in (1980), 10 *American Review of Canadian Studies* 116-117 (No. 1); Richard Jones in (1981), 12 *Études Internationales* 225-227; Peyton V. Lyon in (1980), 13 *Canadian Journal of Political Science* 838-839.
Volume 2: Christopher Young under title: "A Prouder Canada," in (1982), *International Perspectives* 31-33 (Sept./Oct.).

Holmes, John W., and Laroche, Jean-René. "Le Canada et la guerre froide." *In* Painchaud, Paul, ed., *Le Canada et le Québec sur la scène internationale* (Québec, 1977), pp. 275-302. **6457**

Holmes, John W., and others. *The Changing Role of the Diplomatic Function in the Making of Foreign Policy.* Halifax: Centre for Foreign Policy Studies, Dept. of Political Science, Dalhousie University, 1973. 83 p. (Dalhousie University. Centre for Foreign Policy Studies. Occasional Paper) **6458**
Prepared for a seminar held in January 1973.

Horan, James Francis. *Patterns of Canadian Foreign Policy: A Study in the Shaping of Canada's External Relations from Confederation to Suez.* Storrs, Conn., 1972. vi, 482 leaves. **6459**
Thesis (Ph.D.), University of Connecticut, 1972. Abstracted in (1972), 33 *Dissertation Abstracts International* 3001-A. (University Microfilms, Ann Arbor, No. 72-32182).

"International Law and Canadian Foreign Policy in the 1980s / Le droit international et la politique étrangère du Canada au cours des années 80." (1980), 9 *Canadian Council on International Law, Proceedings*, v, 89 p. **6460**
This is the general theme of the ninth annual conference held at Ottawa, October 23-25,

1980. Sponsored jointly with the United Nations Association in Canada. Individual papers are listed separately.

Ismael, Tareq Y. "Canada and the Middle East." (1973-74), 32 *Behind the Headlines* No. 5 (32 p.) **6461**

Johnsen, Julia Emily, ed. *Canada and the Western Hemisphere.* New York: H.W. Wilson, 1944. 295 p. (Reference Shelf, Vol. 17, No. 3) **6462**

Julien, Claude. *Canada: Europe's Last Chance.* Translated from the French by Penny Williams. With introduction by Blair Fraser. New York: St. Martin's Press, 1968. xiii, 178 p., maps. **6463**
Translation of *Le Canada, dernière chance de l'Europe.* First published in French (Paris, B. Grasset, 1965).
Reviews: Michel Brunet in (1969), 50 *Canadian Historical Review* 97-99; Paul Painchaud in (1967-68), 23 *International Journal* 648; Gordon Winter in (1967), 43 *International Affairs* 199-200.

Kattan, Naim. "Le Canada et la France." *In* Penlington, Norman, ed., *On Canada: Essays in Honour of Frank H. Underhill* (Toronto, 1971), pp. 83-94. **6464**

Kavic, Lorne. "Canada and the Pacific: Needs and Challenges." (1969-70), 29 *Behind the Headlines* Nos. 3-4, pp. 1-10. **6465**

Keenleyside, Hugh L., and others. *The Growth of Canadian Policies in External Affairs.* Durham, N.C.: Duke University Press, 1960. x, 174 p. (Duke University. Commonwealth-Studies Center. Publication, No. 14) **6466**
Lectures, with one exception, given as part of the 1959 program of the Center's Summer Seminar and Research Group. Some individual papers are also listed separately.
Contents: "Foreword," by Paul H. Clyde.- 1. "Introduction," by Hugh L. Keenleyside.- 2. "The Origins of Canada's Department of External Affairs," by James Eayrs.- 3. "Canadian External Affairs During World War I," by Gaddis Smith.- 4. " 'A Low Dishonest Decade': Aspects of Canadian External Policy, 1931-1939," by James Eayrs.- 5. "The Treaty Power in Canada," by David R. Deener.- 6. "Le Canada français: du provincialisme à l'internationalisme," by Gérard Bergeron.- 7. "Economic Aspects of Foreign Policy," by Vincent W. Bladen.- 8. "A Middle Power in the Cold War," by Edgar McInnis.- "Selected Readings in Canadian External Policy, 1909-1959," by Gaddis Smith.- Index.
Reviews: H.S. Ferns in (1961), 37 *International Affairs* 415; John Donald Bruce Miller in (1960-61), 16 *International Journal* 185-186; Frederic H. Soward in (1961), 42 *Canadian Historical Review* 162; Frank H. Underhill in (1961), 27 *Canadian Journal of Economics and Political Science* 564.

Kirton, John J. "Les contraintes du milieu et la gestion de la politique étrangère canadienne de 1976 à 1978." (1979), 10 *Études Internationales* 321-349. **6467**

Laut, Agnes Christina. *Canada at the Cross Roads.* Toronto: Macmillan of Canada, 1921. 279 p. **6468**
Review: H. Mitchell in (1922), 3 *Canadian Historical Review* 92-93.

Leacock, Stephen. "Canada and the Monroe Doctrine." (1909), 8 *University Magazine* 351-374. **6469**

Legault, Albert. "Trente ans de politique de défense canadienne." *In* Painchaud, Paul, ed., *Le Canada et le Québec sur la scène internationale* (Québec, 1977), pp. 149-177. **6470**

Legault, L.H. "Canada and the Developing World." (1980), 9 *Canadian Council on International Law, Proceedings* 37-41. **6471**

Le Gris, Claude. *L'entrée du Canada sur la scène internationale (1919-1927).* Préface de John W. Holmes. Paris: Presses universitaires de France, 1966. xii, 96 p. **6472**
Issued as a dissertation, Université de Montréal.
Reviews: H.S. Ferns in (1967), 43 *International Affairs* 414-415; Hilda Blair Neatby in (1967), 48 *Canadian Historical Review* 166.

Louthood, Louise. "Chronique des relations extérieures du Canada et du Québec." (1981), 12 *Études Internationales* 177-199. **6473**
Covers the period from October to December 1980.

Louthood, Louise. "Chronique des relations extérieures du Canada et du Québec." (1981), 12 *Études Internationales* 371-393. **6474**
Covers the period from January to March 1981.

Louthood, Louise. "Chronique des relations extérieures du Canada et du Québec." (1981), 12 *Études Internationales* 549-577. **6475**
Covers the period from April to June 1981.

Lower, Arthur R.M. "Canada and Foreign Policy." (1940), 47 *Queen's Quarterly* 418-427. **6476**

Lower, Arthur R.M. "Foreign Policy and Canadian Nationalism." (1935-36), 15 *Dalhousie Review* 29-36. **6477**

Lower, Joseph Arthur. *Canada on the Pacific Rim.* Toronto, New York: McGraw-Hill Ryerson, c1975. x, 230 p. **6478**

Lyon, Peyton V. "New Directions in Canada's Foreign Policy." (1980), 70 *Round Table* 28-32. **6479**

Lyon, Peyton V. *The Policy Question; a Critical Appraisal of Canada's Role in World Affairs.* Toronto: McClelland and Stewart, 1963. xi, 128 p. **6480**

Lyon, Peyton V., and Tomlin, Brian W. *Canada as an International Actor.* Toronto: Macmillan, 1979. xiii, 209 p. (Canadian Controversies Series) **6481**
Reviews: David Cox in (1980), 13 *Canadian Journal of Political Science* 835-837; Alexander Craig under title: "Lyon and Tomlin on Canada," in (1981) *International Perspectives* 30-31 (July/Aug.); Maureen Appel Molot in (1981), 7 *Canadian Public Policy* 127; John P. Schlegel in (1980), 10 *American Review of Canadian Studies* 119-120 (No. 1)

MacKay, Robert A., ed. *Newfoundland; Economic, Diplomatic, and Strategic Studies.* Foreword by Sir Campbell Stuart. Toronto: Oxford University Press, 1946. xiv, 577 p., maps. **6483**
Issued under the auspices of the Royal Institute of International Affairs.
Reviews: Elias Andrews in (1946-47), 26 *Dalhousie Review* 252-255; François-Albert Angers in (1948-49), 24 *Actualité Économique* 758-759; Eugene Forsey in (1946-47), 2 *International Journal* 84-85; Kenneth Clinton Wheare in (1947), 23 *International Affairs* 581-582.

MacKay, Robert A., and Rogers, E.B. *Canada Looks Abroad.* Foreword by J.W. Dafoe. London, New York etc.: Oxford University Press, 1938. xx, 402 p.
Issued under the auspices of the Canadian Institute of International Affairs. **6484**
Reviews: Raymond Leslie Buell in (1939), 5 *Canadian Journal of Economics and*

Political Science 128-130; A. Berriedale Keith in (1938), 20 *Journal of Comparative Legislation and International Law* 285-286 (3d Ser.); R.W.G. MacKay in (1939), 18 *International Affairs* 106-107; Reginald G. Trotter in (1938-39), 45 *Queen's Quarterly* 259-261.

Macdonald, Ronald St. John. "Fundamentals of Canadian Foreign Policy." (1958), 12 *Year Book of World Affairs* 156-180. **6485**

Madar, Daniel R. "Foreign Policy Objectives, Country Studies and Planning Theory." (1980), 23 *Canadian Public Administration* 380-399. **6486**

Malcolm, K. Blair. *The Roots of John Diefenbaker's Foreign Policy with Special Relation to the Canada, Britain, E.E.C. Controversy of 1961-1962.* Waterloo, Ont., 1974. 133 leaves. **6487**
Thesis (M.A.), Wilfrid Laurier University, 1974.

Martin, Chester B., ed. *Canada in Peace and War: Eight Studies in National Trends since 1914.* London, New York: Oxford University Press, 1941. xix, 244 p.
Issued under the auspices of the Canadian Institute of International Affairs. **6488**
Reviews: Lionel H. Laing in (1942), 36 *American Journal of International Law* 530-531; unsigned in (1941-42), 4 *University of Toronto Law Journal* 440.

Martin, Paul. *Canada and the Quest for Peace.* New York: Columbia University Press, 1967. xi, 96 p. (Jacob Blaustein Lectures in International Affairs, 1st, 1967) **6489**
Review: H.S. Ferns in (1968), 44 *International Affairs* 833-834.

Martin, Paul. *Paul Martin Speaks for Canada; a Selection of Speeches on Foreign Policy, 1964-67.* Toronto, Montreal: McClelland and Stewart, c1967. 158 p.
6490

Massey, Vincent. *On Being Canadian.* Toronto: J.M. Dent, 1948. xiv, 198 p.
6491
Reviews: Norman A.M. MacKenzie in (1949), 30 *Canadian Historical Review* 77-78; Nicholas Mansergh in (1949), 25 *International Affairs* 355.

Matthews, Robert O. "The Churches and Foreign Policy." (1983), *International Perspectives* 18-21 (Jan./Feb.) **6492**

McInnis, Edgar. "A Nation in the Dark." (1936-37), 43 *Queen's Quarterly* 241-249.
6493

McLin, Jon B. *Canada's Changing Defense Policy, 1957-1963; the Problems of a Middle Power in Alliance.* Baltimore: Johns Hopkins Press, 1967. xii, 251 p.
6494
Reviews: H.S. Ferns in (1968), 44 *International Affairs* 620-621; Peyton V. Lyon in (1966-67), 22 *International Journal* 537-538; Harald Von Riekhoff in (1968), 1 *Canadian Journal of Political Science* 226-227.

Miller, Anthony John. "The Functional Principle in Canada's External Relations." (1979-80), 35 *International Journal* 309-328. **6495**

Miller, John A., and Hurst, Donald A. *Challenge of Power: Canada and the World.* Don Mills, Ont.: Academic Press Canada, c1979. 135 p. (Power Series)
6496

Minifie, James M. *Peacemaker or Powder-Monkey: Canada's Role in a Revolutionary World.* Toronto: McClelland and Stewart, c1960. 181 p. **6497**

Reviews: G.S. French in (1961), 27 *Canadian Journal of Economics and Political Science* 297-299; Kenneth McNaught in (1960), 41 *Canadian Historical Review* 339-341.

Morrison, David R. "Canada and International Development." (1979-80), 14 *Journal of Canadian Studies* 133-144. **6498**

Morton, William L. *The Canadian Identity.* Madison: University of Wisconsin Press; Toronto: University of Toronto Press, 1961. ix, 125 p., maps. **6499**

Reviews: Michel Brunet in (1962), 43 *Canadian Historical Review* 68-69; H.S. Ferns in (1962), 38 *International Affairs* 135-136.

Morton, William L. *The Canadian Identity.* 2d ed. Toronto: University of Toronto Press, 1972. xi, 162 p., map. (Canadian University Paperbooks, 1) **6500**

Munro, John A. *The Difficult Art of Canadian Foreign Policy, 1957-1963.* Vancouver, 1965. 161 leaves. **6501**

Thesis (M.A.), University of British Columbia, 1965.

Munro, John A. "Loring Christie and Canadian External Relations, 1935-1939." (1972), 7 *Journal of Canadian Studies* 28-36 (No. 2) **6502**

Munton, Donald J. *External Influences on Canadian Foreign Policy Behavior: Developing and Testing Three Theoretical Models.* Columbus, Ohio, 1973. 381 leaves. **6503**

Thesis (Ph.D.), Ohio State University, 1973. Abstracted in (1974), 34 *Dissertation Abstracts International* 7309-A. (University Microfilms, Ann Arbor, No. 74-11024).

Munton, Donald J. "Les puissances secondaires et l'influence des attributs relationnels: le cas du Canada et de sa politique extérieure." (1979), 10 *Études Internationales* 471-501. **6504**

Newland, John Anthony. *The Rise of the Canadian Presence in France, 1882-1928: A Study in the Growth and Expansion of Overseas Canadian Diplomacy.* Fredericton, 1979. iv, 186 leaves. **6505**

Thesis (M.A.), University of New Brunswick, 1979. (National Library of Canada. Canadian Theses on Microfiche, No. 41083).

Nossal, Kim Richard, ed. *An Acceptance of Paradox: Essays on Canadian Diplomacy in Honour of John W. Holmes.* Toronto: Canadian Institute of International Affairs, 1982. xii, 202 p. (Contemporary Affairs, No. 49) **6506**

Ørvik, Nils. "Our Neighbours to the East: Greenland and Iceland." (1979-80), 59 *Dalhousie Review* 405-425. **6507**

Ogelsby, J.C.M. "A Trudeau Decade: Canadian-Latin American Relations 1968-1978." (1979), 21 *Journal of Inter-American Studies and World Affairs* 187-207. **6508**

Ossman, Albert John. *The Development of Canadian Foreign Policy.* Syracuse, N.Y., 1963. iv, 310 leaves, maps. **6509**

Thesis (D.S.S.), Syracuse University, 1963. Abstracted in (1963), 24 *Dissertation Abstracts* 1681-1682. (University Microfilms, Ann Arbor, No. 63-6752).

Painchaud, Paul, ed. *Le Canada et le Québec sur la scène internationale.* Québec: Centre québécois de relations internationales, Faculté de sciences sociales, Université Laval, distributed by Les Presses de l'Université du Québec, 1977. 643 p. **6510**

Review: Denys Laliberté in (1979), 12 *Canadian Journal of Political Science* 637-638.

Painchaud, Paul. "La nordicité: nouveau mythe canado-québécois de politique étrangère." (1979), 10 *Études Internationales* 614-624. **6511**

Patry, André. "Considérations sur la politique étrangère du Canada." (1946), 52/2 *Revue Dominicaine* 291-300. **6512**

Paul, Alix-Herard. *Relations under Economic Dependency: Mexico and Canada.* Washington, D.C., 1976. 239 leaves. **6513**
Thesis (Ph.D.), American University, 1976. Abstracted in (1976/77), 37 *Dissertation Abstracts International* 589-A.

Pawa, J.M. "Manpower, Diplomacy and Social Maladies: Canada, Britain, the United States and the Recruitment Controversy of 1917-1919." (1980), 11 *Canadian Review of American Studies* 295-311. **6514**

Pearson, Lester B. "Canada's Northern Horizon." (1952-53), 31 *Foreign Affairs* 581-591. **6515**

Pearson, Lester B. "The Development of Canadian Foreign Policy." (1951), 3 *External Affairs* 339-343. **6516**

Pearson, Lester B. "The Development of Canadian Foreign Policy." (1951-52), 30 *Foreign Affairs* 17-30. **6517**

Pearson, Lester B. "Reflections on Inter-War Canadian Foreign Policy." (1972), 7 *Journal of Canadian Studies* 36-42 (No. 2) **6518**

Pratt, Cranford. "Canadian Foreign Policy: Bias to Business." (1982), *International Perspectives* 3-6 (Nov./Dec.) **6519**

Prince, A.E. "The Chamberlain Policy and Canada." (1938-39), 45 *Queen's Quarterly* 245-251. **6520**

Purdie, Raymond J. Lewis. *Canada's Invisible Foreign Policy.* Regina, c1968. vii, 157 leaves. **6521**
Thesis (M.A.), University of Saskatchewan (Regina), 1968. (National Library of Canada. Canadian Theses on Microfilm, No. 10522).

Reford, Robert W. *Canada and Three Crises.* Toronto: Canadian Institute of International Affairs, c1968. xii, 246 p. (Contemporary Affairs, No. 42) **6522**
Review: Gordon Winter in (1970), 46 *International Affairs* 211-213.

Reid, Escott. "Canada and the Threat of War: A Discussion of Mr. Mackenzie King's Foreign Policy." (1936-37), 6 *University of Toronto Quarterly* 242-253. **6523**

Les relations entre la France et le Canada au XIXe siècle. Colloque, 26 avril 1974, Paris, organisé par le Centre culturel canadien. Paris: Centre culturel canadien, 1974. 109 p. (Cahiers du Centre culturel canadien, no 3) **6524**

Reuber, Grant L. "International Interdependence and Canada's Nationalisms." (1979), 17 *Royal Society of Canada, Transactions* 111-120 (4th Ser.) **6525**

Roche, Douglas J. "Canada's Role in the Third World." (1980), 9 *Canadian Council on International Law, Proceedings* 31-35. **6526**

Rotstein, Abraham, and Lax, Gary, eds. *Getting It Back: A Program for Canadian Independence.* Prepared for the Committee for an Independent Canada. Toronto: Clarke, Irwin, 1974. xv, 324 p. **6527**

Sabourin, Louis. "Le Canada et le tiers monde: origine et originalité d'une politique." (1978), 31 *Studia Diplomatica* 527-544. **6528**

Sabourin, Louis. "L'influence des facteurs internes sur la politique étrangère canadienne." (1970), 1 *Études Internationales* 41-63. **6529**

Schneider, Fred D. "Exploring the Third Option: Canadian Foreign Policy and Defense." (1980), 79 *Current History* 121-124. **6530**

Scott, Francis R. *Canada Today; a Study of Her National Interests and National Policy*. Foreword by E.J. Tarr. 2d ed., rev. Prepared for the British Commonwealth Relations Conference, 1938. London, New York, etc.: Oxford University Press, 1939. xii, 184 p., maps. **6531**
Issued under the auspices of the Canadian Institute of International Affairs. First published in July 1938; second edition, revised and enlarged, published in January 1939.
Review: R.W.G. MacKay in (1939), 18 *International Affairs* 106-107, 427-428.

Scott, Francis R. "The Permanent Bases of Canadian Foreign Policy." (1931-32), 10 *Foreign Affairs* 617-631. **6532**

Sébilleau, Pierre. *Le Canada et la doctrine de Monroe, étude historique sur l'influence de l'impérialisme américain dans l'évolution de l'Empire britannique*. Préface de Patrick Bury. Paris: Recueil Sirey, 1937. vii, 219 p. **6533**
Thesis (Doctorat), Université de Paris.
Reviews: Phillips Bradley in (1938), 32 *American Journal of International Law* 893-894; Jean Bruchési in (1938), 19 *Canadian Historical Review* 78-79; G.P. de T. Glazebrook in (1937), 16 *International Affairs* 961-962; Charles Rousseau in (1938), 45 *Revue Générale de Droit International Public* 709-710; Frank H. Underhill in (1939-40), 3 *University of Toronto Law Journal* 230-231; signed J.B. in (1939), 66 *Journal du Droit International* 808; 'Lex' in (1937-38), 16 *Revue du Droit* 445-446; and S.M. in (1938-39), 14/1 *Actualité Économique* 297-298.

Shortt, Adam. "The International Position and Prospects of Canada." (1930), 2 *Canadian Political Science Association, Proceedings* 59-63. **6534**

Smith, Gaddis G. *Nation and Empire: Canadian Diplomacy During the First World War*. New Haven, Conn., 1960. 389 leaves. **6535**
Thesis (Ph.D.), Yale University, 1960.

Smith, Gordon W. *Canadian Attitude to World Affairs as Reflected in 'Hansard,' 1867-1914*. Edmonton, 1948. viii, 204 leaves. **6536**
Thesis (M.A.), University of Alberta, 1948.

Soward, Frederic H. "Some Aspects of Canadian Foreign Policy in the Last Quarter Century." (1966), 4 *Royal Society of Canada, Transactions* 139-153 (4th Ser.) **6537**

Stacey, Charles P. *Canada and the Age of Conflict: A History of Canadian External Policies*. Toronto: Macmillan of Canada, 1977-81. 2 vols. **6538**
Volume 2 published by the University of Toronto Press.
Contents: v. 1. 1867-1921.- v.2. 1921-1948. The MacKenzie King Era.
Reviews:
Volume 1: Hilda Blair Neatby in (1979), 34 *International Journal* 729-730; Richard A. Preston in (1978), 8 *American Review of Canadian Studies* 140-142 (No. 2); Frederic H. Soward in (1978), 59 *Canadian Historical Review* 504-507; P.B. Waite in (1979-80), 33 *Revue d'Histoire de l'Amérique Française* 276-278.
Volume 2: Hilda Blair Neatby in (1981), 62 *Canadian Historical Review* 522-523.

Stacey, Charles P. "From Meighen to King: The Reversal of Canadian External Policies 1921-1923." (1969), 7 *Royal Society of Canada, Transactions* 233-246 (4th Ser.) **6539**

Stacey, Charles P. *Mackenzie King and the Atlantic Triangle.* Toronto: Macmillan of Canada, c1976. xvi, 74 p. (Joanne Goodman Lectures, 1976) **6540**
Contains lectures delivered at the University of Western Ontario in March 1976.
Review: Carman Miller in (1978), 59 *Canadian Historical Review* 253-254.

Stairs, Denis. *The Diplomacy of Constraint: Canada, the Korean War, and the United States.* Toronto: University of Toronto Press, 1974. xv, 373 p. **6541**
Reviews: Robert Bothwell in (1976), 57 *Canadian Historical Review* 220-222; Margaret P. Doxey in (1975), 8 *Canadian Journal of Political Science* 152-153; Allen Levy in (1975), 6 *Études Internationales* 289-291; Peyton V. Lyon in (1974), 17 *Canadian Public Administration* 515-516; Robert O'Neill under title: "Constraint with Honour," in (1973-74), 29 *International Journal* 350-355; Richard A. Preston in (1975), 5 *American Review of Canadian Studies* 162-163 (No. 1).

Stairs, Denis. "The Political Culture of Canadian Foreign Policy." (1982), 15 *Canadian Journal of Political Science* 667-690. **6542**
Presidential address to the Canadian Political Science Association, Ottawa, June 1982.

Stairs, Denis. *The Role of Canada in the Korean War.* Toronto, 1969. xii, 561 leaves. **6543**
Thesis (Ph.D.), University of Toronto, 1969. (National Library of Canada. Canadian Theses on Microfilm, No. 4511).

Stairs, Denis. "Unity, Diversity, and Foreign Policy." (1978), 16 *Royal Society of Canada, Transactions* 89-102 (4th Ser.) **6544**

Takach, George Steven. *Clark and the Jerusalem Embassy Affair: Initiative and Constraint in Canadian Foreign Policy.* Ottawa, 1980. 128 frames. **6545**
Thesis (M.A.), Carleton University, 1980. (National Library of Canada. Canadian Theses on Microfiche, No. 49546). Abstracted in (1981), 19 *Masters Abstracts* 266.

Tanghe, Raymond. *Le Canada dans l'ordre international; tribune d'information sur les problèmes de l'après-guerre.* Montréal: Fides, 1944. 346 p. **6546**
A series of interviews and discussions first conducted over the radio during the winter of 1943-44, with Raymond Tanghe as the chief interlocutor and participant.
Review: André Bergevin in (1945-46), 21/1 *Actualité Économique* 497.

Tarr, E.J. "Canada in World Affairs." (1937), 16 *International Affairs* 676-697.
6547

Taylor, Alastair M. *For Canada - Both Swords and Ploughshares; a Plea for an Integrated Defence and Foreign Policy for Canada.* Toronto: Canadian Institute of International Affairs, 1963. vi, 67 p. (Contemporary Affairs, No. 30)
Cover title: *Both Swords and Ploughshares for Canada.* **6548**

Taylor, Charles. *Snow Job: Canada, the United States and Vietnam (1954 to 1973).* Toronto: Anansi, 1974. ix, 209 p. **6549**
Reviews: Annette Baker Fox in (1975), 5 *American Review of Canadian Studies* 187-190 (No. 2); Donald Martin in (1976-77), 56 *Dalhousie Review* 189-192.

Thakur, Ramesh C. *Canada, India and the Vietnam War: Peacekeeping, Foreign Policy and International Politics.* Kingston, 1978. x, 694 leaves, maps. **6550**
Thesis (Ph.D.), Queen's University, 1978. (National Library of Canada. Canadian

Theses on Microfiche, No. 37550). Abstracted in (1978/79), 39 *Dissertation Abstracts International* 5713-A.

Thomson, Dale C., and Swanson, Roger Frank. *Canadian Foreign Policy: Options and Perspectives.* Toronto, New York: McGraw-Hill Ryerson, 1971. 170 p. (McGraw-Hill Series in Canadian Politics) **6551**

Thordarson, Bruce. *Trudeau and Foreign Policy: A Study in Decision-Making.* Toronto: Oxford University Press, 1972. viii, 281 p. **6552**
Reviews: Audrey D. Doerr in (1972), 5 *Canadian Journal of Political Science* 582-583; Clarence G. Redekop in (1972-73), 28 *International Journal* 375-380.

Tomlin, Brian W. *Canada's Foreign Policy: Analysis and Trends.* Toronto: Methuen, 1977, c1978. xiv, 213 p. **6553**
Some of the papers were originally presented at the 1975-76 Inter-University Seminar on International Relations held in Ottawa.
Reviews: David Cox in (1980), 13 *Canadian Journal of Political Science* 835-837; Kim Richard Nossal in (1979), 34 *International Journal* 732-733.

Trotter, Reginald G. "Which Way Canada?" (1938-39), 45 *Queen's Quarterly* 289-299. **6554**

Trudeau, Pierre Elliott. "Double allégeance du Canada: Francophonie et Commonwealth." (1978-79), *Politique Internationale* 33-42 (no 2) **6555**

Tucker, Michael J. *Canadian Foreign Policy: Contemporary Issues and Themes.* Toronto: McGraw-Hill Ryerson, 1980. xii, 244 p. (McGraw-Hill Ryerson Series in Canadian Politics) **6556**
Reviews: Akira Ichikawa in (1980), 13 *Canadian Journal of Political Science* 837-838; Joseph T. Jockel in (1981), 11 *American Review of Canadian Studies* 103-104 (No. 1); John J. Kirton in (1981), 7 *Canadian Public Policy* 132-133; Peyton V. Lyon under title: "Tucker's Foreign Policy," in (1980), *International Perspectives* 31-32 (July/Aug.); John P. Schlegel in (1981-82), 37 *International Journal* 174-176; Brian W. Tomlin in (1981), 12 *Études Internationales* 229-230.

Vaillancourt, Émile. *Le Canada et les Nations Unies.* Montréal: Éditions Beauchemin, 1942. 145 p. **6557**
Contains a series of open letters, radio talks and editorials.

Von Riekhoff, Harald. "Une analyse des objectifs de la politique étrangère canadienne." *In* Painchaud, Paul, ed., *Le Canada et le Québec sur la scène internationale* (Québec, 1977), pp. 547-574. **6558**

Walker, John R. "Foreign Policy Formulation - A Parliamentary Breakthrough." (1982), *International Perspectives* 10-12 (May/June) **6559**

Watts, C.S. "External Constraints on Canadian Foreign Policy." (1972-73), 2 *Canadian Defence Quarterly* 46-49 (No. 1) **6560**

Wilson, W.A. "Foreign Affairs Survey Reflects Canadian Regionalism." (1980), *International Perspectives* 11-14 (May/June) **6561**

Wrong, George McKinnon. "The Evolution of the Foreign Relations of Canada." (1925), 6 *Canadian Historical Review* 4-14. **6562**

2. COLONIAL PERIOD (BEFORE 1867)

Adair, E.R. "France and the Beginning of New France." (1944), 25 *Canadian Historical Review* 246-278. **6563**

Archer, Christon I. "Retreat from the North: Spain's Withdrawal from Nootka Sound, 1793-1795." (1978), 37 *B.C. Studies* 19-36. **6564**

Arnell, J.C. "The Ports of the Maritimes and Their Trade and Commerce in 1800." (1969), 78 *Canadian Geographical Journal* 12-17. **6565**

Basdeo, S., and Robertson, Harold H. "The Nova Scotia-British West Indies Commercial Experiment in the Aftermath of the American Revolution, 1783-1802." (1981), 61 *Dalhousie Review* 53-69. **6566**

Boissonnault, Charles-Marie. "Mirabeau donne la Colombie 'espagnole' à l'Angleterre." (1972), 10 *Royal Society of Canada, Transactions* 103-113 (4th Ser.) **6567**

Bruchési, Jean. "Les États-Unis et les rébellions de 1837-38 dans le Bas-Canada." (1937), 23 *Revue Trimestrielle Canadienne* 1-20. **6568**

Brunet, Pierre. "Relations diplomatiques entre Anglais et Français au siège de Québec (1759)." (1936), 30 *Royal Society of Canada, Transactions* 83-96 (3d Ser., Sec. 1) **6569**

Buckner, Phillip Alfred. *Colonial Office Government in British North America, 1828-1847.* London, Eng., 420 leaves. **6570**
Thesis (Ph.D.), University of London, 1969.

Burroughs, Peter. *The Canadian Crisis and British Colonial Policy, 1828-1841.* Toronto: Macmillan of Canada, 1972. vi, 118 p. (Foundations of Modern History) **6571**
Review: Sandra S. Clark in (1973), 3 *American Review of Canadian Studies* 111-112 (No. 2).

Burt, Alfred LeRoy. *The United States, Great Britain and British North America from the Revolution to the Establishment of Peace after the War of 1812.* New Haven: Yale University Press; Toronto: Ryerson Press, 1940. vii, 448 p., maps. (Relations of Canada and the United States) **6572**
Running title: *Anglo-American Relations 1775-1820.* Reprinted New York, Russell & Russell, 1961, and Toronto, 1966.
Reviews: Albert B. Corey in (1941), 22 *Canadian Historical Review* 323-326; D.C. Harvey in (1941-42), 21 *Dalhousie Review* 126-127; signed G.S.G. in (1941-42), 48 *Queen's Quarterly* 194-195.

Careless, J.M.S. "Two Rivers Empires: An Historical Analysis." (1975), 5 *American Review of Canadian Studies* 28-47 (No. 2) **6573**

Caron, Ivanhoë. "Influence de la Déclaration de l'indépendance américaine et de la Déclaration des droits de l'homme sur la rébellion canadienne de 1837 et 1838." (1931), 25 *Royal Society of Canada, Transactions* 5-26 (3d Ser., Sec. 1) **6574**

Casgrain, H.-R. "Coup d'oeil sur l'Acadie avant la dispersion de la colonie française." (1888), 1 *Canada-Français* 114-134. **6575**

Clark, Andrew Hill. "The Conceptions of 'Empires' of the St. Lawrence and the Mississippi: An Historico-Geographical View with Some Quizzical Comments on Environmental Determinism." (1975), 5 *American Review of Canadian Studies* 4-27 (No. 2) **6576**

Corey, Albert B. *The Crisis of 1830-1842 in Canadian-American Relations.* New York: Russell & Russell, 1970. xi, 203 p., maps. (Relations of Canada and the United States) **6577**
First published New Haven, Yale University Press; Toronto, Ryerson Press, 1941.
Reviews: S.D. Clark in (1942), 8 *Canadian Journal of Economics and Political Science* 307-311; Charles P. Stacey in (1942), 23 *Canadian Historical Review* 206-207.

Creighton, Donald G. *The Commercial Empire of the St. Lawrence, 1760-1850.* Toronto: Ryerson Press; New Haven: Yale University Press; for the Carnegie Endowment for International Peace, Division of Economics and History, 1937. vii, 441 p., maps. (Relations of Canada and the United States) **6578**
Reviews: D.C. Harvey in (1938-39), 18 *Dalhousie Review* 120-121; Reginald G. Trotter in (1938-39), 45 *Queen's Quarterly* 259-261.

Danglade, James Kirby. *John Graves Simcoe and the United States, 1775-1796: A Study in Anglo-American Frontier Diplomacy.* Muncie, Ind., 1972. vi, 184 leaves. **6579**
Thesis (Ph.D.), Ball State University, 1972. Abstracted in (1972), 33 *Dissertation Abstracts International* 2854-A. (University Microfilms, Ann Arbor, No. 72-30145).

DeRosier, Arthur H. "The Confederates in Canada: A Survey." (1964-65), 3 *Southern Quarterly* 312-324. **6580**

Evans, Howard V. "The Nootka Sound Controversy in Anglo-French Diplomacy -1790." (1974), 46 *Journal of Modern History* 609-640. **6581**

Fraser, D.G.L. "The Origin and Function of the Court of Vice Admiralty in Halifax 1749-1759." (1961), 33 *Nova Scotia Historical Society, Collections* 57-80. **6582**

Frégault, Guy. "L'Empire britannique et la conquête du Canada (1700-1713)." (1956-57), 10 *Revue d'Histoire de l'Amérique Française* 153-182. **6583**

Frégault, Guy. *La guerre de la conquête.* Montréal: Fides, 1955. 514 p. (Collection Fleur de lys) (Études historiques canadiennes) **6584**
Review: Lionel Groulx in (1955-56), 9 *Revue d'Histoire de l'Amérique Française* 579-588.

Frégault, Guy. "La guerre de Sept Ans et la civilisation canadienne." (1953-54), 7 *Revue d'Histoire de l'Amérique Française* 183-206. **6585**
Refers to the years 1756-1763.

Gipson, Lawrence Henry. *Zones of International Friction: The Great Lakes Frontier, Canada, the West Indies, India, 1748-1754.* New York: A.A. Knopf, 1942. xlviii, 352, lix p. (British Empire Before the American Revolution, Vol. 5) **6586**
See also other volumes in this series by L.H. Gipson, especially vols. 6-7: *The Great War For the Empire: The Years of Defeat, 1754-1757,* and *The Victorious Years, 1758-1760.*
Review: Alfred LeRoy Burt in (1942), 23 *Canadian Historical Review* 412-415.

Glazebrook, G.P. de T. "The External Relations of the Province of Canada." (1938), *Canadian Historical Association, Historical Papers* 103-110. **6587**

Glazebrook, G.P. de T. *Sir Charles Bagot in Canada: A Study in British Colonial Government.* London: Oxford University Press, 1929. vi, 160 p. **6588**
Review: D. McArthur in (1929), 10 *Canadian Historical Review* 153-156.

Gould, Ernest Clark. *Relations between Nova Scotia and the United States, 1854-1870.* Toronto, 1934. 137 leaves. **6589**
Thesis (M.A.), University of Toronto, 1934. (National Library of Canada. Canadian Theses on Microfiche, No. 25477).

Graham, Gerald S. *British Policy and Canada, 1774-1791: A Study in 18th Century Trade Policy.* Westport, Conn.: Greenwood Press, 1974. xi, 161 p., 2 leaves of plates, maps. **6590**
Based on the author's thesis (Ph.D.), Cambridge University, 1929 (xxiv, 188, 34 p.). Reprint of the 1930 edition published London, Longmans, Green, issued as No. 4 of Imperial Studies of the Royal Empire Society.
Review: Alfred LeRoy Burt in (1931), 12 *Canadian Historical Review* 202-204.

Graham, Gerald S. *Empire of the North Atlantic; the Maritime Struggle for North America.* 2d ed. Toronto: University of Toronto Press, 1958. xvii, 338 p., maps. **6591**
Issued under the auspices of the Canadian Institute of International Affairs. First edition published in 1950.
Reviews: George F.G. Stanley in (1950), 31 *Canadian Historical Review* 408-410; R.J. Sutherland in (1951), 17 *Canadian Journal of Economics and Political Science* 275-277.

Graham, Gerald S. "The Origin of Free Ports in British North America." (1941), 22 *Canadian Historical Review* 25-34. **6592**

Hodgins, Thomas. *British and American Diplomacy Affecting Canada, 1782-1899. A Chapter of Canadian History.* Toronto: Publishers' Syndicate, 1900. 102 p., map. **6593**

Howay, Frederick H. "The Spanish Settlement at Nootka." (1917), 8 *Washington Historical Quarterly* 163-171. **6594**

Keenleyside, Hugh L. *Canada and the United States; Some Aspects of the History of the Republic and the Dominion.* Introduction by W.P.M. Kennedy. Port Washington, N.Y.: Kennikat Press, 1971. xxi, 396, xlii p., maps. (Kennikat Press Scholarly Reprints; Series in American History and Culture in the Twentieth Century) **6595**
First published New York, Knopf, 1929.
Contents: Introduction.- I. Canada and the American Revolution.- II. The Influence of the United Loyalists.- III. The War of 1812.- IV. Moments of Crisis.- V. Major Boundary Disputes.- VI. Minor Boundary Disputes.- VII. The Fisheries Controversy.- VIII. Commercial Intercourse since 1845.- IX. Immigration and Emigration.- X. The World War and Post-War Relations.- Index.
Reviews: Arthur H.U. Colquhoun in (1929), 10 *Canadian Historical Review* 158-159; H.H. Hemming in (1930), 9 *International Affairs* 254-255; Charles P. Stacey in (1952), 33 *Canadian Historical Review* 285-286; unsigned in (1929), 7 *Canadian Bar Review* 483-487.

Lamirande, Émilien. "L'établissement espagnol de Nootka (1789-1795) et ses aspects religieux." (1978), 48 *Revue de l'Université d'Ottawa* 212-231. **6596**

Lanctot, Gustave. "La Nouvelle-France et sa survivance." (1929), 23 *Royal Society of Canada, Transactions* 71-83 (3d Ser., Sec. 1) **6597**

Laplante, Corinne. *Le traité d'Utrecht et l'Acadie: une étude de la correspondance secrète et officielle qui a entouré la signature du traité d'Utrecht.* Moncton, 1974. 125 leaves. **6598**
Thesis (M.A.), Université de Moncton, 1974.

Le Duc, Thomas H. *The Aroostook War in Canadian-American Relations, 1837-1841.* Toronto, 1935 (c1973). 146 leaves, map. **6599**
Thesis (M.A.), University of Toronto, 1936. (National Library of Canada. Canadian Theses on Microfilm, No. 16645).

MacLachlan, Alastair Donald. *The Great Peace: Negotiations for the Treaty of Utrecht, 1710-1713.* Cambridge, Eng., 1965. vi, 723 leaves. **6600**
Thesis (Ph.D.), Cambridge University, 1965.

Manning, William Ray. *The Nootka Sound Controversy.* New York: Published for University Microfilms, Ann Arbor by Argonaut Press, 1966. 282-484 p. **6601**
Thesis, University of Chicago, 1904. First published in 1905 in the *Annual Report of the American Historical Association* for the year 1904. Refers to the dispute over Nootka Sound in 1789 between Great Britain and Spain, resolved by the Nootka convention of October 28, 1790 (1 BFSP 663), and the agreement of January 11, 1794 (4 Davenport 176).

Martin, Gerald Warren. *Britain and the Future of British North America, 1837-1867.* Cambridge, Eng., 1972. 2 vols. **6602**
Thesis (Ph.D.), University of Cambridge, 1972.

McDonald, Ronald Harold. *Nova Scotia Views the United States, 1784-1854.* Kingston, 1974. iii, 346 leaves. **6603**
Thesis (Ph.D.), Queen's University, 1974. (National Library of Canada. Canadian Theses on Microfiche, No. 20260).

McKegney, James C. "Two Neglected Colonies: New France and the Rio de la Plata in 1750." (1965), 3 *Royal Society of Canada, Transactions* 131-145 (4th Ser.) **6604**

Monet, Jacques. *The Last Cannon Shot; a Study of French-Canadian Nationalism 1837-1850.* Toronto: University of Toronto Press, c1969. x, 422 p. **6605**
Originally issued as a thesis (Ph.D.), University of Toronto, 1964.

Nicholson, Marian Ruth. *Relations of New Brunswick with the State of Maine and the United States, 1837-1849.* Rochester, N.Y.: University of Rochester Press, 1956. 156 leaves. (University of Rochester. Canadian Studies Series, No. 20)
Thesis (M.A.), University of New Brunswick, 1952. **6606**

Rich, E.E. "The Hudson's Bay Company and the Treaty of Utrecht." (1953), 11 *Cambridge Historical Journal* 183-203. **6607**

Robertson, Harold H. *The Commercial Relationship between Nova Scotia and the British West Indies, 1788-1822: The Twilight of Mercantilism in the British Empire.* Halifax, 1975 (c1977). v, 163 leaves. **6608**
Thesis (M.A.), Dalhousie University, 1976. (National Library of Canada. Canadian Theses on Microfiche, No. 28944).

Robitaille, Georges. "Les débuts de la guerre de Sept Ans (1756-1757)." (1941), 35 *Royal Society of Canada, Transactions* 147-160 (3d Ser., Sec. 1) **6609**
Refers to the Seven Years' War between Great Britain and France (1756-1763), for control of the North American continent; terminated by the Treaty of Paris of February 10, 1763 (1 BFSP 422; 1 Hertslet 239; 42 Parry 279), under which France definitively ceded her territories to Great Britain.

Robitaille, Georges. "Nouvel effort vers la paix entre la France et l'Angleterre, de mars à septembre 1761." (1945), 39 *Royal Society of Canada, Transactions* 177-193 (3d Ser., Sec. 1) **6610**

Robitaille, Georges. "Les préliminaires de la guerre de Sept Ans." (1939), 33 *Royal Society of Canada, Transactions* 109-126 (3d Ser., Sec. 1) **6611**

Robitaille, Georges. "Les préliminaires de la guerre de Sept Ans (deuxième partie)." (1940), 34 *Royal Society of Canada, Transactions* 91-99 (3d Ser., Sec. 1) **6612**

Robitaille, Georges. "Les tentatives de paix en 1759-1760." (1946), 40 *Royal Society of Canada, Transactions* 101-110 (3d Ser., Sec. 1) **6613**

Rutledge, Joseph Lister. *Century of Conflict; the Struggle between the French and British in Colonial America.* Toronto: Doubleday Canada, c1956. x, 530 p., maps. (Canadian History Series, Vol. 2) **6614**
Also published, New York, Popular Library, 1956.

Savelle, Max. "Diplomatic Preliminaries of the Seven Years' War in America." (1939), 20 *Canadian Historical Review* 17-36. **6615**

Savelle, Max. *The Origins of American Diplomacy: The International History of Angloamerica, 1492-1763.* With the assistance of Margaret Anne Fisher. New York: Macmillan, 1967. xiii, 624 p., maps. (American Diplomatic History Series) **6616**

Shippee, Lester Burrell. *Canadian-American Relations, 1849-1874.* New York: Russell & Russell, 1970. xi, 514 p., map. (Relations of Canada and the United States) **6617**
First published New Haven, Yale University Press; Toronto, Ryerson Press, 1939.
Reviews: D.C. Harvey in (1940-41), 20 *Dalhousie Review* 260-261; R.W.G. MacKay in (1939), 18 *International Affairs* 883; Charles P. Stacey in (1939), 30 *Canadian Historical Review* 322-325; Reginald G. Trotter in (1939-40), 46 *Queen's Quarterly* 376-378.

Sulte, Benjamin. "Le commerce de France avec le Canada avant 1760." (1906), 12 *Royal Society of Canada, Transactions* 45-63 (2d Ser., Sec. 1) **6618**

Sulte, Benjamin. "France et Canada, 1775-1782." (1917), 11 *Royal Society of Canada, Transactions* 1-16 (3d Ser., Sec. 1) **6619**

Sulte, Benjamin. "La guerre des Iroquois - 1600-1653." (1897), 3 *Royal Society of Canada, Transactions* 65-92 (2d Ser., Sec. 1) **6620**

Sulte, Benjamin. "Guerres des Iroquois, 1670-1673." (1921), 15 *Royal Society of Canada, Transactions* 85-95 (3d Ser., Sec. 1) **6621**

Trudel, Marcel. *Louis XVI, le Congrès américain et le Canada, 1774-1789.* Québec: Éditions du Quartier latin, 1949. xiii, 259 p. (Université Laval. Publications) **6622**
Reviews: Gerald S. Brown in (1950), 31 *Canadian Historical Review* 191-193; Léo-Paul Desrosiers in (1949-50), 3 *Revue d'Histoire de l'Amérique Française* 598-602.

Trudel, Marcel. *La Révolution américaine: pourquoi la France refuse le Canada, 1775-1783.* Rev. ed. Sillery, Québec: Éditions du Boréal Express, 1976. 291 p., maps. (Collection 17/60, 7) **6623**
Previous edition published in 1949 under title: *Louis XVI, le Congrès américain et le Canada, 1774-1789.*

Trudel, Marcel. "Le traité de 1783 laisse le Canada à l'Angleterre." (1949-50), 3 *Revue d'Histoire de l'Amérique Française* 179-199. **6624**
Extract from the author's: *Louis XVI, le Congrès américain et le Canada, 1774-1789.*

Wright, Barbara. *The Hudson Bay in French Colonial Policy, 1670-1715.* Lennoxville, Que., 1973. 129, x leaves. **6625**
Thesis (M.A.), Bishop's University, 1974.

Wrong, George McKinnon. *The Conquest of New France; a Chronicle of the Colonial Wars.* New Haven: Yale University Press, 1921. ix, 246 p., map. (Chronicles of America Series, Vol. 10) **6626**

Wrong, George McKinnon. *The Rise and Fall of New France.* Toronto: Macmillan of Canada; New York: Macmillan, 1928. 2 vols., maps. **6627**

3. RELATIONS WITH THE BRITISH EMPIRE AND THE COMMONWEALTH

See also *"Commonwealth of Nations" (p. 77), and "International Status: British Dominions" (p. 48).*

Allin, C.D. "Colonial Participation in Imperial Wars - Australasia." (1925-26), 33 *Queen's Quarterly* 329-343, 459-465. **6628**

Arnold, Guy. *Economic Co-operation in the Commonwealth.* Oxford, New York: Pergamon Press, 1967. x, 184 p., maps. (Commonwealth and International Library. Commonwealth Affairs Division) **6629**

Attwell, William George. *The Canadian Response to Joseph Chamberlain's Tariff Reform Campaign, 1903-1906.* Ottawa, 1972 (c1973). ix, 218 leaves. **6630**
Thesis (M.A.), Carleton University, 1972. (National Library of Canada. Canadian Theses on Microfilm, No. 14088).

Barkway, Michael. "Canada and the Commonwealth Economic Conference." (1951-52), 7 *International Journal* 245-252. **6631**

Belzile, Thuribe. "La Conférence impériale." (1930-31), 6 *Actualité Économique* 311-320. **6632**

Black, William Harold. *The Ottawa Agreements in Relation to Post-War British Trade Policy.* Providence, R.I., 1940. iii, 161 leaves. **6633**
Thesis (A.M.), Brown University, 1940.

Borden, *Sir* Robert L. *Canada in the Commonwealth, from Conflict to Co-operation.* Oxford: Clarendon Press, 1929. xv, 144 p. **6634**
This is the first series of the "Rhodes Memorial Lectures," Oxford, 1927.
Reviews: E. Ritchie in (1929-30), 9 *Dalhousie Review* 265; W.T. Waugh in (1929), 10 *Canadian Historical Review* 156-158.

Borden, *Sir* Robert L. "The Dominions and Foreign Relations." (1925), 3 *Canadian Bar Review* 513-521. **6635**

Bousquet, Denis. *Les conférences impériales et la création du troisième Empire britannique, 1887-1931.* Montréal, 1954. 393 leaves. **6636**
Thesis (Ph.D.), Université de Montréal, 1954.

Brady, Alexander. "Dominion Nationalism and the Commonwealth." (1944), 10 *Canadian Journal of Economics and Political Science* 1-17. **6637**

British Commonwealth Relations Conference. *Proceedings.* 1st-5th, 1933-1954. Toronto, etc.: Oxford University Press. 5 vols. **6638**
Each volume also has a distinctive title: 1933, *British Commonwealth Relations.*- 1938, *The British Commonwealth and the Future.*- 1945, *The British Commonwealth and World Society.*- 1949, *The Changing Commonwealth.* Issued by the conference under different names: 1938-45, Conference on British Commonwealth Relations; 1949, Commonwealth Relations Conference. Some proceedings are listed separately.

Burt, Alfred LeRoy. *The Evolution of the British Empire and Commonwealth, from the American Revolution.* Boston: Heath, 1956. x, 950 p. **6639**
Reviews: Charles E. Carrington in (1957), 33 *International Affairs* 225-226; D.J. McDougall in (1957), 38 *Canadian Historical Review* 62-64.

Cappon, James. "Canada's Relation to the Empire." (1911-12), 19 *Queen's Quarterly* 85-99. **6640**

Carrington, Charles E. *The Liquidation of the British Empire.* With a Foreword by Watson Kirkconnell. London: Harrap, 1961. 96 p. (Reid Lectures of Acadia University, 2d Ser., 1959) **6641**
Based on three lectures delivered at Acadia University, Wolfville, N.S., October 1959. Also published Toronto, Clarke, Irwin, 1961.
Reviews: Gwendolen M. Carter in (1962), 38 *International Affairs* 240-241; D.J. McDougall in (1961-62), 17 *International Journal* 184-185.

Charteris, A.H. "The British Commonwealth Relations Conference at Toronto, 1933." (1933), 19 *Grotius Society, Transactions* 137-153. **6642**

Chevallier, Jean-Jacques. "Avant la Conférence impériale de 1930." (1931), 7 *Revue de Droit International* 147-251. **6643**

"Commonwealth Prime Ministers' Conference." (1955), 7 *External Affairs* 71-78.
6644

"The Commonwealth Relations Conference: A Canadian View." (1949-50), 40 *Round Table* 21-28. **6645**

Cook, George Leslie. *Canada's Relations with Britain 1911-1919: Problems of Imperial Defence and Foreign Policy.* Oxford, Eng., 1968. 461 leaves. **6646**
Thesis (Ph.D.), Oxford University, 1968.

Cook, Ramsay. "A Canadian Account of the 1926 Imperial Conference." (1965), 3 *Journal of Commonwealth Political Studies* 50-63. **6647**

Cook, Ramsay, and others. *Imperial Relations in the Age of Laurier.* Toronto: University of Toronto Press, 1969. xi, 80 p. (Canadian Historical Readings, 6)
6648

Corbett, Percy E., and Smith, Herbert A. *Canada and World Politics, a Study of the Constitutional and International Relations of the British Empire.* Toronto: Macmillan, 1928. 244 p. **6649**
Reviews: A. Berriedale Keith in a review article under title: "The British Empire," in (1929), 11 *Journal of Comparative Legislation and International Law* 287-290 (3d Ser.); Norman A.M. MacKenzie in (1930), 24 *American Journal of International Law* 432; Norman A.M. MacKenzie in (1928), 9 *Canadian Historical Review* 337-339; George McKinnon Wrong in (1929), 8 *International Affairs* 178-180; unsigned in (1929), 10 *British Year Book of International Law* 265-267; and (1929), 7 *Canadian Bar Review* 483-487.

Creighton, Donald G. "Canada in the English-Speaking World." (1945), 26 *Canadian Historical Review* 119-127. **6650**

Cunningham, Alain MacAlpine. *Canadian Nationalism and the British Connection, 1899-1919.* Burnaby, B.C., 1981. 202 frames. **6651**
Thesis (M.A.), Simon Fraser University, 1981. (National Library of Canada. Canadian Theses on Microfiche, No. 50991).

Dafoe, John W. "The Imperial Conference of 1937." (1937-38), 7 *University of Toronto Quarterly* 1-17. **6652**

Dawson, Robert MacGregor. "The Imperial Conference." (1937), 3 *Canadian Journal of Economics and Political Science* 23-39. **6653**
Reprinted from the author's: *The Development of Dominion Status, 1900-1936.*

Dewey, Alexander Gordon. *The Dominions and Diplomacy: The Canadian Contribution.* London: Longmans, Green, 1929. 2 vols. **6654**
Thesis (Ph.D.), Columbia University, 1935.
Reviews: A. Berriedale Keith in a review article under title: "The Constitution of the Empire," in (1930), 12 *Journal of Comparative Legislation and International Law* 123-126 (3d Ser.); Chester B. Martin in (1930), 11 *Canadian Historical Review* 341-344; H.A. Smith in (1930), 11 *British Year Book of International Law* 251-257; Frederic H. Soward in (1930), 24 *American Journal of International Law* 829-830.

Drummond, Andrew T. "The Commercial Future of the Empire." (1896-97), 4 *Queen's Quarterly* 56-63. **6655**

Drummond, Andrew T. "The Relations of Colonial Britain to the Empire." (1894-95), 2 *Queen's Quarterly* 148-157. **6656**

Drummond, Ian M. *Imperial Economic Policy, 1917-1939: Studies in Expansion and Protection.* Toronto: University of Toronto Press, 1974. 496 p. **6657**
Also published London, Allen & Unwin.

Dyck, Harvey Leonard, and Krosby, Hans Peter, eds. *Empire and Nations, Essays in Honour of Frederic H. Soward.* Toronto: University of Toronto Press in association with the University of British Columbia, c1969. xxi, 228 p. **6658**
Selected essays are listed separately.
Reviews: J.M.S. Careless in (1970-71), 26 *International Journal* 274-276; Roger Graham in (1971), 52 *Canadian Historical Review* 99-101.

Ewart, John S. "Canada, the Empire, and the United States." (1927-28), 6 *Foreign Affairs* 116-127. **6659**

Ewart, John S. "Excerpts from the Imperial Conferences 1923, 1926 and 1929." (1930), 8 *Canadian Bar Review* 91-100. **6660**

Ewart, John S. "Lessons from the Conference." (1908-09), 16 *Queen's Quarterly* 15-31. **6661**

Farr, David M.L. *The Colonial Office and Canada.* Toronto: University of Toronto Press, 1955. xii, 362 p. **6662**
Reprinted Toronto, University of Toronto Press, 1978 (Scholarly Reprint Series).
Reviews: D.G.G. Kerr in (1956), 22 *Canadian Journal of Economics and Political Science* 124-125; Paul Knaplund in (1955), 36 *Canadian Historical Review* 260-261; Arthur R.M. Lower in (1956), 34 *Canadian Bar Review* 353-355.

Frost, Richard Aylmer, ed. *The British Commonwealth and World Society: Pro-*

ceedings of the Third Unofficial Conference. Issued under the auspices of the Royal Institute of International Affairs. London, New York: Oxford University Press, 1947. xii, 204 p. **6663**

Gillies, James McPhail. *The Ottawa Conference of 1932.* Providence, R.I., 1949. vi, 132 leaves. **6664**
Thesis (A.M.), Brown University, 1949. Refers to the Imperial Economic Conference held at Ottawa, July 21-August 20, 1932. See also Ollivier, Maurice, *The Colonial and Imperial Conferences from 1887 to 1937* (Ottawa, 1954), vol. 3, pt. 2, pp. 345-424.

Glazebrook, G.P. de T. "Political and Military Relations of the British Commonwealth and the United States." (1946), 1 *International Journal* 337-348. **6665**

Glazebrook, G.P. de T., and Brady, Alexander. "Canada and the Commonwealth." (1970), 60 *Round Table* 557-564. **6666**

Gordon, Donald C. *The Dominion Partnership in Imperial Defense, 1870-1914.* Baltimore, Md.: Johns Hopkins Press, 1965. xiv, 315 p. **6667**

Greenlee, James G.C. "The ABC's of Imperial Unity." (1979), 14 *Canadian Journal of History* 49-64. **6668**

Greenwood, Thomas. "L'avenir de l'Empire britannique." (1941), 11 *Revue de l'Université d'Ottawa* 7-19. **6669**

Hadfield, *Sir* Robert. "Economic Organization and Development of Empire." (1932-33), 12 *Dalhousie Review* 425-432. **6670**

Hancock, William Keith. *Survey of British Commonwealth Affairs.* London: Oxford University Press, 1937-42. 2 vols. in 3, maps. **6671**
Issued under the auspices of the Royal Institute of International Affairs.
Contents: v. 1. Problems of Nationality, 1918-1936.- v. 2 (pts. 1 and 2). Problems of Economic Policy, 1918-1939.
Reviews: Thomas-A. Birch in (1944-45), 20/2 *Actualité Économique* 89-90 (of vol. 2); Robert MacGregor Dawson in (1938), 4 *Canadian Journal of Economics and Political Science* 271-273 (of vol. 1); Harold A. Innis in (1942), 8 *Canadian Journal of Economics and Political Science* 608-611 (of vol. 2); W.P.M. Kennedy in (1937-38), 2 *University of Toronto Law Journal* 432-435 (of vol. 1).

Harvey, Heather Joan. *Consultation and Co-operation in the Commonwealth; a Handbook on Methods and Practice.* London, New York: Oxford University Press, 1952. viii, 411 p. **6672**
Issued under the auspices of the Royal Institute of International Affairs. First issued to participants in the Fourth British Commonwealth Relations Conference held at Bigwin Inn, Ontario, September 8-18, 1949.
Reviews: J.A. Corry in (1952-53), 8 *International Journal* 52-54; R.F.V. Heuston in (1952), 28 *International Affairs* 379-380.

Hayes, Frank Randall. *The Evolution of Canada's Commonwealth Relations, 1945-1968.* Toronto, 1979. 532 frames. **6673**
Thesis (Ph.D.), University of Toronto, 1979. Abstracted in (1979/80), 40 *Dissertation Abstracts International* 6413-A. (National Library of Canada. Canadian Theses on Microfiche, No. 50273).

Holmested, George S. "Why Not 'Empire?' " (1927-28), 7 *Dalhousie Review* 344-347. **6674**

Hussey, Lyman Andrew. *Anglo-Canadian Relations During the Roosevelt Era, 1901-1908.* Athens, Ga., 1969 (c1970). v, 245 leaves. **6675**

Thesis (Ph.D.), University of Georgia, 1969. Abstracted in (1970), 30 *Dissertation Abstracts International* 3401-A. (University Microfilms, Ann Arbor, No. 70-1167).

"The Imperial Economic Conference, with Particular Reference to the United Kingdom-Canada Agreement." (1934), 13 *International Affairs* 245-252. **6676**
Report of discussions of the Montreal Branch of the Canadian Institute of International Affairs, 1932-1933.

Inglis, Alex I. "Loring C. Christie and the Imperial Idea: 1919-1926." (1972), 7 *Journal of Canadian Studies* 19-27 (No. 2) **6677**

Ingram, J. Clarence. "Inter-Empire Trade." (1932), 40 *Journal of the Canadian Bankers' Association* 60-67. **6678**

Jebb, Richard. *The Empire in Eclipse*. London: Chapman and Hall, 1926. xxxi, 352 p. **6679**

Kendle, John Edward. *The British Empire-Commonwealth, 1897-1931*. London: Warne, 1972. 60 p., maps. (Warne Modern History Monographs) **6680**
Published also Melbourne, Cheshire (Cheshire Modern History Monographs).

Kendle, John Edward. *The Colonial and Imperial Conferences, 1887-1911; a Study in Imperial Organization*. London: Published for the Royal Commonwealth Society by Longmans, 1967. x, 264 p. (Imperial Studies, No. 28) **6681**
A revision of the author's thesis, University of London, 1965.
Review: Robert Kubicek in (1968), 49 *Canadian Historical Review* 308-309.

Kendle, John Edward. *The Round Table Movement and Imperial Union*. Toronto: University of Toronto Press, c1975. xvi, 332 p. **6682**
Review: Ged Martin in (1977-78), 33 *International Journal* 473-476.

Kilduff, Vera R. *The Ottawa Agreements, Their Effect upon the Trade of the British Empire, 1932-34, with Special Reference to the Dominion of Canada*. Saskatoon, 1935. 312 leaves. **6683**
Thesis (M.A.), University of Saskatchewan, 1935. Refers to a series of trade agreements signed by the United Kingdom with the Dominions at the conclusion of the Imperial Economic Conference held at Ottawa July 21-August 20, 1932. For the text of agreements, see 135 BFSP 151, and subs.

Kirk-Greene, Anthony H.M. "Taking Canada into Partnership in 'The White Man's Burden': the British Colonial Service and the Dominion Selection Scheme of 1923." (1981), 15 *Canadian Journal of African Studies* 33-54. **6684**

Lavoie, Paul. "La Conférence impériale de 1930 et la politique des Dominions." (1932), 39 *Revue Générale de Droit International Public* 776-828. **6685**

Leacock, Stephen Butler. *Back to Prosperity; the Great Opportunity of the Empire Conference*. Toronto: Macmillan, 1932. 108 p. **6686**

Lee, R.W. "Canada and the Empire." (1916), 15 *University Magazine* 233-245.
6687

Lhomme, J. "La Conférence économique d'Ottawa et ses résultats." (1933), 40 *Revue Générale de Droit International Public* 181-205. **6688**

Longley, Ronald S. "Cartier and McDougall, Canadian Emissaries to London." (1945), 26 *Canadian Historical Review* 25-41. **6689**

Lyon, Peter, ed. *Britain and Canada: Survey of a Changing Relationship*. London: Cass, 1976. xxix, 191 p. (Studies in Commonwealth Politics and History, No. 4)
6690

Macdonnell, J.M. "After the Ottawa Conference." (1932-33), 11 *Foreign Affairs* 331-346. **6691**

MacKay, Hector. "Deux aspects internationaux des accords d'Ottawa." (1933-34), 9 *Actualité Économique* 21-26. **6692**

MacKay, Robert A. "Imperial Economics at Ottawa." (1932), 5 *Pacific Affairs* 873-885. **6693**

MacKenzie, Norman A.M. "The Second Unofficial British Commonwealth Relations Conference." (1939), 33 *American Journal of International Law* 352-356. **6694**

The first conference was held in Toronto in 1933; the second was held at Lapstone, near Sydney, Australia, September 3-17, 1938.

MacKirdy, Kenneth A. "Canada and the Commonwealth." (1967), 74 *Queen's Quarterly* 452-461. **6695**

Mansergh, Nicholas. *The Commonwealth and the Nations; Studies in British Commonwealth Relations.* London: Royal Institute of International Affairs, 1948. viii, 228 p. **6696**

Reviews: Kenneth Clinton Wheare in (1949), 25 *International Affairs* 215-216; George V. Wolfe in (1950), 44 *American Journal of International Law* 443-444.

Mansergh, Nicholas, ed. *Documents and Speeches on Commonwealth Affairs, 1952-1962.* London, New York: Oxford University Press, 1963. xxi, 775 p. **6697**

Issued under the auspices of the Royal Institute of International Affairs. Continuation of: *Documents and Speeches on British Commonwealth Affairs, 1931-1952.*

Mansergh, Nicholas. *Survey of British Commonwealth Affairs.* London: Oxford University Press, 1952-58. 2 vols. **6698**

Published under the auspices of the Royal Institute of International Affairs.
Contents: v. 1. Problems of External Policy, 1931-1939.- v. 2. Problems of Wartime Co-operation and Post-War Change, 1939-1952.
Reviews: D.J. McDougall in (1952-53), 8 *International Journal* 71-73 (of vol. 1); Alexander Brady in (1960), 41 *Canadian Historical Review* 358-360 (of vol. 2); D.J. McDougall in (1958-59), 14 *International Journal* 219-221 (of vol. 2); Kenneth Clinton Wheare in (1959), 35 *International Affairs* 227 (of vol. 2).

Marriott, J.A.R. *The Evolution of the British Empire and Commonwealth.* London: Nicholson and Watson, 1939. xv, 388 p., maps. **6699**

Review: Edgar McInnis in (1940), 21 *Canadian Historical Review* 73-74.

Martin, Chester B. *Empire & Commonwealth; Studies in Governance and Self-Government in Canada.* Oxford: Clarendon Press, 1929. xxi, 385 p. **6700**

Review: D. McArthur in (1929), 10 *Canadian Historical Review* 153-156.

McFadyean, *Sir* Andrew. "International Repercussions of the Ottawa Agreements." (1933), 12 *International Affairs* 37-59. **6701**

McInnis, Edgar. "Every Nation for Itself." (1936-37), 43 *Queen's Quarterly* 125-133. **6702**

McMinn, Kayron Campbell. *Laurier versus Chamberlain: Anglo-Canadian Relations, 1896-1905.* University, Ala., 1977. vii, 325 leaves, map. **6703**

Thesis (Ph.D.), University of Alabama, 1977. Abstracted in (1978/79), 39 *Dissertation Abstracts International* 408-A. (University Microfilms, Ann Arbor, No. 78-9866).

Miller, John Donald Bruce. *Britain and the Old Dominions*. Baltimore: Johns Hopkins Press, c1966. 286 p. (Britain in the World Today, 7) **6704**

Minville, Esdras. "La Conférence impériale de 1932." (1932-33), 8 *Actualité Économique* 186-193. **6705**

"The Montréal Conference: Few Concrete Achievements." (1958-59), 49 *Round Table* 50-56. **6706**

Morrison, Alfred Eugene. *R.B. Bennett and the Imperial Preferential Trade Agreements, 1932*. Fredericton, 1966 (c1967). vii, 195 leaves. **6707**
Thesis (M.A.), University of New Brunswick, 1966. (National Library of Canada. Canadian Theses on Microfilm, No. 1246).

Morton, Desmond. *A Peculiar Kind of Politics: Canada's Overseas Ministry in the First World War*. Toronto: University of Toronto Press, c1982. xii, 267 p., 8 p. of plates. **6708**

Ollivier, Maurice. *The Colonial and Imperial Conferences from 1887 to 1937*. Ottawa: E. Cloutier, Queen's Printer, 1954. 3 vols. **6709**
Contents: v. 1. Colonial Conferences.- v. 2-3. Imperial Conferences.
Review: Gwendolen M. Carter in (1956), 37 *Canadian Historical Review* 83-85.

"Ottawa and the Trade Agreements." (1932-33), 23 *Round Table* 44-63. **6710**

Page, Robert J.D. "Canada and the Imperial Idea in the Boer War Years." (1970), 5 *Journal of Canadian Studies* 33-49 (No. 1) **6711**

Palmer, Gerald Eustace Howell, ed. *Consultation and Co-operation in the British Commonwealth: A Handbook on the Methods and Practice of Communication and Consultation between the Members of the British Commonwealth of Nations*. Introduction by A. Berriedale Keith on The Constitutional Development of the British Empire in Regard to the Dominions and India from 1887 to 1933. London: Oxford University Press; H. Milford, 1934. lix, 264 p. **6712**
Issued under the joint auspices of the Royal Institute of International Affairs, and the Canadian Institute of International Affairs, on behalf of the first unofficial Conference on British Commonwealth Relations held at Toronto, September 11-21, 1933. Companion volume to the report on the work of the conference.
Reviews: Brooke Claxton under title: "The British Commonwealth and World Peace," in (1934-35), 4 *University of Toronto Quarterly* 259-265; Robert MacGregor Dawson in (1935), 1 *Canadian Journal of Economics and Political Science* 302-305; Lionel H. Laing in (1934), 28 *American Journal of International Law* 825-826; T.W.L. MacDermot in (1934), 15 *Canadian Historical Review* 415-420; Norman A.M. MacKenzie in (1935-36), 1 *University of Toronto Law Journal* 207-209; Robert A. MacKay in (1934-35), 14 *Dalhousie Review* 539-541; unsigned in (1935), 13 *Canadian Bar Review* 123.

Pearson, Lester B. "The Colombo Conference." (1950), 2 *External Affairs* 79-90. **6713**

Preston, Richard A. *Canada and Imperial Defense; a Study of the Origins of the British Commonwealth's Defense Organization, 1867-1919*. Durham, N.C.: Published for the Duke University Commonwealth-Studies Center by Duke University Press, 1967. xxi, 576 p. (Duke University. Commonwealth-Studies Center. Publication, No. 29) **6714**
Reviews: G.P. de T. Glazebrook in (1966-67), 22 *International Journal* 699-700; G.P. de T. Glazebrook in (1967-68), 23 *International Journal* 155-156; Norman Penlington in (1967), 48 *Canadian Historical Review* 380-382; Gordon Winter in (1967), 43 *International Affairs* 806-807.

Prince, A.E. "The Commonwealth Prime Ministers' Conference." (1944), 51 *Queen's Quarterly* 194-203. **6715**

Raleigh, *Sir* Thomas. "Imperial Conference - Or Council?" (1907), 6 *Canadian Law Review* 127-132. **6716**
Reprinted from (1906), 7 *Journal of Comparative Legislation* 12-15 (N.S.)

Richer, Léopold. *Marché de dupes? La Conférence impériale d'Ottawa (1932).* Montréal: Éditions Albert Lévesque, 1933. 208 p. (Documents économiques)
Review: D.C. MacGregor in (1934), 15 *Canadian Historical Review* 90-91. **6717**

Ritchie, T. Kerr. "England or Empire." (1930-31), 10 *Dalhousie Review* 524-534. **6718**

Rowan, Mary Josephine. *The Ottawa Conference and Anglo-Canadian Relations, 1932-37.* Worcester, Mass., 1943. 136 leaves. **6719**
Thesis (A.M.), Clark University, 1943.

Rowell, Newton W. *The British Empire and World Peace; Being the Burwash Memorial Lectures Delivered in Convocation Hall, University of Toronto, November, 1921.* Toronto: Victoria College Press, 1922. xxiii, 307 p. **6720**
Reviews: Arthur H.U. Colquhoun in (1922), 3 *Canadian Historical Review* 380-382; James L. Tryon in (1923), 17 *American Journal of International Law* 416-417; signed G.F.H. in (1923), 1 *Canadian Bar Review* 629.

Salmon, Mark Stephen. *R.B. Bennett and the Imperial Economic Conference, 1932: A Study in Nationalism.* Waterloo, Ont., 1975. iii, 92 leaves. **6721**
Thesis (M.A.), Wilfrid Laurier University, 1976.

Schultz, John A. *Canadian Attitudes Toward the Empire, 1919-1939.* Halifax, 1975 (c1976). 265, (13) leaves. **6722**
Thesis (Ph.D.), Dalhousie University, 1975. (National Library of Canada. Canadian Theses on Microfiche, No. 24954).

Scott, Francis R. *Canada and the Commonwealth.* Toronto: Canadian Institute of International Affairs, 1938. 89 p. **6723**
Prepared for the second British Commonwealth Relations Conference held at Sydney, in 1938.

Scott, Francis R. "A Policy of Neutrality for Canada." (1938-39), 17 *Foreign Affairs* 402-416. **6724**

Shortt, Adam. "The Colonial Conference and Its Functions." (1906-07), 14 *Queen's Quarterly* 319-324. **6725**

Skelton, O.D. "The Imperial Conference of 1923." (1923-24), 31 *Journal of the Canadian Bankers' Association* 153-162. **6726**

Smith, Arnold. "Canada and the Commonwealth." *In* Penlington, Norman, ed., *On Canada: Essays in Honour of Frank H. Underhill* (Toronto, 1971), pp. 111-130. **6727**

Soward, Frederic H. "The Adaptable Commonwealth. (With a Foreword by Nik Cavell)." (1950). 10 *Behind the Headlines* No. 1 (54 p.) **6728**
A report of the proceedings of the 4th Commonwealth Relations Conference held at Bigwin Inn, Ontario, September 1949.

Soward, Frederic H., ed. *The Changing Commonwealth; Proceedings of the*

Fourth Unofficial Commonwealth Relations Conference Held at Bigwin Inn, Ontario, Canada, September 8-18, 1949. Toronto: Oxford University Press, 1950. xiv, 268 p. **6729**
Issued under the auspices of the Canadian Institute of International Affairs.
Review: Max Beloff in (1951), 27 *International Affairs* 372.

Stevenson, John A. "The Imperial Conference at Ottawa." (1932-33), 12 *Dalhousie Review* 429-441. **6730**

Stevenson, John A. "The Other Dominions." (1934), 41 *Queen's Quarterly* 226-240. **6731**

Streeten, Paul, and Corbet, Hugh, eds. *Commonwealth Policy in a Global Context.* Toronto: University of Toronto Press, 1971. viii, 232 p. **6732**
Most essays are based on papers prepared for a seminar arranged in May, 1969, by the Queen Elizabeth House, and the Institute of Commonwealth Studies, University of Oxford, in conjunction with the Trade Policy Research Centre, London.
Review: Frederick J. Fletcher in (1972), 5 *Canadian Journal of Political Science* 470-471.

Toynbee, Arnold Joseph, ed. *British Commonwealth Relations; Proceedings of the First Unofficial Conference at Toronto, 11-21 September 1933.* Foreword by Sir Robert L. Borden. London: Oxford University Press; H. Milford, 1934. 235 p. **6733**
Reviews: Brooke Claxton under title: "The British Commonwealth and World Peace," in (1934-35), 4 *University of Toronto Quarterly* 259-265; Robert MacGregor Dawson in (1935), 1 *Canadian Journal of Economics and Political Science* 302-305; Lionel H. Laing in (1934), 28 *American Journal of International Law* 825-826; T.W.L. MacDermot in (1934), 15 *Canadian Historical Review* 415-420; Norman A.M. MacKenzie in (1935-36), 1 *University of Toronto Law Journal* 207-209; Robert A. MacKay in (1934-35), 14 *Dalhousie Review* 539-541; unsigned in (1935), 13 *Canadian Bar Review* 123.

Troop, William Hamilton. *Canada and the Empire; a Study of Canadian Attitudes to the Empire and Imperial Relationships since 1867.* Toronto, 1934. 231 leaves.
Thesis (Ph.D.), University of Toronto, 1934. **6734**

Troop, William Hamilton. "Canada and the Empire since 1867." (1934-35), 14 *Dalhousie Review* 155-166. **6735**

Trudeau, Pierre Elliott. "The Commonwealth after Ottawa, Looking to the Future." (1974), 64 *Round Table* 35-41. **6736**
Pierre E. Trudeau, Prime Minister of Canada, was Chairman of the Commonwealth Heads of Government Conference held at Ottawa, August 2-10, 1973.

Underhay, F.C. "Sir Robert Borden and Imperial Relations." (1930-31), 10 *Dalhousie Review* 503-517. **6737**

Vézina, François. "Les conférences impériales et la politique de préférence avant 1932." (1932-33), 8 *Actualité Économique* 177-185, 193. **6738**

Walker, Eric Anderson. *The British Empire, Its Structure and Spirit, 1497-1953.* 2d and extended ed. Cambridge, Eng.: Bowes & Bowes, 1953. x, 352 p., map.
6739

Watts, Floyd Elden. *The Imperial Conference of 1911.* Madison, Wis., 1959. 293 leaves. **6740**
Thesis (Ph.D.), University of Wisconsin, 1959. Abstracted in (1959), 19 *Dissertation Abstracts* 2077-2078. (University Microfilms, Ann Arbor, No. 59-730).

Waugh, W.T. "The Development of Imperial Relations." (1927), *Canadian Historical Association, Annual Report* 82-88. **6741**

Webster, A. *Canada at the Imperial Conferences, 1882-1926.* Vancouver, 1928. 175 leaves. **6742**
Thesis (M.A.), University of British Columbia, 1928.

Wigley, Philip G. *Canada and the Transition to Commonwealth: British-Canadian Relations, 1917-1926.* Cambridge; New York: Cambridge University Press, c1977. x, 294 p. (Cambridge Commonwealth Series) **6743**
Reviews: Robert Craig Brown in (1979), 60 *Canadian Historical Review* 231-233; A.D. Gilbert in (1978), 13 *Canadian Journal of History* 338-340; Richard Leach in (1978), 8 *American Review of Canadian Studies* 138-139 (No. 2); Charles P. Stacey in (1977-78), 33 *International Journal* 476-478; Richard Veatch in (1979), 12 *Canadian Journal of Political Science* 184-185.

Wilson, Harold Arnold. *The Imperial Policy of Sir Robert Borden.* Gainesville: University of Florida Press, 1966. 76 p. (University of Florida. Monographs; Social Sciences, No. 29) **6744**
Originally presented as the author's dissertation (Ph.D.), University of Iowa.

Wilson, Harold Arnold. *The Imperial Policy of Sir Robert Borden, 1911-1920: A Study in the Advancement of Dominion Status.* Iowa City, 1961. 270 leaves.
Thesis (Ph.D.), University of Iowa, 1961. **6745**

Winks, Robin W., ed. *The Historiography of the British Empire-Commonwealth; Trends, Interpretations and Resources.* With Twenty-One Essays by George Bennett and others. Durham, N.C.: Duke University Press, 1966. xiv, 596 p.
Review: Patrick C.T. White in (1968-69), 24 *International Journal* 622. **6746**

Woodcock, George. *Who Killed the British Empire: An Inquest.* Toronto: Fitzhenry & Whiteside; London: Cape, c1974. 356 p., maps. **6747**

Zimmern, *Sir* Alfred Eckhard. "The Open Door and Reciprocity, as Illustrated by Developments within the Colonial Empire." (1933), 40 *Queen's Quarterly* 501-515. **6748**

4. RELATIONS WITH THE UNITED STATES

(a) GENERAL

Abrams, Matthew J. *The Canada-United States Interparliamentary Group.* Ottawa: Parliamentary Centre for Foreign Affairs and Foreign Trade; Toronto: Canadian Institute of International Affairs, c1973. x, 148 p. (Contemporary Affairs, No. 47) **6749**
First issued under title: *The Canada-United States Interparliamentary Group, 1959-1969* (New York, 1971 (c1973). ii, 250 leaves). Thesis, Columbia University.
Reviews: André P. Donneur in (1976), 7 *Études Internationales* 289-291; Barbara G. Haskel in (1975), 5 *American Review of Canadian Studies* 178-181 (No. 2); Denis Stairs in (1974-75), 54 *Dalhousie Review* 175-177; William R. Willoughby in (1974), 7 *Canadian Journal of Political Science* 576-577.

Alper, Donald K. "Congressional Attitudes Toward Canada and Canada-United

States Relations." (1980), 10 *American Review of Canadian Studies* 26-36
(No. 2) **6750**

American Assembly. *The United States and Canada.* Edited by John Sloan Dickey. Englewood Cliffs, N.J.: Prentice-Hall, 1964. viii, 184 p. (A Spectrum Book, S-AA-12) **6751**

Angus, Henry F. *British Columbia and the United States; the North Pacific Slope from Fur Trade to Aviation.* By F.W. Howay, Walter N. Sage, and Henry F. Angus. Toronto: Ryerson Press; New Haven: Yale University Press, for the Carnegie Endowment for International Peace, Division of Economics and History, 1942. xv, 408 p. (Relations of Canada and the United States) **6752**

Angus, Henry F., ed. *Canada and Her Great Neighbor; Sociological Surveys of Opinions and Attitudes in Canada concerning the United States.* Introduction by R.M. MacIver. Toronto: Ryerson Press; New Haven: Yale University Press, for the Carnegie Endowment for International Peace, Division of Economics and History, 1938. xxxvi, 451 p. (Relations of Canada and the United States)
Review: J.W. Falconer in (1938-39), 18 *Dalhousie Review* 403-404. **6753**

Arctic Institute of North America. *Alaska in the 70's: Alaskan/Canadian Relationships.* Montreal, 1976. 95 p., maps. **6754**
Papers from a symposium held in Toronto, May 20-21, 1975.

Atlantic Council Working Group on the United States and Canada. *Canada and the United States: Dependence and Divergence.* Cambridge, Mass.: Ballinger, c1982. xiv, 331 p. **6755**
Review: Anthony Westell in (1982), *International Perspectives* 30-31 (July/Aug.).

Balthazar, Louis. "Les relations canado-américaines." *In* Painchaud, Paul, ed., *Le Canada et le Québec sur la scène internationale* (Québec, 1977), pp. 303-328.
6756

Barry, Donald J. "The Politics of 'Exceptionalism': Canada and the United States as a Distinctive International Relationship." (1980-81), 60 *Dalhousie Review* 114-137. **6757**

Berger, Carl C. "Internationalism, Continentalism, and the Writing of History: Comments on the Carnegie Series on the Relations of Canada and the United States." *In* Preston, Richard A., ed., *The Influence of the United States on Canadian Development: Eleven Case Studies* (Durham, N.C., 1972), pp. 32-54.
6758

Bernhagen, Beatrice Mary. *Canadian-American Diplomacy as Revealed in the Debates of the Canadian Parliament, 1867-1889.* Minneapolis, 1933. 108 leaves. Thesis (M.A.), University of Minnesota, 1933. **6759**

Brown, George W. *The Growth of Peaceful Settlement between Canada and the United States.* Prepared for the Canadian-United States Committee on Education. Toronto: Published under the auspices of the Canadian Institute of International Affairs by the Ryerson Press, 1949. 40 p. (Contemporary Affairs, No. 22) **6760**
Reviews: A.G. Bailey in (1949-50), 29 *Dalhousie Review* 457; Gerald S. Graham in (1949), 25 *International Affairs* 354-355.

Brown, Gerald S. "Canadian-American Relations 1900-1939." (1960), 2 *University of Windsor Seminar on Canadian-American Relations, Proceedings* 10-19.
6761

Brown, Robert Craig. *Canada's National Policy, 1883-1900; a Study in Canadian-American Relations.* Princeton, N.J.: Princeton University Press, 1964. xi, 436 p., map. **6762**
Based on the author's thesis (Ph.D.), University of Toronto, 1962.
Reviews: Charles S. Campbell in (1965), 46 *Canadian Historical Review* 253-254; A.E. Campbell in (1964-65), 20 *International Journal* 403-404.

Brown, Robert Craig. *Canadian-American Relations in the Latter Part of the 19th Century.* Toronto, 1962. 2 vols. (679 leaves) **6763**
Thesis (Ph.D.), University of Toronto, 1962. (National Library of Canada. Canadian Theses on Microfilm, No. 6).

Brown, Robert James. *Emergence from Isolation: United States-Canadian Diplomatic Relations, 1937-1941.* Syracuse, N.Y., 1968. iii, 327 leaves. **6764**
Thesis (D.S.S.), Syracuse University, 1968. Abstracted in (1969), 29 *Dissertation Abstracts* 4414-A. (University Microfilms, Ann Arbor, No. 69-7723).

Bruchési, Jean. "Les États-Unis et les rébellions de 1837-38 dans le Bas-Canada." (1937), 23 *Revue Trimestrielle Canadienne* 1-20. **6765**

Burt, Alfred LeRoy. *The United States, Great Britain and British North America from the Revolution to the Establishment of Peace after the War of 1812.* New Haven: Yale University Press; Toronto: Ryerson Press, 1940. vii, 448 p., maps. (Relations of Canada and the United States) **6766**
Running title: *Anglo-American Relations 1775-1820.* Reprinted New York, Russell & Russell, 1961, and Toronto, 1966.
Reviews: Albert B. Corey in (1941), 22 *Canadian Historical Review* 323-326; D.C. Harvey in (1941-42), 21 *Dalhousie Review* 126-127; signed G.S.G. in (1941-42), 48 *Queen's Quarterly* 194-195.

Callahan, James Morton. *American Foreign Policy in Canadian Relations.* New York: Cooper Square Pub., 1967. x, 576 p., maps. **6767**
Reprint of edition published New York, Macmillan, 1937.
Reviews: James P. Baxter in (1937), 31 *American Journal of International Law* 554-555; G.P. de T. Glazebrook in (1938), 17 *International Affairs* 875-876; Charles P. Stacey in (1937), 18 *Canadian Historical Review* 199, 201-202.

Canada. Parliament. Senate. Standing Committee on Foreign Affairs. *Canada-United States Relations.* Ottawa, 1975—. v.1—. **6768**
Also issued in French under title: *Les relations Canada-États-Unis.*
Contents: v. 1. The Institutional Framework for the Relationship. - v. 2-3. Canada's Trade Relations with the United States.
Reviews: Roma Dauphin in (1979), 5 *Canadian Public Policy* 291-292 (of vol. 1; French ed.); John H. Redekop in (1980), 13 *Canadian Journal of Political Science* 169-171 (of vol. 2); Charles Pentland in (1982), 5 *Revue d'Intégration Européenne* 305-307 (of vol. 3).

"Canada-U.S. Relations: Options for the Future. 1. American Reaction." (1973-74), 32 *Behind the Headlines* No. 1 (11 p.) **6769**
Contributions by four authors.

"Canada-U.S. Relations: Options for the Future. 2. Canadian Reaction." (1973-74), 32 *Behind the Headlines* No. 2 (14 p.) **6770**
Contributions by five authors.

Canada-United States Interparliamentary Group. *Report to the Senate on the Meeting*. 1st– , 1959– . Washington: Govt. Print. Off., 1959– . **6771**
Meetings are held annually; the 21st meeting was held in San Diego, California, May 23-27, 1980. Printed for the use of the U.S. Senate, Committee on Foreign Relations.

Canadian-American Business Conference, 6th, 1959. *Canadian-American Business Conference: Proceedings of the 6th Annual Conference*. Chestnut Hill, Mass., 1959. 56 leaves. **6772**
Conference held in Chestnut Hill, Mass., April 21, 1959.

Canadian-American Committee. *Bilateral Relations in an Uncertain World Context: Canada-U.S. Relations in 1978: A Staff Report*. Montreal: Canadian-American Committee, 1978. ix, 102 p., map. **6773**

Clark, Gerald. *Canada: The Uneasy Neighbor*. Toronto: McClelland and Stewart, c1965. xi, 433 p. **6774**
Review: Brian Flemming (1966-67), 46 *Dalhousie Review* 541-543.

Cohen, Maxwell. "Canada and the United States: Framework for the Future." (1964), 58 *American Society of International Law, Proceedings* 225-234. **6775**

Cohen, Maxwell. "Canada and the United States: A Legal Framework for the Future." (1964), 10 *McGill Law Journal* 233-242. **6776**

Cohen, Maxwell. "Canada and the United States - Possibilities for the Future." (1973), 12 *Columbia Journal of Transnational Law* 196-212. **6777**

Cohen, Maxwell. "Constants and Variables in Canada-U.S. Relations." (1980), *International Perspectives* 3-9 (Nov./Dec.) **6778**

Conway, John S. "Canadian-American Relations: Co-operation or Conflict?" (1957-58), 13 *International Journal* 204-212. **6779**

Craig, Gerald Marquis. *The United States and Canada*. Cambridge, Mass.: Harvard University Press, 1968. 376 p., map. (American Foreign Policy Library) **6780**
Reviews: Charles S. Campbell, Jr. in (1969), 50 *Canadian Historical Review* 88; A.F. Madden in (1968-69), 24 *International Journal* 615-616.

Cressy, A. Cheever. *Canadian-American Co-operation in World War II*. Medford, Mass., 1952. 1 vol. **6781**
Thesis (Ph.D.), Tufts University, 1952. Listed in (1951/52), 19 *Doctoral Dissertations Accepted by American Universities* 208.

Cuff, Robert D., and Granatstein, J.L. *Canadian-American Relations in Wartime: From the Great War to the Cold War*. Toronto: Hakkert, 1975. xiii, 205 p. **6782**
Reviews: Robert Craig Brown in (1977), 58 *Canadian Historical Review* 232-233; Michel Brunet in (1976-77), 30 *Revue d'Histoire de l'Amérique Française* 417-418; John H. Redekop in (1976), 9 *Canadian Journal of Political Science* 334-335; Denis Stairs in (1976-77), 56 *Dalhousie Review* 377-379.

Cuff, Robert D., and Granatstein, J.L. *Ties That Bind: Canadian-American Rela-*

tions in Wartime, from the Great War to the Cold War. 2d ed. Toronto: Hakkert, 1977. xxv, 205 p.   **6783**
First edition published in 1975 under title: *Canadian-American Relations in Wartime.*

Danglade, James Kirby. *John Graves Simcoe and the United States, 1775-1796: A Study in Anglo-American Frontier Diplomacy.* Muncie, Ind., 1972. vi, 184 leaves.   **6784**
Thesis (Ph.D.), Ball State University, 1972. Abstracted in (1972), 33 *Dissertation Abstracts International* 2854-A. (University Microfilms, Ann Arbor, No. 72-30145).

Dickey, John Sloan. "Canada Independent." (1971-72), 50 *Foreign Affairs* 684-697.   **6785**

Dickey, John Sloan, and Shepardson, Whitney Hart. *Canada and the American Presence: The United States Interest in an Independent Canada.* New York: New York University Press, 1975. xii, 202 p.   **6786**
Review: Arthur L. Johnson in (1977), 7 *American Review of Canadian Studies* 60-61 (No. 2).

Dobell, Peter C. "Negotiating with the United States." (1980-81), 36 *International Journal* 17-38.   **6787**

Dolan, Michael B.; Tomlin, Brian W.; and Von Riekhoff, Harald. "Integration and Autonomy in Canada-United States Relations, 1963-1972." (1982), 15 *Canadian Journal of Political Science* 331-363.   **6788**

Donnelly, Daniel K. *CanAmerican Union Now!* Toronto: Griffin House, 1978. xiv, 208 p.   **6789**

Donneur, André P. "Le facteur américain dans la politique extérieure canadienne." (1971), 2 *Annales d'Études Internationales* 63-66.   **6790**

Drouin, Marie-Josée, and Malmgren, Harald B. "Canada, the United States and the World Economy." (1981-82), 60 *Foreign Affairs* 393-413.   **6791**

Dziuban, Stanley W. *Military Relations between the United States and Canada, 1939-1945.* Washington: Office of the Chief of Military History, Dept. of the Army, 1959. xv, 432 p. (United States Army in World War II; Special Studies)   **6792**
Reviews: Douglas G. Anglin in (1961), 27 *Canadian Journal of Economics and Political Science* 401-403; Morris Zaslow in (1961), 42 *Canadian Historical Review* 61-63.

Dziuban, Stanley W. *United States Military Collaboration with Canada in World War II.* New York, 1955. 930 leaves.   **6793**
Thesis (Ph.D.), Columbia University, 1955.

Eayrs, James George. "Canadian-American Relations 1939-1960." (1960), 2 *University of Windsor Seminar on Canadian-American Relations, Proceedings* 20-30.   **6794**

English, Harry Edward, ed. "Canada-United States Relations." (1976), 32 *Academy of Political Science, Proceedings*, xii, 180 p. (No. 2)   **6795**
Also reprinted New York, Praeger. Some individual articles are listed separately.

English, Harry Edward. "The Role of Canada-U.S. Relations in the Pursuit of Canada's National Objectives." (1976), 6 *American Review of Canadian Studies* 32-55 (No. 1)   **6796**

Evans, Allan S. *Canadian-American Relations.* Toronto: McGraw-Hill Ryerson, c1981. 115 p., maps. **6797**
Excerpts from the author's: *Canada's Century.*

Feldman, Elliot J., and Feldman, Lily Gardner. "The Special Relationship between Canada and the United States." (1979-80), 4 *Jerusalem Journal of International Relations* 56-85 (No. 4) **6798**

Feldman, Elliot J., and Nevitte, Neil, eds. *The Future of North America: Canada, the United States, and Quebec Nationalism.* Cambridge: Center for International Affairs, Harvard University, 1979. 378 p. (Harvard Studies in International Affairs, No. 42) **6799**
Prepared under the auspices of the Center for International Affairs, Harvard University, and the Institute for Research on Public Policy, Montreal.

Ferguson, George V. "Likely Trends in Canadian-American Political Relations." (1956), 22 *Canadian Journal of Economics and Political Science* 437-448.
6800

Forest, Pierre-Gerlier. "À propos de la 'troisième option' et de la politique américaine de l'État canadien." (1982), 13 *Études Internationales* 305-321. **6801**

Fox, Annette Baker. "Canadian-American Cooperation in Foreign Policy and Defense." (1973), 3 *American Review of Canadian Studies* 173-182 (No. 1)
6802

Fox, Annette Baker. "On Living Together in North America." (1980-81), 36 *International Journal* 1-16. **6803**

Fox, Annette Baker. *The Politics of Attraction: Four Middle Powers and the United States.* New York: Columbia University Press, 1977. viii, 371 p. **6804**
Reviews: E. Donald Briggs in (1978), 11 *Canadian Journal of Political Science* 479-481; Peyton V. Lyon in (1979), 34 *International Journal* 321-323.

Fox, Annette Baker, and Hero, Alfred O. "Canada and the United States: Their Binding Frontier." (1974), 28 *International Organization* 999-1014. **6805**
Reprinted in Fox, Annette Baker, and others, *Canada and the United States* (New York, 1976), pp. 405-420.

Fox, Annette Baker; Hero, Alfred O.; and Nye, Joseph S., eds. *Canada and the United States: Transnational and Transgovernmental Relations.* New York: Columbia University Press, 1976, c1974. xiii, 443 p. **6806**
Reprint of a special issue on Canadian-American relations in (1974), 28 *International Organization* 595-1023 (No. 4). Some individual articles are listed separately.
Reviews: E. Donald Briggs in (1978), 11 *Canadian Journal of Political Science* 479-481; Ronald Ianni in (1977), 15 *Osgoode Hall Law Journal* 515-521; Donald J. Munton in (1979), 52 *Public Affairs* 174-175; Charles Pentland in (1976), 2 *Canadian Public Policy* 277-279; Jean-Pierre Thouez in (1977), 8 *Études Internationales* 662-664.

Gluek, Alvin Charles. *Minnesota and the Manifest Destiny of the Canadian Northwest; a Study in Canadian-American Relations.* Toronto: University of Toronto Press, 1965. xi, 311 p., maps. **6807**
Reviews: George A. Rawlyk in (1966-67), 46 *Dalhousie Review* 555; Lewis H. Thomas in (1967), 48 *Canadian Historical Review* 162-163.

Gotlieb, Allan E., and Kinsman, Jeremy. "Reviving the Third Option." (1981), *International Perspectives* 2-5 (Jan./Feb.), 22-25 (Nov./Dec.) **6808**

Gould, Ernest Clark. *Relations between Nova Scotia and the United States, 1854-1870.* Toronto, 1934. 137 leaves. **6809**
Thesis (M.A.), University of Toronto, 1934. (National Library of Canada. Canadian Theses on Microfiche, No. 25477).

Haglund, David G. "Plain Grand Imperialism on a Miniature Scale: Canadian-American Rivalry over Greenland in 1940." (1981), 11 *American Review of Canadian Studies* 15-36 (No. 1) **6810**

Hamilton, William Eugene, and Drummond, W.M. *Wheat Surpluses and Their Impact on Canada-United States Relations.* Washington: Canadian-American Committee, 1959. xi, 52 p. (Reports on Canada-United States Relations)**6811**
Sponsored by the National Planning Association (U.S.A.), and the Private Planning Association of Canada.

Heeney, Arnold D.P., and Merchant, Livingston T. *Canada and the United States; Principles for Partnership.* Ottawa: Queen's Printer, 1965. ii, 52 leaves. **6812**
First published in the United States under title: *Canada and the United States: Principles for Partnership.* Reprinted from (1965), 53 *U.S. Dept. of State Bulletin* 193-208.

Hodgins, Thomas. *British and American Diplomacy Affecting Canada, 1782-1899. A Chapter of Canadian History.* Toronto: Publishers' Syndicate, 1900. 102 p., map. **6813**

Holmes, John W. "Canada and the United States: Political and Security Issues." (1969-70), 29 *Behind the Headlines* Nos. 1-2 (16 p.) **6814**

Holmes, John W. "Canada and the United States in World Politics." (1961-62), 40 *Foreign Affairs* 105-117. **6815**

Holmes, John W. "Growing Independence in Canadian-American Relations." (1967), 46 *Foreign Affairs* 151-166. **6816**

Holmes, John W. "Heads Across the Border." (1978), 1 *Canada-United States Law Journal* 145-152. **6817**

Holmes, John W. *Life with Uncle: The Canadian-American Relationship.* Toronto: University of Toronto Press, 1981. 144 p. (Bissell Lectures, 1980-81) Also published as Canadian University Paperbacks, 275. **6818**
Reviews: B.C. Cuthbertson in (1982), 63 *Canadian Historical Review* 247-248; John H. Redekop in (1982), 15 *Canadian Journal of Political Science* 610-611.

Holmes, John W. "The Unequal Alliance: Canada and the United States." (1962), 4 *University of Windsor Seminar on Canadian-American Relations, Proceedings* 249-266. **6819**

Holsti, Kal J., and Levy, Thomas Allen. "Bilateral Institutions and Transgovernmental Relations between Canada and the United States." (1974), 28 *International Organization* 875-901. **6820**
Reprinted in Fox, Annette Baker, and others, *Canada and the United States* (New York, 1976), pp. 283-309.

Howe, Stanley Russell. *C.D. Howe and the Americans: 1940-1957.* Orono, Maine, 1977. 286 leaves. **6821**
Thesis (Ph.D.), University of Maine, 1977. Abstracted in (1978/79), 39 *Dissertation Abstracts International* 407-A. (University Microfilms, Ann Arbor, No. 78-10587).

Humphrey, John P. "Canadian-American Friendship. (Review Article)." (1938-39), 8 *University of Toronto Quarterly* 242-246. **6822**

Hutchison, Bruce. *The Struggle for the Border.* Freeport, N.Y.: Books for Libraries, 1970 (c1955). x, 500 p., maps. **6823**
First published Toronto, Longmans, Green, 1955. Also published Don Mills, Ont., Longman Canada, 1970.
Review: Patrick C.T. White in (1956), 37 *Canadian Historical Review* 178-179.

Jacomy-Millette, Annemarie. "David et Goliath: l'équilibre fragile des relations énergétiques canado-américaines à l'aube de la créaction de Petro-Canada." (1982), 13 *Études Internationales* 633-655. **6824**

James, Robert Warren. *Wartime Economic Co-operation; a Study of Relations between Canada and the United States.* Issued under the auspices of the Canadian Institute of International Affairs. Toronto: Ryerson Press, 1949. xiii, 415 p. (Studies in International Affairs, No. 4) **6825**
Reviews: Harry G. Johnson in (1950), 16 *Canadian Journal of Economics and Political Science* 435-438; Frank A. Knox in (1950), 31 *Canadian Historical Review* 189-191.

Kasurak, Peter C. "American 'Dollar Diplomats' in Canada, 1927-1941: A Study in Bureaucratic Politics." (1979), 9 *American Review of Canadian Studies* 57-69 (No. 2) **6826**

Keenleyside, Hugh L. *Canada and the United States; Some Aspects of the History of the Republic and the Dominion.* Introduction by W.P.M. Kennedy. Port Washington, N.Y.: Kennikat Press, 1971. xxi, 396, xlii p., maps. (Kennikat Press Scholarly Reprints; Series in American History and Culture in the Twentieth Century) **6827**
First published New York, Knopf, 1929.
Contents: Introduction.- I. Canada and the American Revolution.- II. The Influence of the United Loyalists.- III. The War of 1812.- IV. Moments of Crisis.- V. Major Boundary Disputes.- VI. Minor Boundary Disputes.- VII. The Fisheries Controversy.- VIII. Commercial Intercourse since 1845.- IX. Immigration and Emigration.- X. The World War and Post-War Relations.- Index.
Reviews: Arthur H.U. Colquhoun in (1929), 10 *Canadian Historical Review* 158-159; H.H. Hemming in (1930), 9 *International Affairs* 254-255; Charles P. Stacey in (1952), 33 *Canadian Historical Review* 285-286; unsigned in (1929), 7 *Canadian Bar Review* 483-487.

Keenleyside, Terence A.; LeDuc, Lawrence; and Murray, J. Alex. "Public Opinion and Canada-United States Economic Relations." (1976-77), 35 *Behind the Headlines* No. 4 (26 p.) **6828**
Review: Paul Pilisi in (1978), 9 *Études Internationales* 137-138.

Koehler, Wallace C., Jr. *Government Dominance and World Politics: Changing Canadian-American Relations in Energy, Trade and Foreign Ownership Policies.* Ithaca, N.Y., 1977. 420 leaves. **6829**
Thesis (Ph.D.), Cornell University, 1977. Abstracted in (1977/78), 38 *Dissertation Abstracts International* 5696 A. (University Microfilms, Ann Arbor, No. 78-1662).

Kottman, Richard N. *The Diplomatic Relations of the United States and Canada, 1927-1941.* Nashville, Tenn., 1958. iv, 526 leaves. **6830**
Thesis (Ph.D.), Vanderbilt University, 1958. Abstracted in (1959), 19 *Dissertation Abstracts* 1730. (University Microfilms, Ann Arbor, No. 58-7590).

Lanctot, Gustave, ed. *Les Canadiens français et leurs voisins du sud.* Montréal: B. Valiquette; New Haven: Yale University Press; pour la Dotation Carnegie pour

la paix internationale, Section d'économie politique et d'histoire, 1941. ix, 322 p. (Relations du Canada avec les États-Unis) **6831**
Review: Signed M.T. in (1941-42), 48 *Queen's Quarterly* 319-320.

Lanctot, Gustave. "Influences américaines dans le Québec." (1937), 31 *Royal Society of Canada, Transactions* 119-125 (3d Ser., Sec. 1) **6832**

Le Duc, Thomas H. *The Aroostook War in Canadian-American Relations, 1837-1841.* Toronto, 1935 (c1973). 146 leaves, map. **6833**
Thesis (M.A.), University of Toronto, 1936. (National Library of Canada. Canadian Theses on Microfilm, No. 16645).

Leyton-Brown, David. "Perspectives on Canadian-American Relations: The Scope of the Literature." (1981), 11 *Canadian Banker* 80-90 (No. 2) **6834**

Little, John Michael. *Canada Discovered: Continentalist Perceptions of the Roosevelt Administration, 1939-1945.* Toronto, 1975. 1 vol. **6835**
Thesis (Ph.D.), University of Toronto, 1975. Abstracted in (1977/78), 38 *Dissertation Abstracts International* 5696-A.

Lyon, Peyton V. "Problems of Canadian Independence." (1960-61), 16 *International Journal* 250-259. **6836**

Marshall, Charles. "Les Canadiens et les Américains." (1872), 9 *Revue Canadienne* 23-32. **6837**
Extract from the author's book published under title: *The Dominion of Canada* (Translated by Joseph Tassé).

Massey, Vincent. *Good Neighbourhood and Other Addresses in the United States.* Toronto: Macmillan, 1930. xiii, 362 p. **6838**

Matson, William Lawrence. *William Lyon Mackenzie King and Franklin Delano Roosevelt: Their Effect on Canadian-American Relations, 1935-1939.* Orono, Maine, 1973. 287 leaves. **6839**
Thesis (Ph.D.), University of Maine, 1973. Abstracted in (1974), 34 *Dissertation Abstracts International* 4161-A. (University Microfilms, Ann Arbor, No. 73-32332).

McDonald, Ronald Harold. *Nova Scotia Views the United States, 1784-1854.* Kingston, 1974. iii, 346 leaves. **6840**
Thesis (Ph.D.), Queen's University, 1974. (National Library of Canada. Canadian Theses on Microfiche, No. 20260).

McInnis, Edgar. *The Unguarded Frontier; a History of American-Canadian Relations.* New York: Russell & Russell, 1970, c1942. 384 p. **6841**
First published Garden City, N.Y., Doubleday, Doran, 1942.
Reviews: John W. Dafoe in (1942-43), 12 *University of Toronto Quarterly* 221-225; Julius W. Pratt in (1943), 24 *Canadian Historical Review* 198-199.

McLaurin, C. Campbell. "American-Canadian Relations." (1943), 22 *Nebraska Law Review* 66-76. **6842**

McLaurin, C. Campbell. "American-Canadian Relations; Economic and Political Union." (1948-49), 3 *Wyoming Law Journal* 29-36. **6843**

Merchant, Livingston T., ed. *Neighbors Taken for Granted; Canada and the United States.* New York: Published for the School of Advanced International Studies, the Johns Hopkins University, Baltimore, by F.A. Praeger, 1966. xv, 166 p. **6844**
Review: H.S. Ferns in (1967), 43 *International Affairs* 414-415.

Minifie, James M. *Open at the Top; Reflections on U.S.-Canada Relations.*
Toronto: McClelland and Stewart, 1964. 194 p. **6845**

Mitchell, James Rowell. *The United States and Canada.* Oxford: Blackwell, 1968.
viii, 220 p. (World Affairs Since 1939, Vol. 2) **6846**
Review: H.S. Ferns in (1968), 44 *International Affairs* 833-834.

Mitchell, Marnie F. *Tension and Understanding in Canadian-American Relations.*
Ottawa, 1975. 121 leaves. **6847**
Thesis (M.A.), Carleton University, 1975.

Morchain, Janet Kerr. *Sharing a Continent; an Introduction to Canadian-American Relations.* Toronto, New York: McGraw-Hill Ryerson, 1973. 248 p.
6848

Munton, Donald J. "Simulating Canadian-American Negotiations: A Boundary Waters Example." (1980), 10 *American Review of Canadian Studies* 37-55 (No. 2) **6849**

Murray, Janice L., ed. *Canadian Cultural Nationalism; The Fourth Lester B. Pearson Conference on the Canada-United States Relationship.* New York: Published for the Canadian Institute of International Affairs and the Council on Foreign Relations by New York University Press, 1977. ix, 139 p. **6850**
Reviews: Réjean Pelletier in (1979), 10 *Études Internationales* 411-413; Allan Smith in (1979), 60 *Canadian Historical Review* 115-116.

Neary, Peter F. "Grey, Bryce, and the Settlement of Canadian-American Differences, 1905-1911." (1968), 49 *Canadian Historical Review* 357-380. **6851**

Nicholson, Marian Ruth. *Relations of New Brunswick with the State of Maine and the United States, 1837-1849.* Rochester, N.Y.: University of Rochester Press, 1956. 156 leaves. (University of Rochester. Canadian Studies Series, No. 20)
Thesis (M.A.), University of New Brunswick, 1952. **6852**

Nye, Joseph S. "Transnational Relations and Interstate Conflicts: An Empirical Analysis." (1974), 28 *International Organization* 961-996. **6853**
Reprinted in Fox, Annette Baker, and others, *Canada and the United States* (New York, 1976), pp. 367-402.

Pearson, Lester B. "Good Neighborhood." (1964-65), 43 *Foreign Affairs* 251-261.
6854

Preston, Richard A. *The Defence of the Undefended Border: Planning for War in North America, 1867-1939.* Montreal: McGill-Queen's University Press, 1977. xiv, 300 p. **6855**
Reviews: Brereton Greenhous in (1979), 60 *Canadian Historical Review* 76-78; George A. Rawlyk in (1979), 86 *Queen's Quarterly* 148-149.

Preston, Richard A., ed. *The Influence of the United States on Canadian Development: Eleven Case Studies.* Durham, N.C.: Duke University Press, 1972. xii, 269 p. (Duke University. Commonwealth-Studies Center. Publication, No. 40)
6856
A selection of papers presented at a conference held at Duke University in April 1971.

Rawlyk, George A. "Canada and the American Revolution: 200 Years of Realizing That Rejection Was Really Acceptance." (1976), 83 *Queen's Quarterly* 377-387.
6857

Redekop, John H. "A Reinterpretation of Canadian-American Relations." (1976), 9 *Canadian Journal of Political Science* 227-243. **6858**

Rothenberg, Stuart. *United States-Canadian Relations, 1950-1973: The Limits of Community.* Storrs, Conn., 1976. xiii, 357 leaves. **6859**
Thesis (Ph.D.), University of Connecticut, 1977. Abstracted in (1977), 38 *Dissertation Abstracts International* 465-A. (University Microfilms, Ann Arbor, No. 77-14501).

Schuster, Leslie. *The Impulse of Independence: Canada's Political Relations with Its Superpower Ally, the United States.* New York, 1979. v, 442 leaves. **6860**
Thesis (Ph.D.), City University of New York, 1979. Abstracted in (1979/80), 40 *Dissertation Abstracts International* 448-A. (University Microfilms, Ann Arbor, No. 79-13164).

Shippee, Lester Burrell. *Canadian-American Relations, 1849-1874.* New York: Russell & Russell, 1970. xi, 514 p., map. (Relations of Canada and the United States) **6861**
First published New Haven, Yale University Press; Toronto, Ryerson Press, 1939.
Reviews: D.C. Harvey in (1940-41), 20 *Dalhousie Review* 260-261; R.W.G. MacKay in (1939), 18 *International Affairs* 883; Charles P. Stacey in (1939), 30 *Canadian Historical Review* 322-325; Reginald G. Trotter in (1939-40), 46 *Queen's Quarterly* 376-378.

Shotwell, James Thomson. "Canadian-American Relations." (1935-36), 42 *Queen's Quarterly* 391-402. **6862**

Shotwell, James Thomson. *The Heritage of Freedom; the United States and Canada in the Community of Nations.* New York, London: C. Scribner, 1934. ix, 136 p. (Pearson Kirkman Marfleet Lectures at the University of Toronto, 1932) **6863**
Review: Reginald G. Trotter in (1935-36), 42 *Queen's Quarterly* 145-148.

Skidmore, Darrel R. *Canadian American Relations.* Toronto: Wiley Publishers of Canada, c1979. 96 p. (Canada, Origins and Options) **6864**

Smythe, Elizabeth. "International Relations Theory and the Study of Canadian-American Relations." (1980), 13 *Canadian Journal of Political Science* 121-147. **6865**

Stevenson, Garth. "Canadian Regionalism in Continental Perspective." (1980-81), 15 *Journal of Canadian Studies* 16-28 (No. 2) **6866**

Stoler, Andrew L. "The Border Broadcasting Dispute: A Unique Case under Section 301." (1980-81), 6 *International Trade Law Journal* 39-54. **6867**

Stursberg, Peter. *Lester Pearson and the American Dilemma.* Toronto: Doubleday Canada, 1980. xii, 333 p., 8 leaves of plates. **6868**
Reviews: Tom Kent in (1980), 61 *Canadian Historical Review* 552-553; Robert W. Reford in (1980-81), 36 *International Journal* 243-245; Denis Smith in (1981), 14 *Canadian Journal of Political Science* 196-197.

Swanson, Roger Frank. *Intergovernmental Perspectives on the Canada-U.S. Relationship.* New York: New York University Press, 1978. xvii, 278 p. **6869**

Swanson, Roger Frank. *State/Provincial Interaction: A Study of Relations between U.S. States and Canadian Provinces.* Washington: Canus Research Institute, 1974. 509 p., maps. **6870**
Prepared for the U.S. Department of State.

Tansill, Charles Callan. *Canadian-American Relations, 1875-1911.* Gloucester, Mass.: P. Smith, 1964 (c1943). xviii, 507 p., map. (Relations of Canada and the United States) **6871**
First published New Haven, Yale University Press; Toronto, Ryerson Press, 1943.
Reviews: D.C. Harvey in (1944-45), 24 *Dalhousie Review* 115-116; A.R.M. Lower in (1944), 25 *Canadian Historical Review* 449-451; Francis R. Scott in (1944), 38 *American Journal of International Law* 516-517.

Tupper, Stanley R., and Bailey, Douglas L. *One Continent—Two Voices; the Future of Canada/U.S. Relations.* Toronto, Vancouver: Clarke, Irwin, 1967. 189 p. **6872**
American edition (New York, Hawthorne Books) has title: *Canada and the United States - the Second Hundred Years.*
Review: Gordon Winter in (1968), 44 *International Affairs* 397-399.

Turner, Robert K., ed. *Partners in the Free World; a Summary Report on the Canadian-American Conference on Foreign Relations, Niagara Falls, Ontario, May 31-June 5, 1951.* Boston: World Peace Foundation, 1952 (c1951). x, 103 p. **6873**

U.S. Congress. House. Committee on International Relations. Subcommittee on International Political and Military Affairs. *United States-Canadian Relations: Hearing, 94th Cong., 2d sess., January 28, 1976.* Washington: Govt. Print. Off., 1976. iii, 26 p., maps. **6874**

U.S. Information Service, Ottawa. *Canadian-American Relations, 1867-1967; a Compilation of Selected Documents concerning the Relations between Canada and the United States During the First Century of Canada's Confederation.* Ottawa, 1967. 3 vols. **6875**

U.S. Information Service, Ottawa. *A List of Selected Publications and Sources of Information on Canadian-American Relations.* Ottawa, 1966. 75, viii p. **6876**

U.S. Information Service, Ottawa. *Selected U.S. and Joint Documentation on Canada-United States Affairs, January 1963-September 1964.* Ottawa, 1964. vi, 135 p. **6877**

Von Riekhoff, Harald; Sigler, John H.; and Tomlin, Brian W. *Canadian-U.S. Relations: Policy Environments, Issues, and Prospects.* Montréal: C.D. Howe Research Institute; Washington: National Planning Association, 1979. vi, 149 p. (Canada-U.S. Prospects, 4) **6878**
Review: Alan S. Alexandroff in (1980), 6 *Canadian Public Policy* 703-704.

Wade, Mason. "Some Aspects of the Relations of French Canada with the United States." (1944), *Canadian Historical Association, Historical Papers* 16-36.
6879

Wagner, James Richard. *Partnership: American Foreign Policy Toward Canada, 1953-1957.* Denver, 1966. 319 leaves. **6880**
Thesis (Ph.D.), University of Denver, 1966. Abstracted in (1966/67), 27 *Dissertation Abstracts International* 1424-A. (University Microfilms, Ann Arbor, No. 66-11768).

Willoughby, William R. "The Canada-United States Interparliamentary Group." *In* Splete, Allen P., ed., *Toward a Better Understanding of Canadian-American Relations* (Canton, N.Y., 1973), pp. 77-83. **6881**

Willoughby, William R. "The Canada-United States Joint Economic Agencies of the Second World War." (1972), 15 *Canadian Public Administration* 59-73.
6882

Winks, Robin W. *The Relevance of Canadian History: U.S. and Imperial Perspectives.* Toronto: Macmillan of Canada, c1979. xv, 99 p. (Joanne Goodman Lectures, 1977) **6883**
Review: Margaret Prang in (1980-81), 36 *International Journal* 247-248.

Winter, Carl George. *American Impetus to Canadian Nationhood: Canadian-American Relations, 1905-1927.* Stanford, Calif., 1951. xii, 391 leaves. (University of Rochester. Canadian Studies Series, No. 7) **6884**
Thesis (Ph.D.), Stanford University, 1951.

Wrong, George McKinnon. *The United States and Canada, a Political Study.* New York, Cincinnati: Abingdon Press, c1921. 191 p. (Wesleyan University. George Slocum Bennett Foundation. Lectures, 2d Ser., 1919-1920) **6885**
Review: Robert L. Borden (1921), 2 *Canadian Historical Review* 272-274.

(b) HISTORICAL

See also *"Acquisition and Loss of Territory" (p. 191), "Airspace and Outer Space" (p. 280), "Arbitration: Specific Cases" (p. 396), "Arctic" (p. 197), "Boundaries of Canada" (p. 166), "Boundary Delimitation and Demarcation" (p. 180), "Foreign Corporations in Canada" (p. 604), "Foreign Investment in Canada" (p. 589), "Inland Waterways" (p. 208), "International Relations of Provinces" (p. 73), "International Taxation" (p. 617), "Judicial Settlement: Specific Cases" (p. 405), "Law of the Sea" (p. 230), "Law of Treaties: Specific Treaties: Trade" (p. 161), "North American Defence" (p. 436), "Trade with the United States" (p. 567), and other aspects of international cooperation (pp. 641, 650, 661, 672, 679, and 682).*

(i) AMERICAN REVOLUTION AND THE TREATY OF PEACE OF 1783

Bemis, Samuel Flagg. "Canada and the Peace Settlement of 1782-3." (1933), 14 *Canadian Historical Review* 265-284. **6886**

Caron, Ivanhoë. "Les Canadiens français et l'invasion américaine de 1774-1775." (1929), 23 *Royal Society of Canada, Transactions* 21-34 (3d Ser., Sec. 1) **6887**

Coffin, Victor. *The Province of Quebec and the Early American Revolution; A Study in English-American Colonial History.* Madison, Wis.: University of Wisconsin, 1896. xvii, pp. 275-562. (University of Wisconsin. Bulletin; Economics, Political Science, and History Series, Vol. 1, No. 3) **6888**
Also published as the author's thesis (Ph.D.), Cornell University.

Everest, Allan Seymour. *Moses Hazen and the Canadian Refugees in the American Revolution.* Syracuse, N.Y.: Syracuse University Press, 1976. xi, 217 p. (New York State Study) **6889**
Published for the New York State American Revolution Bicentennial Commission.
Review: H.N. Muller, III, in (1977), 7 *American Review of Canadian Studies* 61-64 (No. 2).

Lanctot, Gustave. "Le Québec et la Révolution américaine." (1941), 35 *Royal Society of Canada, Transactions* 91-111 (3d Ser., Sec. 1) **6890**

Morin, Victor. "L'échauffourée américaine de 1775-1776 au Canada." (1950), 44 *Royal Society of Canada, Transactions* 33-53 (3d Ser., Sec. 1) **6891**

Morton, H.A. "The American Revolution: A View from the North." (1972), 7 *Journal of Canadian Studies* 43-54 (No. 2) **6892**

Roy, Raoul. *Les Canadiens français et les indépendantistes américains, 1774-1783; une occasion manquée.* Montréal: Éditions du Franc-Canada, 1977. 64 p., maps. (Cahiers de la décolonisation du Franc-Canada, no 7) **6893**

Smith, Justin Harvey. *Our Struggle for the Forteenth Colony: Canada, and the American Revolution.* New York, London: G.P. Putnam, 1907. 2 vols., maps. **6894**

Stanley, George F.G. *Canada Invaded, 1775-1776.* Toronto: Hakkert, 1973. 186 p. (Canadian War Museum. Historical Publications, No. 8) **6895**
Review: Arthur L. Johnson in (1975), 5 *American Review of Canadian Studies* 171-173 (No. 2).

Trudel, Marcel. *Louis XVI, le Congrès américain et le Canada, 1774-1789.* Québec: Éditions du Quartier latin, 1949. xiii, 259 p. (Université Laval. Publications) **6896**
Reviews: Gerald S. Brown in (1950), 31 *Canadian Historical Review* 191-193; Léo-Paul Desrosiers in (1949-50), 3 *Revue d'Histoire de l'Amérique Française* 598-602.

Trudel, Marcel. *La Révolution américaine: pourquoi la France refuse le Canada, 1775-1783.* Rev. ed. Sillery, Québec: Éditions du Boréal Express, 1976. 291 p., maps. (Collection 17/60, 7) **6897**
Previous edition published in 1949 under title: *Louis XVI, le Congrès américain et le Canada, 1774-1789.*

Trudel, Marcel. "Le traité de 1783 laisse le Canada à l'Angleterre." (1949-50), 3 *Revue d'Histoire de l'Amérique Française* 179-199. **6898**
Extract from the author's: *Louis XVI, le Congrès américain et le Canada, 1774-1789.*

Wrong, George McKinnon. *Canada and the American Revolution; the Disruption of the First British Empire.* New York: Macmillan, 1935. xii, 497 p. **6899**
Reviews: H.F. Munro in (1935-36), 15 *Dalhousie Review* 386-387; Reginald G. Trotter in (1935-36), 42 *Queen's Quarterly* 145-148.

(ii) JAY TREATY OF NOVEMBER 19, 1794

Bemis, Samuel Flagg. *Jay's Treaty; a Study in Commerce and Diplomacy.* 2d ed. New Haven: Yale University Press, 1962. xx, 526 p., maps. **6900**
Review: Patrick C.T. White in (1963), 44 *Canadian Historical Review* 244-245.

Clarfield, Gerard. "Postscript to the Jay Treaty: Timothy Pickering and Anglo-American Relations, 1795-1797." (1966), 23 *William and Mary Quarterly* 106-120. **6901**

Combs, Jerald A. *The Jay Treaty; Political Battleground of the Founding Fathers.* Berkeley: University of California Press, 1970. xi, 254 p. **6902**
Review: Jack Sosin in (1971), 52 *Canadian Historical Review* 202-203.

Combs, Jerald A. *Power, Politics and Ideology: A Case Study of the Jay Treaty.* Los Angeles, 1964. 388 leaves. **6903**
Thesis (Ph.D.), University of California, Los Angeles, 1964.

Macdonald, Ronald St. John. "International Law - Jay Treaty of 1794 - Abrogation of Treaties by Outbreak of War - Review of Canadian and Foreign Decisions. *Francis v. The Queen,* (1954) Ex. C.R. 590; (1955) 4 D.L.R. 760). (Case Note)." (1956), 34 *Canadian Bar Review* 602-612, 760-762 (Letter) **6904**

MacKenzie, Norman A.M. "The Jay Treaty of 1794." (1929), 7 *Canadian Bar Review* 431-437. **6905**

Newcomb, Josiah T. "New Light on Jay's Treaty." (1934), 28 *American Journal of International Law* 685-692. **6906**

(iii) WAR OF 1812 AND THE TREATY OF GHENT OF 1814

Boissonnault, Charles-Marie. "Le Québec et la guerre de 1812." (1950-51), 5 *Revue de l'Université Laval* 611-625. **6907**

Gates, Charles M. "The West in American Diplomacy, 1812-1815." (1939-40), 26 *Mississippi Valley Historical Review* 499-510. **6908**

Mahan, A.T. "The Negotiations at Ghent in 1814." (1905-06), 11 *American Historical Review* 68-87. **6909**

Mills, Dudley. "The Duke of Wellington and the Peace Negotiations at Ghent in 1814." (1921), 2 *Canadian Historical Review* 19-32. **6910**

Perkins, Bradford. *Prologue to War; England and the United States, 1805-1812.* Berkeley: University of California Press, 1961. x, 457 p. **6911**
Review: Alfred LeRoy Burt in (1962), 43 *Canadian Historical Review* 151-152.

Updyke, Frank Arthur. *The Diplomacy of the War of 1812.* Baltimore: Johns Hopkins Press, 1915. x, 494 p. (Albert Shaw Lectures on Diplomatic History, 1914) **6912**
Review: John W. Foster in (1915), 9 *American Journal of International Law* 762-765.

Wood, William. "Canada in the War of 1812." *In* Shortt, Adam, and Doughty, Arthur G., eds., *Canada and Its Provinces* (Toronto, 1914-1916), vol. 3, pp. 189-271. **6913**

(iv) NAVAL FORCES ON THE GREAT LAKES (RUSH-BAGOT AGREEMENT OF 1817)

Bédard, Charles. "Les armements sur les Grands Lacs." (1964), 2 *Canadian Yearbook of International Law* 141-152. **6914**

Boutell, H.S. "Is the Rush-Bagot Convention Immortal?" (1901), 173 *North American Review* 331-348. **6915**

Callahan, James Morton. *The Neutrality of the American Lakes and Anglo-American Relations.* Baltimore: Johns Hopkins Press, 1898. 199 p. **6916**
Original edition issued as No. 1-4 of *Anglo-American Relations and Southern History,* which forms the 16th series of Johns Hopkins University Studies in Historical and Political Science. Reprinted New York, Johnson Reprint, 1973.

Cruikshank, E.A. "The Negotiation of the Agreement for Disarmament on the Lakes." (1936), 30 *Royal Society of Canada, Transactions* 151-184 (3d Ser., Sec. 2) **6917**

Eayrs, James George. "Arms Control on the Great Lakes." (1964), 2 *Disarmament and Arms Control* 373-404. **6918**

Foster, John W. *Limitation of Armament on the Great Lakes.* Washington: The Endowment, 1914. vii, 57 p. (Carnegie Endowment for International Peace. Division of International Law. Pamphlet, No. 2) **6919**

Gluek, Alvin Charles. "The Invisible Revision of the Rush-Bagot Agreement, 1898-1914." (1979), 60 *Canadian Historical Review* 466-484. **6920**

Knaplund, Paul. "The Armaments on the Great Lakes, 1844." (1934-35), 40 *American Historical Review* 473-476. **6921**

Levermore, Charles Herbert. *The Anglo-American Agreement of 1817 for Disarmament on the Great Lakes.* Boston: World Peace Foundation, 1914. 28 p. (World Peace Foundation. Pamphlets Series, Vol. 4, No. 4) **6922**

Little, C.H. "Naval Activities on the Great Lakes: Past and Present." (1963), 67 *Canadian Geographical Journal* 203-215. **6923**

Powers, Mabel. "The Disarmament Pact between Canada and the United States." (1930), 32 *Current History* 273-276. **6924**

Scammell, E.H. "The Rush-Bagot Agreement of 1817." (1915), 13 *Ontario Historical Society, Papers and Records* 58-66. **6925**

Stacey, Charles P. "The Myth of the Unguarded Frontier, 1815-1871." (1950-51), 56 *American Historical Review* 1-18. **6926**

(v) WEBSTER-ASHBURTON TREATY OF AUGUST 9, 1842

Adams, Ephraim Douglas. "Lord Ashburton and the Treaty of Washington." (1911-12), 17 *American Historical Review* 764-782. **6927**

Corey, Albert B. *The Crisis of 1830-1842 in Canadian-American Relations.* New York: Russell & Russell, 1970. xi, 203 p., maps. (Relations of Canada and the United States) **6928**
First published New Haven, Yale University Press; Toronto, Ryerson Press, 1941.
Reviews: S.D. Clark in (1942), 8 *Canadian Journal of Economics and Political Science* 307-311; Charles P. Stacey in (1942), 23 *Canadian Historical Review* 206-207.

Current, Richard N. "Webster's Propaganda and the Ashburton Treaty." (1947-48), 34 *Mississippi Valley Historical Review* 187-200. **6929**

Jones, Howard. *To the Webster-Ashburton Treaty: A Study in Anglo-American Relations, 1783-1843.* Chapel Hill: University of North Carolina Press, c1977. xx, 251 p. **6930**
Review: Brian Tennyson in (1978), 59 *Canadian Historical Review* 498-500.

Lenoir, James J. "Treaty Interpretation - A Comparative Study of Views Expressed by the United States and Canadian Courts on the Webster-Ashburton Treaty (1842)." (1934-35), 7 *Mississippi Law Journal* 197-202.
6931

(vi) RECIPROCITY TREATY OF JUNE 5, 1854

Ankli, Robert E. "The Reciprocity Treaty of 1854." (1971), 4 *Canadian Journal of Economics* 1-20. **6932**
Contains a résumé in French under title: "Le traité de réciprocité de 1854."

Biggar, Emerson Bristol. *Reciprocity; the Trade Treaty of 1854-66 between Canada and the United States; How It Came to Be Negotiated and Why It Was Annulled. Economic Aspects of Trade Treaties in Protectionist Countries.* Toronto: Biggar-Wilson, 1911. 38 p. **6933**

Canada. Parliament. *Correspondence on the Subject of the Renewal of the Reciprocity Treaty with the United States, etc.* Ottawa, 1869. 18 p. (Canada. Parliament, 1869. Sessional Papers, No. 47) **6934**

Chapman, James Keith. *Relations of Maine and New Brunswick in the Era of Reciprocity, 1849-1867.* Rochester, N.Y.: University of Rochester Press, c1956. iv, 140 leaves. (University of Rochester. Canadian Studies Series, No. 21)
Thesis (M.A.), University of New Brunswick, 1951. **6935**

Colquhoun, Arthur H.U. "The Reciprocity Negotiations with the United States in 1869. (Notes and Documents)." (1927), 8 *Canadian Historical Review* 233-242. **6936**

Corbett, Walter Edward Hiller. *Nova Scotia under the Reciprocity Treaty of 1854.* Wolfville, N.S., 1941. 117 leaves. **6937**
Thesis (M.A.), Acadia University, 1941.

Cross, Michael Sean. *Free Trade, Annexation and Reciprocity, 1846-54.* Toronto: Holt, Rinehart and Winston of Canada, c1971. viii, 88 p. (Canadian History Through the Press Series) **6938**

Den Otter, A.A. "Alexander Galt, the 1859 Tariff, and Canadian Economic Nationalism." (1982), 63 *Canadian Historical Review* 151-178. **6939**

Désy, Anatole. " 'Le Canada économique sous l'Union' et 'Le traité de réciprocité de 1854.' " (1921), 7 *Revue Trimestrielle Canadienne* 318-329. **6940**

Fuller, G.G. *An Analysis of the 1854 Reciprocity Treaty and Subsequent Canadian-American Reciprocity Attempts.* Kingston, 1934. 228 leaves. **6941**
Thesis (M.A.), Queen's University, 1934.

Harvey, Arthur. *The Reciprocity Treaty: Its Advantages to the United States and to Canada.* Quebec: Hunter, Ross, 1865. 29 p. **6942**

Haynes, Frederick Emory. *The Reciprocity Treaty with Canada of 1854.* Baltimore: American Economic Association, 1892. 70 p. (American Economic Association. Publications. Monographs, Vol. 7, No. 6) **6943**

Hecht, Irene W.D. "Israel D. Andrews and the Reciprocity Treaty of 1854: A Reappraisal." (1963), 44 *Canadian Historical Review* 313-329. **6944**

Hecht, Irene W.D. *Israel De Wolfe Andrews and the Reciprocity Treaty of 1854.* Rochester, N.Y., 1961. 138 leaves. **6945**
Thesis (M.A.), University of Rochester, 1961.

Keefer, Thomas Celtrin. *A Sketch of the Rise and Progress of the Reciprocity*

Treaty; with an Explanation of the Services Rendered in Connection Therewith. Toronto: Lovell and Gibson, 1863. 34 p. **6946**

Kirstein, Ruth. *The Reciprocity Treaty of 1854.* New York, 1939. 82 leaves. **6947**
Thesis (M.A.), New York University, 1939.

La Tulippe, Jean-Guy. "Le traité de réciprocité 1854-1866." (1976), 52 *Actualité Économique* 432-458. **6948**

Lavell, William S. *Early Canadian Ventures in Diplomacy.* Kingston, 1932. 60 leaves. **6949**
Thesis (M.A.), Queen's University, 1932.

Le Duc, Thomas H. "I.D. Andrews and the Reciprocity Treaty of 1854." (1934), 15 *Canadian Historical Review* 437-438. **6950**
This is a letter on W. D. Overman's article published in (1934), 15 *Canadian Historical Review* 248-263.

Masters, Donald C. "A Further Word on I.D. Andrews and the Reciprocity Treaty of 1854." (1936), 17 *Canadian Historical Review* 159-167. **6951**
See also the article by W.D. Overman in (1934), 15 *Canadian Historical Review* 248-263.

Masters, Donald C. *The Reciprocity Treaty of 1854: Its History, Its Relation to British Colonial and Foreign Policy and to the Development of Canadian Fiscal Autonomy.* Toronto: McClelland and Stewart, c1963. xvi, 190 p. (Carleton Library, No. 9) **6952**
First published London, New York, Longmans, Green, 1937.
Reviews: W.A. Mackintosh under title: "Reciprocity," in (1940), 6 *Canadian Journal of Economics and Political Science* 611-620; George A. Rawlyk in (1963-64), 43 *Dalhousie Review* 589-591; Reginald G. Trotter in (1938), 19 *Canadian Historical Review* 74-75; Reginald G. Trotter in (1938), 45 *Queen's Quarterly* 259-261.

Merritt, William Hamilton. *Remarks on the Extension of Reciprocity between Canada and the United States.* St. Catharines, Ont.: H. Leavenworth, 1855. 12 p. **6953**

Officer, Lawrence H., and Smith, Lawrence B. "The Canadian-American Reciprocity Treaty of 1855 to 1866." (1968), 28 *Journal of Economic History* 598-623. **6954**
For a comment by Robert Ankli, and a reply by the authors, see (1970), 30 *Journal of Economic History* 427-431, 432-434.

Overman, William D. "I.D. Andrews and Reciprocity in 1854: An Episode in Dollar Diplomacy." (1934), 15 *Canadian Historical Review* 248-263. **6955**
See also the letter of Thomas H. Le Duc in (1934), 15 *Canadian Historical Review* 437-438, and the article by Donald C. Masters in (1936), 17 *Canadian Historical Review* 156-167.

Overman, William D. "Some Letters of Joshua R. Giddings on Reciprocity." (1935), 16 *Canadian Historical Review* 289-296. **6956**

Pennanen, Gary. "American Interest in Commercial Union with Canada, 1854-1898." (1965), 47 *Mid-America* 24-39. **6957**

Robinson, Chalfant. *History of the Reciprocity Treaty of 1854 with Canada.* Washington: Govt. Print. Off., 1911. 42 p. (U.S. 62d Cong., 1st sess. Senate. Doc. 17) **6958**

Robinson, Chalfant. *A History of Two Reciprocity Treaties: The Treaty with Canada in 1854, the Treaty with the Hawaiian Islands in 1876, with a Chapter on the Treaty-Making Power of the House of Representatives.* New Haven: Tuttle, Morehouse & Taylor Press, 1904. 220 p., map. **6959**

Royal, Joseph. "Le traité de réciprocité." (1864), 1 *Revue Canadienne* 93-103.
6960

Saunders, S.A. "The Maritime Provinces and the Reciprocity Treaty." (1934-35), 14 *Dalhousie Review* 355-371. **6961**

Saunders, S.A. "The Reciprocity Treaty of 1854: A Regional Study." (1936), 2 *Canadian Journal of Economics and Political Science* 41-53. **6962**

Shortt, Adam. "The Reciprocity Treaty." *In* Shortt, Adam, and Doughty, Arthur G., eds., *Canada and Its Provinces* (Toronto, 1914-1916), vol. 5, pp. 242-257.
6963

Tallman, Ronald D. "Reciprocity 1874: The Failure of Liberal Diplomacy." (1973), 65 *Ontario History* 87-105. **6964**

Tansill, Charles Callan. *The Canadian Reciprocity Treaty of 1854.* Baltimore: Johns Hopkins Press, 1922. vii, 9-96 p. (Johns Hopkins University. Studies in Historical and Political Science; Ser. 40, No. 2, pp. 189-276) **6965**
Also issued as the author's thesis (Ph.D.), Johns Hopkins University, 1918.
Review: Arthur H.U. Colquhoun in (1922), 3 *Canadian Historical Review* 373-374.

Trudel, Pierre, and Bélanger, Claude. *Le traité de réciprocité, 1854.* Ottawa: Éditions de l'Université d'Ottawa, 1968. xiii, 121 p. (Cahiers d'histoire de l'Université d'Ottawa, no 1) **6966**
Review: Yves Saint-Germain in (1969-70), 23 *Revue d'Histoire de l'Amérique Française* 332-333.

(vii) AMERICAN CIVIL WAR (1861-65)

Bégin, Dennis Gerald. *The St. Alban's Raid: Reflection of British Neutrality and Anglo-American Relations, 1861-1865.* Saskatoon, c1973. v, 219 leaves. **6967**
Thesis (M.A.), University of Saskatchewan, 1974.

Bovey, Wilfrid. "Confederate Agents in Canada During the American Civil War." (1921), 2 *Canadian Historical Review* 46-57. **6968**

DeRosier, Arthur H. "The Confederates in Canada: A Survey." (1964-65), 3 *Southern Quarterly* 312-324. **6969**

Holmes, John W. *Border Relations between Canada and the United States During the American Civil War.* Toronto, 1933 (c1973). 164 leaves. **6970**
Thesis (M.A.), University of Toronto, 1933. (National Library of Canada. Canadian Theses on Microfilm, No. 16104).

Landon, Fred. "The American Civil War and Canadian Confederation." (1927), 21 *Royal Society of Canada, Transactions* 55-62 (3d Ser., Sec. 2) **6971**

Macdonald, Helen Grace. *Canadian Public Opinion on the American Civil War.* New York, 1926. 239 p. **6972**
Thesis (Ph.D.), Columbia University, 1926. Also published as *Studies in History, Economics and Public Law* (Columbia University).

MacLean, Guy. "The *Georgian* Affair: An Incident of the American Civil War." (1961), 42 *Canadian Historical Review* 133-144. **6973**

Neant, Hubert. "Le Canada et la guerre de Sécession (1860-1865)." (1963), 77 *Revue d'Histoire Diplomatique* 342-361. **6974**

Stouffer, Allen P. "Canadian-American Relations in the Shadow of the Civil War." (1977-78), 57 *Dalhousie Review* 332-346. **6975**

Winks, Robin W. *Canada and the United States: The Civil War Years.* Rev. ed. Montreal: Harvest House, 1971. xxiv, 432 p. **6976**
First published Baltimore, Johns Hopkins Press, 1960.
Reviews: Alice R. Stewart in (1961-62), 41 *Dalhousie Review* 240-241; P.B. Waite in (1961), 42 *Canadian Historical Review* 160-161.

(viii) TREATY OF WASHINGTON OF MAY 8, 1871

Beaty, James. "The Legal Interpretation of the Treaty of Washington." (1872), 1 *Canadian Monthly and National Review* 354-362. **6977**

Canada. Parliament. *Correspondence Respecting the Alleged Violation of the Treaty of Washington.* Ottawa, 1877. 13, 3 p. (Canada. Parliament, 1877. Sessional Papers, No. 14) **6978**

Canada. Parliament. *Messages, Dispatches, and Minutes of the Privy Council Relating to the Treaty of Washington.* Ottawa, 1872. 67 p. (Canada. Parliament, 1872. Sessional Papers, No. 18) **6979**

Chamberlain, Daniel Henry. *Charles Sumner and the Treaty of Washington.* Boston: Riverside Press, 1902. 40 p. **6980**

Cushing, Caleb. *The Treaty of Washington; Its Negotiation, Execution and the Discussions Relating Thereto.* New York: Harper, 1873. viii, 280 p. **6981**
Reprinted Freeport, N.Y., Books for Libraries Press, 1970. Also published in French (Paris, 1874).

Gt. Brit. Foreign Office. *Correspondence with the Government of Canada in Connection with the Appointment of the Joint High Commission and the Treaty of Washington.* London: W. Clowes for H.M. Stationery Off., 1872. 15 p. (Gt. Brit. Parliament. Papers by Command, c. 539) **6982**

Lewis, John. "The Washington Treaty." *In* Shortt, Adam, and Doughty, Arthur G., eds., *Canada and Its Provinces* (Toronto, 1914-1916), vol. 6, pp. 45-52. **6983**

Lindsey, Charles. "The Treaty of Washington." (1872), 1 *Canadian Monthly and National Review* 2-17. **6984**

Mansfield, J. Paris. *New Brunswick and the Treaty of Washington.* Fredericton, 1958. 168, xiii leaves. **6985**
Thesis (M.A.), University of New Brunswick, 1958.

Morrow, Rising Lake. "The Negotiation of the Anglo-American Treaty of 1870." (1933-34), 39 *American Historical Review* 663-681. **6986**

Rogers, Keith R. *French-Canadian Reaction to the Treaty of Washington, 1871.* Lennoxville, Que., 1970. ii, 166 leaves. **6987**
Thesis (M.A.), Bishop's University, 1971.

Sabine, Catharine Mary. *The Treaty of Washington, 1871, from a Canadian Standpoint.* London, Ont., 1923. 211, 7 leaves. **6988**
Thesis (M.A.), University of Western Ontario, 1923.

Showell, Frank. *The Treaty of Washington, 1871, and Its Reception in the Press of Great Britain, Canada and the United States.* Kingston, 1958. 220 leaves.
Thesis (M.A.), Queen's University, 1958. **6989**

Smith, Goldwin A. *The Treaty of Washington; a Chapter in Canadian National Development.* Toronto, 1934. 149 leaves. **6990**
Thesis (M.A.), University of Toronto, 1934.

Smith, Goldwin A. *The Treaty of Washington, 1871: A Study in Imperial History.* Ithaca, N.Y., 1937. vi, 204 leaves. **6991**
Thesis (Ph.D.), Cornell University, 1937.

Smith, Goldwin A. *The Treaty of Washington, 1871: A Study in Imperial History.* New York: Russell & Russell, 1971, c1941. xiii, 134 p. **6992**
First published Ithaca, N.Y., Cornell University Press, 1941.
Reviews: Samuel Flagg Bemis in (1941), 35 *American Journal of International Law* 598; Ronald S. Longley in (1941), 22 *Canadian Historical Review* 206-208; unsigned in (1941-42), 4 *University of Toronto Law Journal* 467.

U.S. Dept. of State. *Papers Relating to the Treaty of Washington.* Washington: Govt. Print. Off., 1872-74. 6 vols., maps. **6993**
This treaty was signed at Washington on May 8, 1871, as the result of the works of a Joint High Commission composed of five British commissioners (including Sir John Alexander Macdonald, Minister of Justice and Attorney General of Canada), and five U.S. commissioners. The treaty deals with the following matters: Alabama claims (Articles 1-17); fisheries in North America (Articles 18-25, and 32); navigation of the St. Lawrence River, etc. (Articles 26-28); reciprocal trade between Canada and the United States (Articles 29-31); and the boundary line west of the Rocky Mountains (Articles 34-42). See text in 61 BFSP 40; 13 Hertslet 970; 17 Stat. 863; TS 133; 12 Bevans 170; 1 Malloy 700; 143 Parry 145. It resulted in four arbitrations: a) the Geneva arbitration (Alabama Claims); b) the Washington arbitration (American-British Mixed Claims Commission); c) the Berlin arbitration (Northwestern boundary), concerned with the proper interpretation of the Oregon Treaty of June 15, 1846, and d) the Halifax Commission (Fishery Commission). (See *Checklist of United States Documents, 1789-1909,* 3d ed., 1911, pp. 913-916). See also implementing legislation (S.C. 1872, c. 2).
Contents: v.1-4. Geneva Arbitration.- v.5. Berlin Arbitration.- v.6. Washington Arbitration, and General Appendix containing the Report of Robert S. Hale.

Weise, Selene Harding Curd. *Negotiating the Washington Treaty, 1871.* Syracuse, N.Y., 1974. 175 leaves. **6994**
Thesis (Ph.D.), Syracuse University, 1976. Abstracted in (1976), 36 *Dissertation Abstracts International* 6469-A. (University Microfilms, Ann Arbor, No. 76-7949).

(ix) RECIPROCITY AGREEMENT OF JANUARY 21, 1911

Allan, John. *Reciprocity and the Canadian General Election of 1911; a Re-Examination of Economic Self-Interest in Voting.* Kingston, 1971. v, 93 leaves. **6995**
Thesis (M.A.), Queen's University, 1971. (National Library of Canada. Canadian Theses on Microfilm, No. 8639).

Bahmer, Robert. *The Movement in the United States for Reciprocity with Canada, 1911*. Boulder, Colo., 1929. 136 leaves. **6996**
Thesis (M.A.), University of Colorado, 1929.

Bayard, Ross Hawthorne. *Anti-Americanism in Canada and the Abortive Reciprocity Agreement of 1911*. Columbia, S.C., 1971. 324 leaves. **6997**
Thesis (Ph.D.), University of South Carolina, 1971. Abstracted in (1972), 32 *Dissertations Abstracts International* 6878-A. (University Microfilms, Ann Arbor, No. 72-18147).

Bourassa, Henri. *The Reciprocity Agreement and Its Consequences as Viewed from the Nationalist Standpoint*. Montreal: Le Devoir, 1911. iv, 43 p. **6998**
This pamphlet is a literal translation of seven articles published in *Le Devoir*, from January 31 to February 7, 1911.

Canada. Parliament. *Correspondence between the British Ambassador at Washington and the Government of Canada in Connection with the Negotiations for a Reciprocity Treaty between Canada and the United States*. Ottawa, 1912. 101 p. (Canada. Parliament, 1912. Sessional Papers, No. 82a) **6999**

Canada. Parliament. *Tariff Relations between the United States and the Dominion of Canada*. Ottawa, 1911. 70 p. (Canada. Parliament, 1911. Sessional Papers, No. 109b) **7000**

Canada. Parliament. *Tariff Relations with the United States; Correspondence Respecting Negotiations, 1910*. Ottawa, 1910. 8 p. (Canada. Parliament, 1910. Sessional Papers, No. 10j) **7001**

Conacher, James B. *Reciprocity and Public Opinion in Canada, 1911*. Kingston, 1939. 255 leaves. **7002**
Thesis (M.A.), Queen's University, 1939.

Ellis, Lewis Ethan. "Canada's Rejection of Reciprocity in 1911." (1939), *Canadian Historical Association, Historical Papers* 99-111. **7003**

Ellis, Lewis Ethan. "The Northwest and the Reciprocity Agreement of 1911." (1939-40), 26 *Mississippi Valley Historical Review* 55-66. **7004**

Ellis, Lewis Ethan. *Reciprocity, 1911; a Study in Canadian-American Relations*. New York: Greenwood Press, 1968, c1939. x, 207 p. **7005**
First published New Haven, Yale University Press; Toronto, Ryerson Press, 1939, in the series: *Relations of Canada and the United States*.
Reviews: S. Bates in (1941-42), 21 *Dalhousie Review* 122-123; Roger Duhamel in (1941-42), 17/2 *Actualité Économique* 288; H.N. Fieldhouse in (1940-43), 19 *International Affairs* 151-152; W.A. Mackintosh under title: "Reciprocity," in (1940), 6 *Canadian Journal of Economics and Political Science* 611-620; Joe Patterson Smith in (1940), 21 *Canadian Historical Review* 217-219; Reginald G. Trotter in (1940), 47 *Queen's Quarterly* 129-131.

Foster, George E. "The Reciprocity Agreement from a Canadian Standpoint." (1911), 193 *North American Review* 663-671. **7006**

Foster, George E. "Reciprocity with the United States." (1910), 9 *University Magazine* 550-562. **7007**

Foster, Joan Mary Vassie. "Reciprocity and the Joint High Commission of 1898-99." (1939), *Canadian Historical Association, Historical Papers* 87-98. **7008**

Forms part of the author's thesis (Ph.D.), Bryn Mawr College, 1937, entitled: *Reciprocity in Canadian Politics*.

Foster, Joan Mary Vassie. *Reciprocity in Canadian Politics from the Commercial Union Movement to 1910*. Bryn Mawr, Pa., 1937. **7009**
Thesis (Ph.D.), Bryn Mawr College, 1937. Listed in (1936-37), 4 *Doctoral Dissertations Accepted by American Universities* 74.

Griffin, Appleton Prentiss Clark, and Meyer, Herman Henry Bernard. *List of References on Reciprocity*. Washington: Govt. Print. Off., 1910. 137 p. **7010**
Prepared at the Library of Congress, Division of Bibliography.

Hammond, M.O. "The Tragedy of Reciprocity." (1911-12), 38 *Canadian Magazine* 84-91. **7011**

Herwig, Aletha Marguerite. *The Farmer and Canadian-American Reciprocity, 1911*. Minneapolis, 1943. 331 leaves. **7012**
Thesis (Ph.D.), University of Minnesota, 1943.

Johnston, Richard, and Percy, Michael B. "Reciprocity, Imperial Sentiment, and Party Politics in the 1911 Election." (1980), 13 *Canadian Journal of Political Science* 711-729. **7013**

Lanham, Percy A. *An Attempt at Reciprocity: A Study of the Tariff Issue in the Election of 1911*. Winnipeg, 1935. vii, 128 leaves. **7014**
Thesis (M.A.), University of Manitoba, 1935.

Lewis, J.S., Jr. "The Recent Tariff." (1909-10), 17 *Journal of the Canadian Bankers' Association* 202-207. **7015**

Lewis, John. "Reciprocity." In Shortt, Adam, and Doughty, Arthur G., eds., *Canada and Its Provinces* (Toronto, 1914-1916), vol. 6, pp. 176-186. **7016**

Maqubela, Sikhumbuzo. *Ontario and the Reciprocity Agreement of 1911*. London, Ont., 1963. vi, 141 leaves. **7017**
Thesis (M.A.), University of Western Ontario, 1963.

McDonald, Ada Jean. *Canada's Rejection of Reciprocity 1911: An Examination of Factors Influencing the Electorate in Southwestern Ontario*. East Lansing, Mich., 1964. iv, 66 leaves. **7018**
Thesis (M.A.), Michigan State University, 1964.

Meyer, Herman Henry Bernard. *Additional References Relating to Reciprocity with Canada*. Washington: Govt. Print. Off., 1911. 44 p. **7019**
Prepared at the Library of Congress, Division of Bibliography.

Mond, *Sir* Alfred. "The Canadian-American Reciprocity Agreement." (1910-11), 7 *English Review* 731-744. **7020**

Mosher, Ralph Lamont. *A Study of the Reciprocity Movement in Canada, 1911-1938*. Wolfville, N.S., 1951. 137 leaves. **7021**
Thesis (M.A.), Acadia University, 1951.

Patton, H.S. "Reciprocity with Canada: The Canadian Viewpoint." (1920-21), 35 *Quarterly Journal of Economics* 574-595. **7022**

Riddell, William Renwick. "International Trade Relations and Reciprocity between Canada and the United States." (1911-12), 19 *Queen's Quarterly* 330-339. **7023**

Robinson, Edward Van Dyke. "Reciprocity and the Farmer." (1911), 19 *Journal of Political Economy* 550-566. **7024**

Schioler, John Pontoppidan. *Western Canada and Reciprocity, 1911.* Rochester, N.Y., 1958. vi, 238 leaves. **7025**
Thesis (M.A.), University of Rochester, 1958.

"Sir Wilfrid Laurier and Tariff Revision." (1910-11), 1 *Round Table* 71-75. **7026**

Skelton, O.D. "Canada's Rejection of Reciprocity." (1911), 19 *Journal of Political Economy* 726-731. **7027**

Skelton, O.D. "The Canadian Reciprocity Agreement." (1911), 21 *Economic Journal* 274-285. **7028**

Skelton, O.D. "Reciprocity: The Canadian Attitude." (1911), 19 *Journal of Political Economy* 77-97. **7029**

Stanwood, Edward. "Trade Reciprocity with Canada." (1913-14), 47 *Massachusetts Historical Society, Proceedings* 141-178. **7030**

Swartz, Willis G. "The Proposed Canadian-American Reciprocity Agreement of 1911." (1930-31), 3 *Journal of Economic and Business History* 118-147. **7031**

Taft, William H. "Reciprocity with Canada." (1911), 19 *Journal of Political Economy* 513-526. **7032**

Taussig, F.W. "Reciprocity with Canada." (1911), 19 *Journal of Political Economy* 542-549. **7033**

"The Trade Agreement." (1910-11), 1 *Round Table* 319-329. **7034**

U.S. Congress. House. Committee on Ways and Means. *Reciprocity with Canada. Hearings, 61st Cong., 3d sess., on H.R. 32216, February 2-9, 1911.* Washington: Govt. Print. Off., 1911. iv, 342 p. **7035**

U.S. Congress. Senate. Committee on Finance. *Reciprocity with Canada. Compilation of Documents Relating to the Proposed Agreement of 1911 and to the Treaty of 1854, and Its Subsequent Operation.* Washington: Govt. Print. Off., 1911. 846 p. (various pagings) **7036**
Contains the special message of President Taft of January 26, 1911, with correspondence; H.R. 32216: "An act to Promote Reciprocal Trade Relations with the Dominion of Canada"; Reports and hearings of the Committee on Ways and Means, etc.

U.S. Congress. Senate. Committee on Finance. *Reciprocity with Canada. Compilation of 1911.* Washington: Govt. Print. Off., 1911. 3 pts. in 5 vols. (5875 p.) (U.S. 62d Cong., 1st sess. Senate. Doc. 80) **7037**
See also *Papers in the Consideration of Bill H.R. 32216, Relating to Reciprocity with Canada*, presented by Thomas H. Carter, printed as S. Doc. 862, 61st Cong., 3d sess. (55 p.).

U.S. Congress. Senate. Committee on Finance. *Reciprocity with Canada: Hearings, 62d Congress, on H.R. 4412, an Act to Promote Reciprocal Trade Relations with the Dominion of Canada, etc.* Washington: Govt. Print. Off., 1911. 2 vols. (1405 p.) (U.S. 62d Cong., 1st sess. Senate. Doc. 56) **7038**

U.S. Congress. Senate. Committee on Finance. *Reciprocity with Canada: Hearings on H.R. 32216, an Act to Promote Reciprocal Trade Relations with the*

Dominion of Canada, etc. Washington: Govt. Print. Off., 1911. 332 p. (U.S. 61st Cong., 3d sess. Senate. Doc. 834) **7039**
Hearings held February 20-23, 1911.

U.S. President. *Canadian Reciprocity: Message from the President of the United States Transmitting Text of the Reciprocal Trade Agreement.* Washington: Govt. Print. Off., 1911. 93 p. (U.S. 63d Cong., 1st sess. House. Doc. 2) **7040**

U.S. President. *Canadian Reciprocity: Special Message of the President of the United States Transmitted to the Two Houses of Congress January 26, 1911; Correspondence Embodying an Agreement between the Department of State and the Canadian Government in Regard to Reciprocal Tariff Legislation; etc.* Washington: Govt. Print. Off., 1911. x, 75 p. (U.S. 61st Cong., 3d sess. Senate. Doc. 787) **7041**

U.S. Tariff Commission. *Reciprocity with Canada: A Study of the Arrangement of 1911.* Washington: Govt. Print. Off., 1920. 114 p. **7042**

Walker, Albert Henry. *'Reciprocity' of William H. Taft: A Historical Sketch.* New York, the Author, 1912. 34 p. **7043**

White, G.C. "The Proposed Agreement as Viewed by the Farmer." (1911), 19 *Journal of Political Economy* 567-573. **7044**

"Why Canada Rejected Reciprocity." (1911-12), 1 *Yale Review* 173-187 (N.S.)
Article signed: "A Canadian." **7045**

Willis, H. Parker. "The International Aspects of Reciprocity." (1911), 19 *Journal of Political Economy* 527-541. **7046**

5. RELATIONS WITH OTHER COUNTRIES (SELECTED)

Adams, Ronald A. *MacKenzie King and the Soviet Trade Mission to Canada, 1924-1927.* Ottawa, 1970. vi, 155 leaves. **7047**
Thesis (M.A.), University of Ottawa, 1970.

Angus, Henry F. "Japan - Our Problem." (1946), 6 *Behind the Headlines* No. 3 (16 p.) **7048**

Balawyder, Aloysius. *Canadian-Soviet Relations, 1920-1935.* Montreal, 1966. i, 234 leaves. **7049**
Thesis (Ph.D.), McGill University, 1966. (National Library of Canada. Canadian Theses on Microfilm, No. 430).

Balawyder, Aloysius. *Canadian-Soviet Relations between the World Wars.* Toronto: University of Toronto Press, c1972. ix, 248 p. **7050**
A revision and enlargement of the author's thesis (Ph.D.), McGill University.
Reviews: Ivan Avakumovic in (1972), 5 *Canadian Journal of Political Science* 463-464; O. Stanek in (1972), 3 *Études Internationales* 558-559; John A. Swettenham in (1973), 54 *Canadian Historical Review* 201-202.

Balawyder, Aloysius, ed. *Canadian-Soviet Relations 1939-1980.* Oakville, Ont.: Mosaic Press, 1981. 222 p. **7051**

Balawyder, Aloysius. *The Maple Leaf and the White Eagle: Canadian-Polish*

Relations, 1918-1978. Boulder: East European Monographs; New York: Distributed by Columbia University Press, 1980. vii, 300 p., plates. (East European Monographs, No. 66) **7052**
Reviews: Adam Bromke in (1981), 16 *Canadian Journal of History* 351-353; H.S. Ferns in (1980-81), 57 *International Affairs* 528-529; C.M. Liebich, and André Liebich in (1981), 12 *Études Internationales* 822-823; Josef Zboralski in (1982), 63 *Canadian Historical Review* 68-69.

Bell, George G. *Canadian Foreign Policy Towards Latin America, 1960-1963: A Study of Selected Foreign Policy Decisions.* Montreal, 1972. 1 vol. **7053**
Thesis (Ph.D.), McGill University, 1972. Abstracted in (1972/73), 33 *Dissertation Abstracts International* 2999-A.

Boutilier, Roger Alan. *Canadian-British West Indian Political Union Overtures, 1911-20.* Kingston, 1973. iii, 223 leaves. **7054**
Thesis (M.A.), Queen's University, 1973. (National Library of Canada. Canadian Theses on Microfiche, No. 17903).

Bowman, Robert James. *Canada's Relations with Latin America, 1963-1968; Integration or Nonintegration?* London, Ont., 1970, c1971. x, 95 (i.e. 101), xi leaves. **7055**
Thesis (M.A.), University of Western Ontario, 1970. (National Library of Canada. Canadian Theses on Microfilm, No. 7195).

Boyer, Harold. *Canada and Cuba: A Study in International Relations.* Burnaby, B.C., c1972. 478 leaves. **7056**
Thesis (Ph.D.), Simon Fraser University, 1973. (National Library of Canada. Canadian Theses on Microfiche, No. 12125). Abstracted in (1973/74), 34 *Dissertation Abstracts Internation* 388-A.

Brecher, Irving, and Brecher, Richard A. "Canada and Latin America: The Case for Canadian Involvement." (1967), 74 *Queen's Quarterly* 462-471. **7057**

Canada. Parliament. Senate. Standing Committee on Foreign Affairs. *Report on Canada-Caribbean Relations / Rapport concernant les relations canado-antillaises.* Ottawa: Queen's Printer, 1970. 62, 62 p. In English and French.
7058

"Canada and Latin America." (1949), 1 *External Affairs* 25-34 (May) **7059**

Chiang, Haven. *Diplomatic Relations between China and Canada.* Ottawa, 1958. vi, 106 leaves. **7060**
Thesis (M.A.), University of Ottawa, 1958.

Chodos, Robert. *The Caribbean Connection.* Toronto: J. Lorimer, 1976. 269 p., map. (Last Post Book) **7061**
Reviews: Alexander Craig in (1979), 34 *International Journal* 523-524; Stephen J. Randall in (1978), 59 *Canadian Historical Review* 113-114.

Couture, Paul M. *The Politics of Diplomacy: The Crisis of Canada-France Relations, 1940-1942.* Toronto, 1981. 410 frames. **7062**
Thesis (Ph.D.), York University, 1981. (National Library of Canada. Canadian Theses on Microfiche, No. 51367).

Couture, Paul M. "The Vichy-Free French Propaganda War in Quebec, 1940-1942." (1978), *Canadian Historical Association, Historical Papers* 200-216.
7063

Di Sanza, Emile. *Canadian Relations with the Caribbean and Latin America: Perspectives on Canada's Role in the World System.* Hamilton, Ont., 1978. x, 186 leaves. **7064**
Thesis (M.A.), McMaster University, 1978. (National Library of Canada. Canadian Theses on Microfiche, No. 39918).

Donneur, André P. "Le système paneuropéen." *In* Painchaud, Paul, ed., *Le Canada et le Québec sur la scène internationale* (Québec, 1977), pp. 329-346. **7065**

Fry, Michael G. "The Development of Canada's Relations with Japan, 1919-1947." *In* Hay, Keith A.J., ed., *Canadian Perspectives on Economic Relations with Japan* (Montreal, 1980), pp. 7-67. **7066**

Gotlieb, Allan E. "Canada-Japan Relations: A Policy Framework." *In* Hay, Keith A.J., ed., *Canadian Perspectives on Economic Relations with Japan* (Montreal, 1980), pp. 1-5. **7067**

Gross Stein, Janice. "La politique étrangère du Canada au Moyen-Orient: stimulus et réponse." *In* Painchaud, Paul, ed., *Le Canada et le Québec sur la scène internationale* (Québec, 1977), pp. 379-419. **7068**

Guy, James John. *Canada's External Relations with Latin America: Environment, Process and Prospects.* St. Louis, Mo., 1975. 306 leaves. **7069**
Thesis (Ph.D.), St. Louis University, 1975.

Hervouet, Gérard. *Le Canada face à l'Asie de l'Est, 1968-1980.* Montréal: Éditions Nouvelle Optique, 1981. 199 p. **7070**
Review: Frank Langdon in (1982), 55 *Pacific Affairs* 279-280.

Hilliker, John F. "The Canadian Government and the Free French: Perceptions and Constraints." (1980), 2 *International History Review* 87-108. **7071**

Himes, Mel. *Interest Groups and Canadian Foreign Policy: The Case of Bangladesh.* Montreal, 1978. x, 360 leaves. **7072**
Thesis (Ph.D.), McGill University, 1978. (National Library of Canada. Canadian Theses on Microfiche, No. 39692).

Houndjahoué, Michel. "La coopération bilatérale entre le Canada et les pays francophones de l'Afrique de l'Ouest: une évaluation de l'offre entre 1961 et 1975." (1981), 15 *Canadian Journal of African Studies* 95-116. **7073**

Houndjahoué, Michel. "Essai sur l'étude de la coopération bilatérale entre le Canada et l'Afrique francophone, 1961-1981." (1982), 13 *Études Internationales* 263-281. **7074**

Kay, Zachariah. *Canada and Palestine: The Politics of Non-Commitment.* Jerusalem: Israel Universities Press, 1978. xii, 218 p. **7075**
Adaptation of the author's thesis, Hebrew University of Jerusalem.
Reviews: David R. Murray in (1982), 63 *Canadian Historical Review* 361-362; Donald C. Story in (1979), 60 *Canadian Historical Review* 516-518.

Keenleyside, Terence A. "Canada and the Pacific: Perils of a Policy Paper." (1973), 8 *Journal of Canadian Studies* 31-49 (No. 2) **7076**

Laforest, Robert William. *The Establishment of Diplomatic Relations between Canada and the U.S.S.R. During the Second World War.* Ottawa, 1978. 139 leaves. **7077**

Thesis (M.A.), University of Ottawa, 1978. (National Library of Canada. Canadian Theses on Microfiche, No. 44054).

Lalande, Gilles. "Le Canada et le Pacifique." *In* Painchaud, Paul, ed., *Le Canada et le Québec sur la scène internationale* (Québec, 1977), pp. 363-378. **7078**

Legge, Garth, and others. "The Black Paper: An Alternative Policy for Canada Towards Southern Africa." (1970-71), 30 *Behind the Headlines* Nos. 1-2 (18 p.) **7079**

Lower, Arthur R.M. *Canada and the Far East-1940.* New York: International Secretariat, Institute of Pacific Relations, 1940. ix, 152 p. (I.P.R. Inquiry Series) **7080**
Reviews: Thomas-A. Birch in (1943-44), 19/2 *Actualité Économique* 99-100; Charles E. Martin in (1941), 35 *American Journal of International Law* 416-417.

Marston, Carroll J. *Canada and the Commonwealth Caribbean: The Other Side of the Coin.* Ottawa, 1976. 1 vol. (various pagings) **7081**
Thesis (M.J.), Carleton University, 1976.

Morelli, Francesco Giusseppi. *Canada and the Middle East.* Ottawa, 1976. v, 220 leaves. **7082**
Thesis (M.A.), Carleton University, 1976. (National Library of Canada. Canadian Theses on Microfiche, No. 28032).

Murray, David R. "The Bilateral Road: Canada and Latin America in the 1980s." (1981-82), 37 *International Journal* 108-131. **7083**

Nef, Jorge, ed. *Canada and the Latin American Challenge.* Guelph: Ontario Co-operative Programme in Caribbean and Latin American Studies, University of Guelph, 1978. viii, 183 p., maps. **7084**

Nossal, Kim Richard. "Business as Usual: Canadian Relations with China in the 1940's." (1978), *Canadian Historical Association, Historical Papers* 134-147. **7085**

Nossal, Kim Richard. *Strange Bedfellows: Canada and China in War and Revolution 1942-1947.* Toronto, 1977. 1 vol. **7086**
Thesis (Ph.D.), University of Toronto, 1977. Abstracted in (1979), 39 *Dissertation Abstracts International* 4482-A.

Ogelsby, J.C.M. *Gringos from the Far North: Essays in the History of Canadian-Latin American Relations, 1866-1968.* Toronto: Macmillan of Canada, 1976. xiv, 346 p., map. **7087**
Reviews: Christon I. Archer in (1976-77), 32 *International Journal* 880-883; Peter Aucoin in (1976-77), 56 *Dalhousie Review* 178-180; William R. Baron in (1976), 6 *American Review of Canadian Studies* 120-122 (No. 2); Graeme S. Mount in (1977), 58 *Canadian Historical Review* 513-515.

Onwumere, Chukwudi Pettson. *At Arm's Length: Canada's Relations with Commonwealth West Africa.* Hamilton, 1978. vii, 177 leaves. **7088**
Thesis (M.A.), McMaster University, 1978. (National Library of Canada. Canadian Theses on Microfiche, No. 39968).

Paragg, Ralph R. *Canada and the Commonwealth Caribbean: The Political Economy of a Relationship in Transition.* Kingston, 1978. xi, 536 leaves. **7089**
Thesis (Ph.D.), Queen's University, 1978. (National Library of Canada. Canadian

Theses on Microfiche, No. 39542). Abstracted in (1979/80), 40 *Dissertation Abstracts International* 447-A.

Raabe, Francis Conrad. *The China Issue in Canada: Politics and Foreign Policy.* University Park, Pa., 1970. 362 leaves. **7090**
Thesis (Ph.D.), Pennsylvania State University, 1970. Abstracted in (1971), 32 *Dissertation Abstracts International* 1052-A. (University Microfilms, Ann Arbor, No. 71-21790).

Redekop, Clarence G. *Canada and Southern Africa, 1946-1975: The Political Economy of Foreign Policy.* Toronto, c1977. xxiv, 1274 leaves. **7091**
Thesis (Ph.D.), University of Toronto, 1977. (National Library of Canada. Canadian Theses on Microfiche, No. 42302).

Ross, Douglas A. "Middlepowers as Extra-Regional Balancer Powers: Canada, India, and Indochina, 1954-62." (1982), 55 *Pacific Affairs* 185-209. **7092**

Schlegel, John P. *The Deceptive Ash: Bilingualism and Canadian Policy in Africa: 1957-1971.* Washington, D.C.: University Press of America, c1978. xviii, 463 p. **7093**
Review: Maureen P. Cronin in (1980), 10 *American Review of Canadian Studies* 96-98 (No. 2).

Schlegel, John P. "Ottawa's Achilles Heel: Formulating Policies in Southern Africa." (1979), 69 *Round Table* 142-153. **7094**

"Some Aspects of Canada's Relations with Latin America." (1953), 5 *External Affairs* 213-217. **7095**

Tennyson, Brian *Canadian Relations with South Africa: A Diplomatic History.* Washington: University Press of America, 1982. 237 p. **7096**
Review: Douglas G. Anglin in (1983), *International Perspectives* 32 (Jan./Feb.)

Winks, Robin W. *Canadian-West Indian Union: A Forty-Year Minuet.* London: Published for the Institute of Commonwealth Studies by Athlone Press, 1968. 54 p. (Commonwealth Papers, 11) **7097**
Reviews: Alice R. Stewart in (1970), 51 *Canadian Historical Review* 194-195; A.P. Thornton in a review article under title: "Small-Island Men," in (1968-69), 24 *International Journal* 590, 592.

Woodsworth, Charles James. *Canada and the Orient; a Study in International Relations.* Issued under the auspices of the Canadian Institute of International Affairs. Toronto: Macmillan of Canada, 1941. xii, 321 p. **7098**
Reviews: Forrest E. La Violettee in (1942), 8 *Canadian Journal of Economics and Political Science* 314-315; signed A.E.P. in (1943), 50 *Queen's Quarterly* 310.

II. INTERNATIONAL ECONOMIC RELATIONS

A. General (Incl. New International Economic Order)

Abbott, George C. "From Rhetoric to Reality." (1978-79), 34 *International Journal* 1-15. **7099**

Abbott, George C. "Size, Viability, Nationalism, and Politico-Economic Development." (1969-70), 25 *International Journal* 56-68. **7100**

Arès, Richard. "De l'aspect international du droit de propriété." (1952-53), 3 *Thémis* 23-35. **7101**

Arnopoulos, Paris J. "New International Order May not Be Mainly Economic." (1977), *International Perspectives* 8-14 (Sept./Oct.) **7102**

Arnopoulos, Paris J. "Socio-Political Implications of the New International Economic Order. (A Framework for Policy Analysis)." (1978), 50 *Canadian Political Science Association, Papers,* 30 p. **7103**

Barrett, Charles A. "The New International Economic Order and Its Implications for Canada." (1976), 3 *Canadian Business Review* 18-21 (No. 1) **7104**

Bernier, Ivan. "Souveraineté et interdépendance dans le nouvel ordre économique international." *In* Macdonald, Ronald St. John, and others, *The International Law and Policy of Human Welfare* (Alphen aan den Rijn, 1978), pp. 425-448. Also published in (1978), 9 *Études Internationales* 361-382. **7105**

Bernier, Ivan. "La survie des entreprises privées en difficulté au regard du droit international économique: le préjudice comme condition d'intervention de l'état." (1981), 22 *Cahiers de Droit* 525-546. **7106**

Bladen, Vincent W. "Economic Aspects of Foreign Policy." *In* Keenleyside, Hugh L., and others, *The Growth of Canadian Policies in External Affairs* (Durham, N.C., 1960), pp. 131-141. **7107**

Boreham, Gordon F. "Economic Cooperation in Southern Africa." (1983), *International Perspectives* 8-13 (Jan./Feb.) **7108**

Burn, Henry Pelham. "Enter a New World Economic Order." (1976), 83 *Canadian Banker and ICB Review* 16-21 (No. 1) **7109**

Colard, Daniel. "La Charte des droits et devoirs économiques des états." (1975), 6 *Études Internationales* 439-461. **7110**

Colloque sur le nouvel ordre économique international, Montréal, 1978. *Les voies*

du tiers-monde: rupture & négociation collectives. Colloque sur le nouvel ordre économique international (NOEI), 1-3 décembre 1978. Montréal: Centre d'étude et de coopération internationale, 1979. 200 p. **7111**
At head of title: Centre d'étude et de coopération internationale C.E.C.I., Conseil consultatif sur la formation, la recherche et la documentation, COFRED.

Cox, Robert W. "Ideologies and the New International Economic Order: Reflections on Some Recent Literature." (1979), 33 *International Organization* 257-302. **7112**

Daly, Donald J. *Canada in an Uncertain World Economic Environment.* Montreal: Institute for Research on Public Policy, c1982. 47 p. (Essays in International Economics) **7113**

Dolan, Michael B., and Tomlin, Brian W. "First World-Third World Linkages: External Relations and Economic Development." (1980), 34 *International Organization* 41-63. **7114**

Doxey, Margaret P. "Strategies in Multilateral Diplomacy: The Commonwealth, Southern Africa, and the NIEO." (1979-80), 35 *International Journal* 329-356.
7115

"Le droit international du développement / The International Law of Development." (1975), 4 *Canadian Council on International Law, Proceedings,* 204 p.
7116
This is the general theme of the fourth annual conference held at Ottawa, October 24-25, 1975. Individual papers are listed separately.

"Le droit international du développement: l'évolution du droit international du développement / The International Law of Development: The Evolving International Law of Development." (1975), 4 *Canadian Council on International Law, Proceedings* pp. 8-67. **7117**
This is a panel. Chairman: Erik Wang (pp. 8-10).- Speaker: Oscar Schachter (pp. 11-34).- Commentators: Gerald K. Helleiner (pp. 34-40), Armand L.C. de Mestral (pp. 41-43), and K.R. Simmonds (pp. 44-50).- General discussion (pp. 51-67).

Dussault, Paul N. "Le tiers-monde, l'ordre économique et la 'restauration' des organisations internationales." (1977), 8 *Études Internationales* 487-499. **7118**

Economic Council of Canada. *For a Common Future: A Study of Canada's Relations with the Developing Countries.* Ottawa: Economic Council of Canada, 1978. ix, 158 p. **7119**
Also issued in French under title: *Pour un commun avenir.*
Reviews: P.K. Kuruvilla in (1979), 22 *Canadian Public Administration* 333-335; Cranford Pratt in (1979), 5 *Canadian Public Policy* 142-144.

Ehrhardt, Roger B. *Canada's Response to the Call for a New International Economic Order.* Edmonton, 1977. viii, 132 leaves. **7120**
Thesis (M.A.), University of Alberta, 1977. (National Library of Canada. Canadian Theses on Microfiche, No. 31967).

Fatouros, Arghyrios A. "International Economic Development and the Illusion of Legal Certainty." (1963), 57 *American Society of International Law, Proceedings* 117-125. **7121**

Galtung, Johan. *Toward Self-Reliance and Global Interdependence.* Ottawa: Environment Canada; Canadian International Development Agency, 1978. ii, 85 p. (Joint Project on Environment and Development, 3) **7122**
Report prepared for the Policy Branch, Canadian International Development Agency and the Advanced Concepts Centre, Department of the Environment.

Genné, Marcelle. "Non-alignement et division internationale du travail: la position des pays en développement. (Review Article)." (1982), 13 *Études Internationales* 173-177. **7123**

Ghosh, Ratna. *Implications of Two Contrasting Strategies for International Development Co-operation.* Calgary, 1976. xii, 306 leaves. **7124**
Thesis (Ph.D.), University of Calgary, 1976. (National Library of Canada. Canadian Theses on Microfiche, No. 28510).

Glasgow, George. "The World in Conference." (1932), 39 *Queen's Quarterly* 633-648. **7125**

Gordon, J. King. "The New International Economic Order." (1975-76), 34 *Behind the Headlines* No. 5 (28 p.) **7126**

Grubel, Herbert G. "Canada's Stake in the New International Economic Order." (1977), 3 *Canadian Public Policy* 324-337. **7127**

Hainsworth, Geoffrey B. "Surviving the New International Economic Disorder. (Review Article)." (1981), 54 *Pacific Affairs* 288-301. **7128**

Helleiner, Gerald K. "Canada and the New International Economic Order." (1976), 2 *Canadian Public Policy* 451-465. **7129**

Helleiner, Gerald K. "Canada's Stake in the New International Economic Order: Comment." (1977), 3 *Canadian Public Policy* 337-343. **7130**

Helleiner, Gerald K. *International Economic Disorder: Essays in North-South Relations.* Toronto: University of Toronto Press, 1981. xii, 245 p. **7131**
Also published London, Macmillan, 1980.
Reviews: George C. Abbott in (1980-81), 36 *International Journal* 916-917; André Martens in (1982), 8 *Canadian Public Policy* 257; Ozay Mehmet in (1982), 15 *Canadian Journal of Economics* 557-559.

Henry, Paul-Marc. "Solutions Without Precedent for a World Without Precedent." (1981), *International Perspectives* 26-31 (Mar./Apr.) **7132**

Hérisson, Charles-D. "Le conflit des intérêts et des idées aux États-Unis en matière de politique économique internationale." (1936-37), 12/2 *Actualité Économique* 201-226. **7133**

Hérisson, Charles-D. "Économie complexe et organisation économique mondiale." (1936), 22 *Revue Trimestrielle Canadienne* 20-39, 173-194. **7134**

Holly, Daniel A. "Les Nations Unies et le nouvel ordre économique mondial." (1977), 8 *Études Internationales* 500-515. **7135**

Holly, Daniel A. "L'O.N.U., le système économique international et la politique internationale." (1975), 29 *International Organization* 469-485. **7136**

Holmes, John W. "The West and the Third World." (1965-66), 21 *International Journal* 20-41. **7137**

"International Economic Law: Canadian Perspectives / Le droit économique international: perspectives canadiennes." (1979), 8 *Canadian Council on International Law, Proceedings*, vii, 366 p. **7138**
This is the general theme of the eighth annual conference held in Ottawa, October 25-27, 1979. Individual papers are listed separately.

Jacomy-Millette, Annemarie. "Anatomie d'un pays en voie de développement à la lumière de ses engagements internationaux: le cas de l'Éthiopie." (1974), 78 *Revue Générale de Droit International Public* 1017-1045. **7139**

Johnson, Harry G. *Canada in a Changing World Economy.* Toronto: Published in co-operation with Carleton University by University of Toronto Press, 1962. 62 p. (Alan B. Plaunt Memorial Lectures, 1962) **7140**
Reviews: Parzival Copes in (1962), 5 *Canadian Public Administration* 517-518; Roger Dehem in (1962), 28 *Canadian Journal of Economics and Political Science* 606-607; Jean McNeil in (1962-63), 38 *Actualité Économique* 480-481.

Johnson, Harry G. *The Canadian Quandary; Economic Problems and Policies.* Toronto, New York: McGraw-Hill, 1963. xx, 352 p. **7141**
Review: H.S. Ferns in (1965), 41 *International Affairs* 588-590.

Johnson, Harry G., ed. *Economic Nationalism in Old and New States.* Chicago: University of Chicago Press, 1967. xi, 145 p. (Comparative Study of New Nations Series) **7142**

Johnson, Harry G. *Economic Policies Towards Less Developed Countries.* London: Allen & Unwin, 1967. xvi, 279 p. (Brookings Institution. Study) **7143**
Reviews: A.L. Keith Acheson in (1968), 75 *Canadian Banker* 63-67 (No. 1); Markos J. Mamalakis in (1968), 1 *Canadian Journal of Economics* 656-657.

Johnson, Harry G. *An Overall View of International Economic Questions Facing Britain, the United States, and Canada During the 1970's.* London: British-North American Committee, 1970. xv, 24 p. **7144**

Johnson, Harry G. "Trade, Development and Dependence." (1976), 83 *Queen's Quarterly* 427-442. **7145**

Kaplansky, Kalmen. "The Economic Policies of a Middle Power: Canada's Contribution to International Economic Cooperation." *In* Gordon, J. King, ed., *Canada's Role as a Middle Power* (Toronto, 1966), pp. 145-166. **7146**

Keirstead, B.S. "Economic Change and the International Order." (1946), 1 *International Journal* 235-242. **7147**

Langdon, S.W. "North/South, West and East: Industrial Restructuring in the World Economy." (1980-81), 36 *International Journal* 766-792. **7148**

Laszlo, Ervin, and Kurtzman, Joel, eds. *The United States, Canada, and the New International Economic Order.* New York: Pergamon Press, 1979. xi, 163 p. (Pergamon Policy Studies in the New International Economic Order) (NIEO Policy Research Library) **7149**
Published for UNITAR and the Center for Economic and Social Studies of the Third World (CEESTEM).
Review: Paris J. Arnopoulos in (1980), 13 *Canadian Journal of Political Science* 647-648.

Lavigne, Marie. "Les relations économiques Est-Ouest 1975-1985: bilan et perspectives." (1981), 12 *Études Internationales* 733-748. **7150**

Leduc, Gaston. "La crise des relations économiques internationales et la chimère de l'état isolé." (1938-39), 14/2 *Actualité Économique* 17-36. **7151**

Locas-Grandchamp, Micheline. *La structure du nouvel ordre politico-économique international vue au travers de la réforme du système monétaire international.* Montréal, 1975. xix, 164 leaves. **7152**
Thesis (M.A.), Université du Québec à Montréal, 1977. (National Library of Canada. Canadian Theses on Microfiche, No. 41592).

Lux, André. "Tradition, systèmes économiques et les contraintes du développement." (1969-70), 25 *International Journal* 1-8. **7153**

Mace, Gordon. "À propos du nouvel ordre économique international. (Review Article)." (1982), 13 *Études Internationales* 365-372. **7154**

Martin, Paul. "The UN Conference on Trade and Development." (1964), 16 *External Affairs* 143-148. **7155**

McMillan, Carl H., and St. Charles, D.P. *Joint East-West Ventures in Production and Marketing: A Three Country Comparison.* Ottawa: Institute of Soviet and East European Studies, Carleton University, 1973. 99 p. (East-West Commercial Relations Series; Working Paper, No. 1) **7156**

McMillan, Carl H., and St. Charles, D.P. *Joint Ventures in Eastern Europe: A Three-Country Comparison.* Montreal: C.D. Howe Research Institute, 1974. xii, 97 p. **7157**
Sponsored by the Canadian Economic Policy Committee, C.D. Howe Research Institute.

McWhinney, Edward. "The International Law-Making Process and the New International Economic Order." (1976), 14 *Canadian Yearbook of International Law* 57-72. **7158**

Mehmet, Ozay. "Global Poverty and the Role of the United Nations." (1976-77), 12 *University of Windsor Review* 47-57 (No. 2) **7159**

Merle, Marcel. "Need for Realistic Approach to New International Order." (1977), *International Perspectives* 3-6 (Nov./Dec.) **7160**

Mills, Joseph C. "The United Nations Conference on Trade and Development." (1965), 72 *Canadian Banker* 57-66 (No. 2) **7161**

North-South Institute. *Test Case for a New Economic Order.* Ottawa: North-South Institute, 1978. viii, 100 p. **7162**
Review: Richard Stubbs in (1980-81), 36 *International Journal* 391-392.

O'Brien, Rita Cruise, and Helleiner, Gerald K. "The Political Economy of Information in a Changing International Economic Order." (1980), 34 *International Organization* 445-470. **7163**

Ouimet, Lise. *La Conférence des Nations Unies sur le commerce et le développement et la théorie fonctionnaliste pour le maintien de la paix.* Ottawa, 1973. xix, 126 leaves. **7164**
Thesis (M.A.), University of Ottawa, 1973.

Parizeau, Jacques. "Note sur l'aménagement des espaces économiques internationaux." (1954-55), 30 *Actualité Économique* 477-488. **7165**

Pearson, Lester B. "The Challenge of Development." (1971), 6 *Stanford Journal of International Studies* 1-3. **7166**

Pearson, Lester B., and others. *International Economic Development in the 1970's.* New York: School of International Affairs, Columbia University, 1970. xiv, 155-344 p. (Journal of International Affairs, Vol. 24, No. 2, 1970) **7167**
Direct outgrowth of the Columbia University Conference on International Economic Development, held in February 1970. The papers relate to the report of the Commission on International Development entitled: *Partners in Development.*

Petersmann, Ernst-U. "The New International Economic Order: Principles, Politics and International Law." *In* Macdonald, Ronald St. John, and others, *The International Law and Policy of Human Welfare* (Alphen aan den Rijn, 1978), pp. 449-469. **7168**

Pratt, Cranford. "From Pearson to Brandt: Evolving Perceptions concerning International Development." (1979-80), 35 *International Journal* 623-645.
7169

Preiswerk, Roy. "Le nouvel ordre économique international est-il nouveau?" (1977), 8 *Études Internationales* 648-659. **7170**

Rajana, Cecil. "Europe and the Third World: A Critical Appraisal of Lomé II." (1979-80), 3 *Revue d'Intégration Européenne* 197-220. **7171**

Ramcharan, B.G. "Legal Policies in International Economic Relations." (1979), 8 *Canadian Council on International Law, Proceedings* 1-90. **7172**

Ramphal, Shridath S. "Global Management Required for New Economic Order." (1981), *International Perspectives* 5-9 (Mar./Apr.) **7173**

Ravenhill, John. "Asymmetrical Interdependence: Renegotiating the Lomé Convention." (1979-80), 35 *International Journal* 150-169. **7174**

Reuber, Grant L. "Steps to Improve International Economic Policy Co-ordination." (1981), 7 *Canadian Public Policy* 596-603. **7175**

Roche, Douglas J. "Politician Applies Human Terms to International Economic Order." (1977), *International Perspectives* 15-18 (July/Aug.) **7176**

Roy, Jacques S. "Recap of UN Special Session on International Development." (1981), *International Perspectives* 2-4 (Mar./Apr.) **7177**

Sabourin, Louis. "International Economic Development: Theories, Methods and Prospects." *In* Macdonald, Ronald St. John, and others, *The International Law and Policy of Human Welfare* (Alphen aan den Rijn, 1978), pp. 399-424.
7178

Sabourin, Louis. "Normes juridiques canadiennes en matière de développement international." *In* Macdonald, Ronald St. John, and others, *Canadian Perspectives on International Law and Organization* (Toronto, 1974), pp. 794-813.
7179

Saddy, Fehmy. "A New World Economic Order: The Limits of Accommodation." (1978-79), 34 *International Journal* 16-38. **7180**

Sajous, Emmanuel, and Abgrall, Jean-François. "Quelques réflexions sur la nécessité d'un nouvel ordre économique international." (1977), 10 *Revue de l'Université de Moncton* 135-138 (no 1) **7181**

Shaw, Timothy M. "The African Condition: Prophecies and Possibilities." (1982), 36 *Year Book of World Affairs* 139-150. **7182**

Shaw, Timothy M. "The Elusiveness of Development and Welfare: Inequalities in the Third World." *In* Macdonald, Ronald St. John, and others, *The International Law and Policy of Human Welfare* (Alphen aan den Rijn, 1978), pp. 81-109. **7183**

Shaw, Timothy M. *Towards an International Political Economy for the 1980s: From Dependence to (Inter) Dependence.* Comments by Robert O. Matthews, Robert McKinnell. Halifax: Centre for Foreign Policy Studies, Dalhousie University, 1980. 90 p. **7184**

Steeves, Jeffrey S. "Challenging the Economic Council's View of the New World Order." (1979), *International Perspectives* 15-20. **7185**

Tindigarukayo, Jimmy Kazaara. *External Economic Dependency and Growth Without Development in Black Africa.* Halifax, 1978 (c1979). iii, 82 leaves.
7186
Thesis (M.A.), Dalhousie University, 1979. (National Library of Canada. Canadian Theses on Microfiche, No. 41244).

Van Dam, André. "Adieu, Bretton Woods!" (1979), 55 *Actualité Économique* 267-272. **7187**

Wallerstein, Immanuel Maurice, ed. *Les inégalités entre états dans le système international: origines et perspectives.* Québec: Centre québécois de relations internationales, 1975. 244 p. (Collection Choix, 8) **7188**
Contains the proceedings of the "Colloque sur le problème de l'inégalité dans le système mondial contemporain, ses origines et perspectives," held at McGill University in 1974. Organized by Centre québécois de relations internationales, in collaboration with Commission de la recherche, mouvements nationaux et impérialisme, de l'Association internationale de sociologie.

B. International Trade

1. GENERAL

Acheson, A.L. Keith. *Some Problems in the Theory of International Trade.* Toronto, 1968. 80 leaves. **7189**
Thesis, University of Toronto, 1968. (National Library of Canada. Canadian Theses on Microfilm, No. 3332).

Adam, Mahomed Ali. *An Inquiry into the Discriminatory Effects of International Trade Law on the Developing Countries.* Edmonton, 1976. xvii, 384 leaves.
7190
Thesis (LL.M.), University of Alberta, 1976. (National Library of Canada. Canadian Theses on Microfiche, No. 27595).

Adams, James H., ed. *Obstacles and Opportunities: Proceedings of the North-South Institute Trade Symposium, Rideau Hall, Ottawa, October, 1980.* Ottawa: North-South Institute, c1981. iv, 48 p. (Canada and Third World Trade, 3) **7191**
Also published in French under title: *Obstacles et perspectives.*

Balassa, Bela. "Tariff Protection in Industrial Nations and Its Effects on the Exports of Processed Goods from Developing Countries." (1968), 1 *Canadian Journal of Economics* 583-594. 7192

Contains a résumé in French under title: "La protection tarifaire des pays industrialisés et ses effets sur les exportations de produits finis par les pays en voie de développement."

Bernier, Ivan. "Les ententes de restriction volontaire à l'exportation en droit international économique." (1973), 11 *Canadian Yearbook of International Law* 48-86. 7193

Biggs, Margaret A. *The Challenge, Adjust or Protect?* Ottawa: North-South Institute, c1980. 157 p. (Canada and Third World Trade, 1) 7194

Also published in French under title: *Le dilemme: reconversion ou protectionnisme?*

Casas, Francisco Ricardo. *Intermediate Goods and the Theory of International Trade.* London, Ont., 1972. viii, 78 leaves. 7195

Thesis (Ph.D.), University of Western Ontario, 1973. (National Library of Canada. Canadian Theses on Microfilm, No. 14028).

Connolly, Michael Bahaamonde, and Swoboda, Alexander K., eds. *International Trade and Money: The Geneva Essays.* Toronto: University of Toronto Press, 1973. 264 p. 7196

Contains papers presented at the Seminar in International Economics for 1970/71, held at the Graduate Institute of International Studies. Published in collaboration with the Graduate Institute of International Studies, Geneva.

Corbet, Hugh. *Trade Strategy and the Asian-Pacific Region.* Toronto: University of Toronto Press, 1970. 221 p. 7197

Review: Jaleel Ahmad in (1973), 4 *Études Internationales* 189-190.

Corry, J.A. "Free Trade in Ideas." (1949-50), 56 *Queen's Quarterly* 1-14. 7198

David, René. "Société des états et droit du commerce international." (1967), 13 *McGill Law Journal* 218-231. 7199

Deutsch, John J. "Changing Trends in World Trade." *In* Clark, Robert M., ed., *Canadian Issues: Essays in Honour of Henry F. Angus* (Toronto, 1961), pp. 134-142. 7200

Diebold, William, Jr. "The New Situation of International Trade Policy." (1962-63), 18 *International Journal* 426-441. 7201

Drummond, W.M. "Trade for Prosperity." (1945), 5 *Behind the Headlines* No. 7 (19 p.) 7202

Elliott, George Alexander. "Transfer of Means-of-Payment and the Terms of International Trade." (1936), 2 *Canadian Journal of Economics and Political Science* 481-492. 7203

Fay, C.R. "Foreign Trade and Merchant Shipping." (1923-24), 31 *Journal of the Canadian Bankers' Association* 223-231. 7204

Frank, Isaiah. "International Trade Policy for the Second Development Decade." (1969-70), 25 *International Journal* 94-108. 7205

Frankson, Pamela Louise. *Towards a Unified International Trade Law: Some Attempts at Universality.* Toronto, c1980. 168 leaves. 7206

Thesis (LL.M.), University of Toronto, 1980.

Galtung, Johan. "La convention de Lomé et le néo-capitalisme." (1978), 9 *Études Internationales* 75-86. **7207**
Refers to the convention of February 28, 1975.

Henry, D.H.W. "International Aspects of Competition Policy." In Macdonald, Ronald St. John, and others, *Canadian Perspectives on International Law and Organization* (Toronto, 1974), pp. 756-793. **7208**

Hérisson, Charles-D. "Commerce international et économie concertée." (1943-44), 19/1 *Actualité Économique* 118-134. **7209**

Hérisson, Charles-D. "Le régime douanier américain." (1937), 23 *Revue Trimestrielle Canadienne* 29-41. **7210**

Iqbal, Munawar. *The Effects of the EEC and the EFTA on Trade Flows: A Cross Sectional Analysis.* Burnaby, B.C., 1979. 211 frames. **7211**
Thesis (Ph.D.), Simon Fraser University, 1979. (National Library of Canada. Canadian Theses on Microfiche, No. 44913).

Jainarain, Iserdeo. *International Trade and the Economic Development of Small Countries, with Special Reference to Guyana.* Winnipeg, 1970. xii, 326 leaves. **7212**
Thesis, University of Manitoba, 1970. (National Library of Canada. Canadian Theses on Microfilm, No. 6270).

Johnson, Harry G. "La théorie du commerce international." (1968-69), 44 *Actualité Économique* 621-637. **7213**

Johnson, Harry G., ed. *Trade Strategy for Rich and Poor Nations.* Toronto: University of Toronto Press; London: Allen and Unwin, c1971. 232 p. **7214**
Contains papers prepared for the Atlantic Trade Study Programme.

Johnson, Harry G.; Wonnacott, Paul; and Shibata, Hirofumi. *Harmonization of National Economic Policies under Free Trade.* Toronto: Published for the Private Planning Association of Canada by University of Toronto Press, c1968. 84 p. (Canada in the Atlantic Economy, Vol. 3) **7215**
Contents: The Implications of Free or Freer Trade for the Harmonization of Other Policies, by H.G. Johnson.- Policy Harmonization in Free Trade Groupings with Special Reference to the European Economic Community, by P. Wonnacott.- Free Trade Areas and Policy Coordination with Special Reference to the European Free Trade Area, by H. Shibata.

Judek, S. "The Evolution of the Keynesian Approach to International Trade." (1960), 30 *Revue de l'Université d'Ottawa* 257-274. **7216**

Kaiser, Gordon E. "Conflict of Laws and the Extraterritorial Effect of Commercial Regulation." (1971-72), 1 *Queen's Law Journal* 384-440. **7217**

Knight, R.E. "Reflections on Foreign Trade and International Finance." (1937-38), 45 *Canadian Banker* 389-400. **7218**

Knox, Frank A. "Empire Trade and British Industry." (1932), 39 *Queen's Quarterly* 46-61. **7219**

Kos-Rabcewicz-Zubkowski, Ludwik. "Le droit commercial international dans les rapports Est-Ouest." (1967), 5 *Canadian Yearbook of International Law* 159-192. **7220**

Kos-Rabcewicz-Zubkowski, Ludwik. "Le droit du commerce international: une nouvelle tâche pour les législateurs nationaux ou une nouvelle 'lex mercatoria.' " (1976), 7 *Revue Générale de Droit* 271-278. **7221**

Lepore, Giuseppe. *International Trade, Its Relevance to Less Developed Countries.* Montreal, 1969 (c1970). iii, 162 leaves. **7222**
Thesis (M.A.), McGill University, 1970. (National Library of Canada. Canadian Theses on Microfilm, No. 6419).

Mackenzie, Kenneth C. *Tariff-Making and Trade Policy in the U.S. and Canada; a Comparative Study.* New York: Praeger, 1968. xvii, 294 p. (Praeger Special Studies in International Economics and Development) **7223**

Maindrault, Marc. "Les crédits à l'exportation." (1977), 8 *Études Internationales* 630-647. **7224**

Marsh, Donald Bailey. *World Trade and Investment; the Economics of Interdependence.* Foreword by Howard S. Ellis. New York: Harcourt, Brace, 1951. xxii, 594 p. **7225**
Reviews: Jean Gérin in (1952-53), 28 *Actualité Économique* 159-160; Charles P. Kindleberger in (1951), 17 *Canadian Journal of Economics and Political Science* 409-412.

Martey, Emmanuel Korley. *International Trade, Structural Changes, and Economic Development in the Context of the Twentieth Century Experience.* Winnipeg, 1965. x, 161 leaves. **7226**
Thesis (M.A.), University of Manitoba, 1965. (National Library of Canada. Canadian Theses on Microfilm, No. 141).

Matthews, Roy A. "Challenge from the Third World: A Threat to Canadian Industry and Workers?" (1980-81), 38 *Behind the Headlines* No. 4 (22 p.) **7227**

McGoun, Archibald. "Imperial Free Trade." (1907), 6 *Canadian Law Review* 214-222. **7228**

Pacific Trade and Development Conference, 4th, Carleton University, 1971. *Obstacles to Trade in the Pacific Area; Proceedings of the Fourth Pacific Trade and Development Conference.* Edited by H.E. English and Keith A.J. Hay. Ottawa: School of International Affairs, Carleton University, 1972. viii, 296 p. Conference held October 7-10, 1971. **7229**

Pestieau, Caroline, and Henry, Jacques. *Non-Tariff Trade Barriers as a Problem in International Development; a Study in Two Parts.* Montreal: Canadian Economic Policy Committee, Private Planning Association of Canada, 1972. xx, 219 p. **7230**
Contents: - Introduction, by R.A. Matthews.- NTBs and the Need for Manufactured-Goods Exports from Developing Countries, by C. Pestieau.- Market Disruption from 'Low-Priced' Imports: The Developed Countries' Case (with Special Reference to Canadian Experience), by J. Henry.
Review: Ralph Kolinski in (1973), 6 *Canadian Journal of Economics* 623-624.

Peterson, James S. "International Regulation of Business Practices: Fact or Fiction?" (1979), 8 *Canadian Council on International Law, Proceedings* 238-249. **7231**

Precht, Paul Lawrence. *New Technology and International Trade.* Edmonton, 1969. v, 96 leaves. **7232**
Thesis (M.A.), University of Alberta, 1969.

Reuber, Grant L. "Balance of Payments and Foreign Trade Problems of the Less Developed Countries." (1965), 72 *Canadian Banker* 20-34 (No. 3) **7233**

Richard, John D. "International Regulation of Business Practices: Fact or Fiction." (1979), 8 *Canadian Council on International Law, Proceedings* 198-225. **7234**

Robinson, J. Lewis. "The Geographical Basis of Foreign Trade." (1950), 40 *Canadian Geographical Journal* 114-123. **7235**

Scammell, W.M. *International Trade and Payments.* London: Macmillan, 1974. xiv, 607 p. **7236**
Review: H.H. Binhammer in (1975), 8 *Canadian Journal of Economics* 637-639.

Scanteie, Eugene. *Les échanges commerciaux entre l'Afrique noire et la C.E.E. créent-ils des effets de domination?* Montréal, 1974. viii, 183 leaves. **7237**
Thesis (M.Sc.), Université de Montréal, 1974.

Schmitthoff, Clive M. "International Business Law: A New Law Merchant." (1961), 2 *Current Law and Social Problems* 129-153. **7238**

Sékaly, Raymond R. *Transnationalization of the Automotive Industry.* Ottawa: University of Ottawa Press, 1981. xi, 294 p., maps. (Institute for International Development and Co-operation. Books and Monographs Series, 4) **7239**

Slater, David W. "World Trade - Trends and Prospects." (1966), 73 *Canadian Banker* 5-19 (No. 4) **7240**

Slosar, Stanislas. *Droit international public: droit des transactions internationales; recueil des textes.* Montréal: Librairie de l'Université de Montréal, 1980. 417 p. Notes de cours, Université de Montréal, Faculté de droit. **7241**

"Steel Dumping into Canada and the United States." (1979), 2 *Canada-United States Law Journal* 17-115. **7242**
Proceedings of a conference of the Canada-United States Law Institute, held September 29 and 30, 1978, at the University of Western Ontario, London.

Sutton, Kenneth C. "Formation of Contract: Unity in International Sale of Goods." (1977), 16 *University of Western Ontario Law Review* 113-162. **7243**

Teng, Chuo-Ying. *An Enquiry into the Causes of International Trade Regulations in Underdeveloped Countries.* Edmonton, 1967. viii, 120 leaves. **7244**
Thesis (M.A.), University of Alberta, 1967.

Tomsa, Branko. "Les relations de la CEE avec les pays de l'Europe de l'Est." (1978), 9 *Études Internationales* 87-105. **7245**

Trakman, Leon E. "The Evolution of the Law Merchant: Our Commercial Heritage." (1980-81), 12 *Journal of Maritime Law and Commerce* 1-24, 153-182. **7246**

Tumlir, Jan. "The Protectionist Threat to International Order." (1978-79), 34 *International Journal* 53-63. **7247**

Uren, Philip E., ed. *East-West Trade; a Symposium.* Introduction by Mitchell W. Sharp. Toronto: Canadian Institute of International Affairs, c1966. 181 p. (Contemporary Affairs, No. 36) **7248**
Review: Abraham Rotstein under title: "East-West Trade," in (1965-66), 21 *International Journal* 527-531.

Urquhart, M.C. "Post-War International Trade Agreements." (1948), 14 *Canadian Journal of Economics and Political Science* 372-385. **7249**

Viner, Jacob. *Trade Relations between Free-Market and Controlled Economies.* Geneva: League of Nations, 1943. 92 p. (League of Nations. Series of Publications, Economic and Financial) **7250**
Review: Gaston Robillard in (1947-48), 23 *Actualité Économique* 176-177.

Wex, Samuel. "A Code of Conduct on Restrictive Business Practices: A Third Option." (1977), 15 *Canadian Yearbook of International Law* 198-235. **7251**

Wonnacott, Ronald J. "The Political Economy of Liberalized Trade." (1973-74), 29 *International Journal* 577-590. **7252**

World Trade and Trade Policy: Comprising Three Studies of the 'Canada in the Atlantic Economy' Series. Research Director: H. Edward English. Toronto: Published for the Private Planning Association of Canada by the University of Toronto Press, 1968. 1 vol. (various pagings) (Canada in the Atlantic Economy, Vols. 1-3) **7253**
Contents: World Trade and Economic Growth: Trends and Prospects with Applications to Canada, by David W. Slater.- Transatlantic Economic Community: Canadian Perspectives, by H.E. English.- Harmonization of National Economic Policies under Free Trade, by Harry G. Johnson, Paul Wonnacott, and Hirofumi Shibata.

Young, Owen D. "The Future of International Trade." (1934), 41 *Queen's Quarterly* 21-28. **7254**

Ziegel, Jacob S., and Graham, William C., eds. *New Dimensions in International Trade Law.* Toronto: Butterworths, 1982. 224 p. **7255**
Papers presented at a seminar on New Dimensions in International Trade Law, held in Toronto, November 14, 1980.

2. MULTILATERAL TRADE (GATT, ETC.)

See also *"Foreign Trade of Canada: Multilateral Trade" (p. 576).*

Addo, Herbert Christian. *International Organizations versus Developing Nations: The Case of the General Agreement on Tariffs and Trade (GATT).* Hamilton, Ont., 1968. vii, 109 leaves. **7256**
Thesis (M.A.), McMaster University, 1968.

"The Annecy Conference on Tariffs and Trade." (1949), 1 *External Affairs* 14-20 (Oct.) **7257**

Barkway, Michael. "GATT Revised." (1954-55), 10 *International Journal* 192-197. **7258**

Bernstein, E.M. "Multilateral Trade in an Unbalanced World." (1950), 16 *Canadian Journal of Economics and Political Science* 340-346. **7259**

Canada. Tariff Board. *A Report of an Inquiry by the Tariff Board Respecting the GATT Agreement on Customs Valuation.* Ottawa: Tariff Board, 1981. 2 vols. 7260
Cover title: *The GATT Agreement on Customs Valuation.* Also issued in French under title: *Rapport d'une enquête par la Commission du tarif ayant trait à l'accord du GATT sur l'évaluation en douane.*

Clark, Robert G. "International Trade Environment in the Post-MTN Period." (1979), *International Perspectives* 7-12 (Sept./Dec.) 7261

Crean, John G. "The Coming Negotiations under GATT." (1973-74), 32 *Behind the Headlines* No. 3 (14 p.) 7262

Curzon, Gerard. "GATT and the Golden Age of Trade Cooperation." *In* Fry, Michael G., ed., *'Freedom and Change': Essays in Honour of Lester B. Pearson* (Toronto, 1975), pp. 190-203. 7263

De Koninck, Rodolphe, and Comtois, Claude. "L'accélération de l'intégration du commerce extérieur des pays de l'ASEAN au marché mondial." (1980), 11 *Études Internationales* 43-63. 7264

Denis, G.A. "New Developments in International Economic Law: The Tokyo Round Results." (1979), 8 *Canadian Council on International Law, Proceedings* 92-114. 7265

Denis, Germain. "Un régime de préférences tarifaires généralisées pour le tiers monde." (1971), 2 *Études Internationales* 231-249. 7266

Finlayson, Jock A., and Zacher, Mark W. "International Trade Institutions and the North/South Dialogue." (1980-81), 36 *International Journal* 732-765. 7267

Fox, Lawrence A. "The Kennedy Round Trade Negotiations: Nature and Prospects." (1964), 6 *University of Windsor Seminar on Canadian-American Relations, Proceedings* 241-252. 7268

"GATT Tariff Conference 1960-61." (1960), 12 *External Affairs* 814-818. 7269

"The GATT To-day." (1955), 7 *External Affairs* 107-115. 7270

Golt, Sidney. *The GATT Negotiations, 1973-75: A Guide to the Issues.* London, England: British-North American Committee, 1974. xii, 82 p. (British-North American Committee. Publications, BN-14) 7271
Sponsored by the British-North American Research Association, the National Planning Association (U.S.A.), and the C.D. Howe Research Institute (Canada).

Golt, Sidney. *The GATT Negotiations, 1973-79: The Closing Stage,* by Sidney Golt, and *A Policy Statement,* by the British-North American Committee. London, England: British-North American Committee, 1978. xviii, 52 p. (British-North American Committee. Publications, BN-22) 7272

Grey, Rodney de C. "The GATT, and All That." (1980), 9 *Canadian Council on International Law, Proceedings* 43-47. 7273

Grubel, Herbert G., and Johnson, Harry G. *Effective Tariff Protection; Proceedings of a Conference.* Geneva: General Agreement on Tariffs and Trade, 1971. vii, 305 p. 7274
Review: W.G. Waters in (1972), 5 *Canadian Journal of Economics* 327-329.

Haugestad, Per Thelin. *Organized Multilateral Trade: Some Aspects of the Struc-*

ture and Operation of the General Agreement on Tariffs and Trade. Montreal, 1959. 175 leaves. **7275**
Thesis (M.A.), McGill University, 1959.

Latimer, Robert E. "The Multi-lateral Approach (the Kennedy Round): Nature and Prospects." (1964), 6 *University of Windsor Seminar on Canadian-American Relations, Proceedings* 253-259. **7276**

Leavy, James. "Quelques aspects juridiques de la libre circulation des marchandises dans les marchés communs canadien et européen." (1979-80), 3 *Revue d'Intégration Européenne* 141-161. **7277**

Low, D. Martin. "The United Nations Commission on International Trade Law: An Overview." (1979), 8 *Canadian Council on International Law, Proceedings* 160-172. **7278**

Macdonald, Donald S. "The Impact of the New Non-Tariff Barrier Codes on GATT and Canada. (Annual Dinner Address)." (1979), 8 *Canadian Council on International Law, Proceedings* 358-366. **7279**

Macdonald, Donald S. "The Multilateral Trade Negotiations - A Lawyer's Perspective." (1980), 4 *Canadian Business Law Journal* 139-163. **7280**

Martyn, Howe. "After the 'Kennedy Round': The Regional Blocs Consolidate." (1968-69), 48 *Dalhousie Review* 312-323. **7281**

Seth, Sanjiv. *The UNCTAD Restrictive Business Practices Code.* Toronto, c1980. 192 leaves. **7282**
Thesis (LL.M.), University of Toronto, 1980.

Slayton, Philip. "Institutional Design Opportunities and the GATT Reforms." (1979), 8 *Canadian Council on International Law, Proceedings* 251-260. **7283**

Slosar, Stanislas. "Nouveaux accords relatifs aux obstacles non-tarifaires conclus dans le cadre du GATT." (1979), 8 *Canadian Council on International Law, Proceedings* 261-283. **7284**

Stanford, Joseph S. "Treaty Amendment: The Problem of the GATT Tariff Schedules." (1969), 7 *Canadian Yearbook of International Law* 255-268. **7285**

"The Torquay Conference." (1951), 3 *External Affairs* 193-197. **7286**

Tovias, Alfred. "Ex-post Studies of the Effects of Economic Integration on Trade: Problems in Measuring Trade-Flow and Welfare Effects." (1981-82), 5 *Revue d'Intégration Européenne* 159-167. **7287**

Vincke, Christian. "Trade Restrictions for Balance of Payments Reasons and the GATT: Quotas v. Surcharges." (1972), 13 *Harvard International Law Journal* 289-315. **7288**

Wagacha, Bernard Mbui. *The Protective Effects of Intra-Customs Union Tariffs.* Winnipeg, 1976. iv, 150 leaves. **7289**
Thesis (M.A.), University of Manitoba, 1976.

Weekes, J.W. "The Emphasis on Non-Tariff Barriers and Dispute Settlement in the Recent GATT Reforms." (1979), 8 *Canadian Council on International Law, Proceedings* 284-292. **7290**

Wex, Samuel. "New Developments in International Economic Law: International Restrictive Business Practices." (1979), 8 *Canadian Council on International Law, Proceedings* 115-138. **7291**

Whalley, John. *An Evaluation of the Recent Tokyo Round Trade Agreement through a General Equilibrium Model of World Trade Involving Major Trading Areas.* London, Ont.: Dept. of Economics, University of Western Ontario, 1980. 53 p. (University of Western Ontario. Centre for the Study of International Economic Relations. Working Paper, No. 8009) **7292**

Winham, Gilbert R. "The Mediation of Multilateral Negotiation." (1979), 13 *Journal of World Trade Law* 193-208. **7293**

Winham, Gilbert R. "Robert Strauss, the MTN, and the Control of Faction." (1980), 14 *Journal of World Trade Law* 377-397. **7294**

Winham, Gilbert R. "The United States Wine Gallon Concession: How the Biggest Chip in the Tokyo Round Was Negotiated." (1980-81), 36 *International Journal* 851-878. **7295**

3. FOREIGN TRADE OF CANADA

(a) GENERAL

Aitken, H.T. "Export Credits Insurance Corporation." (1948), 55 *Canadian Banker* 110-119 (No. 2) **7296**

Aitken, H.T. "Export Credits Insurance Corporation: Assistance for Canadian Exporters." (1966), 73 *Canadian Banker* 72-84 (No. 2) **7297**

Aitken, H.T. "Insuring Export Credits in Canada." (1959), 66 *Canadian Banker* 106-109 (No. 3) **7298**

Anastasopoulos, A. ; Brault, L. ; and Sims, W.A. "The Impact on the Quebec Economy of a Disruption of Trade Relations between Quebec and Its Major Trading Partners." (1980), 6 *Canadian Public Policy* 574-583. **7299**

Anderson, Roger V. *The Future of Canada's Export Trade.* Ottawa: Royal Commission on Canada's Economic Prospects, 1957. 338 p. **7300**

Bannerman, Glen. "The Canadian International Trade Fair: A New Merchandising Technique for Canada." (1952), 44 *Canadian Geographical Journal* 215-225. **7301**

Barrett, Charles A. *Canada's International Trade: Trends and Prospects.* Ottawa: Conference Board in Canada, 1976. 55 p. (Canadian Studies, No. 39) **7302**
A report from the Conference Board in Canada.

Baxter, Ian Francis George, and Feltham, Ivan R., eds. *Export Practice.* Toronto: Osgoode Hall Law School; distributed by Carswell, 1964. 134 p. (Commercial Law Series, No. 1) **7303**

Bernier, Ivan. "La Constitution canadienne et la réglementation des relations économiques internationales." (1979), 8 *Canadian Council on International Law, Proceedings* 324-342. **7304**

Bernier, Ivan. "La Constitution canadienne et la réglementation des relations économiques internationales au sortir du 'Tokyo Round.'" (1979), 20 *Cahiers de Droit* 673-694. **7305**

Bénard, Jean. "Réseau des échanges internationaux et planification ouverte." (1963-64), 39 *Actualité Économique* 537-580. **7306**
Also contains: "Discussion du rapport du professeur J. Bénard" (pp. 568-580).

Bradford, Colin I., and Pestieau, Caroline. *Canada and Latin America: The Potential for Partnership; a Study in Two Parts.* Montreal: Canadian Economic Policy Committee of the Private Planning Association of Canada, 1971. xxi, 228 p. **7307**
Sponsored by the Canadian Association for Latin America, Toronto, and the Canadian Economic Policy Committee, Private Planning Association of Canada, Montreal.
Review: Bruce W. Wilkinson in (1972), 5 *Canadian Journal of Economics* 310, 312-313.

Brewster, Havelock. "Canada and the West Indies: Some Issues in International Economic Relations." (1967), 2 *Journal of Canadian Studies* 25-31 (No. 3) **7308**

Britton, John N.H. "Locational Perspectives on Free Trade for Canada." (1978), 4 *Canadian Public Policy* 4-19. **7309**

Brouillette, Benoît. "Les courants commerciaux de l'Ontario avec l'extérieur." (1969), 7 *Royal Society of Canada, Transactions* 133-156 (4th Ser.) **7310**

Brouillette, Benoît. "Les courants commerciaux de la Colombie Britannique avec l'extérieur." (1965), 3 *Royal Society of Canada, Transactions* 41-51 (4th Ser.) **7311**

Brouillette, Benoît. "Les courants commerciaux des provinces de l'Atlantique avec l'extérieur." (1971), 9 *Royal Society of Canada, Transactions* 63-93 (4th Ser.) **7312**

Brouillette, Benoît. "Les courants commerciaux du Québec avec l'extérieur." (1970-71), 8 *Royal Society of Canada, Transactions* 141-169 (4th Ser.) **7313**

Brouillette, Benoît. "Les courants commerciaux entre l'Île du Prince-Édouard et l'extérieur." (1964), 2 *Royal Society of Canada, Transactions* 63-67 (4th Ser.) **7314**

Brouillette, Benoît. "Les courants commerciaux entre les provinces de la Prairie et l'extérieur." (1968), 6 *Royal Society of Canada, Transactions* 125-141 (4th Ser.) **7315**

Burns, T.M. "The Trade Jungle of Export Credits." (1983), *International Perspectives* 22-24 (Jan./Feb.) **7316**

Canada. Dept. of External Affairs. *Canadian Foreign Trade and Commercial Relations.* Ottawa: Supply and Services Canada, 1980. 26 p. (Canada. Dept. of External Affairs. Reference Series, No. 35) **7317**
Also issued in French under title: *Commerce extérieur et relations commerciales du Canada.*

Canada. Dept. of Finance. *Proposals on Import Policy: A Discussion Paper Proposing Changes to Canadian Import Legislation.* Ottawa: Supply and Services Canada, 1980. 76 p. **7318**

Canada. Dept. of Industry, Trade and Commerce. *Annual Report / Rapport annuel.* 1969/70—. Ottawa. Bilingual. **7319**
This department, reorganized in 1969 (R.S.C. 1970, c. I-11), has jurisdiction over international trade. It operates the Trade Commissioner Service in foreign countries. It is responsible for the administration of the *Foreign Investment Review Act* (S.C. 1973-74, c. 46). The annual reports describe briefly some activities of international interest.

Canada. Parliament. House of Commons. Special Committee on a National Trading Corporation. *Canada's Trade Challenge / Le défi commercial du Canada. Fourth Report.* Ottawa: Supply and Services Canada, 1981. 15, 85, 94, 14 p. **7320**

"Canadian Trade Policy in a World of Economic Nationalism." (1934), 41 *Queen's Quarterly* 81-98. **7321**

Chen, Tung-Pi. "Canadian Export Credits, Guarantee and Insurance Programs." In Fridman, G.H.L., ed., *Studies in Canadian Business Law* (Toronto, 1971), pp. 369-391. **7322**

Chen, Tung-Pi. "Legal Aspects of Canadian Trade with the People's Republic of China." (1973-74), 38 *Law and Contemporary Problems* 201-229. **7323**

Clark, Melvin Gordon. *Canada and World Trade.* Ottawa: Queen's Printer, 1965. 64 p. (Economic Council of Canada. Staff Study, No. 7. 1964) **7324**

Corbo, Vittorio, and Havrylyshyn, Oli. *Canada's Trade Relations with Developing Countries: The Evolution of Export and Import Structures and Barriers to Trade in Canada.* Ottawa: Economic Council of Canada, 1980. x, 136 p. **7325**
Also issued in French under title: *Les relations commerciales entre le Canada et les pays en développement.*

Cousineau, Rosario. *Histoire de la politique commerciale extérieure du Canada de 1602 à 1951.* Ottawa, 1951. 235 leaves. **7326**
Thesis (Ph.D.), University of Ottawa, 1952.

Cousineau, Rosario. "Politique commerciale extérieure du Canada." (1946-47), 22 *Actualité Économique* 17-43. **7327**

Daigle, Benoit Ludovic. *The Possibility of Trade between Canada and Latin America.* Washington, D.C., 1969. xiv, 396 leaves. **7328**
Thesis (Ph.D.), Catholic University of America, 1969. Abstracted in (1969), 30 *Dissertation Abstracts International* 2223-A.

Dauphin, Roma. *The Impact of Free Trade in Canada.* Ottawa: Economic Council of Canada, c1978. xii, 185 p. **7329**
Also issued in French under title: *Les effets de la libéralisation des échanges sur l'économie canadienne.*
Review: Alan M. Rugman in (1978), 4 *Canadian Public Policy* 576-577.

Dauphin, Roma. "Une nouvelle politique économique canadienne." (1979-80), 14 *Journal of Canadian Studies* 118-125. **7330**

Denis, Jean-Émile, and Lindekens, Emmanuel. "Perspectives de coopération industrielle dans le contexte de l'accord cadre entre le Canada et les Communautés européennes." (1977-78), 1 *Revue d'Intégration Européenne* 107-124. **7331**

Dhawan, K.C.; Etemad, Hamid; and Wright, Richard W., eds. *International Business: A Canadian Perspective.* Don Mills, Ont.: Addison-Wesley, c1981. xv, 868 p. **7332**

Dhawan, K.C., and Kryzanowski, Lawrence. *Export Consortia: A Canadian Study.* Montreal: Dekemco, c1978. xi, 249 p. **7333**

Dinsmore, John. "Les échanges internationaux du Québec." (1976), 7 *Études Internationales* 110-115. **7334**

Donnelly, Michael W. "Growing Disharmony in Canadian-Japanese Trade." (1980-81), 36 *International Journal* 879-897. **7335**

Drummond, Andrew T. "The Federal Union of the British West Indies and Commercial Union with Canada." (1916-17), 24 *Queen's Quarterly* 410-420. **7336**

Dubé, Georges. "La réglementation du trafic et du commerce au Canada." (1964-65), 6 *Cahiers de Droit* 55-63 (no 1) **7337**

English, Harry Edward, ed. *Canada and the New International Economy; Three Essays.* Toronto: Published in co-operation with Carleton University by University of Toronto Press, c1961. 75 p. **7338**
Contains three slightly revised public lectures delivered at Carleton University, Ottawa, February 21-23, 1961.
Contents: The Historical Perspective: Nineteenth-Century Trade Theory and Policy, by H.S. Gordon.- The International Perspective: the Emergence of Regional Free Trade Areas, by Harry G. Johnston.- Canada's Policy Problem, by Arthur J. R. Smith.- Summary and Comment, by H.E. English.
Reviews: H. Ian Macdonald in (1961-62), 17 *International Journal* 194-195; Camille Martin in (1962-63), 38 *Actualité Économique* 488-489.

English, Harry Edward. "Canada's International Economic Position." (1963), 70 *Canadian Banker* 31-45 (No. 2) **7339**

English, Harry Edward. *Regional and Adjustment Aspects of Trade Liberalization.* Research Director, H. Edward English. Toronto: Published for the Private Planning Association of Canada by University of Toronto Press, c1973. vi, 203, vi, 144 p. (Canada in the Atlantic Economy, Vol. 5) **7340**
Contains two studies of 'Canada in the Atlantic Economy' series. Also issued separately in paperback as volumes 11 and 12 of the series.
Contents: Trade Liberalization and a Regional Economy, by R.A. Shearer, J.H. Young, and G.R. Munro.- Industrial Viability in a Free Trade Economy, by R.A. Matthews.

English, Harry Edward; Wilkinson, Bruce W.; and Eastman, Harry C. *Canada in a Wider Economic Community.* Toronto: Published for the Private Planning Association of Canada by University of Toronto Press, c1972. viii, 151 p. (Canada in the Atlantic Economy, Vol. 13) **7341**
Review: P.K. Mitra in (1974), 7 *Canadian Journal of Economics* 709-711.

Fullerton, Douglas H. "Eighty Years of Foreign Trade." (1947), 35 *Canadian Geographical Journal* 106-121. **7342**

Fullerton, Douglas H. "Survey of Canadian Foreign Trade." (1947), 253 *Annals of the American Academy of Political and Social Science* 143-149. **7343**

Germain, Claude. "Évolution des exportations canadiennes selon les régions et les zones monétaires." (1960-61), 36 *Actualité Économique* 666-680. **7344**

Gibson, J. Douglas. "Some Problems of Canadian Trading Policy." *In* Clark, Robert M., ed., *Canadian Issues: Essays in Honour of Henry F. Angus* (Toronto, 1961), pp. 110-133. **7345**

Grant, J. Fergus. "Canada's International Trade Fair." (1953), 5 *External Affairs* 250-255. **7346**

Hargrave, John A. "Provincial Initiatives in Foreign Trade." (1970), 5 *University of British Columbia Law Review* 67-90. **7347**

Hawkins, Gordon R.S., ed. *Middle Power in the Market Place; a Discussion of Canadian Trade Policies.* Toronto: Canadian Institute on Public Affairs, 1965. viii, 60 p. **7348**
Contains the proceedings of a conference organized by the Canadian Institute on Public Affairs, in cooperation with the Canadian Broadcasting Corporation.

Hay, Keith A.J., ed. *Canadian Perspectives on Economic Relations with Japan.* Montreal: Institute for Research and Public Policy, c1980. xxi, 383 p. **7349**
Proceedings of a conference sponsored by the University of Toronto-York University Joint Centre on Modern East Asia and the Institute for Research on Public Policy, Toronto, May 1979.
Review: Hiro Matsusaki in (1981), 7 *Canadian Public Policy* 489-490.

Hay, Keith A.J. "Canadian Trade Policy in the 1980s." (1982), *International Perspectives* 16-20 (July/Aug.) **7350**

Henrickson, Maurice Augustus. *The Changing Pattern of Canada-West Indies Trade, 1966-1976.* Calgary, 1978. xv, 202 leaves, maps. **7351**
Thesis (M.A.), University of Calgary, 1978. (National Library of Canada. Canadian Theses on Microfiche, No. 39259).

Hill, Olive Mary. *Canada's Salesman to the World: The Department of Trade and Commerce, 1892-1939.* Toronto: Institute of Public Administration of Canada; Montreal: McGill-Queen's University Press, 1977. 631 p. (Canadian Public Administration Series) **7352**
Reviews: David J. Bellamy in (1978), 21 *Canadian Public Administration* 141-142; Kevin H. Burley in (1977-78), 33 *International Journal* 461-462; Robert A. Shields in (1979), 60 *Canadian Historical Review* 223-224; Glen S. Williams in (1979), 12 *Canadian Journal of Political Science* 413-414.

Hill, Olive Mary. "Canada's Trade with the West Indies." (1959), 58 *Canadian Geographical Journal* 2-9. **7353**

Ho, Samuel P.S., and Huenemann, Ralph W. "Trade with China." (1972), 13 *B.C. Studies* 121-136. **7354**

Holly, Norman E. "Totem and Tabu in Export Trade." (1965-66), 4 *Osgoode Hall Law Journal* 106-112. **7355**

Hunter, William T. "Toward Free Trade? The Dilemma of Canadian Trade Policy. (Review Article)." (1978-79), 13 *Journal of Canadian Studies* 49-62 (No. 1)
7356

Jenkin, Michael. "The Prospects for a New National Policy." (1979-80), 14 *Journal of Canadian Studies* 126-141. **7357**

Jessop, David. *Anglo-Canadian Commercial Relations, 1896-1911.* Halifax, 1974. 306 leaves. **7358**

Thesis (Ph.D.), Dalhousie University, 1974. (National Library of Canada. Canadian Theses on Microfiche, No. 20173).

Johnson, Harry G. "Border Taxes, Border Tax Adjustments, Comparative Advantage, and the Balance of Payments." (1970), 3 *Canadian Journal of Economics* 595-602. **7359**

Contains a résumé in French under title: "Taxes à l'exportation, ajustements de taxes s'il y a exportation, avantage comparatif et balance des paiements."

Johnson, Harry G. "Canada's Foreign Trade Problems." (1959-60), 15 *International Journal* 233-241. **7360**

Keeley, James F. "Canadian Nuclear Export Policy and the Problems of Proliferation." (1980), 6 *Canadian Public Policy* 614-627. **7361**

Knox, Frank A. "Canadian Trade Strategy." (1954), 9 *International Journal* 275-281. **7362**

Knox, Frank A. "Some Aspects of Canada's Post-War Export Problem." (1944), 10 *Canadian Journal of Economics and Political Science* 312-327. **7363**

La Forest, Gerard V. "The Canadian Constitution and the Regulation of International Trade." (1979), 8 *Canadian Council on International Law, Proceedings* 316-323. **7364**

Lalonde, Philippe V. "The Discriminatory Business Practices Act: What Price Symbolism?" (1980), 38 *University of Toronto Faculty of Law Review* 83-105. **7365**

Laureys, Henry. "Le commerce extérieur du Canada." (1922), 8 *Revue Trimestrielle Canadienne* 1-44. **7366**

Lecture given at the 'Cercle Universitaire' of Montreal, January 21, 1922.

Laureys, Henry. *La conquête des marchés extérieurs.* Montréal: Bibliothèque de l'Action française, 1927. 314 p. (Université de Montréal. École des hautes études commerciales. Bibliothèque économique) **7367**

Also translated into English under title: *The Foreign Trade of Canada* (Toronto, 1929).
Review: Alexander Brady in (1928), 9 *Canadian Historical Review* 82-83.

Laureys, Henry. *The Foreign Trade of Canada.* Translated by H.A. Innis, and Alexander H. Smith. Toronto: Macmillan of Canada, 1929. xvi, 325 p. **7368**

First published in French under title: *La conquête des marchés extérieurs* (Montréal, 1927).

Lazar, Fred. *The New Protectionism: Non-Tariff Barriers and Their Effects on Canada.* Toronto: James Lorimer, 1981. xvii, 102 p. (Canadian Institute for Economic Policy Series) **7369**

Published in association with the Canadian Institute for Economic Policy.
Review: Terence F. Winsor in (1982), 8 *Canadian Public Policy* 402.

Le Duc, Albert. "Foreign Trade." (1933), 19 *Revue Trimestrielle Canadienne* 199-211. **7370**

Le Moine, J.M. "Commerce avec les Antilles." (1872), 9 *Revue Canadienne* 184-190. **7371**

Levy, Thomas Allen. "The International Economic Interests and Activities of the Atlantic Provinces." (1975), 5 *American Review of Canadian Studies* 98-113 (No. 1) **7372**

Litvak, Isaiah A. *Obstacles to Imports from Communist Countries: A Canadian Study.* New York, 1965. v, 300 leaves. 7373
Thesis (Ph.D.), Columbia University, 1965. Abstracted in (1966), 26 *Dissertation Abstracts* 5765.

Litvak, Isaiah A. "Trading with the Communists." (1962-63), 22 *Behind the Headlines* No. 6 (21 p.) 7374

Loken, Mark Keith. *The Impact of Effective Commercial Policy on Patterns of Canadian Exports.* Durham, N.C., 1972. 84 leaves. 7375
Thesis (Ph.D.), Duke University, 1972. Abstracted in (1972), 33 *Dissertation Abstracts International* 2599-A.

Looking Outward: A New Trade Strategy for Canada. Ottawa: Economic Council of Canada, 1975. xv, 208 p. 7376
Also issued in French.

Lorrain, Léon. "Le commerce canadien après la guerre." (1918-19), 4 *Revue Trimestrielle Canadienne* 149-156. 7377

MacFadyen, Alan James. *Instability of Canadian Foreign Trade, 1946-1965.* University Park, Pa., 1970. xvi, 344 leaves. 7378
Thesis (Ph.D.), Pennsylvania State University, 1970. Abstracted in (1971), 32 *Dissertation Abstracts International* 63-A.

Manion, James Patrick. "Sixty Years of Foreign Trade." (1953), 5 *External Affairs* 269-273. 7379

Masson, Claude. "Les impératifs économiques de la politique étrangère du Canada." (1970), 1 *Études Internationales* 6-19 (no 2) 7380

Masters, Donald C. "Reciprocity and the Genesis of a Canadian Commercial Policy." (1932), 13 *Canadian Historical Review* 418-428. 7381

Matthews, Roy A. "Canada and Economic Union." (1958-59), 14 *International Journal* 190-201. 7382

Matthews, Roy A. "Canadians for Free Trade; the Political Idea of the Century?" (1967), 57 *Round Table* 141-151. 7383

Matthews, Roy A. "What Canada Needs from International Trade Policy." (1968), 3 *Journal of Canadian Studies* 12-16 (No. 4) 7384

McIvor, R. Craig. "Canadian Foreign Trade and the European Common Market." (1957-58), 13 *International Journal* 1-11. 7385

McMillan, Charles J. "The Pros and Cons of a National Export Trading House." (1981), 7 *Canadian Public Policy* 569-583. 7386

Mitchell, R.M. "Financing Imports and Exports." (1968), 75 *Canadian Banker* 24-38 (No. 2) 7387

Mitchell, R.M. "Financing Imports and Exports: Part II." (1968), 75 *Canadian Banker* 12-15 (No. 3) 7388

Montpetit, Édouard. "Considérations sur la politique commerciale du Canada." (1917-18), 3 *Revue Trimestrielle Canadienne* 113-127. 7389

Morgan, Kenneth Paul. *The Importance of Jamaica-Canada Trade Relations in the Context of Jamaican Dependent Underdevelopment.* Montreal, 1978. ix, 124 leaves. 7390
Thesis (M.A.), McGill University, 1978.

Nappi, Carmine. *Des méthodes quantitatives appliquées au commerce international et interprovincial du Québec.* Montréal, 1974. x, 377 leaves. **7391**
   Short title: *Des méthodes quantitatives et le commerce du Québec.* Thesis (Ph.D.), McGill University, 1974. (National Library of Canada. Canadian Theses on Microfiche, No. 20783).

Neal, Arthur L. "Canada in World Trade." (1945), 30 *Canadian Geographical Journal* 111-125. **7392**

Neal, Arthur L. "Canada's Trade Ties with Latin America." (1945), 31 *Canadian Geographical Journal* 78-95. **7393**

Neal, Arthur L. "Canada's Trade with the British Dominions." (1945), 31 *Canadian Geographical Journal* 154-168. **7394**

Neal, Arthur L. "Commercial Relations between Canada and the United Kingdom." (1945), 30 *Canadian Geographical Journal* 210-231. **7395**

Neal, Arthur L. "Four Million Dollars a Day: A Review of Canada's Export Trade." (1937), 15 *Canadian Geographical Journal* 58-73. **7396**

Parizeau, Jacques. "Le commerce du Canada avec le Commonwealth." (1958-59), 34 *Actualité Économique* 383-399. **7397**

Parizeau, Jacques. "Les traits dominants du commerce extérieur du Canada." (1955-56), 31 *Actualité Économique* 423-444. **7398**

Paumann, Manuel K. *Creating the Export Development Corporation.* Ottawa, 1972 (c1973). 144 leaves. **7399**
   Thesis (M.A.), Carleton University, 1972. (National Library of Canada. Canadian Theses on Microfilm, No. 14098).

Peters, J.E., and Shearer, Ronald A. "The Structure of British Columbia's External Trade, 1939 and 1963." (1970-71), 8 *B.C. Studies* 34-46. **7400**

Postner, Harry H., and Gilfix, Don. *Factor Content of Canadian International Trade: An Input-Output Analysis.* Ottawa: Economic Council of Canada, 1975. ix, 184 p. **7401**
   Also issued in French under title: *Analyse intersectorielle du contenu en facteurs de production du commerce canadien.*
   Reviews: Martin Jaeger in (1977), 3 *Canadian Public Policy* 399-400; James J. McRae in (1978), 11 *Canadian Journal of Economics* 638-639.

Protheroe, David R. *Imports and Politics: Trade Decision-Making in Canada, 1968-1979.* Montreal: Institute for Research on Public Policy, 1980. xxxv, 175 p. **7402**

Reuber, Grant L. *Britain's Export Trade with Canada.* Toronto: University of Toronto Press, 1960. xii, 147 p. (Canadian Studies in Economics, No. 12)
   Based on the author's thesis, Harvard University, 1956. **7403**
   Review: Frederic Benham in (1960-61), 16 *International Journal* 426-427.

Reuber, Grant L. *Canada's Interest in the Trade Problems of Less-Developed Countries.* Montreal: Private Planning Association of Canada, 1964. xiv, 101 p.
7404

Robinson, Thomas Russell. *Foreign Trade and Economic Stability.* Ottawa: Queen's Printer, 1965 (i.e. 1967). xii, 218 p. (Canada. Royal Commission on Taxation. Studies, 5) **7405**

Rotstein, Abraham. "Economic Coexistence: Canada's Trade Relations with the Soviet Bloc." *In* Rotstein, Abraham, ed., *The Prospect of Change: Proposals for Canada's Future* (Toronto, 1965), pp. 245-266. **7406**

Schram, Douglas Charles. *Financing Capital Equipment Exports through the Export Development Corporation.* Vancouver, 1976 (c1977). viii, 176 leaves. **7407**

Thesis (M.Sc.), University of British Columbia, 1976. (National Library of Canada. Canadian Theses on Microfiche, No. 28803).

Semple, R. Keith, and Scorrar, Douglas A. "Canadian International Trade." (1975), 19 *Canadian Geographer* 135-148. **7408**

Shields, Robert A. "Canada, the Foreign Office and the Caribbean Market, 1884-1895." (1978-79), 58 *Dalhousie Review* 703-722. **7409**

Slater, David W. "Canada's International Trade and Payments: An Examination of Recent Trends." (1963), 70 *Canadian Banker* 5-25 (No. 3) **7410**

Slater, David W. "Changes in the Structure of Canada's International Trade." (1955), 21 *Canadian Journal of Economics and Political Science* 1-19. **7411**

Slosar, Stanislas. "Certains aspects juridiques de la politique commerciale internationale du Canada dans les années '80." (1980), 9 *Canadian Council on International Law, Proceedings* 49-55. **7412**

Smith, Arthur J.R. "New Challenges for Canadian Trade Policy." (1961-62), 21 *Behind the Headlines* No. 6 (19 p.) **7413**

Spragins, Robert Franklin. *A Statistical Model of International Trade between Canada and Ten Countries.* Edmonton, 1975. x, 157 leaves. **7414**

Thesis (M.B.A.), University of Alberta, 1975. (National Library of Canada. Canadian Theses on Microfiche, No. 26923).

Stegemann, Klaus. *Canadian Non-Tariff Barriers to Trade.* With appendices by Caroline Pestieau. Montreal: Canadian Economic Policy Committee, Private Planning Association of Canada, 1973. xi, 162 p. **7415**

Review: I.D. Pal in (1974), 7 *Canadian Journal of Economics* 147-149.

Stewart, Larry R. "International Trade: Canada and the Uranium Cartel." (1980), *International Perspectives* 21-25 (July/Aug.) **7416**

Styles, R.G.P. "Export Development Corporation." (1969), 76 *Canadian Banker* 16-19 (No. 5) **7417**

Swiger, Ernest Cullimore, Jr. *'The Big Markets of the Old World': Canadian Commercial Relations with Europe, 1896-1914.* Durham, N.C., 1975. 236 leaves. **7418**

Thesis (Ph.D.), Duke University, 1975.

Taylor, George. "Western Perspectives on the Canadian Constitution and International Trade." (1979), 8 *Canadian Council on International Law, Proceedings* 343-356. **7419**

Thompson, Robert W. *International Trade and Domestic Prosperity: Canada 1926-38.* Toronto: University of Toronto Press, 1970. 139 p. (Canadian Studies in Economics, No. 22) **7420**

Reviews: Paul B. Huber in (1971-72), 51 *Dalhousie Review* 118-119; Rudolf R. Rhomberg in (1971), 4 *Canadian Journal of Economics* 413-414.

Tremblay, Rodrigue. "La politique commerciale et le développement du Canada." *In* Painchaud, Paul, ed., *Le Canada et le Québec sur la scène internationale* (Québec, 1977), pp. 179-195. **7421**

Underhill, Frank H. "Edward Blake, the Liberal Party, and Unrestricted Reciprocity." (1939), *Canadian Historical Association, Historical Papers* 133-141.**7422**

Walsh, Reginald Francis George. *Canadian Trade Negotiations with Eastern Europe: Process and Effect.* Ottawa, 1971. 148 leaves. **7423**
Research essay (M.A.), Carleton University, 1971.

Weeks, E.P. "United Kingdom Trade with Canada." (1950), 40 *Canadian Geographical Journal* 195-205. **7424**

Weihs, Frederick H. *Canadian Trade Policy, 1945-1953.* Vancouver, 1976. v, 171 leaves. **7425**
Thesis (M.A.), University of British Columbia, 1976. (National Library of Canada. Canadian Theses on Microfiche, No. 29981).

Wilkinson, Bruce W. *Canada's International Trade: An Analysis of Recent Trends and Patterns.* Sponsored by the Canadian Trade Committee, Private Planning Association of Canada. Montreal: Private Planning Association of Canada, 1968. xv, 200 p. **7426**
Review: Ronald A. Shearer in (1968), 1 *Canadian Journal of Economics* 836-838.

Williams, Glen S. *The Political Economy of Canadian Manufactured Exports: The Problem, Its Origins and the Department of Trade and Commerce, 1885-1930.* Downsview, Ont., 1978. xi, 342 leaves. **7427**
Thesis (Ph.D.), York University, 1978. (National Library of Canada. Canadian Theses on Microfiche, No. 38505).

Winham, Gilbert R. "Bureaucratic Politics and Canadian Trade Negotiation." (1978-79), 34 *International Journal* 64-89. **7428**

Wonnacott, Ronald J. *Canada's Trade Options.* Ottawa: Economic Council of Canada, 1975. xxii, 218 p. **7429**
Also issued in French under title: *Les options commerciales du Canada.*
Reviews: Jacques Henry in (1977), 53 *Actualité Économique* 117-119; Alan M. Rugman in (1977), 3 *Canadian Public Policy* 405-407.

Wonnacott, Ronald J. "Controlling Trade and Foreign Investment in the Canadian Economy: Some Proposals." (1982), 15 *Canadian Journal of Economics* 567-585. **7430**

Yadav, Gopal Ji. *The Discriminatory Aspects of Canada's Imports of Manufactured Goods from the Less Developed and the Developed Countries.* Kingston, 1969 (c1970). xiv, 227 leaves. **7431**
Half-title: *Canada's Imports.* Thesis (Ph.D.), Queen's University, 1970. (National Library of Canada. Canadian Theses on Microfilm, No. 5754).

Young, John H. *Canadian Commercial Policy: A Study for the Royal Commission on Canada's Economic Prospects.* Ottawa: Queen's Printer, 1957. 265 p. **7432**
Review: Sir Roy Harrod in (1960), 26 *Canadian Journal of Economics and Political Science* 490-492.

(b) TARIFFS AND CUSTOMS

Adamcyk, Leonard F. "A Survey of Tariff Classification - Ironing Out the Creases." (1982), 7 *Canadian Business Law Journal* 101-128. **7433**

Ahmad, Jaleel. "Diversion et création d'échanges commerciaux dans le cadre du système canadien de préférences tarifaires." (1979), 55 *Actualité Économique* 68-81. **7434**

Ahmad, Jaleel. "Les préférences tarifaires canadiennes et la libéralisation des échanges." (1976), 52 *Actualité Économique* 555-565. **7435**

Akin, Thomas B. "The Customs Valuation Agreement in the New GATT and Its Effect on Valuation of Imports into Canada." (1980), 4 *Canadian Business Law Journal* 316-347. **7436**

Annett, Douglas Rudyard. *British Preference in Canadian Commercial Policy.* Toronto: Ryerson Press, 1948. xiv, 188 p., map. (Studies in International Affairs, No. 3) **7437**
Issued under the auspices of the Canadian Institute of International Affairs.
Reviews: Ronald S. Longley in (1950-51), 30 *Dalhousie Review* 105-106; D.J. Morgan in (1949), 25 *International Affairs* 356.

Annis, Charles Arthur. *The Development of Canadian Tariff Policy.* Ithaca, N.Y., 1932. viii, 197 leaves. **7438**
Thesis (A.M.), Cornell University, 1933.

Annis, Charles Arthur. *A Study of Canadian Tariffs and Trade Agreements.* Ithaca, N.Y., 1936. 412 leaves. **7439**
Thesis (Ph.D.), Cornell University, 1936.

Balcom, A.B. "Why All Tariffs Are an Evil." (1924-25), 4 *Dalhousie Review* 476-484. **7440**

Barber, Clarence L. "Canadian Tariff Policy." (1955), 21 *Canadian Journal of Economics and Political Science* 513-530. **7441**

Bernier, Ivan. "La réglementation canadienne en matière de commerce et de douanes." *In* Macdonald, Ronald St. John, and others, *Canadian Perspectives on International Law and Organization* (Toronto, 1974), pp. 726-755. **7442**

Blake, Gordon. *Customs Administration in Canada; an Essay in Tariff Technology.* Toronto: University of Toronto Press, 1957. x, 193 p. (Canadian Studies in Economics, No. 9) **7443**
Review: Jacques Parizeau in (1958-59), 34 *Actualité Économique* 154-155.

Blake, Gordon. "The Customs Administration in Canadian Historical Development." (1956), 22 *Canadian Journal of Economics and Political Science* 497-508. **7444**

Brander, James A., and Spencer, Barbara J. "Tariffs and the Extraction of Foreign Monopoly Rents under Potential Entry." (1981), 14 *Canadian Journal of Economics* 371-389. **7445**

Brown, Robert D. "Customs Valuation: Hidden Barriers and GATT." (1979), 27 *Canadian Tax Journal* 610-618. **7446**

Canada. Anti-Dumping Tribunal. *Annual Report / Rapport annuel.* 1966—.
Ottawa. Bilingual. **7447**
Established in 1969 under the *Anti-Dumping Act* (R.S.C. 1970, c. A-15). It functions as a court of record and makes inquiries about the impact of importation of dumped goods. It reports to Parliament through the Minister of Finance.

Canada. Dept. of Finance. *White Paper on Anti-Dumping / Livre blanc sur l'antidumping.* Ottawa: Queen's Printer, 1968. 101 p. Bilingual. **7448**

Canada. Tariff Board. *Tariff Board Staff Appraisal of the Proposed Legislation to Implement the International Agreement on Customs Valuation.* Ottawa: Tariff Board, 1981. 62 p. (Canada. Tariff Board. Reference, 159) **7449**

Caves, Richard E. "Economic Models of Political Choice: Canada's Tariff Structure." (1976), 9 *Canadian Journal of Economics* 278-300. **7450**
Contains a résumé in French under title: "Modèles économiques de choix politique: la politique douanière au Canada."

Colvin, James A. "Sir Wilfrid Laurier and the British Preferential Tariff System." (1955), *Canadian Historical Association, Historical Papers* 13-23. **7451**

"Customs Tariff Overview." (1977), 29 *Canadian Tax Foundation, Proceedings* 415-472. **7452**
This is a panel. Chairman: Keith G. Dixon.- Speakers: Irving Brecher; J. Peter Connell; Alexander D. Givens; and Pamela A. McDougall.

Dales, John H. "Bi-lateral Canadian and American Approaches: Effects of the Canadian Tariff on Canadian Economic Development." (1964), 6 *University of Windsor Seminar on Canadian-American Relations, Proceedings* 293-300.
7453

Dales, John H. *The Protective Tariff in Canada's Development; Eight Essays on Trade and Tariffs When Factors Move with Special Reference to Canadian Protectionism 1870-1955.* Toronto: University of Toronto Press, c1966. v, 168 p. (Canadian University Paperbooks, 58) **7454**
Reviews: Bernard Bonin in (1967-68), 43 *Actualité Économique* 776-777; Albert Breton in (1967), 33 *Canadian Journal of Economics and Political Science* 461-463; H. Clare Pentland under title: "Canada 1967: Nation or Subsidiary?" in (1967), 48 *Canadian Historical Review* 365-369.

Daly, Donald J., and Globerman, Steven. *Tariff and Science Policies: Applications of a Model of Nationalism.* Toronto: Published for the Ontario Economic Council by University of Toronto Press, c1976. x, 125 p. (Ontario Economic Council. Research Studies, 4) **7455**
Review: A.W. Jenkins in (1977), 3 *Canadian Public Policy* 386-387.

Desgranges, Paul-Yvan. "Le Canada et le monde protectionniste d'après 1918." (1939-40), 15/2 *Actualité Économique* 244-259. **7456**

Eastman, Harry C. "Some Aspects of Tariff Protection in Canada." (1962-63), 18 *International Journal* 353-360. **7457**

Eastman, Harry C., and Stykolt, Stefan. *The Tariff and Competition in Canada.* Toronto: Macmillan, c1967. xvi, 400 p. **7458**
Review: Paul Wonnacott in (1968), 1 *Canadian Journal of Economics* 654-656.

Eaton, Keith E., and Chalmers, Norman A. *Canadian Law of Customs and Excise.* Toronto: Canada Law Book, 1968. xx, 331 p. **7459**
Review: E.J. Mockler in (1967-68), 7 *Alberta Law Review* 166-168.

Elliott, George Alexander. *Tariff Procedures and Trade Barriers; a Study of Indirect Protection in Canada and the United States.* Toronto: University of Toronto Press, 1955. 293 p. **7460**
Reviews: O.J. McDiarmid in (1956), 22 *Canadian Journal of Economics and Political Science* 119-120; Robert W. Thompson in (1955-56), 11 *International Journal* 64-65.

Farley, James M. "'Class or Kind' Interpretation in Relation to Canadian Customs Legislation." (1966), 24 *University of Toronto Faculty of Law Review* 36-47. **7461**

Grey, Rodney de C. *The Development of the Canadian Anti-Dumping System.* Montreal: Canadian Economic Policy Committee, Private Planning Association of Canada, 1973. xi, 112 p. **7462**
Review: Syed N. Alam in (1975), 8 *Canadian Journal of Economics* 128-131.

Hérisson, Charles-D. "Comment rénover la politique commerciale." (1937), 23 *Revue Trimestrielle Canadienne* 448-466. **7463**

Hunter, William T. "The Decline of the Tariff - But Not of Protection." (1979-80), 14 *Journal of Canadian Studies* 111-117. **7464**

"Jurisdiction and Procedure of the Tariff Board." (1960), 14 *Canadian Tax Foundation, Proceedings* 145-163. **7465**
This is a panel. Chairman: Edwin A. Goodwin.- Speakers: George H. Glass; R. W. McKimm; and Richard Lang.

King, Tom. "Tariffs in the United States and Canada." (1930), 37 *Queen's Quarterly* 405-412. **7466**

Lank, Herbert. "Note sur la théorie des droits de douane." (1962-63), 38 *Actualité Économique* 5-19. **7467**

Lindsay, Thomas. *Outline of Customs in Canada.* 4th print., rev. Vancouver: Printed by Elgin Publications, 1975. 223 p. **7468**

Loken, Mark Keith. *Effects of Imperial Preference on Canadian Trade Patterns.* Calgary, 1968. vi, 78 leaves. **7469**
Thesis (M.A.), University of Calgary, 1968. (National Library of Canada. Canadian Theses on Microfilm, No. 2762)

Mackenzie, Kenneth C. "Anti-Dumping Duties in Canada." (1966), 4 *Canadian Yearbook of International Law* 131-160. **7470**

MacPherson, Ronald B. *Tariffs, Markets and Economic Progress; a Re-Appraisal of Trade Policies in the Light of Canada's Productive Capabilities and Long-Term Opportunities.* Toronto: Copp Clark, 1958. xi, 91 p. **7471**

McDiarmid, O.J. "Canadian Tariff Policy." (1947), 253 *Annals of the American Academy of Political and Social Science* 150-157. **7472**

McLean, Simon James. *The Tariff History of Canada.* Toronto: Warwick & Rutter, 1895. 53 p. (University of Toronto. Studies. Political Science Series, No. 4) **7473**

Oberndorfer, Ron H. "Forfeiture Remission: A Comparative Study of British, Canadian, and United States Policy." (1978), 8 *California Western International Law Journal* 586-608. **7474**

Parker, Ian. "The National Policy, Neoclassical Economics, and the Political Economy of Tariffs." (1979-80), 14 *Journal of Canadian Studies* 95-110. **7475**

Patry, André. "Le Canada et le tarif préférentiel britannique." (1947), 53/2 *Revue Dominicaine* 106-110. **7476**

Pinchin, Hugh McAlister. *Canadian Tariff Levels, 1870-1959.* New Haven, Conn., 1970. 585 leaves. **7477**
> Thesis (Ph.D.), Yale University, 1970. Abstracted in (1970/71), 31 *Dissertation Abstracts International* 3145-A. (University Microfilms, Ann Arbor, No. 71-42).

Pinchin, Hugh McAlister. *The Regional Impact of the Canadian Tariff.* Ottawa: Economic Council of Canada, 1979. xiv, 205 p. **7478**
> Also issued in French under title: *L'incidence du régime tarifaire sur les régions.*
> Review: James J. McRae in (1980), 6 *Canadian Public Policy* 689-690.

Rempel, R.A. "Tariff Reform and the Resurgence of the Liberal Party: May 1903 to February 1904." (1967), *Canadian Historical Association, Historical Papers* 156-166. **7479**

Ritchie, Marguerite E. "Experimenting with Canadian Business: Anti-Dumping Protection in Canada." (1979), 3 *Canadian Business Law Journal* 375-397. **7480**

Séguin-Dulude, Louise. "Analyse de la politique commerciale canadienne: rétrospective et synthèse." (1979), 55 *Actualité Économique* 303-341. **7481**

Shaw, J.R. "Why Tariffs Should Be High." (1924-25), 4 *Dalhousie Review* 485-493. **7482**

Slayton, Philip. "The Canadian Anti-Dumping System." (1978), 2 *Canadian Business Law Journal* 438-453. **7483**

Slayton, Philip; Quinn, John J.; and Cassels, James. *The Tariff Board.* Ottawa: Supply & Services Canada, 1981. ix, 154 p. (Canada. Law Reform Commission. Administrative Law Series, No. 17) **7484**
> This is a study prepared for the Law Reform Commission of Canada. Also issued in French under title: *La Commission du tarif.*

"The Tariff - 1957." (1957), 11 *Canadian Tax Foundation, Proceedings* 212-240. **7485**
> This is a panel. Chairman: Walter Lattman.- Speakers: J. Harvey Perry; John H. Young; LeRoy D. Smithers; and Eric Hehner.

"Tariffs and Trade." (1968), 21 *Canadian Tax Foundation, Proceedings* 361-389. **7486**
> This is a panel. Chairman: John H. Dales.- Speakers: Keith E. Eaton; M.G. Clark; H. Edward English; and John R. Petty.

Williams, Glen S. "The National Policy Tariffs: Industrial Underdevelopment through Import Substitution." (1979), 12 *Canadian Journal of Political Science* 333-368. **7487**

Williams, James R. *The Canadian-United States Tariff and Canadian Industry: A*

Multisectoral Analysis. Toronto: University of Toronto Press, 1978. xi, 174 p.
Review: John A. Sawyer in (1979), 12 *Canadian Journal of Economics* 318-320. **7488**

Williams, James R. *Resources, Tariffs, and Trade: Ontario's Stake.* Toronto: Published for the Ontario Economic Council by University of Toronto Press, c1976. viii, 117 p. (Ontario Economic Council. Research Studies, 6) **7489**
Review: I.D. Pal in (1978), 4 *Canadian Public Policy* 150-151.

Wilson, Edwin Everett. *The Tariff Policy of the Dominion of Canada.* Stanford, Calif., 1927. 128 leaves. **7490**
Thesis (A.M.), Stanford University, 1927.

(c) TRADE WITH THE UNITED STATES

See also *"Law of Treaties: Specific Treaties: Trade" (p. 161), "Reciprocity Treaty of June 5, 1854" (p. 526),* and *"Reciprocity Agreement of January 21, 1911" (p. 530).*

(i) GENERAL

Aronsen, Lawrence Robert. *The Northern Frontier: United States Trade and Investment in Canada, 1945-1953.* Toronto, c1981. 369 leaves. **7491**
Thesis (Ph.D.), University of Toronto, 1980. (National Library of Canada. Canadian Theses on Microfiche, No. 46999).

Axline, W. Andrew, and others. *Continental Community?: Independence and Integration in North America.* Toronto: McClelland and Stewart, c1974. 10, 302 p. (Carleton Contemporary) **7492**
Contains papers prepared for a seminar organized by the universities of Carleton and Ottawa.
Reviews: Donald J. Munton in (1975), 8 *Canadian Journal of Political Science* 476-478; Paul Pilisi in (1977), 8 *Études Internationales* 403-404.

Brown, J.J. "Canada-U.S. Trade." (1955), 62 *Canadian Banker* 126-132 (No. 3)
7493

Coffin, Frank M. "Opportunities for North American Economic Statesmanship." (1961), 3 *University of Windsor Seminar on Canadian-American Relations, Proceedings* 19-32. **7494**

Coghlan, Brian C. *Canadian-United States Economic Linkages: 1955-75.* Montreal, 1979. 135 leaves. **7495**
Thesis (M.A.), McGill University, 1979. (National Library of Canada. Canadian Theses on Microfiche, No. 42904).

Conference on Canadian-U.S. Economic Relations, Washington, D.C., 1978. *Conference on Canadian-U.S. Economic Relations: Papers.* Montreal: Institute for Research on Public Policy, c1978. liv, 39 p. (Institute for Research on Public Policy. Occasional Paper, No. 2) **7496**
Joint conference with the Brookings Institution.

Coutts, James A. "Factors Influencing Canadian-American Trade: A Canadian View." (1973-74), 6 *Case Western Reserve Journal of International Law* 56-59.
7497

Cuff, Robert D., and Granatstein, J.L. *American Dollars - Canadian Prosperity: Canadian-American Economic Relations, 1945-1950.* Toronto: Samuel-Stevens, 1978. 286 p. **7498**

Cuff, Robert D., and Granatstein, J.L. "The Rise and Fall of Canadian-American Free Trade, 1947-8." (1977), 58 *Canadian Historical Review* 459-482. **7499**

Curtis, John M., and Moroz, Andrew R. "Canada-United States Trade and Policy Issues - Introduction: Towards a New Relationship / Les problèmes de politiques et du commerce entre le Canada et les États-Unis - Introduction: vers une relation renouvelée." (1982), 8 *Canadian Public Policy* 405-411. **7500**

Dales, John H. "Bi-lateral Canadian and American Approaches: Effects of the Canadian Tariff on Canadian Economic Development." (1964), 6 *University of Windsor Seminar on Canadian-American Relations, Proceedings* 293-300.
7501

Dales, John H. "A Further Comment on Economic Integration." (1967), 2 *Journal of Canadian Studies* 36-39 (No. 3) **7502**
Comment on an article by Harry G. Johnson.

Deutsch, John J. "The Effect of the American Tariff on Canadian Development." (1960), 2 *University of Windsor Seminar on Canadian-American Relations, Proceedings* 31-36. **7503**

Feis, Herbert. "A Year of the Canadian Trade Agreement." (1936-37), 15 *Foreign Affairs* 619-635. **7504**
Refers to the trade agreement between Canada and the United States signed on November 15, 1935 (CTS 1936/9).

Frederick, Glenn D. "Sovereignty and Other Aspects of Canadian-American Economic Interdependence." (1964), 6 *University of Windsor Seminar on Canadian-American Relations, Proceedings* 230-239. **7505**

Gadbaw, Michael. "Recent Developments in the Legal Framework of U.S.-Canadian Trade." (1976-77), 4 *Syracuse Journal of International Law and Commerce* 337-354. **7506**

Gates, Theodore R. "Canadian-American Trade Problems in a Multilateral Context." (1973-74), 6 *Case Western Reserve Journal of International Law* 51-55.
7507

Gilpin, Robert. "Integration and Disintegration on the North American Continent." (1974), 28 *International Organization* 851-874. **7508**
Reprinted in Fox, Annette Baker, and others, *Canada and the United States* (New York, 1976), pp. 259-282.

Greenwood, Ted. "Canadian-American Trade in Energy Resources." (1974), 28 *International Organization* 689-710. **7509**
Reprinted in Fox, Annette Baker, and others, *Canada and the United States* (New York, 1976), pp. 97-118.

Grey, Rodney de C. "Some Issues in Canada-U.S. Trade Relations." (1982), 8 *Canadian Public Policy* 451-457. **7510**
Includes: "A Commentary," by A.J.R. Smith (pp. 457-458).- "Comments," by W.D. Eberle (pp. 459-462).

Grey, Rodney de C. *Trade Policy in the 1980s: An Agenda for Canadian-U.S. Relations.* Montreal: C.D. Howe Institute, 1981. vi, 80 p. (Howe (C.D.) Research Institute. Policy Commentary, No. 3) **7511**
Review: Ramesh C. Kumar in (1982), 8 *Canadian Public Policy* 389-390.

Grey, Rodney de C. *United States Trade Policy Legislation: A Canadian View.* Montreal: Institute for Research on Public Policy, c1982. xvii, 130 p. **7512**

Guido, Robert V., and Morrone, Michael F. "The Michelin Decision: A Possible New Direction for U.S. Countervailing Duty Law." (1974), 6 *Law and Policy in International Business* 237-266. **7513**

Halstead, Donald Paul. *An Analysis of the Economic Effects of Free Trade between Canada and the United States.* Tallahassee, Fla., 1974. vi, 163 leaves. **7514**
Thesis (Ph.D.), Florida State University, 1974. Abstracted in (1975), 35 *Dissertation Abstracts International* 7484-A. (University Microfilms, Ann Arbor, No. 75-12641).

Hastings, Paul Guiler. *A Canada-United States Customs Union; a Study of Trade Relations between Canada and the United States with Particular Reference to the Possibility of a Customs Union between the Two Countries.* Rochester, N.Y.: University of Rochester Press, 1954. 216 leaves. (University of Rochester. Canadian Studies Series, No. 9) **7515**
Thesis, University of Pennsylvania, 1950.

Hazard, John L., ed. *Canadian-American Reciprocity and Regional Development at Mid-Continent.* East Lansing, Mich.: Committee of Canadian-American Studies, Michigan State University, 1968. 192 p. (Writings on Canadian-American Studies, Vol. 3) **7516**

Heilperin, Michael A. "A U.S.-Canadian Partnership for the Revival of Multilateral Trade." (1949-50), 5 *International Journal* 217-229. **7517**

Henry, D.H.W. "Mergers and Joint Ventures as They Affect Canadian-United States Trade Relations - A Look at the Canadian Antitrust Laws." (1966), 32 *Antitrust Law Journal (A.B.A.)* 156-175. **7518**

Hutcheson, John. *Dominance and Dependency: Liberalism and National Policies in the North Atlantic Triangle.* Toronto: McClelland and Stewart, c1978. 182 p. **7519**
Reviews: Walter S.G. Kohn in (1978), 8 *American Review of Canadian Studies* 159-160 (No. 2); Brian Tennyson in (1979), 60 *Canadian Historical Review* 251-252; David A. Wolfe in (1979), 5 *Canadian Public Policy* 288.

Johnson, Harry G. "Canadian-American Economic Integration: A Time for Decision." (1966), 1 *Journal of Canadian Studies* 31-36 (No. 2) **7520**
See also comments by J.H. Dales.

Johnson, Harry G. "Canadian-American Integration in Face of a Changing World Economy." (1962), 4 *University of Windsor Seminar on Canadian-American Relations, Proceedings* 205-215. **7521**

Kindred, Hugh M., and Biggs, William. "Trade and Investment Issues: Patterns of Canadian-American Economic Problems." (1978), 1 *Canada-United States Law Journal* 114-131. **7522**

Kirchschlager, Hellmuth Ludwig. *The New Trade Agreement between the United States and Canada, Signed, November 17, 1938.* Montreal, 1940. xiii, 250 leaves. **7523**
Thesis (M.A.), McGill University, 1940.

Kottman, Richard N. "Herbert Hoover and the Smoot-Hawley Tariff: Canada, a Case Study." (1975-76), 62 *Journal of American History* 609-635. **7524**

Kottman, Richard N. *Reciprocity and the North Atlantic Triangle, 1932-1938.* Ithaca, N.Y.: Cornell University Press, 1968. ix, 294 p. **7525**
Review: Hilda Blair Neatby in (1968-69), 24 *International Journal* 617-618.

Larsen, H.K. "Canada's Economic Problems and the American Connection. (Review Article)." (1979), 8 *Acadiensis* 137-142 (No. 2) **7526**

Lazar, Fred. "Canadian Industrial Strategy: A U.S. Impediment." (1982), 16 *Journal of World Trade Law* 223-235. **7527**

Lea, Sperry. *A Canada-U.S. Free Trade Arrangement; Survey of Possible Characteristics.* Washington, Montreal: Canadian-American Committee, 1963. xi, 115 p. **7528**
Sponsored by the National Planning Association (U.S.A.), and the Private Planning Association of Canada.
Review: Bernard Bonin in (1964-65), 40 *Actualité Économique* 615-617.

Lea, Sperry. "A Canada-U.S. Free Trade Arrangement - Survey of Possible Characteristics." (1964-65), 2 *Atlantic Community Quarterly* 627-641. **7529**

Lea, Sperry. "A Possible Plan for a Canada-U.S. Free Trade Area." (1965-66), 3 *Atlantic Community Quarterly* 102-111. **7530**

Lea, Sperry. "Tariffs and Trade - Bi-lateral Canadian and American Approaches: Probable Characteristics and Rationale." (1964), 6 *University of Windsor Seminar on Canadian-American Relations, Proceedings* 271-284. **7531**

Litvak, Isaiah A., and McMillan, Carl H. "A New United States Policy on East-West Trade - Some Implications for Canada." (1972-73), 28 *International Journal* 297-314. **7532**

Malmgren, Harald B. "Canada and the United States in an Interdependent World: The Evolving Trading System." (1976), 32 *Academy of Political Science, Proceedings* 124-136 (No. 2) **7533**

Masson, Francis, and Whitely, J.B. *Barriers to Trade between Canada and the United States.* Washington: Canadian-American Committee, 1960. xi, 97 p. (Reports on Canada-United States Relations) **7534**
Sponsored by the National Planning Association (U.S.A.), and the Private Planning Association of Canada.

McWhinney, Edward. "Canadian-United States Commercial Relations and International Law: The Cuban Affair as a Case Study." *In* Deener, David R., ed., *Canada-United States Treaty Relations* (Durham, N.C., 1963), pp. 135-150.
7535

Molot, Maureen Appel. *A Common Market for Capital: Indicator of Canada-United States Integration?* Berkeley, Calif., 1972 (c1973). v, 533 leaves. **7536**
Thesis (Ph.D.), University of California, 1972. Abstracted in (1973), 34 *Dissertation Abstracts International* 847-A. (University Microfilms, Ann Arbor, No. 73-18212).

Moroz, Andrew R., and Back, K.J. "Prospects for a Canada-United States Bilateral Free Trade Agreement: The Other Side of the Fence." (1980-81), 36 *International Journal* 827-850. **7537**

Neal, Arthur L. "South of the Border - And North: The U.S. and Canada; Their Relations in Trade and Commerce." (1940), 20 *Canadian Geographical Journal* 211-239. **7538**

O'Brien, Michael John. *The Canadian-American Reciprocal Trade Agreement of 1935 and Its Role in the United States Presidential Election of 1936.* Saskatoon, c1970. v, 119 leaves. **7539**
Thesis (M.A.), University of Saskatchewan, 1971. Refers to the trade agreement of November 15, 1935 (CTS 1936/9).

Pennanen, Gary. "Goldwin Smith, Wharton Barker, and Erastus Wiman: Architects of Commercial Union." (1979-80), 14 *Journal of Canadian Studies* 50-62.
7540

Pestieau, Caroline. *The Sector Approach to Trade Negotiation: Canadian and U.S. Interests.* Montreal: Canadian Economic Policy Committee, 1976. 15 p.
7541

Pollack, Gerald Alexander. *The Effect on Imports from Canada of United States Tariff Reductions under the Reciprocal Trade Agreements Program.* Princeton, N.J., 1958. 488 leaves. **7542**
Thesis (Ph.D.), Princeton University, 1958. Abstracted in (1959), 19 *Dissertation Abstracts* 2789-2790.

Proulx, Pierre-Paul; Dulude, Louise; and Rabeau, Yves. *Étude des relations commerciales, Québec-USA, Québec-Canada: options et impacts, contraintes et potentiels.* Québec: Ministère des affaires intergouvernementales, 1978. (30), 585 p. **7543**

Sarna, A.J. "The Canada-U.S. Free Trade Option." (1979), 13 *Journal of World Trade Law* 303-310. **7544**

Saunders, Ronald S. "Continentalism and Economic Nationalism in the Manufacturing Sector: Seeking Middle Ground." (1982), 8 *Canadian Public Policy* 463-479. **7545**

Shibata, Hirofumi. *Fiscal Harmonization under Freer Trade: Principles and Their Applications to a Canada-U.S. Free Trade Area.* Toronto: Published for the Private Planning Association of Canada by University of Toronto Press, 1969. vi, 88 p. (Canada in the Atlantic Economy, Vol. 9) **7546**
Review: Richard M. Bird in (1970), 3 *Canadian Journal of Economics* 625-627.

Skelton, O.D. "Canada and the American Tariff." (1914), 13 *University Magazine* 45-54. **7547**

Stanwood, Edward. "The American Tariff." (1914), 13 *University Magazine* 35-44.
7548

"Symposium: United States-Canada Trade Liberalization - Possibilities for the Future." (1973-74), 6 *Case Western Reserve Journal of International Law* 50-119. **7549**
Some individual statements are also listed separately.
Contents: Canadian-American Trade Problems in a Multilateral Context, by Theodore

R. Gates (pp. 51-55).- Factors Influencing Canadian-American Trade: A Canadian View, by James A. Coutts (pp. 56-59).- Liberalizing Agricultural Trade between Canada and the United States, by D. Gale Johnson (pp. 60-65).- Agriculture: A Canadian View, by T.K. Warley (pp. 66-73).- Possible Trade Policy Consequences of the Canadian Foreign Investment Policy, by Robert E. Hudec (pp. 74-81).- The Americanization Syndrome in the United States-Canadian Relationship, by John Sloan Dickey (pp. 82-91).- Canadian Foreign Investment Policy, by Roberto D. Gualtieri (pp. 92-98).- The Auto Pact: Precedent or Isolated Phenomenon?, by John Rehm (pp. 99-106).- The Trade Reform Act, by John H. Jackson (pp. 107-115).- Notes on Some Implications of Enlargement of the EEC for Canada, by A.R.A. Gherson (pp. 116-119).

U.S. Congress. Senate. Committee on Governmental Affairs. *United States-Canadian Trade Policies: Impact on Border State Industries: Hearing Before the Subcommittee on Oversight of Government Management, 97th Cong., 1st sess., November 17, 1981.* Washington: Govt. Print. Off., 1982. v, 637 p. **7550**

U.S. Tariff Commission. *Second Trade Agreement between the United States and Canada.* Washington, 1938. 5 vols. **7551**

Wilkinson, Bruce W. "Canada-U.S. Free Trade and Some Options." (1982), 8 *Canadian Public Policy* 428-439. **7552**

Includes: "Commentary on Wilkinson," by Carl E. Beigie (pp. 440-443).- "The Continuing Debate about Freer Trade and Its Effects: A Comment," by Donald J. Daly (pp. 444-450).

Wonnacott, Paul, and Wonnacott, Ronald J. *Free Trade between the United States and Canada: Fifteen Years Later.* London, Ont.: Dept. of Economics, University of Western Ontario, 1980. 57 leaves. (University of Western Ontario. Centre for the Study of International Economic Relations. Working Paper, No. 8011) **7553**

Wonnacott, Paul, and Wonnacott, Ronald J. "Free Trade between the United States and Canada: Fifteen Years Later." (1982), 8 *Canadian Public Policy* 412-427. **7554**

Wonnacott, Ronald J. "Bi-lateral Canadian and American Approaches: Potential Economic Impact of Canadian-U.S. Free Trade." (1964), 6 *University of Windsor Seminar on Canadian-American Relations, Proceedings* 285-292. **7555**

Wonnacott, Ronald J. "Possible Economic Effects of Canadian-U.S. Tariff Elimination." (1965-66), 3 *Atlantic Community Quarterly* 112-119. **7556**

Wonnacott, Ronald J., and Wonnacott, Paul. *Free Trade between the United States and Canada, the Potential Economic Effects.* Cambridge: Harvard University Press, 1967. xx, 430 p., map. (Harvard Economic Studies, Vol. 129) Review: Bernard Bonin in (1967-68), 43 *Actualité Économique* 571-573. **7577**

(ii) HISTORICAL

Butler, George Frederick. *Commercial Relations of Nova Scotia with the United States 1783-1830.* Halifax, 1934. 90 leaves. **7558**
Thesis (M.A.), Dalhousie University, 1934.

Campbell, Robert Ellis. *George Brown's Attempted Reciprocity Treaty in 1874.* Toronto, 1936. 246 leaves. **7559**
Thesis (M.A.), University of Toronto, 1936.

Canada. Parliament. *Tariff Relations with the United States; Correspondence Respecting Negotiations, 1910.* Ottawa, 1910. 8 p. (Canada. Parliament, 1910. Sessional Papers, No. 10j)   7560

Frumhartz, Esther. *Reciprocity; 1860-1880.* Toronto, 1938. 230 leaves.   7561
Thesis (M.A.), University of Toronto, 1938.

Gérin, E. "Relations commerciales entre les États-Unis et le Canada: études historiques." (1865), 2 *Revue Canadienne* 748-757.   7562

Gérin, E. "Relations commerciales entre les États-Unis et le Canada: études historiques." (1866), 3 *Revue Canadienne* 108-122.   7563

Jewell, Patricia. *From Reciprocity to Reciprocity: A Study in the United States-Canadian Trade Relations.* Eugene, Oreg., 1941. 104 leaves.   7564
Thesis (M.A.), University of Oregon, 1941.

LeBourdais, D.M. "Canadian Reciprocity Again?" (1921), 214 *North American Review* 751-760.   7565

Masters, Donald C. "Historic and Contemporary Patterns in Canadian-American Trade Relations." (1962), 4 *University of Windsor Seminar on Canadian-American Relations, Proceedings* 216-239.   7566

Millman, Thomas Reagh. *The Legal Regulation of Trade between Canada and the United States, 1783-1822.* Toronto, 1933 (c1973). 130 leaves.   7567
Thesis (M.A.), University of Toronto, 1933. (National Library of Canada. Canadian Theses on Microfilm, No. 16119).

Pennanen, Gary. "American Interest in Commercial Union with Canada, 1854-1898." (1965), 47 *Mid-America* 24-39.   7568

"Reciprocity with the United States: A Series of Articles Dealing with This Question from the View-Points of Both Countries." (1904), 23 *Canadian Magazine* 407-421.   7569

(iii) SPECIFIC ISSUE: AUTOMOTIVE AGREEMENT

Arnold, Samuel. *The Impact of the Automotive Trade Agreement between Canada and the United States.* Montreal, 1969. xii, 154 leaves.   7570
Half-title: *The Canada-U.S. Automotive Trade Agreement of 1965.* Thesis (M.A.), McGill University, 1969. (National Library of Canada. Canadian Theses on Microfilm, No. 4522). Refers to the agreement signed January 16, 1965 (CTS 1966/14).

Beigie, Carl E. "The Automotive Agreement of 1965: A Case Study in Canadian-American Economic Affairs." *In* Preston, Richard A., ed., *The Influence of the United States on Canadian Development: Eleven Case Studies* (Durham, N.C., 1972), pp. 113-123.   7571

Beigie, Carl E. *The Canada-U.S. Automotive Agreement: An Evaluation.* Washington, Montreal: Canadian-American Committee, 1970. xiii, 173 p.   7572
Sponsored by the National Planning Association (U.S.A.), and the Private Planning Association of Canada.

"Bilateral Adjustment of Trade Problems: The United States-Canadian Automotive Products Agreement of 1965." *In* Chayes, Abram, and others, *International Legal Process* (Boston, 1968), pp. 307-383.   7573

Brewer, Keith J. *The Canadian Automotive Industry and the 1965 Canada-United States Automotive Products Tariff Agreement.* Edmonton, 1967. x, 204 leaves. Thesis (M.A.), University of Alberta, 1967. **7574**

Cowan, Ralph Keith. *Effects of the United States-Canadian Automotive Agreement on Canada's Manufacturing, Trade and Price Posture.* Ann Arbor, 1972. ix, 150 leaves. **7575**

Thesis (Ph.D.), University of Michigan, 1972. Abstracted in (1973), 33 *Dissertation Abstracts International* 4621-A. (University Microfilms, Ann Arbor, No. 73-6808).

Curry, F. Hayden, and Deddish, Michael R., Jr. "The United States-Canadian Automotive Pact: Executive Authority and the Conflict with GATT." (1965-66), 6 *Virginia Journal of International Law* 144-159. **7576**

Deutsch, Antal. "Roll Out the Tariff: The Economics of the Canada-United States Automotive Agreement." (1965-66), 72 *Queen's Quarterly* 169-177. **7577**

Gernant, Paul Leonard. *The International Trade Effects of the 1965 United States-Canadian Automotive Agreement.* Ann Arbor, 1977. vi, 94 leaves. **7578**

Thesis (Ph.D.), University of Michigan, 1977. Abstracted in (1978), 38 *Dissertation Abstracts International* 6844-A. (University Microfilms, Ann Arbor, No. 78-4707).

Gold, Marc Hilary. *The 1965 Canadian-American Automotive Trade Agreement: An Econometric Evaluation.* Detroit, 1976. 81 leaves. **7579**

Thesis (Ph.D.), Wayne State University, 1976. Abstracted in (1977), 37 *Dissertation Abstracts International* 7209-A. (University Microfilms, Ann Arbor, No. 77-9399).

Helmers, Henrik Olaf. *Some Effects of the United States-Canadian Automobile Agreement.* Ann Arbor, 1967. 284 leaves. **7580**

Thesis (Ph.D.), University of Michigan, 1967. Abstracted in (1967-68), 28 *Dissertation Abstracts* 1934-A. (University Microfilms, Ann Arbor, No. 67-15633).

Helmers, Henrik Olaf. *The United States-Canadian Automobile Agreement; a Study in Industry Adjustment.* Ann Arbor: Institute for International Commerce, Graduate School of Business Administration, University of Michigan, 1967. xvi, 188 p., map. (Michigan International Commerce Reports, No. 1) **7581**

Appendix B.: Text of United States-Canadian Agreement and Letters of Undertaking (pp. 161-174).

Helmers, Henrik Olaf; Wood, Donald S.; and Barrow, B.G. "The Canada-U.S. Auto Pact, a Case Study." (1968), 10 *University of Windsor Seminar on Canadian-American Relations, Proceedings* 79-95. **7582**

Jahnke, L. Gordon. "The United States-Canadian Automotive Products Agreement." (1964-66), 2 *University of British Columbia Law Review* 378-400. **7583**

Kirton, John J. "The Politics of Bilateral Management: The Case of the Automotive Trade." (1980-81), 36 *International Journal* 39-69. **7584**

Leyton-Brown, David. "The Mug's Game: Automotive Investment Incentives in Canada and the United States." (1979-80), 35 *International Journal* 170-184. **7585**

Macrory, Patrick F.J. "The United States-Canadian Automotive Products Agreement: The First Five Years." (1970), 2 *Law and Policy in International Business* 1-45. **7586**

Mercer, David William. *Public Policy Applied to the Canadian Automotive Industry; an Examination of the Canada-United States Automotive Agreement.* Kingston, 1966. 211 leaves. **7587**
Thesis (M.A.), Queen's University, 1967.

Metzger, Stanley D. "The United States-Canada Automotive Products Agreement of 1965." (1967), 1 *Journal of World Trade Law* 103-108. **7588**

Murray, J. Alex, and Helmers, Henrik Olaf. "Market Structure and Trade Liberalization: A Case Study. (Automobile Spare Parts in the U.S.-Canadian Market)." (1973), 7 *Journal of World Trade Law* 117-126. **7589**

Neisser, Albert C. *The Impact of the Canada-United States Automotive Agreement on Canada's Motor Vehicle Industry: A Study in Economies of Scale.* New York, c1966. xviii, 393 leaves. **7590**
Thesis (Ph.D.), New School for Social Research, 1966. (University Microfilms, Ann Arbor, 1976, No. 67-4116).

Rehm, John. "The Auto Pact: Precedent or Isolated Phenomenon." (1973-74), 6 *Case Western Reserve Journal of International Law* 99-106. **7591**

Stedman, Charles. "Canada-U.S. Automotive Agreement: The Sectoral Approach." (1974), 8 *Journal of World Trade Law* 176-185. **7592**

Thomson, Duncan Duane. *The Canada-United States Automobile Agreement; Its Effects and Future Canadian-American Trade Relations.* Ottawa, 1969. 76 (i.e. 86), (15) leaves. **7593**
Research essay (M.A.), Carleton University, 1969.

U.S. Congress. House. Committee on Education and Labor. Subcommittee on Labor Standards. *Oversight Hearings on the Impact of the Canadian-American Automotive Agreement on Employment in the United States: Hearings, 94th Cong., 2d sess., Held in Washington, D.C., on April 14 and May 6, 1976.* Washington: Govt. Print. Off., 1976. iii, 777 p. **7594**

U.S. Congress. House. Committee on Ways and Means. *United States-Canada Automotive Products Agreement: Hearings, 89th Cong., 1st sess., on H.R. 6960, the Automotive Products Trade Act of 1965. Held April 27, 28, and 29, 1965.* Washington: Govt. Print. Off., 1965. vii, 312 p. **7595**
The agreement, signed January 16, 1965 (CTS 1966/14), was implemented in the United States by the *Automotive Products Trade Act of 1965*, approved October 21, 1965 (79 Stat. 1016; P.L. 89-283).

U.S. Congress. Senate. Committee on Finance. *United States-Canadian Automobile Agreement: Hearings, 89th Cong., 1st sess.* Washington: Govt. Print. Off., 1965. iv, 491 p. **7596**
Hearings held September 14-21, 1965, on H.R. 9042. See also printed hearings held July 19, 1968 (iii, 98 p.).

U.S. International Trade Commission. *Canadian Automobile Agreement: United States International Trade Commission Report on the United States-Canadian Automotive Agreement, Its History, Terms, and Impact, and the Ninth Annual Report of the President to the Congress on the Operation of the Automotive Products Trade Act of 1965: Committee on Finance, United States Senate.* Washington: Govt. Print. Off., 1976. x, 517 p. **7597**

U.S. President. *Canadian Automobile Agreement; Annual Report of the President to the Congress on the Operation of the Automotive Products Trade Act of 1965.* 1st–, 1966–. Washington: Govt. Print. Off. Annual. **7598**
   The 9th annual report is issued with: *United States International Trade Commission Report on the United States-Canadian Automotive Agreement: Its History, Terms and Impact.*

Wilton, David A. *An Econometric Analysis of the Canada-United States Automotive Agreement: The First Seven Years.* Ottawa: Economic Council of Canada, c1976. viii, 115 p. **7599**
   Review: Carl E. Beigie in (1978), 4 *Canadian Public Policy* 151-153.

Wonnacott, Paul, and Wonnacott, Ronald J. "The Automotive Agreement of 1965." (1967), 33 *Canadian Journal of Economics and Political Science* 269-284. **7600**
   Contains a résumé in French under title: "L'accord canado-américain sur l'industrie de l'automobile de 1965."

(d) MULTILATERIAL TRADE

See also *"Multilateral Trade (GATT, Etc.)" (p. 550).*

Akin, Thomas B. "The Customs Valuation Agreement in the New GATT and Its Effect on Valuation of Imports into Canada." (1980), 4 *Canadian Business Law Journal* 316-347. **7601**

Bernier, Ivan. "Le GATT et le problème du commerce d'état dans les pays à économie de marché: le cas des monopoles provinciaux des alcools au Canada." (1975), 13 *Canadian Yearbook of International Law* 98-155. **7602**

Bonin, Bernard. "Le Canada et le G.A.T.T." (1958-59), 34 *Actualité Économique* 669-679. **7603**

Breithaupt, James Roos. *The European Common Market and Its Probable Effects on Canadian Export Trade.* Toronto, 1957. 113 leaves. **7604**
   Thesis (M.A.), University of Toronto, 1957.

Brizan, George I. *Canada and the Commonwealth Caribbean Economic Relations, 1966-74: An Analysis of Capital and Commodity Flows.* Ottawa, 1975 (i.e.1976). xx, 347 leaves. **7605**
   Thesis (M.A.), Carleton University, 1976. (National Library of Canada. Canadian Theses on Microfiche, No. 26590).

Brown, Robert D. "Customs Valuation: Hidden Barriers and GATT." (1979), 27 *Canadian Tax Journal* 610-618. **7606**

"Canada and the Common Markets." (1961), 15 *Canadian Tax Foundation, Proceedings* 159-179. **7607**
   This is a panel. Chairman: Harvey Perry.- Speakers: H. Ian Macdonald; Carl Bergithon; and Roy A. Matthews.

Carleton University. Institute of Soviet and East European Studies. *Canada in East-West Commerce: Summary of a Round Table at Carleton University, March 22-23, 1974.* Ottawa: Institute of Soviet and East European Studies, Carleton University, 1974. 46 p. (East-West Commercial Relations Series) **7608**

Cermakian, Jean. "Les échanges commerciaux entre le Canada et la Communauté économique européenne." (1972), 16 *Canadian Geographer* 119-127.   **7609**

Clute, Robert E., and Wilson, Robert R. "The Commonwealth and Favored-Nation Usage." (1958), 52 *American Journal of International Law* 455-468.
7610

Colloque sur les relations du Canada et du Québec avec les Communautés européennes, Québec, 1978. *Actes du Colloque sur les relations du Canada et du Québec avec les Communautés européennes.* Québec: Centre québécois de relations internationales; Toronto: Institut canadien des affaires internationales; Québec: Université Laval, 1979. 154 p. (Collection Choix, 10)   **7611**
Organized by Centre québécois de relations internationales (Québec), and Institut européen des hautes études internationales (Nice).

Cunningham, William Bannerman, ed. *Canada, the Commonwealth and the Common Market: Report.* Montreal: McGill University Press, c1962. 142 p.
7612
Report of the 1962 Summer Institute, Mount Allison University, Sackville, N.B. Reviews: Alice Poznanska in (1962-63), 38 *Actualité Économique* 677-678; Paul-Émile Racicot in (1963-64), 17 *Revue d'Histoire de l'Amérique Française* 442.

Curry, F. Hayden, and Deddish, Michael R., Jr. "The United States-Canadian Automotive Pact: Executive Authority and the Conflict with GATT." (1965-66), 6 *Virginia Journal of International Law* 144-159.   **7613**

Deutsch, John J. "Selective Free Trade in the North American Bloc as a Defensive Concept." (1961), 3 *University of Windsor Seminar on Canadian-American Relations, Proceedings* 87-93.   **7614**

English, Harry Edward. "Canada's Economic Interests in Trade Liberalization." *In* Franck, Thomas M., and Weisband, Edward, eds., *A Free Trade Association* (New York, 1968), pp. 191-223.   **7615**

English, Harry Edward. *Transatlantic Economic Community: Canadian Perspectives.* Toronto: Published for the Private Planning Association of Canada by University of Toronto Press, 1968. 70 p. (Canada in the Atlantic Economy, Vol. 2)   **7616**

Fleming, Donald M. "Canada, the United States and Developing Trade Blocs." (1961), 3 *University of Windsor Seminar on Canadian-American Relations, Proceedings* 1-18.   **7617**

Franck, Thomas M., and Weisband, Edward, eds. *A Free Trade Association.* New York: New York University Press; London: University of London Press, 1968. xv, 329 p. (Studies in Peaceful Change, No. 2)   **7618**
Contains a proposal for the formation of a Free Trade Association with the United States, Great Britain and Canada as the core. Includes papers presented at a conference held at New York University February 17-18, 1968, sponsored by the Center for International Studies of New York University. Some individual studies are listed separately.

Gates, Theodore R. "Canadian-American Trade Problems in a Multilateral Context." (1973-74), 6 *Case Western Reserve Journal of International Law* 51-55.
7619

Geiger, Theodore; Volpe, John; and Preeg, Ernest H. *North American Integration and Economic Blocs.* London: Trade Policy Research Centre, c1975. vii, 58 p. (Thames Essay, No. 7) **7620**

Gherson, A.R.A. "Notes on Some Implications of Enlargement of the EEC for Canada." (1973-74), 6 *Case Western Reserve Journal of International Law* 116-119. **7621**

Hawkins, Robert G. "The Economic Impact on the United States of a U.K.-Canada-U.S. Free Trade Association." *In* Franck, Thomas M., and Weisband, Edward, eds., *A Free Trade Association* (New York, 1968), pp. 53-149. **7622**

Heilperin, Michael A. "A U.S.-Canadian Partnership for the Revival of Multilateral Trade." (1949-50), 5 *International Journal* 217-229. **7623**

Inman, M.K. "Canada, the United States and the European Common Market." (1962), 4 *University of Windsor Seminar on Canadian-American Relations, Proceedings* 180-204. **7624**

Johnson, Harry G. "Harmonization of Economic Policies under Free Trading Arrangements: Issues for Canada." (1968), 3 *Journal of Canadian Studies* 16-21 (No. 4) **7625**

Johnson, Harry G. "Trade Challenges Confronting Commonwealth Countries." (1969-70), 25 *International Journal* 109-128. **7626**

Judek, S. "Proposals for Free Trade in Europe and Their Possible Impact on Canada's Foreign Trade." (1958), 28 *Revue de l'Université d'Ottawa* 180-190. **7627**

Kreinin, Mordechai E. "North American Economic Integration." (1981), 44 *Law and Contemporary Problems* 7-31. **7628**

Lasok, Dominik. "Trade with the European Economic Community: A Challenge to Canadian Lawyers." (1978-79), 17 *University of Western Ontario Law Review* 155-168. **7629**

Latimer, Robert E. "Multilateral Trade Negotiations." *In* Hay, Keith A.J., ed., *Canadian Perspectives on Economic Relations with Japan* (Montreal, 1980), pp. 133-138. **7630**
See also "Comment" by Harry C. Eastman (pp. 139-140).

Levitt, Kari, and McIntyre, Alister. *Canada-West Indies Economic Relations.* Montreal: Sponsored by the Canadian Trade Committee, Private Planning Association of Canada and by the Centre for Developing Area Studies, McGill University, 1967. 181 p. **7631**

Lyon, Peyton V. "Second Thoughts on the Second Option." (1974-75), 30 *International Journal* 646-670. **7632**
Discusses the Canada-United States Free Trade Area (CUFTA), and other free trade areas.

Macdonald, H. Ian "Commonwealth Preferences: Canada's Strength at GATT?" (1964), 29 *Business Quarterly* 36-42 (No. 1) **7633**

Martin, Paul. "European Blocs: Their Effect on North American Trade." (1960), 2 *University of Windsor Seminar on Canadian-American Relations, Proceedings* 63-73. **7634**

Matthews, Roy A. "Canada, Britain and the Common Market: A Canadian View." (1962), 18 *World Today* 48-57. **7635**

Mills, Joseph C. "Canada at UNCTAD." (1964-65), 20 *International Journal* 214-220. **7636**

Mitchell, Lionel Anthony. *Canada-Commonwealth Caribbean Trade in the Development of the Commonwealth Caribbean.* Edmonton, 1969. ix, 164 leaves. **7637**
Thesis (M.B.A.), University of Alberta, 1969.

"A North American Market? U.S.-Mexican-Canadian Perspectives on Terms of Trade and Rationalization of Production; Antidumping and Countervailing Duties." (1974), 68 *American Society of International Law, Proceedings* 92-107. **7638**
This is a panel. Robert K. Goldman, Chairman.
Contents: "U.S.-Canadian-Mexican Trade Relations," by Stanley D. Metzger (pp. 93-100).- "Canadian Perspectives on Terms of Trade, Rationalization of Production, Antidumping, and Countervailing Duties," by Ivan R. Feltham (pp. 100-107).

Orr, Patrick. "International and Canadian Quantitative Restrictions on World Textile Trade." (1980), 38 *University of Toronto Faculty of Law Review* 52-82. **7639**

Parizeau, Jacques. "Le Canada et GATT." (1961-62), 37 *Actualité Économique* 238-252. **7640**

Perry, J. Harvey. "Canada and GATT: The Background of Tariff Negotiations This Fall." (1954), 2 *Canadian Tax Journal* 272-279. **7641**

Phillips, W.G. "North American Selective Free Trade." (1961), 3 *University of Windsor Seminar on Canadian-American Relations, Proceedings* 94-102. **7642**

Québec (Province). Ministère de l'industrie, du commerce et du tourisme. Direction des études en relations économiques internationales. *Les négociations commerciales multilatérales du G.A.T.T.: une évaluation préliminaire.* Québec: la Direction, 1979. 54 leaves. **7643**

Sabourin-Hébert, Louise. "De la validité des subventions au regard de l'Accord général sur les tarifs douaniers et le commerce: une application canadienne." (1975), 6 *Revue Générale de Droit* 339-444. **7644**

Sabourin-Hébert, Louise. *De la validité des subventions au regard de l'Accord général sur les tarifs douaniers et le commerce: une application canadienne.* Ottawa, 1976. vii, 210 leaves. **7645**
Thesis (LL.M.), Université d'Ottawa, 1976.

Sinclair, Sol. *The Common Agricultural Policy of the E.E.C. and Its Implications for Canada's Exports.* Montreal: Private Planning Association of Canada, 1964. xii, 101 p. **7646**

Steinberg, David J. "The Meaning of Multi-lateral Negotiations (The Kennedy Round): Its Meaning to Canadian and American Trade." (1964), 6 *University of Windsor Seminar on Canadian-American Relations, Proceedings* 260-268.
7647

Warren, J.H. "Canada's Role in the GATT Negotiations." (1978), 5 *Canadian Business Review* 36-41 (No. 2) **7648**

Wilson, Leslie Alfred James. *Canadian International Trade Policy from the Dunning Budget to the Torquay Agreements.* Toronto, 1956. 102 leaves. **7649**
Thesis (M.A.), University of Toronto, 1956.

Winham, Gilbert R. "Canada at Tokyo Round of Trade Negotiations." (1979), *International Perspectives* 27-30 (Mar./Apr.) **7650**

Wonnacott, Ronald J. "Canada's Future in a World of Trade Blocs: A Proposal." (1975), 1 *Canadian Public Policy* 118-130. **7651**

Zarley, Arvid M. *The Impact of Economic Integration on Third Countries: A Case Study of Canadian Export Shares in the British Market under Alternative Courses of European Integration.* Lafayette, Ind., 1965. 222 leaves. **7652**
Thesis (Ph.D.), Purdue University, 1965. Abstracted in (1966-67), 27 *Dissertation Abstracts* 9-A. (University Microfilms, Ann Arbor, No. 66-5318).

C. Commodities

1. GENERAL

Bauer, P.T. "Commodity Agreements: Aid or Trade?" (1973-74), 29 *International Journal* 610-618. **7653**

Carreau, Dominique. "Le programme intégré pour les produits de base: (une nouvelle approche juridique des matières premières dans l'ordre international)." (1978), 9 *Études Internationales* 194-213. **7654**

Gould, Wesley L. "Metals, Oil, and Natural Gas: Some Problems of Canadian-American Co-operation." *In* Deener, David R., ed., *Canada-United States Treaty Relations* (Durham, N.C., 1963), pp. 151-184. **7655**

Haviland, William Edward. *International Commodity Agreements.* Montreal: Canadian Trade Committee, Private Planning Association of Canada, 1963. xi, 81 p. **7656**
Review: Bernard Bonin in (1964-65), 40 *Actualité Économique* 625.

Hérisson, Charles-D. "Le contrôle des sources de matières premières à l'étranger par les États-Unis." (1938-39), 14/2 *Actualité Économique* 426-439. **7657**

Josling, Tim. "World Trade in Basic Foodstuffs." (1978-79), 34 *International Journal* 39-52. **7658**

Marten, Peter Cornelis. *International Commodity Agreements; an Economic Analysis with Historical Background.* Toronto, 1963. 110 leaves. **7659**
Thesis (M.S.A.), University of Toronto, 1963.

Martin, Robert, and Osberg, Lars. "Producer Cartels: Trade Unions of the Third World." *In* Macdonald, Ronald St. John, and others, *The International Law and Policy of Human Welfare* (Alphen aan den Rijn, 1978), pp. 501-523.**7660**

Roach, E. Hugh. "The Commodities Question Towards a Common Fund - Rhetoric or Reality?" (1977-78), 36 *Behind the Headlines* No. 6 (27 p.) **7661**

Winberg, Alan R. "Raw Material Producer Associations and Canadian Policy." (1975-76), 34 *Behind the Headlines* No. 4 (27 p.) **7662**

2. SPECIFIC PRODUCTS

(a) WHEAT

See also *"Food and Nutrition" (p. 676).*

Cohn, Theodore H. "The 1978-9 Negotiations for an International Wheat Agreement: An Opportunity Lost?" (1979-80), 35 *International Journal* 132-149. **7663**

Doxey, Margaret P. "Oil and Food as International Sanctions." (1980-81), 36 *International Journal* 311-334. **7664**

Ellison, Anthony P. *The Canadian Interest in an International Wheat Agreement.* Prepared for the Centre for the Study of Inflation and Productivity. Ottawa: Economic Council of Canada, 1980. viii, 126 p., charts. (Economic Council of Canada. Discussion Paper, No. 167) **7665**
Includes a summary in French.

Evans, W. Sanford. "Canada and the World's Wheat Trade." (1923-24), 31 *Journal of the Canadian Bankers' Association* 75-78. **7666**

Hamilton, William Eugene, and Drummond, W.M. *Wheat Surpluses and Their Impact on Canada-United States Relations.* Washington: Canadian-American Committee, 1959. xi, 52 p. (Reports on Canada-United States Relations)**7667**
Sponsored by the National Planning Association (U.S.A.), and the Private Planning Association of Canada.

Hevesy, Paul de. "The World Wheat Problem." (1956), 63 *Canadian Banker* 36-43 (No. 1) **7668**

Hudson, S. Claude. "Looking for a New Grain Policy." (1971), 78 *Canadian Banker* 25-28 (No. 6) **7669**

Leslie, Kenneth Ainsworth. *Wheat and Sugar Agreements; a Comparative Study.* Hamilton, Ont., 1965. iv, 83 leaves. **7670**
Thesis (M.A.), McMaster University, 1965.

MacFarlane, David L. "The International Wheat Agreement of 1956: A Canadian View." (1956), 32 *International Affairs* 427-435. **7671**
Refers to the agreement of April 25, 1956 (CTS 1956/5).

MacGibbon, D.A. "The Wheat Problem." (1933-34), 3 *University of Toronto Quarterly* 228-244. **7672**

Mackintosh, W.A. "The Canadian Wheat Pools." (1925-26), 33 *Queen's Quarterly* 115-142. **7673**

Mackintosh, W.A. "The Crisis in Wheat." (1939-40), 46 *Queen's Quarterly* 348-359. **7674**

Menzies, Merril Warren. *The Canadian Wheat Board and the International Wheat Trade (National and International Factors Influencing the Development of Canadian Wheat Policy).* Vancouver, 1957. (9), 483, (85), x leaves. **7675**
Thesis, University of London, 1956.

Parizeau, Jacques. "Les marchés internationaux du blé." (1955-56), 31 *Actualité Économique* 462-471. **7676**

Richardson, B.T. "Canada and the Wheat Agreement." (1952-53), 8 *International Journal* 274-283. **7677**

Rickard, Bruce. "The North Atlantic Triangle and Changes in the Wheat Trade Before the Great War." (1975-76), 55 *Dalhousie Review* 263-271. **7678**

Saba, George C. *An Analysis of Demand for Canadian Wheat under the Common Agricultural Policy of the European Economic Community.* Montreal, 1968. xi, 324 leaves. **7679**
Thesis (M.A.), McGill University, 1968. (National Library of Canada. Canadian Theses on Microfilm, No. 2909).

Sinclair, Sol. "Canada and Wheat in International Trade." (1956-57), 12 *International Journal* 289-299. **7680**

Spry, Graham. "Canadian Wheat and International Wheat Conferences. (Part I)." (1955-56), 11 *International Journal* 93-102. **7681**

Spry, Graham. "Canadian Wheat and International Wheat Conferences. (Part II)." (1955-56), 11 *International Journal* 165-176. **7682**

U.S. Delegation to the Ad Hoc Meeting of the Canada-United States Interparliamentary Group, 1981. *Ad Hoc Meeting of the Canada-United States Interparliamentary Group to Discuss International Wheat Marketing, October 24, 1981: Report by the United States Delegation.* Washington: Govt. Print. Off., 1982. v, 11 p. **7683**
The meeting was held at Washington, D.C.

Warley, Thorald Keith. *Agriculture in an Interdependent World: U.S. and Canadian Perspectives.* Prepared for the Canadian-American Committee. Montreal: C.D. Howe Research Institute, 1977. x, 93 p. (Canadian-American Committee. Publications, CAC 43) **7684**

Western, Maurice, and Nedlin, Ralph. "What's Happening to Wheat?" (1956), 16 *Behind the Headlines* No. 2 (16 p.) **7685**

(b) COFFEE, TEA, SUGAR

Downs, John Richard. *World Trade in Sugar and Its Regulation, with Special Reference to Canada.* Saskatoon, 1953. 172 leaves. **7686**
Thesis (M.A.), University of Saskatchewan, 1953.

Jenness, Robert Allan. *The World Coffee Situation and International Control Measures.* Kingston, 1964. 134 leaves. **7687**
Thesis (M.A.), Queen's University, 1964.

Kravis, Irving B. "International Commodity Agreements to Promote Aid and Efficiency: The Case of Coffee." (1968), 1 *Canadian Journal of Economics* 295-317. **7688**

Contains a résumé in French under title: "Ententes internationales sur les produits en vue de promouvoir l'aide et l'efficacité: le cas du café."

Law, Alton D. "International Commodity Agreements to Promote Aid and Efficiency: The Case of Coffee: A Comment." (1969), 2 *Canadian Journal of Economics* 612-618. **7689**

Leslie, Kenneth Ainsworth. *Wheat and Sugar Agreements; a Comparative Study.* Hamilton, Ont., 1965. iv, 83 leaves. **7690**
Thesis (M.A.), McMaster University, 1965.

Levine, Rhonda Faye. *The Political Economy of the International Coffee Trade, 1930-1975.* Montreal, 1975 (c1976). v, 108 leaves. **7691**
Thesis (M.A.), McGill University, 1975. (National Library of Canada. Canadian Theses on Microfiche, No. 27197).

Magee, David Morris. *The 1962 International Coffee Agreement: Past, Present and Future.* Hamilton, Ont., 1973. vii, 100 leaves. **7692**
Thesis (M.A.), McMaster University, 1973. Refers to the coffee agreement done at New York on September 28, 1962 (469 UNTS 169).

Murray, Trevor William. *An Empirical Analysis of Some Major Impacts of Protectionism in the International Trade in Sugar.* Edmonton, 1980. 141 frames. **7693**
Thesis (M.Sc.), University of Alberta, 1980. (National Library of Canada. Canadian Theses on Microfiche, No. 44787).

(c) OIL AND GAS

See also *"Marine Resources: Oil and Gas Exploitation" (p. 263)*. For pipelines, see also *"Transportation in General" (p. 641)*.

Ayoub, Antoine, ed. *Le nouvel ordre pétrolier, de la firme transnationale aux rapports entre états / The New Petroleum Order, from the Transnational Company to Relations between Governments. IIe colloque international d'économie pétrolière.* Québec: Presses de l'Université Laval, 1976. 234 p.
7694
At head of title: Groupe de recherche en économie de l'énergie. Text in English or French. Proceedings of a conference held at Université Laval, October 2-4, 1975.

Ayoub, Antoine, and Gaudet, Gérard. *Dossier analytique sur l'offre pétrolière de l'OPEP.* Québec: Groupe de recherche en économie de l'énergie (GREEN), Université Laval, 1976. vii, 733 p. **7695**

Ayoub, Antoine, and Nguyen, The-Hiep. "Les incidences économiques et financières des revenus pétroliers: aspects national, régional et international." (1976), 7 *Études Internationales* 516-541. **7696**

Barry, P.S. "The Prolific Pipeline: Finding Oil for Canol." (1977-78), 57 *Dalhousie Review* 205-223. **7697**

Breen, D.H. "Anglo-American Rivalry and the Evolution of Canadian Petroleum Policy to 1930." (1981), 62 *Canadian Historical Review* 283-303. **7698**

Davis, John. *Natural Gas and Canada-United States Relations.* Washington:

Canadian-American Committee, c1959. xii, 32 p., maps. (Reports on Canada-United States Relations) **7699**
Sponsored by the National Planning Association (U.S.A.), and the Private Planning Association of Canada.

Davis, John. *Oil and Canada-United States Relations.* Washington: Canadian-American Committee, c1959. xiv, 36 p., maps. (Reports on Canada-United States Relations) **7700**
Sponsored by the National Planning Association (U.S.A.), and the Private Planning Association of Canada.

Fellows, Catherine. *Continentalism versus Nationalism: The Politics of Oil and Gas.* Windsor, 1973. viii, 163 (i.e. 190) leaves. **7701**
Thesis (M.A.), University of Windsor, 1973. (National Library of Canada. Canadian Theses on Microfiche, No. 19886).

Fisher, Barry D. "The Role of the National Energy Board in Controlling the Export of Natural Gas from Canada." (1971), 9 *Osgoode Hall Law Journal* 553-599.
7702

Haglund, David G. "Canada and the International Politics of Oil: Latin American Source of Supply and Import Vulnerability in the 1980s." (1982), 15 *Canadian Journal of Political Science* 259-298. **7703**

Haglund, David G. "Latin American Oil and the Prospects for Western Hemisphere Self-Sufficiency." (1981-82), 37 *International Journal* 60-75. **7704**

Hanson, E.J. "Natural Gas in Canadian-American Relations." (1956-57), 12 *International Journal* 186-198. **7705**

Hetherington, C.R. "Oil and Gas in the Canadian Arctic." (1975), 2 *Canadian Business Review* 7-10 (No. 4) **7706**

Hubley, Roger. "Why Canadianize the Oil Industry?" (1982), 9 *Canadian Business Review* 15-19 (No. 1) **7707**

Maull, Hanns W. "The Control of Oil." (1980-81), 36 *International Journal* 273-293. **7708**

McDougal, John N. "Canada and the World Petroleum Market." *In* Hillmer, Norman, and Stevenson, Garth, eds., *A Foremost Nation: Canadian Foreign Policy and a Changing World* (Toronto, 1977), pp. 85-125. **7709**

McDougall, John N. *The National Energy Board and Multinational Corporations: The Politics of Pipe Lines and Natural Gas Exports, 1960-1971.* Edmonton, 1975. xii, 236 leaves. **7710**
Thesis (Ph.D.), University of Alberta, 1975. (National Library of Canada. Canadian Theses on Microfiche, No. 24088).

Nguyen, The-Hiep. "La stabilité de l'Opep." (1979), 10 *Études Internationales* 503-526. **7711**
Refers to "Organisation des pays producteurs de pétrole" (OPEP). In English: "Organization of Petroleum Exporting Countries" (OPEC).

Penrose, Edith. "De la dépendance à l'association: la participation du tiers-monde à l'industrie pétrolière internationale." (1971), 2 *Études Internationales* 515-528. **7712**
Translated from the English by Ferry de Kerckhove.

Ritchie, Ronald S. "Oil in World Affairs." (1951), 11 *Behind the Headlines* No. 3 (15 p.) **7713**

Salloum, Gary Michael. *Economic Interdependence and International Politics: The Case of OPEC (Organization of Petroleum Exporting Countries)*. Burnaby, B.C., 1977. viii, 192 leaves. **7714**
Thesis (M.A.), Simon Fraser University, 1977. (National Library of Canada. Canadian Theses on Microfiche, No. 35973).

Schwartz, Warren F., and Kindred, Hugh M. "American Regulation of Oil Imports: Law, Policy and Institutional Responsibility." (1971), 5 *Journal of World Trade Law* 267-302. **7715**

Thompson, Andrew R. "Sovereignty and Natural Resources - A Study of Canadian Petroleum Legislation." (1969), 4 *University of British Columbia Law Review* 161-193. **7716**
Also published in (1966-67), 1 *Valparaiso University Law Review* 284-319.

Waverman, Leonard. "National Policy and Natural Gas: The Costs of a Border." (1972), 5 *Canadian Journal of Economics* 331-348. **7717**
Contains a résumé in French under title: "La politique nationale et le gaz naturel: les coûts d'une frontière."

Waverman, Leonard. "Oil and the Distribution of International Power." (1973-74), 29 *International Journal* 619-635. **7718**

Wirick, Ronald G. "Prospects for the World Petroleum Market and Implications for Canadian Policy." (1982), 8 *Canadian Public Policy* 534-553. **7719**

Wong, Chia Siew. *Political Perspectives on the Economics of Oil: Towards a Model for Forecasting OPEC Policies*. Ottawa, 1978. 307 frames. **7720**
Thesis (M.A.), Carleton University, 1978. (National Library of Canada. Canadian Theses on Microfiche, No. 49557). Abstracted in (1981), 19 *Masters Abstracts* 335.

Zakariya, Hasan S. "Sovereignty, State Participation and the Need to Restructure the Existing Petroleum Concession Regime." (1972), 10 *Alberta Law Review* 218-231. **7721**

(d) OTHER MINERALS

Finlayson, Jock A. "Canada and Strategic Minerals." (1982) *International Perspectives* 18-21 (Sept./Oct.) **7722**

Gray, F.W. "Canada and Coal." (1943), 50 *Queen's Quarterly* 223-233. **7723**

Gray, F.W. "Canada and Coal." (1950-51), 57 *Queen's Quarterly* 444-451. **7724**

Haglund, David G. "La nouvelle géopolitique des minéraux: une étude sur l'évolution de l'impact international des minéraux stratégiques." (1982), 13 *Études Internationales* 445-471. **7725**

Heaton, H. "The Coal Crisis as an International Problem." (1926-27), 34 *Journal of the Canadian Bankers' Association* 24-34. **7726**

Laureys, Henry. "Le problème international du charbon." (1933-34), 9 *Actualité Économique* 61-72. **7727**

Queen's University. Centre for Resource Studies. *Canada's Mineral Trade: Impli-*

cations for the Balance of Payments and Economic Development: Proceedings of the Third CRS Policy Discussion Seminar, September 6-8, 1978. Kingston: Centre for Resource Studies, Queen's University, 1978. v, 113 p. (Queen's University. Centre for Resource Studies. Proceedings, No. 4) **7728**

Queen's University. Centre for Resource Studies. *International Competition and the Canadian Mineral Industries: Proceedings of the Second CRS Policy Discussion Seminar, June 7-9, 1978.* Kingston: Centre for Resource Studies, Queen's University, 1978. v, 109 p. (Queen's University. Centre for Resource Studies. Proceedings, No. 2) **7729**

Redler, Richard. "Aluminum in World Affairs." (1951), 11 *Behind the Headlines* No. 5 (17 p.) **7730**

Stewart, Larry R. "Canada's Role in the International Uranium Cartel." (1981), 35 *International Organization* 657-689. **7731**

Stewart, Miller. "Iron in World Affairs." (1954), 14 *Behind the Headlines* No. 6 (17 p.) **7732**

D. Foreign Investment

1. GENERAL

Adams, James H. "Transnational Investment in the Third World: Issues for Canada." *In* North-South Institute, *In the Canadian Interest?* (Ottawa, 1980), pp. 73-151. **7733**

Angers, François-Albert. "Le problème psychologique et pratique de l'investissement étranger." (1966-67), 42 *Actualité Économique* 339-345. **7734**

Ashton, Roger. "Canadian Investment in U.S. Real Estate for Personal Use." (1981), 29 *Canadian Tax Journal* 702-717. **7735**

Atkey, Ronald G. "Foreign Investment Disputes: Access of Private Individuals to International Tribunals." (1967), 5 *Canadian Yearbook of International Law* 229-240. **7736**

Atkey, Ronald G. "Foreign Investment Disputes: Jurisdiction of International Tribunals." (1968), 7 *Western Ontario Law Review* 111-142. **7737**

Boidman, Nathan. "Canadian Investment in U.S. Real Estate." (1981), 33 *Canadian Tax Foundation, Proceedings* 454-496. **7738**

Castel, Jean-Gabriel, and De Mestral, Armand L.C. *Legal Problems in Foreign Direct Investment: Cases, Notes and Materials.* 2d rev. ed. Toronto: York University, Osgoode Hall Law School, 1978. 258, 397, 111 p. **7739**

Cranston, Ross. "Foreign Investment Restrictions: Defending Economic Sovereignty in Canada and Australia." (1973), 14 *Harvard International Law Journal* 345-367. **7740**

"Development and Foreign Investment / Le développement et les investissements

étrangers." (1975), 4 *Canadian Council on International Law, Proceedings* 129-173. **7741**
This is a panel. Chairman: Max H. Wershof (remarks not printed).- Speaker: K.R. Simmonds (address not printed). - Commentators: Joseph S. Stanford (pp. 129-133); Christian Vincke (pp. 134-142); and Theodore Meron (pp. 143-148).- General discussion (pp. 149-173).

Dickerson, Robert W.V. "Taxation and Foreign Investment by Canadian Corporations." (1959-63), 1 *University of British Columbia Law Review* 483-498.
7742

Eckardt, H.M.P. "The Growth of Our Foreign Investments." (1900-01), 8 *Journal of the Canadian Bankers' Association* 339-347. **7743**

Fatouros, Arghyrios A. "An International Code to Protect Private Investment - Proposals and Perspectives." (1961-62), 14 *University of Toronto Law Journal* 77-102. **7744**

Fatouros, Arghyrios A. "Obstacles to Private Foreign Investment in Underdeveloped Countries." (1961), 2 *Current Law and Social Problems* 194-242. **7745**

Fatouros, Arghyrios A. "The Quest for Legal Security of Foreign Investments - Latest Developments." (1962-63), 17 *Rutgers Law Review* 257-304. **7746**

Garnier, Gérard. "Les investissements directs du Canada à l'étranger." (1973), 49 *Actualité Économique* 211-236. **7747**

Garnier, Gérard. *Les investissements privés à long terme du Canada à l'étranger de 1946 à 1966.* Sherbrooke, 1973. 2 vols. (xiv, 415 leaves) **7748**
Thesis (Doctorat), Université de Genève, Institut universitaire de hautes études internationales.

Glaser, Robert E. "Canadian Investment in the United States: Ohio's Limitations on Foreign Investment." (1981), 4 *Canada-United States Law Journal* 105-108.
7749

Hérisson, Charles-D. "Les placements américains de capitaux à l'étranger." (1939-40), 15/1 *Actualité Économique* 101-121. **7750**

Hérisson, Charles-D. "Les placements étrangers aux États-Unis." (1937-38), 13/2 *Actualité Économique* 124-140. **7751**

Litvak, Isaiah A., and Maule, Christopher J. "Canadian Investment Abroad: In Search of a Policy." (1975-76), 31 *International Journal* 159-179. **7752**

Litvak, Isaiah A., and Maule, Christopher J. "Canadian Outward Investment: Impact and Policy." (1980), 14 *Journal of World Trade Law* 310-328. **7753**

Litvak, Isaiah A., and Maule, Christopher J. "Foreign Investment in Mexico: Some Lessons for Canada." (1970-71), 30 *Behind the Headlines* Nos. 5-6 (16 p.)
7754

McDonald, John G. *Foreign Investment and International Transactions.* Toronto: Butterworths, 1967. 32 p. (Butterworths Carter Report Studies, No. 1) **7755**
At head of title: Canadian Royal Commission on Taxation.

McManus, R. Derek. *Taxation and Canadian Foreign Investment.* Calgary, 1970. xvi, 236 leaves. **7756**

Thesis (M.A.), University of Calgary, 1971. (National Library of Canada. Canadian Theses on Microfilm, No. 10121).

Newby, Robert F. "Acquisition of Exploration and Production Rights Outside of Canada." (1976), 14 *Alberta Law Review* 396-406. **7757**

Pacific Trade and Development Conference, 3d, Sydney, 1970. *Direct Foreign Investment in Asia and the Pacific: The Third Pacific Trade and Development Conference, Sydney, 1970.* Edited by Peter Drysdale. Toronto: University of Toronto Press, 1972. xiii, 360 p. **7758**
Also published Canberra, Australian National University Press.

Peel, David. "New Developments in International Investment Law." (1979), 8 *Canadian Council on International Law, Proceedings* 139-152. **7759**

Rodley, Nigel S. "Some Aspects of the World Bank Convention on the Settlement of Investment Disputes." (1966), 4 *Canadian Yearbook of International Law* 43-63. **7760**

Special Seminar on Canadian Investment in the United States, 1980. *Special Seminar on Canadian Investment in the United States, June 25-26, 1980: Texts of Seminar Papers.* Toronto: Richard De Boo, 1981. 147 p. **7761**
On cover: IFA International Fiscal Association, Canadian Branch.

Spence, James M., and others. "Regulation of Foreign Investment and Trade: Panel Discussion." (1976-77), 4 *Syracuse Journal of International Law and Commerce* 355-376. **7762**

Stanford, Joseph S. "International Law and Foreign Investment." *In* Macdonald, Ronald St. John, and others, *The International Law and Policy of Human Welfare* (Alphen aan den Rijn, 1978), pp. 471-500. **7763**

Tomasky, Eugene Michael. *A Subsidy and Tax Approach to the Repatriation of Canadian Investment Funds.* Edmonton, 1972. viii, 95 leaves. **7764**
Thesis (M.B.A.), University of Alberta, 1972. (National Library of Canada. Canadian Theses on Microfilm, No. 13602).

Triantis, Stephen G. "Obstacles to Canadian Investment Overseas." (1952), 18 *Canadian Journal of Economics and Political Science* 92-95. **7765**

Vo Van, Dat. *L'investissement direct étranger et les politiques commerciales: le cas de la République de Chine, 1950-1976.* Québec, 1978. 133 leaves. **7766**
Thesis (M.Soc.Sc.), Université Laval, 1978. (National Library of Canada. Canadian Theses on Microfiche, No. 39210).

Voghel, Michel C. *Étude comparative des mesures de contrôle de l'investissement étranger au Mexique, en Australie et au Canada.* Montréal, 1979. 175 frames. **7767**
Thesis (M.C.L.), McGill University, 1979. (National Library of Canada. Canadian Theses on Microfiche, No. 50583).

Westell, Anthony. "Canada's Investment Capital Moves South of the Border." (1981), *International Perspectives* 10-14 (Jan./Feb.) **7768**

Williamson, John Peter. "U.S. Foreign Investors Tax Act: Effects on Canadians." (1966), 14 *Canadian Tax Journal* 492-499. **7769**

Wright, Richard W. "Foreign Investment between Neighbours: Canada and

Japan." *In* Hay, Keith A.J., ed., *Canadian Perspectives on Economic Relations with Japan* (Montreal, 1980), pp. 191-202. **7770**

Zaremba, Alois Louis. *Canadian Balance of Payments, 1946-59; Foreign Investment and Economic Development.* Columbus, Ohio, 1960. viii, 209 leaves. **7771**
Thesis (Ph.D.), Ohio State University, 1960. Abstracted in (1961), 21 *Dissertation Abstracts International* 3293. (University Microfilms, Ann Arbor, No. 61-951).

2. FOREIGN INVESTMENT IN CANADA

See also *"Foreign Corporations in Canada" (p. 604).*

Abdel-Malek, Talaat, and Sarkar, Asit K. "An Analysis of the Effects of Phase II Guidelines of the Foreign Investment Review Act." (1977), 3 *Canadian Public Policy* 36-49. **7772**

Aitken, Hugh George Jeffrey. *American Capital and Canadian Resources.* Cambridge: Harvard University Press, 1961. xii, 217 p. **7773**

Arnett, E. James. "The Canadian Foreign Investment Review Act." (1974), 2 *International Business Lawyer* 16-22 (July) **7774**

Arnett, E. James. "Canadian Regulation of Foreign Investment: The Legal Parameters." (1972), 50 *Canadian Bar Review* 213-247. **7775**

Arnett, E. James. "Which Investors Are 'Foreign?' " (1977), 55 *Canadian Bar Review* 231-255. **7776**

Arnold, Brian J. "Restrictions on Foreign Investment in Canadian Financial Institutions." (1970), 20 *University of Toronto Law Journal* 196-235. **7777**

Arnold, Brian J. "U.S. Investment in Canadian Real Estate." (1981), 4 *Canada-United States Law Journal* 112-125. **7778**

Aronsen, Lawrence Robert. *The Northern Frontier: United States Trade and Investment in Canada, 1945-1953.* Toronto, c1981. 369 leaves. **7779**
Thesis (Ph.D.), University of Toronto, 1980. (National Library of Canada. Canadian Theses on Microfiche, No. 46999).

Atkinson, Lloyd. "Recent Trends in American Investment in Canada and Its Relation to the Canadian Trade Situation." (1964), 6 *University of Windsor Seminar on Canadian-American Relations, Proceedings* 355-364. **7780**

Azoulay, Michel. "L'accord cadre et les nouvelles orientations des investissements des pays des Communautés européennes au Canada." (1979-80), 3 *Revue d'Intégration Européenne* 181-196. **7781**

Bachand, Denis J.V. "Une évaluation des investissements américains au Québec." (1971), 2 *Études Internationales* 110-114. **7782**

Barnes, William S. "Foreign Investment in Canada and Mexico: An Agenda for Host Country Screening." (1977), 1 *Boston College International and Comparative Law Journal* 1-10. **7783**

Beaudoin, Gérald. "Le contrôle de l'investissement étranger au Canada." (1978), 32 *Revue Juridique et Politique, Indépendance et Coopération* 283-291. **7784**

Beaudoin, Gérald. "Du mouvement des biens et des capitaux et de la mobilité des personnes au Canada." (1980), 34 *Revue Juridique et Politique, Indépendance et Coopération* 283-290. **7785**

Beck, David. "Law and Policy in the Operation of Canada's Foreign Investment Review Agency." (1980-81), 45 *Saskatchewan Law Review* 183-201. **7786**

Beigie, Carl E. "Foreign Investment in Canada: The Shading Is Gray." (1972), 7 *Columbia Journal of World Business* 23-32 (No. 6) **7787**

Blyth, C.D., and Carty, E.B. "Non-Resident Ownership of Canadian Industry." (1956), 22 *Canadian Journal of Economics and Political Science* 449-460.
7788

Bonin, Bernard. *L'investissement étranger à long terme au Canada: ses caractères et ses effets sur l'économie canadienne.* Paris, 1966. 636 leaves. **7789**
Thesis, Université de Paris, 1966. (National Library of Canada. Canadian Theses on Microfilm, No. 728).

Bonin, Bernard. *L'investissement étranger à long terme au Canada: ses caractères et ses effets sur l'économie canadienne; avec annexe sur les systèmes internationaux de points de base.* Montréal: Presses de l'École des hautes études commerciales, c1967. 462 p. (Problèmes économiques contemporains, 3) **7790**
Based on the author's thesis, Université de Paris, 1966.
Review: Claude Masson in (1968), 75 *Canadian Banker* 68-72 (No. 1).

Bonin, Bernard. "La limitation des investissements directs américains au Canada." (1965-66), 41 *Actualité Économique* 737-746. **7791**

Bonin, Bernard. "M. Walter Gordon et l'investissement étranger au Canada." (1966-67), 42 *Actualité Économique* 345-353. **7792**

Bonin, Bernard. "Le projet de loi C-132 sur l'examen des investissements étrangers." (1973), 49 *Actualité Économique* 141-145. **7793**

Bonney, William H. "Foreign Investment Review Act." (1975), 13 *Alberta Law Review* 83-89. **7794**

Boudreault, Marc. "L'investissement immobilier au Canada par un non-résident." (1979), 10 *Revue Générale de Droit* 385-402. **7795**

Byleveld, Herbert C. "Foreign Investment in Canada: What's the Score?" (1982), 9 *Canadian Business Review* 38-42 (No. 2) **7796**

Cahill, Michael Edward. *Foreign Investment in Canada, and the Foreign Investment Review Act.* Cambridge, Mass., 1978. 124 leaves. **7797**
Thesis (LL.M.), Harvard University, 1978.

Calvet, A.L., and Crener, Maxime A. "Foreign Business Control: The Canadian Experience 1973-1977." (1979), 22 *Canadian Public Administration* 415-438.
7798

Canada. Foreign Investment Review Agency. *A Comparison of Foreign Investment Controls in Canada and Australia / Comparaison des mécanismes australiens et canadiens de réglementation de l'investissement étranger.* Prepared by the Research and Analysis Branch. Ottawa: FIRA, Research and Analysis Branch, 1979. 19, 20 p. (FIRA Papers, No. 5) **7799**
Text in English and French on inverted pages, each with a separate title page and paging.

Canada. Foreign Investment Review Agency. *Foreign Investment Review Act: Annual Report.* 1974/75—. Ottawa. **7800**
Also issued in French under title: *Loi sur l'examen de l'investissement étranger: rapport annuel.* This agency was established in 1974 under the *Foreign Investment Review Act* (S.C. 1973-74, c. 46). It is an autonomous agency reporting to Parliament through the Minister of Industry, Trade and Commerce.

Canada. Foreign Investment Review Agency. *Selected Readings in Canadian Legislation Affecting Foreign Investment in Canada / Aperçu des textes de loi et des règlements visant l'investissement étranger au Canada.* Ottawa: Policy Research Division, Research and Analysis Branch, 1977—. Bilingual. (FIRA Papers, No. 2) **7801**

Canada. Task Force on the Structure of Canadian Industry. *Foreign Ownership and the Structure of Canadian Industry: Report of the Task Force on the Structure of Canadian Industry. January 1968.* Ottawa: Queen's Printer, 1968. 427 p. **7802**
Melville H. Watkins, Chairman.
Review: Harry G. Johnson under title: "Towards a New National Policy," in (1967-68), 23 *International Journal* 615-622.

Canadian Foreign Investment Review Seminar. *Texts of Addresses.* Toronto: Richard De Boo, 1974. 123 p. **7803**
Sponsored by Richard De Boo Ltd., and the Tax Management Inc., April 30-May 1, 1974; contains the text of addresses given by the principal speakers.

Cliche, Denis. *Cadre juridique de l'investissement étranger au Canada.* Montréal, 1975 (c1976). vii, 142 leaves. **7804**
Thesis (LL.M.), McGill University, 1975. (National Library of Canada. Canadian Theses on Microfiche, No. 27105).

Cordell, Arthur J. *The Multinational Firm, Foreign Direct Investment and Canadian Science Policy.* Ottawa: Information Canada, 1971. 95 p. (Science Council of Canada. Special Study, No. 22) **7805**
At head of title: *Background Study for the Science Council of Canada.*

Couture, J. Claude. "L'impact de la réforme fiscale sur les investissements étrangers." (1971), 6 *Revue Juridique Thémis* 291-298. **7806**

Crookell, Harold. "Responding to Foreign Investment." (1972), 37 *Business Quarterly* 22-29 (No. 4) **7807**

Cutler, Maurice. "Foreign Demand for Our Land and Resources." (1975), 90 *Canadian Geographical Journal* 4-19 (No. 4) **7808**

Cutler, Maurice. "The Sale of Canada's Resources." (1975), 91 *Canadian Geographical Journal* 14-25 (Nos. 1 & 2) **7809**

Donaldson, Robert A. "Foreign Investment Review and Canadianization." (1982), *Law Society of Upper Canada, Special Lectures* 461-577. **7810**

Donaldson, Robert A., and Jackson, J.D.A. "The Foreign Investment Review Act: An Analysis of the Legislation." (1975), 53 *Canadian Bar Review* 171-236.
7811

Duval, Jean-Marc. *Japanese Joint Ventures in British Columbia.* Vancouver, 1974 (c1975). viii, 151 leaves. **7812**

Thesis (M.Sc.), University of British Columbia, 1974. (National Library of Canada. Canadian Theses on Microfiche, No. 22068).

Engle, Howard E., Jr. "International Investment - Canadian Bank Act of 1967 - Restrictions Imposed upon Foreign Ownership of Federally Chartered Canadian Banks - Statutes of Canada 1966-67, c. 87." (1968), 9 *Harvard International Law Journal* 305-317. **7813**

English, Harry Edward. "Canada's Domestic Concerns - National Unity and Foreign 'Control': Foreign Investment in Manufacturing." (1976), 32 *Academy of Political Science, Proceedings* 88-99 (No. 2) **7814**

Ernst, Edward R. "Problems of United States Investment in Canada." (1960), 2 *University of Windsor Seminar on Canadian-American Relations, Proceedings* 46-54. **7815**

Espinosa, William H. "The Canadian Foreign Investment Review Act: Red, White, and Gray." (1973), 5 *Law and Policy in International Business* 1018-1041.
7816

Fayerweather, John. *Foreign Investment in Canada: Prospects for National Policy.* Toronto: Oxford University Press, 1974. 200 p. **7817**
Also published White Plains, N.Y., International Arts and Sciences Press.
Reviews: David J. Bellamy in (1975), 8 *Canadian Journal of Political Science* 485-487; John C. Pattison in (1974-75), 30 *International Journal* 804-805.

Feltham, Ivan R., and Rauenbusch, William R. "Economic Nationalism." In Macdonald, Ronald St. John, and others, *Canadian Perspectives on International Law and Organization* (Toronto, 1974), pp. 885-917. **7818**

Franck, Thomas M., and Gudgeon, K. Scott. "Canada's Foreign Investment Control Experiment: The Law, the Context and the Practice." (1975), 50 *New York University Law Review* 76-146. **7819**

French, Robert W. *American Direct Investments in Canada.* Ann Arbor, 1937. 588 leaves. **7820**
Thesis (Ph.D.), University of Michigan, 1937.

Gilpin, Robert. "American Direct Investment and Canada's Two Nationalisms." *In* Preston, Richard A., ed., *The Influence of the United States on Canadian Development: Eleven Case Studies* (Durham, N.C., 1972), pp. 124-143. **7821**

Gilpin, Robert. "Les investissements directs américains et les deux nationalismes au Canada." (1971), 2 *Études Internationales* 44-57. **7822**

Glover, George C., Jr. "Canada's Foreign Investment Review Act." (1973-74), 29 *Business Lawyer* 805-822. **7823**

Godfrey, Dave, and Watkins, Melville H., eds. *Gordon to Watkins to You, Documentary: The Battle for Control of Our Economy.* Toronto: New Press, 1970. 261 p. **7824**
Review: David Corbett under title: "Life with Father," in (1970-71), 26 *International Journal* 44-51.

Gordon, Walter L. "Foreign Control of Canadian Industry." (1966), 73 *Queen's Quarterly* 1-12. **7825**

Gray, Herbert E. *A Citizen's Guide to the Gray Report.* Prepared by the Editors of the Canadian Forum. Toronto: New Press, 1971. 189 p. **7826**

This is an abridgment of a confidential document by Herbert E. Gray, submitted to the Canadian Government, May 1971, under title: *Domestic Control of the National Economic Environment; the Problems of Foreign Ownership and Control.* Reprinted from the *Canadian Forum,* December 1971.

Gray, Herbert E. *Foreign Direct Investment in Canada.* Ottawa: Information Canada, 1972. xi, 523 p. **7827**
Report prepared by a working group. Herb Gray, Chairman.

Gualtieri, Roberto D. "Canada's New Foreign Investment Policy." (1975), 10 *Texas International Law Journal* 46-66. **7828**

Gualtieri, Roberto D. "Canadian Foreign Investment Policy." (1973-74), 6 *Case Western Reserve Journal of International Law* 92-98. **7829**

Guenther, Victor J. *American Investment: Development or Domination?* Don Mills, Ont.: J.M. Dent (Canada), 1971. x, 80 p. **7830**

Hampton, Peter. *Foreign Investment and the Theory of Economic Growth, Examined within the Framework of Canadian Economic Development.* Ottawa, 1963. vii, 244 leaves. **7831**
Thesis (Ph.D.), University of Ottawa, 1963.

Hayden, Peter R., and Burns, Jeffrey H. *Foreign Investment in Canada: A Guide to the Law.* Contributors: Irwin Schwartz, and G. David Quirin. Scarborough, Ont.: Prentice-Hall of Canada, c1974. 1 vol. (loose-leaf) **7832**
Includes the text of the *Foreign Investment Review Act.*

Hayden, Peter R., and Burns, Jeffrey H. "The Foreign Investment Review Act; Xenophobic Folly or not - An Historic Piece of Legislation." (1975), 9 *Law Society of Upper Canada Gazette* 144-153. **7833**

Hayden, Peter R., and Burns, Jeffrey H. *The Regulation of Foreign Investment in Canada.* Scarborough, Ont.: Prentice-Hall of Canada, 1976. 220 p. **7834**

Helliwell, John, and Broadbent, Jillian. "How Much Does Foreign Capital Matter?" (1972), 13 *B.C. Studies* 38-42. **7835**

Howard, Case R. "United States Investments in Canada." (1927-28), 35 *Journal of the Canadian Bankers' Association* 88-91. **7836**

Hudec, Robert E. "Possible Trade Policy Consequences of the Canadian Foreign Investment Policy." (1973-74), 6 *Case Western Reserve Journal of International Law* 64-81. **7837**

Hughes, Graeme C. *A Commentary on the Foreign Investment Review Act: Being an Act to Provide for the Review and Assessment of Acquisitions of Control of Canadian Business Enterprises and of the Establishment of New Businesses in Canada.* Toronto: Carswell, 1975. vii, 214 p. **7838**
Includes the text of the *Foreign Investment Review Act.*
Reviews: Patrick Brode in (1976), 10 *Law Society of Upper Canada Gazette* 70-71; Dirk J. De Vos in (1976), 8 *Ottawa Law Review* 265-269.

Hunter, Michael W. "The Foreign Investment Review Act; (or You, Too, May Be a Non-Eligible Person)." (1974), 32 *Advocate* 148-156. **7839**

Jaffe, Robert A. "After Two Years: Canada's Foreign Investment Review Act." (1978), 3 *North Carolina Journal of International Law and Commercial Regulation* 163-182. **7840**

Janach, Monica Ann. *Foreign Ownership of Land in Canada: The Ontario Case.* Ottawa, 1977. 202 leaves. **7841**
    Research essay (M.A.), Carleton University, 1977.

Karpan, Robin Dale. *Foreign Investment Review Act: A Development in Canadian Foreign Investment Policy.* Ottawa, 1974. 165 leaves. **7842**
    Thesis (M.A.), Carleton University, 1974.

Khan, Mahmood Ali. *Inflow of Foreign Capital into Canada.* Calgary, 1969. xi, 105 leaves. **7843**
    Thesis (M.A.), University of Calgary, 1969. (National Library of Canada. Canadian Theses on Microfilm, No. 4002).

Knapp, Robert Whelan. *United States Direct Investment in Canada, 1950-1960.* Ann Arbor, 1963. vi, 239 leaves. **7844**
    Thesis (Ph.D.), University of Michigan, 1963. Abstracted in (1964), 24 *Dissertation Abstracts* 3131. (University Microfilms, Ann Arbor, No. 64-842).

Koehler, Wallace C., Jr. "Foreign Ownership Policies in Canada: 'From Colony to Nation' Again." (1972), 79 *Canadian Banker* 77-97 (No. 1) **7845**

Kresl, Peter Karl. "Before the Deluge: Canadians on Foreign Ownership, 1920-1955." (1976), 6 *American Review of Canadian Studies* 86-125 (No. 1) **7846**

Lambe, Hugh B. "Foreign Investment in Canadian Real Estate through a Netherlands Corporation." (1980), 28 *Canadian Tax Journal* 343-356. **7847**

Lamont, Douglas F. "Emerging Neo-Mercantilism in Canadian Policy Toward State Enterprises and Foreign Direct Investment." (1974-75), 8 *Vanderbilt Journal of Transnational Law* 121-144. **7848**

Langford, J.A. *Canadian Foreign Investment Controls.* Don Mills, Ont.: CCH Canadian, 1975 (c1974). v, 106 p. **7849**
    This is a study of the *Foreign Investment Review Act.*

Langford, J.A. *Canadian Foreign Investment Controls.* 2d ed. Don Mills, Ont.: CCH Canadian, c1979. v, 225 p. **7850**

Law Society of Upper Canada. Dept. of Continuing Education. *The Foreign Investment Review Act: Edited Proceedings of the Programme Held in May, 1975.* Toronto, c1976. 230 p. (various pagings) **7851**

Leroy, Vély. "Le rapport Gray: prélude d'un nouveau testament." (1972), 48 *Actualité Économique* 211-225. **7852**
    The report by Herbert E. Gray was issued by the Government of Canada under title: *Foreign Direct Investment in Canada* (Ottawa, 1972).

Littell, Norman M. "Legal Aspects and Policy Problems of Foreign Investment in Canada." (1958), *Canadian Bar Association, Papers* 91-114. **7853**

Litvak, Isaiah A., and Maule, Christopher J. "Foreign Investment in Canada." *In* Litvak, Isaiah A., and Maule, Christopher J., eds., *Foreign Investment: The Experience of Host Countries* (New York, 1970), pp. 76-104. **7854**

Litvak, Isaiah A., and Maule, Christopher J. "Interest-Group Tactics and the Politics of Foreign Investment: The Time-Reader's Digest Case Study." (1974), 7 *Canadian Journal of Political Science* 616-629. **7855**
    Contains a résumé in French under title: "La politique canadienne en matière d'investissements étrangers: le cas Time-Reader's Digest."

MacNab, C.T.A. "Constitutionality of Federal Control of Foreign Investment." (1965), 23 *University of Toronto Faculty of Law Review* 95-106. **7856**

Manning, Charles H. "Foreign Investment - The Canadian Foreign Investment Review Act - An Act to Screen Foreign Investment in Canada - Allowing Those Investments of Significant Benefit to Canada." (1973-74), 7 *Vanderbilt Journal of Transnational Law* 725-733. **7857**

McFadyen, Stuart. "The Control of Foreign Ownership of Canadian Real Estate." (1976), 2 *Canadian Public Policy* 65-77. **7858**

McLeod, A.N. "Some Economic Factors Affecting Foreign Investment in Canada." (1958), *Canadian Bar Association, Papers* 115-121. **7859**

McMillan, Charles J. "After the Gray Report: The Tortuous Evolution of Foreign Investment Policy." (1974), 20 *McGill Law Journal* 213-260. **7860**

McMillan, Charles J. "The Regulation of Foreign Investment in Canada: Experience and Prospects." (1977), 6 *Journal of Contemporary Business* 31-51 (No. 4) **7861**

Menezes, Julio. "Economic Nationalism." *In* Menezes, Julio, ed., *Decade of Adjustment* (Toronto, 1980), pp. 78-96. **7862**

Mitchell, Marnie F. "Foreign Investment Policy in the Context of Canadian Federalism." (1978), 50 *Canadian Political Science Association, Papers*, 33 p. **7863**

Munton, Donald J., and Poel, Dale H. "Electoral Accountability and Canadian Foreign Policy: the Case of Foreign Investment." (1977-78), 33 *International Journal* 217-247. **7864**

Murray, J. Alex; Watkins, Melville H.; and Polk, Judd. "Economic Domination or Co-operation." (1970), 12 *University of Windsor Seminar on Canadian-American Relations, Proceedings* 26-50. **7865**

Neher, Philip A. "Capital Movement, Foreign Ownership and Dependence on 'Foreign Investment' in Canada and British Columbia." (1972), 13 *B.C. Studies* 31-37. **7866**

New York University International Institute on Tax and Business Planning, 3d, Toronto, 1974. *1975 Doing Business in Canada: Papers*. Edited by Edward L. Newberger. New York: M. Bender, 1975. xiv, 306 p. **7867**

O'Sullivan, Barry J. "Canada's Foreign Investment Review Act Revisited." (1980-81), 4 *Fordham International Law Journal* 175-198. **7868**

Olson, Thomas H. "Foreign Investment Restrictions on Canadian Energy Resources." (1980), 14 *International Lawyer* 579-612. **7869**

Parizeau, Jacques. "Les investissements américains sont-ils devenus une menace?" (1956-57), 32 *Actualité Économique* 140-156. **7870**

Paterson, Donald G. *British Direct Investment in Canada, 1890-1914: Estimates and Determinants*. Toronto: University of Toronto Press, 1976. xii, 147 p. **7871**

Reviews: Duncan M. McDougall in (1977), 10 *Canadian Journal of Economics* 719-721; A.D. den Otter in (1978), 59 *Canadian Historical Review* 251-253; D.W. Younker in (1978), 8 *American Review of Canadian Studies* 75-77 (No. 1).

Paterson, Donald G. "European Financial Capital and British Columbia: An Essay on the Role of the Regional Entrepreneur." (1974), 21 *B.C. Studies* 33-47.
 7872

Patterson, Donald William. *Canadian Nationalism and the Question of American Direct Investment in Canada.* Ottawa, (c1970). 128 leaves. **7873**
 Thesis (M.A.), Carleton University, 1970. (National Library of Canada. Canadian Theses on Microfilm, No. 7188).

Pattison, John C. *Financial Markets and Foreign Ownership.* Toronto: Ontario Economic Council, 1978. vi, 143 p. (Ontario Economic Council. Occasional Paper, No. 8) **7874**

Potter, K.B. "Recent Developments in the Application of the Foreign Investment Review Act to the Oil Industry." (1977), 15 *Alberta Law Review* 494-517.
 7875

Québec (Province). Comité interministériel sur les investissements étrangers. *Le cadre et les moyens d'une politique québécoise concernant les investissements étrangers.* Québec: Conseil exécutif, 1973. 3 vols. (502 leaves) **7876**
 Chairman: William Tetley.

Québec (Province). Comité interministériel sur les investissements étrangers. *Le cadre et les moyens d'une politique québécoise concernant les investissements étrangers: rapport du Comité interministériel sur les investissements étrangers.* Québec: Conseil exécutif, 1973. 203 p. **7877**
 William Tetley, Chairman. Also issued in English under title: *A Québec Policy on Foreign Investment: Report of the Interdepartmental Task Force on Foreign Investment.*

Reid, Timothy E., ed. *Foreign Ownership: Villain or Scapegoat?* Toronto: Holt, Rinehart and Winston of Canada, c1972. 96 p. **7878**

Richardson, Doug, and Quigley, Tim. "The Resource Industry, Foreign Ownership, and Constitutional Methods of Control." (1974-75), 39 *Saskatchewan Law Review* 92-136. **7879**

Roby, Yves. *Les Québécois et les investissements américains, 1918-1929.* Québec: Presses de l'Université Laval, 1976. xii, 250 p. (Cahiers d'histoire de l'Université Laval, 20) **7880**
 Originally presented as the author's thesis (Ph.D.), University of Rochester.
 Reviews: Robert Armstrong in (1978-79), 32 *Revue d'Histoire de l'Amérique Française* 105-111; Gérard Garnier in (1978), 59 *Canadian Historical Review* 517-521.

Roby, Yves. *Réactions des Québécois aux investissements américains.* Rochester, N.Y., 1974 (i.e. 1975). xxix, 412 leaves. **7881**
 Thesis (Ph.D.), University of Rochester, 1975.

Rothenberg, Stuart. "The Impact of Affluence: Restriction on Foreign Investment in Canada." (1979), 9 *American Review of Canadian Studies* 72-83 (No. 2)
 7882

Rugman, Alan M. "The Foreign Ownership Debate in Canada." (1976), 10 *Journal of World Trade Law* 171-176. **7883**
 Refers to several reports: Watkins, 1968; Wahn, 1970; and Gray, 1972.

Rugman, Alan M. "The Regulation of Foreign Investment in Canada." (1977), 11 *Journal of World Trade Law* 322-333. **7884**

Safarian, Albert E. "Some Myths about Foreign Investment in Canada." (1971), 6 *Journal of Canadian Studies* 3-21 (No. 3) **7885**

Scace, Arthur R.A. "The Degree of Canadian Ownership: An Exercise in Futility?" (1964-65), 3 *Osgoode Hall Law Journal* 295-315. **7886**

Scace, Arthur R.A. "U.S. Investment in Canada: The Foreign Investment Review Act (FIRA) and Provincial Incentives." (1981), 4 *Canada-United States Law Journal* 100-104. **7887**

Sexton, Michael. "Regulation of Direct Foreign Investment: A Case of Delayed Reaction in Australia and Canada." (1974), 2 *Australian Business Law Review* 241-269. **7888**

Shapiro, Daniel M. *Multinational Investment and the Canadian Economy.* Ithaca, N.Y., 1974. viii, 291 leaves. **7889**
Thesis (Ph.D.), Cornell University, 1974. Abstracted in (1975), 35 *Dissertation Abstracts International* 4817-A. (University Microfilms, Ann Arbor, No. 75-4264).

Shearer, Ronald A. *International Investment, Economic Growth and the Case of Canada.* Columbus, Ohio, 1959. viii, 386 leaves. **7890**
Thesis (Ph.D.), Ohio State University, 1959.

"Should Investment Capital Stay Home? Part I. A Canadian-U.S. Dialogue." (1974), 68 *American Society of International Law, Proceedings* 16-38. **7891**
This is a panel. Peter D. Trooboff, Chairman.
Contents: "A Proposal for Rectifying the Present Situation," by Walter Gordon (pp. 17-20).- "Notes on a Working Canadian Relationship," by Vance Hartke (pp. 20-24).- "Foreign Investment - A Quebecois Perspective," by William Tetley (pp. 24-27).- "Toward a New Approach to the Wandering Enterprise," by Andreas F. Lowenfeld (pp. 27-31).- Comments by K. Scott Gudgeon (pp. 31-34).

Skapinker, Joel. *Legal Aspects of Foreign Investment in and Acquisition of Canadian Real Estate.* Montreal, 1978. 120 leaves. **7892**
Thesis (LL.M.), McGill University, 1978.

Smith, J.M. "Foreign Investment in Canada." (1958), 18 *Behind the Headlines* No. 2 (16 p.) **7893**

Spence, James M. "The Foreign Investment Review Act of Canada." (1976-77), 4 *Syracuse Journal of International Law and Commerce* 303-335. **7894**

Stevenson, Garth. "Foreign Direct Investment and the Provinces: A Study of Elite Attitudes." (1974), 7 *Canadian Journal of Political Science* 630-647. **7895**
Contains a résumé in French under title: "Les attitudes des élites provinciales face aux investissements étrangers directs."

Stikeman, Harry Heward. "Foreign Investment Review: Canada's New Medicine." (1974), 39 *Business Quarterly* 77-83 (No. 3) **7896**

Stikeman, Harry Heward. *The Foreign Investment Review Act: The Shape of Things to Come.* Toronto: Richard De Boo, 1974. 74 p. **7897**

Sultan, Ralph G.M. "Canada's Recent Experiment in the Repatriation of American Capital." (1982), 8 *Canadian Public Policy* 498-504. **7898**

Sunil, K.A. *Effect of Foreign Direct Investment on Canada's Balance of Payments, 1950-1965.* Montreal, 1968 (c1969). vii, 192 leaves. **7899**
Half-title: *Direct Investment and Canada's Balance of Payments.* Thesis (M.A.), McGill University, 1969. (National Library of Canada. Canadian Theses on Microfilm, No. 4555).

Tetley, William. "Foreign Investment - A Quebecois Perspective." (1974), 68 *American Society of International Law, Proceedings* 24-27. **7900**

Tremblay, Rodrigue. "Investissements directs étrangers et stratégies industrielles et commerciales: le dilemme canadien." (1972), 48 *Actualité Économique* 226-253. **7901**

U.S. Congress. House. Committee on Energy and Commerce. *Impact of Canadian Investment and Energy Policies on U.S. Commerce: Hearings Before the Subcommittee on Oversight and Investigations and the Subcommittee on Telecommunications, Consumer Protection, and Finance of the Committee on Energy and Commerce, 97th Cong., 1st sess., June 19, July 9, and August 6, 1981.* Washington: Govt. Print. Off., 1981. v, 391 p. (Serial No. 97-41) **7902**

U.S. Congress. Joint Economic Committee. Subcommittee on Inter-American Economic Relationships. *Canadian Foreign Investment Screening Procedures and the Role of Foreign Investment in the Canadian Economy: Hearings, 94th Cong.* Washington: Govt. Print. Off., 1976. iv, 269 p. **7903**
Hearings held December 16, 1975-January 27, 1976.

Wahn, I.G. "Toward Canadian Identity - The Significance of Foreign Investment." (1973), 11 *Osgoode Hall Law Journal* 517-535. **7904**

Walker, R.H.E. "The Carter Revolution: Foreign Investment in Canada." (1967), *Canadian Bar Association, Papers* 183-198. **7905**
Refers to the *Report* of the Royal Commission on Taxation, also known as the *Carter Report.*

Weeks, James K. "The Future of Investment Controls." (1969), 15 *McGill Law Journal* 244-249. **7906**

Wolfe, David A. "Economic Growth and Foreign Investment: A Perspective on Canadian Economic Policy, 1945-1957." (1978-79), 13 *Journal of Canadian Studies* 3-20 (No. 1) **7907**

Wolfe, David A. *Political Culture, Economic Policy and the Growth of Foreign Investment in Canada, 1945-1957.* Ottawa, 1973. iv, 188 leaves. **7908**
Thesis (M.A.), Carleton University, 1973. (National Library of Canada. Canadian Theses on Microfilm, No. 16558).

Wonnacott, Ronald J. "Controlling Trade and Foreign Investment in the Canadian Economy: Some Proposals." (1982), 15 *Canadian Journal of Economics* 567-585. **7909**

E. Multinational and Foreign Corporations

1. GENERAL

Albert, Alain, and Crener, Maxime A. "Stratégie de la firme multinationale: aide liée et cycle de vie du produit." (1975), 6 *Études Internationales* 110-117. **7910**

Angers, François-Albert. "La firme plurinationale et l'état-nation - I." (1970-71), 46 *Actualité Économique* 726-733. **7911**

Armstrong, Jack Irwin. *International Cartels in Modern Industry.* Hamilton, Ont., 1936. 138 leaves. **7912**
Thesis (M.A.), McMaster University, 1936.

Asper, I.H. "The 'Nationality' of Foreign Corporations: The Universal Suez Maritime Canal Company." (1957), 29 *Manitoba Bar News* 71-80. **7913**

Axline, W. Andrew, and Mytelka, Lynn K. "Société multinationale et intégration régionale dans le groupe andin et dans la Communauté des Caraïbes." (1976), 7 *Études Internationales* 163-192. **7914**

Baker, Donald I. "Antitrust Conflicts between Friends: Canada and the United States in the Mid-1970's." (1978), 11 *Cornell International Law Journal* 165-194. **7915**

Baum, Daniel Jay. *The Banks of Canada in the Commonwealth Caribbean: Economic Nationalism and Multinational Enterprises of a Medium Power.* New York: Praeger, 1974. viii, 158 p. (Praeger Special Studies in International Economics and Development) **7916**

Behrman, Jack N. "La firme plurinationale et l'état-nation.-II." (1970-71), 46 *Actualité Économique* 734-751. **7917**

Behrman, Jack N. "Multinational Enterprise: The Way to Economic Internationalism?" (1969), 4 *Journal of Canadian Studies* 12-19 (No. 1) **7918**

Bertin, Gilles. "Expansion à l'étranger et diversification des firmes plurinationales." (1970-71), 46 *Actualité Économique* 637-650. **7919**

Black, Naomi. "Multinational: The World's First Citizens in the Worst Sense." (1973), *International Perspectives* 33-37 (Nov./Dec.) **7920**

Bladen, Vincent W. "Canada and Cartels." (1946), 6 *Behind the Headlines* No. 1 (26 p.) **7921**

Bonin, Bernard. "Attractions Mingled with Fear at Advent of the Multinationals." (1973), *International Perspectives* 37-43 (Nov./Dec.) **7922**

Bonin, Bernard. "La firme plurinationale comme véhicule de transmission internationale de la technologie." (1970-71), 46 *Actualité Économique* 707-725. **7923**

Bright, Christopher R. *International Restrictive Business Practices: A National Legal Response.* Halifax, 1981. v, 396 leaves. **7924**
Thesis (LL.M.), Dalhousie University, 1981.

Burchill, C.S. "The Multi-National Corporation: An Unsolved Problem in International Relations." (1970), 77 *Queen's Quarterly* 3-18. **7925**

Canada. Dept. of Justice. *Canada and International Cartels; An Inquiry into the Nature and Effects of International Cartels and Other Trade Combinations. Report of Commissioner, Combines Investigation Act.* Ottawa: King's Printer, 1945. ix, 72 p. **7926**

F.A. McGregor, Commissioner. Also published in French under title: *Le Canada et les cartels internationaux; enquête sur la nature et les effets des cartels internationaux et autres ententes commerciales.*
Reviews: A.G.B. Fisher in (1946), 22 *International Affairs* 565; C.H. Herbert in (1946), 1 *International Journal* 266-268; Camille Martin in (1946-47), 22 *Actualité Économique* 582-583.

Caron, Yves. "Aspects internationaux de la législation et des précédents judiciaires en matière de pratiques restrictives sur le commerce (anti-trust)." (1966), 1 *Revue Juridique Thémis* 197-232. **7927**

Carstensen, Peter C. "Competition Policy for an Economically Integrated North America." (1981), 44 *Law and Contemporary Problems* 81-103. **7928**

Crener, Maxime A., and Hénault, Georges M. "Administrative Perspective of Transnational Corporations." (1977), *International Perspectives* 18-22 (July/ Aug.) **7929**

Crener, Maxime A., and Hénault, Georges M. "Le rôle paradoxal des entreprises transnationales (ET) dans une ère de tensions protectionnistes." (1977), 8 *Études Internationales* 618-629. **7930**

Crystal, Peter Maurice. *Legal Aspects of Controls on the Entry of U.S. Multinational Companies into the European Economic Community.* Montreal, 1974. vi, 154 leaves. **7931**

Short title: *Legal Controls on Entry of U.S. MNC's into the E.E.C.* Thesis (LL.M.), McGill University, 1974. (National Library of Canada. Canadian Theses on Microfiche, No. 20687).

Deutsch, John J. "International Cartels." (1945), 52 *Canadian Banker* 47-51.
7932

Erriah, Paul Jainarine. *Dependence and Underdevelopment: Multinational Corporations and Economic Nationalism in the Commonwealth Caribbean.* Ottawa, 1976. v, 224 leaves. **7933**
Thesis (M.A.), Carleton University, 1976.

Fatouros, Arghyrios A. "On Domesticating Giants: Further Reflections on the Legal Approach to Transnational Enterprise." (1976), 15 *University of Western Ontario Law Review* 151-177. **7934**

Garnier, Gérard. "Autonomie décisionnelle des filiales françaises d'entreprises américaines multinationales." (1978), 9 *Études Internationales* 214-235. **7935**

Genest, Jean. "Les grandes entreprises internationales." (1972-73), 62 *Action Nationale* 407-431. **7936**

Gordon, Myron J. "A World Scale National Corporation Industrial Strategy." (1978), 4 *Canadian Public Policy* 46-56. **7937**

Gray, Earle. *The Great Uranium Cartel.* Toronto: McClelland and Stewart, c1982. 303 p. **7938**

Guyénot, Jean. *Droit antitrust européen.* Montréal: Presses de l'Université du Québec, 1973. xix, 354 p. **7939**

Hahlo, H.R.; Smith, John Graham; and Wright, Richard W., eds. *Nationalism and the Multinational Enterprise; Legal, Economic and Managerial Aspects.* Leiden: A.W. Sijthoff; Dobbs Ferry, N.Y.: Oceana Publications, 1973. x, 373 p. **7940**

Contains revised and expanded versions of papers presented at an international conference held in Montreal in August, 1971.

Reviews: Maxwell Cohen in (1974), 20 *McGill Law Journal* 330-333; Leon Getz in (1974), 52 *Canadian Bar Review* 486-488; William T. Hunter in (1974), 7 *Canadian Journal of Economics* 348-351; C.S. Kerse in (1975), 13 *Canadian Yearbook of International Law* 450-453; L.P. Singh in (1975), 6 *Études Internationales* 401-402; Bruce W. Wilkinson in (1974), 17 *Canadian Public Administration* 674-676.

Hayashi, Kichiro. "The Role of the Multinational Enterprise in Canada-Japan Relations." *In* Hay, Keith A.J., ed., *Canadian Perspectives on Economic Relations with Japan* (Montreal, 1980), pp. 163-187. **7941**

Haynes, Elliott; Behrman, Jack N.; and Rotstein, Abraham. "The Multi-National Corporation and the Nation State." (1968), 10 *University of Windsor Seminar on Canadian-American Relations, Proceedings* 57-76. **7942**

Helleiner, Gerald K. "Entreprises transnationales, exportations de produits manufacturés et emploi dans les pays moins développés." (1977), 53 *Actualité Économique* 239-279. **7943**

Henry, D.H.W. "Mergers and Joint Ventures as They Affect Canadian-United States Trade Relations - A Look at the Canadian Antitrust Laws." (1966), 32 *Antitrust Law Journal (A.B.A.)* 156-175. **7944**

Henry, D.H.W. "The United States Antitrust Laws: A Canadian Viewpoint." (1970), 8 *Canadian Yearbook of International Law* 249-283. **7945**

Hérisson, Charles-D. "Les migrations internationales d'entreprises américaines ou l'établissement de succursales à l'étranger." (1937-38), 13/1 *Actualité Économique* 117-146. **7946**

Hinnegan, K.A. "The United States Antitrust Doctrine of Potential Competition and Canadian-U.S. Corporate Mergers: The *Labatt-Schlitz* Case." (1968), 7 *Western Ontario Law Review* 60-92. **7947**

Hymer, Stephen. "L'entreprise multinationale." (1971), 2 *Études Internationales* 58-80. **7948**

Hymer, Stephen. "De quelques contradictions relatives à la firme plurinationale et l'efficacité." (1970-71), 46 *Actualité Économique* 651-666. **7949**

Hymer, Stephen, and Rowthorn, Robert. "Les entreprises plurinationales et l'oligopole international: le défi non américain." (1969-70), 45 *Actualité Économique* 639-678. **7950**

Ilersic, A.R. "The Overseas Trade Corporation." (1957), 5 *Canadian Tax Journal* 158-166. **7951**

Ilersic, A.R. "The Overseas Trade Corporation." (1958), 6 *Canadian Tax Journal* 289-293. **7952**

Jain, Jagat Prasad. *The Interface between the Multinational Corporation and the State with Special Reference to Developing Countries.* Thunder Bay, Ont., 1975. vii, 139 leaves. **7953**
Thesis (M.A.), Lakehead University, 1975. (National Library of Canada. Canadian Theses on Microfiche, No. 23678).

Kaufmann, Othmar. "Le contrôle de l'entreprise internationale; l'évolution, des origines à nos jours, du caractère familial du contrôle des entreprises." (1969-70), 45 *Actualité Économique* 780-802. **7954**

Kaufmann, Othmar. "Problèmes structurels de l'internationalisation des entreprises européennes et américaines." (1969-70), 45 *Actualité Économique* 98-104. **7955**

Lavin, Thomas, and Wyatt, Jimmy N. "Concept of Permanent Establishment." (1969), 4 *Revue Juridique Thémis* 219-249. **7956**

Lea, Sperry, and Webley, Simon. *Multinational Corporations in Developed Countries: A Review of Recent Research and Policy Thinking.* London: British-North American Committee, 1973. ix, 77 p. (British-North American Committee. Publications, BN-8) **7957**
Sponsored by the British-North American Research Association, the National Planning Association (U.S.A.), and the C.D. Howe Research Institute (Canada).

Leyton-Brown, David. "Canada, France and Britain as Hosts to Multinationals." (1975), *International Perspectives* 39-43 (Sept./Oct.) **7958**

Leyton-Brown, David. "The Nation-State and Multinational Enterprise: Erosion or Assertion." (1982), 40 *Behind the Headlines* No. 1 (20 p.) **7959**

Litvak, Isaiah A., and Maule, Christopher J. *The Canadian Multinationals.* Toronto: Butterworths, 1981. vii, 184 p. **7960**
Reviews: Edward H. Shaffer in (1982), 8 *Canadian Public Policy* 395-397; Elizabeth Smythe in (1982), 15 *Canadian Journal of Political Science* 622-624.

Litvak, Isaiah A., and Maule, Christopher J. "Canadian Multinationals in the Western Hemisphere." (1975), 40 *Business Quarterly* 30-42 (No. 3) **7961**

Litvak, Isaiah A., and Maule, Christopher J. "Considérations sur la firme plurinationale." (1970-71), 46 *Actualité Économique* 623-636. **7962**

Litvak, Isaiah A., and Maule, Christopher J. "Corporate Metamorphosis: The Case of the Multinational Resource Company." *In* Fry, Michael G., ed., *'Freedom and Change': Essays in Honour of Lester B. Pearson* (Toronto, 1975), pp. 204-241. **7963**

Litvak, Isaiah A., and Maule, Christopher J. "The Multinational Corporation: Some Perspectives." (1970), 13 *Canadian Public Administration* 129-139.
7964

MacLaren, Roy. "A Code of Conduct: First Step in Regulation of Multinationals." (1974), *International Perspectives* 21-24 (May/June) **7965**

Martyn, Howe. "Past Is Future for the Multinational Firm." (1974-75), 54 *Dalhousie Review* 103-111. **7966**

Matthews, Roy A. "The Multinational Corporation and the World of Tomorrow." (1970), 29 *Behind the Headlines* Nos. 3-4, pp. 11-16. **7967**

Matthews, Roy A. "La société plurinationale et le monde de demain." (1970-71), 46 *Actualité Économique* 752-767. **7968**

McDonald, John G. "The Formation and Operation of Foreign Subsidiaries and Branches, Including the Extent to Which Foreign Subsidiaries Are Entitled to Special Treatment under the Law of Their Incorporation or under International Law. II. Canada." (1960-61), 16 *Business Lawyer* 416-450. **7969**

McGurran, H. David. "Overseas Trade Corporations and Foreign Business Corporations." (1957), 5 *Canadian Tax Journal* 323-325. **7970**

McKie, James W. "An Antimonopoly Policy for North America." (1981), 44 *Law and Contemporary Problems* 105-130. **7971**

McManus, John C. "La théorie de l'entreprise plurinationale." (1970-71), 46 *Actualité Économique* 667-690. **7972**

Meredith, Brian. "The Politics of Those Multinational Entities." (1975), *International Perspectives* 43-47 (Sept./Oct.) **7973**

Mikdashi, Zuhayr. "Les industries primaires nationales et la société multinationale: le nouvel environnement international." (1976), 7 *Études Internationales* 67-109. **7974**

Nadelmann, Kurt H. "A Reflection on Bankruptcy Jurisdiction: News from the European Common Market, the United States and Canada." (1982), 27 *McGill Law Journal* 541-555. **7975**

Paquet, Gilles, ed. *The Multinational Firm and the Nation State.* Don Mills, Ont.: Collier-Macmillan Canada, 1972. x, 182 p. **7976**
This is a slightly amended English version of a set of papers presented at a symposium held in Montreal in the Fall of 1969, published in *Actualité Économique,* janvier-mars, 1971.
Review: Harry C. Eastman in (1975), 8 *Canadian Journal of Economics* 127-128.

Pattison, John C. "The Canada Development Corporation." (1971), 5 *Journal of World Trade Law* 461-466. **7977**

Plotkins, Robert Jean. *An Investigation of the Ownership and Control of American Corporations.* Vancouver, 1960. 147 leaves. **7978**
Thesis (M.B.A.), University of British Columbia, 1960.

Popiel, Paul A. "Problèmes structurels dans l'établissement des corporations outre-Atlantique." (1969-70), 45 *Actualité Économique* 499-506. **7979**

Poupart, André. "International Conference on Nationalism and Multi-National Enterprise: Legal, Economic and Managerial Aspects (McGill University)." (1970), 5 *Revue Juridique Thémis* 477-483. **7980**

Roach, E. Hugh. "In Defence of Multinationals: The Myths, the Realities, and the Future." (1976-77), 35 *Behind the Headlines* No. 5 (33 p.) **7981**

Roberts, R. Jack. *Anticombines and Antitrust: The Competition Law of Canada and the Antitrust Law of the United States.* Toronto: Butterworths, 1980. xxx, 799 p. (Canadian Legal Textbook Series) **7982**
Review: Maxwell Cohen in (1982), 27 *McGill Law Journal* 387-392.

Rugman, Alan M. *Inside the Multinationals: The Economics of Internal Markets.* London: C. Helm, c1981. 179 p. **7983**

Rutenberg, David P. "Les avantages de la firme plurinationale." (1970-71), 46 *Actualité Économique* 697-706. **7984**

Safarian, Albert E. "Multinational Policy on Multinational Enterprise." (1978-79), 34 *International Journal* 110-121. **7985**

Safarian, Albert E. "Policy on Multinational Enterprises in Developed Countries." (1978), 11 *Canadian Journal of Economics* 641-655. **7986**

Sobie, Merril. "The Canadian Corporation and Wall Street: Application of United States Securities Laws to Canadian Issuers." (1967), 6 *Western Ontario Law Review* 93-113. **7987**

Stanford, Joseph S. "The Application of the Sherman Act to Conduct Outside the United States: A View from Abroad." (1978), 11 *Cornell International Law Journal* 195-214. **7988**

Stewart, Larry R. "International Cartels and Producer Associations: The Canadian Response." (1981), 61 *Dalhousie Review* 307-324. **7989**

Stone, William Duncan. *Extraterritorial Jurisdiction in the Sphere of Antitrust.* Winnipeg, 1971. v, 287 leaves. **7990**
Thesis (LL.M.), University of Manitoba, 1971.

Susman, A.M. "Diplomatic Protection - Canadian Corporation, Belgian Shareholders - Injury to Corporation's Interests in Spain - Claim by Belgium on Behalf of Shareholders Declared Inadmissible - *Barcelona Traction, Light and Power Company Ltd., Belgium v. Spain.* (Case Note)." (1971), 12 *Harvard International Law Journal* 91-120. **7991**

Zorbas, Basil. *International Licensing Agreements: Antitrust Considerations in the United States, the European Economic Community and Canada.* Toronto, 1976. iv, 203 leaves. **7992**
Thesis (LL.M.), University of Toronto, 1976.

2. FOREIGN CORPORATIONS IN CANADA

See also *"Foreign Investment in Canada" (p. 589).*

Antonides, Harry. *Multinationals and the Peaceable Kingdom.* Toronto: Clarke, Irwin, 1978. 235 p. **7993**
Reviews: Frank De Walle in (1979), 37 *University of Toronto Faculty of Law Review* 271-273; Bruce W. Wilkinson in (1979), 5 *Canadian Public Policy* 578-579.

Armstrong, Willis C. "Thoughts on Canadian Subsidiaries." (1960), 2 *University of Windsor Seminar on Canadian-American Relations, Proceedings* 55-62. **7994**

Bement, Kenneth. "Do American Subsidiary Firms Make Good Canadian Citizens?" (1963), 5 *University of Windsor Seminar on Canadian-American Relations, Proceedings* 176-179. **7995**

Bertrand, R.J. "Canadian Competition Policy Developments and the Multinational." *In* Hawk, Barry E., ed., *International Antitrust* (New York, 1975), pp. 285-299. **7996**

Bonin, Bernard. "Multinational Firms: The Canadian-U.S. Case." (1972), 1 *Journal of Contemporary Business* 19-31 (No. 4)   **7997**

Capon, Frank S. "Problems of Canadian Subsidiaries." (1961), 3 *University of Windsor Seminar on Canadian-American Relations, Proceedings* 105-112.
    7998

Carlisle, Arthur Elliott. *Cultures in Collision: U.S. Corporate Policy and Canadian Subsidiaries.* Ann Arbor: University of Michigan, 1967. xviii, 162 p.   **7999**
A revision of the author's thesis, University of Michigan, 1966.

Clement, Wallace. "Canada and Multinational Corporations: An Overview." In Glenday, Daniel, ed., *Modernization and the Canadian State* (Toronto, 1978), pp. 18-35.   **8000**

Clement, Wallace. *Continental Corporate Power: Economic Elite Linkages between Canada and the United States.* Toronto: McClelland and Stewart, 1977. 408 p.   **8001**
Reviews: John Fayerweather in (1977-78), 33 *International Journal* 464-465; Charles J. McMillan in (1978), 4 *Canadian Public Policy* 409-410; Harvey Rich in (1978), 21 *Canadian Public Administration* 285-289.

Cordell, Arthur J. *The Multinational Firm, Foreign Direct Investment and Canadian Science Policy.* Ottawa: Information Canada, 1971. 95 p. (Science Council of Canada. Special Study, No. 22)   **8002**
At head of title: *Background Study for the Science Council of Canada.*

Crookell, Harold, and Wrigley, Leonard. "Canadian Response to Multinational Enterprise." (1975), 40 *Business Quarterly* 58-65 (No. 1)   **8003**

Etheridge, G.T. "Canadian and American Viewpoints on Problems of Canadian Subsidiaries." (1961), 3 *University of Windsor Seminar on Canadian-American Relations, Proceedings* 113-118.   **8004**

"Extraterritoriality and the Canadian Oil Industry / L'extraterritorialité et l'industrie pétrolière canadienne." (1981), 10 *Canadian Council on International Law, Proceedings,* 85-116.   **8005**
This is a panel. Chairman: Ivan Bernier.
Contents: "Extraterritoriality and the Canadian Oil and Gas Industry," by R.W. Burchill (pp. 85-88).- "Extraterritoriality and the Canadian Oil Industry," by D.W. MacPharlane (pp. 89-104).- Discussion (pp. 105-116).

Farnell, Werner. "American Viewpoints on the Problems of Canadian Subsidiaries." (1961), 3 *University of Windsor Seminar on Canadian-American Relations, Proceedings* 119-126.   **8006**

Feltham, Ivan R., and Rauenbusch, William R. *Multinational Enterprises in Canada: Foreign-Owned Enterprises in Canada.* Toronto: Osgoode Hall Law School of York University, 1971. 109 p.   **8007**
This is a paper prepared for the International Conference on Nationalism and the Multinational Enterprise: Legal, Economic and Managerial Aspects, held at McGill University, August 23-25, 1971.

Filion, Gérard. "L'influence des firmes américaines sur l'économie canadienne et particulièrement celle du Québec." (1973), 11 *Royal Society of Canada, Transactions* 65-73 (4th Ser.)   **8008**

Freeman, Susan. "Canada's Changing Posture Toward Multinational Corporations: An Attempt to Harmonize Nationalism with Continued Industrial Growth." (1974), 7 *New York University Journal of International Law and Politics* 271-315. **8009**

Garnier, Gérard. "Le Canada et l'entreprise américaine à ramifications internationales." (1971), 2 *Annales d'Études Internationales* 147-179. **8010**

Garnier, Gérard. "Les entreprises multinationales et l'indépendance éventuelle du Québec." (1979), 5 *Canadian Public Policy* 59-69. **8011**

Garnier, Gérard. "Facteurs influant sur le partage de la prise de décision entre maisons mères américaines et leurs filiales du Québec." (1974), 5 *Études Internationales* 72-122. **8012**

Garnier, Gérard. "Pouvoirs de décision des filiales québécoises d'entreprises américaines." (1971), 2 *Études Internationales* 11-43. **8013**

Globerman, Steven. *U.S. Ownership of Firms in Canada: Issues and Policy Approaches.* Montreal: C.D. Howe, 1979. vii, 96 p. (Canada-U.S. Prospects) **8014**
Sponsored by the C.D. Howe Research Institute (Canada), and the National Planning Association (U.S.A.).
Reviews: James B. Harries in (1980), 13 *Canadian Journal of Economics* 525-528; William C. Wedley in (1980), 6 *Canadian Public Policy* 411.

Hahlo, H.R. "Fiscalité des entreprises multinationales au Canada." (1973), 8 *Revue Juridique Thémis* 297-303. **8015**

Hitchin, David Edward. *Canadianization of United States-Controlled Corporations in Canada: Authority Relationships and Conflict Resolution.* Los Angeles, 1965 (c1966). xv, 235 leaves. **8016**
Thesis (Ph.D.), University of California, 1965. Abstracted in (1966), 26 *Dissertation Abstracts* 3675. (University Microfilms, Ann Arbor, No. 65-12652).

Hunt, Louise M. *Concentration and Foreign Control in Canadian Manufacturing.* Halifax, 1978. 141 frames. **8017**
Thesis (M.A.), Dalhousie University, 1978. (National Library of Canada. Canadian Theses on Microfiche, No. 44255).

Jackson, Eric, ed. *The Great Canadian Debate: Foreign Ownership.* Toronto: McClelland and Stewart, c1975. 64 p. (Foundations of Contemporary Canada Series) **8018**
A Canada Studies Foundation project.

Kates, Peat, Marwick & Co. *Foreign Ownership: Corporate Behaviour and Public Attitudes; Overview Report.* Toronto: Select Committee on Economic and Cultural Nationalism of the Legislative Assembly of Ontario, 1974. viii, 239 p. **8019**
Prepared for the Select Committee on Economic and Cultural Nationalism of the Legislative Assembly, Province of Ontario.

Kierans, Eric W. "Canadian and American Viewpoints on Problems of Canadian Subsidiaries." (1961), 3 *University of Windsor Seminar on Canadian-American Relations, Proceedings* 127-135. **8020**

Lank, Herbert. "Do American Subsidiary Firms Make Good Canadian Citizens?"

(1963), 5 *University of Windsor Seminar on Canadian-American Relations, Proceedings* 180-184. **8021**

Larkin, Ronald Hughes. *A Study of the Acquisition of Canadian Firms During the Period 1954-1967.* Kingston, 1974 (c1975). v, 143 leaves. **8022**

Half-title: *Acquisition of Canadian Firms.* Thesis (M.A.), Queen's University, 1974. (National Library of Canada. Canadian Theses on Microfiche, No. 22481).

Levin, Malcolm A., and Sylvester, Christine. *Foreign Ownership.* With the assistance of Paula Bourne and Marion Harris. Don Mills, Ont.: PaperJacks, c1962. 109 p. (Canadian Critical Issues Series) **8023**

Levitt, Kari. *Silent Surrender: The Multinational Corporation in Canada.* With a Preface by Mel Watkins. Toronto: Macmillan of Canada, c1970. xxi, 185 p. **8024**

Also published New York, Liveright, 1971. Translated into French by André d'Allemagne under title: *La capitulation tranquille: les multinationales, pouvoir politique parallèle?* (Montréal, Éditions l'Étincelle, c1972. xliii, 220 p.)
Reviews: David J. Bellamy in (1971), 4 *Canadian Journal of Political Science* 421-422; Isaiah A. Litvak in (1972), 5 *Canadian Journal of Economics* 451-453; Joseph Wearing under title: "Foreign Ownership: The True North Strong and Fettered," in (1972), 7 *Journal of Canadian Studies* 51-58 (No. 1); Paul Wonnacott in a review article under title: "United States Investment in the Canadian Economy," in (1971-72), 27 *International Journal* 276, 283-284.

Leyton-Brown, David. "Canada and Multinational Enterprise." *In* Hillmer, Norman, and Stevenson, Garth, eds., *A Foremost Nation: Canadian Foreign Policy and a Changing World* (Toronto, 1977), pp. 63-84. **8025**

Leyton-Brown, David. "Extraterritoriality in Canadian-American Relations." (1980-81), 36 *International Journal* 185-207. **8026**

Leyton-Brown, David. "The Multinational Enterprise and Conflict in Canadian-American Relations." (1974), 28 *International Organization* 733-754. **8027**

Reprinted in Fox, Annette Baker, and others, *Canada and the United States* (New York, 1976), pp. 140-161.

Litvak, Isaiah A.; and Maule, Christopher J. "Canadian-United States Corporate Interface and Transnational Relations." (1974), 28 *International Organization* 711-731. **8028**

Reprinted in Fox, Annette Baker, and others, *Canada and the United States* (New York, 1976), pp. 119-139.

Litvak, Isaiah A.; Maule, Christopher J.; and Robinson, Richard D. *Dual Loyalty: Canadian-U.S. Business Arrangements.* Toronto, New York: McGraw-Hill of Canada, 1971. xi, 242 p. **8029**

Review: Paul Wonnacott in a review article under title: "United States Investment in the Canadian Economy," in (1971-72), 27 *International Journal* 276, 280-282.

Macaulay, Robert. "Do American Subsidiary Firms Make Good Canadian Citizens?" (1963), 5 *University of Windsor Seminar on Canadian-American Relations, Proceedings* 185-194. **8030**

Marchak, M. Patricia. *In Whose Interests: An Essay on Multinational Corporations in a Canadian Context.* Toronto: McClelland and Stewart, 1979. 317 p. Review: Alan S. Alexandroff in (1980), 6 *Canadian Public Policy* 694-696. **8031**

Marshall, Herbert, and others. *Canadian-American Industry: A Study in International Investment.* Toronto: McClelland and Stewart, c1976. xiii, 360 p., maps. (Carleton Library, No. 93) **8032**
First published New Haven, Yale University Press; Toronto, Ryerson Press, 1936.
Reviews: George Alexander Elliott in (1936), 2 *Canadian Journal of Economics and Political Science* 237-239; W.A. Mackintosh in (1936), 17 *Canadian Historical Review* 459; W.A. Mackintosh in (1936-37), 43 *Queen's Quarterly* 335-336.

Mattson, Lawrence Garfield. *The Historic Continentalist-Nationalist Debate and the American Corporation in Canada: Their Relationship in Current Canadian Controversy over American Corporations.* Claremont, Calif., 1976. 227 leaves. **8033**
Thesis (Ph.D.), Claremont Graduate School, 1976. Abstracted in (1976), 37 *Dissertation Abstracts International* 444-A. (University Microfilms, Ann Arbor, No. 76-15772).

McDougall, John N. *The National Energy Board and Multinational Corporations: The Politics of Pipe Lines and Natural Gas Exports, 1960-1971.* Edmonton, 1975. xii, 236 leaves. **8034**
Thesis (Ph.D.), University of Alberta, 1975. (National Library of Canada. Canadian Theses on Microfiche, No. 24088).

Murray, J. Alex, and Gerace, Mary C. "Multinational Business and Canadian Government Affairs." (1973), 80 *Queen's Quarterly* 222-232. **8035**

Patton, Donald J. *The Effect of Foreign Ownership and Control on Government-Business Relations in the Host Country: The Petroleum and Natural Gas Industry in Canada.* Bloomington, Ind., 1972 (c1973). x, 235 leaves, maps. **8036**
Thesis (D.B.A.), Indiana University, 1973. Abstracted in (1974), 34 *Dissertation Abstracts International* 4502-A. (University Microfilms, Ann Arbor, No. 74-2295).

Pikna, Raymond J., Jr. "The Uranium Cartel Saga - Yellowcake and Act of State: What Will Be Their Eventual Fate?" (1980), 12 *Case Western Reserve Journal of International Law* 591-639. **8037**

Rankin, Murray T. "The Supreme Court of Canada and the International Uranium Cartel: Gulf Oil and Canadian Sovereignty." (1981), 2 *Supreme Court Law Review* 411-430. **8038**

Rathwell, John H.W. "Problems Related to the Registration in Western Canada of Foreign Limited Partnerships and the Ownership by Such Partnerships of Interests in Oil and Gas Leases Issued Pursuant to Section 55 of the Canada Oil and Gas Land Regulations." (1972), 10 *Alberta Law Review* 477-486. **8039**

Renwick, James A. "Legal and Other Problems of Foreign Direct Investment in Canada for the Purpose of Establishing a Manufacturing Operation." (1958), *Canadian Bar Association, Papers* 122-138. **8040**

"Rights and Liabilities of Foreign Insurance Companies in Canada." (1906), 5 *Canadian Law Review* 249-259. **8041**

Rugman, Alan M. *Multinationals in Canada: Theory, Performance, and Economic Impact.* Foreword by A.E. Safarian. Boston: M. Nijhoff, c1980. xvi, 197 p. **8042**
Review: Lorraine Eden in (1982), 15 *Canadian Journal of Economics* 562-566.

Safarian, Albert E. "Canada's Domestic Concerns - National Unity and Foreign 'Control': Foreign Investment in Primary Industries." (1976), 32 *Academy of Political Science, Proceedings* 75-87 (No. 2) **8043**

Safarian, Albert E. "Foreign Ownership and Control of Canadian Industry." *In* Rotstein, Abraham, ed., *The Prospect of Change: Proposals for Canada's Future* (Toronto, 1965), pp. 220-244. **8044**

Safarian, Albert E. "Foreign Ownership and Industrial Behavior: A Comment on 'The Weakest Link.' " (1979), 5 *Canadian Public Policy* 318-335. **8045**

Safarian, Albert E. *Foreign Ownership of Canadian Industry.* Toronto: McGraw-Hill of Canada, c1966. xiv, 346 p. **8046**
Reviews: Douglas Copland in (1968-69), 24 *International Journal* 192-194; Craufurd D. Goodwin in (1967), 33 *Canadian Journal of Economics and Political Science* 463-466; H. Clare Pentland under title: "Canada 1967: Nation Subsidiary?," in (1967), 48 *Canadian Historical Review* 365-369.

Safarian, Albert E. *Foreign Ownership of Canadian Industry.* 2d ed. Toronto: University of Toronto Press, 1973. xl, 346 p. (Canadian University Paperbooks, 138) **8047**
Review: Jean Taillon in (1974), 5 *Études Internationales* 717-718.

Safarian, Albert E. "The Task Force Report on Foreign Ownership." (1968), 3 *Journal of Canadian Studies* 50-56 (No. 3) **8048**
Refers to the Gordon Report.

Sherk, Frank. "Do American Subsidiary Firms Make Good Canadian Citizens?" (1963), 5 *University of Windsor Seminar on Canadian-American Relations, Proceedings* 195-204. **8049**

Warner, Malcolm, and Peccei, Riccardo. "Towards 'Participative' Multinationals." (1977), 32 *Relations Industrielles* 172-181. **8050**
Contains a summary in French under title: "Syndicats et multinationales" (pp. 182-183).

Wells, Donald Mclean. *American Multinational Corporations in Canada: Unchallenged Agents of Empire.* Vancouver, 1972. ii, 127 leaves. **8051**
Thesis (M.A.), University of British Columbia, 1972.

Whitham, W.B. "Les investissements américains et les origines de l'industrie pétrolière canadienne." (1968-69), 44 *Actualité Économique* 689-710. **8052**

Williams, W.E. "Problems of Canadian Subsidiaries." (1961), 3 *University of Windsor Seminar on Canadian-American Relations, Proceedings* 136-143. **8053**

Yohe, Robert. "Do American Subsidiary Firms Doing Business in Canada Make Good Canadian Citizens?" (1963), 5 *University of Windsor Seminar on Canadian-American Relations, Proceedings* 205-213. **8054**

F. Nationalization and Expropriation

Berezowski, Cesar. "Quelques aspects internationaux des actes de nationalisation." (1961), 11 *Thémis* 137-147. **8055**

Challies, George Swan. *The Law of Expropriation.* 2d ed. Montreal: Wilson & Lafleur, 1963. xiv, 630 p. **8056**

Dorion, Guy, and Savard, Roger. *Loi commentée de l'expropriation du Québec.* Québec: Presses de l'Université Laval, 1979. xii, 398 p. (Bibliothèque juridique, D-1) **8057**

Giroux, Lorne. "L'expropriation en droit québécois." (1979-80), 10 *Revue de Droit, Université de Sherbrooke* 629-663. **8058**

Harding, John G. "The Nationalization of Canadian Property in Cuba under International Law." (1963), 2 *Western Law Review* 50-63. **8059**

Lajoie, Andrée. *Expropriation et fédéralisme au Canada.* Montréal: Presses de l'Université de Montréal, 1972. xii, 328 p. (Collection Centre de recherche en droit public) **8060**
Reviews: Albert S. Abel in (1972), 7 *Revue Juridique Thémis* 410-412; François Chevrette in (1974), 7 *Canadian Journal of Political Science* 174-177; David Matas in (1973), 19 *McGill Law Journal* 449-452.

Lee, Edward G. "Proposal for the Alleviation of the Effects of Foreign Expropriatory Decrees upon International Investments." (1958), 36 *Canadian Bar Review* 351-359. **8061**

Leermakers, Dirk J. *Compensation for the Expropriation of Alien Property in International Law.* Montreal, 1979. 268 frames. **8062**
Thesis (LL.M.), McGill University, 1979. (National Library of Canada. Canadian Theses on Microfiche, No. 50485).

Manzig, John G.W. *Nationalization under Public International Law and British and Canadian Private International Law.* Halifax, 1968. iv, 197 leaves. **8063**
Thesis (LL.M.), Dalhousie University, 1968.

Mendes, Errol P. "The Canadian National Energy Program: An Example of Assertion of Economic Sovereignty or Creeping Expropriation in International Law." (1981), 14 *Vanderbilt Journal of Transnational Law* 475-507. **8064**

Molot, Maureen Appel, and Laux, Jeanne Kirk. "The Politics of Nationalization." (1979), 12 *Canadian Journal of Political Science* 227-258. **8065**

Srebrnik, Henry Felix. *The Cuban Revolution and the United States: The Case of the Nationalization Procedures, 1959-1960.* Montreal, 1970. iii, 272 leaves. **8066**
Thesis (M.A.), McGill University, 1970. (National Library of Canada. Canadian Theses on Microfilm, No. 5966).

Todd, Eric C.E. *The Law of Expropriation and Compensation in Canada.* Toronto: Carswell, 1976. xxxii, 440 p. **8067**

G. International Finance (Foreign Exchange, Etc.)

Adede, A.O. "Approaches to Bilateral Loan Agreements between Developed and Developing States: Some Lessons from the Practice of Denmark, the United Kingdom and the United States." (1979), 5 *Dalhousie Law Journal* 121-153.
8068

Altman, Oscar L. "Euro-Dollars." (1966), 73 *Canadian Banker* 71-80 (No. 2)
8069

Atala, Charles. *De Bretton Woods à Watergate: où va la monnaie?* Montréal: Leméac, c1973. 244 p. (Dossiers Interlex)
8070

Avison, T.L. "American Dollars Are Hard to Get: The Story of Foreign Exchange Control in Canada." (1940-41), 1 *Behind the Headlines* No. 6 (19 p.)
8071

Avison, T.L. "The Canadian Foreign Exchange Control Board." (1940), 6 *Canadian Journal of Economics and Political Science* 56-60.
8072

Bertin, Gilles. "Nouvelles puissances financières et centres de pouvoir." (1979), 10 *Études Internationales* 719-736.
8073

Blyth, C.D. "Some Aspects of Canada's International Financial Relations." (1946), 12 *Canadian Journal of Economics and Political Science* 302-312.
8074

Bouchette, R.S.M. "Unification internationale des monnaies." (1872), 9 *Revue Canadienne* 96-107.
8075
Paper presented at the meeting of the 'Institut-Canadien-Français' of Ottawa on November 29, 1871; refers to the monetary convention of December 23, 1865, between France, Belgium, Italy and Switzerland (56 BFSP 207; 132 Parry 9).

Cameron, Duncan Charles. "Le Fonds monétaire international, la réforme monétaire et le tiers-monde." (1979), 55 *Actualité Économique* 28-45.
8076

Cameron, Duncan Charles. "The Reform of International Money." (1978-79), 34 *International Journal* 90-109.
8077

Cameron, Duncan Charles. "Special Drawing Rights." (1980-81), 36 *International Journal* 713-731.
8078

Cameron, Duncan Charles. *Le système monétaire international en voie de réforme: les travaux du Comité des vingt.* Ottawa: Éditions de l'Université d'Ottawa, 1977. xiii, 173 p. (Collection des sciences sociales, no 6)
8079
Reviews: Bernard Decaluwé in (1979), 5 *Canadian Public Policy* 137-138; Roger Dehem in (1979), 10 *Études Internationales* 191-192; Denys Laliberté in (1978), 11 *Canadian Journal of Political Science* 687-688.

Cameron, Duncan Charles, and Saint-Germain, Maurice. "Vers un nouvel équilibre monétaire international: un colloque du 46e Congrès de l'ACFAS." (1979), 55 *Actualité Économique* 5-10.
8080

Cechetto, Seth M. *A Comparative Analysis of the Internationalization of United States and Canadian Banks.* Ottawa, 1979. xi, 224 leaves.
8081
Thesis (M.A.), Carleton University, 1979. (National Library of Canada. Canadian Theses on Microfiche, No. 41661).

Clark, E.R. "Canada's Foreign Exchange Problem." (1940-41), 48 *Canadian Banker* 311-324. **8082**

Clayton, G. "The Development of British Exchange Control 1939-45." (1953), 19 *Canadian Journal of Economics and Political Science* 161-173. **8083**

Clendenning, E. Wayne. *The Euro-Currency Markets and the International Activities of Canadian Banks.* Ottawa: Economic Council of Canada, 1977 (c1976). viii, 150 p. **8084**
Also issued in French under title: *Le marché des eurodevises et l'activité internationale des banques canadiennes.*
Review: Ronald A. Shearer in (1977), 3 *Canadian Public Policy* 547-548.

Decaluwé, Bernard. "Quelques enseignements récents de la réforme du système monétaire international." (1979), 55 *Actualité Économique* 18-28. **8085**

Dehem, Roger. "Le mythe de la réforme monétaire internationale." (1972), 3 *Études Internationales* 390-397. **8086**

Dehem, Roger. "Les politiques monétaires." *In* Painchaud, Paul, ed., *Le Canada et le Québec sur la scène internationale* (Québec, 1977), pp. 197-208. **8087**

Dow, Sheila C. *International Monetary Reform and the Distribution of Centrally Created Reserves.* Winnipeg, 1973 (c1974). xii, 140 leaves. **8088**
Thesis (M.A.), University of Manitoba, 1973. (National Library of Canada. Canadian Theses on Microfiche, No. 17304).

Dunn, Robert M., Jr. *The Canada-U.S. Capital Market: Intermediation, Integration and Policy Independence.* Montreal: C.D. Howe Research Institute; Washington: National Planning Association, 1978. viii, 139 p. (Canada-U.S. Prospects, 2) **8089**

"Foreign Currency Transactions: Business and Accounting Aspects." (1978), 30 *Canadian Tax Foundation, Proceedings* 338-358, 490-546. **8090**
This is a panel presented during the thirtieth annual conference of the Canadian Tax Foundation held at Montreal, November 21, 1978.

Frenkel, Jacob A., and Johnson, Harry G., eds. *The Monetary Approach to the Balance of Payments.* Toronto: University of Toronto Press, 1976. 388 p.
8091
Also published London, Allen & Unwin, 1976, and in 1977 as Canadian University Paperbooks, 188.

Friedman, Kenneth J. "The 1980 Canadian Banks and Banking Law Revision Act: Competitive Stimulus or Protectionist Barrier?" (1981), 13 *Law and Policy in International Business* 783-810. **8092**

Galbraith, John Alexander. *Foreign Exchange and Foreign Currency in Canadian Banking.* Don Mills, Ont.: Collier-Macmillan Canada, 1972. 10 p. (Canadian Perspectives in Economics, D4) **8093**

Gardner, William R. *Canada's Postwar Balance of Payments and Exchange Problems.* Eugene, Oreg., 1956. 195 leaves. **8094**
Thesis, University of Oregon, 1956.

Gauthier, Gilles. "À propos de l'Union monétaire anglo-irlandaise." (1979), 55 *Actualité Économique* 262-266. **8095**

Germain, Claude. "La balance des paiements internationaux du Canada." (1960-61), 36 *Actualité Économique* 420-447. **8096**

Gibbons, Alan O. "Foreign Exchange Control in Canada, 1939-51." (1953), 19 *Canadian Journal of Economics and Political Science* 35-54. **8097**

Glazier, Kenneth M. "Banks in Canadian-American Relations." (1979), 10 *Canadian Review of American Studies* 371-377. **8098**

Granatstein, J.L. "The Road to Bretton Woods: International Monetary Policy and the Public Servant." (1981-82), 16 *Journal of Canadian Studies* 174-185. **8099**

Grjébine, André. "Le pouvoir monétaire international: le statut international d'une monnaie est-il un instrument de puissance ou un facteur de fragilité?" (1979), 10 *Études Internationales* 669-717. **8100**

Gupta, Sanjeev. *International Monetary System - Problems and Solutions.* Fredericton, 1977 (c1978). v, 61 leaves. **8101**
Thesis (M.A.), University of New Brunswick, 1977. (National Library of Canada. Canadian Theses on Microfiche, No. 35585).

Herring, Richard John. *International Financial Integration: Capital Flows and Interest Rate Relationships among Six Industrial Nations.* Princeton, N.J., 1973. xv, 331 leaves. **8102**
Thesis (Ph.D.), Princeton University, 1973. Abstracted in (1974), 34 *Dissertation Abstracts International* 4517-A. (University Microfilms, Ann Arbor, No. 74-2334).

Hirschberg, Eliyahu. "Gold Value Clauses and Flight from Currency." (1979), 27 *Chitty's Law Journal* 265-267. **8103**

Hood, William C. "Reflections on the International Monetary System." (1970), 3 *Canadian Journal of Economics* 525-540. **8104**
Contains a résumé in French under title: "Réflexions sur le système monétaire international."

Kertudo, Jean. *Le problème des liquidités internationales de 1958 à 1972.* Montréal, 1973 (c1974). 97, (11) leaves. **8105**
Thesis (M.A.), McGill University, 1974. (National Library of Canada. Canadian Theses on Microfiche, No. 20750).

Kiddy, Arthur W. "The Problem of International Indebtedness." (1921-22), 29 *Journal of the Canadian Bankers' Association* 137-149. **8106**

Kokas, Louis. "Des créances envers l'étranger et de leurs garanties." (1953-54), 29 *Actualité Économique* 696-726. **8107**

Langevin, Pierre. "Le mécanisme du marché de l'euro-dollar et la crise monétaire de mai 1971." (1972), 5 *Revue de l'Université de Moncton* 29-40 (no 2) **8108**

Lee, Boyden Edward. *Canada and the Euro-Dollar Market.* Calgary, 1969. 99 leaves. **8109**
Thesis (M.A.), University of Calgary, 1969. (National Library of Canada. Canadian Theses on Microfilm, No. 4031).

Lelart, Michel. "La mise en place du système monétaire européen." (1979), 55 *Actualité Économique* 568-584. **8110**

Leroy, Vély. "Un résumé des lignes de force du système monétaire international actuel." (1979), 55 *Actualité Économique* 11-17. **8111**

Malach, Vernon W. "The Mechanism of Adjustment in Canada's Balance of Payments, 1921-9." (1952), 18 *Canadian Journal of Economics and Political Science* 303-321. **8112**

McMyn, James. "Trading Foreign Currencies Spells Occupational Hazard." (1974), 81 *Canadian Banker and ICB Review* 18-22 (No. 4) **8113**

Montpetit, Édouard. "Les engagements internationaux et leurs procédés de liquidation." (1923), 9 *Revue Trimestrielle Canadienne* 225-237. **8114**

Montpetit, Édouard. "Le mécanisme du change international." (1919), 5 *Revue Trimestrielle Canadienne* 349-373. **8115**

Morrissette, France. "Le problème de la dette des pays en développement." (1981), 19 *Canadian Yearbook of International Law* 50-131. **8116**
Abridged version of the author's doctoral dissertation, Aix-en-Provence, 1979 (472 leaves).

Mundell, Robert Alexander. *The International Monetary System; Conflict and Reform.* Montreal: Canadian Trade Committee, Private Planning Association of Canada, 1965. ix, 65 p. **8117**

Murphy, Lawrence J. "Recent Developments in Canada's Balance of Payments." (1977), 4 *Canadian Business Review* 32-36 (No. 3) **8118**

Murray, John David. *Tax Differentials and International Capital Flows: The Canadian-United States Experience.* Princeton, N.J., 1978. x, 184 leaves. **8119**
Thesis (Ph.D.), Princeton University, 1978. Abstracted in (1978), 38 *Dissertation Abstracts International* 7470-A. (University Microfilms, Ann Arbor, No. 78-7487).

Nappi, Carmine. "La réforme du système monétaire international: une chronologie et interprétation des événements." (1978), 54 *Actualité Économique* 263-285. **8120**

Ogram, Ernest William. *Canada's Post-War Balance of Payments Adjustments, 1946-1954.* Urbana, Ill., 1957. 226 leaves. **8121**
Thesis, University of Illinois, 1957. Abstracted in (1958), 18 *Dissertation Abstracts* 451. (University Microfilms, Ann Arbor, No. 25263).

Parkinson, Joseph Frederick, ed. *Canadian Investment and Foreign Exchange Problems.* Toronto: University of Toronto Press, 1940. ix, 292 p. (Political Economy Series, No. 6) **8122**
Reviews: T.L. Avison in (1941), 7 *Canadian Journal of Economics and Political Science* 129-130; S. Bates in (1940-41), 20 *Dalhousie Review* 381-382.

Parsy, Luc. *L'impact du marché de l'eurodollar sur la politique monétaire canadienne.* Montréal, 1974. vii, 108 leaves. **8123**
Thesis (M.Sc.), Université de Montréal, 1974.

Pestieau, Caroline. *A Balance of Payments Handbook.* Montreal: Canadian-American Committee, 1974. xiii, 125 p. (Canadian-American Committee. Publications, CAC 38) **8124**

Plumptre, A.F.W. *Three Decades of Decision: Canada and the World Monetary*

System, 1944-75. Toronto: McClelland and Stewart, c1977. xvi, 335 p., 4 leaves of plates. **8125**
Reviews: J.R. Beattie in (1979), 60 *Canadian Historical Review* 112-115; Arthur Blanchette in (1978), *International Perspectives* 31-32 (Sept./Oct.); John C. Pattison in (1978), *Canadian Public Policy* 269-270; W.M. Scammell in (1978-79), 34 *International Journal* 134-135.

Presley, John R., and Dennis, Geoffrey Edwin James. *Currency Areas: Theory and Practice.* Toronto: Macmillan of Canada: Maclean-Hunter Press, c1976. 114 p. Published simultaneously in Great Britain. **8126**

Robertson, Matthew Joseph. *Monetary Policy and the Balance of International Payments.* Hamilton, Ont., 1966. viii, 125 leaves. **8127**
Thesis (M.A.), McMaster University, 1966.

Robinson, H. Lukin. *Canada's Crippled Dollar: An Analysis of International Trade and Our Troubled Balance of Payments.* Toronto: James Lorimer, 1980. 204 p. (Canadian Institute for Economic Policy Series) **8128**
Review: Herbert G. Grubel in (1980), 6 *Canadian Public Policy* 704-706.

Robinson, J. Michael. "Some Legal Problems and Issues Raised by the Recirculation of Petrodollars by Private Lenders." (1979), 8 *Canadian Council on International Law, Proceedings* 173-188. **8129**

Rogstad, Barry Kent. *Long Run International Capital Movements; Impact on the Canadian Economy.* Providence, R.I., 1968 (c1969). vii, 177 leaves. **8130**
Thesis, Brown University, 1968. Abstracted in (1969), 30 *Dissertation Abstracts International* 25-A. (University Microfilms, Ann Arbor, No. 69-10004).

Rolfe, John. "Canadian Euro-Dollar Market Dealers." (1971), 78 *Canadian Banker* 31-33 (No. 3) **8131**

Roome, A.I. "Foreign Exchange." (1966), 73 *Canadian Banker* 19-29 (No. 3) **8132**

Sandwell, B.K. "Canada and the British Loan." (1930), 37 *Queen's Quarterly* 241-246. **8133**

Scammell, W.M. *International Monetary Policy: Bretton Woods and After.* New York: Wiley, 1975. vi, 262 p. (Halsted Press Book) **8134**

Scott, H.D. "Foreign Exchange - Control and Free." (1939-40), 47 *Canadian Banker* 457-463. **8135**

Shearer, Ronald A. "The Continuing International Monetary Crisis: A British Columbia Perspective." (1972), 13 *B.C. Studies* 16-30. **8136**

Shepherd, Sidney A. *Foreign Exchange and Foreign Trade in Canada: An Outline.* 4th ed. Toronto: University of Toronto Press, 1973. xii, 336 p. **8137**
Previous editions published under title: *Foreign Exchange in Canada: An Outline.*

Shepherd, Sidney A. *Foreign Exchange and Foreign Trade in Canada: An Outline of Principles and Precedents.* 5th ed. Victoria, B.C.: Sono Nis Press, c1980. ix, 415 p. **8138**

Shepherd, Sidney A. "Foreign Exchange in Canada." (1959), 66 *Canadian Banker* 38-43 (No. 3) **8139**

Shepherd, Sidney A. *Foreign Exchange in Canada: An Outline.* Toronto: University of Toronto Press, 1953 (i.e. 1954). 232 p. **8140**
Reviews: J.S.M. Allely in (1954), 20 *Canadian Journal of Economics and Political Science* 384-386; Clarence L. Barber in (1954-55), 10 *International Journal* 143-144.

Shepherd, Sidney A. *Foreign Exchange in Canada: An Outline.* Rev. ed. Toronto: University of Toronto Press, c1958. 232 p. **8141**
Review: Jean Mehling in (1958-59), 34 *Actualité Économique* 498-499.

Shepherd, Sidney A. *Foreign Exchange in Canada: An Outline.* 3d ed. Toronto: University of Toronto Press, 1961. 267 p. **8142**

Shepherd, Sidney A. "Foreign Exchange in Canada - Now." (1963), 70 *Canadian Banker* 26-35 (No. 3) **8143**

Slater, David W. "Canada's Foreign Exchange Rates." (1962), 69 *Canadian Banker* 5-25 (No. 2) **8144**

Slater, David W. "Capital Flows, International Liquidity and Recent Changes in International Money Relationships." (1962), 69 *Canadian Banker* 5-19 (No. 4) **8145**

Slater, David W. "International Monetary Arrangements: The Most Recent Two Years of Events, Studies and Talks - A Review." (1965), 72 *Canadian Banker* 5-17 (No. 4) **8146**

Strange, Susan. "The World's Money: Expanding the Agenda for Research." (1980-81), 36 *International Journal* 691-712. **8147**

Tarr, R.H. "The Administration of Foreign Exchange Control in Canada." (1949), 27 *Canadian Bar Review* 625-651. **8148**

Taylor, J.G. "Canada's New Bank Act: Integration of Foreign Banks into the Canadian Banking System." (1981), 11 *Denver Journal of International Law and Policy* 105-113. **8149**

Thomson, Richard M. "The Internationalization of Canadian Banks." (1976), 3 *Canadian Business Review* 19-21 (No. 4) **8150**

Towers, G.F. "International Banking and Foreign Exchange." (1925-26), 33 *Journal of the Canadian Bankers' Association* 529-533. **8151**

Towers, G.F. "International Investment Banking and Its Influence on World Trade." (1930-31), 38 *Journal of the Canadian Bankers' Association* 218-221. **8152**

Turk, Sidney. "The Canadian Foreign Exchange Control Board: Its Genesis and Exodus." (1956), 63 *Canadian Banker* 95-111 (No. 2) **8153**

Turmann, Max. "Les accords de clearing: origines, organisation, fonctionnement et résultats." (1935-36), 11/2 *Actualité Économique* 239-246. **8154**

Viner, Jacob. *Canada's Balance of International Indebtedness, 1900-1913: An Inductive Study in the Theory of International Trade.* Introduction by H.C. Eastman. Toronto: McClelland and Stewart, c1975. xvi, 318 p. (Carleton Library, No. 86) **8155**
Reprint of the edition published Cambridge, Harvard University Press, 1924.
Review: Gilbert E. Jackson in (1924), 5 *Canadian Historical Review* 278-281.

Volcker, Paul A. "The International Exchange Rate System: Problems, Progress and Challenge." (1976), 3 *Canadian Business Review* 23-27 (No. 3) **8156**

Wilford, D. Sykes, and Nattress, W. Dayle. "Monetary and Financial Integration in North America." (1981), 44 *Law and Contemporary Problems* 55-79. **8157**

Willis, H. Parker. "Canadian and American Financial Relations." (1917-18), 25 *Journal of the Canadian Bankers' Association* 102-108. **8158**

Willis, H. Parker. "The Status of the Allied Debts to the United States." (1921-22), 29 *Journal of the Canadian Bankers' Association* 270-276. **8159**

Withers, Hartley. "Problems of International Finance." (1920-21), 28 *Journal of the Canadian Bankers' Association* 329-336. **8160**

Woehrling, Francis. "Vers une théorie du système monétaire international." (1981), 12 *Études Internationales* 475-497. **8161**

Wright, Gerald. *Cooperation and Independence: Canada's Management of Financial Relations with the United States, 1963-1968.* Baltimore, Md., 1976. 299 leaves. **8162**
  Thesis (Ph.D.), Johns Hopkins University, 1976. Abstracted in (1976/77), 37 *Dissertation Abstracts International* 1213-A. (University Microfilms, Ann Arbor, No. 76-16838).

H. International Taxation (Incl. Double Taxation)

Alper, Donald K., and Monahan, Robert L. "Bill C-58 and the American Congress: The Politics of Retaliation." (1978), 4 *Canadian Public Policy* 184-192. **8163**

Alpert, Herbert H. "The Co-ordination between the New Canada-U.S. Treaty and the U.S. Foreign Investment in Real Property Tax Act." (1981), 29 *Canadian Tax Journal* 558-561. **8164**

Alpert, Herbert H. "FIRPTA and Treaties." (1981), 33 *Canadian Tax Foundation, Proceedings* 438-454. **8165**
  Refers to the American *Foreign Investment in Real Property Tax Act (FIRPTA).*

Ashton, Roger. "Canadian Investment in U.S. Real Estate for Personal Use." (1981), 29 *Canadian Tax Journal* 702-717. **8166**

Balogh, Leslie V. "Taxation of Income Earned Outside Canada." *In Essays on Canadian Taxation* (Toronto, 1978), pp. 693-714. **8167**

Balogh, Leslie V. "Taxation of Non-Residents." *In Canadian Taxation* (Toronto, 1981), pp. 937-969. **8168**

Balogh, Leslie V. "Taxation of Non-Residents." *In Essays on Canadian Taxation* (Toronto, 1978), pp. 659-691. **8169**

Bissell, Thomas St.G., and Cleland, E. Gordon. "The New Canadian Tax Treaty: Corporate Implications." (1981), 7 *International Tax Journal* 181-216. **8170**

Bissell, Thomas St.G., and Cleland, E. Gordon. "The New Canadian Tax Treaty: Impact on Individuals." (1981), 7 *International Tax Journal* 379-403. **8171**

Boidman, Nathan. "Canadian Investment in U.S. Real Estate." (1981), 33 *Canadian Tax Foundation, Proceedings* 454-496. **8172**

Boidman, Nathan. "Interpretation of Tax Treaties in Canada." (1980), 34 *Bulletin for International Fiscal Documentation* 388-401. **8173**

Bradford, Hilary P. "Some Canadian-American Income Tax Problems." (1961-62), 11 *Buffalo Law Review* 309-327. **8174**

Brauw, E.A. de. "The New Canada-United Kingdom Double Taxation Convention." (1979), 19 *European Taxation* 291-293. **8175**

Brean, Donald J.S. *Taxing the Multinational Enterprise: Problems of the Host Country.* Toronto, c1979. ix, 204 leaves. **8176**
   Thesis (Ph.D.), University of Toronto, 1979. (National Library of Canada. Canadian Theses on Microfiche, No. 42172).

Broadhurst, David G. "The All New 1983 Foreign Affiliate Regulations - Part I." (1982), 30 *Canadian Tax Journal* 891-898. **8177**

Broadhurst, David G. "The Canada-U.S. Tax Treaty - Part I." (1980), 28 *Canada Tax Journal* 799-809. **8178**
   Refers to the tax treaty signed on September 26, 1980.

Broadhurst, David G. "The Canada-U.S. Tax Treaty - Part II." (1981), 29 *Canadian Tax Journal* 61-70. **8179**

Broadhurst, David G. "Recent Developments Here and There in Taxing International Income." (1979), 27 *Canadian Tax Journal* 201-205. **8180**

Broley, J.A. "The Migrating Executive: Coming to and Transferring within Canada." *In* Canadian Tax Foundation, *Corporate Management Tax Conference, 1979* (Toronto, 1980), pp. 172-188. **8181**

Brown, Robert D., ed. "Canada's Expanding Tax Treaty Network and the Channelling of International Investments." (1977), 25 *Canadian Tax Journal* 637-643. **8182**

Brown, Robert D. "Canada-United States Tax Relations Problems." (1975), 28 *Tax Executive* 1-19. **8183**

Brown, Robert D. "Negotiations for a New Tax Treaty between Canada and the United States - A Long Story with a Happy Ending?" (1981), 4 *Canada-United States Law Journal* 139-150. **8184**

Brown, Robert D. "The United States Turns the Heat on the Canada-U.S. Tax Treaty and Canadian Tax Planners." (1982), 30 *Canadian Tax Journal* 716-727. **8185**

Burge, Marianne, and Broadhurst, David G. "New U.S. Model Income Tax Treaty." (1982), 30 *Canadian Tax Journal* 76-82. **8186**

Burge, Marianne, and Brown, Robert D. "Negotiations for a New Tax Treaty between Canada and the United States - A Long Story." (1979), 27 *Canadian Tax Journal* 94-104. **8187**

"Canada's Income Tax Treaties." (1958), 12 *Canadian Tax Foundation, Proceedings* 222-246. **8188**
   This is a panel. Chairman: D.G. Scott.- Speakers: Neil Phillips; G.H. Allen; and J.F. Harmer.

"Canada's New Tax Treaties." (1976), 28 *Canadian Tax Foundation, Proceedings* 290-338. **8189**
> This is a panel. Chairman: Alexander B. McKie.- Speakers: Gérard Coulombe; Donald J. Johnston; James S. Hausman; and James S. Peterson.

"The Canada-United States Income Tax Treaty." (1980), 32 *Canadian Tax Foundation, Proceedings* 313-428, 698-742. **8190**
> This is a panel presented during the thirty-second annual conference of the Canadian Tax Foundation held at Montreal, October 25 and 26, 1980. Refers to the tax convention signed on September 26, 1980, and the tax convention and protocol of March 4, 1942 (CTS 1942/2), as amended.

"Canadian Taxation of United States Persons." (1975), 27 *Canadian Tax Foundation, Proceedings* 54-122. **8191**
> This is a panel. Chairman: Michael C. Rodney.- Speakers: Norman L. Rapkin; Samuel R. Baker; and David G. Broadhurst.

Caveney, William J. "Extraterritorial Effects of Canadian Tax Laws." (1978), 12 *International Lawyer* 621-624. **8192**

Chaudhuri, Asim. "Relief of Double Taxation in India." (1979), 27 *Canadian Tax Journal* 478-482. **8193**

Chown, John F. "New International Tax Rules in the United Kingdom." (1975), 23 *Canadian Tax Journal* 69-73. **8194**

Côté, Pierre P. *Le droit fiscal canadien et le droit fiscal international face à la double imposition du revenu.* Montréal, 1972. 139, 9 leaves. **8195**
> Thesis (LL.M.), Université de Montréal, 1972.

Crawford, Charles T., and Tikku, Kaushal. "Tax Havens - An Endangered Species?" (1981), 29 *Canadian Tax Journal* 525-535. **8196**

Cumyn, A. Peter. "Can Canada Levy Tax on the Continental Shelf?" (1981), 4 *Canada-United States Law Journal* 165-170. **8197**

Curran, John F. "American Tax Considerations in the Drafting of Canadian Joint Operating Agreements." (1970), 8 *Alberta Law Review* 187-209. **8198**

Dancey, Kevin J.; Friesen, R.A.; and Timbrell, David Y. *Canadian Taxation of Foreign Affiliates.* 3rd ed. Don Mills, Ont.: CCH Canadian, 1982. v, 208 p. **8199**
> The second edition was published under title: *Canadian Taxation of Income Arising in Non-Resident Corporations and Trusts,* by R.A. Friesen, and D.Y. Timbrell.

DeLap, Richard L. "U.S. Taxation of Canadian Investment in U.S. Property Other than Real Estate." (1981), 33 *Canadian Tax Foundation, Proceedings* 124-157. **8200**

Denega, M.A. "The Migrating Executive: Leaving Canada and Working Abroad." *In* Canadian Tax Foundation, *Corporate Management Tax Conference, 1979* (Toronto, 1980), pp. 189-218. **8201**

Dickerson, Robert W.V. "Taxation and Foreign Investment by Canadian Corporations." (1959-63), 1 *University of British Columbia Law Review* 483-498. **8202**

"Doing Business Abroad: Basic Tax and Other Considerations - Part 1." (1977), 29 *Canadian Tax Foundation, Proceedings* 241-278. **8203**

This is a panel. Chairman: Norman L. Rapkin.- Speakers: Norman L. Rapkin; A. Peter Cumyn; Samuel R. Baker; and David Y. Timbrell.

"Doing Business Abroad: Basic Tax and Other Considerations - Part 2." (1977), 29 *Canadian Tax Foundation, Proceedings* 473-509. **8204**
This is a panel. Chairman: Robert P. Simon.- Speakers: John Lees; P. Howard Lyons; and Peter E. McQuillan.

"Effects of Taxes on Trade: Canada, United States and the European Economic Community." (1973), 25 *Canadian Tax Foundation, Proceedings* 6-38. **8205**
This is a panel. Chairman: Denham J. Kelsey.- Speakers: James R. Melvin; Peggy B. Musgrave; and Melvyn B. Krauss.

Etra, Lionel. "Do You Know Whether Your Clients Are U.S. Citizens?" (1980), 28 *Canadian Tax Journal* 841-844. **8206**

Fiorino, John. "The Protocol to the New Canada-U.K. Income Tax Convention." (1981), 29 *Canadian Tax Journal* 698-701. **8207**
Refers to the protocol of April 15, 1980, which came into force on December 18, 1980.

"Foreign Affiliate Regulations." (1975), 27 *Canadian Tax Foundation, Proceedings* 834-892. **8208**
This is a panel. Chairman: R. Alan Short.- Speakers: David Y. Timbrell; James S. Hausman; and Robert J. Dart.

"Foreign Business Corporations." (1959), 13 *Canadian Tax Foundation, Proceedings* 224-249. **8209**
This is a panel. Chairman: Campbell W. Leach.- Speakers: I.G. Wahn; Harold E. Crate; and R. de Wolfe MacKay.

"Foreign Tax Havens for Canadian Business." (1957), 11 *Canadian Tax Foundation, Proceedings* 133-161. **8210**
This is a panel. Chairman: J.A. Renwick.- Speakers: Karl E. Lachmann; W.J. Gibbons; and H. David McGurran.

Frommel, S.N. *Taxation of Branches and Subsidiaries in Western Europe, Canada, and the U.S.A.* 2nd ed. Deventer: Kluwer, c1978. 296 p. **8211**
Review: André Tunc in (1978), 30 *Revue Internationale de Droit Comparé* 1081.

Fuller, David G. "Canadian Tax Planning for the U.S. Citizen." (1973), 21 *Canadian Tax Journal* 149-160. **8212**

Garcia, Charles F., and Shedivy, James H. "Taxation of the U.S. Expatriate Living and Working in Canada." (1978), 26 *Canadian Tax Journal* 523-536. **8213**

Gibson, Roger C. "The New Canada-Australia Income Tax Convention." (1981), 29 *Canadian Tax Journal* 683-697. **8214**
Refers to the tax convention of May 21, 1980, which came into force on April 29, 1981.

Goodman, Wolfe David. "Canadian Tax Aspects of U.S. Decedents' Estates." (1966), 1 *Real Property, Probate and Trust Journal* 227-237. **8215**

Goodman, Wolfe David. "International and Interprovincial Death Duty and Gift Tax Problems." (1974), 12 *Osgoode Hall Law Journal* 191-205. **8216**

Goodman, Wolfe David. *International Double Taxation of Estates and Inheritance.* Toronto, 1976. 364, 64, 3, 10 leaves. **8217**
Thesis (D.Jur.), University of Toronto, 1976.

Goodman, Wolfe David. *International Double Taxation of Estates and Inheritance.* London, Eng.: Butterworths, 1978. xi, 277 p. **8218**

Goodrich, George. "Canada-U.S. Tax Accounting: Competent Authority, Section 482 Transfers and Joint Audits." (1981), 4 *Canada-United States Law Journal* 151-164.   **8219**

Gornick, Alan L. "The Canadian and British Death Tax Conventions." (1946-47), 50 *West Virginia Law Quarterly* 55-74.   **8220**

Grady, Patrick Michael. *The Canadian Exemption from the United States Interest Equalization Tax.* Toronto, 1973. vi, 176 leaves.   **8221**

    Thesis (Ph.D.), University of Toronto, 1973. (National Library of Canada. Canadian Theses on Microfilm, No. 16630).

Hammer, R.M., and Hickey, G.P. "How New U.S.-Canada Treaty Treats Dividends, Interest, Royalties, Double Taxation." (1981), 33 *Tax Executive* 185-194.   **8222**

Hogg, Roy D. "Canadian Taxation of Canadian Investment in U.S. Property Other than Real Estate." (1981), 33 *Canadian Tax Foundation, Proceedings* 157-181.   **8223**

Ilersic, A.R. "Tax Havens and Residence." (1982), 30 *Canadian Tax Journal* 52-56.   **8224**

"Income Tax Treaties: A Canadian Perspective." (1972), 24 *Canadian Tax Foundation, Proceedings* 100-120.   **8225**

    This is a panel. Chairman: H. Arnold Sherman.- Speakers: R. Alan Short; Charles W. Mavor; Max Widmer; Robert J. Patrick, Jr.; and A. Peter Cumyn.

"International Aspects - Part 1." (1970), 22 *Canadian Tax Foundation, Proceedings* 171-187.   **8226**

    This is a panel. Chairman: Harold S. Moffet.- Speakers: R. Alan Short; George J. Brady; and James S. Hausman.

"International Aspects - Part 2." (1970), 22 *Canadian Tax Foundation, Proceedings* 292-351.   **8227**

    This is a panel. Chairman: R. de Wolfe MacKay.- Speakers: Alexander B. McKie; Albert Rädler; Peggy B. Musgrave; and Walter F. O'Connor.

"International Aspects - 1." (1971), 23 *Canadian Tax Foundation, Proceedings* 158-199.   **8228**

    This is a panel. Chairman: R.M. Wingfield.- Speakers: James S. Peterson; Daniel J. Brennan; Samuel R. Baker; and H. Arnold Sherman.

"International Aspects - 2." (1971), 23 *Canadian Tax Foundation, Proceedings* 279-305.   **8229**

    This is a panel. Chairman: John Lees.- Speakers: James S. Hausman; John F. Chown; and David R. Tillinghast.

"International Taxation: Planning by Canadian Business for Operations Abroad." (1973), 25 *Canadian Tax Foundation, Proceedings* 302-342.   **8230**

    This is a panel. Chairman: Neil F. Phillips.- Speakers: Samuel R. Baker; John Lees; David Y. Timbrell; Robert M. Turnbull; and James S. Hausman.

"International Taxation - Current Issues." (1976), 28 *Canadian Tax Foundation, Proceedings* 69-148.   **8231**

    This is a panel. Chairman: M. Arnold Sherman.- Speakers: Robert Couzin; Robert J. Dart; and David A. Ward.

"International Taxation - Recent Developments." (1968), 21 *Canadian Tax Foundation, Proceedings* 407-429.   **8232**

This is a panel. Chairman: Charles McLaughlin.- Speakers: A.B. McKie; R. Alan Short; and Joseph G. McGowan.

"International Taxation and the 1974 Budget." (1974), 26 *Canadian Tax Foundation, Proceedings* 225-274. **8233**
This is a panel. Chairman: Robert P. Simon.- Speakers: J.M. Bradley; A. Peter Cumyn; H. Arnold Sherman; and James S. Peterson.

Jenkins, Glenn P., Misir, Devendranauth, and Glenday, Graham. "The Taxation of Foreign Investment Income in Canada, the United States and Mexico." (1981), 44 *Law and Contemporary Problems* 143-159. **8234**

Johnson, Jon R. "Relief from Double Taxation Arising from Section 482 Allocations." (1968), 26 *University of Toronto Faculty of Law Review* 16-30. **8235**

Johnston, Donald J. "Will Fiscal Reform in Canada Affect United States Interests?" (1968), 14 *McGill Law Journal* 59-83. **8236**
First published in *Taxes,* July 1967.

Jones, David Phillip. "Corporations, Double Taxation and the Theory of Integration." (1979), 27 *Canadian Tax Journal* 405-427. **8237**

Kassell, Mortimer M. "Appraisal of Canada-U.S. Tax Treaty. Solution of Double Taxation Held Questionable." (1945), 80 *Trusts and Estates* 105-107. **8238**

Ketcheson, Bruce. "The Use of Bermuda as a Tax Haven under the Foreign Affiliate Rules." (1981), 6 *Queen's Law Journal* 451-481. **8239**

King, Eldon P. "Income Tax Reciprocity with Canada." (1939), 17 *Taxes* 205-206, 249. **8240**

Koerner, W.R. "United States Citizens in Canada." (1959), 7 *Canadian Tax Journal* 43-47. **8241**

Krishna, Sam Swaminathan. "The New Canada-Federal Republic of Germany Tax Treaty." (1982), 30 *Canadian Tax Journal* 668-681. **8242**

Lahmer, Craig. "Oil and Gas Operations in the United States - Income Tax Implications for Canadian Resource Corporations." (1982), 30 *Canadian Tax Journal* 22-40. **8243**

Lambe, Hugh B. "Will Planning for U.S. Citizens Resident in Canada." (1982), 30 *Canadian Tax Journal* 335-359. **8244**

Lang, Walter. "The Avoidance of International Double Taxation of Income." (1958), 6 *Canadian Tax Journal* 447-452. **8245**

Leduc, Marc. "L'imposition de revenu international: aspects canadiens." (1971), 6 *Revue Juridique Thémis* 177-289. **8246**

Levine, Shelley, and Larter, Ron. *Canada-U.S. Employment Transfers: A Guide to Personal Tax Planning.* Prepared for CCH Canadian Limited by Ernst & Whinney Chartered Accountants. 1979 ed. Don Mills, Ont.: CCH Canadian, c1979. v, 294 p. **8247**

Linch, L.W. Pete. "Current U.S. Tax Developments Affecting Canadian Investors." (1981), 33 *Canadian Tax Foundation, Proceedings* 110-124. **8248**

Lysyk, Kenneth M. "Foreign Revenue Laws: *United States of America v. Harden.*" (1964), 2 *Canadian Yearbook of International Law* 245-257. **8249**

Matsler, Michael. "Capital Gains Treatment under the U.S.-Canadian Income Tax

Convention of 1980: Conflicts with Congressional Policy." (1982), 5 *Boston College International and Comparative Law Review* 461-488. **8250**

McCart, Janice. "Financing U.S. Operations through the Netherlands and the Barbados." (1982), 30 *Canadian Tax Journal* 577-587. **8251**

McDonald, James L., and Chan, William C. "Canadians Investing in the United States." (1979), 27 *Canadian Tax Journal* 714-724. **8252**

McDonald, James L., and Chan, William C. "Canadians Investing in the United States - Part 2." (1980), 28 *Canadian Tax Journal* 68-79. **8253**

McKie, Alexander B. "Canada-Jamaica Tax Treaty: A New Approach." (1971), 78 *Canadian Banker* 13-14 (No. 2) **8254**

McKie, Alexander B. "Canada-Jamaica Tax Treaty: Pattern for Others?" (1971), 19 *Canadian Tax Journal* 41-49. **8255**
Refers to the tax agreement signed on January 4, 1971 (CTS 1971/20).

McKie, Alexander B. "International Tax Agreements: A Matter of Interest." (1966), 14 *Canadian Tax Journal* 71-74. **8256**

Mida, Hymie. "The New U.S. Exclusion Rules and Implications for U.S. Executives in Canada." (1982), 30 *Canadian Tax Journal* 255-271. **8257**

Moore, Philip C. "The Permanent Establishment Concept in Tax Treaties: Old Bottles for New Wine." (1981), 6 *Queen's Law Journal* 482-513. **8258**

Nigro, Don J. "Canadian Taxation and United States Corporations." (1955-56), 33 *University of Detroit Law Journal* 327-334. **8259**
Sub-title: "Tax Aspects and Contrasts in Corporate Taxation of a United States Corporation Doing Business in Canada."

Panzer, Arnold B. "Enforcement of Canadian Tax Judgment by U.S. Courts Denied." (1980), 28 *Canadian Tax Journal* 518-523. **8260**

Perry, David B. "International Comparisons of Tax Levels." (1981), 29 *Canadian Tax Journal* 99-104. **8261**

Peters, Victor. "The Role of Section 17 in the Taxation of Foreign Source Income -Past, Present, and Future." (1982), 30 *Canadian Tax Journal* 501-527. **8262**

Peterson, James S. "Canada's Foreign Tax Credit System." (1971), 19 *Canadian Tax Journal* 89-98. **8263**

Peterson, James S. "Canada's New Tax Treaties." (1975), 23 *Canadian Tax Journal* 315-332. **8264**

Peterson, James S. "Canadian Taxation of Nonresidents." (1973), 12 *Columbia Journal of Transnational Law* 213-259. **8265**

Peterson, James S. *The International Aspects of Canadian Income Taxation.* Montreal, 1970. xxxii, 755 leaves. **8266**
Thesis (D.C.L.), McGill University, 1970. (National Library of Canada. Canadian Theses on Microfilm, No. 6432).

Pilling, A.M. "The Tax Haven Subsidiary." (1975), 23 *Canadian Tax Journal* 467-473. **8267**

Poissant, Charles Albert. *Commentary on Canada-Germany Tax Agreement.* Don Mills, Ont.: CCH Canadian, c1976. 75 p. **8268**

Poissant, Charles Albert. *Taxation in Canada of Non-Residents.* Don Mills, Ont.: CCH Canadian, c1976. v, 289 p. **8269**

Pyrcz, Orville Andrew. *Canadian Taxation of Corporate Foreign Source Income: An Overview.* Toronto, 1972. 234 leaves. **8270**
Thesis (LL.M.), University of Toronto, 1972.

Rapkin, Norman L. "U.S. Employees and Professionals Performing Services in Canada." (1976), 54 *Taxes* 280-305. **8271**

Rendall, James A. "The Impact of Canadian Income Tax Law on Domestic Subsidiaries of U.S. Corporations - B.C. and A.D." (1967), 17 *Buffalo Law Review* 135-144. **8272**

Roberts, Sidney I. "*Great-West Life Assurance Company* v. *United States*: Exploration of the U.S. Interpretation of Treaties." (1982), 30 *Canadian Tax Journal* 759-766. **8273**

Roberts, Sidney I. "Is the Canada-U.S. Estate Tax Treaty in Force?" (1980), 28 *Canadian Tax Journal* 517-518. **8274**
See also the author's remark under title: "The Canada-U.S. Estate Tax Treaty - The Last Word" (p. 845).

Robertson, J.R. "The Use of Tax Evasion and Tax Avoidance by Multinational Companies: A Canadian View." (1977), 25 *Canadian Tax Journal* 513-527.
8275

Scace, Arthur R.A., and Ewens, Douglas S. "Canadian Taxation of Foreign Affiliates." (1972), 10 *Osgoode Hall Law Journal* 325-368. **8276**

Seed, Nicholas J.S., and Pangbourne, David G. "The New Canada/U.K. Tax Convention: A Canadian Perspective." (1979), 27 *Canadian Tax Journal* 17-35.
Refers to the convention signed on September 8, 1978. **8277**

Shibata, Hirofumi. *Fiscal Harmonization under Freer Trade: Principles and Their Applications to a Canada-U.S. Free Trade Area.* Toronto: Published for the Private Planning Association of Canada by University of Toronto Press, 1969. vi, 88 p. (Canada in the Atlantic Economy, Vol. 9) **8278**
Review: Richard M. Bird in (1970), 3 *Canadian Journal of Economics* 625-627.

Short, R. Alan. "The Canada-United Kingdom Tax Agreement." (1966), 14 *Canadian Tax Journal* 39-48. **8279**

Short, R. Alan. "The Comprehensive Canada-U.K. Tax Agreement." (1967), 15 *Canadian Tax Journal* 37-45. **8280**

Short, R. Alan. "Tax Treaties with Developing Countries." (1966), 14 *Canadian Tax Journal* 171-179. **8281**

Smejda, Lucius. "The Proposed Canadian Tax Treaty: Trends and Policies." (1981), 7 *International Tax Journal* 165-180. **8282**

Smith, Ernest H. "Making Canada's Tax Treaties." (1962), 10 *Canadian Tax Journal* 289-297. **8283**

Smith, Lancelot J. "Canadian-U.S. Personnel Movements and Taxes." (1962), 10 *Canadian Tax Journal* 337-346. **8284**

Special Seminar on Analysis of Canada's Tax Conventions and Comparison to the

O.E.C.D. Model Double Taxation Convention, 1979. *Texts of Seminar Papers.*
Toronto: Richard De Boo, 1979. v, 392 p., tables. **8285**
Sponsored by the International Fiscal Association, Canadian Branch.

Special Seminar on Interpreting Tax Treaties, Toronto, 1977. *Texts of Seminar Papers.* Toronto: Richard De Boo, 1977. vii, 65 p. **8286**
Sponsored by the International Fiscal Association, Canadian Branch. Held at the Inn on the Park, Toronto, April 1, 1977.

Special Seminar on the New Treaties and the FAPI Regulations, Montreal, 1975. *Texts of Seminar Papers.* Toronto: Richard De Boo, 1975. ix, 65 p. **8287**
Sponsored by the International Fiscal Association, Canadian Branch. Held at the University of Montreal, June 20, 1975.

Spence, James M. "The Role of the 'Permanent Establishment' Concept in Conventions for the Avoidance of Double Taxation." (1966), 24 *University of Toronto Faculty of Law Review* 82-105. **8288**

Stitt, Hubert J., and Baker, Samuel R. *International Taxation and Canadian Tax Reform.* Don Mills, Ont.: CCH Canadian, c1972. 120 p. **8289**

Stow, William Lewis. *The Potential Impact of Canadian Tax Policy on U.S. Private Direct Investment in Canada.* Kingston, 1971. iii, 65 leaves. **8290**
Half-title: *Canadian Tax Policy.* Thesis (M.A.), Queen's University, 1971. (National Library of Canada. Canadian Theses on Microfilm, No. 8711).

Surrey, Stanley S. "The United States Tax System and International Tax Relationships." (1964), 12 *Canadian Tax Journal* 460-482. **8291**

Switzer, Eric B. "Canadian Taxation of Foreign Affiliate Distributions." (1978), 16 *Osgoode Hall Law Journal* 81-132. **8292**

Switzer, Eric B. *Canadian Taxation of Foreign Affiliate Income.* Toronto, 1976. 261 leaves. **8293**
Thesis (LL.M.), University of Toronto, 1976.

"Tax Considerations for Exporters." (1964), 18 *Canadian Tax Foundation, Proceedings* 182-208. **8294**
This is a panel. Chairman: R. de Wolfe MacKay.- Speakers: William Latimer; R. Alan Short; and Josiah Willard.

"Tax Implications for Canadians Employed, Investing or Carrying on Business in the United States - Part 1." (1976), 28 *Canadian Tax Foundation, Proceedings* 471-536. **8295**
This is a panel. Chairman: Norman J. Munn.- Speakers: Francis J. Oatway; Sanford H. Goldberg; James L. McDonald; and Gary J. Webb.

"Tax Implications for Canadians Employed, Investing or Carrying on Business in the United States - Part 2." (1976), 28 *Canadian Tax Foundation, Proceedings* 650-731. **8296**
This is a panel. Chairman: G. Edward Moul.- Speakers: Walter F. O'Connor; Benjamin Swirsky; and M.I. Stucker.

"Tax Treatment of Foreign Exchange Profits and Losses." (1968), 21 *Canadian Tax Foundation, Proceedings* 287-322. **8297**
This is a panel. Chairman: Edward Saunders.- Speakers: David I. Matheson; Robert M. Turnbull; and Ronald M. Anson-Cartwright.

"Tax Treatment of Foreign Source Income." (1967), 20 *Canadian Tax Foundation, Proceedings* 289-314. **8298**
This is a panel. Chairman: Ivan R. Feltham.- Speakers: R.A. Lachance; Stephan F.F. Kaliski; and E.H. Orser.

"Taxation and Foreign Investments. Part I. Foreign Viewpoints.- Part II. Canadian Viewpoints." (1956), 10 *Canadian Tax Foundation, Proceedings* 1-28. **8299**
This is a panel. Chairman: M. Gerald Teed.- Speakers: Henry S. Bloch; John F. Costelloe; Monteath Douglas; Paul S. Deacon.

"Taxation of Transnational Operations: Recent Developments and Current Issues in Canada and the United States." (1979), 2 *Canada-United States Law Journal* 116-151. **8300**
Proceedings of a conference of the Canada-United States Law Institute, held April 21, 1978, at the Case Western Reserve University School of Law, Cleveland, Ohio.

Taylor, K.W. "Double Taxation." (1931-32), 39 *Journal of the Canadian Bankers' Association* 474-482. **8301**

Thom, Stuart D. "'Permanent Establishment' under the Tax Convention." (1957), 5 *Canadian Tax Journal* 344-348. **8302**

Tikku, Kaushal. "Tax Planning for U.S. Executives in Canada." (1980), 28 *Canadian Tax Journal* 623-646. **8303**

Tillinghast, David R. "Canadian Tax Reform and International Double Taxation: A View from the United States." (1973), 21 *Canadian Tax Journal* 472-493. **8304**

Tuggle, Bernie M. "The Proposed United States-Canada Income Tax Treaty." (1980), 10 *Denver Journal of International Law and Policy* 169-173. **8305**
Refers to the tax treaty signed on September 26, 1980.

Verchères, Bruce. "Extraterritorial Effects of Canadian Tax Law." (1978), 12 *International Lawyer* 624-627. **8306**

Verchères, Bruce. "Tax Havens: Myth or Reality." (1969), 4 *Revue Juridique Thémis* 23-44. **8307**

Ward, David A. "Principles to Be Applied in Interpreting Tax Treaties." (1977), 25 *Canadian Tax Journal* 263-270. **8308**
Also printed in (1980), 34 *Bulletin for International Fiscal Documentation* 545-551.

Weiss, Stanley, and Cohn, Ronald S. "Canadian and U.S. Governments Warn of Potential Double Taxation." (1982), 30 *Canadian Tax Journal* 755-759. **8309**

Williamson, John Peter. *Taxation of U.S. Private Investment in Canada.* Toronto: Canadian Tax Foundation, 1963. vi, 93 p. (Canadian Tax Papers, No. 36) **8310**

Williamson, John Peter. "United States Citizens in Canada." (1964), 12 *Canadian Tax Journal* 231-237, 301-308. **8311**

Willis, Robert. "Double Taxation Relief - The Role of the United Kingdom." (1965), 13 *Canadian Tax Journal* 499-508. **8312**

I. Economic and Technical Assistance

Abraham, Lennox O'Reilly Peter. *A Critique of Canadian Development Assistance to the Commonwealth Caribbean.* Kingston, 1973. v, 155 leaves. **8313**
Half-title: *Canadian Development Assistance.* Thesis (M.A.), Queen's University, 1973. (National Library of Canada. Canadian Theses on Microfilm, No. 16470).

Anglin, Douglas G. "Canada's External Assistance Programme." (1954), 9 *International Journal* 193-207. **8314**

Anglin, Douglas G. "The Canadian Post-War Contribution to International Assistance." (1954), 9 *International Journal* 264-274. **8315**

Barber, Clarence L. "Capital for Underdeveloped Areas." (1955), 62 *Canadian Banker* 69-75 (No. 1) **8316**

Barber, Clarence L. "More Aid to Under-Developed Areas?" (1954-55), 10 *International Journal* 198-209. **8317**

Barton, Brian, and Joyal, André. "L'évaluation des effets de la coopération technique dans les pays moins développés." (1974), 5 *Études Internationales* 439-475. **8318**

Belshaw, Cyril. "Training and Recruitment: Some Principles of International Aid." (1962-63), 18 *International Journal* 43-57. **8319**

Bonin, Bernard. "La participation canadienne au plan de Colombo." (1958-59), 34 *Actualité Économique* 400-413. **8320**

Brecher, Irving. "Canadian Foreign Economic Aid." (1962), 69 *Canadian Banker* 39-50 (No. 4) **8321**

Brecher, Irving. "The Continuing Challenge of International Development: A Canadian Perspective." (1975), 82 *Queen's Quarterly* 323-343. **8322**

Brewin, Francis Andrew. "Canadian Economic Assistance to Underdeveloped Areas." (1949-50), 5 *International Journal* 304-314. **8323**

Briant, Peter Charles. *Canada's External Aid Program.* Montreal: Canadian Trade Committee, Private Planning Association of Canada, 1965. viii, 42 p. **8324**

Bruneau, T.C., and Jorgensen, Jan J. *C.I.D.A.: The Organization of Canadian Overseas Assistance.* Montreal: Centre for Developing Area Studies, McGill University, 1978. 50 p. (McGill University. Centre for Developing Area Studies. Working Paper, No. 24) **8325**

Buckridan, Rakib. *Canadian Attitudes to International Development: A Pilot Study in the National Capital Region.* Ottawa, 1974. ix, 153 leaves. **8326**
Thesis (M.A.), Carleton University, 1974. (National Library of Canada. Canadian Theses on Microfiche, No. 20088).

Byres, T.J., ed. *Foreign Resources and Economic Development: A Symposium on the Report of the Pearson Commission.* London: Cass, 1972. xi, 199 p. **8327**
Refers to the Commission on International Development, set up in 1968 by the International Bank for Reconstruction and Development. The Commission was chaired by Lester B. Pearson, former Prime Minister of Canada.
Review: Thomas Allen Levy in (1973), 4 *Études Internationales* 381-382.

Canada. Dept. of External Affairs. *Canada and the Colombo Plan, 1951-1961.*
Ottawa: Queen's Printer, 1961. 32 p., map.   **8328**

Canada. International Development Agency. *Canada: Strategy for International Development Cooperation, 1975-1980 / Canada: stratégie de coopération au développement international, 1975-1980.* Ottawa: Canadian International Development Agency, 1975. 48, 53 p.   **8329**
Text in English and French on inverted pages, each with a separate title page and paging. Review: Ozay Mehmet in (1976), 19 *Canadian Public Administration* 496-498.

Canada. International Development Agency. *Canada and Development Cooperation: Annual Review.* 1975/76-1979/80. Ottawa: Queen's Printer.   **8330**
Continues: *CIDA Annual Review,* 1967/68-1974/75 (formerly *External Aid Office Annual Review).* Continued by: *Canadians in the Third World. CIDA's Year in Review.* Also issued in French under title: *Le Canada et la coopération au développement.* CIDA started as the Economic and Technical Assistance Branch, Dept. of Trade and Commerce; its functions were transferred to the Dept. of External Affairs, External Aid Office in 1960. It was designated a department in 1968. CIDA is responsible for the administration of official international development assistance programmes in the developing countries of the world. It reports to Parliament through the Secretary of State for External Affairs.

Canada. International Development Agency. *Canadians in the Third World. CIDA's Year in Review.* 1980/81—. Hull, Que.: Minister of Supply and Services Canada, 1982—.   **8331**
Continues: *Canada and Development Cooperation: Annual Review.* Includes *Statistical Annex,* 1980/81—, published separately.

Canada. International Development Agency. *International Development Agency. CIDA: Highlights of the Past Five Years / ACDI: faits saillants des cinq dernières années.* Ottawa: Canadian International Development Agency, 1976. 20, 20 p. In English and French.   **8332**

Canada. International Development Agency. *A Report on Canadians' Attitudes Toward Foreign Aid.* Hull, Que.: Canadian International Development Agency, 1981. 68 p.   **8333**

Canada. International Development Agency. *Taking Stock: A Review of CIDA Activities 1970-1974 / Bilan: rétrospective des activités de l'ACDI 1970-1974.* Ottawa: Canadian International Development Agency, 1974. 43, 45 p.   **8334**
Text in English and French on inverted pages, each with a separate title page and paging.

"Canada and Colombo - A Symposium." (1954-55), 61 *Queen's Quarterly* 319-344.
                                                                         8335
Contents: What We Have Done, by Nik Cavell (pp. 319-328).- The Economics of the Plan, by J.H. Warren (pp. 328-337).- Political Aims and Effects, by Henry F. Angus (pp. 337-344).

"Canada and the Colombo Plan." (1957), 9 *External Affairs* 206-214.   **8336**

"Canada and the Colombo Plan." (1961), 13 *External Affairs* 383-393.   **8337**

"The Canadian International Development Agency." (1968), 20 *External Affairs* 469-474.   **8338**

"Canadian Participation in Technical Assistance Programmes." (1951), 3 *External Affairs* 18-20.   **8339**

"Canadian Technical and Educational Assistance Training Programmes." (1965), 17 *External Affairs* 131-138. **8340**

Carty, Robert, and Smith, Virginia. *Perpetuating Poverty: The Political Economy of Canadian Foreign Aid.* Toronto: Between-the-Lines, 1981. 212 p. **8341**
Prepared with the Latin American Working Group.
Review: Alexa deWiel in (1982), *International Perspectives* 32 (Nov./Dec.).

Cavell, Nik. "The Colombo Plan." (1952), 44 *Canadian Geographical Journal* 203-214. **8342**

Cavell, Nik. "The Colombo Plan: A Progress Report." (1956), 8 *External Affairs* 164-169. **8343**

Cermakian, Jean. "La géographie de l'aide extérieure du Canada." (1969), 13 *Canadian Geographer* 163-168. **8344**

"The Colombo Plan." (1952), 4 *External Affairs* 208-211. **8345**

"The Colombo Plan." (1953), 5 *External Affairs* 102-110, 138-147. **8346**

"The Colombo Plan." (1954), 6 *External Affairs* 273-285. **8347**

"Colombo Plan Council for Technical Co-operation." (1956), 8 *External Affairs* 400-404. **8348**

Commission on International Development. *Partners in Development; Report.* Chairman: Lester B. Pearson. Commissioners: Sir Edward Boyle, and others. New York: Praeger, 1969. xvi, 399 p. (Praeger Paperbacks, P-269) **8349**
Also published London, Pall Mall Press, 1969. This report is known as the *Pearson Report*.
Reviews: Wolfgang G. Friedmann in (1969), 8 *Columbia Journal of Transnational Law* 334-338; Benjamin Higgins in (1971), 4 *Canadian Journal of Economics* 115-117; Ozay Mehmet in (1970-71), 50 *Dalhousie Review* 137-143; Clyde Sanger under title: "Pearson's Elegy," in (1969-70), 25 *International Journal* 178-183; signed P.B.W.R. in (1970), 4 *Journal of World Trade Law* 255-264.

Copland, John Anthony. *The Flow of Official Financial Resources from Canada to the Less-Developed Countries.* Montreal, 1970 (c1971). ix, 211 leaves. **8350**
Short title: *Official Financial Resource Flows from Canada to LDC's.* Thesis (M.A.), McGill University, 1970. (National Library of Canada. Canadian Theses on Microfilm, No. 7023).

Cox, Robert W. "The Pearson and Jackson Reports in the Context of Development Ideologies." (1972), 26 *Year Book of World Affairs* 187-202. **8351**

Cunningham, George. "Australia and Canada as Aid Givers: Putting over the Pearson Report." (1970), 60 *Round Table* 165-171. **8352**

De Bondt, John. "Canada's Aid to Developing Countries." (1972), 85 *Canadian Geographical Journal* 165-171 (No. 5) **8353**

"Le développement: l'aide international et le commerce international / Development: International Aid and Trade." (1975), 4 *Canadian Council on International Law, Proceedings* 26-128. **8354**
This is a panel. Chairman: Albert Legault (pp. 68-69).- Speaker: Pierre Vellas (pp. 69-82).- Commentators: Heribert Golsong (pp. 83-88); Dominique Carreau (pp. 88-97); and Tung-Pi Chen (pp. 98-110).- General discussion (pp. 111-128).

Donahue, William Patrick. *Canadian Foreign Aid Policy, 1965-1974.* Edmonton, 1976. viii, 114 leaves. **8355**
Thesis (M.A.), University of Alberta, 1976. (National Library of Canada. Canadian Theses on Microfiche, No. 27641).

Dover, Margaret Ann. *Criteria of Multilateral Aid Allocation.* Ottawa, 1977. vi, 179 leaves. **8356**
Research essay (M.A.), Carleton University, 1977.

Dudley, Leonard, and Montmarquette, Claude. *The Supply of Canadian Foreign Aid: Explanation and Evaluation.* Ottawa: Economic Council of Canada, c1978. xv, 153 p. **8357**
Review: Sam Lanfranco in (1979), 5 *Canadian Public Policy* 574-575.

Dupuy, Michel. *L'assistance technique et financière aux pays insuffisamment développés.* Paris: A. Pedone, 1956. 271 leaves. **8358**
Based on the author's doctoral dissertation, Université de Paris, Faculté de droit.

"Economic Problems of Developing Nations: UN Trade Conference, Geneva." (1964), 16 *External Affairs* 312-314. **8359**

Ehrhardt, Roger B., and others. *Canadian Aid and the Environment: The Policies and Performance of the Canadian International Development Agency.* By Roger Ehrhardt, Arthur Hanson, Clyde Sanger, and Bernard Wood. Ottawa: North-South Institute; Halifax: Institute for Resource and Environmental Studies, Dalhousie University, 1981. v, 94 p. **8360**
This is a joint study by the Institute for Resource and Environmental Studies, Dalhousie University, and the North-South Institute.
Review: Ralph R. Paragg in (1982), 8 *Canadian Public Policy* 397-398.

Ellis, Howard S. "American Economic Aid to Europe: The Record and the Future." (1951), 11 *Behind the Headlines* No. 2 (24 p.) **8361**

L'expert international: son rôle, son recrutement et sa formation: actes du 2e Colloque international de l'I.C.I. / The International Adviser: His Role, His Selection, and His Training: Proceedings of the 2nd International Conference of the I.C.I. Ottawa: Editions de l'Université d'Ottawa, 1974. 88 p. (University of Ottawa. Institute for International Co-operation. Travaux et documents. Série A, no 2) **8362**
Text in French and English. Conference organized by the Institute for International Co-operation, University of Ottawa / Institut de coopération international, Université d'Ottawa, held March 18-20, 1970.

Fatouros, Arghyrios A., and Kelson, Robert N. *Canada's Overseas Aid.* Toronto: Canadian Institute of International Affairs, 1964. 123 p. (Contemporary Affairs, No. 31) **8363**
A report based on the discussions at the Conference on Canadian Overseas Aid, held in the spring of 1962 at the University of Western Ontario.
Review: D.J. Morgan in (1963-64), 19 *International Journal* 569.

Fromm, Paul, and Hull, James P. *Down the Drain?: A Critical Re-Examination of Canadian Foreign Aid.* Toronto: Griffin House, 1981. x, 165 p. **8364**

Geuber, Grant L. "Why Canadian Foreign Aid?" (1958-59), 14 *International Journal* 11-20. **8365**

Gérin-Lajoie, Paul. "CIDA in a Changing Government Organization." (1972), 15 *Canadian Public Administration* 46-58. **8366**

Gogué, Aimé Tchabouré. *Une fonction d'offre d'aide internationale bilatérale: cas de la France et du Royaume-Uni.* Montréal, 1975. xi, 218 leaves. **8367**
Thesis (Ph.D.), Université de Montréal, 1976.

Gordon, Sheldon E. "Canadian Aid Policy: 'What's in It for Us?.' " (1976), *International Perspectives* 21-25 (May/June) **8368**

Granatstein, J.L., and Cuff, Robert D. "Canada and the Marshall Plan, June-December, 1947." (1977), *Canadian Historical Association, Historical Papers* 197-213. **8369**

Grenier, Raymond. "La 'crise globale' et la coopération canadienne au développement de l'Afrique francophone." (1974), 5 *Études Internationales* 367-375. **8370**

Harvey, Pierre. "L'aide américaine à l'étranger: histoire et perspectives." (1953-54), 29 *Actualité Économique* 351-358. **8371**

Head, Ivan L. "Interview with Ivan Head: Vital Interests at Stake in Crisis of Development." (1980), *International Perspectives* 15-21 (Nov./Dec.) **8372**

Hébert, Jacques, and Strong, Maurice F. *The Great Building Bee: Canada, a Hope for the Third World.* Don Mills, Ont.: General Pub., 1980. 189 p. **8373**
Also issued in French under title: *Le grand branle-bas! Le Canada, espoir du tiers monde.*
Review: Raymond Hudon in (1982), 15 *Canadian Journal of Political Science* 412-414 (of French ed.).

Helleiner, Gerald K. "The Development Business: Next Steps." (1969-70), 25 *International Journal* 158-177. **8374**

Henry, Jacques. "La politique canadienne d'aide à la région soudano-sahélienne." (1976), 2 *Canadian Public Policy* 466-481. **8375**

Higgins, Benjamin. "The Evaluation of Technical Assistance." (1969-70), 25 *International Journal* 34-55. **8376**

Hodge, Gerald. "The Rise and Demise of the U.N. Technical Assistance Administration." (1967), 10 *Canadian Public Administration* 1-24. **8377**

Holly, Daniel A. *L'Unesco, le tiers-monde et l'économie mondiale.* Montréal: Presses de l'Université de Montréal, 1981. 176 p. **8378**
Reviews: Paris J. Arnopoulos in (1982), 15 *Canadian Journal of Political Science* 852-853; Guy Gosselin in (1982), 13 *Études Internationales* 384-386.

Houliston, Peter Robert. *Canadian Aid to Francophone Africa; Its Motives and Potential.* Ottawa, 1969. 92 (i.e. 101), viii leaves. **8379**
Research essay (M.A.), Carleton University, 1969.

Huff, W.G. "Canadian Bilateral Aid: Canadian Content and Balance-of-Payments Cost." (1973), 7 *Journal of World Trade Law* 587-597. **8380**

Ingram, Joseph K. "Canadian Foreign Aid Objectives: Perceptions of Decision-Makers." (1974), 46 *Canadian Political Science Association, Papers,* 29 p. **8381**

Ingram, Joseph K. *A Comparison of Foreign Aid Objectives: Policy-Maker's*

Perceptions, Canada-United States. Hamilton, Ont., 1970. vi, 146 leaves.
Thesis (M.A.), McMaster University, 1970. **8382**

"International Assistance in Public Administration - A United Nations Program." (1958), 1 *Canadian Public Administration* 19-25 (No. 4) **8383**

Jacomy-Millette, Annemarie. "Les accords bilatéraux du Canada en matière d'assistance au développement international avant l'élaboration de la nouvelle stratégie: fluidité et pragmatisme des concepts juridiques." (1975), 6 *Revue Générale de Droit* 165-184. **8384**

Johnson, Harry G. "Pearson's 'Grand Assise' Fails; a Bleak Future for Foreign Aid." (1970), 60 *Round Table* 17-25. **8385**

Juvet, Charles Stanley. *Public Service Training in Canada under the Colombo Plan.* Ottawa, 1958. 126 leaves. **8386**
Thesis (M.P.A.), Carleton University, 1958.

Juvet, Charles Stanley. "Training in Public Administration at Carleton University under Canada's External Aid Program." (1961), 4 *Canadian Public Administration* 396-405. **8387**

Keenleyside, Hugh L. *International Aid: A Summary, with Special Reference to the Programmes of the United Nations.* Toronto, Montreal: McClelland and Stewart, c1966. xiii, 343 p. **8388**
Also published New York, J.H. Heineman.
Review: Wolfgang G. Friedmann in (1966-67), 22 *International Journal* 679-680.

Keenleyside, Hugh L. "The U.N. Technical Assistance Program in Public Administration - A Personal Retrospect." (1961), 4 *Canadian Public Administration* 406-411. **8389**

Keyfitz, Nathan. "Canada and the Colombo Plan." (1960-61), 20 *Behind the Headlines* No. 5 (16 p.) **8390**

Keyfitz, Nathan. "Foreign Aid Can Be Rational." (1961-62), 17 *International Journal* 237-250. **8391**

Kozliner, Marsha. *Commercial Considerations in Canadian Aid: Canada's Aid to India's Power and Transportation Sectors.* Ottawa, 1974. 104, 7 leaves. **8392**
Thesis (M.A.), Carleton University, 1974.

Lachance, Gabrielle. *De l'aide au développement: les organismes non-gouvernementaux de développement et de coopération internationale au Québec* Québec, 1978. xii, 147 leaves. **8393**
Thesis (M.A.), Université Laval, 1978. (National Library of Canada. Canadian Theses on Microfiche, No. 39157).

Larcher, Oswald Wilkinson. *The Politics of Canadian Aid to the Commonwealth Caribbean.* Waterloo, Ont., 1973. 164 leaves. **8394**
Thesis (M.A.), University of Waterloo, 1973.

Latin American Working Group. *Canadian Aid, Whose Priorities?: A Study of the Relationship between Non-Governmental Organizations, Business, and the Needs of Latin America.* Toronto: Latin American Working Group, 1973 61 p. **8395**

Lebel, Ronald. "Foreign Aid Is Big Business." (1966), 39 *Canadian Business* 94-10 (No. 9) **8396**

Leblanc, Hubert. *La pensée politique de l'aide canadienne au développement: motifs, institutions, structures, perspectives.* Toulouse, 1972. xiv, 293 p. **8397**
Thesis, Université de Toulouse.

Lemelin, Claude, and Marion, Jean-Claude. *Le Canada français et le tiers-monde; l'opinion publique au Canada français et l'aide aux pays sous-développés.* Ottawa: Université d'Ottawa, 1963. 81 p. (Cahiers des sciences sociales de l'Université d'Ottawa, no 1) **8398**
Reviews: Jean Angrand in (1975), 6 *Études Internationales* 272-273; Peyton V. Lyon in (1963-64), 19 *International Journal* 249-250.

Leroy, Marcel. "Neo-Malthusianism, Foreign Aid, and International Relations." (1975-76), 31 *International Journal* 26-43. **8399**

Lyon, Peyton V., and Ismael, Tareq Y., eds. *Canada and the Third World.* Toronto: Macmillan of Canada, c1976. 342 p. **8400**
Reviews: William M. Dobell in (1977), 10 *Canadian Journal of Political Science* 640-641; Philip Stuchen in (1977), 84 *Queen's Quarterly* 495-497; Denis Stairs in (1978), 59 *Canadian Historical Review* 257-259.

MacKay, Robert A., and Ritchie, A.E. "The Colombo Plan: Two Years' Experience." (1953), 47 *Royal Society of Canada, Transactions* 33-48 (3d Ser., Sec. 2) **8401**

Marcoux, Serge. *Conception et élaboration de la politique canadienne d'aide aux pays en voie de développement.* Montréal, 1970. xvii, 259 leaves. **8402**
Thesis (M.A.), Université de Montréal, 1970.

Martin, Paul. "The Challenge of Under-Development." (1964), 16 *External Affairs* 525-530. **8403**

Martin, Paul. "Principles and Purposes of Foreign Aid." (1965), 17 *External Affairs* 89-95. **8404**
Address by the Secretary of State for External Affairs, February 9, 1965.

Matthews, Joan. *Canadian Foreign Aid, 1950-1960: Parliamentary Policy, Administration, Content.* Montreal, 1962. vi, 178 leaves. **8405**
Thesis (M.A.), McGill University, 1962.

McBride, James Boyd. *Canadian Aid and Regional Integration.* Ottawa, 1978. 132 leaves. **8406**
Research essay (M.A.), Carleton University, 1978.

McKinley, Kathryn, and Young, Roger. *Technology and the Third World: The Issues and the Role for Canada.* Ottawa: North-South Institute, 1979. vi, 77 p. (North-South Papers, 1) **8407**
Also published in French under title: *La technologie et le tiers-monde.*
Review: Michael MacKenzie in (1980), 6 *Canadian Public Policy* 423.

McLoughlin, Peter F.M. "Rationalizing Foreign Aid." (1962-63), 18 *International Journal* 87-90. **8408**

Mehling, Jean. "Le sous-développement, le plan Colombo, et la contribution canadienne." (1956-57), 32 *Actualité Économique* 604-631. **8409**

Moore, Michael D. *The Foreign Aid Programmes and Policies of the People's Republic of China, 1953-1974.* Ottawa, 1976, c1977. xi, 373 leaves. **8410**
Thesis (M.A.), University of Ottawa, 1976.

Moran, H.O. "Canada's Bilateral Grant Aid Programmes." (1964), 16 *External Affairs* 67-84, 423-440. **8411**

Muhammad, Abdul Hai. *Canadian Aid Policy.* Ottawa, 1968. 149, vi leaves. Thesis (M.A.), Carleton University, 1968. **8412**

Niebyl, Karl H. "Criteria for the Formulation of an Adequate Approach in Aiding the Development of Underdeveloped Areas." (1952), 18 *Canadian Journal of Economics and Political Science* 365-371. **8413**

North-South Institute. *In the Canadian Interest? Third World Development in the 1980s.* Ottawa: North-South Institute, 1980. viii, 190 p. (Canada North-South) Also published in French under title: *L'enjeu canadien.* **8414**
Review: Wayne R. Thirsk in (1982), 8 *Canadian Public Policy* 133-135.

North-South Institute. *North-South Encounter: The Third World and Canadian Performance.* Ottawa: North-South Institute, c1977. ix, 200 p. (Canada North-South) **8415**
Review: Kimon Valaskakis in (1978), 4 *Canadian Public Policy* 410-411.

North-South Institute. *North-South Relations - 1980-85: Priorities for Canadian Policy: A Discussion Paper.* Prepared for the Special Committee of the House of Commons on North-South Relations. Rev. version. Ottawa: The Institute, 1980. ii, 73 p. **8416**

Paragg, Ralph R. "Canadian Aid in the Commonwealth Caribbean: Neo-Colonialism or Development?" (1980), 6 *Canadian Public Policy* 628-641. **8417**

Parizeau, Jacques. "L'aide aux économies sous-développées et leurs transformations de structure." (1954-55), 30 *Actualité Économique* 22-39. **8418**

Pearson, Lester B. "Canada and Technical Assistance to Under-Developed Countries." (1952), 4 *External Affairs* 90-95. **8419**

Pelletier, Irénée. *Le Canada et l'aide au tiers monde.* Toulouse, 1970. 1 vol. **8420**
Thesis (Doctorat), Université de Toulouse, 1970.

Pelletier, Irénée. *La politique canadienne d'aide au développement.* Préface de Pierre Vellas. Paris: Librairie Générale de Droit et de Jurisprudence, 1971. 128 p. (Droit de la coopération économique et sociale internationale, t. 7) **8421**

Peterson, Thomas Edward. *Canada and the Colombo Plan, 1950-1960; a Study in Government Policy and Public Opinion.* Winnipeg, 1962. ii, 169 leaves. **8422**
Thesis (M.A.), University of Manitoba, 1962.

Plumptre, A.F.W. "Perspective on Our Aid to Others." (1966-67), 22 *International Journal* 484-499. **8423**

Québec (Province). Ministère des affaires intergouvernementales. *L'Aide québécoise au développement international.* Québec: le Ministère, Direction des communications, 1981. 22 p. **8424**

Reid, Escott. "A Blueprint for Assisting the World's Poorest People." (1977) *International Perspectives* 3-7 (Sept./Oct.) **8425**

Reuber, Grant L. "Canada's Economic Policies Toward the Less Developed Countries." (1968), 1 *Canadian Journal of Economics* 669-698. **8426**
Contains a résumé in French under title: "La politique économique canadienne à l'égard des pays sous-développés."

Reuber, Grant L. "The Trade-Offs among the Objectives of Canadian Foreign Aid." (1969-70), 25 *International Journal* 129-141. **8427**

Riordan, James Brian. *The Discounting of Foreign Aid Loans to Present Value: The Canadian Situation.* Montreal, 1972. v, 104 leaves. **8428**
Thesis (M.A.), McGill University, 1972. (National Library of Canada. Canadian Theses on Microfilm, No. 12021).

Rivkin, Arnold. "The Role of External Assistance in African Development." (1958-59), 14 *International Journal* 157-167. **8429**

Roche, Douglas J. *Justice not Charity: A New Global Ethic for Canada.* Toronto: McClelland and Stewart, c1976. 123 p. **8430**

Rock, Trevor St.E. *The Political Economy of Canadian Foreign Aid: A Case Study of Jamaica.* Regina, 1979. vii, 194 leaves. **8431**
Thesis (M.A.), University of Regina, 1979. (National Library of Canada. Canadian Theses on Microfiche, No. 39081).

Sabourin, Louis. "Analyse des politiques de coopération internationale du Canada: des projets d'aide à la stratégie de développement." *In* Painchaud, Paul, ed., *Le Canada et le Québec sur la scène internationale* (Québec, 1977), pp. 209-251. **8432**

Sabourin, Louis. "Les programmes canadiens de coopération avec les états de l'Afrique (particulièrement avec l'Afrique francophone)." (1970), 1 *Études Internationales* 73-87. **8433**

Sanger, Clyde. *Half a Loaf; Canada's Semi-Role among Developing Countries.* Toronto: Ryerson Press, c1969. xvii, 276 p., maps. **8434**
Review: Richard Bailey in (1970-71), 26 *International Journal* 288-290.

"Science, Technology and Humanity." (1963), 15 *External Affairs* 163-169. **8435**

Scott, Francis R. "Technical Assistance and Economic Aid through the United Nations." (1953), 47 *Royal Society of Canada, Transactions* 17-31 (3d Ser., Sec. 2) **8436**

Spicer, Keith. "The Administration of Canadian Colombo Plan Aid." (1960-61), 16 *International Journal* 169-182. **8437**

Spicer, Keith. "Clubmanship Upstaged: Canada's Twenty Years in the Colombo Plan." (1969-70), 25 *International Journal* 23-33. **8438**

Spicer, Keith. *External Aid in Canada's Foreign Policy: A Political and Administrative Study of Canada's Assistance under the Colombo Plan.* Toronto, 1962. xii, 594 leaves, map. **8439**
Thesis (Ph.D.), University of Toronto, 1962. (National Library of Canada. Canadian Theses on Microfilm, No. 7).

Spicer, Keith. *A Samaritan State? External Aid in Canada's Foreign Policy.* Toronto: University of Toronto Press, 1966. xiv, 272 p. **8440**
Reviews: J. Duncan Edmonds in (1965-66), 21 *International Journal* 545-547; H.S. Ferns in (1967), 43 *International Affairs* 614-615.

Svoboda, Charles Vincent. "Federal-Provincial Co-operation in Development Assistance." (1979), *International Perspectives* 25-28 (May/June) **8441**

Thomson, Suteera. *Food for the Poor: The Role of CIDA in Agricultural, Fisher-*

ies and Rural Development: A Discussion Paper. Ottawa: Science Council of Canada, 1980. 194 p. (Science Council of Canada. Discussion Paper, D80/1)   **8442**

Torrelli, Maurice. "La C.E.E. et l'aide au développement: renouvellement de la convention de Yaoundé." (1969-70), 45 *Actualité Économique* 240-266.   **8443**

Triantis, Stephen G. "Canada's Interest in Foreign Aid." (1971-72), 24 *World Politics* 1-18.   **8444**

United Nations Association in Canada. *Canada and International Development Programmes: A Conference Held at the University of Toronto, June 1 and 2, 1956.* Ottawa, 1956. 54 p.   **8445**

United Nations Association in Canada. *The Dilemmas of Development.* Toronto: United Nations Association in Canada, Policy Committee, 1966. 52 p. (United Nations Association in Canada. Policy Committee. A Policy Paper)   **8446**

Vinette, André. *Évolution de l'idée d'un système préférentiel généralisé en faveur des pays en voie de développement et analyse de la position du Canada.* Québec, 1973. 195 leaves.   **8447**
Thesis (M.A.), Université Laval, 1973.

Wearing, John Paul. *The Exercise of Evaluation in Canadian International Development Assistance: a Study in Structural Change.* Kingston, 1972. vii, 85 leaves.   **8448**
Thesis (M.P.A.), Queen's University, 1972. (National Library of Canada. Canadian Theses on Microfilm, No. 11724).

Winham, Gilbert R. "Developing Theories of Foreign Policy Making: A Case Study of Foreign Aid." (1970), 32 *Journal of Politics* 41-70.   **8449**

Wright, Hume. "International Aid to Under-Developed Areas." (1951-52), 7 *International Journal* 265-273.   **8450**

Zechel, Bernd. *A Comparative Study of Canadian and West German Foreign Aid Programmes.* Windsor, 1969. ix, 111 leaves.   **8451**
Thesis (M.A.), University of Windsor, 1969.

J. Industrial and Intellectual Property

Allmand, Warren. "Policy Proposals for Change in Patent Law." (1979), 8 *Patent and Trademark Institute of Canada, Bulletin* 133-136.   **8452**

Banner, Donald W. "The Proposals for Revising the Paris Convention." (1979), 5 *Patent and Trademark Institute of Canada, Bulletin* 195-204.   **8453**
Refers to the convention signed at Paris on March 20, 1883, revised six times, and the diplomatic conference to revise the convention, held in Geneva, February-March 1980.

Bereskin, Daniel R. "The Trade Marks Act and the Constitution." (1982), 12 *Patent and Trademark Institute of Canada, Bulletin* 687-711.   **8454**

Bodin, Bernard. "Les brevets, l'entreprise multinationale et la diffusion internationale des innovations." (1974), 50 *Actualité Économique* 96-108.   **8455**

Braithwaite, William J. "Derivative Works in Canadian Copyright Law." (1982), 20 *Osgoode Hall Law Journal* 191-231. **8456**

Clute, A.R. "Canadian Copyright in Its Constitutional and International Aspects." (1904), 24 *Canadian Law Times* 328, 347-384. **8457**

"Copyright." In *Canadian Encyclopedic Digest (Ontario)*, 3d ed., 1974, title 34, vol. 5, 82 p. **8458**

Donegan, E.L. "Importation of Trade-Marked Articles: The 'Interloping Importer.' " (1960), 18 *University of Toronto Faculty of Law Review* 79-93. **8459**

Economic Council of Canada. *Report on Intellectual and Industrial Property.* Ottawa: Information Canada, 1971. x, 236 p. **8460**

Ellis, Shane Alexander. *The Transfer of Proprietary Technology from the Developed Countries to the Developing Nations.* Toronto, c1980. 161 leaves. **8461**
Thesis (LL.M.), University of Toronto, 1980.

Fox, Harold George. *The Canadian Law of Copyright.* Toronto: University of Toronto Press, 1944. lxiv, 770 p. (University of Toronto. Studies. Legal Series. Extra Volume) **8462**
Reviews: Edith E. Ware in (1945), 39 *American Journal of International Law* 365-367; Cecil A. Wright in (1945-46), 6 *University of Toronto Law Journal* 270-272; signed R. O'S. in (1944), 26 *Journal of Comparative Legislation and International Law* 76-77 (3d Ser.).

Fox, Harold George. *The Canadian Law of Copyright and Industrial Designs.* 2d ed. Toronto: Carswell, 1967. lxii, 848 p. **8463**
First edition published in 1944 under title: *The Canadian Law of Copyright.*
Review: Bruce C. McDonald in (1969), 47 *Canadian Bar Review* 142-147.

Fox, Harold George. *The Canadian Law of Trade Marks and Industrial Designs (Including the Law of Trade Names and Unfair Competition).* Toronto: University of Toronto Press, 1940. lxviii, 700 p. (University of Toronto. Studies. Legal Series. Extra Volume) **8464**
Thesis (Ph.D.), University of Toronto, 1940.
Reviews: W.F. Chipman in (1941-42), 4 *University of Toronto Law Journal* 192-194; H.K. Turner in (1941), 23 *Journal of Comparative Legislation and International Law* 106-108 (3d Ser.).

Fox, Harold George. *The Canadian Law of Trade Marks and Unfair Competition.* 2d ed. Toronto: Carswell, 1956. 2 vols. (1338 p.) **8465**
Review: John D. Osborne in (1957), 35 *Canadian Bar Review* 218-225.

Fox, Harold George. *The Canadian Law of Trade Marks and Unfair Competition.* 3d ed. With a Foreword by W.R. Jackett. Toronto: Carswell, 1972. lxxiv, 848 p. **8466**
First edition published in 1940 under title: *The Canadian Law of Trade Marks and Industrial Designs (Including the Law of Trade Names and Unfair Competition).*

Fox, Harold George. "The Law of Industrial and Intellectual Property: 1923-1947." (1948), 26 *Canadian Bar Review* 227-245. **8467**

Freeman, Hadley Fairfield. *The Protection of Trademarks and Tradenames, and Protection Against Unfair Competition, in Canada.* Cleveland: Freeman and Weidman, c1933. 38 p. **8468**

Gault, Thomas Munro. "Aspects of Enforcement of Industrial and Intellectual

Property Rights." (1980), 6 *Patent and Trademark Institute of Canada, Bulletin* 277-286. **8469**

Gérin-Lajoie, Henri. "'Patent Law in Canada: Its Origin and International Aspect.'" (1937), 22 *Canadian Bar Association, Proceedings* 158-174. **8470**

Godinsky, Samuel. "The Industrial Design Act (R.S.C., c. 150) - One Hundred Years After." (1979), 8 *Patent and Trademark Institute of Canada, Bulletin* 137-151. **8471**

Goldsmith, Immanuel. "Patents of Invention." In *Canadian Encyclopedic Digest (Ontario)*, 3d ed., 1981, title 107, vol. 24, 288 p. **8472**

Gowling, E. Gordon. "The New Canadian Trade Marks Act." (1953), 31 *Canadian Bar Review* 664-677. **8473**

Graham, Sir Patrick. "Industrial Property - The Scene in Europe." (1980), 6 *Patent and Trademark Institute of Canada, Bulletin* 247-262. **8474**

Halliday, Walter J. "Inter-American Conventions for Protection of Trade-Marks." (1950), 28 *Canadian Bar Review* 609-634. **8475**

Hanel, Peter. *International Distribution of Patented Inventions*. Halifax, 1976 (c1977). x, 164 leaves. **8476**
Thesis (Ph.D.), Dalhousie University, 1976. (National Library of Canada. Canadian Theses on Microfiche, No. 31501).

Hoen, Egbert 't. *International Copyright and Communication Satellites*. Montreal, 1972 (c1973). vi, 182 leaves. **8477**
Thesis (LL.M.), McGill University, 1972. (National Library of Canada. Canadian Theses on Microfilm, No. 14470).

Huberman, David S.M. "Industrial Foreign Licensing Agreements." (1964), 7 *Canadian Bar Journal* 452-473. **8478**

Jenks, C. Wilfred. "Copyright in Respect of the Publications and Other Documents of Official International Bodies." (1943-44), 5 *University of Toronto Law Journal* 71-94. **8479**

Keyes, A.A., and Brunet, C. *Copyright in Canada: Proposals for a Revision of the Law*. Hull, Que.: Consumer and Corporate Affairs Canada, 1977. xv, 245 p.
Review: R.J. Roberts in (1978), 4 *Canadian Public Policy* 264-266. **8480**

Klar, Lewis N. "An Argument for the Restructuring of the Law of Trade Marks." (1974), 12 *Osgoode Hall Law Journal* 223-234. **8481**

Klar, Lewis N. *The Nature and Function of Trade Marks, with Particular Reference to Licensing and Assignment*. Montreal, c1973. 126 leaves. **8482**
Thesis (LL.M.), McGill University, 1973. (National Library of Canada. Canadian Theses on Microfilm, No. 15895).

Kos-Rabcewicz-Zubkowski, Ludwik. "License Agreements in Canada." *In* Pollzien, Götz M., and Langen, Eugen, eds., *International Licensing Agreements*, 2d ed. (Indianapolis, 1973), pp. 67-88. **8483**

Landry, J. Nelson. "The Protection of Trade Secrets in Canada." (1982), 12 *Patent and Trademark Institute of Canada, Bulletin* 712-744. **8484**

McDonald, Bruce C. "Intellectual Property." *In* Macdonald, Ronald St. John, and others, *Canadian Perspectives on International Law and Organization* (Toronto, 1974), pp. 814-825. **8485**

McDonald, Bruce C. "The Intellectual Property Conference, Stockholm, 1967." (1964-68), 1 *Canadian Legal Studies* 307-310. **8486**

McLeod, Malcolm E. "A Canadian View of the Trademark Registration Treaty and a Preview of Proposed Amendments in Canadian Trademark Law." (1975), *Annual of Industrial Property Law* 98-116. **8487**

McMahon, Thomas J. "Canadian Trademark Law - A Bridge between United States and Foreign Law." (1979-80), 4 *Suffolk Transnational Law Journal* 251-280. **8488**

Montigny, Louvigny de. "Copyright in Canada." (1927), 5 *Canadian Bar Review* 27-43. **8489**

Moss, John H. "Copyright in Canada." (1914), 13 *University Magazine* 194-211. **8490**

Nesgos, Peter D. "Canadian Copyright Law and Satellite Transmissions." (1982), 20 *Osgoode Hall Law Journal* 232-249. **8491**

Ortiz, David Rangel. *Trade Marks: International Protection and Basic Features of the Mexican and Canadian Legal Systems.* Toronto, 1979. iii, 225 leaves. Thesis (LL.M.), University of Toronto, 1979. **8492**

Osborne, John C. "The Heartland of Trade Mark Law." (1980), 6 *Patent and Trademark Institute of Canada, Bulletin* 266-275. **8493**

Parker, George. "The Canadian Copyright Question in the 1980's." (1976), 11 *Journal of Canadian Studies* 43-55 (No. 2) **8494**

Perrault, Antonio. "La propriété littéraire et artistique." (1924), 18 *Royal Society of Canada, Transactions* 49-71 (3d Ser., Sec. 1) **8495**

Pichette, Serge. *Problèmes juridiques de transferts de technologie.* Montréal: Centre d'études en administration internationale, École des hautes études commerciales, 1979. ix, 491 p. **8496**
Study prepared for Centre d'études en administration internationale, École des hautes études commerciales.

Pichette, Serge, and Paquette, Michel. *Le régime canadien de la propriété intellectuelle: excluant les marques de commerce.* Montréal: Centre d'études en administration internationale, École des hautes études commerciales, 1979. ii, 275 p. **8497**
Study prepared for Centre d'études en administration internationale, École des hautes études commerciales.
Review: Andrea Friedman-Rush in (1982), 27 *McGill Law Journal* 613-615.

Ranson, A. Terence. "The Continuing Saga of Europe." (1982), 12 *Patent and Trademark Institute of Canada, Bulletin* 791-795. **8498**

Sandwell, B.K. "The Canadian Copyright Act." (1921-22), 29 *Queen's Quarterly* 182-188. **8499**

Sandwell, B.K. "The Copyright Situation." (1931), 38 *Queen's Quarterly* 335-347. **8500**

Shields, Robert A. "Imperial Policy and the Canadian Copyright Act of 1889." (1980-81), 60 *Dalhousie Review* 634-658. **8501**

Stakes, Wilbur Sylvester, Jr. *Know-How Licensing Agreements and the Antitrust Provisions of the Rome Treaty.* Toronto, 1964. xiv, 163 leaves. **8502**
Thesis (LL.M.), Osgoode Hall Law School, 1964.

Sterling, D.B., and MacLeod, W.J. "International Copyright Control: A Canadian Viewpoint." (1960), 1 *Current Law and Social Problems* 68-106. **8503**

Théberge, Richard. "Les enjeux de la révision de la convention de Paris à la veille de Nairobi." (1981), 12 *Revue Générale de Droit* 83-120. **8504**
Refers to the convention of Paris of March 20, 1883, as amended.

Wilson, *Sir* Daniel. "Canadian Copyright." (1892), 10 *Royal Society of Canada, Transactions* 3-17 (Sec. 2) **8505**

Wise, Frank. "Canadian Copyright." (1911), 10 *University Magazine* 404-413. **8506**

III. INTERNATIONAL TRANSPORTATION AND COMMUNICATION

A. Transportation in General

For marine transportation, see "Law of the Sea: High Seas" (p. 248), and "Marine Navigation and Transportation" (p. 270); see also "Inland Waterways" (p. 208). For air transportation, see "International Air Transportation" (p. 284), and "National Air Law" (p. 311). For pipelines, see also "North American Defence" (p. 436).

Askew, John Coulson. *Continentalism vs. Nationalism: The Party Politics of Oil and Gas Pipelines in Canada, 1949-1976.* London, Ont., 1977. v, 108 leaves. **8507**
  Thesis (M.A.), University of Western Ontario, 1977. (National Library of Canada. Canadian Theses on Microfiche, No. 31551).

Ballem, John Bishop. "International Pipelines: Canada-United States." (1980), 18 *Canadian Yearbook of International Law* 146-160. **8508**

Barry, P.S. "The Prolific Pipeline: Getting Canol under Way." (1976-77), 56 *Dalhousie Review* 252-267. **8509**

Canada. Transport Commission. International Transport Research Group. *Study on International Combined Transport of Goods Convention.* Ottawa: Canadian Transport Commission, Economic and Social Analysis Branch, 1975. 154 p. (ESAB, 75-3) **8510**

Carruthers, Jeff. "The Giant Canada-U.S. Pipeline - the Alaska Highway Project." (1977-78), 1 *Foreign Investment Review* 5-9. **8511**

Diubaldo, Richard J. "The Canol Project in Canadian-American Relations." (1977), *Canadian Historical Association, Historical Papers* 178-195. **8512**

Ells, S.C. "Alaska Highway." (1944), 28 *Canadian Geographical Journal* 104-119. **8513**

Finnie, Richard. "The Epic of Canol." (1947), 34 *Canadian Geographical Journal* 137-139. **8514**

Fischer, Hugo. "The Convention on the Law Applicable to Traffic Accidents." (1971), 9 *Canadian Yearbook of International Law* 189-216. **8515**

FitzGerald, Gerald F. "The Proposed Convention on International Multimodal Transport of Goods: A Progress Report." (1979), 17 *Canadian Yearbook of International Law* 247-279. **8516**

FitzGerald, Gerald F. "The United Nations Convention on the International Multi-Modal Transport of Goods." (1980), 5 *Annals of Air and Space Law* 51-88. **8517**

Grant, Daniel John. *T.D. Pattullo's Northern Empire: The Alaska Highway and the Proposed Annexation of the Yukon Territory, 1933-1941.* Victoria, 1980. 100 frames. **8518**
   Thesis (M.A.), University of Victoria, 1980. (National Library of Canada. Canadian Theses on Microfiche, No. 49409).

Hopkins, Oliver B. "The 'Canol' Project: Canada Provides Oil for the Allies." (1943), 27 *Canadian Geographical Journal* 238-249. **8519**

Kupsch, W.O. "The Wells and Canol: A Visit after 25 Years." (1971), 82 *Canadian Geographical Journal* 134-141. **8520**

Lotz, Jim. "Northern Pipelines and Southern Assumptions." (1977), 30 *Arctic* 199-204. **8521**

Mangematin, Luc. *Contrôle du transport par pipe-line; U.S.A., France, Canada.* Montréal, c1971. v, iii, 138 leaves. **8522**
   Thesis (LL.M.), McGill University, 1971. (National Library of Canada. Canadian Theses on Microfilm, No. 9773).

Munro, John M. *Trade Liberalization and Transportation in International Trade.* Toronto: University of Toronto Press, c1969. x, 203 p. (Canada in the Atlantic Economy, Vol. 8) **8523**
   Published for the Private Planning Association of Canada.
   Reviews: K.W. Studnicki-Gizbert in (1970), 3 *Canadian Journal of Economics* 332-333; Kimon Valaskakis in (1969-70), 23 *Revue d'Histoire de l'Amérique Française* 632-635.

Nerbas, Grant H. "Canadian Transportation Policy, Regulation, and Major Problems." (1967), 33 *Journal of Air Law and Commerce* 242-268. **8524**

Peippo, David J. "Developments in American Antitrust Law: Deregulation under the *Staggers Rail Act* and the Implications for Canadian Railroad Rate-Making." (1982), 27 *McGill Law Journal* 504-526. **8525**

Pineau, Jean. *Droit des transports: transports terrestres, maritimes et aériens.* Montréal: Éditions Thémis, 1977. 254 p. (Cours de Thémis) **8526**

Quirin, G. David, and Wolff, R.N. "The Economics of Oil Transportation in the Arctic." *In* Alexander, Lewis M., and Hawkins, Gordon R.S., eds., *Canadian-U.S. Maritime Problems* (Kingston, R.I., 1972), pp. 32-46. **8527**

Sokolsky, Joel J. "The Canada-U.S. Alaska Highway Pipeline: A Study in Environmental Decision-Making." (1979), 9 *American Review of Canadian Studies* 84-112 (No. 2) **8528**

Stefansson, Vilhjalmur. "Routes to Alaska." (1940-41), 19 *Foreign Affairs* 861-869. **8529**

U.S. Congress. Senate. Committee on Foreign Relations. *Agreement with Canada concerning Transit Pipelines: Report to Accompany Ex. F, 95-1.* Washington: Govt. Print. Off., 1977. 98 p., map. (U.S. 95th Cong., 1st sess. Senate. Ex. Rept. 95-9) **8530**
   Refers to the Alaska pipeline agreement of January 28, 1977 (CTS 1977/29).

B. Telecommunications

See also *"Outer Space" (p. 315)*.

Arcy, Jean d.' "Direct Broadcast Satellites and Freedom of Information." *In* McWhinney, Edward, ed., *The International Law of Communications* (Leyden, 1971), pp. 149-170. **8531**

Biggar, O.M. "The Law Relating to Wireless Communication." (1928), 13 *Canadian Bar Association, Proceedings* 147-157. **8532**

Canada. Dept. of Communications. *Telecommunications and Canada.* Prepared by the Consultative Committee on the Implications of Telecommunications for Canadian Sovereignty. Hull, Que.: Supply and Services, 1979. 98 p. **8533**
Review: Frank Peers in (1979), 5 *Canadian Public Policy* 572-573.

Chapman, John H., and Warren, Gabriel I. "Direct Broadcast Satellites: The ITU, UN and the Real World!" (1979), 4 *Annals of Air and Space Law* 413-432. **8534**

Chayes, Abram. "Unilateralism in United States Satellite Communications Policy." *In* McWhinney, Edward, ed., *The International Law of Communications* (Leyden, 1971), pp. 42-50. **8535**

Christol, Carl Q. "Remote Sensing and International Law." (1980), 5 *Annals of Air and Space Law* 375-426. **8536**

"Conference on International Communications and Institutions, Ottawa, March 23-24, 1973, Proceedings." (1973), 5 *Canadian Communications Law Review* 125-256. **8537**
Individual papers are listed separately.

Cundiff, W.E., and Reid, Mado, eds. *Issues in Canadian/U.S. Transborder Computer Data Flows.* Montreal: Institute for Research on Public Policy; distributed by Butterworth, 1979. v, 89 p. **8538**
Contains proceedings of a conference held in Montreal on September 6, 1978, sponsored by the Institute for Research on Public Policy.

Dalfen, Charles M. "Direct Satellite Broadcasting: International Responses." (1973), 5 *Canadian Communications Law Review* 215-226. **8539**

Dalfen, Charles M. "Direct Satellite Broadcasting: Towards International Arrangements to Transcend and Marshal the Political Realities." (1970), 20 *University of Toronto Law Journal* 366-374. **8540**
Lecture delivered at the Department of Political Economy, University of Toronto, November 21, 1969.

Dalfen, Charles M. "The International Legislative Process: Direct Broadcasting and Remote Earth Sensing by Satellite Compared." (1972), 10 *Canadian Yearbook of International Law* 186-211. **8541**

Dalfen, Charles M. "Telecommunications." *In* Macdonald, Ronald St. John, and others, *Canadian Perspectives on International Law and Organization* (Toronto, 1974), pp. 337-359. **8542**

Dalfen, Charles M. "The Telesat Canada Domestic Communications Satellite System." (1970), 5 *Stanford Journal of International Studies* 84-113. **8543**

Devine, Thomas Joseph. *Towards International Regulation of Telecommunications by Satellite.* Montreal, 1969. 131 leaves. **8544**
Thesis (LL.M.), McGill University, 1969. (National Library of Canada. Canadian Theses on Microfilm, No. 4815).

Dickson, Brian H. "Effect of 1977 I.T.U. World Administrative Radio Conference on the Formulation of U.N. Draft Principles on Direct Broadcast Satellites (DBS)." (1977), 2 *Annals of Air and Space Law* 255-267. **8545**

"Direct Satellite Broadcasting: Legal and Institutional Issues." (1973), 5 *Canadian Communications Law Review* 227-256. **8546**
Panel discussion. Chairman: Olaf Rydbeck.- Speakers: Charles M. Dalfen; Laurent Picard; and Herbert K. Reis.

Doyle, Stephen E. "International Satellite Communications and the Law." (1965), 11 *McGill Law Journal* 137-147. **8547**

DuCharme, Edward D.; Bowen, Robert R.; and Irwin, Matthew J.R. "The Genesis of the 1985/87 ITU World Administrative Radio Conference on the Use of the Geostationary-Satellite Orbit and the Planning of Space Services Utilizing It." (1982), 7 *Annals of Air and Space Law* 261-282. **8548**

Dudoit, Alain. *Une analyse de la politique canadienne en matière de télécommunications spatiales.* Montréal, 1973. v, 383 leaves. **8549**
Thesis (M.A.), Université de Montréal, 1973.

Elias, Taslim Olawale. "The Contribution of Telecommunications and Direct Satellite Broadcasting to Technical Assistance and Nation-Building in the 'New' Countries: An African Viewpoint." *In* McWhinney, Edward, ed., *The International Law of Communications* (Leyden, 1971), pp. 122-137. **8550**

Errera, Roger. "Problems Raised by the Content of Television Programs Transmitted by Telecommunication Satellites." *In* McWhinney, Edward, ed., *The International Law of Communications* (Leyden, 1971), pp. 85-98. **8551**

Fauteux, Paul. "Pour une réglementation internationale de la radiodiffusion directe par satellites." (1980), 5 *Annals of Air and Space Law* 427-447. **8552**

Fauteux, Paul. "Radiodiffusion directe par satellites: adieu au consensus?" (1981), 6 *Annals of Air and Space Law* 345-380. **8553**

Feldman, George J. "International Arrangements for Satellite Communications." *In* Cohen, Maxwell, ed., *Law and Politics in Space* (Montreal, 1964), pp. 23-28. **8554**

Fleming, Sandford. "The Empire Cables." (1904-05), 12 *Queen's Quarterly* 68-73. **8555**

Fleming, Sandford. "The Meaning of the Pacific Cable." (1902-03), 10 *Queen's Quarterly* 301-308. **8556**

Fleming, Sandford. "The Pacific Cable." (1897-98), 5 *Queen's Quarterly* 225-235. **8557**

Frigon, Augustin. "Radio in Wartime." (1939), 25 *Revue Trimestrielle Canadienne* 391-400. **8558**

Galloway, Eilene. "Present Status in the United Nations of Direct Television Broadcast Satellites (June 1977)." (1977), 2 *Annals of Air and Space Law* 269-285. **8559**

Gotlieb, Allan E. "Recent Developments in the Law of Space Communications: Some Current Satellite Questions." (1970), 20 *University of Toronto Law Journal* 359-365. **8560**
Address given at the meeting of the Canadian Institute of International Affairs (New York Branch), January 29, 1970.

Gotlieb, Allan E., and Dalfen, Charles M. "Direct Satellite Broadcasting: A Case Study in the Development of the Law of Space Communications." (1969), 7 *Canadian Yearbook of International Law* 33-60. **8561**

Gotlieb, Allan E.; Dalfen, Charles M.; and Katz, Kenneth. "The Transborder Transfer of Information by Communications and Computer Systems: Issues and Approaches to Guiding Principles." (1974), 68 *American Journal of International Law* 227-257. **8562**

Hage, Robert E. "Communications Satellites and Problems of Copyright in Canada." (1970), 2 *Canadian Communications Law Review* 41-46. **8563**

Herrera de Fraino, Olga. *International Regulation of Direct Broadcasting by Satellites: Its Possible Use for Educational Purposes, Particularly in Latin American Countries.* Montreal, 1978. vii, 169 leaves. **8564**
Thesis (LL.M.), McGill University, 1978.

Hinchman, Walter R. "The Technological Environment for International Communications Law." *In* McWhinney, Edward, ed., *The International Law of Communications* (Leyden, 1971), pp. 21-41. **8565**

Hondius, Frits W. "International Control of Broadcasting Programs in Western Europe." *In* McWhinney, Edward, ed., *The International Law of Communications* (Leyden, 1971), pp. 69-84. **8566**

"The Impact of Satellite Technology on International Telecommunications Operation and International Institutions." (1973), 5 *Canadian Communications Law Review* 140-174. **8567**
Panel discussion. Chairman: Allan E. Gotlieb.- Speakers: B.A. Walker; A.J. Torobin; J.V. Charyk; Bert W. Rein; and Ivan A. Vlasic.

"International Legal Problems of Computer Communications: Automation of the Transnational Information Flow." (1970), 20 *University of Toronto Law Journal* 337-358. **8568**
Part of proceedings of the Conference on the Legal Problems of International Communications, organized jointly by the Canadian Branch, International Law Association, and the Institute for International Co-operation, held at the University of Ottawa, October 24-25, 1969. Chairman: Gerald F. FitzGerald.- Rapporteur: Hugh Lawford (pp. 337-345). Panelists: A.J. de Grandpré (pp. 345-346); William R. Lederman (pp. 346-351); and J.S. Grafstein (pp. 351-355).- Discussion (pp. 355-358).

"International Legal Problems of Direct Satellite Broadcasting." (1970), 20 *University of Toronto Law Journal* 314-332. **8569**
Part of proceedings of the Conference on the Legal Problems of International Communications, organized jointly by the Canadian Branch, International Law Association, and the Institute for International Co-operation, held at the University of Ottawa, October

24-25, 1969. Chairman: Louis Sabourin.- Rapporteur: Charles M. Dalfen (pp. 314-318). Panelists: André Bissonnette (pp. 318-320); Pierre Juneau (pp. 320-321); and Ivan A. Vlasic (pp. 321-323).- Discussion (pp. 323-332).

"International Telecommunications." (1949), 1 *External Affairs* 3-5 (Nov.) **8570**

"The International Telecommunications Consortium: Negotiations for a Permanent Organization." (1971), 23 *External Affairs* 97-100. **8571**

Jakhu, Ram S. "Direct Broadcasting via Satellite and a New Information Order." (1981), 8 *Syracuse Journal of International Law and Commerce* 375-390.
8572

Jakhu, Ram S., and Trecroce, Riccardo. "International Satellite Monitoring for Disarmament and Development." (1980), 5 *Annals of Air and Space Law* 509-527. **8573**

Jasentuliyana, Nandasiri. "The Establishment of an International Maritime Satellite System." (1977), 2 *Annals of Air and Space Law* 323-349. **8574**

Juneau, Pierre. "International Broadcasting: Diversity or Uniformity." (1973), 5 *Canadian Communications Law Review* 206-214. **8575**

Kierans, Eric W. "Legal Problems of International Communications. (Dinner Address)." (1970), 20 *University of Toronto Law Journal* 333-336. **8576**
Address delivered at the Conference on the Legal Problems of International Communications held at the University of Ottawa, October 24-25, 1969.

Kopal, Vladimir. "East-West Cooperation in Space Telecommunications: A Socialist Countries' Viewpoint." *In* McWhinney, Edward, ed., *The International Law of Communications* (Leyden, 1971), pp. 99-112. **8577**

Lee, Edward G. "UNESCO Meeting on Space Communications: Legal Issues." (1970), 20 *University of Toronto Law Journal* 375-379. **8578**

"The Legal Problems of International Telecommunications with Special Reference to Intelsat." (1970), 20 *University of Toronto Law Journal* 287-313. **8579**
Proceedings of a conference organized jointly by the Canadian Branch, International Law Association, and the Institute for International Co-operation, held at Ottawa, October 24, 1969. Chairman: Allan E. Gotlieb.- Rapporteur: J. Alan Beesley.- Panelists: Edward McWhinney; Dallas W. Smythe; and Barry Mawhinney. Dinner address by Eric W. Kierans (pp. 333-336).

Leive, David M. "The Intelsat Arrangements." *In* Matte, Nicolas Mateesco, and DeSaussure, Hamilton, eds., *Legal Implications of Remote Sensing from Outer Space* (Leiden, 1976), pp. 167-172. **8580**

Lyall, Francis. *Law and Space Telecommunications*. Montreal, 1965. 183 leaves. Thesis (LL.M.), McGill University, 1965. **8581**

Mankiewicz, René H. "Intervention with Respect to Satellite-Telecommunication." (1968), 11 *Colloquium on the Law of Outer Space, Proceedings* 226-227. **8582**

Mateesco-Matte, Mircea. "Un *jus communicationis* et un *jus navigationis*." (1981), 6 *Annals of Air and Space Law* 405-438. **8583**

Matte, Nicolas Mateesco. *Aerospace Law: Telecommunication Satellites*. Toronto: Butterworths in cooperation with the Institute of Air and Space Law, McGill University, c1982. xxi, 354 p. **8584**

Also published in French under title: *Droit aérospatial: les télécommunications par satellites.*
Review: Ludwik Kos-Rabcewicz-Zubkowski in (1982), 7 *Annals of Air and Space Law* 622.

Matte, Nicolas Mateesco. *Droit aérospatial: les télécommunications par satellites.* Paris: A. Pedone, 1982. 472 p. **8585**
Also published in English under title: *Aerospace Law: Telecommunication Satellites.*
Review: Michel Bourély in (1982), 7 *Annals of Air and Space Law* 620-622.

McWhinney, Edward. "The Antinomy of Policy and Function in the Institutionalization of International Telecommunications Broadcasting." (1974), 13 *Columbia Journal of Transnational Law* 3-67. **8586**

McWhinney, Edward. "The Development of an International Law of Communications." *In* McWhinney, Edward, ed., *The International Law of Communications* (Leyden, 1971), pp. 11-20. **8587**

McWhinney, Edward, ed. *The International Law of Communications.* Leyden: Sijthoff; Dobbs Ferry, N.Y.: Oceana Publications, 1971. 170 p. **8588**
Contains a collection of 11 essays presented at a special colloquium on the New International Law of Communications held in the Institute of Air and Space Law at McGill University, Montreal, May 25-26, 1970. Individual essays are listed separately.
Reviews: Thomas Joseph Devine in (1972-73), 28 *International Journal* 165-166; David M. Leive in (1972), 66 *American Journal of International Law* 441; Francis Rigaldies in (1972), 3 *Études Internationales* 273-274; E. Roucounas in (1971), 24 *Revue Hellénique de Droit International* 406-407.

Nesgos, Peter D. "Canadian Copyright Law and Satellite Transmissions." (1982), 20 *Osgoode Hall Law Journal* 232-249. **8589**

Nixon, F.G. "Intelsat: A Progress Report on the Move Toward Definite Agreements." (1970), 20 *University of Toronto Law Journal* 380-385. **8590**

Pettey, Bryce H., and Allebes, Edward. "Resurgence of Canadian Nationalism and Its Effect on American-Canadian Communications Relations." (1974), 9 *Journal of International Law and Economics* 149-173. **8591**

Poulantzas, Nicholas M. "Direct Satellite Telecommunications: A Test for Human Rights Attitudes." (1975), 18 *Colloquium on the Law of Outer Space, Proceedings* 157-165. **8592**
Also printed in (1975), 28 *Revue Hellénique de Droit International* 226-237.

Poulantzas, Nicholas M. "Direct Satellite Telecommunications: Recent Legal Developments." (1972), 15 *Colloquium on the Law of Outer Space, Proceedings* 83-87. **8593**

Poulantzas, Nicholas M. "Direct Satellite Telecommunications: State Sovereignty v. Freedom of Information." (1973), 20 *Netherlands International Law Review* 163-181. **8594**
Also published in (1975), 23 *Chitty's Law Journal* 87-98.

Rao, K. Krishna. "The Contribution of Telecommunications and Direct Satellite Broadcasting to Technical Assistance and Nation-Building in the 'New' Countries: An Asian Viewpoint." *In* McWhinney, Edward, ed., *The International Law of Communications* (Leyden, 1971), pp. 113-121. **8595**

Ringereide, Trygve. "Communication Satellites: The New Revolution in Communications." (1963), 67 *Canadian Geographical Journal* 14-21. **8596**

Sagar, David. "International Organizations: INMARSAT." (1981), 6 *Annals of Air and Space Law* 586-591. **8597**

Sagar, David. "International Organizations: INMARSAT." (1982), 7 *Annals of Air and Space Law* 504-509. **8598**

"Satellite Communications." (1964), 16 *External Affairs* 208-210. **8599**

Singh, Indu B. *A Study of Canada-U.S. Cooperation in Space Communications Programs with Special Reference to the Communications Technology Satellite Project*. Athens, Ohio, 1977. 359 leaves. **8600**
Thesis (Ph.D.), Ohio University, 1977. Abstracted in (1978), 38 *Dissertation Abstracts International* 7008-A. (University Microfilms, Ann Arbor, No. 78-07527).

Stevens, Douglas F. *'Pirate' Broadcasting in European Waters: The British Response*. Ottawa, 1968. 60, 11 leaves. **8601**
Research essay (M.A.), Carleton University, 1969.

Stoler, Andrew L. "The Border Broadcasting Dispute: A Unique Case under Section 301." (1980-81), 6 *International Trade Law Journal* 39-54. **8602**

Swinton, Katherine. "Advertising and Canadian Cable Television - a Problem in International Communications Law." (1977), 15 *Osgoode Hall Law Journal* 543-590. **8603**

Valladão, Haroldo. "South American Contributions to Solution of the Juridical Problems of Telecommunications and Direct Satellite Broadcasting." *In* McWhinney, Edward, ed., *The International Law of Communications* (Leyden, 1971), pp. 138-148. **8604**

Verdon, Christiane, and Dalfen, Charles M. "La coopération régionale: nouvelle voie ou impasse dans le développement du droit des satellites de radiodiffusion directe?" (1970), 8 *Canadian Yearbook of International Law* 39-60. **8605**

Vicas, Alexander G. "An Economic Assessment of CCIR's Five Methods for Assuring Guaranteed Access to the Orbit-Spectrum Resource." (1982), 7 *Annals of Air and Space Law* 431-446. **8606**

Walker, B.A., and Torobin, A.J. "Problems Associated with the Creation of Operational Institutions for International Satellite Communications." (1973), 5 *Canadian Communications Law Review* 126-139. **8607**

Warren, Gabriel I. "A Canadian Perspective on Direct Broadcast Satellites and the New World Information and Communication Order." (1981), 8 *Syracuse Journal of International Law and Commerce* 391-396. **8608**

Williams, Sylvia Maureen. "Teleinformatics, the Protection of Privacy and the Law." (1982), 7 *Annals of Air and Space Law* 447-468. **8609**

Ziadat, Adel Awwad. *International Aspects of Direct Broadcasting by Satellite*. Ottawa, 1976. 146 leaves. **8610**
Research essay (M.A.), Carleton University, 1976.

C. Postal Service

Atwater, H.E. "The New Postal Laws." (1907-08), 15 *Queen's Quarterly* 191-201. **8611**
Refers to the postal conventions with the United States of April 1907, and postal relations with Great Britain.

"The New Postal Convention." (1907-08), 15 *Queen's Quarterly* 70-72. **8612**
Refers to the postal convention with the United States of April 1907.

Smith, William. "International Co-operation." (1914), 13 *University Magazine* 444-459. **8613**

IV. INTERNATIONAL SCIENTIFIC AND TECHNOLOGICAL AFFAIRS

A. General

Agblemagnon, N'Sougan. "Mise en place de programmes scientifiques pour le développement." *In* Jacomy-Millette, Annemarie, ed., *Francophonie et Commonwealth: mythe ou réalité?* (Québec, 1978), pp. 169-178.   **8614**

Antoine, Aristide. "Les Nations Unies et la technique." (1948-49), 34 *Revue Trimestrielle Canadienne* 454-458.   **8615**

Arnell, J.C. "International Science and National Technology: A Problem for the 1970's." (1969-70), 25 *International Journal* 667-675.   **8616**

Fairley, H. Scott, and Rowcliffe, Peter J. "The UNCTAD Code of Conduct for the International Transfer of Technology: Problems and Prospects." (1980), 18 *Canadian Yearbook of International Law* 218-247.   **8617**

Ghent, Jocelyn Maynard. *Canadian Government Participation in International Science and Technology*. Ottawa: Science Council of Canada, 1979. 136 p. (Science Council of Canada. Background Study, No. 44)   **8618**
Review: G.D. Garland in (1980), 6 *Canadian Public Policy* 407.

Ghent, Jocelyn Maynard. "Science, Technology; and Trudeau's Foreign Policy." (1977-78), 36 *Behind the Headlines* No. 5 (16 p.)   **8619**

Globerman, Steven. "Canadian Science Policy and Technological Sovereignty." (1978), 4 *Canadian Public Policy* 34-45.   **8620**

Gold, Edgar. "The International Transfer and Promotion of Technology." *In* Macdonald, Ronald St. John, and others, *The International Law and Policy of Human Welfare* (Alphen aan den Rijn, 1978), pp. 549-581.   **8621**

Gordon, J. King, ed. *Canada's Role in Science and Technology for Development: Proceedings of a Symposium Held at the Ontario Science Centre, Toronto, Canada, 10-13 May 1979*. Ottawa: International Development Research Centre, 1979. 136 p.   **8622**

Gotlieb, Allan E. "Technology and Law. (Banquet Address)." (1981), 10 *Canadian Council on International Law, Proceedings*, 194-200.   **8623**
See also the statement by J. Alan Beesley on the Impact of Technology on Development of International Law (pp. 213-219).

Hamilton, Roger Lyne. *Multinational Enterprises and the Transfer of Technology:*

International and Host Country Responses. Downsview, Ont., 1975. xi, 223 leaves. **8624**
Thesis (LL.M.), York University, 1975. (National Library of Canada. Canadian Theses on Microfiche, No. 25717).

"The International Geophysical Year." (1959), 11 *External Affairs* 266-269. **8625**

McKinley, Kathryn, and Young, Roger. *Technology and the Third World: The Issues and the Role for Canada.* Ottawa: North-South Institute, 1979. vi, 77 p. (North-South Papers, 1) **8626**
Also published in French under title: *La technologie et le tiers-monde.*
Review: Michael MacKenzie in (1980), 6 *Canadian Public Policy* 423.

McKnight, Allan. "International Regulation of Science and Technology." (1969-70), 25 *International Journal* 745-753. **8627**

Page, Garnet T. "The Internationalism of Science." (1956-57), 36 *Dalhousie Review* 230-237. **8628**

Pardo, Arvid. "The Impact of Science and Technology on the Development of International Law." (1972), 1 *Canadian Council on International Law, Proceedings* 202-218. **8629**

Precht, Paul Lawrence. *New Technology and International Trade.* Edmonton, 1969. v, 96 leaves. **8630**
Thesis (M.A.), University of Alberta, 1969.

Roach, E. Hugh. "The Transfer of Technology: The Need for Pragmatism." (1978-79), 37 *Behind the Headlines* No. 5 (28 p.) **8631**

Schroeder-Gudehus, Brigitte. "La coopération scientifique; réflexions sur les problèmes d'évaluation de la coopération scientifique bilatérale." (1974), 5 *Études Internationales* 388-398. **8632**

Schroeder-Gudehus, Brigitte. "Les relations internationales culturelles, scientifiques et techniques." *In* Painchaud, Paul, ed., *Le Canada et le Québec sur la scène internationale* (Québec, 1977), pp. 253-272. **8633**

Schroeder-Gudehus, Brigitte. *Les scientifiques et la paix: la communauté scientifique internationale au cours des années 20.* Montréal: Presses de l'Université de Montréal, 1978. 371 p. **8634**
Review: Jean-Pierre Derriennic in (1979), 10 *Études Internationales* 201-202.

"Science, Technology and Humanity." (1963), 15 *External Affairs* 163-169. **8635**

Stoffaes, Christian. "Le pouvoir technologique et nucléaire." (1979), 10 *Études Internationales* 737-756. **8636**

Wilson, J. Tuzo. "Science, ICSU and UNESCO." (1963), 66 *Canadian Geographical Journal* 108-116. **8637**

Zuijdwijk, Anthony J.M. "Three Crucial Aspects of the UNCTAD Code of Conduct on Transfer of Technology." (1979), 8 *Canadian Council on International Law, Proceedings* 226-237. **8638**

Zuijdwijk, Anthony J.M. "The UNCTAD Code of Conduct on the Transfer of Technology." (1978), 24 *McGill Law Journal* 562-587. **8639**

B. Natural Resources

See also *"Commodities" (p. 580), and "Marine Resources" (p. 251).*

Allen, Robert. *How to Save the World: Strategy for World Conservation.* Scarborough, Ont.: Prentice-Hall of Canada, 1980. 144 p. **8640**

Austin, Jack. "Comments on the Legal Status of United States-Canadian Economic Relations in Natural Resource Sharing." (1969), *Canadian Bar Association, Papers,* 25 p. **8641**

Beigie, Carl E. "Canada and the United States in an Interdependent World: The Optimum Use of Canadian Resources." (1976), 32 *Academy of Political Science, Proceedings* 164-175 (No. 2) **8642**

Beigie, Carl E., and Hero, Alfred O., eds. *Natural Resources in U.S.-Canadian Relations.* Boulder, Colo.: Westview Press, 1980-81. 3 vols. **8643**
Published in cooperation with the World Peace Foundation and the C.D. Howe Research Institute.
Contents: v. 1. The Evolution of Politics and Issues.- v. 2. Patterns and Trends in Resource Supplies and Politics.- v. 3. Perspectives, Prospects and Policy Options.
Reviews:
Volume 1: Ronald M. Burns in (1981), 14 *Canadian Journal of Political Science* 645; Raymond Hudon in (1980), 11 *Études Internationales* 564-568; John M. Treddenick in (1980-81), 36 *International Journal* 241-243.
Volume 2: Raymond Hudon in (1982), 13 *Études Internationales* 187-188; John M. Treddenick in (1980-81), 36 *International Journal* 924-926.

Bocking, Richard C. *Canada's Water: For Sale?* Toronto: James Lewis & Samuel, 1972. xii, 188 p. **8644**
Based on a film prepared for the CSC's "Tuesday Night" series.
Review: Neil A. Swainson in (1973), 16 *Canadian Public Administration* 509-510.

Chambers, Winston, and Reid, John. "Limitations on Sovereignty over Natural Resources." (1977), *International Perspectives* 13-19 (Nov./Dec.) **8645**

Clark, Lorne S. "International Law and Natural Resources." (1976-77), 4 *Syracuse Journal of International Law and Commerce* 377-390. **8646**

Clark, Lorne S., and others. "Regulation of Natural Resource Development: Panel Discussion." (1976-77), 4 *Syracuse Journal of International Law and Commerce* 391-405. **8647**

Cram, J.S. "Canadian Water and the United States." *In* Cram, J.S., *Water: Canadian Needs and Resources* (3d ed., Montreal, 1973), pp. 139-152. **8648**

"The Development of Natural Resources: International Law and Policy." (1970), 22 *External Affairs* 398-403. **8649**
Paper given at the annual meeting of the Canadian Bar Association in Halifax, on September 2, 1970.

Dow, Alexander. "International Minerals Policy Should Be Adopted by Canada." (1977), *International Perspectives* 19-25 (Nov./Dec.) **8650**

Gould, Wesley L. "Metals, Oil, and Natural Gas: Some Problems of Canadian-

American Co-operation." *In* Deener, David R., ed., *Canada-United States Treaty Relations* (Durham, N.C., 1963), pp. 151-184. **8651**

Head, Ivan L. "How Will the Present Condition of Resource Scarcity Affect Relations between Europe, North America, and Latin America? A Canadian Point of View." *In* Atlantic Conference, Taormina, 1974, *Resources and International Politics* (Chicago, 1975), pp. 71-85. **8652**

Helliwell, John. "Extractive Resources in the World Economy." (1973-74), 29 *International Journal* 591-609. **8653**

Hurst, C.K. "Water in International Affairs." (1956), 16 *Behind the Headlines* No. 3 (16 p.) **8654**

Innis, Donald Q. "North American Use of Canadian Resources." (1961), 68 *Queen's Quarterly* 316-322. **8655**

Keenleyside, Hugh L. "The International Significance of Canadian Resources." (1949-50), 5 *International Journal* 109-120. **8656**

Lloyd, Trevor. "A Water Resources Policy for Canada." (1966), 73 *Canadian Geographical Journal* 3-17. **8657**
Includes international aspects.

Matte, Nicolas Mateesco. "Limited Aerospace Natural Resources and Their Regulation." (1982), 7 *Annals of Air and Space Law* 379-398. **8658**

McGavin, Robert James. "Canadian-American Relations: Water, Water Everywhere - but Shortages Are Coming." (1978), *International Perspectives* 27-31 (July/Aug.) **8659**

Neate, Frank G. "The Problem of Canadian Fuel Independence." (1929), 36 *Queen's Quarterly* 345-353. **8660**

Nemetz, Peter N., ed. *Resource Policy: International Perspectives.* Montreal: Institute for Research on Public Policy, c1980. xliv, 371 p. **8661**
Review: J.W. Giles in (1981), 24 *Canadian Public Administration* 327-329.

C. Energy Issues

1. GENERAL

See also *"Commodities: Oil and Gas" (p. 583), and "Marine Resources: Oil and Gas Exploitation" (p. 263). For pipelines, see "Transportation in General" (p. 641).*

Adams, Mark S., and Steiner, Barry. "Energy and the North American Community: Canada, Mexico, and the United States." (1980), 3 *Hastings International and Comparative Law Quarterly* 369-434. **8662**

Ayoub, Antoine, ed. *Énergie: coopération internationale ou crise / Energy: International Cooperation or Crisis.* Québec: Presses de l'Université Laval, 1979. viii, 272 p. **8663**
Review: André Joyal in (1981), 12 *Études Internationales* 213-214.

Bourne, Charles B. "Energy and a Continental Concept." (1965), 8 *Canadian Bar Journal* 158-169.   **8664**
Also published in (1964), 6 *University of Windsor Seminar on Canadian-American Relations, Proceedings* 157-169.

Cisler, Walker. "Energy and North American Solidarity." (1963), 5 *University of Windsor Seminar on Canadian-American Relations, Proceedings* 129-135.
8665

Crane, David. "The Pressing Need for Canada to Define Its Energy Policies; a New Dimension to Global Policies." (1973), *International Perspectives* 32-37 (July/Aug.)   **8666**

Creery, Tim. "Energy Resources: the North American Political Context." (1963), 5 *University of Windsor Seminar on Canadian-American Relations, Proceedings* 136-143.   **8667**

Davis, Jack. "Energy and International Trade." (1963), 5 *University of Windsor Seminar on Canadian-American Relations, Proceedings* 144-156.   **8668**

Davis, Jack. "Energy in Its Continental Setting." (1964), 6 *University of Windsor Seminar on Canadian-American Relations, Proceedings* 170-180.   **8669**

Davis, John. "Canadian Energy Policy." (1958), 18 *Behind the Headlines* No. 6 (16 p.)   **8670**

Erickson, Edward W., and Waverman, Leonard, eds. *The Energy Question: An International Failure of Policy.* Toronto: University of Toronto Press, c1974. 2 vols.   **8671**
Contents: v. 1. The World.- v. 2. North America.
Reviews: Alan James MacFadyen in (1975), 1 *Canadian Public Policy* 256-260 (of vol. 1); Ronald S. Ritchie in (1975-76), 31 *International Journal* 358-359 (of vols. 1 and 2); D.A. Seastone in (1975), 1 *Canadian Public Policy* 260-263 (of vol. 2).

Frank, Helmut J., and Schanz, John J., Jr. *U.S.-Canadian Energy Trade: A Study of Changing Relationships.* Boulder, Colo.: Westview Press, 1978. xi, 136 p. (Westview Special Studies in Natural Resources and Energy Management)
8672

Fulford, D.W., and Blackburn, R.G. "Energy and International Economic Welfare." *In* Macdonald, Ronald St. John, and others, *The International Law and Policy of Human Welfare* (Alphen aan den Rijn, 1978), pp. 639-657.   **8673**

Getman, Charles. "Canada's National Energy Program: An Analysis." (1980), 3 *Houston Journal of International Law* 155-178.   **8674**

Grayson, George W. "The Maple Leaf, the Cactus and the Eagle: Energy Trilateralism." (1980-81), 34 *Inter-American Economic Affairs* 49-75 (No. 4)   **8675**

Greenwood, Ted. "Canadian-American Trade in Energy Resources." (1974), 28 *International Organization* 689-710.   **8676**
Reprinted in Fox, Annette Baker, and others, *Canada and the United States* (New York, 1976), pp. 97-118.

Hartwell, Robert. "Energy and North American Solidarity." (1963), 5 *University of Windsor Seminar on Canadian-American Relations, Proceedings* 157-163.
8677

Howe, Ralph W. "Transnational Regionalism: Energy Management in New England and the Maritimes." (1980), 3 *Canada-United States Law Journal* 139-200.
8678

Hunter, Lawson A.W. *Energy Policies of the World: Canada.* Newark: Center for the Study of Marine Policy, College of Marine Studies, University of Delaware, 1975. 64 p., maps. (Energy Policies of the World) **8679**

Jacomy-Millette, Annemarie. "David et Goliath: l'équilibre fragile des relations énergétiques canado-américaines à l'aube de la créaction de Petro-Canada." (1982), 13 *Études Internationales* 633-655. **8680**

Lantzke, Ulf. "Energy: An International Problem." (1979), *International Perspectives* 31-54 (Mar./Apr.) **8681**

Laxer, James. *The Energy Poker Game: The Politics of the Continental Resources Deal.* Toronto, Chicago: New Press, 1970. ii, 72 p. **8682**
Also published in French under title: *Au service des U.S.A.: la politique d'énergie du gouvernement canadien* (Montréal, c1972. 78 p.). Translated by Nicole Sakellaropolo and Odile Hénault.

McDougall, Ian A. "Canadian Energy Development and Trade: The Last Hand of the Poker Game." *In* Dwivedi, O.P., ed., *Protecting the Environment* (Toronto, 1974), pp. 189-210, 315-318. **8683**

McDougall, John N. "Prebuild Phase or Latest Phase? The United States Fuel Market and Canadian Energy Policy." (1980-81), 36 *International Journal* 117-138. **8684**

Mendes, Errol P. "The Canadian National Energy Program: An Example of Assertion of Economic Sovereignty or Creeping Expropriation in International Law." (1981), 14 *Vanderbilt Journal of Transnational Law* 475-507. **8685**

Nickel, Carl; Sharbaugh, H. Robert; and Hurtig, Mel. "A North American Cooperative Energy Policy." (1974), 16 *University of Windsor Seminar on Canadian-American Relations, Proceedings* 121-153. **8686**

Olson, Thomas H. "Foreign Investment Restrictions on Canadian Energy Resources." (1980), 14 *International Lawyer* 579-612. **8687**

"Power to the People: U.S.-Canadian Energy Policy." (1974), 68 *American Society of International Law, Proceedings* 76-92. **8688**
This is a panel. Donald S. Rickerd, Chairman.

Raicht, Lawrence; Maxwell, Judith; and Patterson, G.N. "North American Energy: Facts, Fiction and Perspectives." (1974), 16 *University of Windsor Seminar on Canadian-American Relations, Proceedings* 1-39. **8689**

Ritchie, Ronald S. "Assessing the Energy Issues from a Canadian Perspective." (1974), *International Perspectives* 13-18 (Mar./Apr.) **8690**

Ritchie, Ronald S. "Assessing the Energy Issues from a Canadian Perspective." (1981), *International Perspectives* 19-22 (Nov./Dec.) **8691**

Silverstein, Harvey B. "Canada and Hydrogen Systems: An Energy Policy for a Nation." (1980-81), 36 *International Journal* 294-310. **8692**

Smart, Ian. "Energy and the Public Good." (1980-81), 36 *International Journal* 255-272. **8693**

Sykes, Philip. *Sellout: The Giveaway of Canada's Energy Resources*. Edmonton: Hurtig Publishers, c1973. 235 p., map. **8694**

"Symposium: U.S.-Canadian Energy Resource Development. I. The Future of Canadian Energy Resource Development.- II. Current Views concerning Bilateral Exploitation of North American Energy Resources." (1972-73), 5 *Case Western Reserve Journal of International Law* 36-85. **8695**

Contents: I. Bilateral Exploitation of North American Energy Resources - An Introduction, by David B. Furlong (pp. 36-37).- Many Splendored Possibilities or Hobson's Choice? - Who Made the Policies and What Are the Assumptions, by Richard W. Edwards, Jr. (pp. 39-51).- A View from the North, by Andrew R. Thompson (pp. 52-64).-II. A Continental Energy Policy - An Examination of Some of the Current Issues, by Michael A. Galway (pp. 65-80).- The Effect of Law, Economics, and Politics on Energy Resources Development, by Earl Finbar Murphy (pp. 81-85).

U.S. Congress. Joint Economic Committee. *Canadian Oil Policies and Northern Tier Energy Alternatives: Hearing, 94th Cong., 2d sess., September 13, 1976*. Washington: Govt. Print. Off., 1977. iii, 217 p. **8696**

U.S. General Accounting Office. *Prospects for Cooperation and Trade of Energy Resources between the United States and Canada: Report to the Congress*. Washington: Govt. Print. Off., 1979. iii, 33 p. **8697**

Wonder, Edward F. "The U.S. Government Response to the Canadian National Energy Program." (1982), 8 *Canadian Public Policy* 480-497. **8698**

Includes: "Canadian Views on the U.S. Government Reaction to the National Energy Program," by Roy MacLaren (pp. 493-497).

2. NUCLEAR ENERGY

Allen, Frank. "Atomic Energy and World-Order." (1945-46), 15 *University of Toronto Quarterly* 256-268. **8699**

Bartholomew, Mark Alan. *The Effect of International Interdependence on Foreign Policy Making: Canadian and United States Nuclear Technology Export*. Miami, Fla., 1980. 196 frames. **8700**

Thesis (Ph.D.), University of Miami, 1980. (University Microfilms, Ann Arbor, No. 81-397).

Boardman, Robert. "Canadian Resources and the Contractual Link: The Case of Uranium." (1980-81), 4 *Revue d'Intégration Européenne* 299-325. **8701**

"Canada and the Peaceful Uses of Atomic Energy." (1955), 7 *External Affairs* 294-301. **8702**

"Canada's Agreements on Peaceful Uses of Atomic Energy." (1959), 11 *External Affairs* 156-158. **8703**

Canadian-American Committee. *Safer Nuclear Power Initiatives: A Call for Canada-U.S. Action: A Statement*. Montreal: Canadian-American Committee, 1978. vi, 14 p. (CAC 45) **8704**

Casterton, James Arthur. *The International Dimensions of the Canadian Nuclear Industry*. Ottawa, 1980. 195 frames. **8705**

Thesis (M.A.), Carleton University, 1980. (National Library of Canada. Canadian Theses on Microfiche, No. 49479). Abstracted in (1981), 19 *Masters Abstracts* 264.

Dean, Gordon. "Atoms for Peace: An American View." (1954), 9 *International Journal* 253-260. **8706**

Doern, G. Bruce, and Morrison, Robert W., eds. *Canadian Nuclear Policies: Proceedings of a Conference on Canadian Nuclear Policy.* Montreal: Institute for Research on Public Policy, 1980. xvi, 326 p. **8707**
Conference sponsored by the School of Public Administration and the Norman Paterson School of International Affairs, Carleton University, and the Science Council of Canada; held November 8-10, 1978.
Review: Clive Lloyd Brown-John in (1980), 23 *Canadian Public Administration* 656-658.

Evans, Anne Elizabeth. *Energy Crisis, Canada, and CANDU Reactors.* Ottawa, 1976. vii, 220 leaves. **8708**
Title on convocation programme: *Canadian Nuclear Energy and Its Influence on Foreign Relations.* Thesis (M.A.), Carleton University, 1976. Abstracted in (1978), 16 *Masters Abstracts* 179.

Galarneau, Hélène. *La politique du Canada en matière de contrôle des exportations nucléaires.* Québec, 1979. iii, 157 leaves. **8709**
Thesis (M.A.), Université Laval, 1979. (National Library of Canada. Canadian Theses on Microfiche, No. 41866).

Gorove, Stephen. "Controls over Atoms-for-Peace under Canadian Bilateral Agreements with Other Nations." (1965), 42 *Denver Law Center Journal* 41-51.
8710

Graham, William C. "A Practitioner's View of the Uranium Litigation and Uranium Export Policies." (1979), 8 *Canadian Council on International Law, Proceedings* 294-302. **8711**

Gray, Earle. *The Great Uranium Cartel.* Toronto: McClelland and Stewart, c1982. 303 p. **8712**

Hodgetts, John E. *Administering the Atom for Peace.* New York: Atherton Press, 1964. xi, 193 p. (International Political Science Association Series) (Atherton Press Political Science Series) **8713**
Review: Arthur W. MacMahon, (1963-64), 19 *International Journal* 565-566.

Hunt, Constance D. "Canadian Policy and the Export of Nuclear Energy." (1977), 27 *University of Toronto Law Journal* 69-104. **8714**

Hunter, Lawson A.W. "The Westinghouse Uranium Litigation." (1979), 8 *Canadian Council on International Law, Proceedings* 304-314. **8715**

Infeld, Leopold. "Atomic Energy and World Government." (1946), 6 *Behind the Headlines* No. 4 (20 p.) **8716**

"International Control of Atomic Energy." (1949), 1 *External Affairs* 21-28 (Nov.)
8717

Jennekens, Jon H. *Canadian Involvement in International Nuclear Cooperation.* Ottawa: Atomic Energy Control Board, 1981. 14 leaves. (Canada. Atomic Energy Control Board. Report) **8718**
Includes an abstract in French.

Keeley, James F. "Canadian Nuclear Export Policy and the Problems of Proliferation." (1980), 6 *Canadian Public Policy* 614-627. **8719**

Kintner, Edwin E.; Mooradian, Ara J.; and Rose, David. "Nuclear Power as a Major Energy Source." (1974), 16 *University of Windsor Seminar on Canadian-American Relations, Proceedings* 70-106. **8720**

Legault, Albert. "Arrangements and Techniques to Safeguard Nuclear Material." (1978), *International Perspectives* 24-27 (Sept./Oct.) **8721**

Lewis, W.B. "Atoms for Peace - Canada Goes to Geneva." (1956-57), 63 *Queen's Quarterly* 86-96. **8722**

Mazer, Brian M. "The International Framework of Safeguarding Peaceful Nuclear Energy Programs." (1980-81), 45 *Saskatchewan Law Review* 83-102. **8723**

McIntyre, Hugh C. *Uranium, Nuclear Power, and Canada-U.S. Energy Relations.* Montreal, Washington, D.C.: Canadian-American Committee, 1978. viii, 72 p.
Review: George Bindon in (1979), 5 *Canadian Public Policy* 284-285. **8724**

McKay, Paul. *Exporting Apocalypse: CANDU Reactors and Nuclear Proliferation.* Guelph: Ontario Public Interest Research Group, 1982. 21 p. **8725**

McNaughton, A.G.L. "National and International Control of Atomic Energy." (1948), 3 *International Journal* 11-23. **8726**

Morrison, Robert W., and Wonder, Edward F. *Canada's Nuclear Export Policy.* Ottawa: Norman Paterson School of International Affairs, 1978. 115 p. (Carleton International Studies, 1978/3) **8727**

Noble, John J. "Canada's Continuing Search for Acceptable Nuclear Safeguards." (1978), *International Perspectives* 42-48 (July/Aug.) **8728**

Nyman, James Segvard. *Canadian Atomic Energy Policy.* Berkeley, Calif., 1958. iii, 151 leaves. **8729**
Thesis (M.A.), University of California, 1958.

Palfrey, John. "Energy: the Atomic Concepts." (1964), 6 *University of Windsor Seminar on Canadian-American Relations, Proceedings* 181-185. **8730**

Reiskind, Jason. "Towards a Responsible Use of Nuclear Power in Outer Space - The Canadian Initiative in the United Nations. (With Preceding Note and Commentary by Maxwell Cohen)." (1981), 6 *Annals of Air and Space Law* 461-474. **8731**

Rudd, F.A. "Atomic Energy and World Government." (1946-47), 2 *International Journal* 237-241. **8732**

Stanford, Joseph S. "Nuclear Assistance and Cooperation Agreements: Some Problems in the Application of Safeguards." (1975), 10 *Journal of International Law and Economics* 437-451. **8733**

Stewart, Larry R. "International Trade: Canada and the Uranium Cartel." (1980), *International Perspectives* 21-25 (July/Aug.) **8734**

Stewart, Larry R. *The International Uranium Cartel: A Case Study in Canada's Response to Mineral Cartels and Producer Associations.* Kingston, 1980. 200 frames. **8735**
Thesis (M.A.), Queen's University, 1980. (National Library of Canada. Canadian Theses on Microfiche, No. 50200).

3. OTHER SOURCES OF ENERGY

Bernard, Jean-Thomas. "L'exportation d'électricité par le Québec." (1982), 8 *Canadian Public Policy* 321-333. **8736**

LeMay, Joseph A. "Quebec and Economic Interdependence with the United States: A Focus on Hydro-Quebec." (1980), 10 *American Review of Canadian Studies* 94-109 (No. 1) **8737**

Luce, Charles. "Kilowats Across the Border." (1963), 5 *University of Windsor Seminar on Canadian-American Relations, Proceedings* 164-173. **8738**

Perlgut, Mark. *Electricity Across the Border: The U.S.-Canadian Experience.* Montreal: Canadian-American Committee, 1978. ix, 65 p. (CAC 47) **8739**

Québec (Province). Direction générale de l'énergie. *Les échanges d'électricité entre le Québec et les États-Unis.* Québec: Direction des communications d'Énergie Québec, 1979. 15 p. **8740**
   Also published in English under title: *Electricity: Exchanges between Québec and the United States.*

Smith, Lincoln. "Passamaquoddy Power." (1950-51), 57 *Queen's Quarterly* 312-324. **8741**
   Refers to the International Passamaquoddy Tidal Power Project for New Brunswick and Maine.

D. Weather Information (Meteorology)

"Canada and the World Weather Watch." (1969), 21 *External Affairs* 28-32. **8742**

Hare, F. Kenneth. "Climate: The Neglected Factor?" (1980-81), 36 *International Journal* 371-387. **8743**

Kaplan, Irving E., and Jakhu, Ram S. "Global Climate Space Reflector Systems: Some Legal Issues." (1982), 7 *Annals of Air and Space Law* 353-361. **8744**

Patterson, J. "Meteorology in Peace and War." (1949), 38 *Canadian Geographical Journal* 115-135. **8745**

Samuels, Joseph W. "International Control of Weather Modification Activities." *In* Macdonald, Ronald St. John, and others, *Canadian Perspectives on International Law and Organization* (Toronto, 1974), pp. 360-373. **8746**

Samuels, Joseph W. "International Control of Weather Modification Activities: Peril or Policy?" (1973), 13 *Natural Resources Journal* 327-342. **8747**

Samuels, Joseph W. "International Control of Weather Modification Activities: Peril or Policy?" *In* Teclaff, Ludwik A., and Utton, Albert E., eds., *International Environmental Law* (New York, 1974), pp. 199-214. **8748**

Samuels, Joseph W. "On the International Law Regime to Govern Scientific Weathermaking as It Might Affect Other Nations." (1969), *World Peace Through Law* 521-525. **8749**

Samuels, Joseph W. "Prospective International Control of Weather Modification Activities." (1971), 21 *University of Toronto Law Journal* 222-225. **8750**
Paper prepared for a symposium on the international legal aspects of pollution held in Vancouver, September 1970.

E. Weights and Measures

Canada. Dept. of Industry, Trade and Commerce. *White Paper on Metric Conversion in Canada / Livre blanc sur la conversion au système métrique au Canada.* Ottawa, 1970, reprinted 1972. 22 p. Bilingual. **8751**

Canada. Metric Commission. *Annual Report / Rapport annuel.* 1st—, 1971/73—. Ottawa. Bilingual. **8752**
The Metric Commission, created in 1971, reports to Parliament through the Minister of Industry, Trade and Commerce.

Dupuis, N.F. "'The Metric System.'" (1906-07), 14 *Queen's Quarterly* 163-172.
8753

"Eleventh Conference on Weights and Measures." (1960), 12 *External Affairs* 895-898. **8754**

V. INTERNATIONAL ENVIRONMENTAL COOPERATION

A. General

Akinsanya, A. "Canadian and British Approaches to International Environmental Law: An Overview." (1977), 17 *Indian Journal of International Law* 335-353.
8755

Arctic Institute of North America. *Position Paper: Prepared for the United Nations Conference on the Human Environment, Stockholm, June 1972.* Montreal, 1972. 18 p. **8756**

Bacon, T.C. "The Role of the United Nations Environment Program (UNEP) in the Development of International Environmental Law." (1974), 12 *Canadian Yearbook of International Law* 255-266. **8757**

Beesley, J. Alan. "The Canadian Approach to International Environmental Law." (1973), 11 *Canadian Yearbook of International Law* 3-12. **8758**

Boardman, Robert. *International Organization and the Conservation of Nature.* Bloomington, Ind.: Indiana University Press, 1981. 232 p. **8759**

Canada. Dept. of the Environment. *Canada and the Human Environment; a Contribution by the Government of Canada to the United Nations Conference on the Human Environment, Stockholm, Sweden, June 1972.* Ottawa: Information Canada, 1972. 96 p., maps. **8760**
Includes a summary in French.

Canadian NGO Conference on Human Settlements, Ottawa, 1975. *Report: Canadian NGO Conference on Human Settlements, Ottawa, December 11, 12 and 13, 1975.* Ottawa: Canadian NGO Participation Group, 1976. 106 p. **8761**
Also issued in French. Co-sponsors: the Canadian National Committee for Habitat, the Canadian NGO Participation Group. On Cover: Habitat: United Nations Conference on Human Settlements, Vancouver, 1976.

Carroll, John E. *Environmental Diplomacy: An Examination and a Prospective of Canadian-U.S. Transboundary Environmental Relations.* Ann Arbor: University of Michigan Press, c1983. xix, 382 p. **8762**

Clemens, Walter C., Jr. "Ecology and International Relations." (1972-73), 28 *International Journal* 1-27. **8763**

Common Boundary/Common Problems: The Environmental Consequences of

Energy Production. Proceedings of a Conference held at Banff, Alberta, March 19-21, 1981. Washington, D.C.: American Bar Association, c1982. 116 p.
8764
Sponsored by the Canadian Bar Association, Environmental Law Section, and the American Bar Association, Standing Committee on Environmental Law. Contains 25 brief papers on one of the nine topics of the conference.

Dwivedi, O.P. "The Canadian Government Response to Environmental Concern." (1972-73), 28 *International Journal* 134-152. **8765**

International Banff Conference on Man and His Environment, 2d, 1974. *Man and His Environment: Proceedings of the Second International Banff Conference on Man and His Environment, Held in Banff, Canada, May 19-22, 1974.* Edited by M.F. Mohtadi. 1st ed. Oxford, New York: Pergamon Press, 1976. xvi, 213 p. (Vol. 2) **8766**

Johnston, Douglas M. "International Environmental Law: Recent Developments and Canadian Contributions." *In* Macdonald, Ronald St. John, and others, *Canadian Perspectives on International Law and Organization* (Toronto, 1974), pp. 555-611. **8767**

Katz, Brian. "The Potential Impact of Canada's Environmental Protection Efforts on Canadian-U.S. Relations." (1973), 3 *American Review of Canadian Studies* 39-55 (No. 1) **8768**

Kisicki, Donald Robert. *Environmental Management of the Great Lakes International Boundary Areas: A Case Study of the Niagara Urban Region.* Albany, N.Y.: New York State Sea Grant Program, 1973. xiv, 301 p., maps. (Great Lakes Management Problems Series) **8769**

Knelman, F.H. "What Happened at Stockholm." (1972-73), 28 *International Journal* 28-49. **8770**

Kyba, Patrick. "CCMS: The Environmental Connection." (1973-74), 29 *International Journal* 256-267. **8771**
The Committee on the Challenges of Modern Society (CCMS) is the environmental agency of NATO.

Kyba, Patrick. "Environmental Co-operation to Meet Political Objectives." (1977), 53 *International Affairs* 11-14 (July-Aug.) **8772**

Kyba, Patrick. "Problems of International Environmental Regulation." *In* Dwivedi, O.P., ed., *Protecting the Environment* (Toronto, 1974), pp. 283-297, 325-326.
8773

LeMarquand, David G.; and Scott, Anthony D. "Canada and the United States in an Interdependent World: Canada-United States Environmental Relations." (1976), 32 *Academy of Political Science, Proceedings* 149-163 (No. 2) **8774**

LeMarquand, David G., and Scott, Anthony D. *Canada's Transnational and International Environmental Relations.* Vancouver: University of British Columbia, Dept. of Economics, 1979. 37, 3 p. (University of British Columbia. Dept. of Economics. Resource Paper, No. 37) **8775**

Montigny, Michel de. *Coopération Canada-C.E.E. en matière de politique de l'environnement.* Montréal, 1974. vii, 103 leaves. **8776**
Thesis (M.A.), Université de Montréal, 1974.

Nyamekye, Stephen Kwasi. "The Environmental Issues at the United Nations and the Attitudes of the Less Developed Countries." (1974), 46 *Canadian Political Science Association, Papers,* 26 p. **8777**

Nyamekye, Stephen Kwasi. *Environmental Politics in the United Nations: An Analysis of the Role and Influence of the Less Developed Countries.* Hamilton, Ont., 1975 (c1976). xvi, 540 leaves. **8778**
Thesis (Ph.D.), McMaster University, 1975. (National Library of Canada. Canadian Theses on Microfiche, No. 26186).

Ongay-Perez, Luis Manuel. *The Elements of International Environmental Law.* Halifax, 1977. vi, 200 leaves. **8779**
Thesis (LL.M.), Dalhousie University, 1977. (National Library of Canada. Canadian Theses on Microfiche, No. 36152).

Roohi, Reza. *International Control of Environment with Particular Reference to Marine and Aircraft Pollution.* Montreal, 1976 (c1977). ii, 133 leaves. **8780**
Thesis (LL.M.), McGill University, 1976. (National Library of Canada. Canadian Theses on Microfiche, No. 31870).

Ross, Charles R. "National Sovereignty in International Environmental Decisions." (1972), 12 *Natural Resources Journal* 242-254. **8781**

Ross, Charles R. "National Sovereignty in International Environmental Decisions." *In* Dwivedi, O.P., ed., *Protecting the Environment* (Toronto, 1974), pp. 267-281, 324-325. **8782**

Rowland, Wade. *The Plot to Save the World; the Life and Times of the Stockholm Conference on the Human Environment.* With an Introduction by Maurice Strong. Toronto: Clarke, Irwin, 1973. xi, 194 p. **8783**
Refers to the United Nations Conference on the Human Environment, held in Stockholm, Sweden in 1972.

Sanger, Clyde. "Environment and Development." (1972-73), 28 *International Journal* 103-120. **8784**

Savraides, George B. *The Vancouver Declaration on Human Settlements: History and Interpretation.* Cambridge, Mass., 1977. 68 leaves. **8785**
Thesis (LL.M.), Harvard University, 1977.

Schneider, Jan. *World Public Order of the Environment: Towards an International Ecological Law and Organization.* Toronto: University of Toronto Press, 1979. xiv, 319 p. **8786**
Also issued as the author's thesis (Ph.D.), Yale University, 1979 (ix, 470 leaves).
Reviews: Nigel D. Bankes in (1980), 14 *University of British Columbia Law Review* 388-391; J.E.S. Fawcett in (1981), 97 *Law Quarterly Review* 163-165; John W. Reynolds in (1981), 30 *University of New Brunswick Law Journal* 286-288; John B. Reynolds under title: "The Role of Self-Interest in International Environmental Law," in (1980), 6 *Yale Studies in World Public Order* 497-515; Allen L. Springer in (1981), 75 *American Journal of International Law* 1005-1006.

Spurgeon, David. "The World Environment - It's Not Too Late." (1982), *International Perspectives* 7-10 (May/June) **8787**

Taylor, Alastair M. "Canadian Nationalism and Internationalism: The Ecological Challenge." *In* Dwivedi, O.P., ed., *Protecting the Environment* (Toronto, 1974), pp. 253-266, 323-324. **8788**

United Nations Conference on Human Settlements, Vancouver, 1976. *Report of Habitat-United Nations Conference on Human Settlements, Vancouver, 31 May-11 June 1976.* New York: United Nations, 1976. iv, 183 p. (United Nations. Doc. A/CONF. 70/15) **8789**
United Nations publication. Sales No. E.76/IV.7. Also issued in French and Spanish.

Zalob, David S. "Perspective internationale sur les orientations actuelles du droit et de la procédure en matière d'études d'impact sur l'environnement." (1978-79), 9 *Revue de Droit, Université de Sherbrooke* 516-539. **8790**

B. Pollution

1. GENERAL

Barros, James, and Johnston, Douglas M., eds. *The International Law of Pollution.* New York: Free Press, 1974. xvii, 476 p. **8791**
Also published in Spanish under title: *Contaminación y derecho internacional* (Buenos Aires, Marymar, 1977. 558 p.).
Reviews: Gwilym J. Davies in (1975), 13 *Alberta Law Review* 369-370; Richard A. Frank in (1974-75), 8 *Vanderbilt Journal of Transnational Law* 271-276; Leslie C. Green in (1974-75), 8 *Cornell International Law Journal* 124-126; Christopher C. Joyner in (1974), 68 *American Journal of International Law* 762-763; Patrick Kyba in (1973-74), 29 *International Journal* 661-662; Ralph W. Ochan in (1977-78), 9 *Journal of Maritime Law and Commerce* 141-142; William Samore in (1973-74), 38 *Albany Law Review* 995-997; James R. Wright in (1974), 9 *Journal of International Law and Economics* 179-182.

Beaupré, Bernard. "A Survey of Water and Air Pollution Cases Involving the International Joint Commission (Canada-United States)." In *Environmental Protection in Frontier Regions* (Paris, OECD, 1979), pp. 439-446. **8792**

Beesley, J. Alan. "Pollution of Shared Natural Resources: Of Legal and Trade Implications. (Comments)." (1977), 71 *American Society of International Law, Proceedings* 61-63. **8793**
Comments on a paper presented by Stephen C. McCaffrey.

Bloomfield, Louis M. "The Pollution Problem." (1971), 21 *University of Toronto Law Journal* 175-176. **8794**
Paper prepared for a symposium on the international legal aspects of pollution held in Vancouver, September, 1970.

Bourne, Charles B. "Legal Aspects of Transfrontier Pollution: Canada-United States Experience." (1981), 28 *Netherlands International Law Review* 188-194. **8795**

Carroll, John E., and Mack, Newell B. "On Living Together in North America: Canada, the United States and International Environmental Relations." (1982), 12 *Denver Journal of International Law and Policy* 35-50. **8796**

Davis, Jack, and Jones, Douglas N. "Partners in Pollution." (1970), 12 *University of Windsor Seminar on Canadian-American Relations, Proceedings* 81-102.
8797

De Mestral, Armand L.C. "Pollution Issues: coopération et règlement des différends Canada-États-Unis dans le domaine de la protection de l'environnement." (1978), 1 *Canada-United States Law Journal* 78-97. **8798**

Greene, J.J. "Policy on the Environment." (1971), 21 *University of Toronto Law Journal* 241-246. **8799**
Paper prepared for a symposium on the international legal aspects of pollution held in Vancouver, September 1970.

Ianni, Ronald W. "International and Private Actions in Transboundary Pollution." (1973), 11 *Canadian Yearbook of International Law* 258-270. **8800**

Jordan, Frederick J.E. "Recent Developments in International Environmental Pollution Control." (1969), 15 *McGill Law Journal* 279-301. **8801**

McCaffrey, Stephen C. "Private Remedies for Transfrontier Pollution Damage in Canada and the United States: A Comparative Survey." (1981), 19 *University of Western Ontario Law Review* 35-94. **8802**

McCaffrey, Stephen C. "Trans-Boundary Pollution Injuries: Jurisdictional Considerations in Private Litigation between Canada and the United States." (1973), 3 *California Western International Law Journal* 191-259. **8803**

McNamara, Philip. *The Availability of Civil Remedies to Protect Persons and Property from Transfrontier Pollution Injury.* Montreal, 1980. 381 frames.
8804
Thesis (M.C.L.), McGill University, 1980. (National Library of Canada. Canadian Theses on Microfiche, No. 50498).

Morris, Gerald L. "The Dimensions of the Environmental Problem." (1971), 21 *University of Toronto Law Journal* 177-181. **8805**
Paper prepared for a symposium on the international legal aspects of pollution held in Vancouver, September 1970.

Munton, Donald J. "Dependence and Interdependence in Transboundary Environmental Relations." (1980-81), 36 *International Journal* 139-184. **8806**

Munton, Donald J. "Reagan, Canada, and the Common Environment." (1982), *International Perspectives* 3-6 (May/June) **8807**

Ransome, Jack C.; Fisher, A.D. ; and Caverly, D.S. "Pollution." (1969), 11 *University of Windsor Seminar on Canadian-American Relations, Proceedings* 73-87. **8808**

Scott, Anthony D. "Fisheries, Pollution and Canadian-American Transnational Relations." (1974), 28 *International Organization* 827-848. **8809**
Reprinted in Fox, Annette Baker, and others, *Canada and the United States* (New York, 1976), pp. 234-255.

Thomas, Eileen Mitchell. "The Draft Transfrontier Pollution Treaty Adopted by the American and Canadian Bar Associations Relating to Settlement of International Disputes between Canada and the U.S.A." (1981), 9 *International Business Lawyer* 85-87. **8810**

Yates, John B. "Unilateral and Multilateral Approaches to Environmental Problems." (1971), 21 *University of Toronto Law Journal* 182-192. **8811**
Paper prepared for a symposium on the international legal aspects of pollution held in Vancouver, September 1970.

2. WATER POLLUTION (NON-MARINE)

See also *"Inland Waterways" (p. 208), and "Marine Pollution" (p. 264).*

Arbitblit, Donald Carl. "The Plight of American Citizens Injured by Transboundary River Pollution." (1979-80), 8 *Ecology Law Quarterly* 339-370. **8812**

Bilder, Richard B. "Controlling Great Lakes Pollution: A Study in United States-Canadian Environmental Cooperation." (1971-72), 70 *Michigan Law Review* 469-556. **8813**

Bourne, Charles B. "International Law and Pollution of International Rivers and Lakes." (1971), 21 *University of Toronto Law Journal* 193-202. **8814**
Paper prepared for a symposium on the international legal aspects of pollution held in Vancouver, September 1970.

Bourne, Charles B. "International Law and Pollution of International Rivers and Lakes." (1971), 6 *University of British Columbia Law Review* 115-136. **8815**

Dickstein, H.L. "International Lake and River Pollution Control: Questions of Method." (1973), 12 *Columbia Journal of Transnational Law* 487-519. **8816**

Donnelly, Murray S. "Progress and Problems in Environmental Controls with Special Reference to the Great Lakes." (1979), 17 *Royal Society of Canada, Transactions* 187-200 (4th Ser.) **8817**

Erichsen-Brown, J.P. "Legal Implications of Boundary Water Pollution." (1967), 17 *Buffalo Law Review* 65-69. **8818**

Florio, Franco. "Water Pollution and Related Principles of International Law." (1979), 17 *Canadian Yearbook of International Law* 134-158. **8819**

Hancox, Carol. "Water Pollution in the Great Lakes-St. Lawrence Basin: A Joint Canadian-American Problem." (1964), 6 *University of Windsor Seminar on Canadian-American Relations, Proceedings* 365-373. **8820**

Handl, Günther. "Balancing of Interests and International Liability for the Pollution of International Watercourses: Customary Principles of Law Revisited." (1975), 13 *Canadian Yearbook of International Law* 156-194. **8821**

Hartt, James P. "Water Pollution in the Detroit-Windsor Area in the Year 2000." (1966), 8 *University of Windsor Seminar on Canadian-American Relations, Proceedings* 53-61. **8822**

International Joint Commission. *Safeguarding Boundary Water Quality: A Cooperative Effort between United States and Canada under International Treaty.* Ottawa, Washington, 1961. 32 p. **8823**

Moseley, Frederick E. *The United States-Canadian Great Lakes Pollution Agree-*

ment: *A Study in International Water Pollution Control.* Kent, Ohio, 1978. v, 266 leaves, map. **8824**
Thesis (Ph.D.), Kent State University, 1978. Abstracted in (1978/79), 39 *Dissertation Abstracts International* 3124-A. (University Microfilms, Ann Arbor, No. 78-21087).

"Rehabilitating Our Continental Neighborhood: Rivers, Lakes, Fisheries, and Pollution Zones." (1974), 68 *American Society of International Law, Proceedings* 138-156. **8825**
This is a panel. Robert E. Stein, Chairman.

Saint-Jévin, P. *Protection de la nature et de l'environnement. Aspect international de la gestion des eaux douces au Canada.* Paris, 1976. 499 leaves. **8826**
Thesis (Doctorat), Université de Paris I, 1976.

U.S. General Accounting Office. *A More Comprehensive Approach is Needed to Clean Up the Great Lakes: Report to the Congress by the Comptroller General of the United States.* Washington: General Accounting Office, 1982. v, 137 p., maps. **8827**

3. AIR POLLUTION (TRANSBOUNDARY)

See also *"Transboundary Relations" (p. 183).*

Alhéritière, Dominique. "Les problèmes constitutionnels de la lutte contre la pollution de l'espace atmosphérique au Canada." (1972), 50 *Canadian Bar Review* 561-579. **8828**

Barnett, James K., III. "United States and Canadian Approaches to Air Pollution Control and the Implications for the Control of Transboundary Pollution." (1973-74), 7 *Cornell International Law Journal* 148-170. **8829**

Blackwell, Alan T. "Acid Rain: Corrosive Problem in Canadian-American Relations." (1982-83), 47 *Saskatchewan Law Review* 1-66. **8830**

Canada. Parliament. House of Commons. Standing Committee on Fisheries and Forestry. Subcommittee on Acid Rain. *Still Waters: The Chilling Reality of Acid Rain: A Report.* Ottawa: Supply and Services Canada, 1981. 150 p.
Chairman: Ronald Irwin. **8831**

Carson, Van. "Current Regulatory Framework: The American Legislative Position." (1982), 5 *Canada-United States Law Journal* 72-77. **8832**

Christol, Carl Q. "Aircraft and the International Legal and Institutional Aspects of the Stratospheric Ozone Problem." (1976), 1 *Annals of Air and Space Law* 3-32. **8833**

Cowling, Ellis B. "Acid Rain: An Emerging Ecological and Public Policy Issue." (1982), 5 *Canada-United States Law Journal* 23-31. **8834**

FitzGerald, Gerald F. "Le Canada et le développement du droit international; la contribution de l'Affaire de la fonderie de Trail à la formation du nouveau droit de la pollution atmosphérique transfrontière." (1980), 11 *Études Internationales* 393-419. **8835**

Homer, Janis L. "Controlling Acid Rain: The Challenge Facing the United States and Canada." (1980), 15 *Texas International Law Journal* 489-517. **8836**

Howard, Ross, and Perley, Michael. *Acid Rain: The North American Forecast.* Toronto: Anansi, 1980. 206 p., 6 maps. **8837**
> Also published in French under title: *Pluies acides* (Montréal, Québec/Amérique, 1982. 214 p.).

International Joint Commission. *Transboundary Air Pollution; Detroit and St. Clair River Areas.* Washington: Govt. Print. Off., 1972 (i.e. 1973). 69 p. **8838**
> Reference filed in 1966 (Docket No. 85); completed.

Johnston, Douglas M., and Finkle, Peter Z.R. "Acid Precipitation in North America: The Case for Transboundary Cooperation." (1981), 14 *Vanderbilt Journal of Transnational Law* 787-843. **8839**
> Also reprinted Calgary, Canadian Institute of Resources Law, 1982.

King, William K. "Transboundary Pollution: Canadian Jurisdiction." (1982), 1 *Canadian-American Law Journal* 1-16. **8840**

Lee, Edward G. "International Legal Aspects of Pollution of the Atmosphere." (1971), 21 *University of Toronto Law Journal* 203-210. **8841**
> Paper prepared for a symposium on the international legal aspects of pollution held at Vancouver in September 1970.

Martin, Hans. "Acid Rain from Source to Receptor." (1982), 5 *Canada-United States Law Journal* 16-22. **8842**

Munton, Donald J. "Acid Rain - Silver Clouds Can Have Black Linings." (1981), *International Perspectives* 6-9 (Jan./Feb.) **8843**

Pickering, John, and Swets, Gina L. "Who'll Stop the Rain?: Resolution Mechanisms for U.S.-Canadian Transboundary Pollution Disputes." (1982), 12 *Denver Journal of International Law and Policy* 51-91. **8844**

Rejhon, George. "North American Diplomatic Initiatives." (1982), 5 *Canada-United States Law Journal* 97-101. **8845**

Rempe, George A., III. "International Air Pollution - United States and Canada - A Joint Approach." (1968-69), 10 *Arizona Law Review* 138-147. **8846**

Roberts, John. "The Transnational Implications of Acid Rain: Introductory Remarks." (1982), 5 *Canada-United States Law Journal* 2-9. **8847**

Robinson, Raymond M. "Physical Dimensions and Solutions of the Acid Rain Problem." (1982), 5 *Canada-United States Law Journal* 111-117. **8848**

Rosencranz, Armin. "The Law and Politics of Transboundary Air Pollution: The European Experience." (1982), 5 *Canada-United States Law Journal* 102-108. **8849**

Rosencranz, Armin. "Transboundary Air Pollution: International Law, Agreements, and Other Remedies." *In Common Boundary/Common Problems: The Environmental Consequences of Energy Production* (Washington, D.C., c1982), pp. 95-102. **8850**

Rozalska, Barbara Maria. *Pollution of the Atmosphere and International Environmental Law.* Toronto, 1974. 141, xviii leaves. **8851**
> Thesis (LL.M.), University of Toronto, 1974.

Smith, T. Bradbrooke. "Current Regulatory Framework: The Canadian Legislative Position." (1982), 5 *Canada-United States Law Journal* 66-71. **8852**

U.S. Congress. House. Committee on Interstate and Foreign Commerce. Subcommittee on Oversight and Investigations. *Acid Rain: Hearings, 96th Cong., 2d sess., February 26 and 27, 1980.* Washington: Govt. Print. Off., 1980. iv, 784 p. **8853**

U.S. Congress. Senate. Committee on Foreign Relations. *Acid Rain: Hearing before the Subcommittee on Arms Control, Oceans, International Operations and Environment. 97th Cong., 2d sess., February 10, 1982.* Washington: Govt. Print Off., 1982. iii, 168 p., maps. **8854**

Van Lier, Irene H. *Acid Rain and International Law.* Halifax, 1980. xvii, 369 leaves. **8855**
Thesis (LL.M.), Dalhousie University, 1980. (National Library of Canada. Canadian Theses on Microfiche, No. 48272).

Van Lier, Irene H. *Acid Rain and International Law.* Toronto: Bunsel Environmental Consultants, 1981. xxii, 278 p. **8856**
Originally presented as the author's thesis (LL.M.), Dalhousie University, 1980.
Reviews: Timothy Atkeson in (1982), 76 *American Journal of International Law* 689-690; Charles B. Bourne in (1981), 19 *Canadian Yearbook of International Law* 441-445; Susan M. Cooke in (1982), 23 *Harvard International Law Journal* 187-191.

Weller, Phil. *Acid Rain: The Silent Crisis.* In co-operation with the Waterloo Public Interest Research Group. Kitchener, Ont.: Between the Lines, 1980. 94 p.
8857

4. OTHER FORMS OF POLLUTION (NOISE)

Fink, Lowell S. "Canadian Law and Aircraft Noise Disturbance: A Comparative Study of American, British, and Canadian Law." (1965), 11 *McGill Law Journal* 55-69. **8858**
Also published in (1969), 17 *Chitty's Law Journal* 145-153.

FitzGerald, Gerald F. "Aircraft Noise in the Vicinity of Aerodromes and Sonic Boom." (1971), 21 *University of Toronto Law Journal* 226-240. **8859**
Paper prepared for a symposium on the international legal aspects of pollution held in Vancouver, September 1970.

Kaunda, Gideon H. *The Proposed Multilateral Convention on Noise and Sonic Boom: An Environmental Question.* Montreal, c1977. x, 203 leaves. **8860**
Thesis (LL.M.), McGill University, 1977. (National Library of Canada. Canadian Theses on Microfiche, No. 33312).

Pourcelet, Michel. "La navigation aérienne et le bruit." (1967), 5 *Canadian Yearbook of International Law* 45-67. **8861**

C. International Parks

Bankes, Nigel D. *The International Law of Shared Natural Resources: A Case Study of an International Wildlife Range between Alaska and the Yukon.* Vancouver, 1980. 254 frames. **8862**
   Thesis (LL.M.), University of British Columbia, 1980. (National Library of Canada. Canadian Theses on Microfiche, No. 49894).

Collins, George L. "Background Information for Use in Connection with a Proposal for an Arctic International Wildlife Range." (1971), 6 *University of British Columbia Law Review* 3-11. **8863**

Findlay, John D. "History and Status of the Arctic National Wildlife Range." (1971), 6 *University of British Columbia Law Review* 15-20. **8864**

Oberholtzer, Ernest C. "An International Park." (1935), 10 *Canadian Geographical Journal* 73-80. **8865**

Patton, Edward L. "The Significance of the Proposed Wildlife Range to Industry." (1971), 6 *University of British Columbia Law Review* 47-50. **8866**

Pearse, Peter H. "Some Economic and Social Implications of the Proposed Arctic International Wildlife Range." (1971), 6 *University of British Columbia Law Review* 36-46. **8867**

"Proceedings of the Arctic International Wildlife Range Conference - October 21 and 22, 1970." (1971), 6 *University of British Columbia Law Review* 1-107, map. **8868**
   The conference was held in Whitehorse on October 21 and 22, 1970. Individual articles are listed separately.

Smith, James. "Opening Address to the Arctic International Wildlife Range Conference." (1971), 6 *University of British Columbia Law Review* 12-14. **8869**

Thompson, Andrew R. "A Legal Structure for the Proposed Wildlife Range." (1971), 6 *University of British Columbia Law Review* 51-58. **8870**
   Review: Robert W. Cox in (1978), 11 *Canadian Journal of Political Science* 238-239.

White, Paul S. "Legal Description of the Range." (1971), 6 *University of British Columbia Law Review* 104. **8871**

Willoughby, William R. "The Roosevelt Campobello International Park Commission." (1974-75), 54 *Dalhousie Review* 289-297. **8872**

D. Wildlife Protection (Migratory Birds, Etc.)

Bankes, Nigel D. "A Migratory Caribou Convention." (1980), 18 *Canadian Yearbook of International Law* 285-300. **8873**

Canada. Dept. of Northern Affairs and National Resources. *Migratory Birds*

Convention Act and Migratory Birds Regulations. Ottawa: Queen's Printer, 1965. 33 p. **8874**

Administered by the Canadian Wildlife Service, now part of the Dept. of Fisheries and the Environment.

Canada. Wildlife Service. *Office Consolidation of the Migratory Birds Convention Act: R.S., 1970, c. M-12, and the Migratory Birds Regulations, Established by C.R.C., c. 1035, as Amended.* Ottawa: Canadian Wildlife Service, 1980. 44 p. **8875**

Also issued in French under title: *Loi sur la convention concernant les oiseaux migrateurs.*

Green, Janet. "The Federal Government and Migratory Birds: The Beginning of a Protective Policy." (1976), *Canadian Historical Association, Historical Papers* 207-227. **8876**

LeBlond, Nancy Russell. *Porcupine Caribou Herd: International Agreements on Wilderness Preservation and Wildlife Management: A Study of the Porcupine Caribou.* Ottawa: Canadian Arctic Resources Committee, 1979. 156 p. (Northern Yukon) **8877**

VI. INTERNATIONAL SOCIAL AFFAIRS

A. General

Canada. Health and Welfare Canada. *The Agreement on Social Security between Canada and France: How Does it Affect You?* Ottawa: Health and Welfare Canada, 1981. 22, 22 p. **8878**
Text in English and French on inverted pages. Title in French: *L'Accord entre le Canada et la France sur la sécurité sociale.*
"Development of International Humanitarian Law." (1970), 22 *External Affairs* 369-370. **8879**
Levine, Howard J. "Canada-U.S. Social Security Agreement Near Finalization." (1982), 30 *Canadian Tax Journal* 777-778. **8880**
Samuels, Joseph W. "Humanitarian Relief in Man-Made Disasters: International Law, Government Policy and the Nigerian Experience." (1972), 10 *Canadian Yearbook of International Law* 3-39. **8881**
Samuels, Joseph W. "Humanitarian Relief in Man-Made Disasters: The International Red Cross and the Nigerian Experience." (1975-76), 34 *Behind the Headlines* No. 3 (45 p.) **8882**
Samuels, Joseph W. "Organized Responses to Natural Disasters." *In* Macdonald, Ronald St. John, and others, *The International Law and Policy of Human Welfare* (Alphen aan den Rijn, 1978), pp. 675-690. **8883**

B. Population

Keyfitz, Nathan. "Nation, City, and the World Community: A Demographic Perspective." *In* Macdonald, Ronald St. John, and others, *The International Law and Policy of Human Welfare* (Alphen aan den Rijn, 1978), pp. 585-600. **8884**
Leroy, Marcel. "Neo-Malthusianism, Foreign Aid, and International Relations." (1975-76), 31 *International Journal* 26-43. **8885**
"Population of the Commonwealth." (1960), 12 *External Affairs* 520-524. **8886**

Poznanski, Thaddée. "Quelques problèmes des populations au monde." (1959-60), 14 *Revue de l'Université Laval* 14-29. **8887**

"The Problem of World Population and Food Supply." (1960), 12 *External Affairs* 447-453. **8888**

Sandwell, B.K. "Population and Peace." (1949), 43 *Royal Society of Canada, Transactions* 1-12 (3d Ser., 2d Sec.) **8889**

Seife, Asfaw. *The Legal Implications of the World Population Plan of Action for National Governments of Developing Countries, with Particular Reference to Ethiopia.* Toronto, 1977. iii, 176, 26 leaves. **8890**
Thesis (LL.M.), University of Toronto, 1977.

C. Health

Bélanger, Michel. "Une nouvelle branche du droit international: le droit international de la santé." (1982), 13 *Études Internationales* 611-632. **8891**

Chisholm, Brock, and Bodsworth, C. Fred. "The People's Health: Canada and WHO." (1949), 9 *Behind the Headlines* No. 2 (20 p.) **8892**

FitzGerald, J.G. "International Public Health." (1931), 38 *Queen's Quarterly* 265-279. **8893**

Robinson, George S. *Contamination of Earth's Ecosystem by Extra-Terrestrial Matter; United States Authority to Promulgate and Enforce Quarantine Regulations.* Montreal, 1970 (c1971). vii, 265 leaves. **8894**
Short title: *Earth Exposure to Alien Matter; Quarantine Law.* Thesis (D.C.L.), McGill University, 1970. (National Library of Canada. Canadian Theses on Microfilm, No. 7313).

Ruderman, Peter. "Public Health and the Human Environment." *In* Macdonald, Ronald St. John, and others, *The International Law and Policy of Human Welfare* (Alphen aan den Rijn, 1978), pp. 615-638. **8895**

Smart, Reginald G.; Murray, Glenn F.; and Archibald, H. David, eds. *Psychotropic Substances and Their International Control.* Toronto: Alcoholism and Drug Addiction Research Foundation, 1981. 230 p. **8896**

D. Labour and Trade Unions

See also *"International Labour Organization" (p. 359).*

Bendel, Michael. "The International Protection of Trade Union Rights: A Canadian Case Study." (1981), 13 *Ottawa Law Review* 169-198. **8897**

Bridge, John W. "National and Transnational Regulation of Equal Pay for Equal Work in England and the European Community." (1981-82), 5 *Revue d'Intégration Européenne* 117-144. **8898**

Canada. International Labour Affairs Branch. *Equal Remuneration for Work of Equal Value; a Study of Action Required to Bring Legislation in Each Jurisdiction in Canada into Conformity with International Labour Convention No. 100, concerning Equal Remuneration.* Ottawa: Dept. of Labour, 1971. 55, 12, 8 p. **8899**

The appendix includes the English and French text of convention No. 100, and recommendation No. 90, both adopted by the 34th session of the International Labour Conference, Geneva, June 29, 1951.

Chaison, Gary N. "Union Mergers and International Unionism in Canada." (1979), 34 *Relations Industrielles* 768-776. **8900**

Contains a summary in French under title: "Les fusions syndicales et le syndicalisme international au Canada" (pp. 776-777).

Clark, John. "Canadian Labour Congress as an International Actor." (1980), *International Perspectives* 9-12 (Sept./Oct.). **8901**

Conti, Raymond. *Les relations syndicales canado-américaines.* Montréal, 1959. ii, 164 leaves. **8902**

Thesis (M.A.), Université de Montréal, 1959.

Côté, Marcel. "Le mouvement ouvrier canadien est-il dominé par les grands syndicats internationaux?" (1965-66), 41 *Actualité Économique* 570-577. **8903**

Cox, Robert W. "Labor and Employment in the Late Twentieth Century." *In* Macdonald, Ronald St. John, and others, *The International Law and Policy of Human Welfare* (Alphen aan den Rijn, 1978), pp. 525-548. **8904**

Cox, Robert W., and Jamieson, Stuart M. "Canadian Labor in the Continental Perspective." (1974), 28 *International Organization* 803-826. **8905**

Reprinted in Fox, Annette Baker, and others, *Canada and the United States* (New York, 1976), pp. 210-233.

Crispo, John H.G. *International Unionism; a Study in Canadian-American Relations.* Toronto: McGraw-Hill of Canada, c1967. viii, 327 p. **8906**

Reviews: Brian B. Norton in (1967), 5 *Osgoode Hall Law Journal* 321-323; H. Clare Pentland under title: "Canada 1967: Nation or Subsidiary?," in (1967), 48 *Canadian Historical Review* 365-369; Frank Wildgen in (1969), 2 *Canadian Journal of Economics* 628-630.

Crispo, John H.G. "Multinational Corporations, International Unions and Industrial Relations: The Canadian Case." (1974), 29 *Relations Industrielles* 673-684. **8907**

Crispo, John H.G. *The Role of International Unionism in Canada.* Washington, Montreal: Canadian-American Committee, 1967. xiii, 59 p. **8908**

Sponsored by the National Planning Association (U.S.A.), and the Private Planning Association of Canada.

Després, Jean-Pierre. "Évolution du trade-unionisme international." (1945), 51/1 *Revue Dominicaine* 298-305. **8909**

Dion, Gérard. "L'influence étatsunienne sur le syndicalisme canadien." (1973), 11 *Royal Society of Canada, Transactions* 119-130 (4th Ser.). **8910**

Harker, John. "Canada and the United Nations: Trade Unionism and a New International Economic Order." (1976), *International Perspectives* 11-15 (Sept./Oct.) **8911**

Innis, Harold A., ed. *Labor in Canadian-American Relations: The History of Labor Interaction*, by Norman J. Ware; *Labor Costs and Labor Standards*, by H.A. Logan. New York: Russell & Russell, 1970. xxxviii, 212 p. (Relations of Canada and the United States) **8912**
First published Toronto, Ryerson Press; New Haven, Yale University Press, 1937.
Review: Leonard C. Marsh in (1938), 19 *Canadian Historical Review* 79-80.

"The International Confederation of Free Trade Unions." (1950), 2 *External Affairs* 299-301. **8913**

"International Trade Unionism." (1955), 7 *External Affairs* 225-229. **8914**

Jodoin, Claude. "Canadian and American Trade Unionism - a Unified Whole." (1961), 3 *University of Windsor Seminar on Canadian-American Relations, Proceedings* 169-177. **8915**

Kruger, Arthur. "International Unions and Canadian-American Relations." (1963-64), 23 *Behind the Headlines* No. 5 (23 p.) **8916**

Lavertu, Gaétan. *La participation de la Confédération des syndicats nationaux aux affaires internationales.* Québec, 1968. viii, 124 leaves. **8917**
Thesis (M.Sc.Soc.), Université Laval, 1969.

Montague, J.T. "International Unions and the Canadian Trade Union Movement." (1957), 23 *Canadian Journal of Economics and Political Science* 69-82. **8918**

Scott, Jack. *Canadian Workers, American Unions.* Vancouver: New Star Books, c1978. 242 p. (Trade Unions and Imperialism in America, Vol. 2) **8919**

Swan, Judith. "The Law Relating to Equal Remuneration for Work of Equal Value: International and Canadian Perspectives." *In* Gall, Gerald L., ed., *Civil Liberties in Canada: Entering the 1980s* (Toronto, c1982), pp. 119-149. **8920**

Wellwood, Eleanore J. *Autonomy of Canadian Sections in International Unions in North America: An Analysis of Transnational Organizations in an Asymmetrical Dyadic Environment.* Ottawa, 1973. 153 leaves. **8921**
Thesis (M.A.), Carleton University, 1973.

Westergard-Thorpe, Wayne. "Syndicalist Internationalism and Moscow, 1919-1922: The Breach." (1979), 14 *Canadian Journal of History* 199-234. **8922**

White, Ralph William. *Integration in North America: A Study of Labor Mobility and the Growth of Regional Linkages between Canada and the United States.* Ottawa, 1978. ix, 357 leaves. **8923**
Thesis (M.A.), Carleton University, 1978. Abstracted in (1979), 17 *Masters Abstracts* 223.

Williams, Charles Brian. *Canadian-American Trade Union Relations; a Study of the Development of Binational Unionism.* Ithaca, N.Y., 1964. xii, 488 leaves. **8924**
Thesis (Ph.D.), Cornell University, 1964. Abstracted in (1965), 25 *Dissertation Abstracts* 5003. (University Microfilms, Ann Arbor, No. 65-3143).

Williams, Charles Brian. "The Development of Canadian-American Trade Union Relations: Some Conclusions." (1966), 21 *Relations Industrielles* 332-355.
8925

Williams, Charles Brian. "Development of Relations between Canadian and American National Trade Union Centers, 1886-1925." (1965), 20 *Relations Industrielles* 340-371.
8926

Woodcock, Leonard. "Canadian and American Trade Unionism - a Unified Whole." (1961), 3 *University of Windsor Seminar on Canadian-American Relations, Proceedings* 178-186.
8927

E. Food and Nutrition

See also *"Commodities: Wheat" (p. 581)*.

Barton, G.S.H. "The World Food Supply." (1949), 38 *Canadian Geographical Journal* 228-235.
8928

Booth, J.F. "Our Hungry World." (1948), 8 *Behind the Headlines* No. 7 (16 p.)
8929

Caldwell, Mary Ellen. "The Legal Factor in the Food-Population Equation." *In* Macdonald, Ronald St. John, and others, *The International Law and Policy of Human Welfare* (Alphen aan den Rijn, 1978), pp. 601-614.
8930

Cohn, Theodore H. *Canadian Food Aid: Domestic and Foreign Policy Implications.* Denver, Colo.: University of Denver, School of International Studies, 1979. 118 p. (Monographs Series in World Affairs)
8931
Review: Henry Rempel in (1981), 7 *Canadian Public Policy* 124.

Cohn, Theodore H. "Canadian Food Policy and the Third World." (1980), 79 *Current History* 138-142.
8932

Cohn, Theodore H. "Food Surpluses and Canadian Food Aid." (1977), 3 *Canadian Public Policy* 141-154.
8933
Also published in (1976), 48 *Canadian Political Science Association, Papers,* 30 p.

Fischer, Lewis A. "Canadian Wheat in a Hungry World." (1965-66), 25 *Behind the Headlines* No. 4 (13 p.)
8934

Hay, Keith A.J. "A Plan to Feed the Hungry." (1975), 82 *Canadian Banker and ICB Review* 19-22 (No. 1)
8935

Islam, Nasir. "La crise alimentaire mondiale: quelques implications morales et politiques." (1976), 7 *Études Internationales* 193-214.
8936

Islam, Nasir. "Food Aid: Conscience, Morality, and Politics." (1980-81), 36 *International Journal* 353-370.
8937

Martin, Paul. "Food Relief Discussions at the UN Assembly." (1946-47), 2 *International Journal* 96-101.
8938
Refers to the United Nations Relief and Rehabilitation Administration (UNRRA).

Nicoloff, Olivier. "Value of Food as Weapon More Symbolic Than Real." (1980), *International Perspectives* 19-21 (Sept./Oct.). **8939**

"The Problem of World Population and Food Supply." (1960), 12 *External Affairs* 447-453. **8940**

Reid, Escott. "Canada and the Struggle Against World Poverty." (1969-70), 25 *International Journal* 142-157. **8941**

Richards, A.E. "Canada's Contribution to the Food Supply of the United Nations." (1945), 31 *Canadian Geographical Journal* 50-53. **8942**

Sokol, John F. "Food - Our Next Crisis?" (1977-78), 36 *Behind the Headlines* No. 2 (28 p.) **8943**

Stewart, Andrew. "Canada in a Hungry World." (1941-42), 2 *Behind the Headlines* No. 10 (20 p.) **8944**

Switzer, Clayton M. "Grain and Brain: Weapons in the Hunger War." (1977), 84 *Canadian Banker* 8-10 (No. 5) **8945**

Tosell, W.E. *Partnership in Development: Canadian Universities and World Food.* Ottawa: Science Council of Canada, 1980. 145 p. **8946**
Review: J.W. Grove in (1982), 89 *Queen's Quarterly* 641-643.

Trueman, H.L. "Hunger Unlimited." (1964), 69 *Canadian Geographical Journal* 64-77. **8947**

Weitz, Charles H. "Whatever Became of the World Food Conference?" (1977), *International Perspectives* 14-19 (Sept./Oct.). **8948**

Williams, Douglas, and Young, Roger. "Canadian Food Aid: Surpluses and Hunger." (1980-81), 36 *International Journal* 335-352. **8949**

Williams, Douglas, and Young, Roger. *Taking Stock: World Food Security in the Eighties.* Ottawa: North-South Institute, 1981. vi, 76 p. (North-South Papers, 3) **8950**
Also issued in French under title: *La sécurité alimentaire.*

"The World Food Programme." (1962), 14 *External Affairs* 182-188. **8951**

F. Narcotic Drugs

Charbonneau, Jean-Pierre. *The Canadian Connection.* Translated from the French by James Stewart. Preface by Jean L. Dutil. Ottawa: Optimum, c1976. xvii, 542 p. **8952**
Translation of: *La filière canadienne* (Montréal, Éditions de l'homme, c1975. 597 p.). Deals with Canada and the international traffic in narcotics, from 1930 to date.

Green, Melvyn. "A History of Canadian Narcotics Control: The Formative Years." (1979), 37 *University of Toronto Faculty of Law Review* 42-79. **8953**

Harper, Bruce Alan. *International Narcotics Control.* Vancouver, 1976. 150 leaves. **8954**

Thesis (M.A.), University of British Columbia, 1976. (National Library of Canada. Canadian Theses on Microfiche, No. 32473).

Hossick, Kenneth C. "International Control of Narcotic Drugs." (1955), 7 *External Affairs* 289-293. **8955**

"International Narcotic Control." (1951), 3 *External Affairs* 80-83. **8956**

"Rehabilitating Our Continental Neighborhood: The Problem of Drugs." (1974), 68 *American Society of International Law, Proceedings* 169-189. **8957**
This is a panel. Gary J. Rickner, Chairman.

Samuels, Joseph W. "International Control of Narcotic Drugs and International Economic Law." (1969), 7 *Canadian Yearbook of International Law* 192-223. **8958**

"UN Narcotics Control." (1960), 12 *External Affairs* 710-711. **8959**

"The War on Narcotics: Canada Ratifies Single Convention." (1962), 14 *External Affairs* 27-34. **8960**

G. Alcoholic Beverages

Hayman, Michael. *The Volstead Act as a Reflection of Canadian-American Relations.* Montreal, 1971. v, 206 leaves, maps. **8961**
Thesis (M.A.), McGill University, 1971. (National Library of Canada. Canadian Theses on Microfilm, No. 9356). Refers to the *Volstead Act* of October 28, 1919, enacted in the United States to enforce the prohibition (41 Stat. 305, c. 85).

Kottman, Richard N. "Volstead Violated: Prohibition as a Factor in Canadian-American Relations." (1962), 43 *Canadian Historical Review* 106-126. **8962**

Potter, Pitman B. "Canada and United States in Matter of Trade in Alcoholic Beverages." (1930), 24 *American Journal of International Law* 131-133. **8963**

VII. INTERNATIONAL CULTURAL RELATIONS

See also *"United Nations Educational, Scientific and Cultural Organization" (p. 361).*

A. General

Campbell, Lauren Dawn. *The Politicisation of the Olympics: A Case Study of the XXIst Olympiad.* Fredericton, 1979. v, 86 leaves. **8964**
Thesis (M.A.), University of New Brunswick, 1979. (National Library of Canada. Canadian Theses on Microfiche, No. 41033).

"Canadian Cultural Relations." (1950), 2 *External Affairs* 218-222. **8965**

Cowley, George A. "The Emergence of Culture as a Facet of Foreign Policy." (1976), *International Perspectives* 27-32 (Sept./Oct.) **8966**

Gotlieb, Allan E. "The Transnational Flow of Information: A Canadian Perspective." (1974), 68 *American Society of International Law, Proceedings* 127-134. **8967**
Address delivered at a panel entitled: "Intellectual Reciprocity and Cultural Imperialism: Art Treasures - Media - Data Transfer." John Lawrence Hargrove, Chairman.

Kidd, J.R. "Human Development through Education." *In* Macdonald, Ronald St. John, and others, *The International Law and Policy of Human Welfare* (Alphen aan den Rijn, 1978), pp. 273-290. **8968**

Litvak, Isaiah A., and Maule, Christopher J. "Canadian Multinational Media Firms and Canada-United States Relations." (1981-82), 39 *Behind the Headlines* No. 5 (23 p.) **8969**

Litvak, Isaiah A., and Maule, Christopher J. *Cultural Sovereignty: The Time and Reader's Digest Case in Canada.* New York: Praeger, 1974. viii, 140 p. (Praeger Special Studies in International Politics and Government) **8970**

Litvak, Isaiah A., and Maule, Christopher J. "Interest-Group Tactics and the Politics of Foreign Investment: The Time-Reader's Digest Case Study." (1974), 7 *Canadian Journal of Political Science* 616-629. **8971**
Contains a résumé in French under title: "La politique canadienne en matière d'investissements étrangers: le cas Time-Reader's Digest."

Logaldo, John R. "The Time and Reader's Digest Bill: C-58 and Canadian Cultural Nationalism." (1976-77), 9 *New York University Journal of International Law and Politics* 237-275. **8972**

Martyn, Howe. "Education, Culture, and International Tourism." (1971-72), 51 *Dalhousie Review* 374-389. **8973**

Martyn, Howe. "International Tourism: Public Attitudes and Government Policies." (1970-71), 50 *Dalhousie Review* 40-54. **8974**

McGuinness, Kevin Patrick. *The Legal Implications of Barriers to Entry into the Professional Team Sports Market under North American Competition Law.* Toronto, 1979. iv, 437, 11 leaves. **8975**
Thesis (LL.M.), University of Toronto, 1979.

McNichols, William; Worrall, James; and Rousseau, Roger. "Why Olympics?" (1973), 15 *University of Windsor Seminar on Canadian-American Relations, Proceedings* 23-28. **8976**

McPhail, Thomas L. "A New World Information Order?" (1982), *International Perspectives* 19-20 (May/June) **8977**

Painchaud, Paul. "Canadian Cultural Diplomacy: Its Illusions and Problems." (1977), *International Perspectives* 34-38 (May/June) **8978**

Preston, Richard A. *The Squat Pyramid: Canadian Studies in the United States: Problems and Prospects.* Durham, N.C.: Duke University, Center for International Studies, 1980. iv, 70 p. (Duke University. Center for International Studies. Occasional Papers Series, No. 9) **8979**
Review: Joseph T. Jockel in (1982), 63 *Canadian Historical Review* 87-88.

Richer, A.-M. "Les jeux Olympiques et la paix mondiale." (1949), 55/2 *Revue Dominicaine* 207-212. **8980**

Robertson, Robert T. "Le Commonwealth multiculturel." *In* Jacomy-Millette, Annemarie, ed., *Francophonie et Commonwealth: mythe ou réalité?* (Québec, 1978), pp. 128-136. **8981**

Sabourin, Louis. *La dualité culturelle dans les activités internationales du Canada.* Ottawa: Information Canada, 1970. xiv, 136 p. (Canada. Commission royale d'enquête sur le bilinguisme et le biculturalisme. Documents, 9) **8982**

Schafer, David Paul. *Canada's International Cultural Relations / les relations culturelles du Canada avec l'étranger.* Ottawa: Dept. of External Affairs, 1979. 66, 71 p. **8983**
Text in English and French on inverted pages.

Schroeder-Gudehus, Brigitte. "Problèmes de politique culturelle extérieure: aspects culturels des relations Canada-Europe." (1970), 1 *Études Internationales* 45-60 (no 3) **8984**

Schroeder-Gudehus, Brigitte. "Les relations internationales culturelles, scientifiques et techniques." *In* Painchaud, Paul, ed., *Le Canada et le Québec sur la scène internationale* (Québec, 1977), pp. 253-272. **8985**

Sparkes, Verone. "TV Across the Canadian Border: Does It Matter?" (1977), 27 *Journal of Communications* 40-47 (No. 4) **8986**

Towell, Freeman. "Cultural Affairs: The Canadian Experience in Cultural Relations." (1976), *International Perspectives* 32-38 (Sept./Oct.) **8987**

Wallace, Malcolm W. "Internationalism and Universities." (1949-50), 5 *International Journal* 43-47. **8988**

B. Protection of Cultural Property

Balawyder, Aloysius. *The Odyssey of the Polish Treasures.* Antigonish, N.S.: St. Francis Xavier University Press, 1978. 107 p., plates. **8989**
Review: Edward McWhinney in (1979), 17 *Canadian Yearbook of International Law* 431-434.

Bennett, Peter H. "What Is the World Heritage Convention?" (1977-78), 95 *Canadian Geographical Journal* 22-29 (Dec./Jan.) **8990**

Cameron, Duncan F. *An Introduction to the Cultural Property Export and Import Act: A Report.* Prepared for the Arts and Culture Branch, Department of the Secretary of State, Government of Canada. Ottawa: Dept. of the Secretary of State, 1977. 89 p. **8991**
Also issued in French under title: *Introduction à la Loi sur l'exportation et l'importation de biens culturels.*

Cameron, Duncan F. *An Introduction to the Cultural Property Export and Import Act: A Report / Précisions sur la Loi sur l'exportation et l'importation de biens culturels: document.* Ottawa: Dept. of Communications, 1980. 62 p. **8992**

Castel, Jean-Gabriel. "Polish Art Treasures in Canada - 1940-1960: A Case History." (1974), 68 *American Society of International Law, Proceedings* 121-127. **8993**

L'Heureux, Jacques. "La protection de l'environnement culturel canadien et québécois." (1977), 23 *McGill Law Journal* 306-333. **8994**

Williams, Sharon A. *The International and National Protection of Cultural Property: A Comparative Study.* Downsview, Ont., 1976. xvi, 554 leaves. **8995**
Thesis (D.Jur.), York University, 1976. (National Library of Canada. Canadian Theses on Microfiche, No. 30957).

Williams, Sharon A. *The International and National Protection of Movable Cultural Property: A Comparative Study.* Dobbs Ferry, N.Y.: Oceana Publications, 1978. xvii, 302 p. **8996**
Reviews: Patricia M. Bovan in (1979), 11 *Case Western Reserve Journal of International Law* 216-219; Michel Distel in (1980), 32 *Revue Internationale de Droit Comparé* 274; Leslie C. Green in (1978), 56 *Canadian Bar Review* 361-365; James A.R. Nafziger in (1979), 73 *American Journal of International Law* 532-533; Charles Rousseau in (1978), 82 *Revue Générale de Droit International Public* 1178-1179; Paul Tavernier in (1978), 24 *Annuaire Français de Droit International* 1257-1258; J.C. Woodliffe in (1980), 51 *British Year Book of International Law* 300-301.

Williams, Sharon A. *The Polish Art Treasures in Canada: Legal Problems and Political Realities.* Downsview, Ont., 1974. xi, 164 leaves. **8997**
Thesis (LL.M), York University, 1974. (National Library of Canada. Canadian Theses on Microfiche, No. 22323).

Williams, Sharon A. "The Polish Art Treasures in Canada, 1940-60." (1977), 15 *Canadian Yearbook of International Law* 146-172. **8998**

Williams, Sharon A. "The Protection of the Canadian Cultural Heritage: The Cultural Property Export and Import Act." (1976), 14 *Canadian Yearbook of International Law* 292-306. **8999**

VIII. INTERNATIONAL LEGAL COOPERATION

A. General

Arbitblit, Donald Carl. "The Plight of American Citizens Injured by Transboundary River Pollution." (1979-80), 8 *Ecology Law Quarterly* 339-370. **9000**

Beullac, Roger-A. "De l'interrogatoire à l'étranger en matière pénale." (1966), 26 *Revue du Barreau* 591-603. **9001**

Blom, Joost. "The Enforcement of Foreign Judgments in Canada." (1978), 57 *Oregon Law Review* 399-429. **9002**

Busler, Robert H. "Bankruptcy Reciprocity: A Study as to a Treaty with Canada." (1947), 33 *A.B.A. Journal* 1026-1029, 1071-1073. **9003**

Campbell, B.R. "The Canada-United States Antitrust Notification and Consultation Procedure: A Study in Bilateral Conflict Resolution." (1978), 56 *Canadian Bar Review* 459-495. **9004**

Canada. Dept. of External Affairs. Legal Advisory Division. *International Judicial Co-operation in Civil, Commercial, Administrative and Criminal Matters: Role of the Department of External Affairs*. Ottawa: External Affairs Canada, 1980. viii, 35 p. **9005**
  Also issued in French under title: *Entraide judiciaire internationale en matière civile, commerciale, administrative et criminelle* (vii, 40 p.).

Castel, Jean-Gabriel. "La convention entre les États membres de la Communauté économique européenne sur la compétence judiciaire et l'exécution des décisions en matière civile et commerciale." (1979), 8 *Canadian Council on International Law, Proceedings* 189-196. **9006**

Castel, Jean-Gabriel. "International Civil Procedure." *In* Macdonald, Ronald St. John, and others, *Canadian Perspectives on International Law and Organization* (Toronto, 1974), pp. 842-860. **9007**

Castel, Jean-Gabriel. *The Recognition and Enforcement of Foreign Money Judgments or Decrees in the Anglo-American Common Law System and in the French Civil System*. Montreal, 1957. 505 leaves. **9008**
  Thesis (S.J.D), Harvard University, 1958. Listed in (1957-58), *Index to American Doctoral Dissertations* 103.

Fairley, H. Scott. "Private Remedies for Transboundary Injury in Canada and the United States: Constraints upon Having to Sue Where You Can Collect." (1978), 10 *Ottawa Law Review* 253-272. **9009**

Hardy, Vincent. "Certificats présentés en cour par le Ministère des affaires extérieures: la pratique canadienne." (1977), 15 *Canadian Yearbook of International Law* 236-252.   **9010**

Ianni, Ronald W. "International and Private Actions in Transboundary Pollution." (1973), 11 *Canadian Yearbook of International Law* 258-270.   **9011**

"International Civil and Commercial Procedures: Role of the Department of External Affairs." (1966), 18 *External Affairs* 463-468.   **9012**

"International Civil Procedure: Role of External Affairs." (1962), 14 *External Affairs* 93-97.   **9013**

"International Law and Family Practice / Le droit international et la pratique du droit de la famille." (1981), 10 *Canadian Council on International Law, Proceedings,* 157-196.   **9014**

This is a panel. Chairman: Gerald V. LaForest.
Contents: "The International Abduction of Children: A Problem of Unnecessary Judicial Intervention," by Jeffery Wilson (pp. 157-171).- "L'exécution des obligations familiales à travers les frontières," by Ethel Groffier-Atala (pp. 172-191).- Discussion (pp. 192-193).

Kos-Rabcewicz-Zubkowski, Ludwik, ed. *International Cooperation in Civil and Commercial Procedure: American Continent.* Ottawa: University of Ottawa Press, 1975. xxxiii, 582 p.   **9015**

Published under the auspices of the Canadian Inter-American Research Institute.
Reviews: Philippe Ferland in (1976), 36 *Revue du Barreau* 405-407; González Matamala in (1975), 2 *Anuario de Derecho Internacional* 809-810; Nicolas Mateesco Matte in (1975), 13 *Canadian Yearbook of International Law* 442-444; James P. Taylor in (1976), 14 *Canadian Yearbook of International Law* 403-405; André Tunc in (1976), 28 *Revue Internationale de Droit Comparé* 866-867.

Kos-Rabcewicz-Zubkowski, Ludwik. "Les principaux organes de l'unification du droit et leur mission dans l'hémisphère américain." *In* Popovici, Adrian, ed., *Problèmes de droit contemporain: mélanges Louis Baudouin* (Montréal, 1974), pp. 319-347.   **9016**

Kos-Rabcewicz-Zubkowski, Ludwik. "Quebec (Provincial) and Canadian (Federal) Rules on International Procedure (International Judicial Assistance) in Civil and Commercial Matters." (1964), 13 *International and Comparative Law Quarterly* 270-277.   **9017**

McCaffrey, Stephen C. "Trans-Boundary Pollution Injuries: Jurisdictional Considerations in Private Litigation between Canada and the United States." (1973), 3 *California Western International Law Journal* 191-259.   **9018**

McNamara, Philip. *The Availability of Civil Remedies to Protect Persons and Property from Transfrontier Pollution Injury.* Montreal, 1980. 381 frames.
9019

Thesis (M.C.L.), McGill University, 1980. (National Library of Canada. Canadian Theses on Microfiche, No. 50498).

Moore, Thomas O., III. "Judicial Cooperation in the Taking of Evidence Abroad - The Canada and Ontario Evidence Acts." (1973), 8 *Texas International Law Journal* 57-83.   **9020**

Panzer, Arnold B. "Enforcement of Canadian Tax Judgment by U.S. Courts Denied." (1980), 28 *Canadian Tax Journal* 518-523. **9021**

Read, John E. " 'Analysis of Civil Procedure Conventions.' " (1939), 24 *Canadian Bar Association, Proceedings* 111-122. **9022**
This is annexed to the article entitled: "The Practising Lawyer and External Affairs" (pp. 100-111).

Stevenson, John R. " 'Extraterritoriality' in Canadian-United States Relations." (1970), 63 *U.S. Dept. of State Bulletin* 425-430. **9023**

Weir, John T. "International Judicial Cooperation. (Report of Rapporteur)." (1965), *World Peace Through Law* 429-431. **9024**

B. Execution of Penal Sentences Agreements

Bassiouni, M. Cherif. "Perspectives on the Transfer of Prisoners between the United States and Mexico and the United States and Canada." (1978), 11 *Vanderbilt Journal of Transnational Law* 249-268. **9025**
Refers to the treaty between Canada and the United States of March 2, 1977 (CTS 1978/12).

Bassiouni, M. Cherif. "Treaties on the Execution of Penal Sentences between the United States and Mexico, and the United States and Canada." (1977), 1 *Comparative Law Yearbook* 1-33. **9026**

Nazarevich, Alann J. "The Transfer of Offenders Act and Related Treaties: An Analysis." (1978), 4 *Criminal Reports (3d)* 212-238. **9027**

Paust, Jordan J. "The Unconstitutional Detention of Mexican and Canadian Prisoners by the United States Government." (1979), 12 *Vanderbilt Journal of Transnational Law* 67-72. **9028**

Phillippe, Larry K. "As the Floodgates Open... The Transfer of Offenders Act." (1981), 19 *Criminal Reports (3d)* 289-309. **9029**

Schaffer, Toby Macy. "Justice with Mercy: The Treaties with Canada and Mexico for the Execution of Penal Judgments." (1977-78), 4 *Brooklyn Journal of International Law* 246-268. **9030**

U.S. Congress. Senate. Committee on Foreign Relations. *Penal Treaties with Mexico and Canada: Hearings, 95th Cong., 1st sess., June 15 and 16, 1977.* Washington: Govt. Print. Off., 1977. iii, 279 p. **9031**

C. Commercial Arbitration

Berengaut, Julian. *International Commodity Arbitrage and the Relationships between Foreign and Domestic Prices in Canada and the United States.* Madison, Wis., 1978. iv, 207 leaves. **9032**
Thesis (Ph.D.), University of Wisconsin, Madison, 1978. Abstracted in (1979), 40 *Dissertation Abstracts International* 1598-A. (University Microfilms, Ann Arbor, No. 79-15067).

Brierley, John E.C. "International Trade Arbitration: The Canadian Viewpoint." *In* Macdonald, Ronald St. John, and others, *Canadian Perspectives on International Law and Organization* (Toronto, 1974), pp. 826-841. **9033**

David, René. "L'obligation pour les arbitres de statuer en droit dans les arbitrages du commerce international." *In* Popovici, Adrian, ed., *Problèmes de droit contemporain: mélanges Louis Baudouin* (Montréal, 1974), pp. 305-318. **9034**

Ginsburgs, George. "Execution of Foreign Commercial Arbitral Awards in Post-War Soviet Bilateral Treaty Practice." (1971), 9 *Canadian Yearbook of International Law* 59-101. **9035**

Harvey, L. *Recognition and Enforcement of Foreign Arbitral Awards in Canada.* Cambridge, Mass., 1981. 118 leaves. **9036**
Thesis (LL.M.), Harvard University, 1981.

Kos-Rabcewicz-Zubkowski, Ludwik. "Arbitrage commercial international dans les rapports Est-Ouest." (1975), 35 *Revue du Barreau* 348-363. **9037**

Kos-Rabcewicz-Zubkowski, Ludwik. *East European Rules on the Validity of International Commercial Arbitration Agreements.* Manchester: Manchester University Press; Dobbs Ferry, N.Y.: Oceana Publications, c1970. xii, 332 p.
9038
Reviews: Giovanni Scarangella Arpino in (1972-75), 9 *Jus Gentium (Rome)* 162-163; John E.C. Brierley in (1971), 49 *Canadian Bar Review* 492-494; Humberto Briseno Sierra in (1971), 4 *Boletin Mexicano de Derecho Comparado* 226-230; Rudolf Bystrický in (1971), 5 *Journal of World Trade Law* 475-476; Martin Domke in (1971), 65 *American Journal of International Law* 881; Philippe Ferland in (1971), 12 *Cahiers de Droit* 536-538; Philippe Ferland in (1971), 17 *McGill Law Journal* 803-805; Philippe Ferland in (1970), 5 *Revue Juridique Thémis* 465-466; Kazimierz Grzybowski in (1971), 19 *American Journal of Comparative Law* 399-400; Nicolas Mateesco Matte in (1970), 8 *Canadian Yearbook of International Law* 416-417; Charles Rousseau in (1970), 74 *Revue Générale de Droit International Public* 1147; P. Sanders in (1973), 20 *Netherlands International Law Review* 328-331 (in Dutch); L. Martínez Sanseroni in (1975), 28 *Revista Española de Derecho Internacional* 198-199; David Winter in (1972), 21 *International and Comparative Law Quarterly* 820-821.

Perciballi, Lionello Cappelli. *International Commercial Arbitration as Affected by the New York Convention of 1958.* Toronto, 1975. iii, 220 leaves. **9039**
Thesis (D.Jur.), University of Toronto, 1976.

Wall, J.C. "The Asian-African Legal Consultative Committee and International Commercial Arbitration." (1979), 17 *Canadian Yearbook of International Law* 324-333. **9040**

INDEXES

INDEX OF AUTHORS

References are to numbered entries

Abbondanzio, Francis E. 5061
Abbott, George C. 7099, 7100; (Review) 7131
Abdeh, Ibrahim Ahmad 3712
Abdel-Malek, Talaat 7772
Abel, Albert S. (Review) 8060
Abele, Frances 2546
Abella, Irving 1284
Aberkane, Abès 3906
Abgrall, Jean-François 7181
Abonyi, Arpad 394
Abraham, Claude 3713
Abraham, J.P. 4886
Abraham, Lennox O'Reilly Peter 8313
Abrahamsson, Bernhard J. 3526
Abramovitch, Yehuda 3677, 3678
Abrams, Matthew J. 6749
Accinelli, R.D. 5343
Acheson, A.L. Keith 4678, 7189; (Review) 7143
Adachi, Ken 1234
Adair, E.R. 6563
Adam, Frances Cruchley 6197
Adam, H.T. (Review) 5387
Adam, Mahomed Ali 7190; (Review) 56
Adamcyk, Leonard F. 7433
Adamkiewicz, George 2459, 6382
Adams, Claude 1854
Adams, Ephraim Douglas 6927
Adams, James H. 7191, 7733
Adams, Mark S. 8662
Adams, Ronald A. 7047
Addo, Herbert Christian 7256
Addy, Andrews 1500
Adede, A.O. 5214, 8068
Adelfio, Antonio 3714
Adelman, Maurice 2919
Adler, Gerald M. 4887
Adler, H.H. 3364

Advani, Gotam Motiram 4604
Agblemagnon, N'Sougan 8614
Agrawala, S.K. (Review) 334
Ahmad, Jaleel 7434, 7435; (Review) 7197
Ahmed, Saiyed Ehtasham 3679
Aikin, J. Alexander 2789, 2790
Aikins, G.H. 6303
Aitchison, J.H. 6383; (Reviews) 54, 905
Aitken, H.T. 7296, 7297, 7298
Aitken, Hugh George Jeffrey 7773
Aitken, William B. 2501
Akin, Thomas B. 7436, 7601
Akindele, Rafiu Ayo 4398, 4399, 5136
Akinsanya, A. 8755
Aksim, Rudi Ervin 1020
Alam, Mahmud 3715
Alam, Syed N. (Review) 7462
Albert, Alain 7910
Albert, Joan E. McCabe 3124
Albert, Lionel 788
Albinski, Henry S. 5220
Alcock, Norman Z. 5567, 5790, 5983
Aldridge, James R. 1298
Alexander, Frederick 6384
Alexander, Lewis M. 2994, 2995, 3125; (Review) 3133
Alexander, Yonah 6198
Alexandroff, Alan S. (Reviews) 6878, 8031
Alexandrowicz, G.W. 1298, 3171
Alfaro, Ricardo J. (Review) 5096
Alhéritière, Dominique 3282, 8828
Allan, James H. 5529
Allan, John 6995
Allebes, Edward 8591
Allely, J.S.M. (Review) 8140
Allen, Edward W. 3283; (Review) 3319
Allen, Frank 8699
Allen, G.H. 8188

Allen, Robert 8640
Allett, John 4654
Allin, C.D. 450, 451, 1954, 2502, 6628
Allmand, Warren 8452
Almond, Harry H. 2672, 3456; (Reviews) 52, 6283
Alper, Donald K. 6750, 8163
Alpert, Herbert H. 8164, 8165
Altman, Oscar L. 8069
Altstedter, Norman 5449
Alway, Richard Martin Holden 2276
Ambrose, Paul B. 5612
Amerasinghe, Chittharanjan Felix 4567
Anand, Ram Prakash (Review) 4271
Anastasopoulos, A. 7299
Anderson, Catherine 3195
Anderson, Chandler P. 2335, 2791, 5289
Anderson, Edward 496
Anderson, Isabel B. (Review) 1371
Anderson, J.C. 452
Anderson, John Charles 5791
Anderson, Lee G. 3272
Anderson, Peter Robert P. 4490
Anderson, Roger V. 7300
Anderson, Samuel 2236
Anderson, Violet 6322
Andrassy, Juraj (Review) 2381
Andrén, Nils 5792
Andrew, Arthur J. 1811, 1812, 1813, 6304, 6305; (Reviews) 79, 6418
Andrew, C.M. 1096
Andrew, G.C. 1131
Andrews, Elias (Review) 6483
Andrews, J.A. (Reviews) 3319, 4164, 4291
Angel, Arthur D. 2792
Angers, François-Albert 7734, 7911; (Reviews) 4366, 6483
Anglin, Douglas G. 1501, 4568, 5083, 5165, 6306, 6307, 6385, 8314, 8315; (Reviews) 54, 5842, 6336, 6792, 7096
Angrand, Jean 3172, 3173; (Review) 8398
Angus, Henry F. 1235, 1236, 1237, 1326, 1327, 1328, 1329, 1330, 1502, 4491, 4569, 5984, 6109, 6386, 6752, 6753, 7048, 8335; (Reviews) 54, 539, 1865, 4825, 5212, 6437
Angus, W. David 3619
Ankli, Robert E. 6932
Annett, Douglas Rudyard 7437
Annis, Charles Arthur 7438, 7439
Antoine, Aristide 4492, 8615

Antonides, Harry 7993
Aouedri, Allou Pierre 5137
Appathurai, E. 5157
Appavoo, Patricia J. 701; (Reviews) 23 6385
Appiah, Ebener Evans 5344
Applebaum, B. 3053
April, Serge 1453, 1903
Arbitblit, Donald Carl 8812, 9000
Arbour, Jean-Maurice 603, 1888, 5345 (Reviews) 608, 2331, 2646
Arcand, Arthur 6308
Archbold, Herbert Seymour Chowne 540'
Archer, Christon I. 6564; (Review) 7087
Archer, Ian Dev 3716
Archibald, H. David 8896
Arcy, Jean d' 8531
Arend, Sylvie (Review) 718
Arès, Richard 4366, 7101
Argue, Dorothy F. 4444
Arias, Francisco 4888
Armerding, H.T. 3366
Armour, Eric 1454
Armour, Leslie 1503
Armstrong, Elizabeth 1068
Armstrong, Jack Irwin 7912
Armstrong, Robert (Review) 7880
Armstrong, T.E. 2920
Armstrong, William E. 4445; (Review 4459
Armstrong, Willis C. 5613, 7994
Arnell, J.C. 5826, 6565, 8616
Arnett, E. James 7774, 7775, 7776
Arnold, Brian J. 7777, 7778
Arnold, Guy 6629
Arnold, Samuel 7570
Arnold, Stanley Richard 3680
Arnopoulos, Paris J. 4143, 5221, 6309 7102, 7103; (Reviews) 4806, 7149, 837%
Aronsen, Lawrence Robert 7491, 7779
Arpino, Giovanni Scarangella (Reviews 2331, 4164, 9038
Arthurs, H.W. 1504
Arvay, Joseph 3196
Aryal, Puskar Raj 3717
Ashley, Andrew (Review) 3550
Ashton, Roger 7735, 8166
Askew, John Coulson 8507
Asper, I.H. 7913
Assaly, Louis C. 2091
Asselin, Martial 727

INDEX OF AUTHORS

Assum, Baudouin M.A.J.B. van den 3718
Atala, Charles 6224, 6240, 8070
Atkeson, Timothy (Review) 8856
Atkey, Ronald G. 810, 811, 7736, 7737
Atkinson, Lloyd 7780
Attwell, William George 6630
Atwater, H.E. 8611
Auburn, F.M. 2587, 2588, 2996
Auburtin, Angèle (Review) 5252
Aucoin, Peter (Review) 7087
Audet, Francis-J. 1873
Auger, Robert 2997
Aulis, Hartley L. 69
Austin, Jack 8641
Austin, Jacob 2740, 3107; (Review) 56
Avakumovic, Ivan (Review) 7050
Avery, Donald H. 1177, 1331, 1332, 1333
Avison, T.L. 8071, 8072; (Review) 8122
Avogan, Mathias Kuami 5138
Axline, W. Andrew 7492, 7914
Axworthy, Lloyd (Review) 54
Axworthy, Thomas Sidney 5827
Aylesworth, Allen B. 3586, 5346
Ayoub, Antoine 7694, 7695, 7696, 8663
Ayre, William Burton 70
Azab, Nagulb 607
Azar, Edward E. 6310
Azcárraga, José Luis de 3699
Aziz, Muhammed Abdul 2793
Azoulay, Michel 7781
Azzie, Ralph 3719, 3720

Baar, Ellen (Review) 1234
Babineau, Edmour 5602
Baccelli, Guido Rinaldi 4077, 4078, 4079
Bachand, Denis J.V. 7782
Back, K.J. 7537
Bacon, Robert 5333
Bacon, T.C. 8757
Baeyens, Raymond 617
Bagambiire, Davies Birenzo Namiti 3174
Bahary, Alfred 4035
Bahcheli, Tozun S. 4889
Bahmer, Robert 6996
Bai, Kui-mei 254
Bailey, A.G. (Review) 6760
Bailey, Douglas L. 6872
Bailey, Edwin O. 3907, 3908
Bailey, Lance 4367
Bailey, Paul J. 5198
Bailey, Richard (Review) 8434

Bailey, Thomas Andrew 2277
Bailey-Wiebecke, Ilka 5198
Baillie, C.P.F. 1889
Baird, P.D. 2537, 2589
Baird, W.J. 2590, 3108
Baker, Donald I. 7915
Baker, Marcus 2278
Baker, Philip John Noel 453
Baker, Richard (Review) 5177
Baker, Samuel R. 8191, 8203, 8228, 8230, 8289
Bakotić, Bozidar 1618; (Reviews) 68, 4271
Balachandran, Ponniah 3909
Balassa, Bela 7192
Balawyder, Aloysius 7049, 7050, 7051, 7052, 8989
Balch, Thomas Willing 2279, 2280, 2526, 2969, 2970, 3367
Balcom, A.B. 7440
Baldwin, Gordon B. (Review) 2727
Baldwin, John R. 1097, 1919, 2203
Baldwin, William H. 1455
Ball, Georgiana 2281
Ball, James T. 3284
Ball, M. Margaret 874
Ballem, John Bishop 8508
Balls, Herbert R. (Review) 4723
Balogh, Leslie V. 8167, 8168, 8169
Balthazar, Louis 1586, 6756
Ban-Ethat, José Rigobert 5139
Banker, Stephen 5084
Bankes, Nigel D. 2527, 8862, 8873; (Review) 8786
Banner, Donald W. 8453
Bannerman, Glen 7301
Barandon, P. (Review) 272
Barber, Clarence L. 7441, 8316, 8317; (Review) 8140
Barber, Willard F. (Review) 5560
Bareau, Paul 4821
Barker, Mary L. (Review) 3134
Barkway, Michael 1334, 5892, 6631, 7258
Barlow, F.H. (Review) 3590
Barnaby, Frank (Review) 5746
Barnes, William S. 7783
Barnett, James K. 8829
Barnett, John 1335
Baron, William R. (Review) 7087
Barrea, Jean 6311; (Review) 6358
Barrett, Carol 4400
Barrett, Charles A. 7104, 7302

Barrett, Jane R. 1, 2
Barros, James 3260, 4446, 4447, 4448, 4493, 5166, 5167, 5168, 8791; (Review) 4566
Barrow, B.G. 7582
Barrows, William 2464
Barry, Donald J. 6387, 6388, 6757
Barry, P.S. 5828, 7697, 8509
Barsh, Russell Lawrence 1238, 1505, 2070
Bartholomew, Mark Alan 8700
Barton, Brian 8318
Barton, G.S.H. 8928
Barton, William H. 4494, 4588, 5463
Basdeo, S. 6566
Basdevant, Jules 5291
Bashford, James Whitford 2237
Basmajian, J.V. 6019
Bassiouni, M. Cherif 9025, 9026
Bates, S. (Reviews) 7005, 8122
Batshaw, Harry 1211, 1506, 1507, 1508
Baty, Thomas 1098, 1132
Baudin, Louis 5068
Baudouin, Renée 1685
Bauer, P.T. 7653
Baum, Daniel Jay 7916
Baum, Warren C. 4680
Baumgartner, F.W. 1021
Baxter, Ian Francis George 7303
Baxter, James P. (Review) 6767
Baxter, Neil Himrod 875
Baxter, Richard R. 386, 2794, 5222; (Reviews) 248, 3261, 5652
Bayard, Ross Hawthorne 6997
Bayefsky, Anne F. 1509
Beattie, Clayton E. 5464, 5793
Beattie, J.R. (Review) 8125
Beattie, Laura 4681
Beatty, David Pierce 5829
Beaty, James 6977
Beau, Jean Claude 5085
Beauchamp, K. 3197
Beauchamp, Kenneth P. 34, 2359, 3080, 3126
Beauchesne, Arthur 876
Beaudoin, Gérald 621, 702, 1133, 1510, 1684, 7784, 7785
Beaudoin, Louise 812, 813
Beaudoin, Rosario 255
Beaulieu, Guy (Review) 4987
Beaumont, Jane 1
Beaupré, Bernard 2380, 2433, 2706, 8792

Beauroy, Jacques (Review) 5047
Beck, David 7786
Beck, J. Murray (Reviews) 652, 687
Beck, J. Stafford H. 3257
Beck, Mary Celeste 2795
Beckton, Clare F. 3276; (Review) 674
Bédard, Charles 2707, 2708, 2709, 2710, 2796, 2797, 3763, 3910, 6914
Bédard, Roger Jean 2324
Bedi, Satya Deva 1456
Bedwell, C.E.A. 4368
Beesley, J. Alan 168, 169, 170, 171, 193, 1701, 2591, 2673, 2999, 3000, 3001, 3064, 3198, 3457, 4618, 5568, 6389, 8579, 8623, 8758, 8793
Bégin, Dennis Gerald 6967
Behrman, Jack N. 7917, 7918, 7942
Beichman, Arnold 6225; (Review) 6225
Beigbeder, Yves 4769, 5169
Beigie, Carl E. 7552, 7571, 7572, 7787, 8642, 8643; (Review) 7599
Bélanger, Claude 6966
Bélanger, France 4890
Bélanger, Gérard 732
Bélanger, Michel 8891
Belfie, Michael Arthur 4682
Bell, G.F. 4449
Bell, George G. 5794, 7053
Bell, Joel I. 4570
Bellamy, David J. (Reviews) 7352, 7817, 8024
Belleau, Carole 155
Bellot, Hugh H.L. 6162
Beloff, Max 877; (Reviews) 1729, 6729
Belshaw, Cyril 8319
Belzile, Thuribe 6632
Bement, Kenneth 7995
Bemis, Samuel Flagg 2174, 2190, 6886, 6900; (Review) 6992
Bénard, Jean 7306
Ben-Gal, Talia 6232
Bendel, Michael 8897
Benham, Frederic Charles (Review) 7403
Benjamin, Jacques (Review) 2150
Bennett, D.C.T. 5569
Bennett, Peter H. 8990
Benoit, Marcel Georges Hector 5069
Benson, Kenneth Merrill 2465
Benton, Mark A. 3527
Bentwich, Norman 5570
Berengaut, Julian 9032

INDEX OF AUTHORS 693

Beres, Louis René 395, 1511, 1512, 6199
Bereskin, Daniel R. 8454
Berezowski, Cesar 8055
Berger, Carl C. 6758
Berger, Thomas R. 1513
Bergeron, Désiré 1059, 1814
Bergeron, Gérard 622, 623, 703, 704, 814, 4401, 6312
Bergevin, André (Review) 6546
Bergithon, Carl 7607
Bériault, Yvon 2592
Berle, A.A. 3721
Berlin, Mark L. 4334
Bernard, André 705; (Reviews) 647, 767
Bernard, Jean-Thomas 8736
Bernard, Marc 3614
Bernard, Mathieu A. 232
Bernardin-Haldemann, Verena 4495
Bernhagen, Beatrice Mary 6759
Bernier, Ivan 572, 608, 624, 1617, 7105, 7106, 7193, 7304, 7305, 7442, 7602, 8005; (Review) 5048
Bernier, Robert 4402
Bernstein, E.M. 7259
Berrocal Martin, Luciano 1336
Bertin, Gilles 7919, 8073
Bertrand, Charles-Auguste 497, 6183
Bertrand, Denis 6390; (Review) 1416
Bertrand, R.J. 7996
Best, Geoffrey 6313
Best, J. Calbert 1337
Beullac, Roger-A. 9001
Bevan, George A. 5795
Bevans, Charles I. (Review) 231
Bhatt, S. 4144, 4145; (Review) 68
Bicha, Karel Denis 1338
Bidmead, Harold S. 4369
Bielinski, Eva Halina 6241
Biggar, Emerson Bristol 6933
Biggar, O.M. 3722, 3723, 3724, 3725, 8532
Biggs, Margaret A. 7194
Biggs, William 7522
Bilder, Richard 1550
Bilder, Richard B. 1614, 2674, 2675, 2711, 3458, 8813
Billyou, DeForest (Review) 3833
Bilsland, A.W. 580
Binaghi, Walter 4735, 4736
Binavince, Emilio S. 581, 1514
Bindon, George (Review) 8724
Binet, Henri 4770, 4771

Binet, Henri T.P. 4146, 4147
Binhammer, H.H. (Reviews) 4678, 7236
Birch, Thomas-A. (Reviews) 54, 1102, 4626, 6671, 7080
Bird, Richard M. 4891; (Reviews) 7546, 8278
Birkenhead, Frederick Edwin Smith 356
Birrenbach, Kurt 4822
Birt, Charles 2971
Bishop, Peter V. 5465, 5466, 5530, 5531, 5796; (Review) 4519
Bissell, Claude (Review) 97
Bissell, Thomas St.G. 8170, 8171
Bisson, A.F. (Reviews) 817, 1343
Bissonnette, André 8569
Bissonnette, Lise 815, 816
Bissonnette, Pierre André 4148, 5215, 6242
Blache, Pierre 1515; (Review) 817
Black, Edwin R. 625, 3438
Black, Naomi 4892, 7920; (Review) 6347
Black, Thomas H. 5413
Black, Warren 1339
Black, William Harold 6633
Blackburn, R.G. 8673
Blackwell, Alan T. 8830
Bladen, Vincent W. 7107, 7921
Blaikie, Peter Rutherford 6314
Blair, Gordon 1618
Blake, Gordon 7443, 7444
Blanchette, Arthur E. 148a, 149; (Review) 8125
Blegen, Theodore C. 2503
Bleicher, Samuel A. 4397
Blishchenko, I. 6140
Bloch, Henry S. 8299
Blom, Joost 205, 206, 9002
Blom-Cooper, Louis (Review) 917
Bloomfield, Lincoln P. 2538
Bloomfield, Louis M. 2381, 2741, 3261, 3911, 3912, 5387, 6200, 8794; (Review) 1003
Blue, George Verne 2175, 2466
Blum, Yehuda Z. (Reviews) 242, 2727, 3319
Blumenthal, Mitchell 3913
Blyth, C.D. 7788, 8074
Boak, A.E.R. 6315
Boardman, Robert 3002, 4893, 4894, 8701, 8759; (Review) 4811
Bocking, Richard C. 8644

Boczek, Boleslaw A. (Review) 3550
Bodin, Bernard 8455
Bodsworth, C. Fred 8892
Böckstiegel, Karl-Heinz 3726, 3914, 4149
Boegler-Bogdanow, George W. 4895
Boehm, Peter Michael 878
Boggs, George T. 5425
Boggs, S. Whittemore 2336; (Review) 4825
Bogolasky, José 3727, 3728, 3729, 3730, 3731, 4017, 4134, 4737, 4738
Bogue, Allan G. (Review) 1444
Boidman, Nathan 7738, 8172, 8173
Boissonnault, Charles-Marie 2176, 6567, 6907
Boisvert, Michael A. 4370
Boisvert, René 256
Bolles, Blair 5893
Bolté, Paul-Émile 1516
Bonardelli, Peter M. 1815
Bonavia, George 1340
Bonenfant, Jean-Charles 498, 1517, 2052, 2092; (Reviews) 610, 1685, 1937
Bonin, Bernard 1341, 1342, 7603, 7789, 7790, 7791, 7792, 7793, 7922, 7923, 7997, 8320; (Reviews) 5057, 5093, 5716, 7454, 7528, 7557, 7656
Bonney, William H. 7794
Bonvicini, Gianni 4896
Booth, Charles James 6316
Booth, J.F. 8929
Borchard, Edwin M. 1920, 2798, 5292, 5293; (Review) 454
Borden, Sir Robert L. 879, 6634, 6635; (Review) 6885
Boreham, Gordon F. 1030, 7108
Borgese, Elisabeth Mann 65, 3003, 3004, 3005, 3095, 3175, 3176, 4403, 5187
Bossy, Sanda 6047
Bothe, Michael (Reviews) 56, 709, 6195
Bothwell, Robert 1816, 6392; (Reviews) 96, 1885, 5459, 5965, 6413, 6456, 6541
Boucher, Michel (Review) 798
Bouchette, R.S.M. 8075
Boudin, Leonard B. 374, 2139
Boudreau, Joseph A. 1178, 6079
Boudreault, Marc 7795
Boulanger, Claude 4897, 4898, 4899
Bourassa, Henri 6998
Bourély, Michel 4150, 4151, 4152, 4153, 4154, 4155, 4156, 4371, 4823, 4824; (Reviews) 4278, 8585
Bourne, Charles B. 56, 170, 171, 233, 1584, 2053, 2282, 2742, 2743, 2744, 2745, 2746, 2747, 2748, 2921, 2922, 2923, 2924, 2925, 2940, 5223, 6226, 6265, 8664, 8795, 8814, 8815; (Reviews) 1478, 2268, 2381, 2727, 8856
Bousquet, Denis 6636
Boutell, H.S. 6915
Boutilier, Roger Alan 7054
Bovan, Patricia M. (Review) 8996
Bovey, Wilfrid 6968
Bowen, Robert R. 4180, 8548
Bowie, J.M. (Review) 1551
Bowlby, Kathleen E. 113
Bowman, Alfred Connor (Review) 3259
Bowman, Donald Fox 3528
Bowman, Robert James 7055
Boyce, Peter J. 1702
Boyce, Raymond 5151
Boyd, Andrew 4496, 4497; (Reviews) 6413, 6456
Boyd, Hugh 2799; (Review) 2916
Boyd, John 6393
Boyer, Harold 7056
Boyer, J. MacLeod 1912
Brachet, Bernard 706
Bradford, Colin I. 7307
Bradford, Hilary P. 8174
Bradley, J.M. 8233
Bradley, Martin A. 3587, 3669, 3732, 3882, 4128, 4293; (Review) 4338
Bradley, Phillips (Review) 6533
Brady, Alexander 707, 880, 881, 882, 6317, 6637, 6666; (Reviews) 713, 765, 964, 4825, 6698, 7367
Brady, George J. 8226
Braen, André 3588, 3589
Braithwaite, Max 6048
Braithwaite, William J. 8456
Brander, James A. 7445
Brandon, Michael 2024
Branscombe, Ralph Eugene 6394
Brassard, Hélène 3; (Review) 4277
Brault, L. 7299
Braun, Aurel 5797, 5798
Brauw, E.A. de 8175
Bravo Navarro, Martín (Review) 3259
Brazeau, J.A.R. 1285

INDEX OF AUTHORS

Brazier, Rodney (Review) 6283
Brean, Donald J.S. 8176
Breaux, John B. 2370, 3358
Brebner, John Bartlet 4825; (Review) 54
Brecher, Irving 7057, 7452, 8321, 8322
Brecher, Michael 6128
Brecher, Richard A. 7057
Breen, D.H. 7698
Breen, Urban 1703
Breitfuss, Leonid 2593
Breithaupt, James Roos 7604
Brennan, Daniel J. 8228
Brennan, J. William (Review) 2164
Breton, Albert 708; (Review) 7454
Brewer, Keith J. 7574
Brewin, Andrew (Reviews) 1528, 1826
Brewin, Francis Andrew 8323
Brewster, Havelock 7308
Briant, Peter Charles 8324
Bridge, John W. 4900, 8898
Bridle, Paul 151, 5532
Brière, Jules 3199; (Review) 1343
Brière, Marc 499
Brierley, John E.C. 9033; (Review) 9038
Briggs, E. Donald 2979; (Reviews) 6804, 6806
Briggs, Herbert Whittaker (Review) 240
Bright, Christopher R. 7924
Brinton, Crane 4425
Brinton, Jasper Yeates (Reviews) 272, 3261
Briquet, Pierre E. 4450, 6110
Briseno Sierra, Humberto (Review) 9038
Brissy, Yves 2624
Brittin, Burdick H. (Review) 3259
Britton, John N.H. 7309
Britton, M.E. 2539
Brizan, George I. 7605
Broadbent, Jillian 7835
Broadfoot, Barry 1239
Broadhurst, David G. 8177, 8178, 8179, 8180, 8186, 8191
Broadley, James Ashley 4683
Brock, Peter 5603
Brock, William Ranulf 883
Brode, Michael J. 5614
Brode, Patrick 1315; (Review) 7838
Broeren, Wilma M.J. 3006
Broley, J.A. 8181
Bromke, Adam 1518; (Review) 7052
Brons, Janet Wilkinson 6318

Brookfield, F.M. 582
Brosnan, Vivienne 5467
Brossard, Jacques 626, 627, 709, 710, 711, 817, 1004, 1343, 2150
Brosseau, Richard 441
Brouillette, Benoît 7310, 7311, 7312, 7313, 7314, 7315
Brower, Charles N. 2375; (Review) 6283
Brown, Andrew H. 2800
Brown, Craig 396; (Review) 248
Brown, Dougald 3448
Brown, Douglas McK. 628
Brown, E.A. 5414
Brown, Edward Duncan (Reviews) 3048, 3133, 3319, 5370
Brown, G. Gordon (Review) 1261
Brown, George W. 2178, 2801, 2802, 5894, 6760; (Reviews) 54, 2854, 2878, 5122
Brown, Gerald S. 6761; (Reviews) 6622, 6896
Brown, J.J. 7493
Brown, J. Stanley 5294
Brown, James Milton (Review) 4291
Brown, Mannie 2803; (Review) 2918
Brown, P.S. 3356
Brown, Peter W. (Review) 1927
Brown, Ralph H. (Review) 2182
Brown, Robert Craig 6762, 6763; (Reviews) 3421, 6743, 6782
Brown, Robert D. 7446, 7606, 8182, 8183, 8184, 8185, 8187
Brown, Robert James 6764
Brown, Vera Lee 3369
Brown, Wilson 5199
Brown-John, Clive Lloyd 1457, 5430, 5431, 5998; (Reviews) 608, 1376, 1936, 2331, 8707
Browne, Evan 2594
Browne, Secor D. 3733
Brownlie, Ian (Reviews) 248, 1970, 6195
Bruchési, Jean 71, 6568, 6765; (Review) 6533
Bruha, Thomas (Review) 5691
Brumer, Leon 5170
Brun, Henri 2151; (Review) 2331
Bruncken, Ernest 2749
Bruneau, T.C. 8325
Brunelle, Dorval (Review) 785
Brunet, C. 8480
Brunet, Michel 712; (Reviews) 632, 6463, 6499, 6782

Brunet, Pierre 6569
Bryan, Ingrid A. 3529, 3530
Bryant, William H. (Review) 709
Bryce, James Scott 2540
Bryden, Kenneth (Review) 765
Buchan, Alastair 6319
Buchan, Alastair F. 5468, 5734, 5895; (Reviews) 6413, 6414
Buchet, Edmond Édouard 454
Buckner, Phillip Alfred 6570
Buckridan, Rakib 8326
Buell, Raymond Leslie (Review) 6484
Buick, Glen 1874
Bull, Hedley 5735; (Review) 303
Burchell, Charles J. 500, 884, 3590, 3591, 3592; (Reviews) 460, 508
Burchill, C.S. 7925
Burchill, R.W. 1921, 8005
Burge, Marianne 8186, 8187
Burger, James A. (Review) 6195
Burke, Frank E. 4772
Burke, William T. 3256
Burley, Kevin H. 3531; (Review) 7352
Burn, Henry Pelham 4498, 7109
Burns, Douglas 2712
Burns, Eedson L.M. 5469, 5470, 5471, 5615, 5616, 5736, 5737, 5738, 5799
Burns, Jeffrey H. 7832, 7833, 7834
Burns, Ronald M. 713; (Review) 8643
Burns, T.M. 7316
Buron, Edmond 501
Burpee, Lawrence J. 2179, 2382, 2383, 2384, 2385, 2413, 2713, 5985
Burrage, Henry Sweetser 2205, 2206, 2207
Burrell, Gordon 2071
Burroughs, Peter 6571
Burrows, *Sir* Bernard 5896
Burt, Alfred LeRoy 6572, 6639, 6766; (Reviews) 997, 6586, 6590, 6911
Burton, L.M. (Review) 2576
Burton, T.L. (Review) 2576
Burtt, Judith 4451
Busch, Peter A. 4901
Bush, Edward F. 3532
Busler, Robert H. 9003
Buteux, Paul 5897, 5898, 5899
Butler, Charles F. 6243
Butler, George Frederick 7558
Butler, Harold (Review) 4825
Butler, William E. (Reviews) 230, 4293
Butler, William J. 1586

Button, Roger William 4619
Buzan, Barry G. 3007, 3008, 3009, 3010, 3011, 3012, 3177, 3178, 3179
Byers, R.B. 714, 5617, 5618, 5619, 5620; (Reviews) 54, 5560, 5923
Byleveld, Herbert C. 7796
Byres, T.J. 8327
Byrne, John 2595
Bystrický, Rudolf (Review) 9038

Cacopardo, Massimo 4902
Cadieux, Marcel 72, 257, 1519, 1520, 1704, 1705, 1706, 1817, 1818, 4571, 5621
Cadieux, Rita 1521
Caen, Jacques P. 4157
Cahan, C.H. 2804
Cahill, Michael Edward 7797
Cail, Robert E. 2467
Caix, Robert de 3370
Caldwell, Lawrence T. 5622
Caldwell, Mary Ellen 8930
Callahan, James Morton 2283, 6767, 6916 (Review) 2269
Calvet, A.L. 7798
Calvin, D.D. 2805
Calvo, Charles 232
Camara, José Sette 2025
Camargo, Pedro Pablo (Review) 234
Cameron, David M. 436
Cameron, David R. 629, 715
Cameron, Duncan Charles 4684, 8076 8077, 8078, 8079, 8080
Cameron, Duncan F. 8991, 8992
Cameron, E.R. 3533
Cameron, J.D. 1955
Cameron, John Duncan 1344
Campbell, A.E. (Review) 6762
Campbell, B.R. 9004
Campbell, Betty 1134
Campbell, Charles S. 3371, 5295; (Reviews 2317, 6762, 6780
Campbell, Duncan Darroch 4797
Campbell, John C. (Review) 54
Campbell, Lauren Dawn 8964
Campbell, Robert Ellis 7559
Camps, Miriam 4685
Campsie, John S. 5623, 6320
Candow, James E. 5300
Cantin, Serge A. 3593
Caplan, Kenneth Gary 3735

Caplan, Neil 3200, 3201, 3202
Capon, Frank S. 7998
Capon, Rita R. (Review) 2605
Caporaso, James A. 4907
Cappon, James 5301, 6640
Cardinale, Igino 1060
Careless, J.M.S. 6573; (Reviews) 2523, 6658
Carey, Charles H. 2468
Carey, Thomas C. 716
Carignan, Pierre 259
Carle, François 5626, 5801, 5802
Carlisle, Arthur Elliott 7999
Carlsen, Sigurd Camillo 1353
Carman, F.A. 6073
Carmichael, D.J.C. 6201
Carmichael, Joel 5152
Carnahan, Burt K. 2677, 3459
Caron, Arthur 1061, 2460
Caron, Ivanhoë 6323, 6574, 6887
Caron, Jean-Lucien 6398
Caron, Madeleine 1529
Caron, Maximilien 818
Caron, Yves 7927
Carpenter, *Lord* Boyd 3736
Carpenter, Gloria 6129
Carpenter, Jacqueline Mary 6117
Carr, Wm. K. 5831
Carreau, Dominique 7654
Carrington, Charles E. 6641; (Reviews) 54, 6639
Carroll, Francis M. 10
Carroll, John E. 2753, 8762, 8796
Carrothers, W.A. 1354
Carroz, J.E. 3288, 3289
Carruthers, James R. 1179
Carruthers, Jeff 8511
Carsen, Gary L. 172, 1530
Carson, George Barr 4908
Carson, John 6202
Carson, Van 8832
Carstensen, Peter C. 7928
Carter, Arthur T. 2388
Carter, David J. 6081
Carter, Gwendolen M. 885, 886, 887, 4454, 4633, 5432; (Reviews) 6641, 6709
Carter, Thomas Le Mesurier 4775
Carty, E.B. 7788
Carty, R.K. 4909; (Review) 741
Carty, Robert 8341

Casas, Francisco Ricardo 7195
Casgrain, H.-R. 6575
Cassels, Alan (Review) 5436
Cassels, James 7484
Cassie, Lawrence Peter 5902
Castañeda, Jorge 1069
Castel, Jean-Gabriel 207, 208, 209, 210, 211, 212, 234, 235, 236, 397, 1459, 1531, 2137, 5251, 6141, 6160, 6161, 7739, 8993, 9006, 9007, 9008
Casterton, James Arthur 8705
Castro-Rial, Juan M. 502, 503, 560
Catibog, José Rosa 3737
Cavdar, Arif 3738
Cave, George 357
Cavell, Nik 8335, 8342, 8343
Caveney, William J. 8192
Caverly, D.S. 8808
Caves, Richard E. 4827, 7450
Cayley, Charles Everett 3376
Cazes, P. de 2180
Cechetto, Seth M. 8081
Cederbalk, S. 1878
Cermakian, Jean 4910, 7609, 8344
Chabot, Marc 4911
Chacko, Chirakaikaran Joseph 2389, 2390
Chadwick, Gerald William St. John 687
Chaison, Gary N. 8900
Challener, Richard D. 5903
Challies, George Swan 8056
Chalmers, John W. 2072
Chalmers, Norman A. 7459
Chamberlain, Daniel Henry 6980
Chambers, F.P. (Review) 54
Chambers, L.P. 1532
Chambers, Winston 8645
Chan, William C. 8252, 8253
Chant, John F. 4678
Chapdelaine, Jean 819, 6399
Chapelli, Armando C. 2635
Chapman, James Keith 6935
Chapman, John Doneric 2754
Chapman, John H. 8534
Chappell, Joseph J. 1879
Chaput, Donald 1355
Chaput, Roger 717
Charbonneau, Jean-Pierre 8952
Charles, William H. (Review) 5596
Charteris, A.H. 6642
Chatwood, Andrew 688

Chaudhuri, Asim 8193
Chaumont, Charles M. (Reviews) 3119, 4291
Chaussade, Jean 3290
Chauveau, Paul 3739, 3740, 3915
Chayes, Abram 8535
Cheffins, Ronald I. 2026; (Review) 674
Chen, Tung-Pi 164, 165, 166, 2597, 7322, 7323
Cheng, Bin 3681, 3741, 3916, 3917, 3918, 4036; (Reviews) 4271, 4291
Cheng, Ronald C.K. (Review) 248
Cheng, Seymour Ching-Yuan 888
Cheng, Wei-Lien 3537
Chénier, Pierre 1616
Chesler, Evan R. 3183
Chettle, H.F. 6091
Chevallard, Francine Charbonneau 4828
Chevallier, Jean-Jacques 455, 456, 889, 890, 891, 892, 1822, 1958, 6643
Chevrette, François 3919, 4092; (Review) 8060
Chevrier, Bernard 6400
Chevrier, Lionel 73, 2810, 2811, 2812
Chew, Anne Rose (Cushman) 9
Chia, Lin Sien 3576
Chiang, Haven 7060
Chicanot, E.L. 1356, 1357
Child, Clifton J. (Review) 5122
Chinkin, C.M. (Review) 290
Chipman, W.F. (Review) 8464
Chipman, Ward 2208
Chipman, Warwick 442, 893, 5627
Chisholm, Brock 8892
Chiu, Hungdah 230
Chodos, Robert 7061
Choi, Chung Su 4605
Chopra, Sudhir K. 3452
Choquette, Guy 1922
Chotard, Jean-René (Review) 5922
Chown, John F. 8194, 8229
Christensen, Rolf Buschardt 4912
Christie, Loring C. 504
Christol, Carl Q. 4159, 4160, 4161, 8536, 8833; (Reviews) 4271, 4272
Chu, Anthony Chun-Chang 5832
Churchill, Arthur Chester 9
Cisler, Walker 8665
Clarfield, Gerard 6901
Clark, Andrew Charles 4913
Clark, Andrew Hill 6576

Clark, C.W. 3428
Clark, Dorothy M. 1180
Clark, E.R. 8082
Clark, Gerald 6774
Clark, John 8901
Clark, Lorne S. 6226, 6242, 6244, 6245, 6265, 8646, 8647
Clark, Lovell C. 150
Clark, Margaret 10
Clark, Melvin Gordon 7324
Clark, Robert G. 7261
Clark, Roger S. 1533
Clark, S.D. (Reviews) 6577, 6928
Clark, Sandra S. (Review) 6571
Clarke, A.H. 1139
Clarke, Hugh W. 5127
Clarke, P.F. (Review) 4461
Clarkson, Stephen 6401
Classen, H. George 2153, 2339; (Review) 5839
Claude, Innis L. 4372
Clavet, Adrien 4373
Claxton, Brooke 74, 894, 4374, 5200 (Reviews) 6712, 6733
Claydon, John 370, 566, 1240, 1241, 1358, 1534, 1535, 1614, 5415; (Reviews) 248, 5431
Clayton, G. 8083
Clayton, Graham 4375
Clayton, Richard H. 5739
Cleland, E. Gordon 8170, 8171
Clemens, Walter C. 5628, 8763
Clément, Laurent 358
Clement, Wallace 8000, 8001
Clendenning, E. Wayne 8084
Clerget, Pierre 3538
Clermont, André-J. (Review) 3830
Clermont, Bernard-L. 5347
Cliche, Denis 7804
Clift, Dominique 718
Clingan, Thomas A. 3127
Clokie, H. McD. 505, 5904; (Reviews) 1269, 5096, 5202, 6436
Clouden, Anselm Bertram 3016
Clute, A.R. 2598, 8457
Clute, Robert E. 1176, 7610
Cocca, Aldo Armando 4162, 4163
Codding, George A., Jr. (Review) 3667
Coffey, Peter 4914
Coffin, Frank M. 7494
Coffin, Victor 6888

Coffin, William F. 1923, 6402
Coghlan, Brian C. 7495
Coghlan, F.A. 1715
Cohen, Bernard Lande 6092
Cohen, Martin Bernard 1823
Cohen, Maxwell 11, 260, 261, 262, 263, 264, 265, 266, 267, 585, 631, 719, 1124, 1359, 1528, 1536, 1537, 1538, 1539, 1540, 1716, 1924, 2375, 2391, 2392, 2393, 2394, 2543, 2755, 2813, 2927, 2930, 2931, 2932, 2933, 4164, 4165, 4322, 4572, 4573, 5158, 5159, 5472, 5473, 6775, 6776, 6777, 6778, 8731; (Reviews) 253, 303, 5246, 5596, 7940, 7982
Cohn, Ronald S. 8309
Cohn, Theodore H. 7663, 8931, 8932, 8933; (Review) 4717
Colard, Daniel 1541, 5571, 6093, 7110
Colas, Émile 1542, 3920
Colby, Elbridge (Review) 249
Coldwell, M.J. 1287
Cole, Charles V. 1461, 3203, 4606, 5226
Cole, Douglas 2291
Cole, M. Sanford D. 3017
Cole, R. Taylor (Reviews) 617, 632
Colliard, Claude Albert (Review) 917
Collin, A.E. 2544
Collins, Edward, Jr. (Review) 3048
Collins, George L. 8863
Colombos, C. John (Reviews) 156, 3076, 3119, 3833
Colquhoun, Arthur H.U. 6936; (Reviews) 6595, 6720, 6827, 6965
Colson, David 3129
Colton, Timothy 5986
Colvin, James A. 7451
Combs, Jerald A. 6902, 6903
Comeau, Roger 3377
Commager, Henry 2469
Comstock, Rudolph Swayne 2814
Comtois, Claude 7264
Comtois, Jean (Review) 3421
Comtois, Robert 4500
Conacher, James B. 7002
Conant, Melvin A. 5833, 5834, 5835, 5905, 6021
Conboy, Martin 3110
Conklin, William E. 1544; (Review) 1637
Conley, Marshall W. 3539
Conn, J.R. 1360

Connell, J. Peter 7452
Connelly, Alpha M. 359
Conner, Barbara Ann 4634
Connolly, Michael Bahaamonde 7196
Connor, John T. (Review) 5652
Conroy, Pat 4776
Constas, Dimitrios C. 1925, 4829, 4916
Conti, Raymond 8902
Conway, John S. 896, 897, 898, 1062, 5629, 6779; (Reviews) 1060, 1796
Conway, Myrtle R. 4800
Cook, George Leslie 6646
Cook, Ramsay 720, 721, 6404, 6647, 6648; (Reviews) 150, 157
Cooke, Susan M. (Review) 8856
Coombs, Maurice J. 5416
Cooper, H.H.A. 6203, 6204, 6205, 6206, 6207, 6208, 6209, 6210, 6246
Cooper, John 3140
Cooper, John A. 567
Cooper, John Cobb 3660, 3682, 3921, 4166, 4167
Copes, Parzival 3151, 3152, 3292, 3293, 3294, 3295, 3296, 3297, 3298; (Review) 7140
Copithorne, M.D. 173, 174, 175, 176, 1140, 1546, 1547, 1548, 5216, 5227, 5348
Copland, Douglas 899; (Review) 8046
Copland, John Anthony 8350
Corbet, Hugh 6732, 7197
Corbett, David C. 1361, 1362, 1363, 1364; (Reviews) 1376, 7824
Corbett, Edward M. 722
Corbett, Percy E. 268, 269, 270, 271, 272, 273, 274, 398, 429, 443, 900, 901, 1718, 4376, 4404, 5086, 5252, 5433, 6324, 6325, 6326, 6405, 6406, 6649; (Reviews) 290, 460, 472, 508, 1952, 2592, 5202
Corbett, Walter Edward Hiller 6937
Corbo, Vittorio 7325
Corcelle, Charles 6051
Corcoran, James I.W. 6076, 6077
Cordell, Arthur J. 7805, 8002
Corey, Albert B. 6577, 6928; (Reviews) 156, 2198, 6572, 6766
Cornell, P.G. (Review) 157
Corradini, Alessandro 5630
Corrigan, Beatrice 1031
Corrigan, John M. 3922, 4080

Corriveau, Patrice 4830, 6327
Corry, J.A. 723, 5906, 7198; (Reviews) 613, 6672
Cosford, Edwin G. 3205, 3206
Costelloe, John F. 8299
Costigan, Richard F. 360
Côté, Ernest-A. 4501
Côté, Marcel 8903
Côté, Pierre G. 3620
Côté, Pierre P. 8195
Côté, Yvon 75
Cotler, Irwin 1549, 1618, 6228
Coudevylle, Andrée 4917
Coulibaly, Seydou 3742
Coulombe, Gérard 8189
Coupar, Doug (Review) 5717
Couper, Alistair D. 3273
Courtis, Kenneth S. 4918
Cousin, Marie-Elisabeth 1005
Cousineau, René 1365
Cousineau, Rosario 1719, 7326, 7327
Coutts, James A. 7497, 7549
Couture, J. Claude 7806
Couture, Paul M. 7062, 7063
Couzin, Robert 8231
Cowan, G.S. (Review) 249
Cowan, Helen 1366
Cowan, Ralph Keith 7575
Cowen, Zelman (Review) 613
Cowie, Donald 6328
Cowley, George A. 8966
Cowling, Ellis B. 8834
Cox, David 5560, 5837; (Reviews) 54, 6450, 6481, 6553
Cox, R. Gregory 3594, 3595, 3596, 3600
Cox, Robert W. 4377, 4405, 4406, 7112, 8351, 8904, 8905; (Reviews) 4398, 8870
Crabitès, Pierre 457, 5349
Crackanthorpe, Montague 5228
Craig, Alexander (Reviews) 6481, 7061
Craig, Gerald Marquis 6780
Craig, Sydney G. 2815
Cram, J.S. 8648
Crane, Brian 572, 1617, 5631
Crane, David 8666
Cranston, Ross 7740
Crate, Harold E. 8209
Crawford, Charles T. 8196
Crawford, Horace Donald 5087
Crawford, Malcolm 4919
Crean, Frank Leo van de 561

Crean, G.G. 5803
Crean, John G. 5088, 7262
Creery, Tim 8667
Creighton, Donald G. 4825, 6578, 6650
Crelinsten, Ronald D. 6211, 6212, 6213, 6235, 6247
Crener, Maxime A. 7798, 7910, 7929, 7930
Crenna, Dave 724
Crépeau, Paul André 632
Cressy, A. Cheever 6781
Cricher, Aaron Lane 2825
Crispo, John H.G. 8906, 8907, 8908
Critchley, W. Harriet 2545, 3018, 5838
Crofton, F. Blake 506
Croisat, Maurice 725, 726
Crommelin, Michael 3180, 3197, 3207, 3208
Cronin, Maureen P. 507, 5907; (Review) 7093
Cronkite, F.C. (Review) 1199
Crookell, Harold 7807, 8003
Crosby, D.G. 3204
Cross, Hartley William 458, 459
Cross, J.A. 902
Cross, Michael Sean 2504, 6938
Cruickshank, David A. 2599
Cruikshank, E.A. 6917
Cruttwell-Vaughn, Adrian 6407
Crystal, Peter Maurice 7931
Cuff, Robert D. 5577, 5847, 6782, 6783, 7498, 7499, 8369
Culkin, W.E. 2238
Culver, Howard L. 3743
Cumming, Peter A. 1242, 1272
Cumming, R. Stanley 2816
Cumyn, A. Peter 3209, 8197, 8203, 8225, 8233
Cundiff, W.E. 8538
Cunningham, Alain MacAlpine 6651
Cunningham, George 8352
Cunningham, J.R. (Review) 3637
Cunningham, William Bannerman 7612
Curran, John F. 8198
Current, Richard N. 6929
Currey, Charles Herbert 903
Currie, A.W. 2817
Curry, F. Hayden 7576, 7613
Curtis, G.F. (Reviews) 5252, 6397
Curtis, John M. 7500
Curzon, Gerard 7263

Cushing, Caleb 6981
Cushman, Dawn 3540
Cuthbertson, B.C. (Review) 6818
Cuthbertson, Brian 5839
Cutler, Maurice 7808, 7809
Cutler, Phil 6163
Cuyvers, Luc 2340, 3210

Dabbs, R. Paul 5804
Dacks, Gurston 633; (Review) 2086
Da Costa, Richard Cochrane 4407
Dafoe, John W. 4455, 4456, 6408, 6652; (Reviews) 5202, 6436, 6841
Daggett, Athern P. 2054, 3378
Dahamni, Ahmed 1720
Dahl, Christen Sverdrup 4129
Dai, Poeliu 586, 1033, 4607, 5185, 5537, 5538, 5539, 5540, 5541, 5542, 5740
Daigle, Benoit Ludovic 7328
Dale, Norman G. 3134
Dale, William 904
Dales, John H. 7453, 7454, 7501, 7502
Dalfen, Charles M. 371, 372, 4168, 4209, 5229, 5350, 5351, 8539, 8540, 8541, 8542, 8543, 8561, 8562, 8569, 8605
Dallas, Alexander Grant 2261
Daly, Donald J. 7113, 7455, 7552
D'Amato, Anthony A. 276
Damiano, Piercarlo 4037
Dan Dicko, Dankoulodo 1006
Dancey, Kevin J. 8199
Dandurand, Raoul 552
Danglade, James Kirby 6579, 6784
Danielian, N.R. 2904
Daniels, Roger (Review) 1283
Danielsson, Sune 4169
D'Aquino, Susan 1368
Darling, H.J. 3541
Darling, H. Maurice 4457
Dart, Robert J. 8208, 8231
Das, Kamleshwar 1550
Das, S.K. 1959
Dauphin, Roma 4378, 4920, 7329, 7330; (Review) 6768
D'Auteuil, Maurice 6409
David, Eric (Reviews) 709, 3259
David, Jacques 6142
David, René 7199, 9034
Davidson, Donald C. 2292
Davidson, George 2293

Davies, Gareth John 3460
Davies, Gwilym J. (Review) 8791
Davis, David John 3379
Davis, George B. 6130
Davis, Glen White 5475
Davis, Jack 8668, 8669, 8797
Davis, Jerome D. 5908
Davis, John 7699, 7700, 8670
Davis, John W. 2181
Davis, Morris 1181; (Review) 4518
Davy, Grant R. 4502, 5632
Dawson, Frank Griffith 1182
Dawson, Robert MacGregor 54, 460, 508, 6653; (Reviews) 495, 6671, 6712, 6733
Dawson, Samuel Edward 6329
Dawson, Will 2262
Day, Brigham 1551, 4574
Day, J. Graham 3536, 3542
Deacon, Paul S. 8299
Deák, Francis 3744
Dealey, J.Q. 2756
Dean, Arthur H. (Review) 5652
Dean, Edgar Packard 5987
Dean, Gordon 8706
Dean, Patrick 4551
Dean, Reginald Scott 5280
DeBane, Pierre 727
De Blois, Denis Grégoire 1926
De Boer, Gerrit B. 4038
De Bondt, John 8353
Decaluwé, Bernard 4921, 8085; (Review) 8079
Deddish, Michael R. 7576, 7613
DeDongo, Paul J. 3745
Deener, David R. 12, 1927, 1960, 1961; (Reviews) 1970, 4164
De Grandpré, A.J. 8568
Dehem, Roger 4922, 8086, 8087; (Reviews) 7140, 8079
Dehner, Joseph W. 2600
De Koninck, Rodolphe 7264
Delafield, Joseph 2182
De La Fuente, Manuel 5070
DeLap, Richard L. 8200
DeLisle, Kenneth Edward 5633
Delisle, R.J. 1463, 1962
Dellapenna, Joseph W. 2601
Delpuer, Jean 3621
Demain, Bernard 5217
Dembling, Paul G. 4170, 4171

Demers, Henri 13
De Mestral, Armand L.C. 178, 179, 180, 181, 182, 183, 184, 185, 186, 237, 253, 3019, 3181, 3211, 3299, 3300, 3439, 3461, 3462, 3463, 7117, 7739, 8798; (Reviews) 246, 5652
De Montigny, Yves 1243
Dempsey, Hugh A. 2073
Denega, M.A. 8201
Denis, G.A. 7265
Denis, Germain 7266
Denis, Jean-Émile 4923, 7331
Dennis, Geoffrey Edwin James 8126
Dennis, William C. 5267
Den Otter, A.A. 6939
De Pauw, Richard James 1721
De Planelles, Margarita 4833
De Ricci, James Herman 2505, 3380
DeRosier, Arthur H. 6580, 6969
Derriennic, Jean-Pierre 6214; (Review) 8634
De Salvia, Michel 1619
DeSaussure, Hamilton 4039, 4172, 4173, 4288, 6038, 6039, 6040; (Review) 4287
Deschênes, Pierre-A. 4174
Desgranges, Paul-Yvan 7456
Desjardins, Alice 1183, 1552, 1553, 1619, 2055
Desjardins, Louis Georges 2506
Desmarais, Ginette 4924
De Smith, Stanley A. 905, 990; (Reviews) 613, 1002
Després, Jean-Pierre 4777, 4778, 4779, 8909
Desrosiers, Léo-Paul (Reviews) 6622, 6896
Dessauer, F.E. 5572
Dessaulles, Louis Antoine 2507
Désy, Anatole 6940
Désy, Jean 4458
Dethan, G. (Review) 1885
Deutsch, Antal 7577
Deutsch, Harold C. 1034
Deutsch, Herman J. 2239, 2240, 2341
Deutsch, John J. 7200, 7503, 7614, 7932
Deutsch, Karl W. 361
Devine, D.J. 3274
Devine, Thomas Joseph 8544; (Review) 8588
De Vos, Dirk J. (Review) 7838
De Walle, Frank (Review) 7993

Dewey, Alexander Gordon 906, 1724, 6654
DeWiel, Alexa (Review) 8341
Dhawan, K.C. 7332, 7333
Dial, Roger L. 6330, 6331
Dickason, Olive Patricia 6332
Dickerson, Robert W.V. 7742, 8202
Dickey, John Sloan 6751, 6785, 6786, 7549
Dickie, Lloyd Merlin 3278, 3301
Dickson, Brian H. 8545
Dickson, J.D. 5840
Dickson, Lovat (Review) 97
Dickstein, H.L. 8816
Diebold, William 7201
Diederiks-Verschoor, Isabella H.Ph. 3923, 3924, 4175, 4176, 4177, 4178; (Reviews) 52, 3667, 3669, 3814, 3833, 4061, 4271, 4277
Diefenbaker, John G. 2936
Diersch, Wolfdieter 3746
Di Marzo, Luigi 1963, 1964
Dimitriu, Paul 4834
Dinsmore, John 7334
Dinstein, Yoram 1554; (Review) 6195
Dinwoodie, D.H. 2602, 5281
Dion, Gérard 8910
Dion, Léon 728
Diop, Charles M. 3683
Dirks, Gerald E. 1288, 1289, 1290, 1291, 1292, 4801; (Review) 1376
Dirks, Gerry (Review) 5616
Di Sanza, Emile 7064
Distel, Michel (Reviews) 303, 709, 1937, 5370, 8996
Diubaldo, Richard J. 2603, 5841, 8512; (Review) 2571
Dixit, R.K. 5408; (Review) 241
Djalal, Hasjim 3543
Dobell, Peter C. 76, 1368, 1725, 6410, 6787; (Review) 90
Dobell, William M. 1035, 1036, 1037, 1726, 1727; (Review) 8400
Dodd, Rosemarie A. 4925
Doe, John 4589
Doehring, Karl 4741; (Review) 3119
Doern, G. Bruce 8707
Doerr, Audrey D. (Review) 6552
Dogra, Hari Krishan 5352
Dohan, David J. 3684

INDEX OF AUTHORS

Doherty, Edward J. 2470
Dohle, Gordon Carl 907
Dolan, Michael B. 6788, 7114
Dollot, René 2528
Domanski, Robert P. 1293
D'Ombrain, Nicholas (Review) 6410
Domke, Martin (Review) 9038
Donahue, William Patrick 8355
Donaldson, John 3302
Donaldson, Robert A. 7810, 7811
Donegan, E.L. 8459
Donnelly, Brian Eugene 3464
Donnelly, Daniel K. 6789
Donnelly, Michael W. 7335
Donnelly, Murray S. 2715, 8817
Donneur, André P. 14, 15, 1825, 4835, 6790, 7065; (Reviews) 6452, 6749
Doran, Joseph Ingersoll 3381
Dorcey, Anthony H.J. 3128
Dorion, Guy 8057
Dorion, Henri 2325, 2326
Dorion-Robitaille, Yolande 2604
Dorland, Arthur G. 908
Dorscht, Axel 1022
Dosman, Edgar J. 2546, 2605
Douglas, A. Vibert 4802
Douglas, Colin 3212
Douglas, Dudley G.W. 1913
Douglas, Monteath 8299
Douglas, W.A.B. 5543
Dover, Margaret Ann 8356
Dow, Alexander 8650
Dow, Sheila C. 8088
Downs, John Richard 7686
Doxey, G.V. 1070
Doxey, Margaret P. 562, 909, 910, 911, 1070, 1555, 4379, 4408, 5434, 5435, 5436, 5437, 5438, 5439, 6411, 7115, 7664; (Reviews) 100, 4717, 5459, 6541
Doxford, C.F. (Review) 5560
Doyle, Stephen E. 4179, 8547; (Review) 4291
Drago, Luis M. 5302
Draper, G.I.A.D. (Review) 290
Dreisziger, Nandor A.F. 2229, 2396, 2757
Drieger, Elmer A. 1556
Drion, Huibert 3925
Drouet, Ludovic O. 4157
Drouin, Marie-Josée 6791
Drummond, Andrew T. 1369, 6655, 6656, 7336

Drummond, Ian M. 6657
Drummond, W.M. 6811, 7202, 7667
Drysdale, Peter 7758
Dubé, Georges 277, 4575, 7337
Dubé, Paul-André 2508
Ducatenzeiler, Graciela 5070
DuCharme, Edward D. 4180, 8548
DuCrest, Maxime M. 3747
Dudley, Leonard 8357
Dudoit, Alain 8549
Duff, Wilson 2074
Dufour, André 238, 634, 1894, 1895, 6238; (Reviews) 321, 713, 1936
Dufour, J.A. 2056
Dugard, C.J.R. (Review) 5652
Duhamel, Roger 1728, 5604; (Reviews) 1269, 2592, 4376, 7005
Dulude, Louise 7543
Dumon, Laurence 461
Dumont, Georges 729
Dumouchel, Jean 510, 511, 512, 912, 913, 914, 1965, 1966
Dunbar, M.J. 2547, 2560
Duncan, Bingham 3429
Duncan, James S. 1914, 2818
Duncan, Lewis 4380
Dunlop, Charles Clifford 2397
Dunn, Frederick Sherwood 462
Dunn, James David 3465
Dunn, Lewis A. 5742
Dunn, Robert M. 8089
Dunne, Michael (Review) 6456
Dunton, Davidson 730
Duplisea, Gerald Hugh 5089
Dupras, Maurice 915, 1007
Dupré, Maurice 5637
Dupuis, Lionel-Alain 4081
Dupuis, N.F. 8753
Dupuy, Michel 8358
Dupuy, Pierre 77
Dupuy, René-Jean 3020, 3182, 4181; (Review) 234
Durocher, René (Review) 783
Duroselle, Jean Baptiste 4836
Dussault, Paul N. 4803, 7118
Duthiel de la Rochère, J. (Review) 248
Duthoit, Eugène 362
Duval, Jean-Marc 7812
Dwivedi, O.P. 2398, 8765
Dworsky, Leonard B. 2716
Dyck, Harvey Leonard 6658

Dyer, Louis 1141
Dziuban, Stanley W. 5842, 5843, 6792, 6793

Eagleton, Clyde 2758, 2759, 2937, 4636; (Reviews) 1199, 5387
Easson, Alex J. 4926, 4927, 4928
Easterhay, Carl A. 2717
Eastman, Harry C. 7341, 7457, 7458, 7630; (Reviews) 5967, 7976
Eastman, Samuel Mack 4459, 5476; (Reviews) 54, 4366, 4445, 4482, 4778, 5212
Eaton, Keith E. 7459
Eayrs, James George 54, 1729, 1730, 1731, 1732, 1826, 1827, 4503, 4837, 4838, 5090, 5743, 5805, 6002, 6333, 6412, 6413, 6414, 6794, 6918; (Reviews) 79, 4626
Ebenstein, William 6094
Eberle, W.D. 7510
Eby, John C. 5091
Eckardt, H.M.P. 7743
Eckhardt, William 5573, 5605
Eden, Lorraine (Review) 8042
Edeson, W.R. (Review) 3059
Edge, Frederick 4742
Edmonds, J. Duncan 6415; (Review) 8440
Edmonds, William L. 1967
Edmondson, Locksley G.E. 1558, 4590
Edwardh, Marlys 1459
Edwards, A.B. (Review) 290
Edwards, Everett Eugene 9, 16
Edwards, F.B. 1142
Edwards, G.L. 3141
Edwards, Gary (Review) 3550
Edwards, Richard W. 8695
Edwards, Wayne 5477
Egerton, George W. 4460, 4461
Eggleston, Ellen K. 2342
Eggleston, Wilfrid 689, 2606; (Review) 648
Ehrhardt, Roger B. 7120, 8360
Ehrlich, Thomas (Review) 3319
El-Amin, Abdel-Salam 6248
Elashiv, Arlazar 3926
Elias, Taslim Olawale 8550
Elkin, Alexander B. 1968
Elliott, Charles Burke 5303
Elliott, George Alexander 7203, 7460; (Review) 8032
Elliott, T.C. 2241

Elliott, W.Y. 916
Ellis, Howard S. 8361
Ellis, James (Review) 253
Ellis, Lewis Ethan 7003, 7004, 7005
Ellis, Shane Alexander 8461
Ellison, Anthony P. 7665
Ells, S.C. 8513
Eltscher, Louis Robert, III 1828
Emanuelli, Claude C. 239, 1209, 2038, 2155, 3021, 3466, 3467, 3468, 3469, 3470, 5230, 5638, 6249, 6250, 6251; (Reviews) 236, 709
Embolo, Essama A. 5140
Emerson, David L. 799
Engelhardt, Ed 5304
Engle, Howard E. 7813
English, Harry Edward 6795, 6796, 7229, 7253, 7338, 7339, 7340, 7341, 7615, 7616, 7814
English, John (Reviews) 100, 856, 4488, 5965, 6413
Enomoto, Lawrence M.G. 3491
Epstein, Martin 2938
Epstein, William 5639, 5640, 5641, 5642, 5643, 5744, 5745, 5746, 5747, 5748, 5779
Erades, Lambertus (Reviews) 56, 234, 241, 1927, 1970
Erichsen-Brown, J.P. 8818
Erickson, Edward W. 8671
Erler, Jochen 3544, 4381, 4743, 4744; (Review) 3259
Ernst, Edward R. 7815
Errera, Roger 8551
Erriah, Paul Jainarine 7933
Ervin, Linda 17
Espinosa, William H. 7816
Estall, Martyn 6321
Estorick, Eric 6015
Etemad, Hamid 7332
Etheridge, G.T. 8004
Etra, Lionel 8206
Ettinger, Michael L. 187, 3545
Eubank, John A. 3685
Eustace, Marilyn D. 6252
Evans, Allan S. 6797
Evans, Alona E. 6226, 6265; (Review) 4061
Evans, Anne Elizabeth 8708
Evans, Donald 5574
Evans, Howard V. 6581

Evans, J.A.S. 1039
Evans, J.J. (Review) 3530
Evans, W. Sanford 2980, 7666
Everest, Allan Seymour 6889
Ewart, John S. 463, 513, 514, 515, 516, 525, 1143, 2294, 3546, 3748, 5231, 6416, 6659, 6660, 6661; (Reviews) 471, 490
Ewart, T.S. 526
Ewens, Douglas S. 8276
Eyre, Kenneth C. 2607, 5544

Fairley, H. Scott 635, 3303, 3304, 5417, 8617, 9009; (Reviews) 303, 3048
Fairman, Charles (Review) 611
Fairweather, Gordon 636
Fairweather, R. Gordon L. 1740
Falconer, J.W. (Review) 6753
Falconer, Thomas 2471
Falk, Richard A. 278, 279
Famula, Paul F. 3645
Farand, André 4182
Faris, Nabil Ahmed 1071
Farley, James M. 7461
Farmer, Margaret E. 4183
Farnell, Werner 8006
Farr, David M.L. 6417, 6662
Farrell, Robert Barry 1741, 6418
Farris, W.B. 5354, 5355
Fatouros, Arghyrios A. 7121, 7744, 7745, 7746, 7934, 8363
Fauteux, Paul 4184, 4185, 8552, 8553
Fawcett, J.E.S. 917, 1144, 1929; (Reviews) 68, 615, 1927, 4291, 8786
Fay, C.R. 7204; (Review) 1102
Fayerweather, John 7817; (Review) 8001
Fayon, Pierre (Review) 56
Feaver, H.F. 5388
Fedele, Frank 3686
Feder, Barnaby J. 2608
Feis, Herbert 7504
Feld, Werner J. 4931, 4932
Feldman, Arlene Butler 4072
Feldman, Elliot J. 6419, 6798, 6799
Feldman, George J. 8554
Feldman, Lily Gardner 6798
Feldman, Mark B. 3129
Fellows, Catherine 7701
Feltham, Ivan R. 7303, 7638, 7818, 8007
Fenema, Peter van 4186

Fenrick, W.J. 3022, 6003, 6004
Fenston, John 4039
Fenwick, Charles G. 5092; (Reviews) 268, 917, 5117, 6307
Fera, Norma M. 1466
Ferguson, Alan John 3130
Ferguson, George V. 4382, 5909, 6800
Ferland, Philippe (Reviews) 9015, 9038
Ferns, H.S. (Reviews) 54, 1013, 1927, 2916, 5834, 6401, 6413, 6414, 6440, 6466, 6472, 6489, 6494, 6499, 6844, 6846, 7052, 7141, 8440
Fieldhouse, H.N. 5440; (Review) 7005
Fieldhouse, Noel 6334
Filion, Gérard 8008
Filion, Louis Jacques 6420
Finan, J.S. 5644
Findlay, John D. 8864
Fingland, F.B. 2548
Fink, Lowell S. 8858
Finkelstein, Lawrence S. 5645
Finkle, Peter Z.R. 3305, 3306, 3307, 3308, 8839; (Reviews) 1182, 1567
Finkleman, J. 1200
Finlay, Robert Bannatyne 363, 6005
Finlayson, Jock A. 7267, 7722
Finnie, Richard 8514
Finnie, Robert S. 3440
Fiorino, John 8207
Fischer, Dana D. (Review) 5370
Fischer, Georges 5749
Fischer, Hugo 1559, 8515
Fischer, Lewis A. 4933, 8934
Fish, Andrew 2263
Fisher, A.D. 8808
Fisher, A.G.B. (Review) 7926
Fisher, Barry D. 7702
Fisher, Margaret Anne 6616
Fisher, Roger (Review) 320
Fisher, Tobias (Reviews) 54, 6413
Fistié, Pierre 6335
Fittro, Mary E. 2509
FitzGerald, Gerald F. 517, 1969, 2027, 2381, 2760, 3661, 3662, 3749, 3750, 3751, 3752, 3753, 3754, 3755, 3756, 3757, 3758, 3927, 3928, 3929, 3930, 3931, 3932, 3933, 3934, 4040, 4041, 4042, 4043, 4044, 4045, 4093, 4187, 4745, 4746, 4747, 4748, 5282, 5389, 6200, 6226, 6253, 6254, 6255, 6256,

6265, 8516, 8517, 8568, 8835, 8859; (Reviews) 234, 236, 1002, 3119, 3667, 3777, 4166, 6160, 6161
FitzGerald, J.G. 8893
Fitzhardinge, L.F. 464
Fitzmaurice, G.G. 5268
Flackett, John M. (Review) 272
Fleming, Donald J. 399; (Review) 253
Fleming, Donald M. 7617
Fleming, James MacLean 6422
Fleming, Sandford 8555, 8556, 8557
Flemming, Brian 2678, 3023, 3024, 3471, 5390, 5391, 5392; (Reviews) 917, 1002, 2646, 2727, 3073, 6440, 6774
Flenley, Ralph 18
Fletcher, Frederick J. (Review) 6732
Fletcher-Cooke, *Sir* John 1072
Fleury, Serge 1829, 1830, 1831
Flint, John (Review) 874
Flinterman, Cees 5418
Florio, Franco 8819
Flory, Maurice 1008
Flournoy, Richard W. 1145
Flynn, Frank Joseph 3687
Focsaneanu, Lazar 280
Foerkel, Jens (Review) 303
Foley, Edward C. 3213
Forbes, Frederic J. 4462
Forbes, Gordon W. 6184, 6185
Forbes, Wm.O.M. 3646
Forest, Pierre-Gerlier 4934, 6801
Forest, Réal 1560, 2057
Forget, Claude E. 2609
Forsey, Eugene 637, 731, 918; (Reviews) 653, 765, 4778, 6483
Fortier, Jean-Marc 4046
Fortin, L. Yves 4935
Fortin, Pierre 732
Foster, *Sir* George 4409
Foster, George E. 7006, 7007
Foster, Joan Mary Vassie 7008, 7009
Foster, John (Review) 272
Foster, John W. 2295, 2296, 5306, 6919; (Review) 6912
Foster, Leslie A. 51
Foster, William Fraser 4188, 5356, 5357
Fotheringham, Peter 4637
Fowler, R.M. 281
Fowlie, E.L. 4804
Fox, Annette Baker 437, 5910, 6336, 6424,
6802, 6803, 6804, 6805, 6806; (Reviews) 6304, 6456, 6549
Fox, Francis 4189
Fox, Harold George 8462, 8463, 8464, 8465, 8466, 8467
Fox, Lawrence A. 7268
Fox, Paul 733
Fox, William Thornton Rickert 5910
Fraino, Carlos 3759
Francis, Daniel 2610
Francis, George R. 2716
Francis, R. 465
Francis, Thomas L. 2819
Franck, Christian 4840
Franck, Thomas M. 568, 919, 1743, 3183, 3184, 6228, 7618, 7819;(Reviews) 248, 615, 1000, 5411
Frank, Helmut J. 8672
Frank, Isaiah 7205
Frank, Pierre 3760
Frank, Richard A. (Review) 8791
Franks, C.E.S. (Review) 2550
Frankson, Pamela Louise 7206
Frappier, Monique DesRochers 5646
Fraser, A.M. 690
Fraser, Blair 734, 1833
Fraser, Charles Frederick 1146, 1184, 1185, 1744, 4805
Fraser, D.G.L. 6582
Fraser, F.M. (Review) 998
Frazer, Keener C. 5269
Frederick, Glenn D. 7505
Frédérick, Michel 2343, 2344, 3214, 3215
Freedman, Max 4591, 5911
Freeman, Hadley Fairfield 8468
Freeman, Linda 6425
Freeman, R.E. 2820
Freeman, Susan 8009
Frégault, Guy 6583, 6584, 6585; (Review) 1551
Freifeld, Sidney A. 1745, 1896
Freitas, Jorge Alberto de Sousa 4047
French, G.S. (Reviews) 54, 6497
French, Robert W. 7820
Frenette, Claude 587
Frenkel, Jacob A. 8091
Freudenberg, Reinhardt (Review) 3261
Freymond, Bernard 1746
Freymond, Jacques 6337
Friede, Wilhelm (Review) 249

Friedlander, Robert A. 569, 5419, 6215; (Reviews) 1479, 6195
Friedman, Julian R. (Review) 303
Friedman, Kenneth J. 8092
Friedman-Rush, Andrea (Review) 8497
Friedmann, Wolfgang G. 282, 283, 920, 1370, 4505, 4506, 4841, 5912, 5913; (Reviews) 56, 1927, 4665, 8349, 8388
Friesen, George (Review) 5011
Friesen, R.A. 8199
Frigon, Augustin 8558
Frith, Elizabeth Aldon (Stewart) 518
Fromm, Paul 8364
Frommel, S.N. 8211
Frost, Richard Aylmer 6663
Frowein, J. (Reviews) 1927, 3833
Frowein, Jochen A. 4507
Frumhartz, Esther 7561
Fry, Michael G. 5420, 6338, 6426, 7066; (Review) 49
Fujita, Katsutoshi 4082
Fukatsu, Ei'ichi 5358
Fulford, D.W. 8673
Fuller, David G. 8212
Fuller, G.G. 6941
Fullerton, Douglas H. 735, 7342, 7343
Fumoleau, René 2075
Furlong, David B. 8695

Gadbaw, Michael 7506
Gaggero, Eduardo D. 4190
Gagné, Maud 2611
Gagné, Paul (Review) 5431
Gagné, Roland-Yves 4130
Gagnon, Guy 2058
Gagnon, Jean Dunis 2093
Gagnon, Onésime 519
Galarneau, Hélène 6427, 6428, 6429, 6430, 6431, 8709; (Reviews) 1, 5756
Galbraith, J. William 4842
Galbraith, John Alexander 8093
Galbraith, John S. 1834, 2472, 5201
Galicki, Zdzislaw Waclaw 4191
Gall, Gerald L. 1561; (Review) 1678
Gallatin, Albert 2209, 2210, 2473, 2474
Galloway, Eilene 4192, 4193, 4194, 4195, 4196, 4197, 4198, 8559; (Review) 31
Galtung, Johan 7122, 7207
Galway, Michael A. 2612, 8695
Gamacchio, Giampiero 3762
Gannon, Thomas M. (Review) 6195

Ganong, William F. 2211
Garcia, Charles F. 8213
Gardner, Daniel L. 4048
Gardner, Gérard 2327, 2549
Gardner, William R. 8094
Gariépy, Henri 820
Garigue, Philippe 5914
Garland, G.D. (Review) 8618
Garner, James W. 5270
Garner, Joseph John Saville 78
Garnier, Gérard 7747, 7748, 7935, 8010, 8011, 8012, 8013; (Review) 7880
Garraty, John A. 2297
Garrow, D. Bruce 4098
Garstin, L.H. 6164
Gates, Charles M. 6908
Gates, Theodore R. 7507, 7549, 7619
Gaudet, Gérard 7695
Gault, Ian Townsend 3216, 3441
Gault, Thomas Munro 8469
Gauthier, François 736
Gauthier, Gilles 8095
Gautier, Pierre 3763
Geffcken, H. 3382
Geiger, Theodore 7620
Geise, Conrad David 4937
Gelber, Lionel 4638, 4843, 6432; (Review) 6397
Gelber, Marvin 1073, 6433; (Reviews) 1791, 4435, 5977
Gellner, John 5479, 5844, 5915, 5916, 5917; (Reviews) 5616, 6413
Gendron, François 5750; (Review) 5799
Genest, Jean 7936
Genné, Marcelle 7123
George, James 1041
George, Pierre 4780
Georgiades, Euthymène (Reviews) 3119, 3667, 3669, 3833, 4061, 4164, 4166, 4276
Gerace, Mary C. 8035
Gérin, E. 7562, 7563
Gérin, Jean (Review) 7225
Gérin-Lajoie, Henri 8470
Gérin-Lajoie, Paul 8366
Gerity, F.O. 2822, 3615
Germain, Claude 7344, 8096
Germain, Victorin 4463
Gernant, Paul Leonard 7578
Gertler, Z. Joseph 3764
Getman, Charles 8674

Getz, Leon (Review) 7940
Geuber, Grant L. 8365
Gey van Pittius, Ernst F.W. 1147, 1148
Ghent, Jocelyn Maynard 821, 5751, 8618, 8619
Gherson, A.R.A. 4938, 7549, 7621
Ghosh, Ratna 7124
Ghouse, Mohammad (Review) 56
Gibbon, W.A. 6165
Gibbons, Alan O. 2230, 8097
Gibbons, George 2231, 2413
Gibbons, W.J. 8210
Gibson, Dale 1562
Gibson, F.W. 2298
Gibson, J. Douglas 4576, 7345
Gibson, James A. 520, 6434
Gibson, Roger C. 8214
Gibson, Roy 4199
Gil, Enrique 5072
Gilbert, A.D. (Review) 6743
Gilbert, Sidney Norman 438
Giles, J.W. (Review) 8661
Gilfix, Don 7401
Gill, W.B. 588
Gillanders, D.E. 3555
Gillespie, G.J. 3309
Gillies, James McPhail 6664
Gillilland, Whitney 3765, 4131
Gilmore, Iris 5884
Gilmore, William C. 4464, 6083
Gilpin, Robert 7508, 7821, 7822
Giner, Marcel M. 5752
Gingold, Edward Gerald 6143
Ginsburg, Norton 65
Ginsburgs, George 1149, 2123, 9035; (Reviews) 230, 326
Gipson, Lawrence Henry 6586
Girard, Charlotte 54; (Review) 6307
Girard, Roger 4697
Giroux, Lorne 822, 8058
Gist, Francis J. 6257
Gittens, Thoms Wilton 5128
Givens, Alexander D. 7452
Glaser, Robert E. 7749
Glasgow, George 5647, 5648, 7125
Glass, David 2299
Glazebrook, G.P. de T. 19, 2700, 4465, 4508, 5202, 6095, 6096, 6435, 6436, 6437, 6438, 6587, 6588, 6665, 6666; (Reviews) 39, 1865, 4626, 6397, 6533, 6714, 6767

Glazier, Kenneth M. 8098
Glenday, Graham 8234
Glenn, H. Patrick (Review) 234
Glenn, Jane 1563
Globerman, Steven 7455, 8014, 8620
Glover, George C., Jr. 7823
Glubb, John 6339
Gluek, Alvin Charles 2212, 2475, 2510, 3430, 5309, 6439, 6807, 6920; (Review) 2268
Godechot, Thierry (Reviews) 817, 1343, 4488
Godfrey, Dave 7824
Godinsky, Samuel 8471
Goedhuis, Daniel 4200, 4201
Goetze, Bernd A. 5649, 5650
Goffart, Lionel J. 4844
Goforth, William Wallace 2823
Gogué, Aimé Tchabouré 8367
Gold, Edgar 3025, 3026, 3027, 3028, 3029, 3030, 3031, 3032, 3033, 3034, 3035, 3060, 3081, 3144, 3248, 3472, 3473, 3474, 3475, 3476, 3500, 3547, 3548, 3549, 3550, 3551, 3552, 3553, 3576, 3616, 8621
Gold, Marc Hilary 7579; (Review) 56
Goldberg, Arthur 4509
Goldberg, Charlotte K. 2761
Goldberg, Sanford H. 8295
Golden, David A. 4202
Goldenberg, H. Carl 2117, 6113
Goldenberg, Sydney L. 6166
Goldie, D.M.M. 2762, 2763, 4510
Goldie, L.F.E. (Reviews) 3319, 4271
Goldsman, Alvin 5845
Goldsmith, Immanuel 188, 8472
Golsong, Heribert 1564, 1619
Golt, Sidney 7271, 7272
Gonzales-Rodas, Aster 3766
Gonzalez, Manuel Pérez (Review) 326
Good, J.W. 6340
Goodhart, A.L. 5575
Goodman, Carl F. 5277
Goodman, Wolfe David 8215, 8216, 8217, 8218
Goodrich, Carter 4781
Goodrich, George 8219
Goodrich, Leland M. 4511, 5441; (Review) 5177
Goodwin, Craufurd D. (Review) 8046
Goodwin, Frances K. 5310

Gordenker, Leon 4383, 4410, 5172
Gordon, Daniel 1074
Gordon, Donald C. 5545, 6667
Gordon, H.S. 7338
Gordon, J. King 4639, 4673, 5480, 5481, 5482, 5806, 6440, 7126,8622
Gordon, Myron J. 7937
Gordon, Sheldon E. 1747, 8368
Gordon, Shirley Saul 4466
Gordon, Walter L. 7825, 7891
Goreish, Ishaq R. 4049
Gormley, W. Paul 1565; (Reviews) 3259, 3668, 4288
Gornick, Alan L. 8220
Gorove, Stephen 4203, 4204, 4205, 4206, 4207, 4208, 8710; (Review) 4272
Gosnell, R.E. 2300
Gosselin, Guy (Reviews) 4806, 4811, 8378
Gosztonyi, Paul Marie Joseph 4815
Gotlieb, Allan E. 189, 190, 191, 192, 193, 371, 372, 1294, 1566,1567, 1585, 1748, 1930, 1970, 1971, 3036, 3153, 3185, 4209, 4592,5651, 5652, 5653, 5753, 6022, 6041, 6341, 6441, 6442, 6443, 6808,7067, 8560, 8561, 8562, 8567, 8579, 8623, 8967
Gottlieb, Manuel 6114
Gottlieb, Paul Herbert 921
Gough, Barry M. 1120, 2264, 2476
Gould, Ernest Clark 6589, 6809
Gould, Wesley L. 7655, 8651; (Reviews) 236, 253, 272
Goundrey, D.J. 2687, 3502
Gow, James Iain 4845, 5576; (Review) 2151
Gowling, E. Gordon 8473
Goyer, Jean-Pierre 823, 5483
Grady, Patrick Michael 8221
Graebner, Norman A. 2477, 2478
Grafstein, J.S. 8568
Graham, A.M. 1931
Graham, Gerald 2701
Graham, Gerald Francis 2679, 3477
Graham, Gerald S. 3383, 6590, 6591, 6592; (Reviews) 54, 2592, 6760
Graham, Sir Patrick 8474
Graham, Roger (Reviews) 6413, 6658
Graham, Wallace 3384
Graham, William C. 7255, 8711
Granatstein, J.L. 20, 62, 79, 1838, 4698, 5484, 5560, 5577, 5846,5847, 6444, 6445, 6446, 6782, 6783, 7498, 7499, 8099, 8369; (Reviews) 150, 1278, 6413
Granger, C. (Reviews) 68, 4166, 4271
Granier, Elisabeth Mireille 4210
Grant, Christina Phelps 1075
Grant, Daniel John 8518
Grant, J. Fergus 7346
Grant, Madeline 37
Grauer, Christopher 5359
Gray, Colin S. 5654, 5655, 5848, 5849, 5988; (Review) 5616
Gray, Earle 7938, 8712
Gray, F.W. 7723, 7724
Gray, Herbert E. 7826, 7827
Gray, Mary A. 5232
Gray, Robert Reed (Review) 4271
Grayson, George W. 8675
Green, Alan G. 1371
Green, Colin A. 5850
Green, Howard C. (Reviews) 5574, 6401
Green, Janet 8876
Green, Leslie C. 21, 22, 121, 122, 144, 240, 241, 242, 243, 285,286, 287, 288, 289, 290, 291, 400, 430, 431, 563, 564, 570, 589, 590, 604, 922, 923, 1042, 1043, 1056, 1057, 1076, 1077, 1121, 1125, 1244, 1245, 1246, 1247, 1248, 1249, 1250, 1468, 1469, 1470, 1471, 1472, 1473, 1474, 1475, 1568, 1569, 1570, 1571, 1572, 1573, 1574, 1575, 1616, 1897, 1898, 1899, 1900, 2076, 2613, 2614, 3037, 3038, 3111, 3217, 3249, 3310, 3478, 3479, 4512, 4513, 4514, 4515, 4593, 4594, 4595, 4596, 4608, 4609, 4610, 4611, 4612, 4613, 4614, 4782, 4846, 5173, 5174, 5175, 5233, 5360, 5393, 5394, 5395, 5396, 5421, 5422, 5454, 5455, 5989, 5999, 6006, 6007, 6008, 6009, 6010, 6011, 6042, 6052, 6053, 6054, 6055, 6056, 6057, 6058, 6084, 6085, 6097, 6115, 6118, 6119, 6144, 6145, 6146, 6147, 6167, 6168, 6169, 6170, 6171, 6172, 6173, 6192, 6193, 6194, 6195, 6216, 6217, 6218, 6219, 6220, 6221, 6222, 6223, 6238, 6258, 6259, 6260, 6261, 6342; (Reviews) 50, 52, 56, 231, 234, 236, 248, 270, 271, 320, 444, 608, 617, 874, 1003, 1182, 1242, 1275, 1479, 1685,

1776, 1937, 2049, 3259, 3319, 4164, 5066, 5215, 5370, 5411, 5431, 5691, 6159, 6161, 6283, 8791, 8996
Green, Lewis 2345
Green, Melvyn 8953
Greene, J.J. 8799
Greene, Stephen 3311
Greenhous, Brereton (Review) 6855
Greening, W. 1372
Greenlee, James G.C. 6668
Greenspan, Brian H. 6148
Greenwald, Joseph 4847
Greenwood, F. Murray 737
Greenwood, J.W. 1835
Greenwood, Ted 7509, 8676
Greenwood, Thomas 1063, 4516, 4517, 5754, 6343, 6669
Gregg, Eugene Stuart 2825
Gregor, Richard 4411
Gregorio, V. di (Reviews) 709, 4288
Grenier, Bernard 1576
Grenier, Fernand (Review) 2326
Grenier, Raymond 8370
Grenon, Jean-Yves 1577, 2028, 2118, 4848, 4939, 4940, 4941, 4942
Grey, Julius H. 1186, 1373
Grey, Rodney de C. 7273, 7462, 7510, 7511, 7512
Grieves, Forest L. (Review) 56
Griffin, A.K. (Review) 2918
Griffin, Appleton Prentiss Clark 7010
Griffin, Elizabeth Anne 738
Griffin, Watson 2511
Griffin, William L. 2232, 2764, 2964; (Review) 2381
Griffith, N. Patrick 4943
Griffiths, Franklyn 2550, 5656, 5657, 5658, 5755, 5756
Griffiths, Stuart 6447
Grima, J. Peter 4944
Grimal, Henri 924
Grimes, David A. 5442
Grjébine, André 8100
Groffier-Atala, Ethel 6224, 9014
Gross Stein, Janice 7068
Gross, Ernest A. 4551
Gross, Leo (Review) 241
Groulx, Lionel (Reviews) 49, 6584
Grove, J.W. (Review) 8946
Grubel, Herbert G. 7127, 7274; (Review) 8128
Gruszczynski, Alfred J. 3935
Gryger, Elizabeth M. 1078
Grzybowski, Kazimierz (Reviews) 321, 9038
Gualtieri, Roberto D. 7549, 7828, 7829
Gudgeon, K. Scott 7819, 7891
Gudmundsson, Thordur Ingvi 3154
Guenther, Victor J. 7830
Guerreri, Giuseppe 3936, 3937, 4050
Guichard, Léon 3385
Guido, Robert V. 7513
Guillaume, Gilbert 3767, 4018
Guinchard, Michel (Review) 4288
Guldimann, Werner 3663, 3768, 3769; (Review) 3669
Gunatilaka, Visty Charles 3688
Gunther, Peter 1374
Gupta, Aditya N. 4640
Gupta, Sanjeev 8101
Gushue, Raymond 3112
Gutiérrez, Juan José López (Review) 3119
Guy, James John 5073, 7069
Guyénot, Jean 7939

Haagerup, Niels J. (Review) 4996
Haanappel, Peter P.C. 3770, 3771, 3772, 3773, 3774, 3775, 3776, 3777, 3778, 3938, 3939, 4094, 4171, 4211, 4212, 4213, 4214, 4215, 4216, 4217, 4218; (Reviews) 3814, 4288, 4289
Hackett, W.T.G. 4412
Hackford, R.R. 3779
Hackworth, Green Haywood 1932, 2156, 3312, 5311
Hadfield, Sir Robert 6670
Hadjidimoulas, Constantine C. 401
Hadjis, Dimitris 3647, 3940
Hadwen, John G. 4518, 4519
Hafner, Gerhard (Review) 3048
Hage, Robert E. 8563
Haglund, David G. 6810, 7703, 7704, 7725
Hagy, James William 739, 740
Hahlo, H.R. 7940, 8015
Haifa, Said Jamil 5153
Haight, G.W. (Review) 3276
Hailbronner, Kay 3689; (Reviews) 52, 3669, 4061, 4277, 4288, 6283, 6286
Hainsworth, Geoffrey B. 7128
Hajnal, Peter I. 23, 24
Haley, Andrew G. 4219
Halim, Md. Abdul 4699

INDEX OF AUTHORS

Hall, Hessel Duncan 466, 467, 925, 926, 955
Hall, Walter Phelps 927
Hallett, Mary E. 1375
Halliday, Walter J. 8475
Halstead, Donald Paul 7514
Hambleton, H.G. (Review) 5051
Hamel, Philippe 2826
Hamelin, Louis-Edmond (Review) 3263
Hamelin, Marcel 4467
Hamilton, Alvin 3039
Hamilton, Roger Lyne 8624
Hamilton, William Baskerville 928
Hamilton, William Eugene 6811, 7667
Hammarskjöld, Knut 3780
Hammer, R.M. 8222
Hammond, M.O. 7011
Hammond, Thomas 5757
Hampton, Peter 7831
Han, Chin Tack 5807
Hancock, William Keith 6671
Hancox, Carol 8820
Handl, Günther 8821; (Review) 3506
Hanel, Peter 8476
Hanff, George 1295
Hanham, H.J. 571
Hankin, Janet G. 591
Hanna, William 6344
Hanson, Arthur 8360
Hanson, E.J. 7705
Hanson, Stan D. 2184
Happy, J.R. (Review) 789
Harbottle, Michael 5485
Harbron, John D. 592, 741, 5093; (Review) 5117
Harding, John G. 8059
Hardy, Allison Taylor 1837; (Review) 150
Hardy, Edith H. 4783
Hardy, J.E.G. 2119
Hardy, Vincent 9010
Hare, F. Kenneth 8743
Hargrave, John A. 3465, 7347
Harker, John 8911
Harmer, J.F. 8188
Harper, Bruce Alan 8954
Harries, James B. (Review) 8014
Harrington, Lyn 2765
Harrington, Richard 2765
Harris, David John (Review) 242
Harrison, Albert 3124

Harrison, Eric 4413, 4849, 5918; (Review) 5977
Harrison, Peter 3040, 3124
Harrison, Rowland J. 3218, 3219
Harrison, W. 3480
Harrison, W.E.C. 54, 402, 4468, 5851
Harrod, *Sir* Roy Forbes (Review) 7432
Hart, Albert Bushnell 5316
Hart, John Edward 5852
Hartke, Vance 7891
Hartmann, Gunther 1972; (Review) 5431
Hartt, James P. 8822
Hartwell, Robert 8677
Hartzer, Craig E. 4945
Harvey, Arthur 6942
Harvey, D.C. 3387; (Reviews) 1865, 2198, 4825, 6572, 6578, 6617, 6766, 6861, 6871
Harvey, Heather Joan 929, 6672; (Review) 1865
Harvey, L. 9036
Harvey, Pierre 8371
Haskel, Barbara G. 4865; (Review) 6749
Hasse, A.R. 2213
Hassner, Pierre 5659, 5919
Hastings, Lionel Ismay 5920
Hastings, Paul Guiler 7515
Haugestad, Per Thelin 7275
Hausman, James S. 8189, 8208, 8226, 8229, 8230
Haviland, William Edward 7656
Havrylyshyn, Oli 7325
Hawkins, Freda E. 1376, 1377, 1378, 1379, 1380, 1381; (Review) 1289
Hawkins, Gordon R.S. 2995, 3040a, 3186, 7348
Hawkins, Robert G. 7622
Hawthorn, H.B. (Review) 1261
Hay, Keith A.J. 7229, 7349, 7350, 8935
Hayakawa, S. Ichiye 1251
Hayashi, Kichiro 7941
Hayden, Gene 3041
Hayden, Peter R. 7832, 7833, 7834
Hayes, Frank Randall 6673
Hayman, Michael 8961
Haynes, Elliott 7942
Haynes, Frederick Emory 6943
Hayter, *Sir* William (Review) 1817
Haythorne, George V. 4784
Hazard, Henry B. (Review) 1154

Hazard, John L. 7516
Hazard, John N. (Reviews) 326, 334
Head, Ivan L. 292, 639, 1182, 1187, 1188, 1189, 1190, 1578, 2615,2616, 3187, 3220, 3221, 3690, 5361, 8372, 8652
Healey, Denis 4850
Healey, Derek 4700
Healy, Nicholas J. 3617
Heasman, Donald J. 930, 1044; (Review) 997
Heathcote, Nina 4520
Heaton, H. 4414, 7726
Heaton, Herbert (Review) 3392
Heaver, Trevor D. (Review) 3550
Hébert, Jacques 8373
Hecht, Irene W.D. 6944, 6945
Heckscher, Kay 4851
Heeney, Arnold D.P. 80, 2399, 2400, 2401, 5853, 6812
Heeney, William Brian Danford 80
Heere, Wybo P. (Reviews) 3777, 4061, 4077, 4110
Hehner, Eric 7485
Heilperin, Michael A. 7517, 7623
Heine, William 5486
Heinselman, Robert E. 6043
Heintzman, Ralph 742
Helleiner, Gerald K. 7117, 7129, 7130, 7131, 7163, 7943, 8374
Heller, Paul Peter 3781
Helliwell, John 7835, 8653; (Review) 4678
Helmers, Henrik Olaf 7580, 7581, 7582, 7589
Hemming, H.H. (Reviews) 6595, 6827
Hénault, Georges M. 7929, 7930
Henderson, J.M. 2827
Henderson, James Youngblood 1238, 1505, 2070
Henderson, Michael D. 1749, 1750, 4852, 4853
Hendry, James M. 293, 294, 1973, 1974, 2138, 4415
Henein, Jean-Claude 4220
Henkin, Louis 2680, 3481
Hennigar, W.J. 931
Henrickson, Maurice Augustus 7351
Henry, D.H.W. 7208, 7518, 7944, 7945
Henry, Jacques 7230, 8375; (Review) 7429
Henry, Paul-Marc 7132
Henry, Philip W. 2828
Héraud, Guy 4946; (Review) 793

Herbert, C.H. (Review) 7926
Herchak, Gayle 4701
Hérisson, Charles-D. 1579, 5141, 7133, 7134, 7209, 7210, 7463,7657, 7750, 7751, 7946
Herman, Lawrence L. 521, 1079, 3113, 3222, 3255, 3453, 3554, 5397,5398
Herman, Valentine 4972
Hermoso, Justino 4051
Hero, Alfred O. 6805, 6806, 8643; (Review) 1806
Herperger, Donald John 123
Herrera de Fraino, Olga 8564
Herrero y Rubio, Alejandro (Review) 368
Herring, Richard John 8102
Herrington, William C. 3313
Hertz, Allen Zangwil 640, 6448
Hertzman, Lewis 5854, 5921
Hervouet, Gérard 5154, 7070
Herwig, Aletha Marguerite 7012
Herz, Martin F. 1838
Hesse, Nicky E. 3782, 3941
Hetherington, C.R. 7706
Hettinger, James Frederick 6449
Heuston, R.F.V. (Review) 6672
Hevesy, Paul de 7668
Hewison, George 3314
Hewson, John P. 5660
Heywood, Robert W. 4947
Hickey, G.P. 8222
Higgins, Benjamin 8376; (Review) 8349
Higgins, Larratt T. 2939, 2940; (Review) 2754
Higgins, Rosalyn (Reviews) 56, 5588, 6361
Higgs, G.R.L. 3555
Higiro, Jean-Marie Vianney 1100
Hignette, Marcel 3388
Hildred, Sir William 4749
Hill, A.J. 2242
Hill, Edward Albert 1975
Hill, Olive Mary 7352, 7353
Hill, Roger J. 5546, 5661, 5922
Hill-Norton, Sir Peter 5923
Hilliker, John F. 150, 6098, 7071
Hillmer, Norman 1751, 6392, 6450; (Review) 150
Hills, Theodore Lewis 2829; (Review) 2916
Himes, Mel 7072
Hinchman, Walter R. 8565
Hind, Henry Youle 5317

INDEX OF AUTHORS

Hinnegan, K.A. 7947
Hirschberg, Eliyahu 8103
Hirst, Francis W. 5662
Hiscocks, C. Richard 1580, 6099; (Review) 4626
Hitchin, David Edward 8016
Hitt, William R. 4221
Hjalsted, Finn 3942
Ho, Samuel P.S. 7354
Hoan, Daniel W. 2830
Hoar, Victor 6120
Hockin, Thomas A. 5854, 5921, 6451
Hodge, Gerald 8377
Hodgetts, John E. 4521, 8713
Hodghead, Helen Marr 3389
Hodgins, Bruce W. 743
Hodgins, Frank E. 6030
Hodgins, Thomas 1191, 1192, 1976, 2041, 2042, 2301, 2302, 2303, 2304, 2305, 2306, 3042, 3390, 3391, 6593, 6813
Hodson, Henry V. 932
Hoen, Egbert 't 8477
Hoffman, Paul 568
Hogg, Peter W. 641; (Review) 608
Hogg, Roy D. 8223
Hohmann, W. 3555
Holborn, Louise W. 1296, 1382, 1383
Holbraad, Carston (Review) 444
Holcombe, Arthur N. 4469
Holgate, Henry 2831
Holland, *Sir* Robert E. 933, 1080, 4577, 5487, 6345
Hollick, Ann L. 3043, 3044
Holly, Daniel A. 4522, 4806, 7135, 7136, 8378
Holly, Norman E. 7355
Holmes, J.D. 2059
Holmes, John W. 642, 934, 935, 936, 937, 4384, 4416, 4523, 4524, 4641, 4948, 5094, 5203, 5234, 5488, 5489, 5490, 5924, 6346, 6452, 6453, 6454, 6455, 6456, 6457, 6458, 6814, 6815, 6816, 6817, 6818, 6819, 6970, 7137; (Reviews) 5910, 6307, 6444
Holmested, George S. 938, 2307, 6674
Holsti, Kal J. 6347, 6820
Holt, Wayne G. 2551
Homer, Janis L. 8836
Hommel, Maurice W. 1581
Hondius, Frits W. 8566
Honig, F. (Reviews) 240, 241, 1002

Hood, William C. 8104
Hope, Ronald 3556
Hopkins, C.A. (Review) 248
Hopkins, E. Russell (Reviews) 1185, 2025
Hopkins, John (Review) 242
Hopkins, Oliver B. 5855, 8519
Horan, James Francis 6459
Hore, Satchidananda 939
Horney, Esther 1452
Horowitz, Irving Louis 6174
Horvitz, Joanne F. 6263, 6264
Hosenball, S. Neil 4222, 4223
Hossick, Kenneth C. 8955
Hough, Barbara 5400, 5771
Hougham, George Millard 522
Houliston, Peter Robert 8379
Hoult, David P. 3482
Houndjahoué, Michel 7073, 7074
Howard, Case R. 7836
Howard, Michael (Review) 6413
Howard, Rhoda 1297, 1582
Howard, Ross 8837
Howard, William Ralph 2832
Howay, F.W. 6752; (Reviews) 2263, 2269, 2353
Howay, Frederick H. 6594
Howe, Ralph W. 8678
Howe, Stanley Russell 6821
Howell, Alfred 1150, 3557, 3597
Howell, John M. 373
Howley, M.F. 2329
Hoy, Gerald E. 4949
Hoyles, N.W. 1151
Hsiao, Frank S.T. 1045
Huband, Charles R. 6186
Huber, Paul B. (Review) 7420
Huberman, David S.M. 8478
Hubert, Jean-Paul 5095
Hubley, Roger 7707
Hubscher, Frank Frederick 4095
Hucker, John 1298, 1384, 1385, 1386, 1583
Huculak, Michael 2308
Hudec, Robert E. 7549, 7837
Hudon, Edward G. 1252; (Review) 56
Hudon, Raymond (Reviews) 8373, 8643
Hudson, G.F. 940
Hudson, Manley O. 295, 468, 941, 5362, 5363; (Reviews) 249, 1148
Hudson, S. Claude 7669
Huenemann, Ralph W. 7354

Huff, W.G. 8380
Hughes, Charles E. 5578
Hughes, Graeme C. 7838
Hughes, John Jay (Review) 1060
Hugon, Philippe 1009
Huisken, Ron (Review) 5756
Hull, Douglas Gordon 5129
Hull, James P. 8364
Hulmes, Frederick George 5176
Humphrey, John P. 296, 1253, 1587, 1588, 1589, 1590, 1591, 1592,1593, 1594, 1595, 1596, 1597, 1598, 1600, 1601, 1602, 1603,1604, 1605, 1606, 1607, 1608, 1609, 1610, 1611, 1614, 1615, 1637,1933, 4417, 4525, 4526, 5096, 5097, 6822; (Reviews) 1544, 6325
Humphreys, David 4854
Huner, Jan 4019
Hunt, Constance D. 5780, 8714
Hunt, Harry E. 2718
Hunt, Kenneth 5663
Hunt, Louise M. 8017
Hunter, Ian A. 1387, 1392, 1612, 1613
Hunter, Lawson A.W. 8679, 8715
Hunter, Louis Clare 4950
Hunter, Michael W. 7839
Hunter, William T. 7356, 7464; (Review) 7940
Hurd, W. Burton 1388
Hurley, James Ross (Review) 682
Hurry, Margaret Isabel 2833
Hurst, C.K. 8654
Hurst, *Sir* Cecil 942, 5579
Hurst, Donald A. 6496
Hurt, Leslie John 4951
Hurtig, Mel 8686
Hurtubise, René 1389
Hussey, Lyman Andrew 6675
Hutcheson, John 7519
Hutchison, Bruce 6823
Hyde, Charles Cheney 2094, 2309, 2529, 2766
Hyde, James N. (Review) 1182
Hymer, Stephen 25, 7948, 7949, 7950
Hyndman, Patricia 3618

Ianni, Ronald W. 1977, 8800, 9011; (Review) 6806
Ibrahim, Muhammad Khalil 611
Ichikawa, Akira 5547; (Review) 6556
Ignatieff, George 81, 1752, 4597, 5664, 5665, 5666, 5758, 5927,5928, 6023; (Reviews) 54, 4398, 4493
Ilersic, A.R. 7951, 7952, 8224
Illich, Michael John 3783
Imai, Shin 1390
Imam, Abbas Imam Ibrahim 3784
Immarigeon, Antoine-Elie (Review) 1361
Inch, Donald R. 2617
Infeld, Leopold 8716
Ing, Alexius S. 6348
Inglis, Alex I. 89, 90, 124, 150, 5493, 6677
Inglis, Peter 2941
Ingram, Derek 943
Ingram, J. Clarence 6678
Ingram, Joseph K. 8381, 8382
Inions, Noela J. 3223
Inman, M.K. 7624
Innis, Donald Q. 8655; (Review) 2916
Innis, Harold A. 3392, 3393, 8912; (Reviews) 2592, 3396, 3403, 6671
Inohana, Terue 4952
Intravia, L.R. 4132
Ionescu, Ghita 6131
Ippolito, Joseph T. 3224
Iqbal, Munawar 7211
Ireland, Gordon 3316
Ireland, Tom 2834
Ireland, Willard E. 2243; (Review) 2251
Irish, Maria M. 2214
Irvine, Dallas D. 3394
Irving, John A. (Review) 1261
Irwin, Clare J. 3943
Irwin, Matthew J.R. 4180, 8548
Irwin, W. Arthur 5098
Isajiw, W.W. 1254; (Review) 1376
Isham, Charles 3395
Islam, Nasir 8936, 8937
Ismael, Tareq Y. 6461, 8400
Isnard, H. 1101
Israel, Milton (Review) 94
Iwi, Edward F. 944

Jackman, W.T. 2835
Jackson, Eric 8018
Jackson, *Sir* Geoffrey 1838
Jackson, Gilbert E. (Review) 8155
Jackson, J.D.A. 7811
Jackson, John H. 7549
Jackson, Robert H. 6187
Jacobs, F.G. (Review) 3319
Jacobs, Gunther 365

Jacobs, Jane 744
Jacobson, Harold K. 4406, 4706, 5856
Jacomy-Millette, Annemarie 299, 643, 824, 825, 826, 1010, 1620,1934, 1935, 1936, 1937, 1978, 1979, 4642, 6227, 6228, 6349, 6824,7139, 8384, 8680; (Reviews) 236, 246, 608, 709, 4398
Jacquemin, Alex 4953
Jacquemin, Georges 4224, 6240
Jaeger, Martin (Review) 7401
Jaffe, Robert A. 7840
Jahnke, L. Gordon 233, 4954, 7583; (Review) 1970
Jain, Jagat Prasad 7953
Jainarain, Iserdeo 7212
Jakhu, Ram S. 3785, 4225, 4226, 4232, 5667, 8572, 8573, 8744
James, Robert Rhodes 4527
James, Robert Warren 6825
Jamieson, Don 1621
Jamieson, Stuart M. 8905
Janach, Monica Ann 1195, 7841
Janis, Mark W. (Review) 3048
Jankowitsch, Peter 4227
Jansen, Gordon W.V. 5548
Janssen, Friedrich-Wilhelm 439
Janzen, William 1392
Jarry, G. Michel 1393
Jasentuliyana, Nandasiri 4228, 4229, 4230, 4751, 8574
Jaworski, Adam 4020
Jay, John 5319
Jebb, Hubert Miles Gladwyn (Review) 5965
Jebb, Richard 2310, 6679
Jenkin, Michael 7357
Jenkins, A.W. (Review) 7455
Jenkins, Glenn P. 8234
Jenks, C. Wilfred 1980, 2029, 2030, 2095, 2096, 2097, 2098, 2099,8479
Jennekens, Jon H. 8718
Jennes, Desmond 1255, 1256
Jenness, Robert Allan 7687
Jennings, R.Y. 945
Jennings, Sir William Ivor 946, 947, 1938
Jensen, Kurt F. 6132
Jenson, Jane 4955
Jessen, Sabine 2562
Jessop, David 7358
Jessup, Philip C. 2836
Jewell, Patricia 7564

Jewett, M.L. 374, 2139
Jiménez de Aréchaga, Eduardo 3786
Jiranek, Slavomir 5062
Jockel, Joseph T. 5857, 5858; (Reviews) 6556, 8979
Jodoin, Claude 8915
Johannson, Peter Roff 827, 828, 829, 830; (Reviews) 1806, 2960
Johnsen, Julia Emily 6462
Johnson, Arthur L. (Reviews) 6786, 6895
Johnson, Barbara 3011, 3012, 3046, 3047, 3048, 3049, 3142, 3155,3156, 3317, 3318
Johnson, Caswell Lewington 1394
Johnson, D.H.N. (Reviews) 56, 242, 3319, 4164, 4271, 4291
Johnson, Harry G. 7140, 7141, 7142, 7143, 7144, 7145, 7213, 7214, 7215, 7253, 7274, 7338, 7359, 7360, 7520, 7521, 7625, 7626, 8091, 8385; (Reviews) 6825, 7802
Johnson, Harry R. (Review) 56
Johnson, John A. 4231
Johnson, Jon R. 8235
Johnson, Ralph W. 2769, 2944, 2945
Johnson, Walter S. 2129
Johnston, Donald J. 8189, 8236
Johnston, Douglas M. 34, 230, 248, 300, 301, 303, 304, 305, 306, 408, 1939, 1940, 2359, 2681, 2682, 2683, 3050, 3051, 3052, 3053, 3054, 3055, 3056, 3057, 3058, 3059, 3060, 3064, 3080, 3081, 3106, 3131, 3132, 3133, 3134, 3135, 3143, 3144, 3146, 3276, 3319, 3320, 3321, 3322, 3323, 3324, 3325, 3326, 3348, 3454, 3476, 3483, 3484, 3485, 3486, 3487, 3488, 3489, 3490, 3491, 3492, 3499, 3500, 3558,6350, 8767, 8791, 8839; (Review) 3048
Johnston, George A. (Review) 6179
Johnston, Richard 7013
Johnston, V. Kenneth 469, 470, 2618, 2972
Jolicoeur, André 593
Jonah, James O.C. 5497
Jones, Barton T. (Review) 6286
Jones, David Phillip 8237
Jones, David R. (Review) 5424
Jones, Dorothy Wendy 5859
Jones, Douglas N. 8797
Jones, Douglas W. 1196

Jones, F.C. (Review) 1261
Jones, George Mallory 2502
Jones, Howard 6930
Jones, John, Jr. 1901
Jones, Kenneth 2619
Jones, Richard (Reviews) 5965, 6456
Jones, Wesley L. 2413
Jones, Wilbur Devereux 2215
Jordan, Frederick J.E. 2436, 2719, 8801
Jordan, Robert S. 5929; (Review) 5910
Jordon, Mabel E. 2265
Jorgensen, Jan J. 8325
Josling, Tim 7658
Jost, Isabelle 2185
Joyal, André 8318
Joyner, Christopher C. (Review) 8791
Joynt, Carey B. 5761
Juda, L. (Review) 3526
Judah, Charles Barnet 3396
Judek, S. 7216, 7627
Juliani, T.J. (Review) 6213
Julien, Claude 6463; (Review) 720
Juneau, Pierre 8569, 8575
Juvet, Charles Stanley 8386, 8387
Juvet, David C. 4096

Kachanov, V.A. 831
Kaida, Lawrence 573
Kaiser, Gordon E. 7217
Kakkar, Gul Mohammed 3787
Kalbach, Warren E. 1348, 1395, 1396
Kaliski, Stephan F. 2982, 4956, 8298
Kallen, Evelyn 1257
Kalogeropoulos, George A. 1047
Kalshoven, Frits (Reviews) 3259, 5691, 6195
Kanaan, Issam Y. 3788
Kanamby, Paul Mulemeri 5142
Kanya-Forstner, A.S. 1096
Kaplan, Irving E. 4232, 8744
Kaplansky, Kalmen 7146
Kapp, Richard Ward 6351
Kapur, Ashok 5762, 5763, 5764, 5765, 5766
Karpan, Robin Dale 7842
Karpishka, Roman B. 4021
Kass, Stephen L. 5409
Kassell, Mortimer M. 8238
Kasta, Donald 2437
Kasurak, Peter C. 1839, 6826
Kattan, Naim 6464

Katz, Brian 8768
Katz, Kenneth 8562
Katz, Leslie (Review) 682
Kaufmann, Johan 4518, 4519
Kaufmann, Othmar 7954, 7955
Kaunda, Gideon H. 8860
Kavass, Igor I. (Review) 231
Kavic, Lorne 948, 6465
Kay, Zachariah 7075; (Reviews) 6418, 6445
Kean, Arnold W.G. 4052, 4133; (Reviews) 3833, 3962
Kear, Allan R. 644
Kearley, Laurence (Reviews) 203, 1166, 1437
Keating, Bern 2552
Keating, Thomas 3311
Keating, Thomas F. 4643
Keefer, Thomas Celtrin 6946
Keeley, James F. 7361, 8719
Keenan, John T. 3789, 4053
Keenleyside, Hugh L. 82, 1397, 1755, 1756, 2553, 2946, 5160, 5860, 6466, 6595, 6827, 8388, 8389, 8656
Keenleyside, Terence A. 1757, 1758, 1840, 4643, 6828, 7076;(Review) 96
Keeton, George W. 5581
Keirstead, B.S. 54, 7147
Keirstead, W.C. (Review) 2918
Keith, A. Berriedale 471, 472, 473, 474, 475, 516, 523, 524, 525, 949, 1981, 3250; (Reviews) 249, 454, 460, 508, 942, 6484, 6649, 6654
Keith, B.C. 1476
Keith, Kenneth James (Review) 1936
Keller, Joseph 3188
Kelly, Ian F. 1197, 1387
Kelly, John Joseph 6063, 6064
Kelly, Mark Stewart 832
Kelsen, Hans 5443
Kelsey, Brian A. 2140
Kelson, Robert N. 8363
Kendall, John C. (Review) 4488
Kendle, John Edward 6680, 6681, 6682
Kennedy, J. de N. 2078
Kennedy, Thomas M. 3184
Kennedy, W.P.M. 476, 477, 526, 645, 950, 1153; (Reviews) 460, 490, 495, 508, 523, 942, 955, 1148, 1154, 6393, 6671
Kenny, L.M. 5498
Kenny, Stephen (Review) 780

INDEX OF AUTHORS

Kent, Tom (Review) 6868
Kent, William 4528
Kenworthy, William E. 2770
Keppel-Jones, Arthur 951
Kerig, D.V. (Review) 56
Kerley, Ernest L. 5277
Kerr, A.C. 952
Kerr, D.G.G. (Review) 6662
Kerr, Donald A. 2837, 3648
Kerr, John Andrew 2079
Kerr, Philip Henry 952
Kerr, Robert W. 3598
Kerr, William Hastings 3397
Kerse, C.S. (Review) 7940
Kertudo, Jean 8105
Kester, William Cameron 2973
Ketcham, Earle H. (Reviews) 2853, 2918
Ketcheson, Bruce 8239
Kettner, Bonni Raines 833
Keyes, A.A. 8480
Keyfitz, Nathan 8390, 8391, 8884
Keyser, Charles Frank 2907
Keyserlingk, Robert H. 834; (Review) 5204
Keyston, J.E. 5668
Khalid, El Rashid Osman 4707
Khan, Mahmood Ali 7843
Khan, Mumtaz Ahmed 5669
Kidd, J.R. 4807, 8968
Kiddy, Arthur W. 8106
Kidwai, M.H.M. 478, 479
Kiefe, Robert 1154
Kierans, Eric W. 8020, 8576, 8579
Kierstead, Stella 4470
Kiervin, Jack Orval 5099
Kilduff, Vera R. 6683
Kilgour, Arthur R. 403
Killam, Ronald W.B. 4816
Killey, J.M. 3442
Kim, L. Junchul 6352
Kimminich, O. (Review) 5066
Kindleberger, Charles P. 6353; (Review) 7225
Kindred, Hugh M 244, 245, 375, 376, 2141, 3622, 7522, 7715;(Reviews) 236, 3637
King, Eldon P. 8240
King, Francis 2838
King, Marlene Irma 6354
King, Tom 7466
King, William Frederick 2596
King, William K. 8840
King, William Lyon Mackenzie 4644
Kingham, J.D. 3061, 4418
Kingston, C.S. 2480
Kingstone, H. Courtney 4233
Kinsman, Jeremy 4645, 6341, 6442, 6808
Kintner, Edwin E. 8720
Kirchschlager, Hellmuth Ludwig 7523
Kirk-Greene, Anthony H.M. 6684
Kirkham, D. Barry 1048
Kirsch, Philippe 3189
Kirstein, Ruth 6947
Kirton, John J. 1759, 1760, 2449, 5861, 5862, 6467, 7584; (Reviews) 1806, 2960, 6556
Kisicki, Donald Robert 8769
Kiss, Alexandre Charles 2720; (Review) 4293
Kitazawa, Kimiko 4708
Kitsikis, Dimitri 5204
Kitsinger, Otto C. (Review) 1003
Kiwanuka, Richard Ntege 1622
Klaassen, Walter 5990
Klang, Daniel (Review) 444
Klar, Lewis N. 8481, 8482
Kleffens, Eelco N. van 302
Klein, Jean 5670, 5671, 5930; (Reviews) 326, 5640
Klein, Robert A. 444
Klemm, Cyrille de 3492
Klepak, H.P. 5100
Klitscher, K.R. 2186
Klotz, John C. 3493
Klotz, Otto 2244, 2245, 2356
Kly, Yussuf Naim 1623
Knaplund, Paul 6921; (Review) 6662
Knapp, Robert Whelan 7844
Knapton, E.J. 6355
Knelman, F.H. 8770
Knicely, James J. (Review) 3259
Knight, R.E. 7218
Knopff, Rainer 646; (Review) 1637
Knorr, Klaus E. 1102, 5931
Knox, Frank A. 2839, 7219, 7362, 7363; (Review) 6825
Knox, *Sir* Geoffrey 1941
Knudson, Charles A. 1023
Knuth, Harald Wolfgang W. 4957
Koch, Eric 1258
Koehler, Wallace C. 6829, 7845
Koenigsberg, M. 1477

Koerner, W.R. 8241
Koffi, Aoussou 3790
Kogan, Norman 4857
Kohler, Gernot 26, 5672, 5673
Kohler, Larry Robert 1761
Kohn, Hans 6356
Kohn, Walter S.G. (Review) 7519
Kokas, Louis 1398, 8107
Kolinski, Ralph (Review) 7230
Koller, Philip Alexander 3559
Konan, Raymond H. 2620
Kopal, Vladimir 4234, 4235, 8577; (Review) 4293
Kos-Rabcewicz-Zubkowski, Ludwik 2060, 2142, 2143, 4022, 4236, 4237,5101, 5254, 5582, 6149, 6150, 6151, 6152, 6153, 7220, 7221, 8483,9015, 9016, 9017, 9037, 9038; (Reviews) 4273, 4723, 5066, 6195, 8584
Kose, Yasuyuki 3944
Kotaite, Assad 3791, 3792, 4752, 4753
Kotani, Hidejiro 5499
Kotowitz, Yehuda 3530
Kottman, Richard N. 2840, 6830, 7524, 7525, 8962
Kovach, A.J. 3225
Koval, Josef 3793
Kovrig, Bennett 5063
Kozliner, Marsha 8392
Krauss, Melvyn B. 8205
Krauss, Michel 1058, 6122
Krauter, Joseph F. 1181, 1259
Kravis, Irving B. 7688
Kreindler, Lee S. 4023
Kreinin, Mordechai E. 7628
Kresl, Peter Karl 7846
Krieger, David 3062
Krishna, Sam Swaminathan 8242
Kronby, Malcolm 1399
Krosby, Hans Peter 4858, 6658
Krueger, Robert B. 3063
Kruger, Arthur 8916
Kruijtbosch, E.D.J. 4859
Krutilla, John V. 2947, 2948
Kryzanowski, Lawrence 7333
Kuash, Timothy John 6266
Kubicek, Robert (Review) 6681
Kuhn, Arthur K. 5283, 5284
Kuhn, Tillo E. (Review) 5053
Kumar, Ramesh C. (Review) 7511

Kunen, James L. 2841
Kung, S.W. 1400
Kunz, Josef L. (Review) 2025
Kupsch, W.O. 8520
Kurtzman, Joel 7149
Kuruvilla, P.K. (Review) 7119
Kushnin, Slava M. 1103
Kusi, Jonathan Atta 574
Kwavnick, David 745, 746
Kyba, Patrick 8771, 8772, 8773; (Review) 8791
Kyer, Clifford Ian 1841
Kyte, George William 2438

Laabi, Abdelhai 4958, 6357
Laberge-Altmejd, Danielle 6211, 6212, 6247
Labrie, Arthur 3327
Lacasse, Jean-Paul 2159, 3226, 3227, 3228; (Reviews) 709, 2151
Lacey, A. 691
Lachance, Gabrielle 8393
Lachance, Louis 1624
Lachance, Monique 5674, 5675; (Review) 856
Lachance, R.A. 8298
Lachapelle, Andrée 1629
Lachmann, Karl E. 8210
Lachs, Manfred 1625, 4238, 4239
Lacoste, Paul (Review) 1624
Ladner, Leon J. 2949, 2950
La Fay, Howard 5863
Lafleur, Eugene 5991
Lafleur, Gérard 3794, 3945
La Forest, Gerard V. 605, 835, 1478, 1479, 2100, 2233, 2357, 2771,2772, 3114, 3115, 3262, 7364, 9014; (Reviews) 248, 1937
Laforest, Robert William 7077
Laforet, Joseph 4097
Lahmer, Craig 8243
Laidlaw, John B. 2721
Laing, Lionel H. 249, 480, 3398, 3599, 4860, 6175; (Reviews) 4665, 6488, 6712, 6733
Lajoie, Andrée 8060
Lakhtine, W. 2621
Lalande, Gilles 647, 1762, 7078; (Review) 6418
Lalande, Léon (Reviews) 3076, 3636

INDEX OF AUTHORS

Laliberté, Denys (Reviews) 6510, 8079
Lallier, Adalbert 747
Lalonde, Philippe V. 5366, 7365
Lamarche, Thomas 1155
Lamb, John 5676
Lambe, Hugh B. 7847, 8244
Lamberson, R. 3428
Lambert, Julien-Maurice (Review) 5204
Lambrechts, Claude 2720
Lamirande, Émilien 6596
Lammasch, Henri 5320, 5321
Lamont, Douglas F. 7848
Lamontagne, Maurice A. 648, 649
Lamontagne, Roland 3263
Lamontagne, Roland J. (Reviews) 632, 5482
La Morandière, Charles de 3399
Lanctot, Gustave 6597, 6831, 6832, 6890
Lande, Ellen Beth 836
Lande, Eric P. 5074
Landey, Deborah 837
Landheer, B. (Review) 5691
Landis, Henry 2722
Landon, Fred 1316, 6971
Landry, J. Nelson 8484
Lane, Eric M. 4098
Lane, Robert C. 4959
Lanfranco, Sam (Reviews) 5716, 8357
Lang, Walter 8245
Langdon, Frank 3047, 3155; (Review) 7070
Langdon, S.W. 7148
Langer, S. Joshua 2133; (Review) 5652
Langevin, Pierre 8108
Langford, J.A. 2920, 7849, 7850
Langis, Pierre-Paul 5102
Langlais, Antonio 366, 390, 1626, 4529, 4530, 4531, 4532, 4578, 4579, 4788
Langley, James 4960
Langlois, Elisabeth 2624
Langlois, Juan Pablo 4134
Langlois, Micheline 27
Langlois, P. 692
Langlumé, Patrice Michel 238
Lanham, Percy A. 7014
Lank, Herbert 7467, 8021
Lansing, Robert 5322
Lantzke, Ulf 8681
Lapenna, Ivo (Reviews) 334, 5588, 6361
LaPierre, Laurier L. 1982
Laplante, Corinne 2187, 6598

Lapointe, Ernest 527, 528, 4471
Lapointe, L.-A. 529
Lapointe, Paul A. 3065, 3066, 3067, 3109
Laponce, Jean A. (Review) 1283
La Pradelle, Paul de (Reviews) 68, 3833, 4276
Larcher, Oswald Wilkinson 8394
Larkin, Ronald Hughes 8022
Larmour, W.T. 2622
Laroche, Jean-René 6457
Larose-Aubry, Huguette 3795, 3796, 3797, 3798, 3799, 3800, 3801
Larsen, H.K. 7526
Larsen, Paul B. 4024
Larter, Ron 8247
La Serre, Françoise de 4961
Lash, Z.A. 3600, 5323
Laski, H.J. 650
Laskin, Bora 651, 1902, 1983; (Reviews) 539, 632, 1185
Lasok, Dominik 4962, 4963, 4964, 7629
Lass, William E. 2246
Lasserre, Jean-Claude 2842
Lasswell, Harold D. 4291, 4292
Laszlo, Ervin 7149
Latchford, Stephen 3802
Latey, Maurice 4861
Latimer, Robert E. 7276, 7630
Latimer, William 8294
Latouche, Daniel 748, 749
Latouche, Daniel Gustave 5423
La Tulippe, Jean-Guy 6948
Laulicht, Jerome 4385, 5677
Laureys, Henry 5188, 7366, 7367, 7368, 7727
Laut, Agnes Christina 6468
Lauterpacht, Sir Hersh (Reviews) 156, 271
Laux, Jeanne Kirk 5809, 8065
Lauzon, Yves 3623
Lavell, William S. 6949
Lavenir, Hervé 1842
Lavertu, Gaétan 8917
Lavigne, D.M. 3431
Lavigne, Marie 7150
Lavin, Thomas 7956
La Violette, Forrest E. 1260, 1261, 1262, 1263; (Review) 7098
Lavoie, Paul 530, 6685
Law, Alton D. 7689
Law, Carl Edgar 3251

Lawes, A.L. 3560
Lawford, Hugh J. 194, 195, 196, 197, 1942, 2046, 2843, 2844,8568
Lawler, James 4385
Lawler, William Ralph 5678
Lawrence, Donald Arthur 5103
Lawrence, Henry 2773
Lawrence, Ivy M. 6196
Lawrence, William Beach 2216
Lawson, Karin L. 2358, 2623, 3229
Lawson, Murray G. 2512
Lawton, William N. 377
Lax, Gary 6527
Laxer, James 8682
Lay, S. Houston (Review) 68
Laylin, John G. (Review) 2774
Lazar, Fred 7369, 7527
Lazarev, Marklen I. 4240
Lea, Sperry 7528, 7529, 7530, 7531, 7957
Leach, Richard (Review) 6743
Leach, Richard A. 953
Leach, Richard H. 838, 839, 859; (Review) 674
Leacock, Stephen 6469
Leacock, Stephen Butler 954, 6686
Leavy, James 4965, 7277
LeBaron, Bentley (Review) 3518
Lebel, Michel 246, 247, 1584, 1614, 1627, 1628
Lebel, Ronald 8396
Leblanc, Hubert 8397
LeBlanc, Napoleon 4808
LeBlanc, Romeo 3157
LeBlond, Nancy Russell 8877
LeBourdais, D.M. 7565
Lebov, Richard Ned 6202
Leclerc, Marc 1843
Leddy, John Francis 4809
Lederer, Ivo J. (Review) 6363
Lederman, William R. 378, 2061, 8568
Le Duc, Albert 7370
Leduc, Gaston 7151
LeDuc, Lawrence 6828
Leduc, Marc 8246
Le Duc, Thomas H. 2217, 6599, 6833, 6950, 6955
Lee, Adah L. 2854
Lee, Boyden Edward 8109
Lee, Carol F. 1264
Lee, Chae-Jin 6100
Lee, Edward G. 198, 199, 1480, 1903, 1904, 4534, 6228, 8061, 8578, 8841; (Reviews) 56, 4271
Lee, Luke T. (Review) 230
Lee, R.W. 445, 6687
Lee, Roy S.K. 3803
Lee, T.R. 2723
Leener, Georges de 1104
Leermakers, Dirk J. 1198, 8062
Lees, John 8204, 8230
Leeson, Howard A. 652, 840
Lefebvre, Olivier 2845, 2846
Le Garignon, John P. 28
Legault, Albert 29, 2624, 5500, 5674, 5675, 5679, 5680, 5767,5768, 5769, 5810, 5811, 5932, 6358, 6470, 8721
Legault, L.H. 200, 201, 1901, 1905, 2684, 3019, 3071, 3190, 3494,6443, 6471; (Review) 253
Léger, Brigitte 4243
Leger, Georges Antoine 3145, 3328, 3329
Léger, Jean-Marc 1011; (Review) 5117
Legge, Garth 7079
Legget, Robert Ferguson 2847
Le Gris, Claude 6472
Lehart, Michel 4966
Lehoux, Grégoire 3072, 5238
Leigh, Monroe 4241
Leighton, Gertrude C.K. 1961
Leisner, Walter 612
Leister, Valnora 4242
Leitenberg, Milton 5681
Leive, David M. 8580; (Review) 8588
Lelart, Michel 8110
LeMarquand, David G. 2774, 8774, 8775
LeMay, Joseph A. 8737
Lemay, Valère 750
Lemelin, Claude 8398
Lemieux, Denis 1629
Lemieux, Rodolphe 531
Lemieux, Vincent 841
Lemineur-Toumson, C. 4886
Le Moine, J.M. 7371
Lenentine, Charlotte 2218
Lenoir, James J. 2039, 6931
Lenoir, Robert L. 1156
Lenschow, Gerhard 2983
Lentner, Howard H. 751, 5933
Lentz, Theodore Ferdinand 5573
Leopold, G. Vernon (Review) 4291
LePan, Douglas 83
Lepore, Giuseppe 7222

Leroy, Marcel 8399, 8885
Leroy, Vély 7852, 8111
Leshem, Moshe 3804
Leslie, E. 5501
Leslie, Kenneth Ainsworth 7670, 7690
Lester, A.P. 2047
Letalik, Norman G. 3035, 3081, 3495, 3500, 3553, 3558, 3576, 3601, 3616
Letemendia, Miren A. 4967; (Review) 4869
Levadie, Meyer 532
Levermore, Charles Herbert 6922
Lévesque, René 752, 753
Lévesque, Suzanne 1629
Levie, Howard S. (Review) 3259
Leville, G. 1630
Levin, Malcolm A. 8023
Levine, Herbert M. 6198
Levine, Howard J. 8880
Levine, Martin 1401
Levine, Rhonda Faye 7691
Levine, Shelley 8247
Levirs, Franklin P. 2481
Levitt, Kari 7631, 8024
Levy, Allen (Reviews) 5459, 6541
Levy, Gary 5189, 5190
Levy, Thomas Allen 839, 842, 843, 844, 845, 846, 847, 848, 6820,7372; (Reviews) 608, 652, 8327
Lewis, D.E. 2685, 3496
Lewis, David Charles 5770
Lewis, Edward Norman 3561
Lewis, J.S. 7015
Lewis, John 3400, 6983, 7016
Lewis, Malcolm M. 481, 1985, 3401
Lewis, W.B. 8722
Leys, Colin (Review) 4717
Leyton-Brown, David 714, 6834, 7585, 7958, 7959, 8025, 8026, 8027
L'Heureux, Eugène 5583
L'Heureux, Jacques 8994
Lhomme, J. 6688
Li, Kuo Lee 30, 31, 3691
Liang, Irene Ai-Yum 3805
Liebich, André (Review) 7052
Liebich, C.M. (Review) 7052
Liesemer, Donald P. 5934
Lillich, Richard B. 1631, 5279
Lillie, Harry R. 2530, 3432
Linch, L.W. Pete 8248
Lindekens, Emmanuel 4923, 7331

Linden, Allen M. 1403
Lindgren, William 4419
Lindsay, Thomas 7468
Lindsey, Charles 6984
Lindsey, George R. 2554, 5769
Lingard, Charles Cecil 54
Linton, Neville 5130
Lipson, Leslie (Review) 5979
Lisein Norman, Margaretha 4968
Lissitzyn, Oliver J. 3806, 6267; (Reviews) 52, 334, 3936, 4164, 5588,6361
Lithwick, N.H. 754
Littell, Norman M. 7853
Little, C.H. 3443, 6923
Little, John Michael 6835
Litvak, Isaiah A. 7373, 7374, 7532, 7752, 7753, 7754, 7854, 7855,7960, 7961, 7962, 7963, 7964, 8028, 8029, 8969, 8970, 8971; (Review) 8024
Livada, Valentin R. (Reviews) 2605, 3048
Lleonart y Amselem, Alberto José (Review) 321
Lloyd, Lorna (Review) 5177
Lloyd, Trevor 54, 2555, 2556, 2557, 2558, 2625, 5864, 8657
Locas-Grandchamp, Micheline 7152
Lockwood, George H. 6123
Lodenstein, John Peter 4969
Lodge, Juliet 4970, 4971, 4972
Lodrup, P. 32
Loftas, Tony 3158, 3331
Logaldo, John R. 8972
Logan, Harold Amos 8912
Logan, Roderick M. 2753, 3073
Logsdon, John M. 4244, 4245
Loken, Mark Keith 7375, 7469
Lombard, Phyllis Ruth 5367
Lonergan, Stephen J. 2531, 3692
Long, Gavin (Review) 6413
Long, John S. 2080
Long, John W. 2266, 2267
Long, Morden H. 1764
Longley, Ronald S. 3402, 6689; (Reviews) 5122, 6992, 7437
Loomis, D.G. 5549
Looper, Robert B. (Review) 1974
Loranger, Louis J. 126
Loriot, François 2848, 3264, 3693, 4246, 4247
Loriot, Gérard (Review) 767
Lorrain, Léon 7377

Los, Laurence John 1081
Lotz, Jim 3330, 8521
Louis, Jean-Victor 4973, 4974
Lounsbury, Ralph Greenlee 3403
Loutfi, M.A. 3444
Louthood, Louise 6473, 6474, 6475; (Review) 4289
Lovell, R.I. 5255
Low, D. Martin 6154, 7278
Lowe, A.V. (Review) 3485
Lowe, Edith (Johnston) 16
Lowell, Abbott Lawrence 955, 1986
Lowenfeld, Andreas F. 3807, 7891; (Reviews) 242, 3669
Lower, Arthur R.M. 653, 755, 1404, 5075, 5205, 5682, 6476, 6477, 7080; (Reviews) 4665, 6662, 6871
Lower, Joseph Arthur 6478
Lowry, Bullitt 2311
Lowry, P. Donovan 3497, 3498
Loy, Frank E. 3808
Lucas, Alastair R. 2626
Lucas, F.G.T. 3562
Lucas, Kenneth C. 3158, 3331
Luce, Charles 8738
Lucey, William L. 2219
Lucy, R.V. 1049
Ludz, Peter Christian 5935
Luk, Kenneth 6229
Lund, T.G. 6188
Lureau, Daniel 3946
Lustgarten, Lionel S. 4248
Lux, André 7153
Lyall, Francis 8581
Lyon, J. Noel (Review) 4291
Lyon, James T. 3674, 3809, 3864, 4249
Lyon, Noel (Review) 1637
Lyon, Peter 5812, 6690
Lyon, Peyton V. 54, 594, 4975, 5936, 5937, 5938, 6479, 6480, 6481, 6836, 7632, 8400; (Reviews) 1289, 5459, 6333, 6395, 6456, 6494, 6541, 6556, 6804, 8398
Lyons, A.B. (Review) 240
Lyons, P. Howard 8204
Lysyk, Kenneth M. 654, 1265, 2081, 8249

Mabbutt, James M. (Review) 2331
MacArthur, D.A. 2177, 2312
Macaulay, A.M. 5122
Macaulay, Robert 8030
Macaulay, Wallace D. 3649

MacBrayne, Sheila F. 3694, 3695, 3947
MacCallum, J.L. 2439
MacChesnay, Brunson (Review) 4164
MacDermot, Niall 1632
MacDermot, T.W.L. 54, 1844; (Reviews) 6712, 6733
MacDonald, David 1585, 4250
Macdonald, Donald S. 5239, 7279, 7280; (Review) 2727
MacDonald, Elliott B. 3948, 3989, 3990
Macdonald, Flora 1765
Macdonald, H. Ian 4976, 4977, 7607, 7633; (Reviews) 5053, 7338
Macdonald, Helen Grace 6972
MacDonald, Hugh 5939
MacDonald, John A.G. 1299
Macdonald, R.D.S. 3335
Macdonald, Ronald St. John 248, 303, 304, 305, 306, 379, 380, 381, 404, 405, 406, 407, 408, 1050, 1615, 1633, 1634, 1635, 1636, 1637, 1766, 2043, 2062, 2144, 2559, 3064, 3135, 3333, 3499, 4420, 4533, 4534, 5104, 5105, 5240, 5368, 5399, 5400, 5444, 5445, 5771, 6485, 6904; (Reviews) 1974, 3261
MacDonald, Vincent C. 1987
MacDonald, W.C. (Review) 3590
Macdonnell, H.W. 4789
Macdonnell, J.M. 6691
MacDougall, A.R. 367
Mace, Gordon 1767, 5076, 5077, 7154
MacFadyen, Alan James 7378; (Review) 8671
MacFarlane, David L. 7671
Macfarlane, R.O. 655
MacGibbon, D.A. 2849, 4709, 7672; (Review) 2918
MacGregor, D.C. (Review) 6717
MacGregor, James Patrick 1481
MacGuigan, Mark 656, 1619
MacGuigan, Mark R. 3074
MacInnes, Charles S. 2413
MacIntyre, Malcolm M. 446
MacIver, Robert Morrison 6753
Mack, Newell B. 8796
MacKay, Hector 6692
MacKay, R. de Wolfe 8209
MacKay, R.W.G. (Reviews) 6484, 6531, 6617, 6861
MacKay, Robert A. 150, 155a, 956, 957, 1105, 2413, 2440, 3334, 4646, 5126,

5584, 5683, 5684, 5813, 6133, 6134, 6483, 6484, 6693, 8401; (Reviews) 54, 888, 942, 2389, 4488, 5096, 6712, 6733
MacKay, William Andrew (Review) 234
MacKenzie, Charles H.C. 3563
Mackenzie, Kenneth C. 2775, 7223, 7470
MacKenzie, Michael (Reviews) 8407, 8626
MacKenzie, Norman A.M. 54, 127, 249, 307, 308, 309, 310, 391, 409, 958, 959, 1126, 1157, 1199, 1200, 1943, 1988, 1989, 1990, 2130, 3107, 3116, 3252, 3810, 4100, 4386, 5272, 5685, 6359, 6694, 6905; (Reviews) 156, 453, 474, 1185, 1952, 2105, 2389, 2878, 4472, 5252, 6491, 6649, 6712, 6733
MacKenzie, W.C. 3335
Mackenzie, W.J.M. (Review) 5252
MacKinnon, B.J. 2104
MacKinnon, Frank (Review) 54
MacKinnon, W.B. (Review) 54
Mackintosh, W.A. 4535, 7673, 7674; (Reviews) 6952, 7005, 8032
MacKirdy, Kenneth A. 960, 4536, 6695; (Reviews) 998, 1114
Mackneson, Stephen Wayne 3253, 3696
MacLachlan, Alastair Donald 6600
Maclaren, J.J. 2188
MacLaren, Roy 5424, 7965, 8698
MacLauchlan, H. Wade 3230
MacLean, A.H. (Reviews) 1261, 4626
MacLean, Donald A. 4421
MacLean, Guy 6973
MacLeod, W.J. 8503
MacMahon, Arthur (Review) 8713
Macmaster, *Sir* Donald 5324
MacNab, C.T.A. 7856
Macphail, Andrew 2189
MacPharlane, D.W. 8005
Macpherson, Crawford Brough 632
Macpherson, Marion A. 595
MacPherson, Ronald B. 7471
Macquarrie, Heath 4647, 5106, 5107
MacRae, A.O. 2513
Macrory, Patrick F.J. 7586
MacWhite, M. (Review) 454
MacWilliam, D.A. 3445
Madar, Daniel R. 1768, 1769, 1770, 6486
Madden, A.F. 482; (Reviews) 964, 6780
Maduro, Morris F. 2984, 2985, 3265
Maes, Albert 4537, 4978
Magdelénat, Jean-Louis 3811, 3812, 3813, 3814, 3815, 3816, 4054, 4055, 4135, 4136, 4251, 4252, 4253; (Reviews) 3777, 3962, 4061
Magee, David Morris 7692
Magnusson, N.L. 5865
Magone, C.R. 1482
Mahan, A.T. 6909
Mahant, E.E. 4387, 4979, 4980, 4981
Mahler, Gregory (Review) 735
Mahoney, Terry 4655
Mahood, Harry Richard 2850
Maindrault, Marc 7224
Mainwaring, John 2101, 4790, 4791, 4792
Maitland, R.L. 5585
Malabard, Jean 1845, 3817
Malach, Vernon W. 8112
Malcolm, K. Blair 6487
Malik, Charles 1638, 1639
Malik, Sushma 4254
Mallen, Pierre-Louis 756
Mallory, James R. 483, 757, 5814; (Reviews) 102, 674
Malmgren, Harald B. 6791, 7533
Malone, Christopher Paul 849
Maltais, Eugene LeRoy 5772
Mamalakis, Markos J. (Review) 7143
Manchester, Lorne 3336
Mandell, Brian 5676
Mangematin, Luc 8522
Mangoldt, Hans von (Review) 4276
Manheim, Frank J. 1106
Mani, V.S. (Review) 3178
Manigat, Leslie F. 961, 1012
Manion, James Patrick 84, 7379
Mankabady, S. (Review) 3550
Mankiewicz, René H. 68, 2063, 3664, 3818, 3819, 3820, 3821, 3822, 3823, 3824, 3949, 3950, 3951, 3952, 3953, 3954, 3955, 3956, 3957, 3958, 3959, 3960, 3961, 3962, 3963, 3964, 3965, 3966, 3967, 3968, 3969, 3970, 3971, 3972, 3973, 4025, 4056, 4057, 4058, 4059, 4255, 4256, 4257, 4258, 4259, 4260, 4261, 4262, 4263, 4264, 4265, 4754, 4755, 4756, 4757, 4758, 4759, 6268, 6269, 6270, 6271, 6272, 6273, 6274, 6275, 6276, 6277, 6278, 8582; (Reviews) 290, 1937
Mann, F.A. (Reviews) 240, 3259
Manning, Charles Anthony Woodward 4472

Manning, Charles H. 7857
Manning, William Ray 156, 6601
Manny, Carter 128
Manoogian, Peter R. 4982
Manor, F.S. 5550
Mansergh, Nicholas 962, 963, 964, 6696, 6697, 6698; (Reviews) 54, 946, 997, 6437, 6491
Mansfield, J. Paris 6985
Manzig, John G.W. 8063
Mapelli, Enrique 3825, 3826, 3974
Mapp, Wayne Daniel 3564
Maqubela, Sikhumbuzo 7017
Maranda, Jean-Gabriel 6176
Marasinghe, M.L. 2145
March, Roman Robert 1771
Marchak, M. Patricia 8031
Marchand, Jean 1405
Marcoff, Marco G. (Review) 4277
Marcoux, J. Michel (Review) 2646
Marcoux, Laurent 6155
Marcoux, Serge 8402
Marcus, Stephen 1406
Margalioth, Eliahu 3975
Margo, Roderick David 4137
Marion, Jean-Claude 8398
Marmier, Xavier 1107
Marr, Norman 2951
Marr, William L. 1407, 1408, 1409
Marriott, J.A.R. 484, 6699
Marsh, A.H. 2044
Marsh, Donald Bailey 7225
Marsh, Leonard C. (Review) 8912
Marshall, Charles 6837
Marshall, Herbert 8032
Marshall, Richard Eugene 4862, 5940
Marshall, William Isaac 2482
Marston, Carroll J. 7081
Marston, Geoffrey 3602
Marten, Peter Cornelis 7659
Martens, André (Review) 7131
Martens, F. de 5325
Martey, Emmanuel Korley 7226
Martial, Jean A. 3117, 3697, 4101
Martig, Ralph Richard 2247
Martin, Cabot 3231
Martin, Camille (Reviews) 4626, 4778, 7338, 7926
Martin, Charles E. 2952, 2953, 6101; (Review) 7080

Martin, Chester B. 533, 965, 6488, 6700; (Review) 6654
Martin, Donald (Review) 6549
Martin, Ged (Review) 6682
Martin, Gerald Warren 6602
Martin, Hans 8842
Martin, Kingsley 5941
Martin, L.W. 5942
Martin, Lawrence 2190
Martin, Paul 311, 312, 313, 657, 1772, 1991, 3118, 3665, 3666,4422, 4648, 5206, 5502, 5503, 5504, 5505, 5506, 5507, 5551, 5686,5687, 5943, 6489, 6490, 7155, 7634, 8403, 8404, 8938
Martin, Peter 3976, 3977
Martin, Robert 1619, 7660; (Review) 290
Martinelli, Jean-Claude 3827
Martinez Ruiz, L.F. 2064
Martyn, Howe 7281, 7966, 8973, 8974
Marwitz, Gustav Peter Axel 5944
Marx, Herbert (Review) 1678
Marzari, Frank 5688, 5689, 5945; (Review) 6401
Masse, Barthélémy 3828
Masse, Marcel 850
Massey, Vincent 85, 5108, 6491, 6838
Masson, Claude 7380; (Review) 7790
Masson, Francis 7534
Massy, Philippe R. de 2931
Masters, Donald C. 54, 6951, 6952, 6955, 7381, 7566
Matamala, González (Review) 9015
Matas, David 758, 1901, 4983; (Review) 8060
Matas, R.J. 1992
Mateesco-Matte, Mircea 3978, 3979, 4266, 4267, 4268, 4269, 4270,4289, 8583
Mathie, William 658
Mathur, Athakattu Mathew 1127
Mathys, François (Review) 253
Matsler, Michael 8250
Matson, William Lawrence 6839
Matsusaki, Hiro (Review) 7349
Mattar, Gamil A. 5508
Matte, Nicolas Mateesco 52, 314, 368, 3075, 3076, 3119, 3667, 3668, 3698, 3699, 3829, 3830, 3831, 3832, 3833, 3980, 3981, 3982, 3983, 4060, 4061, 4062, 4102, 4103, 4271, 4272, 4273, 4274, 4275, 4276, 4277, 4278, 4279,

4280, 4281, 4282, 4283, 4284, 4285, 4286, 4287, 4288, 4289, 4423, 5586, 8584, 8585, 8658; (Reviews) 3814, 9015, 9038
Matthews, Joan 8405
Matthews, Robert O. 565, 1300, 6492, 7184
Matthews, Roy A. 4984, 4985, 7227, 7340, 7382, 7383, 7384, 7607, 7635, 7967, 7968
Mattson, Lawrence Garfield 8033
Maule, Christopher J. 7752, 7753, 7754, 7854, 7855, 7960, 7961, 7962, 7963, 7964, 8028, 8029, 8969, 8970, 8971
Maull, Hanns W. 7708
Maurette, Fernand 4793
Mavor, Charles W. 8225
Mawhinney, Barry 3077, 8579
Maxey, Edwin 6032
Maxim, James M. 2627
Maxwell, Judith 8689
Maxwell, Norman James 2851
Maybee, J.R. 1210
Maybee, Jack 1846
Mayer, R.A. 759
Mayers, Edward Courtenay 3603
Mayhew, Daniel Richard 4986
Maynard, Bruce H.E. 5509
Mayo, H.B. 693, 5946
Mayo, Lawrence Shaw 2221
Mayrand, Léon 315, 1301, 1847, 1848, 2160, 5218
Mazer, Brian M. 534, 5773, 5774, 8723
Mazzeo, Domenico 1108, 1109
McAllister, Ian 4987
McArthur, D. (Reviews) 6588, 6700
McArthur, Ernest 1640
McBride, James Boyd 8406
McCabe, James O. 2248, 2268, 2483
McCaffrey, Stephen C. 8802, 8803, 9018
McCarney, Rosemary A. 5241
McCart, Janice 8251
McClymont, Ian (Review) 2374
McConchie, Roger D. 3266
McConnell, William H. 2628, 2629, 3267, 6135; (Review) 765
McCracken, George W. 1641
McCracken, John E. 2684
McCready, Douglas J. (Review) 4717
McCullough, W.S. 1082
McCurdy, C.A. 6033

McDermott, Gordon Bryan 1317
McDiarmid, O.J. 7472; (Review) 7460
McDonald, Ada Jean 7018
McDonald, Bruce C. 1583, 8485, 8486; (Review) 8463
McDonald, David C. 1642
McDonald, James L. 8252, 8253, 8295
McDonald, John G. 7755, 7969
McDonald, Ronald Harold 6603, 6840
McDonald, Susan A. 1993, 2065
McDorman, Ted L. 33, 34, 2031, 2359, 3078, 3079, 3080, 3081, 3500, 3565
McDougal, John N. 7709
McDougal, Myres S. 3256, 4290, 4291, 4292
McDougall, D.J. (Reviews) 6639, 6641, 6698
McDougall, Duncan M. 1410; (Review) 7871
McDougall, Ian A. 2376, 2954, 3134, 8683
McDougall, John N. 7710, 8034, 8684
McDougall, Pamela A. 7452
McElroy, Robert McNutt 2182
McFadyean, *Sir* Andrew 6701
McFadyen, Stuart 1201, 7858
McFarlane, William James 4988
McGavin, Robert James 8659
McGillicuddy, Owen E. 86
McGinnis, David 1411
McGoun, Archibald 7228
McGrath, *Sir* Patrick T. 694, 2330, 2974, 5207, 5326
McGregor, Fred A. 7926
McGuinness, Kevin Patrick 8975
McGurran, H. David 7970, 8210
McInnes, Hector 3624
McInnes, R.W. 2082
McInnis, Edgar 1643, 4473, 4474, 4649, 4665, 6102, 6360, 6493, 6702, 6841; (Reviews) 54, 6365, 6699
McIntyre, Alister 7631
McIntyre, Hugh C. 8724
McIvor, R. Craig 4989, 7385
McKay, Paul 8725
McKay, Raoul J. 2083
McKean, W.A. (Reviews) 1678, 6195
McKee, Samuel 2852
McKegney, James C. 6604
McKelvey, E. Neil 3268
McKenna, Frank J. 3232
McKenry, Carl E.B. (Review) 4293

McKercher, Brian 4475
McKie, Alexander B. 8227, 8254, 8255, 8256
McKie, James W. 7971
McKim, Anson C. 3834
McKinley, Kathryn 8407, 8626
McKinnell, Robert 7184
McKinsey, Lauren S. 760
McKitterick, T.E.M. 2532
McKnight, Allan 8627
McLaren, John P.S. (Review) 292
McLaren, Robert I. 851, 3501, 4538, 5177; (Review) 1806
McLaurin, C. Campbell 6842, 6843
McLean, Simon James 7473
McLeod, A.N. 7859
McLeod, Malcolm 2484
McLeod, Malcolm E. 8487
McLin, Jon 4388, 4389
McLin, Jon B. 6494; (Review) 54
McLoughlin, Peter F.M. 8408
McMahon, Thomas J. 8488
McManus, John C. 7972
McManus, R. Derek 7756
McMaster, Glen F. 3835
McMenemy, Frank S. 2461
McMenemy, John Murray 2955
McMillan, Anthony J. 1412
McMillan, Carl H. 7156, 7157, 7532
McMillan, Charles J. 7386, 7860, 7861; (Review) 8001
McMinn, Kayron Campbell 6703
McMurrich, J. Playfair 6065
McMyn, James 8113
McNairn, Colin H. 3836
McNally, George Frederick 87
McNamara, Philip 8804, 9019
McNaught, Kenneth 1773, 1774, 4539; (Reviews) 54, 6497
McNaughton, A.G.L. 81, 2956, 4710, 8726
McNaughton, John T. 5690
McNeil, Jean (Review) 7140
McNichols, William 8976
McNutt, W.S. (Review) 3421
McPhail, Thomas L. 8977
McPherson, Ian E. 3837, 3838, 4026
McQuillan, Peter E. 8204
McRae, Donald M. 129, 130, 131, 132, 133, 447, 1644, 1944, 2040, 2146, 2282, 2360, 2687, 3061, 3082, 3083, 3159, 3233, 3502, 4418, 4424, 4817, 5256, 5401, 5402; (Reviews) 51, 248, 1182, 3134
McRae, James J. (Reviews) 7401, 7478
McRae, K.D. 1266, 1645
McRoberts, Kenneth 761; (Reviews) 741, 789
McShane, King G. 5109
McTaggart, David Fraser 5775
McTaggart, Don 6177
McTavish, Mary 2
McWhinney, Edward 88, 134, 316, 317, 318, 319, 320, 321, 322, 323, 324, 325, 326, 327, 328, 329, 330, 331, 332, 333, 334, 335, 336, 337, 412, 413, 432, 440, 485, 575, 613, 614, 615, 616, 617, 659, 660, 661, 662, 762, 763, 764, 765, 1994, 1995, 1996, 1997, 3084, 3085, 3669, 3700, 4293, 4540, 4541, 4580, 4615, 4990, 4991, 5219, 5369, 5370, 5403, 5587, 5588, 5589, 5590, 5591, 5592, 5691, 5692, 5693, 5694, 5776, 6279, 6280, 6281, 6282, 6283, 6284, 6285, 6286, 6361, 7158, 7535, 8579, 8586, 8587, 8588; (Reviews) 248, 290, 653, 947, 3831, 5652, 8989
Meagher, Arthur J. 3604, 3605, 3650
Meeker, Leonard C. 4294
Meekison, J. Peter 852
Mehling, Jean 8409; (Review) 8141
Mehmet, Ozay 7159; (Reviews) 7131, 8329, 8349
Meisel, John 5947; (Review) 54
Meissner, Boris 576
Melko, Matthew 5593
Melvin, A. Gordon 2134
Melvin, James R. 8205
Mendes, Errol P. 1646, 8064, 8685; (Review) 56
Mendez, Joseph-M. 4992, 4993
Menefee, Ferdinand Northrup 2853
Menezes, Julio 7862
Menon, P.K. 4138, 4139
Menter, Martin 4295
Menzies, Merril Warren 7675
Mercer, David William 7587
Merchant, Livingston T. 6812, 6844
Mercier, Jean 1413, 1414
Meredith, Brian 2630, 7973
Meret, Livia 1083

Mérignhac, A. 3404
Merillat, Herbert Christian Laing 1775, 1776
Merk, Frederick 2249, 2250, 2485, 2486, 2487, 2488, 2489, 2490,2491
Merle, Marcel 5695, 7160
Meron, Theodor 2124
Merrick, John Robert 4650
Merrills, J.G. 596, 5242; (Reviews) 1936, 3048
Merriman, *Sir* Boyd 3606
Merritt, William Hamilton 6953
Mesaritis, Panayiotis 3234
Mestier du Bourg, Hubert de 3235, 3236, 3446, 3447
Mesznik, Roger 3277
Metz, Homer 4542
Metzger, Stanley D. 7588, 7638
Meunier, M. 1202
Meyer, Adolph Frederick 2412
Meyer, Cord 4425
Meyer, Herman Henry Bernard 7010, 7019
Meyer, Stephen M. 5696
Meyers, John E. 2631
M'Gonigle, R. Michael 2686, 3503, 3504, 3505, 3506
Mhun, Henry 4863, 4994
Michell, H. (Review) 1439
Michelmann, Hans J. 4995
Mickenberg, Neil H. 1242
Mida, Hymie 8257
Middlemiss, Danford W. 3086, 3156, 3179, 5866
Mignault, P.B. 535, 2441
Mikdashi, Zuhayr 7974
Milani, Michael 1998
Milde, C. Michael 3670, 3671, 3984, 4760, 4761, 4762, 4763, 4764; (Review) 4271
Miles, Edward 3087; (Review) 3073
Miljan, Toivo 4864, 4996
Millar, Thomas B. 135, 1777, 4651
Miller, Abraham H. 6230
Miller, Anthony John 3839, 4390, 4652, 4711, 6495
Miller, Carman (Review) 6540
Miller, D.M. 6066
Miller, David Hunter 2251, 2269, 2313, 2632
Miller, Eugene H. 5110
Miller, Georgette M. 6287

Miller, John A. 6496
Miller, John Donald Bruce 966, 967, 6704; (Review) 6466
Millman, Thomas Reagh 7567
Mills, Dudley 6910
Mills, George Hampden Stanley 2514
Mills, Hal 3081, 3237, 3500
Mills, Joseph C. 7161, 7636
Millstone, Maurice Shelly 1158, 1159
Milsten, Donald E. 2633, 3088, 5552
Milton, William Fitzwilliam 2270
Minghi, Julian Vincent 2161
Minifie, James M. 6497, 6845
Minotto, Claude 2561
Minshew, Velon H. (Review) 4288
Mintah, Gloria 202
Minville, Esdras 6705
Misener, R.S. 2856
Mishra, Shantnu 3672
Misir, Devendranauth 8234
Misra, K.P. 606
Miszerak, Martin A. 3856
Mitchell, Bruce (Review) 2753
Mitchell, C. Clyde 5458
Mitchell, C.L. 3337
Mitchell, David Joseph 2462
Mitchell, H. (Review) 6468
Mitchell, Harvey 695
Mitchell, James Rowell 6846
Mitchell, John Stirling 766
Mitchell, Lionel Anthony 7637
Mitchell, Marnie F. 6847, 7863
Mitchell, R.M. 7387, 7388
Mitra, P.K. (Review) 7341
Mizouni, Mohamed Hédi 4599
Moch, Jules 5697
Mockler, E.J. (Review) 7459
Modak, N.D. 4997
Mohammed, Franklyn 4543
Mohtadi, M.F. 8766
Molot, Henry L. 2147
Molot, Maureen Appel 4865, 7536, 8065; (Review) 6481
Monahan, Robert L. 8163
Moncharville, M. 3405
Mond, *Sir* Alfred 7020
Monet, Jacques 2515, 6605
Monk, Richard C. 4544
Monlaü, Michel B. 3840
Monnet, François Marie 767
Monsma, Edward Bodus 5178
Montague, J.T. 8918

Montigny, Louvigny de 8489
Montigny, Michel de 8776
Montigny, Yves de 1267
Montmarquette, Claude 8357
Montpetit, Édouard 7389, 8114, 8115
Monture, G.C. 1268
Mooradian, Ara J. 8720
Moore, A. Milton 768
Moore, Dorothy Louise 2442
Moore, George Bissland 5867
Moore, Joan E. 2533
Moore, John Bassett 2162, 2314, 2724, 5258, 5259, 5327, 5328
Moore, Michael D. 8410
Moore, Philip C. 8258
Moore, Rodney Ernest 968
Moore, Thomas O. 9020
Moore, Sir William Harrison 1999, 4476
Moran, H.O. 8411
Morchain, Janet Kerr 6848
More, Eric W. (Review) 4459
Morel, André 1160
Morelli, Francesco Giusseppi 7082
Morgan, Charles Stillman 2854
Morgan, D.J. (Reviews) 7437, 8363
Morgan, J.H. 486
Morgan, Kenneth Paul 7390
Morgan, Lucy Ingram 1415
Morillo-Ferrer, Consuelo 4545
Morin, Claude 853, 854
Morin, Jacques-Yvan 250, 369, 618, 1647, 2000, 2001, 2002, 2688, 3089, 3120, 3160, 3161, 3507, 3508, 5111
Morin, Rosaire 1416
Morin, Victor 2084, 6891
Morin, Wilfrid 769, 770, 1269
Morin, William 3566, 3567, 3607, 3651, 3652, 3653
Morine, Alfred B. 3406, 3407
Morison, J.L. (Reviews) 885, 925
Morley, Jeremy D. 5992
Morley, Lawrence W. 4296, 4297
Moroz, Andrew R. 7500, 7537
Morris, Alexander 2085
Morris, Gerald L. 248, 303, 304, 305, 306, 382, 408, 572, 663, 771, 1617, 2003, 3135, 3499, 8805; (Review) 1003
Morris, Grace Parker 2252
Morris, Hugh G. 3238
Morris, Margaret W. 2634
Morrison, Alfred Eugene 6707

Morrison, David R. 6498; (Review) 6401
Morrison, Jean 1013
Morrison, Robert W. 8707, 8727; (Review) 5756
Morrison, Stephen R. 1483
Morrissette, France 8116
Morrone, Michael F. 7513
Morrow, Rising Lake 6986
Morse, Anita 2776
Morse, Charles 338, 487, 536, 1203, 1484, 2131, 3408, 5208, 5371, 6034
Morton, Desmond 1204, 1778, 6708
Morton, H.A. 6892
Morton, William L. 4546, 6499, 6500; (Reviews) 54, 885
Moseley, Frederick E. 2725, 8824
Mosher, Ralph Lamont 7021
Mosler, Hermann 5372
Moss, John H. 8490
Moss, Robert 6231
Mostafa, Khairy H.Y. 5191
Motiuk, Laurence 37
Moulton, Harold Glenn 2854
Mount, Graeme S. (Review) 7087
Moursi, Fouad Kamel 3841
Mousaw, Ralph Edgar 1110
Mowat, H.M. 537
Moyse, Robert 5948
Mroz, Edward (Review) 3830
Mueller, Volkmar 4998
Münch, F. (Reviews) 334, 3119, 3259
Muhammad, Abdul Hai 8412
Muir, R.C. 3445
Mukherjee, P.K. 3625
Muli'aumaseali'i, Saverivi 3090, 3673
Muller, H.N., III (Review) 6889
Mulligan, Wm. Orr 2191
Mundell, Robert Alexander 8117
Munro, Donald W. 3091
Munro, Gordon R. 2377, 3146, 3162, 3163, 3164, 3165, 3338, 3339
Munro, H.F. (Review) 6899
Munro, Hector A. 5594, 6178
Munro, Henry F. 2986
Munro, John A. 89, 90, 150, 1417, 2315, 2316, 4772, 6501, 6502
Munro, John M. 8523
Munton, Donald J. 847, 848, 5698, 6362, 6503, 6504, 6849, 7864, 8806, 8807, 8843; (Reviews) 158, 6806, 7492
Murchison, John Taylor 3701

Murphy, Earl Finbar 8695
Murphy, Ewell E. 5993
Murphy, John F. (Review) 6200
Murphy, Lawrence J. 8118
Murphy, Lin (Review) 231
Murphy, Margaret 6067
Murphy, Orville T. 3409
Murphy, Wallace S. 2957
Murray, Alexander L. 1318, 1485
Murray, David R. 150, 1849, 7083; (Review) 7075
Murray, Geoffrey S. 5510
Murray, Glenn F. 8896
Murray, Graham (Reviews) 5854, 5921
Murray, Howard 969
Murray, J. Alex 6828, 7589, 7865, 8035
Murray, Janice L. 6850
Murray, John Darrach 5553
Murray, John David 8119
Murray, Keith A. 5285
Murray, Ronald Charles 3092, 4999
Murray, Trevor William 7693
Musgrave, Peggy B. 8205, 8227
Mushkat, Marion 5815
Myerson, Moses Hyman 6179
Myhal, Patricia J. 1648
Myrand, Marie-Louise 162
Mytelka, Lynn K. 7914

Nadal, François 5000, 5001
Nadeau, G.W. 4104
Nadeau, Gilbert 2813
Nadeau, Jean-Marie 2855
Nadelmann, Kurt H. 7975
Nadon, Marc 3637
Nafziger, James A.R. (Reviews) 3319, 8996
Naidu, Mumulla Venkat Rao 4547, 4548
Namaliu, Rabi Langanai 1111
Nanda, Ved P. (Review) 303
Nanes, Allan 4866
Nappi, Carmine 7391, 8120
Nathan, Manfred 488
Nattress, W. Dayle 8157
Navarro, Mariano Aguilar (Review) 5652
Nazarevich, Alann J. 9027
Ndongko, Wilfred Awung 5002
Neal, Arthur L. 7392, 7393, 7394, 7395, 7396, 7538
Neant, Hubert 6974
Neary, Peter F. 1333, 3410, 3411, 6851

Neatby, Hilda Blair (Reviews) 6472, 6538, 7525
Neate, Frank G. 8660
Nedlin, Ralph 7685
Nef, Jorge 6202, 7084
Neher, Philip A. 7866
Neisser, Albert C. 7590
Nelles, H.V. (Reviews) 2960, 2967
Nellestyn, A. 5777
Nelson, Harold I. 6363; (Review) 5204
Nelson, Herbert Ira 489
Nelson, James Gordon 2562
Nemeth, John 4063
Nemetz, Peter N. 8661
Nerbas, Grant H. 4105, 8524
Nergaard, Paul 2563
Nesgos, Peter D. 3191, 3842, 4106, 4107, 4298, 8491, 8589
Nesham, E.W. 2361
Nettl, J.P. 2066
Neville, W.F.W. (Review) 6401
Nevitte, Neil 6419, 6799
Newberger, Edward L. 7867
Newberry, Patience Josephine Ruth 5606
Newbury, Philip 2689, 3509
Newby, Robert F. 7757
Newcomb, Josiah T. 6906
Newcombe, Alan G. 4656
Newcombe, Hanna 4400, 4426, 4600, 4653, 4654, 4655, 4656, 4657
Newell, I. 696
Newland, John Anthony 6505
Newman, Parley W. 5929
Nguyen, The-Hiep 7696, 7711
Nicholas, Barry (Review) 240
Nicholas, H.G. 145, 4549
Nicholson, Francis J. (Review) 290
Nicholson, Marian Ruth 6606, 6852
Nicholson, Norman L. 2163, 2164, 2165, 2253
Nicholson, T.A.C. 3843
Niciu, Martian 4299
Nickel, Carl 8686
Nicol, Eric Patrick 4867
Nicoloff, Olivier 8939; (Review) 52
Niebyl, Karl H. 8413
Nied, G. David 2362, 5404
Niedermeier, Lynn 1270
Nigro, Don J. 8259
Nisan, Mordechai 6086
Nish, Cameron 5047; (Review) 6307

Nish, Elizabeth (Review) 632
Nishigori, Hou 3985
Nisot, Joseph 597
Nixon, Elliott B. (Review) 3550
Nixon, F.G. 8590
Nkiwane, Solomon Moyo 4477
Noble, John J. 8728
Noble, Paul C. 5410
Noble, W.R. (Review) 5387
Noel, Albert John 5143
Noel, Roderick Aldwin David 3844
Nogaro, Bertrand 4427
Nomikos, Eugenia V. 6364
Noor Muhammad, Haji N.A. (Review) 303
Nord, Douglas C. 1419, 1420; (Review) 6413
Nordon, Charles L. 5373
Normand, Wilfrid Guild 136
North, Robert C. 6364
Northey, John F. 2004
Norton, Augustus R. 6232
Norton, Brian B. (Review) 8906
Norton, Virgil 3125
Nossal, Kim Richard 1651, 1779, 2443, 2449, 2777, 6506, 7085, 7086; (Reviews) 148a, 6553
Noto, Mario T. 1486
Nowak, Tadeusz Cieplak 4064
Nyamekye, Stephen Kwasi 8777, 8778
Nye, Joseph S. 6806, 6853
Nyiri, Nicolas A. 6001
Nyman, James Segvard 8729

Oak, G. Brian 5003
Oatway, Francis J. 8295
Oberholtzer, Ernest C. 8865
Oberndorfer, Ron H. 7474
O'Brien, John David 3986
O'Brien, Michael John 7539
O'Brien, Rita Cruise 7163
O'Brien, William V. 2635
Ochan, Ralph W. 3094; (Review) 8791
O'Connell, Daniel Patrick 970, 2135; (Reviews) 1970, 3319
O'Connor, Walter F. 8227, 8296
O'Connor, William E. (Review) 4061
Odubayo, Wilberforce O. 3845
Oelofsen, Pieter Daniel 6103
Ørvik, Nils 2565, 5816, 5954, 5955, 5956, 6507; (Review) 2605

Oetting, R.B. 2778
Officer, Lawrence H. 6954
Ogden, Suzanne 4581
Ogelsby, J.C.M. 5112, 6508, 7087
Oglesby, R.R. (Review) 314
Ogley, Roderick C. (Review) 3175
O'Grady, William 773
Ogram, Ernest William 8121
Ogunbanwo, Ogunsola Olaniyi 3254, 3702
O'Hearn, W.J. 1487
O'Hearn, Walter 4550, 4665
O'Higgins, Paul 1488
Okidi, C. Odidi 3147
Ollivier, Maurice 538, 539, 540, 541, 2005, 6709
Olson, Thomas H. 7869, 8687
O'Marra, Alfred Joseph Clifford 6233
O'Neill, Robert (Reviews) 5459, 6541
Ongay-Perez, Luis Manuel 8779
Onorato, William T. 3510
Onwuku, Ralph Iheanyi 6024
Onwumere, Chukwudi Pettson 7088
Orban, Edmond 774, 4869
Orr, Patrick 7639
Orser, E.H. 8298
Ortega, Manuel Medina (Review) 4291
Ortiz, David Rangel 8492
Osbaldeston, Gordon 1781
Osberg, Lars 7660
Osborn, Chase Salmon 2192
Osborn, Stella Brunt 2192
Osborne, John C. 8493
Osborne, John D. (Review) 8465
Ossman, Albert John 6509
Ostlund, Raymond E. 3988
O'Sullivan, Barry J. 7868
Ottenheimer, Gerald R. 3343
Otter, A.D. den (Review) 7871
Ouellet, Fernand 775
Ough, John P. 2566
Ouimet, Lise 5210, 7164
Overman, William D. 6955, 6956
Owen, Walter S. 5699
Owugah, Lemuel 5004
Ozere, S.V. 3344

Pace, F.C. 6025
Paddock, Harold 776
Padjen, Ivan 340
Pagé, Carole 777

Page, Donald M. 39, 40, 137, 146, 150, 4478
Page, Garnet T. 4810, 8628
Page, Robert J.D. 6711
Paget, D. 3192
Painchaud, Paul 414, 664, 855, 971, 1014, 6510, 6511, 8978; (Review) 6463
Paint, Henry M. 2857, 2858, 2859
Paisant, Marcel 5330
Pal, I.D. (Reviews) 5436, 7415, 7489
Palfrey, John 8730
Palk, William L. 5005, 5006, 5007
Pallone, Frank 2534
Palmer, Gerald Eustace Howell 6712
Palmer, Howard (Review) 1289
Pandya, Rajnikant 4027
Pangbourne, David G. 8277
Pange, Jean de 542
Pantaleo, Peter 2444
Panting, G.E. (Review) 151
Panzer, Arnold B. 8260, 9021
Papacostas, A.N. (Review) 334
Paquet, Gilles 732, 7976
Paquet, L.A. 1319
Paquette, Michel 8497
Paquette, Richard 4083, 4108, 4109, 4110
Paradis, Roger 2193
Paragg, Ralph R. 7089, 8417; (Review) 8360
Parai, Louis 1348, 1421, 1422
Pardo, Arvid 3095, 8629
Parent, Georges-Henri 1851
Parizeau, Jacques 778, 7165, 7397, 7398, 7640, 7676, 7870, 8418; (Review) 7443
Parizeau, Micheline 3693
Park, Choon-ho 3275
Parker, George 8494
Parker, Ian 7475
Parkinson, Joseph Frederick 54, 8122
Parks, Alex L. (Review) 3637
Parry, Clive 1161
Parry, D. Hughes 415
Parry, Jack O. 1945
Parsons, John E. 2364
Parsons, R.A. 3345
Parsy, Luc 8123
Partan, Daniel G. (Reviews) 3048, 5652
Partsch, Karl Josef 6068
Paslawski, Lou 6069
Passaris, Constantine 1302, 1423, 1424

Patenaude, Luce 2331
Paterson, Alastair R. 3846, 3847
Paterson, Donald G. 7871, 7872
Paton, G.W. (Review) 1199
Patriarche, V.H. 2567
Patrick, Robert J. 8225
Patry, André 341, 817, 856, 972, 1064, 1852, 1853, 1882, 2779, 2780, 5008, 6512, 7476; (Review) 503
Patry, Richard 779
Patsalides, John George 5554
Patterson, Bruce 1112
Patterson, Donald William 7873
Patterson, G.N. 8689
Patterson, J. 8745
Patterson, Kirk R. 2565
Patterson, Walter T. 3989, 3990
Pattison, John C. 7874, 7977; (Reviews) 7817, 8125
Patton, Donald J. 3276, 8036
Patton, Edward L. 8866
Patton, H.S. 7022
Paul, Alix-Herard 6513
Paul, Gurbachan Singh 1425
Paul, John 5677
Paullin, Charles O. 2254
Paumann, Manuel K. 7399
Paust, Jordan J. 6238, 9028
Pavlasek, Tomas J.F. 3672
Pawa, J.M. 6514
Pearcy, G. Etzel 3239
Pearse, Peter H. 3291, 3346, 8867
Pearson, G.A.H. (Review) 5709
Pearson, Geoffrey 1652
Pearson, Lester B. 90, 342, 343, 2568, 4428, 4551, 4658, 4872, 5512, 5513, 5957, 5958, 6104, 6365, 6426, 6515, 6516, 6517, 6518, 6713, 6854, 7166, 7167, 8349, 8419
Pease, Theodore Calvin 2194
Peccei, Riccardo 8050
Peel, David 2860, 7759
Peers, Frank (Review) 8533
Peippo, David J. 3583, 8525
Pelkmans, Jacques 5009
Pell, Claiborne 1113
Pelland, Léo 543, 2102, 5994
Pellet, Alain (Reviews) 321, 4276
Pelletier, Georges 1426
Pelletier, Irénée 8420, 8421

Pelletier, Jean 1854
Pelletier, Luc 1024
Pelletier, Réjean (Review) 6850
Pellonpää, Matti Päävo 1205
Pemberton, Ian Cleghorn Blanshard 1320
Pemberton, J.S.B. 5868
Penegar, Kenneth L. (Review) 4291
Peng, Ming-Min 3704, 4073
Penisson, Bernard 1855
Penlington, Norman 2317; (Reviews) 2153, 6714
Pennanen, Gary 6957, 7540, 7568
Pennington, A.C. 2920
Penny, Arthur G. 2516
Penrose, Edith 7712
Pentland, Charles, 4391, 4818, 5010, 5011, 5012, 5013; (Reviews) 793, 4370, 4914, 4996, 5436, 6338, 6768, 6806
Pentland, H. Clare (Reviews) 7454, 8046, 8906
Pépin, Eugène 41, 416, 417, 3705, 3848, 3849, 4302, 4303, 4304, 4305, 4306; (Reviews) 68, 3833, 4164, 4276
Pepper, Donald A. 3347
Perciballi, Lionello Cappelli 9039
Percy, Michael B. 7013
Perez-Jimenez, Fabian 1653
Perkins, Bradford 6911
Perley, Michael 8837
Perlgut, Mark 8739
Perrault, Antonio 344, 973, 8495
Perrault, Joseph-Édouard 2445
Perron, Jean Roch (Review) 94
Perron, Martin 4935
Perry, David B. 8261
Perry, J. Harvey 7485, 7641
Pérusse, S. 1202
Pescatore, Pierre 617
Pestieau, Caroline 7230, 7307, 7541, 8124
Peters, J.E. 7400
Peters, Victor 8262
Petersmann, Ernst-U. 7168
Peterson, Courtland H. (Review) 4291
Peterson, James S. 7231, 8189, 8228, 8233, 8263, 8264, 8265, 8266
Peterson, M.J. (Reviews) 243, 5691
Peterson, Thomas Edward 8422
Petrenko, Alex 1654
Petrie, J.R. (Review) 4441
Petrusa, Seraph M. 4659

Pettey, Bryce H. 8591
Pharand, Donat 167, 922, 2535, 2569, 2636, 2637, 2638, 2639, 2640, 2641, 2642, 2643, 2644, 2645, 2646, 2647, 2648, 2649, 2650, 2651, 2652, 2653, 2654, 2690, 2691, 2692, 3064, 3096, 3097, 3098, 3137, 3138, 3240, 3241, 3269, 3511, 3512, 3513, 4582, 5376, 6228
Phelan, G.B. 1065
Phelan, Vincent C. 1427, 4795
Phillippe, Larry K. 9029
Phillips, Neil 8188
Phillips, R.A.J. 1271, 2570, 2571
Phillips, W.G. 7642
Picard, Roger 4873, 5211, 6366
Pichette, Serge 8496, 8497
Pick, Alfred 5114
Pickering, John 8844
Pickersgill, J.W. 91
Pickett, James (Review) 4717
Pierce, Clifford James 544
Pierce, S.D. 5870
Piggott, Eleanora 1428
Pijoan, J. 4479
Pike, Gordon C. 3434
Pikna, Raymond J., Jr. 8037
Pilisi, Paul 5064; (Reviews) 54, 6828, 7492
Pillai, Nilakandan Perumal 4480
Pilling, A.M. 1655, 8267
Pilon, Raphaël 1856
Pimlott, Douglas H. 3448
Pinchin, Hugh McAlister 7477, 7478
Pineau, Jean 3568, 3569, 3850, 8526; (Reviews) 3637, 3814, 3997, 4276
Pineo, C.C. 4712
Pinsonnault, Marcel 3626
Pinto, Roger (Reviews) 241, 2381
Piotrowski, G. 665
Piper, Donald C. 1782, 2446, 2726, 2727; (Review) 2916
Piplani, S.S. 4430
Piscopo, Franco A. 1162
Plain, Richard Hayward McVicar 2958
Plaut, W. Gunther (Review) 1528
Plischke, Elmer 2655
Plosz, D.J. 4713
Plotkins, Robert Jean 7978
Plumptre, A.F.W. 4714, 5870, 8125, 8423
Plumptre, Timothy 1783
Podea, Iris S. 5115

Poel, Dale H. 7864
Poissant, Charles Albert 8268, 8269
Polanyi, John C. 5700, 5756
Polk, Judd 7865
Pollack, Gerald Alexander 7542
Pollack, Irving M. 1495
Pollak, Walter 5377
Pollock, David H. (Review) 5177
Pollock, Sidney 4392
Pomerance, Michla 577
Pomerant, Joseph Baer 1489
Poncelet, Maurice (Reviews) 704, 709
Pondaven, Philippe 2729
Pontavice, Emmanuel du 3991, 4084; (Review) 3814
Pontecorvo, Giulio 3277, 3302, 3348
Poole, A.F.N. 2167
Pope, Maurice Arthur 92
Popescu, Dumitra 3851, 4140
Popiel, Paul A. 7979
Popovici, Adrian (Review) 5048
Popp, Alfred H.E. 3570, 3571, 3992
Popple, A.E. 1490
Porritt, Edward 490
Portes, Jacques 1883
Posner, Richard (Review) 4291
Postner, Harry H. 7401
Potholm, Christian P. 5144
Potter, G.A. 5701
Potter, K.B. 7875
Potter, Pitman B. 974, 8963
Poulantzas, Nicholas M. 1128, 1656, 1906, 3166, 3258, 3259, 4307, 4308, 4309, 4310, 4311, 4312, 4313, 4314, 4315, 4316, 4317, 6234, 6288, 6289, 6290, 6291, 6367, 8592, 8593, 8594; (Review) 3119
Poupart, André 7980
Pourcelet, Michel 3572, 3627, 3628, 3654, 3852, 3993, 3994, 3995, 3996, 3997, 3998, 3999, 4111, 4318, 6292, 6293, 8861; (Review) 3833
Powell, R. 3655
Power, Michael F. 3563
Power, W. Kent 1657, 6035
Powers, Mabel 6924
Poznanska, Alice (Review) 7612
Poznanski, Thaddée 8887
Prabhu, M.A. 3573
Prachowny, Martin F.J. 4678
Prager, Carol A.L. (Review) 444
Prang, Margaret (Review) 6883
Prat, Henri 4393
Pratt, Cranford 6519, 7169; (Review) 7119
Pratt, Geoffrey N. 420, 421, 3674, 3675, 3864
Pratt, Gibson E. 2730
Pratt, Julius W. 2492; (Review) 6841
Pratt, R.C. (Review) 997
Precht, Paul Lawrence 7232, 8630
Preeg, Ernest H. 7620
Preiswerk, Roy 7170
Presley, John R. 8126
Preston, Richard A. 54, 1051, 5595, 5702, 5871, 5959, 5995, 6714, 6855, 6856, 8979; (Reviews) 5459, 6538, 6541
Price, Richard 2071, 2086
Price, Trevor 1785
Prince, A.E. 1084, 1085, 6520, 6715
Pritchard, David A. 4716
Probst, Samuel E. 4319
Pross, A. Paul 3134
Protheroe, David R. 7402
Proulx, Daniel 1658, 1659
Proulx, Pierre-Paul 666, 7543
Provencher, Jean (Review) 2331
Prowse, D.W. 3415, 3416
Prud'Homme, L.A. 2195, 2196, 2197, 2975, 2976, 2977
Prussing, Eugene E. 3574
Pryce, Roy 5014
Przetacznik, Franciszek 1907
Pugsley, William Howard 4431
Pullen, T.C. 2572, 2583
Purdie, Raymond J. Lewis 6521
Purver, Ronald G. 3193, 5703, 5704, 5705
Pyrcz, Orville Andrew 8270

Qing-nan, Meng 3514
Quenneville, Jean-Guy R. 781
Quigley, Harold S. (Review) 5252
Quigley, Tim 7879
Quinn, John J. 7484
Quirin, G. David 7832, 8527

Raabe, Francis Conrad 7090
Rabeau, Yves 732, 7543
Raby, S. 2087
Racicot, Paul-Émile (Review) 7612
Radzinowicz, Leon 6156
Rädler, Albert 8227
Raffo, Peter 138

Rahman, A.T.M. Siddiquer 5192
Raicht, Lawrence 8689
Rainbow, Edwin D. 2861
Rainville, J.-H. 2862
Rajana, Cecil 7171; (Review) 4914
Rajkhan, Siraj Mohammad 4000
Rajotte, Jacques 4112
Rajski, Jerzy 4765; (Review) 4272
Raleigh, *Sir* Thomas 6716
Ralph, Michael 4432
Raman, K. Venkata 1616, 5411, 5412; (Reviews) 68, 253, 3259
Ramcharan, B.G. 1660, 1661, 5446, 7172
Ramphal, Shridath S. 7173
Ramsay, Robert A. 2168
Ranadive, Ramesh V. 3853
Rand, Michael C. 858, 2006
Randall, Stephen J. (Review) 7061
Ranger, Robin 5706, 5707, 5708, 5709, 5710, 5711, 5781, 5960, 6026
Rankin, Bruce 93
Rankin, Murray T. 8038
Ransome, Jack C. 8808
Ranson, A. Terence 8498
Rao, K. Krishna 8595
Rao, K. Narayana (Review) 241
Rao, T.S. Rama (Review) 334
Rapkin, Norman L. 8191, 8203, 8271
Rasmussen, Eric K. 2731
Rathwell, John H.W. 8039
Ratiner, Leigh 2684
Rauenbusch, William R. 7818, 8007
Ravenhill, John 7174
Rawlyk, George A. 1429, 6857; (Reviews) 6807, 6855, 6952
Raworth, Philip 5015
Raynauld, André 5193, 5194
Razanamparany, Voahangy Vaonindrina 4065
Re, Edward D. 5243
Rea, Kenneth (Review) 2559
Read, Horace E. 1908, 2007, 5378
Read, John E. 346, 347, 1788, 1789, 1946, 5244, 5286, 5379, 5380, 5381, 5596, 6014, 6368, 9022
Reboud, Louis 4874
Redding, Forest William 3349
Redekop, Clarence G. 1086, 7091; (Reviews) 155a, 6410, 6451, 6552
Redekop, John H. 6858; (Reviews) 6768, 6782, 6818

Redgwell, J.F. 4001
Redler, Richard 6116, 7730
Reed, Walter Dudley 4320
Reese, Trevor R. 975
Reeves, J.S. (Review) 2389
Reeves, William George 3417
Reford, Robert W. 4660, 5514, 5712, 5713, 5714, 5782, 5817, 6522; (Review) 6868
Rehm, John 7549, 7591
Reid, Escott 94, 95, 1859, 4717, 5447, 5961, 5962, 5963, 5964, 5965, 6136, 6523, 8425, 8941; (Reviews) 460, 508
Reid, G.L. 4950
Reid, John 8645
Reid, Mado 8538
Reid, Patrick 976
Reid, R.L. 2222
Reid, *Sir* Robert 5260
Reid, Robert S. 2656, 3266
Reid, Timothy E. 7878
Reijnen, G.C.M. 4321
Reiskind, Jason 4322, 6148, 8731
Rejhon, George 8845
Rémillard, Gil 667
Rempe, George A. 8846
Rempel, Henry (Review) 8931
Rempel, R.A. 7479
Renault, L. 5331
Rendall, James A. 4583, 8272
Rendel, A.M. 1790
Renouf, Alan 4433, 5161, 5382
Renton, A. Wood 1884
Renwick, James A. 8040
Reny, Jean Pierre 5017
Reschenthaler, G.B. 4113
Reuber, Grant L. 6525, 7175, 7233, 7403, 7404, 8426, 8427
Reukema, Barbara 4114
Revel, G. (Review) 890
Reycraft, L.S. 3515, 3629, 3630, 3631
Reymond, Henri (Reviews) 4446, 5166
Reynolds, John B. (Review) 8786
Reynolds, John W. (Review) 8786
Rhee, Sang-Myon 3139, 3351
Rhinelander, John B. 6294
Rhomberg, Rudolf R. (Review) 7420
Rice, A. Clayton (Review) 248
Rice, William Gorham 2008, 2103
Rich, E.E. 6607
Rich, Harvey (Review) 8001

Richard, Ghislaine 4028, 4115
Richard, John 4661
Richard, John D. 7234
Richards, A.E. 8942
Richards, J. Howard 2169, 2573
Richards, Pauline N. (Review) 51
Richards, Peter Godfrey 1791
Richardson, B.T. 977, 4601, 7677
Richardson, B.V. 3854, 4116, 4117, 4118, 4119, 4120, 4121
Richardson, David Blair 2271
Richardson, Doug 7879
Richardson, J.L. (Reviews) 5709, 5979
Richardson, Jack E. 3706, 3707, 4066; (Review) 4166
Richer, A.-M. 8980
Richer, Léopold 978, 6717
Richmond, Anthony H. 1430
Rickard, Bruce 7678
Rickner, Gary J. 8957
Ricour, Pierre 6369
Riddell, Walter Alexander 157, 5212; (Review) 4626
Riddell, William Renwick 545, 546, 1163, 1321, 5245, 5261, 7023; (Review) 5259
Ridder, H. (Review) 1161
Rie, Robert 6370; (Review) 4665
Rieber, Roger A. 5018
Riesenfeld, Stefan A. (Review) 3319
Rigaldies, Francis 155, 246, 247, 383, 434, 2365, 3099, 3100, 3101, 3102, 3242, 3516; (Reviews) 1936, 2646, 8588
Riggs, Thomas 2182, 2366
Riley, Richard B. 859
Ringereide, Trygve 8596
Riordan, James Brian 8428
Rioux, Marcel 782
Ripoll, Roberto Puceiro 4190
Rippon, Clive L. 4074
Ristelhueber, René 1303
Ritchie, A.E. 1792, 8401
Ritchie, Charles 96, 97, 1860
Ritchie, E. (Review) 6634
Ritchie, Jean Harris 3708
Ritchie, Marguerite E. 4067, 7480
Ritchie, Ronald S. 5818, 5966, 5967, 7713, 8690, 8691; (Review) 8671
Ritchie, T. Kerr 6718
Rivkin, Arnold 8429
Rizos, E.J. 1793
Roach, E. Hugh 7661, 7981, 8631

Robbins, Charles E. 4002
Robbins, John E. 1066
Robert, Jean-Claude 783
Robert-Andino, Luis Fernando 3855
Roberts, Brian Birley 2574
Roberts, Bruce 4113
Roberts, Debra 42
Roberts, E.M. 3121
Roberts, James Alan 98
Roberts, John 8847
Roberts, R.J. (Review) 8480
Roberts, R. Jack 7982
Roberts, Sidney I. 8273, 8274
Robertson, Harold H. 6566, 6608
Robertson, J.R. 8275
Robertson, Matthew Joseph 8127
Robertson, Robert T. 8981
Robichaud, Hédard J. 3436
Robillard, Gaston (Review) 7250
Robinson, Chalfant 6958, 6959
Robinson, Edward Van Dyke 7024
Robinson, George S. 4323, 4324, 4325, 4326, 8894
Robinson, H. Lukin 6105, 8128
Robinson, J. Lewis 2537, 2575, 7235
Robinson, J. Michael 8129
Robinson, J.P. Perry 5715
Robinson, Kenneth Ernest 1114
Robinson, Marvin 4327, 4552
Robinson, Raymond M. 8848
Robinson, Richard D. 8029
Robinson, Thomas Russell 7405
Robinson, W.G. 1286
Robitaille, Georges 6609, 6610, 6611, 6612, 6613
Robitaille, Paul (Review) 4276
Roby, Yves 7880, 7881
Roche, A.G. 3289
Roche, Douglas J. 6526, 7176, 8430
Rock, Trevor St.E. 8431
Roddick, Paul M. 1431, 1432
Rodgers, Raymond S. 2009
Rodière, René (Reviews) 2646, 3637
Rodley, Nigel S. 7760
Rogers, A.W. 2067
Rogers, E.B. 6484
Rogers, George W. 2693
Rogers, Keith R. 6987
Rogers, Norman McL. 2010; (Review) 476
Rogstad, Barry Kent 8130

Rohmer, Richard Heath 2576
Rohn, Peter H. 1947
Rolfe, John 8131
Rolin, Henri 5597
Rolston, Susan J. 3103
Romanelli, Gustavo 3856
Ronhovde, Andreas G. 2579, 2657, 2694
Roohi, Reza 8780
Roome, A.I. 8132
Root, Elihu 5332, 5333
Roper, Albert 4029
Ropp, Theodore 5819; (Review) 6413
Rose, David 8720
Roseman, Daniel 43, 5019
Rosen, S. McKee 5872
Rosenau, James N. 4394
Rosenbaum, Naomi 1052, 4553
Rosenbloom, Donald J. (Review) 1479
Rosenbluth, Gideon 5716
Rosencranz, Armin 8849, 8850
Rosenne, Shabtai 5383
Rosenow, Beverly J. 3352
Rosenthal, Abraham Michael 4554
Rosevear, A. Beatty 422, 423, 3857, 4003, 4068, 4122, 4328; (Reviews) 68, 3833
Ross, Charles R. 448, 2375, 2433, 2447, 8781, 8782
Ross, David J. 979
Ross, Douglas A. 5555, 5873, 7092
Ross, Eleanor 2223
Ross, Michael 4656
Ross, Patricia Dorothy 6027
Ross, William Michael 3517, 3518
Rossignol, Gilles 5054
Rossignol, Michel 5874
Rothenberg, Stuart 6859, 7882
Rothney, Gordon O. 2332
Rotstein, Abraham 6527, 7406, 7942; (Review) 7248
Rotvand, Georges 5968
Roucounas, E. (Reviews) 3669, 8588
Rouméliotis, Panayotis 5020
Rouquet La Garrigue, Victor 5021, 5022
Rousseau, A. 1087, 1115
Rousseau, Charles 2658; (Reviews) 56, 234, 236, 241, 248, 321, 334, 454, 461, 709, 917, 924, 1927, 1936, 2381, 2646, 2709, 3119, 3259, 3485, 3833, 4164, 4277, 4291, 5370, 5691, 6195, 6533, 8996, 9038
Rousseau, Roger 8976

Roussin, Marcel 5116, 5117, 5118, 5820
Rowan, John Patrick August 5598
Rowan, Mary Josephine 6719
Rowat, Donald C. 784
Rowcliffe, Peter J. 8617
Rowell, F.N.A. 4030
Rowell, Newton W. 547, 980, 5384, 5385, 6720
Rowland, Wade 8783
Rowley, G.W. 2577
Rowthorn, Robert 7950
Roy, Jacques S. 7177
Roy, Jean-Denis 4085, 4123
Roy, Jean-Louis 785, 860
Roy, Patricia E. 1273, 1274; (Review) 1234
Roy, Raoul 6893
Roy, Richard 668
Royal, Joseph 6960
Rozalska, Barbara Maria 8851
Rubinoff, Arthur G. (Review) 94
Rudd, F.A. 8732
Ruddick, Valley 3194
Ruderman, Peter 8895
Rugman, Alan M. 7883, 7884, 7983, 8042; (Reviews) 7329, 7429
Russell, Benjamin 548
Russell, Bertrand 5607
Russell, Peter H. (Review) 613
Russell, Ruth B. 4555, 4556
Rutan, Gerard F. 861, 862
Rutenberg, David P. 7984
Rutledge, Joseph Lister 6614
Rutter, Michael F. (Reviews) 56, 2646
Ryan, Edward F. 3608
Ryan, H.R.S. 1322, 1662
Ryan, Michael H. 1916, 5023
Ryan, Selwyn D. 6125
Ryan, Stuart 6028
Ryan, William F. 2781
Ryback, P. 110

Saba, George C. 7679
Saba, John 669
Saba, John E. 3858, 4069
Sabia, M.J. 5515
Sabine, Catharine Mary 6988
Sabourin, Louis 670, 786, 787, 863, 864, 865, 1015, 1016, 1663, 4395, 6371, 6528, 6529, 7178, 7179, 8432, 8433, 8569, 8982

Sabourin-Hébert, Louise 7644, 7645
Saddy, Fehmy 7180
Safarian, Albert E. 7885, 7985, 7986, 8043, 8044, 8045, 8046, 8047, 8048
Sagar, David 8597, 8598
Sagaseta de Ilúrdoz, Miguel Sáenz (Review) 3833
Sage, Walter N. 2493, 2517, 6752; (Review) 2485
Saint-Germain, Maurice 8080
Saint-Germain, Yves (Review) 6966
Saint-Jévin, P. 8826
Saint-Lager, Olivier de 4329
Saint-Louis, Michel A. 6126, 6127
Sajous, Emmanuel 7181
Saleh, Saleh Tewfik 4330
Saleh, Samir 3859
Salim, Ziad 6372
Saljooqi, Hamid S. 3860
Salloum, Gary Michael 7714
Salmon, Mark Stephen 6721
Sam, Kenneth P. 3448
Samarrai, Alauddin 6373
Samek, Robert A. 1664
Samore, William (Review) 8791
Sampaio de Lacerda, J.C. 3861, 4766
Sampat-Mehta, Ramdeo 1122, 1275, 1434
Samson, Jean-K. (Reviews) 2331, 2709
Samuelli, Antoine Louis 4331
Samuels, Joseph W. 139, 1616, 1665, 5425, 6106, 8746, 8747, 8748, 8749, 8750, 8881, 8882, 8883, 8958; (Reviews) 236, 253, 1567, 1970, 2049, 3669, 4166
Sand, Peter H. 3674, 3675, 3862, 3863, 3864
Sandell, Harold 4124
Sanders, P. (Review) 9038
Sandwell, B.K. 549, 671, 1435, 1436, 1666, 2011, 2863, 2864, 2865, 4875, 5213, 6137, 8133, 8499, 8500, 8889; (Reviews) 5202, 6436
Sanger, Clyde 100, 5717, 8360, 8434, 8784; (Review) 8349
Sanguin, André Louis 3148
Sanon, Pierre J. 1667
Sanseroni, L. Martínez (Review) 9038
Santiago, Zeno Marques 5119
Sarbadhikari, Pradip 348
Sargant, E.B. 1164
Sarkar, Asit K. 7772
Sarna, A.J. 7544

Sastry, K.R.R. 2045
Sater, John E. 2578, 2579
Sattler, James F. 5718
Saunders, Ronald S. 7545
Saunders, S.A. 6961, 6962; (Review) 3403
Sautier, Jérôme 3519, 4718
Sauveplanne, J.G. (Review) 4164
Savard, Pierre 1017, 1861, 1885
Savard, Roger 8057
Savary, Alan 1018
Savelle, Max 2198, 2255, 6615, 6616; (Review) 2194
Savraides, George B. 8785
Sawicki, Manuela Lila 5179
Sawyer, John A. (Review) 7488
Sayre, Paul 4585
Saywell, John Tupper 5448
Scace, Arthur R.A. 7886, 7887, 8276
Scafuri, Allison L. (Review) 4291
Scammell, E.H. 6925
Scammell, W.M. 4719, 7236, 8134; (Review) 8125
Scanteie, Eugene 5024, 7237
Scarman, Leslie George 1668
Schachter, Oscar 4332, 7117
Schafer, David Paul 8983
Schafer, Joseph 2494
Schaffer, Toby Macy 9030
Schanz, John J., Jr. 8672
Scheinman, Lawrence 5783
Schellenberger, Milton Arthur 5025
Schentag, T.R. 5875
Scheuner, Ulrich (Review) 885
Schick, F.B. 6180
Schioler, John Pontoppidan 7025
Schlegel, John P. 672, 7093, 7094; (Reviews) 1806, 6481, 6556
Schlochauer, Hans-Jürgen (Reviews) 240, 241, 242, 243, 290, 4291
Schmeiser, Douglas A. (Review) 1567
Schmitthoff, Clive M. 5026, 5027, 7238
Schnee, Jerome E. 4333
Schneider, Fred D. 6530
Schneider, Jan 8786
Schopen, Lynn 4662
Schram, Douglas Charles 7407
Schroeder-Gudehus, Brigitte 8632, 8633, 8634, 8984, 8985
Schultz, John A. 6722
Schuster, Leslie 6860
Schwartz, Bryan 4334

Schwartz, Irwin 7832
Schwartz, Mildred A. 1165
Schwartz, Warren F. 7715
Schwebel, Stephen M. (Review) 5167
Schwenk, Walter 4086, 4141, 6295
Scobie, W.E. (Reviews) 3028, 3029, 3035
Scorrar, Douglas A. 7408
Scott, Anthony D. 2378, 3353, 8774, 8775, 8809; (Review) 2948
Scott, Duncan C. 1123
Scott, Francis R. 491, 653, 981, 982, 2104, 4558, 5180, 6531, 6532, 6723, 6724, 8436; (Reviews) 54, 1865, 6871
Scott, H.D. 8135
Scott, Jack 8919
Scott, James Brown 983, 2659, 5333, 5334
Scott, Janet V. 203, 1166, 1437
Scott, Robert Day 2234
Seastone, D.A. (Review) 8671
Sébilleau, Pierre 6533
Sedweek, T.M. 2880
Seed, Nicholas J.S. 8277
Séguin-Dulude, Louise 7481
Seidel, Heinz-Dieter 6191
Seidl-Hohenveldern, Ignaz (Reviews) 3259, 4665
Seife, Asfaw 8890
Seiler, Daniel Louis 5028, 5029
Sékaly, Raymond R. 7239
Selak, Charles B. 3354
Seldon, Zena Aronoff 3865
Sellen, Robert W. 5426
Semple, R. Keith 7408
Senécal, Nicole 2012
Senkiko-Kasara, Pauline 4004
Séranne, Catherine 5065
Serbyn, Rowan 610
Seth, Sanjiv 7282
Sewell, James P. 4434, 4811
Sewell, W.R. Derrick 2959
Sexton, Michael 7888
Seymour-Ure, Colin 5030
Shaffer, Edward H. (Review) 7960
Shapiro, Daniel M. 7889
Shapiro, Samuel 5335
Sharbaugh, H. Robert 8686
Sharma, Surya P. (Review) 334
Sharp, John M. 6296
Sharp, Mitchell 349, 350, 1794, 1862, 5784
Shatzky, Boris 984
Shaw, J.R. 7482

Shaw, Timothy M. 5146, 5147, 6385, 7182, 7183, 7184
Shaw, William F. 788
Shdanov, N. 6140
Shea, Albert A. 6015; (Review) 4626
Shearer, I.A. (Review) 1479
Shearer, Ronald A. 7340, 7400, 7890, 8136; (Reviews) 7426, 8084
Shearman, Hugh 985
Shedivy, James H. 8213
Sheffy, Menachem 4767
Shefrin, Frank 4720
Sheikh, Ahmed 5556
Shenstone, Michael 4877
Shepardson, Whitney Hart 6786
Shepherd, Sidney A. 8137, 8138, 8139, 8140, 8141, 8142, 8143
Sherfield, Roger Mellor Makins 99
Sheridan, Paul Robert 5031
Sheridan, Ronald T. 5032
Sherk, Frank 8049
Sherman, H. Arnold 8228, 8233
Sherman, Michael E. 5719, 5785, 5786, 5787
Sherrin, Jeffrey J. 2695, 3520
Shibata, Hirofumi 7215, 7253, 7546, 8278
Shields, Robert A. 550, 1886, 1948, 2120, 2121, 7409, 8501; (Review) 7352
Shiels, Sir Drummond 986
Shilling, Nancy Adams 5156
Shinn, Ridgway Foulks 987
Shippee, Lester Burrell 2495, 6617, 6861
Short, David E. 1669
Short, R. Alan 8225, 8226, 8279, 8280, 8281, 8294
Shortt, Adam 2013, 5821, 6534, 6725, 6963
Shotwell, James Thomson 6862, 6863
Showell, Frank 6989
Shumate, Roger Vernon 4481
Sichilongo, Mengo D.F. 5247
Siddiqui, Norma 4396
Siegel, Arthur (Review) 784
Siegfried, André 551
Sien, Chia Lin (Review) 3526
Siewert, Clark C. (Review) 303
Sigler, John H. 6878; (Review) 5011
Sik, Ko Swan (Review) 248
Silcox, Claris Edwin 1088
Silver, Jan 5181
Silverburg, Sanford R. 6070

Silverstein, Harvey B. 3577, 3578, 4721, 8692
Simeon, Richard 789, 790
Simmonds, K.R. 2148, 7117; (Reviews) 56, 234, 243, 303
Simmonds, Robert H. 1901
Simon, H. Paul 4335, 5720, 5822
Simon, Pierre A. 4663
Simoneau, Pierre 673
Simoni, Arnold 4435
Simpson, James M. 6071, 6238; (Review) 6195
Simpson, Robert Vernon 4616
Sims, W.A. 7299
Simsarian, James 2782
Sinclair, Adelaide 4722
Sinclair, Clayton 2867
Sinclair, Sol 7646, 7680
Singal, Ramesh 4226
Singer, Howard Lewis 791
Singer, J. David 4397, 4436, 4442, 5721
Singer, Norman J. (Review) 290
Singh, Indu B. 8600
Singh, L.P. (Reviews) 6410, 7940
Sinha, S. Prakash 435, 578, 1492, 1493, 1670, 6157
Siotis, Jean 5033
Sirag-Eldin, Yahya 4070
Sissons, C.B. 1276
Skapinker, Joel 7892
Skelton, O.D. 2122, 5608, 6726, 7027, 7028, 7029, 7547
Skidmore, Darrel R. 6864
Skilling, H. Gordon 1671, 1672, 1863, 1864, 1865, 1866, 1867, 5823; (Reviews) 885, 1834
Skinner, Gerald R. 5722, 5723
Slack, Michael 5698
Slater, David W. 7240, 7253, 7410, 7411, 8144, 8145, 8146
Slater, Jerome 5120
Slattery, Brian 2199
Slayton, Philip 7283, 7483, 7484
Sleight, Reuben Benjamin 2825
Sletmo, Gunnar K. 3579
Slimman, Donald J. 3104
Sloane, John H. 5034
Slonim, S. 1089
Slosar, Stanislas 251, 374, 424, 1167, 2038, 2139, 5780, 7241, 7284, 7412; (Reviews) 248, 253, 709
Sloup, George Paul 4336
Smart, I.M.H. 6236
Smart, Ian 8693
Smart, Reginald G. 8896
Smedresman, Peter S. 2448
Smejda, Lucius 8282
Smiley, Donald V. 674, 792, 1673; (Reviews) 682, 715, 6404
Smirnoff, Michel (Review) 3259
Smith, A.J.R. 7510
Smith, Allan (Review) 6850
Smith, Arnold 100, 988, 989, 1795, 6727
Smith, Arthur J.R. 7338, 7413
Smith, Brian D. 2580, 2660
Smith, David (Review) 874
Smith, David E. 1090, 1917, 5121
Smith, Denis 743; (Reviews) 674, 675, 6868
Smith, Ernest H. 1909, 5162, 8283
Smith, Gaddis G. 45, 2318, 5427, 6535; (Review) 84
Smith, Goldwin 2014
Smith, Goldwin A. 2272, 2518, 6990, 6991, 6992
Smith, Gordon S. 46
Smith, Gordon W. 2661, 2662, 2663, 2664, 6536
Smith, Herbert A. 492, 553, 2015, 2132, 2783, 2784, 2868, 6649; (Review) 6654
Smith, I. Norman 4559, 4602; (Review) 2559
Smith, J.M. 7893
Smith, James 8869
Smith, James J. 4087, 4088
Smith, Jean Edward 1025, 1026
Smith, Joe Patterson 2519; (Review) 7005
Smith, John Graham 7940
Smith, Justin Harvey 6894
Smith, Lancelot J. 8284
Smith, Lawrence B. 6954
Smith, Lincoln 8741
Smith, R.H. 2732
Smith, Rufus Z. 1838
Smith, Sidney A. 3580
Smith, Sydney E. 5969
Smith, T. Bradbrooke 8852
Smith, Virginia 8341
Smith, William 2333, 8613
Smith, William George 1439

Smith, William H. 2413
Smithers, LeRoy D. 7485
Smithers, *Sir* Peter 4878
Smouts, Marie-Claire 4560
Smythe, Dallas W. 8579
Smythe, Elizabeth 6865; (Review) 7960
Snow, Rodney A. 3167
Sobie, Merril 7987
Sözer, Bülent 4005
Sokol, John F. 8943
Sokolov, H. 6181
Sokolsky, Joel J. 8528
Soldatos, Panayotis 793, 4437, 5035, 5036, 5054; (Reviews) 800, 1685, 4869, 6450
Solem, Erik 2581
Soloveytchik, George 4879
Soraghan, Joseph R. 4337
Sosin, Jack (Review) 6902
Sousa Freitas, Jorge de 3675
Soward, Frederic H. 54, 101, 653, 991, 1116, 1796, 2496, 4482, 4483, 4484, 4664, 4665, 5122, 6374, 6537, 6658, 6728, 6729; (Reviews) 150, 1729, 1817, 1865, 3260, 4518, 4825, 5212, 6333, 6397, 6466, 6538, 6654
Spaak, Paul-Henri 5970
Sparkes, Verone 8986
Speaight, Robert 102
Spence, James M. 7762, 7894, 8288
Spencer, Barbara J. 7445
Spencer, John 1206
Spencer, Robert 2449; (Review) 98
Spencer, Robert A. 54, 1027, 5971
Spicer, Keith 1797, 8437, 8438, 8439, 8440
Spicer, W. Wylie 3449, 3581
Spiliakos, Panos C. (Review) 4287
Spitzer, Tadeusz B. 4561
Spowart, Ann 1440
Spragins, Robert Franklin 7414
Spraight, J.M. 5599
Springer, Allen L. (Review) 8786
Sprokkreeff, Hans Pieter 3866
Sprudzs, Adolf (Review) 51
Spry, Graham 5557, 7681, 7682
Spurgeon, David 8787
Srebrnik, Henry Felix 8066
St.-Aubin, Michel 866
St. Charles, D.P. 7156, 7157
St. John, Peter 6237
St. Laurent, Louis S. 4586
St. Laurent, Renault 351

St. Pierre, Paul 2665
Stacey, Charles P. 148, 2170, 2497, 5876, 5877, 6017, 6036, 6538, 6539, 6540, 6926; (Reviews) 150, 6577, 6595, 6617, 6743, 6767, 6827, 6861, 6928
Staines, David (Review) 1289
Stairs, Denis 103, 1770, 4562, 5459, 5460, 5461, 6541, 6542, 6543, 6544; (Reviews) 90, 4488, 5979, 6452, 6453, 6749, 6782, 8400
Stakes, Wilbur Sylvester, Jr. 8502
Stambrook, F. 1869
Stanek, O. (Review) 7050
Stanfield, R.L. 6134
Stanford, Gerald B. 3149
Stanford, Joseph S. 392, 1950, 1951, 7285, 7763, 7988, 8733
Stanley, George F.G. 2374, 5462, 6895 (Review) 6591
Stanton, Stephen B. 992, 5336, 5337
Stanwood, Edward 7030, 7548
Star, Spencer 1441; (Review) 1371
Starnes, John 867; (Reviews) 79, 1854
Stead, Gordon W. 2582
Stead, Robert J.C. 2877
Stedman, Charles 7592
Steele, J.A. 5788
Steeves, Jeffrey S. 7185
Stefansson, Vilhjalmur 8529
Stegemann, Klaus 7415
Steiger, A.G. (Review) 5428
Stein, Michael (Reviews) 682, 722, 753
Stein, Murray 2379
Stein, Robert E. 8825
Steinberg, David J. 7647
Steiner, Barry 8662
Steiner, Zara 1798
Stephens, D.M. 2450
Stephens, George Washington 2878
Stepler, D.H. (Review) 6453
Sterling, D.B. 8503
Stevens, Douglas F. 8601
Stevenson, Garth 675, 1799, 4666, 6450, 6866, 7895; (Review) 674
Stevenson, John A. 556, 6730, 6731
Stevenson, John R. 9023
Stewart, Alice R. (Reviews) 6976, 7097
Stewart, Andrew 8944
Stewart, Beverley Ann 5972
Stewart, Bryce Morrison 2105
Stewart, Herbert L. 2992

Stewart, Larry R. 7416, 7731, 7989, 8734, 8735
Stewart, Miller 7732
Stewart, Patrick Grattan 5878
Stewart, Robert B. 1952, 2016, 2017, 2018, 2106, 2107, 2108
Stewart, Robert William 3278
Stigger, Philip 1870
Stikeman, Harry Heward 7896, 7897
Stingelin, Peter 5037
Stinson, Robert David 5038
Stitt, Hubert J. 8289
Stoebner, André W. 4339
Stoffaes, Christian 8636
Stoler, Andrew L. 6867, 8602
Stone, A.J. 3521, 3522, 3582
Stone, Julius (Review) 271
Stone, William Duncan 7990
Stonehouse, Robert C. 203, 204, 1166, 1437, 1494
Storrs, A.H.G. 2583
Story, Donald C. 4485, 4486, 5039; (Reviews) 54, 82, 4488, 6450, 7075
Stouffer, Allen P. 6975
Stow, William Lewis 8290
Strange, Susan 8147
Straus, Richard 2136
Strebel, Helmut (Reviews) 234, 241
Streeten, Paul 6732
Stripinis, Daniel 1674
Strome, W. Murray 4340
Strong, Maurice F. 352, 353, 8373
Stubbs, Richard (Review) 7162
Stuchen, Philip 1091, 1305, 1306; (Reviews) 100, 8400
Stucker, M.I. 8296
Studnicki-Gizbert, K.W. (Review) 8523
Sturmthal, Adolf 4796
Stursberg, Peter 676, 6868
Stuyt, Alexander Marie (Review) 334
Stykolt, Stefan 7458
Styles, R.G.P. 7417
Suaiko, Elia 4657
Suffling, Roger (Review) 2550
Sugarman, Robert J. 2451
Sugimoto, Howard Hiroshi 1442
Sukonthapan, Pisawat 4006
Sullivan, Lawrence R. 1045
Sultan, Ralph G.M. 7898
Sulte, Benjamin 6618, 6619, 6620, 6621
Sumichrast, Frederick Caesar de 2019
Sunahara, Ann Gomer 1277, 1278
Sundberg, Jacob 3867
Sunil, K.A. 7899
Suratgar, David (Review) 1182
Surette, Ralph 3355
Surrey, Stanley S. 8291
Susman, A.M. 7991
Sussman, Edmond 4880
Sussman, Gennifer 2879
Sutherland, R.J. 5879; (Reviews) 5834, 6591
Sutton, Gary 2696, 3523
Sutton, Kenneth C. 7243
Suy, Erik 354
Svarlien, Oscar 2666
Svoboda, Charles Vincent 5163, 8441
Swain, Robert Eckles 5280
Swainson, Neil A. 2960, 2961; (Review) 8644
Swan, George S. 2367, 3243, 3244, 3245, 3246
Swan, John Harold 3868
Swan, Judith 8920
Swann, F. Richard (Review) 1371
Swanson, Roger Frank 158, 868, 869, 1871, 1887, 5880, 5881, 5882, 5883, 6551, 6869, 6870; (Reviews) 5854, 5921
Swartz, Willis G. 7031
Sweeney, Joseph 493
Swets, Gina L. 8844
Swettenham, John A. 5428; (Review) 7050
Swezey, Charles F. 2716
Swiger, Ernest Cullimore, Jr. 7418
Swinton, Katherine 8603
Swirsky, Benjamin 8296
Switzer, Clayton M. 8945
Switzer, Eric B. 8292, 8293
Swoboda, Alexander K. 7196
Sykes, Philip 8694
Sylvain, Ivan J. 394
Sylvester, Christine 8023
Sylvestre, Guy 1872
Symmons, C.R. 3168
Szablowski, G.J. 2020
Szabó, Denis 6212, 6213
Szabó, Joseph (Review) 613
Szasz, Paul C. 5779; (Review) 3506
Szawlowski, Richard 1675, 4723, 5066

Tabor, Hans 4563
Tackaberry, R.B. 5558, 5559

Tadros, Michel-Charles 4617
Taft, William H. 4487, 7032
Tager, Thomas Edward 6044
Taillon, Jean (Review) 8047
Tait, W.McD. 2368
Takach, George Steven 6545
Tallamy, Bertram Dailey 2880
Tallin, G.P.R. (Review) 56
Tallman, Ronald D. 2520, 3419, 6964
Talmadge, Marian 5884
Tamaki, George T. 1168, 1169, 1170, 1171
Tamm, John R. 3709, 4341
Tammelo, Ilmar 355
Tancelin, Maurice (Reviews) 52, 3637, 4277
Tang, Chin-Shih 4342, 4343; (Reviews) 52, 4272, 4287, 4288
Tanghe, Raymond 2881, 6546
Tanguay, Guy 2173
Tanguay, J.F. 4667, 4668
Tanner, Susan 172, 1530
Tansill, Charles Callan 3437, 6871, 6965
Tapia Salinas, L. 5078
Tardu, Maxime 1129, 1676
Tarnopolsky, Walter S. 1677, 1678, 1679, 1680, 1681, 1682, 1683, 1684
Tarnovecky, Joseph 2463
Tarr, E.J. 6547
Tarr, R.H. 8148
Taubenfeld, Howard J. (Reviews) 68, 6286
Taussig, F.W. 7033
Tavernier, Paul (Review) 8996
Taylor, A.J.P. 1053
Taylor, Alastair M. 4438, 4669, 5560, 6548, 8788
Taylor, Andrew 2584
Taylor, Charles 6549
Taylor, Claude 3869
Taylor, George 7419
Taylor, Hannis 5263
Taylor, J.G. 8149
Taylor, James P. (Review) 9015
Taylor, K.W. 8301
Taylor, Kenneth 1901, 1910
Taylor, Kenneth W. 5973
Taylor, Martin R. 677
Taylor, Paul 5040
Taylor, Phillip 5041, 5042
Tearney, Thomas W. 2882
Teclaff, Ludwik A. (Review) 3506
Teilhac, Ernest 5724

Tellier, Luc-Normand 870; (Review) 4370
Teng, Chuo-Ying 7244
Tennyson, Brian 7096; (Reviews) 6930, 7519
Terry, John Charles 5824
Tetley, William 3583, 3584, 3585, 3609, 3610, 3611, 3612, 3632, 3633, 3634, 3635, 3636, 3637, 3638, 3639, 3640, 3641, 3642, 3657, 3658, 7876, 7877, 7891, 7900
Tezapsidis, Leonidas 5043
Thaher, Abu Kasim 4075
Thakur, Ramesh C. 5561, 5562, 6550
Thanos, Panagiotis G. 3613
Thapa, Dhruba Bar Singh 5429
Thatcher, Max B. 678
Théberge, Richard 8504
Theuman, Richard 598
Thibault, Claude J. 47
Thibodeau, Marc Arthur 794
Thirsk, Wayne R. (Review) 8414
Thom, Adam 2498
Thom, Stuart D. 8302
Thomas, Brinley (Review) 1444
Thomas, David Martin 5885
Thomas, Eileen Mitchell 5248, 8810
Thomas, Lewis H. (Review) 6807
Thomka-Gazdik, Julian G. 3870, 3871, 3872, 3873, 4007, 4008
Thompson, Andrew R. 2697, 3197, 7716, 8695, 8870
Thompson, Bram 557, 558, 3123
Thompson, Dale Edward 4724
Thompson, Dennis (Review) 613
Thompson, Dwayne Thomas 2883
Thompson, Frederic Fraser 3420, 3421
Thompson, G. (Review) 4277
Thompson, Ralph 2884
Thompson, Robert W. 5974, 7420; (Review) 7460
Thomson, Dale C. 104, 6551
Thomson, Duncan Duane 7593
Thomson, Georges 4344; (Review) 4288
Thomson, James S. 5600
Thomson, Jennifer 48, 3105
Thomson, Lesslie R. 2885, 2886, 2887
Thomson, Richard M. 8150
Thomson, Suteera 8442
Thordarson, Bruce 105, 6552; (Reviews) 90, 91, 6426
Thorne, E.S. 4071

Thornton, A.P. 106, 1117, 1118; (Review) 7097
Thorson, Joseph T. 993, 5195, 5196
Thouez, Jean-Pierre (Review) 6806
Tien-Hsi, Cheng (Review) 1199
Tienhaara, N. 1348
Tikku, Kaushal 8196, 8303
Tillinghast, David R. 8229, 8304
Tillman, Seth P. (Review) 6363
Timbers, William H. 1495
Timbrell, David Y. 8199, 8203, 8208, 8230
Timlin, Mabel F. 1443, 1444, 1445
Tindigarukayo, Jimmy Kazaara 7186
Titus, Norman Frederick 2825
Tobolewski, Aleksander 3874, 4009, 4010, 4011, 4768; (Review) 3831
Todd, Eric C.E. 8067
Toepper, Anton 3875
Tolle, Paulo Ernesto 4142
Tomalin, Beth 4670
Tomasky, Eugene Michael 7764
Tomkinson, Grace 4725
Tomlin, Brian W. 394, 4671, 6481, 6553, 6788, 6878, 7114; (Reviews) 4811, 6556
Tomlinson, J.W.C. 3356, 3357
Tompkins, Stuart R. 2319
Tomsa, Branko 5044, 7245
Tomson, Edgar (Review) 4276
Toogood, J.D. 6375, 6376
Torobin, A.J. 8607
Torrelli, Maurice 871, 1685, 2088, 5045, 5046, 5047, 5048, 5049, 5050, 5051, 5052, 8443
Tosell, W.E. 8946
Touré, Amadou 5148
Touret, Bernard 1279
Touscoz, Jean 1019, 4882; (Reviews) 326, 3119, 5652
Tovias, Alfred 7287
Towell, Freeman 8987
Towers, G.F. 8151, 8152
Townsend, David A. (Review) 1637
Toxey, Walter W. 1172, 1446
Toynbee, Arnold Joseph 6733
Toyoda, Toshiyuki 5643
Traavik, Kim (Review) 2646
Trakman, Leon E. 7246
Traquair, Ramsay 5975
Travis, Ralph 3169
Travis, Samuel L. 4012
Trecroce, Riccardo 5667, 8573

Treddenick, John M. 795; (Review) 8643
Tremblay, André 796
Tremblay, Arthur 679
Tremblay, Guy 1686
Tremblay, Marc-Adélard 797
Tremblay, Paul 1687, 5516
Tremblay, Rodrigue 798, 5149, 7421, 7901
Trembley, William A. 5123
Tremeear, W.J. 3659
Trend, Burke (Review) 79
Triantis, Stephen G. 5053, 7765, 8444
Trinko, Curtis V. 3184
Tripet, André 1130
Tritt, Robert Walter 4439
Troncoso, Francisco M. 3876, 4072
Troop, William Hamilton 6734, 6735
Troper, Harold M. 1284, 1447
Trotman, Gene Thornton Torron 5124
Trotman, J.H. 5976
Trotter, Reginald G. 54, 680, 994, 995, 996, 2171, 4440, 5125, 5126, 6138, 6554; (Reviews) 5096, 6484, 6578, 6617, 6861, 6863, 6899, 6952, 7005
Trudeau, André 619
Trudeau, Pierre Elliott 681, 682, 1688, 6555, 6736
Trudeau-Bérard, Nicole 2667
Trudel, Marcel 1323, 6622, 6623, 6624, 6896, 6897, 6898
Trudel, Pierre 6966
Trueman, H.L. 8947
Trumpener, Ulrich (Review) 4448
Tryon, James L. (Review) 6720
Tsai, Shaopan 3877, 4013
Tschirgi, Robert Daniel 1092
Tsotsou, Georgia (Review) 5167
Tsoutsos, Athos G. (Review) 5977
Tucker, Albert Victor 2888
Tucker, Michael J. 5726, 5727, 6556
Tuggle, Bernie M. 8305
Tumlir, Jan 7247
Tunc, André (Reviews) 8211, 9015
Tunem, Alfred 2273
Tupper, Charles Hibbert 559, 1119, 2022
Tupper, Stanley R. 6872
Turack, Daniel C. 1214, 1215, 1216, 1217, 1218, 1219, 1220, 1221, 1222, 1223, 1224, 1225, 1226, 1227, 1228, 1229, 1230, 1231, 1232, 1233, 5164; (Reviews) 236, 248
Turcat, André 4031

Turcotte, Edmond 683, 4812
Turewich, Larry Andrew 699
Turi, Giuseppe 4672
Turk, Sidney 8153
Turlington, Edgar (Review) 271
Turmann, Max 8154
Turnbull, Robert M. 8230
Turner, Allan R. 2369
Turner, Arthur C. 5977
Turner, H.K. (Review) 8464
Turner, John H.F. 1918
Turner, Robert K. 6873
Turner, Wesley Barry 1804
Turnquest, Harcourt Lowell 3270
Turp, Daniel 155
Twiss, *Sir* Travers 2499
Tynan, Thomas M. 2585, 2668

Udokang, Okon 2048, 2049, 2050, 2051
Ullman, Richard H. (Review) 5428
Underhay, F.C. 6737
Underhill, Frank H. 997, 6377, 7422; (Reviews) 964, 1361, 6466, 6533
Updyke, Frank Arthur 6912
Upton, L.F.S. 1280
Urbano, Henrique (Review) 6349
Uren, Philip E. 7248
Urquhart, M.C. 7249
Usher, Abbott Payson (Review) 3392
Usher, D. 799
Utton, Albert E. 2669, 2698, 2965, 3524; (Reviews) 1927, 2948, 3319

Vachon, G.K. 5100, 5728
Vagts, Detlev (Review) 303
Vaillancourt, Benoit 1911
Vaillancourt, Émile 6557
Valaskakis, Kimon 800, 801, 5052, 5055; (Reviews) 8415, 8523
Valencia, Mark J. 3576
Valentine, D.G. (Review) 241
Valero, Juan J. 1691, 1692
Valiquette, André 1067
Valladão, Haroldo 6298, 6299, 8604
Vallat, Frank A. 1173, 2069
Vallejo Sàenz, Arturo 4032
Valpy, Dumaresq Richardson 5609
Van Allen, L.C. 2579
Van Allen, W.H. 2910
Van Dam, André 7187

Vanderelst, Wilfrid 652
Van der Esch, Bastiaan 684
Vander Zwaag, David L. 3362
Vanek, D.C. 384, 426
Van Lier, Irene H. 8855, 8856
Van Praagh, David 4674
Van Wijk, Alfons Pieter 5056
Variawa, Mohamed 1094
Varty, David L. 4089, 4125
Vary, Michel Jacques 4126
Vasseur, Pierre 5197
Vassil, Patricia Louise (Review) 3506
Vaugeois, Denis 872
Veatch, Richard 4488; (Reviews) 4448, 5167, 5965, 6426, 6743
Vechsler, Michael J. 1904, 5779
Velay, Clément C. 4883
Vellas, Pierre 3878, 8354
Vencatassin, J.L. 4346
Verchères, Bruce 8306, 8307
Verdon, Christiane 4729, 8605
Vereshchetin, V.S. 4347, 4348, 4349, 4350
Verhoeven, Joe (Review) 2331
Verma, Dhirendra P. 4587
Verplaetse, Juliaan G. (Review) 4164
Verploeg, Elias Alexander G. 3879
Verreau, Hospice 2200, 2201
Vertinsky, I. 3357
Vexler, Robert Irwin 2320
Vézina, François 6738
Vicas, Alexander G. 4351, 4352, 8606
Videla Escalada, Federico 3880
Vierdag, Egbert W. (Review) 290
Vignes, Daniel 2911
Villamin, Maria Luisa 6300
Villeneuve, Jacques G. de 4014
Vince, Donald M.A.R. 2126
Vincent, Jack E. 4675
Vincke, Christian 252, 1693, 2149, 7288
Viner, Jacob 4441, 7250, 8155
Vinette, André 8447
Visscher, Paul de 6238
Vlasic, Ivan A. 3256, 3881, 3882, 4166, 4291, 4292, 4353, 4354, 4355, 4356, 4357, 4358, 4359, 5729, 6226, 6265, 8569; (Reviews) 3701, 3833, 4271
Voaden, Herman 4813
Vogel, Robert 49
Voghel, Michel C. 7767
Voisset, Michèle (Review) 6286

Volcker, Paul A. 8156
Volpe, John 7620
Von Riekhoff, Harald 5978, 5979, 6558, 6788, 6878; (Review) 6494
Vo Van, Dat 7766

Waart, P.J.I.M. de (Review) 303
Waddington, George Edwin 5730
Wade, E.C.S. (Review) 500
Wade, F.C. 2321
Wade, Mason 802, 6879; (Review) 54
Wagacha, Bernard Mbui 7289
Wagenberg, Ronald Harvey 599; (Review) 54
Wager-Smith, Elizabeth 2521
Wagner, Helmut 4932
Wagner, J. Richard (Review) 6450
Wagner, James Richard 6880
Wahn, I.G. 7904, 8209
Waite, G. Graham 2453
Waite, P.B. (Reviews) 713, 6538, 6976
Waite, Peter (Review) 2170
Walker, Albert Henry 7043
Walker, B.A. 8607
Walker, Donald E. 838, 839
Walker, Eric Anderson 6739
Walker, John R. 6559
Walker, R.H.E. 7905
Walker, Robert Brian James 5182
Wall, J.C. 9040
Wall, Rachel F. (Review) 157
Wallace, Edward J. 2500
Wallace, Elisabeth 5131, 5132; (Reviews) 874, 928, 1000
Wallace, Malcolm W. 8988
Wallace, Michael D. 4397, 4436, 4442, 5997
Wallace, R.C. 4814
Wallerstein, Immanuel Maurice 7188
Walmsley, Norma Eleanor 1311
Walmsley, Percival B. 4489
Walsh, David Francis 873
Walsh, Kevin B. 4360
Walsh, Reginald Francis George 7423
Walton, F.P. 1174
Wanczycki, Jan K. 2109
Wang, Erik B. 392, 3170, 4361, 5249, 5264, 5886; (Review) 2605
Warbrick, Colin 3450
Warburg, J.P. 1028
Ward, David A. 8231, 8308

Ward, Donald William S. 4076, 6045
Ward, Les 3643, 3644
Ward, Norman (Review) 681
Ward, William Peter 1281, 1282, 1283
Wardroper, Kenneth 2738
Ware, Edith E. (Review) 8462
Ware, Norman Joseph 8912
Warley, Thorald Keith 7684
Warner, Donald F. 2522, 2523, 2524
Warner, Fayette S. 2912
Warner, Malcolm 8050
Warnock, John W. 427, 5854, 5887, 5888, 5921; (Review) 5716
Warren, Gabriel I. 1618, 6301, 8534, 8608
Warren, J.H. 7648, 8335
Warren, Jake 4884
Warren, Reginald A. 5980
Warwick, Donald P. 6378
Washburn, Israel 2224
Wassenbergh, H.A. 3676, 3883, 3884, 3885, 4362; (Reviews) 3777, 3962
Waterfiled, Donald Cresswell 2967
Waters, Maurice 4676
Waters, W.G. (Review) 7274
Watkins, Ernest 2968
Watkins, Melville H. 7802, 7824, 7865; (Review) 84
Watson, Lorna 5731
Watt, D.C. (Review) 6307
Watt, Donald C. (Review) 3506
Watt, Lewis 5601
Watts, C.S. 6560
Watts, Floyd Elden 6740
Watts, Ronald L. 803, 998
Waugh, W.T. 6741; (Reviews) 927, 6634
Waultrin, René 2670
Waverman, Leonard 7717, 7718, 8671
Wearing, John Paul 8448
Wearing, Joseph (Review) 8024
Weatherbe, R.L. 2225
Webb, Gary J. 8295
Weber, Ludwig 1694, 3886, 3887, 3888, 3889, 3890, 3891, 3892, 3893, 3894, 3895, 3896, 4033; (Reviews) 31, 4289
Webley, Simon 7957
Webster, A. 6742
Webster, Daniel 2209
Wedley, William C. (Review) 8014
Weekes, J.W. 7290
Weeks, E.P. 7424
Weeks, James K. 7906

Weeks, Kathleen 2373
Wehringer, Cameron K. (Review) 4291
Weihs, Frederick H. 7425
Weiler, Paul C. 1695
Weinfeld, Abraham Chaim 2110
Weinroth, Howard 5610; (Review) 444
Weir, John T. 9024
Weis, Paul 140, 1497
Weisband, Edward 1743, 7618
Weise, Selene Harding Curd 6994
Weiser, Elisabeth 817
Weiss, Friedl (Reviews) 253, 303
Weiss, Stanley 8309
Weitz, Charles H. 8948
Welch, Ronald M. 2739
Weller, Phil 8857
Wells, Donald Mclean 8051
Wells, Samuel F. (Review) 6338
Wellwood, Eleanore J. 8921
Wengler, Wilhelm 6139
Westell, Anthony 7768; (Review) 6755
Westergard-Thorpe, Wayne 8922
Western, Maurice 4677, 7685
Wex, Samuel 2454, 7251, 7291
Whalen, Hugh 804
Whalley, John 7292
Wharton, Francis 5338
Wheare, Kenneth Clinton 495, 999; (Reviews) 472, 6483, 6696, 6698
White, Arthur V. 2412
White, G.C. 7044
White, James 2202, 2257, 2258, 2322, 2323, 2334, 5339
White, Patrick C.T. (Reviews) 2523, 6746, 6823, 6900
White, Paul S. 8871
White, Philip Meltan 5133
White, Ralph William 8923
Whitehead, G.R.B. 2090
Whiteley, A.S. 1448
Whiteley, William H. 3423, 3424
Whitely, J.B. 7534
Whiteman, Marjorie M. 2172
Whitham, W.B. 8052
Whitney, Harriet Eleanor 2235, 2455
Whitton, Charlotte 1449
Whyte, John D. (Reviews) 765, 1678
Wickersham, George W. 393
Widmer, Max 8225
Widstrand, Carl 6385
Wigley, Philip G. 6743

Wihlborg, Clas G. 4363
Wijesinha, Samson Sena 3897
Wijk, Aart van 3898, 3899, 3900, 3901, 3902, 3903, 3904, 4034; (Reviews) 52, 3667, 3668, 3962
Wijkman, Per Magnus 4363
Wiktor, Christian L. 50, 51, 163, 231, 2173
Wilberforce, Richard Orme 1696
Wilder, Shael H. 6239
Wildgen, Frank (Review) 8906
Wildhaber, Luzius 620
Wilford, D. Sykes 8157
Wilgress, Dana 4885
Wilgress, L.D. 5057
Wilkes, Daniel 2699
Wilkinson, Bruce W. 7341, 7426, 7552; (Reviews) 7307, 7940, 7993
Wilkinson, Maurice 3348
Wilkinson, W.E. 1175, 6037
Willard, Josiah 8294
Williams, Anne M. (Review) 303
Williams, Charles Brian 8924, 8925, 8926
Williams, Colin H. 579
Williams, D. Colwyn 5563, 5564; (Reviews) 242, 4164
Williams, Douglas 8949, 8950
Williams, Gardner S. 2785
Williams, Glen S. 7427, 7487; (Review) 7352
Williams, James R. 7488, 7489
Williams, John S. 4730
Williams, R. Hodder 6108
Williams, Ray 4127
Williams, S. 6148
Williams, Sharon A. 213, 214, 215, 216, 217, 237, 253, 1479, 6141, 6158, 6159, 6160, 6161, 8995, 8996, 8997, 8998, 8999; (Review) 6200
Williams, Sylvia Maureen 8609
Williams, W.E. 8053
Williams, William 5340
Williamson, John Peter 7769, 8310, 8311
Willis, H. Parker 7046, 8158, 8159
Willis, John (Review) 249
Willis, R.B. 2913
Willis, Robert 8312
Willison, *Sir* John S. 2023
Willmann, Hildegard 2786
Willmore, Larry N. 5134
Willmot, Robert 76
Willms, Abraham Martin 107

Willoughby, William R. 1805, 1806, 2456, 2914, 2915, 2916, 2917, 5889, 5890, 5981, 6881, 6882, 8872; (Review) 6749
Wilson, *Sir* Charles William 2374
Wilson, *Sir* Daniel 8505
Wilson, Edwin Everett 7490
Wilson, F.J. 805
Wilson, Frank L. 806
Wilson, H.J. 2127
Wilson, Harold Arnold 6744, 6745
Wilson, J. Tuzo 8637
Wilson, Jeffery 9014
Wilson, Kenneth R. 4731
Wilson, Leslie Alfred James 7649
Wilson, Robert R. 1000, 1001, 1002, 1003, 1176, 1953, 7610; (Reviews) 56, 234, 917, 1970
Wilson, W.A. 6561
Wilton, David A. 7599
Winberg, Alan R. 7662
Winchell, Alexander N. 2259
Windsor, Philip 5058
Wine, Joseph Raymond 6046
Winer, Stanley L. 754
Wingler, Wilhelm 385
Winham, Gilbert R. 1807, 5250, 6379, 6380, 7293, 7294, 7295, 7428, 7650, 8449
Winks, Robin W. 6746, 6883, 6976, 7097
Winsor, Justin 2226
Winsor, Terence F. (Review) 7369
Winston, Milton W. 1498
Winter, Carl George 2227, 2457, 6884
Winter, David (Review) 9038
Winter, Gordon (Reviews) 720, 2559, 4665, 6413, 6463, 6522, 6714, 6872
Winterowd, Charles Gregory 5611
Wionczek, Miguel S. 5067, 5079, 5080
Wiper, James 1808
Wirick, Ronald G. 7719
Wise, Frank 8506
Wise, S.F. 5789
Wiseman, Henry 428, 5521, 5522, 5523, 5524, 5525, 5526, 5565; (Review) 5412
Wishart, Andrew 5341
Withers, Hartley 8160
Withrow, W.H. 1324
Woehrling, Francis 8161
Woehrling, José 246, 247, 383, 2037; (Review) 303

Woetzel, Robert K. (Reviews) 68, 4166, 4291
Wojcik, Tadeusz L. 4015
Wolfe, David A. 7907, 7908; (Review) 7519
Wolfe, George V. (Review) 6696
Wolfe, J.P. 6018, 6072
Wolfe, Larry Dennis Sturm 2787
Wolff, R.N. 8527
Wonder, Edward F. 3451, 8698, 8727
Wong, Chia Siew 7720
Wong, Yau Kwan 5566
Wonnacott, Paul 7215, 7253, 7553, 7554, 7557, 7600; (Reviews) 7458, 8024, 8029
Wonnacott, Ronald J. 7252, 7429, 7430, 7553, 7554, 7555, 7556, 7557, 7600, 7651, 7909
Wood, Andrew Dartnell B. 5527
Wood, Bernard 8360
Wood, Donald S. 7582
Wood, John R. 449, 1450
Wood, William 6913
Woodcock, George 6747
Woodcock, Leonard 8927
Woodliffe, J.C. (Review) 8996
Woodside, Willson 4564
Woodsworth, Charles James 7098
Woolsey, Lester H. (Review) 249
Woolsey, Theodore S. 600
Wormwith, N.B. 5342
Worrall, James 8976
Worswick, Noel Denis 6381
Wouk, Jonathan (Review) 5616
Wright, Barbara 2978, 6625
Wright, Cecil A. (Review) 8462
Wright, Conrad Payling 2918; (Review) 5212
Wright, Gerald 5982, 8162; (Review) 6450
Wright, H.R.C. (Review) 4678
Wright, Hume 8450
Wright, James R. (Review) 8791
Wright, Peter (Reviews) 2709, 2727, 3319
Wright, Richard W. 7332, 7770, 7940
Wright, Scott 4127
Wrigley, Leonard 8003
Wrong, Dennis H. (Review) 1361
Wrong, George McKinnon 6562, 6626, 6627, 6885, 6899; (Review) 6649
Wyatt, Derrick (Review) 243
Wyatt, Jimmy N. 7956

Wydrzynski, Christopher J. 1207, 1314, 1451; (Review) 1937

Yachetti, Roger D. 1208
Yadav, Gopal Ji 7431
Yadi, Melchiade 5150
Yannopoulos, G.N. 5059
Yates, George W. 2788
Yates, John B. 8811
Yee, Herbert Sun-Jun 601, 602
Yogis, John A. 2671, 3363, 3425; (Review) 3319
Yohe, Robert 8054
Young, Brian (Review) 772
Young, Charles A. 3525
Young, Christopher 4657; (Review) 6456
Young, Elizabeth 5732; (Review) 3133
Young, George Renny 3426
Young, John H. 7432, 7485
Young, Owen D. 7254
Young, Richard (Review) 2995
Young, Robert 2071
Young, Robert Andrew 807, 808
Young, Roger 8407, 8626, 8949, 8950
Younker, D.W. (Review) 7871

Zacher, Mark W. 111, 3048, 3049, 3504, 3505, 3506, 4565, 4566, 5183, 5184, 5825, 7267; (Reviews) 4405, 4406, 4493, 4811
Zakariya, Hasan S. 7721
Zalob, David S. 8790
Zama, Charles Cho 3150
Zaremba, Alois Louis 7771
Zarley, Arvid M. 7652
Zaslow, Morris 2586; (Reviews) 5842, 6792
Zboralski, Josef (Review) 7052
Zebroff, George 809
Zechel, Bernd 8451
Zhukov, Gennady P. 3711, 4364, 4365
Ziadat, Adel Awwad 8610
Ziegel, Jacob S. 5060, 7255
Zimmern, *Sir* Alfred Eckhard 6748
Ziskind, David 1452
Zorbas, Basil 7992
Zorn, Roman J. 1325, 1499
Zuijdwijk, Anthony J.M. 1095, 1697, 1698, 1699, 8638, 8639
Zussman, Ephraim Ahron 6302
Zylberberg, Jacques 5081, 5082; (Review) 793

INDEX OF CORPORATE NAMES, CONFERENCES AND SERIES

References are to numbered entries

Acadia University, Wolfville, N.S. 6641
Accent Québec, AQ11 2879
Addiction Research Foundation of Ontario 8896
Adelphi Papers, No. 143 3010
Adlai Stevenson Institute of International Affairs 4717
Administrative Law Series 1387
Alan B. Plaunt Memorial Lectures, 1962 7140
Alaska History, No. 18 2313
Alaskan Boundary Tribunal 2274
Alaskan-Canadian Boundary Commission 2275
Albert Shaw Lectures on Diplomatic History, 1914 6912
American Assembly 5734, 6751
American Bar Association 5246
American Bar Association. Standing Committee on Environmental Law 8764
American Commonwealth, Vol. 2 2464
American Diplomatic History Series 6616
American Economic Association. Publications. Monographs, Vol. 7, No. 6 6943
American Foreign Policy Library 6780
American History Leaflets, No. 6, November, 1892 5316
American Society of International Law 1775, 1776, 6286
Anglo-American Association 3365
Arctic Development and the Environment Program 2657
Arctic Institute of North America 2559, 2578, 2579, 2657, 2694, 6754, 8756
Arctic Institute of North America. Technical Papers, No. 27 2694
Association des études internationales 618
Association des études internationales. Cours, 1956/57, no 3 2658

Association internationale de sociologie 7188
Association of Canadian Law Teachers 632
Assuranceforeningen Gard, Arendal, Norway 3474
Atherton Press Political Science Series 8713
Atlantic Council of Canada 6202
Atlantic Council Working Group on the United States and Canada 6755
Atlantic Institute for International Affairs 5935
Atlantic Institute Studies, 1 5935
Atlantic Trade Study 7214
Autonomismes-nationalités 783

Background Study for the Science Council of Canada. Special Study, No. 16 3278
Banff Conference on Law and Order in the International Community, Banff, Alta., 1965 292
Banff Conference on World Development, 3d, 1965 6440
Berkshire Studies in European History 995
Bibliothèque de droit international, t. 61 1936
Bibliothèque de philosophie contemporaine 1624
Bibliothèque juridique, D-1 8057
Bibliothèque juridique, D-2 1576
Bissell Lectures, 1980-81 6818
Books That Matter 2794
Britain in the World Today, 7 6704
British and American Joint Commission for the Final Settlement of the Claims of the Hudson's Bay and Puget's Sound Agricultural Companies 5224

British Commonwealth Relations Conference 6638
British Commonwealth Relations Conference, 2d, Sydney, 1938 6531, 6723
British Commonwealth Relations Conference, 3d, London, 1945 6663
British Commonwealth Relations Conference, 4th, Bigwin Island, Ont., 1949 6728, 6729
British Commonwealth Series, Book 1 883
British Empire Before the American Revolution, Vol. 5 6586
British-North American Committee 7144, 7271, 7272, 7957
British-North American Committee. Publications, BN-8 7957
British-North American Committee. Publications, BN-14 7271
British-North American Committee. Publications, BN-22 7272
British-North American Research Association 7957
Brookings Institution 7496
Brookings Institution. Institute of Economics. Publication, No. 33 2854
Brookings Institution. Study 7143
Bunsel Environmental Consultants 8856
Butterworth Basic Text Series 253
Butterworths Carter Report Studies, No. 1 7755

CAC, 37 3073
CCH Canadian Limited 8199, 8247, 8268, 8269, 8289
CEDE, Note de recherches, no 1 4888
CFP, 122 6049
Cahiers d'histoire de l'Université d'Ottawa, no 1 6966
Cahiers d'histoire de l'Université d'Ottawa, no 4 5204
Cahiers d'histoire de l'Université Laval, 20 7880
Cahiers de l'Institut d'histoire, 15 1885
Cahiers de l'Université du Québec, C-27 610
Cahiers de la décolonisation du Franc-Canada, no 7 6893
Cahiers des sciences sociales de l'Université d'Ottawa, no 1 8398
Cahiers du Centre culturel canadien, no 3 6524
Cahiers du Québec, 38 4869
Cambridge Commonwealth Series 6743
Canada. Anti-Dumping Tribunal 7447
Canada. Atomic Energy Control Board 8718
Canada. Atomic Energy Control Board. Report 8718
Canada. Bureau of Competition Policy. Research Branch 3530
Canada. Bureau of Competition Policy. Research Branch. Research Monograph, No. 2 3530
Canada. Civil Aeronautics Directorate 4090
Canada. Commission royale d'enquête sur le bilinguisme et le biculturalisme. Documents, 9 8982
Canada. Defence Research Board 46
Canada. Dept. of Communications 8533, 8992
Canada. Dept. of Employment and Immigration 1286
Canada. Dept. of Energy, Mines and Resources 2541
Canada. Dept. of External Affairs 4, 61, 63, 150, 151, 152, 153, 159, 160, 258, 403, 630, 657, 685, 689, 1522, 1707, 1708, 2750, 2751, 2806, 2926, 2927, 3013, 3014, 4452, 4625, 4626, 4627, 4628, 4629, 4630, 4631, 4632, 4686, 4687, 4688, 4689, 4739, 4772, 4903, 4904, 4906, 5265, 5266, 5451, 5452, 5533, 5624, 5625, 5800, 6395, 6396, 7317, 8328, 8983
Canada. Dept. of External Affairs. Conference Series, 1945, No. 2 4632
Canada. Dept. of External Affairs. Conference Series, 1948, No. 2 685
Canada. Dept. of External Affairs. Conference Series, 1955, No. 1 5800
Canada. Dept. of External Affairs. Legal Advisory Division 9005
Canada. Dept. of External Affairs. Reference Series, No. 12 4688
Canada. Dept. of External Affairs. Reference Series, No. 13 4739
Canada. Dept. of External Affairs. Reference Series, No. 14 4687

INDEX OF CORPORATE NAMES, ETC. 751

Canada. Dept. of External Affairs. Reference Series, No. 15 4686
Canada. Dept. of External Affairs. Reference Series, No. 16 4689
Canada. Dept. of External Affairs. Reference Series, No. 17 1708
Canada. Dept. of External Affairs. Reference Series, No. 21 4631
Canada. Dept. of External Affairs. Reference Series, No. 35 7317
Canada. Dept. of Finance 4690, 7318, 7448
Canada. Dept. of Fisheries and Oceans 3285
Canada. Dept. of Fisheries and the Environment 3286
Canada. Dept. of Indian Affairs and Northern Development 2590, 3108
Canada. Dept. of Indian and Northern Affairs 2604
Canada. Dept. of Industry, Trade and Commerce 7319, 8751 1525
Canada. Dept. of Justice 7926
Canada. Dept. of Manpower and Immigration 1340, 1345, 1346, 1347, 1348, 1349
Canada. Dept. of Marine 3534
Canada. Dept. of Mines and Technical Surveys 2163
Canada. Dept. of Mines and Technical Surveys. Geographical Branch. Memoir, 2 2163
Canada. Dept. of National Defence 26, 5672, 6049
Canada. Dept. of Northern Affairs and National Resources 2926, 2927, 8874
Canada. Dept. of the Environment 3444, 8760
Canada. Dept. of the Interior 2596
Canada. Dept. of the Secretary of State 1135, 1136, 1458, 1523, 1524,
Canada. Dept. of the Secretary of State. Arts and Culture Branch 8991
Canada. Dept. of Trade and Commerce 161
Canada. Directorate of Strategic and Air Defence Operational Research. Operational Research Division 5546
Canada. Economic Council 7325
Canada. External Aid Office 110
Canada. Fisheries and Marine Service 3280, 3287
Canada. Foreign Investment Review Agency 7799, 7800, 7801
Canada. Health and Welfare Canada 8878
Canada. Human Rights Commission 5, 1526, 1527
Canada. Hydrographic Service 3014
Canada. Indian and Northern Affairs Canada 2661
Canada. Inland Waters Directorate 3134
Canada. International Development Agency 3350, 7122, 8329, 8330, 8331, 8332, 8333, 8334
Canada. International Labour Affairs Branch 4773, 8899
Canada. Law Reform Commission 1387, 7484
Canada. Law Reform Commission. Administrative Law Series, No. 17 7484
Canada. Marine Transportation Administration 3535
Canada. Metric Commission 8752
Canada. Ministry of Transport 3535
Canada. National Advisory Committee, St. Lawrence Waterway 2806
Canada. National Commission for UNESCO 4798, 4809
Canada. Parliament 154, 227, 228, 229, 686, 1137, 1956, 2111, 2112, 2113, 2114, 2115, 2116, 2152, 2284, 2285, 2286, 2287, 2288, 2289, 2337, 2338, 2386, 2752, 2807, 2808, 2809, 3372, 3373, 3374, 3375, 3427, 4453, 5296, 5297, 5298, 5299, 6089, 6934, 6978, 6979, 6999, 7000, 7001, 7560
Canada. Parliament. House of Commons. Parliamentary Task Force on North-South Relations 8416
Canada. Parliament. House of Commons. Special Committee on a National Trading Corporation 7320
Canada. Parliament. House of Commons. Standing Committee on Banking and Commerce 4691
Canada. Parliament. House of Commons. Standing Committee on External Affairs 2928
Canada. Parliament. House of Commons. Standing Committee on External Af-

fairs and National Defence 1709, 5534
Canada. Parliament. House of Commons. Standing Committee on Fisheries and Forestry. Subcommittee on Acid Rain 8831
Canada. Parliament. Senate. Standing Committee on Foreign Affairs 1710, 4905, 6768, 7058
Canada. Parliament. Special Joint Committee on Immigration Policy 1350, 1351
Canada. Parliament, 1869. Sessional Papers, No. 47 6934
Canada. Parliament, 1870. Sessional Papers, No. 81 3374
Canada. Parliament, 1871. Sessional Papers, No. 12 3373
Canada. Parliament, 1872. Sessional Papers, No. 18 6979
Canada. Parliament, 1874. Sessional Papers, No. 54 1137
Canada. Parliament, 1876. Sessional Papers, No. 110 2287
Canada. Parliament, 1877. Sessional Papers, No. 14 6978
Canada. Parliament, 1878. Sessional Papers, No. 125 2289
Canada. Parliament, 1880. Sessional Papers, No. 26 2115
Canada. Parliament, 1887. Sessional Papers, No. 48 5298
Canada. Parliament, 1888. Sessional Papers, Nos. 65a, 65b, and 65c, pp. 12-114 5297
Canada. Parliament, 1892. Sessional Papers, Nos. 24, and 24a 2114
Canada. Parliament, 1893. Sessional Papers, Nos. 51 to 51c 2111
Canada. Parliament, 1893. Sessional Papers, No. 52 154
Canada. Parliament, 1895. Sessional Papers, No. 48 686
Canada. Parliament, 1897. Sessional Papers, No. 77 2288
Canada. Parliament, 1898. Sessional Papers, No. 16a 2808
Canada. Parliament, 1898. Sessional Papers, No. 39 5296
Canada. Parliament, 1899. Sessional Papers, No. 99 2284
Canada. Parliament, 1903. Sessional Papers, No. 65 2337
Canada. Parliament, 1903. Sessional Papers, No. 149 2286
Canada. Parliament, 1906. Sessional Papers, Nos. 19b, and 19d 2703
Canada. Parliament, 1907-1908. Sessional Papers, No. 10a 2112
Canada. Parliament, 1907-1908. Sessional Papers, No. 10b 2113
Canada. Parliament, 1907-1908. Sessional Papers, Nos. 19b, and 19c 2704
Canada. Parliament, 1907-1908. Sessional Papers, No. 54 2285
Canada. Parliament, 1907-1908. Sessional Papers, Nos. 54a, and 54b 2338
Canada. Parliament, 1907-1908. Sessional Papers, Nos. 215, and 215a 3375
Canada. Parliament, 1909. Sessional Papers, Nos. 101, and 102 2116
Canada. Parliament, 1910. Sessional Papers, No. 10j 7001, 7560
Canada. Parliament, 1910. Sessional Papers, No. 19c 2705
Canada. Parliament, 1910. Sessional Papers, No. 19e 2152
Canada. Parliament, 1911. Sessional Papers, Nos. 97a, and 97b 5299
Canada. Parliament, 1911. Sessional Papers, No. 109b 7000
Canada. Parliament, 1911. Sessional Papers, No. 208, pp. 344-350 1956
Canada. Parliament, 1912. Sessional Papers, No. 82a 6999
Canada. Parliament, 1912. Sessional Papers, No. 84 3427
Canada. Parliament, 1912. Sessional Papers, No. 119 2386
Canada. Parliament, 1913. Sessional Papers, No. 19a 2702
Canada. Parliament, 1922. Sessional Papers, No. 47 227
Canada. Parliament, 1922. Sessional Papers, No. 89a 2807
Canada. Parliament, 1923. Sessional Papers, No. 35 228
Canada. Parliament, 1923. Sessional Papers, No. 111a 3372
Canada. Parliament, 1924. Sessional Papers, Nos. 35, 37, and 37a 229

INDEX OF CORPORATE NAMES, ETC. 753

Canada. Parliament, 1924. Sessional Papers, Nos. 101c, 101d, 101e, 101f, 101g, 157 and 180 2809
Canada. Parliament, 1924. Sessional Papers, No. 232 6089
Canada. Parliament, 1925. Sessional Papers, No. 116 4453
Canada. Parliament, 1928. Sessional Papers, No. 227 2752
Canada. Polar Continental Shelf Project 2541
Canada. Royal Commission on Bilingualism and Biculturalism 1762, 8982
Canada. Royal Commission on Bilingualism and Biculturalism. Studies, 3 1762
Canada. Royal Commission on Canada's Economic Prospects 7300, 7432
Canada. Royal Commission on Conditions of Foreign Service 1819
Canada. Royal Commission on Dominion-Provincial Relations 1984
Canada. Royal Commission on Illegal Warfare Claims and for Return of Sequestrated Property in Necessitous Cases 6050, 6111
Canada. Royal Commission on Taxation 7405, 7755
Canada. Royal Commission on Taxation. Studies, 5 7405
Canada. Special Committee on Hate Propaganda in Canada 1528
Canada. Tariff Board 7260, 7449
Canada. Tariff Board. Reference, 159 7449
Canada. Task Force on Immigration Practices and Procedures 1286
Canada. Task Force on the Structure of Canadian Industry 7802
Canada. Transport Canada 3579, 3583
Canada. Transport Canada. Marine, TP 3891E 3579
Canada. Transport Canada. Marine, TP 3892E 3583
Canada. Transport Commission 4091
Canada. Transport Commission. Directorate of Transport Industries Analysis. Research Branch 3644
Canada. Transport Commission. International Transport Research Group 8510
Canada. War Claims Commission (World War II) 6112
Canada. Wartime Information Board 3734
Canada. Water Resources Branch 2387
Canada. Wildlife Service 8875
Canada, Origins and Options 6864
Canada and Third World Trade, 1 7194
Canada and Third World Trade, 3 7191
Canada in the Atlantic Economy, Vols. 1-3 7253
Canada in the Atlantic Economy, Vol. 2 7616
Canada in the Atlantic Economy, Vol. 3 7215
Canada in the Atlantic Economy, Vol. 5 7340
Canada in the Atlantic Economy, Vol. 8 8523
Canada in the Atlantic Economy, Vol. 9 7546, 8278
Canada in the Atlantic Economy, Vol. 13 7341
Canada North-South 8414, 8415
Canada Studies Foundation 8018
Canada-U.S. Prospects 2753, 8014
Canada-U.S. Prospects, 2 8089
Canada-U.S. Prospects, 4 6878
Canada-United States Institute 5225
Canada-United States Interparliamentary Group 6771, 7683
Canada-United States University Seminar, 1971-1972 2714
Canadian Air Line Pilots Association 4053
Canadian Arctic Resources Committee 2542, 2560, 2562, 3448, 8877
Canadian Association for Adult Education 1418
Canadian Association for American Studies 5577
Canadian Association for Latin America 7307
Canadian Bar Association 5246
Canadian Bar Association. Committee on International Law 114
Canadian Bar Association. Environmental Law Section 8764
Canadian Bar Association. Nova Scotia Branch. Maritime Law Section 3028, 3029, 3035
Canadian Broadcasting Corporation 326

Canadian Commission for UNESCO 4799
Canadian Controversies Series 675, 715, 6481
Canadian Council on International Law 50, 115, 116, 6460, 7138
Canadian Critical Issues Series 8023
Canadian Cultural Centre 6524
Canadian Economic Policy Committee 7157, 7307, 7462, 7541
Canadian Foreign Investment Review Seminar 7803
Canadian Forum 7826
Canadian Historical Association 1796, 2170
Canadian Historical Association. Booklets, No. 1 2170
Canadian Historical Association. Booklets, No. 7 1796
Canadian Historical Readings, 6 6648
Canadian History Series, Vol. 2 6614
Canadian History Through the Press Series 2504, 6938
Canadian Human Rights Foundation 1615
Canadian Immigration and Population Study 1346
Canadian Institute for Economic Policy 7369, 8128
Canadian Institute for Economic Policy Series 7369, 8128
Canadian Institute of International Affairs 1, 18, 37, 39, 40, 54, 60, 62, 117, 403, 772, 885, 1010, 1261, 1361, 1444, 1567, 1817, 1865, 2550, 2559, 2995, 4412, 4459, 4665, 4906, 4915, 5096, 5122, 5202, 5560, 5640, 5652, 5734, 5787, 5922, 5932, 5967, 5977, 5979, 6026, 6304, 6349, 6360, 6403, 6436, 6437, 6440, 6484, 6488, 6522, 6531, 6548, 6712, 6729, 6749, 6760, 6825, 6850, 7098, 7248, 7437, 7611, 8363
Canadian Institute of International Affairs. Special Series 4644
Canadian Institute of Resources Law 8839
Canadian Institute on Public Affairs 6321, 6322, 6397, 7348
Canadian Inter-American Research Institute 9015
Canadian Legal Casebook Series 236
Canadian Legal Manual Series 3637
Canadian Legal Textbook Series 7982

Canadian Lives 105
Canadian Maritime Law Association 3035
Canadian NGO Conference on Human Settlements, Ottawa, 1975 8761
Canadian NGO Participation Group 8761
Canadian National Committee for Habitat 8761
Canadian Peace Research Institute 3062, 4385, 4400, 4426, 4662, 4675, 5500, 5573, 5731, 5990
Canadian Perspectives in Economics, D4 8093
Canadian Political Science Association 632
Canadian Public Administration Series 1376, 2960, 7352
Canadian Studies, No. 39 7302
Canadian Studies in Economics, No. 9 7443
Canadian Studies in Economics, No. 12 7403
Canadian Studies in Economics, No. 22 7420
Canadian Studies in History and Government, No. 2 3421
Canadian Studies in History and Government, No. 5 2268
Canadian Tax Foundation 8310
Canadian Tax Papers, No. 36 8310
Canadian University Paperbooks, 1 6500
Canadian University Paperbooks, 49 1729
Canadian University Paperbooks, 58 7454
Canadian University Paperbooks, 138 8047
Canadian University Paperbooks, 212 3392
Canadian War Museum. Historical Publications, No. 8 6895
Canadian-American Business Conference, 6th, 1959 6772
Canadian-American Committee 2929, 3073, 5093, 6773, 6811, 7528, 7534, 7572, 7667, 7684, 7699, 7700, 8124, 8704, 8739, 8908
Canadian-American Committee. Publications, CAC 38 8124
Canadian-American Committee. Publications, CAC 43 7684
Canadian-American Conference on Foreign Relations, Niagara Falls, Ont., 1951 6873
Canadian-United States Committee on

INDEX OF CORPORATE NAMES, ETC.

Education 6760
Canadiana avant 1867 2507
Carleton Contemporary 6401, 6450, 7492
Carleton International Studies, 1978/3 8727
Carleton Library, No. 9 6952
Carleton Library, No. 49 6452
Carleton Library, No. 81 158
Carleton Library, No. 83 1678
Carleton Library, No. 86 8155
Carleton Library, No. 93 8032
Carleton Library, No. 98 6453
Carleton Library, No. 103 148a
Carleton Library, No. 115 2164
Carleton Library, No. 118 149
Carleton University 42
Carleton University. Dept. of Political Science 784
Carleton University. Institute of Canadian Studies 148a, 149, 2164
Carleton University. Institute of Soviet and East European Studies 7156, 7608
Carleton University. Norman Paterson School of International Affairs 1, 7, 17, 48, 57, 684, 4865, 5681, 5689, 5862, 6083, 6385, 7229, 8707, 8727
Carleton University. Norman Paterson School of International Affairs. Bibliography Series, 2 17
Carleton University. Norman Paterson School of International Affairs. Bibliography Series, 4 48
Carleton University. Norman Paterson School of International Affairs. Occasional Papers, 14 5689
Carleton University. Norman Paterson School of International Affairs. Occasional Papers, 15 684
Carleton University. Norman Paterson School of International Affairs. Occasional Papers, 21 5862
Carleton University. Norman Paterson School of International Affairs. Occasional Papers, 24 4865
Carleton University. School of Public Administration 8707
Carnegie Endowment for International Peace 2198, 4554, 4665, 6572, 6752, 6753, 6766
Carnegie Endowment for International Peace. Division of Economics and History 4825
Carnegie Endowment for International Peace. Division of Economics and History. Publications 490
Carnegie Endowment for International Peace. Division of International Law 156
Carnegie Endowment for International Peace. Division of International Law. Pamphlet, No. 2 6919
Carnegie Endowment for International Peace. Division of International Law. Publications 156, 5259
Carnegie Endowment for International Peace. Studies in the Administration of International Law and Organization, No. 10 4441
Center of Planning and Economic Research. Research Monograph Series, 14 5053
Centre for the Study of Inflation and Productivity (Canada) 7665
Centre international d'études et de recherches européennes 617
Centre international de recherches sur le bilinguisme. Travaux, 6 1279
Centre québécois de relations internationales 8, 60, 119, 772, 1010, 2624, 4915, 5077, 5811, 6349, 6358, 6403, 6510, 7188, 7611
Centre québécois de relations internationales. Notes de recherche, nos 1, 3 2624
Chronicles of America Series, Vol. 10 6626
Coles Canadiana Collection 2077, 2085
Collection Centre de recherche en droit public 2331, 8060
Collection Choix, 4 5811
Collection Choix, 7 772
Collection Choix, 8 7188
Collection Choix, 9 1010
Collection Choix, 10 4915, 7611
Collection Choix, 12 6349
Collection Choix, 13 6403
Collection Constantes, vol. 10 682
Collection d'études théoriques et pratiques de droit étranger, de droit comparé et de droit international, no 4 1154

Collection des sciences sociales, no 6 8079
Collection 17/60, 7 6623, 6897
Collection Fleur de lys 6584
Collection Les idées du jour, D-39 2324
Collection Les idées du jour, D-56 798
Collection Politique 728
Collection Science politique 4869
Collection U2, 142 924
Colloque sur le nouvel ordre économique international, Montréal, 1978 7111
Colloque sur les relations du Canada et du Québec avec les Communautés européennes, Québec, 1978 4915, 7611
Columbia University. School of International Affairs 7167
Columbia University. Studies in International Organization, No. 7 4566
Commercial Law Series, No. 1 7303
Commission of the European Communities 4903, 4906
Commission on International Development 8327, 8349
Commission on Pacific Fisheries Policy 3291
Committee for an Independent Canada 6527
Commonwealth and International Library. Commonwealth Affairs Division 6629
Commonwealth Papers, 11 7097
Comparative Study of New Nations Series 7142
Conference Board in Canada 7302
Conference on 'Canada and the Northern Rim,' Queen's University, 1977 5836
Conference on Canadian-American Affairs 58
Conference on Canadian Overseas Aid, University of Western Ontario, 1962 8363
Conference on Canadian-U.S. Economic Relations, Washington, D.C., 1978 7496
Congrès des relations internationales du Québec, 11th, 1979 6349
Congrès des relations internationales du Québec, 12th, 1980 6403
Conservation Council of New Brunswick 3136
Contemporary Affairs, No. 20 4459
Contemporary Affairs, No. 21 5122
Contemporary Affairs, No. 22 6760

Contemporary Affairs, No. 24 5977
Contemporary Affairs, No. 25 5967
Contemporary Affairs, No. 30 6548
Contemporary Affairs, No. 31 8363
Contemporary Affairs, No. 34 5652
Contemporary Affairs, No. 35 6440
Contemporary Affairs, No. 36 7248
Contemporary Affairs, No. 37 5932
Contemporary Affairs, No. 38 5979
Contemporary Affairs, No. 39 5560
Contemporary Affairs, No. 40 5787
Contemporary Affairs, No. 42 6522
Contemporary Affairs, No. 43 1567
Contemporary Affairs, No. 44 6304
Contemporary Affairs, No. 45 5640
Contemporary Affairs, No. 47 6749
Contemporary Affairs, No. 49 6506
Council on Foreign Relations 5834, 6850
Cours de Thémis 8526
Current Comment, 11 6083

Dalhousie Continuing Legal Education Series, No. 12 3028
Dalhousie Continuing Legal Education Series, No. 18 3029
Dalhousie Continuing Legal Education Series, No. 20 3035
Dalhousie Ocean Studies Programme 51, 64, 2682, 3081, 3500, 3622
Dalhousie University. Canadian Marine Transportation Centre 3526, 3563
Dalhousie University. Canadian Marine Transportation Centre. Research Report, No. 6 3563
Dalhousie University. Centre for African Studies 6385
Dalhousie University. Centre for Foreign Policy Studies 6330, 6362, 6458 7184
Dalhousie University. Centre for Foreign Policy Studies. Occasional Paper 6458
Dalhousie University. Centre for International Business Studies 3276
Dalhousie University. Faculty of Law 51, 245, 3028, 3029, 3035, 3553, 3616
Dalhousie University. Faculty of Law. Public Services Committee 3276
Dalhousie University. Institute for Resource and Environmental Studies 8360
Dalhousie University. Institute of Public Affairs 3134
Dalhousie University. School of Business

INDEX OF CORPORATE NAMES, ETC.

Administration 3276
Dent's Canadian Texts 6320
Ditchley Paper, No. 37 2574
Documents économiques 6717
Documents politiques 538
Dossiers Interlex 6224, 6240, 8070
Droit de la coopération économique et sociale internationale, t. 7 8421
Droit et science politique, 6 2151
Duke University. Center for International Studies 8979
Duke University. Center for International Studies. Occasional Papers Series, No. 9 8979
Duke University. Commonwealth-Studies Center 997, 2727, 6466
Duke University. Commonwealth-Studies Center. Publication, No. 7 947
Duke University. Commonwealth-Studies Center. Publication, No. 8 964
Duke University. Commonwealth-Studies Center. Publication, No. 9 653
Duke University. Commonwealth-Studies Center. Publication, No. 14 6466
Duke University. Commonwealth-Studies Center. Publication, No. 19 1927
Duke University. Commonwealth-Studies Center. Publication, No. 25 928
Duke University. Commonwealth-Studies Center. Publication, No. 27 1003
Duke University. Commonwealth-Studies Center. Publication, No. 29 6714
Duke University. Commonwealth-Studies Center. Publication, No. 30 2727
Duke University. Commonwealth-Studies Center. Publication, No. 33 1002
Duke University. Commonwealth-Studies Center. Publication, No. 38 1000
Duke University. Commonwealth-Studies Center. Publication, No. 39 874
Duke University. Commonwealth-Studies Center. Publication, No. 40 6856
Duke University. Commonwealth-Studies Center. Publications 997

ESAB, 75-3 8510
East European Monographs, No. 66 7052
East-West Center 3487
East-West Commercial Relations Series 7608
East-West Commercial Relations Series; Working Paper, No. 1 7156
East-West Environment and Policy Institute 3487
East-West Environment and Policy Institute. Research Report, No. 10 3487
Economic Council of Canada 3339, 7119, 7324, 7329, 7401, 7429, 7478, 7665, 8084, 8357, 8460
Economic Council of Canada. Discussion Paper, No. 167 7665
Economic Council of Canada. Staff Study, No. 7. 1964 7324
Éditions Thémis. Notes et documents 246, 247
Energy Policies of the World 8679
Ernst & Whinney Chartered Accountants 8247
Essays in International Economics 7113
Études et documents, no 7 3
Études historiques canadiennes 6584

FIRA Papers, No. 2 7801
FIRA Papers, No. 5 7799
Financial Post Conferences 2866
Foundations of Contemporary Canada Series 8018
Foundations of Modern History 6571
Frontenac Library, No. 5 2317
Fur Seal Arbitration 5307

Galleon Book 1478
Graduate Institute of International Studies, Geneva. Publications, No. 3 4472
Gt. Brit. Commissioners for Adjusting the Boundaries for the British and French Possessions in America 2183
Gt. Brit. Foreign Office 2479, 6982
Gt. Brit. Parliament. Papers by Command, c. 539 6982
Gt. Brit. Privy Council. Judicial Committee 2328
Great Events in World History 2262
Great Lakes Fishery Commission 218
Great Lakes Management Problems Series 8769

Hague. Permanent Court of Arbitration 5312, 5313
Halifax Commission, 1877 5314, 5315

Halsted Press Book 8134
Harris Foundation Lectures, 1927 942
Harvard Economic Studies, Vol. 129 7557
Harvard Historical Monographs, 23 2485
Harvard Studies in East Asian Law, 3 230
Harvard Studies in International Affairs, No. 42 6419, 6799
Harvard University. Center for International Affairs 6419, 6799
Howe (C.D.) Research Institute 2753, 2879, 3073, 6878, 7511, 7684, 7957, 8014, 8089, 8643
Howe (C.D.) Research Institute. Policy Commentary, No. 3 7511
Hutchinson's Library; Politics, No. 4 946

I.P.R. Inquiry Series 4376, 7080
IUCN Environmental Policy and Law Paper, No. 18 3485
Illinois State Historical Library. Collections, Vol. 27; French Series, Vol. 2 2194
Imperial Studies, No. 28 6681
Indian-Eskimo Association of Canada. Legal Committee 1242
Institut européen des hautes études internationales 4915, 7611
Institut français des relations internationales 6349, 6403
Institute for International Development and Co-operation. Books and Monographs Series, 4 7239
Institute for Research on Public Policy 436, 2086, 4113, 4987, 6419, 6799, 7113, 7349, 7402, 7496, 7512, 8538, 8661, 8707
Institute for Research on Public Policy. Occasional Paper, No. 2 7496
Institute of Pacific Relations 1261
Institute of Pacific Relations. International Research Committee 1199
Institute of Public Administration of Canada 1342, 2960, 7352
International Assembly on Nuclear Weapons, Scarborough, 1966 5734
International Banff Conference on Man and His Environment, 2d, 1974 8766
International Boundary Commission 2157, 2347, 2348, 2349, 2350, 2351, 2352, 2353, 2354, 2355
International Boundary Commission. Special Report, No. 1 2355
International Boundary Commission. Special Report, No. 2 2157
International Columbia River Engineering Board 2943
International Commission for the Northwest Atlantic Fisheries 219, 220
International Commission of Jurists 6000, 6121
International Commission of Jurists. Canadian Section 1615
International Conciliation, No. 487 929
International Conference on Human Rights, Tehran, 1968 1525
International Conference on Nationalism and the Multinational Enterprise: Legal, Economic and Managerial Aspects, McGill University, 1971 8007
International Development Research Centre 8622
International Fiscal Association. Canadian Branch 7761, 8285, 8286, 8287
International Fisheries Commission 222
International Information Center on Peace-Keeping Operations 29
International Institute for the Unification of Private Law 1193, 1194
International Joint Commission 2402, 2403, 2404, 2405, 2406, 2407, 2408, 2409, 2410, 2411, 2412, 2413, 2414, 2415, 2416, 2417, 2418, 2419, 2420, 2421, 2422, 2423, 2424, 2425, 2426, 2427, 2428, 2429, 2430, 8823, 8838
International Labour Organization 4794
International Law Association. Canadian Branch 56, 6286
International North Pacific Fisheries Commission 221
International Ocean Institute 3175
International Ocean Institute. Occasional Papers, No. 4 3095
International Ocean Institute. Occasional Papers, No. 6 3175
International Pacific Halibut Commission 222
International Pacific Salmon Fisheries Commission 223
International Political Science Association Series 8713

INDEX OF CORPORATE NAMES, ETC. 759

International Studies Conference, 8th, London, 1935 5808
International Union for Conservation of Nature and Natural Resources 3485
International Waterways Commission 2702, 2703, 2704, 2705
Inter-University Seminar on International Relations, Ottawa, 1971-72 7492
Irish University Press Series of British Parliamentary Papers. Colonies. Canadian Boundary, 3 2154
Issues in Canadian History 2315, 6392, 6445, 6446

Jacob Blaustein Lectures in International Affairs, 1st, 1967 6489
Joanne Goodman Lectures, 1976 6540
Joanne Goodman Lectures, 1977 6883
Joanne Goodman Lectures, 1981 6313
Johns Hopkins University. School of Advanced International Studies, Washington, D.C 6844
Johns Hopkins University. Studies in Historical and Political Science; Ser. 40, No. 2, pp. 189-276 6965
Joint Centre on Modern East Asia 7349
Joint Program in Transportation 3529
Joint Project on Environment and Development, 3 7122
Journal of International Affairs, Vol. 24, No. 2, 1970 7167

Kates, Peat, Marwick & Co. 8019
Kennikat Press Scholarly Reprints; Series in American History and Culture in the Twentieth Century 6595, 6827

Last Post Book 7061
Latin American Working Group 8341, 8395
Laurentian Library, 54 6404
Law Institute of the Americas 5111
Law of the Sea Institute 2682, 2995, 3011, 3059, 3144
Law of the Sea Institute. Occasional Paper, No. 17 3144
Law of the Sea Institute. Occasional Paper, No. 29 3011
Law Society of Upper Canada. Dept. of Continuing Education 7851

League of Nations Society in Canada 1984
League of Nations. Series of Publications, Economic and Financial 7250
Lehigh University, Bethlehem, Pa. Dept. of International Relations. Research Monograph, No. 1 268
Library of World Affairs, No. 17 240, 241, 242
Library of World Affairs, No. 61 917
Ligue des droits de l'homme, Montréal 1402
London Institute of World Affairs 240, 242

McGill Conference on the Law of Outer Space, 1st, Montreal, 1963 4164
McGill University. Centre for Developing Area Studies 7631, 8325
McGill University. Centre for Developing Area Studies. Working Paper, No. 24 8325
McGill University. Centre for Research of Air & Space Law 4338
McGill University. Faculty of Law 4164
McGill University. Faculty of Law. Library 35
McGill University. Institute and Centre of Air and Space Law 52, 68, 4099
McGill University. Institute of Air and Space Law 31, 35, 410, 411, 3667, 3668, 3669, 3682, 3814, 3831, 3864, 3882, 4077, 4152, 4164, 4273, 4287, 4289, 4293, 8584
McGill University. Institute of Air and Space Law. Publication, No. 1 3682
McGill University. Institute of Air and Space Law. Publication, No. 6 3936
McGill University. Institute of Air and Space Law. Publication, No. 7 3864
McGill University. Library. Reference Dept. 36
McGill University. Office of Industrial Research 3444
McGraw-Hill Ryerson Series in Canadian Politics 674, 6556
McGraw-Hill Series in Canadian Politics 6551
Madawaska Historical Society (Maine) 2218

Maine Historical Society. Collections, Vol. 8, pp. 1-106 2224
Maine. Legislature. Committee on Northeastern Boundary 2220
Manitoba. Legislative Assembly. Library 10
Maritimes' Coastal Zone Seminar, Mount Allison University, 1973 3136
Memorial University of Newfoundland. Extension Service 3350
Michigan. State University, East Lansing. Committee of Canadian-American Studies 7516
Michigan International Commerce Reports, No. 1 7581
Monographs Series in World Affairs 8931
Mount Allison University, Sackville, N.B., Summer Institute, 1962 7612

NIEO Policy Research Library 7149
National Conference on Immigration Policy, Victoria College, University of Toronto, 1975 1418
National Japanese Canadian Citizens Association 1234
National Planning Association 2753, 3073, 6878, 7528, 7957, 8014, 8089
National Security Series, No. 1 5798
National Security Series, No. 3 5649
National Security Series, No. 6 5836
National Security Series, No. 6, 1976 6252
National Studies on International Organization 4665
National Tripartite Conference, Ottawa, 1969 4794
New Brunswick. Human Rights Commission 1649, 1653
New Educational Library 986
New Perspectives in Political Science, 26 5603
New York Historical Society. Proceedings for the Year 1843. Appendix 2209
New York State American Revolution Bicentennial Commission 6889
New York State Sea Grant Program 8769
New York State Study 6889
New York University. Center for International Studies 7618
New York University International Institute on Tax and Business Planning,
3d, Toronto, 1974 7867
North American Air Defense Command 5884
North American Boundary Commission, 1872-1876 2363
North Pacific Fur Seal Commission 224
North-South Institute 3093, 7162, 7191, 7194, 8360, 8407, 8414, 8415, 8416, 8626, 8950
North-South Institute. Briefing, 2 3093
North-South Papers, 1 8407, 8626
North-South Papers, 3 8950
Northern Yukon 8877
Northwest Atlantic Fisheries Organization 225, 226
Nova et Vetera Iuris Gentium. Series A: Modern International Law, No. 5 3259
Nova Scotia Resources Council 3136

ORAE Extra-Mural Paper, No. 15 26, 5672
ORD Report, No. 68/R5 5546
Oceans Policy Study, 1:1 2580
Ontario. Legislative Assembly. Select Committee on Economic and Cultural Nationalism 8019
Ontario. Mineral Resources Branch 3455
Ontario. Ministry of Natural Resources. Mineral Policy Background Paper, No. 10 3455
Ontario. Provincial Great Lakes/Seaway Task Force 2856
Ontario Co-operative Programme in Latin American and Caribbean Studies 7084
Ontario Economic Council 1409, 1673, 7489, 7874
Ontario Economic Council. Discussion Paper Series 1673
Ontario Economic Council. Occasional Paper, No. 8 7874
Ontario Economic Council. Research Studies, 4 7455
Ontario Economic Council. Research Studies, 6 7489
Ontario Economic Council. Working Paper Series, No. 1/76 1409
Ontario Public Interest Research Group 8725
Ouvrages historiques 856
Oxford Paperbacks, 268 5436

INDEX OF CORPORATE NAMES, ETC. 761

Oxford Paperbacks, 277 6410
Oxford University. Institute of Commonwealth Studies 6732

Pacific Trade and Development Conference, 3d, Sydney, 1970 7758
Pacific Trade and Development Conference, 4th, Carleton University, 1971 7229
Papers of Woodrow Wilson; Supplementary Volumes 4461
Parliamentary Centre for Foreign Affairs and Foreign Trade 6749
Peace Research Institute 4600, 4654
Peace Research Institute-Dundas 4655
Peace Research Reviews, Vol. 1, No. 2 5731
Peace Research Reviews, Vol. 1, No. 5 5573
Peace Research Reviews, Vol. 2, No. 2 4400
Peace Research Reviews, Vol. 2, No. 4 5500
Peace Research Reviews, Vol. 3, No. 4 4385
Peace Research Reviews, Vol. 5, No. 6 3062
Peace Research Reviews, Vol. 6, Nos. 4-6 4426
Peace Research Reviews, Vol. 7, No. 4 4675
Peace Research Reviews, Vol. 7, No. 6 5990
Peace Research Reviews, Vol. 8, No. 3 4600
Pearson Kirkman Marfleet Lectures at the University of Toronto, 1932 6863
Pensée chrétienne, 1 1516
Pergamon Policy Studies in the New International Economic Order 7149
Philosophie et problèmes contemporains, 2 1269
Policy Studies Institute (London, England) 436
Political Economy Series, No. 6 8122
Political Pamphlets, Vol. 83, No. 4 2500
Power Series 6496
Praeger History of Civilization 962
Praeger Paperbacks, P-269 8349
Praeger Scientific 3279

Praeger Special Studies 3279
Praeger Special Studies in International Economics and Development 7223, 7916
Praeger Special Studies in International Politics and Government 3178, 5431, 5764, 6200, 8970
Princeton University. Center for International Studies 272
Private Planning Association of Canada 7215, 7230, 7253, 7340, 7341, 7404, 7528, 7546, 7616, 7646, 8117, 8278, 8523
Private Planning Association of Canada. Canadian Economic Policy Committee 7415
Private Planning Association of Canada. Canadian Trade Committee 5057, 7426, 7631, 7656, 8324
Problèmes économiques contemporains, 3 7790
Procedural Aspects of International Law Series, Vol. 10 1182
Pugwash Symposium, 25th, Kyoto, 1975 5643
Pugwash Symposium, 30th, Toronto, 1978 5756

Québec (Province). Assemblée législative. Comité de la Constitution 817, 1343
Québec (Province). Civil Code Revision Office 3656
Québec (Province). Civil Code Revision Office. Report, Vol. 47 3656
Québec (Province). Comité interministériel sur les investissements étrangers 7876, 7877
Québec (Province). Conseil exécutif 780, 7876, 7877
Québec (Province). Direction générale de l'énergie 8740
Québec (Province). Ministère de l'immigration. Direction de la recherche 3
Québec (Province). Ministère de l'industrie et du commerce. Centre de documentation 13
Québec (Province). Ministère de l'industrie, du commerce et du tourisme. Direction des études en relations économiques internationales 7643

Québec (Province). Ministère des affaires intergouvernementales 800, 870, 4828, 7543, 8424
Québec (Province). Ministère des affaires intergouvernementales. Direction générale de la coopération internationale 857
Queen Elizabeth House 6732
Queen's University. Centre for International Relations 2565, 5649, 5798, 5836, 5922, 6252
Queen's University. Centre for Resource Studies 7728, 7729
Queen's University. Centre for Resource Studies. Proceedings, No. 2 7729
Queen's University. Centre for Resource Studies. Proceedings, No. 4 7728
Queen's University. Industrial Relations Centre 4950
Queen's University. Industrial Relations Centre. Research Series, No. 9 4950
Questions of the Day, No. 41 3395

Reference Shelf, Vol. 17, No. 3 6462
Reid Lectures of Acadia University, 2d Ser., 1959 6641
Reid Lectures of Acadia University, 4th Ser., 1963 1114
Relations du Canada avec les États-Unis 6831
Relations of Canada and the United States 249, 4825, 5252, 6572, 6577, 6578, 6617, 6752, 6753, 6766, 6861, 6871, 6928, 8912
Reports on Canada-United States Relations 5093, 6811, 7534, 7667, 7699, 7700
Research Strategies for the Study of International Political Terrorism, Evian, France, 1977 6235
Resources for the Future 2947, 2948
Resources for the Future. Reprint, No. 42 2947
Resources of the Sea Conference, Fish and Oil, St. John's, Nfld., 1973 3350
Revue générale de droit international public; Publications, Nouv. sér., no 16 2729
Royal Commonwealth Society 6681
Royal Institute of International Affairs 6483, 6671, 6698, 6712

Ryerson Paperbacks, 35 5915

SAG Memorandum, 64/M.2 46
Scandinavian Institute of African Studies 6385
Science Council of Canada 3278, 7805, 8002, 8442, 8618, 8707, 8946
Science Council of Canada. Background Study, No. 44 8618
Science Council of Canada. Discussion Paper, D80/1 8442
Science Council of Canada. Special Study, No. 22 7805, 8002
Self-Counsel Series 1134
Séminaire St-Augustin. Bibliothèque 28
Séminaire St-Augustin. Bibliothèque. Document, 221 28
Seminar on the Development and Administration of the International River Basin, University of British Columbia, 1961 2754
Série Études anglo-américaines 924
Short Studies in Political Science, 22 398
Simon Fraser University. Dept. of Economics and Commerce 3294, 3298
Simon Fraser University. Dept. of Economics and Commerce. Discussion Paper, 79-3-1 3294
Simon Fraser University. Dept. of Economics and Commerce. Discussion Paper, 79-7-2 3298
Simon Fraser University. School of Business Administration and Economics 3296
Simon Fraser University. School of Business Administration and Economics. Discussion Paper, 81-08-01 3296
Société québécoise de droit international 155
South African Institute of International Affairs, Johannesburg 500
Southern Legal Foundation 5111
Special Seminar on Canadian Investment in the United States, 1980 7761
Special Seminar on Interpreting Tax Treaties, Toronto, 1977 8286
Special Seminar on the New Treaties and the FAPI Regulations, Montreal, 1975 8287
Spectrum Book, S-AA-12 6751
Spectrum Book, S-AA-19 5734

INDEX OF CORPORATE NAMES, ETC. 763

St. Lawrence Seaway Authority 2847, 2874
Studia Collegii Maximi Immaculatae Conceptionis 4366
Studies in Commonwealth Politics and History, No. 4 6690
Studies in History, Economics and Public Law, No. 278 2105
Studies in History, Economics and Public Law, No. 335 888
Studies in History, Economics and Public Law, No. 358 2389
Studies in International Affairs, No. 1 1865
Studies in International Affairs, No. 3 7437
Studies in International Affairs, No. 4 6825
Studies in International Politics 5011
Studies in Peaceful Change 1743
Studies in Peaceful Change, No. 2 7618
Studies in Political History 6363
Studies in the Structure of Power; Decision Making in Canada, 1, 3, 6, 8 6413

TP-1676 3535
Tariff Commission, London 494
Thames Essay, No. 7 7620
Toronto Committee on Immigration and Migration 1418
Trade Policy Research Centre 6732, 7620
Trade Unions and Imperialism in America, Vol. 2 8919
Trilateral Commission 3106
Trilateral Commission. Triangle Papers, 9 3106

UNITAR Peaceful Settlement Study, No. 8 5412
United Church of Canada. Board of Evangelism and Social Service 5574
United Nations 8789
United Nations. Doc. A/CONF. 70/15 8789
United Nations Association in Canada 425, 1689, 1692, 4673, 5518, 6460, 8445, 8446
United Nations Association in Canada. Policy Committee. A Policy Paper 5518, 8446
United Nations Association in Canada. Reference Paper, No. 1 1689
United Nations Conference on Human Settlements, Vancouver, 1976. 8761, 8789
United Nations Conference on the Human Environment, Stockholm, 1972 8756
United Nations Conference on the Law of the Sea, 3d, 1974-1982 3011
United Nations Institute for Training and Research 7149
U.S. Bureau of Mines. Bulletin, 453 5280
U.S. 20th Cong., 1st sess. House. Ex. Doc. 43 2906
U.S. 44th Cong., 2d sess. Senate. Ex. Doc. 41 2363
U.S. 45th Cong., 2d sess. House. Ex. Doc. 89 5314
U.S. 58th Cong., 2d sess. Senate. Doc. 162 2274
U.S. 61st Cong., 3d sess. Senate. Doc. 787 7041
U.S. 61st Cong., 3d sess. Senate. Doc. 834 7039
U.S. 61st Cong., 3d sess. Senate. Doc. 870 5313
U.S. 62d Cong., 1st sess. Senate. Doc. 17 6958
U.S. 62d Cong., 1st sess. Senate. Doc. 56 7038
U.S. 62d Cong., 1st sess. Senate. Doc. 80 7037
U.S. 63d Cong., 1st sess. House. Doc. 2 7040
U.S. 67th Cong., 2d sess. Senate. Doc. 114 2427
U.S. 67th Cong., 2d sess. Senate. Doc. 179 2428
U.S. 73d Cong., 2d sess. Senate. Doc. 110 2908
U.S. 73d Cong., 2d sess. Senate. Doc. 116 2909
U.S. 79th Cong., 2d sess. Senate. Rept. 1499 2898
U.S. 82d Cong., 2d sess. Senate. Ex. Rept. 5 1496
U.S. 83d Cong., 1st sess. Senate. Rept. 441 2899
U.S. 83d Cong., 2d sess. House. Rept. 1215 2893
U.S. 83d Cong., 2d sess. Senate. Doc. 165 2907

U.S. 85th Cong., 2d sess. Senate. Doc. 118 2964
U.S. 87th Cong., 1st sess. Senate. Ex. Rept. 2 2963
U.S. 95th Cong., 1st sess. House. Rept. 95-193 3359
U.S. 95th Cong., 1st sess. Senate. Ex. Rept. 95-9 8530
U.S. Congress. House. Committee on Education and Labor. Subcommittee on Labor Standards 7594
U.S. Congress. House. Committee on Energy and Commerce 7902
U.S. Congress. House. Committee on Foreign Affairs 3422
U.S. Congress. House. Committee on Foreign Affairs. Subcommittee on Inter-American Affairs 2733
U.S. Congress. House. Committee on International Relations. Subcommittee on International Political and Military Affairs 6874
U.S. Congress. House. Committee on Interstate and Foreign Commerce 2889
U.S. Congress. House. Committee on Interstate and Foreign Commerce. Subcommittee on Oversight and Investigations 8853
U.S. Congress. House. Committee on Merchant Marine and Fisheries 2370, 3358, 3359
U.S. Congress. House. Committee on Public Works 2890, 2891, 2892, 2893
U.S. Congress. House. Committee on Rivers and Harbors 2894
U.S. Congress. House. Committee on Ways and Means 7035, 7595
U.S. Congress. Joint Economic Committee 8696
U.S. Congress. Joint Economic Committee. Subcommittee on Inter-American Economic Relationships 7903
U.S. Congress. Senate. Committee on Commerce 2895, 2896
U.S. Congress. Senate. Committee on Commerce, Science, and Transportation 3360
U.S. Congress. Senate. Committee on Finance 7036, 7037, 7038, 7039, 7596, 7597

U.S. Congress. Senate. Committee on Foreign Relations 1496, 2371, 2372, 2452, 2734, 2735, 2897, 2898, 2899, 2900, 2901, 2902, 2903, 2962, 2963, 3361, 5405, 5406, 6771, 7683, 8530, 8854, 9031
U.S. Congress. Senate. Committee on Governmental Affairs 7550
U.S. Delegation to the Ad Hoc Meeting of the Canada-United States Interparliamentary Group, 1981 7683
U.S. Dept. of Agriculture. Library 9
U.S. Dept. of Agriculture. Library. Bibliographical Contributions, No. 30 16
U.S. Dept. of Agriculture. Library. Bibliographical Contributions, No. 30, Ed. 2 9
U.S. Dept. of Commerce 2904
U.S. Dept. of Commerce. Bureau of Foreign and Domestic Commerce. Domestic Commerce Series, No. 4 2825
U.S. Dept. of State 2256, 2905, 2906, 2964, 5273, 6993
U.S. Dept. of State. Publication, No. 347 2905
U.S. Dept. of State. Publication; Arbitration Series, No. 2 5273
U.S. General Accounting Office 2736, 8697, 8827
U.S. Great Lakes Basin Commission 2737
U.S. Information Service, Ottawa 6875, 6876, 6877
U.S. Interdepartmental Board on the Great Lakes-St. Lawrence Project 2908
U.S. International Trade Commission 7597
U.S. Library of Congress. Legislative Reference Service 2907
U.S. President 2908, 2909, 7040, 7041, 7598
U.S. Tariff Commission 7042, 7551
United States Army in World War II; Special Studies 5842, 6792
Université d'Ottawa. Faculté de droit. Collection des travaux. Monographies juridiques, no 7 2646
Université d'Ottawa. Faculté de droit. Collection des travaux. Monographies juridiques, no 8 1937
Université d'Ottawa. Publications sériées, 59 5117

Université de Montréal 5016, 7111, 8496, 8497
Université de Montréal. Centre de recherche en développement économique 5149
Université de Montréal. Centre de recherche en droit public 2331, 8060
Université de Montréal. Centre international de criminologie comparée 6211, 6235, 6247
Université de Montréal. École des hautes études commerciales. Bibliothèque économique 7367
Université de Montréal. École des hautes études commerciales. Centre d'études et de documentation européennes 66, 4888, 5047, 5051, 5054, 7367
Université de Montréal. École des hautes études commerciales. Centre d'études et de documentation européennes. Annals 5047
Université de Montréal. École des hautes études commerciales. Centre d'études et de documentation européennes. Annals, 1 5051
Université de Montréal. École des hautes études commerciales. Centre d'études et de documentation européennes. Cahiers, 5 5054
Université de Montréal. Faculté de droit 250, 251, 252, 2150, 3572, 7241
Université de Paris. Institut des hautes études internationales 618, 2658
Université de Sherbrooke. Faculté de droit 239
Université du Québec à Montréal. Département de science politique 14, 15
Université du Québec à Montréal. Département de science politique. Notes de recherche, no 1 14
Université du Québec à Montréal. Département de science politique. Notes de recherche, no 14 15
Université internationale de sciences comparées. Faculté internationale de droit comparé 617
Université Laval 772, 4915, 6349, 6403, 7611
Université Laval. Centre d'études nordiques 2326
Université Laval. Centre d'études nordiques. Travaux et documents, 1 2326
Université Laval. Centre international de recherches sur le bilinguisme 1279
Université Laval. Département de science politique 5811
Université Laval. Groupe de recherche en économie de l'énergie 7694, 7695, 8663
Université Laval. Institut d'histoire 1885
Université Laval. Institut de géographie 2326
Université Laval. Publications 6622, 6896
University League for Social Reform 6401
University Lecture Series 4551
University of Alberta. Dept. of Political Science 6220
University of Alberta. Dept. of Political Science. Occasional Paper, 1 6220
University of British Columbia 233
University of British Columbia. Dept. of Economics 8775
University of British Columbia. Dept. of Economics. Resource Paper, No. 37 8775
University of British Columbia. Institute of International Relations 111, 112
University of British Columbia. Publications; Lecture Series, No. 27 2768
University of California. Publications in History, Vol. 41 1834
University of Chicago. Committee for the Comparative Study of New Nations 7142
University of Delaware. College of Marine Studies 8679
University of Florida. Monographs; Social Sciences, No. 29 6744
University of Florida, Gainesville 6744
University of Guelph, Ont. Dept. of Political Studies 428
University of Illinois. Illinois Studies in the Social Sciences, Vol. 18, Nos. 3-4 3396
University of Manitoba. Libraries. Reference Series, No. 8 10
University of Manitoba. Library 10
University of Maryland. Institute of Criminal Justice and Criminology 6211, 6235, 6247
University of Michigan. Institute for International Commerce 7581
University of New Brunswick. Centre for

Conflict Studies 59
University of Ottawa 8398
University of Ottawa. Dept. of Geography and Regional Planning 3124
University of Ottawa. Faculty of Law 1937, 2646, 4897
University of Ottawa. Institute for International Development and Co-operation 7239
University of Ottawa. Institute for International Co-operation 8362
University of Ottawa. Institute for International Co-operation. Travaux et documents. Série A, no 2 8362
University of Ottawa. Publications, 15 2592
University of Ottawa. Research Notes, Geography and Regional Planning, No. 4 3124
University of Rhode Island. Center for Ocean Management Studies 3279
University of Rochester. Canadian Studies Series, No. 7 6884
University of Rochester. Canadian Studies Series, No. 9 7515
University of Rochester. Canadian Studies Series, No. 18 2514
University of Rochester. Canadian Studies Series, No. 20 6606, 6852
University of Rochester. Canadian Studies Series, No. 21 6935
University of Toronto. Centre for International Studies 2449, 6441
University of Toronto. Faculty of Law 2995
University of Toronto. Library 2
University of Toronto. Library. Reference Dept. 24
University of Toronto. Library. Reference Series, No. 20 24
University of Toronto. Library. Reference Series, No. 25 2
University of Toronto. Studies. Legal Series. Extra Volume 8462, 8464
University of Toronto. Studies. Political Science Series, No. 4 7473
University of Toronto/York University Joint Program in Transportation. Transportation Paper, No. 3 3529
University of Virginia. Center for Oceans Law and Policy 2580
University of Washington. Publications in the Social Sciences, Vol. 13, No. 1 2251
University of Waterloo. Dept. of Man-Environment Studies 2714
University of Waterloo. Faculty of Environmental Studies 2562
University of Western Ontario. Centre for the Study of International Economic Relations 7292, 7553
University of Western Ontario. Centre for the Study of International Economic Relations. Working Paper, No. 8009 7292
University of Western Ontario. Centre for the Study of International Economic Relations. Working Paper, No. 8011 7553
University of Western Ontario. Dept. of Economics 7292, 7553
University of Windsor Seminar on Canadian-American Relations 67
University of Winnipeg. Library 10
University of Wisconsin. Bulletin; Economics, Political Science, and History Series, Vol. 1, No. 3 6888

Valiant Series 2861

W.M. Martin Lectures, 1960 5596
Warne Modern History Monographs 6680
Waterloo Public Interest Research Group 8857
Wellesley Papers, 5 6026
Wellesley Papers, 6 5922
Wellesley Papers, 7 2550
Wesleyan University. George Slocum Bennett Foundation. Lectures, 2d Ser., 1919-1920 6885
West Virginia University. Studies in American History. Series 1, Diplomatic History, Nos. 2 and 3 2283
Westview Replica Edition 3578, 4721
Westview Special Studies in Natural Resources and Energy Management 8672
Westwater Research Centre 2774
William L. Clayton Lectures on International Economic Affairs and Foreign Policy, 1958 6365

Winnipeg Air Law Committee 3905
World Affairs Since 1939, Vol. 2 6846
World Law Foundation 292
World Peace Foundation 6349, 6403, 8643
World Peace Foundation. Pamphlets Series, Vol. 4, No. 4 6922
World Peace Foundation. Pamphlets Series, Vol. 10, No. 6 955
World Peace Through Law Center 6289
World Peace Through Law Center. Pamphlets Series, No. 18 6289

World's Classics 475
Writings on Canadian-American Studies, Vol. 3 7516

Yale Historical Publications; Miscellany, 27 3403
Yale University. Institute of International Studies 271
York University. Osgoode Hall Law School 235, 8007

Ref. NOV 1 1984
Z
6465
C2
W54
1984